THE OXFORD HANDBOOK OF

LATER MEDIÆVAL ARCHAEOLOGY IN BRITAIN

Contributors

Abby Antrobus, Grenville Astill, James H. Barrett, Terry B. Barry,
Jelena Bekvalac, James Bond, Niall Brady, Peter J. Brown,
Jill Campbell, Matthew Champion, Sally Crawford,
Oliver H. Creighton, Christopher Daniell, Gareth Dean, Piers Dixon,
Simon A. Draper, Holly Dugan, Christopher Dyer, Richard Fawcett,
Glenn Foard, Michael Fradley, Mark Gardiner, Christopher M. Gerrard,
Louisa Gidney, Kate Giles, Rebecca L. Gowland, C. P. Graves,
Alejandra Gutiérrez, J. Avelino Gutiérrez-González, Mark A. Hall,
Claire Hanusse, David A. Hinton, Martin Huggon, Michael J. Huxtable,
Tom Beaumont James, Richard Kelleher, Susan Kilby, Keith D. Lilley,
Aleksandra McClain, Maureen Mellor, Stephen Mileson, Lisa Moffett,
Richard Morris, Ronan P. O'Donnell, David Parsons,
Bennjamin J. Penny-Mason, Aleks Pluskowski, Rebecca Redfern,
Amanda Richardson, Stephen Rippon, Charlotte A. Roberts,
Else Roesdahl, Simon Roffey, Colin Rynne, John Schofield,
Bob Silvester, Eleanor R. Standley, Richard Suggett,
Emma J. Wells, Hugh Willmott, Peter Yeoman

Oxford Handbooks offer authoritative and up-to-date surveys of original research in a particular subject area. Specially commissioned essays from leading figures in the discipline give critical examinations of the progress and direction of debates, as well as a foundation for future research. *Oxford Handbooks* provide scholars and graduate students with compelling new perspectives upon a wide range of subjects in the humanities, social sciences, and sciences.

Also published by
OXFORD UNIVERSITY PRESS

The Oxford Handbook of Roman Britain
Edited by Martin Millett, Louise Revell, and Alison Moore

The Oxford Handbook of Neolithic Europe
Edited by Chris Fowler, Jan Harding, and Daniela Hofmann

The Oxford Handbook of the European Bronze Age
Edited by Harry Fokkens and Anthony Harding

The Oxford Handbook of Anglo-Saxon Archaeology
Edited by Helena Hamerow, David A. Hinton, and Sally Crawford

THE OXFORD HANDBOOK OF

LATER MEDIEVAL ARCHAEOLOGY IN BRITAIN

Edited by
CHRISTOPHER M. GERRARD
and
ALEJANDRA GUTIÉRREZ

OXFORD
UNIVERSITY PRESS

OXFORD
UNIVERSITY PRESS

Great Clarendon Street, Oxford, OX2 6DP,
United Kingdom

Oxford University Press is a department of the University of Oxford.
It furthers the University's objective of excellence in research, scholarship,
and education by publishing worldwide. Oxford is a registered trade mark of
Oxford University Press in the UK and in certain other countries

© Oxford University Press 2018

The moral rights of the authors have been asserted

First Edition published in 2018
First published in paperback 2020

Impression: 1

All rights reserved. No part of this publication may be reproduced, stored in
a retrieval system, or transmitted, in any form or by any means, without the
prior permission in writing of Oxford University Press, or as expressly permitted
by law, by licence or under terms agreed with the appropriate reprographics
rights organization. Enquiries concerning reproduction outside the scope of the
above should be sent to the Rights Department, Oxford University Press, at the
address above

You must not circulate this work in any other form
and you must impose this same condition on any acquirer

Published in the United States of America by Oxford University Press
198 Madison Avenue, New York, NY 10016, United States of America

British Library Cataloguing in Publication Data

Data available

Library of Congress Cataloging in Publication Data

Data available

ISBN 978–0–19–874471–9 (Hbk.)
ISBN 978–0–19–885804–1 (Pbk.)

Printed and bound by
CPI Group (UK) Ltd, Croydon, CR0 4YY

Links to third party websites are provided by Oxford in good faith and
for information only. Oxford disclaims any responsibility for the materials
contained in any third party website referenced in this work.

Preface

CHRISTOPHER M. GERRARD
AND ALEJANDRA GUTIÉRREZ

The later Middle Ages in Europe are a rich and exciting period for the archaeologist in which there have been very significant recent advances in knowledge. In fact, most of what we have learnt about the material culture of our medieval past has been discovered in the past two generations and an inspiring cross-section of finds is now on display in Britain in the newly re-fitted galleries at the Ashmolean in Oxford (Anglo-Saxon and Medieval), the British Museum (Medieval Europe), and the Victoria and Albert Museum (Medieval and Renaissance), not to mention the award-winning £27m *Mary Rose* museum in Portsmouth which opened its doors in 2013. Major exhibitions of medieval objects including the *Age of Chivalry* (Royal Academy of Arts 1987), medieval relics (*Treasures of heaven*, British Museum 2011), *Opus Anglicanum* (Victoria and Albert Museum 2016), and Medieval Europe AD 400–1500 (British Museum international touring exhibition) have all attracted large numbers of visitors.

The popularity and profile of medieval monuments is also striking. Among the UK's thirty UNESCO World Heritage Sites in 2016 there are castles (of Gwynedd, Durham, and the Tower of London), two cathedrals (Canterbury and Durham), a palace, and an abbey (Westminster). Its castles and monasteries in particular are a mainstay of cultural tourism: the top five medieval visitor attractions in 2015 were the Tower of London (2.7 million), Westminster Abbey (1.6 million), Edinburgh Castle (1.5 million), Canterbury Cathedral (957k), and Leeds Castle (500k). These are enormous numbers worth £20 billion of GDP annually and supporting nearly 200,000 jobs all told. Then again, across most of Europe we never need to travel that far to come into contact with the later Middle Ages. The way the rooms are arranged in some of the houses we live in, the layout of a village or a town, the castle on the hill, the shapes of the fields we see out of the train window, the way the light shines through stained glass in a local church: all of these are everyday experiences in our modern lives which may be shaped by the Middle Ages. With rare exceptions, almost all the places we live in today already existed in the medieval period. Parliament and democratic government, monarchy and royal courts, universities and their libraries; all these are medieval institutions which are still familiar to us today.

The Society for the Public Understanding of the Middle Ages, founded in 2010, aims to focus on how the general public views this period through literature, movies, TV, and video games, all of which claim to take us one step closer to the medieval past. Every genre finds its place there, from drama to comedy and from satire to mystery and political intrigue. Like it or not, *Robin Hood: prince of thieves* grossed $390 million worldwide, Umberto Eco's historical whodunit *The name of the rose* has been in print for over thirty years, and C. J. Samson's Shardlake series has over two million copies in print; the Middle Ages are one of our most popular collective historical playgrounds. Quite why this should be so is harder to say but the medieval period has something to offer the curious as well as the specialist, a world which is at once familiar and yet at once strangely distant. There are everyday items of dress which we recognize instantly, others which we turn over in our hands in silent bafflement, and while there are medieval practices we seem to grasp quite readily, others can leave us feeling remote.

In Britain there have been major field archaeology projects which have long remained in the public eye. In 1982 the spectacular lifting of the *Mary Rose* was watched on television by twenty million viewers, while the highest profile project of recent years has been the discovery of the remains of Richard III (d. 1485) under a Leicester car park. The king's skeleton was dated by radiocarbon to 1455–1540 (95 per cent), and the mitochondrial DNA matched that of two independent and genealogically verified modern matrilineal descendants of Richard III's sister, Anne of York (Buckley et al. 2013). This story had global media reach and has become a symbol of local pride as well as having a direct economic impact on the city of Leicester: a £4-million visitor centre opened on the site in 2014.

This *Handbook* provides an overview of the contribution of archaeology to our developing understanding of the later Middle Ages in Britain between 1066 and *c*.1550. In all there are sixty entries, divided into ten thematic sections, and intended to be attractive to a broad audience of undergraduates, postgraduates, and researchers as well as those in the broader heritage sector working in commercial units and local authorities. We will cover medieval objects, standing buildings, sites such as castles and monasteries, as well as the extensive relict landscapes of the Middle Ages. Our ambition is that this volume should act as a point of departure for future scholarship and provide a 'way in' for anyone grappling with the challenge of specialized research literature. There have been several previous syntheses, beginning with Colin Platt's *Medieval England: a social history and archaeology from the Conquest to 1600*, first published in 1978. John Steane's *The archaeology of medieval England and Wales* and Helen Clarke's *The archaeology of medieval England*, which both appeared in 1984, are still valued today, thirty years on, as is David Hinton's survey with its longer chronology (1990). Many contributors to this *Handbook* make reference to those volumes. Within the range of medieval academic titles the *Handbook* bridges the gap between a standard undergraduate text such as *The archaeology of Britain* (with its three later medieval chapters), single-topic monographs such as *Monastic landscapes* (Bond 2004) or *Beyond the medieval village* (Rippon 2008), the historiographical insights of *Medieval archaeology: traditions and contemporary approaches* (Gerrard 2003), and *Reflections: 50 years of medieval archaeology* (Gilchrist and Reynolds 2009). There would be little merit in repeating the industry-by-industry breakdown of *English medieval industries* (Blair and Ramsay 1991) or the regional approach adopted in *Medieval rural settlement* (Christie and Stamper 2012), essential though these synthetic volumes are. Every effort has also been made to minimize overlap with *The archaeology of medieval Europe, Vol. 2: twelfth to sixteenth centuries* (Carver and Klápště 2011), although this does provide a valuable companion volume.

WHY AN *OXFORD HANDBOOK* OF LATER MEDIEVAL ARCHAEOLOGY?

Every editor of a *Handbook* of this sort needs to ask themselves, why now? Is there a need for a volume of this kind? We would answer that question in two ways. First, later medieval archaeology is still a relatively young discipline. We would hazard a guess that it would still have been possible in the mid-1950s for a one individual (possibly John Hurst) to know all there was to know about the subject in Britain, to have visited most of the sites, and grasp the detail as well as the wider agenda. Today such a claim would be unthinkable and in 2015, when Colin Platt passed away, many felt in some unseen way that the mantle had passed to another generation. For that reason, special effort has been made to include a range of scholars from England, Scotland, and Wales and to involve younger contributors who will shape the future of the subject. This is absolutely in line with the wider ethos of the *Oxford Handbooks* series. Second, following the economic crisis of recent years, state funding for archaeology and centralized professional capacity has been slashed and there is now further uncertainty about the role of UK research councils following the Brexit referendum. The European funding which had become steadily more important in recent years may well not be available in the future and this will doubtless change once again the kind of research which archaeologists undertake. Now is therefore a good moment to take stock and to produce something which might serve as a reference point for further study. We also hope very much that colleagues working across Europe will find useful parallels (and differences) with their own narratives.

Some basic parameters may be useful. First, the period between 1066 and c.1550 is referred to here throughout as 'later medieval' but other terms can be found in the scholarly literature, among them 'post-Conquest', often used by archaeologists in reference to the Norman Conquest of 1066, and 'Late Middle Ages' or 'High Middle Ages'. Few contributors, however, have chosen to ignore either the preceding centuries or those which followed: the chronological threads of our subject are woven into a bigger picture. Second, our contributors do not entirely stick to British material and we would not have wanted them to do so. Indeed, we have firmly stuck by our promise to make explicit the rich cultural and commercial associations with other parts of Europe and Part X is explicitly designed to do just that. Third, we have not tried to be comprehensive; this is not an encyclopaedia, we have encouraged authors to synthesize current knowledge but also to 'poke the hive' a little and explore newer debates. For that reason the contents list does not read as a list of categories of material culture (there is no separate chapter here on pottery, for example); instead we have focused on topics and themes which archaeology has the power to illuminate. Finally, as will quickly become clear, this is very much a multi-disciplinary volume. Archaeology, and later medieval archaeology in particular, is a team game and these days few can afford to work in ignorance of other disciplines. On that basis, we hope that even the most experienced archaeological researcher may be tempted to read beyond their own research topics and that the *Handbook* will be of interest to those working in related specialisms across disciplines such as history, anthropology, historical geography, and the sciences.

Research Outlook

Later medieval archaeology is taught at most, if not all, UK universities and widely across Europe and the world. Its teachers may not be as numerous as prehistorians or Romanists but there is no lack of interest in undergraduate and postgraduate courses, topics for doctoral students or volunteers for medieval excavations. At the outset of a *Handbook* like this one, it may be useful to rehearse the reasons why this should be so:

- later medieval archaeology makes full use of all the modern *archaeological techniques* available to study the past. Most practitioners lie at different points within a triangle drawn between the complementary archaeologies of the humanities, sciences, and professional practice. Fieldwork, excavation, data collection, and synthesis lie at the heart of the subject and post-excavation should embrace, for example, the study of environmental and biomolecular archaeology, just as it does for other periods. There are, however, some important differences to note with archaeologists of other periods. Even relatively modern maps, such as nineteenth-century tithe maps, can be of use for the information they provide on field boundaries and field-names, and the later medieval archaeologist may be as much at home in the Record Office as in the field. Some dating techniques are also preferred over others, such as dendrochronology (and now dendro-provenancing), whereas radiocarbon dating has traditionally been less commonly applied because it is considered imprecise. AMS (Accelerator Mass Spectrometry) and Bayesian statistics are reducing this range of error but later medieval archaeologists prefer to work at a higher chronological resolution than their counterparts in other periods;
- while there may be differences of emphasis, later medieval archaeology should make full use of the toolkit of *theoretical perspectives* open to an archaeologist of any other period;

- the social and economic context for later medieval British archaeology is widely regarded as *European* and, to a large extent, Christian and feudal. However, these generalizations rightly invite comparison between regions and, indeed, some criticism;
- *multi-disciplinarity*: typically, the later medieval archaeologist must be prepared to familiarize themselves with the work of historical geographers, economic historians, architectural historians, and historical ecologists. Their sources are often complementary and may reveal different facets of the medieval past. In particular, later medieval archaeology is especially attractive because it interacts with the study of written sources. Although this may not imply any training in palaeography or an understanding of Latin and French, it does demand an appreciation of the strengths and weaknesses of historic documents and cartography and pictorial evidence (for example, few towns possess written records before the thirteenth century and the documentary record can be socially and geographically selective) and an awareness of the different themes which are of interest to medieval historians. For clarity, although there may be overlaps in historical, social, and theoretical interests, the study of history does not generally apply scientific techniques (for example, to investigate the movement of human populations or human diet) or involve fieldwork (nor is it generally interested in human prehistory). For this reason, major projects will often draw together multi-disciplinary teams;
- many later medieval buildings such as churches and domestic houses are still in use today and, although rarely exactly in their original condition, they are superficially *familiar* to us in some respects. In some ways this can be useful: we all understand in outline what the purpose of a church is, for example. However, the later medieval archaeologist must always be prepared to unlearn the familiar and engage with contemporary perspectives which may be very different from our own, not least in the nature of religious practice and belief;
- 'medievalism', that is, a loose confection of fictionalized and adapted quasi-medieval themes in literature, the world of gaming, and on screen, from *Monty Python and the Holy Grail* to *The Lord of the Rings* to *Game of Thrones*, has many millions of followers. This public appreciation can be a point of entry for more serious interest;
- *survival and volume of the evidence*: like standing buildings, the field evidence of medieval earthworks such as ridge and furrow and deserted rural settlements can be extensive. Taken together, these provide an intimate understanding of the medieval environment but they will often require particular field skills such as standing building recording, architectural dating, and topographical survey to a greater extent. In general, though not always, the same is true of artefacts; later medieval pottery is generally more abundant than Neolithic pottery, for example. It can also be true of stratigraphy, especially the depth of urban deposits beneath towns and cities. In spite of this, the material evidence for later medieval life is uneven and requires nuanced interpretation;

- *threats to the evidence*: the inevitable flip-side to the relative abundance of physical evidence for the Middle Ages is that it remains a fragile resource unless procedures and legislation are in place for its protection. Although it may be widely considered an old-fashioned point of view, there will always be those who argue that archaeology of the later historic periods is in some way less valuable because of the evidence provided by the written record;
- the study of later medieval archaeology is, in many ways, *relatively young*. There are many further questions to be asked and new insights can be at once revealing, surprising, and thought-provoking.

Themes

In reading through the papers presented here we have identified three cross-cutting themes which characterize the later medieval archaeology of today. The first of these is the impact of science-based archaeology, materials analysis such as X-radiography, chemical analysis (ICPS), ceramic petrology, and residue analysis, and not to mention botanical and biological analyses of seeds and faunal remains. Sometimes results come from the most unexpected sources, as is the case for medieval crops and weeds which have been unexpectedly discovered beneath later re-thatching on medieval buildings. Nevertheless, no dating technique has had the same impact on the subject than dendrochronology, both for buildings and for timbers obtained from waterfronts. Meanwhile, the 'landscape' approach underlined here by several contributors may at least in part be attributed to the increased use of remote-sensing prospection techniques such as magnetometry, GPR, and UAVs. New applications such as isotopes and aDNA are now very much part of the agenda too but, as we shall see, there are concerns that these should address meaningful questions rather than being condemned to the novelty drawer.

The second theme to be highlighted is the use of theory. A generation ago, Helen Clarke (1984, 12) spoke of medieval archaeology being set in a 'traditional' mould in spite of New (or processual) Archaeology 'insinuating' its way into the discipline. The choice of language is telling. Today many of the papers in this volume reflect the centrality of archaeological theory to their approach, particularly post-processual perspectives. A third theme which is particular to Britain is the legislative context in which all archaeology now takes place. Planning policy guidance, formalized in the early 1990s, requires archaeology to be taken into consideration where appropriate in local plans (for housing and infrastructure) and as part of what is now called 'development control'. Archaeology, at least archaeology at any scale, therefore tends to be found where redevelopment is taking place (more investigation in south-east England than the north-east, for example) while the cost of excavation and conservation falls to the private developer. Over the years this has not only transformed the number of sites being dug but also brought about a new emphasis on non-destructive survey methods, the quarrying of archived 'meta-data', and the preservation of sites *in situ*. Likewise, the obligation to report finds from metal-detecting through the Portable Antiquities Scheme has greatly increased the number and range of metal objects being recorded. Some of these discoveries have permitted significant reinterpretations, for example of coin use and distributions (Chapter 32).

Summary of Contents

This *Handbook* is divided into ten thematic parts, each containing several chapters. Part I establishes the background to the historical development of the discipline (Chapter 1), the field techniques used in the study of later medieval archaeology (Chapter 2), its theoretical underpinning (Chapter 3), and the main types of available written evidence (Chapter 4). These chapters are all specifically referenced to lead into more specialist literature if the reader wishes to pursue a topic in greater depth. In each case we present thematic summaries of research from excavation, artefact studies, building recording, and environmental archaeology and outline the current challenges of research, including the latest methodological and theoretical developments. At a time when later Medieval Archaeology is becoming more interpretative, we hope that this *Handbook* will be a marker of the achievements and maturity of the subject.

Part II, introduced by Grenville Astill (Chapter 5) presents six chapters covering aspects of the medieval countryside from field systems (Chapter 6), animals (Chapter 7), archaeobotany (Chapter 8), fish and fishing (Chapter 9), to wild mammals, birds, and exotics (Chapter 10), rounding off with a chapter by Peter Brown which describes a litany of natural disasters and the archaeological evidence for the different ways in which medieval communities sought to cope with risk (Chapter 11). We return to two of the themes raised in Part II, those of medieval risk and the environment, in the final chapter of this *Handbook* where future agendas come under consideration.

The introduction to Part III emphasizes the diversity of settlement across England, Scotland, and Wales (Chapter 12) and just how far the pattern of villages and open fields was the exception. Chris Dyer (Chapter 13) describes medieval settlements in more detail, drawing attention to the kinds of artefacts routinely found on rural sites, while the following chapter examines how people in later medieval Britain perceived their surroundings, from castles and peasant dwellings to sacred places such as holy wells and hermitages (Chapter 14). Two chapters then follow on peasant housing (Chapter 15) and elite housing (Chapter 16). Niall Brady completes Part III with a discussion of agricultural buildings (Chapter 17).

Part IV shifts the discussion from the countryside into towns, a theme which is introduced by Keith Lilley (Chapter 18) and followed by chapters on urban housing (Chapter 19), and medieval shops and shopping (Chapter 20). Of particular importance to these chapters is the multidisciplinary combination of historical, architectural, and archaeological evidence and the complications of fieldwork when so many structures have been restored or altered. Chris Dyer's second contribution, on the dynamic relationship between towns and countryside, invites contrasts in housing and material cultural, as well as in contact, exchange, and the distribution of goods (Chapter 21). Finally, Gareth Dean (Chapter 22) examines the primary infrastructure of the urban environment: roads, bridges, waterways, and their associated structures.

Part V explores the archaeological evidence for the display of power in the later Middle Ages. Oliver Creighton (Chapter 23) introduces this topic with an assessment of key debates around medieval castles and the structured viewing of their settings. This paper enmeshes with topics already raised, such as the ecological signature of elite landscapes mentioned by Pluskowski in Chapter 10, as well as highlighting two further 'grand challenges' for later medieval archaeology identified in Chapter 60, those of 'social complexity' and 'identity'. Four chapters then follow which consider medieval palaces (Chapter 24), elite recreational landscapes of the forest, park, and warren (Chapter 25), the relatively new field of battlefield archaeology (Chapter 26), and the artefactual evidence for high-status activities, from royal regalia to insignia such as badges and seals (Chapter 27).

Maureen Mellor (Chapter 28) begins Part VI with an overview of industry, commerce, and the study of objects in the Middle Ages. The richness of the archaeological record here reflects the fact that this has been a well-established field of research for the past fifty years and more. Six papers appraise the extractive industries (Chapter 29), the archaeological evidence for workshops (Chapter 30), windmills and watermills (Chapter 31), coinage (Chapter 32), and pastimes (Chapter 33). These authors summarize recent important discoveries, some of which have transformed our understanding, and introduce new approaches to the evidence. Coins, for example, are considered not just for their contribution to dating but also the different ways in which they were adapted for other uses and placed into specific burial contexts.

Part VII, introduced by Richard Morris (Chapter 34), reflects on the evidence for churches and belief in the medieval landscape. Three chapters then discuss the major monument categories of monasteries (Chapter 35), cathedrals (Chapter 36), and churches (Chapter 37). The nature of the evidence for these three is subtly different, not least because so many churches survive as standing buildings and an understanding of architectural history and art history may be required to decipher their fabrics and furnishings. Mark Hall (Chapter 38) then takes a holistic view of sacrality, including relics and other sacred objects, and introduces the theme of pilgrimage discussed next by Peter Yeoman (Chapter 40). This article evaluates the physical evidence for medieval pilgrimage in the form of infrastructure for travel, shrines, and the material culture of pilgrimage souvenirs. Part VII is completed by a discussion of later medieval graffiti (Chapter 39), whose study has flourished in recent years due to the availability of inexpensive digital cameras and the enthusiasm of community groups, and by a discussion of the images painted on the walls, depicted in stained glass, and carved in wood, alabaster, or metal (Chapter 41). Most of these images have disappeared in Britain but the authors show what can be pieced together from contemporary sources and restoration projects.

Introduced by Emma Wells (Chapter 42), Part VIII explores a series of medieval contributions to sensual culture studies. An interest in the senses in human experience and in the experiential is now widespread in archaeology and across the social sciences and humanities subjects. Chapters on taste (Chapter 43), sound (Chapter 44), smell (Chapter 45), and sight (Chapter 46) describe how medieval people experienced places, landscapes, and material culture, in short the sensory profile of a culture as understood through food remains, refuse disposal, health, architecture, and the structuring of landscapes. Taking care not to impose their own sensory bias, these five chapters set out possible methodologies for sensual studies, sometimes involving close attention to textual sources and at other times field experiments (as it does here for sound). The interplay of the senses, or synaesthesia, provides great potential to examine how medieval people used all their senses to evaluate their surroundings, for example the fusion of senses experienced in churches through wall paintings, readings, the ringing of bells, and the smells of liturgy.

Part IX is dedicated to aspects of the medieval life course from infancy (Chapter 48), through health and adulthood (Chapter 49), to death and burial (Chapter 53), and through to the afterlife (Chapter 54). With the introduction of new scientific techniques and more rigorous standards of recovery and recording, the contribution of bioarchaeology to our understanding of the Middle Ages has flourished over the past decade. As the introduction by Rebecca Gowland and Benn Penny-Mason explains (Chapter 47), a thorough understanding of context has proved central to this progress and it is the integration of historical, archaeological, architectural, and bioarchaeological evidence for the medieval life course, from infancy to old age, which has proved so fruitful as well as a maturing theoretical framework in which to reflect on the results. In the spirit of interdisciplinarity, interspersed with this framework of four chapters are three more which consider the archaeological evidence for growing up and growing old, on medieval dress (Chapter 49), gender (Chapter 50), and medicine and public health (Chapter 52). All three benefit from some of the new approaches to the archaeology of behaviour and identity which feature in Chapter 60.

Part X, introduced by Alejandra Gutiérrez (Chapter 55), fixes attention on the wider geographical context for developments in Britain along the seaboards of Atlantic Europe and the North and Baltic Seas. In the historic past, as today, these coastlines were a major artery for navigation and contributed significantly to the development and economy of bordering countries, offering transportation as well as trade, communication, and routes for settlement and conquest. Here we not only examine the evidence for contact in the Middle Ages but also scrutinize the different strengths of the archaeological record which explain, to some extent, an unfortunate tendency towards national 'compartmentalization'. Anglo-Norman and Gaelic Ireland are examined by Terry Barry (Chapter 56), France by Claire Hanusse (Chapter 57), southern Scandinavia by Else Roesdahl (Chapter 58), and Spain and Portugal by Christopher M. Gerrard and Avelino Gutiérrez-González (Chapter 59). What emerges is a major resource for examining regional identities and practices in the later Middle Ages, one whose potential we hope can still be fulfilled in spite of recent political events. The future is the theme of a final chapter which draws together some of the current infrastructural issues being faced by later medieval archaeologists, though by no means unique to them, and sets out what are here called 'the grand challenges'. With luck, all these will soon be out of date.

References

Alexander, J. and Binski, P. (eds) 1987 *Age of Chivalry: art in Plantagenet England 1200-1400*, Royal Academy of Arts/Weidenfeld and Nicolson, London

Bagnoli, M., Klein, H. A., Mann, C. G., and Robinson, J. (eds) 2011 *Treasures of heaven: saints, relics and devotion in medieval Europe*, British Museum Press, London

Blair, J. and Ramsay, N. (eds) 1991 *English medieval industries: craftsmen, techniques, products*, The Hambledon Press, London

Bond, J. 2004 *Monastic landscapes*, Tempus, Stroud

Buckley, R., Morris, M., Appleby, J., King T., O'Sullivan, D., and Foxhall, L. 2013 ' "The king in the car park", new light on the death and burial of Richard III in the Grey Friars church, Leicester, in 1485', *Antiquity* 87(336), 519-38

Carver, M. O. H. and Klápště, J. (eds) 2011 *The archaeology of medieval Europe, Vol. 2: twelfth to sixteenth centuries*, Aarhus University Press, Aarhus

Christie, N. and Stamper, P. (eds) 2012 *Medieval rural settlement: Britain and Ireland, AD 800-1600*, Windgather Press, Oxford

Clarke, H. 1984 *The archaeology of medieval England*, British Museum Publications, London

Gerrard, C. M. 2003 *Medieval archaeology: understanding traditions and contemporary approaches*, Routledge, London

Gilchrist, R. and Reynolds, A. (eds) 2009 *Reflections: 50 years of medieval archaeology 1957-2007*, The Society for Medieval Archaeology Monograph 30, Leeds

Hinton, D. 1990 *Archaeology, economy and society: England from the fifth to the fifteenth century*, Seaby, London

Hunter, J. and Ralston, I. 1999 *The archaeology of Britain: an introduction from the Upper Palaeolithic to the Industrial Revolution*, Routledge, London

Platt, C. 1978 *Medieval England: a social history and archaeology from the Conquest to 1600*, Routledge and Kegan Paul, London

Rippon, S. 2008 *Beyond the medieval village: the diversification of landscape character in southern Britain*, Oxford University Press, Oxford

Steane, J. 1984 *The archaeology of medieval England and Wales*, Guild Publishing, London

Acknowledgements

The editors are grateful to Clare Kennedy for supervising the production of this *Handbook* and to the authors for their collaboration and patience. Special thanks are due to all those individual and institutions who have generously allowed us to use their images, especially to:

Øyvind Aasen, Nat Alcock, Geoff Arnott, Steve Ashby, Gary Bankhead, James Barrett, Valentín Barroso, Teddy Bethus, Frank Blackwell, Jim Brown, Chris Caple, C. Chapelain de Séreville-Niel, Andy Chapman, Benoît Clavel, Peter Claughton, Oliver Creighton, Stephen Driscoll, Lionel Duigou, Stephen Eastmead, Dave Evans, David Griffith, Robert Higham, Derek Keene, Jim Knowles, R. F. Hartley, Xavier de Jauréguiberry, Helen Lubin, R. W. Parker, Sarah Pearson, Nicolas Prouteau, Daniele Quercia, Tony Randall, Steve Rippon, Simon Roffey, Mike Searle, David Simon, Catherine Smith, Paul Stamper, Adam Stanford, Charlotte Stanford, Kris Strutt, Naomi Sykes, M. C. Truc, Tom Vaughan, Graeme Young, Aerial-Cam Ltd, Arqueocanaria SL, Ashmolean Museum (Oxford), Bordesley Abbey Project, Buckinghamshire Archaeological Society, Clwyd-Powys Archaeological Trust, Cotswold Archaeology, Fife Council Archaeological Unit, Fitzwilliam Museum (Cambridge), Kent Archaeological Society, Leicestershire Fieldworkers, Lincoln Cathedral, McDonald Institute of Archaeology (Oxford), Museum of London Archaeology, The National Gallery of Art (Washington), Norfolk County Council, Norfolk Historic Environment Service, Norwich Castle Museum and Art Gallery, Moesgaard Museum (Denmark), Oxbow Books, Perth Museum and Art Gallery, Portable Antiquities Scheme, Salisbury Cathedral, Salisbury Museum, The Society for Medieval Archaeology, State and University Library Dresden, Sydvestjyske Museer (Denmark), The Walters Art Museum (Baltimore), Thomas Fisher Rare Book Library, University of Toronto, West Lothian Archaeological Trust, Worcestershire Archaeology, and York Museums Trust.

Contents

List of Figures   xxiii
List of Contributors   xxxiii

PART I WRITING LATER MEDIEVAL ARCHAEOLOGY

1 Overview: people and projects   3
   Christopher M. Gerrard

2 Methods in medieval archaeology   20
   Michael Fradley

3 Embracing new perspectives   38
   C. P. Graves and Christopher M. Gerrard

4 The written evidence for the later Middle Ages   52
   Simon A. Draper

PART II THE MEDIEVAL COUNTRYSIDE

5 Overview: geographies of medieval Britain   69
   Grenville Astill

6 Field systems and the arable fields   86
   Ronan P. O'Donnell

7 The animal in late medieval Britain   102
   Louisa Gidney

8 The archaeobotany of late medieval plant remains: the resource and the research   116
   Lisa Moffett

9	Medieval fishing and fish trade JAMES H. BARRETT	128
10	The medieval wild ALEKS PLUSKOWSKI	141
11	Coping with disaster PETER J. BROWN	154

PART III RURAL SETTLEMENT AND BUILDINGS

12	Overview: the form and pattern of medieval settlement STEPHEN RIPPON, PIERS DIXON, AND BOB SILVESTER	171
13	Rural living 1100–1540 CHRISTOPHER DYER	193
14	Perceptions of medieval settlement MARK GARDINER AND SUSAN KILBY	210
15	Peasant houses RICHARD SUGGETT	226
16	The medieval manor house and the moated site JILL CAMPBELL	242
17	Agricultural buildings NIALL BRADY	259

PART IV LIVING IN TOWNS AND PORTS

18	Overview: living in medieval towns KEITH D. LILLEY	275
19	Urban housing JOHN SCHOFIELD	297
20	Medieval shops ABBY ANTROBUS	312
21	Town and countryside CHRISTOPHER DYER	325

22	Urban infrastructure Gareth Dean	340

PART V POWER AND DISPLAY

23	Overview: castles and elite landscapes Oliver H. Creighton	355
24	Medieval palaces and royal houses Tom Beaumont James	371
25	Royal and aristocratic landscapes of pleasure Stephen Mileson	386
26	Medieval battlefield archaeology Glenn Foard	401
27	Symbols of power David A. Hinton	418

PART VI CRAFTS, INDUSTRY, AND OBJECTS

28	Overview: medieval industry and commerce Maureen Mellor	435
29	Quarrying and extractive industries David Parsons	455
30	The medieval workshop David A. Hinton	475
31	Water and wind power Colin Rynne	491
32	Old money, new methods: coins and later medieval archaeology Richard Kelleher	511
33	Play and playfulness in late medieval Britain: theory, concept, practice Mark A. Hall	530

PART VII THE ARCHAEOLOGY OF RELIGION AND BELIEF

34 Overview: church and landscape c.1100–1550   545
    RICHARD MORRIS

35 The medieval monastery and its landscape   565
    JAMES BOND

36 The cathedral   581
    RICHARD FAWCETT

37 The medieval parish church: architecture, furnishings, and fittings   597
    RICHARD FAWCETT

38 Approaching medieval sacrality   614
    MARK A. HALL

39 Medieval graffiti inscriptions   626
    MATTHEW CHAMPION

40 An archaeology of pilgrimage   641
    PETER YEOMAN

41 The devotional image in late medieval England   658
    KATE GILES AND ALEKSANDRA MCCLAIN

PART VIII AN ARCHAEOLOGY OF THE SENSES

42 Overview: the medieval senses   681
    EMMA J. WELLS

43 Cooking, dining, and drinking   697
    HUGH WILLMOTT

44 Sound and landscape   713
    STEPHEN MILESON

45 London smellwalk around 1450: smelling medieval cities   728
    HOLLY DUGAN

46 Medieval colour   742
    Michael J. Huxtable and Ronan P. O'Donnell

PART IX GROWING UP AND GROWING OLD

47 Overview: archaeology and the medieval life course   759
    Rebecca L. Gowland and Bennjamin J. Penny-Mason

48 Birth and childhood   774
    Sally Crawford

49 Dressing the body   789
    Eleanor R. Standley

50 Gender and space in the later Middle Ages: past, present,
    and future routes   805
    Amanda Richardson

51 Health and well-being: the contribution of the study of human
    remains to understanding the late medieval period in Britain   819
    Charlotte A. Roberts, Jelena Bekvalac, and
    Rebecca Redfern

52 Medieval medicine, public health, and the medieval hospital   836
    Martin Huggon

53 Later medieval death and burial   856
    Christopher Daniell

54 The medieval afterlife   868
    Simon Roffey

PART X A WIDER CONTEXT: TRADE AND EXCHANGE, EUROPE AND BEYOND

55 Overview: trade and other contacts in late medieval Britain   887
    Alejandra Gutiérrez

56 Looking west: Ireland in the Middle Ages   909
    Terry B. Barry

57 Looking south-east: France in the Middle Ages 925
   Claire Hanusse

58 Looking north-east: Southern Scandinavia in the Middle Ages 941
   Else Roesdahl

59 Looking south: Spain and Portugal in the Middle Ages 964
   Christopher M. Gerrard and J. Avelino Gutiérrez-González

60 A last word: the study of later medieval archaeology 982
   Christopher M. Gerrard

Index 997

List of Figures

1.1	'A View of the Abbey Church at Llantony, from within the West Door', 1780, by Samuel Grimm	4
1.2	A trench dug at Bamburgh Castle in 2004 exposed a sand-filled post-medieval trench which paralleled the medieval foundations	6
1.3	Excavations at the medieval village of Faxton in 1967 by Lawrence Butler	9
1.4	Mick Aston (1946–2013), John Hurst (1927–2003), and Maurice Beresford (1920–2005) in 1989 at Wharram Percy	10
2.1	A hachured earthwork survey of Newhall Tower in Cheshire	26
2.2	A 3D LiDAR model of the deserted medieval village of Walburn, North Yorkshire	28
2.3	Magnetometry survey in practice below Corfe Castle, Dorset	29
2.4	Teampall na Trionaid ('Trinity church'), Carinish, North Uist in the Western Isles of Scotland	30
4.1	Conjectural reconstruction of the layout and principal features of Glastonbury Abbey's manor house at Shapwick, Somerset, in the later medieval period	57
4.2	The barn at Manor Farm, Kingston Deverill, Wiltshire, built c.1408	59
6.1	The region of two- or three-field systems	88
6.2	The distribution of field system types in East Anglia	89
6.3	The approximate boundary between Midland open fields and irregular field systems in the West Country	90
6.4	The village of Elsdon in the Northumberland uplands, showing the minimal extent of the former open fields	92
7.1	Burial pit for cattle, excavated at Shapwick, Somerset, where bones have been dated to AD 980–1160	107
7.2	Goat horn cores found during excavations at Perth	110
8.1	Excavations in the monastic kitchen at Durham Cathedral in 2014	121
10.1	Wild animal bones as recovered in excavations	143

10.2	A misericord from St Mary's, Enville, Staffordshire, representing bear baiting (fifteenth century)	149
11.1	The steps descending into St Nicholas's Church, New Romney, Kent, made necessary by sediments brought in by a storm surge in 1287/8	157
11.2	Schematic diagram showing the estimated spread of the fire at Glasgow Cathedral	158
11.3	A folded silver coin from the reign of Edward I or Edward II (1272–1327) from Flintshire, Wales	160
11.4	A fourteenth- to sixteenth-century lead *ampulla* from the Vale of Glamorgan, Wales	162
12.1	Test-pitting in the burh at Lyng, Somerset, as part of the community project Lost Islands of Somerset	173
12.2	The Priest's House, Muchelney, Somerset, a priest's lodging of the fourteenth century and later	174
12.3	A medieval turf building at Kiltyrie, on the slopes of Ben Lawers, Scotland	176
12.4	Example of a Welsh girdle settlement: Ty-uchaf in Llanwddyn	179
12.5	Medieval reclamation of land on the Gwent Levels	183
13.1	Croft F at Great Linford (Buckinghamshire)	194
13.2	Multi-phase peasant building at West Cotton (Northamptonshire)	195
13.3	Copper-alloy buckles and buckle plates from Tattenhoe and Westbury (Buckinghamshire)	203
13.4	House at Quoygrew, Orkney, *c.*1200	206
14.1	Scolland's Hall, Richmond Castle (North Yorkshire)	214
14.2	Tofts at Great Linford (Buckinghamshire), showing the brewhouses also used for the sale of ale set towards the street	217
15.1	Map showing the distribution of houses with crucks in England and Wales	227
15.2	An excavated stone-walled two-unit dwelling on St Tudwal's Island, Caernarvonshire, which retained unusually clearly the principal features of the hall	231
15.3	Recreation of the furnished home of Robert Dene of Stoneleigh, Warwickshire, based on his probate inventory (1552) and surviving three-bayed, cruck-framed house	233
15.4	Tyddyn Llwydion (Pennant Melangell, Montgomeryshire): cut-away of a cruck-framed upland hall-house/long-house	233
15.5	Tyddyn Llwydion: the building sequence of a late medieval hall-house on a new site	234
15.6	A peasant hall with dais canopy: Upper Hem, Forden, Montgomeryshire	236

LIST OF FIGURES

16.1	Oakham Castle, showing aisled hall and the two blocked up service doors	245
16.2	An idealized tripartite plan	246
16.3	Athelhampton, showing the oriel window at the high end of the hall	247
17.1	A large structure excavated by Worcestershire Archaeology north of St James' Church in Southam, Worcestershire, comparable with the major medieval barns of the Cotswold region	260
17.2	Swalcliffe Tithe Barn in Oxfordshire	264
17.3	Sandonbury, Hertfordshire, ground plan	267
17.4	General plan of Barton Farm, Bradford-on-Avon, Wiltshire	269
18.1	A plan-analysis of Coventry (Warwickshire) showing 'plan-units' that each represent, potentially, discrete stages of accretion in the medieval urban landscape	277
18.2	The layout of New Winchelsea (Sussex) at the time of its foundation (c.1283)	278
18.3	Using a Geographical Information System (GIS) to combine archaeological site plans and data with historic 1:2500-scale Ordnance Survey maps	282
18.4	The layout of later medieval Chester	286
18.5	The Gough Map of Great Britain (dated c.1360–1400)	287
18.6	The positions of settlements and places that are represented by the Gough Map	287
18.7	The hinterland of medieval Coventry, c.1450	292
19.1	A twelfth-century lane in the City of London	299
19.2	39 Strand Street, Sandwich, of the 1330s, partly reconstructed	303
19.3	Brook Street, Winchester, in the fourteenth century	304
19.4	Swan Lane, London: lead cames forming a pane or quarry from a window, with a fragment of blue glass, from a waterfront dump of 1270–1350	305
20.1	The restored early sixteenth-century shop adjacent to St Mary's Guildhall in Lavenham Market Place	313
20.2	A customer in a perfumer's shop, after a fifteenth-century illumination adorning John Lydgate's *The pilgrimage of the life of man*	314
21.1	A town plan: Bewdley in Worcestershire	327
21.2	A town house: a three-storey corner shop at Ludlow	328
21.3	A hinterland: Stratford-upon-Avon	330
21.4	Stone mortars from King's Lynn	333
22.1	Old Ouse Bridge in York packed with buildings, including St William's chapel	347

23.1	Hen Domen: excavations within the bailey	359
23.2	Norwich Castle, showing the positioning of the Norman castle within the Anglo-Saxon townscape	360
23.3	Wallingford: castle kitchens under excavation in 1972	362
23.4	Chepstow Castle: the Great Tower	364
23.5	The King's Knot, Stirling	367
24.1	Lyddington Bede House in Leicestershire, part of a medieval bishop's palace	372
24.2	A map of royal palaces during the Middle Ages	374
24.3	Westminster palace and abbey, as depicted by Wenceslaus Hollar in 1647	379
24.4	A reconstruction of the thirteenth-century palace floor from the king's apartments at Clarendon Palace, Wiltshire	381
25.1	The great royal park of Clarendon (Wiltshire) with its palace, inner park, multiple compartments, and several gates	389
25.2	The distribution of woodland and parks in medieval England	390
25.3	The park at Willey (Shropshire), first documented in the late thirteenth century	392
25.4	Kennington Palace in Surrey	395
26.1	Map of all medieval battles	403
26.2	Graph of battles in Britain by half century	404
26.3	The distribution of artefacts and mass graves on Towton battlefield, set against the historic terrain	407
26.4	Distribution of battle archaeology on Bosworth battlefield	409
26.5	A lead-iron composite round shot of $c.39$ mm diameter with an area of lead lost	412
27.1	Harold's coronation depicted on the Bayeux Tapestry	420
27.2	Gilt copper-alloy badge from London, fourteenth–fifteenth centuries, depicting a standing boar on a twisted rope	422
27.3	The Pusey horn as recorded in the eighteenth century for *Archaeologia*	424
27.4	Effigy of Brian Fitzalan, Lord of Bedale, in St Gregory's church, Bedale, North Yorkshire, early fourteenth century	426
28.1	The leat tunnel in Shillamill Wood, near Tavistock, Devon	437
28.2	Quarry for steatite, or soapstone, at Catpund near Cunningsburgh in Shetland, Scotland	440
28.3	Silver matrix seal of the city of Exeter with the craftman's signature LUCAS ME FECIT, $c.1200$–1208	442

28.4	Bulkington, Wiltshire, tiny hamlet drawing on pottery from a variety of production centres in the medieval period	445
28.5	Dragon Hall, Norwich, a warehouse built by Robert Toppe, a mercer and sheriff of Norwich 1430	447
29.1	Selected English sites using Caen stone	459
29.2	Metal-working sites on Exmoor	461
29.3	The Bere Ferrers silver/lead extraction sites	462
29.4	Leicestershire coalfield: aerial photograph showing landscape features	466
29.5	Leicestershire coalfield: reconstruction diagram of mineshaft and pillar-and-stall workings	467
30.1	Excavations at 17, Redcliff Street, Bristol, revealed the remains of a hearth of fourteenth century date with a pitched stone base and a stoking chamber	480
30.2	Recent finds of twelfth-century antler carving found during excavation in Northampton	483
31.1	Reconstruction of horizontal-wheeled watermill at Cloontycarthy, Co. Cork, Ireland	492
31.2	Reconstruction of fourteenth-century undershot watermill at Patrick Street, Dublin, Ireland	494
31.3	Undershot waterwheel paddle floats	495
31.4	Ground plans of later medieval watermills	498
31.5	Mill-pond drain at Bordesley Abbey, dendro-dated to AD 1227	499
31.6	Machinery from later medieval watermills	500
31.7	Reconstruction of the later medieval post windmill at Great Linford, Buckinghamshire	504
31.8	A suggested evolution of English windmill foundations	505
32.1	A range of medieval coins found in Britain	514
32.2	Periodization scheme for analysing medieval coins 1066–1544	516
32.3	Finds of medieval coin hoards (1066–1544) made in England and Wales per decade	518
32.4	PAS single find evidence from England and Wales to 2008	521
32.5	Map illustrating the sources of non-English coins found in England and Wales	522
33.1	One of the Nine Men's Morris boards, with playing piece, from Nevern Castle, Wales	532
33.2	A selection of medieval dice from the Perth High Street excavations, Perth, Scotland	534

33.3	The tomb of St Osmund, Salisbury Cathedral, Wiltshire, with detail of one of the gaming boards (for alquerque)	536
35.1	The gatehouse of Cleeve Abbey, Somerset: elevation drawing with building phases interpreted	566
35.2	The water-powered iron mill within the precinct of the Cistercian abbey of Bordesley, Worcestershire	568
36.1	Some English cathedral plans	583
36.2	Durham Cathedral, nave interior built between 1093 and 1133	587
36.3	Nave of Salisbury Cathedral	588
36.4	Glasgow Cathedral during excavation	592
37.1	Parish church plans	599
37.2	Moulding profiles attributable to a single master mason	601
37.3	Examples of window designs found in parish churches	603
37.4	Fotheringhay Church, Northamptonshire, an example of the 'Perpendicular' style	604
37.5	St Mary, Happisburgh, Norfolk. Octagonal baptismal font of the fifteenth century	609
37.6	The footings of the twelfth-century apse at Pennant Melangell, Montgomeryshire	611
37.7	St Mary, North Shoebury in Essex	611
38.1	The holy well or healing spring and chapel of St Gwenfrewi (Winefride) at Holywell, Flintshire, Wales	618
38.2	A Rogationtide procession in the conceptualized city of Constantinople as depicted in the Luttrell Psalter *c.* 1320–40	621
39.1	Lidgate, Suffolk. Latin inscription that translates as 'John Lidgate made this, with licence, on the feast of Saints Simon and Jude', dated on stylistics grounds to *c.*1400–*c.*1550	627
39.2	Inscriptions, including late medieval text, from the church of St Mary, Troston, Suffolk	631
39.3	Pelta design in the nave of St John's church, Duxford, Cambridgeshire	633
39.4	Elaborate compass-drawn design in St Mary's church, Lidgate, Suffolk	634
39.5	Incised late medieval North Sea cog at St Margaret's church, Cley-next-the-Sea, Norfolk	636
40.1	Lincoln Cathedral carving of a pilgrim *c.*1400	642
40.2	Artist's reconstruction of the church, hostel, and harbour for pilgrims en route to St Andrews across the Firth of Forth	644

40.3	Reconstruction drawing of St Mary's Hospital, Ospringe, Kent, in its developed form *c.*1250	645
40.4	Fragment of mould for casting Walsingham Annunciation badges and a mould-match badge from the Thames foreshore in London	650
40.5	Late twelfth-century burial of male leper pilgrim with scallop shell at his hip, St Mary Magdalen's Hospital, Winchester	652
40.6	Burial of young man *c.*1300 from St Ethernan's Priory, May Island, Fife, with a Compostela shell inserted into his wedged-open mouth soon after death	653
40.7	The Worcester Cathedral pilgrim, as excavated and reconstructed	654
41.1	Three-dimensional digital model of the guild chapel at Stratford-upon-Avon	661
41.2	The Corporal Works of Mercy window, All Saints North Street, York, early fifteenth century	662
41.3	The cadaver tomb of Archbishop Henry Chichele, Canterbury Cathedral, *c.*1425	666
41.4	The Middleham Jewel, fifteenth century, featuring an engraving of the Trinity, inset sapphire, and inscription	667
41.5	Christ enthroned and holding the Crucifixion, with patrons depicted praying below. Folio 33 recto from the Bolton Book of Hours, early fifteenth century	669
41.6	St Mary's guild chapel, St Botolph's, Boston, Lincolnshire	671
42.1	Star pattern made by the vault cross-ribs above the feretory in which St Cuthbert's shrine was housed, Durham Cathedral	682
42.2	Prayer niches of the shrine of St Werburgh, Chester Cathedral	684
42.3	Part of a pilgrim sign, possibly a badge, made of pewter and showing a man swinging a censer for burning incense, fourteenth to fifteenth centuries	687
42.4	The rood screen at Binham Priory, Norfolk, showing sixteenth-century whitewash and text over the fifteenth-century figural depictions	688
43.1	Ceramic cooking jars from Deansway, Worcester; copper-alloy skillet and flesh hook from Pottergate, Norwich; skimmer from London	700
43.2	Wooden dishes from St Mary Spital, London; wooden bowl from High Street, Southampton; pewter saucers from Southampton and Leicester Austin Friars; pewter spoon from Barentin's Manor, Oxfordshire	703

43.3	Glass jug from Southampton; ceramic 'face jug' from Hallgate, Doncaster; leather 'black jack' from Watling Street, London; glass goblet from High Street, Southampton; glass beaker from Southampton; ceramic drinking jug from Woolwich; pewter tankard from Tonbridge Castle, Kent	706
44.1	A small copper-alloy bell of the kind used as a dress accessory, found in Lewknor (Oxfordshire)	716
44.2	The heavily restored Norman font at Belton church (Lincolnshire), showing a bell-ringer in action	718
44.3	Ewelme hundred in south Oxfordshire, based on nineteenth-century maps	721
44.4	Selected bell soundmarks in Ewelme hundred	722
44.5	Dorchester Abbey's tenor bell of $c.1380$, weight 843 kg	724
45.1	Urban smell wheel	729
45.2	Civic smell perceptions	736
45.3	Smell perceptions	737
45.4	Positive civic smells	738
45.5	Negative civic smells	738
46.1	Wall painting in All Saints and St Andrews Church, Kingston, Cambridgeshire	746
46.2	Traces of white paint at Fountains Abbey, North Yorkshire	747
46.3	A striking pottery vessel made in the fifteenth century in the Valencia area, Spain, decorated with gold and blue colours	752
47.1	Defining chronological, biological, and social age, in relation to medieval language commonly used to describe those under the age of 21 years old	764
48.1	Copy of the brass of the infant Nicholas Wadham (dated 1508), St Peter's Church, Ilton, Somerset	777
48.2	The deserted medieval village of Widford, Oxfordshire	782
48.3	Finger-pinched decoration on a sherd of medieval pottery	785
49.1	The right-hand hawking glove believed to have belonged to Henry VIII	792
49.2	Hair-covering of embroidered silk net with braid edging dated to $c.1300$, excavated from Rig VI, High Street, Perth	793
49.3	Gold, amethyst, and enamel reliquary ring from the hoard found near Thame, $c.1350–1400$	794
49.4	Gold seal ring set with a reused sapphire intaglio carved with the veiled head of a woman	796
49.5	*AVE MARIA* inscribed buckle plates	798

49.6	Copper-alloy buckle of gaping-mouth beast type	799
50.1	The Templar preceptory at South Witham in Lincolnshire as reconstructed after excavation by Philip Mayes in 1965–7	809
51.1	A late medieval skeleton in a grave prior to excavation: Hull Magistrates Court site	820
51.2	Stature trends over the four phases of burials at the site of the hospital and priory of St Mary Spital	824
51.3	Stable isotope plot showing mobility histories of skeletons with evidence of treponemal disease buried at the site of Hull Magistrates Court	828
52.1	Lead sheet wrapped around the right shin of a 26–35 year old female, Sk 7186 (*c*.1250–*c*.1400), and a copper-alloy plate found between the knees of skeleton 12441, a 36–45-year-old male (*c*.1120–*c*.1200), both from St Mary Spital, London	839
52.2	The Black Death cemetery at East Smithfield	842
52.3	An example of rhino-maxillary syndrome seen on Sk 48 from St Mary Magdalen, Winchester	844
52.4	St Mary Magdalen chapel in Ripon, North Yorkshire, built in the first half of the twelfth century	845
52.5	Plan of St Mary Spital, London, showing the known layout of the site at the time of the Dissolution	848
54.1	Doom painting, North Leigh Church, Oxfordshire	869
54.2	Medieval wall painting from South Leigh Church, Oxfordshire, showing the Virgin Mary and St Michael weighing a soul	871
54.3	The Markham Chapel, Newark Church, Nottinghamshire	873
54.4	The elaborately decorated porch and chantry chapel of John Greenway (*c*.1517), Tiverton, Devon	874
54.5	Chantry chapels of Bishop William Wayneflete, Winchester Cathedral (late fifteenth century) and Sir Edward Despenser, Tewkesbury Abbey (late fourteenth century)	875
54.6	Reconstructed pre-Reformation view-sheds at Stoke Charity Parish church, Hampshire, and Holy Trinity Bradford-on-Avon, Wiltshire	879
55.1	Main places mentioned in the text and sea routes around Great Britain in the medieval period	888
55.2	Main places and sea routes around Europe in the medieval period	890
55.3	Some of the main medieval trading routes, links, and places mentioned in the text beyond the Mediterranean	892

55.4	A range of imported items found in British contexts	896
56.1	Aerial photograph of an early medieval ringwork castle at Danesfort, Co. Kilkenny	910
56.2	Trim Castle, Co. Meath	912
56.3	Plan of the deserted medieval village of Piperstown, Co. Louth	917
56.4	Earthworks of the Pale at Kilteel, Co. Kildare	921
57.1	Frequency of large fish groups and their distance to shore in north-west of France in the fourteenth and fifteenth centuries	928
57.2	The east tower of a urban fortification at Talmont, Vendée, France	931
57.3	A leper's grave at Saint-Thomas d'Aizier, Eure, France	934
58.1	Denmark and part of Norway and Sweden with main place-names mentioned in the text	942
58.2	North portal of Lime church, northern Jutland, Denmark, c.1100	952
58.3	Part of a 'dancing girl' jug from Ragnhildsholmen Castle in south-western Sweden, c.1250–1310; and an English jug of Grimston Ware, found in Ribe, thirteenth to fourteenth century	954
58.4	Reconstruction of the crown of Philippa of England	956
59.1	Main medieval routes to Santiago de Compostela and places mentioned in the text	965
59.2	Staff or *bordón* fragments found during excavations in Oviedo, and Compostela pilgrims as depicted in the *Book of Trades* of 1568	967
59.3	Ironworks excavated at Bagoeta, Álava (seventh to fourteenth centuries)	969
59.4	A fifteenth-century sugar factory under excavation in Agaete, Las Palmas de Gran Canaria	970
59.5	Alabaster figures from an altarpiece made in England c.1440–60 and originally installed at the church of Campo del Tablado, Castropol, Asturias	973

List of Contributors

Abby Antrobus, Suffolk County Council Archaeological Service, is a senior local government archaeologist. Her PhD thesis, *Urbanisation and the urban landscape: building medieval Bury St Edmunds* (University of Durham, 2009), combined archaeological, historical, landscape, and architectural evidence to explore how, why, and by whose agency one pilgrimage centre developed, within the context of the phenomenon of rapid urban growth in twelfth-century Europe. She particularly specializes in the management of the archaeological resource of Suffolk's towns—from the major port of Ipswich to small market centres—advising on the impacts of development, approaches in the field, research frameworks, and approaches to development management and heritage promotion.

Grenville Astill is professor in the Department of Archaeology at Reading University. He is a specialist in the archaeology of the medieval countryside and landscape, monasticism, and industry. He is a director of the Bordesley Abbey Project.

James H. Barrett is a medieval archaeologist with a background in the analysis of fish bones from archaeological sites and an interest in the intersection of economic and environmental history. He studied at the Universities of Toronto, Sheffield, and Glasgow. He taught at the University of York before moving to the University of Cambridge, where he is now a Reader in Medieval Archaeology. James has worked in both the field and the laboratory, publishing widely across the spectrum of the humanities and sciences. He has directed a variety of interdisciplinary research projects, including The Medieval Origins of Commercial Sea Fishing, funded by the Leverhulme Trust.

Terry B. Barry is Emeritus Fellow of Trinity College, Dublin, where he specialized in teaching medieval archaeology. His research interests centre on the settlement archaeology of Ireland, Britain, and Western Europe in the Middle Ages, particularly its castles and defensive earthworks. He is the author of many articles and books, including The *Archaeology of medieval Ireland* (2004), and in 2000 he edited *A history of settlement in Ireland*, also for Routledge.

Jelena Bekvalac is Curator of Human Osteology, Centre for Human Bioarchaeology, Museum of London. Her main research interests are: bioarchaeological studies; health and disease patterns in the medieval and post-medieval periods, particular focus on London collections; biographical and documentary source research with post-medieval collections, with particular reference to St Bride's, London; application of digital radiography investigating patterns of disease and impact of industrialization on health. She is currently Acting Chair of the Subject Specialist Network Human Remains group.

James Bond is a freelance landscape archaeologist dedicated to the study of the historic landscape, with special interest on monasteries. He has written extensively on the subject, including the book *Monastic landscapes* (2004).

Niall Brady has a specialist interest in medieval agrarian technology and has studied medieval ploughing in Ireland and medieval barns across southern England. He has been project director for the Discovery Programme's (Ireland), Medieval Rural Settlement Project (2002–10) and is working on the publication of two monographs arising from excavation and fieldwork on that project. Niall is founding director of The Archaeological Diving Company Ltd, Ireland's leading maritime archaeological consultancy.

Peter J. Brown is currently studying for a PhD at Durham University, UK. His research considers the archaeological and historical evidence for natural disasters during the later medieval period, primarily in the British Isles. He is particularly interested in how society was impacted by catastrophic events, what measures were taken to mitigate damage and provide protection from future recurrence as well as the different ways in which these events were perceived and commemorated. He has published and contributed to conferences on a number of related topics and themes.

Jill Campbell is a post-doctoral researcher at Queen's University Belfast. A buildings archaeologist, she is interested in houses from the late and post-medieval periods across the United Kingdom.

Matthew Champion is a freelance archaeological consultant, specializing in early graffiti inscriptions and aspects of medieval faith and belief. As well as being Project Director of the Norfolk and Suffolk Medieval Graffiti Surveys, he acts as an advisor and consultant to a number of national organizations including the National Trust and Churches Conservation Trust. His other research interests include medieval church wall paintings and medieval architectural construction techniques. He is also a Fellow of the Society of Antiquaries of London.

Sally Crawford is based at the University of Oxford. She writes and researches on archaeology, including childhood in the early medieval period. She is a founder member of the *Society for the Study of Childhood in the Past*, and is general editor of its Monograph Series, as well as being its current President. Author of many articles on early medieval childhood, burial ritual, disease, and disability, she is a regular contributor to the international journal *Childhood in the Past*. Books on the early medieval period include *Childhood in Anglo-Saxon England* (Sutton Press), *Daily life in Anglo-Saxon England* (Greenwood Press), and *Early medieval England* (Shire). She is co-editor of *Children, childhood and society* (Archaeopress), *Oxford University Press handbook of Anglo-Saxon archaeology* (OUP), and *Oxford University Press handbook of the archaeology of childhood* (OUP).

Professor **Oliver H. Creighton**'s research interests focus on medieval buildings, landscapes and townscapes in Britain and Europe. His work has a strong interdisciplinary dimension and he has particular interests in the study of medieval castles in their wider settings; in elite landscapes; in urban archaeology and town defences; and in archaeological heritage management. His books include *Castles and landscapes: power, community and fortification in medieval England* (2002 and 2005), *Designs upon the land: elite landscapes of the Middle Ages* (2009), *Early European castles: aristocracy and authority, AD 800–1200* (2012), (with Robert Higham) *Medieval town walls: an archaeology and social history of urban defence* (2005), and (with Neil Christie et al.) *Transforming townscapes. From burh to borough: the archaeology of Wallingford, AD 800–1400* (2013).

Christopher Daniell has written extensively about medieval death and burial practices, including *Death and burial in the Middle Ages 1066–1550*. He worked for many years for York Archaeological Trust as an archaeologist and historian and was a Visiting Research Fellow with the Centre for Medieval Studies in York. He now works for the Ministry of Defence as the Senior Historic Building Advisor. His primary research interests are in death and burial practices, and modern and historic graffiti.

Gareth Dean is an interdisciplinary scholar and researcher, drawing on approaches developed in archaeology, historical geography, and history. His research focuses on the integration of information from different sources, ranging from objects to tenements and their relationship to the wider urban landscape, and how this facilitates understanding of the development and character of medieval urban space. He has published on medieval York, GIS and the analysis of archaeological, historical, and cartographic data, the social uses of the street and the urban environment, and approaches to mapping medieval cities. He is a research fellow of the Universities of York and Nottingham.

Piers Dixon is an Operations Manager in Survey and Recording at Historic Environment Scotland, formerly RCAHMS. A committee member of Ruralia (an international association for the archaeology of medieval settlement and rural life) his interests include rural settlement, castles, monasteries, and landscape. His publications include *Excavations in the fishing town of Eyemouth* (1986), *Excavations at Jedburgh Friary* (2000), *Puir labourers and busy husbandmen* (2002), *But the walls remain'd* (2002), 'The medieval landscape' in RCAHMS, *In the shadow of Bennachie* (2007), editor of *Buildings of the land* (2008), and co-author of *A history of Scotland's landscapes* (forthcoming 2017).

Simon A. Draper is Assistant Editor for the Victoria County History in Oxfordshire and Editor of *Transactions of the Bristol and Gloucestershire Archaeological Society*. He read archaeology at Durham University and completed a doctorate there published in 2006 as *Landscape, settlement and society in Roman and early medieval Wiltshire* (British Archaeological Reports British Series 419). He is particularly interested in the relationship between place-names and landscape archaeology and has published a number of articles on the subject. He is also a tutor at Cambridge University's Institute of Continuing Education.

Holly Dugan is an Associate Professor of English at the George Washington University, in Washington, DC. She is the author of *The ephemeral history of perfume: scent and sense in Early Modern England*, co-editor (with Lara Farina) of 'Intimate senses', a special issue of *Postmedieval: a journal of medieval culture studies*, and author of numerous articles on the history of olfaction.

Christopher Dyer is Emeritus Professor of History at the University of Leicester, and has recently held fellowships at the University of Birmingham and the Institute of Historical Research. He has served as President of the Society for Medieval Archaeology. His best-known work has been on living standards, but he has researched the history and archaeology of villages and towns, and has pursued studies in landscape history and material culture.

Richard Fawcett who is an Emeritus Professor of the School of Art History at the University of St Andrews, spent much of his previous career in the Ancient Monuments Inspectorate of Historic Scotland. He is a Fellow of the Royal Society of Edinburgh and of the Societies of Antiquaries of London and Scotland, and was appointed OBE in 2008. His main research interests are in the field of medieval architecture, on which he has published extensively, including an award-winning survey of Scottish church architecture.

Glenn Foard is Reader in Battlefield Archaeology at the University of Huddersfield. He has researched and written extensively on battles and sieges in Britain and Flanders. Particular interests include reconstruction of historic landscape to explore the interaction of terrain and action, the use of metal detectors to recover artefact scatters, and the analysis of lead projectiles from early gunpowder weapons. Major projects completed include studies of Naseby, Edgehill, Bosworth, and Oudenaarde, and a resource assessment of battlefields in England. His current research is on the battles of the Wars of the Roses and a survey of Barnet battlefield.

Michael Fradley is a Research Assistant on the Endangered Archaeology in the Middle East and North Africa (EAMENA) Project at the University of Oxford, exploring the heritage of the region through the use of satellite imagery. He has worked in commercial archaeology in the UK and as a landscape surveyor for English Heritage (now Historic England), and has worked on research projects in Europe, Africa, South America, and the Middle East. As a landscape archaeologist, Michael's interests include medieval landscapes, survey methods, applied archaeology, and the history of water management.

Mark Gardiner is a Senior Lecturer at Queen's University Belfast and has worked widely on the medieval landscapes of Britain and Ireland, examining marshlands, woodlands and uplands, and more generally on aspects of society and settlement. His more recent studies have considered the role of transhumance as a means of transforming the countryside. In other work, he has examined the way in which the interior space was organized and imagined in the late medieval house, the subject of a book in progress.

Christopher M. Gerrard is Professor of Medieval Archaeology at Durham University. His eight books include *Medieval Archaeology: understanding traditions and* *contemporary approaches* (2003) and *Interpreting the English village: landscape and community at Shapwick, Somerset* which won the Best Archaeological Book of the Year award in 2014. His fieldwork includes excavations in Spain and the Azores and projects on qanats, natural disasters in the Middle Ages, and, most recently, the discovery of mass graves of seventeenth-century Scottish soldiers under one of Durham University's libraries.

Louisa Gidney is a freelance faunal remains specialist. Her research interests are practical livestock husbandry in relation to the interpretation of archaeological data; dwarfism in cattle and sheep, especially chondrodysplasia in Dexter cattle and the Ancon sheep mutation; polycerate sheep, particularly Manx Loaghtan and Hebridean; skeletal anatomy of modern primitive cattle and sheep breeds.

Kate Giles is a Senior Lecturer in Buildings Archaeology at the University of York. She specializes in the study of pre-modern 'public buildings' including guildhalls and churches and has undertaken major projects on guildhalls in York, Boston (Lincolnshire), and Stratford-upon-Avon (Warwickshire). Her wider research interests include transition and periodization, antiquarianism and the historiography of recording, documenting and interpreting late medieval wall paintings. She is Deputy Director of the Humanities Research Centre at the University of York.

Rebecca L. Gowland (Department of Archaeology, Durham University) is a senior lecturer in human bioarchaeology, whose research focuses on the analysis of evidence for social identity and body/society interactions from the human skeleton, with a particular emphasis on the life course and health. She has co-authored *Human identity and Identification* (CUP) and co-edited the *Social Archaeology of Funerary Remains* (Oxbow).

C. P. Graves is Senior Lecturer in the Department of Archaeology, Durham University. Her research interests are urban archaeology and the development of a mercantile culture in Northern Europe, religious practice and architecture in both the medieval and post-medieval periods; medieval window glass; and archaeological theory, especially the analysis of ritual.

Alejandra Gutiérrez is a Research Fellow at Durham University. Her interests lie in the study of medieval and later material culture, particularly the movement of goods, trade, and exchange, and European contact with Britain in the Middle Ages. She writes about ceramics and other archaeological finds and has authored numerous articles on the subject, including a book, *Mediterranean pottery in Wessex households*, and an accompanying web-guide for the identification of medieval and later Spanish pottery (www.dur.ac.uk/spanish.pottery).

J. Avelino Gutiérrez-González is Professor of Medieval Archaeology at Oviedo University. He is a specialist on medieval settlement, landscape, and material culture from northern Spain. He has published extensively on these subjects and is currently the director of the Research Group 'ARQUEOS: Ancient and Medieval Archaeology: Territory, Society and Material Culture'.

Mark A. Hall is an archaeologist, medievalist, and museum curator based at Perth Museum and Art Gallery, Perth and Kinross, Scotland, and currently on secondment in the Outer Hebrides working on the Udal Project for Comhairle nan Eilean Siar. He has long-standing research interests in the archaeology of board games and play, the cult of saints, Pictish sculpture, cultural biography, and cinematic re-imaginings of the past, of archaeology, and of museums.

Claire Hanusse is Maître de conférences en histoire et archéologie du Moyen Âge, Centre de recherches archéologiques et historiques anciennes et médiévales, Université de Caen Normandie, France. Her research is based on the study of villages and pattern of habitats, together with material culture and medieval Normandy, where she is currently excavating with students.

David A. Hinton is an Emeritus Professor of Archaeology at the University of Southampton. He was co-editor of the companion volume in this series, *The Oxford handbook of Anglo-Saxon archaeology* (2011).

Martin Huggon is currently completing his PhD at the University of Sheffield, and is Associate Tutor in Archaeology and Heritage at Bishop Grosseteste University, Lincoln. His thesis examines the archaeology of medieval hospitals in England and Wales between the years 1066 and 1546. This work is mainly focusing on architecture and material culture from a range of sites, but is also attempting to include a wide range of evidence that includes zooarchaeological remains, cemetery studies, and geographical distribution. His research interests include medieval hospitals and almshouses, medieval medicine, and the interconnection of spirituality, diet, and physical activity to health, and the archaeology of the Military Orders, especially in regard to the provision of hospitality to pilgrims.

Michael J. Huxtable is Lecturer in Medieval Literature in the Department of English Studies at Durham University. He is a member of Durham's Institute of Medieval and Early Modern Studies and Ordered Universe Research Project. He has written on medieval natural philosophy, theology, and the history of ideas concerning visual culture. He is currently researching medieval heraldic writing and its influences and influence upon other genres and types of discourse from the thirteenth to mid-fifteenth century.

Tom Beaumont James is Professor Emeritus in Archaeology and History at Winchester University. His main areas of interest are medieval buildings, especially medieval palaces, and also the Black Death of 1348–50, having written books on Clarendon Park, Wiltshire, and Winchester, among others.

Richard Kelleher is Assistant Keeper in the Department of Coins and Medals at the Fitzwilliam Museum, Cambridge. He specializes in the coinage of medieval and early modern Europe, particularly that of Britain and the Latin East. His research interests include the role of coins in archaeology, the use of metal-detector finds for mapping monetization and coin use, the secondary use of coins, and the coinage of the Crusader

States of Edessa and Antioch. He is the author of *A history of coinage in medieval England*, winner of the Royal Numismatic Society's Lhotka Prize.

Susan Kilby is a Research Associate at the Centre for English Local History, University of Leicester, and is currently involved in the Leverhulme Trust funded project, 'Flood and Flow: Place-Names and the Changing Hydrology of River-Systems'. Her main interests lie in the complexities of medieval relationships with local landscape, with a particular focus on the lower orders. This ranges from economic interests through to more culturally informed ideas, including conceptual notions of the landscape, the survival of cultural memory, and the landscape as a repository for local cultural capital.

Keith D. Lilley is Professor of Historical Geography at Queen's University Belfast. He specializes in the mapping and analysis of medieval urban landscapes, with interests in town-planning and urban morphology. His books include *Urban life in the Middle Ages* (Palgrave, 2002), *City and cosmos: the medieval world in urban form* (Reaktion, 2009), and *Mapping medieval geographies* (Cambridge, 2013). He has pioneered the use of Geographical Information Systems (GIS) in the study of medieval urban landscapes and led the creation of online resources to map medieval towns and cities, such as Chester and Swansea. He is currently Chair of the Historic Towns Trust.

Aleksandra McClain is a Senior Lecturer in Medieval Archaeology at the University of York. She specializes in the study of churches, commemoration, and the Anglo-Norman period in England and northern Europe. Her wider research interests include transition periods and cultural contact, social, cultural, and spatial identities, the material expression of religious and secular authority, and the patronage of ecclesiastical material culture. She sits on the committees of the Society for Church Archaeology and the Society for Medieval Archaeology, and is currently deputy editor of *Medieval Archaeology*.

Maureen Mellor is an archaeologist with a special interest in the material culture of interiors and in medieval diet. She has over thirty years professional experience working with the products of English and European clay industries in field archaeology and in museums. She teaches and lectures at the University of Oxford's Department for Continuing Education and is currently researching an image-conscious medieval queen and medieval food and foodways, the latter in collaboration with the Department of Archaeology and Anthropology, University of Bristol. She acts as Reader for Historic England on relevant medieval projects. She is also a Fellow of the Society of Antiquaries, London.

Stephen Mileson is a social historian specializing in the interdisciplinary study of the medieval landscape. He is author of *Parks in medieval England* (OUP, 2009) and, with Stuart Brookes, of a forthcoming book about peasant perceptions of the material environment, based on research funded by the Leverhulme Trust. He works for the Oxfordshire Victoria County History and is a Research Fellow in the Centre for Medieval History at the University of Oxford.

Lisa Moffett is Regional Advisor for Archaeological Science, Historic England. She is a specialist on botanical remains from the medieval period, and has written extensively on the subject, especially on the archaeology of food.

Richard Morris is Professor at Huddesfield University. He has written extensively on the archaeological study of churches and buildings, and on the historical geography of parish churches. In recent years he is investigating approaches to the archaeology of medieval and early modern battles. He has also has worked as an historical biographer, and on themes relating to aviation and warfare.

Ronan P. O'Donnell is an archaeologist specializing in theoretical approaches, notably Non-Representational and Actor-Network Theories, to the medieval and post-medieval periods, particularly to landscapes. His recent work has included investigations of enclosure in North-East England, and the development of open-field agriculture in Midland England.

David Parsons is Emeritus Reader in Church Archaeology in the University of Leicester. His principal research site is All Saints' Church, Brixworth, Northamptonshire, where the survey of the standing fabric revealed some forty different building stone types. The analysis of these by geologist Dr Diana Sutherland coupled with enquiries into the stone sources has led to a general reappraisal of the building stone industry in the Anglo-Saxon—and by extension the later medieval periods. He now lives in Sussex, where the historic extraction of both iron and salt has intensified his interest in medieval industries.

Bennjamin J. Penny-Mason (Department of Archaeology, Durham University) is currently a PhD student, researching non-adult bioarchaeology, the history of paediatric medicine and medieval childhood.

Aleks Pluskowski is Associate Professor in Medieval Archaeology at the University of Reading. He completed his PhD at the Department of Archaeology in the University of Cambridge on a comparison of diachronic responses to the wolf in medieval Britain and Scandinavia, subsequently published as *Wolves and the wilderness in the Middle Ages* (Boydell, 2006). In 2010–14 he directed the Ecology of Crusading Project, which investigated the environmental impact of crusading, colonization and religious transformation in the medieval eastern Baltic. He continues to work on the relationship between ecological and cultural dynamics in medieval frontier societies, particularly associated with crusading and multiculturalism.

Rebecca Redfern is Curator of Human Osteology, Centre for Human Bioarchaeology, Museum of London, and Honorary Research Fellow at Durham University. Her research interests are: bioarchaeology, history of medicine, biomolecular analyses of population mobility and diet.

Amanda Richardson is senior lecturer in late medieval history at the University of Chichester and a Fellow of the Society of Antiquaries. She has worked on social space and gender in late medieval England and has written extensively on medieval forests and deer parks, which she has explored as gendered spaces. Her most recent research includes the 'post-history' of deer parks, especially their role as signifiers of early modern English national identity. She plans in the future to combine her main research interests by researching the estates of thirteenth- and fourteenth-century queens consort of England.

Stephen Rippon is Professor of Landscape Archaeology at the University of Exeter (UK), and a past President of the Medieval Settlement Research Group. His interests include wetland landscapes, regional variation in landscape character, and the Roman-medieval transition. His books include *The Gwent levels* (1996), *The transformation of coastal wetlands* (2000), *Historic landscape analysis* (2004; 2012), *Beyond the medieval village* (2008; 2014), *Making sense of an historic landscape* (2012), and *The fields of Britannia* (2015).

Professor **Charlotte A. Roberts** Department of Archaeology, Durham University, is a Fellow of the Wolfson Research Institute for Health and Wellbeing. Her research interests are: Bioarchaeological approaches to the history of disease and medicine worldwide and any period, especially infectious disease; the application of biomolecular techniques to answer archaeological questions; application of evolutionary medicine, medical geography and anthropology to palaeopathology. She is President of the British Association of Biological Anthropology and Osteoarchaeology.

Else Roesdahl is Professor (emerita) of Medieval Archaeology at Aarhus University, Denmark. She is also Honorary doctor at Trinity College Dublin and the University of York. Her research interests include Viking-Age Trelleborg-type fortresses and their context; conversion and cultural change; Scandinavia's international relations; artefact studies; housing culture; and the economic importance of walrus ivory. She has also written, edited, and organized synthetic books, including handbooks, and has been involved in major international exhibitions and their catalogues.

Simon Roffey is Reader in Medieval Archaeology at the University of Winchester. His research interests include the archaeology of the medieval church, religion and ritual, and medieval leprosy hospitals. He has conducted archaeological research on a number of ecclesiastical sites, more recently being the Co-Director of excavations at the medieval hospital of St Mary Magdalen, Winchester. He has written numerous articles, as well as two books, on the subject of the archaeology of the medieval afterlife and chantry chapels. Dr Roffey is a Fellow of the Society of Antiquaries, London, and the Royal Historical Society.

Colin Rynne is a senior lecturer in the Department of Archaeology, University College Cork, Ireland. He is the author of several books on the industrial archaeology of Ireland and has published widely on the archaeology of water power in early medieval Ireland and Europe.

John Schofield was an archaeologist at the Museum of London from 1974 to 2008. He has written several books about medieval buildings and urban archaeology, including *The building of London from the Conquest to the Great Fire* (3rd ed, 1999), *Medieval London houses* (rev. edn, 2003), *St Paul's Cathedral before Wren* (2011), *London 1100–1600: the archaeology of a capital city* (2011) and with Alan Vince, *Medieval towns* (rev edn, 2005). His interests include the form of London from 1100 to 1700, and St Paul's Cathedral, where he is Cathedral Archaeologist.

Bob Silvester was until his recent retirement the Deputy Director of the Clwyd-Powys Archaeological Trust. He is the current President of the Medieval Settlement Research Group and his other interests include historic landscapes of the Welsh borderlands, church archaeology, and seventeenth- and eighteenth-century estate mapping. His publications include two volumes on the Fenland Project in Norfolk (1988 and 1991), the co-editorship of *Life in medieval landscapes: people and places in the Middle Ages* (2012), and of *Reflections on the past* (2012), and a long sequence of articles on a wide range of subjects that commenced in 1976.

Eleanor R. Standley is Associate Professor of later medieval archaeology in the School of Archaeology, and Assistant Keeper of the medieval archaeology collections in the Ashmolean Museum, at the University of Oxford. Having studied dress accessories for her doctoral thesis, her research continues to focus on non-ceramic small finds and aspects of dress of the later medieval and early post-medieval periods. Themes of daily life, including devotion, magic, sexuality, gift-giving, memory, and hoarding, feature in her work.

Richard Suggett is Senior Investigator at the Royal Commission on the Ancient and Historical Monuments of Wales (RCAHMW) specializing in historic buildings. He is the author of several studies of medieval and post-medieval housing culture, including *Houses and history in the March of Wales* (2005) and (with Margaret Dunn) *Discovering the historic houses of Snowdonia* (2014). His *History of magic and witchcraft in Wales* (2008) is part of a broader study of crime and popular culture.

Emma J. Wells is Associate Lecturer and Programme Director in Parish Church Studies and English Building History at the University of York. Her research interests fall within the field of the religious and cultural history of late medieval and early modern Britain and focus on the art, architecture, and material culture of the period set within their broader Western European context. Her wider interests include pilgrimage, cult and commemoration, the changing nature of sacred space (particularly during the longue durée of the Reformation), sensory experience, and the application of interdisciplinary approaches. Her book, *Pilgrim routes of the British Isles* was published by Robert Hale in 2016. She is a former executive committee member and social media manager of the Ecclesiastical History Society and currently sits on the editorial board of *Royal Studies Journal*.

Hugh Willmott is a Senior Lecturer in European Historical Archaeology at the University of Sheffield, a post he has held since 2004. As well as being the co-editor of the volume *Consuming passions: dining from Antiquity to the eighteenth century* (2005), he has published widely on the archaeology of glass and drinking culture.

Peter Yeoman is now an independent archaeologist and heritage consultant, following a long career with Historic Scotland. His main research interests are the archaeology of Iona, medieval pilgrimage, along with the display and interpretation of early medieval sculpture.

PART I

WRITING LATER MEDIEVAL ARCHAEOLOGY

CHAPTER 1

OVERVIEW

People and Projects

CHRISTOPHER M. GERRARD

This first part of this *Handbook* considers the foundation stones of theory and methodology in later medieval archaeology. It includes a summary of applications of theory co-written with Pam Graves with illustrative examples and a chapter apiece by Michael Fradley and Simon Draper on archaeological field techniques and the written evidence respectively. As an introduction to these companion pieces, this overview traces the history of later medieval archaeology through a selection of people and projects across England, Scotland, and Wales.

EARLY IDEAS

During the eighteenth and nineteenth centuries engagement with the medieval past shifted from a largely literary and sensory appreciation, one characterized by a relative indifference to both archaeological sites and artefacts, towards a greater desire for historical context and scholarship. This change is firmly rooted in the impact of the Gothic Revival in architecture and a re-shaping of national identities at a time of social and political upheaval when many European countries opted to locate their origins during the Middle Ages. In turn, the peculiar nature of these interests led to growing imbalances in the understanding of individual artefact types and monument classes which were not corrected in Britain until well into the twentieth century (Gerrard 2003).

Very briefly, four themes are central to the early part of this story: the Landscape Movement in gardens, Romanticism in poetry and fiction, the Picturesque in painting, and the Gothic Revival in architecture. Arguably, two turning points can be identified, the first being the last 30 years of the eighteenth century when architectural recording reached the highest standards in the work of draughtsmen like John Carter and Samuel Grimm (Figure 1.1) and editors and publishers like Richard Gough (Badham 1987; Frew

FIGURE 1.1 'A View of the Abbey Church at Llantony, from within the West Door'. An engraving of 1780 by Samuel Grimm. The Swiss artist was much in demand, producing some nine hundred scenes for the county of Sussex alone (The National Library of Wales, public domain)

1980; 1982) and Francis Grose (Bending 2002). This was a time of escalating concern about the preservation and inappropriate restoration of medieval buildings and greater connoisseurship in archaeological artefacts (Frew 1979; Miele 1996; Sweet 2004). The *spolia* of the French Revolution, then being traded across the Channel, was to include medieval stained glass, carved wood, and even weighty architectural fragments such as the windows from the château at Écouen, outside Paris, which can today be seen in the Lord Mayor's Chapel in Bristol (e.g. Lafond 1964). Given the many dangers of foreign travel, the notion of a picturesque itinerary through the Scottish Highlands and Lowlands, for example, was becoming an increasingly attractive proposition (Andrews 1989, 85–108) and the discourse of travel itself encouraged greater understanding and knowledge of archaeological monuments. The ruins of abbeys like Tintern on the River Wye in Wales were one draw for these early tourists, the great medieval castles of Wales another; Beaumaris (Anglesey), according to Samuel Johnson, 'corresponds with all the representation of romancing narratives' (Johnson 1816, 101–2).

The mid-point of the nineteenth century marks a second turning point in the development of later medieval archaeology; the number of archaeological campaigns in the first half of the century rose fourfold over the next 50 years in England alone. There were several reasons for this. Sites with links to national history held great appeal and there was a particular emphasis on castles and monasteries for excavation, for example at Bamburgh Castle in Northumberland (Figure 1.2). Elsewhere, this surge in activity is explained by the numerous Gothic Revival restoration programmes underway at cathedrals, churches, and chapels (Brooks 1999; Buchanan 2002). The establishment of archaeological societies too was undoubtedly important in broadening the range of sites under investigation (Levine 1986) while the Museums Act of 1845 encouraged the establishment of local collections, for example, the Museum of County Antiquities at Lewes Castle created by the Sussex Archaeological Society in 1850. Since the turn of the century there had been an appetite for finds such as coins, armour, and seals but, under the influence of the Gothic Revival, this range was now extended to include window glass, church bells, and plate; papers on artefacts made up 16.8 per cent of the contributions to the *Archaeological Journal* in the period 1844–99. By the middle of the century Charles Roach Smith's *Catalogue of the Museum of London antiquities* (1854) contained sections on medieval sculpture and carving, pottery, embossed leather (shoes, purses, etc.), pilgrim badges, seals, dress accessories, and lead tokens. Roach Smith had collected these during 'watching briefs' across London. Like other antiquarians of his age, he protested loudly at the 'heedless neglect and destruction' he saw around him: the cartloads of decorated floor tiles from Eynsham Abbey (Oxfordshire) being sold off to repair roads (AJ 1851, 211), the removal of stones from Llanthony Priory (Monmouthshire) whose north aisle apparently made such a fine skittle ground (AJ 1845, 82), threats from new railway lines, the pulling down of churches, and the white-washing over of their wall paintings.

What held later medieval archaeology back from progressing as prehistory and Roman archaeology did at the end of the nineteenth century and the first decades of the twentieth century? The first problem was that chronologies of everyday medieval material were extremely uncertain. In 1847 members of the British Archaeological

FIGURE 1.2 A trench dug at Bamburgh Castle in 2004 exposed a sand-filled post-medieval trench which paralleled the medieval foundations (foreground with ranging rod). This is an unusually well-documented example of late eighteenth-century antiquarian digging which first identified the outline of the chapel. The discovery was commented upon a century later by Northumberland historian Cadwallader

(© Graeme Young)

Association asserted that 'specimens of medieval pottery are supposed to be of very rare occurrence' (AJ 1847, 79); even Roach Smith thought it to be 'comparatively rare, and completely void of beauty, taste, or sightliness' (Roach Smith 1854, 113). This perception put off collectors and the situation was not helped by the lack of readily accessible national collections, at least until 1866 when the Department of British and Medieval Antiquities and Ethnography was formed at the British Museum (Cherry 1997). A second reason is the overwhelming focus of scholars on ecclesiastical architecture and documentary history. During the nineteenth century Gothic style was everywhere, from railways to manor houses, from Canada to New Zealand. And while all this building certainly brought about significant advances in our understanding of ecclesiastical architecture through the contributions of architect Thomas Rickman, Robert Willis, and others (see Chapter 36), and boosted interest in the medieval 'decorative arts', there was a less certain grasp of the contribution that archaeology might make more generally, particularly in spheres such as the study of rural settlement, industry, and peasant housing. As John Hurst put it: 'all the work on the Medieval period was concerned with the upper classes, with churches, abbeys, castles, and manor houses, and even there it was mainly architectural' (Smith 2006, 60).

Organizations and Institutions

The Society for Medieval Archaeology was established in 1957 but the seeds of later medieval studies had been sown well before the Second World War, first by Pitt-Rivers and later during publically funded clearance programmes at castles and abbeys. Once their layouts had been established, grassy lawns and guidebooks quickly followed; a grand exercise in public education and the ideals of a common national heritage (Mandler 1997, 225–64). In Wales alone more than a quarter of a million pounds (12 million today) was spent on the excavation and consolidation of monuments in the care of the Ministry of Works, much of it on medieval castles (O'Neil 1946). The study of finds also advanced in different ways, for example through research into badges and jettons (Barnard 1916) and a landmark overview of medieval finds from London by John Ward-Perkins (1940). By 1948 the Council for British Archaeology's policy for field research was being extended into the historic periods, The Roman London Excavation Council had inserted 'and Medieval' into its name, and medieval and post-medieval archaeology was said 'to have arrived' (Bruce-Mitford 1948). While urban archaeology and industrial and rural sites remained largely unexplored, by 1957 things were beginning to change with promising excavations underway at Great Beere (Devon) (Jope and Threlfall 1958) and the deserted Yorkshire village of Wharram Percy (see Smith 2006 for an interview with John Hurst), among others.

As Maurice Beresford (1986, 36) put it: 'nothing from the world of archaeology was then allowed to tarnish an historical education'; nevertheless, from the very start the possibilities of later medieval archaeology had attracted some unlikely allies. One of these was Oxford Professor of European Archaeology Christopher Hawkes, who drew attention to deserted villages in the Lincolnshire Wolds (Hawkes 1946, 100–1) and promoted their excavation, another was Cambridge economic historian Michael Postan, who, though never one for field archaeology, sought evidence for a contraction in population before the Black Death through deserted villages (e.g. Postan 1973). In 1957 Oxford bachelor don Billy Pantin was the only academic titled as University Lecturer in Medieval Archaeology and History and it was to be Pantin who followed Rupert Bruce-Mitford, Keeper of British and Medieval Antiquities at the British Museum, as the Society's President at the end of 1959 (Gerrard 2009). Late in his career the irrepressible Pantin was chosen for a BBC documentary to illustrate the typical tutorial hour at Oxford but the result was considered too improbable and mystifying to be convincing to viewers (Knowles 1975). Indeed, with Eisenhower in the White House and Lennon meeting McCartney for the first time in 1959, this might seem to be another age. That said, even in the absence of social media, people were astonishingly well connected. When the Deserted Medieval Village Research Group (DMVRG, now the Medieval Settlement Research Group) was formed after discussions at Wharram Percy in October 1952, other disciplinary interests were coerced into action. In 1954, by which time there were 29 members, the Group included archaeologists such as

Gerald Dunning, John Hurst (both Inspectorate of Ancient Monuments), Leo Biek (of the Ancient Monuments Laboratory), Brian Hope-Taylor (Council for British Archaeology), former research biochemist Martyn Jope (Queen's Belfast), Charles Phillips (Ordnance Survey), and William Grimes (Director London Museum); historians Trevor Aston (Oxford), Beresford (Leeds), Howard Colvin (Oxford), W. G. Hoskins (Oxford), and Postan (Cambridge); geographers Karl Sinnhuber (UCL), Harry Thorpe (Birmingham), and Clifford ('HCD') Darby (UCL), author of the seven monumental volumes of analysis of Domesday Book, together with flyer Kenneth St Joseph and a smattering of people with museums, architecture, and town planning interests. As Jack Golson, co-founder of the Group put it, later medieval archaeology still had no great profile in Britain at the time (ANU 2008), but all of these men (and there was just one female member of the DMVRG in 1954) might be considered to have been at the core of the formation of the discipline of later medieval archaeology while the Wharram Percy excavations were, in their own way, a benchmark of exactly that kind of inter-disciplinary collaboration (Wrathmell 2012).

Aerial photography was key to recognizing new sites on the ground. The main task of the DMVRG in those early days was to buy RAF air photographs from the Air Ministry and St Joseph's obliques, build up card indexes of deserted sites with all their details, and plot them onto quarter inch maps, as well as publishing and lecturing (for which lantern slides were purchased). Local correspondents were engaged and recommendations made subsequently to protect identified sites from golf courses, housing estates, road widening, reservoirs, cemetery extensions, and ploughing. Excavations on the recommendation of the DMVRG included those at Faxton in Northamptonshire in 1966–8 (Figure 1.3) where the site was progressively being bulldozed in favour of 'agricultural improvement'. Reading through the early annual reports, the sense of activity and urgency is palpable, especially from Hurst and Beresford (Figure 1.4). Later, other specialized interests subsequently also came to be catered for by 'groups' such as the Medieval Pottery Research Group (in which Hurst was also deeply involved) and the Castle Studies Group. Other regional groups have also been established such as the Historic Rural Settlement Group in Scotland in 2007.

Other institutions played their part in the growth of the subject. From a lengthy post-War list of bodies whose functions have since been absorbed or cut away, the National Buildings Record gave us a reliable description of the medieval building stock for the first time and led to the introduction of 'listing', while the revival of the archaeology branch of the Ordnance Survey (OS) after 1947 accurately located and surveyed many field monuments until its demise in 1978. Many of us still regularly use the excellent field reports of the various Royal Commissions for Historic Monuments which led, for example, to the discovery of the earthwork remains of later medieval gardens. From today's matrix of heritage bodies the later medieval archaeologist might highlight their colleagues embedded in local authorities who developed (and continue to develop) the old OS cards and Sites and Monuments Records (SMR) data into Historic Environment Records (HERs), now such a formidable tool for development-control and research, or the opening up of national and county record offices, and the continuing work of the

FIGURE 1.3 Excavations at the medieval village of Faxton in 1967 by Lawrence Butler. Squares (8 ft or 2.4 m) were dug before the site was opened out into an open-area excavation to reveal several phases of housing

(© Lawrence Butler Faxton archive)

Victoria County History and the Council for British Archaeology, the latter so often at the forefront of research policy and lobbying over the past 50 years. Among more recent initiatives is the Portable Antiquities Scheme which began to record finds of archaeological interest made by the members of the public in 1997, especially those finds made by metal-detectorists which fall outside the terms of the Treasure Act 1996 (Worrell et al. 2010). Finds Liaison Officers (FLOs) identify and record details of the finds brought to them, 13,500 in the scheme's first year and now over 1.1 million in all, most of which can be searched for online where high-resolution images are available for download under a Creative Commons Share-Alike licence. A selection of the most important finds of later medieval date is also reported upon in the journal *Medieval Archaeology* and includes items such as post-Conquest coinage, seal matrices, religious accessories such as pilgrim badges, as well as dress accessories such as belt buckles and strap ends.

One particularly influential organization has been the Ancient Monuments and Historic Buildings Directorate in its various guises. Several of its inspectors such as Stuart Rigold and Bryan O'Neil both had medieval interests; Gerald Dunning, a founding father of medieval archaeology, published no less than 305 scholarly articles between 1926 and his death in 1981 while Hurst's careful selection of rescue sites for investigation

FIGURE 1.4 From left to right: Mick Aston (1946–2013), John Hurst (1927–2003), and Maurice Beresford (1920–2005) in 1989 at the presentation at Wharram Percy of a volume to celebrate Hurst and Beresford's achievements in medieval rural settlement

(© Paul Stamper)

was crucial to the development of the subject. Medieval archaeology is fortunate that he spent 35 years in the same post in various ministries and departments at a time when there was so much new building and agricultural development. The interests of Leo Biek and John Musty too were, from the earliest days of the Ancient Monuments Laboratory, as much directed towards resolving medieval questions as they were to any other period of the past. Other significant initiatives since the 1980s have included the introduction of project planning and research designs, the shift from core funding of organizations to the funding of specific projects, the Monuments Protection Programme which accelerated the process of protecting important medieval archaeological remains and led onto the more rigorous mapping of rural settlement (Roberts and Wrathmell 2000; Schofield 2000), the development of Historic Landscape Characterization (e.g. Rippon 2013), running the 'Heritage at Risk' programme, and funding for the latest generation of national and regional research frameworks (e.g. Petts and Gerrard 2006). Today the Royal Commission on the Ancient and Historical Monuments of Wales (RCAHMW), Historic Environment Scotland (HES), and CADW, the Welsh government's historic environment service, all maintain their own archives; for example Coflein is the free online digital archive of RCAHMW.

UK universities have also had an important role to play in the development of the subject. Inspired in part by the writing of Hoskins and Beresford and the revival of local history there has been a long tradition of extra-mural or continuing education among later medieval archaeologists: Mick Aston, Peter Fowler, Trevor Rowley, and Christopher Taylor among them. During the 1960s and 1970s, university archaeologists were also funded to take on research excavations; Peter Addyman at Ludgershall Castle (Wiltshire) is one example of this. Today it is increasingly difficult to find space and time in a university context for fieldwork and post-excavation commitments for which there may be little money, although several do continue to manage this. With the emphasis on 'research excellence' and 'grant capture', medieval archaeologists have had to adapt to new challenges and financial environments. A glance at the grants awarded by the Leverhulme Trust since 2005, for example, reveals project funding for topics such as medieval commercial sea fishing, the composition and corrosion of stained glass, the buildings of Scotland, landscape traditions, and the bioarchaeology of medieval adolescents. Among the projects awarded funds by the Arts and Humanities Research Council are those on the backlog of twentieth-century excavations at Glastonbury Abbey, medieval rural settlement, mapping medieval Chester, Cistercian houses on medieval borders, and marine flooding in medieval London. Almost all UK universities now have modules and courses on later medieval archaeology.

Some 21 per cent of all recorded archaeological investigations are now funded by initiatives such as the Heritage Lottery Fund, universities, and local groups (Darvill 2016); never before has there been such an active public commitment and engagement with the historic environment (Simpson and Williams 2008). The Heritage Lottery Fund, which derives its funds from the National Lottery established in 1994, has dispersed in excess of £150 million to 'heritage' causes. Of the many community-style projects now bearing fruit, the Norfolk Medieval Graffiti Survey was established in 2010 by volunteers to record graffiti in 650 medieval churches across the county. There have been regular publications of the results (e.g. Champion 2012) as well as talks and conference presentations to showcase new discoveries and the idea has now been rolled out in several other counties. A second example of a community project with the later medieval theme is the Currently Occupied Rural Settlements (CORS) project developed by Carenza Lewis which is using test-pitting to recover datable finds, mainly pottery, in an attempt to map the evolution of settlements (Lewis 2007). Multiple test-pits spread right across a settlement allow its footprint to be defined over time and so to identify periods of contraction and growth where excavation is often impractical. Some of this work has been undertaken by self-funded community projects, summaries of results being published online as well as in *Medieval Settlement Research*. Finally, the Cromarty Medieval Burgh Community Archaeology Project came about when storms in the north of Scotland in 2012 exposed archaeological deposits and artefacts. This Project provides training and excavation to learn more about the origins of the town in the middle of the thirteenth century as well as trade and commerce.[1] Public involvement, needless to say, brings all kinds of logistical assistance and knowledge to a project and crowd-funding is one of the ways in which new opportunities are being opened up for people to participate and contribute. One example of what can be achieved and how projects can be brought alive through attractive online delivery, the use of social media, intelligent digital reconstructions, drone work, and well-targeted trenches is the DigVentures excavation at Leiston Abbey in Suffolk.[2] The benefits of co-production with a local community can extend from the simple sharing of information to advocacy for heritage, the redefinition of local identities, and, in a limited number of cases, to very positive contributions to tourism and the local economy.

RESCUE AND DEVELOPER-LED ARCHAEOLOGY

Much like Roach Smith in the 1850s, in 1937 Martyn Jope and Rupert Bruce-Mitford could be found salvaging the buried evidence of medieval Oxford from the huge hole being excavated for the basement of the New Bodleian Library extension (Bruce-Mitford 1939). From this came the first sequence of medieval pottery for the Oxford region and, in 1964, Bruce-Mitford's enthusiasm for the Reference Collection of Medieval Pottery at the British Museum. Today most of the excavation work being carried out in Britain is by commercial units employed by developers and it is perhaps worthwhile rehearsing how this came to be. After the War, bomb-damaged city centres were investigated with limited public and charity money, among them London and Bristol: the campaigns of William Grimes and the Roman and Medieval London Excavation Council are the best examples of sustained campaigns. State funds only began to be deployed in a serious way once urban regeneration schemes began in the mid-1960s and the cores of historic towns were threatened with wholesale clearance. As a result, many English towns saw excavation on a large scale, among them King's Lynn, Southampton, and Winchester, all campaigns whose results feature heavily throughout this *Handbook*. Away from the

---

[1] www.medievalcromarty.org.
[2] digventures.com/leiston-abbey/timeline/.

pressures of urban 'rescue', less well understood monument classes could also be investigated to establish the extent of a site for the purposes of scheduling or in advance of conservation work, the results being used to make sites more visible and understandable. Launceston Castle (Cornwall), excavated by Andrew Saunders, was one site which benefited from this policy. With the formation of the organization RESCUE archaeology gained a higher media profile, the State contribution to archaeology began to rise, and several major units were established such as those in Norwich (1971) and York (1972). When this funding stream was withdrawn in the early 1980s other sources became available, such as the job-creation programmes which sponsored the Elgin and Perth High Street excavations and at Hulton Abbey in Staffordshire among many others. Although major developers had also begun to take on the burden of archaeological costs, most sites remained vulnerable until the introduction of Planning Policy Guidance Note 16 (PPG16) in February 1990. PPG16, commonly misconstrued as a piece of legislation (and therefore not passed by parliament), introduced the principle of 'the polluter pays', the polluter in this instance being identified as the private or public developer.

PPG16 was succeeded by Planning Policy Statement 5 Planning for the Historic Environment in 2010 and then by the National Planning Policy Framework (NPPF) in 2012 and 25 years on we are now in a better position to evaluate just how archaeology in the UK has been affected (Aitchison 2012; Flatman and Perring 2012). On the positive side, the 'polluter pays' principle allows more money to find its way into archaeology, reliance on State funding has reduced, archaeology has merged with the wider interests of the 'historic environment', creative strategies for sampling are now more sophisticated, standards for archaeological work are set by the Chartered Institute for Archaeologists (CIfA received its Royal Charter in 2014), numbers of professional archaeologists rose from 2200 in 1991 to 6865 in 2007 (in 2016 numbers are considered insufficient), and the geographical range and variety of sites under excavation are extensive, sometimes permitting the investigation of past landscapes at a large scale with provision for both analysis and publication. In Scotland it is now 21 years since the introduction of planning guidance (NPPG5) in 1994 and a useful summary of the far-reaching achievements of planning-led archaeology can be found online (CIfA 2015); undoubtedly PPG16 heralded fundamentally important changes in archaeology. On the negative side, there were early frustrations when commercial interests so rarely matched academic priorities as to where and what to dig; as Martin Biddle (1994, 7) put it on behalf of developers: 'You mean you don't want to know, even if I pay you for it?'. Particularly worrying is the severely limited finds analysis for some sites (e.g. the study of pottery merely for the purpose of stratigraphic calibration) and the restricted circulation of results: a vast body of data now exists which is not easily available to the discipline (though see the Archaeological Investigations Project 1990–2010, OASIS, the English Heritage Excavations Index, and others). Only 6 per cent of the investigations undertaken between 1990 and 1994 had been published by 2006 (Fulford 2011), in part because only a small proportion merited full publication. More recently there has been a reduction in the numbers of local authority archaeologists which inevitably diminishes access to Historic Environment Records and, in some cases, threatens their very existence. At a time of austerity, there have also been museum closures and issues around archive storage as well as the re-structuring and re-branding of our statutory and executive agencies (e.g. in 2015 Historic Scotland to Historic Environment Scotland, English Heritage to Historic England and the English Heritage Trust). In this environment the stated wish of current governments to de-regulate in order to increase the numbers of houses being built must be taken very seriously. The Housing and Planning Bill 2015–16 introduces for the first time the concept of 'permission in principle' (PiP) and a 'technical details consent', a two-stage planning application process for brownfield and local plan allocations onto which archaeological procedures will have to be mapped if developments are not to go ahead without adequate assessment. Not everyone believes that archaeology is so important.

Recent Projects and Publications

Many projects and publications stand out over the past 15 years. These include major urban projects in London (e.g. at Spitalfields), Bristol (e.g. Alexander 2016; Watts 2011), Norwich (Shelley 2005), with case studies of medieval topography, archaeology, and building stock such as Sandwich (Clarke et al. 2010), the London Guildhall (Bowsher et al. 2007), medieval townscapes (e.g. Lilley et al. 2007), together with important surveys of art and architecture published by the British Archaeological Association (e.g. Geddes 2016 for Aberdeen and Moray; Rodwell and Tatton-Brown 2015 for Westminster). Small towns and burghs have seen greater attention, among them Beverley, Hull, Monmouth, and Trellech, ports such as Hartlepool, and previous excavations have been published, such as those for Shrewsbury and Hereford. Many synthetic urban surveys are also available, such as those for Scottish burghs (e.g. Govan; Dalglish and Driscoll 2009). Of the major categories of later medieval monument there are some major new case studies including for castles (e.g. Austin 2007 for Barnard Castle, Co. Durham; Caple 2007 for Dryslwyn Castle, Llangathen; Driscoll 1997 for Edinburgh Castle; Impey 2008 for the White Tower at the Tower of London; Turner and Johnson 2006 for Chepstow Castle, Monmouthshire), moated sites (e.g. Brown 2006), elite housing (e.g. Emery 1996), sacred spaces (e.g. Norwich Cathedral close; Gilchrist 2005), and religious houses (e.g. at Eynsham, Oxfordshire; Hardy et al. 2003; Hall 2006; Robinson and Harrison 2006). In London alone there have been major excavations at Clerkenwell nunnery, Merton Priory, Bermondsey Abbey, St Marys Hospital, and elsewhere. Rural settlement too has been well served (e.g. Whittlewood in East Midlands; Jones and Page 2006) and there is an excellent summary of recent progress which includes seasonal settlements and farmsteads which have previously been less well studied (Christie and Stamper 2012). Typologies, distributions, and chronologies of medieval housing have been overhauled, combing archaeological evidence and vernacular buildings into a new narrative. Peasant houses are now thought of in a very different way, not flimsy and frequently replaced, but often robust and long-lived (e.g. Wrathmell 1989).

The topic of landscapes continues to attract a wide range of interests (e.g. Silvester and Turner 2011 for a range of themes from waterways to transhumance; Rippon 1996 for the Gwent Levels; RCAHMS 2002 for the First Edition Survey Project and Dixon 2002, both for Scotland; Creighton 2009 for elite landscapes) with some recent and remarkable applications of GIS methodology (e.g. Partida et al. 2013). There have been advances in our understanding of industry (e.g. Betts 2002 for floor tiles; Goodall 2011 for ironwork; Young et al. 2006 for pottery), the artefacts of everyday life (e.g. the Lewis chessmen, Caldwell et al. 2009; for a recent major finds catalogue, see Griffiths et al. 2007), and some remarkable shipwrecks (e.g. Newport medieval ship, Roberts 2004; and the Magor Pill wreck, Nayling 1998, both in Wales), with some multi-period projects being conducted at enormous scale such as the High Speed 1 railway through Kent (Andrews et al. 2011). Some of the most striking progress has been made in the field of human remains and burial activity (e.g. Connell et al. 2012 at the Augustinian priory and hospital of St Mary Spital, London; Hindmarch and Crone 2016; Gilchrist and Sloane 2005), as well as biomolecular archaeology, for example in the study of medieval food (Woolgar et al. 2006). At the same time, new theoretical perspectives refresh and reinvigorate older debates (e.g. Gilchrist 2012 for the life course; Johnson 2002 for castles; 2007 for landscapes), period boundaries are interpreted more flexibly (e.g. Gaimster and Gilchrist 2003), and long-awaited reports and excavations have been brought through to publication such as Glastonbury Abbey (Somerset) (Green and Gilchrist 2015) and the urban archaeology of Linlithgow (West Lothian), first excavated 1966–77 (Hunter et al. 2015). All of this wealth of recent information is drawn upon by the many contributors to this volume as they approach their themes and we will return to broader agendas and some of the gaps in our knowledge in the final chapter of the *Handbook*.

REFERENCES CITED

Aitchison, K. 2012 *Breaking new ground: how archaeology works*, Landward Research Ltd, Kindle Locations 4907–10

AJ, 1845 'Proceedings of the Central Committee of the British Archaeological Association', *The Archaeological Journal* 2, 72–92

AJ, 1847 'Archaeological Intelligence', *The Archaeological Journal* 4, 72–83

AJ, 1851 'Proceedings at the meetings of the Archaeological Institute', *The Archaeological Journal* 8, 91–214

Alexander, M. 2016 *Medieval and post-medieval occupation and industry in the Redcliffe suburb of Bristol: excavations at 1–2 and 3 Redcliff Street, 2003–2010*, Cotswold Archaeology, Cirencester

Andrews, M. 1989 *The search for the Picturesque: landscape aesthetics and tourism in Britain, 1760–1800*, Stanford University Press, Stanford

Andrews, P., Mepham, L., Schuster, J., and Stevens, C. J. 2011 *Settling the Ebbsfleet Valley. High Speed 1 excavations at Springhead and Northfleet, Kent: the late Iron Age, Roman, Saxon and medieval landscape. Volume 4: Saxon and later finds and environmental reports*, Oxford Wessex Archaeology Monograph, Salisbury

ANU 2008 'Interview with Emeritus Professor Jack Golson, Archaeologist', Emeritus Faculty Oral History, The Australian National University, www.anu.edu.au/emeritus/ohp/interviews/jack_golson.html

Austin, D. 2007 *Acts of perception: a study of Barnard Castle in Teesdale*, Architectural and Archaeological Society of Durham and Northumberland Research Reports 6, Durham

Badham, S. 1987 'Richard Gough and the flowering of romantic antiquarianism', *Church Monuments* 2, 32–43

Barnard, F. P. 1916 *The casting-counter and the counting board: a chapter in the history of numismatics and early arithmetic*, Clarendon Press, Oxford

Bending, S. 2002 'Every man is naturally an antiquarian: Francis Grose and polite antiquities', *Art History* 25(4), 520–30

Beresford, M. W. 1986 'Forty years in the field: an exaugural lecture', *The University of Leeds Review* 29, 27–46

Betts, I. M. 2002 *Medieval 'Westminster' floor tiles*, Museum of London Archaeology Service, London

Biddle, M. 1994 *What future for British archaeology? The opening address at the Eighth Annual Conference of the Institute of Field Archaeologists, Bradford, 13–15 April 1994*, Oxbow Lecture 1, Oxford

Bowsher, D., Howell, I., and Holder, N. 2007 *The London Guildhall: an archaeological history of a neighbourhood from early medieval to modern times*, Museum of London Archaeology Service, London

Brooks, C. 1999 *The Gothic Revival*, Phaidon, London

Brown, N. R. 2006 *A medieval moated manor by the Thames estuary: excavations at Southchurch Hall, Southend, Essex*, Essex County Council, Chelmsford

Bruce-Mitford, R. L. S. 1939 'The archaeology of the site of the Bodleian Extension in Broad Street, Oxford', *Oxoniensia* 4, 89–146

Bruce-Mitford, R. L. S. 1948 'Medieval archaeology', *The Archaeological Newsletter* 6, 1–4

Buchanan, A. 2002 'Interpretations of medieval architecture, c.1550–c.1750', in M. Hall (ed.), *Gothic architecture and its meanings 1550–1830*, Spire, Reading, 27–50

Caldwell, D., Hall, M., and Wilkinson, C. 2009 'The Lewis hoard of gaming pieces: a re-examination of their context, meanings, discovery and manufacture', *Medieval Archaeology* 53, 155–203

Caple, C. 2007 *Excavations at Dryslwyn Castle 1980–95*, The Society for Medieval Archaeology Monograph 26, Leeds

Champion, M. 2012 'Architectural inscriptions: new discoveries in East Anglia', *Church Archaeology* 16, 65–80

Cherry, J. 1997 'Franks and the medieval collections', in M. Caygill and J. Cherry (eds), *A. W. Franks: 19th-century collecting and the British Museum*, British Museum Press, London, 184–200

Christie, N. and Stamper, P. 2012 *Medieval rural settlement: Britain and Ireland, AD 800–1600*, Windgather, Oxford

CIfA 2015 *21 years of planning-led archaeology in Scotland—and 21 years more?*, Chartered Institute for Archaeologists, Reading

Clarke, H., Pearson, S., Mate, M., and Parfitt, K. 2010 *Sandwich, the 'completest medieval town in England': a study of the town and port from its origins to 1600*, Oxbow Books, Oxford

Connell, B., Gray Jones, A., Redfern, R., and Walker, D. 2012 *A bioarchaeological study of the medieval burials on the site of St Mary Spital: excavations at Spitalfields Market, London E1, 1991–2007*, Museum of London Archaeology Monograph 60, London

Creighton, O. H. 2009 *Designs upon the land: elite landscapes of the middle ages*, Boydell Press, Woodbridge

Dalglish, C. and Driscoll, S. 2009 *Historic Govan: archaeology and development*, The Scottish Burgh Survey, Historic Scotland, Edinburgh

Darvill, T. C. 2016 'What's been going on? Archaeological investigations in England since 1990', *The Archaeologist* 98, 97–8

Dixon, P. J. 2002 *Puir labourers and busy husbandmen: the countryside of Lowland Scotland in the Middle Ages*, Birlinn, Edinburgh

Driscoll, S. 1997 *Excavations within Edinburgh Castle*, The Society of Antiquaries of Scotland, Edinburgh

Emery, A. 1996 *Greater medieval houses of England and Wales 1300–1500, Vol. I*, Cambridge University Press, Cambridge

Flatman, J. and Perring, D. 2012 'The National Planning Policy Framework and Archaeology: a discussion', *Papers from the Institute of Archaeology* 22, 4–10

Frew, J. M. 1979 'Richard Gough, James Wyatt, and late eighteenth-century preservation', *Journal of the Society of Architectural Historians* 38, 366–74

Frew, J. M. 1980 'An aspect of the Early Gothic Revival: the transformation of medievalist research, 1770–1800', *Journal of the Warburg Courtauld Institute* 43, 174–85

Frew, J. M. 1982 'Gothic is English: John Carter and the revival of the Gothic as England's national style', *Art Bulletin* 64(2), 315–19

Fulford, M. 2011 'The impact of commercial archaeology on the UK heritage', in B. Cunliffe (ed.), *History for the taking? Perspectives on material heritage*, British Academy, London, 33–53

Gaimster, D. and Gilchrist, R. (eds) 2003 *The archaeology of Reformation 1480–1580*, The Society for Post-Medieval Archaeology Monograph 1, Leeds

Geddes, J. (ed.) 2016 *Medieval art, architecture and archaeology in the Dioceses of Aberdeen and Moray*, British Archaeological Association Conference Transactions 40, Routledge, Abingdon

Gerrard, C. M. 2003 *Medieval archaeology: understanding traditions and contemporary approaches*, Routledge, London

Gerrard, C. M. 2009 'The Society for Medieval Archaeology: the early years (1956–62)', in R. Gilchrist and A. Reynolds (eds), *Reflections: 50 years of Medieval Archaeology 1957–2007*, The Society for Medieval Archaeology Monograph 30, Leeds, 23–46

Gilchrist, R. 2005 *Norwich Cathedral Close: the evolution of the English cathedral landscape*, Boydell, Woodbridge

Gilchrist, R. 2012 *Medieval life: archaeology and the life course*, The Boydell Press, Woodbridge

Gilchrist, R. and Sloane, W. 2005 *Requiem: the medieval monastic cemetery in Britain*, Museum of London Archaeology Service, London

Goodall, I. H. 2011 *Ironwork in medieval Britain: an archaeological study*, The Society for Medieval Archaeology Monograph 31, Leeds

Green, C. and Gilchrist, R. 2015 *Glastonbury Abbey: archaeological investigations 1904–79*, The Society of Antiquaries, London

Griffiths, D., Philpott, R. A., and Egan, G. 2007 *Meols: the archaeology of the North Wirral Coast, discovery and observation in the nineteenth and twentieth centuries*, Oxford University School of Archaeology Monograph 68, Oxford

Hall, D. W. 2006 *Scottish monastic landscapes*, Tempus, Stroud

Hardy, A., Dodd, A., and Keevill, G. D. 2003 *Ælfric's Abbey: excavations at Eynsham Abbey, Oxfordshire, 1989-92*, Thames Valley Landscapes 16, Oxford

Hawkes, C. F. C. 1946 'Anglo-Danish Lincolnshire and the deserted villages of the Wolds', in J. N. L. Myres, C. F. C. Hawkes, R. L. S. Bruce-Mitford, J. W. F. Hill, and C. A. Ralegh Radford, 'The archaeology of Lincolnshire and Lincoln: Anglian and Anglo-Danish Lincolnshire', *The Antiquaries Journal* 103, 85–101

Hindmarch, E. and Crone, A. 2016 *Living and dying at Auldhame: the excavation of an Anglian monastic settlement and medieval parish church*, The Society of Antiquaries of Scotland, Edinburgh

Hunter, D., Brooks, C., Caldwell, D., Stell, G., and Middleton, M., compiled by Smith, S. 2015 ARO16: *Digging Linlithgow's past: early urban archaeology on the High Street, 1966–1977*, Archaeology Reports Online, Glasgow

Impey, E. 2008 *The White Tower*, Yale University Press, London and New Haven

Johnson, M. 2002 *Behind the castle gate: from medieval to Renaissance*, Routledge, London

Johnson, M. 2007 *Ideas of landscape*, Blackwell, Oxford

Johnson, S. 1816 *A diary of a journey into North Wales in the year 1774*, Robert Jennings, London

Jones, R. and Page, M. 2006 *Medieval villages in an English landscape: beginnings and ends*, Windgather Press, Macclesfield

Jope, E. M. and Threlfall, R. I. 1958 'Excavation of a medieval settlement at Beere, North Tawton, Devon', *Medieval Archaeology* 2, 112–40

Knowles, M. D. 1975 'William Abel Pantin 1902–1973', *Proceedings of the British Academy* 60, 447–58

Lafond, J. 1964 'The traffic in old stained glass from abroad during the eighteenth and nineteenth centuries in England', *Journal of the British Society of Master Glass-Painters* 14(1), 58–71

Levine, P. 1986 *The amateur and the professional: antiquarians, historians and archaeologists in Victorian England, 1838–1886*, Cambridge University Press, Cambridge

Lewis, C. 2007 'New avenues for the investigation of currently-occupied rural settlement: preliminary observations from the Higher Education Field Academy', *Medieval Archaeology* 51, 133–63

Lilley, K. D., Lloyd, C. D., and Trick, S. 2007 'Designs and designers of medieval "new towns" in Wales', *Antiquity* 81, 279–93

Mandler, P. 1997 *The fall and rise of the stately home*, Yale University Press, New Haven

Miele, C. 1996 'The first conservation militants: William Morris and the Society for the Protection of Ancient Buildings', in M. Hunter (ed.), *Preserving the past: the rise of heritage in modern Britain*, Stroud, Alan Sutton, 17–37

Nayling, N. 1998 *The Magor Pill medieval wreck*, Council for British Archaeology Research Report 120, York

O'Neil, B. H. 1946 'The castles of Wales', in V. E. Nash-Williams (ed.), *A hundred years of Welsh archaeology*, Cambrian Archaeological Association, centenary volume 1846–1946, Gloucester, 129–40

Partida, T., Foard, G., and Hall, D. 2013 *An atlas of Northamptonshire: the medieval and early-modern landscape*, Oxbow Books, Oxford

Petts, D. with Gerrard, C. M. 2006 *Shared visions: the North East Regional Research Framework for the Historic Environment*, Durham County Council, Durham

Postan, M. M. 1973 *Essays on medieval agriculture and general problems of medieval economy*, Cambridge University Press, Cambridge

RCAHMS 2002 *But the walls remained: a survey of unroofed rural settlement depicted on First Edition of the Ordnance Survey 6-inch map of Scotland*, Royal Commission on the Ancient and Historical Monuments of Scotland, Edinburgh

Rippon, S. 1996 *Gwent Levels: the evolution of a wetland landscape*, Council for British Archaeology Research Report 105, York

Rippon, S. 2013 'Historic Landscape Characterisation: its role in contemporary British Archaeology and landscape history', *Landscapes* 8(2), 1–14

Roach Smith, C. 1854 *Catalogue of the Museum of London antiquities collected by, and the property of, Charles Roach Smith*, T. Richards, London

Roberts, B. K. and Wrathmell, S. 2000 *An atlas of rural settlement in England*, English Heritage, London

Roberts, O. T. P. 2004 'Llong Casnewydd: the Newport Ship—a personal view', *International Journal of Nautical Archaeology* 33(1), 158–63

Robinson, D. M. and Harrison, S. 2006 'Cistercian cloisters in England and Wales', *Journal of the British Archaeological Association* 159, 131–207

Rodwell, W. and Tatton-Brown, T. W. T. 2015 *Westminster: the art, architecture and archaeology of the royal palace and abbey, Part 1*, British Archaeological Association Conference Transactions volume 39, Leeds

Schofield, J. 2000 *MPP 2000: a review of the Monuments Protection Programme, 1986–2000*, English Heritage, London

Shelley, A. 2005 *Dragon Hall, King Street, Norwich: excavation and survey of a late medieval merchant's trading complex*, East Anglian Archaeology 112, Norwich

Silvester, B. and Turner, S. 2011 *Life in medieval landscapes: people and places in the Middle Ages*, Windgather Press, Stroud

Simpson, F. A. and Williams, H. 2008 'Evaluating community archaeology in the UK', *Public Archaeology* 7(2), 69–90

Smith, P. J. 2006 'Roots and origins: archaeology and Wharram. An interview with John G. Hurst', *Medieval Settlement Research Group Annual Report* 21, 59–64

Sweet, R. 2004 *Antiquaries: the discovery of the past in eighteenth-century Britain*, Hambledon, London

Turner, R. and Johnson, A. 2006 *Chepstow castle: its history and buildings*, Almeley, Logaston

Ward-Perkins, J. B. 1940 *London Museum medieval catalogue 1940*, Museum of London, London

Watts, M. 2011 *Medieval and post-medieval development within Bristol's inner suburbs*, Costwold Archaeology, Cirencester

Woolgar, C. M., Serjeantson, D., and Waldron, T. (eds) 2006 *Food in medieval England: diet and nutrition*, Oxford University Press, Oxford

Worrell, S., Egan, G., Naylor, J., Leahy, K., and Lewis, M. (eds) 2010 *A decade of discovery: Proceedings of the Portable Antiquities Scheme Conference 2007*, British Archaeological Reports British Series 520, Oxford

Wrathmell, S. 1989 *Wharram. A study of settlement on the Yorkshire Wolds, vol. 6: domestic settlement 2: medieval peasant farmsteads*, York University Archaeological Publications 8, York

Wrathmell, S. 2012 *A history of Wharram Percy and its neighbours*, York University, York

Young, J., Vince, A., and Naylor, V. 2006 *A corpus of Anglo-Saxon and medieval pottery from Lincoln*, Lincoln Archaeology Studies, Oxford

CHAPTER 2

METHODS IN MEDIEVAL ARCHAEOLOGY

MICHAEL FRADLEY

The key trends in methodological practice in later medieval archaeology in Britain largely follow those seen elsewhere in the discipline of archaeology. Where distinctions arise this is usually due to the abundance of documentary data available, the survival of buildings and landscapes, and the relationship of medieval archaeology to the discipline of history, which can allow a very different narrative to develop than tends to be constructed for earlier periods (see Chapter 4). For instance, the enigmatic diasporas of the earlier medieval period have inspired large-scale DNA studies of cemetery sites, but there is less impetus for this form of research in the later medieval period where societal changes are recorded in greater detail in a wide variety of historical documents. The practice of medieval archaeology, however, has certainly not occurred in isolation, and ultimately it has benefitted methodologically from studies focused on earlier periods and remains in robust health.

Excavation

Archaeological excavation is a key means of obtaining data and often the principal source of major new discoveries in later medieval archaeology. The volume and range of finds can be high, large urban sites may produce upwards of 100,000 sherds of pottery and cemeteries in particular can be densely packed: 1041 individuals were recorded at St Helen-on-the-Walls in York, for example (Dawes and Magilton 1980). Excavations at Ludgershall Castle (Wiltshire) produced 3000 kg of animal bone (Ellis and Addyman 2000, 243) so finds registers for even relatively modest sites can challenge Roman field campaigns for volume. That said, some data-sets are less well served than others. There is little in the way of faunal data from monastic sites, for instance, and well-stratified material from rural settlement sites is harder to come by than it is for medieval towns.

Later medieval archaeology has sometimes stood at the forefront of innovations on-site, notably when open-area excavation was introduced at Wharram Percy in North Yorkshire in 1953 (Hurst 1971), or at Winchester in the 1960s and 1970s where drawing film, planning in colour, and the metric system made an early appearance (Biddle and Kjølbye-Biddle 1969). Other advances included the use of vertical tripod-mounted cameras to record the plan at the Templar preceptory at South Witham (Mayes 2002) and the excavation in 1964–73 of the moat at Sandal Castle in rolling 1 m sections so that pottery and other artefacts could be precisely plotted (Moorhouse 1983). Archaeologists with links to medieval archaeology have produced some of the leading textbooks on archaeological excavation (Barker 1993; Carver 2009; Roskams 2001). All three of these authors cited traversed the professional and academic sectors of the discipline in some way, and it is notable that the practice of excavation has shifted dramatically toward the developer-funded commercial sector since the introduction of PPG16 in 1991 (Gerrard 2009, 95–6). The increasing economic burden of archaeological excavation means that we are unlikely to see the sort of long-term, research-led studies of medieval sites, such as Hen Domen in Powys, that were the high points in the development of medieval archaeology in the latter half of the twentieth century (Beresford and Hurst 1990; Higham and Barker 2000).

Today, the development of professional standards in excavation and many other forms of survey is spearheaded through the relationship between commercial excavation units and heritage managers at a local and national level. While academic departments continue to undertake annual summer excavations as part of their undergraduate teaching programmes, it is unsurprising that it is the developer-funded teams operating all year round who are setting the bar in terms of quality and quantity of results, in spite of the frequent limitations in funding within the development process. While some would argue that academic-led excavations have the advantage of being research-led, it is difficult to argue that the sector could match the scale, standards, and insights of the major excavations of sites such as Norwich Castle (Popescu 2009).

A trend has therefore developed for academic research to focus on the synthesis and contextualization of data produced in the developer-funded sector, and increasingly on a national scale. From an academic perspective this is arguably to capitalize on an often unpublished dataset (Gardiner and Rippon 2009, 65), frequently due to a lack of adequate funding in the developer-funded process. The gap in terms of skills and resources within university departments is also relevant, although increasing numbers of postgraduates in the UK are spending a portion of their career working in the commercial sector, which has helped assist communication and the cross-fertilization of skills and research interests. Regardless of the origin and context of excavation data, this is an exciting time in terms of the development of partnerships across the commercial, academic, and custodial sectors in which the various groups operate on an equal footing. Major projects have developed in recent years for the periods spanning the later prehistoric through to the early medieval which have begun synthesizing the massive bodies of grey literature relating to sites across England (e.g. Gosden and Ten Harkel 2011), and a comparable 'big data' study of the later medieval period will undoubtedly follow in the near future.

One novel advance in the field over the last decade has been the development of intensive test-pitting strategies. This method has a long history in medieval archaeology, for example 1000 0.5 x 1 m test-pits were dug at 10 m intervals at Royston Grange in Derbyshire to track the spread of finds across the landscape (Hodges 1991). Test-pitting was also used to great effect at Shapwick (Aston and Gerrard 2013, 45–6), at Whittlewood (Jones and Page 2006, 25–6), as well as in various projects for *Time Team* during which their community appeal became clear. More recently, the same method has been employed in rural villages across East Anglia and the East Midlands (e.g. Lewis 2011). This strategy, utilizing hand-dug 1 x 1 m test units, has enabled research into historic settlements where modern development, and therefore commercially funded excavation, is relatively rare. By obtaining ceramic sequences from garden plots and other open areas across these villages, it offers a new, relatively inexpensive and unobtrusive perspective on the development sequence of medieval villages. A key and very positive component of this model has also been the involvement of the communities local to the modern village (Gardiner and Rippon 2009, 73), and it has proved a very powerful tool in terms of heritage outreach and public engagement with medieval archaeology. On a less positive note, critiques of test-pitting have begun to appear (Wright 2015, 11–14), and while the method has been attempted in urban contexts, its use in contexts where there is a high probability of encountering deep, complex stratigraphy is questionable.

Field Survey

Field-walking, a traditional mainstay of archaeological fieldwork, has contributed to some significant projects across the UK, including the Vale of the White Horse Survey (Tingle 1991), the Raunds Area Project (Cadman and Foard 1984), and the Whittlewood Project (Jones and Page 2006). Guidelines, several with well-worked later medieval examples, can be found online. Rather than identifying new sites for the first time, as is so often the case for the prehistoric and Roman periods, field-walking in later medieval archaeology has been effective in clarifying site chronologies: at Lillingstone Dayrell (Buckinghamshire), for example, pottery evidence helped to unpick the process of desertion of the medieval village (Jones 2010, 25). It can also help to pick out patterns of artefact distribution on extensive sites such as battlefields (Sutherland and Schmidt 2003; see Chapter 26). Elsewhere, field-walking results unravel patterns of land-use and thus the development of the landscape in the longue durée. High- and low-density pottery concentrations have been found to reflect manuring patterns which in turn permit the detailed mapping of medieval arable zones and help distinguish between farming strategies such as infield/outfield cultivation, assarts, and so on (Jones 2004). There is often merit in combining field-walking with other prospection techniques such as geophysics and test-pitting in order to elucidate the character and date of any archaeological remains.

While field-walking is now frequently a component of Heritage Lottery funded projects because it can engage the local community to great effect (e.g. Suffolk Archaeology's

'Managing a Masterpiece' Project at Stoke by Nayland), the technique is now less commonly applied in commercial archaeology, largely due to the intensification of arable cultivation which has led to a significant closing of the window between periods of time between the ploughing and sowing of fields. As a result it may not be feasible to put an effective team together when field-walking opportunities arise because, for example, a crop has just been sown or there is still stubble on the field which restricts visibility of the ground surface. In contrast, and largely due to the admirable efforts of the Portable Antiquities Scheme (PAS), material recovered by users of metal detectors is increasingly available as a means of identifying areas of occupation and activity. The ethics of using this material still remains controversial for some archaeologists, but in some areas it is becoming a more accepted element of archaeological research (see Chapters 32 and 49). Particular challenges to interpretation include the lack of systematic recovery methods by detectorists and differing access to land which may involve constraints such as lack of permissions to enter land and preferential searching on fields close to accessible road networks. On a positive note metal-detecting has enabled a different regional perspective on late medieval landscape, in that it offers insights into largely aceramic regions, such as parts of the West Midlands, which were largely invisible to the ceramic-focused methodology of field-walking.

Archaeo-topographical survey, or 'analytical earthwork survey' as it is also termed, has been one of the great traditions of British medieval archaeology (e.g. Taylor 1974). The features recorded are the surface topographies created by the past physical actions of people on the ground, whether the levelling of an area on which to build or the digging of a ditch around a field. The stratigraphic relationships between different earthwork forms can often be confidently identified, allowing complex site narratives to be proposed without recourse to archaeological excavation. The key contributors to the development of practice in Britain have been the national teams from the various Royal Commissions of Scotland, Wales, and England, with the latter subsequently merging with English Heritage (now Historic England). Influential figures from these institutions through the years, such as Christopher Taylor and Paul Everson, have made major contributions to our understanding of medieval settlements and other landscapes (e.g. Everson 1998; Taylor 1981). For instance, work led by Everson at Bodiam Castle in West Sussex was a key catalyst in moving discourse on medieval castles beyond a military-centred model (Taylor et al. 1990). The majority of the data produced by these groups has been published in monographs, articles, and report series (the Royal Commissions abandoned their parish-by-parish inventories of earthworks in favour of a more selective regional and thematic approach in the 1970s), but some projects have only been published in part, such as the study of dispersed medieval settlement in Shropshire (e.g. Everson and Stamper 1987). This unpublished but archived data, like the grey literature of the commercial sector, would be worth revisiting.

Traditional practice in Britain has been to map earthwork complexes as patterns of sloping ground which are generally depicted with hachures, mirroring those often used to depict the plan form of features from archaeological excavation. However, with the development of New Archaeology in the 1960s and 1970s came a rejection of this 'subjective' approach and an insistence of objective methods. Unfortunately, the objective recording of earthwork forms as contour models proved ineffective (Barker 1993, 60), with the result that earthwork survey was largely abandoned as a field practice (though for a recent example at Wigmore Castle see Rátkai 2015, 14). The traditional practice of hachure survey continued to evolve and achieve major successes in a number of national agencies, but investment in skills and research has now dwindled (Bowden and McOmish 2012), which is a particular tragedy given the degradation of archaeological earthwork complexes over this same period. The prolific and high-quality output of the Royal Commission groups and English Heritage that was apparent in the later twentieth century is now no more than a trickle, and there has been little to replace it within the wider heritage sector. The development of laser-scanning technologies may reverse this trajectory in the near future, offering a means of constructing high-resolution objective survey models, although whether its users can match the rigorous interpretations of earlier surveyors is yet to be seen.

Place-, Field-, and Personal Names

Settlement place-names were largely established in the early medieval period but continued to be coined after the Norman Conquest in AD 1066. Newcastle-under-Lyme in Staffordshire is one such addition. While some names were abandoned, supposedly because they were hard to pronounce, others were adapted to reflect tenurial authority, for example Leighton Buzzard from the Busard family, Hurstpierpoint from the de Pierpoint family, and Temple Guiting in Gloucestershire which refers to a period of ownership under the Knights Templar. These 'manorial affixes' aside, personal names have also been used more widely as a guide to settlement patterns. In the west of Somerset, the 1327 Lay Subsidies list the names of tenants as well as the subsidy paid. These names frequently refer to farmsteads which either still survive or have long since been deserted (Aston 1983). At a regional scale, and in combination with Historic Landscape Characterization (HLC, see below), place-names have also proved central to the analysis of Cornish settlement patterns between the late Romano-British period and the thirteenth/fourteenth century (Turner 2006) and it is here, in an area where few early medieval settlement sites have come to light and our understanding of the evolution of settlement is more constrained, that place-name interpretation is particularly effective.

In urban environments, street and district names are of significant value in reconstructing medieval townscapes. These may denote aspects of trade such as the sites and functions of markets or the presence of long-vanished institutions, for example the various Blackfriars, Whitefriars, and Greyfriars whose names often survive in some form in towns across England. In particular, medieval street names may survive into the present, giving an indication of trades or activities that were conducted in those areas. In the medieval town of Newcastle upon Tyne there was a Flesher Row, a Butcher Bank, and a Fishergate, all purveyors of commodities concentrated in different parts of town (Graves and Heslop 2013, 130).

Arguably of greatest value for research on the late medieval period are those references to vanished aspects of the landscape embedded in historic field-names. These can provide insight into medieval land-use, for example Chesteynwode (now Chestnut Wood) in Borden on the North Downs was indeed notable for the sweet chestnuts which grew there (Gardiner 2012, 102), while 'Town Field' is sometimes an indicator of deserted settlement earthworks on estate plans (Beresford 1989 using Warwickshire examples), and terms such as 'laund' and 'park' reflect the later medieval passion for hunting (see Chapter 25). By extracting the field-names recorded on nineteenth-century tithe maps and apportionments it is often possible to add substantially to the archaeological record (for the mapping of parish boundaries on tithe maps, see Kain and Oliver 2001), as in the case of the fortified site of 'Warandashales' in north Shropshire (Fradley 2006, 15) or to the south-west of Corfe Castle, Dorset, where Vineyards Farm indicates a number of earthwork terraces, potentially gardens and cultivation linked to the adjacent fortification. Caution is required, however. Few 'Castle Fields' relate to genuine castle sites and it is all too easy to make assumptions. A group of fields called 'College Fields' in Buerton, Cheshire, would seem on first glance to refer to a medieval collegiate church, but more detailed research indicates the land was granted in the seventeenth century to the English College in Douai in Flanders (TNA C205/19/17).

Aerial Survey

The potential of aerial survey in archaeology has been long recognized (Crawford 1924). As well as offering the means through which to identify and interpret the forms of archaeo-topography discussed above, aerial photography also provides the opportunity to detect additional archaeological signatures such as cropmarks and soil-marks. Imagery can be divided into two broad categories: vertical, with shots taken looking straight down from a bird's-eye perspective, and oblique, where photographs are taken at an angle to the ground. Copies of aerial photographs showing features of archaeological interest can often be found in local Record Offices or Local History or Heritage Centres as well as at Historic Environment Records (HERs) in England and Wales attached to local government offices. The key practitioners, however, have often been based in national agencies and it is the Historic England Archive at Swindon, Wiltshire, which holds the largest archive of aerial photos, over 4 million in all, including RAF photographs from the 1940s. Another significant archive is the Centre for Aerial Photography at Cambridge University (CUCAP), not least because Kenneth St Joseph, who was appointed curator there in 1948, flew from Cambridge to take some of pioneering shots of later medieval sites and landscapes (Knowles and St Joseph 1952; Beresford and St Joseph 1979). The major public archive of aerial photography for Wales is the Royal Commission on the Ancient and Historical Monuments of Wales (RCAHMW) while the most significant collection for Scotland (1.6 million images) is the National Collection of Aerial Photography (NCAP) maintained by Historic Environment Scotland.

As in so many areas of the discipline, the growing availability of archive material online could enable a corresponding level of site identification, particularly for aerial photographic collections dating back to the mid-twentieth century before the more widespread impact of mechanized agriculture. The potential for the discovery of major late medieval archaeological sites through the analysis of aerial photograph collections remains high, as in the case of Newhall Tower in Cheshire (Fradley 2005; 2009) (Figure 2.1),

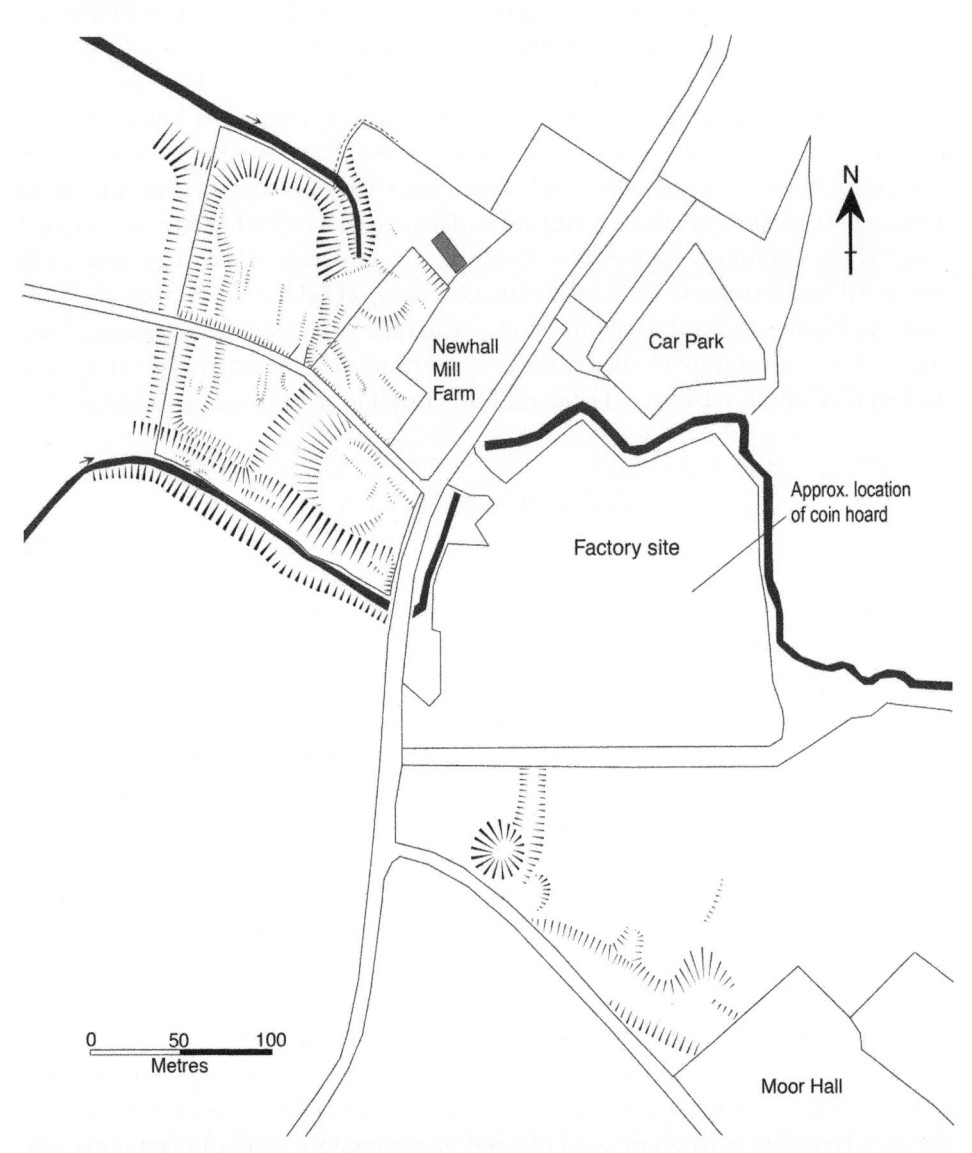

FIGURE 2.1 A hachured earthwork survey of Newhall Tower in Cheshire. The site is documented from the thirteenth century and a large twelfth-century coin hoard was reported from the survey area in the late 1950s, yet the fortified complex was only identified in 2005 through an inspection of historic aerial photographs

(© Michael Fradley)

although there are also unfortunate cases in which the importance of major complexes have not been recognized and the site has subsequently suffered irreparable damage, as at Ridgewardine in Shropshire (Fradley 2006, 12–14). There is still a huge potential for future work on the full range of later medieval monuments across the country.

LiDAR

Continuing the remote-sensing theme, Light Detection and Ranging (LiDAR) has become increasingly important in archaeological practice in Britain. As a reconnaissance tool, it has a number of distinct attributes in terms of the detection of subtle archaeo-topographical features, in that it can be used to penetrate extensive woodland cover and can also pick up broad, subtle earthwork features that are near invisible to the naked human eye on the ground. Along with the public availability of Ordnance Survey mapping and aerial photograph collections discussed above, the UK has also benefitted from the release by the Environment Agency of LiDAR data of varying coverage and precision, although the restriction of access to university and public body groups have limited this potential.

The use of LiDAR has significant potential as a tool, although it is very much an evolutionary step in the wider development of aerial reconnaissance survey in archaeology. LiDAR survey of Savernake Forest identified a number of new features of potential medieval date, primarily tracks and features associated with the medieval hunting forest (Crutchley et al. 2009, 29–36), but it is notable that there have been no major later medieval discoveries as a result of LiDAR interpretations, at least in the UK. In part this may be due to high densities of modern population at or near medieval centres, but it may also be attributed to previous research investment (for example in the recognition of deserted medieval settlements) and the relative accessibility of woodland areas which has reduced the numbers of major new sites yet to be discovered. Outside of isolated landscapes in upland Wales and Scotland, the impact of LiDAR on later medieval archaeology is likely to add local detail and be more incremental in its value, as in the example of Sudeley Castle (Gloucestershire) or Walburn (North Yorkshire), where a deserted medieval village with its ridge and furrow is clearly visible (Figure 2.2).

Geophysical Survey

Geophysical survey techniques have been a commonplace of all large-scale pre-development investigations since the early 1990s (Gerrard 2009, 96–7). Resistance metres and magnetometers (Figure 2.3), the two types of instrument most commonly used, offer the non-destructive assessment of sub-surface features and allow targeted excavation to follow. Resistivity is somewhat slower and reveals differences in relative

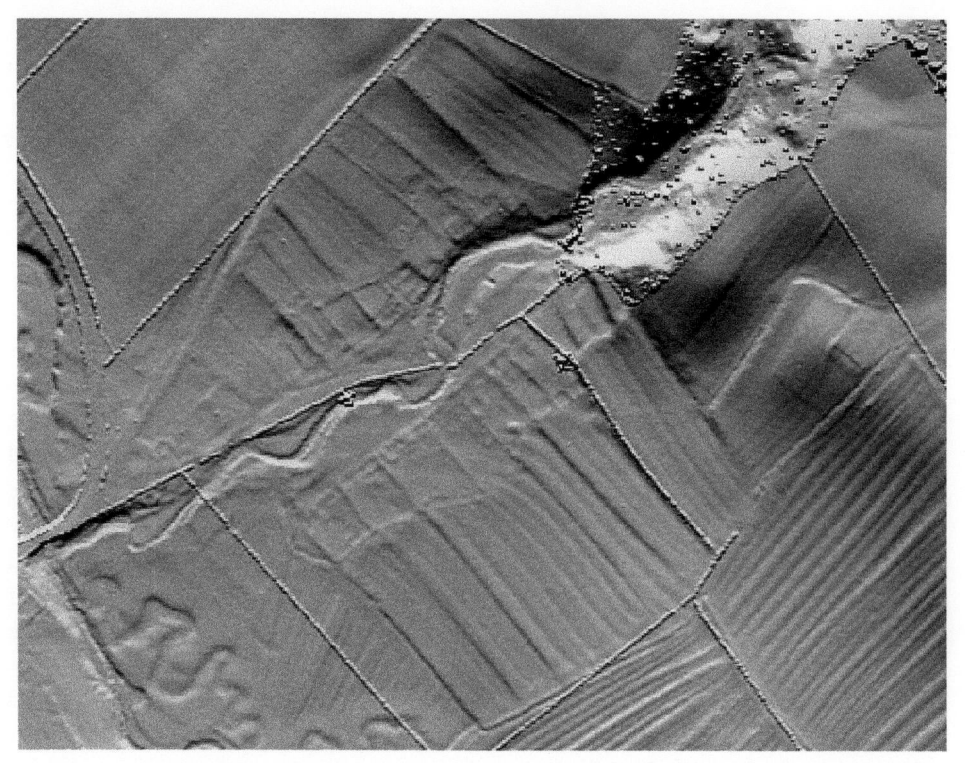

FIGURE 2.2 A 3D LiDAR model of the deserted medieval village of Walburn, North Yorkshire
(© Stephen Eastmead, altogetherarchaeology.org)

resistance through ditches and wall footings while magnetometry (fluxgate gradiometry) provides rapid assessments of larger areas. It is especially good at picking out ditches, pits, building remains, and anything burnt such as kilns and hearths. Just as field-walking has declined so geophysical survey has grown in popularity, with the added benefit that it is effective in geographical areas or archaeological periods where there are low levels of ceramic use. While geophysics has become relatively standard as a methodology ahead of any form of excavation, it is at its most effective when utilized systematically across wide areas. The Wallingford Burh to Borough project is a notable example in which the application of techniques across the eponymous town and its environs allowed an impressive non-destructive analysis of buried archaeology across the landscape (Christie and Creighton 2013). Another published case study is from Trelech, once one of the largest towns in Wales, where resistivity survey revealed the well-defined walls of a large building complex with a possible cloister at its heart. This was interpreted as the site of a possible medieval hospice (Hamilton and Howell 2000).

Ground-penetrating radar (GPR) is another technique that has attracted attention; recent GPR work undertaken at Old Sarum, just outside Salisbury (Wiltshire), by the University of Southampton, for example, has revealed details of the plan of a

FIGURE 2.3 Magnetometry survey in practice below Corfe Castle, Dorset, by staff from the University of Exeter

(© Michael Fradley)

twelfth-century town there. The method offers the exciting possibility of penetrating man-made surfaces such as tarmac and concrete, as well as providing an impression of depth-specific stratigraphic variations. GPR therefore has a distinct advantage over alternative geophysical techniques because it can be used in built-up urban areas and across other artificially surfaced areas. That said, early excitement over the potential of GPR has proved ill founded and there is a need now for more critical research into the effectiveness of the technique. On the same note, while there are centres of excellence in terms of the use of and research into geophysical techniques, notably the University of Bradford, there is a wider need for research institutions to invest in expertise and maintenance in order to ensure that the use of geophysical techniques remain consistent and effective.

Standing Buildings

The wealth of standing buildings has ensured that the study of structural fabric continues to make a fundamental contribution to medieval archaeology (see Chapter 15). Due to their quality of construction, most surviving structures tend to be religious in origin or were built by wealthier members of society (Figure 2.4). Excellent work has been published by researchers such as Tim Tatton-Brown for Lambeth Palace (2000)

FIGURE 2.4 Teampall na Trionaid ('Trinity church'), Carinish, North Uist in the Western Isles of Scotland. Ruin of a monastery and college, including two chapels connected by a passage, founded and built in the fourteenth century. The burial ground (left) is enclosed by an eighteenth-century wall. The buildings have been laser scanned to produce elevation drawings and two trial trenches were dug here in 2012 to inform future management plans (Canmore ID 10265)

(© West Lothian Archaeological Trust)

and with John Crook at Salisbury Cathedral (2009), while Edward Impey's edited volume on the White Tower in London is a comprehensive account of a complex that has been in use for nearly a millennium (Impey 2008).

A significant proportion of the basic analysis of vernacular standing structure has been undertaken by committed regional specialists, such as Madge Moran's research on the timber-framed houses of Shropshire (e.g. Moran 1999), and for which advances in dendrochronology dating techniques have often been of paramount importance. Standing medieval structures continue to be discovered encased in later buildings; for instance recent work at Wallingford Castle (Oxfordshire) has identified walls of a probable gatehouse linked to the thirteenth-century extension of the fortified complex encased in the Coach House, otherwise built in the early nineteenth century (Christie and Creighton 2013, 167). New identifications are more common in the theatre of domestic architecture, where timbers are enclosed or re-used within a later building, and where dating through dendrochronology has become an essential tool (Grenville 1997). There have also been significant theoretical advances in terms of the analysis of the form of standing structures, enabling complex interpretations of the motivations and reasons for the choices made by their original builders and patrons (Johnson 1996).

Characterization

While not strictly an archaeological methodology, plan analysis has provided useful and varied insights, particularly on the form and development of urban settlements. Pioneered by Conzen (1960) in his analysis of Alnwick, Northumberland, and further developed through subsequent research by academics such as Terry Slater and Keith Lilley, this method aims to analyze variations in property plot forms dating back to the medieval period. The technique has not been taken up more widely by the archaeological community, however, and as the detailed but flawed studies of Gloucester and Worcester have demonstrated, there are challenges in its application (Baker and Holt 2004; Griffin et al. 2004). Nevertheless, as a means of identifying distinctions and anomalies within a complex urban plan layout, plan analysis is still of great value, and there is potential for its application in future archaeological studies of urban environments. Comparable studies of less complex rural settlement forms have also been undertaken by historical geographers (Roberts 2008), but this has arguably had even less impact on current archaeological methods.

The principles of plan analysis have been taken further in the archaeological sector through the development of Historic Landscape Characterization (HLC) or Historic Land-Use Assessment, as it is known in Scotland. This cartographic approach explores wider patterns in the countryside in the form of field patterns and morphologies, processing these data alongside other forms of historic evidence through a GIS platform. While the development and funding of HLC has been undertaken largely in the heritage management sector, it has also been promoted as a distinct research tool (Rippon

2008; 2009, 242–5). There has been notable criticism of the technique (e.g. Williamson 2007), particularly when only modern maps are incorporated, and it could be argued that in its current form as a methodology HLC creates an overly sterile picture of the historic landscape.

Scientific Methods and Ecology

In his analysis of the development of medieval archaeology Chris Gerrard singled out the application of dendrochronology as the dating method which has made the single most important contribution (Gerrard 2003, 202). The ability to date ceramic sequences closely, usually from the well-stratified deposits found in sequences of riverside reclamation in urban environments, has undoubtedly had a major knock-on impact on the ability of archaeologists across the country to date and interpret excavated medieval archaeology rapidly and confidently. But the archaeological sciences have achieved far more than simply assisting in the analytical process as an appendage to the principal methodology of excavation. One of the most important recent advances in medieval archaeology, as in the discipline as a whole, is the emergence of rigorous scientific studies as stand-alone methodologies in their own right, with wide-ranging studies of subjects as diverse as fine-residue analysis of ceramics, complex research on faunal assemblages, and research of vegetation history through the examination of botanical remains (Gerrard 2003, 202–4).

This process of 'stepping out' from the appendices, in which these forms of analysis are no longer simply an appendage, has become a cause for celebration in medieval archaeology. Extensive studies of subjects such as diet and human remains are enabling the construction of exciting new narratives of life in the medieval world (Müldner 2009; Roberts 2009). The study of the St Bees Lady remains from Cumbria presents a particularly effective example in which multiple forms of archaeological data are combined, with a notable scientific lead, to produce an exceptionally rich account (Knüsel et al. 2010). Archaeological scientists have also made important and challenging contributions to broader theoretical debates in the discipline as can be seen, for instance, in the work of the late John G. Evans (2003, 90–3, 192–200).

One aspect of research that has also attracted a significant amount of interdisciplinary interest is historical ecology (e.g. Beswick and Rotherham 1993). As a greater appreciation of the importance of conservation in the modern landscape has developed, this area of study has a significant contribution to make to concepts of sustainable living and agriculture in the present. Many woods in Britain were present in the medieval period and exploited for fuel and timber, by charcoal-burners, grazing stock, hunters and trappers, and many others besides. Medieval woods were in fact much busier places than they generally are today. Historic landscape features preserved in woodland may include green ways, boundary banks and ditches, canalized streams, charcoal hearth-pits, saw-pits, and stone quarrying. The standard in terms of understanding of the medieval arboreal landscape was set by the work of Oliver Rackham, whose publications on the species diversity of trees and management techniques, such as coppicing, remain key texts (Rackham 1980; 1986). At Hayley Wood in Cambridgeshire (Rackham 1975) Rackham demonstrated how far the history of the site could be reconstructed from an understanding of its woodland flora, historic maps, and texts. Trees survive because of decisions made by local inhabitants and the reasoning behind allowing a tree to grow and which species were selected in the first instance are both questions whose answers add to the understanding of the history of any parish.

Another controversial contribution from historical ecology was made by Max Hooper and his colleagues (1970) who suggested that the flora of hedges could be used to calculate their ages. His 'rule' was that the number of species in a length of hedgerow 30 yards long (27.3 m) rises with age by about one species roughly each century that passes. Several botanical studies set out to test his theory (e.g. Williams and Cunnington 1985; a good summary can be found in Barnes and Williamson 2006, 24–41) and found that there are considerable regional differences in the composition of hedgerows, not least because hedges can be replanted or deliberately planted up as a mixed hedge. Soil types and conditions also have a bearing on botanical diversity while species extinctions may occur because of drought, local management of the hedges, and through competition with other species. Various landscape surveys with archaeological objectives have reflected on this, most notably on the Weld estate in Dorset (Keen and Carreck 1987), at Shapwick in Somerset (Hill 2007), and in Norfolk (Barnes and Williamson 2006), and drawn the conclusion that Hooper's 'rule' tells us very little about the precise age and origins of hedges. That said, the diversity of species *can* indicate the reorganization of parts of the landscapes (e.g. phases of enclosure) and is useful additional evidence for the landscape archaeologist when combined with other means of assessment. Among these are the study of historic maps which may help to establish when hedges are first recorded as well as the orientation and shape of field boundaries, excavation which can establish the earliest evidence of a field boundary, and field-walking, which identifies the evolving pattern of land-use. Like so many other techniques applied to later medieval archaeology, single strands of evidence are strengthened through multi-disciplinary collaboration. The Shapwick Project, for example, also included a contribution on the invertebrate faunas of hedgerows with particular reference to the presence of so-called 'Ancient Woodland Indicator Species' (AWIS), mainly saproxylic Coleoptera and Diptera (Clements and Alexander 2007). Previous studies elsewhere had shown that many species in these groups are restricted to long-established woodland habitats which have not been significantly disturbed or replanted and therefore there might be a link between the age of the hedgerow and the range and numbers of invertebrate AWIS in the samples collected from hedgerows. Once again, there is clearly a coincidence of interest here between historical archaeologists and ecologists which might be taken further, especially in the context of large-scale landscape projects. Formed in 1979, the Society for Landscape Studies is an important forum for research of this sort.

Conclusion

Later medieval archaeology involves the application of a broad range of practical methodologies. As excavation becomes increasingly difficult due to the resources required to take a dig successfully through to publication, so there has been a greater emphasis on exploring alternative, non-destructive techniques. While archaeological excavation still stands at the heart of the data-gathering process, it is proof of the health of the discipline that such a broad range of methods, in many cases innovatively and ingeniously applied, are involved in the research process. It is those projects that successfully select and combine multiple techniques that will achieve the most in terms of effective data gathering and interpretation.

Abbreviation

TNA   The National Archives, Kew, UK.

References cited

Aston, M. 1983 'Deserted settlements on Exmoor and the Lay Subsidy of 1327 in west Somerset', *Proceedings of the Somerset Archaeological and Natural History Society* 127, 71–104

Aston, M. and Gerrard, C. M. 2013 *Interpreting the English village: landscape and community at Shapwick, Somerset*, Windgather, Oxford

Baker, N. and Holt, R. 2004 *Urban growth and the medieval Church: Gloucester and Worcester*, Ashgate, Aldershot

Barker, P. A. 1993 *Techniques of archaeological excavation*, Batsford, London (3rd edn)

Barnes, G. and Williamson, T. 2006 *Hedgerow history: ecology, history and landscape character*, Windgather, Macclesfield

Beresford, M. 1989 'A review of historical research (to 1968)', in M. Beresford and J. G. Hurst (eds), *Deserted medieval villages*, Sutton, Gloucester, 3–75

Beresford, M. and Hurst, J. G. 1990 *Wharram Percy deserted medieval village*, Batsford, London

Beresford, M. W. and St Joseph, J. K. 1979 *Medieval England: an aerial survey*, Cambridge University Press, Cambridge

Beswick, P. and Rotherham, I. D. (eds) 1993 *Ancient woodlands, their archaeology and ecology: a coincidence of interest*, Landscape Conservation Forum, Sheffield

Biddle, M. and Kjølbye-Biddle, B. 1969 'Metres, areas and robbing', *World Archaeology* 1, 208–19

Bowden, M. and McOmish, D. 2012 'A British tradition? Mapping the archaeological landscape', *Landscapes* 12(2), 20–40

Cadman, G. and Foard, G. 1984 'Raunds, manorial and village origins', in M. Faull (ed.), *Studies in Late Anglo-Saxon settlement*, Oxford University, Oxford, 81–100

Carver, M. O. H. 2009 *Archaeological investigation*, Routledge, London

Christie, N. and Creighton, O. H. (eds) 2013 *Transforming townscapes. From burh to borough: the archaeology of Wallingford, AD 800–1400*, The Society for Medieval Archaeology Monograph 35, London

Clements, D. and Alexander, K. 2007 'A comparative study of the invertebrate faunas of hedgerows of differing ages', in C. M. Gerrard with M. Aston (eds), *The Shapwick Project, Somerset: a rural landscape explored*, The Society for Medieval Archaeology Monograph 25, Leeds, 332–41

Conzen, M. R. G. 1960 *Alnwick, Northumberland: a study in town-plan analysis*, Institute of British Geographers 27, London

Crawford, O. G. S. 1924 *Archaeology and air survey*, Her Majesty's Stationery Office, London

Crutchley, S., Small, F., and Bowden, M. 2009 *Savernake Forest: a report for the National Mapping Programme*, English Heritage Research Report Series 29-2009, English Heritage, Swindon

Dawes, J. D. and Magilton, J. R. 1980 *The cemetery of St Helen-on-the-Walls, Aldwark*, The Archaeology of York: the medieval cemeteries 12/1, Council for British Archaeology, York

Ellis, P. and Addyman, P. 2000 *Ludgershall Castle, Wiltshire: a report on the excavations by Peter Addyman, 1964-1972*, Wiltshire Archaeological and Natural History Society, Devizes

Evans, J. G. 2003 *Environmental archaeology and the social order*, Routledge, London

Everson, P. 1998 ' "Delightfully surrounded with woods and ponds": field evidence for medieval gardens in England', in P. Pattison (ed.), *There by design: field archaeology in parks and gardens*, British Archaeological Reports British Series 267, Oxford, 32–7

Everson, P. and Stamper, P. 1987 'Berwick Maviston and Attingham Park', *Transactions of the Shropshire Archaeological Society* 55, 64–9

Fradley, M. 2005 'Newhall Tower: the identification of the medieval castle and a nearby earthwork from aerial photographs', *Journal of the Cheshire Archaeological Society* 80, 91–7

Fradley, M. 2006 'Monastic enterprise in town and country: two case-studies from north-east Shropshire', *Landscape History* 28, 5–20

Fradley, M. 2009 'Field Investigation at Newhall Tower, Newhall CP, Cheshire', *Medieval Settlement Research* 24, 59–67

Gardiner, M. 2012 'South-east England: forms and diversity in medieval rural settlement', in N. Christie and P. Stamper (eds), *Medieval rural settlement: Britain and Ireland, AD 800-1600*, Windgather, Oxford, 100–17

Gardiner, M. and Rippon, S. 2009 'Looking to the future', in R. Gilchrist and A. Reynolds (eds), *Reflections: 50 years of medieval archaeology 1957-2007*, The Society for Medieval Archaeology Monograph 30, Leeds, 65–75

Gerrard, C. M. 2003 *Medieval archaeology: understanding traditions and contemporary approaches*, Routledge, London

Gerrard, C. M. 2009 'Tribes and territories, people and places', in R. Gilchrist and A. Reynolds (eds), *Reflections: 50 years of medieval archaeology 1957-2007*, The Society for Medieval Archaeology Monograph 30, Leeds, 79–112

Gosden, C. and Ten Harkel, L. 2011 'English landscapes and identities. The early medieval landscape: a perspective from the past', *Medieval Settlement Research* 26, 1–10

Graves, C. P. and Heslop, D. 2013 *Newcastle upon Tyne, the eye of the north: an archaeological assessment*, Oxbow, Oxford

Grenville, J. 1997 *Medieval housing*, Leicester University Press, London

Griffin, S., Jackson, R., Atkin, S., Dinn, J., Griffin, L., Hughes, P., Hurst, D., Pearson, E., and Vince, A. 2004 'Excavations at City Arcade, High Street, Worcester', *Transactions of the Worcestershire Archaeological Society* 19, 45–109

Hamilton, M. and Howell, R. 2000 'Trelech: the geophysical survey of a possible hospice site', *Medieval Archaeology* 44, 229–33

Higham, R. and Barker, P. A. 2000 *Hen Domen, Montgomery: a timber castle on the English-Welsh border, a final report*, Exeter University Press, Exeter

Hill, D. J. 2007 'Hedgerows, woods, trees and the historic landscape', in C. M. Gerrard with M. Aston (eds), *The Shapwick Project, Somerset: a rural landscape explored*, The Society for Medieval Archaeology Monograph 25, Leeds, 323–32

Hodges, R. 1991 *Wall-to-wall history: the story of Roystone Grange*, Duckworth, London

Hooper, M. D. 1970 'Dating hedges', *Area* 4, 63–5

Hurst, J. G. 1971 'A review of archaeological research (to 1968)', in M. W. Beresford and J. G. Hurst, *Deserted medieval villages*, Lutterworth Press, Woking, 76–144

Impey, E. (ed.) 2008 *The White Tower*, Yale University Press, London

Johnson, M. 1996 *An archaeology of Capitalism*, Oxford, Blackwell

Jones, R. 2004 'Signatures in the soil: the use of pottery in manure scatters in the identification of medieval arable farming regimes', *The Archaeological Journal* 161, 159–88

Jones, R. 2010 'Contrasting patterns of village and hamlet desertion in England', in C. Dyer and R. Jones (eds), *Deserted villages revisited*, University of Hertfordshire Press, Hatfield, 8–27

Jones, R. and Page, M. 2006 *Medieval villages in an English landscape: beginnings and ends*, Windgather, Macclesfield

Kain, R. J. P. and Oliver, R. R. 2001 *Historic parishes of England and Wales*, History Data Service, Colchester

Keen, L. and Carreck, A. (eds) 1987 *Historic landscape of Weld: the Weld Estate, Dorset*, Lulworth Heritage, East Lulworth

Knowles, D. M. and St Joseph, J. K. 1952 *Monastic sites from the air*, Cambridge University Press, Cambridge

Knüsel, C., Batt, C. M., Cook, G., Montgomery, J., Müldner, G., Ogden, A. R., Palmer, C., Stern, B., Todd, J., and Wilson, A. S. 2010 'The identity of the St Bees Lady, Cumbria: an osteobiographical approach', *Medieval Archaeology* 54, 271–311

Lewis, C. 2011 'Test pit excavation within currently occupied rural settlements: results of the HEFA CORS Project 2010', *Medieval Settlement Research* 26, 48–59

Mayes, P. 2002 *Excavations at a Templar Preceptory: South Witham, Lincolnshire 1965–67*, The Society for Medieval Archaeology Monograph 19, Leeds

Moorhouse, S. 1983 'The medieval pottery', in P. A. Mayes and L. A. S. Butler (eds), *Sandal Castle excavations 1964–73: a detailed archaeological report*, Wakefield, West Yorkshire Archaeology, 83–212

Moran, M. 1999 *The vernacular buildings of Whitchurch and area and their occupants*, Logaston Press, Almeley

Müldner, G. 2009 'Investigating medieval diet and society by stable isotope analysis of human bone', in R. Gilchrist and A. Reynolds (eds), *Reflections: 50 years of medieval archaeology 1957–2007*, The Society for Medieval Archaeology Monograph 30, Leeds, 327–46

Popescu, E. S. 2009 *Norwich Castle: excavations and historical survey 1987–98*, East Anglian Archaeological Monograph 132, Dereham

Rackham, O. 1975 *Hayley Wood: its history and ecology*, Cambridgeshire and Isle of Ely Naturalist's Trust, Cambridge

Rackham, O. 1980 *Ancient woodland*, Cambridge University Press, Cambridge

Rackham, O. 1986 *The history of the countryside*, Dent, London

Rátkai, S. 2015 *Wigmore Castle, North Herefordshire: excavations 1996 and 1998*, The Society for Medieval Archaeology Monograph 34, London

Rippon, S. 2008 *Historic landscape analysis: deciphering the countryside*, Council for British Archaeology, York

Rippon, S. 2009 'Understanding the medieval landscape', in R. Gilchrist and A. Reynolds (eds), *Reflections: 50 years of medieval archaeology 1957-2007*, The Society for Medieval Archaeology Monograph 30, Leeds, 227-54

Roberts, B. K. 2008 *Landscapes, documents and maps: villages in northern England and beyond, AD 900-1250*, Oxbow, Oxford

Roberts, C. A. 2009 'Health and welfare in medieval England: the human skeletal remains contextualised', in R. Gilchrist and A. Reynolds (eds), *Reflections: 50 years of medieval archaeology 1957-2007*, The Society for Medieval Archaeology Monograph 30, Leeds, 307-25

Roskams, S. 2001 *Excavation*, Cambridge University Press, Cambridge

Sutherland, T. and Schmidt, A. 2003 'Towton, 1461: an integrated approach to battlefield archaeology', *Landscapes* 4(2), 15-25

Tatton-Brown, T. W. T. 2000 *Lambeth Palace: a history of the archbishops of Canterbury and their houses*, SPCK, London

Tatton-Brown, T. W. T. and Crook, J. 2009 *Salisbury Cathedral: the making of a medieval masterpiece*, Scala, London

Taylor, C. C. 1974 *Fieldwork in medieval archaeology*, Batsford, London

Taylor, C. C. 1981 'The role of fieldwork in medieval settlement studies', *Medieval Village Research Group Annual Report* 29, 29-31

Taylor, C. C., Everson, P., and Wilson-North, R. 1990 'Bodiam Castle, Sussex', *Medieval Archaeology* 34, 155-7

Tingle, M. 1991 *The Vale of the White Horse Survey: the study of a changing landscape in the clay lowlands of southern England from Prehistory to the present*, British Archaeological Report British Series 218, Oxford

Turner, S. (ed.) 2006 *Medieval Devon and Cornwall: shaping an ancient countryside*, Windgather Press, Bollington

Williams, L. R. and Cunnington, W. 1985 'Dating a hedgerow landscape in Middlesex: Fryent Country Park', *London Naturalist* 64, 7-22

Williamson, T. 2007 'Historic Landscape Characterisation: some queries', *Landscapes* 8(2), 64-71

Wright, D. W. 2015 *Middle Saxon settlement and society*, Archaeopress, Oxford

CHAPTER 3

EMBRACING NEW PERSPECTIVES

C. P. GRAVES AND CHRISTOPHER M. GERRARD

THIS chapter considers the application of archaeological theory to later medieval archaeology. Critical overviews have appeared before (e.g. Gerrard 2003; Gilchrist 2009a; McClain 2012) and it might be argued that further exposition is unnecessary. After all, it is axiomatic that theory underpins all archaeological practice, observation, and interpretation, and perhaps what divides those who consciously use 'theory' from those who do not is merely the presence of some critical and explicit statement of purpose. Nevertheless, readers (and writers) of this *Handbook* will wish to ensure that their perspectives are both self-critical and make allowance for the fullest possible toolkit of approaches. With that in mind, what follows is a selective review of the different approaches offered by archaeologists of the Later Middle Ages set into a wider historiographical framework.

MODELS IN LEGOLAND?

In the first half of the twentieth century, 'common sense' or 'functionalist' approaches to archaeological evidence were the norm. For example, the establishment of a monastery might be seen as an accumulation of decisions taken by donors of land rather than adopting a longer-term perspective which emphasized changing attitudes towards the ideals of monasticism (Mytum 1989). In other words, explanation at that time tended towards historical particularism.

In the post-War period archaeologists with medieval interests began to venture beyond the 'what', 'where', and the 'when' questions. During the 1960s, the social sciences across Europe made greater use of numerical methods in research, promoting models and generalizing laws of human behaviour. David Clarke's ground-breaking *Analytical archaeology* was published in 1968 and early applications of these new ideas were to include Martin Jope's thoughts on model-building in medieval archaeology (Jope 1972). Nearly a decade later in 1981, Philip Rahtz was still arguing passionately for 'the generation and testing of hypotheses in a rigorous manner' and pushing medieval archaeologists to 'discern repeated patterns which may lead to the definition of generalising laws of human behaviour' (Rahtz 1983). Rahtz's Wharram Percy Data Sheets, first drawn up in 1980, showed how such an approach might be applied in practice. By breaking down the objectives of the long-running excavation project at Wharram Percy into component themes such as technology and craft, trade and economy, past lifeways, environment, religion, aristocratic nuclei, settlement history, farming and food, Rahtz aimed to highlight the long-term processes of change (Rahtz 1980; see also Arnold 1986). This emphasis on the long-term remains central to many medieval landscape studies today, though it is usually re-framed in the terminology of *Annales* history as *longue durée* (Astill and Davies 1997 in Brittany; Beaumont James and Gerrard 2007, 201–8 for Clarendon royal house and park).

Among the medieval archaeologists who made use of the deductive approach were Martin Carver (1983), who championed the value of sampling procedures in urban excavation, Roger Leech (1981), who advocated new themes such as social organization, subsistence, and technology for the study of medieval towns in north-west England, and geographer Brian Roberts (1977), who researched settlement hierarchies. The influence of human geography was especially important (e.g. Chorley and Haggett 1967) and spatial analysis was set to become an important area of take-up by later medieval archaeologists. Guy Halsall, for example, overlaid the distribution of monastic houses in North Yorkshire with Thiessen polygons to demonstrate their 'spheres of influence' (Halsall 1989, 123–4). Eager to avoid 'subjective analysis', pottery specialists like Alan Vince were also willingly experimental in their adoption of new statistical and spatial approaches. Frequencies of pottery of different kinds were plotted, fall-off curves examined, and mechanisms of distribution 'predicted' (e.g. Vince 1977). Behind all this was the belief that cultural behaviour in the past was strongly patterned, that there were underlying trends in the routine movement of goods and people. Only through New Archaeology, it was argued, could medieval archaeology become a more objective, science-based discipline freed from its dependency on historical readings of the past and on 'kings and queens' history (Biddick 1993).

Reactions to processual perspectives from collaborating disciplines outside the social sciences could be frosty. The processualist vocabulary of 'data', 'flow diagrams', 'systems analysis', and 'problem orientation' was a particular hurdle. Medieval archaeologists found themselves in the crosshairs of criticism from all angles: while prehistorians accused them of disciplinary inferiority (Bintliff 1986), historians found their language to be 'status-seeking' because they stressed the scientific nature of the discipline (Hobsbawm 1979). Even within the wider 'family' of later medieval archaeologists there were many, the majority in fact, who silently shared these views. A disappointed Rahtz described the reactions to his Wharram Data Sheets as 'apathy' and 'hostility' (Rahtz 1981), while at the Society for Medieval Archaeology's conference in April 1981 there were accusations of 'incomprehensible jargon', 'annoying and controversial remarks', and, in the final line of John Hurst's summing up, he urged his colleagues to 'play with reality, not play with models in Legoland' (Hinton 1983).

In fact, by the time 'processual' approaches found a shaky toehold in later medieval archaeology they were already falling out of fashion. By 1984 theorists were challenging systems theory and scientific approaches, and Steve Driscoll referred to Rahtz's call for a 'new medieval archaeology' as 'casual and misdirected' (Driscoll 1984). The main criticisms of processual archaeology are by now well rehearsed (e.g. Johnson 1999, 98–115) and will not be repeated here. Those interested in seeking out an accessible later medieval case study in theoretical critique and counter-critique might refer to Fleming (2006) and associated references to the writing of prehistorian Julian Thomas and medievalist Mick Aston.

The Impact of Structuralism

An important debate for medieval archaeology concerned the relationship between history and archaeology as disciplines, and more specifically how to regard texts in relation to archaeological interpretation (e.g. Austin and Thomas 1990; see also Chapter 4 in this *Handbook*). Driscoll (1984; 1988) argued for the recognition of texts as part of a symbolic system: as technologies with specific properties (Clanchy 1979; Goody and Watt 1963) which were strategically deployed in the reproduction of institutions and specific historical conditions. This idea, of material culture as meaningful, as part of a symbolic code, had first gained impetus in archaeological interpretation through structuralist anthropology.

For archaeologists working in historical periods, the most inspirational structuralist scholarship came out of America and often dealt with everyday objects, housing, for example—the very stuff of ordinary lives (e.g. Deetz 1977). Applications to later medieval archaeology ranged from castles (Coulson 1979) to religious architecture (e.g. Fergusson 1989 for designs of Cistercian refectories; Gilchrist 1988 for nunnery plans). For example, the plan form and architecture of the fourth-century *Anastasis Rotunda* of the Church of the Holy Sepulchre in Jerusalem, one of the holiest sites in Christianity, has a long history of artistic representation and architectural mimesis. The chapels of Military Orders houses belonging to the Templars and Hospitallers were noted for their distinctive layouts with a central rotunda, an encircling aisle, and a chancel to the east. The aim here was to place the visitor into a 'multimedia' representation of core elements of the sacred topography of Jerusalem so as to be able to recall the architecture of a specific building (Kühnel 1987; Kühnel et al. 2014).

Among the most important applications of structuralist concepts are those by Glassie (1975) and Hillier and Hanson (1984), both based on the Chomskyan concept of a 'generative grammar'. The primary axiom of structuralism is that human perception is ordered by fundamental cognitive structures, and that all social communication proceeds from those principles. Glassie discerned an architectural grammar through whose concrete manifestations relations between members of a household, and between the household and visitors from outside, were controlled. He could also relate major changes to those patterns and relations, through transformations in the layout and the linkage of domestic spaces, the presentation of façades, and new conceptions of social order regarding gender rules, privacy, and status. Hillier and Hanson, meanwhile, reduced patterns of access between spaces to ideographic formulae which they termed 'permeability diagrams'.

Generally speaking, the concept of 'spatial depth' within a building can be a useful tool to demonstrate the relative physical exclusion of one space from another (Hillier and Hanson 1984, 181). The technique has been used to good effect by later medieval archaeologists (e.g. Fairclough 1992; Richardson 2003). There are challenges to deploying these approaches and methods of presentation, however, as its advocates are well aware. Even if the layout of a building can be precisely phased and measured, space is necessarily reduced to an essentially planar dimension. Once more, society is conceptualized as a homogeneous entity and presumes normative responses. This is inadequate because many of the nuances of social behaviour are lost, such as servants with admission to deeper, more exclusive, private spaces or seasonal changes to rules regarding access. The system is equally ill adept at systematizing spaces that split and cohere again, something which is common in Christian liturgy, for instance. Further refinements to these spatial analysis techniques were suggested by Markus (e.g. 1993) who introduced sight lines, but even this cannot account for visual acuity or the presence of other people, among other concerns.

Post-Processual Archaeology

Many papers in this volume make use of post-processual approaches. Here we consider three ways in which these theoretical agendas have been influential.

Phenomenology and the Experiential

There are now many applications of a phenomenological approach to later medieval monuments. In his volume *Housing culture*, Matthew Johnson (1993) explored approaches to the medieval rural house in western Suffolk between 1400 and 1700. The title is significant, and the content takes the reader into the mentality of the houses' occupants and their changing use of space. Another example is Karin Altenberg's investigation of the responses of medieval inhabitants of Dartmoor and Bodmin Moor to the landscapes around them (Altenberg 2003; and see Chapter 14 in this *Handbook*). However, much of the trajectory in theoretical applications and focus of research with regards to later medieval architecture and landscape settings can be followed through what might be called 'The castles debate'. A 'traditionalist school', succinctly summarized by Stocker (1992), once emphasized military function as the pre-eminent consideration in the development of castles, largely influenced by the military backgrounds and war experiences of the earliest advocates of castle studies. These were royal, noble, lordly residences, but essentially fortresses, designed to be defensive and adapted in response to changing military technologies. This could be characterized as a functionalist approach. The work of Charles Coulson (e.g. 1979) and his students then initiated a 'revisionist' series of analyses, in search of the symbolic and the ideological as much as the practical. According to this interpretation, the architecture of defence was as much about expressing prowess, wealth, dominance, separation, and consumption as military functionality. Though not explicitly theoretical, the later work of Philip Dixon and Pam Marshall (Marshall 2002) on twelfth-century stone keeps and donjons explored these spaces as theatres for the construction not only of identity, but of profoundly psychological asymmetrical conditions of encounter between petitioners, those seeking or at the receiving end of justice, guests, and the castle's principal inhabitants.

Several case studies of castles and their designed landscapes are available, often inspired by analytical earthwork surveys which have revealed fresh detail. That for the fifteenth century pleasure garden at Kenilworth Castle in Warwickshire is especially interesting for what it tells us about the physical movement of the appreciative visitor through staged landscapes, in this case by barge or boat (Jamieson and Lane 2015). It was Bodiam Castle in Sussex, however, built in 1385, which became the 'poster child' for revisionist arguments (see Chapter 23). Its appearance of defensiveness was argued to belie the reality that the moat could be dug through and drained in one night, the mirror-like reflection in the water being intended only to make the castle seem more substantial. Arrow and artillery loops, it was said, simply did not provide sufficient range or interlocking coverage of the approach to the castle, and offered only a false impression of its military capabilities; substantial earthworks in the immediate landscape were not platforms for artillery attack but garden features essential to the visual appreciation of the site. This approach has been taken further by Matthew Johnson (2002), explicitly informed by post-processual theory. In essence, the idea is that spaces were used to create a series of impressions in the mind of the visitor, almost like theatrical experiences. Idiomatic to this approach was the understanding that aspects of formal life in castles was heavily ritualized, that spaces, chambers, and the manipulated landscape settings were, effectively, magnificent stage sets for the reproduction of social relations.

When it seemed that an unfortunate and artificial impasse might possibly emerge between these two approaches (Platt 2007), new directions were called for which would capitalize on the best of traditional approaches, combined with the social and historical nuances afforded by post-processual theory, and with the new potential for both detail, and the analysis in breadth and depth of scale afforded by modern archaeological landscape recording techniques in particular (Creighton and Liddiard 2008). The *Lived experience in the Later Middle Ages* project (2017), by Matthew Johnson and his teams at Northwestern University and Southampton University, has sought to locate Bodiam in a landscape also exploited for industrial purposes, exposing how the castle could not have been built without ties into a wider network of industrial production and evolving mercantile capitalism linking the site to the commercial and distributive activity of the Cinque Ports.

The imperative to understand how the entirety of environment, material culture, and practice has contributed to the creation of identities in any given context in the past has led to the development of an archaeology of the senses (Skeates 2010). One complete part of this *Handbook* is dedicated to the medieval sensory world. Late medieval archaeological applications have been influenced by pioneering work in medieval history (e.g. Woolgar 2006), as well as the extensive, theoretically robust developments in sociology and anthropology (see Chapter 42). Programmatic calls for a sensory archaeology of the Middle Ages have been made by Giles (2007) and Graves (2007), whilst Wells (2013) created possibly the first sustained, exceptionally detailed application in respect of medieval pilgrimage sites at Durham, Canterbury, and York Cathedrals, and the small cult centre of St Neot (Cambridgeshire). Grounded in archaeological and other material observation, this work drew out both the extent of immersion and variety of sensory experiences, whereby each individual's religious experience resulted from a nuanced and multi-dimensional set of interactions between the pilgrim's own life experiences and expectations, on the one hand, and the extent to which institutional design could control a desired outcome, on the other hand. Consequently, changes in fabric, route, and any aspect of the 'sensorium', as Wells defined it, could potentially produce quite different experiences.

With respect to domestic environments, Cumberpatch (1997) stresses the colour, texture, and decoration of medieval artefacts and their environments. Pottery is imagined against a backdrop of cloths, bedding, and cushions, in other words the complete sensory environment. The most important space for display in a high status medieval household was the hall, either on the first or second floor, with its walls hung with large patterned textiles, blackened silver, recessed cupboards, decorated tiles, or stone mosaic floors (Brown et al. 1997) but the bedchamber also offered privacy and might be furnished with cushions, covers, rugs and tapestries, and mirrors. Visual reconstruction forces the archaeologist to consider the balance of all kinds of medieval artefacts in the domestic home but it also marks an important conceptual break. Rather than thinking of pottery in terms of general trends in their consumption or changes in form, the focus is on individual objects available at any one time within the household. Unsurprisingly, the case has been made for publishing multi-material groups by phase, so that objects can be seen in groups as they may once have been (Mellor 2004). There is also a renewed interest in table manners (e.g. Hadley 2005) and the rituals surrounding the preparation, serving, and eating of food. Manuals of etiquette, like that of Petrus Alphonsi at the turn of the twelfth century which emphasize the importance of good manners and gentility, show just how complex customs were and their immense symbolic importance. Manuscript illustrations and panel paintings too have come under renewed scrutiny (Gaimster 1997).

The Archaeology of Identity

The understanding of identity is, like so many other topics in later medieval archaeology, an interdisciplinary pursuit which ranges out in different directions. Childhood is belatedly receiving attention, for example through the study of artefacts and toys pioneered by the late Geoff Egan (Egan 1998; and Chapter 48 in this *Handbook*), but archaeologists still lag behind historians (e.g. Hanawalt 1993; Shahar 1992). A recent study of the skeletal remains of adolescents is revealing, however, new evidence about their health and working life (Lewis 2016), while the social identity of the buried dead has also been considered (Gilchrist and Sloane 2005). Expressions of identity have particularly been explored in monastic contexts by scholars from different disciplines. Their themes have included imagery and the arts, dress, writing, food and nutrition, foundation legends, liturgy and devotional practices, organizational practices, religious women, and environment and settlement, among other attributes (e.g. Arnold 2012; Boynton 2006; Frizzard 2007). The social construction of gender, as opposed to examining the space and actions of women, has been very effectively explored through the archaeology of medieval religious women (e.g. Gilchrist 1994; 1999; 2009b; Hadley 1999).

Mercantile identity has similarly been examined from differing perspectives, particularly through pottery which can be dated and whose point of manufacture may be known (Gaimster 1999; Immonen 2007; see Chapter 55 in this *Handbook*). Hinton (Chapter 27), examines the artefacts associated with status and has previously proposed that material culture may be one means of excluding individuals from access to a social group (Hinton 2005). Another perspective on the production and maintenance of authority is taken by Johnson (2015) in a study of medieval moated sites in southeast England. Building on work by Graves (1989) and Gilchrist (1994) in other contexts, he investigates the relationship between lived experience and social power both in the imagination and as a set of stratified spaces. By altering the physical and symbolic landscape, the owners of moated sites came to reinforce social boundaries by making their status visible and restricted in terms of access.

Biography and the Life Course

The detailed study of objects also opens windows into how medieval people interacted with and understood the world that they inhabited. This is an interdisciplinary undertaking that requires the collation of many different sources including history, art history, and anthropology. Roberta Gilchrist, for example, has used the sociological continuum of the 'life course', from conception to the afterlife, as a framework to place and then unwrap particular social customs (Gilchrist 2007; 2012). We learn, for example, about apotropaic rings for pregnant women and the positioning of shoes of the dead in chimneys, as well as more obviously biographical items such as wedding rings. As Gilchrist links people to their 'things' and their stages of life, she reveals the lived experience of medieval Europe.

The purpose of the biography, when applied to artefacts, is that the archaeologist should study the full 'life' of an artefact from production, through exchange to 'consumption' and discard (Kopytoff 1986). This approach is well understood in prehistory and among American historical archaeologists (e.g. Deetz 1977) and can be applied to individual artefacts. The aim here is to trace the cultural contexts which produced the artefacts and those people through whose hands they moved during their life history. Gerrard (2007), for example, considers the life histories of mundane household items from a medieval rural settlement site, while Hall (2001) narrates the story of a fourteenth-century ivory knife handle with Green Man imagery from Perth. Stress is usually laid on the active role of artefacts in emphasizing the identity of their users and owners which, in the case of some medieval artefacts, could extend well beyond the expected one, two, or three generations.

Studies of iconoclasm have sought to base an understanding of the breakage and disfigurement of religious images, a significant aspect of the biography of these artefacts, in contemporary practices relating to the biographies of ordinary people, in particular the construction of medieval personhood, identities, and social relations (Graves 2008). It is noticeable just how many medieval rituals and practices pay attention to the head and hands, from the loose hair which identified maidens on wall paintings to the beard as an indicator of male virility on pottery face jugs. This repeated convergence on head and hands in social life, material culture, contemporary religious thought, and scientific and political theory gives the context in which focused attacks on religious images make historical and cultural sense. Moreover, social systems of patronage, livery and maintenance, and in particular the role of gifts of cloth and clothing to express and secure social relationships provide a context in which saints might be perceived to have defaulted on the reciprocity of social obligations. From this perspective, iconoclasm may be read as the meting out of corporal punishment on the physical representations of treacherous saints. Most iconoclasm was, and remains, the act of ordinary, undocumented people caught up in extraordinary religious convulsions. Their actions resulted from, and lead us to appreciate, a far wider context of social practices and conventions which gave them a vocabulary with which to speak in physical terms, and transform the appearance of churches to be inherited by subsequent generations.

The more detailed study of artefact damage and wear surely has further potential as we attempt to understand the involvement of artefacts in medieval social life (e.g. McCracken 1990). In the meantime, the materiality of medieval heirlooms has been the subject of a recent study which draws attention to their place in both the medieval home and parish church (Gilchrist 2013). This work emphasizes that heirlooms are not merely commemorative or biographical but that they can be transformed by ritual process. Evidently, the memories they evoke may change through time, they may not be as originally intended by their creator, and they can be intentionally removed altogether from the biographical cycle by a family or institution. The potential for interdisciplinary analysis of historical documents and material culture is considerable, as one recent regional assessment has demonstrated (Jervis et al. 2015).

In this respect, medieval archaeologists are finding that some deposits are 'special' in their nature and that 'structured deposition' is no longer an alien concept of interest only in earlier periods (Bradley et al. 2015; Gilchrist 2008 for magic; Hill 1995; Willis 1997). The purposeful concealment of coins in Scotland, for example, has been discussed by Hall (2012). Another recent case study concerns the chessmen found in sand dunes on the Isle of Lewis. The 93 Scandinavian gaming pieces found in 1831 were long believed to be a chance loss sometime between the second half of the twelfth century and into the thirteenth century (Caldwell et al. 2009). At least four different chess sets are represented and these have been the subject of several art historical investigations. Re-examination of every aspect of their deposition and cultural associations now suggests that they were not necessarily lost merchant's stock but far more likely to be the prized possession of a local prince, nobleman, or senior churchman, and then later deliberately deposited as a hoard. In a later context, the gold rings and silver coins deposited in the Thame hoard have been persuasively argued to be associated with the closure of the monasteries and the destruction of a shrine at Caversham belonging to Notley Abbey. This is deduced from a careful re-evaluation of the objects themselves and the social and spiritual context of the time. In this case the contemporary geography of the hoard, at the convergence of three parish boundaries, is likely to be significant in determining the hoard's place of burial (Standley 2016).

Conclusion

Some understanding of archaeological theory is important to every student of later medieval archaeology because the application of theory challenges orthodoxies and encourages, metaphorically at least, the excavation of past practices which might otherwise be lost in the presumption of normative behaviour. Later medieval archaeology, at least as it is now practised in the Anglo-Saxon world, has undergone a more radical transformation in its scope and approaches than many give it credit for. There is now a broad swathe of new interpretation around theoretical debate which, while it is neither consistent nor coherent in its coverage and rhetoric, affects all the topics outlined in this *Handbook*. We would go further. Some recent work, and here we are thinking particularly of Gilchrist's 2012 volume, exceeds related scholarship in other periods. Certainly, much modern writing overrides disciplinary boundaries in a way that was once unthinkable.

References cited

Altenberg, K. 2003 *Experiencing landscapes: a study of space and identity in three marginal areas of medieval Britain and Scandinavia*, Almqvist and Wiksell, Stockholm

Arnold, C. J. 1986 'Archaeology and history: the shades of confrontation and cooperation', in J. L. Bintliff and C. F. Gaffney (eds), *Archaeology at the interface: studies in archaeology's relationships with history, geography, biology and physical science*, British Archaeological Reports International Series 300, Oxford, 32–9

Arnold, E. F. 2012 *Negotiating the landscape: environment and monastic identity in the Medieval Ardennes*, University of Pennsylvania Press, Philadelphia

Astill, G. and Davies, W. 1997 *A Breton landscape*, UCL Press, London

Austin, D. and Thomas, J. 1990 'The "proper study" of medieval archaeology: a case study', in D. Austin and L. Alcock (eds), *From the Baltic to the Black Sea: studies in medieval archaeology*, Unwin Hyman, London, 43–78

Beaumont James, T. and Gerrard, C. M. 2007 *Clarendon: landscape of kings*, Windgather Press, Macclesfield

Biddick, K. 1993 'Decolonizing the English past: readings in medieval archaeology and history', *Journal of British Studies* 32, 1–23

Bintliff, J. L. 1986 'Archaeology at the interface: an historical perspective', in J. L. Bintliff and C. F. Gaffney (eds), *Archaeology at the interface: studies in archaeology's relationships with history, geography, biology and physical science*, British Archaeological Reports International Series 300, Oxford, 4–31

Boynton, S. 2006 *Shaping a monastic identity: liturgy and history at the Imperial Abbey of Farfa, 1000–1125*, Cornell University Press, Ithaca, NY

Bradley, R., Lewis, J., Mullin, D., and Branch, N. 2015 'Where water wells up from the earth: excavations at the findspot of the late Bronze Age hoard from Broadward, Shropshire', *The Antiquaries Journal* 95, 21–64

Brown, D. H., Chalmers, A., and MacNamara, A. 1997 'Light and the culture of colour in medieval pottery', in G. De Boe and F. Verhaege (eds), *Method and theory in Historical Archaeology*, Pre-printed papers of the Medieval Europe Brugge 1997 Conference, vol. 10, Zellik, 145–7

Caldwell, D. H., Hall, M. A., and Wilkinson, C. M. 2009 'The Lewis hoard of gaming pieces: a re-examination of their context, meanings, discovery and manufacture', *Medieval Archaeology* 53, 155–203

Carver, M. O. H. 1983 'Forty French towns: an essay on archaeological site evaluation and historical aims', *Oxford Journal of Archaeology* 2, 339–78

Chorley, R. J. and Haggett, P. (eds) 1967 *Models in geography*, Methuen, London

Clanchy, M. 1979 *From memory to written record: England 1066–1307*, Arnold, London

Coulson, C. 1979 'Structural symbolism in medieval castle architecture', *Journal of the British Archaeological Association* 132, 73–90

Creighton, O. H. and Liddiard, R. 2008 'Fighting yesterday's battle: beyond war or status in castle studies', *Medieval Archaeology* 52, 161–9

Cumberpatch, C. G. 1997 'Towards a phenomenological approach to the study of medieval pottery', in C. G. Cumberpatch and P. W. Blinkhorn (eds), *Not so much a pot, more a way of life*, Oxbow Monograph 83, Oxford, 125–52

Deetz, J. 1977 *In small things forgotten: the archaeology of early American life*, Anchor Press/Doubleday, Garden City, NY

Driscoll, S. T. 1984 'The new medieval archaeology: theory vs. history', *Scottish Archaeological Review* 1984, 104–8

Driscoll, S. T. 1988 'The relationship between history and archaeology: artefacts, documents and power', in S. T. Driscoll and M. R. Nieke (eds), *Power and politics in early medieval Britain and Ireland*, Edinburgh University Press, Edinburgh, 162–87

Egan, G. 1998 *The medieval household: daily Living c.1150–c.1450*, Medieval finds from excavations in London 6, Museum of London, London

Fairclough, G. 1992 'Meaningful constructions: spatial and functional analysis of medieval buildings', *Antiquity* 66, 348–66

Fergusson, P. 1989 'The refectory at Easby Abbey: form and iconography', *The Art Bulletin* 71, 334–51

Fleming, A. 2006 'Post-processual landscape archaeology: a critique', *Cambridge Archaeological Journal* 16(3), 267–80

Frizzard, A. 2007 'Shoes, boots, leggings and cloaks: the Augustinian canons and dress in Later Medieval England', *Journal of British Studies* 46(2), 245–62

Gaimster, D. 1997 'Distant voices, still-lifes: late medieval religious panel painting as a context for archaeological ceramics', in G. De Boe and F. Verhaege (eds), *Method and theory in Historical Archaeology*, Pre-printed papers of the Medieval Europe Brugge 1997 Conference, vol. 10, Zellik, 37–46

Gaimster, D. 1999 'The Baltic ceramic market, c.1200–1600: an archaeology of the Hansa', *Fennoscandia Archaeologica* 16, 59–69

Gerrard, C. M. 2003 *Medieval archaeology: understanding traditions and contemporary approaches*, Routledge, London and New York

Gerrard, C. M. 2007 'Not all archaeology is rubbish: the elusive life histories of three artefacts from Shapwick, Somerset', in M. Costen (ed.), *People and places: essays in honour of Mick Aston*, Oxbow, Oxford, 166–80

Gilchrist, R. 1988 'The spatial analysis of gender domains: a case study of medieval English nunneries', *Archaeological Review from Cambridge* 7(1), 21–9

Gilchrist, R. 1994 *Gender and material culture: the archaeology of religious women*, Routledge, London

Gilchrist, R. 1999 *Gender and archaeology: contesting the past*, Routledge, London

Gilchrist, R. 2007 'Archaeology and the life course: a time and age for gender', in L. Meskell and R. W. Preucel (eds), *A companion to Social Archaeology*, Blackwell, London, 142–60

Gilchrist, R. 2008 'Magic for the dead? The archaeology of magic in later medieval burials', *Medieval Archaeology* 52, 119–59

Gilchrist, R. 2009a 'Medieval archaeology and theory: a disciplinary leap of faith', in R. Gilchrist and A. Reynolds (eds), *Reflections: 50 years of Medieval Archaeology 1957–2007*, The Society for Medieval Archaeology Monograph 30, Leeds, 385–408

Gilchrist, R. 2009b 'Rethinking later medieval masculinity: the male body in death', in D. Sayer and H. Williams (eds), *Mortuary practices and social identities in the Middle Ages*, Exeter University Press, Exeter, 236–52

Gilchrist, R. 2012 *Medieval life: archaeology and the life course,* Boydell, Woodbridge

Gilchrist, R. 2013 'The materiality of medieval heirlooms: from biographical to sacred objects', in H. P. Hahn and H. Weiss (eds), *Mobility, meaning and transformations of things: shifting contexts of material culture through time and space*, Oxbow Books, Oxford, 170–82

Gilchrist, R. and Sloane, B. 2005 *Requiem: the medieval monastic cemetery in Britain*, Museum of London Archaeology Service, London

Giles, K. 2007 'Seeing and believing: visuality and space in pre-modern England', *World Archaeology* 39(1), 105–21

Glassie, H. 1975 *Folk housing in middle Virginia: a structural analysis of historic artefacts*, University of Tennessee Press, Knoxville

Goody, J. and Watt, I. 1963 'The consequences of literacy', *Comparative studies in society and history* 5(3), 304–45

Graves, C. P. 1989 'Social space in the English medieval parish church', *Economy and Society* 18(3), 297–322

Graves, C. P. 2007 'Sensing and believing: exploring worlds of difference in pre-modern England: a contribution to the debate opened by Kate Giles', *World Archaeology* 39, 515–31

Graves, C. P. 2008 'From an archaeology of iconoclasm to an anthropology of the body: images, punishment and personhood in England, 1500–1660', *Current Anthropology* 49(1), 35–57

Hadley, D. M. (ed.) 1999 *Masculinity in medieval Europe*, Longman, London and New York

Hadley, D. M. 2005 'Dining in disharmony in the Later Middle Ages', in M. Carroll, D. M. Hadley, and H. Willmott (eds), *Consuming passions: dining from Antiquity to the eighteenth century*, Tempus, Stroud, 101–19

Hall, M. A. 2001 'An ivory knife handle from the High Street Perth, Scotland: consuming ritual in a medieval borough', *Medieval Archaeology* 45, 169–88

Hall, M. A. 2012 'Money isn't everything: the cultural life of coins in the medieval burgh of Perth, Scotland', *Journal of Social Archaeology* 12(1), 72–91

Halsall, G. 1989 'Coverham Abbey: its context in the landscape of late medieval North Yorkshire', in R. Gilchrist and H. Mytum (eds), *The archaeology of rural monasteries*, British Archaeological Reports British Series 203, 113–39

Hanawalt, B. 1993 *Growing up in medieval London*, Oxford University Press, Oxford

Hill, J. D. 1995 *Ritual and rubbish in the Iron Age of Wessex: a study on the formation of a specific archaeological record*, Tempus Reparatum, Oxford

Hillier, B. and Hanson, J. 1984 *The social logic of space*, Cambridge University Press, Cambridge

Hinton, D. A. (ed.) 1983 *Twenty five years of medieval archaeology*, Department of Archaeology and Prehistory, University of Sheffield, Sheffield

Hinton, D. A. 2005 *Gold and gilt, pots and pins: possessions and people in medieval Britain*, Oxford University Press, Oxford

Hobsbawn, E. 1979 'An historian's comments', in B. C. Burnham and J. Kingsbury (eds), *Space, hierarchy and society*, British Archaeological Reports International Series 59, 247–52

Immonen, V. 2007 'Defining a culture: the meaning of Hanseatic in medieval Turku', *Antiquity* 81, 720–32

Jamieson, E. and Lane, R. 2015 'Monuments, mobility and medieval perceptions of designed landscapes: the Pleasance, Kenilworth', *Medieval Archaeology* 59, 255–71

Jervis, B., Briggs, C., and Tompkins, M. 2015 'Exploring text and objects: escheators' inventories and material culture in medieval English rural households', *Medieval Archaeology* 59, 168–92

Johnson, E. 2015 'Moated sites and the production of authority in the eastern Weald of England', *Medieval Archaeology* 59, 233–54

Johnson, M. 1993 *Housing culture: traditional architecture in an English landscape*, Smithsonian Institution Press, Washington, DC

Johnson, M. 1999 *Archaeological theory*, Blackwell, Oxford

Johnson, M. 2002 *Behind the castle gate: from the Middle Ages to the Renaissance*, Routledge, London

Johnson, M. (ed.) 2017 *Lived experience in the Later Middle Ages: studies of Bodiam and other elite landscapes in south-eastern England*, Oxbow, Oxford

Jope, E. M. 1972 'Models in medieval studies', in D. L. Clarke (ed.), *Models in archaeology*, Methuen & Co Ltd, London, 963–90

Kopytoff, I. 1986 'The cultural biography of things: commodification as process', in A. Appadurai (ed.), *The social life of things: commodities in cultural perspective*, Cambridge University Press, Cambridge, 64–91

Kühnel, B. 1987 *From the earthly to the heavenly Jerusalem: representations of the Holy City in Christian art of the first millennium*, Herder, Freiburg im Breisgau

Kühnel, B., Noga-Bnai, G., and Vorholt, H. (eds) 2014 *Visual constructs of Jerusalem*, Brepols, Turnhout

Leech, R. H. 1981 'Medieval urban archaeology in the northwest: problems and response', in P. Clack and S. Haselgrove (eds), *Approaches to the urban past*, Department of Archaeology, University of Durham Occasional Paper 2, Durham, 55–64

Lewis, M. 2016 'Work and the adolescent in medieval England AD 900–1550: the osteological evidence', *Medieval Archaeology* 60(1), 138–71

Markus, T. A. 1993 *Buildings and power: freedom and control in the origin of modern building types*, Routledge, London

Marshall, P. 2002 'The ceremonial function of the donjon in the twelfth century', *Château Gaillard* 20, 140–51

McCracken, C. 1990 *Culture and consumption*, University of Indiana Press, Bloomington

McClain, A. 2012 'Theory, disciplinary perspectives and the archaeology of later medieval England', *Medieval Archaeology* 56, 131–70

Mellor, M. 2004 'Changing rooms', *Medieval Ceramics* 28, 125–35

Mytum, H. 1989 'Functionalist and non-functionalist approaches in monastic archaeology', in R. Gilchrist and H. Mytum (eds), *The archaeology of rural monasteries*, British Archaeological Reports British Series 203, 339–61

Platt, C. 2007 'Revisionism in castle studies', *Medieval Archaeology* 51, 83–102

Rahtz, P. A. 1980 *Wharram Percy Data Sheets*, University of York, York

Rahtz, P. A. 1981 *Wharram Percy Data Sheets*, University of York, York

Rahtz, P. A. 1983 'New approaches to medieval archaeology, part 1', in D. A. Hinton (ed.), *Twenty five years of medieval archaeology*, Department of Archaeology and Prehistory, University of Sheffield, Sheffield, 12–23

Richardson, A. 2003 'Gender and space in English royal palaces c.1160–c.1547: a study in access analysis and imagery', *Medieval Archaeology* 47, 131–65

Roberts, B. K. 1977 *Rural settlement in Britain*, Dawson, Folkestone

Shahar, S. 1992 *Childhood in the Middle Ages*, Routledge, London

Skeates, R. 2010 *An archaeology of the senses: prehistoric Malta*, Oxford University Press, London

Standley, E. 2016 'Hid in the earth and secret places: a reassessment of a hoard of later medieval gold rings and silver coins found near the River Thame', *The Antiquaries Journal* 96, 117–42

Stocker, D. 1992 'The shadow of the general's armchair', *The Archaeological Journal* 149, 415–20

Vince, A. 1977 'The medieval and post-medieval ceramic industry of the Malvern region: the study of a ware and its distribution', in D. P. S. Peacock (ed.), *Pottery and early commerce*, Academic Press, London, 257–305

Wells, E. 2013 *An archaeology of sensory experience: pilgrimage in the medieval Church c.1170–c.1550*, unpublished PhD thesis, University of Durham

Willis, S. 1997 'Samian: beyond dating', in K. Meadows, C. Lemke, and J. Heron (eds), *TRAC 96: Proceedings of the 6th Theoretical Roman Archaeology Conference*, Oxbow, Oxford, 38–54

Woolgar, C. M. 2006 *The senses in late medieval Britain*, Yale University Press, New Haven

CHAPTER 4

THE WRITTEN EVIDENCE FOR THE LATER MIDDLE AGES

SIMON A. DRAPER

THE period 1100–1500 saw a boom in writing of all kinds in Britain, from literary works such as romances and treatises to legal and administrative documents including charters, registers, and accounts. A key driving force was the growth in the production of official records, both at a national and regional level for the Crown and Church, but also locally for institutions such as manors, boroughs, and guilds (Clanchy 2013). Many of those records have survived in archives and it is the range of those documents and the kinds of information contained within them that I propose to explore in this chapter with particular reference to recent research in later medieval archaeology.

In a short essay such as this it is not possible to cover the topic in depth. I do not propose to examine manuscript illustrations or medieval maps, of which barely 30 local examples survive from Britain (all of them English) before 1500: the cartographic representation of space was not something widely practised or even considered before the sixteenth century (Skelton and Harvey 1986). Rather, I offer this chapter as an archaeologist-turned-historian with practical experience of working with both material and written evidence in southern and midland England. I wish to share my experiences of finding and interpreting medieval sources, as well as highlight some areas where documentary history and archaeology can interact in mutually beneficial ways to enhance our understanding of the medieval past. Lastly, I will consider the relationship between history and archaeology and the current state of collaboration between the two disciplines.

FINDING WRITTEN EVIDENCE

Any archaeologist or historian looking for medieval records about a particular locality or theme may be forgiven for being daunted. There is a bewildering array of source material available for study, some of which has been transcribed and printed, although a great deal remains only in manuscript form. Long-running societies dedicated to publishing scholarly editions of medieval sources have undoubtedly improved access to, and knowledge of, several of the more important ones. The Early English Text Society (founded in 1864) has published a good proportion of the surviving Middle English literary texts, including all of the medieval drama, most of the romances, and much prose and poetry, such as sermons, treatises, letters, and cookery books. Other literary works in Latin and other languages have been published as part of the Rolls Series (1858–1911), including almost all the great medieval chronicles, as well as hagiographical works and some major monastic cartularies. A wide range of source materials illustrative of English medieval political, religious, and social life can also be found in four volumes of the English Historical Documents series (Douglas and Greenaway 1981; Myers 1969; Rothwell 1975; Williams 1967).

National government records have been published at different dates and in different formats. Some of the earliest editions of material currently held at The National Archives (TNA) are those of the Record Commission in the early nineteenth century, of which the Hundred Rolls (*Rotuli Hundredorum*) of 1274–5 and 1279–80 and the *Valor Ecclesiasticus* (a valuation and survey of Church possessions) of 1535 remain particularly useful. Also at TNA are records of the Chancery, the department at the heart of medieval royal administration in England and Wales. Its most important records include the Charter, Close, Patent, Liberate, and Fine Rolls, detailing the day-to-day business of government, and Inquisitions *Post Mortem*, which are enquiries into the possessions of people who held property directly from the king. Those records have been 'calendared' or summarized by historians and published in volumes which are increasingly being made available online through websites such as British History Online and Medieval Genealogy. Some equivalent Scottish Chancery records housed in the National Archives of Scotland (NAS) are published in the series *Registrum Magni Sigilli Regum Scotorum*.

Records of the Exchequer (the government department responsible for the king's finances) at TNA include surveys, such as Domesday Book (published in multiple editions), taxation lists (lay subsidies and poll taxes: Fenwick 1998–2005), and Pipe Rolls—accounts for lands in royal possession beginning in the mid-twelfth century—which are being serialized by the Pipe Roll Society. Exchequer Rolls for Scotland 1326–1600 in NAS have also been printed in 23 volumes. Some records of the English royal courts of justice are useful for both historians and archaeologists. Feet of Fines—records of land transactions from the court of Common Pleas—have mostly been published by county record societies, and some abstracts are available online. The workings of the court of King's Bench have also partly been calendared as the *Curia Regis* Rolls, and the Selden Society has published additional medieval legal records.

Church records can be divided broadly into those relating to the papacy, Church jurisdictions (e.g. parishes and dioceses), and religious houses. Papal records have been calendared as Papal Registers and Papal Letters, whilst the majority of medieval bishops' registers with other diocesan records (including registered copies of early wills) have been published by societies such as the Canterbury and York Society (Smith 1981; 2004). The charters and other official documents issued by medieval English bishops are being serialized as English Episcopal *Acta*. Records of individual parish churches generally do not survive from before the Reformation, but occasionally churchwardens' accounts extend back before 1500 (e.g. Hobhouse 1890) and information taken from bishops' registers and archdeacons' visitations can be important for church surveys. Chief amongst monastic records are the books of charters (cartularies) and other records (registers) relating to monastic estates, several of which have been published by national and local societies (Davis 1958). Sir William Dugdale's *Monasticon Anglicanum* contains transcriptions of numerous monastic charters, including some for which manuscripts have since been lost (Dugdale 1817–30).

Local records mainly comprise those of institutions, such as manors, boroughs, and guilds, and individuals, including letters and land charters. Most of these remain unpublished, but some have been printed by county or national record societies (e.g. Pugh 1970) and excerpts often appear in secondary literature (e.g. Ault 1972). The Paston Letters is perhaps the best known collection of medieval correspondence, comprising the private letters of members of the Paston family of Norfolk gentry between 1422 and 1509, and offer rich pickings for historians and archaeologists alike (Beadle and Richmond 2005; Davis 2004). Manorial records broadly comprise three classes of records: accounts (detailing manorial income and expenditure on a yearly basis), court rolls (records of the manor court, which regulated tenancies and customs on the manor), and surveys of tenants and their holdings, which can be subdivided into rentals (focused on the rents and labour services owed) and terriers (usually describing the name, size, and owner or occupier of each parcel of land). Some manorial records survive in national repositories such as TNA, particularly for periods during which those manors were in Crown custody, but otherwise they are mainly to be found in county record offices or archives of private or institutional landowners, such as Berkeley Castle in Gloucestershire (Wells-Furby 2004) or the various colleges of Oxford and Cambridge universities. Both Oxford's Bodleian Library and the British Library in London also house extensive collections of medieval manorial records and charters. Occasionally medieval local records will be found in overseas repositories: for example, the fourteenth-century court rolls for Bromesberrow in Gloucestershire are held by Harvard University Law School (Draper 2010).

Studying medieval manuscripts is an exercise for which time and patience is needed, as well as some skill in reading old handwriting (palaeography) and translating medieval Latin (occasionally also Middle English and Anglo-Norman French); although the fact that most official records are formulaic means it is often not too hard to gain a basic understanding. Increasingly archival catalogues and finding aids are becoming available online, enabling documents to be located more easily, but it still worth seeking the help of an archivist, particularly for smaller archives where cataloguing may be less than comprehensive. TNA's website facilitates searches across multiple English archives and county record offices, as well as TNA itself, and provides access to the Manorial Documents Register, a database listing the whereabouts of all known documents for English manors. Shortcuts to locating original records are often provided by good local histories, such as those published by the Victoria County History for England, and themed studies by modern academic historians (e.g. Dyer 2002).

INTERPRETING WRITTEN EVIDENCE

As with archaeological remains, written evidence must be interpreted with great care; it almost never provides a clear window onto the past. Texts and records were created by many different people for a wide variety of reasons, few of which can be fully recovered by modern individuals. An element of bias will be inherent in almost every one, whether conscious or unconscious, and there will often be frustrating gaps, omissions, or inconsistencies which are hard, if not impossible, to compensate for (see Harvey 1991 on the pitfalls of using documents for landscape studies). The languages and handwriting of the period present their own challenges, meaning that the original sense of a text may become obscured or altered in later transcription and translation. The vagaries of document production and preservation also have to be taken into account: documents tend to be more plentiful for high-status people and pursuits, as well as for places in which the Crown, aristocracy, or Church had a particular interest. Manorial records frequently do not survive for manors in lay ownership. Furthermore, scribal error was not uncommon. Accounts were often based on those of the preceding year, from which place-names and personal names were simply copied (or miscopied) from one year to the next (e.g. TNA, SC 6/HENVIII/2853–2879), and descriptions of property in deeds and court rolls were sometimes repeated from one transaction to the next, leading to a building or structure being described as 'new' long after the term had ceased to be accurate.

Perhaps the greatest interpretational difficulty facing both historians and archaeologists is reconciling written evidence with reality. Very often documents tell us what was intended to happen, rather than what necessarily did happen. This is particularly the case with wills, whilst treatises are often idealistic with a strong moral or religious component. Licences are particularly problematic. The number issued for chantry chapels 'almost certainly exceeds the actual foundations themselves' (Roffey 2007, 32), whilst the royal licensing of deer parks may not have been as rigorous as the documents alone appear to suggest (Mileson 2009, 121–45). Similarly, licences to crenellate (usually found in the Patent Rolls) did not always result in the building of a fortified manor house or castle (Davis 2007). Such a licence lies at the heart of the so-called 'battle for Bodiam', a long-running academic debate in which some have taken Sir Edward Dalyngrigge's 1385 licence to crenellate 'for the defence of the adjacent country' as direct evidence of a primarily military function for Bodiam Castle in East Sussex (Platt 2007). As Liddiard (2005, 9) has pointed out, however, 'the licence to crenellate did not confer the "right" of fortification onto Dalyngrigge and its wording cannot be taken literally. Licences were actively sought out by the recipient as a marker of a particular social relationship with the king'. Therefore written evidence cannot be taken at face value, and it is for this reason that archaeology is crucial to our understanding of the medieval past, often complementing the historical perspective, but at times, as at Bodiam, challenging it.

Written Evidence
and Later Medieval Archaeology

The following discussion is designed to represent a snapshot of how written evidence is being used by late medieval archaeologists and archaeological evidence by late medieval historians. Rather than attempting to survey the whole field of research, it will instead focus on a small number of select case studies: it is not intended to be comprehensive.

The Shapwick Project in Somerset provides a good example of a major landscape archaeology project that has made full use of documentary and cartographic evidence alongside physical remains. In particular, a technique known as regressive map analysis—working backwards in time through all available maps of an area and redrawing them to a common scale so that changes between them can be observed and measured—has shed new light on the origins and plan of the medieval village. Whilst the maps used were not medieval in date (starting with the Ordnance Survey and working back through the 1839 tithe survey and various eighteenth-century enclosure and estate maps), they provided an accurate picture of the village plan back to *c.*1750 and, when combined with architectural, archaeological, and documentary evidence (particularly a detailed manorial survey of 1515), presented a reasonable impression back to the late fifteenth century. The technique also revealed that the village had been laid out to a plan resembling a ladder using multiples of a unit known as a 'rope' (20 feet), an event which may have taken place as early as the tenth century (Gerrard with Aston 2007, 44–74).

Another innovative use of documentary and cartographic evidence at Shapwick was the attempt to reconstruct the layout of the medieval open fields using the descriptions and field-names contained in the 1515 survey. As well as giving a detailed understanding of the geography of the medieval landscape, including field and furlong boundaries, tracks, quarries, and mill sites, it also enabled archaeologically suggestive field-names to be located and targeted for fieldwork (including *Oldechurche*, where the remains of the pre-1330 parish church were revealed) as well as providing insights into medieval perceptions of landscape; for example, *Swetefurlong* evidently brought greater pleasure than *Shytbrok* (Gerrard with Aston 2007, 74–101; Aston and Gerrard 2013, 22–5). As Aston and Gerrard observe (2013, 22) field-names 'are a severely under-researched resource for most parts of Britain', but medieval archaeologists are gradually becoming aware of their potential (Mileson 2012, 92).

A final example of written and archaeological evidence coming together at Shapwick is provided by the 'new' manor house site, where a combination of archaeological, architectural, and documentary research has enabled a reconstruction to be made of the layout of Glastonbury Abbey's *curia* or manorial complex (Figure 4.1). The moat—hitherto unexpected, but located by excavation—was documented in the 1515 survey, along with rooms and buildings such as the hall, chamber, storeroom, kitchen, stable, and barton, all inside the moat. Additional information was provided by fourteenth-century account rolls, which listed amongst other features a dovecote, ox-house, postern, great

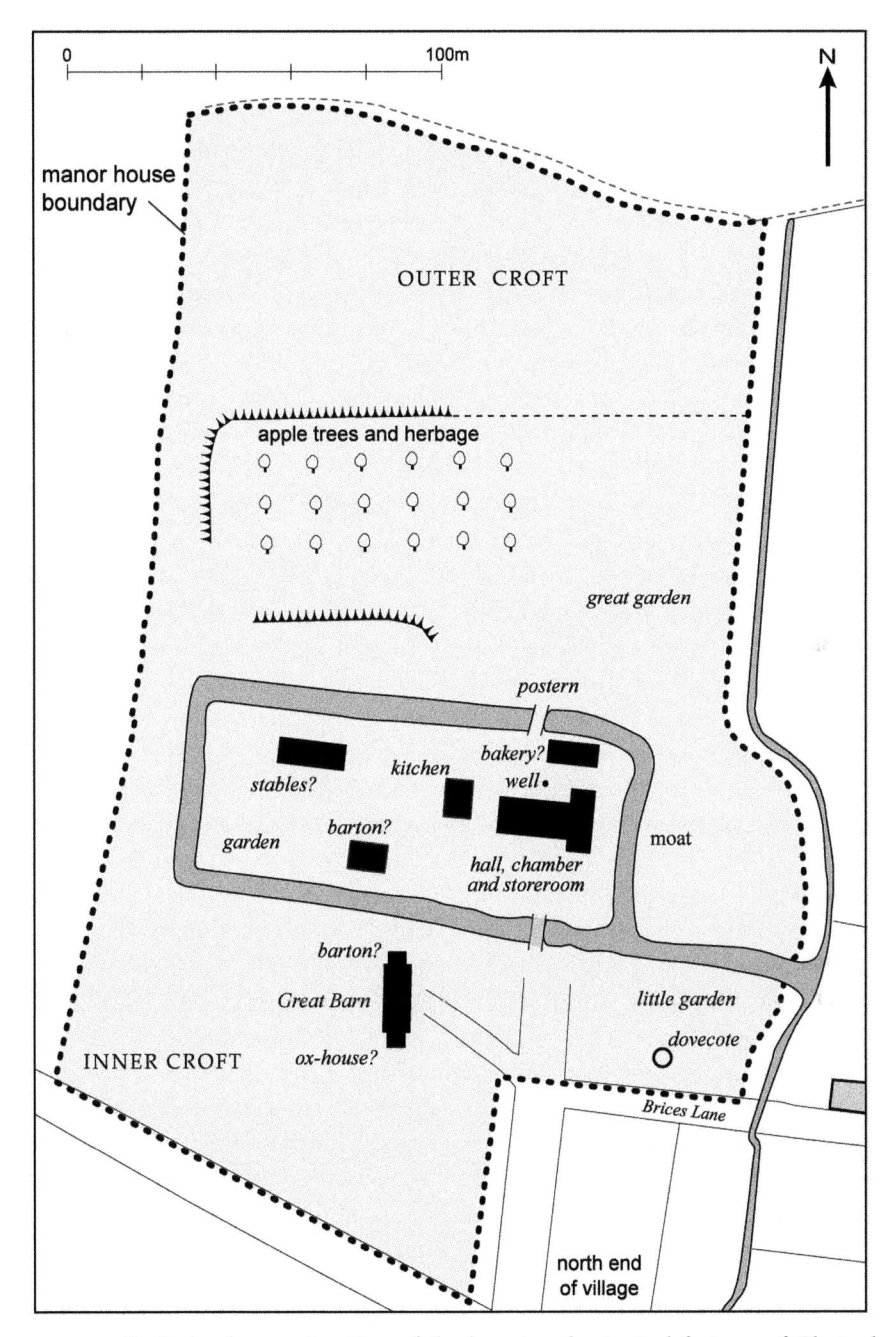

FIGURE 4.1 Conjectural reconstruction of the layout and principal features of Glastonbury Abbey's manor house at Shapwick, Somerset, in the later medieval period. Buildings as for *c*.1500. In italics are terms used in medieval documents (Gerrard with Aston 2007, 992)

(drawn by Alejandra Gutiérrez © Christopher Gerrard)

and little gardens, and inner and outer crofts. The medieval kitchen and hall both survive within the fabric of Shapwick House, dated by dendrochronology to 1428 and 1489 respectively (Aston and Gerrard 2013, 227–39).

At another medieval English village, Wharram Percy in North Yorkshire, the archaeology was scrutinized for more than 60 years, yet it was only in the latter stages of research that the physical evidence was reassessed in the light of the village's complex manorial history. As a result of the documentary research it was possible, with reasonable confidence, to ascribe major changes to the two manor houses, parish church, and village lands to changes in seisin (possession or occupancy, rather than absentee ownership) of the manors in 1166 and 1254 (Wrathmell 2012, 262–77). The late twelfth century in particular saw 'considerable architectural elaboration of St Martin's [church], accompanied by the erection of the South Manor buildings and the creation of the open-field ridge and furrow, all signifying the arrival of the Percys as lords in demesne' (Wrathmell 2012, 221). As this example shows, even if manorial records (court rolls, accounts, etc.) do not survive, manorial history (reconstructed largely from national records) can still inform medieval archaeology.

In the absence of manorial records at Wharram Percy medieval peasant life was studied by combining the excavated evidence for buildings, gardens, fields, crops, animals, and possessions with written evidence from neighbouring communities with better surviving documentary records (Wrathmell 2012, 312–40). Particularly informative were early probate inventories (a class of document generally rare before 1530), from which that of William Acklum of neighbouring Wharram le Street dated 1481 was studied in detail, enabling (when considered alongside the archaeological evidence) detailed reconstruction drawings of the furnishings of one peasant farmhouse to be made. Such a method 'helps us in many ways visualize aspects of the peasant economy' (Dyer 2012, 347) and graphically represents the coming together of written evidence and archaeology.

Another recent study of medieval peasant housing in midland England employs the same technique with the inventory of Robert Dene of Stoneleigh in Warwickshire dated 1552 (Alcock and Miles 2013, 157–9), but the project is also notable for its integration of architectural, archaeological, and documentary evidence in the study of more than 100 buildings across five counties. A significant result is that archaeological techniques (particularly dendrochronology) have challenged historians' views of later medieval peasant housing, which have so far largely been based on documents alone and have given the impression of a post-Black Death 'peasant housing crisis' characterized by decaying houses and the struggle (recorded in court rolls) between lords and tenants over their repair. Instead, it is now clear that numerous new or renewed high-quality timber-framed houses were erected by peasants during this period, several of which still survive as standing buildings. 'The new information from dated cruck buildings makes an important contribution to our knowledge. It helps to correct the bias of our written sources, which give a very one-sided account of the history of houses in the period 1380–1510' (Dyer 2013, 117).

A further example of the benefits of combining the archaeological study of standing buildings with documentary research comes from Wiltshire, where the Wiltshire

Dendrochronology Project has succeeded in dating 12 buildings across the county, including a seven-bay barn at Manor Farm, Kingston Deverill (Figure 4.2), containing timbers felled *c.*1407, *c.*1408, and in the winter of 1409–10 (Lloyd 2013). Armed with these dates it was then possible for a historian to locate within the surviving manorial account rolls a detailed entry for the building of the barn in the financial year 1408–9 which listed the materials used, their costs, and the wages and expenses of the craftsmen employed (Wiltshire and Swindon Archives, 192/32/vii). Had it not been for the dendrochronology, this important piece of historical evidence may have been overlooked, since the extensive collection of medieval accounts for Kingston Deverill spanning the period 1396–1502 had previously only been sampled by researchers (Alex Craven pers. comm.).

High-status buildings are increasingly being studied in an interdisciplinary manner. The challenge issued to the document-led militaristic interpretation of castles by their archaeology-driven reinterpretation as symbols of status and lordship has already been alluded to in discussion of the 'battle of Bodiam' above, and some recent castle excavation reports succeed in interweaving written and archaeological evidence to create altogether richer narratives. The report on Dryslwyn Castle in Carmarthenshire combines the archaeological evidence for its construction and the diet, economy, and daily lives of its inhabitants with the written evidence, both for its military and political history, drawn principally from English and Welsh chronicles, but also its garrisoning and provisioning, as detailed in various account rolls (Caple 2007). A similar approach has

FIGURE 4.2 The barn at Manor Farm, Kingston Deverill, Wiltshire, built *c.*1408, as demonstrated by both dendrochronology and documentary evidence

(© Alex Craven)

been taken at Wallingford Castle in Oxfordshire, where the evidence of chronicles (particularly *Gesta Stephani*) as well as various national and local records is considered together with the evidence from excavations, geophysics, and earthworks. In particular, the documents identified several phases of expansion of the castle, which were reflected in the archaeology (Christie and Creighton 2013, 145–218). An unusual source of written evidence for Wallingford Castle was three references in medieval romance literature: 'scholars have sometimes marginalized such material as a source of valid information, but references to castles in medieval romances should be registered as an important reflection of contemporary perceptions of these places' (Creighton 2013, 160). Post-medieval written and cartographic sources were not neglected at Wallingford and provided useful topographical details concerning the medieval castle and borough, including the location of a prison called 'Cloere Brien' (Christie and Creighton 2013, 36).

The use of written evidence in later medieval archaeology is not confined to investigations of landscapes, settlements, and buildings. Zooarchaeologists studying animal bones often turn to literary or documentary sources, either for comparison with the archaeological record, or for help when interpreting it. An example of the former is the recent comparison of bone assemblages from the kitchen middens of religious houses with textual evidence for medieval Christian doctrine on fasting. The result—no clear archaeological signal for fasting—raises questions as to the strictness of observance (O'Connor 2007, 4). A similar comparison of theory with practice has been made with medieval hunting, where studies of deer bone assemblages in England indicate that the rigid protocol for aristocratic hunting as described in various thirteenth- and fourteenth-century hunting manuals appears to have been increasingly followed in practice. In particular, the scarcity of certain deer bones compared to others is seen as evidence for the documented 'unmaking' ritual, whereby the quarry was cut up and certain joints of meat gifted to participants or fed to the hounds (Thomas 2007).

An example of written evidence aiding the interpretation of animal bones is a recent study of medieval butchery which examines cut and chop marks in the context of documentary evidence for the establishment of the Guild of Butchers in the fourteenth century and the guild's increasing refinement of butchery practice through the development of new tools and the training of butchers through apprenticeships (Seetah 2007). Similarly, zooarchaeologists have turned to historical evidence to explain why a peacock's foot bone from Carisbrooke Castle on the Isle of Wight and a crane's foot bone from Lincoln exhibit cut marks indicative of the birds' toes having been removed: such a procedure was advocated in later medieval recipe books as a method of dressing game birds for the table (Sykes 2009, 353).

Bioarchaeologists studying human bones do so with the aid of historical information (see Chapter 51). In relation to determining health from skeletal remains we are reminded that 'disease that only affects the soft tissues, such as plague and childhood diseases such as measles and chicken pox, will not be detected unless contemporary historical data is accessed' (Roberts 2009, 320). Thus modern study of the Black Death relies on a combination of archaeological and written evidence. The recently excavated East Smithfield cemetery in London is a case in point, which the excavators conclude 'without the written sources… would just be yet another possible Black Death burial ground, archaeologically identified only as an emergency cemetery probably of the mid-14th century or later' (Grainger et al. 2008, 33).

Bioarchaeology and written evidence also complement one another in the study of medical treatment and diet. Trepanation, or making a hole in the skull to treat a range of medical complaints, is well documented both textually and archaeologically in the later medieval period, whilst the widespread famines and harvest failures recorded in numerous fourteenth-century documents across Britain appear to be reflected in the general increase in enamel defects (or hypoplasias) seen in teeth over the period (Roberts 2009, 316–19). Increasingly bioarchaeologists are taking a 'biocultural' approach to their research, incorporating evidence from several academic spheres. A recent study of childhood epidemiology in Britain interprets skeletal remains in the contexts of written and pictorial evidence, including an analysis of childhood accidents based on accounts in medieval coroners' rolls and hagiographies (Penny-Mason and Gowland 2014; and see Chapter 48 in this *Handbook*).

The study of artefacts in later medieval Britain has traditionally been the domain of archaeology, particularly since a whole raft of everyday or household objects lay outside the scope of routine medieval documentation, whilst most personal possessions mentioned in written sources belonged to a small segment of the medieval population: the richest or most powerful. One recent study of possessions in medieval Britain, however, gives archaeological and historical evidence equal billing and 'tries to avoid giving priority to one sort of data over any other' (Hinton 2005, 3). Written evidence is cited from sources as diverse as poems, chronicles, inventories, tax lists, and legislation. For example, the chronicler Gerald of Wales's comments about the absence of tables from Welsh princes' halls are countered by the example of a thirteenth-century aquamanile from Nant Col in Gwynedd, which 'suggests a very different level of social behaviour', whilst gemstone rings are studied in the knowledge from romantic poetry that each gem was popularly associated with a different quality: 'coral of godnesse', 'rubye of rightfulnesse', and 'crystal of cleannesse' (Hinton 2005, 185, 213; see Chapter 49 in this *Handbook*). Hinton (2005, 3) believes that 'if a question is worth asking, it is worth answering with the use of all the information that is available, be it material survival or textual statement'.

Conclusion: History and Later Medieval Archaeology

The preceding discussion has focused on handpicked examples of 'best practice' in the integration of written and archaeological evidence from across later medieval Britain, thereby presenting a healthy view of the relationship between the academic disciplines of archaeology and history. However, not all practitioners share my optimism: 'medieval archaeologists do not deal with texts enough; they regard them as historians' business.

But that means they will remain stuck in paradigms that historians have invented for them, without being able to critique their internal structuration. Historians face the same problem if they do not engage with archaeology from the inside; and far from enough historians do it' (Wickham 2010, 431).

Wickham's first point, that archaeologists on the whole do not engage enough with written evidence, is illustrated by the recent 'backlog' publication of the mostly deserted medieval village at Caldecote in Hertfordshire excavated between 1973 and 1977 (Beresford 2009), which prompted one historian to publish a critique bemoaning not only the lack of integration of historical material, but (more seriously) the almost complete ignorance of the wealth of evidence contained in the surviving manor court rolls, 'the most detailed documentary source available' to students of the medieval village (Dyer 2009, 1). As Dyer observed, the information contained within the court rolls would not only have greatly enriched discussion of peasant life and economy, but also would have reframed discussion of the fabric and layout of the village: 'reading the Caldecote court rolls suggests that some of the conclusions in the excavation report need to be revised' (Dyer 2009, 5). Unfortunately, no further funds for additional historical study could be made available during the write-up process. From my own perspective, I remain concerned that far too many excavation reports barely make use of documentary evidence, and those that do often present it in isolation from the archaeology, usually in a chapter of its own. The reverse view, that medieval historians do not engage enough with archaeology, has been commented on by McClain (2012, 157), who has singled out two overview volumes on the medieval economy and the Anglo-Norman Church for criticism in this regard. The Victoria County History has also come under fire for its apparent inconsistency in the treatment and mapping of medieval townscapes, which 'potentially propagates a view that landscapes are themselves problematic (and even untrustworthy) sources for historical analysis and study' (Lilley 2012, 73).

Part of the problem appears to lie with the disciplinary 'pigeon holes' that researchers find themselves being placed in. Johnson (2010, 10–11) has parodied the differing approaches of historians, architectural historians, folk-life enthusiasts, and archaeologists to the study of vernacular buildings, observing that 'a particular disciplinary training... gives the scholar not just a set of spectacles but a set of blinkers as well'. Gardiner and Rippon (2009, 71–2) have discussed the problems of dealing with the sheer quantity of evidence available: 'we are asking medieval archaeologists to be experts in their own field, and also to have more than a passing acquaintance with numerous other disciplines. Few other subjects make such a demand upon their practitioners'. Another problem is historians and archaeologists 'talking past' each other (Gardiner and Rippon 2009, 71; Johnson 2010, 10); 'there is the sense of two cultures talking together, but not necessarily *to* each other' (O'Connor 2008, 90).

According to Gilchrist and Reynolds (2009, 6) 'the elephant in the room' is medieval archaeology's seeming lack of confidence in its ability to forge distinctive narratives. Wickham (2010, 431), however, has replied to this concern by arguing that 'archaeology can easily write its own grand narratives of all aspects of the past, if it takes textuality by the horns and interrogates it properly, from a material direction. This has not been done much yet; but my sense ... is that it will not be long before it is'. There is an increasing sense, then, that medieval archaeology in Britain is nearing maturity and that its stages of development thus far have to a significant degree been defined by its relationship to history. 'Childhood' saw a resentment of medieval archaeology's perceived status as the 'handmaiden of history' and calls for a clean break with the discipline (e.g. Austin 1990; see Moreland 2010). This was followed by 'adolescence', when historical archaeology was redefined as something more than text-aided archaeology (e.g. Andrén 1998; Moreland 2001) and there were calls for medieval archaeology's inclusion within a wider 'interdisciplinary cultural history' (Hines 2004). Now, in early 'adulthood', there is widespread acceptance of the inherently interdisciplinary nature of medieval archaeology and this is reflected in an increasingly distinct research agenda. Clearly much remains to be done in further integrating the two disciplines and forms of evidence, and there is an almost entirely new relationship to be explored with art history (McClain 2012), but at least historians and archaeologists are now by and large working towards a common goal; 'not competing to provide an interpretation of the past, but ... offering alternative and preferably complementary routes to it' (Gardiner and Rippon 2009, 71).

References cited

Alcock, N. and Miles, D. 2013 *The medieval peasant house in midland England*, Oxbow, Oxford

Andrén, A. 1998 *Between artifacts and texts: historical archaeology in global perspective*, Plenum, New York

Aston, M. and Gerrard, C. M. 2013 *Interpreting the English village: landscape and community at Shapwick, Somerset*, Windgather, Oxford

Ault, W. O. 1972 *Open-field farming in medieval England*, Allen and Unwin, London

Austin, D. 1990 'The "proper study" of medieval archaeology', in D. Austin and L. Alcock (eds), *From the Black Sea to the Baltic: studies in medieval archaeology*, Unwin Hyman, London, 9–42

Beadle, R. and Richmond, C. (eds) 2005 *Paston letters and papers of the fifteenth century III*, Early English Text Society 22, London

Beresford, G. 2009 *Caldecote: the development and desertion of a Hertfordshire village*, The Society for Medieval Archaeology Monograph 28, Leeds

Caple, C. 2007 *Excavations at Dryslwyn Castle, 1980–95*, The Society for Medieval Archaeology Monograph 26, Leeds

Christie, N. and Creighton, O. H. 2013 *Transforming townscapes. From burh to borough: the archaeology of Wallingford, AD 800–1400*, The Society for Medieval Archaeology Monograph 35, Leeds

Clanchy, M. T. 2013 *From memory to written record: England 1066–1307*, Wiley-Blackwell, Chichester (3rd edn)

Creighton, O. H. 2013 'Romance Wallingford: literary perspectives on the castle', in N. Christie and O. H. Creighton, *Transforming townscapes. From burh to borough: the archaeology of Wallingford, AD 800–1400*, The Society for Medieval Archaeology Monograph 35, Leeds, 160–1

Davis, G. R. C. 1958 *Medieval cartularies of Great Britain: a short catalogue*, Longmans, London

Davis, N. (ed.) 2004 *Paston letters and papers of the fifteenth century I–II*, Early English Text Society 20–1, London (2 volumes)

Davis, P. 2007 'English licences to crenellate 1199–1567', *Castle Studies Group Journal* 20, 226–45

Douglas, D. C. and Greenaway, G. W. (eds) 1981 *English historical documents II c.1042–1189*, Eyre Methuen, London (2nd edn)

Draper, S. A. 2010 'Bromesberrow', in A. R. J. Juřica (ed.), *The Victoria History of the County of Gloucester XII*, Boydell, Woodbridge, 95–122

Dugdale, Sir W. (revd J. Caley, H. Ellis, and B. Bandinel), 1817–30 *Monasticon Anglicanum*, James Bohn, London (6 volumes)

Dyer, C. 2002 *Making a living in the Middle Ages*, Yale University Press, London

Dyer, C. 2009 'Excavations and documents: the case of Caldecote, Hertfordshire', *Medieval Settlement Research* 24, 1–5

Dyer, C. 2012 'The inventory of William Akclum and its context', in S. Wrathmell (ed.), *A history of Wharram and its neighbours* (Wharram, a study of settlement on the Yorkshire Wolds 13), York University Archaeological Publications 15, York, 342–9

Dyer, C. 2013 'Medieval peasant buildings 1250–1550: documents and historical significance', in N. Alcock and D. Miles, *The medieval peasant house in midland England*, Oxbow, Oxford, 105–18

Fenwick, C. (ed.) 1998–2005 *The poll taxes of 1377, 1379 and 1381*, Oxford University Press, Oxford (3 volumes)

Gardiner, M. and Rippon, S. 2009 'Looking to the future of medieval archaeology', in R. Gilchrist and A. Reynolds (eds), *Reflections: 50 years of medieval archaeology 1957–2007*, The Society for Medieval Archaeology Monograph 30, Leeds, 65–75

Gerrard, C. M. with Aston, M. 2007 *The Shapwick Project: a rural landscape explored*, The Society for Medieval Archaeology Monograph 25, Leeds

Gilchrist, R. and Reynolds, A. 2009 'Introduction: "the elephant in the room" and other tales of medieval archaeology', in R. Gilchrist and A. Reynolds (eds), *Reflections: 50 years of medieval archaeology 1957–2007*, The Society for Medieval Archaeology Monograph 30, Leeds, 1–7

Grainger, I., Hawkins, D., Cowal, L., and Mikulski, R. 2008 *The Black Death cemetery, East Smithfield, London*, Museum of London Archaeology Service Monograph 43, London

Harvey, P. D. A. 1991 'The documents of landscape history: snares and delusions', *Landscape History* 13, 47–52

Hines, J. 2004 *Voices in the past: English literature and archaeology*, D. S. Brewer, Woodbridge

Hinton, D. A. 2005 *Gold and gilt, pots and pins: possessions and people in medieval Britain*, Oxford University Press, Oxford

Hobhouse, E. (ed.) 1890 *Church-wardens' accounts of Croscombe, Pilton, Yatton, Tintinhull, Morebath, and St Michael's, Bath, ranging from AD 1349 to 1560*, Somerset Record Society 4, London

Johnson, M. 2010 *English Houses 1300–1800: vernacular architecture, social life*, Longman, Harlow

Liddiard, R. 2005 *Castles in context: power, symbolism and landscape 1066–1500*, Windgather, Macclesfield

Lilley, K. 2012 'Review article: the Victoria County History and the landscape of towns: a review and critique', *Landscapes* 13(1), 70–4

Lloyd, A. 2013 'The Wiltshire Dendrochronology Project 2009–2011: a summary of results', *Vernacular Architecture* 44, 62–73

McClain, A. 2012 'Theory, disciplinary perspectives and the archaeology of later medieval England', *Medieval Archaeology* 56, 131–70

Mileson, S. A. 2009 *Parks in medieval England*, Oxford University Press, Oxford

Mileson, S. A. 2012 'The South Oxfordshire Project: perceptions of landscape, settlement and society, c.500–1650', *Landscape History* 33(2), 83–98

Moreland, J. 2001 *Archaeology and text*, Duckworth, London

Moreland, J. 2010 *Archaeology, theory and the Middle Ages*, Duckworth, London

Myers, A. R. (ed.) 1969 *English historical documents IV 1327–1485*, Eyre and Spottiswoode, London

O'Connor, T. 2007 'Thinking about beastly bodies', in. A Pluskowski (ed.), *Breaking and shaping beastly bodies: animals and material culture in the Middle Ages*, Oxbow, Oxford, 1–10

O'Connor, T. 2008 'Review of *Food in medieval England: diet and nutrition*', *Environmental Archaeology* 13(1), 89–90

Penny-Mason, B. J. and Gowland, R. L. 2014 'The children of the Reformation: childhood palaeoepidemiology in Britain, AD 1000–1700', *Medieval Archaeology* 58, 162–94

Platt, C. 2007 'Revisionism in castle studies: a caution', *Medieval Archaeology* 51, 83–102

Pugh, R. B. (ed.) 1970 *Court Rolls of the Wiltshire manors of Adam de Stratton*, Wiltshire Record Series 24, Devizes

Roberts, C. 2009 'Health and welfare in medieval England: the human skeletal remains contextualized', in R. Gilchrist and A. Reynolds (eds), *Reflections: 50 years of medieval archaeology 1957–2007*, The Society for Medieval Archaeology Monograph 30, Leeds, 308–25

Roffey, S. 2007 *The medieval chantry chapel: an archaeology*, Boydell, Woodbridge

Rothwell, H. (ed.) 1975 *English historical documents III 1189–1327*, Eyre and Spottiswoode, London

Seetah, K. 2007 'The Middle Ages on the block: animals, guilds and meat in the medieval period', in A. Pluskowski (ed.), *Breaking and shaping beastly bodies: animals and material culture in the Middle Ages*, Oxbow, Oxford, 18–31

Skelton, R. A. and Harvey, P. D. A. 1986 *Local maps and plans from medieval England*, Clarendon Press, Oxford

Smith, D. M. 1981 *Guide to Bishops' Registers of England and Wales*, Royal Historical Society Guides and Handbooks 11, London

Smith, D. M. 2004 *Supplement to the guide to Bishops' Registers of England and Wales*, Canterbury and York Society, York

Sykes, N. 2009 'Animals, the bones of medieval society', in R. Gilchrist and A. Reynolds (eds), *Reflections: 50 years of medieval archaeology 1957–2007*, The Society for Medieval Archaeology Monograph 30, Leeds, 347–61

Thomas, R. 2007 'Chasing the ideal? Ritualism, pragmatism and the later medieval hunt in England', in A. Pluskowski (ed.), *Breaking and shaping beastly bodies: animals and material culture in the Middle Ages*, Oxbow, Oxford, 125–48

Wells-Furby, B. 2004 *A catalogue of the medieval muniments at Berkeley Castle*, Bristol and Gloucestershire Record Series 17–18, Bristol (2 volumes)

Wickham, C. 2010 'Review of *Reflections: 50 years of medieval archaeology, 1957–2007*', *Medieval Archaeology* 54, 430–1

Williams, C. H. (ed.) 1967 *English historical documents V 1485–1558*, Eyre and Spottiswoode, London

Wrathmell, S. (ed.) 2012 *A history of Wharram and its neighbours* (Wharram, a study of settlement on the Yorkshire Wolds 13), York University Archaeological Publications 15, York

PART II
THE MEDIEVAL COUNTRYSIDE

CHAPTER 5

OVERVIEW
Geographies of Medieval Britain

GRENVILLE ASTILL

The 'geographies' in this title is partly an homage to the disciplinary training of many pioneers who started the study of the medieval countryside (Gerrard 2003). But, more particularly, it raises a major methodological concern about the scale of the units in which the countryside has been studied. Most projects have been based on elements of the administrative structure, such as the parish, which featured in the lives of country people. To a certain extent this is a pragmatic response as the basic information for some surveys, the cartographic and archive material and the archaeological inventories, for example, has been curated in county heritage services. And while the parish, for example, always had a clear meaning and identity for those in the countryside, its purpose and significance changed during the later phases of its formation in the twelfth century and particularly during the late fifteenth and sixteenth centuries, and this is rarely acknowledged in the fieldwork based on this unit (Whyte 2009). And although the fieldwork is essentially parish-based, it is often focused on elements within the parish, such as a particular settlement and its fields which may raise the matter of typicality for the parish let alone a larger area.

Defining Regions

It is sometimes difficult to integrate the geographically based archaeological surveys with those rural analyses of the historians which, because of the character and distribution of agrarian records, are often based on the study of an institution's or family's estates. The constituent lands of such estates were often widely distributed and straddled administrative boundaries, although in some cases, particularly those concerned with the fifteenth and sixteenth centuries, a unit of study based on groups of townships or districts has been possible. Such approaches are often in contrast to other parts of Europe where more extensive and coherent blocks of countryside are considered and often with a greater time depth, as for example in France, often associated with the *Annales* school (e.g. Fournier 1962; 2014; Zadora-Rio 2008). Although the *Annales* has been influential in British agrarian research, such larger-scale approaches were rarely adopted by archaeologists or historians—few historians followed Hilton's example in his study of *A medieval society: the West Midlands at the end of the thirteenth century* (1966). However, there has been a notable move towards the study of larger geographic areas such as the Whittlewood Project, based on twelve parishes (briefly part of Whittlewood Forest, but without the coherence to be regarded as a *pays*; Jones and Page 2006) and stimulated by the more extensive survey of the East Midlands (Lewis et al. 1997) and this followed such surveys of the Clwydian Hills, Wales (Brown 2004), and the thematic projects initiated by the Royal Commissions and their successors in all three countries, such as the two-volume Perth survey (RCHAMS 1990; 1994) and North-West Lincolnshire (Everson 1991), the Malverns (Bowden 2005), and the Mendips (Jamieson 2015).

However, the idea of distinctive environmental and cultural entities, the *pays*, was adopted as a way of classifying and characterizing the territory of Britain and marks a refinement of the earlier division between highland and lowland zones (Fox 1932). Originating from the Department of Local History in Leicester, the successive leaders and staff adopted the *pays* as a tool with which to understand the variability of Britain's rural character. One of the most influential has been Thirsk's classification of England (and Wales by Emery) in terms of farming regions for the sixteenth and early seventeenth centuries which were shaped by how communities responded to the market within the parameters presented/determined by the agricultural and cultural attributes of the region in which they lived and worked. Despite Thirsk's reservations that her work was 'very tentative' (1967, 4), this model has been adopted on many occasions as a way of understanding the complex agrarian character of medieval England.

Pays, however, are not universally accepted as an appropriate unit or scale with which to study the countryside. This form of characterization is most often described as a 'top-down' approach because although it recognizes the complexity of individual locales, the purpose for which it is used is broader and designed to understand the countryside in a much wider context and so cannot reflect the individual or communal concerns of the resident population.

But *pays* have been used to define regions in other ways than farming practice. For example, Phythian-Adams (1987) has argued strongly that we can better understand the cultural development of this country if we divide it using watersheds so that the drainage systems of major river valleys become the key units. In his work on East Anglia and the East Midlands Williamson (2006) argues for a similar technique in order to understand the processes of early medieval settlement and colonization. However, it is noticeable that of all the main geographic units studied for the character of their medieval land-use and settlement, the major river valleys remain comparatively unknown.

Units such as *pays* do not seem to have formed the appropriately sized area for detailed fieldwork in Britain; there has been a preference for small administrative units like the parish or township, or themes. *Pays* seem to be used to bring a coherence to independently generated datasets, but there is little discussion about how this information might be integrated—at a basic level it is often more visible in distributions of building types or varieties of field system (see Chapter 6). Indeed, although attempts to construct cultural regions of Britain have a long history, the results are often not generally accepted because the regions seem only to be significant in terms of the distribution of one class of material culture and there is a lack of geographic coincidence in the extents of major cultural markers such as ceramics, vernacular architecture, or settlement and field types (e.g. Jope 1963; for a historiography of *pays*, Rippon et al. 2014).

The parish- or township-based studies formed the foundation of our reconstruction of the medieval countryside and some therefore have commented on the essentially anecdotal and atheoretical nature of the methodology (Johnson 2007). Some attempts to move away from an empirical approach and offer a new context for the interpretation of a collection of case studies have been made stemming from a collaboration between archaeologists working on maritime societies both sides of the Channel. Loveluck, for example, in a survey of north-west Europe between the seventh and twelfth centuries, has chosen to emphasize specific living environments as a context for the creation of wealth and social networks so that materiality is privileged as a prime mover over socio-economic status. In this case, it is the European coastal regions, with their riverine, marsh, and creek systems which, despite being marginal in traditional agricultural terms, prioritized specialized production and trade to give it a distinctive independent society free from central and tenurial interference and so capable of generating and disposing of wealth, aided by a developing urban patriciate, to a much greater extent than the inland European areas. While this description emphasizes the overall socio-economic context, the work is archaeology-led and draws on case studies to highlight their overall material and social implications to demonstrate distinctive regional identities (Loveluck 2014). And while this reinterpretation is very much focused on the east-coast connections, it could be applied to the south and west littorals. Barrett's discussion of the fish industry charts its expansion from the east to the west coasts during the later Middle Ages.

One characteristic of these maritime regions is the use of distinctive modes of communication which offer an alternative view of trade as being essentially hierarchical. The Fens and the south-east coastal areas, for example, had generated small-scale and informal exchange systems that did not rely on higher order or central places with their roads, but instead were articulated through 'dendritic' networks based on the waterways and creeks peculiar to these areas (Gardiner 2007; Spoerry 2005).

While the study of coastal regions offers one way to place detailed case studies in context and to test the relevance and significance of the often small sample, other approaches have developed over the last twenty years that aim to study larger geographic areas and these have been stimulated by a combination of technology-led methodologies such as GIS and the increasingly available country-wide databases such as LiDAR. There are, however, counties such as Northamptonshire whose medieval landscape is one of the most studied in the country, where there is both a legacy of long-term excavation and survey programmes such as Raunds and major studies of settlements, open fields, and more specialized landscapes such as the forest area of Rockingham and brought together in historical atlases (Audouy and Chapman 2009; Brown and Foard 1998; Chapman 2010; Deegan and Foard 2007; Hall 1995; Parry 2006; Partida et al. 2013). Indeed, models developed in the county for settlement sequences, and nucleation in particular, have been widely discussed and adopted for larger areas of the country, although of course such detail does not preclude continued debate (e.g. Brown and Foard 1998). However, a GIS-based county-wide assessment of the county's (largely medieval) settlement pattern and land-use has made a further important contribution in showing that a classic champion landscape was far more varied than the expected villages and open fields and that even this typical Midland settlement and field type was much more confined in extent and distribution, limited as they were to some of the major river valleys in the county (Williamson et al. 2013). One suspects such new results will be one of the consequences of the current 'big data' projects which assemble for the first time the products of Historic Environment Records (HERs) and grey literature, often in a cross-temporal and cultural way. As a result of these new surveys we therefore not only have to reconsider the sample bias of what have become 'classic' case studies, but also to rethink the very processes of settlement and land-use that have entered into the general discourse.

Other national insights into elements of the medieval landscape have been commissioned for the purposes of heritage management. One of the most influential has been Roberts' and Wrathmell's use of map-based datasets to provide a characterization of rural settlement, mainly in terms of geographic regions or 'provinces'. The focus in particular is that which is dominated by the champion landscape, the central province which, it is argued, had deep roots that could extend back to the Roman or even later prehistoric periods and essentially founded on a land-use of extensively cleared woodland (Roberts and Wrathmell 2000; 2002). Concerns have been raised about the overdrawing of such provinces and while such regions can include some of the attributes associated with the culture of champion areas they do not by any means include all those attributes, and particularly those which in the past have been regarded as fundamental in their creation, such as population densities (Hinton 2005; Page and Jones 2007). Lowerre's (2014) conversion of Robert's and Wrathmell's *Atlas* maps shows that while there is a general justification for the three main provinces, the potential for a higher level of settlement heterogeneity within these regions deserves further investigation. And there have been important correctives to the bias towards the midland champion area, even though there is a prospect of an increasing similarity between regions/provinces (Rippon 2008).

What is perhaps more interesting, however, is that the overall methodology has not been subject to a sustained scrutiny (although major concerns have been voiced; Austin 2007) perhaps because it incorporates techniques that remain at the heart of the practice of British historic landscape reconstruction. Fundamental to Roberts's and Wrathmell's approach is the use of the nineteenth-century map cover, the earliest available for the whole country, in order to characterize not just the pre-industrial countryside but, by a recognized retrogressive approach, to demonstrate that such rural landscapes had at least extensive medieval or earlier framework. This morphological approach privileges the easily accessible cartographic information about settlement and field form based on the patterns of field boundaries (but less in the case of Scotland where the medieval landscape is more difficult to identify because of extensive later change; Dixon 2000; 2007a). The assumption is that the meaning and purpose of such boundaries have remained constant and were the preeminent attributes which gave the medieval countryside its character.

Historic Landscape Characterization

A combination of a morphological approach using early cartographic material with GIS lies at the core of the Historic Landscape Characterization (HLC) initiative, started over 25 years ago, which aims to provide a chronological depth or historical dimension to the Landscape Character Assessment of present-day landscapes which informs decisions regarding the planning process (Aldred and Fairclough 2003; Fairclough and Herring 2016; Herlin 2016). Arranged on a county/local administrative unit basis, the HLC has been adopted in England, Wales (Alfrey 2007), and Scotland (as Historic Land-Use Assessment; Dixon 2007b) and is intended to be value-free and treats all landscape types of equal importance. The typical attributes used in more recent iterations of this exercise include current land-use, field shape and size, boundary types, shape and type of routes, woodland and water, building types and settlement patterns, place-names, topography, and geology. The landscape types, which can number up to around 20 for each county, are intended to accept that habitats and biodiversity are cultural. The academic use of such an exercise continues to be debated and discussion remains focused on adopting a morphological approach using late maps and the way that GIS creates over-simplistic boundaries to produce an excessive depiction of the 'blocky' character of landscape types (Austin 2007; Williamson 2007). HLC can also ignore what were important landscape elements that represented important cultural behaviour, but these elements did not coincide with the scale of the existing landscape type units to be identified, such as the midland fox hunting 'shires' (Finch 2007). And neither can the identification of related or similar landscape types be assumed to have a common origin. In order to respond to some of these criticisms, a distinction between HLC and 'historic landscape analysis' has been suggested where the latter uses more varied sets of data that could include, for example, patterns of land-ownership and occupancy which would acknowledge the dynamic nature of the countryside (Rippon 2007; and see Chapter 6 in this *Handbook*).

The characterization of the medieval countryside also involves the discussion of more specialized activities that left their mark on the landscape. Pluskowski draws attention to the distinctive areas given over to the aristocratic culture of hunting, which accelerated after the Norman Conquest, with its own distinctive ceremonial and symbolism. The regulated nature of the activity required specifically managed extensive landscapes that were protected under forest law and, on a smaller scale, chases. The fullest extent of these reserves was reached by the later thirteenth century, by which time the wild ungulate population had been depleted, even in the wooded and least settled marcher areas of Wales and Scotland which were managed in the context of political conquest.

Most of the specialized activities so far indentified, however, were to do with agricultural activities and it is always important to integrate with our other evidence because specialized sites can only be understood as a part of a wider system. The most common cases involve seasonal activities such as fishing with distinctive beach activities (see Chapter 9 in this *Handbook*; Fox 2001) and transhumance (Fox 1996; and a major theme of research in the Welsh uplands, e.g. Roberts 2006). Sheepcotes (or bercaries) have been identified as a particular form of long, narrow building on the uplands, especially on the remote uplands of the wolds. Built mainly to overwinter the sheep, they were also used for lambing and dairying and so had a contact with the main farms in the lowlands, for provisions and the supply of hay, for example (Dyer 1995; Hurst 2005). Vaccaries were also centres for cattle breeding and many had a distinctive location, as in the north-west where they were sited at the head of small river valleys which gave access to lowland meadows and the main farms, but the animals could also graze the rough pastures of the uplands, especially during the summer (Atkin 1985). These sites probably provided the bloodstock for distant parts of the country, and so an important element to both the sheepcote and vaccary sites were the distinctive trackways with constrictions that allowed greater control when the animals were moved and provided connections to the wider route system.

Most evidence for the industrial character of the countryside appears to be associated with high-status properties, including stone and mineral extraction and metal processing, sometimes in combination with ceramic production (Bond 2004; Moorhouse 1989; Rippon et al. 2009). The grouping of such activities is notable; for example in the northwest, within complex water systems, fulling mill sites have been identified associated with tenter banks and potash pits. Such fulling sites were often close by to flax-retting ponds (Higham 1989), so it is possible that linen-making was included in demesne wool production and so may not have been specified in manorial accounts.

Chronological Changes

One of the legacies of a morphological approach is the variety of plan forms and changes identified, but it is only possible to place them in a relative chronological sequence usually based on cartographic material. To a certain extent this matter is being addressed by the integration of excavation results and large-scale survey, or the practice of ground-truthing in an attempt to provide absolute dates for change in particular landscapes. It is surprising, however, that the chronologies of change in the countryside have yet to be finally established (Astill 2010 for following paragraphs). Most attention has been given to the process of nucleation and associated field systems. Between the 1970s and 1990s there was a preference for a long chronology that ranged from the ninth to the twelfth or thirteenth centuries, and the long time span was used to accommodate regional differences, but also to include the development of dispersed settlement that was then seen as occurring during the twelfth century. Village formation was also thought to have taken place at one particular time as a stage in the settlement sequence—the 'village moment'.

More recently there is a tendency to telescope village and field formation into a shorter and earlier chronology, with an emphasis on major change in the long eighth century, and nucleation starting at that time and continuing in the ninth century with another change in the tenth century—the 'Great Replanning'. This sequence assumes that the main framework of the rural landscape was in place early on and that any changes that subsequently happened were 'ongoing modifications'. So the twelfth and thirteenth centuries, the time which historians identify as a profound period of agricultural intensification and population increase, had little place in the new chronology. As mentioned above, many of these models were based on individual case studies for which a general relevance was claimed. With the larger-scale, GIS-assisted, work a much longer gestation of rural settlement is proposed that extended beyond the twelfth century (see Chapter 6). The character of the chronological sequence has also become much more complex: for example whereas village creation was always seen as happening hand in hand with the creation of the field system, settlement and fields could now have their own, independent, development so that a village was formed while the older field system was retained. It also allows the copious evidence for settlement change generated by the earthwork surveys done from the 1960s (mainly by the Royal Commissions in England, Scotland, and Wales) to be incorporated into the debate. This evidence also highlights the extent and character of late medieval changes, particularly visible in the contraction of the 'ends' in dispersed settlements. The extensive development of test-pitting as a means to understand currently occupied villages has also demonstrated the profound change and often contraction in such settlements in the century after *c.*1350. We are also becoming more aware of settlement change and relocation that took place as a result of the leasing of demesnes, particularly on monastic estates during the earlier sixteenth century, where new and often distinctive farms were built to replace their inconveniently sited predecessors (Astill et al. 2004; Bond 2004).

The potential to identify regional, even local, change has led to a similar shift in emphasis in our explanations for them, from national or regional, such as state development, urbanization, or estate fragmentation, to the more local which brought cultural and local environmental considerations to the fore as major influences.

THEORETICAL APPROACHES

The emphasis on an essentially functionalist interpretation of the countryside which privileges its productive capabilities characterizes the British approach towards the study of the rural landscape. Some critiques note that medieval archaeologists continued to use this essentially document-led and empirical methodology at a time when archaeologists of other periods, particularly prehistorians, and former collaborators such as cultural geographers, were choosing to study landscapes in terms of how they were perceived and in particular their symbolic, ritual, or conceptual significance (Johnson 2007). This was also associated with a phenomenological approach which drew attention to the experiential aspects of the countryside which in one sense introduced more sense of the dynamic by considering the means by which people moved through the countryside; this also had the advantage of making connections between the units in which archaeologists traditionally studied rural areas and drew attention to the importance of communication and the routes used. While some employed such approaches to the comparative research of some medieval rural societies (Altenberg 2003), others have chosen to try to explain why relict elements of earlier landscapes were incorporated into the medieval landscapes, for example prehistoric burial mounds. The deep history of such features and their embedded meaning or the appreciation of the symbolic purpose of some aspects of medieval landscapes have also come from a more archaeologically or 'practice-led' methodology that has been used in thematic studies of monastic or seigneurial landscapes (Creighton 2009; Everson and Stocker 2011; Liddiard 2005). The combination of looking at the countryside from both empirical and conceptual points of view may have most impact in the study of frontier societies where there is an opportunity to confront ethnic and religious interactions as well as the management and environmental change of such regions and this would deepen our appreciation of the significance of the Welsh and Scottish marcher and border regions (Pluskowski et al. 2011a; 2011b).

The Potential of Environmental Archaeology

Environmental archaeology has made a huge impact on the study of the medieval countryside, but its true potential may yet to be achieved (Bell 1989). Although environmental change has been invoked in many discussions about landscape character, the evidence has largely been indirect, non-scientific, and has not initiated many environmental projects to test the validity of the interpretations. For example, the earlier discussions about the impact of climate change or more recently the micro-environmental reasons for the siting of villages have not been considered in terms of the geoarchaeological data or indeed as part of an ecosystem (see Chapter 11). To a certain extent this might be an issue of scale: the biggest impact has been made at a site level with faunal analyses and macrobotanic work, but recent reviews have demonstrated the greater landscape potential of such work (e.g. Van der Veen et al. 2013; and see Chapter 8 in this *Handbook*).

Attempts to add an environmental element to landscape analysis has been sadly lacking for many of the medieval projects. In some cases the evidence for land-use coming from the cartographic material (and in some cases in combination with Domesday data) has been regarded as sufficient to provide a broad picture, based on the assumption (as with the morphology) that the pre-industrial countryside was a direct and constant legacy from the Middle Ages and there was no need to seek an independent source of information. In other cases actual environmental evidence in the past has just not been available in sufficient quantities or from locations to make a significant impact. For example, the tendency for palynological and molluscan work to be concentrated on particular soil types to exploit optimum preservation, combined with the relative neglect of arable core areas, has limited our environmental understanding of the medieval countryside. However, one of the big data projects collecting grey literature used environmental material to assess the archaeological validity of farming regions (Rippon et al. 2014). But it is interesting that there have been few attempts to follow up on the environmentally led Ystad, Sweden, survey where scientific methodologies were extended in order to deal with the more fragmented preservation coming from historic sites (Berglund 1991). A notable exception is the Quoygrew survey which combines the fullest exploitation of the environmental data with the archaeology of that part of Orkney (Barrett 2012).

Often the indirect, documentary evidence for environmental conditions are of a very broad scale and it is difficult to know if that environmental regime had any relevance for particular localities and so there is a need for a finer-grain approach that would give a better resolution. This is particularly relevant in discussions about agricultural intensification. The latest survey of agrarian Northamptonshire, for example, shows that at Domesday there was a much higher proportion of pasture in relation to arable than had been previously realized and morphological work suggested that this resource did not occur in obvious blocks but were distributed in ribbon-like extents between fields and on township boundaries (Williamson et al. 2013). This challenges one of the general explanations for village formation, that people started to live in larger groups as a means to manage scarce resources, which in this case was the pasture which had been depleted from being turned over to arable, thus reducing the capacity to support livestock; it also potentially dilutes the distinctiveness of the central province. Yet this impression remains quite coarse-grained and may also need to be reconciled with the evidence for increasing sedimentation in some of the large river valleys from the later tenth century that is thought to indicate more intensive cultivation; for example that from the Thames at Oxford may reflect greater ploughing in the upper Thames and the Cotswolds (Robinson and Wilkinson 2003).

Similarly the nature and character of 'marginal' lands has been rehabilitated in the sense that these areas' productive capabilities had been underestimated as had the local population's ability to diversify and sustain a more varied and less cereal-based economy than that which existed in the champion areas and so was better equipped to survive a late medieval crisis (Bailey 1989; Dyer 1989). The archaeological evidence has extended the period over which these margins were used so, for example, central Devon and the south edge of Exmoor, the Fens and Northumbrian valleys were brought into use during the eighth century, a considerable time before the documentary evidence for their exploitation (Astill 2010). The environmental data, particularly the pollen analyses from sites close to arable areas (rather than the more usual upland blanket bogs) in Devon/Exmoor, showed the development of a distinctive agricultural regime, convertible husbandry that was introduced in the eighth century and was continued throughout the Middle Ages. This farming used a distinctive form of rotational cropping where the majority of fields were subject to short periods of cultivation followed by a longer grass ley, a method which was particularly suited to the soils and terrain of the area and designed for sustainable, long-term use. This type of farming system was arranged in the landscape to accommodate, and indeed exploit, existing routes that facilitated connections throughout the south-west (Rippon et al. 2006).

In Dartmoor, the pollen analyses from the Houndtor area showed extensive cultivation of oats and rye in combination with extensive upland pasture for livestock grazing. However, the construction of field boundaries and cultivation changed the drainage systems which contributed to the onset of peat growth and some regeneration of trees and ultimately the abandonment of arable cultivation during the early fourteenth century (Austin and Walker 1985). This environmental evidence from Devon considerable deepens our view of 'marginal' agriculture and how in some areas it was more sustainable than others; it also serves to emphasize the variety of responses possible within comparable landscapes.

Another case of pronounced environmental change is seen largely as a consequence of the severe reduction of the population after the mid-fourteenth century. The shift from the more labour-intensive arable cultivation to the increased pasturing of livestock is regarded as having dramatic effect on the use and appearance of the countryside. The shrinkage of settlements, often combined with the amalgamation of holdings for some of the survivors, are testified in both excavation reports and earthwork surveys (Dyer 1997). We are less clear about the extent to which the regional character of areas of the country was maintained or modified: the distribution and intensity of permanent enclosure for example needs further investigation and the extent to which there may have been woodland generation or a more complex management of hedgerow resources. Similarly, we need more information about field reorganization, including the change from open field to infield. The potential contribution of environmental work is high, but may require the refinement of methodologies to deal with former arable cores of the country.

While the late medieval change in land-use did not seem to increase the wild ungulate population, but spurred the creation of more managed hunting landscapes, the parks, it did however stimulate further specialization in the countryside which may have made regional identities more distinctive. The intensification of rabbit breeding for meat and fur, coney culture, particularly in East Anglia, produced further specialized landscape elements, often associated with the pillowmound earthworks and enclosures (see Chapter 10). The greater emphasis of animal husbandry made the crewyards for the overwintering of cattle a familiar addition to village crofts, and those that continued to grow cereals often built larger barns for more efficient storage (Astill 1997).

The activities of butcher-graziers are relatively well documented for the fifteenth and sixteenth centuries, including the long-distance transportation of livestock from the Marcher regions partly to meet the demand for meat and partly in an attempt to improve breeding stock (e.g. most recently Dyer 2012). The details of the animal management are however currently inadequately understood and would benefit from further research. It is important to model for various husbandry strategies, and the potential for the isotopic analysis of faunal assemblages needs to be realized. On the face of it, the plentiful supply of pasture coming after a time when that resource may have been limited could have resulted in changes in the conformation and size of livestock. Normally this is achieved either through genetic change, by the introduction of new bloodstock, or by making improvements in the upkeep of the animals, or a combination of both. Zooarchaeologists have commented on the significant change in the size of sheep in sixteenth-century assemblages from Launceston Castle and Lincoln (Albarella and Davis 1994; Dobney et al. 1995). While this development is often presented as anticipating the better-known developments of the eighteenth century, it is also worth considering why there was a significant interval between the increased availability of pasture from the mid-fourteenth century and the change in size. We are in danger of confusing the scale of the various types of information: an assumption that increased pasture was a national phenomenon compared to the detailed evidence coming from individual herds.

The recent discussion of pigs from Dudley Castle, West Midlands, involved both zoological and isotopic analysis (Hamilton and Tomas 2012). A significant increase in the size of pigs occurred in phase 6 (1321–97) compared to the previous phase 5 (1262–1321), but that was associated with a relative decrease in pig numbers. A different form of pig management appears to have been introduced that involved a greater control over breeding and feeding and this involved making extensive use of enclosures (confinement); the isotope results suggested a reduction in the diversity of the animals' diet (a result of limited or no access to natural resources, for example pasture or woodland) and a possible increase in legume consumption. This limited dietary range was not evident from the isotopic signatures of the contemporary cattle. Overall, the management indicated a combination of genetic improvement of the bloodstock with a confinement and a more limited and possibly specialized feeding regime, perhaps indicating a greater control of the pastures by excluding the pigs' damaging behaviour. We need to know the extent of the catchment or resource area of Dudley Castle in the thirteenth and fourteenth centuries in order to assess the results' real significance, but they have a relevance beyond the castle and indicate the potential for the development of this research. A further aspect of livestock management is to compare the documentary evidence for increased protein consumption, particularly meat, with the zooarchaeological evidence for the maintenance of herd size and whether it supports the increasing preference for the consumption of younger animals (Albarella 1997).

The other important contribution environmental work needs to make us aware of is how weather events can be incorporated into our overall dynamic model of medieval agrarian society. We have only approached this problem in the past by invoking the shift in the European climatic patterns, such as the Little Ice Age, as an explanation of overall socio-economic change in the same way as we have used macroeconomic models. We have yet to discuss the consequences of such general change in terms of what effects it had on local societies. It is a matter of scale (a leitmotiv of this piece): of trying to reconcile or understand the relationship between global and local events and what that meant in terms of local communities. At the moment we are largely at the stage of realizing we can recognize such periods of crisis, mainly in terms of flooding or coastal erosion, or outbreaks of disease (Griffiths 2015; and see Chapter 11 in this *Handbook*). We need to find a way of assessing impact. Historians are reconsidering the effects of bad weather in terms of crop production and cereal prices and on a different scale the general consequences of particularly intense periods of wet weather and disease, as with 1315–17 (Campbell 2010; 2016). But the increasingly sophisticated and regional dendrochronological analysis is placing us in a position to recognize relatively minor weather events and the same is true of the more detailed dating of cemeteries which allow us to identify periods of short-term crisis, some of which largely escaped the chroniclers' attention but were nevertheless of immense importance to the localities (Connell et al. 2012).

How to build in an environmental dimension to our assessment of the character of rural life has encouraged some to return to the idea of modelling medieval rural societies in terms of ecosystems (e.g. Schreg 2014). Others have also wanted to incorporate a greater sense of the dynamic by estimating the resilience of settlements and their territories. Resilience is seen as the ability of a particular rural community or system to absorb stress caused by internal tensions as well as external factors. So in the interaction between exogenous (climate, disease, floods) and endogenous factors, the latter are dominant in determining a settlement's ability to survive or recover from crises. The lower the resilience of the society, the more vulnerable it is. The most sustained European survey by Curtis (2014) uses population trends, loss or degradation of lands, and destruction of housing and goods as the three main criteria which determine resilience and vulnerability, but this to a certain extent reflects the documentary basis of his study which ranges from the thirteenth to nineteenth centuries. The quality and the maintenance of soil condition with the material culture, however, are those aspects which need to be incorporated into any archaeological discussion of this theme, as indeed they have in a Scandinavian case study (Svensson et al. 2012).

Conclusion

The prospect then for a greater understanding of the medieval countryside is encouraging, especially if we can develop practice-led approaches that integrate our powerful datasets and combine information that currently exists at different geographic scales and levels of intensity, in particular the archaeological and environmental material.

References cited

Albarella, U. 1997 'Size, power, wool and veal: zooarchaeological evidence for late medieval innovations', in G. De Boe and F. Verhaeghe (eds), *Environment and subsistence in medieval Europe*, Papers of the 'Medieval Europe Brugge 1997' Conference, Volume 9, Institute for the Archaeological Heritage of Flanders, Bruges, 19–30

Albarella, U. and Davis, S. 1994 'Mammals and birds from Launceston Castle, Cornwall: decline in status and rise of agriculture', *Circaea* 12, 1–156

Aldred, O. and Fairclough, G. 2003 *Historic Landscape Characterisation: taking stock of the method*, English Heritage and Somerset County Council, London

Alfrey, J. 2007 'Contexts for Historic Landscape Characterisation in Wales', *Landscapes* 8, 84–91

Altenberg, K. 2003 *Experiencing landscapes: a study of space and identity in three marginal areas of medieval Britain and Scandinavia*, Almqvist and Wiksell, Stockholm

Astill, G. 1997 'An archaeological approach to the agricultural technologies in medieval England', in G. Astill and J. Langdon (eds), *Medieval farming and technology: the impact of agricultural change in Northwest Europe*, Brill, Leiden, 193–224

Astill, G. 2010 'The long and the short: rural settlement in medieval England', in R. Goddard, J. Langdon, and M. Müller (eds), *Survival and discord in medieval society*, Brepols, Turnhout, 11–28

Astill, G., Hirst, S., and Wright, S. 2004 'The Bordesley Abbey Project reviewed', *The Archaeological Journal* 161, 106–58

Atkin, M. 1985 'Some settlement patterns in Lancashire', in D. Hooke (ed.), *Medieval villages*, Oxford University Committee for Archaeology Monograph 5, Oxford, 171–85

Auduoy, M. and Chapman, A. 2009 *Raunds: the origins and growth of a Midland village, AD 450–1500. Excavations in North Raunds, Northamptonshire, 1977–87*, Oxbow Books, Oxford

Austin, D. 2007 'Character or caricature? Concluding discussion', *Landscapes* 8, 92–105

Austin, D. and Walker, M. 1985 'A new landscape context for Houndtor, Devon', *Medieval Archaeology* 29, 148–52

Bailey, M. 1989 *A marginal economy? East Anglian Breckland in the Later Middle Ages*, Cambridge University Press, Cambridge

Barrett, J. H. (ed.) 2012 *Being an islander: production and identity at Quoygrew, Orkney, AD 900–1600*, McDonald Institute, Cambridge

Bell, M. 1989 'Environmental archaeology as an index of continuity and change in the medieval landscape', in M. Aston, D. Austin, and C. Dyer (eds), *The rural settlements of medieval England*, Blackwell, Oxford, 269–86

Berglund, B. (ed.) 1991 *The cultural landscape during 6000 years in Southern Sweden: the Ystad Project*, Munksgaard International Booksellers and Publishers, Copenhagen

Bond, J. 2004 *Monastic landscapes*, Tempus, Stroud

Bowden, M. 2005 *The Malvern Hills: an ancient landscape*, English Heritage, London

Brown, A. and Foard, G. 1998 'The Saxon Landscape: a regional perspective', in P. Everson and T. Williamson (eds), *The archaeology of landscape*, Manchester University Press, Manchester, 67–94

Brown, I. 2004 *Discovering a Welsh landscape: archaeology and the Clwydian Hills*, Windgather Press, Macclesfield

Campbell, B. 2010 'Nature as historical protagonist: environment and society in pre-industrial England', *Economic History Review* 63, 281–314

Campbell, B. 2016 *The great transition: climate, disease and society in the late medieval world*, Cambridge University Press, Cambridge

Chapman, A. 2010 *West Cotton, Raunds: a study of medieval settlement dynamics AD 450–1450. Excavations of a deserted medieval hamlet in Northamptonshire 1985–89*, Oxbow Books, Oxford

Connell, B., Jones, A., Redfern, R. and Walker, D. 2012 *A bioarchaeological study of medieval burials on the site of St Mary Spital: excavations at Spitalfields Market, London E1, 1991–2007*, Museum of London Archaeology, London

Creighton, O. H. 2009 *Designs upon the landscape: elite landscapes of the Middle Ages*, Boydell, Woodbridge

Curtis, D. 2014 *Coping with crisis: the resilience and vulnerability of pre-industrial settlements*, Ashgate, Farnham

Deegan, A. and Foard, G. 2007 *Mapping ancient landscapes in Northamptonshire*, English Heritage, London

Dixon, P. 2000 'Nuclear and dispersed medieval rural settlement in southern Scotland', in J. Klápště (ed.), *Ruralia IV: the rural house from the Migration Period to the oldest still standing buildings*, Institute of Archaeology, Prague, 252–72

Dixon, P. 2007a 'Reaching beyond the clearances: finding the medieval—based upon recent survey work by RCAHMS in Strath Don, Aberdeenshire', in M. Gardiner and S. Rippon (eds), *Medieval landscapes: landscape history after Hoskins, Volume 2*, Windgather Press, Macclesfield, 153–69

Dixon, P. 2007b 'Conservation not reconstruction: Historic Land-Use Assessment (HLA), or characterising the historic landscape in Scotland', *Landscapes* 8, 72–83

Dobney, K., Jaques, S., and Irving, B. 1995 *Of butchers and breeds: report on vertebrate remains from various sites in the City of Lincoln*, City of Lincoln Archaeological Unit, Lincoln

Dyer, C. 1989 '"The retreat from marginal land": the growth and decline of medieval rural settlements', in M. Aston, D. Austin, and C. Dyer (eds), *The rural settlements of medieval England*, Blackwell, Oxford, 45–57

Dyer, C. 1995 'Sheepcotes: evidence for medieval sheep farming', *Medieval Archaeology* 39, 136–66

Dyer, C. 1997 'Peasants and farmers: rural settlements in an age of transition', in D. Gaimster and P. Stamper (eds), *The Age of Transition: the archaeology of English culture 1400–1600*, Oxbow Monograph 98, Oxford, 61–76

Dyer, C. 2012 *A country merchant 1495–1520: trading and farming at the end of the Middle Ages*, Oxford University Press, Oxford

Everson, P. 1991 *Change and continuity: rural settlement in North-West Lincolnshire*, Her Majesty's Stationery Office, London

Everson, P. and Stocker, D. 2011 *Custodians of continuity? The Premonstratensian abbey at Barlings and the landscape of ritual*, Lincolnshire Archaeology and Heritage Reports Series 11, Sleaford

Fairclough, G. and Herring, P. 2016 'Lens, mirror, window: interactions between Historic Landscape Characterisation and Landscape Character Assessment', *Landscape Research* 41, 186–98

Finch, J. 2007 '"Wider framed countries": Historic Landscape Characterisation in the midland shires', *Landscapes* 8, 50–63

Fournier, G. 1962 *Le peuplement rural en Basse Auvergne durant le haut Moyen Âge*, Presses Universitaires de France, Paris

Fournier, G. 2014 *Les villages fortifiés et leur évolution: contribution à l'histoire du village en Auvergne et sur ses marges*, Le Sauvetat, Clermont-Ferrand

Fox, C. 1932 *The personality of England*, National Museum of Wales, Cardiff

Fox, H. 1996 *Seasonal settlement*, University of Leicester Vaughan Papers 39, Leicester

Fox, H. 2001 *The evolution of the fishing village: landscape and society along the South Devon coast, 1086–1550*, Leopard's Head Press, Oxford

Gardiner, M. 2007 'Hythes, small ports and other landing places in later medieval England', in J. Blair (ed.), *Waterways and canal-building in medieval England*, Oxford University Press, Oxford, 85–109

Gerrard, C. M. 2003 *Medieval archaeology: understanding traditions and contemporary approaches*, Routledge, London

Griffiths, D. 2015 'Medieval coastal sand inundation in Britain and Ireland', *Medieval Archaeology* 59, 103–21

Hall, D. 1995 *The open fields of Northamptonshire*, Northamptonshire Record Society 38, Northampton

Hamilton, J. and Thomas, R. 2012 'Pannage, pulses and pigs: isotopic and zooarchaeological evidence for changing pig management practices in later medieval England', *Medieval Archaeology* 56, 234–59

Herlin, I. 2016 'Exploring the national contexts and cultural ideas that preceded the landscape character assessment method in England', *Landscape Research* 41, 175–85

Higham, M. 1989 'Some evidence for twelfth- and thirteenth-century linen and woollen textile processing', *Medieval Archaeology* 33, 38–52

Hilton, R. 1966 *A medieval society: the West Midlands at the end of the thirteenth century*, Weidenfield and Nicholson, London

Hinton, D. 2005 'Debate: South Hampshire, "East Wessex" and the *Atlas of Rural Settlement in England*', *Landscape History* 27, 71–5

Hurst, D. 2005 *Sheep in the Cotswolds: the medieval wool trade*, Tempus, Stroud

Jamieson, E. 2015 *The historic landscape of the Mendip Hills*, Historic England, London

Johnson, M. 2007 *Ideas of landscape*, Blackwell, Oxford

Jones, P. and Page, M. 2006 *Medieval villages in an English Landscape*, Windgather Press, Macclesfield

Jope, M. 1963 'The regional cultures of medieval Britain', in I. L. Foster and L. Alcock (eds), *Culture and environment*, Routledge, Kegan and Paul, London, 327–50

Lewis, C., Mitchell-Fox, P., and Dyer, C. 1997 *Village, hamlet and field: changing medieval settlements in central England*, Manchester University Press, Manchester

Liddiard, R. 2005 *Castles in context: power, symbolism and landscape, 1066–1500*, Windgather Press, Macclesfield

Loveluck, C. 2014 *Northwest Europe in the Early Middle Ages, c. AD 600–1150*, Cambridge University Press, Cambridge

Lowerre, A. 2014 *Rural settlement in England: analysing environmental factors and regional variation in historic rural settlement organisation using regression and clustering techniques*, Research Report Series 72-2014, English Heritage, Portsmouth

Moorhouse, S. 1989 'Monastic estates, their composition and development', in R. Gilchrist and H. Mytum (eds), *The archaeology of rural monasteries*, British Archaeological Reports British Series 203, Oxford, 29–82

Page, M. and Jones, R. 2007 'Stability and instability in medieval village plans: case-studies in Whittlewood', in M. Gardiner and S. Rippon (eds), *Medieval landscapes: landscape history after Hoskins, Volume 2*, Windgather Press, Macclesfield, 139–52

Parry, S. 2006 *Raunds Area Survey: an archaeological study of the landscape of Raunds, Northamptonshire 1985–94*, Oxbow Books, Oxford

Partida, T., Hall, D., and Foard, G. 2013 *An atlas of Northamptonshire: the medieval and early-modern landscape*, Oxbow Books, Oxford

Phythian-Adams, C. 1987 *Rethinking English local history*, Leicester University Press, Leicester

Pluskowski, A., Boas, A., and Gerrard, C. M. 2011a 'The ecology of crusading: investigating the impact of holy war and colonisation at the frontiers of medieval Europe', *Medieval Archaeology* 55, 192–225

Pluskowski, A., Brown, A., Shillito, L.-M., Seetah, K., Makowiecki, D., Jarzebowski, M., Kļaviņš, K., and Kreem, J. 2011b 'The ecology of Crusading project: new research on medieval Baltic landscapes', *Antiquity* 85, 328

RCAHMS 1990 *North-East Perth: an archaeological landscape*, Her Majesty's Stationery Office, Edinburgh

RCAHMS 1994 *South-East Perth: an archaeological landscape*, Her Majesty's Stationery Office, Edinburgh

Rippon, S. 2007 'Historic Landscape Characterisation: its role in contemporary British archaeology and landscape history', *Landscapes* 8, 1–14

Rippon, S. 2008 *Beyond the medieval village: the diversification of landscape character in Southern Britain*, Oxford University Press, Oxford

Rippon, S., Claughton, P., and Smart, C. 2009 *Mining in a medieval landscape: the royal silver mines of the Tamar Valley*, Exeter University Press, Exeter

Rippon, S., Fyfe, R., and Brown, A. 2006 'Beyond villages and open fields: the origins and development of a historic landscape characterised by dispersed settlement in south-west England', *Medieval Archaeology* 50, 31–70

Rippon, S., Wainwright, A., and Smart, S. 2014 'Farming regions in medieval England: the archaeobotanical and zooarcharchaeological evidence', *Medieval Archaeology* 58, 195–255

Roberts, B. and Wrathmell, S. 2000 *An atlas of rural settlement in England*, English Heritage, London

Roberts, B. and Wrathmell, S. 2002 *Region and place*, English Heritage, London

Roberts, K. 2006 *Lost farmsteads: deserted rural settlements in Wales*, Council for British Archaeology Research Report 148, York

Robinson, M. and Wilkinson, D. 2003 'The "Oxenford": detailed studies of the Thames Crossing in St Aldates', in A. Dodd (ed.), *Oxford before the University: the Late Saxon and Norman archaeology of the Thames crossing, the defences and the town*, Oxford University, Oxford, 65–134

Schreg, R. 2014 'Ecological approaches in medieval rural archaeology', *European Journal of Archaeology* 17, 83–119

Spoerry, P. 2005 'Town and country in the medieval Fenland', in K. Giles and C. Dyer (eds), *Town and country in the Middle Ages: contrasts, contacts and interconnections, 1100–1500*, The Society for Medieval Archaeology Monograph 22, Leeds, 85–110

Svensson, E., Petersson, S., Nilsson, S., Boss, L., and Johansson, A. 2012 'Resilience and medieval crises at five rural settlements in Sweden and Norway', *Lund Archaeological Review* 18, 89–106

Thirsk, J. 1967 'The farming regions of England', in J. Thirsk (ed.), *The agrarian history of England and Wales Volume IV*, Cambridge University Press, Cambridge, 1–112

Van der Veen, M., Hill, A., and Livarda, A. 2013 'The archaeobotany of medieval Britain (c. AD 450–1500): identifying research priorities for the 21st century', *Medieval Archaeology* 57, 151–82

Williamson, T. 2006 *England's landscape: East Anglia*, English Heritage, London

Williamson, T. 2007 'Historic Landscape Characterisation: some queries', *Landscapes* 8, 64–71

Williamson, T., Liddiard, R., and Partida, T. 2013 *Champion: the making and unmaking of the English medieval landscape*, Liverpool University Press, Liverpool

Whyte, N. 2009 *Inhabiting the landscape: place, custom and memory, 1500–1800*, Windgather Press, Macclesfield

Zadora-Rio, E. 2008 *Des paroisses de Touraine aux communes d'Indre-et-Loire: la formation des territoires*, CNRS, Tours

CHAPTER 6

FIELD SYSTEMS AND THE ARABLE FIELDS

RONAN P. O'DONNELL

The Middle Ages were a turbulent period for the rural economy, resulting in major changes to arable landscapes (Platt 2012). Despite this, later medieval arable landscapes have suffered a surprising neglect. Archaeologists have tended to place medieval events in *longue durée* narratives. This is a valid approach, but in practice has led to medieval arable landscapes being overshadowed by those of the early medieval period, in which open-field systems originated, or the early modern period in which their decline gained momentum. This means that the medieval period is often viewed as a period of stasis between periods of change. It will be argued here that this is a misconception. Upheavals of the arable landscape did occur in the twelfth and thirteenth centuries and again in the mid-fourteenth and fifteenth centuries. These events result from population growth in the first half of the period followed by demographic collapse due to a number of crises in the early fourteenth century. While these events are well known (e.g. Schofield 2003), they have rarely been examined by landscape archaeologists and consequently any regional variation in their effects is poorly understood.

Regional Variation

Before moving on to how field systems changed we must first discuss their regional variation. This variation is well understood because it has often been viewed as an important element in models of open-field origins (e.g. Hall 2013; Rippon 2008). Early discussions, such as the pioneering work of Grey (1915), tended to see variation as a departure from the Midland Field System, which was regarded as particularly fully developed. Other forms were thus seen as precursors of the Midland System. Most modern work has set out to attack this by demonstrating the advantages and complexity of other systems (e.g. Bailey 2009; Rippon 2008). Consequently, it is possible to present a reasonably balanced picture of medieval field systems in England and Wales, though Scotland is less well understood as a result of a paucity of medieval historical sources. Scholarship to date has revealed a geographical framework in which the highly formal Midland Field System occurs in a band stretching from Durham in the north-east to Somerset in the south-west (Figure 6.1). This was first outlined by Grey in 1915, but is similar to the 'champion' countryside which was recognized by sixteenth-century county historians. This idea has been remarkably persistent, being roughly equivalent to Roberts and Wrathmell's (2000) Central Province. There is a great deal of variation in the field systems to either side, and indeed within this Central Province.

There are a few generic observations which apply to medieval arable land right across Britain. Arable agriculture was based on the township within which several farmers worked. These townships were small, roughly equivalent to a village and occasionally co-terminus with a parish or manor. The holdings of any one tenant within a field system were rarely ring-fenced, nearly always consisting of a number of strips distributed across the township. In most instances, but not all, some form of common grazing right existed across fallow arable or after the harvest.

The long tradition of research on the Midlands has led to a particularly good understanding of field systems in this region. Typically, a township contained two or three fields divided into furlongs which were in turn divided into selions or strips. Each selion was held by one person who held several others too. A significant minority of townships contained more than three fields though in some cases these were grouped into seasons to allow three-course rotations (Lewis et al. 2001, 145). One field was fallowed each year, while the other two were cropped following rotations decided by the manor court. Grazing was allowed on the fallow and after harvest. The holdings of one tenant were evenly distributed between the three fields and often followed a regular cycle (Hall 1995, 117). Very little land was enclosed, usually no more than a halo of pasture closes surrounding each village (Foard et al. 2005, 12). Generally, demesnes were dispersed among the peasant holdings (e.g. Jones and Page 2006, 135). The Midland Field System extends into Yorkshire where typical Midland open-fields have been revealed in the Vale of Pickering (Hall 2012), though on higher areas there is more common waste and the terms 'field' and 'furlong' are used interchangeably suggesting more informal cropping. Midland open-field systems were common in most of the West Midlands (Roberts 1973). However one area in the north called the Arden contained irregular field systems in which there were no fields, only individual furlongs, and in which holdings were not evenly distributed across the township (Dyer 1991). Midland Field Systems extend, in some form, into south Wales where they were imposed on the landscape by Norman and English lords between the eleventh and thirteenth centuries (Davies 1973, 527; Rippon 2008, 201–21). Three-course rotations have been demonstrated in some areas, including Llantrissent in Glamorgan (Davies 1973, 488). However, there may be some differences between south Welsh field systems and typical Midland fields; at Monmouth, for example, no holding was distributed across all of its four fields (Davies 1973, 491).

Outside the Midland zone fields systems are often termed 'irregular' in reference to the lack of cropping control exercised by manor courts. These field systems often lacked the fields of the Midlands, and usually had many cropping units roughly equivalent to Midland furlongs (Bailey 2009; Herring 2006a). Often, each holding within these fields

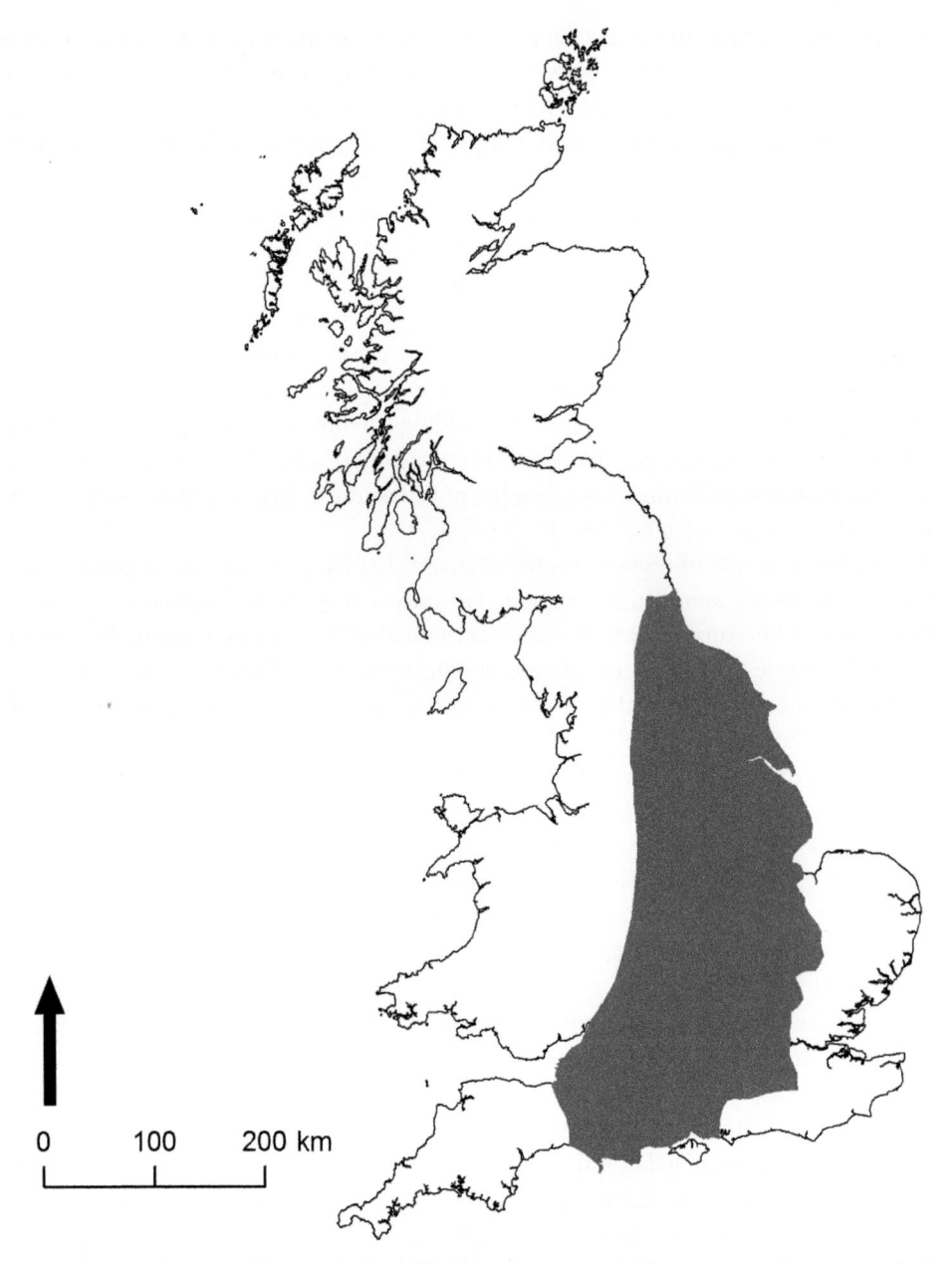

FIGURE 6.1 The region of two- or three-field systems (in grey). This region is the area in which strip holdings were grouped into furlongs and fields which were used to regulate cropping. It is equivalent to the 'champion' countryside recognized by sixteenth-century historians and is similar to the 'Central Province' defined by Roberts and Wrathmell (2000)

(© Ronan O'Donnell)

was clustered in one part of the field system (Bailey 2009; Barker 1973, 391–5; Hunter 2003; Rippon 2008, 179, 130), and there were usually large areas of enclosed land.

In East Anglia the most formal systems occur in the north-west of the region and in a thin strip along the Suffolk coast (Figure 6.2). Here sandy heaths provided extensive

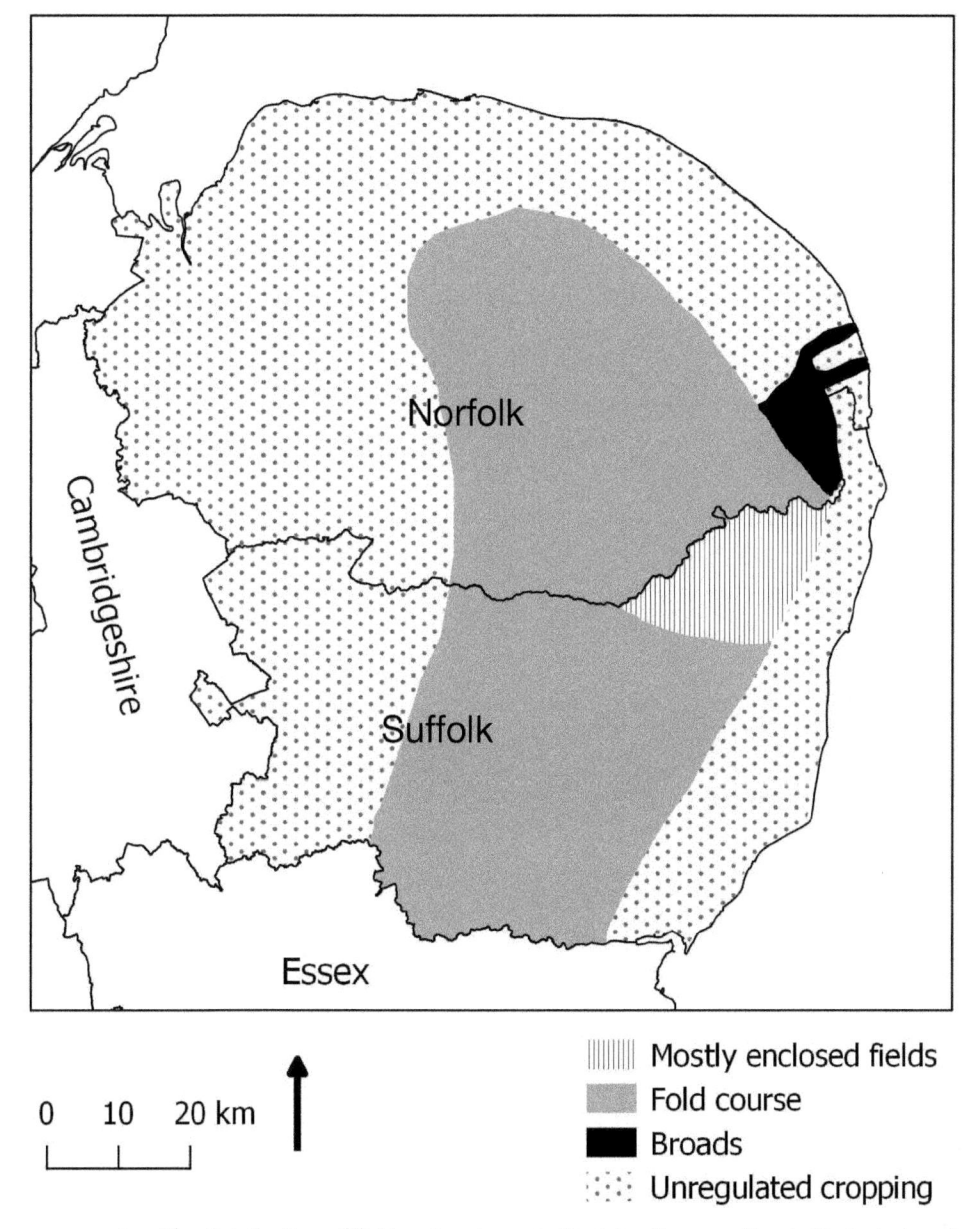

FIGURE 6.2 The distribution of field system types in East Anglia according to Postgate (1973) and Bailey (2009). The centre of the region is home to the fold-course system, while less closely regulated agriculture was practised to either side

(© Ronan O'Donnell)

sheep pasture, but were easily leached. The solution to leaching was to graze sheep on common waste during the day and fold them on the fallow arable overnight. The right to do this was called a 'fold course'. The distribution of manure was controlled by penning the sheep in a wattle fold. These were strictly controlled by manorial lords. Usually villein tenants had to put their sheep in the lord's fold so that they would manure the demesne land (Bailey 2007, 105) but in some cases free tenants did operate their own folds. In order to create compact blocks of fallow for the fold the strips were grouped into *quarentia* which are further grouped into 'shifts'. These shifts were not fixed and do not equate to Midland fields. In the middle of the East Anglia region there were neither fold courses nor shifts. In Essex extensive common fields are found in the north and west (Rippon 2008, 179) but in south and east Essex enclosed fields were much more common (Hunter 2003).

The West Country is also well understood. In East Somerset regular Midland Field Systems are found while further west field systems are more irregular (Figure 6.3) (Gerrard 2007, 996–7; Rippon 2008, 50–1). Recently, there has been some controversy over the extent of subdivided fields in West Somerset and Devon, with an Historic Landscape Characterization by Turner (2007, 41–5) showing most of Devon under open fields while Rippon (2008, 125) was unable to find substantial evidence for them in the

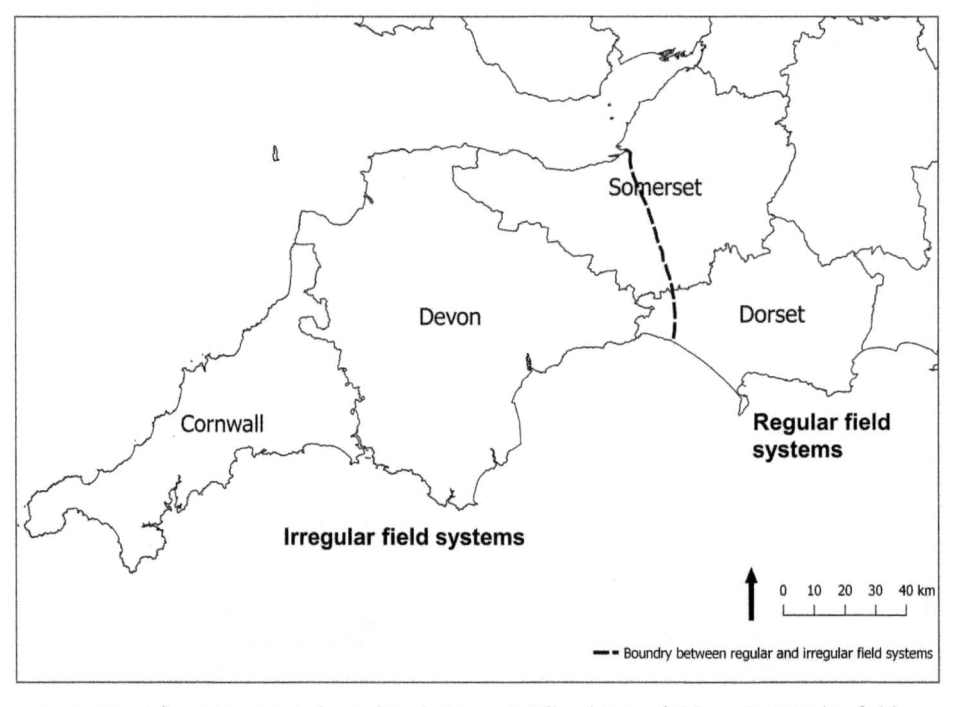

FIGURE 6.3 The approximate boundary between Midland open fields and irregular field systems in the West Country according to Rippon (2008) and Roberts and Wrathmell (2000). The majority is an irregular field region but the eastern end includes typical Midland fields

(© Ronan O'Donnell)

Blackdown Hills on the Somerset-Devon border. There is good evidence that ley farming, that is putting areas of arable down to grass for a number of years before ploughing them up again, was used as it has been observed in pollen cores (Rippon 2008, 130). The field systems of Cornwall are much better understood as a result of the work of Herring (2006a) who has shown that field systems there consisted of between 6 and 17 cropping units. At most two or three were cropped each year; every year one was prepared for sowing and grass planted under the crop of another which was to be put down to pasture.

Little recent work has been done on the south-east, but research carried out in the 1960s and early 1970s allows some remarks to be made. In Kent there was no common grazing or rotations; the fields were divided into units called 'yokes', but these appear to have been fiscal with no relationship to either landscape or cropping (Barker 1973, 387, 407). Sheep folding was used by tenants but formal fold courses did not exist (Barker 1973, 412). In Sussex cropping was more closely regulated with furlongs used as the cropping unit. These furlongs were grouped into 'leynes' in order to create contiguous fallows, which necessitated cropping regulation (Barker 1973, 422–9).

The north of England is more poorly understood. Britnell (2004) has examined County Durham. He found that while there is evidence for three-course rotations these were probably not of a Midland type. At Castle Eden, which is well documented, there was a three-field system in which holdings were evenly divided between the fields. In these ways it was quite similar to the Midland system although it differed as holdings were quite compact within each of the fields. Northumberland is even less well understood. Three-field systems are reasonably common in the low-lying east of the county (Butlin 1973, 111–32), which are superficially similar to Midland Field Systems but include large areas of common waste (Lomas 1996, 73; O'Donnell 2014, 108–13). Field systems in the uplands of the county tend to be very irregular, with hamlets within one township often possessing their own open-field systems (Figure 6.4). The north-west of England is particularly poorly understood. Youd (1962) found one field systems among Lancashire town-fields, and there is some evidence of infield-outfield cultivation (Hall 2013, 87). At Holme-Cultram the outfield was divided into areas called 'reines', each of which was cultivated for three years then left fallow for six. Infield-outfield was also used in north Wales where the permanently cultivated infield was called *Tir Cordllan* which was also a defined fiscal unit (Jones 1973, 435); there are some sixteenth-century references for the use of paring and burning to prepare north Welsh outfield (Jones 1973, 444). Finally, Scotland is very poorly understood as a result of a paucity of medieval documentation. In most of Scotland infield-outfield systems existed. These were probably of quite late origins (Dodgshon 1973). The fields were ploughed into ridges called 'run-rigg', a term which also refers to the subdivision of holdings within the systems.

It seems that there was a great variety of field systems in Britain during the Middle Ages. The systems described above, particularly those of Scotland, were far from static, and as we shall see some of their features developed under specific later medieval conditions.

FIGURE 6.4 The village of Elsdon in the Northumberland uplands, showing the minimal extent of the former open fields (O'Donnell 2014). The more lightly coloured improved pasture roughly corresponds to the area of open fields (A) which are surrounded by extensive commons (B). A small hamlet called Hudspath (C), which lay within Elsdon parish, had a small separate open field system

(© Ronan O'Donnell)

Changes and Narratives

Discussions of regional variation unintentionally give the impression of stasis; however, all arable landscapes were subject to major changes throughout the Middle Ages. The clearest overarching narrative for these is provided by economic history. Rapid population growth during the twelfth and thirteenth centuries led to expansion of arable cultivation. It also increased the price of grain and decreased the price of labour, meaning that it became economic for lords to farm demesnes directly using peasant labour services. In the fourteenth century this began to change. Bad harvests from 1315 to 1322, followed by the Black Death, halved the population. This reduced the price of land and grain while increasing the price of labour. Lords were forced to lease their demesnes to peasants. At the same time, land surpluses allowed peasants to increase their estates, fuelling engrossment and enclosure. These trends continued beyond the sixteenth century. There is ample scope for archaeological examination as the effects of both periods are clearly revealed by archaeological surveys. However, because most examinations focus on either the early medieval period when open field originated or the early modern period in which enclosure became significant, the developments of the Middle Ages are downplayed as incidental to the 'important' narratives.

Pre-Black Death

From an archaeological perspective the pre-Black Death period is characterized by assarting; that is, the process of reclaiming arable land from waste. Typically, we imagine assarting occurring in uplands and there is certainly archaeological evidence for this. For instance earthworks at Brown Willy, Dartmoor, show that the original two-field system was expanded between the eleventh and thirteenth centuries (Herring 2006b). Similarly in the Quantocks in Somerset assarting went so far as to create new settlement in the eleventh and thirteenth centuries (Riley 2006, 106). In the Peak District many granges or monastic farms were established during the twelfth and thirteenth centuries on the limestone plateau. In some cases it appears that the assarting which created these formed open fields as these are revealed by boundary shapes, while in other cases they were large enclosed pastures (Barnet and Smith 2004, 63–76). Field-walking in the Vale of the White Horse has revealed an increase in the quantity of pottery (from manuring) between the twelfth and fourteenth centuries suggesting population growth (Tingle 1991, 98). At Fyfield, thirteenth-century lynchets are found on north-facing slopes (Fowler 2000, 234) and new fields begin to be mentioned for the first time in the thirteenth and fourteenth centuries. This expansion allowed the medieval settlement of Raddun in Wiltshire to expand from a single shepherd's hut in the twelfth century (Fowler 2000, 124–5). In north Wales the process of assarting is partly driven by partible inheritance which makes holdings too small to farm and thus encroachment on commons is forced (Jones 1973, 454–5). Consequently, a wide range of landscape evidence from upland areas across Britain reveals that arable expanded dramatically, in line with historical understanding, but that the precise dating of this expansion may have varied between different areas.

Although we typically associate assarting with upland areas there is also good evidence for it from the lowlands. At Gillingham in northern Kent such assarting is revealed by lands with modern English names and with which no labour services are associated (Barker 1973, 394). Similarly, peasant families assarted consolidated blocks of land during the twelfth and thirteenth centuries on the manor of Havering in Essex (McIntosh 1986). Dyer (1991, 43) demonstrated significant assarting at Hanbury in Worcestershire between the twelfth and thirteenth centuries which reclaimed around one-fifth of the land in that township. Though even after this more land remained under grass than in the East Midlands. At Yarnton, Oxfordshire, eleventh- to fourteenth-century pottery is found on floodplains where no Saxon pottery is recovered and this has been interpreted as evidence of expansion (Hey 2004, 205). At Shapwick, Somerset, expansion was limited in the twelfth century but became more significant in the thirteenth while references in documents show that this continued into the early fourteenth century (Gerrard 2007, 997). The only major survey to fail to find evidence for extensive assarting is that at

Wharram Percy, North Yorkshire, where the eight and a half carucates of 1323 are similar to the size of the manor at Domesday (Hall 2013, 292).

Royal Forests provided some of the best areas for lowland assarting. More than 6,000 acres of Rockingham, Salcey, and Whittlewood Forests was assarted between 1200 and 1350 (Lewis et al. 2001, 142). The parishes with the greatest evidence for assarting also have the greatest population growth. Clearance at Rockingham led to the division of parishes and the creation of entirely new ones up to 1390 (Foard et al. 2005, 9–12); at Whittlewood there was also enough clearance for the creation of new settlements (Jones and Page 2006, 131). Pottery seems to be concentrated on assarts and some names may indicate ley cultivation of assarted land, but otherwise their cultivation is not unusual. At Wychwood there was also extensive assarting between the twelfth and thirteenth centuries (Schumer 1984, 45–6).

In recent years a number of investigations of wetland landscapes have demonstrated that these were some of the most important areas of reclamation during the first half of the Middle Ages. In the Fens reclaimed land was divided into 'doles' and allotted in a tenurial cycle. These were created between the twelfth and thirteenth centuries. Reclaimed land was first divided between neighbouring communities. Most of this land was used for meadow, but it was possible for people to withdraw their strips from common grazing after mowing to allow arable cultivation in some years (Gardiner 2009). This was, then, something between severalty holdings and standard open fields. Hall and Coles (1984) have examined the reclamation of the silt fen during the same period. Here earlier strips were short, but later longer strips were created. Usually these form blocks of parallel strips equivalent to a Midland furlong, however they do not appear to have been cropped communally as they were in the Midlands. In the Humber estuary there was also large-scale reclamation (Van de Noort 2004, 139–49). In this area monasteries were important and some granges were created in the wetlands. Moated sites were also formed on reclaimed land suggesting that secular lords were involved. In the Somerset Levels areas which had been defended from the sea in the early medieval period saw more intensive drainage during the later Middle Ages (Rippon 1997, 209). In addition, a small amount of enclosure occurred in front of the sea walls. To the north of the Severn the Gwent Levels were drained shortly after 1066 and largely by monastic lords (Rippon 1997, 218). Finally, at Romney Marsh reclamation occurred up to the mid-thirteenth century and may only have been halted by flooding. Again, this was driven by monasteries but also by tenants acting with seigniorial permission (Gardiner 1988, 114).

Another feature of this period is the division of existing holdings. In Gillingham, Kent, holdings seem to have become more fragmented as inheritance led to division, while rising grain prices made smaller farms viable. At Marham in Norfolk, Campbell (2005, 206) has found that mean holding size fell from ten acres to three between the twelfth and thirteenth centuries. This was probably driven by the same population rise as that which drove assarting. Similarly, Lewis et al. (2001, 145–6) have shown that many East Midlands field systems gained additional fields in the twelfth and thirteenth centuries which may be an intensification of arable farming.

The changes described above often led to novel ways of holding land for which archaeologists have observed evidence, although little patterning is yet apparent. For instance, at Brown Willy in Cornwall a field added during the thirteenth century has less regular strip sizes than the original two fields suggesting that the shareholding system emerged at the same time as the expansion. This was a novel type of tenure, in which each township paid a fixed rent to which each tenant contributed according to his/her means. Similarly, Roberts (1973, 224) has suggested that the Statute of Merton caused a change in the way assarting worked in the West Midlands. In the south of the West Midlands open fields had expanded to the limits of technology when the Statute was enacted. In the Arden, later assarting created fields held in severalty as a result of the Statute. At Stoneleigh Abbey in Warwickshire a range of different tenures arose from assarting. Some assarts were created by peasants as there is a *cultura* which is divided between peasants yet has an assarting name. Alongside these there were also enclosed assarts including the land of granges (Hilton 1960, 44–50). Conversely, at Wakefield in West Yorkshire assarting occurred throughout the twelfth and thirteenth centuries, but usually created severalty holdings as this was required by the manor (Moorhouse 1981, 662). At Wychwood in Gloucestershire, assarting created closes held in severalty, small pieces of open fields at the edges of townships, and large subdivided fields which may have been the most frequent (Schumer 1984, 50). Finally, in Scotland run-rigg originated during the thirteenth century as a result of the imposition of feudalism; earthwork evidence demonstrates that it overlies earlier medieval enclosed fields (Dixon 1994).

In addition to landscape development, rising grain prices also led to agricultural improvement. In most of the country this was a revolution in methods rather than technology (Campbell 2000; Dyer 1997) but some improvements have been identified. Mate (1985) has shown that marl and nightsoil were spread in Kent and Norfolk while marling has also been identified in documents relating to Hanbury in Warwickshire (Dyer 1991, 47). At Whittlewood, the increasing amount of pottery recovered from arable fields from 1250 onwards suggests more intensive manuring during direct demesne farming (Jones and Page 2006, 132). Mate (1985) has also shown that seeding rates varied spatially suggesting that these were carefully considered. Postles (1989) revealed that both weeding and fallow stirring were used for weed control. At Holywell in Oxfordshire expenditure varied between different years suggesting that the amount of weed growth was taken into account; weeding appears to have taken place at the times suggested by Walter of Henley and seems to have covered most of the demesne. Campbell (1988) discusses the use of vetches, a legume which adds nitrogen to soils, and shows that they appear early in the Winchester account rolls and were initially cultivated across the chalk uplands. They reach Norfolk by 1299 and only become widespread by the fourteenth century, mostly in Norfolk, Kent, Berkshire, Oxfordshire, and Hertfordshire. The use of vetches has been identified in archaeobotanical assemblages from Shapwick (Straker et al. 2007, 879).

To sum up, there is a very clear expansion of arable farming during the twelfth and thirteenth centuries. This is to be expected as the phenomenon has long been known to historians. However, it is clear that it may be observed through a wide range of archaeological techniques including field-walking, historic landscape characterization, and aerial photography. This may, in time, allow an understanding of the regional variation of these processes as fine-grained as that of the field systems themselves. At the present time it appears that, while forest and upland landscapes have the most extensive evidence, assarting was a potent force across the entire British lowland. Perhaps the most interesting aspect of the process is the variety of tenures created by assarting which may have led to a particularly complex legal landscape on the eve of the Black Death. Lands of different tenures were created alongside each other in nearly every case which has been studied in detail, and it is unclear why different tenures were selected. The reasons for this will form an important avenue for future research. It is also interesting that almost all social groups are represented among assarters from peasants to secular lords and monasteries. While future research may reveal that certain groups were more important in some areas than others it is clear that this can only be a difference of degree. The trends came to an abrupt halt in the mid-fourteenth century but there was no strict reversal of the changes, as we shall see.

Post Black-Death

The upheaval that resulted from a long period of famine and a disastrous plague caused a change in trajectory for the medieval landscape. A lower price of grain and higher price of labour meant that lords abandoned direct farming and leased demesnes to peasants. Peasants were also able to increase their estates as population collapse left holdings vacant. This allowed consolidation and piecemeal enclosure of open fields, alongside a general retraction of arable agriculture and settlement desertion.

One of the most obvious developments of this period is the contraction of the arable area. For instance, Wharram Percy glebe terriers suggest that the poorest land in the south and west of Wharram Percy township was abandoned (Hall 2012, 295). The timing of this appears to vary regionally, as in the Vale of the White Horse contraction appears to have occurred only from the sixteenth century as cloth production became more important; the initial shocks of early fourteenth-century crises do not appear to have led to long-term changes. Contraction was greatest at those settlements with the greatest recovered quantities of medieval pottery and thus perhaps those with the greatest commitment to arable agriculture (Tingle 1991, 98).

Some of the land which went down to grass was newly enclosed from the open fields. In the irregular field areas of Suffolk there was much piecemeal enclosure, which was hastened by the clustering of holdings that had always been a feature of these regions (Bailey 2009, 25–6). Much of this was carried out by yeoman farmers who removed most of the open-field systems of these areas before 1550. In Cornwall and Devon piecemeal enclosure had been practised since the thirteenth century at least (Herring 2006a; Turner 2007, 48), but in this period became more intensive. This meant that large blocks were enclosed in each event creating rectangular fields rather than the thin strips that were made before the fourteenth century. At Shapwick piecemeal enclosure and enclosure of upland areas are very much in evidence and continue to be up to 1515 (Gerrard

2007, 998). Unlike earlier assarting, piecemeal enclosure is not uniform across the country, as for instance, at Rockingham Forest in the Midlands there is little piecemeal enclosure, but large areas are put down to sheepwalk (Foard et al. 2005, 16). In south Wales the Glyn Dŵr revolt of 1400-15 also led to piecemeal enclosure (Davies 1973, 528). In north Wales the combination of land being put down to pasture and continuing partible inheritance forced some tenants to leave their holdings and this subsequently provided new opportunities for consolidation and piecemeal enclosure (Jones 1973, 451–5).

One alternative to the enclosure of field systems was their reorganization, which continued the trend towards increasing tenurial complexity of the preceding period. In Suffolk the response to the crises took the form of more tightly controlled fold course in the hope of increasing wool production as wool prices held up. This neglected some the manuring aspects of fold course but more strongly enforced the use of stints (Bailey 2009, 22); elsewhere, tenants consolidated their holdings. At Whittlewood field systems were reorganized so that at Deans Hanger a fourth field was added to an existing three-field system between 1336 and 1566 (Jones and Page 2006, 143). At Havering, now in London, a new attitude to land developed as tenants increasingly treated their estates as manors (McIntosh 1986, 145–6). At Wharram Percy an infield-outfield system developed after enclosure had removed the open-field system. This also developed in neighbouring parishes. Finally, it was during this period that newly enclosed land in Scotland stopped being added to the open fields, thereby allowing the creation of the outfield; this was at least partly a fiscal distinction as outfield paid different rents to the infield (Dodgshon 1994).

The demise of direct demesne farming is evident in many archaeological surveys. At West Cotton, Northamptonshire, the old manor house enclosure was divided in two and part was transferred to a tenant in the mid-thirteenth century. Both of these tenements were well appointed so the demesne tenants were wealthy. In 1300 the manor house was abandoned completely (Chapman 2010, 243). In the Peak District monasteries abandoned some of their direct farming; Needham Grange in Derbyshire, for example, was leased to tenants in the fourteenth and fifteenth centuries (Barnett and Smith 2004, 72).

Finally, agricultural decline led to changes to crops and methods. Thirsk (1997) has suggested that this was a period of alternative agriculture in which new crops and methods were developed. For lords this included dovecotes and warrens and for the less wealthy hemp and flax replaced some wheat production though both were cultivated on a smaller scale prior to the Black Death. Many of these crops diffused from areas of the Continent, particularly the climatically similar Low Countries and, as a result, most crops initially appear in East Anglia. Mate (1992) has also shown this to be an important period of innovation in the south-east where vetches, marling, and higher seeding rates become more prominent.

While it is not yet possible to determine clear regional patterns in post-Black Death landscape developments there is clearer regional differentiation than in the earlier phase of expansion. In some areas there is no piecemeal enclosure while in others it is a major force. Similarly, reorganization is common in some areas but absent in others. Regional chronologies also exist with piecemeal enclosure being important in the thirteenth-century West Country long before it became common elsewhere. As with the earlier phase the changes created new tenures and attitudes to land ownership, most clearly in Scotland, which existed alongside more ancient tenures.

Conclusions

We have seen that far from being a period of stasis in the development of agricultural landscapes between the early medieval and the early modern periods, the Middle Ages are in fact a lively period of landscape development. The first phase in which expansion of the arable area occurred across the country led to a proliferation of new land tenures and an increasingly legally complex landscape. Change in this period was driven by a heterogeneous group of people from whom we have yet to identify particularly important social groups if such groups exist. There is as yet no clear regional patterning though this may be expected to emerge with closer study. The following phase of contraction displays more regional variation particularly in the prevalence of piecemeal enclosure which increased the proportion of land in severalty, though always alongside open-field tenures. These post-Black Death changes added to the developments of the previous two centuries to create new layers to the arable landscape rather than simply reversing earlier change. There is clearly much work still to be done and it is hoped that future work will uncover much of the detail missing from the broad narrative presented here.

References cited

Bailey, M. 2007 *Medieval Suffolk: an economic and social history, 1200–1500*, Boydell Press, Woodbridge

Bailey, M. 2009 'The form, function and evolution of irregular field systems in Suffolk, c.1300 to c.1550', *Agricultural History Review* 57, 15–36

Barker, A. R. H. 1973 'Field systems of South East England', in A. R. H. Barker and R. A. Butlin (eds), *Studies of field systems in the British Isles*, Cambridge University Press, Cambridge, 377–430

Barnet, J. and Smith, K. 2004 *The Peak District: landscapes through time*, Windgather Press, Macclesfield

Britnell, R. 2004 'Fields, farms and sun-division in a moorland region, 1100–1400', *Agricultural History Review* 52, 20–37

Butlin, R. A. 1973 'Field systems of Northumberland and Durham', in A. R. H. Barker and R. A. Butlin (eds), *Studies of field systems in the British Isles*, Cambridge University Press, Cambridge, 93–144

Campbell, B. M. L. 1988 'The diffusion of vetches in medieval England', *Economic History Review* 41, 193–208

Campbell, B. M. L. 2000 *English seigniorial agriculture, 1250–1450*, Cambridge University Press, Cambridge

Campbell, B. M. L. 2005 'The land', in R. Horrox and W. M. Ormrod (eds), *A social history of England 1200–1500*, Cambridge University Press, Cambridge

Chapman, A. 2010 *West Cotton, Raunds: a study of medieval settlement dynamics AD 450–1450. Excavation of a deserted medieval hamlet in Northamptonshire, 1985–89*, Oxbow, Oxford

Davies, M. 1973 'Field systems of South Wales', in A. R. H. Barker and R. A. Butlin (eds), *Studies of field systems in the British Isles*, Cambridge University Press, Cambridge, 480–529

Dixon, P. J. 1994 'Field systems, rig and other cultivation remains in Scotland: the field evidence', in S. Foster and T. C. Smout (eds), *The history of soils and field systems*, Scottish Cultural Press, Aberdeen, 26–52

Dodgshon, R. A. 1973 'The nature and development of infield-outfield in Scotland', *Transactions of the Institute of British Geographers* 59, 1–23

Dodgshon, R. A. 1994 'Rethinking Highland field systems', in S. Foster and T. C. Smout (eds), *The history of soils and field systems*, Scottish Cultural Press, Aberdeen, 53–65

Dyer, C. 1991 *Hanbury: settlement and society in a woodland landscape*, University of Leicester Press, Leicester

Dyer, C. 1997 'Medieval farming and technology: conclusion', in G. Astill and J. Langdon (eds), *Medieval farming and technology: the impact of agricultural change in North-West Europe*, Koninklijke Brill, Leiden, 293–312

Foard, G., Hall, D., and Partida, T. 2005 'Rockingham Forest, Northamptonshire: the evolution of a landscape', *Landscapes* 2, 1–29

Fowler, P. J. 2000 *Landscape plotted and pieced: landscape history and local archaeology in Fyfield and Overton, Wiltshire*, The Society of Antiquaries of London, London

Gardiner, M. 1988 'Medieval settlement and society in the Broomhill area, and excavations at Broomhill Church', in J. Eddison and C. Green (eds), *Romney Marsh: evolution, occupation and reclamation*, Oxford University Committee for Archaeology, Oxford, 112–62

Gardiner, M. 2009 'Dales, long lands and the medieval division of land in Eastern England', *Agricultural History Review*, 57, 1–14

Gerrard, C. M. 2007 'The late medieval landscape', in C. M. Gerrard with M. Aston (eds), *The Shapwick Project, Somerset: a rural landscape explored*, The Society for Medieval Archaeology Monograph 25, Leeds, 981–98

Grey, H. L. 1915 *English field systems*, Harvard University Press, Cambridge, MA

Hall, D. N. 1995 *The open fields of Northamptonshire*, Northamptonshire Record Society, Northampton

Hall, D. N. 2012 'Field systems and land-holdings', in S. Wrathmell (ed.), *Wharram XIII: a history of Wharram Percy and its neighbours*, University of York, York, 278–89

Hall, D. N. 2013 *The open fields of England*, Oxford, Oxford University Press

Hall, D. N. and Coles, J. 1984 *Fenland Survey: an essay in landscape and persistence*, English Heritage, Swindon

Herring, P. 2006a 'Cornish strip fields', in S. Turner (ed.), *Medieval Devon and Cornwall: shaping an ancient countryside*, Windgather, Macclesfield, 44–77

Herring, P. 2006b 'Medieval strip fields at Brown Willy, Bodmin Moor', in S. Turner (ed.), *Medieval Devon and Cornwall: shaping an ancient countryside*, Windgather, Macclesfield 78–103

Hey, G. 2004 *Yarnton: Saxon and medieval settlement*, Oxford Archaeology, Oxford

Hilton, R. 1960 *The Stoneleigh Leger Book*, The Dugdale Society, Stratford-upon-Avon

Hunter, J. 2003 *Field Systems in Essex*, Essex Society for Archaeology and History, Colchester

Jones, G. R. L. 1973 'Field systems of North Wales', in A. R. H. Barker and R. A. Butlin (eds), *Studies of field systems in the British Isles*, Cambridge University Press, Cambridge, 430–91

Jones, R. L. C. and Page, M. 2006 *Medieval villages in an English landscape*, Windgather, Macclesfield

Lewis, C., Mitchell-Fox, P., and Dyer, C. 2001 *Village, hamlet and field: changing medieval settlements in central England*, Windgather, Macclesfield

Lomas, R. A. 1996 *County of conflict: Northumberland from Conquest to Civil War*, Tuckwell Press, Edinburgh

Mate, M. 1985 'Medieval agrarian practices: the determining factors', *Agricultural History Review* 33, 22–31

Mate, M. 1992 'The agrarian economy of south-east England before the Black Death: depressed or buoyant?', in B. M. S. Campbell (ed.), *Before the Black Death: studies in the 'crisis' of the early fourteenth century*, Manchester University Press, Manchester

McIntosh, M. K. 1986 *A community transformed: the manor and liberty of Havering 1500–1620*, Oxford University Press, Oxford

Moorhouse, S. A. 1981 'The rural medieval landscape', in M. Faull and S. A. Moorhouse (eds), *West Yorkshire: an archaeological survey to 1500*, West Yorkshire Metropolitan County Council, Leeds

O'Donnell, R. P. 2014 *Landscape, agency and enclosure: transformations in the rural landscape of North-East England*, unpublished PhD thesis, University of Durham

Platt, C. 2012 'Archaeology and the "agrarian crisis" in England 1315–22', *Medieval Archaeology* 56, 292–97

Postgate, M. R. 1973 'Field systems of East Anglia', in A. R. H. Barker and R. A. Butlin (eds), *Studies of field systems in the British Isles*, Cambridge University Press, Cambridge, 281–324

Postles, D. 1989 'Cleaning the medieval arable', *Agricultural History Review* 37, 130–43

Riley, H. 2006 *The historic landscape of the Quantock Hills*, English Heritage, Swindon

Rippon, S. 1997 *The Severn Estuary: landscape evolution of a wetland landscape*, Council for British Archaeology, York

Rippon, S. 2008 *Beyond the medieval village: the diversification of landscape character in southern Britain*, Oxford University Press, Oxford

Roberts, B. K. 1973 'Field systems of the West Midlands', in A. R. H. Barker and R. A. Butlin (eds), *Studies of field systems in the British Isles*, Cambridge University Press, Cambridge, 188–231

Roberts, B. K. and Wrathmell, S. 2000 *Region and place: a study of English rural settlement*, English Heritage, Swindon

Schofield, P. R. 2003 *Peasant and community in medieval England 1200–1500*, Palgrave Macmillan, Basingstoke

Schumer, B. 1984 *The evolution of Wychwood to 1400: pioneers frontiers and forests*, University of Leicestershire Press, Leicester

Straker, V., Campbell, G., and Smith, W. 2007 'The charred plant macrofossils', in C. M. Gerrard with M. Aston (eds), *The Shapwick Project, Somerset: a rural landscape explored*, The Society for Medieval Archaeology Monograph 25, Leeds, 869–88

Thirsk, J. 1997 *Alternative agriculture: a history from the Black Death to the present day*, Oxford University Press, Oxford

Tingle, M. 1991 *Vale of the White Horse Survey: the study of a changing landscape in the clay lowlands of southern England from Prehistory to the present*, British Archaeological Reports British Series 218, Oxford

Turner, S. 2007 *Ancient country: the historic character of rural Devon*, Devon Archaeological Society, Exeter

Van de Noort, R. 2004 *The Humber wetlands: the archaeology of a dynamic landscape*, Windgather, Macclesfield

Youd, G. 1962 'The common fields of Lancashire', *Transactions of the Historic Society of Lancashire and Cheshire* 113, 1–40

CHAPTER 7

THE ANIMAL IN LATE MEDIEVAL BRITAIN

LOUISA GIDNEY

THE systematic study of later medieval faunal assemblages largely grew out of the New Archaeology of the 1960s and 1970s, with its emphasis on scientific and quantitative studies (Gerrard 2003, 159–60 and, for later studies, see 202–3). Such approaches were greatly facilitated by the support of English Heritage in establishing regional laboratories for the analysis of biological finds, in addition to the Ancient Monuments Laboratory in London. This scientific approach of the 1970s also saw the founding of the Association for Environmental Archaeology (AEA), and the International Council for Archaeozoology (ICAZ); the fourth ICAZ conference was hosted in London in 1982. In Britain, the AEA journal *Circaea* provided an outlet for publication of, for example, the seminal late medieval faunal assemblage from Launceston Castle (Albarella and Davies 1996), fully 20 years before the final site report was published (Saunders 2006).

The 1970s saw an increase in large-scale excavations and a concomitant increase in large faunal assemblages available for analysis according to rigorous scientific principles. In an era before computerized data-capture, Mark Maltby's (1979) pioneering work on the urban faunal assemblages from Exeter remains an invaluable resource for comparative studies because of the detailed paper publication of tables not only of fragment counts but also ageing and, in particular, metrical data. The adoption of microfiche saw much comparable data relegated to this medium, which is now difficult to access. Though Exeter was the first monograph to be published solely on British archaeozoological data, there have been few subsequent comparable works, with the fascicule series from York (Bond and O'Connor 1999) and Lincoln (Dobney et al. 1996; O'Connor 1982) being the prime examples which include later medieval assemblages. Rather, as Maltby observed (1979, xi), faunal studies tend to remain doomed as an appendix to the main site report.

The advent of computerization saw an initiative by English Heritage and leading archaeozoologists (Jones et al. 1980) to develop a standardized computer recording system in order to enhance the compatibility of inter-site comparisons of data recorded by different specialists. This programme was used to record and analyse the assemblage spanning the twelfth to seventeenth centuries from Barnard Castle, County Durham (Jones et al. 1985) but the time lag from excavation between 1974 and 1981, analysis of the faunal remains from 1981 to 1985, to final publication some 20 years later is commonplace in the dissemination of faunal data (Austin 2007), and still presents challenges in how and where data and interpretation should be published in a timely fashion. The Ancient Monuments Laboratory Report series remains an accessible archive resource. Internet publishing, for example SAIR (the Scottish Archaeology Internet Report series) and the data-hosting site ADS (the Archaeology Data Service at the University of York) are enhancing the dissemination of data. However, much information from commercially funded, rather than research, excavations remains in the paper 'grey literature' with little prospect of full publication. The integration of scientific analyses common to both human and animal remains saw the launch firstly of the International Journal of Osteoarchaeology and secondly of the International Journal of Paleopathology. While these are undoubtedly invaluable outlets for promoting the results of research projects and new techniques of scientific analysis to an international audience, the topics covered are rarely within the remit of commercially funded assemblages from later medieval sites.

Other major topics to be tackled were taphonomy and the interpretation of environmental data, both themes of the 1993 AEA conference (Huntley and Stallibrass 2000). Previously, Gautier (1984) had drawn attention to the problems of quantifying archaeozoological data, while Stallibrass (1984) demonstrated the impact of small carnivore scavenging on the composition of surviving faunal remains. Such studies were still inspired by assemblages from time periods pre-dating the late medieval. In contrast, Jones and Ruben (1987) demonstrated the methodological challenges of recording fragments smaller than 6 cm in hand-excavation at Goltho medieval manor in Lincolnshire.

Continuing excavation in the 1980s in advance of ongoing urban re-development retrieved vast assemblages of animal bones. Such datasets stimulated the conference held in 1986 to discuss the themes of 'diet and crafts in towns' (Serjeantson and Waldron 1989), and thereby began to redress the fact that most previous work on the theoretical aspect of the analysis of animal bones had been based on rural, prehistoric sites. The fact that later medieval urban assemblages required explicit research designs to cope with the volume of faunal-remains data resulted in O'Connor's (2003) handbook for archaeologists, based on the experience of analysing animal bones from several decades of excavation in York. Albarella's (2005) comparative synthesis of meat production and consumption in medieval towns and villages demonstrates the remarkable potential of this material to address themes ranging from species frequency to age at slaughter and carcass processing.

More recently, a major initiative of the twenty-first century has been the critical evaluation and integration of zooarchaeological and historical data, such as recipes, husbandry manuals, and estate records into analysis and this, for example, was the approach taken by Thomas (2005) for the Dudley Castle assemblage and Gidney (2013) for cattle management.

Beyond Food and Agriculture

The majority of the animal bones found on later medieval archaeological sites represent refuse from the consumption of meat from cattle, sheep, and pigs. The proportions of cattle to sheep bones change from the eleventh to fifteenth centuries, reflecting wider economic pressures and changes in the perceived social status of particular meats. Pluskowski (Chapter 10) documents the expression of social status shown by access to hunted native species and managed, introduced, wild species such as rabbit and fallow deer. Even so, the increasing social complexity of later medieval Britain is reflected in the composition of faunal assemblages that indicate exploitation patterns not primarily driven by meat production, as the following five themes will illustrate.

Calf Slaughter (Why Kill Calves?)

The presence of bones from infant calves on archaeological sites has become enshrined as standard zooarchaeological evidence for a dairy-based cattle-herding strategy. This interpretation is based on the premise that a herd or flock kept primarily for milking will generate a surplus of young males which are neither needed for breeding nor useful for milking (O'Connor 2000, 89). The integration of historical sources, new scientific techniques, and new comparative collections challenges this position with regard to male calves, at least for later medieval assemblages. In the first instance, male calves were needed to supply draught oxen for arable areas lacking breeding cows. Furthermore, the indispensable nature of rennet for the production of hard, keeping cheeses requiring in turn an annual spring slaughter of calves to produce rennet from the stomach bags is a concept that has yet to be widely considered among those zooarchaeologists particularly interested in the faunal evidence for dairy herds. Earlier medieval historical sources re-iterated in the sixteenth century, such as Markham (Best 1986, 168), indicate that the best time to calve cows for the dairy was late March and all April, but that all the calves born then should be slaughtered.

Infant calf bones are generally sparse on medieval urban and castle sites prior to the fifteenth century, even when preservation is good. Thereafter, infant calf bones occur in numbers at sites all over England, for example Barnard Castle (Jones et al. 2007), Hartlepool (Daniels 2010, 192), Leicester (Gidney 1991a; 1991b), and Launceston Castle, where Albarella and Davis (1996, 34) discuss this as a national phenomenon. All the standard interpretations covered by Albarella and Davis concentrate on the dairy exploitation of the dam and the concomitant consumption of veal as a response to the decline of draught cattle, in turn linked to the rise of horse power. While these were doubtless important considerations, the calf hides would also have value. Gidney (1991a) considered the use of vellum in Leicester, given the proximity of Parchment Lane to the excavated site. Vellum was used for bookbinding as well as for writing and a wealth of surviving medieval parchment is now being studied by the BioArCh team at York University, using both DNA and mass spectrometry (ZooMS) to identify the species (Teasdale et al. 2015). Sheep parchment has been the principle topic of interest to date but the techniques are also applicable to calf vellum. It is notable that the abundant finds of cobbling waste recovered from deposits dated c.1475–1515 from the moat at Barnard Castle were principally of calf skin (Austin 2007, 540–52). Greater numbers of later medieval calfskin shoes have also been observed in London (Grew and Neergaard 1988, 44–6), where it is suggested that production of English cordwain from calfskin was a response to disruption of supplies from Spain (see Chapter 59).

The quality of calfskins for leather working is influenced by diet, sex, and season. Reed (1972, 38–41) categorizes the qualities of veal and calf skins, making a significant distinction between very young and older calves. The best skins are from milk-fed calves rather than those weaned on to solid food. Heifer calf skins are more valuable, being tougher and finer grained than those of bull calves. In Europe, calfskins are at their best from April to June. Unfortunately, zooarchaeological discussion of calf cull patterns tends not to consider the quality of the skin as a primary reason for slaughter, yet this could have been an important incentive for the slaughter of spring-born milk-fed calves, including heifers. DNA studies by the BioArCh team at York may prove able to establish independent evidence for the sex ratio of the calf skins used in individual manuscript books (Matthew Collins pers. comm.).

The sudden appearance nationally in the late medieval archaeological record of a significant cull of calves is an event that might be considered to lead to change in the morphology of the cattle by selection of those calves to rear. Hall and Hall (1988, 491) point out that, under artificial selection, only the 'better' 50 per cent of the annual calf crop should be retained for breeding but that the natural calf mortality in the Chillingham herd mirrors this optimum cull. A blanket cull of spring-born later medieval calves may have resulted in a change in phenotype but this would have been an inadvertent side effect rather than a deliberate strategy.

Selection Pressures

The lack of stature seen for pre-fifteenth century medieval cattle has attracted negative comment from historians (Dyer 2002, 25). In fact, this may represent a natural response to the benign weather of the Medieval Warm Period (see Chapter 11); miniaturization can happen without any input from human selection. Ozgul et al. (2009) have identified the processes resulting in a recent decline in the body size of the feral Soay sheep on St Kilda. Here, the less frequent occurrence of long harsh winters has increased the survivability of small slow-growing individuals, who are breeding at a younger age and producing lambs of lighter body weight. Consequently, there is now a reduction in the mean body weight of the population. The St Kilda example demonstrates the speed with which such a shift in parameters of size and weight can occur when driven by environmental change.

Conversely, Albarella and Davis (1996, 42–57) discuss the appearance of larger cattle at Launceston Castle, Cornwall, between the fifteenth century and the sixteenth century to 1650. The change in both size and shape of cattle bones is described as 'dramatic'. Albarella and Davis consider a range of possible causes for this change in phenotype, including changes in sex ratio, and castration, and conclude that a change in genotype is indicated. Evidence for similar change on a range of contemporary sites in England is presented. The literary evidence for both cross-breeding between indigenous regional cattle types and the import of Dutch cattle are discussed, together with the opinions of agrarian historians. The consensus is in favour of deliberate 'improvement' by the more stable period of Elizabeth's reign.

While this is a thorough discussion of the evidence, one point was not explicitly considered, specifically as a response to the Little Ice Age (see Chapter 11). This is Bergmann's Rule, observed in the nineteenth century as an inverse correlation between latitude and body size, related to temperature (Davis 1981, 110). Armitage (1994, 236–8) drew attention to the 'extraordinarily large size' of black rat bones found on later medieval and early Tudor archaeological sites in Britain and both the large size and black pelage are believed to be an adaptive response to the cold of the Little Ice Age. No one would describe this sudden and dramatic increase in the size of rat bones as evidence for 'improvement' or selective breeding on the part of humans, yet this change is contemporary to that documented for the cattle bones. Rats obviously have a far faster reproductive rate than cattle and so might be anticipated to show a more contemporary morphological response to the deteriorating weather of the Little Ice Age.

Fourteenth-century records demonstrate the mortality of out-wintered cattle resulting from severe winter weather (Austin 2007, 105). Tusser's sixteenth-century recommendations for February's husbandry indicate continued out-wintering of cattle (Hartley 1969, 132). Increased mortality of out-wintered small and lean cattle would, of itself, enhance the representation of larger cattle in the breeding pool. Observation of this fact and selection for it, either by deliberate retention of larger calves or natural mortality of puny calves, and importation of larger Dutch cattle may have been part of the dynamic stimulating the increase in cattle size observed by Albarella and Davis. It is therefore possible that this size 'improvement' was initially driven by natural selection, operating under Bergmann's rule as a response to the Little Ice Age, and a pragmatic reaction to mortality of smaller breeding stock, rather than the inception of conscious breeding of larger animals for enhanced carcass return.

Disease

Peter Brown (Chapter 11) discusses the rarity of archaeological evidence for short-lived catastrophic events caused by natural phenomena. Mortality of out-wintered cattle in extreme winter weather has been alluded to above. In addition, murrain, or contagious disease, regularly decimated cattle herds, culminating in the early fourteenth-century pandemic (Newfield 2009; Slavin 2010).

Large-scale rural excavations at Shapwick in Somerset revealed an example of a pit filled with articulated cattle skeletons (Gerrard 2007, 425), which may represent such a localized catastrophe. This burial pit was not fully excavated but parts of at least seven cattle bodies were recovered (Figure 7.1). Bones from two separate individuals produced a calendar C^{14} date range of AD 980–1160 for this event. The pit that the carcasses were deposited in was a disused lime kiln close to the *curia*, or manorial administrative centre of Shapwick. The use of the old lime kiln may be significant in the disposal of the bodies, as lime is still used as an agricultural disinfectant. The proximity to the *curia* suggests official disposal of manorial property, along similar precepts to those subsequently detailed in Walter of Henley and associated treatises of the thirteenth century, whereby fallen stock were inspected by the manorial officials to ascertain the cause of death (Oschinsky 1971, 423). No evidence for the salvage of the hides was observed on the bones, which suggests that the bodies were tainted. In the 1319 outbreak of cattle murrain, bodies were buried shortly following their death on account of their stench (Newfield 2009, 166). As might be expected with a sudden catastrophic mortality, no pathological changes indicative of the cause of death were observed on the cattle bones.

Tempting though it was to equate the Shapwick find with murrain (Gidney 2007a, 901–3; Newfield 2015, 16), another explanation also deserves consideration. The worst winter in current living memory, in 1947, commenced with blizzards in February and March. Traditionally one should have 'half one's hay left in February', but in 1947 drought the previous year had reduced the hay crop and downpours had spoiled the cereal harvest, so fodder was already in short supply. The impact on the Chillingham herd of semi-feral park cattle was a reduction from 33 to 13 head, with only the older and stronger animals surviving (Whitehead 1953, 49–50). The corpses of the 20 fallen stock

FIGURE 7.1 Burial pit for cattle, excavated at Shapwick, Somerset, where bones have been dated to AD 980–1160

(© Christopher Gerrard)

were buried in one pit, after the thaw had revealed all the bodies. This example provides a further possible interpretation of the Shapwick burial pit and indicates the difficulty of elucidating the causative effect of a mass fatality, when the response in both cases would be a single burial event of the carcasses. A similar cycle of bad weather causing fodder and crop failure, leading to malnourishment and therefore increased susceptibility to infectious disease of the famine survivors, was a feature of the early fourteenth century agrarian crisis and the cattle plague which commenced in 1319 (Newfield 2009, 176; Slavin 2010).

Opportunities to test these hypotheses about the diagnostic presence or absence of pathological conditions against unequivocal archaeological finds of oxen bones are rare. The surviving demesne accounts for Shapwick (Martin Ecclestone pers. comm.) for 21 years between 1258 and 1334 indicate the manor maintained an average of 49 oxen, castrated males used primarily for ploughing arable. It was therefore anticipated that the majority of the cattle buried in this feature could derive from such oxen. Extrapolating the number of bodies represented to include the unexcavated half of the pit suggests that the equivalent of two plough teams of eight oxen could have been buried here. The morphology of the pelves indicate the presence of one female, with the remainder male and therefore possibly oxen. The ageing data from the teeth suggested that the heads appeared to derive from older animals than indicated by the stages of epiphysial fusion of the limb bones. The hypothesis proposed was that the bodies might be of castrates, hence a delay in the fusion of the later fusing skeletal elements compared to the stages of tooth wear (Gidney 2007a, 902). Unlike the modern oxen studied by Bartosiewicz et al. (1997), there is a total absence of pathological changes in the Shapwick cattle skeletons. This finding appears to negate simple assumptions of correlation between use for draught work and morphological changes to the skeleton. In part, this may be because the skeletons in the pit represent a snapshot in time of the composition of the live cattle herd, rather than the deliberately culled cattle that entered the human food chain.

Cats, Dogs, Horses, Goats

While cat bones are generally infrequent finds in medieval deposits, there are some instances of unusual concentrations. One such deposit was at Causeway Lane, Leicester (Gidney 1999, 327), where cat bones contributed some 18 per cent of the identified fragments from one pit within one of the seven property boundaries identified on the site. Some two-thirds of the cat limb bones were from immature animals with unfused epiphysial ends, and mandibles with the deciduous dentition were also present. Skinning marks were seen on mandibles with both deciduous and permanent dentition. The interpretation was of waste from processing cat skins, which would have produced furs of suitable lowly status for the local residents (Veale 1966). Similar concentrations of immature cat bones at King's Lynn (Noddle 1977) and Exeter (Maltby 1979, 86) have also been interpreted as evidence for the exploitation of cats for fur skins (Serjeantson 1989, 131) while comparable evidence for skinning marks on the basal border of cat mandibles was identified at Perth High Street (Smith 1998, 877). Recognition of such small-scale, back-yard urban fur farming is entirely dependent on the chance of locating such discrete features within the confines of urban excavations. An unusual assemblage from Cambridge concludes that cats were also consumed by humans, presumably during periods of food shortage: 79 cats recovered from a thirteenth-century well had had their throats slit and they had been skinned and dismembered (Luff and Moreno 1995). Certainly, the medieval urban cat was seen as having an economic value beyond rodent control and human companionship.

Dog bones are generally larger than those of cat and more easily retrieved by hand during excavation. Smith (1998, 862–70) provides a detailed overview of the dog remains recovered from medieval Scottish towns. The commonest was the 'plain dog' type, with a broad face and long snout, probably of slim build, but of varying height. Also represented was a strong, bow-legged type, with a very strongly developed, downward-angled sagittal crest to the skull and heavily built mandibles. The final type of dog was small and fine-boned with a round, domed skull. Although a range of hunting dogs and hounds were considered, Smith judges their remains most likely to represent householders' guard dogs, and herders' and butchers' dogs. Several examples of dogs deposited as intact bodies are given, which may represent valued companion animals. Conversely, Smith (1998, 877) presents evidence that dog carcasses were skinned in Perth, Aberdeen, Dundee, and Elgin. A traditional Scottish use of such skins was to make fishing floats and some cut marks on the dog bones were more akin to butchery than skinning. Dead dogs certainly appear to have been used to feed live dogs at Witney Palace, Oxfordshire (Wilson and Edwards 1993) and Gidney (1996) considered the cosmetic and healing uses of dog fat.

Among the most intriguing examples of horse remains are the 76 skinned animals, both articulated and dismembered, recovered from 31 pits in Westminster (Cowie and Pipe 1998), in an area known to have been occupied by skinners and leather-working craftsmen, such as cordwainers, saddlers, and a bookbinder (Yeomans 2006, 117). Smith (1998, 876) documents examples of butchery marks on horse bones from Aberdeen and points out that, while horseflesh was proscribed as human food by the medieval church, evidence suggestive of human consumption of horseflesh was also found at Dunbar, Perth, and St Andrews. Rural sites can also produce high proportions of horse bones, for example Hallhill, Dunbar (Smith 2011), but this reflects the presence of horse breeding stock and natural mortalities rather than the cull of working animals.

Horn cores and other skull fragments, metapodials, and third phalanges can provide conclusive evidence for the presence of goat (Figure 7.2). Goat horn cores, but no other skeletal elements, were abundant at Jennings Yard, Windsor. The sex ratio of 46 male horn cores to 21 female (Bourdillon 1993, 73–4) appears to reflect the greater utility of the larger male horn for craft work. Similar concentrations of goat horns cores from medieval towns, with a predominance of male examples, were discussed by Noddle (1994, 119–20), who presented evidence that goat skins were traded with the horns attached and that male skins were preferred for tanning. Concentrations of goat horn cores have generally been found either in trading ports, such as Southampton and King's

FIGURE 7.2 Goat horn cores found during excavations at Perth
(photo by David Bowler, © Alder Archaeology)

Lynn, or on the fringes of upland areas, such as the Welsh borders and Scottish burghs, for example in fourteenth-century Perth (Hodgson et al. 2011). The meat of goats, as opposed to kids, does not appear to have been a popular commodity.

The Wild and Barbarous Fringes

The practicalities of livestock husbandry in the uplands have hitherto attracted less attention than the arable cultivation centred on lowland settlements (Dyer 2002), partly reflecting the attitude of central authority to what were perceived as the wild and barbarous fringes of medieval England. Winchester (2000) has addressed the historical and landscape evidence for this topic in Northern England and the Scottish Borders, for the latter part of the period under review. Common to all the upland areas was seasonal exploitation of upland grazing, whether the *hendre* and *hafod* of Wales or the shielings of northern England and Scotland. Besides the normal movements of cattle to and from pasture and to market, the earlier tradition of cattle-raiding remained a dynamic activity, adding to the perception of the wildness and barbarity of these regions.

The lack of complementary faunal evidence for these activities is largely a product of the upland soil conditions, which are not conducive to the survival of bone. For example, despite excellent historical records for the thirteenth century vaccary at Gatesgarth, Buttermere (Winchester 2003), subsequent excavation of the site failed to recover any animal bone (Railton 2009). While the historical evidence can indicate the important role of cows in the uplands, tangible faunal evidence may only survive in the manors, castles, and towns supplied from such hinterlands. Consumption at high-status castle sites in the late thirteenth century tail-end of the Medieval Warm Period shows considerable divergence, depending on local resources. Barnard Castle is notable for the high proportions of pig and red deer bones, reflecting the neighbouring woodland resources. Sheep remains were common at Launceston, while cattle bones were abundant at Dryslwyn (Gidney 2007b, 300). Dryslwyn is also noteworthy for the evidence for consumption of very young veal calves in the thirteenth century (Gidney 2007b, 301–2), two centuries before this becomes a national phenomenon in the English archaeological record.

The unique commercial status of the Scottish burghs in relation to the marketing of meat and export of hides, skins, wool, and wool-fells has been highlighted by Hodgson et al. (2011) with regard to the large assemblage spanning the twelfth to fourteenth centuries recovered from Perth High Street. The abundance of goat horn cores hints at both the size of goat herds in the hinterland and the impact of the export trade for goat hides and horns. Meanwhile, the demands of the export trade for cattle hides may have impinged on the selection of cattle for slaughter, which were generally found to be at least 4 years old. A very similar story was revealed by both the analysis of a late medieval midden at the bishop's manor at Old Rayne, Aberdeenshire (Smith 2012) and by faunal remains from Rattray, Aberdeenshire (Hamilton-Dyer et al. 1993) where the faunal assemblages were dominated by fragments of cattle bone from adult animals, with no evidence found for veal calves, suggesting that the quality of the hides was an important consideration in the selection of stock for slaughter.

Conclusion

Looking at faunal assemblages from a viewpoint that is not constrained by simple economics of meat production can provide different insights into animal-keeping strategies. Calf slaughter can be viewed as specific evidence for cheese production requiring rennet, rather than merely removing competition for the dam's milk. The transition from the Medieval Warm Period to the Little Ice Age could, in itself, explain changes in the size and build of domestic livestock, without invoking suppositions of planned livestock breeding programmes for 'improvement'. In urban situations cats and dogs could be viewed as fur bearers rather than companion animals, while horse carcasses required some ingenuity in disposal. The fringes of medieval England and Wales demonstrate differing patterns of faunal consumption, partly reflecting the local topography. In contrast, the unique legal and commercial status of the Scottish burghs was seen to have a unifying effect on the faunal assemblages from both rural and urban sites. The possible ramifications of the Scottish export of goat hides were seen as far south as Windsor and provide an example where isotope analysis has the potential to complement the historical evidence for trade links.

REFERENCES CITED

Albarella, U. 2005 'Meat production and consumption in town and country', in K. Giles and C. Dyer (eds), *Town and country in the Middle Ages: contrasts, contacts and interconnections, 1100–1500*, The Society for Medieval Archaeology Monograph 22, Leeds, 131–48

Albarella, U. and Davis, S. J. M. 1996 'Mammals and birds from Launceston Castle, Cornwall: decline in status and the rise of agriculture', *Circaea* 12(1), 1–156

Armitage, P. L. 1994 'Unwelcome companions: ancient rats reviewed', *Antiquity* 68, 231–40

Austin, D. 2007 *Acts of perception: a study of Barnard Castle in Teesdale*, Architectural and Archaeological Society of Durham and Northumberland Research Report 6, Durham

Bartosiewicz, L., van Neer, W., and Lentacker, A. 1997 *Draught cattle: their osteological identification and history*, Annales Sciences Zoologiques 281, Tervuren

Best, M. R. (ed.) 1986 *Gervase Markham: the English housewife*, McGill-Queen's University Press, Kingston

Bond, J. M. and O'Connor, T. P. 1999 *Bones from medieval deposits at 16–22 Coppergate and other sites in York*, The Archaeology of York 15/5, Council for British Archaeology, York

Bourdillon, J. 1993 'Animal bone', in J. W. Hawkes and M. J. Heaton, *A closed-shaft garderobe and associated medieval structures at Jennings Yard, Windsor, Berkshire*, Wessex Archaeology Report 3, Salisbury, 67–79

Cowie, R. and Pipe, A. 1998 'A late medieval and Tudor horse burial ground: excavations at Elverton Street, Westminster', *The Archaeological Journal* 155, 226–51

Daniels, R. 2010 *Hartlepool: an archaeology of the medieval town*, Tees Archaeology Monograph Series 4, Hartlepool

Davis, S. J. M. 1981 'The effects of temperature change and domestication on the body size of Late Pleistocene to Holocene mammals of Israel', *Paleobiology* 7(1), 101–14

Dobney, K. M., Jaques, S. D., and Irving, B. G. 1996 *Of butchers and breeds: report on vertebrate remains from various sites in the City of Lincoln*, Lincoln Archaeological Studies 5, Lincoln

Dyer, C. 2002 *Making a living in the Middle Ages: the people of Britain 850–1520*, Yale University Press, London

Gautier, A. 1984 'How do I count you, let me count the ways? Problems of archaeozoological quantification', in C. Grigson and J. Clutton-Brock (eds), *Animals and archaeology: 4. Husbandry in Europe*, British Archaeological Reports International Series 227, 237–51

Gerrard, C. M. 2003 *Medieval archaeology: understanding traditions and contemporary approaches*, Routledge, London

Gerrard, C. M. 2007 'Excavations at and near Church Field', in C. M. Gerrard with M. Aston (eds), *The Shapwick Project, Somerset: a rural landscape explored*, The Society for Medieval Archaeology monograph 25, Leeds, 405–47

Gidney, L. J. 1991a *Leicester, the Shires, 1988 excavations: the animal bones from the medieval deposits at Little Lane*, Ancient Monuments Laboratory Report 57/91, London

Gidney, L. J. 1991b *Leicester, the Shires, 1988 excavations: the animal bones from the medieval deposits at St Peter's Lane'*, Ancient Monuments Laboratory Report 116/91, London

Gidney, L. J. 1996 'The cosmetic and quasi-medicinal use of dog fat', *ORGAN The Newsletter of the Osteoarchaeological Research Group* 11, 8–9

Gidney, L. J. 1999 'The animal bones', in A. Connor and R. Buckley, *Roman and medieval occupation in Causeway Lane, Leicester*, Leicester Archaeology Monographs 5, 310–29

Gidney, L. J. 2007a 'The animal bone', in C. M. Gerrard with M. Aston (eds), *The Shapwick Project, Somerset: a rural landscape explored*, The Society for Medieval Archaeology Monograph 25, Leeds, 895–922

Gidney, L. J. 2007b 'Animal and bird bones', in C. Caple, *Excavations at Dryslwyn Castle 1980–95*, The Society for Medieval Archaeology Monograph 26, Leeds, 295–314

Gidney, L. J. 2013 *Offspring of the Aurochs: a comparison of a reference collection of Dexter cattle skeletons with archaeological and historical data*, unpublished PhD thesis, Durham University

Grew, F. and de Neergaard, M. 1988 *Shoes and pattens: medieval finds from excavations in London 2*, The Stationery Office, London

Hall, S. J. G. and Hall, J. G. 1988 'Inbreeding and population dynamics of the Chillingham cattle (*Bos taurus*)', *Journal of Zoology* 216, 479–93

Hamilton-Dyer, S., McCormick, F., Murray, H. K., and Murray, J. C. 1993 'The bone assemblage and animal husbandry', in H. K. Murray and J. C. Murray, 'Excavations at Rattray, Aberdeenshire; a Scottish deserted burgh', *Medieval Archaeology* 37, 203–5

Hartley, D. (ed.) 1969 *Thomas Tusser: his good points of husbandry*, Cedric Chivers Ltd, Bath

Hodgson, G. W. I., Smith, C., and Jones, A. 2011 'The mammal bone', in G. W. I. Hodgson, C. Smith, and A. Jones (eds), *Perth High Street archaeological excavation 1975–1977: living and working in a medieval Scottish Burgh. Environmental remains and miscellaneous finds.* Fascicule 4, Perth, 5–44

Huntley, J. P. and Stallibrass, S. 2000 *Taphonomy and interpretation*, Symposia of the Association for Environmental Archaeology 14, Oxford

Jones, R. T. and Ruben, I. 1987 'Animal bones, with some notes on the effects of differential sampling', in G. Beresford, *Goltho: the development of an early medieval manor c.850–1150*, English Heritage Archaeological Report 4, 197–206

Jones, R. T., Sly, J., Simpson, D., Rackham, J., and Locker, A. 1985 *The terrestrial vertebrate remains from the castle, Barnard Castle*, Ancient Monuments Laboratory Report 4630, London

Jones, R. T., Sly, J., Simpson, D., Rackham, J., and Locker, A. 2007 'Animal bones', in D. Austin, *Acts of perception: a study of Barnard Castle in Teesdale*, Architectural and Archaeological Society of Durham and Northumberland Research Report 6, Durham, 589–606

Jones, R. T., Wall, S. M., Locker, A. M., Coy, J., and Maltby, M. 1980 *Computer based osteometry data capture user manual*, Ancient Monuments Laboratory Report 3342, London

Luff, R. M. and Moreno, M. 1995 'Killing cats in the medieval period: an unusual episode in the history of Cambridge, England', *Archaeofauna* 4, 93–114

Maltby, M. 1979 *The animal bones from Exeter 1971–1975*, Exeter Archaeological Reports 2, Sheffield

Newfield, T. P. 2009 'A cattle panzootic in early fourteenth-century Europe', *Agricultural History Review* 57(2), 155–90

Newfield, T. P. 2015 'Human-bovine plagues in the Early Middle Ages', *Journal of Interdisciplinary History* XLVI:I, 1–38

Noddle, B. 1977 'Mammal bone', in H. Clarke and A. Carter (eds), *Excavations in King's Lynn 1963–70*, The Society for Medieval Archaeology Monograph 7, London, 378–98

Noddle, B. 1994 'The under-rated goat', in A. R. Hall and H. K. Kenward (eds), *Urban-rural connexions: perspectives from environmental archaeology*, Symposia of the Association for Environmental Archaeology 12, 117–28

O'Connor, T. 1982 *Animal bones from Flaxengate, Lincoln c.870–1500*, The Archaeology of Lincoln XVIII-1, London

O'Connor, T. P. 2000 *The archaeology of animal bones*, Sutton Publishing Ltd, Stroud

O'Connor, T. P. 2003 *The analysis of urban animal bone assemblages: a handbook for archaeologists*, The Archaeology of York Principles and Methods 19/2, York

Oschinsky, D. 1971 *Walter of Henley and other treatises on estate management and accounting*, Clarendon Press, Oxford

Ozgul, A., Tuljapurkar, S., Benton, T. G., Pemberton, J. M., Clutton-Brock, T. H., and Coulson, T. 2009 'The dynamics of phenotypic change and the shrinking sheep of St Kilda', *Science* 325, 464–7

Railton, M. 2009 'Archaeological investigation of the remains of a medieval vaccary at Gatesgarth Farm, Buttermere', *Transactions of the Cumberland and Westmorland Antiquarian and Archaeological Society* 3rd Series IX, 57–67

Reed, R. 1972 *Ancient skins, parchments and leathers*, Seminar Press, London

Saunders, A. 2006 *Excavations at Launceston Castle, Cornwall*, The Society for Medieval Archaeology Monograph 24, Leeds

Serjeantson, D. 1989 'Animal remains and the tanning trade', in D. Serjeantson and T. Waldron (eds), *Diet and crafts in towns*, British Archaeological Reports British Series 199, Oxford, 129–46

Slavin, P. 2010 'The fifth rider of the Apocalypse: the great cattle plague in England and Wales and its economic consequences, 1319–1350', in S. Cavaciocchi (ed.), *Economic and biological interactions in pre-industrial Europe from the 13th to the 18th centuries*, Firenze University Press, Firenze, 165–80

Smith, C. 1998 'Dogs, cats and horses in the Scottish medieval town', *Proceedings of the Society of Antiquaries of Scotland* 128, 859–85

Smith, C. 2011 'Animal bone', in S. Mitchell and S. Anderson, 'A rural medieval settlement and Early Iron Age funerary remains at Hallhill, Dunbar, East Lothian', *Scottish Archaeological Internet Report* 50, 26–9

Smith, C. 2012 'The animal bone', in H. K. Murray and J. C. Murray, 'Excavations at the Bishop's Manor, Old Rayne, Aberdeenshire in 1990 and 2008', *Scottish Archaeological Internet Report* 52, 25–7

Stallibrass, S. 1984 'The distinction between the effects of small carnivores and humans on post-glacial faunal assemblages: a case study using scavenging of sheep carcases by foxes', in C. Grigson and J. Clutton-Brock (eds), *Animals and archaeology: 4. Husbandry in Europe*, British Archaeological Reports International Series 227, 259–69

Teasdale, M. D., Van Doorn, N. L., Fiddyment, S., Webb, C. C., O'Connor, T., Hofreiter, M., Collins, M. J., and Bradley, D. G. 2015 'Paging through history: parchment as a reservoir of ancient DNA for next generation sequencing', *Philosophical Transactions of the Royal Society of London Series B: Biological Sciences* 370, 1660

Thomas, R. 2005 *Animals, economy and status: integrating zooarchaeological and historical data in the study of Dudley Castle, West Midlands (c.1100–1750)*, British Archaeological Reports British Series 392, Oxford

Veale, E. M. 1966 *The English fur trade in the later Middle Ages*, Clarendon Press, Oxford

Whitehead, G. K. 1953 *The ancient white cattle of Britain and their descendants*, Faber and Faber Ltd, London

Wilson, B. and Edwards, P. 1993 'Butchery of horse and dog at Witney Palace, Oxfordshire, and the knackering and feeding of meat to hounds during the post-medieval period', *Post-Medieval Archaeology* 27, 43–56

Winchester, A. J. L. 2000 *The harvest of the hills: rural life in Northern England and the Scottish Borders 1400–1700*, Edinburgh University Press, Edinburgh

Winchester, A. J. L. 2003 'Demesne livestock farming in the Lake District: the vaccary at Gatesgarth, Buttermere, in the later thirteenth century', *Transactions of the Cumberland and Westmorland Antiquarian and Archaeological Society* 3rd Series III, 109–18

Yeomans, L. M. 2006 *A zooarchaeological and historical study of the animal product based industries operating in London during the post-medieval period*, unpublished PhD thesis, University College London

CHAPTER 8

THE ARCHAEOBOTANY OF LATE MEDIEVAL PLANT REMAINS

The Resource and the Research

LISA MOFFETT

PEOPLE depend on plants for survival. We use plants for food, medicine, building materials, household furnishings, animal food, textiles, lubricants, dyes, and much more. Archaeobotany studies the remains of plants preserved on archaeological sites and attempts to understand the uses and relationships between people and plants in the past. Some plant remains can also be used as proxy indicators of past environments and environmental changes. This chapter looks briefly at the methods of archaeobotany, highlights some of the plant remains that have been found from the late medieval period in Britain, with reference to a few selected sites, and then attempts to summarize some of the key issues in current research and look briefly at possible research directions in future. No attempt will be made to provide a directory of the large number of late medieval sites that have produced plant remains, but much of this information for England is covered by the Historic England regional reviews for archaeobotany (Carruthers and Hunter in prep.; Hall and Huntley 2007; Pelling in prep.). In Wales this multi-period summary coverage is provided by Caseldine (1990). There is also an excellent summary for Scotland (Dickson and Dickson 2000). All of these reviews are necessarily out of date the moment they are written but are nevertheless a useful source of information about which sites have produced archaeobotanical remains and serve as an overview of the archaeobotany resource in the areas covered.

METHODOLOGY

Plant remains have been occasionally retrieved from archaeological sites since the nineteenth century, but only since the 1980s has it become standard on archaeological excavations in Britain to sample for plant remains. The quality of information gained from studying plant remains is only as good as the sampling that retrieved the material from the site. Plant remains are usually too small to see in the soil, so retrieval usually relies on taking soil samples from the archaeological deposits and processing to separate the plant remains from the soil. The identification and interpretation of plant materials requires specialist expertise and access to appropriate equipment. The most basic equipment is a low-power microscope and a reference collection of modern plant material with which to compare the archaeological plant remains for identification. Traditional microscopy is still the most commonly used method of studying plant remains, but increasingly other scientific methods are also being applied. These include isotopes (Fraser et al. 2011) and ancient DNA (aDNA; Schlumbaum et al. 2008) with no doubt other techniques to come in future. Applying new techniques in addition to traditional microscopy is increasing the information gained and the range of questions we can ask.

Plant materials are fragile and subject to biological decay. They usually disappear very quickly in ordinary well-drained burial conditions. Understanding the processes of preservation, therefore, is important when interpreting plant remains. In Britain, plant materials are most commonly preserved by charring, waterlogging (anoxic conditions), and mineralization. These are special conditions resulting from environmental circumstances and human actions. They preserve only a fraction of the original plant material used on a site, and generally not a representative sample because most preservation introduces a bias.

Charring burns away most of the organic component of the plant material, leaving a carbon skeleton which is not subject to decay, but which is very vulnerable to mechanical damage. Cereals and weeds associated with them are the most commonly charred items as cereals tend to have a higher risk of exposure to fire than other plant materials due to processing, use of chaff for tinder, malting, cooking, etc.

Mineral replacement requires dissolved minerals in the burial environment and sufficient moisture to transport the minerals into the plant materials. Depending on the conditions the minerals sometimes fill the voids in the material rather than actually replacing the organic material, creating a cast of the inside of the seed which can be very difficult to identify. Mineralization is most common in cess pits and tanning pits.

Anoxic burial conditions preserve organic materials because most microorganisms that cause decay need oxygen to survive. Anaerobic bacteria also cause decay but at a much slower rate. Waterlogging in stagnant conditions is the most common anoxic burial environment but deposits do not always have to be fully waterlogged to preserve organic remains if conditions are sufficiently anoxic. Wells, cess pits, cut features of any kind below the water table, old river channels, and some quay deposits are all examples of waterlogged features that could preserve waterlogged/anoxic remains. Well-sealed highly organic deposits can be preserved above the water table as the organic material can act as a sponge to hold moisture. Stone-built garderobes are the most common example of this.

Desiccation and smoke blackening occur less commonly, but also inhibit organic decay. Desiccated plant remains may be found in daub and interior cavities in buildings (Ernst and Jacomet 2005). Smoke-blackened thatch is a rare but important material for the late medieval period (Letts 1999).

The most commonly studied plant parts on late medieval sites are 'seeds' in the broadest vernacular sense (including true seeds, fruits, achenes, caryopses, mericarps, nutlets, etc.), chaff parts of cereal plants, fruits, stems, wood, and wood charcoal. Generally these are the densest plant parts and the most likely to be preserved under the conditions mentioned above, but flower parts, cereal bran, buds, and cuticle fragments are sometimes preserved, usually in waterlogged deposits. Pollen and spores are also common. They are generally tough and decay more slowly than other plant materials but still disappear over time unless they are buried in an anoxic, acidic environment. Phytoliths are silica bodies produced by some plants. A number of temperate crops can be identified by their phytoliths as can some tropical imported species. There are currently no published studies of phytoliths from late medieval Britain, but there is potential in future (McParland pers. comm.) as phytoliths may be preserved where other remains are not.

Most of the plants remains focused on here are those that relate to economic activities rather than environmental change.

Late Medieval Plants and Archaeology

The range of species known from archaeobotanical remains in the late medieval period is greater than that from early medieval, but probably still much less than actually used. Historical and pictorial records are also important in obtaining a more comprehensive picture (e.g. Dyer 2006; Sillasoo 2006; Stone 2006). An indicative list of late medieval food plants is given in Moffett (2006, 44).

The most common late medieval remains are cereals. Bread wheat (*Triticum aestivum*), rivet wheat (*Triticum turgidum*), rye (*Secale cereale*), 6-row barley (*Hordeum sativum*), 2-row barley (*Hordeum sativum*), common oat (*Avena sativa*), and bristle oat (*Avena strigosa*) were all cultivated. Legumes have less chance of exposure to fire than cereals so their record is poorer, but there are finds of pea (*Pisum sativum*), bean (*Vicia faba*), and vetch (*Vicia sativa* ssp. *sativa*), the latter probably used for fodder rather than human food.

Fruit and nut remains, mainly waterlogged and mineralized, are also common. These include sloe (*Prunus spinosa*), bullace and damson (both forms of *Prunus domestica* ssp. *insititia*), cherry (*Prunus cerasus*), fig (*Ficus carica*), hazel (*Corylus avellana*), walnut (*Juglans regia*), grape (*Vitis vinifera*), apple (*Malus* sp.), pear (*Pyrus* sp.), medlar (*Mespilus germanica*), almond (*Prunus dulcis*), and peach (*Prunus persica*). Some species such as olive (*Olea europaea*) and citrus (*Citrus* sp.) cannot grow in Britain and must be imported. Grape, fig, walnut, and peach were probably imported but may have been locally grown as well. Vineyards were cultivated on monastic and high-status sites, probably mainly in the south and Midlands as reflected in the distribution of monastic vineyards known from documents (Bond 2004, 166–77). The cultivation of marginal fruit crops such as fig and peach were well within the capability of skilled medieval gardeners employed by the wealthy who had the space and resources to devote to luxuries. Many fruits could have been collected wild, but some may also have been brought within gardens for convenience. These include bilberry (*Vaccinium myrtillus*), bramble (*Rubus fruticosus* agg.), raspberry (*Rubus ideaus*), wild strawberry (*Fragaria vesca*), rosehips (*Rosa* sp.), hawthorn (*Crataegus monogyna*), sloe, bullace, damson, and hazel. The large-seeded plums (*Prunus domestica* ssp. *domestica*) are mostly found on post-medieval sites, but may have been cultivated earlier.

Vegetables and herbs are poorly represented on archaeological sites because the actual vegetables are plant parts such as leaves, roots, and flower shoots which are rarely preserved. Epidermis fragments which could be leek, onion, or garlic (*Allium* sp.) are sometimes found, as at Aberdeen and York (Dickson and Dickson 2000, 183; Hall and Huntley 2007, 126). At Beverley, East Riding of Yorkshire, some partly charred garlic cloves (*Allium sativum*) were found in a thirteenth-century deposit (Hall and Huntley 2007, 135). Seeds of possible leek (*Allium* cf. *porrum*) were found at Leicester (Moffett 1993, 7). Seeds of other plants which could have been grown as vegetables, such as carrot (*Daucus carota*), parsnip (*Pastinaca sativa*), celery (*Apium graveolens*), and cabbage/mustard (*Brassica* spp. and *Brassica/Sinapis*) are fairly common, but the seeds of the cultivated plants are indistinguishable from those of the native wild plants. Vegetables and herbs were usually harvested well before they set seed, so finding seeds is no indication of vegetable growing, though it may be suggestive if the plant is found outside its natural habitat.

Some very rich assemblages of plant remains come from wet deposits in ports. Ports are among the more likely places to find exotic species, not just because the exotics were being traded through ports but also because ports often supported a wealthy class who could afford to buy them. Exotic plants from London in the sixteenth century included cucumber/melon (*Cucumis* sp.) and marrow/pumpkin (*Cucurbita* sp.). Further plants from that date in London include strawberry, apple/pear, mulberry (*Morus nigra*), barberry (*Berberis* sp.), hazel, walnut, carrot, fennel (*Foeniculum vulgare*), parsley (*Petroselinum crispum*), opium poppy (*Papaver somniferum*), and rosemary (*Rosmarinus officinalis*) (Giorgi 1997). Other plants will have been brought into ports inadvertently as packing material and contaminants in other products. Ports rarely include the ships themselves, but at Newport a fifteenth-century ship was found buried in tidal mud on the banks of the River Usk in south-east Wales. Exotic food plants include millet (*Panicum miliaceum*), stone pine (*Pinus pinea*), almond, olive, pomegranate (*Punica granatum*), and peach, in addition to a range of other food plants. Packing material suggests the ship's voyage may have begun in the Iberian Peninsula (Carruthers 2013, 14). Imported exotics also found their way inland to high-status sites like Shrewsbury Abbey where twelfth- to fourteenth-century deposits contained almond and stone pine as well as a range of fruit (Greig 2002, 165).

Towns, not surprisingly, tend to have the most diverse types of archaeobotanical assemblages. Many towns were built in fairly low-lying areas near rivers so waterlogging of at least deeper archaeological deposits is not uncommon. At Worcester, for example, the site at Newport Street lies near the Severn and had layers of waterlogged organic deposits. These produced seeds of plants likely to have been growing on or near the riverbanks, mixed with species likely to represent dumping of household waste, such as strawberry, summer savoury (*Satureja hortensis*), flax (*Linum usitatissimum*), carrot, and dyer's rocket (*Reseda luteola*) (Pearson 2015, 209). The latter may have been a weed, but was, as its name suggests, also much used in dyeing. Urban sites did not just receive the products of the countryside. Town residents will have often produced their own fruits and vegetables from urban gardens (Dyer 2006, 33). Gardens may have included both fruit trees and a vegetable patch that may also have included herbs. Herbs could be used for medicine, flavouring, and aesthetic pleasure. Herbs such as pot marigold (*Calendula officinalis*), opium poppy, and fennel are found in towns but rarely in the countryside.

Towns often produce abundant charred cereal remains such as the crop- and weed-rich deposits that had been dumped mainly into cut features at Deansway in Worcester (Moffett 2004, 551–2). It is not always clear why the grain has been charred. Grain drying seems a more rural activity, though it is possible that grain was sometimes roasted to improve the flavour before using it in pottage. It is possible that in some cases charred grain and weed seeds actually represent the remains of threshing waste being used as fuel where the chaff has burned away and the dense grains and weed seeds are all that survives. De Moulins (2007) suggests that thatch may also find its way into domestic fires and that some assemblages that seem mainly to be grains and weeds may actually be all that is left of burned thatch.

Building materials and industrial waste are also found in urban deposits. Possible thatch has been suggested from Walmgate in York (Hall and Huntley 2007, 127) and from the late fifteenth or early sixteenth century at Stone in Staffordshire (Moffett and Smith 1996). Industrial waste is mostly found in towns, such as the dyebath waste at York from two sites at Piccadilly. Further evidence for textile dyeing was found at Beverley along with retting of flax and hemp (Hall and Huntley 2007, 135 and 146). Tanning is not easily identified from archaeobotanical remains, but the presence in pits of concentration of bark, especially oak bark, is suggestive (Hall and Kenward 2003, 121–4).

Animals were housed in towns so fodder, and bedding materials for both humans and animals, will have been brought into towns in large quantities. A rich deposit of stable manure probably incorporating animal bedding was found at Fish Street in Worcester (Miller et al. 2002). Stable manure and hay were found at York along with burned peat and turves, suggesting that many different resources of the countryside were being brought into the town (Hall and Huntley 2007, 141).

The ditches of town defences were sometimes large enough and deep enough to be waterlogged, or deliberately kept partly full of water, especially if it was near a river or stream. As the town ditch was a convenient place to dispose of rubbish, excavations can produce lots of plant remains, as well as leather, textiles, and other organic materials. At Perth the town ditch was used for dumping cereal waste, roofing, and faeces (Dickson and Dickson 2000, 182). One section of the town ditch at Coventry was very rich in animal waste from the households and industries of the town, but the botanical remains reflected the local environment of the ditch (Fryer 2007) with very little sign of household waste. Town ditch deposits were often lost as the town expanded and built over the ditch, filling it up with less organic soils, and sometime isolating it from its water sources so that the ditches became drier.

Elite sites such as castles, manors, and monasteries sometimes also have abundant plant remains (Figure 8.1). Ashy kitchen floor deposits from Eynsham Abbey, Oxfordshire, varied from producing just wood charcoal to layers rich in cereal remains of bread wheat and rivet wheat, with small amounts of barley, rye, oat, pea, and bean (Pelling 2003). The presence of probable fodder crop remains such as vetch and lentil (*Lens culinaris*) suggests that not all of this waste was directly related to food being cooked, and may in fact be derived from fuel. Very similar remains were found at Dean Court Farm, a grange farm of Abingdon Abbey (Moffett 1994). Latrines, such as the one at Dryslwyn Castle in Wales (Huntley and Daniell 2007), commonly have fruit remains. Fig, apple/pear, and grape are common. Herbs, such as the cumin (*Cuminum cyminum*) found at Dryslwyn are much less abundant but probably under-represented for the reasons given above. Moats are also often waterlogged, and, like town ditches, may contain the waste representing different activities, but may also preserve only the remains of the local vegetation. Much may depend on what part of the ditch or moat happens to be excavated. At Acton Court household, Gloucestershire, food waste included fig, grape, apple, strawberry, sloe, bullace,

FIGURE 8.1 Excavations in the monastic kitchen at Durham Cathedral in 2014 produced a very large assemblage of medieval fish, birds (including goose and pheasant), marine shells (including crab), and animal bone, together with pottery and window glass dating from the twelfth century onwards. Among the charred plant macrofossils were cereals such as oats and barley as well as pea, beans, and hazelnut fragments

(© Durham University)

raspberry, fennel, and black mustard, mixed with plants likely to have been derived from different sources such as woods or hedges, damp meadows, and disturbed ground, as well as aquatic plants from the wet moat itself (Robinson and Straker 2004). At Shapwick, Somerset, charred cereal remains were dumped into the moat, while the waterlogged remains included wood, both worked and unworked, and seeds of plants reflecting the local vegetation near and in the moat (Smith and Campbell 2007). Pollen from the moat also included cereals, and probably a mix of local and regional pollen that indicated a largely open landscape with a few trees and possibly hedgerows (Tinsley 2007).

The evidence from lower-status rural sites is generally of a different character, mainly because waterlogged deposits are much rarer, and cess pits usually absent or difficult to recognize. Charred plant remains, however, are sometimes abundant and, where this is the case, may provide evidence for some of the economic activities taking place on site. Mixing and redeposition may be less, so the assemblage is potentially more interpretable.

At Stratton in Bedfordshire there was continuity of occupation from the early to the late medieval period, and there was little evidence of change of agricultural practice despite whatever changes of landownership and landscape reorganization may have been taking place higher up the social ladder as a result of the Conquest. The early medieval crops of bread wheat, rivet wheat, barley, and oat continued to be cultivated, although rye and oat may have had greater importance in the late early medieval and into the late medieval. The number of late medieval samples, however, was much less than for the early medieval, so this conclusion is tentative. The weed species were also very consistent through time, suggesting that the soils cultivated and the husbandry practices used may also have been consistent (Smith forthcoming).

The early medieval settlement and late medieval manor and hamlet at West Cotton, Northamptonshire, shows a similar picture but much more clearly (Campbell and Robinson 2010). There is little material from the very earliest phases of the settlement, but from the late early medieval onwards there is abundant evidence for bread wheat, rivet wheat, flax, bean, vetch, and possibly a cabbage-type vegetable or mustard. Pea and lentil were also found in the later medieval period. The weed flora was diverse, and there was slight evidence for association between some species of weeds and particular crops, but little indication of change through time. Although many variations in arable husbandry practice might not be detectable from the archaeobotanical record, major changes in soils, tillage, or harvest methods would be expected to produce some change in the weed flora (Jones et al. 2005). Ovens rich in chaff fragments with some sprouted grains may have been used for malting.

Research

There has been much research on medieval settlement, agriculture, and peasant material culture (ably summarized in Dyer 2014). However, despite the large number of excavations of late medieval sites, there has been little focus on the archaeobotany other than as a source of information about diet. Partly this is because of now outdated assumptions that the relatively abundant historical records can provide all the information needed. Late medieval plant remains receive relatively little research effort and funding compared with prehistoric or Roman plant remains, and yet the potential to utilize multi-disciplinary lines of evidence to address research questions for the late medieval period is considerable.

As an example, West Cotton and Stratton both present a striking contrast to the manor at Perceton in Scotland, where wheat is only barely present and the cereal assemblage is dominated by barley and oat (Hastie 2004). In contrast to the free-threshing wheat found at many (but not all) English sites, the main cereal at Dryslwyn Castle appeared to be oat, possibly bristle oat, which is hardier than wheat and one of the hardiest of all temperate climate cereals. Differences like these are often noted in site reports with comments about particular crops being better suited to certain types of soils or local climates. However, understanding of local variation in archaeobotanical cereal remains has rarely been studied beyond the level of individual site observation. An exception is the study by Rippon et al. (2014) which compared the archaeobotanical record of crop species, the pollen record, domestic animals, and distribution of basic soil types across a transect from south-west England to East Anglia. The aim was to see if there were differences across the area studied and how this compared with both the geology and the historical record. Their results showed that different cereals predominated on different soil types, but other cereals, not just the predominate ones were also cultivated. This compared with what is known from some of the estate records of the eleventh to fourteenth centuries in their transect. Further studies are needed to provide this kind of information from other areas of the country.

One aspect of local arable husbandry is utilization of landraces and their relationship to local conditions. Landraces do not have the uniformity of modern varieties, nor are they as clearly distinct in terms of their characteristics. Despite having substantial genetic diversity, however, a landrace has a predominance of certain traits that have often evolved under cultivation to adapt to local conditions and practices. Local landraces of cereals have not been studied so far, as estate documents generally do not record this information, and it is not identifiable from charred or waterlogged cereal remains. There is potential with further study of smoke-blackened thatch, where variation in characteristics is visible (Letts 1999). Colour is generally lost, but morphological features such as size and length of ears, presence or absence of awns, presence of hairs, shape of chaff parts, whether the ears are erect or pendulous, and other characteristics potentially could be recorded. Since the thatch in a roof is likely to represent a single year's crop from a particular supplier (or even a particular field) there is considerable potential for studying the diversity of a single crop from a particular place at a particular point in time. Ethnographic evidence from traditional farmers suggests that there is likely to have been considerable diversity within a single crop, and that the characteristics of local crops would vary substantially from place to place.

Support for this is suggested by samples of later crop plants in herbaria and in post-medieval documents, but the hypothesis is untested at present. Testing it by recording crop variation in surviving smoke-blackened thatch could greatly enhance our understanding of medieval crops and farming practice. Another potential line of evidence is to study the DNA of medieval crops. DNA survives poorly in plant remains, especially charred plant remains, but techniques have developed considerably in recent years and it is now possible to sequence much smaller fragments of DNA than ever before. In genetically well-studied crops such as wheat and barley it may even be possible to detect genes or groups of genes associated with a specific characteristic, such as drought tolerance. Research in ancient plant DNA is still in its early stages, but it is not too early to begin to formulate appropriate questions that future studies may be able to address.

Van der Veen et al. (2013) surveyed 385 records of late medieval archaeobotanical datasets from a wide range of site classifications as part of a larger survey covering the whole of Britain AD 450–1500. Their results show that for the later medieval period the data from urban sites are much greater than from rural ones. The number of samples analysed for each site varied considerably, but only on 32 late medieval sites had 30 or more samples been analysed. Even on archaeological sites that have been well sampled, the number of samples that represents a given period may be small, and the number that can be compared between similar contexts of a similar period even smaller. This makes it very difficult to observe changes through time on most sites.

The same authors recommend using samples with 300–500 identifications as ideal, and a minimum of 100. This potentially involves collecting and processing substantially bigger samples from some contexts than is current practice but would certainly much improve our datasets, especially for questions such as looking at continuity and change through time. Many commercial archaeological excavations are very limited in scope, however, and do not produce large numbers of samples or collect large samples. Some sites may be well sampled during excavation, but the number of samples processed and assessed is curtailed due to resource restrictions, and the number of samples actually analysed and reported on is even smaller. Rippon et al. (2014) suggest combining results from small sites to produce a bigger picture. This is one way forward, and for the purposes of their study was adequate if not ideal. With other kinds of studies, however, this use of small datasets may not be adequate.

Whether sampling is adequate depends very much on the questions we ask and, sadly, many sites are still being excavated with hardly any research aims at all. The difficulty is we lack sufficient synthetic research in late medieval archaeobotany to be able to effectively formulate site-based research questions that can be placed in a wider research context. Collaborative work between archaeobotanists and historians is greatly needed to make the most of the substantial data we already have as well as inform the collection of data in future. The relationship between people and plants is both fundamental and wide ranging. Understanding late medieval plant-related activities such as crop husbandry, horticulture, trade, and industry needs to become a more multidisciplinary process.

Acknowledgements

I am grateful to Wendy Carruthers and Alejandra Gutiérrez for useful information and references. This chapter was supported by Historic England.

References cited

Bond, J. 2004 *Monastic landscapes*, Tempus, Stroud

Campbell, G. and Robinson, M. 2010 'The environmental evidence', in A. Chapman, *West Cotton, Raunds: a study of medieval settlement dynamics AD 450–1450*, Oxbow, Oxford, 427–515

Carruthers, W. 2013 'Newport medieval ship project specialist report: waterlogged plant remains', online archive Archaeology Data Service [viewed 30 November 2016] http://archaeologydataservice.ac.uk/archiveDS/archiveDownload?t=arch-1563-1/dissemination/pdf/Newport_Medieval_Ship_Specialist_Report_Waterlogged_Plant_Remains.pdf

Carruthers, W. and Hunter, K., in preparation *A review of archaeological plant remains from the Midland Counties*, Historic England, London

Caseldine, A. 1990 *Environmental archaeology in Wales*, St David's University College, Lampeter

De Moulins, D. 2007 'The weeds from the thatch roofs of medieval cottages from the south of England', *Vegetation History and Archaeobotany* 16, 385–98

Dickson, C. and Dickson, J. 2000 *Plants and people in ancient Scotland*, Tempus, Stroud

Dyer, C. 2006 'Gardens and garden produce in the later Middle Ages', in C. M. Woolgar, D. Serjeantson, and T. Waldron (eds), *Food in medieval England: diet and nutrition*, Oxford University Press, Oxford 27–40

Dyer, C. 2014 'The material world of English peasants, 1200–1540: archaeological perspectives on rural economy and welfare', *Agricultural History Review* 62(1), 1–22

Ernst, J. and Jacomet, S. 2005 'The value of the archaeobotanical analysis of desiccated plant remains from old buildings: methodological aspects and interpretation of crop weed assemblages', *Vegetation History and Archaeobotany* 15, 45–56

Fraser, R. A., Bogaard, A., Heaton, T., Charles, M., Jones, G., Christensen, B. T., Halstead, P., Merbach, I., Poulton, P. R., Sparkes, D., and Styring, A. K. 2011 'Manuring and stable nitrogen isotope ratios in cereals and pulses: towards a new archaeobotanical approach to the inference of land use and dietary practices', *Journal of Archaeological Science* 38, 2790–804

Fryer, V. 2007 'Plant macrofossils and other remains', in P. Mason and I. Soden, 'An archaeological excavation of the medieval town ditch, Belgrade Plaza, Coventry', Northamptonshire Archaeology Report 07/72, 25–7, online archive Archaeology Data Service [viewed 18 December 2016] http://archaeologydataservice.ac.uk/archiveDS/archiveDownload?t=arch-703-1/dissemination/pdf/northamp3-157338_1.pdf

Giorgi, J. 1997 'Diet in late medieval and early modern London: the archaeobotanical evidence', in D. Gaimster and P. Stamper (eds), *The Age of Transition: the archaeology of English culture 1400–1600*, Oxbow Monograph 98, Oxford, 197–213

Greig, J. R. A. 2002 'The 13th–18th century plant remains', in N. Baker (ed.), *Shrewsbury Abbey*, Shropshire Archaeological and Historical Society Monograph Series 2, 163–77

Hall, A. R. and Huntley, J. P. 2007 *A review of the evidence for macrofossil plant remains from archaeological deposits in northern England*, English Heritage Research Department Report Series 87/2007, York

Hall, A. and Kenward, H. 2003 'Can we identify biological indicator groups for craft, industry and other activities?', in P. Murphy and P. E. J. Wiltshire, (eds), *The environmental archaeology of industry*, Symposia of the Association for Environmental Archaeology 20, Oxford, 114–30

Hastie, M. 2004 'The plant remains', in S. Stronach, 'The evolution of a medieval Scottish manor at Perceton, near Irvine, North Ayrshire', *Medieval Archaeology* 48(1), 164–6 (143–66)

Huntley, J. and Daniell, J. 2007 'Plant remains', in C. Caple, *Excavations at Dryslwyn Castle 1980–95*, The Society for Medieval Archaeology Monograph 26, Leeds, 321–35

Jones, G., Charles, J., Bogaard, A., Hodgson, J. G., and Palmer, C. 2005 'The functional ecology of present-day arable weed floras and its applicability for the identification of past crop husbandry', *Vegetation History and Archaeobotany* 14, 493–504

Letts, J. 1999 *Smoke blackened thatch*, English Heritage and the University of Reading, London and Reading

Miller, D., Darch, E., and Pearson, E. 2002 *Archaeological watching brief at 15/19 Fish Street, Worcester*, Worcestershire County Council Archaeological Service internal report 964, Worcester

Moffett, L. 1993 *Macrofossil plant remains from Leicester Shires*, English Heritage Ancient Monuments Laboratory Report 31/93, London

Moffett, L. 1994 'Charred plant remains', in T. Allen, 'A medieval grange of Abingdon Abbey at Dean Court Farm, Cumnor, Oxon', *Oxoniensia* 59, 219–447

Moffett, L. 2004 'Botanical remains', in H. Dalwood and R. Edwards, *Excavations at Deansway, Worcester, 1988–89: Romano-British small town to late medieval city*, Council for British Archaeology Report 139, York, 537–56

Moffett, L. 2006 'The archaeology of medieval plant foods', in C. M. Woolgar, D. Serjeantson, and T. Waldron (eds), *Food in medieval England: diet and nutrition*, Oxford University Press, Oxford, 41–55

Moffett, L. and Smith, D. 1996 'Insects and plants from a late medieval and early post-medieval tenement in Stone, Staffordshire, UK', *Circaea* 12(2), 157–75

Pearson, E. 2015 'Plant remains', in P. Davenport, *Excavations at Newport Street, Worcester, 2005*, Cotswold Archaeology and Worcester Archive and Archaeology Service, Cirencester, 201–16

Pelling, R. 2003 'Archaeobotanical remains', in A. Hardy, A. Dodd, and G. D. Keevill, *Ælfric's Abbey: excavations at Eynsham Abbey, Oxfordshire, 1989–92*, Thames Valley Landscapes 16, Oxford 439–48

Pelling, R. in preparation *A review of archaeological plant remains from the Southern Region: Anglo-Saxon to post-medieval*, Historic England, London

Rippon, S., Wainwright, A., and Smart, C. 2014 'Farming regions in medieval England: the archaeobotanical and zooarchaeological evidence', *Medieval Archaeology* 58, 195–255

Robinson, E. and Straker, V. 2004 'Plant and animal macro-fossils from period 4.2–4.3 contexts in the moat', in K. Rodwell and R. Bell, *Acton Court: the evolution of an early Tudor courtier's house*, English Heritage, London, 411–15

Schlumbaum, A., Tensen, M., Jaenicke-Despres, V. 2008 'Ancient plant DNA in archaeobotany', *Vegetation History and Archaeobotany* 17, 233–44

Sillasoo, U. 2006 'Medieval plant depictions as a source for archaeobotanical research', *Vegetation History and Archaeobotany* 16, 61–70

Smith, W. forthcoming 'The vegetational history of Stratton', in D. Shotliff and D. Ingham, *Stratton, Biggleswade, Bedfordshire: the evolution of a rural settlement from the early Saxon to the post-medieval period*

Smith, W. and Campbell, G. 2007 'Medieval plant macrofossils and waterlogged wood', in C. M. Gerrard with M. Aston (eds), *The Shapwick Project, Somerset: a rural landscape explored*, The Society for Medieval Archaeology Monograph 25, Leeds, 857–64

Stone, D. 2006, 'The consumption of field crops in late medieval England', in C. M. Woolgar, D. Serjeantson, and T. Waldron (eds), *Food in medieval England: diet and nutrition*, Oxford University Press, Oxford, 11–26

Tinsley, H. 2007 'Pollen analysis of sediment samples', in C. M. Gerrard with M. Aston (eds), *The Shapwick Project, Somerset: a rural landscape explored*, The Society for Medieval Archaeology Monograph 25, Leeds, 852–7

Van der Veen, M., Hill, A., and Livarda, A. 2013 'The archaeobotany of medieval Britain (c. AD 450–1500): identifying research priorities for the 21st century', *Medieval Archaeology* 57, 151–82

CHAPTER 9

MEDIEVAL FISHING AND FISH TRADE

JAMES H. BARRETT

Fishing and fish trade were important components of economy and society in medieval Britain. Their roles were varied. Fish could provide means to pay obligatory renders and opportunities to amass considerable wealth. They were an important source of storable protein and also facilitated expressions of social identity. Moreover, the large fishing industries of the late Middle Ages were important determinants of shifts in political economy at regional and inter-regional scales, and in the emergence of an increasingly global trade in commodities. This *Handbook* contribution surveys a selection of archaeological (primarily fish-bone) and historical evidence, outlining major patterns in fishing and fish trade in medieval Britain. The balance of emphasis is on the five centuries from AD 1050 to 1550, but first it is essential to address a major period of transition during the preceding Viking Age. The main taxa to be discussed are herring, cod, and related marine species, but trends in the consumption of freshwater and migratory fish are also considered.

THE FISH EVENT HORIZON AND FISHING AD 850–1050

The years between AD 850 and 1050 were characterized by an increase in the importance of sea fishing, and perhaps the beginning of decline in the natural availability of freshwater fish. This shift, informally dubbed the 'fish event horizon' (Barrett et al. 2004), is evident in differing detail in many countries around the North, Baltic, and Irish Seas. Aspects of the original argument have been questioned on the basis of new evidence for some sea fishing in early and middle Anglo-Saxon England (e.g. Carver and Loveluck 2013, 122–4) on one hand, and the limited historical evidence for commercial gadid fishing prior to the thirteenth century on the other (Kowaleski 2016). The possibility that the 'fish event horizon' was influenced by Christian fasting practices has also come under scrutiny, based on the study of historical evidence (Frantzen 2014, 232–45). Nevertheless, it remains the case that more sea fish bones (in both absolute numbers and vis-à-vis freshwater and migratory species) occur at more sites starting around the year AD 1000.

The English evidence is diverse, but York provides one of the most informative time-series of fish-bone data, now fully published (Harland et al. 2016). The relevant assemblages are large and well recovered using sieving. They range in date from the seventh century to beyond the end of the Middle Ages. Here the fish remains were first dominated by migratory and freshwater species (such as eel, cyprinids, and pike), but show a major increase in the abundance of herring from the mid-tenth century. Concurrently, cod became more than a trace taxon for the first time. By the middle of the eleventh century, gadids actually became more frequent than any freshwater or migratory species other than eel. London tells a similar story. The relative abundance of herring increased around the turn of the first and second millennia, with flatfish also occurring in large numbers and gadids (e.g. cod and whiting) appearing at more than trace levels for the first time (Locker 1997; Orton et al. 2014). In the south, sea fish (mostly herring) replaced freshwater and migratory species (mostly eel) as the most abundant fish in Hamwic/Southampton by AD 1030 (e.g. Hamilton-Dyer 1997). These are only selected examples of a general trend across England.

Equally informative is the fact that stable isotope analysis of human skeletal material shows that the sea fish consumed in earlier centuries—at Bishopstone in East Sussex for example—do not correspond with measureable quantities of marine protein in human diet (Müldner 2016; Thomas 2010). The exceptions showing even limited evidence of a marine diet in England before the eleventh century are either burials of possible Scandinavian migrants (e.g. Pollard et al. 2012) or cemeteries from coastal Norfolk, where herring are a particularly abundant local resource (Hull and O'Connell 2011). In fact, the earliest unambiguous stable isotope evidence for sea-fish consumption in medieval England relates to a minority of young men buried at St Andrew, Fishergate, in the mid-/late eleventh or early twelfth centuries. Müldner (2009, 336) suggests that they may have been fishermen.

Was this shift to the sea motivated at least in part by a decline in the availability of freshwater fish caused by human impacts on aquatic ecosystems? To address this question we remain very reliant on the time-series of fish-bone evidence from York. The absolute abundance of freshwater fish remains declined through time and the average total length (TL) of one of the most abundant obligate freshwater species (pike) also decreased. Large individuals (50 to 80 cm TL) were well represented until the middle of the eleventh century, but almost absent after that. These patterns raise the possibility of overfishing, and it has also been suggested that the disappearance of grayling (*Thymallus thymallus*) and burbot (*Lota lota*) from the York fauna was due to increasing water pollution (O'Connor 1989, 198). What is not yet known is the degree to which we can generalize from the picture of a single city. As one moves forward in time through the Middle

Ages, however, historical evidence suggests that freshwater fish were increasingly monopolized by the elite, often by cultivation in fishponds (Serjeantson and Woolgar 2006). Thus it seems likely that they had become rare in the wild. Further zooarchaeological research on this important question is clearly merited.

There is little historical evidence regarding any aspect of English sea fishing in the years around AD 1000, leading to some source-based disagreements between zooarchaeologists and historians (cf. Barrett et al. 2004; Frantzen 2014). Accepting the danger of anachronism, one must infer the organization of England's growing sea fisheries of c. AD 950–1050 by extrapolating backwards from the Domesday Book and even later sources. Domesday provides well-known examples of herring renders from both rural estates and coastal ports—particularly the now submerged town of Dunwich in Suffolk (Campbell 2002; Kowaleski 2016). Campbell (2002, 9) estimates an annual East Anglian catch of at least 3,298,000 herring. These fish were salted and dried or salted and smoked—barrelling herring with brine was only introduced to England in the late fourteenth century (see Barrett 2016a and references therein). A variety of sources, including Domesday, demonstrate that the necessary salt was produced on a large scale in eastern England (Campbell 2002).

Based on finds of herring bones, the resulting products were brought to centres such as York and London for consumption. But were these English herring also serving distant markets in the years around AD 1000? It may be reasonable to speculate that many were shipped up the Rhine and Seine, the conduits of Continental wine to England prior to the thirteenth century. This inference is based on the important and well-documented trade of East Anglian herring for wine during the thirteenth and fourteenth centuries, by which time the main source was Gascony (cf. Littler 1970, 203, 224–5; Rose 2011; Saul 1982), combined with the observation that fish were the first item in Henry of Huntingdon's list of English exports to Germany c.1130 (Oksanen 2013, 179). Rather than wool, which became a major export in the course of the twelfth and thirteenth centuries, the wealth of late Anglo-Saxon and early Anglo-Norman England may have hinged in large measure on its herring fishery (contra Sawyer 2013).

Cod-family fish, unlike herring, do not appear in Domesday (Kowaleski 2016). Nevertheless, as noted above, their bones do occur in tenth- and eleventh-century archaeological assemblages. Some of the excavated cod specimens have been the subject of stable isotope analysis indicating that, prior to the thirteenth century, most were probably local catches from the southern North Sea rather than (for example) imports of Scandinavian stockfish (Barrett et al. 2008; 2011; see below). Anatomical patterning in the cod bones from London tells a similar story (Orton et al. 2014; 2016). Thus there was an increase in English cod fishing around AD 1000—serving growing urban populations—rather than the introduction of a new imported product. On balance, the rising consumption of cod can now be interpreted as a matter of increasing demand rather than changing long-range networks of supply (cf. Barrett et al. 2004; 2011).

In light of the discussion thus far, what was the relationship between herring and cod fishing, and why is there a discrepancy between historical and archaeological evidence for the latter? There are no answers from tenth- to eleventh-century textual sources, but latter accounts may provide some clarity. For example, in the Dunwich Bailiffs' *Minute Book* of 1404–30 (Bailey 1992) it is clear that the main herring season was supplemented with smaller fisheries for cod and other species. For much of the Middle Ages, at least in eastern and south-eastern England, gadids and other sea fish may have been secondary catches in a cycle of activity, payments, and record-keeping dictated by herring.

For different reasons, parts of Scotland also experienced a major increase in sea fishing between AD 850 and 1050. A new importance was attached to the catching and consumption of herring and/or large gadids in areas of the country that were influenced by the Scandinavian diaspora of the Viking Age (Barrett et al. 2001; Cerón-Carrasco 2005; Sharples et al. 2015). In the Western Isles, both herring and gadids were targeted, whereas in the Northern Isles (Orkney and Shetland), it was cod and the related gadids saithe and ling that were prioritized (cf. Barrett et al. 1999; Cerón-Carrasco 2011; Serjeantson 2013; Sharples et al. 2015). The contrast cannot be explained based on natural fish distributions, nor the character of fishing grounds, but must instead reflect differing communities of practice in the Western and Northern Isles.

The initial ninth/tenth-century increase in sea fishing is demonstrated by fish bones from sites such as Old Scatness (Nicholson 2010), Pool (Nicholson 2007), Quoygrew (Harland and Barrett 2012), and Bornish (Sharples et al. 2015). Moreover, by the eleventh to twelfth centuries there was a further increase in sea fishing in northern Scotland, evidenced by both zooarchaeology (Barrett 1997; 2012; Barrett et al. 2004) and stable isotope analysis of human bone (Barrett and Richards 2004; Müldner 2016). By this date it is probable that cod were being dried (without salt) to produce stockfish—used to pay local renders and possibly also for small-scale export (Barrett 1997; 2012; Harland 2007). It must also be asked whether the fishery for herring in the Western Isles developed in part for trade, perhaps to the Hiberno-Scandinavian town of Dublin. Unlike gadids, however, the oily herring cannot be preserved for any length of time without salt; it is unclear where Hebridean islanders could have acquired large supplies of this preservative prior to the availability of solar salt in the late Middle Ages (Sharples et al. 2015, 253; see below).

Fishing in England and Scotland AD 1050–1350

Moving forward in time, many regions of both England and Scotland witnessed further increases in the importance of sea fishing between AD 1050 and 1350. They were also drawn into an increasingly pan-European network of fish trade, involving both British exports and the import of North Atlantic stockfish and (near the end of the period) barrelled herring from the western Baltic. This network had many participants, but from the early fourteenth century it was dominated by towns of the German Hansa, especially Lübeck.

In England, the herring fisheries of the east and south-east coasts were growing in the eleventh century according to historical sources (Kowaleski 2016). Both rural estates and ports were active participants, with the significance of different centres changing through time. Great Yarmouth replaced Dunwich as the most important focus of the East Anglian herring fishery during the twelfth and thirteenth centuries. Yarmouth was already frequented by Continental fishermen in the twelfth century (Campbell 2002, 6) and in 1295 those from Holland, Zeeland, and Friesland received royal protection (Unger 1978, 341). By the early fourteenth century as many as c.1000 fishing boats may have converged on Yarmouth during the herring season (Saul 1982, 78). King's Lynn and Boston emerged as new coastal ports in the late eleventh and early twelfth centuries, albeit more as centres of fish trade than of fishing itself (Nedkvitne 2014, 31, 55). Grimsby, at the mouth of the Humber, fulfilled both functions in the twelfth and thirteenth centuries, but faced growing competition from Hull during the thirteenth century—and from the short-lived Ravenserodd (across the Humber estuary near what is now Spurn Head), from the 1230s until it was washed away in the middle of the fourteenth century (Rigby 1993, 7–12, 31–3; see Chapter 11 in this *Handbook*). Fishing was also an important activity further north, in Bridlington, Whitby, and Scarborough, Yorkshire, for example (Kowaleski 2016). In the south, herring fishing was conducted in Kent and Sussex (Tsurushima 2006), and the Cinque Ports held rights in the East Anglian herring fishery—by charter from the thirteenth century and in practice already from the twelfth or even the eleventh century (Kowaleski 2016). The herring from all these fisheries were eaten across England: in towns, monasteries, and rural settlements (e.g. Barrett et al. 2004; Colson 2014; Serjeantson and Woolgar 2006). It was argued above that some were also exchanged for Continental wine in the eleventh and twelfth centuries; certainly this was the case by the thirteenth century, at which point the main trade shifted from northern towns such as Rouen to La Rochelle and then Gascony (Littler 1970, 203, 224–5; Rose 2011, 61–2).

What of herring imports, especially of the iconic barrelled product from the Danish Scanian fishery of the High Middle Ages? Its first documented appearance in England dates to 1308, but large-scale trade only became common in the second half of the fourteenth century (Nedkvitne 2014, 517–18). English fishermen also attempted to participate in the Scanian catch, but with limited success given the protectionist policies of the German Hansa—an organization that was partly brought into existence by the herring trade (Jahnke 2009; and see Part X of this *Handbook*). Thus it is not surprising that medieval fish-bone assemblages from England lack evidence for the distinctive Scanian cure (in which specific parts of the skeleton are removed during processing).

Returning to the subject of cod and related species, gadid fisheries continued and expanded between AD 1050 and 1350 (Barrett et al. 2004; cf. Kowaleski 2016). Some of the catch was marketed fresh, but there is also evidence of preservation for longer storage. At Cartergate in Grimsby, Humberside, cod bones dating between the late twelfth and mid-fourteenth century show the manufacture of a product in which the head and anterior vertebrae had been removed on-site (Russ 2011). This is analogous to how one variety of stockfish was made (Barrett 1997). In northern Scandinavia this product was dried without salt. At Grimsby's latitude, however, one must assume that the fish were both dried and salted, like West Country and later Newfoundland cures (see below). Based on thirteenth-century zooarchaeological evidence, pre-processed decapitated cod were consumed in York, a journey upriver from Grimsby (Harland et al. 2016).

England also became an important market for imports of stockfish proper, from Norway and perhaps other areas of the North Atlantic (Barrett et al. 2011; Orton et al. 2014). Some of the ports discussed above, Grimsby and Ravenserodd for example, became centres for this trade (Nedkvitne 2014; Rigby 1993). Others, such as King's Lynn and Boston, served as foci for the transhipment of diverse goods, including stockfish. Major population centres such as London consumed much imported fish, often acquired by internal trade with transhipment ports (Colson 2014). Stockfish were also consumed in the countryside—at Wharram Percy in North Yorkshire, for example (Barrett et al. 2008).

When did the stockfish trade first begin? Anecdotal historical evidence is known from the late eleventh and early twelfth centuries (Nedkvitne 2016; Nielssen 2016), but zooarchaeological data from London suggest that the main shift from local (whole) to imported (decapitated) cod may have been later—in the early-thirteenth century (Orton et al. 2014). Similarly, analysis of a small sample of medieval cod bones from archaeological sites in England shows that almost all specimens predating the thirteenth century have stable isotope signatures consistent with relatively local catches in the southern North Sea, the English Channel, or the Irish Sea (Barrett et al. 2011; see Hutchinson et al. 2015 for comparative data regarding the isotope values to be expected in the Irish Sea). It is specimens of thirteenth- to fourteenth-century date that better match Arctic Norwegian or North Atlantic sources. Using these methods, London presently shows the best evidence for northern imports. Nevertheless, a few thirteenth- to fourteenth-century cod bones from York and Wharram Percy also have stable isotope signatures characteristic of stockfish-producing regions (Barrett et al. 2011). Stockfish imports were initially mainly in the hands of Norwegian and English merchants, but became increasingly monopolized by the German Hansa from the second decade of the fourteenth century (Nedkvitne 2014).

We do not yet know the precise source of all the stockfish consumed in medieval England. Stable isotope evidence cannot separate northern Norway, Iceland, and northern Scotland with confidence (Barrett et al. 2011; Hutchinson et al. 2015). Moreover, by AD 1294 (a few years before the beginning of systematic English customs records regarding fish trade) the Norwegian crown enforced the role of Bergen as a staple transhipment port for northern exports (*DN* 1849, 23). Thus historical sources seldom reveal the origin of English imports prior to their departure from this town.

We do know, however, that stockfish production in Arctic Norway was attracting royal attention by the turn of the eleventh and twelfth centuries and that Iceland first began to export dried cod at some point in the thirteenth century (Thór 2009, 329). It has also been argued that the Scandinavianized earldom of Orkney in northern Scotland was exporting stockfish in the eleventh to twelfth centuries (Barrett 1997; 2012; Harland

and Barrett 2012). It may be relevant that Orcadians are noted as visiting Grimsby in the early twelfth century (Guðmundsson 1965, 130), and that one of the parishes dominated by London's medieval stockfishmongers was dedicated to Magnus the Martyr, patron saint of Orkney (Colson 2014). If the Orkney hypothesis is correct, however, Orcadian imports of the eleventh to twelfth centuries were not sufficiently numerous to have yet been recognized in the fish-bone record from England (see above). Ironically, the cod fishery of Orkney was in decline by the thirteenth century, when northern trade with England increased. Some small-scale producers—including those in Orkney—may have been marginalized vis-à-vis Arctic Norway as the stockfish trade became increasingly commercialized (Barrett 2012; 2016b).

What of fishing in other parts of Scotland during the eleventh to fourteenth centuries? Herring were an important catch in some areas. Their bones continue to be abundant finds in the Western Isles (e.g. Ingrem 2005, 192–3), and also appear in zooarchaeological assemblages from the new burghs of the Lowland east (e.g. Hodgson et al. 2011). There is surprisingly little fish-bone evidence for the consumption of salmon, another of Scotland's major traditional resources, but cod and related species (especially ling) were clearly important (Bailey et al. 2015). In some cases, as in twelfth- to fourteenth-century Perth and thirteenth- to fourteenth-century Aberdeen, relatively even representation of different skeletal elements suggests local consumption of fresh or lightly cured catches (Harland 2010, 32; Hodgson et al. 2011, 53–7). In other instances cured gadid products may have been manufactured locally. At Leith, a thirteenth-century assemblage of cranial bones and anterior vertebrae from large cod and ling suggests that a stockfish-like product was being made—either for nearby consumption (in Edinburgh for example) or export (Stronach 2002). A similar assemblage of cod and ling, of thirteenth- to fourteenth-century date, is known from the burgh of Eyemouth, in the Scottish Borders (Dixon 1986, 83). Certainly some Scottish fish were being exported by the thirteenth-century, to England and the Continent. As discussed below, however, it is only in the late fourteenth and fifteenth centuries that customs accounts record this activity systematically.

England's east coast herring fishery probably peaked with medieval demographic and economic expansion in the years around AD 1300, prior to the many crises of the fourteenth century (cf. Campbell 2010). It subsequently declined, to be replaced with imports of barrelled herring and the emergence of increasingly long-range fisheries that culminated in annual expeditions to Newfoundland in the sixteenth century. To provide one example, Great Yarmouth was the fourth highest-taxed provincial town (after Bristol, York, and Newcastle) in 1334, whereas by 1377 it was eighteenth (Saul 1982, 76). As noted above, imported barrelled herring, initially from the Baltic, began to compete on the English market during the fourteenth century (Nedkvitne 2014, 517–18). However, the problems facing the east coast fishery were varied and complex (Kowaleski 2003, 193–8). The fourteenth century witnessed unprecedented siltation and/or destruction of pre-existing harbours, and persistent warfare discouraged Continental boats from landing fish in England. Fishermen from the Low Countries instead began to salt their catch on board, a development culminating in a superior product barrelled at sea. England's herring fleet also suffered through military requisition. Moreover, new fisheries of the English West Country were better placed to be intermediaries in the French wine trade that had previously been important to Great Yarmouth. This advantage can only have increased in the context of rising labour costs after the Black Death, which reduced the viability of large-scale salt production in eastern England. The cheap solar salt from Atlantic Europe that filled the gap was more accessible in the south-west (Kowaleski 2003, 226).

Confronted with these developments, some east coast fishermen shifted their efforts to catching other species (especially cod) from new waters: in the North Sea (e.g. Dogger Bank), off the coasts of Denmark and Norway, and around Iceland (Childs and Kowaleski 2000). English fishermen reached Iceland in the first decade of the fifteenth century, to purchase stockfish from the locals and to make their own catches which were both salted and dried. The merchants of Hull (and of Bristol in the south-west) played the biggest part, but many small ports were also involved (Childs 1995). Icelandic dried cod probably contributed to some of the provisions on the *Mary Rose* when it sank in 1545 (Hutchinson et al. 2015), and continued to supply the English market into the seventeenth century (Jones 2000).

The new West Country fisheries of the late Middle Ages were also active in both local and distant waters, harvesting species such as cod, hake, and ling (Kowaleski 2000; 2003). Ireland was a favoured destination and Iceland was also visited. On at least one occasion (in 1438) fishermen from Cornwall were fined for an unlicensed trip to Finnmark in Arctic Norway (Childs 1997, 285). Temporary fishing stations were established in the West Country starting in the thirteenth century, but the main growth of the fishery was from the late fourteenth century. It was not until the late fifteenth and sixteenth centuries that permanent fishing villages developed (e.g. Fox 2001; Kowaleski 2014, 47). The Black Death is known to have reduced the number of fishermen in some settlements, but the long-term trend was one of expansion in the scale of trade and the distances sailed (Kowaleski 2014). As the Middle Ages ended, West Country fishermen expanded their efforts to Newfoundland (Candow 2009; Kowaleski 2003).

The late medieval fisheries of Devon and Cornwall were not the only competitors of England's declining east coast herring industry. Wales has not yet figured in this text— given a paucity of fish-bone evidence—but it hosted a major herring fishery in the late fifteenth and sixteenth centuries (Kowaleski 2003, 219–20). The antecedent of this development, a coastal herring fishery in Anglesey, is recorded as early as the late eleventh or early twelfth centuries (Kowaleski 2016). Archaeological finds of coastal and estuarine fish traps also imply the exploitation of marine and migratory fish in medieval Wales (e.g. Turner 2002).

Many of Scotland's sea fisheries were also prosperous in the late Middle Ages. Although salmon are almost invisible in the zooarchaeological record they were taxed, incidentally from 1398 and systematically from 1425 (Rorke 2001, 182–3). Herring attracted royal customs levies from 1424, allowing us to see that the volume of exports rose dramatically in the mid-sixteenth century (Rorke 2001, 197; 2005, 153). By the 1460s cod were unambiguously added to the Scottish customs system, but they had probably also been taxed earlier based on anecdotal sources (Rorke 2001, 197). The documented export of all these species in the late Middle Ages is likely to have been facilitated by the increasing availability, from the 1360s, of solar salt from western France. The Scottish situation was not uniform, however, as evidenced by the decline in cod fishing in Orkney (see above). As was the case with the English east coast and West Country fisheries, shifting patterns of trade brought differing economic outcomes to different regions.

Acknowledgements

I thank Christopher Gerrard and Alejandra Gutiérrez for inviting me to contribute this text, which draws on elements of a previous study of sea fishing in medieval northern Europe (Barrett 2016b). The research was funded by the Leverhulme Trust and the COST Action Oceans Past Platform, supported by COST (European Cooperation in Science and Technology).

References cited

Bailey, L., Holden, T., Franklin, J., Smith, C., and Cerón-Carrasco, C. 2015 'An archaeological excavation of a medieval fishermen's midden at Castle Hill Pumping Station, Banff', *Scottish Archaeological Journal* 36–37, 1–35

Bailey, M. (ed) 1992 *The Bailiffs' Minute Book of Dunwich, 1404–1430*, The Boydell Press/Suffolk Records Society, Woodbridge

Barrett, J. H. 1997 'Fish trade in Norse Orkney and Caithness: a zooarchaeological approach', *Antiquity* 71, 616–38

Barrett, J. H. 2012 'Being an islander', in J. H. Barrett (ed.), *Being an islander: production and identity at Quoygrew, Orkney, AD 900–1600*, McDonald Institute for Archaeological Research, Cambridge, 275–92

Barrett, J. H. 2016a 'Studying medieval sea fishing and fish trade: how and why', in J. H. Barrett and D. C. Orton (eds), *Cod and herring: the archaeology and history of medieval sea fishing*, Oxbow, Oxford, 1–12

Barrett, J. H. 2016b 'Medieval sea fishing AD 500–1550: chronology, causes and consequences', in J. H. Barrett and D. C. Orton (eds), *Cod and herring: the archaeology and history of medieval sea fishing*, Oxbow, Oxford, 250–72

Barrett, J. H., Beukens, R. P., and Nicholson, R. A. 2001 'Diet and ethnicity during the Viking colonisation of northern Scotland: evidence from fish bones and stable carbon isotopes', *Antiquity* 75, 145–54

Barrett, J. H., Johnstone, C., Harland, J., van Neer, W., Ervynck, A., Makowiecki, D., Heinrich, D., Hufthammer, A. K., Enghoff, I. B., Amundsen, C., Christiansen, J. S., Jones, A. K. G., Locker, A., Hamilton-Dyer, S., Jonsson, L., Lõugas, L., Roberts, C., and Richards, M. 2008 'Detecting the medieval cod trade: a new method and first results', *Journal of Archaeological Science* 35(4), 850–61

Barrett, J. H., Locker, A. M., and Roberts, C. M. 2004 '"Dark Age Economics" revisited: the English fish bone evidence AD 600–1600', *Antiquity* 78, 618–36

Barrett, J. H., Nicholson, R. A., and Cerón-Carrasco, R. 1999 'Archaeo-ichthyological evidence for long-term socioeconomic trends in northern Scotland: 3500 BC to AD 1500', *Journal of Archaeological Science* 26, 353–88

Barrett, J. H., Orton, D., Johnstone, C., Harland, J., Neer, W. V., Ervynck, A., Roberts, C., Locker, A., Amundsen, C., Enghoff, I. B., Hamilton-Dyer, S., Heinrich, D., Hufthammer, A. K., Jones, A. K. G., Jonsson, L., Makowiecki, D., Pope, P., O'Connell, T. C., de Roo, T., and Richards, M. 2011 'Interpreting the expansion of sea fishing in medieval Europe using stable isotope analysis of archaeological cod bones', *Journal of Archaeological Science* 38, 1516–24

Barrett, J. H. and Richards, M. P. 2004 'Identity, gender, religion and economy: new isotope and radiocarbon evidence for marine resource intensification in early historic Orkney, Scotland', *European Journal of Archaeology* 7, 249–71

Campbell, B. M. S. 2010 'Nature as historical protagonist: environment and society in pre-industrial England', *The Economic History Review* 63, 281–314

Campbell, J. 2002 'Domesday herrings', in C. Harper-Bill, C. Rawcliffe, and R. G. Wilson (eds), *East Anglia's history*, Boydell, Woodbridge, 5–17

Candow, J. E. 2009 'Migrants and residents: the interplay between European and domestic fisheries in northeast North America, 1502–1854', in D. J. Starkey, J. T. Thór and I. Heidbrink (eds), *A history of the North Atlantic fisheries volume 1: from early times to the mid-nineteenth century*, Verlag H. M. Hauschild GmbH, Bremen, 416–52

Carver, M. and Loveluck, C. 2013 'Early medieval, AD 400 to 1000', in J. Ransley and F. Sturt (ed.), *People and the sea: a maritime archaeological research agenda for England*, Council for British Archaeology, York, 113–37

Cerón-Carrasco, R. 2005 *Of fish and men ('De iasg agus dhaoine'): a study of the utilization of marine resources as recovered from selected Hebridean archaeological sites*, British Archaeological Reports British Series 400, Oxford

Cerón-Carrasco, R. 2011 'The ethnography of fishing in Scotland and its contribution to icthyoarchaeological analysis in this region', in U. Albarella and A. Trentacoste (eds), *Ethnozooarchaeology: the present and past of human-animal relationships*, Oxbow, Oxford, 58–72

Childs, W. R. 1995 'England's Icelandic trade in the fifteenth century: the role of Hull', *Northern Seas Yearbook* 5, 11–31

Childs, W. R. 1997 'The commercial shipping of south-western England in the later fifteenth century', *The Mariner's Mirror* 83, 272–92

Childs, W. R. and Kowaleski, M. 2000 'Fishing and fisheries in the Middle Ages', in D. J. Starkey, C. Reid, and N. Ashcroft (eds), *England's sea fisheries: the commercial sea fisheries of England and Wales since 1300*, Chatham, London, 19–28

Colson, J. 2014 'London's forgotten company? Fishmongers, their trade and their networks in later medieval London', in C. Barron and A. F. Sutton (eds), *Proceedings of the 2012 Harlaxton Medieval Symposium: the medieval merchant*, Shaun Tyas, Donington, 20–40

Dixon, P. 1986 *Excavations in the fishing town of Eyemouth 1982–1984*, Borders Architects Group, Edinburgh

DN Diplomatarium Norvegicum 1849 *Diplomatarium Norvegicum volume 5*, Dokumentasjonsprosjektet, P.T. Malling, Oslo

Fox, H. 2001 *The evolution of the fishing village: landscape and society along the south Devon coast, 1086–1550*, Leopard's Head Press, Oxford

Frantzen, A. J. 2014 *Food, eating and identity in early medieval England*, Boydell, Woodbridge

Guðmundsson, F. 1965 *Orkneyinga Saga*, Hið Islenzka Fornritafélag, Reykjavik

Hamilton-Dyer, S. 1997 *The Lower High Street Project, Southampton: the faunal remains*, unpublished report for Southampton City Archaeological Unit

Harland, J. F. 2007 'Status and space in the "Fish Event Horizon": initial results from Quoygrew and Earl's Bu, Viking Age and medieval sites in Orkney, Scotland', in H. H. Plogmann (ed.), *The role of fish in ancient time*, Verlag Marie Leidorf, Rahden, 63–8

Harland, J. F. 2010 *Technical report: the fish bone from Bon Accord, Aberdeen (site code 20215)*, Centre for Human Palaeoecology Report 2010/02, York

Harland, J. F. and Barrett, J. H. 2012 'The maritime economy: fish bone', in J. H. Barrett (ed.), *Being an islander: production and identity at Quoygrew, Orkney, AD 900–1600*, McDonald Institute for Archaeological Research, Cambridge, 115–38

Harland, J. F., Jones, A. K. G., Orton, D. C., and Barrett, J. H. 2016 'Fishing and fish trade in medieval York: the zooarchaeological evidence', in J. H. Barrett and D. C. Orton (eds), *Cod and herring: the archaeology and history of medieval sea fishing*, Oxbow, Oxford, 172–204

Hodgson, G. W. I., Smith, C., Jones, A., Fraser, M., Jones, A. K. G., Heppel, D., Cerón-Carrasco, R., Clarke, A. S., Smart, I. H. M., Longmore, R. B., and McKay, D. 2011 *Perth High Street archaeological excavation 1975–1977 fascicule 4: living and working in a medieval Scottish burgh, environmental remains and miscellaneous finds*, Tayside and Fife Archaeological Committee, Perth

Hull, B. D. and O'Connell, T. C. 2011 'Diet: recent evidence from analytical chemical techniques', in H. Hamerow, D. A. Hinton, and S. Crawford (eds), *The Oxford handbook of Anglo-Saxon archaeology*, Oxford University Press, Oxford, 667–87

Hutchinson, W. F., Culling, M., Orton, D. C., Hänfling, B., Lawson Handley, L., Hamilton-Dyer, S., O'Connell, T. C., Richards, M. P., and Barrett, J. H. 2015 'The globalization of naval provisioning: ancient DNA and stable isotope analyses of stored cod from the wreck of the Mary Rose, AD 1545', *Royal Society Open Science* 2, 150–99

Ingrem, C. 2005 'Fish', in N. Sharples (ed.), *A Norse farm in the Outer Hebrides: excavations at Mound 3, Bornais, South Uist*, Oxbow, Oxford, 192–4

Jahnke, C. 2009 'The medieval herring fishery in the western Baltic', in L. Sicking and D. Abreu-Ferreira (ed.), *Beyond the catch: fisheries of the North Atlantic, the North Sea and the Baltic, 900–1850*, Brill, Leiden, 157–86

Jones, E. 2000 'England's Icelandic fishery in the early modern period', in D. J. Starkey, C. Reid, and N. Ashcroft (eds), *England's sea fisheries: the commercial sea fisheries of England and Wales since 1300*, Chatham, London, 105–10

Kowaleski, M. 2000 'The expansion of the southwestern fisheries in late medieval England', *The Economic History Review* 53, 429–54

Kowaleski, M. 2003 'The commercialization of the sea fisheries in medieval England and Wales', *International Journal of Maritime History* 15, 177–231

Kowaleski, M. 2014 'Coastal communities in medieval Cornwall', in H. Doe, A. Kennerly, and P. Payton (eds), *A maritime history of Cornwall*, University of Exeter Press, Exeter, 43–59

Kowaleski, M. 2016 'The early documentary evidence for the commercialisation of the sea fisheries in medieval Britain', in J. H. Barrett and D. C. Orton (eds), *Cod and herring: the archaeology and history of medieval sea fishing*, Oxbow, Oxford, 23–41

Littler, A. S. 1970 *Fish in English economy and society down to the reformation*, unpublished PhD thesis, University College of Swansea, Swansea

Locker, A. 1997 'The fish bones', in P. Mills, 'Excavations at the Dorter Undercroft, Westminster Abbey', *Transactions of the London and Middlesex Archaeological Society* 46, 111–13

Müldner, G. 2009 'Investigating medieval diet and society by stable isotope analysis of human bone', in R. Gilchrist and A. Reynolds (ed.), *Reflections: 50 years of medieval archaeology, 1957–2007*, The Society for Medieval Archaeology Monograph 30, Leeds, 327–46

Müldner, G. 2016 'Marine fish consumption in medieval Britain: the isotope perspective from human skeletal remains', in J. H. Barrett and D. C. Orton (eds), *Cod and herring: the archaeology and history of medieval sea fishing*, Oxbow, Oxford, 239–49

Nedkvitne, A. 2014 *The German Hansa and Bergen 1100-1600*, Böhlau Verlag, Cologne

Nedkvitne, A. 2016 'The development of the Norwegian long-distance stockfish trade', in J. H. Barrett and D. C. Orton (eds), *Cod and herring: the archaeology and history of medieval sea fishing*, Oxbow, Oxford, 50–9

Nicholson, R. A. 2007 'The fish remains', in J. Hunter, J. M. Bond, and A. N. Smith (eds), *Investigations in Sanday, Orkney, vol. 1: excavations at Pool, Sanday. Multi-period settlement from Neolithic to Late Norse times*, The Orcadian Ltd/Historic Scotland, Kirkwall, 263–79

Nicholson, R. A. 2010 'Fish and fishing from the Pictish to the Norse centuries', in S. J. Dockrill, J. M. Bond, V. E. Turner, L. D. Brown, D. J. Bashford, J. E. Cussans, and R. A. Nicholson (eds), *Excavations at Old Scatness, Shetland, vol. 1: the Pictish and Viking settlement*, Shetland Heritage Publications, Lerwick, 156–67

Nielssen, A. R. 2016 'Early commercial fisheries and the interplay among farm, fishing station and fishing village in North Norway', in J. H. Barrett and D. C. Orton (eds), *Cod and herring: the archaeology and history of medieval sea fishing*, Oxbow, Oxford, 42–9

O'Connor, T. P. 1989 *Bones from Anglo-Scandinavian levels at 16-22 Coppergate*, Council for British Archaeology, London

Oksanen, E. 2013 'Economic relations between East Anglia and Flanders in the Anglo-Norman period', in D. Bates and R. Liddiard (eds), *East Anglia and its North Sea world in the Middle Ages*, Boydell, Woodbridge, 174–87

Orton, D. C., Morris, J., Locker, A., and Barrett, J. H. 2014 'Fish for the city: meta-analysis of archaeological cod remains and the growth of London's northern trade', *Antiquity* 88, 516–30

Orton, D. C., Locker, A., Morris, J., and Barrett, J. H. 2016 'Fish for London', in J. H. Barrett and D. C. Orton (eds), *Cod and herring: the archaeology and history of medieval sea fishing*, Oxbow, Oxford, 205–14

Orton, D. C., Makowiecki, D., de Roo, T., Johnstone, C., Harland, J., Jonsson, L., Heinrich, D., Enghoff, I. B., Lougas, L., Neer, W. V., Ervynck, A., Hufthammer, A. K., Amundsen, C., Jones, A. K. G., Locker, A., Hamilton-Dyer, S., Pope, P., MacKenzie, B. R., Richards, M., O'Connell, T. C., and Barrett, J. H. 2011 'Stable isotope evidence for late medieval (14th–15thC) origins of the eastern Baltic cod (*Gadus morhua*) fishery', *PLoS ONE* 6(11), e27568

Pollard, A. M., Ditchfield, P., Piva, E., Wallis, S., Falys, C., and Ford, S. 2012 '"Sprouting like cockle amongst the wheat": the St Brice's Day massacre and the isotopic analysis of human bones from St John's College, Oxford', *Oxford Journal of Archaeology* 31, 83–102

Rigby, S. H. 1993 *Medieval Grimsby: growth and decline*, University of Hull Press, Hull

Rorke, M. 2001 *Scottish overseas trade, 1275/86-1597*, unpublished PhD, University of Edinburgh, Edinburgh

Rorke, M. 2005 'The Scottish herring trade, 1470-1600', *The Scottish Historical Review* 84, 149–65

Rose, S. 2011 *The wine trade in medieval Europe 1000-1500*, Continuum, London

Russ, H. 2011 'Fish remains', in M. Rowe (ed.), *Land to the east of Cartergate Grimsby, north east Lincolnshire*, unpublished report for Preconstruct Archaeological Services Ltd, Lincoln

Saul, A. 1982 'English towns in the late Middle Ages: the case of Great Yarmouth', *Journal of Medieval History* 8, 75–88

Sawyer, P. 2013 *The wealth of Anglo-Saxon England*, Oxford University Press, Oxford

Serjeantson, D. 2013 *Farming and fishing in the Outer Hebrides AD 600 to 1700: the Udal, North Uist*, The Highfield Press, Southampton

Serjeantson, D. and Woolgar, C. M. 2006 'Fish consumption in medieval England', in C. M. Woolgar, D. Serjeantson, and T. Waldron (eds), *Food in medieval England: diet and nutrition*, Oxford University Press, Oxford, 102–30

Sharples, N. M., Ingrem, C., Marshall, P., Mulville, J., Powell, A., and Reed, K. 2015 'The Viking occupation of the Hebrides: evidence from the excavations at Bornais, South Uist', in J. H. Barrett and S. J. Gibbon (eds), *Maritime societies of the Viking and medieval world*, The Society for Medieval Archaeology Monograph 37, Leeds, 237–58

Stronach, S. 2002 'The medieval development of South Leith and the creation of Rotten Row', *Proceedings of the Society of Antiquaries of Scotland* 132, 383–423

Thomas, G. 2010 *The later Anglo-Saxon settlement at Bishopstone: a downland manor in the making*, Council for British Archaeology, York

Thór, J. T. 2009 'Icelandic fisheries, c.900–1900', in D. J. Starkey, J. T. Thór, and I. Heidbrink (eds), *A history of the North Atlantic fisheries volume 1: from early times to the mid-nineteenth century*, Verlag H. M. Hauschild GmbH, Bremen, 232–349

Tsurushima, H. 2006 'The eleventh century in England through fish-eyes: salmon, herring, oysters, and 1066', *Anglo-Norman Studies* 29, 193–213

Turner, R. 2002 'Fish weirs and fish traps', in A. Davidson (ed.), *The coastal archaeology of Wales*, Council for British Archaeology, York, 95–108

Unger, R. W. 1978 'The Netherlands herring fishery in the late Middle Ages: the false legend of Willem Beukels of Biervliet', *Viator* 9, 335–56

CHAPTER 10

THE MEDIEVAL WILD

ALEKS PLUSKOWSKI

WILD species, whether mammals or birds (fish are treated separately, see Chapter 9), typically make up a small proportion of any faunal assemblage from late medieval sites in Britain. Their meat did not represent a nutritional staple and hunting was more often conducted by professional retinues than by individual aristocrats. Identification of certain species, particularly wolves, wild boar, and wild cats is also compounded by their skeletal similarities to their domestic counterparts, and alongside the possibilities of hybridity most cases reported in the literature are difficult to positively verify (see Albarella 2006; O'Connor 2007; Pluskowski 2006a). Along with the fragmentary documentary record, the process of extinction of some of the most important wild species in Britain which took place during or in the centuries after the late medieval period remains obscure. A combination of habitat loss, prey depletion, and hunting are frequently cited as the causes of these gradual extinctions, the final stages of which would have seen regionally discrete populations of wolves, lynx, wild boar, and beaver isolated and genetically fragmented. This is based on a combination of the last documented presence of these species and their reported absence from the archaeological record. The final refuges of these populations, such as the Yorkshire Moors, the Peak Forest, or the Cairngorms, are relatively poorly known in terms of the environmental archaeology of late medieval settlements, and this lack of data prevents us from moving beyond the established, albeit sporadic and vague, documentation. Of course, the absence or reduction of a species in the archaeological record may reflect a reduction in human exploitation as much as an actual decline in the population. Our understanding of this process will only be developed further with genetic and stable isotope studies on positively identified bone recovered from well-dated contexts, but it is clear that the late medieval period represented a time of significant ecological transformation in Britain and accelerated the cumulative long-term human impact on these species (for summaries see O'Connor and Sykes 2010; Yalden 1999; Yalden and Albarella 2009). The exploitation of wild animals was closely tied to how the landscape was organized and managed (see Chapter 25), and the extent to which an aristocratic paradigm developing after the

Norman Conquest facilitated the preservation of certain species and their habitats, and caused the depletion of others.

Wild Mammals and Their Habitats

There is a close synchronicity between the development of royal authority and aristocratic identity from the late eleventh century and the exploitation of wild species, as reflected in faunal assemblages. The decades following the Norman Conquest of England in 1066 saw the transformation of the ownership and management of the landscape. A new law was nominally introduced which designated whole swathes of the country as *foresta*, although the first official legislation (the Assize of the Forest) dates to 1184. Forests varied in shape and size, but could encompass significant parts of counties. Within their bounds, disturbing or hunting deer and other defined game became a punishable offence, along with damage to their preferred habitat, woodland. Special courts were established to deal with offenders, and although the proceedings reveal an emphasis on finance rather than judicial concerns, they functioned completely outside the commercial economy. Forests, and their diminutive equivalents—chases—supplied royal and aristocratic households with significant quantities of venison; between 1311 and 1315, Edward II requested 1798 deer—red (*Cervus elaphus*) and fallow (*Dama dama*)—from 36 forests and chases across the realm (Langton 2010, 18). This system was adopted in Scotland from the mid-twelfth century, although it was only ever applied to the lowlands (Gilbert 1979, 13). It was also incrementally applied to Wales, associated with Anglo-Norman land ownership, initially restricted to the Marches but more widely applied after the Edwardian Conquest was completed in 1283. The majority of forests in Wales, however, covered very small territories. Grants of 'free warren' enabled landholders such as monasteries and knightly families to hunt smaller game, particularly hare (*Lepus europeaus*) and roe deer (*Capreolus capreolus*). The hunting culture developing after the Norman Conquest emphasized visual display focused on a ceremony of dismemberment of the deer carcass referred to as 'the unmaking'. This is not clearly evident before the late eleventh century (Sykes 2006, 170–1; 2007b). Venison, part of the 'economy of the regard' in late medieval Britain, had no recorded cash value, although the costs of hunting and salting the meat were regularly noted (Langton and Jones 2010, 11; Offer 1997). The impact of this regulated hunting culture is clearly visible in the composition of faunal assemblages recovered from late medieval sites. The quantity of wild mammal remains in English archaeological assemblages significantly rises between the mid-eleventh and mid-twelfth century on high-status sites, and increases again at all social levels from the mid-twelfth to mid-fourteenth century whilst retaining the earlier contrasts between social groups (Sykes 2006, 164–5; for a comprehensive survey see Sykes 2007a) (Figure 10.1). The relative representation of the three most hunted wild ungulates also changes during this same period. At high-status sites, the ratio of red deer to roe deer increases, whilst from the

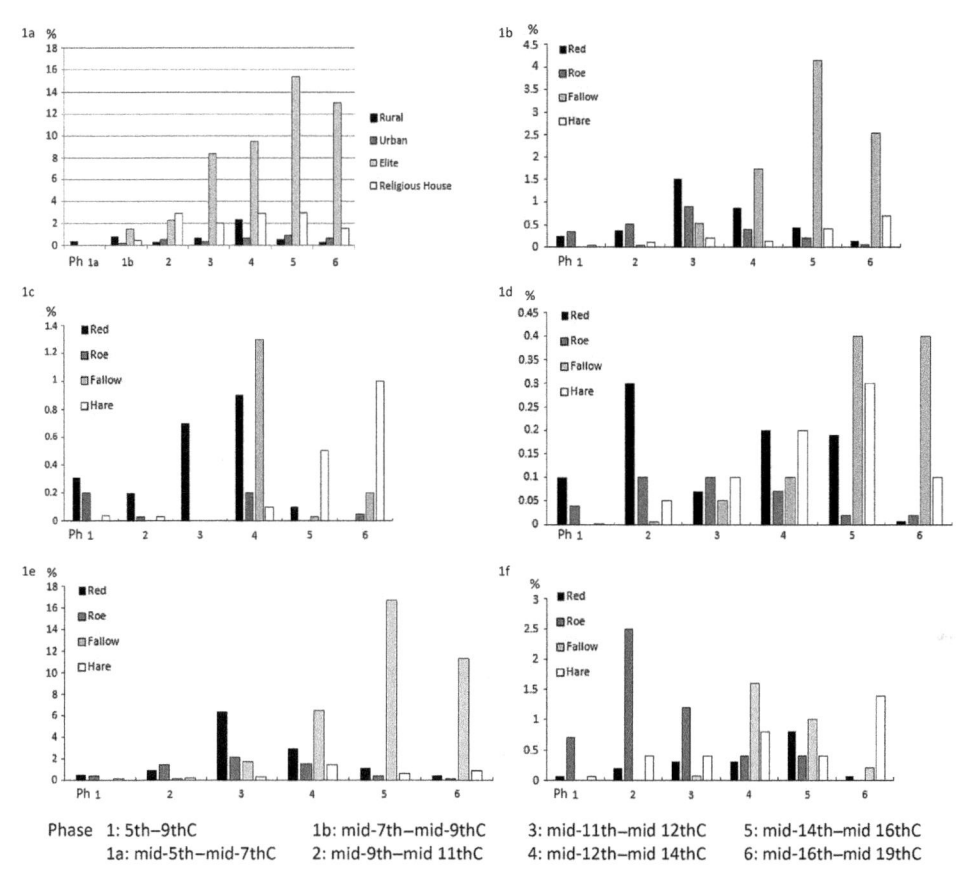

FIGURE 10.1 Wild animal bones as recovered in excavations (data provided by Naomi Sykes): 1a: The representation of wild mammals in medieval English sites, as a percentage of the total bone assemblage excluding fish; 1b: Relative percentage of wild mammals in different periods; 1c: Relative percentage of wild mammals on rural sites; 1d: Relative percentage of wild mammals on urban sites; 1e: Relative percentage of wild mammals on high-status sites; 1f: Relative percentage of wild mammals on religious sites

mid-twelfth century quantities of fallow deer, re-introduced most probably from Sicily after the Conquest, are much higher than the two indigenous cervids. The presence of hare and higher numbers of roe deer on monastic sites has been interpreted as reflecting lesser hunting rights, although numbers of the latter steadily decreased over time until they dropped sharply between the mid-twelfth and mid-fourteenth century. Although hunting was a regulated aristocratic activity, it enveloped late medieval rural society and should be regarded as an inclusive, albeit hierarchical, practice (Judkins 2013; Sykes 2007b).

Whilst these ratios reflect social choices to exploit specific prey species, the hunting culture developed by the Normans and accentuated under the Angevins had profound ecological consequences. The system of provisioning venison contributed to the significant depletion of wild ungulate populations across much of Britain. By the fifteenth century, the most abundant populations were found in the Scottish Highlands. Roe deer populations were extirpated from East Anglia, severely depleted in southern England, and only remained intact in parts of northern England and the Scottish Highlands, where the remnant population exhibits relatively high genetic diversity (Baker and Hoelzel 2013). Wild boar populations steadily decreased as a combined result of hunting, habitat degradation, and in-breeding with domestic pigs, and there is no evidence for their presence outside of select enclosures after the end of the thirteenth century; their last free-roaming territory appears to have been the Forest of Dean, where the species vanished from the documentary record between *c*.1282 and the reign of Edward II a few decades later (Albarella 2010, 64). In Scotland, at around the same date, their rarity is attested by the need to feed and manage the surviving population. Occasional fragments of bone from later contexts have been interpreted as imports, and subsequently the species was reintroduced, particularly from the sixteenth century onwards. The most important shift in how wild animals were valued came in 1389, however, when a royal decree of Richard II restricted the right to hunt to those earning over 40s per year, and designated all other hunting as poaching, irrespective of whether it took place within the bounds of a Forest or chase. Poaching, nonetheless, continues to be documented throughout the fifteenth and sixteenth centuries.

The Exploitation of Wild Birds

The procurement of wild birds from the twelfth century required a level of resources and experience which limited it to wealthier social groups. The remains of wild birds are infrequently found on medieval archaeological sites, but they are more common on high-status sites than in urban or rural contexts. They can be sub-divided into three groups: raptors, used exclusively for falconry by the aristocracy (Cherryson 2002); those species defined as game and found in a broader range of social contexts; and accidental finds of scavenging species, particularly corvids, with regional diversity reflecting local environmental variability as well as social preferences and accessibility (Albarella and Thomas 2002). The diachronic composition of bird-bone assemblages from medieval sites in Britain indicates a shift in the diversity of species exploited from the latter half of the fourteenth century, reflecting improvements in living standards and purchasing power amongst the lower social classes. With the greater availability of meat, the aristocracy responded by increasing the diversity of wild birds served at their tables, and by creating a regular supply of large and visually striking species through the managed breeding of swans (*Cygnus* sp.), pheasants (*Phasianus colchicus*), peafowl (*Pavo cristatus*), and herons (*Ardea cinera*) (Albarella and Thomas 2002; Stone 2006). The changing diversity of species is a sensitive gauge of aristocratic presence at high-status sites; the gradual reduction in activity and the presence of high-status residents at Launceston castle from the mid-thirteenth century is reflected in the increasing monotony of the diet, particularly represented by bird and fish bones (Albarella and Thomas 2002, 26).

As in the case of wild ungulates, reliable supplies of wild birds became associated with controlled populations kept in enclosures, alongside dovecotes (Woolgar 1999, 13). The specific circumstances of the pheasant's introduction into Britain remain unclear, but from the twelfth century large numbers are referred to in written sources. Their remains are not found frequently, although they typically appear in association with high-status sites connected with parks (e.g. King John's Hunting Lodge at Writtle in Essex; Bramwell 1969). By the late fifteenth century, along with the rabbit, populations of pheasants were breeding in the wild and as a result were given royal protection (Poole 2010, 160). Peafowl were re-introduced after the Norman Conquest, and their remains are found almost exclusively on high-status sites (Poole 2010, 160; Sykes 2007a, 63). From the latter half of the fourteenth century, they feature as display pieces at lavish banquets. The peacock's well-established Christian symbolism is, at this time, accentuated within the political context of fifteenth-century visual culture in emphasizing dynastic longevity. Swans are increasingly represented on high-status sites from the fourteenth century, a trend mirrored by their frequent mention in contemporary documents as one of the commonest birds consumed by the elite (Albarella and Thomas 2002, 34), as well as in the appearance of specialized swanneries and swanherds, paralleled by heronries (Stone 2006, 156). As in the case of wild ungulates, the growing popularity of reared and contained birds contrasted with the gradual depletion of certain species, such as bustards (*Otis tarda*), migrating white storks (*Ciconia ciconia*), cranes (*Grus grus*), and perhaps grey partridges (*Perdix perdix*) (Albarella and Thomas 2002, 33; Serjeantson 2010). By the early sixteenth century, legislation was passed to restrict the hunting of a range of wild bird species and forbid the taking of their eggs (Stone 2006, 160).

Wild Animals at the Fringes of Control

The three major mountainous regions of Britain—central Wales, north-west Scotland, and the Peak District—remained sparsely settled throughout the Middle Ages. Attempts to designate these areas as Forests were only implemented in the Peak. The Edwardian conquest of Wales at the end of the thirteenth century did not result in the significant extension of Forests beyond the Dean and the existing domains in the Marches. These regions, with their relatively extensive corridors of woodland and limited human activity, sustained extensive populations of deer until the fifteenth century, which in turn attracted the largest surviving indigenous carnivores: wolves. Wolves had been protected within the bounds of royal *foresta* but permission to hunt them was usually granted, though this was not always the case. Conan, Duke of Brittany, provided the Abbey of Fors (Jervaulx) in Wensleydale (from the place-name, a landscape long associated with wolves) pasture for cattle in his private *foresta* of Richmond in Yorkshire c.1160–71, but forbade them to use any mastiffs to drive wolves from their pastures (Clay 1942, no. 67). His concern was that the hunting dogs might compromise the valuable herds of deer inhabiting the Forest. It was also evident that successful wolf hunting was best left to professionals, who had the time, resources, and experience to eradicate whole packs rather than isolated individuals.

By the later thirteenth century, as the attention of English kings increasingly turned towards Scotland and Wales, the wilder frontiers of the kingdom came under fresh scrutiny (Lieberman 2010, 231–2). In 1281, one of the most prominent Marcher lords, Peter Corbett, was charged by Edward I with exterminating all wolves in a series of adjacent counties: Worcestershire, Herefordshire, Gloucestershire, Shropshire, and Staffordshire. Similar royal initiatives were evident in Scotland shortly after, with the appointment of professional wolf hunters at Stirling in 1288–90 (Stuart and Burnett 1878, 38). The effectiveness of these hunting campaigns is extremely difficult to judge. Very few wolf remains have been reported from medieval British archaeological contexts, although the two best-known examples from Aberdeen and Rockingham were situated within or close to royal hunting landscapes (see Pluskowski 2006b). Quite probably the result of sustained hunting was the isolation of discrete populations followed by a loss of genetic variability and a reduction in fitness over a few generations. If positively identifiable medieval wolf remains are found in future excavations, genetic analysis combined with high-resolution dating may be able to shed new light on the extinction of the species in Britain.

The only other large carnivore potentially still surviving in the wilder regions of the British landscape by the twelfth century may have been the lynx (*Lynx lynx*). With more specific habitat preferences, the decline and extinction of the species can be linked to cumulative deforestation and limited prey availability, rather than sustained hunting. Indeed there is very little direct archaeological evidence for the species, but the last population may have been confined to the Grampian Mountains in north-east Scotland (Hetherington 2010, 81). The smaller wild cat, also dependent on wooded habitats, survived for longer, but rarely features in medieval zooarchaeological assemblages (Kitchener and O'Connor 2010). The indigenous bear (*Ursus arctos*) had vanished from the British landscape during the early medieval period, although live brown bears and occasional body parts were subsequently imported from Continental Europe (Hammon 2010, 100–1; see below). These carnivores could be exploited for their pelts, but smaller species of fur-bearing mammals were much more commercially valuable by the twelfth century. These consisted of various mustelids, red squirrels (*Sciurus vulgaris*), and beavers (*Castor fiber*). Their remains are found very infrequently on medieval sites, for the reason that fur-working was a concentrated activity, associated with a well-established industry (Baxter and Hamilton-Dyer 2003). A few assemblages can be linked to waste from fur-working (see Chapter 7). Where they feature in other contexts, they represent opportunistic catches, as can be linked to occasional hunting in a free warren. The late medieval fur trade was international, well organized, and dominated by specific regional suppliers (Delort 1978). In England, rabbits (and lambs) were bred for the fur market, although the former were ultimately sourced from a network of aristocratic and monastic warrens. Rabbit hunting became associated with domesticated ferrets, with suggestions that both may have been introduced into Britain as part of a 'coney culture' package (Van Dam 2001, 162). The other varieties of fur on the market were more readily sourced, in bulk, from the Baltic Sea region and Russian Taiga. The evidence for the survival of beaver populations is as obscure as the wolf or lynx, with remains not reported in archaeological contexts dating after the twelfth century. Nonetheless, arguments, based on tentative documentary sources, have been made for their survival as late as the early nineteenth century (Coles 2010, 115).

The final category of wild mammals at the fringes of human management in late medieval settlements is that of small commensals. The largest assemblages of smaller vertebrates have been recovered from urban contexts, where they tend to be interpreted as 'predator debris' or other natural expirations, rather than the result of human economic activities (Armitage et al. 1985, 121–3; O'Connor 2003, 197). Their remains are typically used as ecological proxies, contributing to the reconstruction of local ecosystems, situated within the broader context of urban ecology. Black rats (*Rattus rattus*) and certain species of mice recovered from urban contexts have been used as indicators of nearby rubbish dumps and houses; voles and shrews of more rural landscapes; moles and hedgehogs of open spaces such as gardens (Nicholson 2004, 535). Urban gardens, together with churchyards and waste ground, were virtually 'habitat islands' separated by areas of dense human occupation with little greenery (Armitage 1985). Excavations have revealed how some urban tenements could go through periods of abandonment, becoming overgrown and resulting in the development of relatively bio-diverse patches of wilderness (Arnold et al. 2006). An assemblage from a well in the garden of the Franciscan friary in London, dating to *c*.1480–1500, included the remains of an estimated 64 individuals, representing three species of mice, two species of vole, three species of shrew, black rat, hedgehog, and weasel (Armitage et al. 1985). The remains of these small animals had accumulated as a pit-fall deposit over as much as a 50-year period, and suggested the surrounding garden was overgrown and contained a rich variety of habitats: thick grassland, scrub, water-filled ditches and/or ponds, perhaps even hedges and orchards.

One species which appears to have gone largely unrecorded by contemporaries in late medieval Britain, but which has been the focus of an ongoing debate in modern scholarship, is the black rat. Rats were a ubiquitous urban fauna in England by the eleventh and twelfth centuries, with evidence for an increasing population spreading beyond major towns to a broader range of settlements in the thirteenth and fourteenth centuries (Rielly 2010, 143). The Black Rat has traditionally been regarded as the major vector for the pathogen which caused the mid-fourteenth century Black Death pandemic, with ongoing scholarly disagreements focusing on the identity of the disease (for contrasting perspectives, see Benedictow 2010 and Hufthammera and Walløe 2013). Wild mammals are widely recognized as disease vectors, with the most terrifying in medieval Britain represented by sporadic episodes of rabies, such as in 1166, when the *Annales Cambriae* recorded that a rabid wolf had bitten twenty-two people in the town of Carmarthen, in south Wales (Ithel 1860, 51–2).

Importing Exotics

Late medieval hunting culture, as outlined above, increasingly revolved around those exotics imported in the later eleventh and early twelfth century, particularly fallow deer, rabbits, and pheasants. All three species were confined in guarded enclosures, where they could be managed: parks. Along with warrens, dovecotes, and fishponds they became quintessential symbols of lordship (Williamson 2006, 7). This culture of confinement was extended to rarer exotics that were imported into Britain from the frontiers of Latin Christendom. Henry I's park at Woodstock which contained lions, leopards, and camels, may have been based on Sicilian models, a cultural emulation more evident in the proliferation of enclosed fallow deer (Sykes 2004, 80–1; see Chapter 25 in this *Handbook*). Most of what is known about these exotics comes from written sources, and the most spectacular were always monarchical gifts; Henry III had received an elephant from the French King Louis IX and a polar bear from the Norwegian King Haakon in 1252. Both animals were kept within the precincts of the Tower of London; both died within a few years of arriving. More effort went into the maintenance of lions, which are listed in a number of European royal, aristocratic, and later urban patrician sites (for a full survey, see Loisel 1912). The regal status of the lion in the West had already been established in the *Physiologus* and by the latter half of the twelfth century, in both Latin and vernacular 'beast literature', the lion was, by default, the ruler of their metaphorical animal kingdoms (Haist 2000). Chrétien de Troyes' influential *Le Chevalier au Lion* (*Yvain*) written c.1175–81, used the lion to symbolize Christ alongside nobility, and its rescue by Yvain represented the resurrection of spiritual love within the knight (Harris 1949). In England, the motif of the grateful lion was adopted for the quintessential English hero, Guy of Warwick (Brodeur 1924). This association between Christian knights and lions may partly explain the animal's popularity in medieval European heraldry from the latter half of the twelfth century (Pastoureau 2000, 25–30), and in England the exotic cats housed within the Tower would have also functioned as living heraldic emblems (Shenton 2002). Two lion skulls, along with the partial skull of a leopard, were recovered from excavations in the moat of the Tower in the early twentieth century. Subsequently radiocarbon dated to c.1280–1385 and c.1420–1480, they belonged to young animals aged three to four years, and evidently kept in cramped conditions (O'Regan et al. 2006).

Given the higher purchasing power of urban households, captive wild animals were more likely to be found in towns. Pet monkeys met contemporary demands for the exotic and marvellous, and at least two examples have been found in medieval Britain (in Southampton and London; for a recent archaeological summary see Brisbane et al. 2007), whilst the other common living wild mammals brought into the urban environment—brown bears used for baiting—reinforced the ideology of a controlled and segregated space. The evidence for bear baiting as a popular, commercialized activity is limited before the sixteenth century, with excavated examples of bear remains

FIGURE 10.2 A misericord from St Mary's, Enville, Staffordshire, representing bear baiting (fifteenth century)

(© Mike Searle, CC BY-SA 2.0)

associated with known arenas or 'bear gardens' also dating from this time (Gaimster et al. 1990, 184). In England, commercialization and popularization is particularly evident from the last quarter of the fifteenth century, with 'bearwards' touring their masters' bears (and apes) around manors to test the prowess of dogs owned by the local gentry (Brownstein 1969, 244). However, earlier bear baiting and dancing is attested in sporadic written and artistic sources, and appears to have been visible in both urban and rural settings (Figure 10.2). Unlike the pursuit of bears in the mountains and forests of Continental Europe, widely recognized as one of the most dangerous types of hunt, the restrained bear was more easily overcome and emblematic of human control over the dangerous wild.

Conclusion

By the beginning of the fourteenth century, many wild mammal species had already been severely depleted and their habitats fragmented. Wolf (and perhaps lynx) populations were confined to more remote areas of Britain, wild boars were restricted to one small range, beavers vanish from the archaeological record, and the extirpation of roe deer from the Midlands and southern England was accelerated by their declassification as a beast of the forest in 1339 (Young 1979, 4). Red deer populations had shrunk to the extent that in the fifteenth century it was difficult to sustain hunts in certain forests. Any dependence on native wild fauna was gradually replaced by more reliable stocks of game in parks. These were not the hunting wildernesses of aristocratic fantasy, but concentrated species of deer, particularly fallow deer. These herds would be maintained and hunted by professional retinues, with staged hunts featuring as unusual, striking, and highly choreographed theatre.

Alongside fallow deer, the rabbit's popularity steadily increased, particularly in the later fourteenth century, as a form of agricultural diversification, and the proliferation of mainland warrens paralleled that of parks (Bailey 1988). This, in turn, fuelled a booming fur industry in the fourteenth and fifteenth centuries. The limited number of ferret and polecat remains before the thirteenth century can also be linked to this trend (Sykes and Curl 2006, 123–4). Wild species became more accessible over the course of the fourteenth century too. As incomes improved, upwardly mobile individuals could afford previously restricted meat (and indeed fur), which accounts for the presence of food preparation waste from game mammals and birds in a broad range of social contexts. This cannot all be attributed to poaching, despite the documented presence of a significant black market in venison. As the growing market economies of towns enabled their populations to acquire a diverse range of game, the aristocratic class reacted by diversifying their diet. Since the suite of wild mammals was limited, this involved procuring a greater range of wild bird species. This, in turn, resulted in the rising popularity of falconry, particularly amongst the knightly class. But again, the demand for a reliable supply prompted the creation of swanneries and peacock enclosures, whose consumption was even more carefully controlled than that of rabbits. As a result, the game dishes found on the tables of the most powerful nobility in Britain from the fourteenth century were dominated by fallow deer, rabbits, swans, and peacocks, a trend that continued into the sixteenth century.

The final categories of wild species, and the last exclusive preserve of the late medieval aristocracy, were exotics. Again, a ranking of species is evident, from the live North African monkeys available to clerics and merchants to the elephants, polar bears, and white gyrfalcons presented as gifts to monarchs. Exotics were widely recognized currency within medieval European courtly circles, and some of the most powerful magnates created enclosures where they could be housed, what would later be referred to as *ménageries*. In England, the park at Woodstock, Oxfordshire, initially served as the main royal enclosure for exotics, but in the mid-thirteenth century this became a virtual farm for the royal herd of white fallow deer and the exotics were moved to the Tower of London. At this time, when the heraldic lion was becoming increasingly used as a symbol of English monarchy, it is not surprising that a group of lions was deliberately maintained into the fourteenth and fifteenth centuries, whilst other exotics (including other big cats such as leopards) came and went. It is telling that by the sixteenth century the wolf was deemed exotic enough to be housed in the Tower. This animal represented the long-term legacy of the Norman Conquest; the depletion and eradication of native fauna and their replacement with imported and curated exotics. The story of 'the wild' in late medieval Britain is therefore one of ecological transformation, and of the pragmatic and responsive implementation of an evolving paradigm of aristocratic dominion.

References cited

Albarella, U. 2006 'Pig husbandry and pork consumption in medieval England', in E. M. Woolgar, D. Serjeantson, and T. Waldron (eds), *Food in medieval England: diet and nutrition*, Oxford University Press, Oxford, 72–87

Albarella, U. 2010 'The wild boar', in T. O'Connor and N. J. Sykes (eds), *Extinctions and invasions: a social history of British fauna*, Oxbow, Oxford, 59–67

Albarella, U. and Thomas, R. 2002 'They dined on crane: bird consumption, wild fowling and status in medieval England', *Acta zoologica cracoviensia* 45, 23–38

Armitage, P. L. 1985 'Small mammal faunas in later medieval towns: a preliminary study in British urban biogeography', *The Biologist* 32(2), 65–71

Armitage, P. L., West, B., Clark, B. T., Dyson, T., Festing, M. F. W., and Locker, A. 1985 'Faunal evidence from a late medieval garden well of the Greyfriars, London', *Transactions of the London and Middlesex Archaeological Society* 36, 107–36

Arnold, P. G., Sadler, J. P., Hill, M. O., Pullin, A., Rushton, S., Austin, K., Small, E., Ward, B., Wadsworth, R., Sanderson, R., and Thompson, K. 2006 'Biodiversity in urban habitat patches', *Science of the Total Environment* 360, 196–204

Bailey, M. 1988 'The rabbit and the medieval East Anglian economy', *Agricultural History Review* 36, 1–20

Baker, K. H. and Hoelzel, R. 2013 'Evolution of population genetic structure of the British roe deer by natural and anthropogenic processes (*Capreolus capreolus*)', *Ecology and Evolution* 3(1), 89–102

Baxter, I. L. and Hamilton-Dyer, S. 2003 'Foxy in furs? A note on evidence for the probable commercial exploitation of the red fox and other fur bearing mammals in Saxo-Norman Hertford, Hertfordshire', *Archaeofauna* 12, 87–94

Benedictow, O. 2010 *What disease was plague? On the controversy over the microbiological identity of plague epidemics of the past*, Brill, Leiden

Bramwell, D. 1969 'Identification of bird bones', in P. A. Rahtz (ed.), *Excavations at King John's hunting lodge, Writtle, Essex, 1955–57*, The Society for Medieval Archaeology Monograph 3, London, 115

Brisbane, M., Hambleton, E., Maltby, M., and Nosov, E. 2007 'A monkey's tale: the skull of a macaque found at Ryurik Gorodishche, near Novgorod', *Medieval Archaeology* 51, 185–91

Brodeur, A. G. 1924 'The grateful lion', *Publications of the Modern Language Association of America* 29, 485–524

Brownstein, O. 1969 'The popularity of baiting in England before 1600: a study in social and theatrical history', *Educational Theatre Journal* 21(3), 237–50

Cherryson, A. D. 2002 'The identification of archaeological evidence for hawking in medieval England', *Acta zoologica cracoviensia* 45, 307–14

Clay, C. T. (ed.) 1942 *Early Yorkshire Charters IV*, Printed for the Yorkshire Archaeological Society, Leeds

Coles, B. 2010 'The European beaver', in T. O'Connor and N. J. Sykes (eds), *Extinctions and invasions: a social history of British fauna*, Oxbow, Oxford, 104–15

Delort, R. 1978 *Le commerce des fourrures en occident á la fin du Moyen âge (vers 1300–vers 1450)*, 2 volumes, Ecole française de Rome, Rome

Gaimster, D., Margeson, S., and Hurley, M. 1990 'Medieval Britain and Ireland in 1989', *Medieval Archaeology* 134, 162–252

Gilbert, J. M. 1979 *Hunting and hunting reserves in medieval Scotland*, Donald, Edinburgh

Haist, M. 2000 'The lion, bloodline and kingship', in D. Hassig (ed.), *The mark of the beast: the medieval bestiary in art, life, and literature*, Routledge, New York, 18–19

Hammon, A. 2010 'The bear', in T. O'Connor and N. J. Sykes (eds), *Extinctions and invasions: a social history of British fauna*, Oxbow, Oxford, 95–103

Harris, J. 1949 'The role of the lion in Chrétien de Troyes "Yvain"', *Publications of the Modern Language Association of America* 64, 1143–63

Hetherington, D. 2010 'The lynx', in T. O'Connor and N. J. Sykes (eds), *Extinctions and invasions: a social history of British fauna*, Oxbow, Oxford, 75–82

Hufthammera, A. K. and Walløe, L. 2013 'Rats cannot have been intermediate hosts for *Yersinia pestis* during medieval plague epidemics in Northern Europe', *Journal of Archaeological Science* 40(4), 1752–9

Ithel, J. W. 1860 *Annales Cambriae*, Longman, London

Judkins, R. R. 2013 'The game of the courtly hunt: chasing and breaking deer in late medieval English literature', *Journal of English and Germanic Philology* 112(1), 70–92

Kitchener, A. C. and O'Connor, T. 2010 'Wildcats, domestic and feral cats', in T. O'Connor and N. J. Sykes (eds), *Extinctions and invasions: a social history of British fauna*, Oxbow, Oxford, 83–94

Langton, J. 2010 'Medieval forests and chases: another realm?', in J. Langton and G. Jones (eds), *Forests and chases of medieval England and Wales, c.1000–c.1500*, St John's College Research Centre, Oxford, 14–35

Langton, J. and Jones, G. 2010 'Deconstructing and reconstructing the forests: some preliminary matters', in J. Langton and G. Jones (eds), *Forests and chases of medieval England and Wales, c.1000–c.1500*, St. John's College Research Centre, Oxford, 1–13

Lieberman, M. 2010 *The medieval March of Wales*, Cambridge University Press, Cambridge

Loisel, G. 1912 *Histoire des ménageries de l'antiquité à nos jours*, 2 volumes, Octave Doin, Paris

Nicholson, R. A. 2004 'Animal husbandry and exploitation', in H. Dalwood and R. Edwards (eds), *Excavations at Deansway, Worcester 1988–89: Romano-British small town to late medieval city*, Council for British Archaeology Research Report 139, York, 94–6

O'Connor, T. 2003 *The analysis of urban animal bone assemblages: a handbook for archaeologists*, Council for British Archaeology, York

O'Connor, T. 2007 'Wild or domestic? Biometric variation in the cat *Felis silvestris* Schreber', *International Journal of Osteoarchaeology* 17, 581–95

O'Connor, T. and Sykes, N. J. (eds) 2010 *Extinctions and invasions: a social history of British fauna*, Oxbow, Oxford

Offer, A. 1997 'Between the gift and the market: the economy of regard', *Economic History Review* 50(3), 450–76

O'Regan, H., Turner, A., and Sabin, R. 2006 'Medieval big cat remains from the Royal Menagerie at the Tower of London', *International Journal of Osteoarchaeology* 16(2), 385–94

Pastoureau, M. 2000 'Pourquoi tant de lions dans l'occident medieval', *Micrologus* 8(1), 11–30

Pluskowski, A. G. 2006a 'Where are the wolves? Investigating the scarcity of European Grey Wolf (*Canis lupus lupus*) remains in medieval archaeological contexts and its implications', *International Journal of Osteoarchaeology* 16, 279–95

Pluskowski, A. G. 2006b *Wolves and the wilderness in the Middle Ages*, Boydell, Woodbridge

Poole, K. 2010 'Bird introductions', in T. O'Connor and N. J. Sykes (eds), *Extinctions and invasions: a social history of British fauna*, Oxbow, Oxford, 156–65

Rielly, K. 2010 'The black rat', in T. O'Connor and N. J. Sykes (eds), *Extinctions and invasions: a social history of British fauna*, Oxbow, Oxford, 134–45

Serjeantson, D. 2010 'Extinct birds', in T. O'Connor and N. J. Sykes (eds), *Extinctions and invasions: a social history of British fauna*, Oxbow, Oxford, 146–55

Shenton, C. 2002 'Edward III and the symbol of the leopard', in P. Coss and M. Keen (eds), *Heraldry, pageantry and social display in medieval England*, Boydell, Woodbridge, 69–81

Stone, D. J. 2006 'The consumption and supply of birds in late medieval England', in E. M. Woolgar, D. Serjeantson, and T. Waldron (eds), *Food in medieval England: diet and nutrition*, Oxford University Press, Oxford, 148–61

Stuart, J. and Burnett, G. (eds) 1878 *The Exchequer Rolls of Scotland*, vol. 1, Edinburgh, General Register House

Sykes, N. J. 2004 'The introduction of fallow deer to Britain: a zooarchaeological perspective', *Environmental Archaeology* 9, 75–83

Sykes, N. J. 2006 'The impact of the Normans on hunting practices in England', in E. M. Woolgar, D. Serjeantson, and T. Waldron (eds), *Food in medieval England: diet and nutrition*, Oxford University Press, Oxford, 162–75

Sykes, N. J. 2007a *The Norman Conquest: a zooarchaeological perspective*, Archaeopress, Oxford

Sykes, N. J. 2007b 'Taking sides: the social life of venison in medieval England', in A. G. Pluskowski (ed.), *Breaking and shaping beastly bodies: animals as material culture in the Middle Ages*, Oxbow, Oxford, 149–60

Sykes, N. J. and Curl, J. 2010 'The rabbit', in T. O'Connor and N. J. Sykes (eds), *Extinctions and invasions: a social history of British fauna*, Oxbow, Oxford, 116–26

Van Dam, P. J. E. M. 2001 'Status loss due to ecological success: landscape change and the spread of the rabbit', *Innovation* 14(2), 157–70

Williamson, T. 2006 *The archaeology of rabbit warrens*, Shire, Princes Risborough

Woolgar, C. M. 1999 *The great household in late medieval England*, Yale University Press, New Haven

Yalden, D. W. 1999 *The history of British mammals*, T. & A. D. Poyser, London

Yalden, D. W. and Albarella, U. 2009 *The history of British birds*, Oxford University Press, Oxford

Young, C. R. 1979 *The Royal Forests of medieval England*, Leicester University Press, Leicester

CHAPTER 11

COPING WITH DISASTER

PETER J. BROWN

THE medieval period was punctuated by catastrophic events. Wars, political unrest, famines, and plagues all took their toll on an agrarian society that largely depended on the success of the harvest. The difficulties that these types of events could engender is perhaps best illustrated by episodes of particularly sharp economic decline such as the famine of 1315–22 or the outbreak of plague three decades later (1348–52). The widespread effect of the 1315–22 famine drove living standards to an all-time low and it took many years for the livestock market to fully recover from the accompanying panzootic (Campbell 2010a, 289–90; Kershaw 1973). The effect of the Black Death was even more profound with unprecedented mortality, evidenced by mass graves, suddenly reversing the economic and demographic growth of the previous centuries (Campbell 2010b, 29; Gowland and Chamberlain 2005). Although these events were certainly exceptional, many smaller-scale disasters also rocked medieval society over the course of the Middle Ages. This chapter analyses one category of event, natural hazards, which in Britain are mainly weather-related (flooding, lightning, windstorms, and wind-blown sand). Given that weather is heavily influenced by climatic fluctuations, a brief overview of this topic is presented first.

CLIMATE AND WEATHER

Climatic change over the medieval period has been a major focus for climatologists since the mid-twentieth century. Through disparate strands of evidence, including historical records, ice cores, glaciology, and dendrochronology, this has led to the recognition of two epochs: the Medieval Climate Anomaly *c.*900–*c.*1300 (also called the Medieval Warm Period), and the Little Ice Age *c.*1300–*c.*1900. The Medieval Climate Anomaly has long been characterized as a time of warmer conditions which saw the occupation of Iceland, viniculture in southern England, and a boom in British medieval population and economic activity while, conversely, the Little Ice Age was a time of deterioration and contraction with colder summer temperatures, increased winter storm intensity, and advancing glaciers (Hughes and Diaz 1994; Matthews and Briffa 2005). Certainly for Northern Europe this picture retains some value but a growing number of proxy records are demonstrating that significant temporal and regional fluctuations occurred throughout both periods (e.g. Dawson et al. 2007; Trouet et al. 2012), highlighting the complexity behind the often over-simplistic model which has been applied to historical and archaeological interpretations. This picture is likely to become increasingly nuanced as more data are amassed and new techniques are developed to study the changing climate of the past.

The impact of environmental forces such as gradual climatic change, annual-decadal fluctuations, and short-term weather events on past populations has frequently been treated with scepticism by historians and archaeologists. While some studies (Parry 1975, 11) have demonstrated a possible link between climatic and cultural change, researchers have been careful to emphasize the marginal impact of climate compared to endogenous forces such as economy and demography (Campbell 2010b, 282; Parry 1981, 16). In a much-debated case study from medieval archaeology, Guy Beresford faced heavy criticism for linking increased rainfall with abandonment at Barton Blount, Derbyshire, and (the village identified as) Goltho, Lincolnshire. The local clay soils, he argued, would have become unworkable following episodes of extreme precipitation, presumed to have become more frequent with the onset of the Little Ice Age, forcing populations to migrate (Beresford 1975, 51–2). Detractors pointed to the fact that neighbouring villages experienced no comparable depopulation, proving that climate was unlikely to have been a major factor, as 'raindrops [are not] locally selective' (Beresford and Hurst 1971, 21), with the post-Black Death economic and demographic situation cited as a more plausible explanation (Wright 1976). Beresford (1981, 36) countered that the variation could be explained by minimal differences in local soil composition and indeed soil chemistry and geology are now beginning to be recognized as major determining factors in the development of medieval villages (Rippon et al. 2014, 200–1; Williamson et al. 2013, 79–80) although it remains to be proved whether this contributed to village desertion in Beresford's case studies. While it is probably true that economic and demographic concerns were the fundamental factors behind abandonment, as some have since conceded (Stern 2000, xlix–l), Beresford's argument probably holds some value which has largely gone unappreciated.

If connecting environmental change to cultural developments is a controversial topic, then the challenge of linking climatic data with archaeological and historical evidence compounds the problem. While climatic data, depending on the type of proxy, often operates at an annual scale, archaeological remains can rarely be tightly dated (Cooper and Peros 2010, 1226–7) although this problem can be mediated for historic periods through documentary evidence, where it is available. Even when climatic and cultural changes can be shown to be simultaneous, however, it must be remembered that correlation does not imply causation (Coombes and Barber 2005, 305). An important consideration must be the degree to which climatic changes were perceptible in pre-instrumental periods (Bell 2012). Outside of particularly harsh or ameliorable seasons, gradual climatic changes may not have been noticeable. Short-term extreme weather events, however, which could become more frequent and/or more intense in times of fluctuating climate (Trouet et al. 2012), must have been a very real concern. It is therefore probable that the impact of climate and weather, in common with the theory of punctuated equilibrium which envisages periods of stability and consistency interrupted by sudden episodes of change (Gould 1999, xviii–xix), was felt most when populations were struck by sudden extreme meteorological hazards. The catastrophic impact of such events in Britain has been exemplified by more recent disasters such as the North Sea storm surge of 1953, the windstorm of 1987, and the floods of winter 2013/14, to name only a select few. Although similar events are well known from the medieval period (e.g. Bailey 1991), their impact has only rarely been a focus for archaeologists (Brown 1997, 140–1; Hall and Price 2012, 55). The remainder of this chapter, therefore, considers the effect of these events on medieval society and the reactions they provoked.

The Moment of Disaster

The physical impact of meteorological hazards is usually limited to a short span of time, although the social repercussions can continue for months, years, or even decades. Identifying evidence for the occurrence of these events, however, can pose problems. While floods deposit sediments and wind-blown sand is usually preserved in discrete stratigraphic layers, these can be cleared subsequently by anthropogenic or natural forces while windstorms and lightning strikes rarely leave identifiable signatures. Some case studies though, do provide tantalizing evidence for the short-term effect of hazards in the past. One such example comes from the burnt remains of a thirteenth-century house at Pennard, Swansea, Wales, discovered beneath a layer of wind-blown sand. The excavators recovered broken pottery from the floor which appeared to be *in situ*, having fallen from a height, probably from hooks or furniture during the fire (Moorhouse 1985, 5). It seems unlikely that a burnt-out house in a settlement would have gone undisturbed unless the wind-blown sand had almost immediately covered over its remains, suggesting the fire and aeolian sand accumulation were near-contemporaneous events. A parallel, at Fuller's Hill, Great Yarmouth, Norfolk, where burnt layers were interspersed with blown sand was interpreted by the excavators as the result of the pressure of wind and sand on structures which collapsed in onto open hearths (Rogerson 1976, 159) which also convincingly explains the formation of the site at Pennard. A likely scenario is therefore that a storm together with aeolian sand destabilized the house which collapsed in upon itself setting alight the building, incinerating furniture, and sending ceramics onto the floor where they smashed only to be rapidly covered over by encroaching sand. Presumably, as no skeletal remains were encountered, the inhabitants were able to escape to safety.

In some cases, entire settlements bear the mark of changes brought about by the action of natural hazards over the short term. This can be seen at New Romney, Kent, where sediments of sand and shingle brought in by storm surge floods over the winter of 1287/8 caused widespread damage (Gardiner and Hartwell 2006; Tatton-Brown 1988, 108), altering the morphology of the town to the extent that the church of Saint Nicholas has ever since been entered by descending a flight of stairs from the post-storm street level (Figure 11.1). Although the chancel was subsequently replaced, the event can be traced within the surviving Norman nave where the murky flood waters permanently stained the pillars (Grimson 1978, 34). Nearby at Old Winchelsea, although a series of earlier storms had already caused damage to the extent that the town had been relocated by Royal Decree some 2 km inland, the storms of 1287/8 completely submerged the site of the mainly abandoned settlement (Martin and Martin 2004, 2–6). Comparable losses can be seen at many medieval coastal sites such as Dunwich, Suffolk, where storms throughout the thirteenth and fourteenth centuries (and later) eroded the coastline sending a large proportion of the town into the sea (Sear et al. 2011). Similarly, at Ravenser Odd, East Yorkshire, the town was engulfed by the sea in *c*.1310–*c*.1360 as the morphology of Spurn Head responded to storms and wave action (De Boer 1964, 82–3).

FIGURE 11.1 The steps descending into St Nicholas's Church, New Romney, Kent, made necessary by sediments brought in by a storm surge in 1287/8

(© Tony Clark, CC BY-SA 2.0)

Prior to these events, both places were thriving mercantile ports and their decline substantially altered the regional economic landscape allowing nearby ports to benefit from increased trade (Bailey 1991, 197–8) while their own inhabitants faced material loss, expensive repairs, and even homelessness.

Where historical records are available, particularly detailed reconstructions of the effects of extreme events can be traced through the standing remains of medieval structures. The timber spire of Glasgow Cathedral, for example, was ignited by lightning shortly before 1406. Although excavations inside the cathedral failed to detect any evidence for the fire, perhaps due to the relaying of the floor in the eighteenth century (Driscoll 2002, 8, 161), structural evidence does attest to the damage. While the roof bosses in the south choir aisle from the time of Bishop Wardlaw (1367–87) pre-date the fire, those in the north choir aisle date from 1508–23 and the ribs and vaulting in the same area show evidence of later repairs (Ralegh Radford 1970, 23). In the chapter house, only the lower courses consist of original thirteenth-century stonework, with later reparations above (Fawcett 1996, 65, 70, fig. 20) and the vestry, located above the thirteenth-century treasury on the north side of the cathedral, may also have been damaged as documentary evidence indicates its repair after the time of the fire and its location is consistent with the other damage (McRoberts 1966, 40–2). If this damage pattern was a result of the lightning-induced fire (Figure 11.2), the swarm of repairs 'fossilized' within

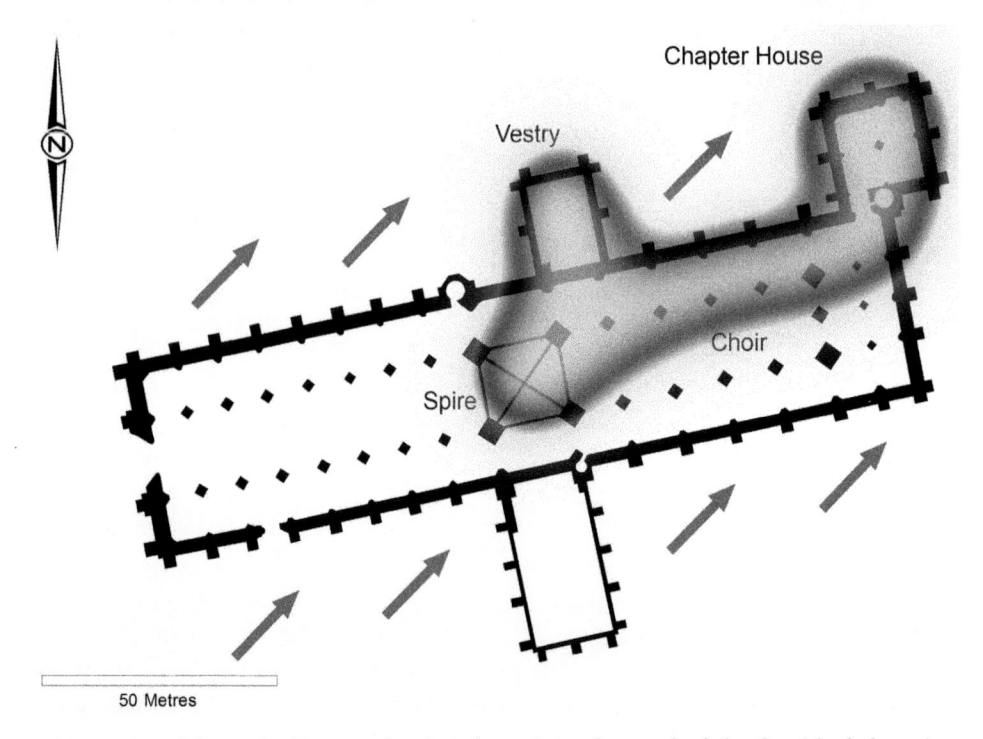

FIGURE 11.2 Schematic diagram showing the estimated spread of the fire (shaded area) at Glasgow Cathedral. Arrows indicate inferred wind direction

(© Peter J. Brown)

the current structure suggests that a south-westerly wind, Glasgow's prevailing wind, spread the flames from the central spire towards the north-east corner of the cathedral (Durkan 1975, 90–1). A cautionary tale to a structural biography such as this, however, comes from the Abbey of Strata Florida, Ceredigion, in Wales where lightning is also reported to have burnt large parts of the Cistercian church in 1284 (Christie 1887, 115–17). While excavations in the nineteenth century uncovered melted lead roofing (Williams 1889a, 153), a detail specifically mentioned in the written sources describing the fire, it is impossible to confirm whether the melted lead recovered in the excavations was a product of the lightning strike of 1284 because the historical record is rich with other conflagrations, all of which are candidates (e.g. Williams 1889b, 26–7).

Mitigating the Damage

In most cases, medieval society was poorly equipped to mitigate the effects of natural hazards (Gerrard and Petley 2013). Then as now, there was no practical way to lower flood levels or lessen the force of the wind. Lightning-induced fires could be extinguished but fire-fighting technology was basic. A list given by the seventeenth-century surveyor and mathematician George Atwell (1662, 95), which equally applies to the medieval period, describes the most effective tools for fighting fires as 'pikes, forks, ladders, buckets, wet blankets, sand, ashes, horse manure, dust and dirt'. So ill-equipped were populations that when fires were extinguished it was viewed as miraculous. This occurred at Keyingham, East Yorkshire, when the church of Saint Nicholas was ignited by a lightning strike but the suppression of the fire and the fact that no harm befell the volunteer fire-fighters was attributed to the intercession of the former rector Philip Inglebard, whose tomb had been found to exude a sweet oil in the blaze and was later held responsible for a number of miracles (Bond 1868, 194–5).

Where the impact of hazards was severe and divine intercession provided no respite, medieval populations had no option but to flee. Floods certainly provoked short-term abandonment at some monastic houses such as the Franciscans of Reading, Berkshire (Martin 1885, 911–12), and the nuns of Crabhouse Priory, Norfolk (Page 1906, 408). As already mentioned, a number of coastal settlements were depopulated as a result of storms and storm surges but sand inundations also sparked abandonments (Brown 2015). At Forvie, Aberdeenshire, a settlement was engulfed by aeolian sand when a southerly storm coincided with an extreme low tide in 1413, exposing an especially large body of sand to fierce storm conditions (Lamb 1982, 185). Survivors were forced to abandon the town, a fact which is supported by the archaeological evidence (e.g. Kirk 1957, 4) as well as the subsequent appearance of a chapel dedicated to Saint Adamnan, the same dedication as Forvie's parish Church, some 5 km to the north, probably attesting to a short-distance migration of the population after the storm event (MacGibbon and Ross 1897, 388). Similarly, the coastal settlement at Meols, Merseyside, was abandoned in the late fifteenth or early sixteenth century, most likely due to a catastrophic wind-blown sand event. Sequences of historic maps suggest that most of the population moved inland to a new site known as Great Meols which had formerly been marginal land within the parish but was later re-organized to provide a new home for the beleaguered inhabitants (Griffiths et al. 2007, 409–11, 414).

Besides escaping to safety, mitigation primarily took the form of spiritual supplications to God, the saints, or reliance on folk beliefs, and as a result they leave little trace in the material record. The popularity of prayers as a method of accruing protection in the face of natural disasters, in common with other difficulties including disease or famine, can be seen in widespread documentary evidence from across Europe (Hanska 2002, 91–3). In 1289, for example, the Bishop of Chichester encouraged parish priests to conduct prayers and processions whenever adverse weather conditions loomed without seeking prior permission from the archdeacon (Powicke and Cheney 1964, 1086). Similarly, in 1293, the Archbishop of York ordered special prayers for calm weather *pro serenitate aeris* to be said throughout the diocese (Raine 1873, 100–1). Likewise, the fifteenth-century Welsh poet Dafydd Nanmor records how the people of Y Ferwig, Ceredigon, turned to their patron saint, Petrog, to blow away the sands that had inundated their lands (Roberts and Williams 1923, 15–17, 132). While patron saints protected particular localities, other saints were invoked in the face of particular hazards. Saint Barbara, for example, was well regarded as a defender against lightning (Buzwell 2005, 17). One material manifestation for protective prayers may be found in folded coins (Figure 11.3), a practice in which a vow was made to a saint for deliverance from danger in a 'contract' between saint and supplicant (Duffy 1992, 184). Although this practice

FIGURE 11.3 A folded silver coin from the reign of Edward I or Edward II (1272–1327) from Flintshire, Wales

(© Portable Antiquities Scheme Object ID: NMGW-1223EC, CC BY)

was not exclusively employed in the mitigation of extreme weather, also providing cures from illness and good luck, their dense and widespread distribution, representing almost 1 per cent of all medieval numismatic finds from England and Wales in the database of the Portable Antiquities Scheme (Kelleher 2011, 1499; and see Chapter 32 in this *Handbook*), attests to the universality of the practice.

Rituals were also important methods for preventing or reducing damage from natural hazards. During a severe storm at Burton, Staffordshire, for example, 'As soon as the shrine of the holy virgin was placed on the ground, as if the saint was prostrating herself ... before the Lord on behalf of the church, all that wild storm abated immediately' (Bartlett 2002, 211). That this was a common practice is demonstrated by its inclusion in the late eleventh-century guidelines of Abbot William of Hirsau which prescribe that, in the event of a storm, the sacristan should set up the processional cross along with saintly relics and holy water at the side of the monastery's cloister closest to the approaching storm (Herrgott 1726, 524). In the popular compendium of hagiography *The golden legend*, Jacobus de Voragine elaborates that 'when storms come up, the cross is brought out of the church and held up against the tempest ... and the bells are rung that the demons who are in the air may flee in fright and desist from harassing us' (Ryan 1993, 288). This final detail, that the peel of church bells was believed to avert storms and lightning, is corroborated by church warden's accounts from Spalding, Lincolnshire, which record payments made to bell ringers in 1519 for ringing during a tempest (North 1882, 657). Beyond the monastic and ecclesiastical setting, lay people participated in similar rituals. In 1543, for instance, the reforming Protestants branded the parishioners of Northgate in Canterbury, Kent, heretical for dousing their homes with holy water during a thunderstorm (Gairdner and Brodie 1902, 300). Comparably, holy water was applied to fields to protect crops from threats including weather and disease, a fact which has been confirmed archaeologically through the distribution of *ampullae* in rural, agricultural settings (Anderson 2010, 199–200; Thomas 1971, 30) (Figure 11.4). Although popular beliefs and saintly cults were regionally variable, attempts to mitigate disaster appear to have adhered to a common framework.

PROTECTION AND ADAPTATION

As well as providing relief from disasters in the short term, spiritual and folk practices took on an important role in providing protection from future danger. This was especially the case with lightning as, due to an ignorance of electrical energy, medieval populations had no reliable physical defence, making spiritual protection the only viable option. Personal safety, for instance, could be accrued through possession of certain artefacts or materials. Emeralds, for example, were believed to protect against storms and lightning (Evans and Serjeantson 1933, 40, 85) and where real gems were unobtainable coloured glass may have been substituted (Standley 2013, 89–90). Similarly, as fossils, prehistoric lithics, and sea urchins were thought to be products of lightning

FIGURE 11.4 A fourteenth- to sixteenth-century lead *ampulla*, a container for holy water, oil, or ashes from the shrine of a saint, usually obtained through pilgrimage. This example was found in a rural context in the Vale of Glamorgan, Wales

(© Portable Antiquities Scheme Object ID: NMGW-514FAB, CC BY)

strikes, they were believed to protect individuals and structures from harm. As a result, they were sometimes curated beneath floors, in roof-spaces, or worn as pendants (Blinkenberg 1911; Gilchrist 2012, 247). Amulets and charms bearing the *Agnus Dei* symbol (e.g. Enticott 1996) probably also bestowed protection as Matthew Paris describes how a Papal *Agnus Dei*, a wax disc blessed by the Pope, was affixed to the tower at St Albans in the hope of averting future damage from lightning (Riley 1867, 313).

Although medieval populations had no protection from lightning, there were certainly material responses to other meteorological hazards. While medieval scholars were generally ignorant of the underlying factors behind extreme weather events, invariably explaining them in relation to the classical elements and the movement of celestial bodies (Jones 2013, 41), populations were well aware of their implications for society. As flooding was a recurrent hazard, those at risk undoubtedly became well aware of seasons, weather conditions, and local areas prone to floods. Bowler (2004, 14–19) hypothesized that flood-risk at Perth may even have resulted in land-value and social status becoming connected to topography, with the most important buildings and institutions occupying the highest ground while the poverty stricken endured low-lying land which was inundated relatively regularly. Where possible, floodplains and wetlands would have been avoided for permanent settlement but these remained extremely valuable resources, providing game, fish, plants, timber, and salt as well as rich pasture (Gardiner 2007) although livestock could easily perish in rapid-onset floods if shepherds were unable to herd them to safety (Whyte 2009, 70). Those floods which were sudden, unseasonal, and high magnitude probably led to the most devastating losses (Rohr 2005, 77), a fact which can be visualized archaeologically, for example, on the Trent where a succession of bridges were damaged, washed away, and rebuilt as extreme flood events led to channel migration (Brown 2009, 89). To protect against these inundations, defences were commonly built in areas where memory of recurrent floods persisted. Such was the case at Thornton Abbey, Lincolnshire, where excavation uncovered a dyke which had been overtopped by two layers of alluvium, demonstrating that these measures were not always successful (Willmott and Townend 2012, 19). Similar flood defences were revealed through topographical survey at Bordesley Abbey, Worcestershire, where the floor of the south transept was raised by 20-26 cm following inundation to prevent further damage (Aston 1972, 134–5; Hirst et al. 1983, 54–5). Reclaimed land was particularly vulnerable, although the increased agricultural yields made the risk worthwhile (Galloway 2012, 70), leading to expensive losses when dykes were overtopped and repairs were needed (e.g. Gardiner and Hartwell 2006, 155–6). Although the highest magnitude events could still precipitate disaster, material defences and social adaptations permitted a degree of resilience in the face of routine flooding.

Some evidence for adaptation can also be seen in medieval structures damaged in storm events where repairs and modifications attempted to minimize the effect of future storms. The damage inflicted to the south-western tower at Chichester Cathedral, West Sussex, by a windstorm in 1210 not only provoked extensive repairs but also the enlargement of the supporting buttress (Tatton-Brown 1996, 49). Similarly, the 1362 windstorm which swept through southern England prompted the insertion of an internal wooden scaffold to support the spire at Salisbury Cathedral, Wiltshire, in the event of high winds (Miles et al. 2004, 20). The same storm also destroyed the gatehouse at the Abbey of St Albans which was afterwards reconstructed, reusing masonry from the previous structure, with a strong lead roof (RCHME 1982, 31; Riley 1869, 387) which was perhaps intended to be more resilient to severe weather. That attempts to protect against future loss were rare is probably a reflection of cost. Far from reducing risk, many repairs cut financial corners, the structural measures taken to secure Norwich Cathedral's spire after 1463 being one example (Feilden 1996, 730–1).

While defences and adaptations to floods and storms were largely organized by individuals or local landowners, higher authorities did play a role. This was particularly the case in reclaimed wetlands where, for example, in the case of Romney Marsh, between Kent and East Sussex, local authorities emerged to manage the financial and practical arrangements for the construction and maintenance of flood defences (Bankoff 2013, 30). Town councils too, often legislated to keep municipal waterways free of refuse and industrial waste that might clog the riverbed and bring on an inundation (Jørgensen 2010). Authorities also frequently intervened in the aftermath of disaster. Following the windstorm of 1362, for example, a Royal Decree forbade workmen and roof-tilers from inflating their prices to take advantage of the widespread damage (Maxwell Lyte

1909, 238). Similarly, in the aftermath of flooding, reactionary Royal Commissions on walls and ditches (*de walliis et fossatis*) were formed to force landholders and tenants to contribute money and labour towards the repair and upkeep of flood defences in order to speed the return to normality. The increase in these commissions during the fourteenth century brings us back to the initial debate; Galloway and Potts (2007, 376–7) suggest that this was linked to the increased storminess of the Little Ice Age, although the upheaval of the Black Death probably also made some centralized intervention more necessary than in earlier times.

Conclusion

The impact of climate and weather in the later medieval period has sometimes been downplayed in favour of endogenous forces but short-term extreme weather events were certainly stimuli for bursts of localized change. Scientific evidence confirms that major climatic shifts occurred throughout the later Middle Ages but the impact of these fluctuations on populations and individuals has rarely been fully considered. While gradual changes were probably almost imperceptible, short-term fluctuations and extreme weather events must have been a very real concern. Although care should be taken not to exaggerate the impact of natural disasters in medieval Britain, when sudden, unpredictable, and high-intensity meteorological hazards did occur, they frequently determined the immediate future of individuals, institutions, structures, and settlements. In the most extreme events, whole or partial settlements, as at Forvie, Dunwich, and Pennard, were abandoned when floods, storms, or sand encroached onto areas of human habitation. In the moment of disaster, while material evidence of the event is sometimes preserved, the historical record demonstrates the wide range of, mainly spiritual, defences which are largely but not totally invisible to the archaeologist. In the interim between events, spiritual protection remained paramount but, particularly against flooding, medieval populations developed structural defences to prevent loss or damage and the resilience of communities was promoted through social adaptation and the intervention of authorities. The combination of archaeological and historical evidence, therefore, provides an unparalleled insight into the relationship between past human society and environmental change, a subject which despite the rapid growth in climate-related research has not yet been fully addressed.

References cited

Anderson, W. 2010 'Blessing the fields? A study of late-medieval ampullae from England and Wales', *Medieval Archaeology* 54, 182–203

Aston, M. 1972 'The earthworks of Bordesley Abbey, Redditch, Worcestershire', *Medieval Archaeology* 16, 133–6

Atwell, G. 1662 *The faithfull surveyour*, William Nealand, Cambridge

Bailey, M. 1991 '*Per impetum maris*: natural disaster and economic decline in eastern England, 1275-1350', in B. M. S. Campbell (ed.), *Before the Black Death: studies in the 'crisis' of the early fourteenth century*, Manchester University Press, Manchester and New York, 184-208

Bankoff, G. 2013 'The "English Lowlands" and the North Sea Basin system: a history of shared risk', *Environment and History* 19, 3-37

Bartlett, R. (ed.) 2002 *Geoffrey of Burton, life and miracles of St Modwenna*, Oxford University Press, Oxford

Bell, M. 2012 'Climate change, extreme weather events and issues of human perception', *Archaeological Dialogues* 19(1), 42-6

Beresford, G. 1975 *The medieval clay-land village: excavations at Goltho and Barton Blount*, The Society for Medieval Archaeology Monograph 6, London

Beresford, G. 1981 'Climatic change and its effect upon the settlement and desertion of medieval villages in Britain', in C. Delano Smith and M. Parry (eds), *Consequences of climatic change*, University of Nottingham, Nottingham, 30-9

Beresford, M. and Hurst, J. G. 1971 *Deserted medieval villages*, Lutterworth Press, London

Blinkenberg, C. 1911 *The thunderweapon in religion and folklore: a study in comparative archaeology*, Cambridge University Press, Cambridge

Bond, E. A. (ed.) 1868 *Chronica monasterii de Melsa, Volume III*, Her Majesty's Stationery Office, London

Bowler, D. P. 2004 *Perth: the archaeology and development of a Scottish burgh*, Tayside and Fife Archaeological Committee Monograph 3, Perth

Brown, P. J. 2015 'Coasts of catastrophe? The incidence and impact of aeolian sand on British medieval coastal communities', *Post Classical Archaeologies* 5, 127-48

Brown, T. 1997 'Clearances and clearings: deforestation in Mesolithic/Neolithic Britain', *Oxford Journal of Archaeology* 16(2), 133-46

Brown, T. 2009 *The environment and aggregate-related archaeology*, Oxbow Books, Oxford

Buzwell, G. 2005 *Saints in medieval manuscripts*, University of Toronto Press, Toronto

Campbell, B. M. S. 2010a 'Nature as historical protagonist: environment and society in pre-industrial England', *The Economic History Review* 63(2), 281-314

Campbell, B. M. S. 2010b 'Physical shocks, biological hazards, and human impacts: the crisis of the fourteenth century revisited', in S. Cavaciocchi (ed.), *Le interazioni fra economia e ambiente biologico nell'Europa preindustriale secc. XIII-XVIII*, Istituto Internazionale de Storia Economica 'F. Datini', Prato, 13-32

Christie, R. C. (ed.) 1887 *Annales Cestrienses: or Chronicle of the Abbey of S. Werburg, at Chester*, The Record Society, London

Coombes, P. and Barber, K. 2005 'Environmental determinism in Holocene research: causality or coincidence?', *Area* 37(3), 303-11

Cooper, J. and Peros, M. 2010 'The archaeology of climate change in the Caribbean', *Journal of Archaeological Science* 37(6), 1226-32

Dawson, A. G., Hickey, K., Mayewski, P. A., and Nesje, A. 2007 'Greenland (GISP2) ice core and historical indicators of complex North Atlantic climate changes during the fourteenth century', *The Holocene* 17(4), 427-34

De Boer, G. 1964 'Spurn Head: its history and evolution', *Transactions and Papers (Institute of British Geographers)* 34, 71-89

Driscoll, S. 2002 *Excavations at Glasgow Cathedral 1988-1997*, The Society for Medieval Archaeology Monograph 18, London

Duffy, E. 1992 *The stripping of the altars: traditional religion in England c.1400–c.1580*, Yale University Press, New Haven and London

Durkan, J. 1975 'The Great Fire at Glasgow Cathedral', *The Innes Review* 26, 89–92

Enticott, D. 1996 'Medieval pendant from Gleaston', *Contrebis* 21, 10

Evans, J. and Serjeantson, M. S. 1933 *English medieval lapidaries*, Oxford University Press, Oxford

Fawcett, R. 1996 'Current thinking on Glasgow Cathedral', in T. W. T. Tatton-Brown and J. Munby (eds), *The archaeology of cathedrals*, Oxford University Committee for Archaeology Monograph 42, Oxford, 57–72

Feilden, B. M. 1996 'Restorations and repairs after World War II', in I. Atherton, E. Fernie, C. Harper-Bill, and H. Smith (eds), '*Norwich Cathedral: church, city and diocese, 1096–1996*, The Hambledon Press, London, 728–44

Gairdner, J. and Brodie, R. H. (eds) 1902 *Letters and papers, foreign and domestic, of the reign of Henry VIII*, Her Majesty's Stationery Office, London

Galloway, J. A. 2012 'Tempests of weather and great abundance of water: the flooding of the Barking marshes in the later Middle Ages', in M. Davies and J. A. Galloway (eds), *London and beyond: essays in honour of Derek Keene*, Institute of Historical Research, London, 67–83

Galloway, J. A. and Potts, J. S. 2007 'Marine flooding in the Thames Estuary and tidal river c.1250–1450: impact and response', *Area* 39(3), 370–9

Gardiner, M. 2007 The transformation of marshlands in Anglo-Norman England', in C. P. Lewis (ed.), *Anglo-Norman studies XXIX: proceedings of the Battle Conference 2006*, Boydell Press, Woodbridge, 35–50

Gardiner, M. and Hartwell, B. 2006 'Landscapes of failure: the archaeology of flooded wetlands at Titchwell and Thornham (Norfolk) and Broomhill (East Sussex)', *Journal of Wetland Archaeology* 6, 137–60

Gerrard, C. M. and Petley, D. 2013 'A risk society? Environmental hazards, risk and resilience in the later Middle Ages in Europe', *Natural Hazards* 69(1), 1051–79

Gilchrist, R. 2012 *Medieval life: archaeology and the life course*, The Boydell Press, Woodbridge

Gould, S. J. 1999 'Introduction: the scales of contingency and punctuation in history', in J. Blintiff (ed.), *Structure and contingency: evolutionary processes in life and human society*, Leicester University Press, London, ix–xxii

Gowland, R. L. and Chamberlain, A. T. 2005 'Detecting plague: palaeodemographic characterisation of a catastrophic death assemblage', *Antiquity* 79, 146–57

Griffiths, D., Philpott, R. A., and Egan, G. 2007 *Meols: the archaeology of the North Wirral Coast*, Oxford University School of Archaeology Monograph 68, Oxford

Grimson, J. 1978 *The Channel coasts of England*, Hale, London

Hall, M. and Price, N. (eds) 2012 'Medieval Scotland: a future for its past', *Scottish Archaeological Research Framework* [www.scottishheritagehub.com]

Hanska, J. 2002 *Strategies of sanity and survival: religious responses to natural disasters in the Middle Ages*, Finnish Literature Society, Helsinki

Herrgott, M. 1726 *Vetus disciplina monastica*, Caroli Osmont, Paris

Hirst, S. M., Walsh, D. A., and Wright, S. M. 1983 *Bordesley Abbey II: second report on the excavations at Bordesley Abbey, Redditch, Hereford-Worcestershire*, British Archaeological Reports British Series 111, Oxford

Hughes, M. K. and Diaz, H. F. 1994 'Was there a "Medieval Warm Period", and if so, when and where?', *Climate Change* 26, 109–42

Jones, R. 2013 *The medieval natural world*, Routledge, Abingdon and New York

Jørgensen, D. 2010 'Local government responses to urban river pollution in late medieval England', *Water History* 2, 35–52

Kelleher, R. 2011 'Interpreting single finds in medieval England: the secondary lives of coins', in N. Holmes (ed.), *Proceedings of the XIV International Numismatic Congress, Glasgow, Vol. II*, International Numismatic Council, Glasgow, 1492–9

Kershaw, I. 1973 'The Great Famine and the agrarian crisis in England 1315–1322', *Past and Present* 59, 3–50

Kirk, W. 1957 'Sands of Forvie', *Discovery and Excavation Scotland*, 4

Lamb, H. H. 1982 *Climate, history and the modern world*, Methuen, New York

MacGibbon, D. and Ross, T. 1897 *The ecclesiastical architecture of Scotland, Vol. III*, David Douglas, Edinburgh

Martin, C. T. (ed.) 1885 *Registrum epistolarum Fratris Johannis Peckham, Archepiscopi Cantuariensis, Vol. III*, Her Majesty's Stationery Office, London

Martin, D. and Martin, B. 2004 *New Winchelsea, Sussex: a medieval port town*, Heritage Marketing and Publications Ltd, King's Lynn

Matthews, J. A. and Briffa, K. R. 2005 'The "Little Ice Age": re-evaluation of an evolving concept', *Geografiska Annaler* 87A, 17–36

Maxwell Lyte, H. C. (ed.) 1909 *Calendar of the Close Rolls, Edward III, vol. XI, AD 1360–1364*, Her Majesty's Stationery Office, London

McRoberts, D. 1966 'Notes on Glasgow Cathedral', *The Innes Review* 17, 40–7

Miles, D. W. H., Howard, R. E., and Simpson, W. G. 2004 *The tree-ring dating of the tower and spire at Salisbury Cathedral, Wiltshire*, Centre for Archaeology Report 44/2004, English Heritage

Moorhouse, S. 1985 'The ceramic contents of a 13th century timber building destroyed by fire at Pennard, Gower', *Medieval and Later Pottery in Wales* 8, 1–9

North, T. 1882 *The church bells of the county and city of Lincoln*, Samuel Clarke, Leicester

Page, W. (ed.) 1906 *A history of the County of Norfolk, Vol. 2*, Archibald Constable and Co., London

Parry, M. L. 1975 'Secular climatic change and marginal agriculture', *Transactions of the Institute of British Geographers* 64, 1–13

Parry, M. L. 1981 'Evaluating the impact of climatic change', in C. Delano Smith and M. Parry (eds), *Consequences of climatic change*, University of Nottingham, Nottingham, 3–16

Powicke, F. M. and Cheney, C. R. (eds) 1964 *Councils and synods, with other documents relating to the English Church, II, AD 1205–1313*, Oxford University Press, Oxford

Raine, J. (ed.) 1873 *Historical papers and letters from the Northern Registers*, Her Majesty's Stationery Office, London

Ralegh Radford, C. A. 1970 *Glasgow Cathedral*, Her Majesty's Stationery Office, Edinburgh

RCHME, 1982 *A guide to Saint Albans Cathedral*, Her Majesty's Stationery Office, London

Riley, H. T. (ed.) 1867 *Gesta abbatum monasterii Sancti Albani, Volume I, AD 793–1290*, Her Majesty's Stationery Office, London

Riley, H. T. (ed.) 1869 *Gesta abbatum monasterii Sancti Albani, Volume III, AD 1349–1411*, Her Majesty's Stationery Office, London

Rippon, S., Wainwright, A., and Smart, C. 2014 'Farming regions in medieval England: the archaeobotanical and zooarchaeological evidence', *Medieval Archaeology* 58, 195–255

Roberts, T. and Williams, I. (eds) 1923 *The poetical works of Dafydd Nanmor*, University of Wales Press Board, Cardiff and London

Rogerson, A. 1976 'Excavations on Fuller's Hill, Great Yarmouth', in A. J. Lawson, H. Richmond, A. Rogerson, R. Taylor, K. Wade, P. Wade-Martins, and D. A. Edwards, *Norfolk: various papers*, East Anglian Archaeology Report 2, Gressenhall, 131–234

Rohr, C. 2005 'The Danube floods and their human response and perception (14th to 17th C)', *History of Meteorology* 2, 71–86

Ryan, W. G. (ed.) 1993 *Jacobus de Voragine, the golden legend, vol. 1*, Princeton University Press, Princeton

Sear, D. A., Bacon, S. R., Murdock, A., Doneghan, G., Baggaley, P., Serra, C., and LeBas, T. P. 2011 'Cartographic, geophysical and diver surveys of the medieval town site at Dunwich, Suffolk, England', *The International Journal of Nautical Archaeology* 40(1), 113–32

Standley, E. R. 2013 *Trinkets and charms: the use, meaning and significance of dress accessories 1300–1700*, Oxford University School of Archaeology Monograph 78, Oxford

Stern, D. V. 2000 *A Hertfordshire demesne of Westminster Abbey: profits, productivity and weather, vol. 1*, University of Hertfordshire Press, Hatfield

Tatton-Brown, T. W. T. 1988 'The topography of the Walland Marsh area between the eleventh and thirteenth centuries', in J. Eddison and C. Green (eds), *Romney Marsh: evolution occupation, reclamation*, Oxford University Committee for Archaeology, Oxford, 105–11

Tatton-Brown, T. W. T. 1996 'Archaeology and Chichester Cathedral', in T. W. T. Tatton-Brown and J. Munby (eds), *The archaeology of cathedrals*, Oxford University Committee for Archaeology Monograph 42, Oxford, 47–55

Thomas, K. 1971 *Religion and the decline of magic*, Charles Scribner's Sons, New York

Trouet, V., Scourse, J. D., and Raible, C. C. 2012 'North Atlantic storminess and Atlantic Meridional Overturning Circulation during the last millennium: reconciling contradictory proxy records of NAO variability', *Global and Planetary Change* 84–5, 48–55

Whyte, I. 2009 'Floods and their impact on the landscape: flood histories from Cumbria', *Landscapes* 10(1), 61–76

Williams, S. W. 1889a *The Cistercian Abbey of Strata Florida: its history, and an account of the recent excavations made on its site*, Whiting and Co., London

Williams, S. W. 1889b 'On further excavations at Strata Florida Abbey', *Archaeologia Cambrensis* 6(21), 24–58

Williamson, T., Liddiard, R., and Partida, T. 2013 *Champion: the making and unmaking of the English Midland landscape*, Liverpool University Press, Liverpool

Willmott, H. and Townend, P. 2012 *Thornton Abbey Project, 2nd Interim Report 2012*, unpublished report, available at: http://www.thorntonabbeyproject.com [accessed 13 April 2015]

Wright, S. M. 1976 'Barton Blount: climatic or economic change?', *Medieval Archaeology* 20, 148–52

PART III

RURAL SETTLEMENT AND BUILDINGS

CHAPTER 12

OVERVIEW

The Form and Pattern of Medieval Settlement

STEPHEN RIPPON, PIERS DIXON,
AND BOB SILVESTER

During the later medieval period, the vast majority of the British population lived in rural settlements whose primary means of subsistence was agriculture. This section of the *Handbook* explores five different aspects of these rural settlements including Richard Suggett's paper on regional variations in peasant houses (vernacular architecture), Jill Campbell's contribution on the higher-status manorial houses and moated sites, and Niall Brady's study of agricultural buildings. Chris Dyer explores daily life in rural settlements, and Mark Gardiner and Susan Kilby examine contemporary perceptions. For those wishing to explore further, an excellent collection of papers on medieval rural settlement can be found in *Medieval rural settlement: Britain and Ireland, AD 800–1600* (Christie and Stamper 2012) while the Roberts and Wrathmell (2002) volume *Region and place* provides the most comprehensive discussion of regional variations within the English landscape. For Scotland, other than the collection of edited papers already mentioned, the best summary of the variety of rural settlement is still the conference papers in Govan (2003), though Barrett (2008) covers the Norse parts of the north and west. For Wales the edited volume *Lost farmsteads* (Roberts 2006) offers a wide-ranging assessment of Welsh settlement; the best individual site report of recent times is that for Cefn Graeanog (Kelly 1982), while for the tribulations that can beset a single settlement site, the story of Hen Caerwys is recommended (Davies and Silvester 2015). In this introduction, however, the three authors pull back from the detail of life within individual settlements and examine the broader picture of local and regional variation in the form and pattern of medieval rural settlement.

Studying Medieval Settlement Patterns

Later medieval settlement patterns can be researched in a variety of ways. Field-walking has proved to be particularly successful in those regions that currently experience extensive arable cultivation, such as in East Anglia where the progressive migration of settlement—away from pre-Conquest sites associated with parish churches towards the edges of remote greens and commons—is repeatedly seen (Lawson 1983; Rogerson et al. 1987; Wade-Martins 1980). In the Norfolk Marshland, for example, field-walking has enabled the expansion and contraction of settlement into the lower-lying parts of the Fenland to be mapped in detail, reflecting a classic 'push into the margins', followed by a retreat (Rippon 2002; Silvester 1988). On a smaller scale, the intensive investigation of individual parishes has allowed the creation and abandonment of tenement plots to be mapped alongside the reconstruction of land-use zones and the changing patterns of arable cultivation reflected in manure scatters, for example at Raunds (Northamptonshire; Parry 2006) and Shapwick (Somerset; Aston and Gerrard 2013; Gerrard with Aston 2007). Where deserted settlements and their associated field systems are preserved as earthworks after areas were put down to pasture in the late medieval period, they can be studied by mapping the evidence from early air photographs and on the ground (e.g. Croft and Mynard 1993; Everson et al. 1991). In upland regions abandoned settlements have sometimes survived as earthworks and tumbled stone walls, untouched by any later cultivation (e.g. Johnson and Rose 1994; Roberts 2006).

On a smaller scale there is a long history of excavation on medieval settlements whose early focus was on deserted villages that were threatened with destruction, although in recent years the emphasis has changed to investigations within currently occupied medieval settlements both in the context of development-led work and programmes of community-based test-pitting (e.g. Figure 12.1) (Lewis 2007; for a historiography see Dyer and Everson 2012; Rippon 2009). Some areas have seen detailed surveys of standing late medieval buildings, and in recent years these have started to be integrated with programmes of archaeological survey and excavation, documentary research, and historic landscape analysis, in order to unravel the evolution of settlement patterns (e.g. Puxton and Shapwick in Somerset: Rippon 2006; Aston and Gerrard 2013; and see Rippon 2012; 2014). In contrast to England, few permanently occupied settlements have been excavated in Wales despite the advent of developer-funding, although a recent advance has seen investigations of seasonal settlements and excavation within standing houses, coupled with the assessment of their surrounding landscapes (e.g. Britnell 2001; Britnell et al. 2008).

In Scotland the study of medieval rural settlement has been bedevilled by the difficulty of recognizing and locating medieval settlement remains in field survey and excavations, especially in the Highlands. Excavations have been mainly research-based and small in scale here, and almost invariably they have only revealed post-medieval buildings. Field-walking in the Lowlands regularly produces finds of medieval pottery, but few discoveries have led on to excavations of medieval settlements (but see Dixon 1998). Developer-funding has provided the opportunity to investigate some lowland medieval settlements but this has often been limited in extent. A significant change in the recording and analysis of rural settlement happened as a result of new afforestation policy in 1989 which dictates that important archaeological sites should not be planted. At the same time a strategic programme of archaeological mapping—the Afforestable Land

FIGURE 12.1 Test-pitting in the burh at Lyng, Somerset, as part of the community project Lost Islands of Somerset

(© South West Heritage Trust)

Survey—was established and included analytical studies of medieval and later rural settlement (e.g. RCAHMS 2001), complementing the National Archaeological Survey of 1987–2007 (RCAHMS 2007). The more intensive Ben Lawers Landscape Project is discussed in the following section.

Settlement Patterns

Although there were some specialized rural settlements, most of the rural population were primarily engaged in agriculture. Within these villages, hamlets, and farmsteads most people participated in both arable cultivation and animal husbandry although the balance between the two varied considerably from region to region. There was also considerable variation in the composition of medieval rural settlement. In midland England, for example, most settlement within a parish or township was nucleated into a single village with farmsteads standing alongside cottages of the landless poor, service provision such as a smithy or mill, communal buildings such as the church (and its associated priest's house) (Figure 12.2), and the residence of the manorial lord. Although archaeological attention has often focused on peasant tofts and manorial enclosures (e.g. at Caldecote, Hertfordshire; Beresford 2009), these other components

FIGURE 12.2 The Priest's House, Muchelney, Somerset, a priest's lodging of the fourteenth century and later, built of local lias with Ham stone dressings and thatched roof. The upper two-light window on the right is possibly fourteenth century and the house is first mentioned in 1308

(© Paul Stamper)

have been investigated too, for example the mills at Wharram Percy (Yorkshire) and Raunds (Northamptonshire) and a probable priest's house at Shapwick (Somerset). These villages were associated with a small number of vast open fields, the most comprehensive study of which is in Northamptonshire (Partida et al. 2013; Williamson et al. 2013). Elsewhere—across most of Britain in fact—rural settlement patterns were more dispersed. In some places isolated farmsteads were common (e.g. on the boulder clays of north-west Essex: Cooke et al. 2008; Rodwell and Rodwell 1986; 1993; Timby et al. 2007), although elsewhere archaeological and documentary research has shown that what in the nineteenth century were isolated farmsteads had in the later medieval period been small hamlets (e.g. in Cornwall and Devon: Beresford 1964; Fox 1989; Henderson and Weddell 1994).

These broad regional differences in settlement patterns and their associated field systems have been mapped across England, for example the distribution of documentary evidence for the existence of open fields (e.g. Gray 1915), near contemporary observations of the landscapes (references to 'champion' landscapes in John Leland's itinerary: Slater 1907, 47; Rippon 2014, fig. 1.1), enclosure maps of the post-medieval period (Gonner 1912), and using characterization of later sources such as the nineteenth-century Ordnance Survey First Edition maps (Rackham 1986; Roberts 1987; Roberts and Wrathmell 2000; 2002). A consistent picture is emerging in England of a three-fold division between, firstly, the south-east, with its predominantly dispersed settlement and enclosed fields; secondly, a central zone (stretching from the south coast in Dorset and Hampshire, up through the Midlands, and to the coast of north-east England) within which settlement was nucleated into villages and the agricultural land organized in open fields; and, thirdly, the west and south-west of England with predominantly dispersed settlement and enclosed fields. Whilst useful as a starting point, however, it must be remembered that within each of these three broad regions there was considerable variation, with localized areas of more dispersed settlement within the central zone (e.g. Whittlewood in Buckinghamshire and Northamptonshire: Jones and Page 2006), and areas with nucleated villages and small-scale open fields in parts of the south-east and the south-west (e.g. Herring 2006). Local variations in landscape character such as these can arise through a variety of processes, such as the relatively late colonization of former waste land, the shrinkage of formerly large villages, or the extra-ordinary growth of a particular hamlet as a result of local circumstances such as the exploitation of local mineral resources (e.g. Bere Ferrers in Devon when a planned settlement was created to house workers from the royal silver mines: Rippon et al. 2009).

Medieval rural settlement in Scotland can be divided into three zones: the Norse areas of northern and western Scotland, the Highlands, and the Lowlands. The Lowlands can themselves be divided into two zones: firstly, the low-lying coastal and valley terrain; and secondly, the hill ground of the Southern Uplands and other lowland ranges such as the Ochils and Campsies. There is, however, relatively little understanding of medieval settlement since few sites have been successfully identified and confirmed by excavation. It has proved difficult to distinguish medieval buildings from post-medieval ones, especially in the Highlands, in the absence of distinguishable plan-forms, and owing to the use of perishable building materials such as turf and timber (Figure 12.3) (e.g. Fairhurst and Dunbar 1971). This gap in the evidence has been alleviated most successfully in the Western and Northern Isles where Norse settlements have been identified and excavated (Barrett 2012; Parker Pearson et al. 2004; Sharples 2005; Turner et al. 2013), and in lowland Scotland where a handful of excavations complement a settlement model based upon field survey and documentary research (Barrow 1962; Dixon 1998; 2003; Hindmarsh and Oram 2013; Murray and Murray 1993). Despite the concerted efforts of a large-scale multi-disciplinary project at Ben Lawers in the central Highlands (Turner 2003), however, our knowledge of highland medieval settlement patterns remains patchy, and is largely dependent on extrapolating from medieval documents and post-medieval remains (Lelong 2003). The recognition of large turf-walled long houses of the early medieval period (c. AD 600–1000) in highland Perthshire has put this gap into sharp relief, especially as they were replaced by scatters of huts in the high medieval period (c. AD 1020–1220), possibly summer shielings, or, as has been suggested, cottars' huts, interleaved with episodes of rig cultivation (Carver et al. 2013).

In lowland Scotland there were two settlement types: a mixture of large and small row villages and moated manors in the low-lying areas, and farmsteads and shielings on the higher ground (Dixon 2003). It has been argued that the Lowlands were 'champagne country' with villages and intermixed strip fields that originated in twelfth

FIGURE 12.3 A medieval turf building at Kiltyrie, on the slopes of Ben Lawers, Scotland
(© Crown Copyright: RCAHMS. Licensor www.rcahms.gov.uk)

and thirteenth centuries, if not before, in the extreme south-east (formerly part of Northumbria), and this traditional view has recently been reiterated by Dalglish (2012). Excavations at Eldbotle (Hindmarsh and Oram 2013), for example, have revealed late first-millennium occupation on the same site as the later village with ditches and gullies on a similar orientation suggesting a continuity of settlement that has previously eluded settlement studies in the Lowlands. In contrast, analysis of settlements in Aberdeenshire suggests a more nuanced pattern in the north-east. Here there were two main elements in the settlement pattern of townships (or *touns* in Scots). The first are row villages (and small burghs) settled by Anglo-French incomers in the Garioch, comprising ordered rows of adjacent yards and houses, and the second clustered townships of less ordered form in which the yards were closely grouped, but not in streets or rows, although the houses often obeyed a dominant axis (Dixon and Fraser 2007). A subsidiary, but dynamic, element in the late medieval settlement pattern peculiar to the north-east are the smallholdings, known locally as 'crofts', that were created through the intake of new land and which sometimes developed into small nucleated agricultural settlements that may have supported a mill, brewery, or a smithy. An analysis of unroofed and abandoned settlement on first edition Ordnance Survey 6-inch maps suggests that such clustered townships predominated not only in lowland Aberdeenshire, but also more widely along the fringes of the highlands, providing a marked contrast to the row-plan villages of the Lowlands (RCAHMS 2002).

Dalglish (2012) has argued that this pattern of townships emerged in the post-medieval period in both the Highlands and Lowlands, consonant with a dispersal of settlement. Confusingly, however, Dodgshon (1981) has argued on the one hand that late and post-medieval settlement was increasingly dispersed as a result of what he termed 'township splitting' in lowland Scotland, while on the other hand he has argued that the imposition of feudal landholding led to clustering of settlement and strip-field farming in the western Highlands and Islands (Dodgshon 1993). The presence of place-names with the prefix 'Old', however, supports the case that there was a real change in the pattern of settlement of Aberdeenshire over the course of the medieval period for the practical purpose of providing better access to distant outfields (Dixon and Fraser 2007), rather than just an administrative change to a dispersed settlement pattern. Two examples of small *touns* in the Southern Uplands have been partly excavated, complementing field survey and documentary evidence of eastern Dumfriesshire that suggested a pattern of small hamlets of two to five buildings was typical for the late medieval and early modern period (RCAHMS 1997). Dowglen, in Eskdale, was excavated as an example of the *touns* which documentary sources indicated had origins in the fourteenth century if not before (RCAHMS 1997). The lack of datable artefacts suggested it pre-dated the seventeenth century, but it was otherwise undated. At Shootinglee, a stead in the royal forest of Ettrick near Traquair, in the Scottish Borders, excavations within a row of five houses and yards revealed a byre-house overlying a clay oven. Pottery suggests the site originated as early as the thirteenth century, and the last use of the oven has been radiocarbon-dated from the late fifteenth to the early seventeenth century (Durham and Dixon 2015; 2016). Both were upland settlements poorly supplied with available arable land, only a few hectares in extent, and with an economy biased towards pastoral farming.

Two Scotland-wide studies have shed new light on rural settlement over the last twenty years. The First Edition Survey Project (1995–2001) took a different approach to that adopted by Roberts and Wrathmell in England, recording unroofed structures depicted on the Ordnance Survey 6-inch maps, the majority of which lay in the Highlands and Galloway (RCAHMS 2002). Whilst this has added immensely to our distribution of post-medieval settlement, with an additional 3217 townships recorded (an increase of 88 per cent), the question that remains is whether or not these sites are indicative of medieval precursors. It should be emphasized that the First Edition Ordnance Survey map cannot be used as a proxy for medieval rural settlement in Scotland in the way it has in England because of the clearance of settlement for sheep farming in the Highlands and for improved farms in the Lowlands, which research in Aberdeenshire has shown are not necessarily on the same sites as the pre-improvement *touns* (Dixon and Fraser 2007). The Historic Land-Use Assessment Project (1996–2015), characterizing past influences on the modern landscape, has confirmed that in places, however, there is a pattern of row or street villages of potential medieval origin complementing the fossilized reverse-S-shaped strip fields, as well as the cropmarks of ploughed-out ridges in arable farmland in the Lowlands (HLAmap nd).

For the Highlands, even modern excavation techniques have proved unsuccessful in locating medieval settlement, perhaps because the excavation strategy has been limited to individual buildings or parts of buildings rather than whole settlements, or even farmsteads, reducing the potential to locate earlier phases of occupation. Despite the ease with which post-medieval settlement can be located, excavation was of limited success in identifying medieval structures in the multi-disciplinary Ben Lawers Project. The most notable achievement was the excavation of a small sub-rectangular turf building, and the fragmentary trace of another, under two turf shieling huts on the fringe of the post-medieval outfield and the upper limit of rig cultivation that was dated to the twelfth and thirteenth centuries (Atkinson 2016): it has been argued that this is a sign of expanding settlement at the time.

Survey and excavation programmes in Shetland, Orkney, and the Outer Hebrides suggest a pattern of dispersed farmsteads with occasional larger groupings (Crawford 1988; Hamilton 1956; Morris 1991; Sharples 2005). These settlements originate in the Viking period, sometimes with Pictish antecedents. They occupy the *machar* shell sand of the west coast on the Uists, which in the late medieval and post-medieval periods were abandoned and replaced by township clusters further inland. On Unst, in Shetland, they were replaced by townships with rectangular stone or stone-and-turf gabled buildings in the post-medieval period (Tait 2012). Dodgshon (1993) argued that on Uist the move inland to clustered townships on the peat-lands was under the influence of feudal landholding in the western Highlands, and that the unenclosed lazy-bed rigged fields replaced small enclosed globular-shaped fields which they appear to overlie. In contrast, Dixon (1993, 10) has argued that this model is based upon a mis-reading of the evidence and that survey work at Waternish, on the Isle of Skye, shows that the sub-circular enclosures, *c*.1 ha in extent, were found throughout the peninsula as an integral part of field systems and can be interpreted as outfield enclosures.

Regional variations in settlement forms and patterns undoubtedly exist in Wales, but have been little researched with more work by historical geographers than by archaeologists (e.g. Sylvester 1969). Historical geographers have long maintained that hamlets of bond tenants provided the support for the numerous courts of the Welsh princes in the pre-Conquest era, fading out by the later Middle Ages to leave only an isolated church or a single farm; this theory is persuasive but has yet to be validated by excavation (Jones 1985; Longley 1997). The Welsh lowlands—the southern and northern coastal belts and their fringes, and the valleys of the Marches—experienced varying degrees of nucleated settlement formation after the Conquest, though the archaeological evidence to support their development is hardly abundant other than in the Vale of Glamorgan. It is settlement morphology throughout most of the lowland areas and relict earthwork complexes in the Wye and Usk catchments in the more southerly reaches of central Wales that provide the most convincing examples of nucleation rather than excavation (Silvester 1997; Thomas and Dowdell 1987). Differentiation between Anglo-Norman nucleated villages with their open fields and dispersed Welsh settlement with their much smaller arable common fields provides an easy but potentially over-simplistic model. In regions where recent studies have examined the two settlement forms bordering each other, as in the wetlands adjacent to the Severn

Estuary in Monmouthshire and in the northern and southern parts of Pembrokeshire (Rippon 2008), this appears to be a reasonably valid distinction, but it has yet to be tested in other areas where the English faced the Welsh. Dispersed settlement predominated in the medieval era over much of Wales, although this sweeping statement needs to be tempered by an appreciation that much of the field survey and the very small amount of excavation that has taken place have been directed towards the more marginal uplands. Where excavation has occurred, the results point to relatively short-lived occupation (as at Cefn Graeanog, Gwynedd: Kelly 1982; and Hen Caerwys, Flintshire: Davies and Silvester 2015). Systematic field survey on the lower lands has occurred only sparsely, and more in eastern Wales than elsewhere (Roberts 2006). It suggests that farms were strung out in favoured locations, though the identification of deserted sites is heavily reliant on the recognition of the artificial platforms on which the houses were erected, and without doubt underplays the presence of house sites where surface traces are absent. Peculiar to Wales is the girdle settlement (Figure 12.4) where the arable sharelands lay at the centre of a ring of scattered houses: this was initially articulated as a historical concept but field remains have now been recognized in several places (Butler 1996; Silvester 2006, 24). Retraction of settlement in the fourteenth century appears to have been reversed in the fifteenth century, and earthwork evidence points to the emergence of new farms encompassed by several enclosures, paralleling the emergence of newly constructed houses in many parts of Wales which are still standing and have been dated by dendrochronology (Silvester and Kissock 2012; Suggett 2004). Generally though, most lowland farmsteads have been examined only as single entities and there has been little research on the wider landscapes in which they lay.

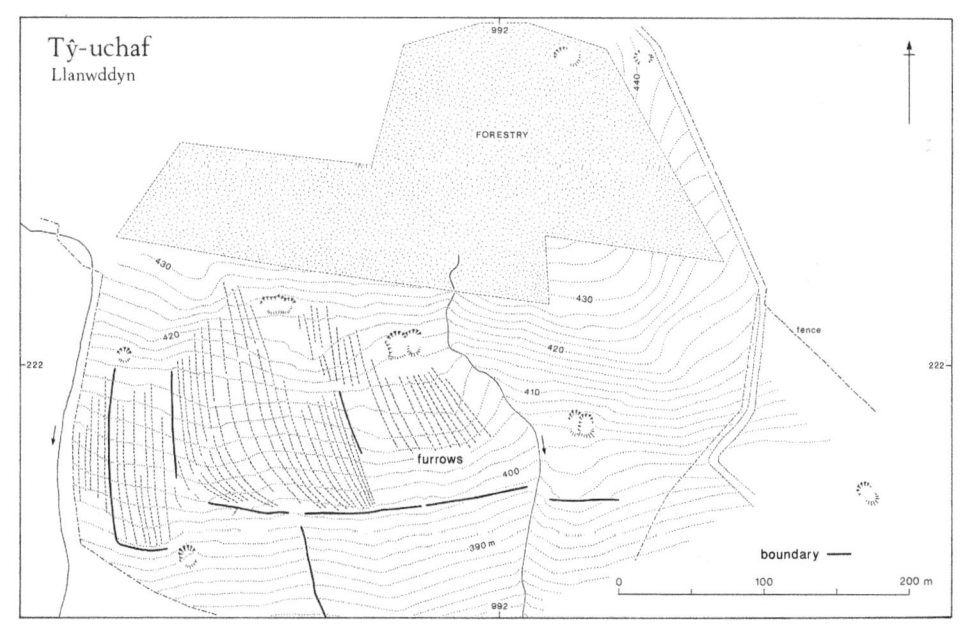

FIGURE 12.4 Example of a Welsh girdle settlement: Ty-uchaf in Llanwddyn (from Roberts 2006, fig 2.4)

(© Clwyd-Powys Archaeological Trust)

Planned Villages

Another facet of medieval settlement character that shows marked regional variation is in the organization of space within settlements and in particular the extent to which planning may be associated with immigrant populations. The origins of nucleated villages in England has excited much discussion both in terms of chronology and process, and until recently the prevailing view has been that the processes of settlement nucleation and the laying out of villages began well before the Norman Conquest (e.g. Lewis et al. 1997; Partida et al. 2013; Rippon 2014; Roberts and Wrathmell 2002; Williamson 2003). It has generally been assumed that the laying out of villages—and the open fields with which they are associated—involved some degree of planning, although Tom Williamson et al. (2013) have recently noted that the regularity in some village plans results from tenements having been laid out over former open field strips. There are, however, several categories of later medieval villages that clearly do result from careful planning, most notably the regular-row plan settlements of northern England that may in part relate to the recolonization that followed the 'Harrying of the North', but which still appears to have being used as a way of laying out new settlements well into the twelfth century or even later (Creighton and Rippon 2017).

Another, rarer, type of post-Conquest planned village is that created by Flemish colonists, of which there are several examples in south-west Wales (e.g. Letterston in Pembrokeshire: Kissock 1997; Rippon 2014, fig. 6.21). In Scotland, although planned villages of potential medieval origin have been identified in various places, and attributed to Anglo-French incomers in Aberdeenshire, Flemish settlement is best seen as part of the wider immigration of settlers from northern Europe in the twelfth and thirteenth centuries. They were encouraged to settle as traders in the new burghs as well as small feudal landlords in south Lanarkshire and Aberdeenshire (Duncan 1975; Oram 2011). In the former, the place-names Covington, Thankerton, Symington, Roberton, Lamington, Biggar, and Wiston originate as the fiefs held by Flemish incomers, and row or street villages are evident today at Thankerton, Wiston, and Biggar which may be of medieval origin. In the Garioch, a dale in central Aberdeenshire, Flemish incomers were undoubtedly part of the mix of new small landlords, for example at Old Flinder (Flandres in thirteenth-century charters of Lindores Abbey), where a small street village was depicted on a mid-eighteenth-century estate plan, or Wardhouse where Bartholmew the Fleming settled and built a moated manor, but no village is extant (Dixon and Fraser 2007).

Specialized Grazing Settlements

Although some lowland areas supported specifically pastoral settlements, reflected for example by the place-names '-den' found across the Weald of Kent, Surrey, and Sussex where mostly famously pigs but also cattle were grazed (Everitt 1986), it was upland areas that supported the largest numbers of specialized grazing settlements. The seasonal movement of livestock was widespread in upland areas. In south-west England, for example, a combination of place-name research, archaeological survey, documentary research, and historic landscape analysis has revealed the network of droveways along which livestock were driven from lowland areas up onto the granite uplands across which seasonal settlements were scattered (Dudley 2011; Fox 1996; 2012; Johnson and Rose 1994).

In Scotland medieval documents frequently mention 'scalingas' in the twelfth and thirteenth centuries (Barrow 1971). These were temporary shelters, or shieling huts, built by graziers on the summer pastures. Whether this refers to the practice of transhumance is not explicit. Indeed, they might equally have been built by shepherds looking after the monastic flocks of abbeys such as Kelso, Dryburgh, and Melrose, or by cattle herdsmen. A shieling was typically some distance from the core settlement, as suggested by the *dabhaichean* in Moray which included distant grazings (Ross 2011). Samsonshelis in Channelkirk, where Dryburgh Abbey acquired a toft and croft, arable, and common grazing for three hundred sheep, sixty oxen, and two horses may be an example of transhumance carried out by the abbey (Oram 2011, 258), but the toft, croft, and arable belie this, suggesting this was a permanent settlement at a former shieling site, a process of settlement colonization that occurred in other dales in the Southern Uplands, such as Liddesdale (Dixon 2009). The establishment of hunting forests in the twelfth and thirteenth centuries limited access to grazing in much of southern Scotland, and thus the summer resource. Gilbert (1979) has noted that shieling grants occur in the late medieval period in Ettrick forest, but it is also evident that shielings were abandoned in the Lowlands during the seventeenth century (Winchester 2000). The turf or turf-and-stone huts that are found in groups in upland areas of southern Scotland and the Highlands and Islands (excluding Orkney and Shetland where the practice does not occur) are the visible evidence of the practice of transhumance, which is well documented in the post-medieval period, continuing until the nineteenth and even twentieth century in the Isle of Lewis. Excavations, however, suggest that the medieval origin needs further research. Those excavated in the central highlands on Ben Lawers have been radiocarbon-dated to the late medieval and post-medieval periods (Atkinson 2016), while a shieling hut at Camp Shiel Burn in Peeblesshire was also radiocarbon-dated to the late medieval period (Durham 2009). Pottery from a group of huts at Slackshaw Burn near Mauchline suggests a late medieval date (Fairbairn 1927). Only one site on the Hebrides has produced any trace of an earlier period of occupation where a turf shieling hut was excavated under a stone figure-of-eight hut of post-medieval date, with radiocarbon dates of the eleventh century at Torrin on the Isle of Skye (Canmore nd ID 11454).

In the Welsh hills, large numbers of simple rectangular huts, and also platforms with and without hut remains visible on them, have been recorded in recent years. Some have small enclosures attached, and very occasionally there are traces of cultivation beds. Mostly they are randomly scattered and isolated in upland valleys and on hillsides, but sometimes small groups of up to eight to ten huts are encountered, particularly in mid-Wales. Distinguishing between those dwellings that were occupied on a permanent basis and the many others which were only resorted to on a seasonal basis (*hafotai/hafodydd*), when stock were grazed on the upland pastures, has engendered an on-going debate that not even excavation has been able to resolve (Locock 2006; Silvester and Kissock 2012). Where topographical and height factors combined with the simplicity of the remains favour the interpretation as summer settlement, dating still remains a problem. Like the 'medieval or later rural settlement' concept that was developed in Scotland (Foster and Hingley 1994), it is frequently impossible to date field remains that could fall anywhere within the medieval era or even into the post-medieval centuries. Only at rare sites such as Hafod Nant y Criafolen on the Denbigh Moors (Denbighshire) do middens provide a narrow date range in the sixteenth century (Allen 1979). Most of the extensive Welsh uplands supported seasonal settlement, but physical remains and written references are less common in the eastern uplands than further west from which it might be inferred that transhumant practice gradually faded out during the Middle Ages in areas closer to England while continuing in north-west Wales as late as the eighteenth century (Silvester 2006).

Specialized Settlements in Coastal Landscapes

The reclamation of coastal marshes for agricultural use is well studied and was undertaken extensively around the coast of England (Rippon 2000), although in a few places saltmarshes were left unreclaimed: in the case of the Thameside marshes, this may have been because proximity to the large urban market of London meant that adequate profits could be made from grazing sheep and producing cheese without the capital and recurrent cost of embanking and draining the marshes and then maintaining those flood defences (Rippon 2013a; 2013b). In Scotland, reclamation of coastal saltmarshes for arable is also well documented in the Carse of Gowrie (Perthshire), where it was carried out by the monks of Couper Angus Abbey at 'Edderpolles' (a place now called the Grange), and in an area near the loch of Spynie in the Laich of Moray by Freskin as Lord of Duffus, while inland marsh at Blairgowrie (Perthshire) was drained for arable and pasture (Duncan 1975; Oram 2011). In Wales, the largest coastal wetland—the Gwent Levels—was also reclaimed from the late eleventh and twelfth centuries (Figure 12.5) with markedly differing settlement patterns and field systems resulting from the different patterns of lordship that were responsible (Rippon 1996; 2008).

The occupants of coastal settlements also exploited other resources. In south-west England, for example, Fox (2001) has shown how the churches and primary settlements within coastal parishes were located inland, and that the shoreline fishing villages that are so characteristic of the region today only started to emerge in the late medieval period, initially as seasonal sites. The extent to which this happened elsewhere has yet to be established, although anecdotal evidence in counties such as Essex suggests that it was also the case there (e.g. Leigh-on-Sea in Essex). In Scotland, river and coastal fisheries

FIGURE 12.5 Medieval reclamation of land on the Gwent Levels

(© Stephen Rippon)

are documented in the monastic cartularies of abbeys such as Kelso and Coldingham, as one of the items in the rental of a number of villages, but to date one of the largest medieval deposits of fish bones in the Lowlands has been from the port and fishing village of Eyemouth in Berwickshire (Dixon 1986). The gadoids such as cod and ling were strongly represented, but so was herring, which was referred to as red or white in the records of Coldingham Priory in 1374, presumably being dried and smoked fish respectively. Gadoids were fished by line, with hooks baited by winkles and limpets that were found in large quantity. Similar deposits were also found at Eldbotle (East Lothian), another seaside village (Hindmarsh and Oram 2013). In the Northern Isles and Caithness, large fish-bone assemblages have been recovered from the Norse coastal settlements such as Freswick Links in Caithness (Batey 1982), and Quoygrew, in Orkney (Barrett 2012; and see Chapter 9 in this *Handbook*). Fishing with seine nets, or with traps of wickerwork (e.g. in the River Conan, Easter Ross) or stone (the only surviving feature), provide a barrier to the fish escaping as the tide runs out, and have been recorded in excess of four hundred places along the coast (Canmore nd), while traps or 'yairs' were built across rivers (Hale 2003), including major ones such as the Forth.

Industrial Settlements

The vast majority of later medieval rural settlements were associated with agriculture, although there were some rural communities which specialized in exploiting other resources. Another facet of coastal wetlands, for example, was the opportunity they afforded for producing salt, and the specialist settlements associated with its exploitation are still reflected in place-names (e.g. Saltcot in Essex). In Scotland, salterns are documented along the River Forth when they were acquired by several of the bigger monasteries in Scotland (Jedburgh, Newbattle, Holyrood, Kelso, Dunfermline, and Cambuskenneth), and are also recorded at Aberdeen and St Andrews (Duncan 1975). Unfortunately, the only dated excavated examples of salterns have been post-medieval in date (e.g. St Monance in Fife: Canmore nd, ID 34266; and on the Sutherland coast at Brora: Hambley and Aitken 2011). Some forty-seven salt-working sites around the coast have been recorded in the Canmore database, usually in areas with coal-bearing rocks that provide the fuel for burning to evaporate the sea water, and although for the most part these are post-medieval in date, they may be continuing a medieval tradition.

Away from the coast, specialist industrial settlements will have been rare as most communities engaged in industry were also part-time farmers, although at Bere Alston, in Devon, a small planned village was created for workers at the royal silver mines in the Tamar valley (Rippon et al. 2009). Lyveden, in Northamptonshire, is an example of a community specializing in pottery production (Steane and Bryant 1975). Industrial settlements of medieval date in Wales and Scotland are rare, the only obvious examples depending on fourteenth-century documentary evidence for communities of lead miners established in the north-east of Wales, though their archaeological remains have yet to be recognized (Rees 1968).

Specialist High-Status Settlements

The landscape of medieval Britain contained a variety of high-status settlements and it should not be forgotten that, in addition to being centres for administration and displaying social status, they also performed some of the same basic functions as lower-status rural settlements. Castles and manor houses, for example, lay at the centre of agricultural estates and a proportion of local produce was collected, processed, and stored there (see Chapters 16 and 23). Some settlements were highly specialized in that they were related to particular aspects of countryside management such as recreation—the lodges associated with parks and forests (e.g. Writtle in Essex: Rahtz 1969; Old Lodge in Chepstow Park, Monmouthshire: Turner and Johnston 2006, 194)—and the administration of royal and baronial forests (e.g. Simonsbath on Exmoor: Hegarty and Wilson-North 2014; Colwyn Castle, Powys: Silvester 2010). Although not really settlements in the traditional sense, some lodges were residences for parkers and foresters, while others were for the periodic accommodation of hunting parties (i.e. not really settlements in the strict sense; see Chapter 25). In Scotland, King David (1124–53) introduced the concept of hunting forests as a royal prerogative establishing, for example, the royal forests of Ettrick and Jedburgh in the Scottish Borders, while granting fiefs to his chosen followers with the right of free forest, as he did for Robert de Brus in Annandale.

Earthwork castles are the visible statement of this new form of lordship, but dedicated hunting lodges from the twelfth and thirteenth centuries are not easy to separate from them. Hermitage in Liddesdale (Roxburghshire) is an example of what may be a hunting lodge. The lordship of Liddesdale was granted to Ranulf de Soulis by King David and appears to have included the right of free forest. Initially based at Liddel, near Castleton, where there is an earthwork castle (Canmore nd, ID 67934), a new focus was created to the north-west at Hermitage in the thirteenth century. Although better known for its late medieval stone castle, this sits within an earthwork castle which lies at the focus of a deer park, and also a moated site and earthen-dyked deer trap that pre-dates the park pale. The moated site comprises two adjacent ditched enclosures, the larger of which contains the footings of two rectangular buildings, one of which is a substantial mortared stone structure that measures 20 x 11 m overall, and the smaller a thirteenth-century chapel of squared ashlar similar to that of the primary phase of the stone castle (Canmore nd, ID 67915). Another possible hunting lodge has been excavated, comprising a large rectangular building with stone footings, some 36 x 9 m overall, on a ridge immediately overlooking Buzzart Dykes park in Perthshire (Hall et al. 2011; Hall 2013).

The occupation of crannogs, artificial islands, or island dwellings in freshwater lakes has its origins in prehistory (Lenfert 2011), but continued into the post-medieval period with castles and elite dwellings occupying these locations. These are paralleled by the occupation of islands in the sea, with elite foci such as Kisimul Castle in Castlebay, and the Isle of Barra, belonging to the MacNeils of Barra, in the late medieval period. Recent research by Shelley (2009) indicates a range of functions for freshwater loch settlements, both secular and religious, and concludes that the island location emphasized the authority of lordship, as well as the natural strength of water as a barrier. Typical structures to be found on these sites are one or more rectangular buildings, which can include towers from the late medieval period or enclosure walls where it has pretensions as a castle. Creighton (2002; and see Chapter 23 in this *Handbook*) has identified the importance of ornamental landscapes to castles (and see Liddiard 2007) and artificial lakes, such as that created at Kenilworth (Warwickshire) at the upper end of the social scale and Stokesay (Shropshire) at the other, in providing an aesthetically pleasing landscape. The creation of a large pond beside Invernochty Castle (Aberdeenshire) by damming a burn suggests this may be a feature in Scotland too, as early as the late twelfth century, and that it may be a factor in the continued popularity of island settlements amongst the aristocracy. Shelley's analysis of islands occupied by settlements on Pont's maps (*c.*1590s) and that of other early map makers revealed 118 potential loch settlements, and concluded that their general absence in the north-east and south-east lowlands is a genuine distribution resulting from the lack of freshwater lochs rather than a different sensibility.

The overall distribution of crannogs and other loch settlements is mainly to the north and west of Scotland, but examples do occur even in the lowland south-east (e.g. Loch Leven Castle in Fife, Loch Clunie in Perthshire, and Loch Doon in Dumfries and Galloway). To the north and west, Finlaggan Castle and settlement on two islands in Loch Finlaggan, Islay, was the seat of the lord of the Isles in the late medieval period, and Lochindorb Castle in Moray, built by the Comyn lords of Badenoch in the thirteenth century, is a first-rank castle of enclosure, and shows the importance of such locations to major landowners. They also served as estate centres for ecclesiastical lordship, such as the bishop of Aberdeen's dwelling at Bishop's Loch, Loch Goil, Aberdeenshire (Dixon and Fraser 2007), and provided suitable locations for monastic houses (St Serf's in Loch Leven), churches, chapels, and burial grounds (Shelley 2009).

Conclusions

The vast majority of the rural population in later medieval Britain were primarily engaged in agriculture, although the ways that they structured their landscape varied dramatically. The 'Central Province' of England, with its tightly nucleated villages and vast open fields, was very much the exception (although very similar landscapes could also be found in the lowlands of southern Wales), and across most of Britain communities lived in landscapes characterized by a wide variety of settlement patterns and field systems. Whilst the majority of the population spent most of their time practising mixed agriculture, there were some parts of the landscape where rural occupations were more diverse, most notably on the coast, in uplands, and in those areas rich in natural resources. The landscape was also dotted with a variety of higher-status settlements that in addition to being residences of the elite were also engaged in the management of the countryside. This chapter has hopefully shown some of the many commonalities between the different regions and nations of medieval Britain, although it will also be apparent that there have been separate research traditions in England, Scotland, and Wales. A challenge for the future will be to break down this compartmentalization and explore these issues more thematically across the three nations.

References Cited

Allen, D. 1979 'Excavations at Hafod y Nant Criafolen, Brenig Valley, Clwyd, 1973–4', *Post-Medieval Archaeology* 13, 1–59

Aston, M. and Gerrard, C. M. 2013 *Interpreting the English village: land and community at Shapwick, Somerset*, Windgather Press, Oxford

Atkinson, J. 2016 'Ben Lawers: An archaeological landscape in time. Results from the Ben Lawers Historic Landscape Project, 1996–2005', *Scottish Archaeological Internet Reports* 62 (http://doi.org/10.9750/issn.1473-3803.2016.62)

Atkinson, J. forthcoming 'The Ben Lawers Landscape Project', *Scottish Archaeological Internet Reports*, The Society of Antiquaries of Scotland

Barrett, J. H. 2008 'The Norse in Scotland', in S. Brink and N. Price (eds), *The Viking world*, Routledge, Oxford, 411–27

Barrett, J. H. (ed.) 2012 *Being an islander: production and identity at Quoygrew, Orkney, AD 900–1600*, McDonald Institute Monograph, Cambridge

Barrow, G. W. S. 1962 'Rural settlement in central and eastern Scotland: the medieval evidence', *Scottish Studies* 6(2), 123–44

Barrow, G. W. S. (ed.) 1971 *Regesta regum Scottorum, II, Acts of William I*, Edinburgh University Press, Edinburgh

Batey, C. 1982 'The late Norse site of Freswick', in J. R. Baldwin (ed.), *Caithness: a cultural crossroads*, Scottish Society for Northern Studies, Edinburgh, 45–59

Beresford, G. 2009 *Caldecote: the development and desertion of a Hertfordshire village*, The Society for Medieval Archaeology Monograph 28, Leeds

Beresford, M. W. 1964 'Dispersed and grouped settlement in medieval Cornwall', *Agricultural History Review* 12(1), 13–27

Britnell, W. J. (ed.) 2001 *Tŷ-mawr, Castle Caereinion*, Montgomeryshire Collections 89, Powysland Club

Britnell, W. J., Silvester, R. J., Suggett, R., and Wiliam, E. 2008 'Tŷ-draw, Llanarmon Mynydd Mawr, Powys, a late-medieval cruck-framed hallhouse-longhouse', *Archaeologia Cambrensis* 157, 157–202

Butler, L. 1996 'Medieval settlement in Wales', in J. Fridrich, J. Klápště, Z. Smetánka, and P. Sommer (eds), *Ruralia I*, Institute of Archaeology, Prague, 119–23

Canmore nd, *The online catalogue to Scotland's archaeology, buildings, industrial and maritime heritage*, http://canmore.rcahms.gov.uk/

Carver, M., Barrett, J., Downes, J., and Hooper, J. 2013 'Excavations at the early medieval settlement of Pitcarmick, Perthshire', *Proceedings of the Society of Antiquaries of Scotland* 142, 145–200

Christie, N. and Stamper, P. (eds) 2012 *Medieval rural settlement: Britain and Ireland, AD 800–1600*, Windgather Press, Oxford

Cooke, N., Brown, F., and Phillpotts, C. 2008 *From hunter gatherers to huntsmen: a history of the Stansted landscape*, Framework Archaeology Monograph II, Oxford and Salisbury

Crawford, I. 1988 'The Udal, North Uist', in R. Mason (ed.), *Settlement and society in Scotland*, Scotland Association for Scottish Historical Studies, St Andrews, 1–34

Creighton, O. H. 2002 *Castles and landscapes: power, community and fortification in medieval England*, Equinox, London

Creighton, O. H. and Rippon, S. 2017 'Conquest, colonisation and the countryside: archaeology and the mid-11th- to mid-12th-century rural landscape', in D. M. Hadley and C. Dyer (eds), *The archaeology of the 11th century: continuities and transformations*, The Society for Medieval Archaeology Monograph 38, London, 57–87

Croft, R. A. and Mynard, D. C. 1993 *The changing landscape of Milton Keynes*, Buckinghamshire Archaeological Society Monograph 5, Aylesbury

Dalglish, C. 2012 'Scotland's medieval countryside: evidence, interpretation, perception', in N. Christie and P. Stamper (eds), *Medieval rural settlement: Britain and Ireland, AD 800–1600*, Windgather Press, Oxford, 270–87

Davies, W. R. and Silvester R. J. 2015 'Hen Caerwys: a historiography of the first fifty years', *Transactions of the Flintshire Historical Society* 40, 17–40

Dixon, P. J. 1986 *Excavations in the fishing town of Eyemouth*, Borders Architects Group Monograph 1, Edinburgh

Dixon, P. J. 1993 *Waternish, Skye and Lochalsh: an archaeological landscape*, RCAHMS, Edinburgh

Dixon, P. J. 1998 'A rural medieval settlement in Roxburghshire: excavations at Springwood Park, Kelso, 1985–6', *Proceedings of the Society of Antiquaries of Scotland* 128, 671–751

Dixon, P. J. 2003 'Champagne country: a review of medieval rural settlement in Lowland Scotland', in S. Govan (ed.), *Medieval or later rural settlement in Scotland, ten years on*, Historic Scotland, Edinburgh, 53–64

Dixon, P. J. 2009 'Hunting, summer grazing and settlement: competing land use in the uplands of Scotland', in J. Klápště (ed.), *Medieval rural settlement in marginal landscapes*, Ruralia 7, Brepols, Tournhoult, 27–46

Dixon, P. J. and Fraser, I. 2007 'The medieval landscape', in RCAHMS (ed.), *In the shadow of Bennachie*, The Society of Antiquaries of Scotland Monograph, Edinburgh, 137–214

Dodgshon, R. A. 1981 *Land and society in early Scotland*, Clarendon Press, Oxford

Dodgshon, R. A. 1993 'West Highland and Hebridean settlement prior to crofting and the Clearances: a study in stability of change', *Proceedings of the Society of Antiquaries of Scotland* 123, 419–38

Dudley, P. 2011 *Goon, Hall, Cliff and Croft: the archaeology and landscape history of west Cornwall's rough ground*, Cornwall County Council, Truro

Duncan, A. A. M. 1975 *Scotland: the making of the kingdom*, Oliver and Boyd, Edinburgh

Durham, J. 2009 'Camp Shiel Burn', in *Discovery and Excavation in Scotland* 10, 165

Durham, J. 2012 'Shootinglee, Scottish Borders', *Discovery and Excavation in Scotland* 13, 166

Durham, J. and Dixon, P. J. 2015 'Shootinglee', *Discovery and Excavation in Scotland* 15, 178

Durham, J. and Dixon, P. J. 2016 'Shootinglee', *Discovery and Excavation in Scotland* 16, n.p.

Dyer, C. and Everson, P. 2012 'The development of the study of medieval settlements, 1880–2010', in N. Christie and P. Stamper (eds), *Medieval rural settlement: Britain and Ireland, AD 800–1600*, Windgather Press, Oxford, 11–30

Everitt, A. 1986 *Continuity and colonization: the evolution of Kentish settlement*, Leicester University Press, Leicester

Everson, P., Taylor, C. C., and Dunn, C. J. 1991 *Change and continuity: rural settlement in north-west Lincolnshire*, Her Majesty's Stationery Office, London

Fairbairn, A. 1927 'Notes on excavation of prehistoric and later sites at Muirkirk, Ayrshire, 1913–1927', *Proceedings of the Society of Antiquaries of Scotland* 61, 283–4

Fairhurst, H. and Dunbar, J. 1971 'Rural settlement in Scotland', in M. W. Beresford and J. G. Hurst (eds), *Deserted medieval villages: studies*, Lutterworth Press, London

Foster, S. and Hingley, R. 1994 'Medieval or later rural settlement in Scotland: defining, understanding and conserving an archaeological resource', *Medieval Settlement Research Group Annual Report* 9, 7–11

Fox, H. S. A. 1989 'Peasant farmers, patterns of settlement and pays: transformations in the landscapes of Devon and Cornwall', in R. A. Higham (ed.), *Landscape and townscape in the South West*, University of Exeter Press, Exeter, 41–75

Fox, H. S. A. 1996 *Seasonal settlement*, Vaughan Papers in Adult Education No. 39, University of Leicester, Leicester

Fox, H. S. A. 2001 *The evolution of the fishing village: landscape and society along the south Devon coast, 1086–1550*, Leopard's Head Press, Oxford

Fox, H. S. A. 2012 *Dartmoor's alluring uplands: transhumance and pastoral management in the Middle Ages* (edited by M. Tompkins and C. Dyer), University of Exeter Press, Exeter

Gerrard, C. M. with Aston, M. 2007 *The Shapwick Project, Somerset: a rural landscape explored*, The Society for Medieval Archaeology Monograph 25, Leeds

Gilbert, J. 1979 *Hunting and hunting reserves in Scotland*, John Donald, Edinburgh

Gonner, E. C. K. 1912 *Common land and enclosure*, Macmillan, London

Govan, S. (ed.) 2003 *Medieval or later rural settlement in Scotland: 10 years on*, Historic Scotland, Edinburgh

Gray, H. L. 1915 *English field systems*, Cambridge, Massachusetts

Hale, A. G. C. 2003 'Fish-traps in Scotland: construction, supply, demand and destruction', in J. Klápště (ed.), *Water management in the medieval rural economy*, Ruralia V, Brepols, Tournhoult, 119–26

Hall, D. 2013 'Buzzart Dikes', *Discovery and Excavation in Scotland* 14, 156

Hall, D., Oram, R., and Malloy, K. 2011 'A hunting we will go? Stirling University's Deer Parks Project', *Tayside and Fife Archaeological Journal* 17, 59–67

Hambley J. and Aitken, J. 2011 'Back Beach Brora, Highland (Clyne parish), excavation', *Discovery and Excavations in Scotland* 12, 99–101

Hamilton, J. R. C. 1956 *Excavations at Jarlshof, Shetland*, Her Majesty's Stationery Office, Edinburgh

Hegarty, C. and Wilson-North, R. 2014 *The archaeology of hill farming on Exmoor*, English Heritage, London

Henderson, C. G. and Weddell, P. J. 1994 'Medieval settlement on Dartmoor and in West Devon: the evidence from excavations', *Proceedings of the Devon Archaeological Society* 52, 119–40

Herring, P. 2006 'Cornish strip fields', in S. Turner (ed.), *Medieval Devon and Cornwall: shaping an ancient countryside*, Windgather Press, Macclesfield, 44–77

Hindmarsh, E. and Oram, R. 2013 'Excavations at the medieval settlement of Eldbotle, East Lothian', *Proceedings of the Society of Antiquaries of Scotland* 142, 245–300

HLAmap nd, Scotland-wide view of land use in modern and past times, http://hla.rcahms.gov.uk/

Johnson, N. and Rose, P. 1994 *Bodmin Moor. An archaeological survey, vol. 1: the human landscape to c.1800*, English Heritage, London

Jones, G. R. J. 1985 'Forms and patterns of medieval settlement in Welsh Wales', in D. Hooke (ed.), *Medieval villages: a review of current work*, Oxford University Committee for Archaeology, Oxford, 155–69

Jones, R. and Page, M. 2006 *Medieval villages in an English landscape*, Windgather Press, Macclesfield

Kelly, R. S. 1982 'The excavation of a medieval farmstead at Cefn Graeanog, Clynnog, Gwynedd', *Bulletin Board Celtic Studies* 29, 859–908

Kissock, J. A. 1997 '"God made nature and men made towns": post-Conquest and pre-Conquest villages in Pembrokeshire', in N. Edwards (ed.), *Landscape and settlement in medieval Wales*, Oxbow Books, Oxford, 123–37

Lawson, A. J. 1983 *The archaeology of Witton, near North Walsham, Norfolk*, East Anglian Archaeology 18, Norwich

Lelong, O. 2003 'Rural settlement in the Highlands', in S. Govan (ed.), *Medieval or later rural settlement in Scotland, ten years on*, Historic Scotland, Edinburgh, 7–16

Lenfert, R. 2011 *Long-term continuity and change within Hebridean and mainland Scottish island dwellings*, unpublished PhD, University of Nottingham

Lewis, C. 2007 'New avenues for the investigation of currently occupied medieval rural settlement: preliminary observations from the Higher Education Field Academy', *Medieval Archaeology* 51, 133–64

Lewis, C., Mitchell-Fox, P., and Dyer, C. 1997 *Village, hamlet and field*, Manchester University Press, Manchester

Liddiard, R. 2007 'Medieval designed landscapes: problems and possibilities', in M. Gardiner and S. Rippon (eds), *Medieval landscapes*, Windgather Press, Macclesfield, 201–14

Locock, M. 2006 'Deserted rural settlements in south-east Wales', in K. Roberts (ed.), *Lost farmsteads: deserted rural settlements in Wales*, Council for British Archaeology, York, 41–6

Longley, D. 1997 'The royal courts of the Welsh princes of Gwynedd', in N. Edwards (ed.), *Landscape and settlement in medieval Wales*, Oxbow Books, Oxford, 41–54

Morris, C. 1991 'The Viking and Early Settlement Archaeological Research Project', *Current Archaeology* 11, 298–9

Murray, H. and Murray, J. C. 1993 'Excavations at Rattray, Aberdeenshire: a Scottish deserted burgh', *Medieval Archaeology* 37, 109–218

Oram, R. 2011 *Domination and lordship: Scotland 1070–1230*, Edinburgh University Press, Edinburgh

Parker Pearson, M., Sharples, N. and Symonds, J. 2004 *South Uist: the archaeology and history of a Hebridean Island*, Tempus, Stroud

Parry, S. 2006 *Raunds area survey*, Oxbow Books, Oxford

Partida, T., Hall, D., and Foard, G. 2013 *An atlas of Northamptonshire: the medieval and early-modern landscape*, Oxbow Books, Oxford

Rackham, O. 1986 *The history of the countryside*, J. M. Dent and Sons, London

Rahtz, P. A. *Excavations at King John's hunting lodge, Writtle, Essex, 1955–57*, The Society for Medieval Archaeology Monograph 3, London

RCAHMS 1997 *Eastern Dumfriesshire: an archaeological landscape*, Her Majesty's Stationery Office, Edinburgh

RCAHMS 2001 *'Well shelterd and watered': Menstrie Glen, a farming landscape near Stirling*, Royal Comission on the Ancient and Historical Monuments of Scotland, Edinburgh

RCAHMS 2002 *'But the walls remained': the First Edition Survey Project*, Her Majesty's Stationery Office, Edinburgh

RCAHMS 2007 *In the shadow of Bennachie: a field archaeology of Donside, Aberdeenshire*, The Society of Antiquaries of Scotland Monograph in association with the Royal Commission on the Ancient and Historical Monuments of Scotland, Edinburgh

Rees, W. 1968 *Industry before the Industrial Revolution*, University of Wales Press, Cardiff

Rippon, S. 1996 *Gwent Levels: the evolution of a wetland landscape*, Council for British Archaeology Research Report 105, York

Rippon, S. 2000 *The transformation of coastal wetlands: exploitation and management of marshland landscapes in North West Europe during the Roman and medieval periods*, British Academy, London

Rippon, S. 2002 'Adaptation to a changing environment: the response of marshland communities to the late medieval "crisis"', *Journal of Wetland Archaeology* 1, 15–39

Rippon, S. 2006 *Landscape, community and colonisation: the North Somerset Levels during the 1st to 2nd millennia AD*, Council for British Archaeology Research Report 152, York

Rippon, S. 2008 *Beyond the medieval village: the diversification of landscape character in southern Britain*, Oxford University Press, Oxford

Rippon, S. 2009 'Understanding the medieval landscape', in R. Gilchrist and A. Reynolds (eds), *Reflections: 50 years of Medieval Archaeology 1957–2007*, The Society for Medieval Archaeology Monograph 30, Leeds, 227–54

Rippon, S. 2012 *Making sense of a historic landscape*, Oxford University Press, Oxford

Rippon, S. 2013a 'Historic landscape character and sense of place', *Landscape Research* 38(2), 179–203

Rippon, S. 2013b 'Human impact on the coastal wetlands of Britain in the medieval period', in E. Thoen, G. J. Borger, A. M. J. de Kraker, T. Soens, D. Tys, L. Vervaet, and J. T. Weerts (eds), *Landscapes or seascapes? The history of the coastal environment in the North Sea area reconsidered*, Comparative Rural History of the North Sea Area Publication 13, Brepols, Turnhout, 333-51

Rippon, S. 2014 *Beyond the medieval village: the diversification of landscape character in southern Britain*, Oxford University Press, Oxford (2nd edn)

Rippon, S., Claughton, P., and Smart C. 2009 *Mining in a medieval landscape: the royal silver mines of the Tamar Valley*, University of Exeter Press, Exeter

Roberts, B. K. 1987 *The making of the English village*, Longman, London

Roberts, B. and Wrathmell, S. 2000 *An atlas of rural settlement in England*, English Heritage, London

Roberts, B. and Wrathmell, S. 2002 *Region and place*, English Heritage, London

Roberts, K. (ed.) 2006 *Lost farmsteads: deserted rural settlements in Wales*, Council for British Archaeology, York

Rodwell, W. J. and Rodwell, K. A. 1986 *Rivenhall: investigations of a villa, church and village 1950-1977*, Council for British Archaeology Research Report 55/Chelmsford Archaeological Trust Report 4, London

Rodwell, W. J. and Rodwell, K. A. 1993 *Rivenhall: investigations of a villa, church and village 1950-1977, vol. 2: specialist studies and index to volumes 1 and 2*, Council for British Archaeology Research Report 80/ Chelmsford Archaeological Trust Report 4.2, London

Rogerson, A., Davison, A., Pritchard, D., and Silvester, R. 1997 *Barton Bendish and Caldecote: fieldwork in south-west Norfolk*, East Anglian Archaeology 80, Norwich

Ross, A. 2011 *The Kingdom of Alba: c.1000-c.1130*, Birlinn, Edinburgh

Sharples, N. 2005 *A Norse farmstead in the Outer Hebrides, excavations at mound 3, Bornais, South Uist*, Oxbow Books, Oxford

Shelley, M. J. H. 2009 *Freshwater Scottish loch settlements of the late medieval and early modern periods, with particular reference to northern Stirlingshire, central and northern Perthshire, northern Angus, Loch Awe and Loch Lomond*, unpublished PhD thesis, University of Edinburgh

Silvester, R. J. 1988 *The Fenland Project, number 3: Norfolk Survey, Marshland and Nar Valley*, East Anglian Archaeology 45, Norwich

Silvester, R. J. 1997 'Historic settlement surveys in Clwyd and Powys', in N. Edwards (ed.), *Landscape and settlement in medieval Wales*, Oxbow Books, Oxford, 113-21

Silvester, R. J. 2006 'Deserted rural settlements in central and north-east Wales', in K. Roberts (ed.), *Lost farmsteads: deserted rural settlements in Wales*, Council for British Archaeology, York, 13-39

Silvester, R. J. 2010 'Historical concept to physical reality; forests in the landscape of the Welsh borderlands' in J. Langton and G. Jones (eds), *Forests and chases of medieval England and Wales c.1100-c.1500*, St John's College Research Centre, Oxford, 141-54

Silvester, R. J. and Kissock, J. 2012 'Wales: medieval settlements, nucleated and dispersed, permanent and seasonal', in N. Christie and P. Stamper (eds), *Medieval rural settlement. Britain and Ireland, AD 800-1600*, Windgather Press, Oxford, 151-71

Slater, G. 1907 'The inclosure of common fields considered geographically', *Geographical Journal* 29(i), 35-55

Steane, J. M. and Bryant, G. F. 1975 'Excavations at the deserted medieval settlement at Lyveden: Fourth report', *Journal of Northampton Museum and Art Gallery* 12, 2-160

Suggett, R. 2004 'The interpretation of late medieval houses in Wales', in R. R. Davies and G. H. Jenkins (eds), *From medieval to modern Wales. Historical essays in honour of Kenneth O. Morgan and Ralph A. Griffiths*, University of Wales Press, Cardiff, 81–103

Sylvester, D. 1969 *The rural landscape of the Welsh Borderland*, Macmillan, London

Tait, I. 2012 *Shetland vernacular buildings 1600–1900*, The Shetland Times Ltd, Lerwick

Thomas, H. J. and Dowdell, G. 1987 'A shrunken medieval village at Barry, Glamorgan', *Archaeologia Cambrensis* 136, 94–137

Timby, J., Brown, R., Biddulph, E., Hardy, A., and Powell, A. 2007 *A slice through rural Essex: archaeological discoveries from the A120 between Stansted Airport and Braintree*, Wessex Archaeology Monograph 1, Salisbury

Turner, R. T. 2003 'The Ben Lawers Landscape Project', in S. Govan (ed.), *Medieval or later rural settlement in Scotland, ten years on*, Historic Scotland, Edinburgh

Turner, R. and Johnston, A. (eds) 2006 *Chepstow Castle: its history and buildings*, Logaston Press, Almeley

Turner, V. E., Bond, J. M. and Larsen, A.-C. 2013 *Viking Unst: excavation and survey in Northern Scotland 2006–2010*, Shetland Amenity Trust, Lerwick

Wade-Martins, P. 1980 *Fieldwork and excavation on village sites in Launditch Hundred, Norfolk*, East Anglian Archaeology 10, Norwich

Williamson, T. 2003 *Shaping medieval landscapes*, Windgather Press, Macclesfield

Williamson, T., Liddiard, R., and Partida, T. 2013 *Champion: the making and unmaking of the English medieval landscape*, Liverpool University Press, Liverpool

Winchester, A. 2000 *The harvest of the hills: rural life in Northern England and the Scottish Borders, 1400–1700*, Keele University Press, Keele

CHAPTER 13

RURAL LIVING 1100–1540

CHRISTOPHER DYER

FOUR-FIFTHS of the population of medieval Britain were country dwellers below the ranks of the aristocracy. The most important single group were the small-scale cultivators, conveniently described by us as peasants, but also under scrutiny are the landless, and rural people who often combined non-agricultural activities (such as cloth-making, mining, fishing) with some cultivation. The material conditions of country people varied with the quantity and quality of land that they held, their opportunities in the market, and their obligations in rents and taxes. They experienced changes in fortune over time: the period up to about 1300 saw the growth of new settlements, both villages and hamlets; in the next two centuries the shrinkage and abandonment of settlements are symptoms of troubles and challenges. Regions varied greatly, and in this chapter the first part will deal with the English lowlands in the north-east, the Midlands, East Anglia, and the south from Devon to Kent. Much land in the lowlands was devoted to growing crops in large open fields, farmed from nucleated villages, but the wooded, pastoral, and wetland landscapes with their dispersed settlements often with enclosed fields and irregular open fields accounted for a greater area (see Chapter 12). The rural scene to the west and north will receive attention in the later part of the chapter. Britain's peasant past is well recorded in numerous documents, but great quantities of data have emerged from excavations and surveys, enabling a full picture of rural life to emerge from material evidence.

Rural settlements were made up of a series of tofts, crofts, closes, or plots (modern archaeological vocabulary varies). A typical plot often consisted of a dwelling house and outbuildings which included at least a single barn, but sometimes there were two, three, or even more structures, contained within an enclosure that was usually rectangular, with an entrance out onto a street. To take an example, Croft F at Great Linford (Buckinghamshire) has a dwelling house, built with a timber frame resting on low stone foundation walls, identified by its hearths and its latrine, and much altered in its relatively long life (Figure 13.1) (Mynard and Zeepvat 1992, 67–73). A large barn lay to the east, and two smaller buildings, one almost square to the north, ranged around the cobbled yard. At least one of the outbuildings had probably

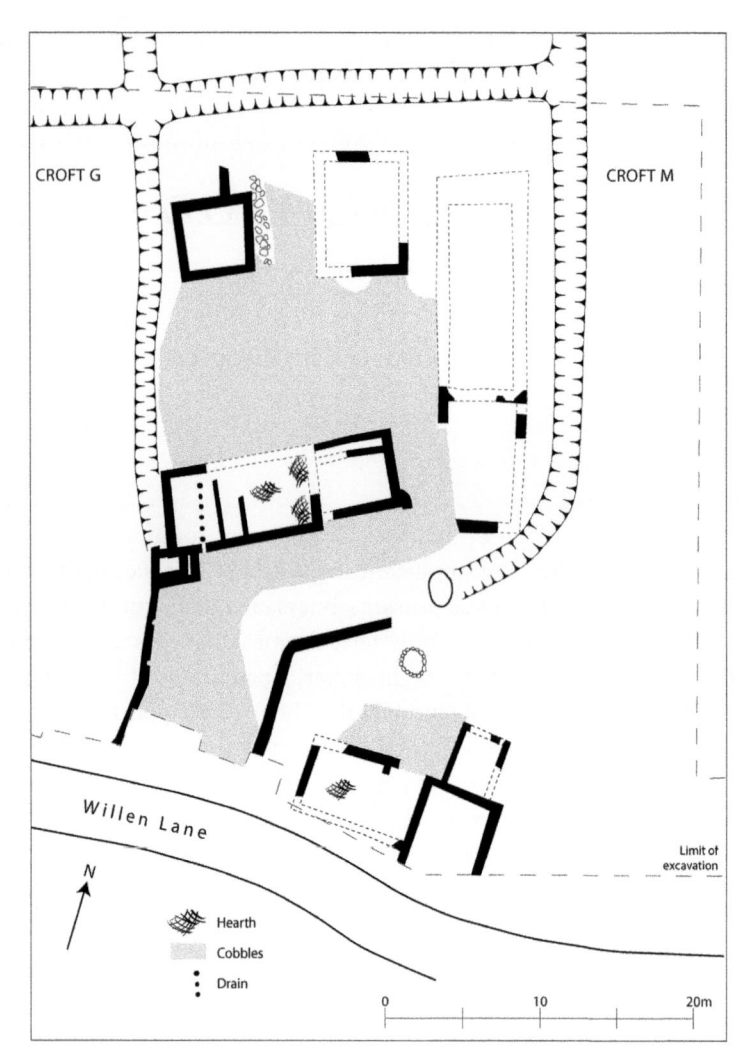

FIGURE 13.1 Croft F at Great Linford (Buckinghamshire): dwelling, barn and other buildings in an enclosed croft, 1250–1400

(redrawn by Alejandra Gutiérrez after Mynard and Zeepvat 1992, 70)

been used to shelter livestock. All of these were built, like the dwelling, with stone foundations and timber frames. Access to the buildings and yard was gained by an entrance off the road later called Willen Lane, which was wide enough to contain a pit for water, presumably to enable animals to drink. These structures belonged to a phase dated to c.1250–c.1400. At the entrance from the road the boundaries were marked by stone walls, doubtless intended to impress, but the rest of the boundary was marked by a ditch.

Such houses and outbuildings provided spaces for habitation and production for a small domestic group, a single household containing parents and children and sometimes one or two living-in servants. Each family occupied a dwelling of limited size, often 5 metres wide, with a length of 10 or 15 metres, which was just capable of accommodating four, five, or six people. This supports the conclusion drawn from documents that country people lived in nuclear families. If a new family was formed by the marriage of the heir to land, we sometimes find that the surviving retired couple, widow, or widower were given separate accommodation. The need to provide space for the older generation, or other relatives, and the constantly changing needs of the main household as children were born, grew up, and then departed, must explain the alteration of houses which is revealed by their excavated foundations. For example, in tenement D at the hamlet of West Cotton (Northamptonshire) a kitchen or bakehouse was built in the thirteenth century, serving a nearby house (Chapman 2010, 176–81). It was large enough (9.5 x 5.5 m internal measurements) to be converted into a dwelling, which involved some rebuilding of the stone foundation walls, and the insertion of partitions to make three very small rooms, one of which had a hearth (Figure 13.2). Later a small fourth room was added to the corner of the house, with its own doorway, perhaps for an elderly relative.

Households gathered together in hamlets and villages were usually distinguished clearly from their neighbours by enclosures, defined by ditches associated with hedges

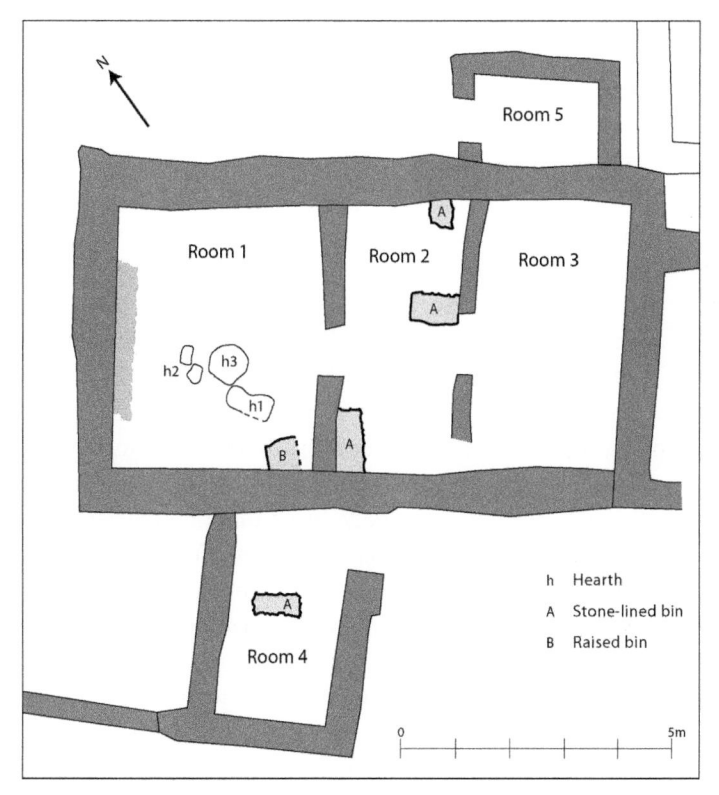

FIGURE 13.2 Multi-phase peasant building at West Cotton (Northamptonshire) (from Chapman 2010, 179)

(© MOLA Northampton, courtesy of MOLA and Oxbow Books)

or fences, or walls of mud or (more rarely) stone. The ditches were often cleaned and renewed, as at Holworth in Dorset in the thirteenth to fifteenth centuries, partly because they had an important function for drainage, but also because they marked a property boundary, and might deter potential thieves (Rahtz 1958). Quite frequent finds of locks and keys, and iron door fittings, add to the picture of peasants' desire for security. Villagers clearly had a sense of privacy, and while they co-operated with their neighbours on matters of common interest, they were careful to mark the limits of their closes in relation both to adjacent households and the public space of the street and village green.

The buildings, the yard, and the enclosed space of the plot where they stood formed the centre of a unit of production which gained its livelihood from the meadows, fields, pastures, and woods that stretched for 2 or 3 km from the settlement. The house and its buildings sheltered the workers: all members of the family who could contribute, and servants if these were employed. Women were engaged in heavy tasks in the fields alongside the men judging from the similarity of the adult male and female arm bones observed in the burials in the churchyard at Wharram Percy (Yorkshire) (Mays et al. 2007, 122–3). In or near the buildings would be kept the implements such as carts and ploughs, though these leave few traces in the finds from excavations. The only plough coulter excavated from a late medieval settlement site ironically comes not from the arable heartlands of the Midlands, but from a hamlet on the edge of moorland at Alnhamsheles in Northumberland (Dixon 2014). The iron rims of cart wheels and the tines of harrows are also scarce as such large pieces of iron, if worn or broken, would have been reworked by smiths. The draught animals which hauled the implements have left evidence in the form of iron shoes, ox-goads, buckles, and harness fittings, and the bones of horses and the mature cattle some of which would have worked as oxen. Byres and stables can be recognized in excavation by their drains and troughs, and sometimes from a scatter of animal shoes. Wheeled vehicles have signalled their presence by leaving their ruts on stretches of roads in or near settlements (Spoerry and Atkins 2015, 57). The most abundant material evidence for field cultivation comes from the smaller tools, including spade shoes (the blade of the spade was made of wood), spuds and weeding hooks for removing larger weeds such as thistles from the growing corn, and sickles or reaping hooks (Goodall 2011). Pieces of scythe blade are encountered less often, again because the large size of the complete blade made them difficult to lose and valuable enough to recycle. Whetstones (some imported from Norway) for sharpening these tools figure among the more common finds on settlement sites. An essential contribution to the fertility of the fields came from the dung heaps kept near the peasant buildings, which are sometimes detectable in excavation, but leave more enduring traces in the scatter of pottery in the fields, resulting from the inclusion of domestic refuse, including broken pottery, with the manure (Jones 2004).

After the harvest, crops would be brought back to the plot for protection and storage in a barn or in stacks (with thatched roofs) in the yard. Barns are identified by their lack of hearths, internal partitions, and other signs that they accommodated either people or animals. In a hamlet near Okehampton in Devon, again sited on the edge of moorland but nonetheless cultivating land in fields in the thirteenth century, houses were associated with buildings probably used as barns which measured 11.5 and 11.6 m in length (Austin 1978). Everywhere safe storage of the sheaves was so important that sometimes the barns were as large or larger than the dwelling houses, and the structures, judging from their stone foundations (from the thirteenth century and subsequently), resembled in quality those of the dwellings. The actual crops can also be analysed from the grains and sometimes other parts of the plant which were charred, usually by accident during the process of drying corn, or from the burning of straw (Carruthers 2005; Moffett 2006, 43–53; Rippon et al. 2014; see Chapter 8 in this *Handbook*). The proportion of different grains varied from site to site, though wheat, barley, and oats are most commonly encountered, with rye in specific localities. Documents record the proportions of different grains harvested by the lord, or a whole village in the case of tithe accounts, but deposits of carbonized grains tell us about the use of crops by a particular household. The grains themselves can be identified as belonging to bread wheat, or rivet wheat, or two-row or six-row barley. Each of these varieties had different characteristics in resistance to disease, ability to discourage birds, and suitability for consumption, as bread or as ale in the case of different types of barley. The types of wood which were brought into the village for building timber or to be burnt as fuel have been identified, as have the useful plants that grew on the commons, such as rushes, and the weeds that caused nuisance in the corn fields (Hillman et al. 2005).

Within the enclosure around the peasant house and its buildings some space was available for production of pigs, poultry, honey, garden produce, and extra grazing. At Holworth the square enclosures in which the buildings lay measured 30 x 30 m, and the much larger separate croft behind this was about 90 m long (Rahtz 1958). Most households had much less space. Garden products leave few material remains, though smaller and less substantial buildings, at Wharram Percy for example, may well have been used as pigsties and poultry houses. Spaces along a stone wall at Great Linford probably sheltered bee skeps (Mynard and Zeepvat 1992, 72). Pollen and seeds reveal some of the garden crops, notably an abundance of cabbage and mustard cultivation at West Cotton, and many sites produce evidence for flax and hemp, which were commonly grown in gardens alongside fruit and vegetables (Chapman 2010, 164). Fruit has left traces on rural sites, though the best evidence for rural production comes from urban cess pits. These contain an abundant variety of pips, seeds, and stones which would often have come from rural gardens, orchards, and hedgerows (Greig 1981).

Larger peasant holdings are known from documents to have kept small herds of cattle and flocks of sheep. Some of the cattle could have been kept in byres, which occasionally lay under the same roof as the human living space in a long-house, but indoor space was limited, and it has been argued that in the East Midlands, in such villages as Barton Blount (Derbyshire) cattle were kept overnight and in bad weather in yards (Beresford 1975, 13–18). These were often sited next to the buildings, with surfaces worn down by the hoofs of cattle and removal of dung. Sheep spent much of their time on the pastures, but could be put into sheepcotes capable of holding a few dozen animals as have been identified from building foundations at Roel and Lower Harford (Gloucestershire)

(Dyer 1995, 159). An alternative was to use the croft behind the houses for wintering sheep—the dimensions of such enclosures have already been indicated for Holworth, but they were a feature on the Yorkshire Wolds, the Cotswolds, and other regions.

The house, its buildings, yards, gardens, and orchards was not just the base from which cultivators set out to do their work in the fields, meadows, and woods. Much of the working lives of the family, and especially the females, was devoted to processing the crops both for household consumption and for sale. Food preparation has left traces in the settlements, including pieces of hand-mill for home grinding of grain and malt in the home, though a local mechanical mill, whether powered by water, wind, or a horse was usually available. The advantage of the large mill was the saving of labour through its speed and efficiency, but this came at a cost in tolls paid to the miller and ultimately for the profit of the lords of the manor who owned most mills. In addition, time could be wasted in queuing, and the mills did not work consistently if water or wind were lacking or the machinery went wrong, so there were good reasons to have the option of hand-milling. Using the lord's mill was usually compulsory, so hand-milling might lead to payment of a fine to the manorial court (Holt 1988, 36–53). Some households had their own oven, which again may have been preferred in some circumstances to the common oven provided by the manorial lord. Most households had the means of brewing their own ale, but the equipment rarely survives, because the vessels in which water was heated were made of expensive recyclable metal, and wooden tubs and barrels have decayed in normal soil conditions.

The most frequently encountered objects connected with dairying were shallow pottery pans, as the mainly wooden utensils have not survived. Meat production led households into slaughtering and butchering their own animals, as is suggested by the presence among the animal bones in villages of the bones from the head, that is butchers' waste. Rural butchery techniques suggest a lower level of skill and specialization than is found in towns (Richardson 2005, 164–7). The food and drink produced in the peasant households were consumed partly by the household members, and partly by neighbours by some form of exchange. Here the evidence comes from documents, because those who produced written records had an interest in regulating trade and creaming off some of its profits. The commercial sale of ale led to accusations of over pricing, illicit measures, and unwholesome ale. Some of the household's produce—bread, cheese and butter, eggs, fruit and vegetables, and poultry—was taken to local towns for sale, often by the female producers, who were subject to the towns' controls on hucksters.

To what extent were the rural cultivators aiming to satisfy household needs, or were they producing for the market? The material evidence sometimes supports a commercial interpretation. At West Cotton peasant houses were provided with well-built malt kilns, large enough to convert their surplus of barley into malt intended for sale, and extra acres were presumably planted with barley to meet the demand (Chapman 2010, 225–9). Samples of burnt grain seem to be heavily slanted towards particular crops, such as wheat in proximity to London where the inhabitants usually ate wheat bread (Rippon et al. 2014, 236). Animals and animal products (cheese, wool, and hides) were commonly sold. The best evidence for the trade in animals for slaughter comes from the accumulations of bones in towns which had a rural origin, mostly from peasants as their livestock (according to the documents) cumulatively outnumbered those kept and sold by the lords of manors. Towns consumed beef in quantity, encouraging peasants to rear animals to satisfy that demand. Many of the bones of cattle and sheep found in towns came from mature or even elderly animals, suggesting that a high proportion of rural animals were kept mainly for their milk, wool, and capacity to haul heavy loads, and were sold when they ceased to perform these useful functions (see Chapter 7).

The rural population were often involved in part-time craft production, and contributed to making cloth, metal implements, leather goods, pottery, and foodstuffs, and performing such services as building work (see Part VI). These activities have left their mark on rural settlements, in the form of heckle teeth and spindle-whorls (for combing and spinning wool and flax fibres), slags, hammerscale and hearths left by smiths, pottery and tile kilns with heaps of wasters, and specialist tools such as chisels. Away from the settlements the waste heaps and diggings mark the site of iron, lead, tin, and coal mines in which peasants often played a part. In woodlands, where materials and skilled labour could be brought together, charcoal was burnt, leaving distinct residues, glass furnaces were active in a few localities, and specialist workers turned wooden cups and bowls on lathes, or constructed barrels and other wooden vessels from staves (e.g. Foard 2001). On the coast a salt industry often depended on the employment of country people in extracting turf or peat to boil the brine. Fishing industries could be found in peasant settlements both near the sea (at Romney Marsh for example) and inland near rivers and meres (e.g. Barber and Priestley-Bell 2008, 183–7, 188–90, 224–7). Craft activities would have been practised directly for the benefit of the household, such as the rather clumsy repetitive mending of a child's shoe at Wharram Percy (Mould 2005), but often the goods were being made for sale. Urban weavers used yarn prepared in the country, for example, and shoes were made in towns from leather sometimes tanned in a nearby village.

Peasants must have gained surpluses from production, but the extent of their profits is difficult to assess. They handled money, though this is not fully apparent from the few coins found on settlements. Of a sample of thirty-three widely scattered sites mainly occupied between the twelfth and fifteenth centuries, no coins at all were found on half of them, and the remaining seventeen yielded a total of sixty coins, mainly silver pennies, halfpennies, and farthings (Dyer 1998). Finds of coins made throughout the countryside, mostly from fields, by metal detectorists who reported their finds to the Portable Antiquities Scheme are much more plentiful (see Chapter 32). For example, those minted in 1279–1351 numbered 5886 according to one count, but of course this still does not amount to a great number for each household, as the coin finds were spread over the territories of hundreds of villages. The coins must have been lost by people ploughing and harvesting, or more likely were mislaid near houses and spread on the land as part of the manure heap. These finds have been used, in combination with other figures, to make an ingenious calculation of the total of money in circulation, such as a figure of £2 million in 1319, which would suggest for each individual about seventy to eighty pence (Allen 2015, 19–23). The coins that are found now, many of them worn by frequent handling, represent a small percentage of the large numbers in circulation, many of which passed often through the hands of peasants.

An indirect approach to understanding peasant income might be to consider their acquisitions and expenditure. Much of their food came from their holding of land, but sea fish formed at least a small part of inland peasant diet, and would have been bought usually in preserved form as red and white herring from the North Sea and stockfish (dried cod) from Arctic Norway as is suggested by bones found at Wharram Percy (Barrett 2005; Chapter 9 in this *Handbook*). Cloth and clothing, household textiles such as bedding, and also shoes, were purchased by households which lacked the skill, equipment, and time to make them themselves. They rarely leave any material trace (apart from remnants of linen shrouds in graves in churchyards) but metal dress accessories (usually of copper alloy) survive in some numbers, both from settlement sites and in the fields, having been lost or discarded. These buckles, belt ends, decorative plaques, and belt fittings were usually of urban manufacture and were presumably bought as part of the belts and garments to which they were attached (see Chapter 49). Many domestic furnishings and items of kitchen equipment were made entirely of wood, and have not survived, but non-organic materials were more often used for utensils for cooking and serving food. These include cast bronze or sheet bronze cooking vessels of which only fragments are found, as the bulk of the vessels that were broken or discarded were taken to the urban founder for recycling, but also chains and other fittings for hanging pots over a fire, metal spoons and knives, candle holders, and many other smaller items. Hand-mills were usually obtained from distant quarries, as were the stone mortars, for grinding food into a paste. Fuel, most often wood or turf, was sometimes obtained from a distance, and might have to be purchased by households who lacked rights of common in woods or on peat deposits. The market would have been the usual source of charcoal and mineral coal.

Houses were built at considerable cost to those who lived in them. A tenant might have the good fortune to be granted trees by the lord, but much building timber was purchased, together with laths and nails for the roof and relatively expensive items such as the hinges and locks for doors and window shutters. Above all, peasants hired specialist craftsmen, masons to build the foundations, and thatchers for the roof, but most important were the carpenters who cut the timbers and raised the frame (Dyer 2013, 19–20). Buildings, both houses and barns, represented the single largest item of expenditure ever made by a peasant household, though fortunately for them as buildings became more durable and sophisticated in the thirteenth century they lasted for many generations if kept in repair. Some of the Great Linford houses were in use (with alterations) for more than two centuries, and throughout England hundreds of houses built in the period 1380–1500 are still standing and inhabited (see Chapter 15).

Fragments of pottery are the most common find from excavations of medieval rural sites, and they are found scattered on associated fields. To take a single example, part of a deserted village at Goldicote in Warwickshire, including two buildings, was excavated when a pipeline cut through the site. A total of 2687 sherds of pottery were recovered, dating from the eleventh to the fifteenth centuries, with a majority between 1100 and

1400 (Rátkai 2012, 100–13). All of the pots that they represent had travelled some distance to reach the small and quite remote village, with wares made at Chilvers Coton, Deritend, Coventry, and Warwick in north Warwickshire, and others from the south in Northamptonshire, from Boarstall and Brill in western Buckinghamshire, and from the north Cotswolds. Pottery was carried from centres of manufacture to the west at Hanley Castle in Worcestershire and the city of Worcester, and also from a less remote kiln at Alcester. Not all of the manufacturing centres can be located precisely, and a proportion of the pottery found probably came from kilns within 10 or 20 km, but those that can be identified precisely from the analysis of the geology of their fabric mostly lay at a distance of about 40 km. Potters may sometimes have sold their wares directly to consumers, but in the great majority of cases the pots were handled by middlemen, and the Goldicote peasants would have bought their cooking pots, bowls, jugs, and pitchers from traders in the nearest market town, Stratford-upon-Avon, or from itinerant pedlars.

The medieval countryside was full of consumers who could afford to spend money on a wide range of goods and services because they derived income from production. What were the motives and aims of peasant consumption? It was once thought that they were relatively poor and very practical people, so their expenditure can be regarded as mainly functional. They invested in barns to conserve their harvested crops, and spent much of their money on useful utensils and implements. There is much to support this view, but some objects were decorative and impractical like the colourfully glazed jugs in which ale might be served at table. Occasional finds are pewter flasks for holy water (*ampullae*) which were bought at a shrine visited on a pilgrimage, reflecting piety and perhaps also status-seeking (see Chapter 40). Another approach to peasant consumption is to regard it as a symptom of emulation. It is said that peasants knew of the superior way of life of the aristocracy, and imitated it as much as their resources allowed. Accordingly a peasant house contained a hall resembling a lord's main room where meals were taken and guests received, and its upper end and dais with carved beams portrayed the household's internal hierarchy (see Chapter 43). Architecturally elaborate halls are especially apparent in still-standing peasant houses in fifteenth-century Kent (Pearson 1994, 90–5). This idea that peasants followed their superiors has some justification, and one notes the stone mortar used in the kitchen, or the occasional find of a chafing dish for keeping food warm at table, both of which would be found in gentry households.

Emulation alone is unlikely to have been the chief driving force, as peasants with limited means would surely have had more plausible and realistic goals, which related to competition within the community. Houses were given features which would convey to neighbours and observers the superior status of the household. These might include an abundance of timber in the framing of the walls, especially on the side of the house visible from the street, or houses with upper floors would be jettied out beyond the ground floor, a style borrowed from town houses. Some peasants owned metal seal matrices (recovered from fields, not usually from settlements) with which they authenticated documents. These might suggest another case of emulation, but they may have been status symbols for the more acquisitive peasants who often transferred land by charters to which wax seals were attached. A significant minority of metal dress accessories were decorated and would have helped to establish the superior status of the wearer (Figure 13.3). In a similar category were the ornamental fittings designed to hang visibly (and audibly) from the harness of horses used for riding, and the spurs on the boots of the riders. To confirm the pretentiousness and attention-seeking of these metal artefacts, a few were gilded (Smith 2009). Such features suggest that peasants saw themselves as individuals, seeking to outdo and impress their neighbours. This view has to be modified in the light of the widespread sense of a collective interest, expressed in everyday routines in the management of common land. Communal buildings required heavy and regular contributions from the villagers, most costly being the parish church, of which the nave, tower, and porch were the responsibility of the laity of the parish. In addition a church house or a guildhall (the meeting place of a religious fraternity) could be built. Consumption was also driven by a growing desire for comfort and domesticity, apparent in the repositioning of the hearth from the centre of the hall to a place against an internal wall, with a smoke hood to allow the fumes to escape. Private rooms, chambers, increased in number towards the end of our period.

Rural life was not dominated entirely by the necessities of daily subsistence, or by competitive and acquisitive impulses. There are hints among the finds from rural settlements of time spent in pleasure, like the musical instruments notably pipes carved from bones, or the nine mens' morris boards scratched on stone. Simple entertainment came from 'buzz bones' in which a hole drilled in a pig's bone through which a cord was threaded allowed the cord to be twisted and then released to create a satisfying whirring noise (Dyer 2014, 20–1). Finally, we should allow for a specifically peasant outlook that was reflected in their consumption. They lived with a shifting balance between the well-being and identity of individual households and communal concerns. They sometimes expressed their hierarchical tendencies by showing off their wealth to neighbours, but houses in a village had a similar design and were built from the same materials. Peasant material culture had local roots, so that fields and settlements observed customary local forms, whereby houses were built with crucks in the north and west, and used box framing in the south and east.

Surely a discussion of peasant consumption is unrealistic because it ignores widespread poverty in the countryside? In support of this view are the analyses of the bones from the churchyard at Wharram Percy, which provides a large sample of 687 burials of rural people (Mays et al. 2007, 77–192). The skeletons are not precisely dated, but the majority belong to people who lived between 1100 and 1450. Their bones show that 45 per cent of the sample died before they reached the age of 16, and that probably is too low a figure because children's smaller and more fragile bones are difficult to find. Babies were breast fed, which gave them a good nutritional start in life, but the poor diet of teenagers meant that they gained height slowly. Bone conditions such as porotic hyperostosis which was found in 125 individuals suggested that they had experienced some serious episode of stress, from infectious disease or hunger. On the other hand, almost half of those who survived into adulthood could expect to live beyond the age of 50, and most of the individuals had not suffered sufficiently severe deprivation to affect their

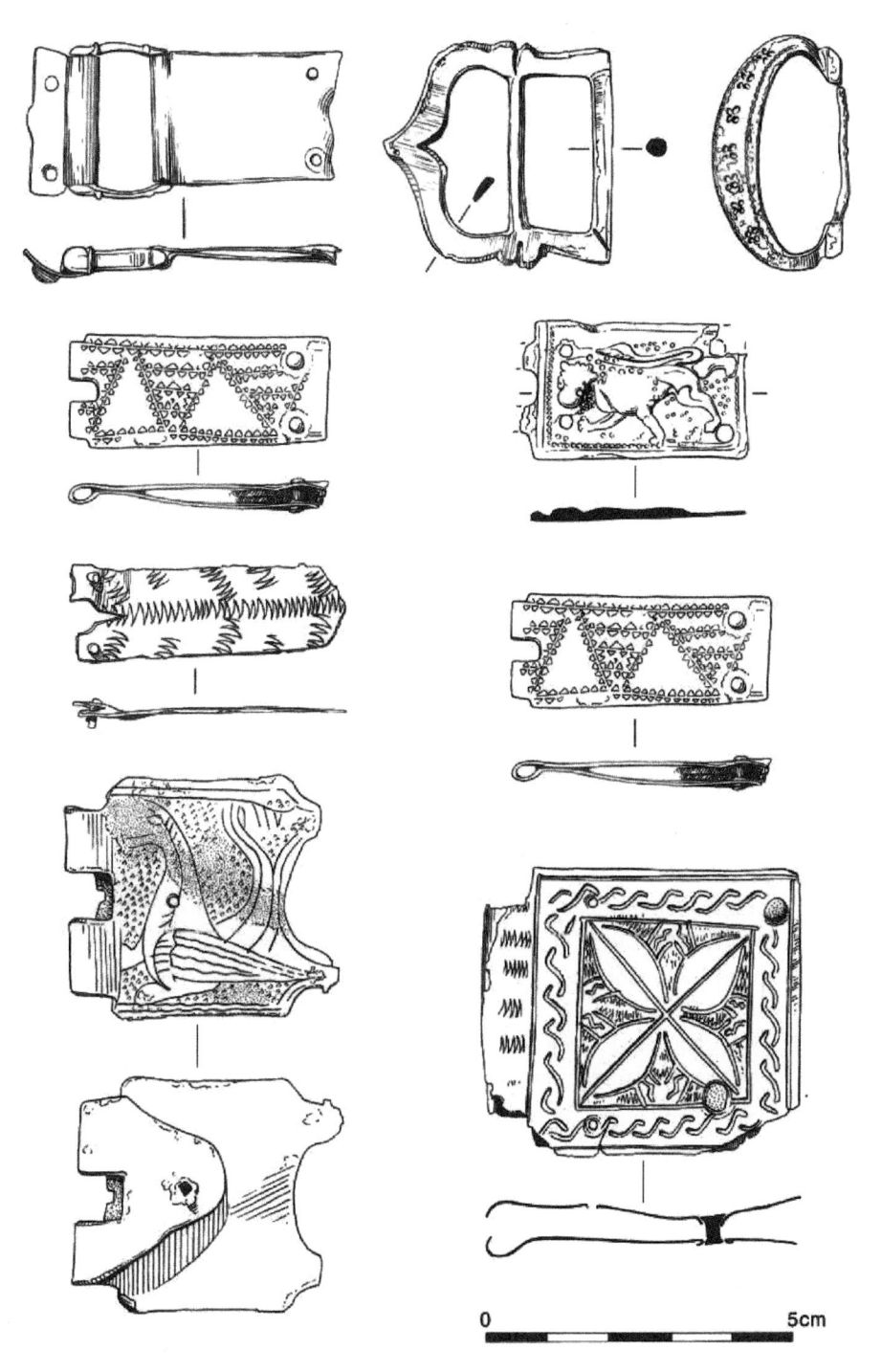

FIGURE 13.3 Copper-alloy buckles and buckle plates from Tattenhoe and Westbury (Buckinghamshire), some with decoration, including a lion, twelfth to fifteenth century

(from Ivens et al. 1995, 354)

bones. Less direct indications of poverty come from the minority of houses in villages and hamlets in every region, which from 1200 to 1500, persisted in using the earthfast building method, in which the ends of vertical timbers were embedded in post-holes, or in trenches, and were not founded on stone walls or at least on padstones.

The limited resources of some rural households are suggested by the repairs carried out on ceramic pots, even mundane and cheap ones. Perhaps these took place in brief episodes of deprivation, but the ups and downs of life cannot explain why some settlements, such as those in the Weald of south-east England, although they were inhabited for a century or two, apparently used very little pottery and left few artefacts for excavators to find (Gardiner 1998). In most villages better-off peasants—those with 15 acres (6 ha) or more—lived alongside smallholders and cottagers, though they often occupied different parts of the settlement. At Shapwick (Somerset) in a long narrow village the smallholders lived in the northern end and the wealthier tenants in the south (Aston and Gerrard 2013, 173–5).

Reference has been made to the overall expansion in settlements up to the late thirteenth century, and their tendency subsequently to shrink. The explanation of these changes used to focus on rising birth rates in the thirteenth century and epidemic mortality after 1348, but more complex changes were involved. The plagues were preceded by the abandonment of settlements, even as early as 1300, and villages collapsed not in the 1350s and 1360s but decades, even a century, after that catastrophe. Artefacts, especially pottery, show growth in manufactures and rural consumption in the thirteenth century, which was also a period of increasing single coin finds. Commercial expansion must have stimulated an agricultural boom and the formation of new households, but that was not necessarily followed by a trade slump in the period when population was falling. Houses were abandoned in a process of restructuring, in which the survivors took on more land and increased production from each household, leading to new house building. A handful of rural houses have been dated by dendrochronology to 1250–1350, but larger numbers were built in a rising surge which began in 1380 and reached a building boom in the period 1430–1520. The houses were more numerous, but also represented higher living standards, as more of them had two-storey wings which contained two or three rooms (Alcock and Miles 2012). The standard of construction rose, and at least a few had tiled or slated roofs. There is even a rare discovery that a peasant house had a glazed window (Andrews and Milne 1979, 73, 115, 130).

The northern and western regions of England and the countryside of Wales and Scotland were not a world apart, but they are sufficiently different to merit some separate discussion. Their agriculture tended towards the pastoral: their cultivated land lay in small open fields and separate enclosures, and many of the cultivators had access to large open pastures. Settlements tended to be dispersed, though nucleated villages are found in river valleys in north-west England, and in parts of south Wales and southern Scotland (see Chapter 12). The great majority of settlements cultivated grain, which according to the botanic samples included a high proportion of barley and oats. To maintain fertility they sometimes practised infield-outfield cultivation, in which part of the arable was cropped intensively, but the rest only occasionally. In parts of the western and northern isles organic material was concentrated to form high-quality 'plaggen' soils. Animals were commonly driven to graze on remote pastures, and if the distances were too great for daily journeys, temporary seasonal settlements, shielings, or hafods were built for the herdsmen and dairy maids. Many communities or individuals were drawn into non-agricultural activities, such as fishing, collecting shellfish and birds' eggs, and extracting minerals. An isolated farmstead at Brassington in the Peak District of Derbyshire has evidence from excavation of lead mining and smelting, and extensive iron working was a feature of a settlement site at Hen Caerwys in Flintshire (Makepeace 2001; Davies and Silvester 2015).

Did the people of the west and north gain much wealth from their potentially lucrative pastoralism and by-occupations? Their housing is not so different from the rest of Britain, except that the building traditions of the native population and Norse settlers had a strong influence in the western and northern isles. A higher proportion of houses belonged to the long-house type in which cattle and humans were accommodated under the same roof (Figure 13.4). In the Solway plain the houses of the end of the fifteenth century known as clay dabbins used sparse supplies of timber and locally available earth to build on the basis of cruck frames resembling those of the Midlands (Jennings 2002), and in the same period some very impressive timber-framed houses were being built in parts of Wales. On some sites the main structure was made entirely of timber, without stone foundations, throughout the late medieval period, and even at Tatton in Cheshire, which belongs to the north-west Midlands rather than the true north, houses of the thirteenth and fourteenth centuries were based on earthfast posts (Higham 1998–9, 79–101). Excavations, like those at Eldbottle in East Lothian, produced limited evidence for material possessions, with quite small quantities of pottery which tended to come from local sources, and metal small finds seem scarce (e.g. Hindmarsh and Oram 2012).

The people of these regions should not be considered backward, as they made skilful adaptations to their environment. Their fields and pastures were aimed at maximizing productivity in country where extensive and continuous cultivation would have ruined the soil. In some areas urban markets were too remote for regular use to be made of them, so that (in the Hebrides, for example) pottery was made locally to not very high standards (Armit et al. 2008). However, they did not always choose a 'low technology' solution to their problems, as for example the tin industry of Cornwall applied water power systematically to the various processes of preparing ore and smelting (Gerrard 2000).

The people of the north and west were aware of the great opportunities presented by expanding markets. At Quoygrew on the northern tip of the most northern island of the Orkneys a small community exploited the resources of land and sea to produce food and goods for their own use, but also sent dried cod, fish oil, butter, and coarse cloth into distant markets in the south, which their location on the coast and sailing skills made possible. They bought soapstone vessels for cooking from Norway, and pottery from Scotland and England (Barrett 2012). At Tyddyn Llwydion in Montgomeryshire (Powys) stood an isolated long house, undated but probably built around 1500. Its skilled carpenter deserved a handsome reward. The peasant who had it built did not

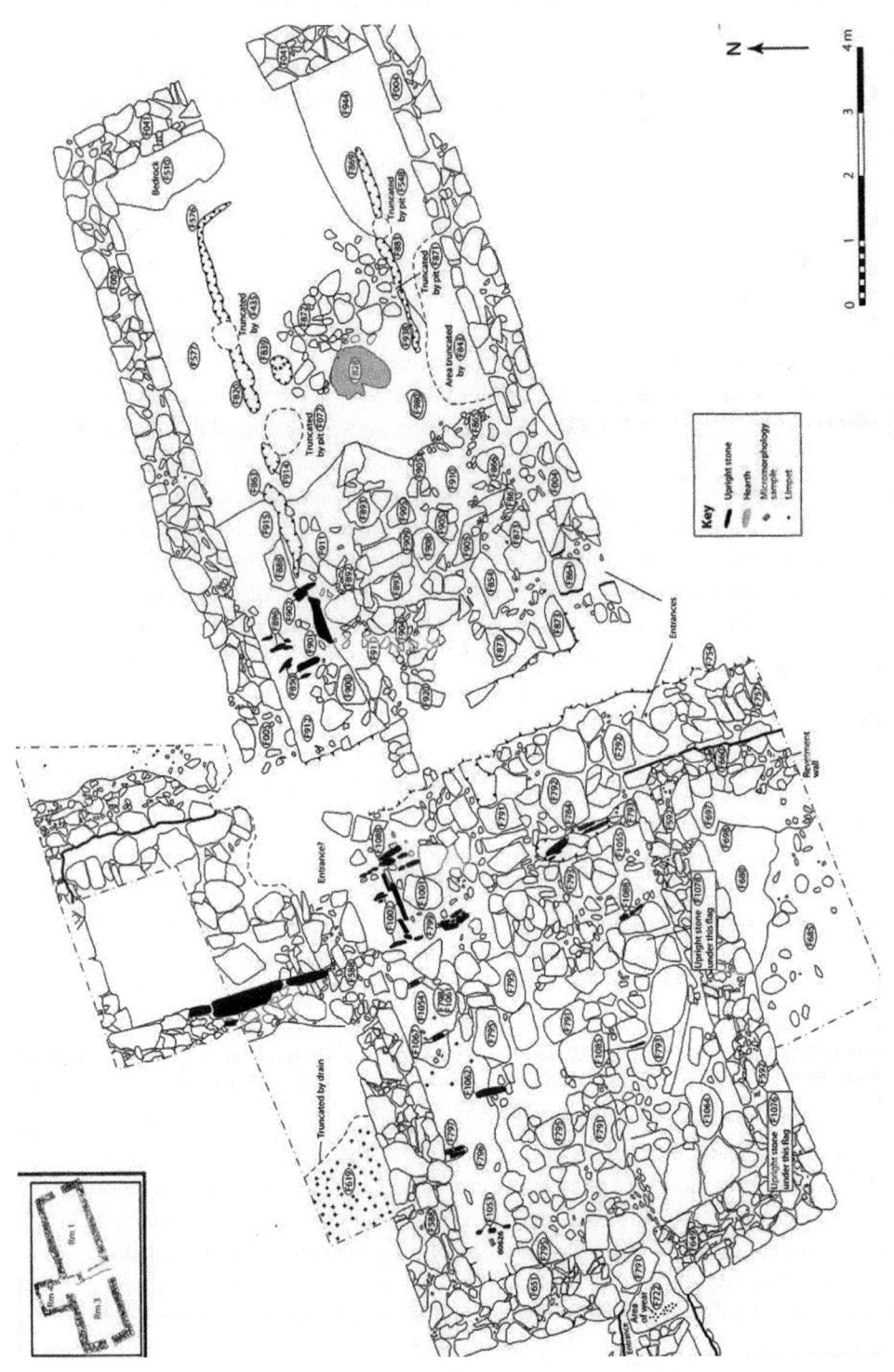

FIGURE 13.4 House at Quoygrew, Orkney, with substantial stone foundations. To the east a room with a hearth, a hall, and at the western end a byre with a drain and stalls for cattle, c.1200

(from Barrett 2012, 65)

aspire to consume in the style of his equivalents in midland and southern England, as excavation under and around the house produced no pottery or small finds (Britnell and Suggett 2002). Yet he had wealth enough to pay for a fine house, perhaps obtained by rearing cattle to be sold into England to satisfy the demand for beef in Coventry or London.

References cited

Alcock, N. and Miles, D. 2012 *The medieval peasant house in the Midlands*, Oxbow, Oxford

Allen, M. 2015 'Coin finds and the English money supply, c.973–1544', in M. Allen and D. Coffman (eds), *Money, prices and wages: essays in honour of Professor Nicholas Mayhew*, Palgrave Macmillan, Basingstoke, 7–23

Andrews, D. and Milne, G. 1979 *Wharram: a study of settlement on the Yorkshire wolds. Domestic settlement, 1: area 10 and 6*, The Society for Medieval Archaeology Monograph 8, London

Armit, I., Campbell, E., and Dunwell, A. 2008 'Excavation of an Iron Age, early historic and medieval settlement and metalworking site at Eilean Olabhat, North Uist', *Proceedings of the Society of Antiquaries of Scotland* 138, 27–104

Aston, M. and Gerrard, C. M. 2013 *Interpreting the English village: landscape and community at Shapwick, Somerset*, Windgather, Oxford

Austin, D. 1978 'Excavations at Okehampton Park, Devon, 1976–78', *Proceedings of the Devon Archaeological Society* 36, 191–239

Barber, L. and Priestley-Bell, G. 2008 *Medieval adaptation, settlement and economy of a coastal wetland: the evidence around Lydd, Romney Marsh, Kent*, Oxbow, Oxford

Barrett, J. H. 2005 'The fish bone', in C. Treen and M. Atkin (eds), *Water resources and their management*, Wharram. A Study of Settlement on the Wolds, York University Archaeological Publication 12, York, 169–75

Barrett, J. H. (ed.) 2012 *Being an islander: production and identity at Quoygrew, Orkney, AD 900–1600*, McDonald Institute Monograph, Cambridge

Beresford, G. 1975 *The medieval clay-land village: excavations at Goltho and Barton Blount*, The Society for Medieval Archaeology Monograph 6, London

Britnell, W. J. and Suggett, R. 2002 'A sixteenth-century peasant hallhouse in Powys: survey and excavation of Tyddyn Llwydion, Pennant Melangell, Montgomeryshire', *The Archaeological Journal* 159, 142–69

Carruthers, W. J. 2005 'Environment and economy at Wharram Percy: evidence from pond and dam samples', in C. Treen and M. Atkin (eds), *Water resources and their management*, Wharram. A study of settlement on the Wolds, York University Archaeological Publication 12, York, 214–19

Chapman, A. 2010 *West Cotton, Raunds: a study of medieval settlement dynamics AD 450–1450*, Oxbow, Oxford

Davies, W. R. and Silvester, R. J. 2015 'Hen Caerwys: an historiography of the first fifty years', *Flint Historical Society Journal* 40, 17–40

Dixon, P. 2014 'Survey and excavations at Alnhamsheles deserted medieval village, on the Rowhope Burn, Alnham Moor, Northumberland', *Archaeologia Aeliana*, 5th ser. 43, 169–220

Dyer, C. 1995 'Sheepcotes: evidence for medieval sheepfarming', *Medieval Archaeology* 39, 136–64

Dyer, C. 1998 'Peasants and coins: the uses of money in the Middle Ages', *The British Numismatic Journal* 67, 30–47

Dyer, C. 2013 'Living in peasant houses in late medieval England', *Vernacular Architecture* 44, 19–27

Dyer, C. 2014 'The material world of English peasants, 1200–1540', *Agricultural History Review* 62, 1–22

Foard, G. 2001 'Medieval woodland agriculture and industry in Rockingham Forest, Northamptonshire', *Medieval Archaeology* 45, 65–95

Gardiner, M. 1998 'The characterization of medieval Wealden settlements: excavations at Ivenden, Combe Farm, Mayfield, East Sussex', *Sussex Archaeological Collections* 136, 95–110

Gerrard, S. 2000 *The early British tin industry*, Tempus, Stroud

Goodall, I. H. 2011 *Ironwork in medieval Britain: an archaeological study*, The Society for Medieval Archaeology Monograph 31, Leeds

Greig, J. 1981 'The investigation of a medieval barrel-latrine from Worcester', *Journal of Archaeological Science* 8, 265–82

Higham, N. J. 1998–9 'The Tatton Park project, part 2', *Journal of the Chester Archaeological Society* 75, 61–133

Hillman, G., Arthur, J. R. B., Carruthers, W. J., and Jones, J. 2005 'Charred plant remains from Site 30' and 'Plant microfossil remains from Site 71', in C. Treen and M. Atkin (eds), *Water resources and their management*, Wharram: a study of settlement on the Wolds, York University Archaeological Publication 12, York, 185–200

Hindmarch, E. and Oram, R. 2012 'Eldbottle: the archaeology and environmental history of a medieval rural settlement in East Lothian', *Proceedings of the Society of Antiquaries of Scotland* 142, 245–99

Holt, R. 1988 *The mills of medieval England*, Blackwell, Oxford

Ivens, R., Busby, P., and Shepherd, N. 1995 *Tattenhoe and Westbury: two deserted medieval settlements*, Buckinghamshire Archaeological Society Monograph Series 8, Aylesbury

Jennings, N. 2002 'The building of the clay dabbins of the Solway plain: materials and man-hours', *Vernacular Architecture* 33, 19–27

Jones, R. 2004 'Signatures in the soil: the use of pottery in the identification of medieval farming regimes', *The Archaeological Journal* 161, 159–88

Makepeace, G. A. 2001 'Report on the excavations of a medieval farm at Hill Top Farm, Aldwark, near Brassington, Derbyshire 1992–5', *Derbyshire Archaeological Journal* 121, 162–89

Mays, P., Harding C., and Heighway, C. 2007 *Wharram: a study of settlement on the Yorkshire Wolds XI: the churchyard*, University of York Archaeological Publications 13, York

Moffett, L. 2006 'The archaeology of medieval plant foods', in C. M. Woolgar, D. Serjeantson, and T. Waldron (eds), *Food in medieval England: diet and nutrition*, Oxford University Press, Oxford, 41–55

Mould, Q. 2005 'The leather', in C. Treen and M. Atkin (eds), *Water resources and their management*, Wharram: a Study of Settlement on the Wolds, York University Archaeological Publication 12, York, 145–8

Mynard, D. C. and Zeepvat, R. J. 1992 *Excavations at Great Linford 1974–80*, Buckinghamshire Archaeological Society Monograph 3, Aylesbury

Pearson, S. 1994 *The medieval houses of Kent: an historical analysis*, Royal Commission on the Historical Monuments of England, London

Rahtz, P. 1958 'Holworth, medieval village excavations, 1958', *Proceedings of the Dorset Natural History and Archaeological Society* 81, 127–46

Rátkai, S. 2012 'Medieval pottery', in P. Thompson, 'Medieval settlement at Goldicote', *Transactions of the Birmingham and Warwickshire Archaeological Society* 116, 72–139

Richardson, J. 2005 'The animal remains', in C. Treen and M. Atkin (eds), *Water resources and their management*, Wharram: a study of settlement on the Wolds, York University Archaeological Publication 12, York, 153–69

Rippon, S., Wainwright, A., and Smart, C. 2014 'Farming regions in medieval England: the archaeobotanical and zooarchaeological evidence', *Medieval Archaeology* 58, 195–255

Smith, S. 2009 'Materializing resistant identities among the English peasantry: an examination of dress accessories from English settlement sites', *Journal of Material Culture* 14, 309–32

Spoerry, P. and Atkins, R. 2015 *A Late Saxon village and medieval manor: excavations at Botolph Bridge, Orton Longueville, Peterborough*, East Anglian Archaeology Report 153, Bar Hill

CHAPTER 14

PERCEPTIONS OF MEDIEVAL SETTLEMENT

MARK GARDINER AND SUSAN KILBY

The approach to the perception of landscape and settlement adopted by medieval archaeologists has been rather different to those of their colleagues working on the prehistoric period. To a large extent such differences can be attributed to the quality of the evidence. Many of the medieval buildings studied still survive, albeit often as ruins. The landscape with its pattern of roads, fields, and farms can be largely reconstructed in broad terms, and sometimes in detail. This sort of material both informs our understanding of past perceptions of landscape, but also serves to constrain the way we might interpret it. The type of imaginative reconstruction advocated, for example by Tilley (2010, 30–1), in which archaeologists place themselves within the landscape and respond to the experience, has been practised only rarely for the historic period. It is not that medievalists lack the imagination of prehistorians, but rather they do not feel the need to embark upon discussions of their particular experience of place when it is possible instead to reflect upon how those in the Middle Ages may have perceived their surroundings.

A simple contrast between the medievalists' and the prehistorians' approaches to the perception of landscape is, however, misleading. Embodiment or the 'experience of place' using the senses of the body occupying and moving through a place has been practised by both groups, but with different emphases. To stand in a medieval building and look out at the vista beyond is to adopt a phenomenological approach. It does not become less so if the appreciation of the view is informed by the knowledge that in the late Middle Ages the area in the foreground would have been occupied by gardens and that in the distance by woodland. That information adds a depth to the experience. The medieval archaeologists can further enrich their understanding of the meaning of the landscape and the experience which may have been evoked if there is also some knowledge of the stories associated with places—the *lieux de mémoire*—locations which evoke social memory. Such a rich reading of the landscape has been given, for example, for Peak Castle in Derbyshire. The castle stood on the hill above a cave listed amongst the four wonders of England, according to the twelfth-century historian, Henry of Huntingdon. It was said that the wind from the cave blew with such force that it could strip clothing off people and blow it up into the sky. The castle was constructed on top of this rather magical place and its design contrived to make the greatest impact. The position of the great tower, and its 'angle, design and fenestration were carefully manipulated'. Its windows were orientated to Mam Tor on one side and Hope church on another (Barnwell 2007, 22–33). The legend and the building itself fed off one another to produce a stronger sense of the power of place.

This preamble situates the particular approaches of late medievalists to the perception of settlement within the wider archaeological interest in phenomenology. The richness of the medieval record has allowed the embodied response to place to be augmented by an understanding of context, not so that one might replace the other, but might add to the experience. The value of a combined approach can be best appreciated by looking at a further castle site. Cooling Castle in the north of Kent has recently been discussed by an historian and English scholar, Cristina Maria Cervone (2008), and an archaeologist, Matthew Johnson (2002, xiii–xix)—the former taking a literary, if wide-ranging approach to one aspect of the site, the unusual plaque attached to the outside of the gatehouse, and the latter adopting a rhetorical view of their appreciation of the building. For Cervone, who is concerned with texts, the key element of the castle is the plaque which reads:

> Knouwyth that beth and schul be
> That i am mad in help of the cuntre
> In knowyng of whyche thyng
> Thys is chartre and wytnessyng

The plaque takes the form of a charter with appendant seals and the initial words echo the common opening of such a document (*Sciant presentes et futuri* ...), as a medieval reader would have immediately appreciated, and alludes to a licence to crenellate. The text, however, unlike such a licence, is in the vernacular and is cast in the form of a poem which makes it clear that it is by no means a simple quotation of a legal text. The most striking thing about the wording is that it gives the building a persona ('I am made ...'). The building seems to speak to the viewer.

Another, more succinct text appears on the nearly contemporary Pipewell Gate at the entrance to Winchelsea (East Sussex), and reads 'I. Helde'. This has been interpreted, as no doubt was expected by those who placed it there, as a reference to John Helde, mayor of Winchelsea in 1399 and 1404 (Salzman 1937, 63). But equally it was also intended to be read as 'I held', a reference to the survival, either of the gatehouse, or perhaps the town more generally, when it was attacked by the French in 1380 (Martin and Martin 2004, 62). The persona of this building was the endurance of the town. Both Cooling Castle and Pipewell Gate were given voices which make explicit that these were not to be seen as merely inanimate objects, but were intended to serve as personifications of their builders, in the first case of John de Cobham and in the second of the town of

Winchelsea. Their inscriptions speak of an increasingly literate population which might be addressed with texts intended to intrigue through their ambiguities. More generally, these buildings provide evidence for the argument that late medieval settlements and their settings were intended to convey complex messages, rarely 'vocalized' as in these examples, but always present.

Lordly Farmsteads

Medieval houses were planned both as places to be seen by the approaching or passing visitor (the reflective view), and as places from which to look out from (the projective view). The careful contrivance of the appearance of buildings to impress the visitor is evident from at least the ninth century onwards, when the angles of the walls and the roof of major halls were subtly altered to make them appear both longer and taller than they really were (Gardiner 2013, 63–9). By the twelfth century the emphasis in contriving an appropriate appearance for lordly buildings had moved to placing the hall towards the front of the site, so that it or the gatehouse in front of it was clearly visible to those approaching and passers-by (Gardiner 2017). At Wharram Percy (North Yorkshire), for example, the mid-twelfth-century hall was located so that it appeared on the skyline when viewed from the green below (Everson and Stocker 2010, 265), while at Castle Acre, Norfolk, the enclosure was provided with a gatehouse and subsequently the 'country house' set within it was converted into a great tower which dominated the site of the town below (Coad and Streeten 1982, 191–3). Apart from castles, however, there have been few studies of the means by which later lordly dwellings were constructed to impress the visitor. There is no doubt that the arrangement of a suitable approach to the entrance door was a major consideration in the plan of a gentry hall, just as it was to a castle. Campbell (2014, 178–9) has argued that even seemingly irregular designs, such as Hextalls (Surrey), were in fact carefully and metrically laid out. Yet, contriving a design which served to provide an impressive façade and worked as a satisfactory internal space was a difficult task. The interior of the late medieval hall had a plan which did not allow much scope for variation. The entrance was conventionally located at one end of the hall, while the largest windows had to be set at the other in order to illuminate the lord's seat at the table. Campbell has shown that one means of resolving the desire to produce a balanced façade and the need for these features in the interior was to treat them as equal elements in the design. The large window illuminating the lord's seat was commonly projected forward in the fifteenth-century house to form an oriel window and designed so that it echoed the two-storeyed porch of the main entrance. Similarly, at one end of the house beyond the hall, the services containing the kitchen and stores might be constructed to reflect the chamber set at the opposite end (Campbell 2014, 179–81). In that way the front of a gentry house could be designed to present a show-façade to the visitor.

Castles offered an image of martial strength which also conveyed a strong sense of social status (see Chapter 23). Even for lesser lords who could not afford the expense of a grand fortified building, the castle form carried such prestige that it might be imitated in more modest, if scarcely defensible structures. The Old Manor House in Walmer (Kent), constructed perhaps in the early twelfth century, appears to be a copy in miniature of the nearby great tower at Rochester Castle (Fernie 2000, 84). Turrets were constructed at the four corners of the Walmer house, though three of them were so small that they served little apparent purpose while the fourth housed only a stairwell. The building was entered, as at Rochester, from a projecting staircase, first built in timber and later replaced in stone (Philp 2011). Weeting 'Castle' (Norfolk) built some fifty years later less obviously evoked martial forms, since it balanced 'lordly and domestic functions within a single architectural structure' (Heslop 2000, 54). The aisled hall is wholly domestic, but the attached chamber block seems to mimic the form of a great tower. It was entered at first-floor level by an external staircase which unusually could not be reached directly from the interior of the hall. On either side of the interior of the entrance were deep niches which have been compared with those in the gateway of Castle Acre Castle (Norfolk). The chamber block was three stories high, creating a building of imposing grandeur, but this was in fact an entirely domestic building, as the projecting latrine block concealed at the rear indicates (Heslop 2000).

Both the houses at Walmer and Weeting were set within large moats, or at least ditched enclosures since it was unclear whether they were water-filled. Such ditches provided a framing device for the buildings set within, and visitors approached the entrance over a bridge which provided further opportunities for managing the display of the façade. Fenwick (2012, 290) has noted that in the Humber lowlands moats were often located besides waterways and it is possible that these were intended to be viewed by travellers along the rivers. The extraordinary density of moated sites in some areas of the country, particularly parts of Worcester, Essex, and Suffolk, argue that they were not only dug around the houses of the wealthy gentry (Aberg 1978, fig. 1). They also served the aspirant peasants as a mark of status. Roberts characterized these people in the Forest of Arden (Warwickshire) as 'a group of wealthy freeholders who accumulated land to create sub-manors, and who demonstrated this wealth in the construction of large moated farmsteads' (Roberts 1968, 112). Although the value of security offered by moated sites was no doubt also in the minds of the builders, this hardly seems the sole or even main consideration in their construction (*cf.* Platt 2010). The moat was evocative of the idea of a fortified residence, even if it was not defensive.

Houses were not merely buildings to be seen, but also places to look out from, as has already been noted. Window seats, which were common in stone buildings from the early thirteenth century, suggest how much time must have been given to watching and presumably enjoying the view (Wood 1965, 346–7). In one of the earliest surviving examples, the windows with their seats on the first floor of Moyse's Hall (*c.*1180) in Bury St Edmunds (Suffolk) look out directly on to activity in the market place. A century earlier a timber balcony had been constructed at Scolland's Hall in Richmond Castle (North Yorkshire) to look down the Swale valley and perhaps also into a garden immediately beneath (Figure 14.1). That balcony was accessible only from the main chamber, but a second longer one ran the length of the hall and seems to have been reached directly

FIGURE 14.1 Scolland's Hall, Richmond Castle (North Yorkshire) from the south. The position of the balcony overlooking the River Swale is marked by the row of joist holes below the lower tier of windows. The building on the left was constructed in the later twelfth century and blocked access to the balcony

(© Mark Gardiner)

from the bailey, and therefore may have been accessible to a greater range of occupants with the castle. It provided a dramatic view across the Swale valley, the sides of which fell sharply away beneath (Peers 1953, 19–20). The elevated position occupied by castles and the views from tall towers were appreciated as much in the late Middle Ages as they are now. McNeill (2006, 123) has examined five towers of the period around 1300 which have evidence for stairs leading from private quarters to the roof and concluded that they were intended for the enjoyment of the view by the lord. Girouard reached a similar conclusion about the broad walk around the battlements on the fifteenth-century tower at Tattershall (Lincolnshire). This, he suggested, was intended 'more for after-dinner strollers than for soldiers' (Girouard 1978, 78). Perhaps the most remarkable of viewing places is Longthorpe Tower (Northamptonshire) in which the great chamber was decorated internally, not only with biblical and allegorical figures, but also with birds 'mostly of a type likely to be found in the nearby fenland ... bittern curlew and various kinds of goose or swan' (Rouse 1964, 10). McNeill (2006, 126) comments that while it may not be credible to suggest that Sir Robert Thorpe, the lord of Longthorpe, was a keen bird-watcher, he may well have been an acute observer of wildlife in the countryside around.

When we consider these buildings, the argument that the capacity to perceive and enjoy landscape was a development of the fifteenth century, as claimed by Cosgrove (1985) and others, seems unpersuasive. The medieval eye may have perceived a different landscape from that which we see, for our view has been influenced by the concepts of the Romantic Movement. That is quite different, however, from arguing that people in the late Middle Ages did not enjoy the elevated views which were offered from the upper rooms and roofs.

Peasants' Experience of Space

Establishing the way in which peasants thought about and viewed their surroundings is considerably more problematic than considering the elite perspectives on the world. Peasants rarely wrote about their understanding of their world, but their actions are often written about in the vast corpus of manorial documentation that survives for this period in England. Since peasants were not the authors of these myriad documents, it is argued, there is little to be gained in using them to elucidate peasant mentalities. In recent years, however, historians and archaeologists have begun to reconsider approaches to the study of the late medieval settlement, to the extent that the scholarly pursuit of peasant mentalities, in particular concerning their conception of their environment, is now being taken up more widely (Altenberg 2003; Gardiner 2012; Jones 2011; Kilby 2010; Mileson 2012; Müller 2001; Olson 2009; Smith 2010; Stone 2005; Whyte 2003).

Manorial sources were produced on behalf of lords, but it is possible to detect and isolate the peasant voices therein (Kilby 2013, 72–7). Scholars have suggested that, in particular, names—both personal names and those bestowed upon the landscape—can offer a gateway into the mental world of the lower orders (Gardiner 2012, 17; Jones 2012, 260; Kilby 2010, 72; Mileson, 2012, 92). It is generally accepted that field-names were conceived by peasant farmers, with the earliest evidence for these appearing in the late Anglo-Saxon period. Archaeologists and linguists have long identified the mutual benefits to be gained in assessing local field-names, and in current scholarship, field-names and other minor landscape names are being used as a means of accessing peasant mentalities. Assessing the changing nature of the perception of prehistoric burial mounds across a long chronological period, Semple and Whyte used place-names as part of a wider range of evidence (Semple 1998, 111–12; Whyte 2003, 6). Following the work of anthropologists and ethnographers, archaeologists and historians are beginning to view the landscape—and the names associated with it—as a repository for history and folklore, and therefore closely associated with collective memory. Although at present this emerging field of enquiry is dominated by scholars of the Early Modern period—for which a greater quantity of documentation survives—medievalists are beginning to show that similar attitudes prevailed in the late medieval period (Gardiner 2012, 17; Kilby 2013, 138–65).

For many peasants throughout England, but most especially serfs living in highly manorialized areas, their obligations to labour on the lord's land meant that they enjoyed largely open access to the fields beyond the settlement, through a system of roads, paths, and headlands; although certain areas of the lord's home farm (the demesne) and private resources, such as parks, warrens and fisheries, might be subject to more rigorous controls concerning access (Creighton 2009, 111–12, 160; Chapter 25 in this *Handbook*). Walled, gated, and moated elite residences have been interpreted in a number of ways: as a means of conveying information about status and power, for defensive purposes, and to ensure privacy (Liddiard 2005; Creighton 2009, 53–7; Platt 2010, 125). By contrast, little has been written about peasant notions of privacy, although Astill noted that numerous surveyed English peasant tofts showed a tendency for ditched, fenced, or walled boundaries, suggesting that it might be an important factor. Set behind hedges, he suggested, it would have been difficult to see into most tofts (Astill 1994, 53; Dyer 1994, 139). This is supported by documentary evidence in many instances: the homestead of a prominent Castor (Northamptonshire) freeman was described in 1319 as being walled, hedged, and ditched; and a plot of villein land 'enclosed with hedges and ditches' in Winslow (Buckinghamshire) was granted out in 1335 for the purposes of building a house (NRO F(M) Charter 254; Noy 2011, 57). However, a more complex recent analysis by Mileson and Brookes (2017) has suggested that houses set close together in the centre of a village more often had immediate access to the road, while isolated houses and those set in smaller clusters may have been less visible from the road. Privacy was more rigorously protected in places where it already existed, but in the centre of a village where houses were already set close together, there was less effort to establish it.

Privacy is both about the freedom to be alone and remote from public gaze, but also freedom from intrusion. John Horold of Lakenheath (Suffolk), who was almost certainly unfree, seems to have been particularly determined to delineate the bounds of his tenement, suggesting his interest was in recording the limits of his private property, despite the fact that, notionally at least, servile peasants' property legally belonged to the lord. In 1325 he paid a fine for an inquisition to assess the perimeter, and to place bounds between himself and his neighbour. After a further incident a few years later involving the theft of several trees from his yard by another neighbour, he once again requested that the court set the bounds (CUL/EDC/7/16/II/1/8/15, 1/9/7, 1/6/38). This concern to establish boundaries between quarrelsome neighbours is echoed in court cases at Sevenhampton (Wiltshire), where it was granted that bounds should be placed between the properties of two men, following a trespass committed by one of them; there is a similar case from Walsham (Suffolk) (Kilby 2015, 83; Pugh 1970, 44). Even in those instances where boundaries are not expressly mentioned, it is clear that in a number of neighbourly spats at Lakenheath, long-running disputes lasting several years often resulted in peasants entering neighbouring properties and causing deliberate damage to gates, fences, and walls (CUL/EDC/7/16/II/1/6/24 and 41, 1/9/13). In these cases, there was no record of any theft, but the fact that peasants brought court action against this kind of unneighbourly behaviour does emphasize that breaking a neighbour's boundary was considered to be a breach of their privacy. This is supported by evidence contained in land transfers: even where tofts and messuages were being transferred or shared within families, there was often a clause recognizing that the new tenant ought to have 'free ingress and egress' to and from the toft, indicating that this did not always happen, and that attempts were made to regulate, and in some instances, restrict access (Kilby 2013, 256; Smith

1982, 35). It was inevitable, of course, that peasants might enter each others' tenement at some times, but they sought to create a distinction between the space into which any visitor might come on business and the more private space of the house. This is apparent at Great Linford (Buckinghamshire) where the brewhouses from which ale might be sold were placed to the front by the street and the houses set back behind (Figure 14.2), and a similar arrangement can be seen in the late fourteenth- or early fifteenth-century smithy and house at Goltho (Lincolnshire) (Beresford 1975, fig. 5; Mynard and Zeepvat 1991, 51–91).

Perhaps we should be unsurprised that boundaries were of great interest. Local peasants were seen as the custodians of the memory and knowledge of the parish boundaries, and prominent and elderly residents were expected to be able to convey information concerning boundaries should it be required, sometimes in order to settle disputes. In some instances where villages shared resources across a boundary, older men were usually selected to set or re-establish frontiers, since their memory extended beyond that of younger men. This is demonstrated in the division of a Lincolnshire fen in the twelfth century, where one assessor was described as 'an old and wore out man' (Hallam 1965, 167). Many disputes are recorded concerning shared resources. Once again, it can be seen that prominent, older men were called upon to re-apportion a Suffolk fen between Wangford and Lakenheath (CUL/EDR/G3/28/Liber M). There is limited evidence for

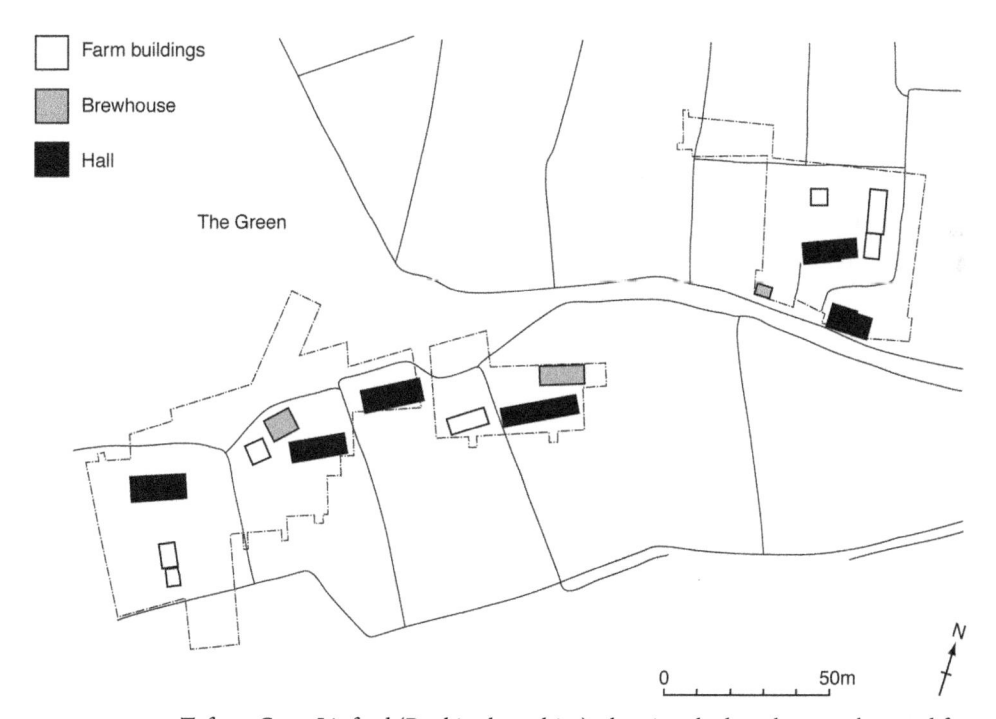

FIGURE 14.2 Tofts at Great Linford (Buckinghamshire), showing the brewhouses also used for the sale of ale set towards the street, with the houses and farm buildings set behind (based on Mynard and Zeepvat 1991, fig. 12)

(© Mark Gardiner)

Rogation processions in this period, but it was the time of year when knowledge about the bounds and the local environment was transmitted and remembered (Blair 2005, 487–8). At Elmley Castle (Worcestershire) in 1449, the court ordered all tenants over the age of 12 to participate in the Rogation procession 'to survey and make anew all the metes and bounds of th[e] lordship' (Field 2004, 122). This rare evidence for a late medieval Rogation procession suggests that, in this case, too few tenants were taking part and that generally these ceremonies passed without any need for the court's involvement. The need for a clear agreement of the line of parish boundaries is evident in those cases where such knowledge was lacking. At Elton (Huntingdonshire), the jurors presented a number of encroachments made by the tenants of adjacent villages on to their meadow—a problem that remained unresolved after more than twenty years, although clearly remaining a significant issue (Ratcliff and Gregory 1946, 96). Similarly, at Great Cressingham (Norfolk), the court attempted to penalize men from the neighbouring parish of Hilborough for damaging their common; and the parishioners of Mildenhall (Suffolk) built an embankment in Lakenheath one league long and ten feet wide, and diverted a watercourse and causing grievous damage to Lakenheath peasant land (Chandler 1885, 23; CUL/EDC/7/16/II/1/9/20).

The separation of private land and public space may have been clearly understood, but the ways in which communal areas might be used were sometimes a cause of contention. Medieval court rolls abound with countless cases involving peasant self-interest. Many thought nothing of blocking roads and paths. At the Wakefield (West Yorkshire) court in November 1332, thirteen men were fined for obstructing rights of way with dungheaps, logs, and heaps of tan (tree bark) (Walker 1983, 127). In some instances, peasants dug up the common highway. In Stanley (West Yorkshire), Adam Isbell sank pits in the road to dig for coal; similarly at Elton, Hugh Prest excavated a pit in the road outside his house (Walker 1983, 110; Ratcliff and Gregory 1946, 119). At Sevenhampton, Walter Tailor built a wall that encroached on the king's highway, and at Brandon (Suffolk), John Crowe dug a trench in the road that he was ordered to repair (Pugh 1970, 79; Bailey 2002, 228). In some instances, it is clear that the court presentments outline the licensing—and, in effect therefore, the sanctioning—of peasant actions on common or demesne land. At Ossett (West Yorkshire), Hugh Sonman paid a fine of a shilling to dig an iron mine in one of his selions, and here, as elsewhere, clearly the lord was keen to benefit financially from a potentially revenue-generating enterprise (Walker 1983, 121).

Areas of land which served for communal activities were to be found in many villages. They might be used for sports and recreation, for commerce, and for other gatherings. In 1481 in Bethersden (Kent) a group of local men, led by their vicar, refused to accept that a piece of land alleged by them to be common ground and used as their football pitch, was to be appropriated and ploughed up by the lord's new tenant. On the day that the pitch was to be ploughed, the unruly gang prevented access to the farmer, and 'riotously' played football for almost the whole day, destroying the plough, and scattering it across the field (TNA/KB/9/365). Similar places for playing camp-ball, a combination of football and handball, have been identified across East Anglia (Dymond 1990). Such areas were often situated close to the churchyard and may also have been used for archery practice and maypole dancing (Hutton 1994, 30–1). Some churchyards served for sports, drama, and, in Scotland at least, for archery practice. The struggle between the competing conceptions of the parish churchyard as a sacred space and a place for communal uses of all sorts continued throughout the later Middle Ages and beyond (Dymond 1999, 467–83).

Peasant behaviour on demesne land, or in woods, warrens, parks, and fisheries is more difficult to interpret. Undoubtedly, some peasant access was licensed, but it is possible to detect other acts that give the impression that many local peasants may have been aware that certain parts of the manorial environment were out of bounds, but that this did not deter them from gaining access regardless—the most obvious acts relating to poaching. Undoubtedly, the group of Lakenheath boys caught setting snares and traps in the doorway of the lord's dovecote in 1332 knew that they were trespassing (CUL/EDC/7/16/II/1/9/9). And yet, where peasants' own land—whether notionally private, or communal—was under threat, remedial action was often taken.

Unravelling peasant mentalities regarding the local landscape requires us to assess different aspects of the landscape separately. Peasants had different attitudes to spaces within the settlement, regarding some as strictly private and rarely to be entered. These included the lord's farmstead and some of the tofts of the more wealthy peasants. The tofts of other peasants, though viewed as private space, and often ditched, hedged, and gated, might be entered in certain circumstances. Despite the strong assertions of ownership displayed when considering interests that were most clearly personal or communal, it was not uncommon for late medieval peasants to overlook temporarily the fact that they might need permission in order to access certain other areas, to appropriate additional land, or to use resources that they had rented for purposes other than those already agreed. Where these more selfish acts impacted the whole community and were seen as a nuisance to all, such as digging holes in the road, or building walls upon it, they were usually brought swiftly to the court's attention.

PERCEPTIONS OF THE SPIRITUAL IN THE COUNTRYSIDE

By the time of the Reformation the countryside of Britain was permeated with places of sanctity (Walsham 2011, 40–8). These extended far beyond the established sacred spaces—churches, chapels, and monasteries—to places associated with saints, sites which were still or had once been occupied by hermits, and also holy wells. The progressive accretion of contemporary holy sites and remembered places provided late medieval Britain with numerous locations which were sacralized. Most of these types of holy site are discussed elsewhere in this volume by Hall (Chapter 38). It is necessary here only to comment on the range of places associated with saints and to consider the role of hermits in establishing a sacred landscape.

Saints' cults attracted pilgrims and, in what has been described as a symbiotic relationship, local details were added to saints' lives exploiting the topographic associations and providing further cultic places for the pilgrims to visit (James 1993, 105). In the countryside around the town of St David's (Pembrokeshire) were a series of chapels which provided additional sites for the pilgrims journeying to the cathedral. Amongst these was the chapel and holy well at Porth Strinian. The cove below the chapel was named after Justinian who had come from Brittany to join David on Romsey Island. He was killed by his servants and a spring appeared on the spot which by the fourteenth century was noted for miraculous cures. The body of the murdered Justinian was initially buried in the chapel close to the spring, but his remains were later translated to St David's Cathedral (James 1993, 106–7). In additional to the various chapels around the cathedral town, Rhygyfarch's eleventh-century *Life of St David* includes reference to a large number of other places localizing the saint's cult: *Portus Magnus* (Porth Mawr), *Vetus Rubus* (unlocated near St David's), *Vallis Rosina* (the valley of St David's), *flumen quod dicitur Alun* (River Alun), *Martirium Dunaut* (unlocated spring near St David's), and Porthlysgi was evidently connected with Lisci, a local aristocrat who killed an opponent of St David (Sharpe 2007 on the text; place-names identified in Sharpe and Davies 2007). The whole countryside around St David's was filled with holy places or sites with a close connection to the life of the saint.

It was not only the area around pilgrimage centres which produced cultic sites. Many, probably most, Anglo-Saxon minsters were the burial place of saints and there were many significant places in the local landscape connected with their lives (Blair 1997; 2002). Memory of some of these persisted into the late medieval period, but in addition there developed many more sacralized sites across Britain, some at natural locations, such as springs, and others at shrines or crosses which had shown miracle-working properties. The ecclesiastical authorities did not so much repress these cultic places as seek to manage the enthusiasm which they engendered, putting down only those which threatened their authority (Walsham 2011, 67; Watkins 2007, 96–7, 108). But if much of the countryside of late medieval England had places with holy associations, there were other areas which were deemed less firmly within the orbit of God's grace. These were places at the margins, particularly woodlands and marshes, and more generally environments far from human habitation (Gardiner 2008, 299–300; Rippon 2009, 47–9). Unlike the well-settled lands where sanctity was concentrated in numerous but particular places, the locations on the margins where malevolent forces might be present were diffuse and extensive. These areas were deemed to be the haunt of ghosts and demons in the Middle Ages, such as the woodland between Peterborough (Cambridgeshire) and Stamford (Linconshire)—where in the twelfth century, a wild, spectral hunt with black horses, hounds, and even goats was regularly witnessed—and locations at which suicides and executed criminals might be buried (Mellows and Mellows 1966, 54–5; Reynolds 2009, 247–8). Surviving minor names, such as the field-names *thirspitt* (demon's or giant's pit) in Ailsworth (Northamptonshire) and *drakecrundell* (dragon's pit) in South Creake (Norfolk) also identify places associated with the supernatural (BL/Cotton MS Nero C. vii/14; Hesse 1998, 80–4). And in some instances, major place-names indicate the setting for both the demonic and the miraculous: at Drakelow in Derbyshire, two peasants apparently struck down by St Modwenna arose as revenants to terrorize the neighbourhood. Drakelow means 'dragon burial mound/hill', and so here the landscape provided the obvious setting for the local legend, and the conjunction of place-name and folklore is unlikely to have been accidental (Harte 2003, 180; Watkins 2007, 183).

One means of neutralizing such godless spaces was to settle them with holy men and establish centres of Christianity which might sanctify such regions and make them safe for lay people. The model for such activity was the early eighth-century hermit and saint, Guthlac, who established a monastery on the demon-haunted site at Crowland (Lincolnshire). By the eleventh and twelfth centuries, hermits were choosing to live not so much in the utter wilderness, but just beyond the margins of settlement, not least because hermitages in very remote locations were unlikely to attract alms. We can suggest that one of the (unacknowledged) roles of the hermit was to establish sanctity at the margins of settlement, effectively beginning the process of the sacralization of the landscape. A hermit on his own was a minor force in the preparation of land in this way, but a well-regarded eremite could attract followers, and in time these might take on the more formal character of a religious community, sometimes developing into a monastery (Herbert 1985; Licence 2003; 2011, 97–105). The site on the edge of an area of peat moss and beside the sea at Cockersand in Lancashire near the mouth of the River Lune was occupied first in the early 1180s by a hermit, Hugh Garth. He attracted sufficient alms and followers that the site was transformed in due course into a hospital and by 1190 into a priory, later raised to the status of an abbey (Farrer 1898, ix–x).

In archaeological terms we could envisage that the role of such pioneers was to establish the outlines of a particular form of encultured landscape in which it was deemed safe to settle. The landscape was sacralized, made safe for occupation because in the foundation of a hermitage it had acquired its first religious outposts. However, that pioneering work of hermits was largely done by the thirteenth century, as settlement had been pushed into even remote areas of Britain and by the fourteenth century hermits had largely left their wilderness sites to occupy positions on roads and by bridges where they took on the task of their repair, such as the hermit who lived near bridges adjacent to the River Cam in Cambridge in the late fourteenth century (Cam 1959, 114; Jones 1998, 53–5). The historian Wace was surely right when he wrote that the mysteries of the wood of Barenton in Brittany had disappeared with the spread of settlement, although in many places, field-names recorded in the late medieval period suggest the continued memory of both sacred and demonic sites for a time (Burgess and van Houts 2004, 162).

Conclusions

Our understanding of how people in late medieval Britain perceived their landscape is still at an early stage. While much attention has been devoted to seigneurial perceptions of space, largely confined to the rather narrow field of castles, much less work has been devoted to the way in which peasants conceptualized the landscape which they occupied. The study of the perception of the spiritual has been almost entirely limited to established religious sites, which fails to reflect the thorough penetration of the sacred into the mundane world. If these aspects of late medieval archaeology have remained underdeveloped, it is because approaching the way the world was experienced by people in the past is bound to prove challenging. In recent years archaeology has increasingly turned to think in greater detail about perception as it has become clearer that the thought-about world and the experienced world, two interlinked aspects of perception, played a significant role in behaviour. There remains much scope for future work in understanding the way in which people viewed their surroundings.

Acknowledgements

We are grateful to the late Lesley Boatwright for supplying the reference to the late fifteenth-century football pitch at Bethersden.

Abbreviations

BL   The British Library
CUL   Cambridge University Library
TNA   The National Archives, Kew
NRO   Northamptonshire Record Office

References cited

Aberg, F. A. 1978 'Introduction', in F. A. Aberg (ed.), *Medieval moated sites*, Council for British Archaeology, London, 1–4

Altenberg, K. 2003 *Experiencing landscapes: a study of space and identity in three marginal areas of medieval Britain and Scandinavia*, Almqvist and Wiksell, Stockholm

Astill, G. 1994 'Rural settlement: the toft and croft', in G. Astill and A. Grant (eds), *The countryside of medieval England*, Blackwell, Oxford, 36–61

Bailey, M. 2002 *The English manor c.1200–c.1500*, Manchester University Press, Manchester

Barnwell, P. 2007 'The power of Peak Castle: cultural contexts and changing perceptions', *Journal of the British Archaeological Association* 160, 20–38

Beresford, G. 1975 *The medieval clay-land village: excavations at Goltho and Barton Blount*, The Society for Medieval Archaeology Monograph 6, London

Blair, J. 1997 'Saint Cuthman, Steyning and Bosham', *Sussex Archaeological Collections* 135, 173–92

Blair, J. 2002 'A saint for every minster? Local cults in Anglo-Saxon England', in A. Thacker and R. Sharpe (eds), *Local saints and local churches in the early medieval West*, Oxford University Press, Oxford, 455–94

Blair, J. 2005 *The Church in Anglo-Saxon society*, Oxford University Press, Oxford

Burgess, G. S. (trans.) and van Houts, E. (ed.) 2004 *The history of the Norman people: Wace's 'Roman de Rou'*, Boydell, Woodbridge

Cam, H. M. 1959 'The city of Cambridge: bridges', in J. P. C. Roach (ed.), *A history of the county of Cambridge and the Isle of Ely*, 3, Oxford University Press, London, 114

Campbell, J. 2014 'A house is not just a home: means of display in English medieval gentry buildings', in M. Svart Kristansen and K. Giles (eds), *Dwellings, identities and homes: European housing culture from the Viking Age to the Renaissance*, Jutland Archaeological Society, Moesgaard, 175–84

Cervone, C. S. 2008 'John de Cobham and the Cooling Castle's charter poem', *Speculum* 83, 884–916

Chandler, H. W. 1885 *Five court rolls of Great Cressingham in the county of Norfolk*, Eyre and Spottiswoode, London

Coad, J. G. and Streeten, A. D. F. 1982 'Excavations at Castle Acre Castle, Norfolk, 1972–77: country house and castle of the Norman earls of Surrey', *The Archaeological Journal* 139, 138–301

Cosgrove, D. 1985 'Prospect, perspective and the evolution of the landscape idea' *Transactions of the Institute of British Geographers* 10, 45–62

Creighton, O. H. 2009 *Designs upon the land: elite landscapes of the Middle Ages*, Boydell, Woodbridge

Dyer, C. 1994 *Everyday life in medieval England*, Hambledon, London

Dymond, D. 1990 'A lost social institution: the camping close', *Rural History* 1, 165–92

Dymond, D. 1999 'God's disputed acre', *Journal of Ecclesiastical History* 50, 467–97

Everson, P. and Stocker, D. 2010 'Who at Wharram?', in S. Wrathmell (ed.), *Wharram: a study of settlement on the Yorkshire Wolds. XIII: a history of Wharram Percy and its neighbours*, York University Archaeological Publications 15, York, 262–77

Farrer, W. 1898 *The Chartulary of Cockersand Abbey of the Premonstratensian Order*, Chetham Society, Manchester

Fenwick, H. 2012 'Medieval moated sites in the Humber lowlands of England: landscape transformation, utilisation and social emulation', *Medieval Archaeology* 56, 283–92

Fernie, E. 2000 *The architecture of Norman England*, Oxford University Press, Oxford

Field, R. K. 2004 *Court Rolls of Elmley Castle, Worcestershire, 1347–1564*, Worcestershire Historical Society, Worcester

Gardiner, M. F. 2008 'The wider context', in L. Barber and G. Priestley-Bell (eds), *Medieval adaptation, settlement and economy of a coastal wetland: the evidence from around Lydd, Romney Marsh, Kent*, Oxbow Books, Oxford, 297–304

Gardiner, M. F. 2012 'Oral tradition, landscape and the social life of place-names', in R. Jones and S. Semple (eds), *Sense of place in Anglo-Saxon England*, Shaun Tyas, Donington, 16–30

Gardiner, M. F. 2013 'The sophistication of Late Anglo-Saxon timber buildings', in M. D. J. Bintley and M. G. Shapland (eds), *Timber, trees and woodland in Anglo-Saxon England*, Oxford University Press, Oxford, 45–77

Gardiner, M. F. 2017 'Manorial farmsteads and the expression of lordship before and after the Norman Conquest', in D. M. Hadley and C. C. Dyer (eds), *The archaeology of the 11th century: continuities and transformations*, The Society for Medieval Archaeology 38, London, 88–103

Girouard, M. 1978 *Life in the English country house: a social and architectural history*, Yale University Press, New Haven

Hallam, H. E. 1965 *Settlement and society: a study of the early agrarian history of South Lincolnshire*, Cambridge University Press, Cambridge

Harte, J. 2003 'Hell on earth: encountering devils in the medieval landscape', in B. Bildhauer and R. Mills (eds), *The monstrous Middle Ages*, University of Toronto Press, Toronto, 177–95

Herbert, J. 1985 'The transformation of hermitages into Augustinian priories in twelfth-century England', in W. J. Shiels (ed.), *Monks, hermits and the ascetic tradition*, Studies in Church History 22, Oxford, 131–45

Heslop, T. A. 2000 'Weeting "Castle", a twelfth-century hall house in Norfolk', *Architectural History* 43, 43–57

Hesse, M. 1998 'Medieval field systems and land tenure in South Creake, Norfolk', *Norfolk Archaeology* 43, 79–97

Hutton, R. 1994 *The rise and fall of merry England: the ritual year 1400–1700*, Oxford University Press, Oxford

James, H. 1993 'The cult of St David in the Middle Ages', in M. Carver (ed.), *In search of cult: archaeological investigations in honour of Philip Rahtz*, Boydell, Woodbridge, 105–12

Johnson, M. 2002 *Behind the castle gate: from medieval to Renaissance*, Routledge, London

Jones, E. A. 1998 'The hermits and anchorites of Oxfordshire', *Oxoniensia* 63, 51–77

Jones, R. 2011 'Elemental theory in everyday practice: food disposal in the later medieval English countryside', *Ruralia* 8, 57–75

Jones, R. 2012 'Thinking through the manorial affix: people and place in medieval England', in S. Turner and B. Silvester (eds), *Life in medieval landscapes: people and places in the Middle Ages*, Windgather, Oxford, 251–67

Kilby, S. 2010 'A different world? Reconstructing the peasant environment in medieval Elton', *Medieval Settlement Research* 25, 72–7

Kilby, S. 2013 *Encountering the environment: rural communities in England, 1086–1348*, unpublished PhD thesis, University of Leicester

Kilby, S. 2015 'Mapping peasant discontent: trespassing on manorial land in fourteenth-century Walsham-le-Willows', *Landscape History* 36(2), 69–88

Licence, T. 2003 'The Benedictines, the Cistercians and the acquisition of a hermitage in twelfth-century Durham', *Journal of Medieval History* 29, 315–29

Licence, T. 2011 *Hermits and recluses in English Society, 950–1200*, Oxford University Press, Oxford

Liddiard, R. 2005 *Castles in context: power, symbolism and landscape, 1066–1500*, Windgather Press, Macclesfield

Martin, D. and Martin, B. 2004 *New Winchelsea, Sussex: a medieval port town*, Heritage Marketing, King's Lynn

McNeill, T. E. 2006 'The view from the top', *Les Cahiers de l'Urbanisme*, hors série, Mélanges d'archéologie médiévale: liber amicorum en hommage à André Matthys, 122–5

Mellows, C. and Mellows, W. T. 1966 *The Peterborough chronicle of Hugh Candidus*, Peterborough Museum Society, Peterborough

Mileson, S. 2012 'The South Oxfordshire Project: perceptions of landscape, settlement and society, c.500–1650', *Landscape History* 33(2), 83–98

Mileson, S. with a contribution by Brookes, S. 2017 'Openness and closure in the later-medieval village', *Past and Present* 234(1), 3–37

Müller, M. 2001 *Peasant mentalities and cultures in two contrasting communities in the fourteenth century; Brandon in Suffolk and Badbury in Wiltshire*, unpublished PhD thesis, University of Birmingham

Mynard, D. C. and Zeepvat, R. J. 1991 *Excavations at Great Linford, 1974–80*, Buckinghamshire Archaeological Society, Aylesbury

Noy, D. (ed. and trans.) 2011 *Winslow Manor Court books, part one, 1327–1377*, Buckinghamshire Record Society, Aylesbury

Olson, S. 2009 *A mute gospel, the people and culture of the medieval English common fields*, Pontifical Institute of Mediaeval Studies, Toronto

Peers, C. 1953 *Richmond Castle, Yorkshire*, Her Majesty's Stationery Office, London

Philp, B. 2011 *Upper Walmer, Kent: the Norman fortified manor-house*, Kent minor sites series 21, Dover

Platt, C. 2010 'The homestead moat: security or status?', *The Archaeological Journal* 167, 115–33

Pugh, R. B. 1970 *Court Rolls of the Wiltshire manors of Adam de Stratton*, Wiltshire Record Society, Devizes

Ratcliff, S. C. (ed.) and Gregory, D. M. (trans.) 1946 *Elton manorial records, 1279–1351*, The Roxburghe Club, Cambridge

Reynolds, A. 2009 *Anglo-Saxon deviant burial customs*, Oxford University Press, Oxford

Rippon, S. 2009 '"Uncommonly rich and fertile" or "not very salubrious"? The perception and value of wetland landscapes', *Landscapes* 1, 39–60

Roberts, B. 1968 'A study of medieval colonization in the Forest of Arden, Warwickshire', *Agricultural History Review* 16, 101–13

Rouse, E. C. 1964 *Longthorpe Tower*, Her Majesty's Stationery Office, London

Salzman, L. F. (ed.) 1937 *The Victoria History of the County of Sussex 9: Rape of Hastings*, Oxford University Press for the Institute of Historical Research, Oxford

Semple, S. 1998 'A fear of the past: the place of the prehistoric burial mound in the ideology of middle and later Anglo-Saxon England', *World Archaeology* 30(1), 109–26

Sharpe, R. 2007, 'Which text is Rhygyfarch's Life of St David?', in J. W. Evans and J. M. Wooding (eds), *St David of Wales: cult, church, and nation*, Boydell, Woodbridge, 90–105

Sharpe, R. and Davies, J. R. (ed. and trans.) 2007 'Rhygyfarch's life of St David', in J. W. Evans and J. M. Wooding (eds), *St David of Wales: cult, church, and nation*, Boydell, Woodbridge, 107–55

Smith, R. 1982 'Rooms, relatives and residential arrangements: some evidence in manor court rolls 1250–1500', *Annual Report of the Medieval Settlement Research Group* 30, 34–5

Smith, S. V. 2010 'Houses and communities: medieval peasant experience', in C. Dyer and R. Jones (eds), *Deserted villages revisited*, University of Hertfordshire Press, Hatfield, 64–84

Stone, D. 2005 *Decision-making in medieval agriculture*, Oxford University Press, Oxford

Tilley, C. 2010 *Explorations in landscape phenomenology 3. Interpreting landscapes: geologies, topographies, identities*, West Coast Press, Walnut Creek, CA

Walker, S. S. 1983 *The court rolls of the manor of Wakefield from October 1331 to September 1333*, Yorkshire Archaeological Society, Leeds

Walsham, A. 2011 *The Reformation of the landscape: religion, identity and memory in early modern Britain and Ireland*, Oxford University Press, Oxford

Watkins, C. S. 2007 *History and the supernatural in medieval England*, Cambridge University Press, Cambridge

Whyte, N. 2003 'The after-life of barrows: prehistoric monuments in the Norfolk landscape', *Landscape History* 25, 1–16

Wood, M. 1965 *The English medieval house*, Phoenix House, London

CHAPTER 15

PEASANT HOUSES

RICHARD SUGGETT

The discovery that thousands of durable medieval peasant dwellings have survived for half a millennium or more is relatively recent and still astonishes. Many are fragmentary today, of course, but there are survivals, especially of detail, that one would not have thought possible. It is now realized, for example, that basal layers of medieval thatch can persist, providing an extraordinary resource for archaeobotanists (Letts 1999). It is still unclear how many peasant houses actually survive; the pleasurable work of discovery continues. Over three thousand domestic sites with cruck-trusses have been recorded to date, the majority of which were once peasant dwellings (Figure 15.1), and there are probably an even greater number of box-framed peasant and sub-gentry halls in southern and eastern England. These are generally houses without a history in the sense that very few are documented (but with exceptions: Alcock and Miles 2013) but the houses themselves embody the choices and ambitions of their builders: peasants who are otherwise anonymous. Durability (a pre-condition of survivability) is central to the discussion of the choices involved in building peasant houses. Permanence—building for the future as well as the present—was a distinguishing feature of the peasant hall-house in late medieval England and Wales but not in large areas of Scotland.

In Scotland, the rubble-walled blackhouses of the Hebrides, as well as the 'fermetouns' of the mainland, probably belong to a relatively late eighteenth-century phase of improved housing associated with tenurial modernization. They are not the survivors of the medieval peasant building tradition as was once believed. Instead, medieval peasants in Scotland built houses with walls that were regularly renewed, and which must have coexisted with masonry traditions of tower and church building. Documentary references to pre-modern Highland peasant houses show that, despite abundant building stone, 'almost invariably' walling materials other than stone were used, especially turf or peat and clay (Turner 1998). These dwellings were referred to in Anglo-Scots as 'creel houses' or 'basket houses' from the lavish use of woven wattle to line the turf walls internally (Noble 2000). Creel houses were thatched, generally hipped, and many had cruck-trusses which were often regarded as separately owned from the walls (belonging

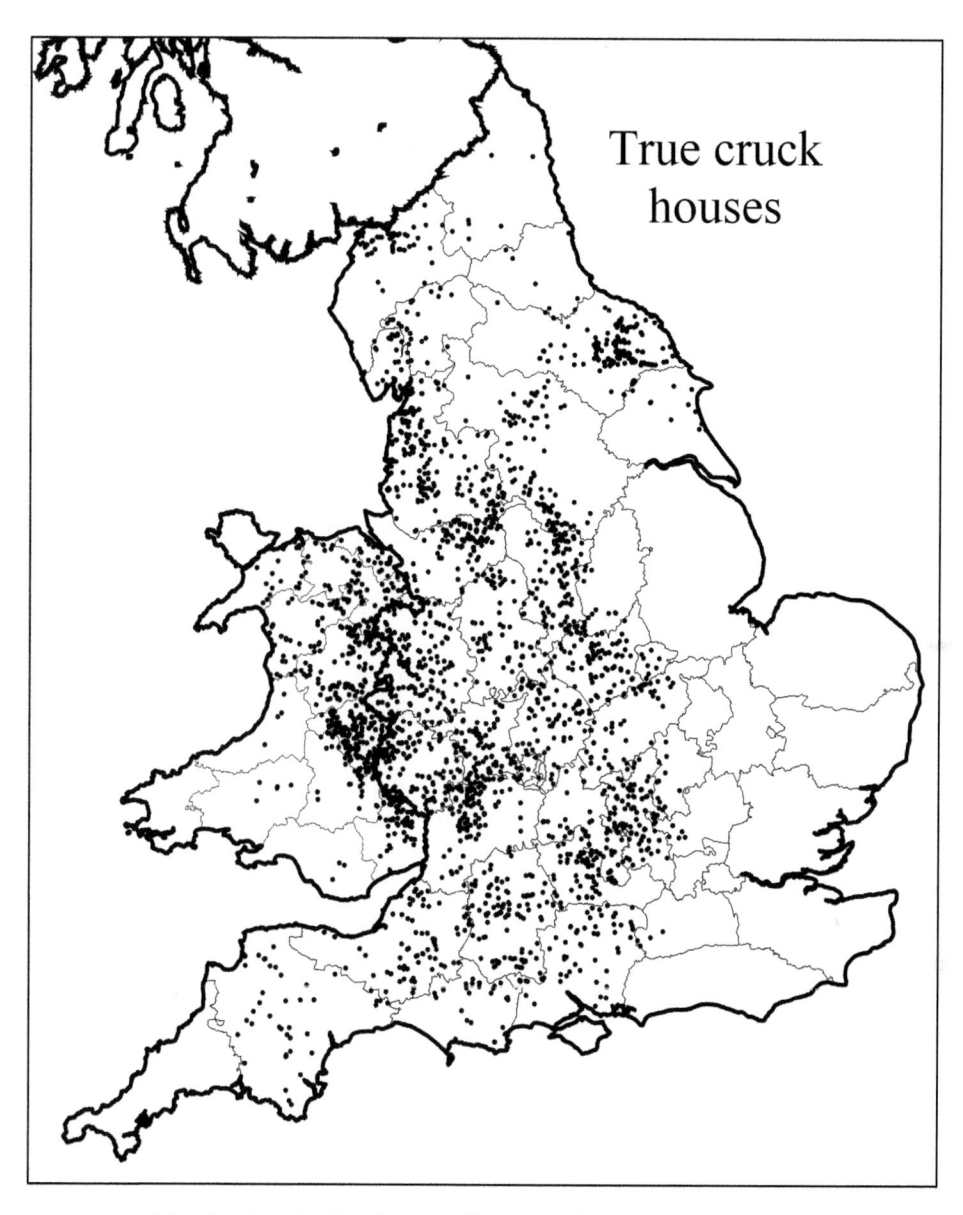

FIGURE 15.1 Map showing the distribution of houses with crucks in England and Wales. A total of 3143 examples are plotted. Update by Nat Alcock of the map published in Alcock and Miles (2013, 8)

(© Nat Alcock)

to laird rather than tenant or vice versa) and were therefore removed and re-used when houses came to be vacated or rebuilt (Fenton and Walker 1981, 44–51).

The archaeology of creel houses is fugitive because the walls were impermanent and, as a result, their historical depth is uncertain. However, one little-known description provides information about these peasant houses in the late seventeenth century before they became antiquarian curiosities (Campbell 1975, 25): 'Their houses for the most part sheilds [= sheals or cottages] made of earth or stone and clay and riveted with rivets [= roofed with divots or roofing turves]. In Loch Aber [west Highlands] the walls of their houses is of juniper and such like pletted together. The chimney [is] in the middle of the house, to which the vent answers. The company sits round about the ground [where] it burns'. These were pre-modern dwellings in the open hall tradition but they were certainly not permanent houses and were periodically rebuilt or re-sited re-using the trusses. Various rituals were observed when a new house was built. In particular, 'at the setting up of the couples' or trusses 'a woman is necessary to put to her hand.' This seems to have been an acknowledgement of the fundamental importance of the gender division of labour characteristic of the peasant household.

By contrast, in the English–Scottish borderlands and contemporary with the renewable houses of the Highlands, there were numerous durable towers and defensible houses (pele houses, peel towers, bastles) built 'for defence against sudden risings' (Campbell 1975, 25). They were a response to border raiding and generally occupied by leading families. But if living in association with livestock is a mark of a peasant dwelling some may be considered superior peasant houses and were occupied by customary tenants. The bastles of the northern borderland remain a fascinating architectural solution to a social problem: a kind of vertical long-house in which hall and chamber were located above the beast-house and generally reached only by a moveable ladder (Ramm et al. 1970).

In the greater part of England and Wales, by contrast, peasant houses were not only undefended but timber- rather than stone-built. They were also permanent rather than temporary. Their survival depends not only on the durability of building materials but also on the capacity to adapt structures to new requirements and fashions. Late medieval houses still form the structural core of numerous farmhouses and cottages today, and are often recognized by the presence of a cruck-truss. The suggestion that cruck-trusses might be survivals from late medieval peasant dwellings was first made by Charles Innocent (1916), a Yorkshire architect and antiquary, who observed that 'crooks' or 'siles' occurred only in the older farmhouses, cottages, and barns of northern England, the Midlands, and Wales. The truncated cruck blades sometimes found in storeyed houses showed that crucks became obsolete in the sixteenth and seventeenth centuries.

Identifying crucks (and by extension, peasant housing) became a preoccupation of a new sub-discipline—vernacular architecture—which first came of age with the publication of a reflective regional study of medieval houses in Monmouthshire (Fox and Raglan 1951). Later, the mapping of surviving cruck-trusses revealed a thought-provoking distribution (Alcock 1981; Smith 1970) which showed that crucks were widely but unevenly distributed across Britain, from Cardigan Bay to the East Midlands, and from Devon to Cumbria (Figure 15.1). Across mainland Scotland, full crucks ('siles') had a general distribution and co-existed with the renewable walling tradition, but none has so far been dated. The surviving cruck-trusses (some dated to the fifteenth and sixteenth centuries) in the clay 'dabbins' of the Solway Plain are in the same tradition and show a marked history of re-use (Jennings 2003, 123–37). In Ireland full crucks have also been noted but the scarfed or jointed cruck tradition, present also in west Wales and late medieval Devon, predominated. In England, crucks were conspicuously absent from eastern and southeastern regions, their distribution apparently stopping abruptly along a so-called 'cruck line' with few outliers. Here cruck construction met the alternative box-framing timber tradition. The box-framing tradition was rich and varied, urban as well as rural, and, while initially regionally restricted, it increasingly supplanted crucks in the countryside, especially when storeyed ranges were required.

Significantly, the chronology of cruck construction is more or less coeval with the durable medieval peasant house. It must be emphasized that crucks were not a 'primitive' form of construction but the product of sophisticated carpentry by professional craftsmen. Though they varied in refinement, cruck construction became a high craft, particularly in the Welsh Marches, and the heavily bayed cruck-framed hall was built to impress. Belonging to the European Gothic aesthetic and reaching from ground to ridge, crucks were translations into timber of the pointed Gothic stone arch (Suggett 2005, 21–2) which had first developed in the twelfth century and became widespread in church, castle, and manor-house in the thirteenth century. A small number of scientifically dated cruck-trusses, as well as documentary references, are consistent with their emergence during this period, although their chronology has been the matter of debate (Hill and Alcock 2007). The earliest cruck-trusses have a scattered distribution and belong to the second half of the thirteenth century, and the first unambiguous documentary reference to a cruck (rather than a 'fork') is from Harlech Castle kitchen in 1305–6. In the fourteenth century cruck construction was widely adopted and there are numerous late medieval documentary references to crucks and siles as carpenters were contracted by peasants to build houses and other buildings (Alcock 1981, 28–36). Although crucks have a distinctive chronology and distribution, however, they did not belong to a particular walling tradition. Crucks are found in stone walls, with timber (Wales and the west Midlands) and clay (especially Devon, Norfolk, and Cumbria) walls, and in association with renewable walls (Scotland). The distinctive arched profile of the cruck-truss even had its counterpart in the central arch-braced trusses of halls constructed in the box-framed tradition.

Archaeology and Peasant Houses

How do standing structures relate to archaeology? How representative are surviving standing structures in terms of construction and plan? Was there a vernacular threshold, a change in construction that favoured the survival of houses? What material culture is associated with peasant houses? These are some of the questions that archaeology is best placed to resolve. To begin with, the sheer scale and complexity of the archaeological resource needs to be appreciated. In England the classic 'county gazetteers of deserted medieval villages (known in 1968)' listed a resource of over 2263 settlements (Beresford and Hurst 1971, 182–212). Many more sites have since been identified, but only a small fraction has been surveyed let alone excavated. The importance of dispersed upland settlements has been established. Systematic recording in upland Wales has located nearly three thousand structures loosely categorized as platforms, long-huts, and long-huts with platforms (Roberts 2006; see Chapter 12 in this *Handbook*). These include many deserted medieval dwellings but few have been excavated and their date range is problematic. In Scotland, an astonishing twenty-five thousand deserted settlements have been located from the early six-inch maps but it has proved impossible to distinguish the medieval antecedents of settlements cleared in the nineteenth century despite the continuity of some place-names. In the upland margins of southern Scotland, however, the platforms and earthworks of dwellings akin to deserted medieval settlements in other parts of Britain have been identified (Dixon 2002; 2006).

Of these numerous deserted medieval settlements, the best preserved are the masonry dwellings of the south-west and west (Figure 15.2). In particular, some deserted upland long-houses fringing Dartmoor and Exmoor have survived with considerable stretches of upstanding masonry. Excavation at several sites (notably at Hound Tor, Devon) has yielded unambiguous intercommunicating house-and-cowhouse plans complete with 'shippon' drains (Beresford 1979). A thirteenth-century origin is claimed for the plan-type, and the social and agricultural contexts of these houses, as well as their relationship to standing structures, have been the subject of continuing discussion (summarized by Grenville 1997, 134–51). Nonetheless, the authentic peasant house has proved rather elusive. The variability of building techniques and materials has become increasingly apparent and does not necessarily correspond to the distribution of the post-medieval vernacular. Building in clay was widespread, for example, and timber-framing frequently gave way to stone. House sites are often difficult to interpret, and the reconstruction of above-ground features problematic. The excavation of Wharram Percy, a deserted medieval village in the Yorkshire Wolds, has been particularly instructive because the duration of the project was long enough for excavators to change their mind about fundamental issues relating to the interpretation of buildings and assessments of their durability. The foundations of the buildings at Wharram were rather nondescript walls of chalk. The excavators first interpreted these as the remains of self-build houses that were periodically renewed, perhaps every generation. Comparison with surviving vernacular buildings later suggested that the dwarf walls actually supported substantial cruck-framed structures. These issues have been reviewed by Grenville (1997, 129), who tellingly observes: 'It is an object lesson to archaeologists; looking for flimsy buildings at Wharram, we see no padstones; looking for cruck frames, we observe the same drawing, and we see the positions of robbed out padstones'. The final assessment (Wrathmell 2012, 340–2) acknowledged that the problems of interpretation are severe, both in distinguishing houses from ancillary buildings and when assessing their durability.

Wharram and other excavations showed the difficulties of constructing a purely archaeological narrative for peasant houses. The shift to viewing peasant dwellings as substantial houses was largely prompted by an influential article which considered documentary sources in relation to the archaeology (Dyer 1986). Dyer's subsequent work (1989; 1994; 2002; 2005) has led to an interdisciplinary approach by historians and archaeologists which has transformed the study of medieval peasant culture. There is now greater

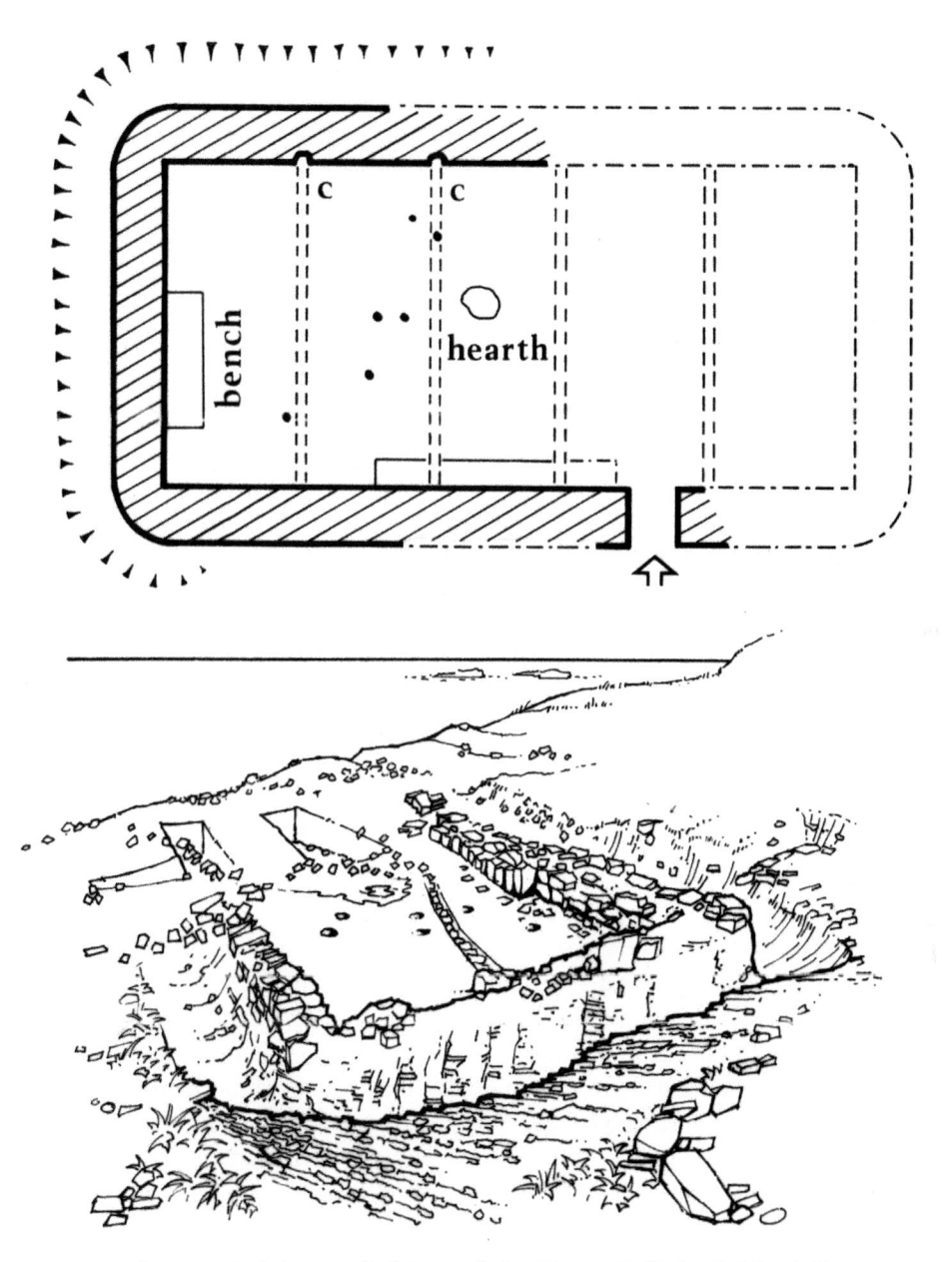

FIGURE 15.2 An excavated stone-walled two-unit dwelling on St Tudwal's Island, Caernarvonshire, which retained unusually clearly the principal features of the hall: the hearth, stone benches flanking the hearth, a wider upper-end sleeping platform, as well as several post-holes of uncertain significance. The walls, partly cut from the living rock, had rounded corners and sockets for the (cruck-)trusses. Reported by D. Hague, who suggested a mid-fourteenth-century occupation date from the pottery finds (Wilson and Hurst 1964, 246–8)

(© Crown Copyright: Royal Commission on the Ancient and Historical Monuments of Wales)

appreciation of the range of buildings on peasant farmsteads and their different survivability: peasant houses co-existed with barns, stables, cowhouses, detached kitchens, and other buildings which all required investment and had different standards of construction. Temporary buildings co-existed with permanent buildings. In particular, the long-houses of the north and west co-existed with renewable shielings and dairy-houses on the summer pastures. Increasingly, dwellings are regarded contextually as a component among others of the wider historic landscape, and the maturity of medieval rural settlement studies has recently been marked by the publication of a collection of nuanced regional studies (Christie and Stamper 2012). Peasants are now acknowledged as active consumers rather than passively enduring unrelenting poverty, and there is continuing study of the artefacts found at excavated sites and their significance (see Chapter 13).

Increasingly powerful dating techniques have helped refine the chronology of the peasant hall-house. The archaeological evidence suggests that multi-bayed hall-houses may have developed by the early thirteenth century. The durability of these houses was helped by the adoption of the ground wall and sill-beam in place of earthfast timbers which rotted over time. This change in building technique did not necessarily lead to wholesale rebuilding and a fall in real wages may have encouraged peasants to repair rather than replace buildings in the thirteenth century (Gardiner 2000; 2014). However, a combination of wage recovery and lower commodity costs, particularly after the Black Death, prompted a prolonged phase of rebuilding beginning in the latter part of the fourteenth century. As a result, the chronology of surviving peasant houses is now reasonably well understood from dendrochronology and demonstrates that only a few exceptional survivors of peasant houses in England date from before 1380. The majority date from the late fourteenth to the late fifteenth centuries and after with building peaks that vary from region to region: these houses are generally well carpentered with a distinctive three- or four-bay plan.

Dyer (2013) ponders the paradox that while surviving houses show that there was prolonged rebuilding between c.1350 and c.1500, the documentary and archaeological evidence for the same period relates to the decay of buildings and the contraction and extinction of settlements: 'the standing buildings tell us of new construction, but the documents of houses falling down'. However, it is clear that economic depression brought new opportunities for building with the rationalization of holdings, lower rents, and the falling cost of materials. A distinctive multi-bayed hall-house plan developed in this period with each bay having increasingly specialized functions. The earlier peasant halls of the west Midlands generally had three bays open to the roof with a two-bay hall and inner-room. Houses built after the mid-fifteenth century (Figure 15.3) usually had a single-bayed hall between floored chamber and service-rooms (Alcock and Miles 2013, 156). In fourteenth-century north-east Wales there is documentary evidence for three-bay dwellings akin to the west Midlands peasant houses (Suggett 2013). None has survived, apparently because of replacement by a specialized four-bay hall-house/long-house in the late fifteenth and early sixteenth centuries.

Tyddyn Llwydion, a cruck-framed peasant hall-house in Powys (Britnell and Suggett 2002), exemplifies the mature late medieval peasant hall-house in upland Wales (Figure 15.4). This was a four-bayed hall-house with a platformed siting

FIGURE 15.3 Recreation of the furnished home of Robert Dene of Stoneleigh, Warwickshire, based on his probate inventory (1552) and surviving three-bayed, cruck-framed house

(drawing by Pat Hughes © Nat Alcock)

FIGURE 15.4 Tyddyn Llwydion (Pennant Melangell, Montgomeryshire): cut-away of a cruck-framed upland hall-house/long-house showing cowhouse, cross-passage, single-bayed hall, and inner-room

(© Crown Copyright: Royal Commission on the Ancient and Historical Monuments of Wales)

which excavation confirmed as having a cowhouse-passage-hall-chamber plan. The lower-end bay was undoubtedly a cowhouse, the tips from the stakes of stall dividers remained in the subsoil and some cattle were evidently stalled facing the passage partition and fed from the passage between outer bay and hall. The location of the hall was confirmed by the presence of the hearth. The focus of the hall was the upper-end partition, which was box-framed rather than cruck-framed, and the special status of

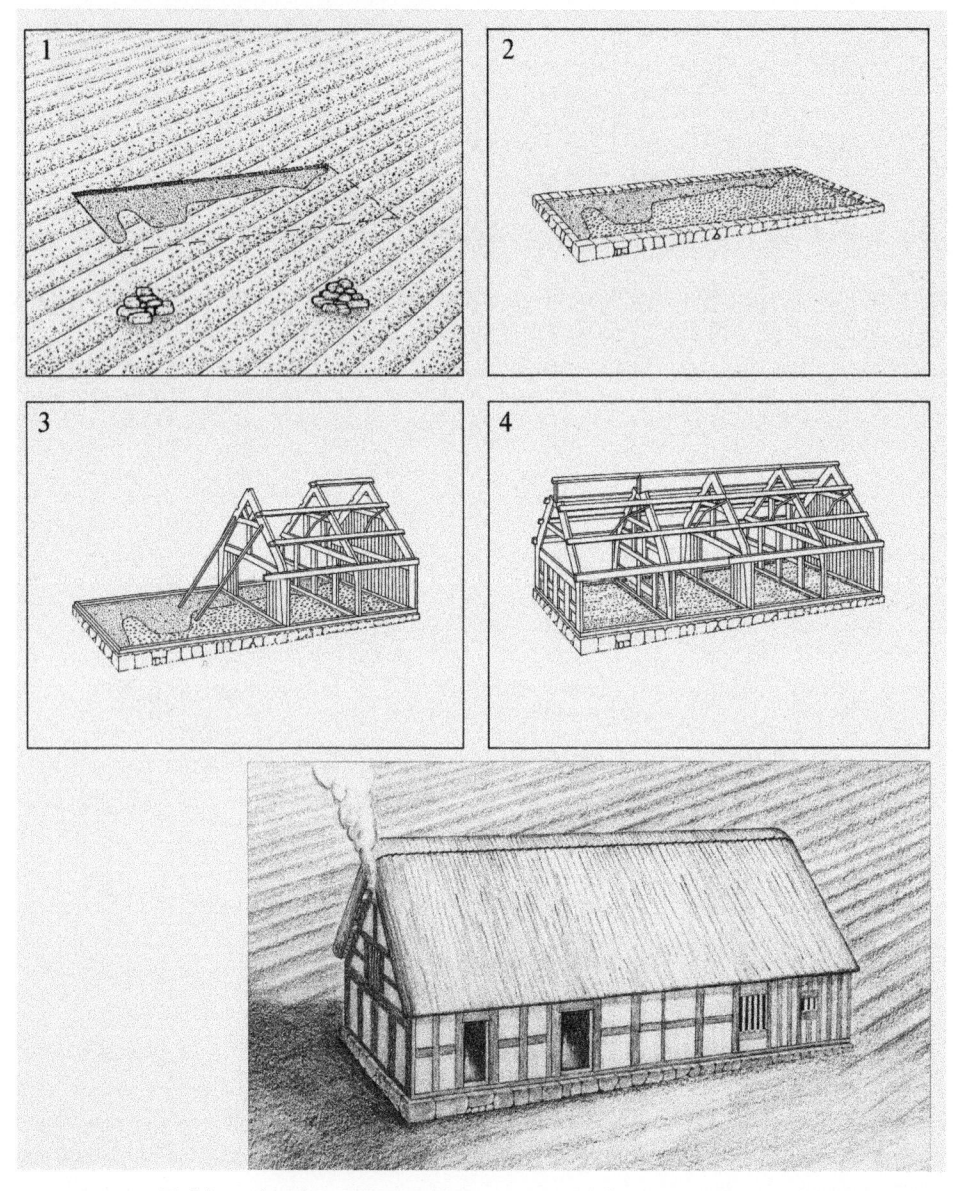

FIGURE 15.5 Tyddyn Llwydion: the building sequence of a late-medieval hall-house on a new site

(© Crown Copyright: Royal Commission on the Ancient and Historical Monuments of Wales)

the upper end bay was signalled by a change in wall-framing from large panels to close studding. Dated to 1554, the date when a living tree was felled to make a cruck-truss for the dwelling, Tyddyn Llwydion proved to be a new house on a new site: there was no evidence for earlier occupation and the house contained no re-used timber. But while excavation was able to establish the sequence of construction (Figure 15.5) there were no significant finds, possibly because the house was swept clean or because the material culture was primarily wood-based. Whatever the case, the absence of finds serves to emphasize that the house itself was the principal item of material culture, and its plan structured the everyday routines of the peasant household.

INSIDE THE PEASANT HOUSE

Several thousand peasant dwellings survive from 1350 to 1550, mostly with three- or four-bay plans. The centrality of the hall is striking but while variation occurs in the use of the outer bays (cowhouse, kitchen, or other service-rooms), the inner bays are uniformly hall and chamber. Complementary archival and archaeological discoveries combine to give a fairly full picture of the plan and furnishing of the late medieval peasant hall-house (Dyer 2013; Field 1965; Hinton 2010). Numerous finds of coins in the countryside suggest that peasants habitually carried money in purse and pocket as consumers in a cash economy (see Chapter 32). These coins are mostly of small denominations but silver and (exceptionally) gold coins have been excavated. Peasants became consumers in fourteenth-century England and Wales. Chroniclers sharply observed that the Welsh had been tamed not by the Edwardian conquest but from fear of losing their goods (Suggett 2013). Peasant wills have survived in some numbers recording monetary bequests for pious uses, much as favoured by the land-owning class. Inventories listing the contents of peasant houses are much rarer, but some survive for the diocese of York c.1500. Additionally, and somewhat earlier, manorial records occasionally list the principal goods (*principalia*) of peasants who had quitted (left, retired, or died) their holdings.

Peasant houses were not randomly sited. The dispersed houses of upland settlements occupied the boundary between enclosed fields and open pasture. Village houses were often demarcated from their neighbours by a ditched and hedged toft. This gave a hierarchy of increasingly private spaces—street, yard, and house—where different forms of interaction took place. The toft gave some seclusion but the disputes inseparable from village life sometimes involved eavesdroppers, who listened under the low eaves of the house to the concerns of their neighbours. The house itself was entered from the long walls through the doorways of a cross-passage. The uses of this cross-passage, to which there was great attachment, are not fully understood but it had some agricultural functions, especially in a long-house. Opposed doorways meant that the cross-passage could act as a threshing floor. In some long-houses the passage bay was demonstrably a feeding passage for the cattle stalled in the lower-end bay (Figure 15.4); the passage partition was sometimes framed with open panels for feeding the cattle stalled in the downhouse. Beams with sockets for tethering posts have occasionally survived in the hall-house/long-houses of the Welsh Marches so that the passage was essentially part of the house. In Wales it was sometimes referred to as 'the floor end' (W. *penllawr*) indicating the separation between the domestic and more agricultural parts of the building. In the four-bay peasant houses of the Marches the large passage bay probably functioned as a general work area. Excavation at Tyddyn Llwydion showed that fires were sometimes lit here and that temporary partitions were erected there.

The long-house was essentially an upland plan-type. If the outer bay was not a cowhouse it had a service function (Figure 15.6). Named service-rooms included the 'spence' or pantry for dry foods and the 'buttery' or cellar for drink. If cooking did not take place in the hall then the kitchen occupied the outer bay or a detached building. The cooking utensils were kept here and the iron cooking-pot (cauldron) was suspended over the kitchen fire. Inventories recorded metal pans, but the earthenware pots revealed by excavation were generally ignored by appraisers. The range and quantity of surviving pottery is very variable, and some house sites yield virtually no sherds. Field-walking reveals that in many cases broken pottery was consigned to the midden and conveyed to the fields.

The hall lay between inner and outer rooms. The hall is sometimes referred to as the 'firehouse' (from the principal hearth) or the 'insethouse' (from its position). As the house was entered from the long wall, there was an architectural pause as visitors turned to enter the hall and sometimes the entrance to the hall was marked by a screen or partition truss. In Welsh peasant halls the hall-partition truss was generally finely carpentered, occasionally decorated, and sometimes with spere-posts defining the entry to the hall (Figures 15.4 and 15.6) (Suggett 2005, 84–111, 273). Once inside, it is usually the archaeological discovery of the open hearth that locates the hall. The hall fire was not necessarily laid on an elaborate base (though sometimes it was)—a scattering of stones

FIGURE 15.6 A peasant hall with dais canopy: Upper Hem, Forden, Montgomeryshire
(© Crown Copyright: Royal Commission on the Ancient and Historical Monuments of Wales)

would do. Excavation has shown that the hearth could wander over time creating a large area of reddened floor. Smoke from the open hearth sometimes emerged from a louver but more often than not it escaped through one of the gable ends, creating a thoroughly sooted roof from its passage along the house. The fire might have a 'reredos', that is a fireback of stone or clay, and the fire was additionally constrained by the double-ended firedogs that carried the spits for roasting meat.

At the upper end of the hall, beyond the fire, was the hall seat and table (Figures 15.3, 15.4, and 15.6). Mortises show that the long bench was often fixed to the upper-end partition, which might be of superior post-and-panel construction, especially in the west. The bench was essentially a plank which terminated in shaped ends, as is shown by a few surviving examples in Devon and Breconshire, but it was often provided with 'bankers' or long cushions and might be enhanced by a timber canopy, especially in the Welsh Marches, southern England, and in Devon (where it was sometimes a modification oversailing a low partition). This structure is sometimes interpreted functionally as an 'internal jetty' designed to increase the accommodation of the solar above. However, as medieval furniture demonstrates, the canopy was symbolic rather than functional and intended to signify status (Figure 15.6). Beneath it, a moveable table top was set on trestles in front of the fixed bench (for dining, see Chapter 43). The table-board was distinctively long and narrow; those sitting at the table faced the hall and its fire (as depicted in the Luttrell Psalter) rather than other diners (as sometimes erroneously depicted in reconstruction drawings). Above all, the hall was for eating in and peasant inventories record the dining accoutrements of the hall and its table. The board-cloth which covered the table during meals is frequently mentioned, as are hand-towels, ewers, and basins used for hand-washing before meals and between courses; these items undoubtedly demonstrate the formal nature of meals in the peasant hall. Some peasant inventories also include a cupboard ('almary') in which the accoutrements of the table were probably kept. This was a substantial item of furniture, if it was like the armoire of the elite, and probably displayed pewter dishes (also inventoried) on its flat top. The hall was to an extent a public room, where visitors were received and betrothals and other life-cycle events occurred, and even a peasant hall might have an element of display beyond its furniture. In high-status halls the dais partition was enhanced by a tapestry or painted decoration. Peasant inventories sometimes refer to painted cloths ('dorsers') and fabric 'hallings' which, one assumes, enhanced the upper-end partition and bench. Weapons were also inventoried and presumably hung on the wall, as in aristocratic halls, a reminder that a peasant might have followed his lord into battle.

The inner-room was generally called the 'chamber' and sometimes the 'bower'. Two-doorway partitions show that the inner bay was often divided to provide a service-room alongside the chamber (in a long-house), or to accommodate a ladder-stair to a loft (solar) over the chamber, probably a relatively late development. Whereas the hall was a public room; the chamber was more private and functioned as a parlour-bedroom. Peasants had mattresses, blankets, coverlets pillows, and sheets; the Welsh *brethyn* and Scottish *plaid* were highly valued. The special status of the inner-room was sometimes signalled by a change in wall-framing (as at Tyddyn Llwydion, Figure 15.4). Men and women kept their more personal and valuable possessions (primarily money and clothes) in the chamber in locked chests or coffers, which are frequently mentioned in inventories and were sometimes stolen. Some foodstuffs were also kept securely in hutches in the chamber.

Reconstructions of hall-house interiors tend to show (probably correctly) relatively uncluttered floors. Peg-holes (unrelated to mortises) indicate that many items, including foodstuffs, were suspended from projecting pegs or hooks. 'His hall rofe was full of bakon flytches' runs a description of a wealthy peasant's house, and his chamber had hutches 'full of egges, butter and chese' (Hanawalt 1986, 57). Hams and flitches were an agreeable sight but could be noxious during the curing process. Head ulcers which afflicted infants were attributed to the 'droppyngs of restye bacon and salte beefe on their bare heades' (Pinchbeck and Hewitt 1969, 6). Despite this disadvantage, it was sensible to keep food away from exploratory vermin. The cat, of course, was resident in the hall and allowed to sit 'nyhe the fyre' although she 'brenneth ofte hire hippes' (Owst 1961, 35). Dogs waited for scraps and sometimes devoured the contents of unattended cooking pots.

Excavations have often proved disappointing in terms of finds, but as the hall was regularly swept clean this should not be unexpected. One sermon described how a woman 'clenseth hur hous': 'she taketh a besom and dryveth togethur all the unclennes of the household; and, lest that the duste ascende and encwmber the place, she spryngeth it [with] water; and whan that she hath gadred all to-thether, she casteth it with gret violence owte of the dore' (Owst 1961, 35). The dish-shaped floor depressions sometimes observed archaeologically can be attributed to frequent sweeping. However, every Easter (according to one homily) the old hearth was cleared out of the hall. The hearth, which had burnt all winter and 'blakyd [the hall] wyth smoke', was renewed, and the floor freshly strewn with rushes and flowers in place of the old straw (Owst 1961, 35).

The routines of the hall reflected the gender division of labour, and there may have been parts of the house particularly associated with men or with women. However, one cannot read into the hall-house plan the all-pervasive symbolism encountered in some housing cultures. Neither is it helpful to read into the lines and circles randomly scribed on walls and trusses an 'apotropaic' or protective significance. This makes our rather pragmatic ancestors appear more superstitious than they actually were. The organizing principles of the medieval hall-house were social and explicitly hierarchical. Houses were organized into high and low ends from the lower-end kitchen/cowhouse to the upper-end hall and chamber. The downslope siting of many houses deliberately emphasized the hierarchy implicit in the plan so that the high ends were physically as well as socially higher than the low ends.

Houses and Consumption

Houses were an aspect of consumption, and indeed the most expensive consumer item that a peasant might acquire in a lifetime (see Chapter 13). That element of choice must be re-emphasized: the peasant was not compelled to build a durable home. The hall-house—built for the future as well as the present—has special significance because it embodies the preferences and priorities of the peasant. These were professionally built houses, and the peasant had to pay the builders with money that had been accumulated over many years or specially borrowed for the purpose. In many respects they were miniature versions of the hierarchically arranged gentry hall-house complete with high and low ends. Although late medieval Welsh poetry conventionally contrasted the delights of the fair, gentry hall with the wretched (home-made) turf-roofed peasant house, this topos was part of an elite European literary tradition that generally mocked the rusticity of peasants, especially their food, dress, and dwellings (Freedman 1999). Prosperous peasants could challenge these social markers, especially after the mid-fourteenth century. 'The villeins very often have silver and gold' was one of the complaints in a millenarian poem dating from the eve of Owain Glyndŵr's revolt (Livingston and Bollard 2013, 20–1). The peasant with money to spend was a disturbing figure who confused social categories and challenged hierarchy. Officials ('justicis, sherreves and bailifs'), when they noticed an ambitious peasant, might say aggressively, 'Loo, he is a carle, and wolde be moore than his syr was! Late us take fro him the richesse' (Owst 1961, 370n).

The peasant's decision to build a new hall was probably inseparable from the need to show that he was as good as his neighbours. There was surely a competitive element in house building and it is noticeable how often peasant hall-houses form clusters, notably in cruck villages like Long Crendon (Buckinghamshire) and Stoneleigh (Worcestershire) but also in the more dispersed settlements of, for example, Powys and Devon. It is not only the appearance of these new halls that is impressive but also their steady accumulation. Collectively the thousands of durable peasant hall-houses built after the Black Death and Peasants' Revolt amounted to an assertion of free identity: the peasant sitting at his own table in his own hall was undoubtedly his own master (Figure 15.6). The new peasant hall-house challenged the distinctiveness of gentry housing culture. However, peasant hall-houses were never simple emulations of aristocratic dwellings but adapted to the needs of the peasant economy. Nevertheless, peasants appropriated—perhaps unexpectedly—the hall as an architectural setting for household hierarchy and its expression in formal dining. The widespread adoption by peasants of a version of the housing culture of the gentry eroded the markers of difference between them. The development of the Wealden house in parts of south-east England was a striking example of a high-status house-type adopted and adapted by the higher peasantry (Pearson 1994, 132–4). The reaction of the gentry in the fifteenth century to peasant houses which mirrored their own was to build ever grander hall-houses, but in the first half of the sixteenth century the gentry hall-house was abandoned for a new type of house, generally storeyed and increasingly stone- or brick-built, and with fireplaces rather than the open hearth. In early-modern Britain regional diversity progressively displaced the uniformity of the late medieval hall-house plan.

References cited

Alcock, N. 1981 *Cruck construction: an introduction and catalogue*, Council for British Archaeology Research Report 42, London

Alcock, N. and Miles, D. 2013 *The medieval peasant house in Midland England*, Oxbow, Oxford

Beresford, G. 1979 'Three deserted medieval settlements on Dartmoor: a report on the late E. Marie Minter's excavations', *Medieval Archaeology* 23, 98–158

Beresford, M. and Hurst, J. (eds) 1971 *Deserted medieval villages*, Lutterworth Press, London

Britnell, W. and Suggett, R. 2002 'A sixteenth-century peasant hallhouse in Powys: survey and excavation of Tyddyn Llwydion, Pennant Melangell, Montgomeryshire', *The Archaeological Journal* 159, 142–69

Campbell, J. (ed.) 1975 *A collection of Highland rites and customes*, The Folklore Society, Cambridge

Christie, N. and Stamper, P. (eds) 2012 *Medieval rural settlement: Britain and Ireland, AD 800–1600*, Windgather Press, Oxford

Dixon, P., Govan, S., and MacInnes, L. 2002 *But the walls remained: a survey of unroofed rural settlement depicted on the first edition of the Ordnance Survey 6-inch map of Scotland*, Royal Commission on the Ancient and Historical Monuments of Scotland, and Historic Scotland, Edinburgh

Dixon, P. 2006 *Puir labourers and husbandmen: the countryside of lowland Scotland in the Middle Ages*, Birlinn with Historic Scotland, Edinburgh

Dyer, C. 1986 'English peasant buildings in the later Middle Ages (1200–1500)', *Medieval Archaeology* 30, 19–45

Dyer, C. 1989 *Standards of living in the Later Middle Ages: social change in England, c.1200–1520*, Cambridge University Press, Cambridge

Dyer, C. 1994 *Everyday life in medieval England*, The Hambledon Press, London

Dyer, C. 2002 *Making a living in the Middle Ages: the people of Britain, 850–1520*, Yale University Press, London

Dyer, C. 2005 *An age of transition? Economy and society in England in the Later Middle Ages*, Clarendon Press, Oxford

Dyer, C. 2013 'Living in peasant houses in late medieval England', *Vernacular Architecture* 44, 19–27

Fenton, A. and Walker, B. 1981 *The rural architecture of Scotland*, John Donald Publishers, Edinburgh

Field, R. 1965 'Worcestershire peasant buildings, household goods and farming equipment in the later Middle Ages', *Medieval Archaeology* 9, 105–45

Fox, C. and Lord Raglan, 1951 *Monmouthshire houses, part I: medieval houses*, National Museum of Wales, Cardiff

Freedman, P. 1999 *Images of the medieval peasant*, Stanford University Press, Stanford

Gardiner, M. 2000 'Vernacular buildings and the development of the later medieval domestic plan in England', *Medieval Archaeology* 44, 159–79

Gardiner, M. 2014 'An archaeological approach to the development of the late medieval peasant house', *Vernacular Architecture* 45, 16–28

Grenville, J. 1997 *Medieval housing*, Leicester University Press, London

Hanawalt, B. 1986 *The ties that bound: peasant families in medieval England*, Oxford University Press, Oxford

Hill, N. and Alcock, N. 2007 'The origins of crucks: new ideas revisited and a rejoinder', *Vernacular Architecture* 38, 8–14

Hinton, D. 2010 'Deserted medieval villages and the objects from them', in C. Dyer and R. Jones (eds), *Deserted villages revisited*, University of Hertfordshire Press, Hatfield, 85–108

Innocent, C. 1916 *The development of English building construction*, Cambridge University Press, Cambridge

Jennings, N. 2003 *Clay dabbins: vernacular buildings of the Solway Plain*, Cumberland and Westmorland Antiquarian and Archaeological Society Extra Series 30, Kendal

Letts, J. 1999 *Smoke-blackened thatch: a unique source of late medieval plant remains from southern England*, English Heritage, London

Livingston, M. and Bollard, J. 2013 *Owain Glyndŵr: a casebook*, Liverpool University Press, Liverpool

Noble, R. 2000 'Creel houses of the Scottish highlands', in T. Owen (ed.), *From Corrib to Cultra: folklife essays in honour of Alan Gailey*, Institute of Irish Studies, Belfast

Owst, G. 1961 *Literature and pulpit in medieval England*, Basil Blackwell, Oxford

Pearson, S. 1994 *Medieval houses of Kent: an historical analysis*, Royal Commission on Historical Monuments England, London

Pinchbeck, J. and Hewitt, M. 1969 *Children in English society, vol. I: from Tudor times to the eighteenth century*, Routledge and Kegan Paul, London

Ramm, H. G., McDowall, R. W., and Mercer, E. 1970 *Shielings and bastles*, Royal Commission on Historical Monuments England, London

Roberts, K. (ed.) 2006 *Lost farmsteads: deserted rural settlements in Wales*, Council for British Archaeology Research Report 148, York

Smith, J. 1970 'The evolution of the English peasant house to the seventeenth century: the evidence of the buildings', *Journal of the British Archaeological Association* 33, 122–47

Suggett, R. 2005 *Houses and history in the March of Wales: Radnorshire, 1400–1800*, Royal Commission on the Ancient and Historical Monuments of Wales, Aberystwyth

Suggett, R. 2013 'Peasant houses and identity in medieval Wales', *Vernacular Architecture* 44, 6–18

Turner, D. 1998 'Peasant housing and holdings in a marginal area: medieval settlement in the West Highlands, Scotland', *Ruralia* 2, 71–7

Wilson, D. M. and Hurst, G. 1964 'Medieval Britain in 1962 and 1963', *Medieval Archaeology* 8, 231–99

Wrathmell, S. (ed.) 2012 *A history of Wharram Percy and its neighbours*, York Archaeological Publications 15, York

CHAPTER 16

THE MEDIEVAL MANOR HOUSE AND THE MOATED SITE

JILL CAMPBELL

SINCE the 1990s, there has been growing interest amongst archaeologists in medieval manor houses. Modern scholars recognize that these buildings are central to furthering our understanding of the relationships between the medieval manor, economy, landscape, social, and cultural history of late medieval England (Bailey 2002, 2). The houses of the elite not only provided the basic functions of any shelter, but were designed by a self-conscious class with purpose and meaning: to display status and act as symbols of authority within a designed landscape. They were truly the 'power houses' of medieval England and a reflection of a society expressing standing, taste, and style (Emery 2007, 5; Girouard 1993; King 2003, 104). Yet the medieval manor did not just serve as the lord's home; it was also the administrative heart of their agricultural estate and represented the jurisdiction of the lord, exercised through the manorial courts.

The earliest studies on the medieval manor house were driven by architectural historians, among them T. Hudson Turner (1851), Faulkner (1958), and Wood (1965) who were principally concerned with the fabric, features, and chronology of the architecture they observed. The outcome was an expansive body of extremely detailed building surveys which paid little attention to the social and cultural influences in their design, the way in which they were used at the time of construction and in subsequent years, and the surrounding landscape. On the whole, despite the excavation of a number of sites such as Penhallam (Cornwall) and Joydens Wood (Kent), early investigations also focused on furthering our understanding of architectural history by recording the development of the buildings (Beresford 1974; Colvin 1948; Hogg 1941; Tester and Caiger 1959). While these approaches provided a useful 'snapshot' of the manor house at a particular time, they failed to address critical questions about how space was created and used (Emery 2006, 3; King 2003, 104). Even today, scholars tend to focus on their own specialist fields rather than consider the topic of the manor house more holistically. The result is detailed research into the composition of the manor (Bailey 2002), the lives of the gentry (Given Wilson 1996; Goldberg 2004; Radulescu and Truelove 2005) and architectural analyses of buildings, and yet a failure to capture the wider relationship between the medieval manor and society and to understand how the buildings themselves were used to display identity, status, and wealth. Recent exceptions to this are the comprehensive studies produced by Anthony Emery, who recognized that medieval houses were not built within a 'vacuum', but were a consequence of external factors such as the economy, fashion, politics, and society (Emery 1996; 2000; 2006).

Generally speaking, archaeological interest in the medieval manor house has not been as extensive as it has for other major medieval monuments such as castles, churches, and cathedrals. Very few manor house or moated sites have been excavated in their entirety or near entirety. Notable exceptions include the Manor of Hextalls (Surrey), Sydenhams Moat (Warwickshire), East Haddesley (Yorkshire), Old Abbey Farm (Cheshire), and the manor houses at Wharram Percy (North Yorkshire) and Goltho (Lincolnshire), which were located within the settlement site (Beresford 1987; Beresford and Hurst 1990; Heawood et al. 2004; Le Patourel 1973; Poulton 1998; Smith 1990). A number of individual sites have also been examined as part of research excavations or developer-led investigations such as Old Abbey Farm (Cheshire), Southchurch Hall (Essex), Mount House (Oxfordshire), Acton Court (Gloucestershire), Tempsford Park (Bedfordshire), Barentin's Manor (Oxfordshire), and the Manor of Hextalls (Surrey) (Heawood et al. 2004; Helliwell 1975; Brown 2006; Allen and Hiller 2002; Rodwell and Bell 2004; Maull and Chapman 2005; Shotliff 1996; Page et al. 2005; Poulton 1998). Nevertheless, synthesis has been lacking and this chapter will address key areas of debate within the field as well as possible directions for future research.

Halls and Chamber Blocks

Despite the acknowledgement that manorial residences, and in particular moated sites, formed an essential part of the settlement pattern of England (Creighton and Barry 2012, 65), there has been almost no discussion regarding the architectural language of display in manor houses of the late medieval period. This includes how these buildings were intended to be seen and how they portrayed contemporary attitudes, social organization, and tastes, particularly as their form, function, and meaning changed over time. These statements may have been clear at the point of construction, 'but to whose language we may have lost the code' (Cooper 2002, 28).

Much like the manorial complex which varied in form, size, and composition, the manor house of the post-Conquest period was itself fluid in form and character. The earliest surviving domestic buildings in England date to the twelfth and thirteenth centuries, and this period is considered as to be of increasing standardization and integration in domestic planning (Blair 1993, 15; Emery 2007, 44). Prior to this, manorial sites were made up of free-standing components grouped around a kitchen, hall, and sometimes a chapel, often constructed of timber. Spearheaded by architectural historians such as Wood and Faulkner, early interpretations of surviving buildings centred upon ground-floor open halls (aisled or unaisled) and first-floor halls, which were considered to be an alternative to the open ground-floor hall of earlier and later houses (Blair 1993, 1; Faulkner 1958; Wood 1965). During the 1990s, John Blair challenged this long-held view after analysing the results of a number of excavated manorial sites, coupled with detailed analysis of the documentary evidence. Blair proposed that the terminology used by scholars to describe two-storeyed stone-built blocks was 'anachronistic and misleading'. Instead he suggested that first-floor halls were in fact heated chamber blocks, once associated with timber-framed or stone-built ground floor halls which had themselves not survived (Blair 1993, 1–2). More than twenty two-storeyed stone-built blocks still stand from the Anglo-Norman period including Donington-Le-Heath (Leicestershire), Old Soar (Kent), Burton Agnes (Yorkshire), Hemingford Grey Manor House (Cambridgeshire), and Boothby Pagnell (Lincolnshire) (Blair 1993, 8; Emery 2000, 180; 2006, 381–2; 2007, 30; Impey and Harris 2002). Blair used Boothby Pagnell, which had long been celebrated as a typical example of a first-floor hall, as his case study. Drawing upon documentary sources and re-interpreting the plan and design of the building, he convincingly argued that buildings such as Boothby Pagnell were in fact free-standing chamber blocks (Blair 1993, 8). Blair's argument is now widely accepted by scholars and has emphasized the need to study manor houses using every available strand of evidence and not just to focus on architectural features.

These two-storeyed chamber blocks did not stand in isolation. Rather, they were accompanied by a free-standing open hall, of which fewer examples have survived. Notable exceptions are the early thirteenth-century examples at Balsall (Warwickshire) and Barnack (Nothamptonshire) (Alcock 1982; Blair 1993, 8–9). A resistivity survey undertaken in 1995 at Boothby Pagnell to test Blair's argument discovered a large rectangular building measuring approximately 24.5 x 17 m to the east of the surviving structure, located within the presumed position of the moat. The well-constructed stone footings and deep foundation trench suggested that they once carried a substantial stone structure, almost certainly the missing hall dating to $c.$1200 (Impey and Harris 2002, 252–3). Blair points out that no examples with unambiguous remains of both elements (hall and chamber) survive together on one site in England, with the possible exception of Leicester Castle (Leicestershire), but mentions comparable examples in France such as Beaumont-le-Richard and Briquebec (Alcock and Buckley 1987; Blair 1993, 9; Impey 1993). Despite the small sample size, it is now widely accepted that two-storeyed stone-built blocks were not first-floor halls, rather, they were chamber blocks that once co-existed alongside ground-floor halls.

Only a small number of ground-floor open halls survive from the twelfth century and only a few of these from a secular manorial context. All are partial or fragmentary in their survival such as Penhallam (Cornwall), Farnham Castle (Surrey), and Old Sarum (Wiltshire) with one notable exception, Oakham Castle (Rutland) (Beresford 1974; Emery 2000, 178–80; 2006, 614–15; Hill 2013). Oakham Castle (Figure 16.1) dates to the late twelfth century and is a remarkably complete example. The hall, which is defined

FIGURE 16.1 Oakham Castle, showing aisled hall and the two blocked up service doors

(© Jill Campbell)

by an exceptional stone-built aisle arcade, consists of four bays and measures 19.9 x 13.2 m. The gable ends have two prominent buttresses crowned by carved finials, and the eastern gable has two blocked doorways which would once have connected to the services (Hill 2013, 168–70; Holland Walker 1924). During a recent study, Hill argued that the hall had supported a timber lean-to structure at either end, perhaps a forerunner to the cross-wing, which likely housed the services and other lesser rooms (Hill 2013, 172). Oakham Castle stands at an important juncture in the development of the tripartite plan (see the following section) in English medieval houses. Despite the fact there was no cross passage at the east or low end of the hall, something which became a fairly standard feature in the following centuries, the presence of original blocked doorways indicates that a service end which had once been attached is a development of the later twelfth century.

Hill's assessment of Oakham Castle was the first scholarly interpretation of the site since Wood's examination in 1935. His analysis demonstrated that Oakham Castle is an example of an early English hall and fits into the model proposed by Blair (Blair 1993; Hill 2013, 197). The development of lavish halls and chamber blocks, such as Boothby Pagnell and Oakham Castle, demonstrate the wealth of the growing gentry class under the Plantagenet kings. Blair and Hill's reassessment of these buildings highlights the need for archaeologists to re-examine manor houses as part of a wider assessment of how medieval buildings contributed to a symbolic language used to display identity, and this must be considered in future research projects. It is clear that one of the key factors driving developments in the style, plan, and materials used in manorial residences was an increased desire to display wealth, power, and status (Blair 1993, 13). The study of late medieval manorial sites has been little debated in the literature since the Blair's challenge nearly thirty years ago, and as a consequence has advanced little. This reinforces the importance of revisiting sites, particularly those of the lesser gentry such as the Manor of Hextalls (Surrey) or the medieval moated manor site at Boreham Airfield (Essex) which are often only examined as a consequence of developer-led excavations (Clarke 2003; Poulton 1998).

Hall, Chamber, and Services: The Tripartite Plan

Between the thirteenth and fifteenth centuries, building design from the grandest of houses to relatively impoverished rural cottages drew upon the same elements of a tripartite plan: the central open hall, the chamber or solar, and services (Figure 16.2). This 'standard' plan was flexible and easily adapted to reflect the status and personal taste of the owner while working to the physical constraints of the site. It was a means of

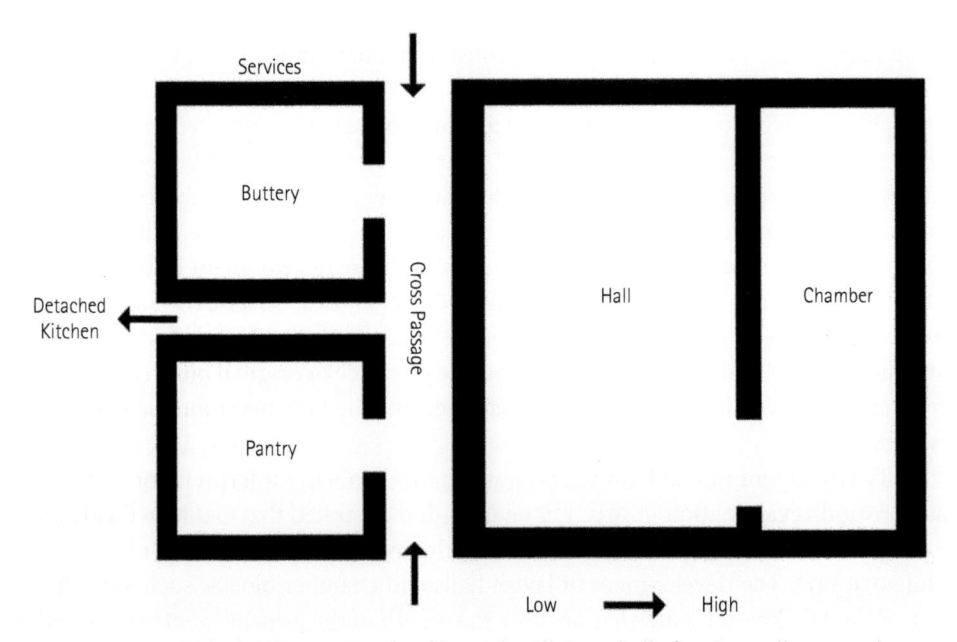

FIGURE 16.2 An idealized tripartite plan (drawn by Jill Campbell after Grenville 1997, 90)

organizing physical space while adhering to a formal arrangement which held hierarchical and symbolic meaning (Gardiner 2008, 37; Grenville 1997, 89–92; King 2003, 105; and see Chapter 15 in this *Handbook*). Through the size and disposition of rooms, their architecture and embellishment, a very particular 'spatial syntax' was communicated which expressed social distinctions, identities, power, and status. This also established a convention for managing both external appearance and internal space. A visitor moving towards a medieval manor house could 'read' the building during their approach using architectural features. For example, large windows such as the oriel windows at Athelhampton (Dorset) and the heraldic stained glass windows at Ockwells Manor (Berkshire) were placed at the high end of the hall (Figure 16.3) to illuminate the lord and to emphasize his status in comparison to those who were only admitted to the low end of the hall (Cooke 2010; Emery 2006, 488; Wood 1965, 113–14). Once inside the hall, a medieval peasant understood the function and layout of the space they had entered and the behaviour that was expected of them: indeed, this was probably part of the appeal behind using the same design at all social levels (Johnson 2010, 68).

Despite this standardization of the plan, however, there was no rigid blueprint for medieval builders to follow; no two houses are in fact precisely the same (Emery 2006, 2). This period was one of increasing social mobility amongst the upper levels of society and, as a consequence, established families needed to reinforce their position, while the nouveaux riches wished to demonstrate their new wealth. The study of late medieval building contracts reveals that house-builders strove to equal, if not to exceed, their neighbours and deployed new houses as deliberate visual references to their status. The building accounts

FIGURE 16.3 Athelhampton, showing the oriel window at the high end of the hall

(© Jill Campbell)

of 1506 and 1509 from Little Saxham (Suffolk) mention payments to skilled workmen, the carpenter, and glazier, to enable them to travel 30 miles (48 km) to Horham Hall (Essex), to view work already completed there (Airs 1978; Emery 2000, 114–16; Howard 1987, 12–15). Presumably this was work to be imitated or bettered.

The entrance to the hall was through opposing doorways into a cross passage, commonly separated from the hall by a screen or wall. From the passage, two doorways led into the service rooms known as the buttery (for the storage of wine and ale) and to the pantry (for the storage of dried goods); if there were three doorways, the central door led to the kitchen which was commonly detached from the main house (Gardiner 2008, 40; Grenville 1997, 89). The hall was a large open space, heated by a central hearth the smoke from which escaped through a louvre. At the opposite end of the hall to the services was a high table, often raised on a dais with a moulded beam or hood to frame those sitting there (Gardiner 2008, 37). Beyond the dais was the entrance to the lord's private chamber or 'solar', a term used to describe the ground-floor and first-floor rooms, the latter of which is presumed to be the 'best chamber'. Gardiner (2000, 162) has suggested that the chamber served not only as a space for sleeping but for storing personal items and valuables. He refers to the Paston letters which illustrate that chambers in manorial houses accommodated chests containing deeds, money, and account books as well as a counting board (Davis 1971; Gardiner 2000, 162). The tripartite plan was not just a practical way of organizing space, it was also full of symbolism and meaning and clearly defined social grading. It comes as no surprise that the service area was known as the 'low' end and the opposite end with the dais and chamber was the 'high' end, demarcating social distinctions. Despite a common entrance, there was a clear hierarchy with servants operating in the low end of the hall and the lord operating at the high end, from which access to the chambers was controlled. Guests were expected to negotiate their way from a common entrance, through the low end of the hall to the high end to the chamber beyond if permitted (Grenville 1997, 89).

During the late medieval period, features which were to become fixed in the tripartite plan were consolidated and this development can be traced in surviving buildings. For example, at the late twelfth century manorial sites Oakham Castle and Penhallam (Cornwall), the cross passage did not have an opposing door, something which became standard by the second half of the thirteenth century. The early thirteenth-century Nassington Prebendal manor house (Northamptonshire) had opposing cross passage doors, though conversely only had one door leading to the services rather than the more common two or three doors (Emery 2000, 279–82; Hill 2001). One of the earliest houses to favour the full tripartite plan was Southchurch Hall (Essex), a moated timber-framed manor house which dates to the mid-fourteenth century (Brown 2006, 3; King 2003, 108). The open hall here is a two-and-a-half bay timber-framed building with a chamber at one end and a cross passage at the other which contained a pair of central doors that led to the buttery and pantry (Emery 2000, 9; Rackham 1986, 43).

By the end of the late medieval period architecture had reached levels of excess not previously seen before. Political and social status both demanded visible public expression whether it was through great houses, clothing, or the number of liveried retainers in service (Cooper 2002, 293). Maddern (2005, 31) suggested that, in order to be part of this society, the gentry were 'acting out a role'. This could mean showing the appropriate hospitality or building a house that displayed the right kind of message. From the fifteenth century, society witnessed some of the most important architectural and structural developments of the manor house, with a growing emphasis on domestic comfort. There was a gradual abandonment of the typical medieval plan, which was viewed by now as old-fashioned and restrictive, and a corresponding expansion in the space devoted to private living accommodation (Cooper 1999, 16, 55; Thompson 1987, 44–5). Houses became larger. No-one of gentry-standing would be expected to sleep in a hall, and the provision of new rooms coupled with architectural devices such as contrived symmetry, the creation of courtyards, and the addition of large expanses of windows all helped to demonstrate status. At the same time, while the hall remained central to spatial organization, its form and function were updated. The aisled hall was no longer fashionable, with the preference for a large uninterrupted space. Other changes included the abandonment of the central hearth and the introduction of large bay windows, wall fireplaces, and screens (Emery 2007, 47; Wood 1965, 56–62).

A post-processual framework enables archaeologists to explore the idea that the gentry invested in their houses and the surrounding landscape in order to display their identity, social prestige, and wealth (Cooper 1999; Creighton 2009). It is precisely this interaction with the physical environment and material culture which enabled the medieval elite to present their position in society by imitating patterns of display exhibited by those at the top of the social scale. It is clear that the gentry shared similar ideologies with the nobility, with both groups striving to display those qualities that made them 'gentle', such as refinement, good manners, and honourable behaviour. During the late medieval period therefore space acquired meaning and identity, and this was emulated and displayed through material culture and buildings. The design of buildings, the use of architectural features, the choice of materials, and the creation of a designed setting which surrounded the house all contributed to a symbolic language which was easily read during the late medieval period. These ideas are accepted for the post-medieval period, yet have been rarely discussed for houses and landscapes of the preceding centuries. There are essential similarities which must be considered as an area of future research within the field.

Future Research

So what does the future research in to the study of the late medieval manor house hold? The construction or modification of existing manorial sites, and the use of material culture were used deliberately to develop a cultural identity and reinforce status, and this is something that future investigations must consider. Perhaps the way to move forward is for archaeologists to consider buildings as artefacts. This will enable scholars to investigate their design, style, and use during the period in which they were built as well as to understand how people responded to buildings over time, something which many previous approaches have failed to consider. Identity and status has always involved the consumption and display of material culture, which also shines a light on how people of the late medieval period viewed themselves (Grassby 2005, 596). The examination of artefacts and environmental evidence must also be included in all future research into the medieval manor house and moated sites. Moated sites have the potential to produce a number of high quality artefacts and to provide an important insight into day-to-day life, as well as recording the changes to the site over the centuries. At Wood Hall (Yorkshire) excavations produced high-quality leather items such as shoes and finely decorated gloves, as well as wooden items such as lathe-turned bowls and items of glass such as an enamelled and gilded glass goblet, possibly originating from Bohemia (Metcalf 2001, 28; 1993, 19). At Acton Court (Gloucestershire) important amounts of pottery and building materials were recovered as well as a large quantity of vessel glass including many imported examples, tobacco pipes, textiles, leather, including six shoes, and two wooden staves from longbows (Rodwell and Bell 2004, 294–414). Timbers also survive well in waterlogged sites. At Southchurch Hall (Essex) several pieces of fourteenth-century boat planking were discovered below the trestle of a timber bridge (Hutchinson 2006, 136). Remains of bridges also survive at sites including Penhallam (Cornwall), Acton Burnell (Shropshire), Lewmote (Kent), Southchurch Hall (Essex), and Hen Gwrt (Monmouthshire), among others (Rigold 1975; Thornhill 1973; Wilson and Hurst 1964, 272–4).

In the last twenty years, the number of archaeobotanical samples analysed has slowed. This is perhaps due to budgetary constraints which can slow the post-excavation process and the rise in developer-led investigations which are focused on being cost-effective (see Chapter 8). In many instances there is little attempt to compare results with the national archaeobotanical dataset or to address questions that are at the core of research-led excavations. Recent papers such as Rippon et al. (2014) indicate the advantages of using zooarchaeological and archaeobotanical evidence on a much broader scale to investigate regional variation in landscape character, particularly in undocumented periods. Unfortunately, much of the valuable information gathered from archaeobotanical reports remains as 'grey literature', and may not feature fully in published excavation reports (Van der Veen et al. 2013, 169–70).

Botanical data from excavations can provide an invaluable insight into the diets, agriculture, trade practices, and environment of the period; however, reliable reconstructions are dependent on the quality of datasets and their recovery from a secure context (Van der Veen et al. 2013, 151). The sediment from moat ditches has often remained wet, making it appear ideal for radiocarbon dating and environmental study. Yet the fact that flora and fauna assemblages are preserved in a moat does not mean that they can necessarily produce the desired picture of an environmental record of the period. This is because the ditches of medieval moats were regularly cleaned and drained not only at the time they were in use, but also during subsequent centuries. This was demonstrated at Perceton (Ayrshire), for example, where the preservation of deposits and features was poor due to horticultural mixing and bioturbation and this proved a challenge for the construction of reliable stratigraphic and chronological sequences (Stronach 2004, 148).

Analysis of the 11,105 animal bones and 2265 shells of marine molluscs recovered at Barentins Manor (Oxfordshire) produced significant insights into the economy and change of husbandry at the manor. Management of cattle for meat was initially the principal use of animals on the site; however, there was a change to an arable economy as dairying become more important. An abundance of pig and deer bones suggested the exploitation of local woodland and scrub, unusual in a Thames Valley context. The number of sea fish and shellfish, including edible crab, is also a clear indication of trade (Wilson et al. 2005). On the other hand, the preservation of organic remains from the moat was poor, and they were only recovered from one sample from the very bottom of the moat. This may have resulted from the drainage of the moat after the site was abandoned (Robinson 2005, 153).

Our understanding of space must also be carefully considered in future research. In recent years scholars have began to consider the process of seeing, particularly how past spaces were used to portray identity, power, and wealth. Giles (2007, 106) has argued, however, that current approaches to the relationship between landscapes, buildings, and material culture impose a modern way of thinking and seeing. She believes that archaeologists must address the debates occurring in other disciplines regarding the historicity of visuality and spatiality, in order to understand how communities retained a connection with the past (Giles 2007, 117–18; Chapter 14 in this *Handbook*). Sensory perception and connotations of the late medieval household must also be critically considered by archaeological investigations in the future, in order that we can begin to understand experiences of the day-to-day life such as eating and drinking (Brears 2008; Woolgar 2006, 273; see Chapter 43 in this *Handbook*). Material culture such as furniture and furnishings and the reorganization of space were delicate tools that individuals deliberately and interactively used to develop their own cultural identity and standing (De Clercq et al. 2007, 1). These complex ideas must be an essential part of all future research and reiterate the point that studies of the late medieval manor house must adopt a comprehensive approach and incorporate different disciplines and strands of evidence.

Another key theme emerging in the study of medieval archaeology is the role of the landscape. For example, a recent investigation of forty-five pre-thirteenth century nucleated settlements has challenged the idea that manor houses and parish churches lay at their focal points (Dyer 2003, 11; Jones and Page 2006, 79). Some 47 per cent of manor houses were found to be over 250 m from the nearest settlement and 91 per cent were over 100 m away (Campbell 2013, 274). Generalizations should not be made based on such a small sample size, but this suggests that where the manor house was positioned within the landscape and the resources which surrounded it were both an important part of display. Manors were not isolated country houses; rather, they were agrarian and administrative centres of the lord's estates and surrounded by buildings which were essential in running a farmstead such as barns, stables, dovecotes, bakehouses, and brewhouses (Gardiner 2007, 170–3). Farmyards were an important part of a medieval manorial house and were displayed, not hidden away, as at many post-medieval gentry house sites.

Moats

It is clear that those constructing manor houses found landscape features such as fishponds, deer parks, and moats appealing and used them as part of a 'designed medieval landscape' (Creighton 2009; Liddiard and Williamson 2008, 533; see also Chapters 23 and 25 in this *Handbook*). Dominance over the landscape and resources showed a considerable degree of social control and authority and, despite challenges in dating landscape features and the requirement for more rigorous testing, perhaps through GIS analysis, further investigation is required. Moats in particular have largely been ignored in the literature in recent years despite the fact that over five thousand sites were recorded in England by members of the Moated Sites Research Group during the late 1970s and 1980s. This is perhaps due to the fact that the group approached these monuments typologically, categorizing moats by their size and shape. These observations failed to capture the symbolism of these monuments and did not adequately question why so many of them were constructed, and why their construction largely ceased after *c*.1350.

Moated sites in England are spread across the country with the majority constructed in the more fertile region of central England (Aberg 1978, 2). Conversely, research into moated sites in Scotland and Wales is much more limited in scope and size. To date, approximately 120 moated sites have been identified in Scotland and only a handful have been subject to archaeological investigation. Early studies such as Dunrod and Bombie (Kircudbrightshire) did not advance the subject as excavations primarily focused on a small area of the moat. More recent interventions, as at Wallaces's House, Elderslie (Renfrewshire), and Perceton (Ayrshire), examined the site in its entirety while also considering the role of moats as a status symbol in Scottish medieval society (Alexander 2000; Anderson 1946; Burdon-Davies 1966; Stronach 2004, 147, 159–60). A similar number of sites, approximately 130, have been recorded in Wales, primarily concentrated in the low-lying areas and Marches. Like England, this area contained some of the most fertile land and moats were likely used as part of the display of wealth and political and cultural status, perhaps related to the Edwardian conquest in the mid-1280s (RCHAM 1982, 69–71). Much like Scotland, there has been very little scholarly research, perhaps because very few moats actually contain standing remains of structures. Notable exceptions include Horseman's Green and Althrey Hall (both Flintshire) as well as Llay Hall and Lower Berse (both Denbighshire) which were associated with high-status aisle-trussed halls (Cole 1991; Emery 2000, 667; Hubbard 1986, 110, 248–9; Smith 1988, 96–126, 321). Medieval structural remains have been found at Hen Gwrt (Monmouthshire), Horseland and Highlight (Glamorgan) with post-medieval buildings replacing earlier remains at Llay Hall, New Hall (both Denbighshire), and Halghton Hall (Flintshire)

(Craster and Lewis 1963; Hurst 1988, 940; RCHAM 1982; Spurgeon and Thomas, 1978, 30). Overall, sites in Scotland and Wales are difficult to date, but it is likely that the majority were built during the long thirteenth century, as in England. Excavations at Llys Edwin (Flintshire) and Highlight suggest a construction date of the late twelfth or early thirteenth century, while excavations of the moat at Hen Gwrt suggest the primary occupation was from the first half of the thirteenth century, although construction of the moat did not take place for another century (Craster and Lewis 1963). Moated sites in Wales are often associated with the place-names 'Llys' or 'Plas' (mansion, hall, or palace), such as Llysworney and Gadlys (Glamorgan) and Llys Edwin (Flintshire), the latter of which is one of three possibly fortified sites.

Moats were used in the medieval period for a variety of functions, but most were likely to have enclosed an island upon which a house was built, the location of which varied. It has been suggested that by the time the hall and chamber had become integrated the house was usually located towards the centre of the enclosure (Rigold 1978, 33). Moreover, the house was often orientated so that the length of the building ran across the longer axis of the island, creating a forecourt while also leaving room for a back yard, as is seen at Lower Brockhampton or Southchurch Hall (Brown 2006; Emery 2000, 558; Rigold 1978, 33). Later houses may be planned so that three or four sides of the building are built on the edge of the moat, with each range appearing to rise up out of the water, as at Acton Court (Gloucestershire). This reflective quality magnified the structure and created the illusion that the building was floating as at Acton Court (Gloucestershire) and more famously Bodiam Castle (Sussex).

Moats were not just a feature of high-status sites, but were also found on manorial sites of the lesser gentry and indeed non-manorial sites (Platt 2010, 115). The traditional interpretation of the role of moats is that of defence or drainage but, as Creighton has argued, this can only take us so far (Creighton 2009, 88–115); moats vary in shape, size, and depth and are found in variety of topographical locations. Moats were used to contain garden compartments and orchards and house livestock and dovecotes so it is likely that some moats also had an ornamental role. The moated manor house of Lower Brockhampton (Herefordshire) has a second moat filled by a small drain which carried the overflow from the principal moat (British Library Add. MS 36415; Morriss and Hoverd 1994; Poulton 1998). The subsidiary island itself is too small to have supported a domestic building, but may have had room for an orchard, garden, or possibly a small banqueting house as at Kenilworth (Warwickshire) (Creighton 2009, 79; Henderson 1992, 117; Johnson 2002, 137; Woodhouse 1999, 10). The moat may also have been used for breeding fish, for fishing, and as a place for boating. A secondary moat attached to the principal moat was also recorded at Barentin's Manor (Oxfordshire). Excavations on the second island produced no evidence for any structures and it too may have served as an enclosure for animals or as a garden or orchard (Page et al. 2005, 16–17).

Water has a unique ability to transform the human experience, particularly through its reflective qualities. Creighton (2009, 77–90) has suggested that we must look beyond the functionalist approach to watery landscapes traditionally undertaken in medieval landscape studies and consider the meaning. Water is symbolic and was used to seclude or create access to buildings. It was also used to magnify and have a stunning visual impact. A watery backdrop impacted the way in which the building and landscape was experienced. Future research must seek to examine the symbolism of these monuments and place moats into their European context. It must re-assess how landscape features such as moats, dovecotes, fishponds, and deer parks were used to display lordly dominance as part of medieval designed landscapes, not just in lowland England but across the British Isles (see also Chapters 23 and 25).

In conclusion, houses and landscapes were a conspicuous statement of elite identity in the late medieval period. This is not something that was exclusive to Britain; direct parallels can be drawn with manorial sites in France, Belgium, Scandinavia, and elsewhere. Future research must look now beyond national borders and explore commonalities and cultural influences in sites across Europe.

References Cited

Aberg, A. (ed.) 1978 *Medieval moated sites*, Council for British Archaeology Report 17, Oxford

Airs, M. 1978 'The designing of five East Anglian country houses, 1505–1637', *Architectural History* 21, 58–67

Alcock, N. W. 1982 'The hall of the Knights Templars at Temple Balsall, W. Midlands', *Medieval Archaeology* 25, 155–8

Alcock, N. W. and Buckley, R. J. 1987 'Leicester Castle: the great hall', *Medieval Archaeology* 31, 73–9

Alexander, D. 2000 'Excavation of a medieval moated site in Elderslie, Renfrewshire', *Scottish Archaeology Journal* 22, 155–77

Allen, T. G. and Hiller, J. 2002 *The excavation of a medieval manor house of the Bishops of Winchester at Mount House, Witney, Oxfordshire*, Oxford Archaeology, Oxford

Anderson, W. A. 1946 'Report on excavations at Bombie', *Transactions of the Dumfriesshire and Galloway Natural History Antiquaries Society* 25, 27–35

Bailey, M. 2002 *The English manor c.1200–c.1500*, Manchester University Press, Manchester

Beresford, G. 1974 'The medieval manor of Penhallam, Jacobstow, Cornwall', *Medieval Archaeology* 18, 90–145

Beresford, G. 1987 *Goltho: the development of an early medieval manor c.850–1150*, Historic Buildings and Monuments Commission for England, London

Beresford, M. and Hurst, J. 1990 *Wharram Percy: deserted medieval village*, Batsford, London

Blair, J. 1993 'Hall and chamber: English domestic planning 1000–1250', in G. Meirion-Jones and M. Jones (eds), *Manorial domestic building in England and northern France*, The Society of Antiquaries of London Occasional Papers 15, London, 1–21

Brears, P. 2008 *Cooking and dining in medieval England*, Prospect Books, Totnes

British Library Add. MS 36415 MS, Notebooks of J. C. Buckler: Site of Lower Brockhampton, Herefordshire

Brown, N. R. 2006 *A medieval moated manor by the Thames Estuary: excavations at Southchurch Hall, Southend, Essex*, East Anglian Archaeology Report 115, Chelmsford

Burdon-Davies, E. F. 1966 'The moated manor at Dunrod, Kircudbrightshire', *Transactions of the Dumfriesshire and Galloway Natural History Antiquaries Society* 93, 121–36

Campbell, J. 2013 'Understanding the relationship between manor house and settlement in medieval England', *Ruralia* IX, 273–85

Clarke, R. 2003 *A medieval moated site and windmill: excavations at Boreham Airfield, Essex 1996*, East Anglian Archaeology Occasional Paper 11, Chelmsford

Cole, J. R. 1991 *Althrey Hall, Bangor-is-y-coed, Clwyd: excavations September 1991*, Clwyd-Powys Archaeological Trust Report 22

Colvin, H. M. 1948 'Excavations in Joyden's Wood, Bexley', *Archaeologia Cantiana* 61, 133–5

Cooke, P. 2010 *Athelhampton house and gardens*, Athelhampton House, Dorchester

Cooper, N. 1999 *Houses of the gentry 1480–1680*, Yale University Press, London

Cooper, N. 2002 'Display, status and the vernacular tradition', *Vernacular Architecture* 33, 28–33

Craster, O. E. and Lewis, J. M. 1963 'Hen Gwrt moated site, Llantilio Crossenny, Monmouthshrie', *Archaeologia Cambrensis* 112, 159–83

Creighton, O. H. 2009 *Designs upon the land: elite landscapes of the Middle Ages*, The Boydell Press, Woodbridge

Creighton, O. H. and Barry, T. 2012 'Seigneurial and elite sites in the medieval landscape', in N. Christie and P. Stamper (eds), *Medieval rural settlement: Britain and Ireland, AD 800–1600*, Oxbow Books, Oxford, 63–80

Davis, N. 1971 *Paston letters and papers of the fifteenth century, part I*, Clarendon Books, Oxford

De Clerq, W., Dumolyn, J., and Haemers, J. 2007 '"Vivre noblement": material culture and elite identity in late medieval Flanders', *Journal of Interdisciplinary History* 38, 1–31

Dyer, C. 2003 *Making a living in the Middle Ages: the people of Britain 850–1520*, Penguin Books, London

Emery, A. 1996 *Greater medieval houses of England and Wales 1300–1500, Vol. I*, Cambridge University Press, Cambridge

Emery, A. 2000 *Greater medieval houses of England and Wales 1300–1500, Vol. II*, Cambridge University Press, Cambridge

Emery, A. 2006 *Greater medieval houses of England and Wales 1300–1500, Vol. III*, Cambridge University Press, Cambridge

Emery, A. 2007 *Discovering medieval houses*, Shire Publications, Princes Risborough

Faulkner, P. A. 1958 'Domestic planning from the twelfth to the fourteenth centuries', *The Archaeological Journal* 115, 150–83

Gardiner, M. 2000 'Vernacular buildings and the development of the later medieval domestic plan in England', *Medieval Archaeology* 44, 159–79

Gardiner, M. 2007 'The origins and persistence of manor houses in England', in M. F. Gardiner and S. Rippon, (eds), *Medieval landscapes: landscape history after Hoskins, Vol. II*, Windgather Press, Macclesfield

Gardiner, M. 2008 'Butttery and pantry, and their antecedents: idea and architecture in the English medieval house', in M. Kowaleski and P. J. P. Goldberg (eds), *Medieval domesticity: home, housing and household in medieval England*, Cambridge University Press, New York, 37–65

Giles, K. 2007 'Seeing and believing: visuality and space in pre-modern England', *World Archaeology* 39(1), 105–21

Girouard, M. 1993 *Life in the English country house*, Yale University Press, New Haven and London

Given-Wilson, C. 1996 *The English nobility in the late Middle Ages*, Routledge, Oxford

Goldberg, P. J. P. 2004 *Medieval England: a social history 1250–1550*, Hodder Arnold Publication, London

Grassby, R. 2005 'Material culture and cultural history', *Journal of Interdisciplinary History* 35(4), 591–603

Grenville, J. 1997 *Medieval housing*, Leicester University Press, London

Heawood, R., Howard-Davis, C., Drury, D., and Krupa, M. 2004 *Old Abbey Farm, Risely: building survey and excavation at a medieval moated site*, Oxford Archaeology North, Lancaster

Helliwell, L. 1975 *Southchurch Hall: an illustrated guide*, Museum Publications, Southend

Henderson, P. 1992 'Sir Francis Bacon's water gardens at Gorhambury', *Garden History* 20(2), 116–31

Hill, N. 2001 'The manor house, Medbourne: the development of Leicestershire's earliest manor house', *Transactions of the Leicestershire Archaeological and Historical Society* 75, 36–61

Hill, N. 2013 'Hall and chambers: Oakham Castle reconsidered', *The Archaeological Journal* 93, 163–216

Hogg, A. H. A. 1941 'Earthworks in Joyden's Wood, Bexley, Kent', *Archaeologia Cantiana* 54, 10–27

Holland Walker, J. 1924 'Oakham Castle', *Transactions of the Thoroton Society Nottinghamshire* 28, 29–45

Howard, M. 1987 *The early Tudor country house: architecture and politics 1490–1550*, George Philip, London

Hubbard, E. 1986 *Clwyd: Denbighshire and Flintshire*, Penguin Books, Harmondsworth

Hudson Turner, T. 1851 *Some account of domestic architecture in England*, J. H. Parker, Oxford

Hurst, J. G. 1988 'Rural building in England and Wales', in H. E. Hallam (ed.), *The agrarian story of England and Wales. Vol. II 1042–1350*, Cambridge University Press, Cambridge, 854–966

Hutchinson, G. 2004 'Boat timbers', in N. R. Brown, *A medieval moated manor by the Thames Estuary: excavations at Southchurch Hall, Southend, Essex*, East Anglian Archaeology Report 115, Chelmsford, 136–9

Impey, E. 1993 'Seigneurial domestic architecture in Normandy 1050–1350', in G. Meirion-Jones and M. Jones (eds), *Manorial domestic building in England and northern France*, The Society of Antiquaries of London Occasional Papers 15, London, 82–120

Impey, E. and Harris, R. 2002 'Boothby Pagnell revisited', in G. Meirion-Jones, E. Impey, and M. Jones (eds), *The seigneurial residence in western Europe AD c.800–1600*, British Archaeological Reports International Series 1088, Oxford, 245–69

Johnson, M. 2002 *Behind the castle gate: from medieval to Renaissance*, Routledge, London

Johnson, M. 2010 *English houses 1300–1800: vernacular architecture, social life*, Pearson Education, Harlow

Jones, R. and Page, M. 2006 *Medieval villages in an English landscape: beginnings and ends*, Windgather Press, Macclesfield

King, C. 2003 'The organization of social space in late medieval manor houses: an East Anglian study', *The Archaeological Journal* 160(1), 104–24

Le Patourel, J. H. E. 1973 *The moated sites of Yorkshire*, The Society for Medieval Archaeology Monograph 5, London

Liddiard, R. and Williamson, T. 2008 'There by design? Some reflections on medieval elite landscapes', *The Archaeological Journal* 165(1), 520–35

Maddern, P. C. 2005 'Gentility', in R. Radulescu and A. Truelove (eds), *Gentry culture in late medieval England*, Manchester University Press, Manchester, 18–34

Maull, A. and Chapman, A. 2005 *A medieval moated enclosure in Tempsford Park*, Bedfordshire Archaeology Monograph 5, Bedford

Metcalf, V. 1993 'The Wood Hall Moated Manor Project: excavations 1989-92', *Yorkshire Archaeological Society* 22, 15-22

Metcalf, V. 2001 *Wood Hall Moated Manor Project: interim report*, unpublished report for the Wood Hall Archaeological Trust Ltd

Morriss, R. K. and Hoverd, T. 1994 *Lower Brockhampton nr Bromyard Herefordshire: an outline analysis*, Hereford Archaeology Series 201 (unpublished)

Page, P., Atherton, K., and Hardy, A. (eds) 2005 *Barentin's Manor: excavations of the moated manor at Harding's Field, Chalgrove, Oxfordshire 1976-79*, Oxford University School of Archaeology, Oxford

Platt, C. 2010 'The Homestead Moat: Security or Status?', *The Archaeological Journal* 167, 115-33

Poulton, R. 1998 *The lost manor of Hextalls Little Pickle, Bletchingley*, Surrey Archaeology Unit, Woking

Rackham, O. 1986 *The ancient woodland of England: the woods of south-east, Essex*, Rochford District Council, Rochford

Radulescu, R. and Truelove, A. 2005 *Gentry culture in late medieval England*, Manchester University Press, Manchester

RCAHM 1982 *An inventory of the ancient monuments in Glamorgan, Vol. 3: medieval secular monuments, part 2: non-defensive*, Her Majesty's Stationary Office, Cardiff

Rigold, S. E. 1975 'Structural aspects of medieval timber bridges', *Medieval Archaeology* 19, 48-91

Rigold, S. E. 1978 'Structures within English moated sites', in F. A. Alberg (ed.), *Medieval moated sites*, Council for British Archaeology Research Report 17, 29-36

Rippon, S., Wainwright, A., and Smart, C. 2014 'Farming regions in medieval England: the archaeobotanical and zooarchaeological evidence', *Medieval Archaeology* 58, 195-255

Robinson, M. 2005 'Environmental evidence', in P. Page, K. Atherton, and A. Hardy (eds), *Barentin's Manor: excavations of the moated manor at Harding's Field, Chalgrove, Oxfordshire 1976-79*, Oxford University School of Archaeology, Oxford, 153-5

Rodwell, K. and Bell, R. 2004 *Acton Court: the evolution of an early Tudor courtier's house*, English Heritage, London

Shotliff, D. 1996 'A moated site in Tempsford Park, Tempsford', *Bedfordshire Archaeology* 22, 96-128

Smith, L. 1990 'Sydenhams Moat: a thirteenth-century moated manor-house in the Warwickshire Arden', *Transactions for the Birmingham and Warwickshire Archaeological Society* 96, 27-64

Smith, P. 1988 *Houses of the Welsh countryside: a study in historical geography*, Her Majesty's Stationary Office, London

Spurgron, C. J. and Thomas, H. J. 1978 'Medieval Glamorgan: an interim report on recent fieldwork', *Morgannwg* 22, 14-41

Stronach, S. 2004 'The evolution of a medieval Scottish manor at Perceton, near Irvine, North Ayrshire', *Medieval Archaeology* 48, 143-66

Tester, P. J. and Caiger, J. E. L. 1959 'Medieval buildings in the Joyden's Wood square earthwork', *Archaeologia Cantiana* 72, 18-40

Thompson, M. W. 1987 *The decline of the castle*, Cambridge University Press, Cambridge

Thornhill, L. 1973 'A double moated site at Beckenham', *Archaeologia Cantiana* 91, 145-64

Van der Veen, M., Hill, A., and Livarda, A. 2013 'The archaeobotany of medieval Britain (c. AD 450-1500): identifying research priorities for the 21st century', *Medieval Archaeology* 57, 151-82

Wilson, B., with Allison, E., Atherton, K., and Wilkinson, M. 2005 'Animal bones and shells', in P. Page, K. Atherton, and A. Hardy (eds), *Barentin's Manor: excavations of the moated manor at Harding's Field, Chalgrove, Oxfordshire 1976-79*, Oxford University School of Archaeology, Oxford, 125-53

Wilson, D. M. and Hurst, G. 1964 'Medieval Britain in 1962 and 1963', *Medieval Archaeology* 8, 231-299

Wood, M. 1965 *The English medieval house*, Batsford, London

Woodhouse, E. 1999 'Spirit of the Elizabethan garden', *Garden History* 27(1), 10-31

Woolgar, C. M. 2006 *The senses in late medieval England*, Yale University Press, London

CHAPTER 17

AGRICULTURAL BUILDINGS

NIALL BRADY

The study and understanding of the medieval agricultural economy has been guided in large measure by surviving documentary sources, which are particularly numerous for this period. Manorial accounts, inventories, and court records are all illuminating about land management and the different components of agrarian complexes (see Chapter 4). This range of written records is largely comparable across the medieval world, but in England they survive in particularly large numbers. It is why European researchers will often refer to England as a sounding board for insight to their own particular regions, and it can explain why research into medieval economic history is sometimes less developed outside England in areas where such records are fewer and less continuous, as they are in Scotland and Ireland.

The pre-occupation with written sources has led to a situation where archaeological sources are studied less, and where the impact of material remains on wider narratives is correspondingly reduced. Material remains from across Britain have tended to occupy a passive role in wider discussions, in which archaeological information is absorbed to illustrate discussions that are dominated by paradigms defined by historians. So, for instance, the discovery of a ploughshare may be regarded as evidence for ploughing rather than as an opportunity to consider the particular type of ploughing that was practised and how this knowledge might agree with or challenge prevailing views. Rather than focusing on new discoveries of ploughing implements, medievalists, for too long perhaps, have preferred to consider the records of ploughteams noted in, for instance, Domesday Book. Research in Denmark led by Steensberg and then by Lerche revealed how useful it is to study the artefact, but Denmark is a region where plough frames as well as plough irons and cultivation furrows survive in relative abundance (Lerche 1994). More recent research in Sweden led by Myrdal focuses on the investment into iron that such implements reflects, and perhaps shows the potential for work in a region like Britain where the physical remains of ploughs and agricultural tools more generally is poor (Myrdal 1997; Myrdal and Sapoznik 2016).

Agricultural buildings can be difficult to identify in excavation but survive above ground in large numbers especially in England, both as timber structures and as stone buildings (Figure 17.1). The work of the Vernacular Buildings Group and related studies has helped to reveal regional styles of construction and is a vital means for collating the essential datasets. Attention has highlighted particular building techniques used and, where timberwork survives, the type and range of joints employed (for example, Stenning 1993). Such analysis tends to be absorbed into wider discussions in rather simple ways, where the building information is used to illustrate what, for instance, a granary or a barn might look like. It is rare to find a study of these structures within the context of an independent perspective on the wider narratives (Dyer 1995; Platt 1969). Perhaps it explains the curious observation from a recent paper celebrating the role of castle complexes within the context of seigneurial landscapes that archaeologists need to be careful about attributing symbolic characteristics to manorial facilities and landscapes (Creighton and Barry 2012, 78). It suggests that the proper way to assess agricultural complexes is within the framework of the ordered estate management of the period; issues associated with 'design' should not apply. Yet it is the case that landscape

FIGURE 17.1 A large structure excavated by Worcestershire Archaeology north of St James' Church in Southam, Worcestershire, aligned roughly east to west, c. 20 m x 14.5 m, constructed of limestone blocks, with associated pottery of thirteenth- to fourteenth-century date. The form of this structure and its internal dimensions make it comparable with the major medieval barns of the Cotswold region, so it is thought to have had a similar function, associated with the Prior of Coventry. An early post-medieval pit adjacent contained a large amount of burnt grain, which indicates the probable continued agricultural use of the site, although the barn is not visible on the first detailed map of 1778

(© Aerial-Cam Ltd)

perspectives on the economic foundation of Britain in the Middle Ages have been largely ignored, and the opportunity remains for the new scholar to apply such approaches to a largely unexplored area. The present chapter offers some direction. It begins with a descriptive account of the archaeological sources that exist for study, and it concludes by outlining some ideas for future research.

The Agrarian Assemblage

The range of material available for study is vast, and includes the full spectrum of tools and implements used to facilitate arable husbandry, vegetable growing, livestock management (dairying and beef, cattle, sheep, pigs, and fowl), woodland management, viticulture and nurturing the wilderness (parklands and hunting), and buildings and structures for storage, maintenance, and processing of products. There are useful studies on many of these components, and surveys of the principal elements as well as essays on particular components (e.g. Astill and Grant 1988; Astill and Langdon 1997; Bond 2004; Brady 1997; Stenning 1993). The archaeological evidence arising from excavation tends to be the most challenging to assemble (e.g. Gardiner 2014). For example, the trenching tools and other devices that were used to assist in the ditching and dyking for land reclamation schemes remain largely invisible.

Manual tools were used to help prepare land for cultivation, but the principal devices for cultivation were animal-drawn, and include the plough for cutting through and turning the sod, and the harrow for breaking the clods of earth and preparing the topsoil for sowing (Goodall 2011). The numbers of plough pieces recovered from the period are quite small, and those for harrows even fewer (Astill 1997; see Chapter 13 in this *Handbook*). The recent discovery of an intact plough coulter from a seventh-century context at Lyminge, Kent, has created interest (Thomas et al. 2016), but there are no comparable new archaeological discoveries from the later Middle Ages. In Scotland, plough pebbles were used during the early medieval period and these are known from some thirteenth/fourteenth-century contexts, albeit as 'old finds'. Plough pebbles are small field stones that were inserted into the base of a plough's timber frame to act as an anti-wear device, and they are found *in situ* with plough frame fragments in Denmark (Lerche 1994). Plough pebbles are the most conspicuous evidence for advanced ploughing in Ireland during the thirteenth century, where they are associated with the economic boom that marks the period of High Farming (Brady 2009; 2016). However, and with the exception of Scotland, they are not yet known from elsewhere in Britain. Despite extensive field-walking during the Whittlewood project, not a single plough pebble was observed (Jones and Page 2006; Chris Dyer pers. comm.). Archaeologists may be left to study the relicts of the cultivated fields (Dixon 2016; Liddiard 1999; see Chapter 6 in this *Handbook*). Contemporary written sources, however, do record a range of plough types (heavy and light) and also the use of different teams of traction animals, with oxen changing to horse in the course of the thirteenth century, and the use of four- and eight-animal traction teams (Langdon 1986). Various manuscript illuminations and sculptural representations of ploughing also reveal the variety of ploughs in use; the most cited example of medieval ploughing is the scene from the Luttrell Psalter (1334), which shows a wheel-less or swing plough in operation, complete with a mouldboard to invert the cut sod. The plough is being pulled by a team of four oxen and operated by a team of two people; the ploughman who steers the device, and a second man who is herding the team (Backhouse 2000). The Psalter is a very useful source for many aspects of the agricultural regime because of the detail applied to its illustrations, but there is still some debate about its provenance.

Archaeologists can expect to recover pruning hooks and knives used for weeding, along with sickles for harvesting (Goodall 2011). The occurrence of scythes is rare; it seems they were used quite late and reflect the need to increase efficiency during the harvest at a time when labour had become scarcer. Depopulation is an aspect of the fourteenth-century crises that also saw a shift away from the dominance of arable-based regimes across much of Britain (Langdon 1997). In their place, the new regimes better reflected the natural productive capacities of the ambient soils than the forced and opportunistic markets of former years.

Dyer's work on sheepcotes is an important study that shows how archaeological remains can be studied in conjunction with the written sources to inform wider narratives on husbandry systems (Dyer 1995). The buildings in his Gloucestershire study area housed sheep over the winter months and are long narrow structures. Earthwork remains can vary in length between 23 and 65 metres, and are usually 6–8 metres wide, with entrances placed in the long side walls. Excavation confirms the presence of stone walls under the earthworks, while manorial accounts indicate the use of timber internally to support the roof and to provide internal divisions, some of which were used to store hay and fodder for the animals. Thatch was used typically as roofing material but there is some indication of slates being used later. As with other buildings, sheepcotes were located often within the main work yard at the manor, and sometimes they seem to have been located to one side. The purpose of the sheepcote was to assist in the wider task of maintaining healthy sheep flocks whose wool was especially sought after.

Cattle stalls are a subject for future study, and while dovecotes are another important building type within the manorial complex, they too could repay research enquiry based on landscape analysis. Environmental research has the potential to illuminate many aspects of the agrarian regime (Astill and Grant 1988; and see Chapters 7 and 8 in this *Handbook*). Livestock in the medieval period were generally smaller than modern equivalents, and the study of faunal remains may help ultimately to understand stocking densities in the various livestock buildings, as well as the realities of ploughing and drawing wheeled vehicles. In tandem, studies of plant and seed remains have tended to highlight the range of cultivated and weed species present in floral assemblages, and it becomes possible to see patterns of use and growth on general levels. Looking to the future, individual studies should provide more detailed insights, making it possible to assess whether certain plant strains were considered more versatile than others in different environments, such as coastal landscapes, wetlands, and across the wide variety of different soil groupings. The findings from work of this kind would help to understand more clearly the nature and extent of the principal agricultural systems, and how these might have changed through time.

Detailed knowledge of plant species will also inform questions associated with storage and processing. The contemporary treatise on estate management by Walter of Henley (c.1276) advises that a surplus of grain should be turned into coin quickly (Oschinsky 1971, 309). Walter's advice, predicated on the basis of good management, reflects a sense of the precarious nature of storing or banking grain over any length of time. Grain and food crops were stored in a variety of ways. The purpose was to dry the harvested food product and to store it securely before it was needed to be processed further prior to eating. Once harvested between Michaelmas and Martinmas (29 September and 11 November), grain would be gathered into sheaves and stacked in small heaps, or stooks, in the field to begin the drying process. After several days, the stooks would be transported out of the field. On manors and estates, such work was done under the vigilant eye of the reeve, and the harvesters and gleaners might be checked to be sure they were not taking grain for their own use (Ault 1965). The harvest was brought into the haggard (different regional terms apply), where it might be piled into heaps and left in the open air to complete the drying process. Such heaps were constructed carefully. They were raised onto stilts or padstones to prevent rodents infesting them at the base, and the uppermost sheaves were arranged to ensure a weather-resistant seal on the top, to prevent spoiling by weevils. The archaeological footprint of these heaps is enigmatic although the padstones used to deter rodents are commonly seen around farmyards and were used in this way into the early twentieth century. On smaller holdings and smaller peasant lands, sheaves might be brought into the living house and stored in the rafters, where the grain would air-dry over time.

Barns were also used to store the harvest. There are many barns surviving across England, and excavations sometimes interpret series of post-holes and building plans as barns (for example at West Whelpington; Wrathmell 2012, 252). There are both large barns and small barns, and barns were built from stone construction and from timber or from both, and could employ crucks in their design where regionally appropriate. Each barn type shares certain elements in common. Barns are rectangular in plan and will have an entry door placed centrally on one long wall. A second doorway might be placed opposite. Both doorways will be wide enough to accept the harvest. In small barns, the doorways can be narrow enough. In most barns, however, the doorways facilitated waggons and carts (Figure 17.2). The harvest could be made into heaps within the barn building, or it could fill bays within the building, and these would lie away from the central entranceway. The manorial records of St Paul's Cathedral, London, are particularly informative; they describe operations on a large scale, and they provide insight to the nature and size of the harvest. At Belchamp in Essex, for example, a lease for 1174–80 records a wheat barn (*grangia frumentaria*) and an oats barn (*grangia avenaria*). The wheat barn was an aisled structure with a hipped roof, measuring four perches and seven feet long in its main section with end aisles extending the length by 5 feet in each direction (c.25.5 m in overall length). The barn was 1 perch 8 feet high (7.42 m) and was

FIGURE 17.2 Swalcliffe Tithe Barn (now a museum) in Oxfordshire

(© Des Blenkinsopp, CC BY-SA 2.0)

aligned east–west. The central nave measured 1 perch 7 feet wide (7.12 m), and each side aisle was 7 feet wide (2.1 m), giving an overall width of *c*.9.22 m. The east side of the wheat barn and much of the west side was filled with wheat, while the north aisle of the west side was filled with maslin (a rye and wheat mixture). The oats barn was also aisled and hipped, measuring approximately 24 m long, 10.7 m wide, and 9.4 m high. The west side of the barn was filled with oats, the east-end aisle with oats and barley up to the tie-beam, and its south-side aisle with barley. The remainder of the barn remained empty (Hale 1858, 138–9).

Such accounts are not common but they show how barns were used. It is noteworthy in these instances that the barns are restricted to storing grain and related crops only. Indeed, these barns were used to store unthreshed grain only. When the grain was deemed to be dry enough (over the course of the winter months), the heap would be opened, its sheaves removed as needed and threshed. Threshing might occur within the barn. Some barns retain a series of corrugated stones that served as the threshing floor. The threshing floor was located between the barn's entrance doors. The doors would be swung open to create a draught to assist in separating the grain from the chaff as the team of threshers beat the sheaves with wooden threshes, with the grain falling into the troughs of the corrugated surface.

At St Paul's, as at other larger complexes, there were separate buildings for animals and machinery. These barns were purpose-built specialized buildings, and they are part of the assemblage of agricultural buildings associated with manors across England. The term 'tithe barn' has become synonymous with the larger grain barns in England, but it is a misnomer and applies more correctly to those specific grain barns (*grangia ad decimas*) that served to retain the one-tenth portion of the manor's crop set aside specifically as payment of the Church tax. In other regions, to the north, the specialized use of barns for storage of the unthreshed grain is not so common. In Scotland, a barn may serve a dual purpose as the granary as well. In other instances, barns were combined with livestock buildings. The variety of barn types and uses reflects the regionalism of the agricultural systems that existed, and further work could usefully be done to illustrate this further.

The granary was where the threshed crop was stored prior to its consumption. In the large manors across southern England, granaries were separate buildings within the manorial enclosure, and were inevitably watched carefully because of the valuable commodity that lay within. Like barns and other agricultural buildings, granaries would be locked for fear of theft. In some instances, the roofs of granaries were tiled rather than shingled, and tiling would be more fire-resistant. Granaries could be quite small buildings, ideally square in shape and raised off the ground. At Shaftsbury Abbey's manor at Barton Farm, Bradford-on-Avon, Wiltshire, the stone-built structure is quite a lavish three-bay design, built in stone with ashlar façades and a timber-framed cruck-built roof that held stone tiles (Historic England listing 1036096).

When needed, the stored grain in the granary would be removed. A portion would be set aside as seed-corn for the next year's crop, while the remainder would be processed further; it could be sent to the mill to be ground into flour, or it could be processed for beer-making. The oast houses of Kent typify the processing of grain for beer, where the kernels would be dried and roasted to suit the particular end product. Simpler corn-drying kilns are typical of the northern lands, where sheaves of grain are spread over a hurdle of withies enclosed within a stone-lined pit that was attached to a flue. A fire was set outside the flue and the smoke ascended through the flue to heat, dry, and roast the grain. Although some corn-drying kilns can be quite large, many are less than 3 m in size, with the kiln itself being under 2 m in diameter (Dixon 2002).

The medieval watermill and windmill are discussed elsewhere in this *Handbook* (see Chapter 31). However, it is worth stressing in this context that lords were prepared to invest significant sums to maintain them; a point best made in relation to tidal mills, which were subject to the destructive forces of high seas. Henry of Eastry, Prior of Christ Church, Canterbury, was prepared to invest £143 13s to replace a tidal mill on the Isle of Thanet in Kent that had been destroyed in 1290 (Holt 1988, 88–9). The mill achieved an annual rent of twenty-five quarters of wheat, but was destroyed once again in 1316 by floods. The prior was committed to the mill and spent another £74 13s 4d in its relocation and rebuilding. However, the mill was destroyed once again in 1326 by high tides. At this stage Henry had had enough. He abandoned the tidal location thirty-six years after his first recorded rebuild, and built a windmill as a replacement for a mere £12 19s. Windmills had additional benefits in that they did not rely on access to moving water and this freed up their location, bringing the milling process closer to where grain was stored. Their structures were also infinitely manoeuvrable, with a long post extending from the rear of the superstructure that could be swung around to allow the mill's sails to intercept the wind.

Agricultural Buildings and Landscape

Much is known already about the character of the medieval agricultural complex. When considering the trajectory of future research, there is a need to distinguish more clearly the nature of agriculture on peasant and lower-order holdings. The bulk of attention has been given to seigneurial sites, and to ecclesiastical sites in particular. Archaeological work can address these gaps, as archaeologists are more likely to encounter a peasant holding, while the sources that historians can access will not typically refer to peasant holdings *per se*. It is also the case that new insight can be gained from a landscape perspective. There is, for example, a pattern to the layout of estate manors in England, and the premise of this author is that the pattern is not explained simply within the context of ordered estate management. The standing buildings hold a key because they permit the visual appreciation of the manors as they existed when in use (see Chapter 4). The ordered arrangement of estate centres comes across, but so too does a physical massing or hierarchy of structure that is not so easily explained within the context of rational economics. In closing this chapter, we may return to the grain barn to reflect on this issue.

When looked at as a complex, manors are arranged into a series of courtyards, or *curiae*. The residential area is a separate location, housing the manor house, its kitchen and related buildings being managed by the household staff. The work yards lie to one side and are distinct from it. Within the arable areas of southern England, there is often a clear division between livestock and crops, with each having its own distinct *curia*. This is quite clear, for instance, at the St Paul's manor of Sandonbury, Hertfordshire (Figure 17.3). Here the arrangement of units is defined and clear. The later layers of use need to be peeled back to reveal the medieval manor, and the St Paul's accounts can assist in this (Hale 1858; see also Faith 1994 on how economic aspects of the wider context can be addressed). Other examples are also evident. It would be most useful to trace these layouts more systematically, and to assess the degree of variation across the wider landscape and gauge why differences exist. It would also be instructive to see whether there is a similar ordering of units on smaller holdings.

Even in today's landscape, the large grain barn dominates the local skyline, as noted at Great Coxwell in Oxfordshire. It is tempting to explain this in terms of the space required to store the bulky harvest, complete with intact sheaves heaped into great mounds and filling the bays. But there are certain indicators to suggest that these buildings may have served a wider narrative of power and prestige display (Brady 1997). On the one hand, the investment in barn-building and barn maintenance represented a significant financial outlay on most manors and estates. At the rectory of Swalcliffe, Oxfordshire, for instance, monies spent on the construction of a stone barn in the early 1400s accounted for more

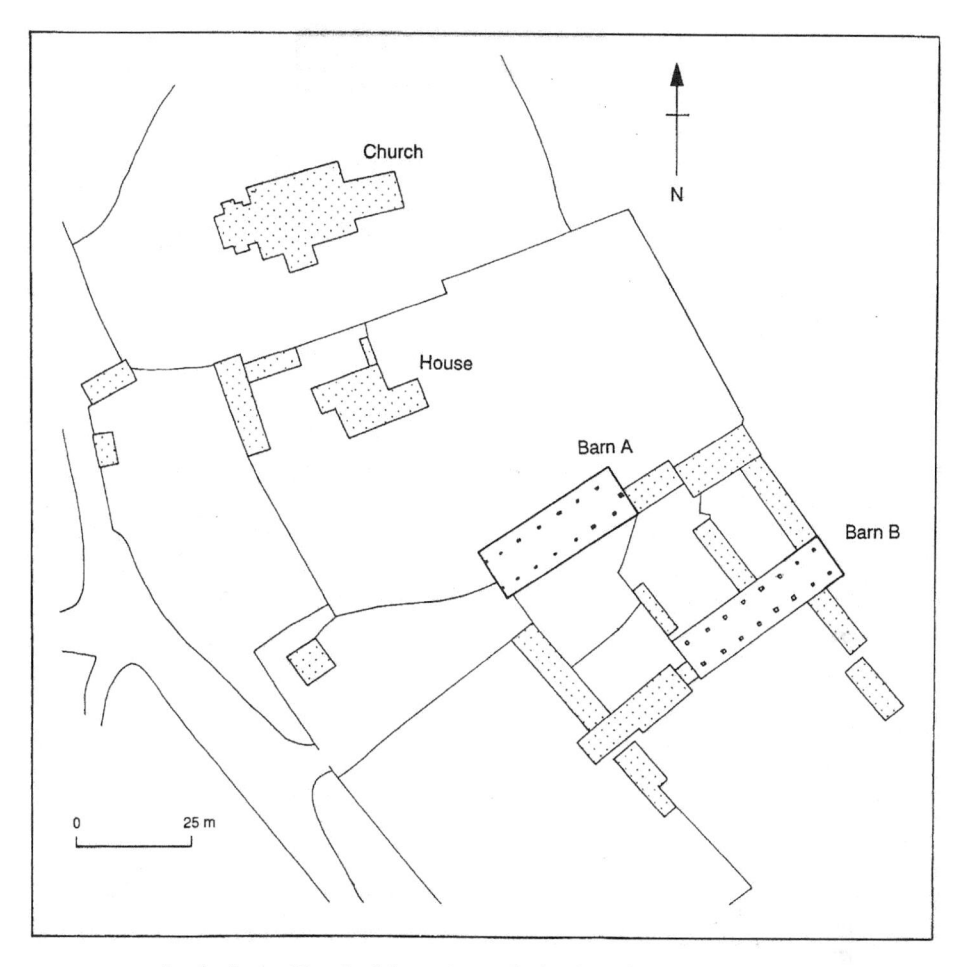

FIGURE 17.3 Sandonbury, Hertfordshire. Ground plan based on Ordnance Survey base map and field inspection. The work yard of this manor of St Paul's contains a series of barns and is distinct and separate from the residential *curia*

(© Niall Brady)

than 42 per cent of all the monies spent on buildings there over almost four decades. The rectory was acquired by New College, Oxford, in 1389 and it generated an annual income of about £50. A fine stone barn stands there today, one of two on the site (Figure 17.2). It is a ten-bay construction, measuring 39 m long and 7 m wide internally, with walls that reach 5 m high, supporting a cruck-framed timber roof whose ridge is almost 10 m above the ground. Although built with local Banbury ironstone for the most part, a non-local oolitic limestone is used in the copings and string courses. It is an elegant building, and the annual accounts record its construction between 1400–1 and 1406–7 and indicate that it cost at least £123 to build. When comparing building costs with other structures, the grain barn is clearly quite an expensive investment. The building of sheepcotes, for instance, required considerably less money, even though the £20 or £30 required for those in Gloucestershire was deemed to represent a goodly sum (Dyer 1995, 156).

There are instances where it is possible to calculate the storage space required for the crops in a given year and this information can help when looking at the storage capacity of a barn. At Temple Cressing in Essex, for example, the Knights Templar preceptory had two large aisled timber barns built in the thirteenth century (the following is described more fully in Brady 1997, 90–2). In 1309, the estate comprised 1287 acres of which 1115 were profitable. The gross acreage devoted to arable would have been 781 acres. Allowing for fallow land (one-third of the acreage), it is possible the estate harvested some 521 acres annually. Average sheaf size is thought to occupy approximately 2 cubic feet (0.566 m^3) and an acre of land might produce eighty sheaves. The space required to store the harvested sheaves from an acre would have been in the order of 4.5 m^3, and the space required to store the harvest from 521 acres would be 2344.5 m^3. The standing barns both preserve much of their original construction, and this allows one to see how much space each barn would have to store the grain. The two barns respectively measure 36.6 m and 39.9 m long internally, 13.6 m and 12.2 m wide, 7 m and 6.4 m high to the tie-beams, and 11.7 m and 11 m high to the ridge. The side walls are 3 m and 2.6 m high. The cubic capacity of the barns can be calculated from these measurements, and it is 6852 m^3. Documentary sources, such as the St Paul's inventories, record how these buildings were stored to capacity when needed, with stacks of grain placed in the aisles and the main bays, and reaching as high as the tie-beams and even to the ridge pole on occasion. In short, the two barns at Cressing Temple had far more capacity to store grain than was produced annually on the estate.

A view of seigneurial attitudes to their lands was founded on a rational economic approach, where only what was absolutely needed was built or invested in (Postan 1973). In other words, we should not expect over-building or extravagances as this expenditure would not be recovered. However, it is more usual today to recognize the investment that medieval lords made in the display of wealth as a necessary foundation to any claims of power and authority (Dyer 1989). It helps to explain why, for example, the wealthy Abbey of Glastonbury might have adorned the gables of its barns at Glastonbury and Pilton, Somerset, with the symbols of the evangelists, or why New College Oxford used expensive stone to dress its copings and string courses at Swalcliffe.

Rural manors could be remote from the estate centres but even here it would be necessary to assert authority. Indeed, in the absence of a formal castle complex or ecclesiastical centre, the opportunity to declare one's authority may well have been invested in the largest structure within the complex. Residences were not the most striking buildings, but grain barns were. The burden of labour obligations was known to all, and where better to assert authority than within an agricultural building that had to be visited in the course of fulfilling those duties? Harvest time was the busiest moment in the agricultural year and everyone was engaged in taking in the product of the year's work and the food required to endure the winter months. Tenants and peasants alike would be keen to tend to their own plots at this time, and labour obligations were an additional burden. Economic and social historians today believe that the greatest spirit of innovation in agricultural techniques may have been with the peasantry, while the seigneurial estates were conservative and slow-moving, preferring to maintain their control over resources and profit (Langdon 1997). It is possible that an archaeological approach founded in landscape analysis could inform this view. One example might be the work yards at Barton Farm, Bradford-on-Avon (Figure 17.4). Access to this curial complex is from across the bridge at the north end of the complex on lower ground. As one enters the work yards having passed the gatehouse and the manor house, there remains an uphill procession that passes the granary and also the byre before reaching the barn with its magnificent, almost triumphant gabled entrances at the top end of the complex. The carriage of Shaftsbury Abbey's crops through the work yard into the barn must have been a ritual that permitted a reaffirmation of authority if ever such was required.

If there remains doubt about whether archaeologists should limit their appreciation of the complex of agricultural buildings to the singular and rather sober attitude of the

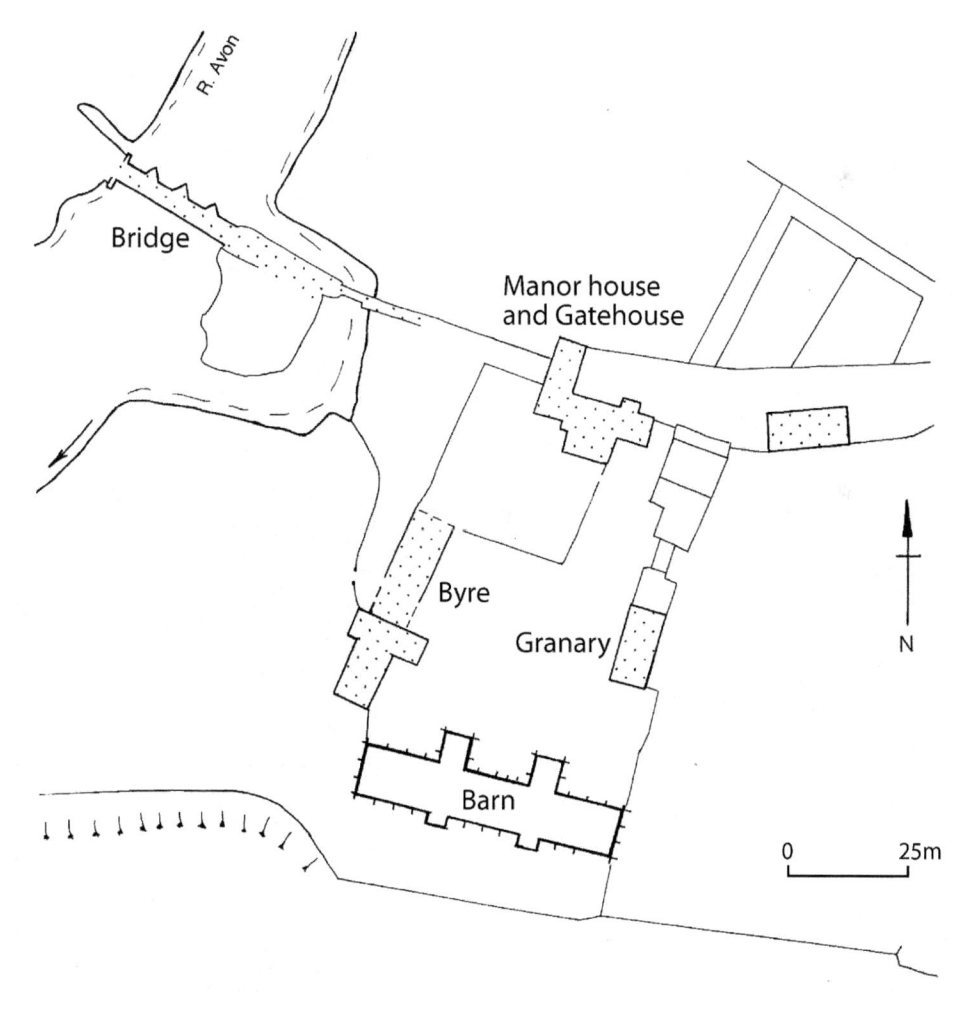

FIGURE 17.4 General plan of Barton Farm, Bradford-on-Avon, Wiltshire (after Haslam 1984), showing access to the manor, the location of the barn, and distribution of other buildings

medieval accountant, namely to the ordered layout encouraged by good estate management, it is useful to remind readers of the closing moments of Piers Plowman (Passus XIX–XX in the B-text), where William Langland has chosen a barn as the setting for the climax of his social critique (Brady 1997, 100–4; Talbot Donaldson 1990). Langland describes his barn, *unitas*, as an allegory of Christ and the Church; the timber frame is made from the True Cross, the mortar for its foundations is prepared from Christ's baptism and the blood he bled on the cross; the wattle-and-daub walls are from Christ's pain and passion, while the roof is covered by the Bible (Holy Writ). This sanctuary is where Langland's hero, Piers the simple ploughman, is to find peace and fulfilment. After filling the barn with the harvest, Piers goes away to plough again, but the barn becomes a refuge for wider society as it is attacked by Pride. Various transformations take place, and the voices of society's consumers are heard (a brewer, vicar, lord and king, supported later by Friar Flatterer) over those of society's producers, those who sweat and toil in the fields, who remain quite silent. In the end, *unitas* fails; for Langland at least, the barn might present itself as an image of stability and well-being, but it had become symbolic of the widespread corruption within the prevailing social institutions during the turbulent and impoverished world of the later fourteenth century. To him, the barn epitomized social evil and was itself an impediment to progress.

Conclusion

Despite the apparent wealth of information that exists on agricultural buildings and the implements used to help cultivate the land and manage the livestock, there is still great potential for future research but medieval archaeologists need to be interested in agriculture to take this forward. Excavation remains a key source for the discovery of objects and assemblages in sealed datable contexts, while the study of standing buildings and excavated remains should develop more within the context of landscape analysis to take their research onto the next level. Only then will archaeologists be better able to contribute to and develop the wider discussions that are currently focused on understanding the regional identities that created the variety of medieval countrysides, which define the landscape of medieval Britain.

References Cited

Astill, G. 1997 'An archaeological approach to the development of agricultural technologies in medieval England', in G. Astill and J. Langdon (eds), *Medieval farming and technology: the impact of agricultural change in Northwest Europe*, Brill, Leiden, 193–223

Astill, G. and Grant, A. (eds) 1988 *The countryside of medieval England*, Blackwell, Oxford

Astill, G. and Langdon, J. (eds) 1997 *Medieval farming and technology: the impact of agricultural change in Northwest Europe*, Brill, Leiden

Ault, W. 1965 'Open-field husbandry and the village community', *Transactions of the American Philosophical Society* 55(7), 1–102

Backhouse, J. 2000 *Medieval life in the Luttrell Psalter*, Toronto Univeristy Press, Toronto

Bond, J. 2004 *Monastic landscapes*, Tempus, Stroud

Brady, N. 1997 'The gothic barn of England: icon of prestige and authority', in E. Smith and M. Wolfe (eds), *Technology and resource use in medieval Europe: cathedrals, mills and mines*, Ashgate, Aldershot, 76–105

Brady, N. 2009 'Just how far can you go with a pebble? Taking another look at ploughing in medieval Ireland', in J. Fenwick (ed.), *Lost and found II: rediscovering Ireland's past*, Wordwell, Bray, 61–70

Brady, N. 2016 'The plough pebbles from Bective Abbey', in G. Stout and M. Stout (eds), *The Bective Abbey project, Co. Meath: excavations 2009-12*, Wordwell, Dublin, 103–9

Creighton, O. H. and Barry, T. 2012 'Seigneurial and elite sites in the medieval landscape', in N. Christie and P. Stamper (eds), *Medieval rural settlement: Britain and Ireland, AD 800-1600*, Windgather Press, Oxford, 63–80

Dixon, P. 2002 *Puir labourers and busy husbandmen: the countryside of lowland Scotland in the Middle Ages*, Birlinn, Edinburgh

Dixon, P. 2016 'Mukked and folded land: the evidence of field data for medieval cultivation techniques in Scotland', *Ruralia* 7, 107–23

Dyer, C. 1989 *Standards of living in the later Middle Ages: social change in England c.1200-1520*, Cambridge University Press, Cambridge and New York

Dyer, C. 1995 'Sheepcotes: evidence for medieval sheepfarming', *Medieval Archaeology* 39, 136–64

Faith, R. 1994 'Demesne resources and labour rent on the manors of St Paul's Cathedral, 1066-1222', *Economic History Review* 47, 657–78

Gardiner, M. 2014 'The distribution and adoption of the byre-house (longhouse) in late medieval Britain', in I. Boháčová and P. Sommer (eds), *Medieval Europe in motion, in honour of Jan Klápště*, Archaeological Institute, Prague, 145–62

Goodall, I. H. 2011 *Ironwork in medieval Britain: an archaeological study*, The Society for Medieval Archaeology Monograph 31, Leeds

Hale, W. (ed.) 1858 *The Domesday of St Paul's of the year M CC XXII, or, registrum de vistatione maneriorum per Robertum Decanum*, Camden Society, London

Haslam, J. 1984 'Excavations at Barton Farm, Bradford-on-Avon, 1983: interim report', *Wiltshire Archaeological and Natural History Magazine* 78, 120–1

Holt, R. 1988 *The mills of medieval England*, Blackwell, Oxford

Jones, R. and Page, M. 2006 *Medieval villages in an English landscape*, Windgather Press, Macclesfield

Langdon, J. 1986 *Horses, oxen and technological innovation*, Cambridge University Press, London and New York

Langdon, J. 1997 'Was England a technological backwater in the Middle Ages?', in G. Astill and J. Langdon (eds), *Medieval farming and technology: the impact of agricultural change in Northwest Europe*, Brill, Leiden, 275–312

Lerche, G. 1994 *Ploughing implements and tillage practices in Denmark from the Viking period to about 1800, experimentally substantiated*, Royal Danish Academy of Sciences and Letters' Commission for Research on the History of Implements and Field Structures. Publication 8, Poul Kristensen, Herning

Liddiard, R. 1999 'The distribution of ridge and furrow in East Anglia: ploughing practice and subsequent land use', *Agricultural History Review* 47, 1–6

Myrdal, J. 1997 'The agricultural transformation of Sweden, 1000–1300', in G. Astill and J. Langdon (eds), *Medieval farming and technology: the impact of agricultural change in Northwest Europe*, Brill, Leiden, 147–71

Myrdal, J. and Sapoznik, A. 2016 'Spade cultivation and intensification of land use 1000–1300: written sources, archaeology and images', *Ruralia* 10, 203–33

Oschinsky, D. 1971 *Walter of Henley and other treatises on estate management and accounting*, Clarendon Press, Oxford

Platt, C. 1969 *The monastic grange in medieval England: a reassessment*, Fordham University Press, New York

Postan, M. M. 1973 *Essays on medieval agriculture and general problems of medieval economy*, Cambridge University Press, Cambridge

Stenning, D. 1993 'The Cressing barns and the early development of barns in south-east England', in D. Andrews (ed.), *Cressing Temple: a Templar and Hospitaller manor in Essex*, Chelmsford, 51–75

Talbot Donaldson, E. (ed. and trans.) 1990 *Piers Plowman*, Norton, New York and London

Thomas, G., McDonnell, G., Merkel, J., and Marshall, P. 2016 'Technology, ritual and Anglo-Saxon agriculture: the biography of a plough coulter from Lyminge, Kent', *Antiquity* 90, 742–58

Wrathmell, S. 2012 'Northern England: exploring the character of medieval rural settlements', in N. Christie and P. Stamper (eds), *Medieval rural settlement: Britain and Ireland, AD 800–1600*, Windgather Press, Oxford, 249–65

PART IV
LIVING IN TOWNS AND PORTS

CHAPTER 18

OVERVIEW

Living in Medieval Towns

KEITH D. LILLEY

In this part of the *Handbook* we present four chapters which discuss urbanization and commercialization, both defining characteristics of the later Middle Ages across Europe. Of course the pattern and distribution of urban life was not geographically uniform, and neither was urbanization a process that affected everywhere the same way, but broadly speaking the period between 1150 and 1540 saw insular Britain become more urban than it had ever been before. As well as the creation of wholly new towns, such as Salisbury and Roxburgh, the period witnesses the expansion of already-existing urban centres, such as Bristol, Norwich, and York (Lobel 1969; 1975; Martin and Oram 2007). The formation and transformation of later medieval townscapes left its traces on the material and physical form of towns and cities across England, Wales, and Scotland, and today provide a basis for archaeological evaluation and assessment of urban life in the later Middle Ages (Astill 2009; Lynch et al. 1988; Schofield and Vince 2003). Their cultural significance is recognized through nationwide programmes, such as Historic England's Extensive Urban Surveys (EUS), and valuing the imprint and legacies of medieval urbanism on the layout and character of towns and cities is at the heart of heritage management efforts to characterize historic townscapes, for example through mapping Historic Urban Character Areas (HUCAs) (Thomas 2006).

THE ANALYSIS OF URBAN LANDSCAPES

Inherited medieval urban forms are important and revealing in what they can tell us about urbanism in later medieval Britain. Studying urban forms indicates the former extent of medieval towns and cities, suggests patterns of growth and development, and provides a spatial context for situating more localized archaeological work on particular urban sites (see Baker et al. 1992; Cameron and Stones 2001; Jones et al. 2003). Yet there is still a tendency, both among historians and archaeologists of the Middle Ages, to generalize about medieval urban forms, in particular to use small-scale plans to characterize their layouts and differentiate between those with 'regular' form from those with 'irregular' form, a somewhat arbitrary judgement (Schofield and Vince 2003, 37–46). More detailed examination of the plans of medieval urban landscapes reveals instead greater complexity, and if studied closely can be helpful in revealing the various stages that shaped towns and cities in the Middle Ages, adding to the understanding of the processes of urbanization (Conzen 1968). This is especially useful for studying those aspects of medieval urbanism that are typically poorly documented, including the phasing of townscape formation and transformation. For the period prior to the thirteenth century particularly, before urban written records become more widespread and detailed, the tangible traces of urban development revealed by the patterns of streets and plots offers insights into what was going on, on the ground, during a key period that was particularly important for the physical development of towns and cities in Britain (Lilley 2002, 138–76).

The wide variety of shapes and forms revealed by analysing medieval town-plans is a material record of the activities of those groups and individuals, so often unrecorded in contemporary written records, who were responsible for forming new urban landscapes in the later Middle Ages. In studying medieval town-plans, past scholars have tended to see 'regularity' in form as a sign of 'town planning', and conversely have taken 'irregular' forms to reflect 'organic' or 'unplanned' urban growth (Nicholas 2003). Archaeologists and geographers, however, have latterly taken a different view, arguing instead that urban planning in the Middle Ages gave rise to many different urban forms, not just regular plans, while irregularities in form often reflect distinct phases of 'planned' urban development (Bond 1990; Slater 1990). A case in point is Coventry, a major provincial capital in later medieval England, and often seen as a typical 'organic' growth city with an irregular plan, whereas detailed analysis of its form using a method of town-plan analysis revealed a pattern of expansion in distinct phases, from the late eleventh to the late thirteenth century, led by the two key local landholders, the Earls of Chester and the Priors of the Benedictine Abbey of St Mary's in Coventry (Lilley 1998; 2000) (Figure 18.1). Similar examples of towns with organized, planned urban development have been widely identified elsewhere across Britain, again using similar morphological approaches and detailed plan-analyses. The same approach has also revealed that those towns long considered as having 'planned' origins, such as Ludlow in Shropshire, are likewise actually the product of not one single phase of development but a series of multiple phases, with stages of expansion taking place again over decades and centuries (Conzen 1988; Lilley 1999; Slater 1990). Thus even 'new towns' of the Middle Ages have layouts, almost without exception, that are 'composite' in form. Similar arguments have been put forward by geographers studying medieval 'new towns' across Britain, including work undertaken in Scotland, on St Andrews for example, as well as in Wales, for places such as Conwy, Pembroke, and Rhuddlan, and in England too (Brooks and Whittington 1977; Lilley et al. 2007). Thus what were for many years seen to be 'classic' examples of 'new towns', such as Winchelsea in Sussex, Salisbury in Wiltshire, and Hedon in Yorkshire, on closer inspection and analysis of street and plot patterns, reveal clear and distinct stages of formation, spanning centuries in most cases, of various urban forms (Martin and Martin 2004; Slater 1985; 1999) (Figure 18.2). This is somewhat

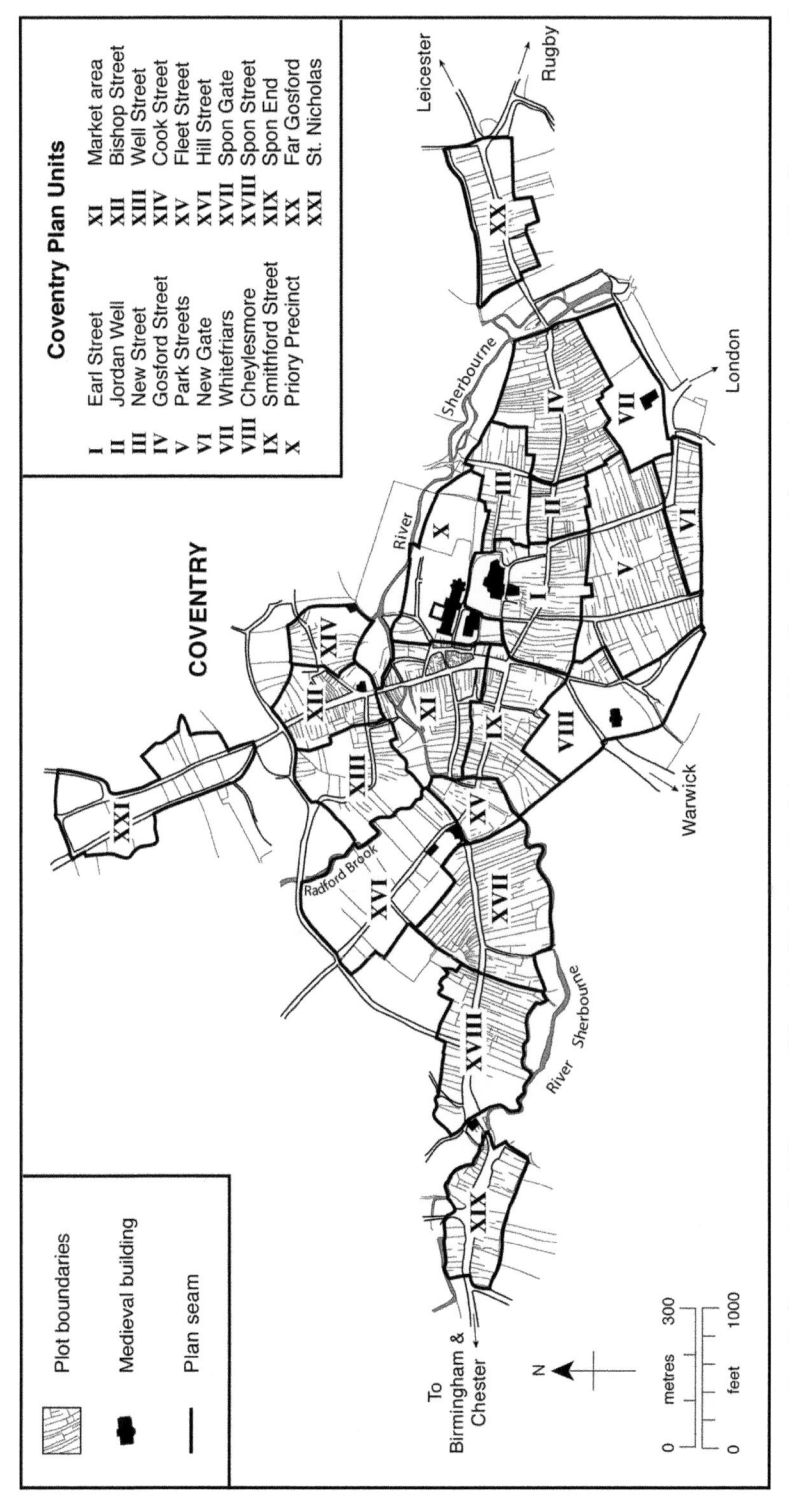

FIGURE 18.1 A plan-analysis of Coventry (Warwickshire) showing 'plan-units' (numbered areas) that each represent, potentially, discrete stages of accretion in the medieval urban landscape

(© Keith Lilley)

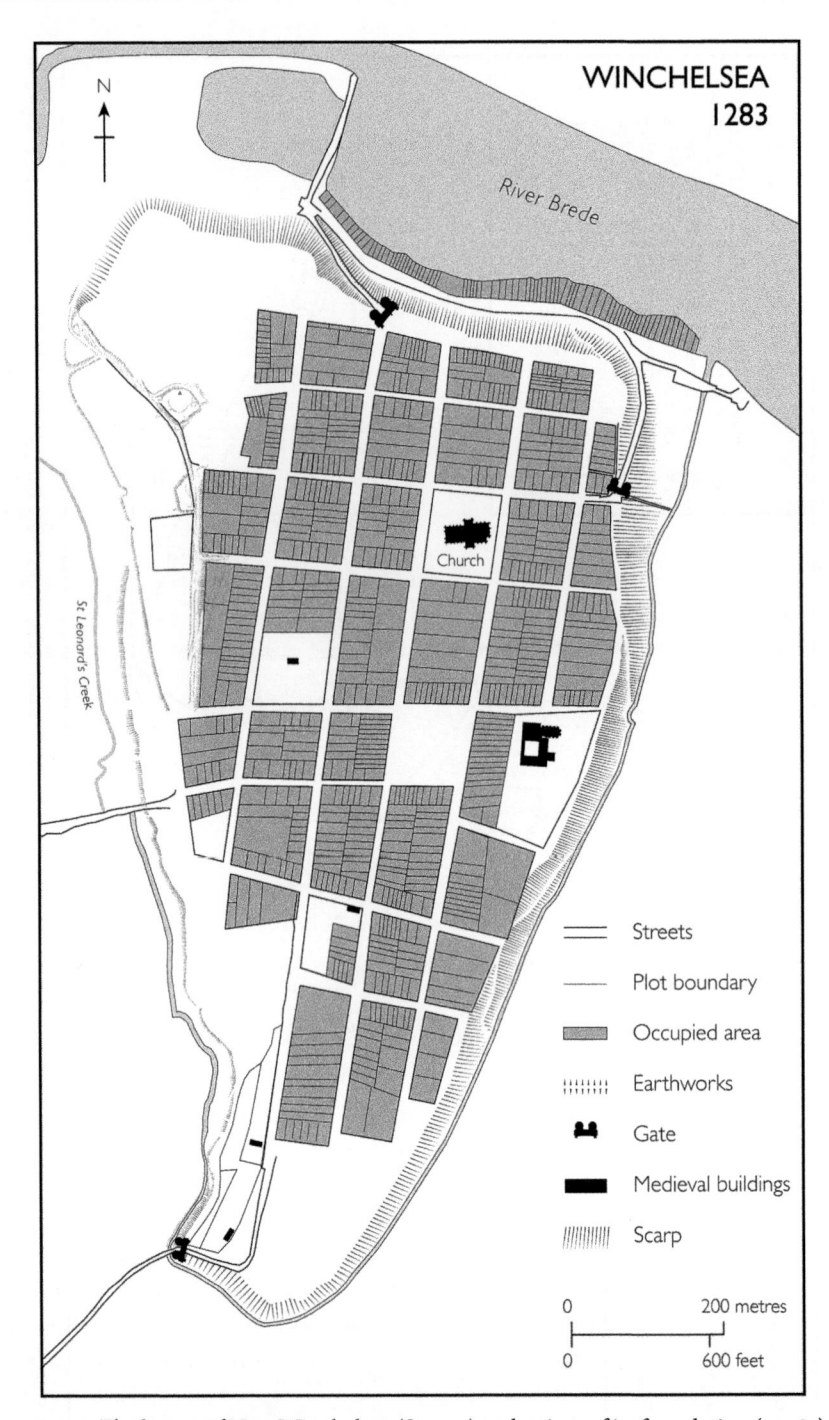

FIGURE 18.2 The layout of New Winchelsea (Sussex) at the time of its foundation (c.1283), mapping derived from the *Mapping the medieval urban landscape* research project funded by the Arts and Humanities Research Council

(© Keith Lilley)

at odds with the views often still put forward by historians based on typologies of urban forms that hinge on dividing towns according to their regularity, often as a result of using small-scale historic plans to do so, such as those of John Speed (1610) which inevitably exaggerate the impression of irregularity (see Morris 1994). The need for detailed morphological study is thus clear, though 'regular' and 'planned' new towns were less common in occurrence than 'organic-growth' towns of 'irregular' form, the former still predominate in some textbooks on medieval urbanism despite the mounting evidence to the contrary.

One particular aspect of the urban landscape that attracted particular attention and interest during the 1970s and 1980s was the waterfront. So many of the larger medieval towns and cities owed their prosperity to maritime and coastal trade and commerce in Britain, and the archaeological imprint of this through the survival of waterlogged structures and deposits has provided a good insight into the forms and formation of urban waterfronts during the Middle Ages (see Good et al. 1988). As a result of this, the development of quaysides in Bristol and London, for example, has been found to reflect distinct phases as lines of wooden revetments were pushed ever further outwards into the waters of the Avon and Thames respectively (Jones 1988; Milne and Goodburn 1990). The dendrochronology of timbers used in these revetments provides close dating of the process of quayside development, coupled with the environmental deposits well preserved by anaerobic conditions which can yield such incredible insights into the foodstuffs and items that were being traded and exchanged along what were essential arteries through medieval urban landscapes, the navigable rivers and waterways on which so many of the greatest towns and cities stood.

Medieval New Towns

There is no doubt that the face of the English countryside, more so than Scotland's and Wales's, was changed significantly in the two centuries following the Norman Conquest through the creation of new towns of one form or another. While their shapes and sizes might have varied, their origins often share much in common. Promoted particularly through local lords seeking to channel commerce and trade through their markets, the commercialization of the medieval countryside invariably involved adding an urban settlement nucleus to an existing minster church, a castle, or abbey (Blair 2005; Britnell 1993). Although no systematic study of medieval towns beyond some county or regional studies has been undertaken, those that have do reveal one particular dominant and widespread urban form used time and time again by local lords on their estates from the 1100s through to the 1300s: the 'castle-town' (Lilley 2017). Characterized by having in most cases a castle and market place in close proximity, often adjoining, castle-towns can be found everywhere in England in the later Middle Ages, sometimes associated with 'frontier' colonization, in areas where incoming lords, most noticeable with the change-over to Norman lordship after 1066, sought to extend their influence around the borders of Norman England, but they were equally evident too in areas of 'interior' colonization, the English Midlands and East Anglia, for example. From the Anglo-Scottish border, with towns such as Alnwick, to the Welsh Marches, and towns such as Bridgnorth, and across lowland England, with places such as Brinklow and Saffron Walden, the 'castle-town' could be found, each sharing a common model of urban form (Lilley 1999; 2017). The ubiquity of this model deserves further analysis. Here some detailed regional studies would provide a starting point for comparative research, looking for example at potential influences on shape and design, aspects of urban planning, and linking these to certain 'agents of change', including local lords.

Right through the late Middle Ages, lords and political elites created towns as part of the economic development of their estates and landholdings, encouraging incomers to take up residence there and so generate revenues for their lords through trade and rents (Beresford 1967). How far particular lords had a direct influence on medieval urban form and design is still poorly understood (Lilley 2001). Yet a comparative study of medieval urban form across Britain—adopting both synchronic and diachronic approaches—has the potential to reveal the roles of such lords, monastic and lay, royal and aristocratic, testing how far their agency in forming new towns was a factor in comparison to the role that others played in promoting urbanism in the later Middle Ages. Recent detailed archaeological studies of 'new towns', such as Wallingford (Oxfordshire), has demonstrated the importance of excavations within the towns for assessing the progress of the development of a town following its foundation (see Christie and Creighton 2013). For although areas in a new town may have been laid out *de novo* with new streets and plots, as one episode of 'town planning' to provide building plots for those migrants coming to take up residence there, the occupation of these plots and house sites could actually take a long period of time to gain physical, built structures, such as domestic buildings. Indeed, in some cases, plots could lie empty for years, as in the case of New Winchelsea in Sussex, before being built upon, or sometimes the plots were never developed (see Martin and Martin 2004).

The Importance of Archaeology

Understanding the processes of urban formation and transformation in the later Middle Ages continues to occupy the attention of medievalists and is a key area where archaeology is making a substantive contribution. This is in part due to the relatively poorly documented nature of medieval urban development, with archaeological research and especially urban excavations providing crucial information not only on the fabric and form of medieval townscapes but on chronology (Astill 1985; Barley 1976; Carver 1980). Through archaeological investigation of urban sites stratified deposits and structures help identify when an area of a town was first occupied and had definably 'urban' activity occurring within it, thus then offering some insight into periodizing, in effect 'dating', the morphological phases of urban development that are revealed through plan-analysis. The importance of archaeological investigation in confirming continuity of urban features has been demonstrated in cases of even the largest of medieval towns, such as Norwich and York (see Ayers 1994; Ottaway 1992). Here the longevity of morphological features such as property boundaries, over centuries, confirms that plots and streets shown on maps and plans surveyed and drawn by later cartographers (such as those of the Ordnance Survey of the nineteenth century) are features that are in many cases medieval in origin (see Ottaway 1992, 149).

Though much later in date, the large-scale Ordnance Survey (OS) plans that are available for all British towns and cities (the 1:2500 scale series for example) can serve as a proxy for mapping out the layouts and forms of their medieval antecedents because townscape continuity is widely found (Lilley 2000). Moreover, since the nature of urban archaeology—especially developer-led excavations—is spatially discrete, with excavated sites typically dotted across an urban landscape, in dispersed locations, the local study of urban form, and using maps to locate excavated medieval features in relation to the wider patterns of streets and plots, is helpful in extrapolating out from particular sites features in the medieval urban landscape (Lilley 2000 provides a detailed example). This might include, for example, establishing the alignments of urban defences, such as ditches and walls, and confirming the orientation of relict plot patterns and streets, and not just determining the structural positions and forms of buildings in the landscape, domestic and institutional. In the case of medieval Swansea, for example, the pattern of defences can be deduced from the layout of streets and plots, providing a basis for understanding the town's evolution from the eleventh century onwards (Lilley and Dean 2015) (Figure 18.3).

In all mapping of medieval urban landscapes and townscapes there is particular advantage in using Geographical Information Systems (GIS), which not only help to visualize a locality in cartographic form but also can provide a systematic way of integrating a wide variety of historical, cartographic, and archaeological material, from maps and plans to individual artefacts and features (Dean 2012; Lilley 2012). Recent archaeological studies of medieval towns and cities using GIS have in fact revealed in two and sometimes three dimensions the layout of entire urban landscapes for particular periods in time, as in the case of Swansea and Chester (Lilley and Dean 2015; Lilley 2012). Not only is the wider urban landscape made visible but also, through some sophisticated analytical work, the stratigraphic sequences for particular areas of a town or city can be unpicked, so providing a deeper understanding of the social and economic fabric and structure within the townscape and revealing particular localities and neighbourhoods with certain characteristics or traits as revealed through their artefact assemblages, as has been shown at York for the later Middle Ages (Dean 2012). The quantities of archaeological data—much of it in the form of 'grey literature' such as site reports and watching briefs—provides enormous scope for undertaking similar detailed studies, letting the material culture 'speak' with its own voice rather than relying on the stories told by documentary sources, which often have little to say about the cultural aspects of life in medieval towns and cities, especially for the lower social orders and marginalized groups in urban society (Gilchrist 1999).

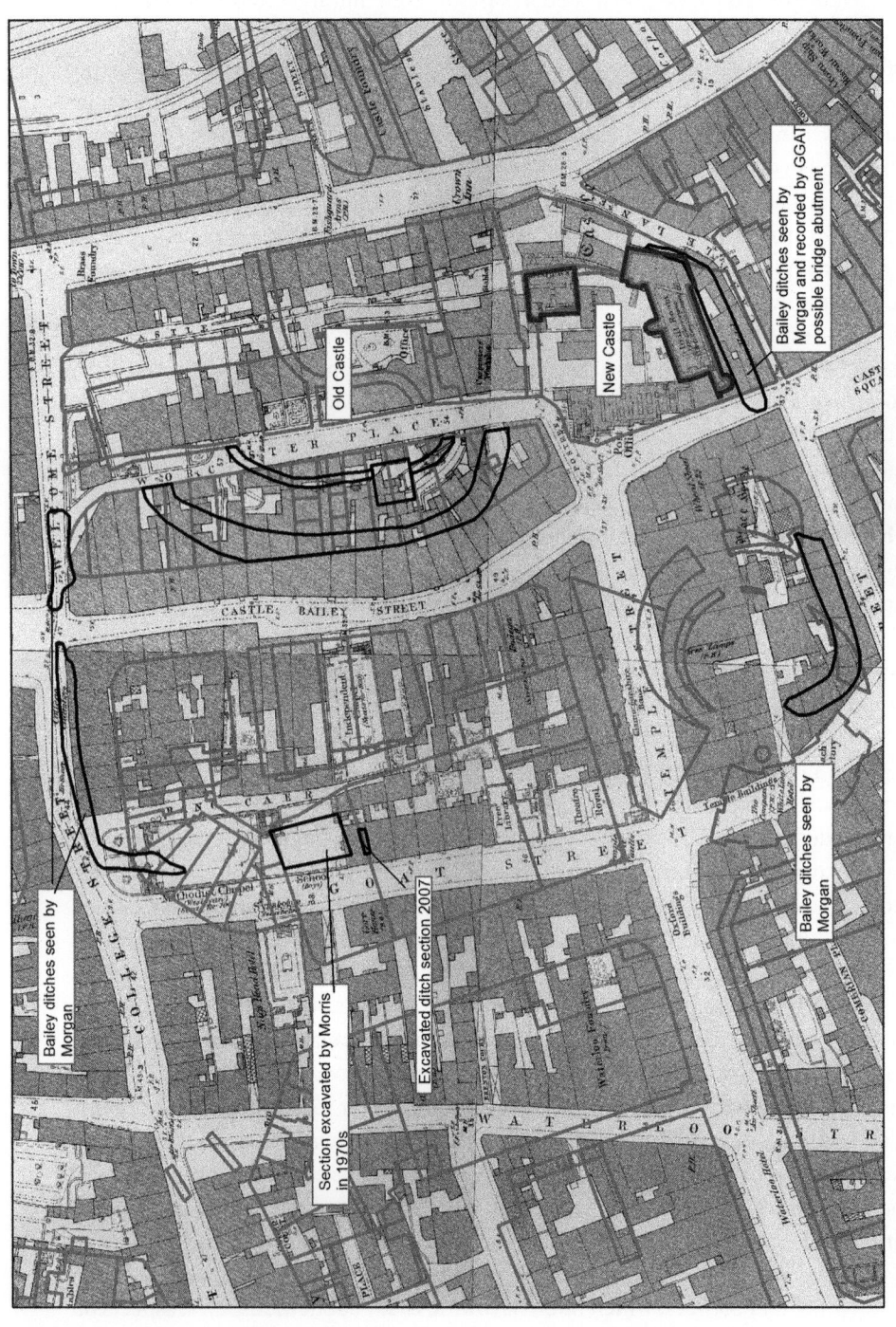

FIGURE 18.3 Using a Geographical Information System (GIS) to combine archaeological site plans and data with historic 1:2500-scale Ordnance Survey maps, from the *City witness: place and perspective in medieval Swansea* research project, funded by the Arts and Humanities Research Council

(© Keith Lilley and Gareth Dean)

What people ate, how they prepared their food, what they wore, how their materials were made, how they died, and what environmental conditions they lived in are all aspects of urban life in the Middle Ages better represented in the urban archaeological record than in written sources (see Chapter 22; and Schofield and Vince 2003, 212–42). The surviving written accounts from towns tend to reflect instead the lives of social elites: the civic officials, ecclesiastical communities, and of course seigneurial and royal households, each important in shaping urban life but on the whole just one relatively small part of urban living in the later Middle Ages. The most revealing recent studies of single medieval towns and cities are thus those that combine both archaeological and historical material, a feature of all the chapters in this Part of the *Handbook*. For Great Britain there is a wealth of such work at varying scales, from single areas of a town to city-wide analyses (Schofield et al. 1981; Schofield and Leech 1987).

Integrated and cross-disciplinary studies of parts of towns include work undertaken on Cheapside in London, for example, not only mapping out the structural changes that took place in this area during the later Middle Ages, but also, through combining written accounts with excavated archaeological material, insights into how the people of Cheapside lived and worked (Keene 1985a; Schofield et al. 1990). Since the 1980s, a range of such detailed studies have been led through cooperation between historians and archaeologists, allowing much greater understanding of urban life in the later Middle Ages in the more populated parts of Britain, in the south-east of the country (in the case of the work undertaken on Wallingford, for example), but more widely too, in Scotland for instance in a study of the now decayed medieval town of Roxburgh, and in Wales in a continued programme of archaeological investigation in Swansea (Christie and Creighton 2013; Lilley and Dean 2015). Individually such studies provide an immensely rich body of high-quality research that is ripe for reflection and synthesis at national and regional scales, particularly for comparative study, as well as forming a sound basis for informing future research agendas in urban and medieval archaeology in Britain.

The comparative archaeological approach to late medieval urbanism has however yet to really take root in UK, apart from some synthetic overviews of the topic, such as Colin Platt's *The English medieval town* (1976), Maurice Barley's volume of the same year entitled *Plans and topography of medieval towns in Britain*, and more recently John Schofield and Alan Vince's *Medieval towns* (1994/2003), and Patrick Ottaway's *Archaeology in British towns* (1992). The challenge for scholars today, in drawing together case studies of individual places, is the sheer volume of material that has accumulated, especially 'grey literature' resulting from development-led archaeology of the 1990s and 2000s (for further reflection see Chapter 1). One solution to this though is to focus on towns of particular types or periods and adopting a comparative approach.

Comparative Approaches

The comparative study of medieval towns and cities requires a systematic and consistent empirical framework and here archaeology also has an important role to play.

Some assessment and evaluation of the physical forms of medieval urban landscapes, for example in mapping out the layouts of towns and their phases of development, is often a basis to archaeological assessment. A number of such studies were undertaken in the 1970s, with significance still today, such as Wiltshire, Oxfordshire, and Sussex (Aldsworth and Freke 1976; Haslam 1976; Rodwell 1975). The premise for this work was the realization that plans and maps had the scope to identify and help explore research questions and themes which could then inform archaeological and historical enquiry.

Addressing why it is that some medieval towns have more similar layouts than others has preoccupied historical geographers and urban morphologists too, likewise using a comparative approach to examine the processes that formed urban landscapes in the Middle Ages, as exemplified by the work of M. R. G. Conzen (1968) and Terry Slater (1990), among others. A series of studies of Norman towns in England and Wales also took a 'Conzenian' approach to find commonalities in urban form, using a plan-analysis approach and identifying, for example, the widespread use of 'castle-town' complexes associated especially with earlier phases of conquest and colonization in Norman England and Wales (Lilley 1999). The same strategy was adopted by King Edward I in Wales in the later thirteenth century, with towns such as Conwy and Caernarfon, where fortification of town walls and castles were constructed at the same time, and the layouts of the streets and plots intimately linked morphologically with the towns' castles. Placing the towns' plans side by side, reproduced at the same scale and using the same cartographic conventions, reveals that the Edwardian new towns were not all laid out to the same design, but some certainly were, such as Beaumaris and Conwy, and Holt and Flint (Lilley et al. 2007).

A further basis for comparative study of medieval towns and cities, using mapping as a common denominator, is the long-established British Historic Towns Atlas (HTA), first published in 1969, with detailed and large-scale (1:2500) plans for each place covered by the atlas series (part of an international, pan-European enterprise), much of which is now online (at historictownsatlas.org.uk). The HTA maps each consistently project the location and form of known medieval buildings and structures onto a redrawn detailed nineteenth-century town-plan, so enabling users to place, side by side, maps of towns to explore their local topographies and archaeologies but with the scope also to do so comparatively (see Addyman 2015; Lobel 1969; 1975). With the HTAs of York and other provincial medieval English cities such as Coventry, Norwich, and Bristol all now available, there is scope to use this archaeologically informed urban mapping to frame and situate new archaeological research and enquiry for particular types of medieval town or city, or for comparing features of medieval urban landscapes for particular periods or for selected locations such as market places and suburbs.

From both detailed individual study of certain medieval towns as well as comparative studies of groups of towns, the overall impression gained from studying the material culture of medieval urban sites in Britain is one of largely organized and orderly townscapes, with streets in the inner urban areas dominated by domestic and commercial properties built-up along the street-frontages, sometimes formed of buildings constructed in stone, either in part or whole, or else timber-framed. In

England a transition to buildings of more substantial construction is evident from the middle of the twelfth century, buildings of one, two, or more storeys high, thus forming definable 'urban' townscapes and building façades, certainly in the larger urban centres such as London, York, and Bristol, but more widely too (see Chapter 19). The rise in size and permanence of urban buildings reflected growing prosperity and commerce in towns and cities across Britain. Some sense of this localized urban wealth is evident from the physical extent of the built up areas of towns and cities, which often encompassed an area that extended from the urban core to the suburbs that lay beyond. By 1300, for example, Coventry extended more than 3 km from east to west, while at Chester the Bishop's suburb to the east of the walled city was as extensive as the area within the city's walls (Lilley 1998; 2017) (Figures 18.1 and 18.4). Historians have tended to measure urban size through proxy indicators based on records of taxation, especially those of the fourteenth and fifteenth centuries such as the Lay Subsidies (1334 for example), available for England, and also the Poll Tax (1377) (Dyer 2000). Population figures are not absolute for this period but relative, and with this in mind it is possible to produce urban hierarchies for later medieval England. London invariably occupies first place in these hierarchies, followed by provincial urban centres, such as York, Bristol, Norwich, and Coventry. A recent estimate of York's population in around 1300 is 20,000, a figure that the city did not again reach in the post-Black Death period until the early nineteenth century, while London's population is estimated to have been around 80,000 by 1400 (Rees Jones 2013; Barron 2004).

Mapping Urban Britain

Medieval material culture of course embraces more than simply unearthed finds and standing field-monuments. For antiquarians writing in the eighteenth and nineteenth centuries equally important were contemporary artefacts and *objects d'art*, or 'memorials' and 'antiquities' as they were often described. For example, in 1755 a then newly discovered medieval map was put on display at the Society of Antiquaries in London, a map that would soon come into the possession of Richard Gough, one of the country's leading antiquarian figures of the time (Millea 2007) (Figure 18.5). Gough described this as a 'most curious map' and it still survives, now named after him as the 'Gough Map' of Great Britain, following his bequest of the map to the Bodleian Library, Oxford, in 1833. The Gough Map is especially significant as a 'memorial' to later medieval English mapmaking, but it also represents a unique contemporary overview of Britain's settlement geography at the time of its making, probably in the reign of Edward III (*c*.1360) (Lilley and Lloyd 2009) (Figure 18.6).

A hierarchy of urban centres across Britain is evident in how the (unknown) map maker (or makers) of the Gough Map depicted towns and cities with differing symbols, or icons, according to their particular urban status and functions. Thus the two largest and most significant (English) urban centres shown on the Gough Map are London and

Key to townscape features

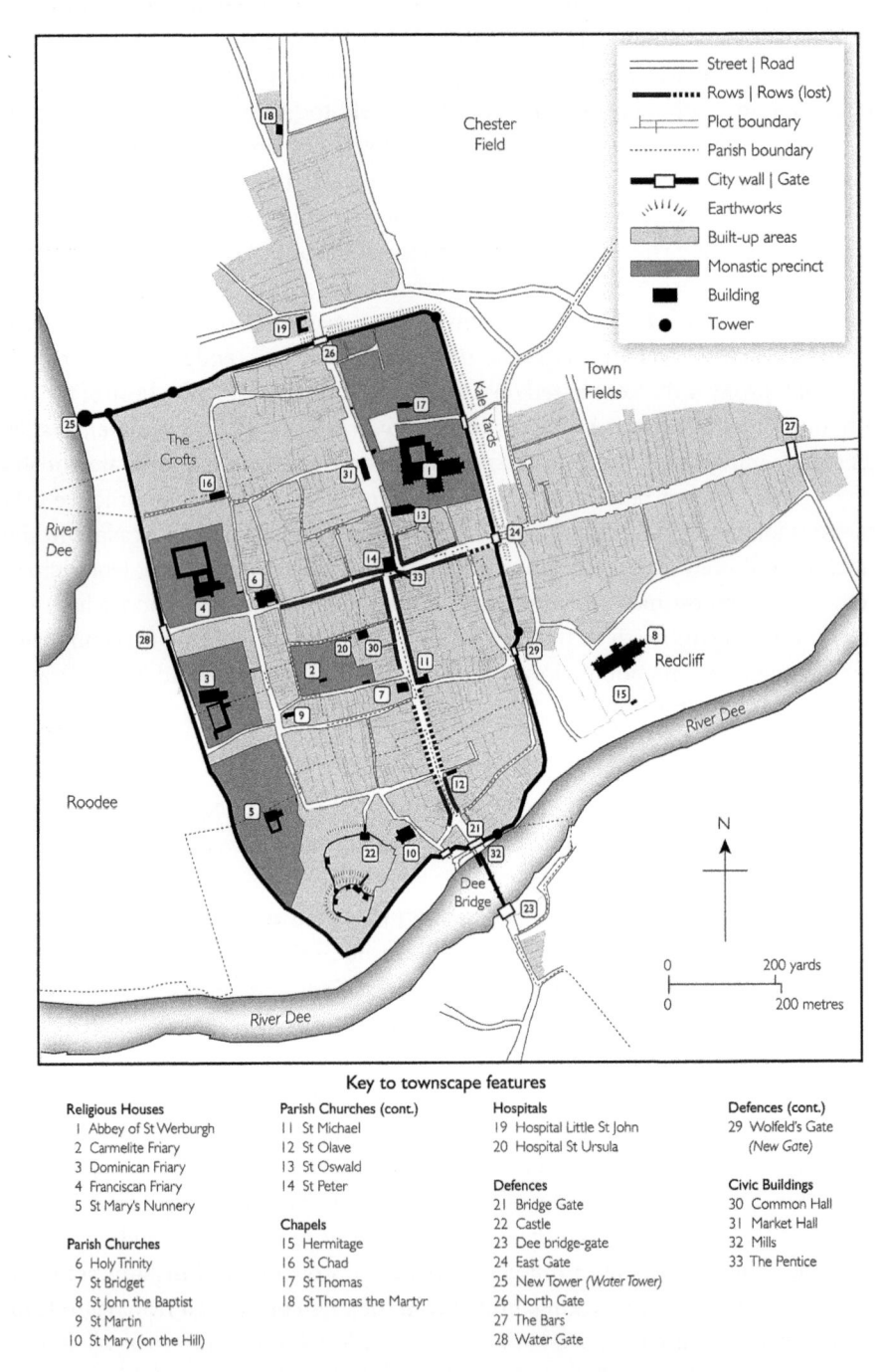

Religious Houses
1 Abbey of St Werburgh
2 Carmelite Friary
3 Dominican Friary
4 Franciscan Friary
5 St Mary's Nunnery

Parish Churches
6 Holy Trinity
7 St Bridget
8 St John the Baptist
9 St Martin
10 St Mary (on the Hill)

Parish Churches (cont.)
11 St Michael
12 St Olave
13 St Oswald
14 St Peter

Chapels
15 Hermitage
16 St Chad
17 St Thomas
18 St Thomas the Martyr

Hospitals
19 Hospital Little St John
20 Hospital St Ursula

Defences
21 Bridge Gate
22 Castle
23 Dee bridge-gate
24 East Gate
25 New Tower *(Water Tower)*
26 North Gate
27 The Bars
28 Water Gate

Defences (cont.)
29 Wolfeld's Gate *(New Gate)*

Civic Buildings
30 Common Hall
31 Market Hall
32 Mills
33 The Pentice

FIGURE 18.4 The layout of later medieval Chester showing the extensive suburb east of the walled city and the large areas occupied by institutions, from the *Mapping medieval Chester* research project, funded by the Arts and Humanities Research Council

(© Keith Lilley)

FIGURE 18.5 The Gough Map of Great Britain (dated c.1360–1400)

(© Bodleian Library, Oxford)

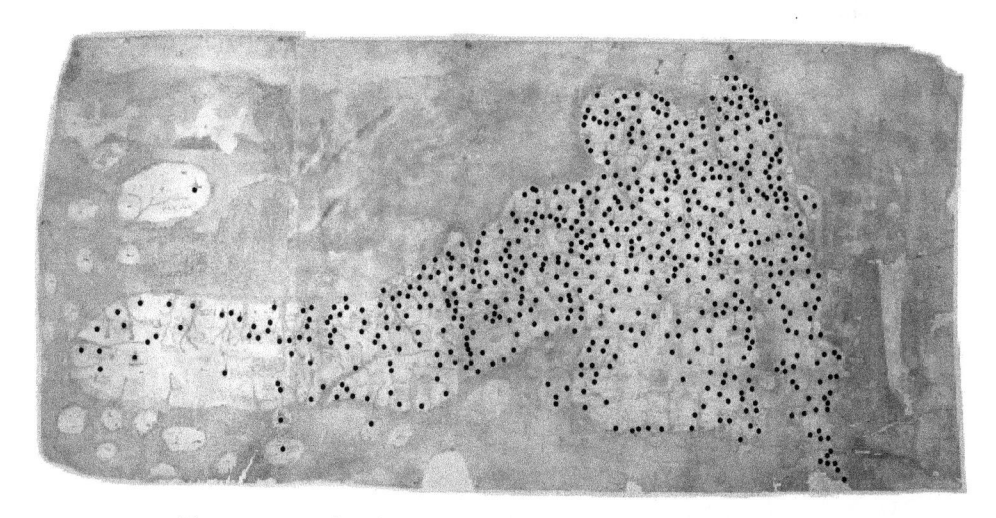

FIGURE 18.6 The positions of settlements and places (shown as black dots) that are represented by the Gough Map, from the *Mapping the realm* research project, funded by The British Academy

(© Bodleian Library and Keith Lilley)

York, both singled out by being drawn with equally impressive-looking walls and buildings crammed within them, and they are also the only two places named on the map in letters picked out in gold (Millea 2007). Other places of higher urban status and seemingly shown by their icons to be places of national importance are Norwich, Bristol, and Coventry, reflecting their leading positions in the fourteenth century English urban hierarchy. For Wales, the 'new towns' of Edward I, such as Caernarfon and Conwy, are shown, but nowhere in Wales is depicted with those higher-status symbols that are seen in England, perhaps in part a reflection of the Anglocentric perspective of the map, but also a pattern revealed by modern studies of Welsh medieval towns (Lilley and Lloyd 2009). Similarly Scotland, apart from Edinburgh, is not well endowed with urban places according to the Gough Map, perhaps for the same reasons as Wales, though again recent work, on places such as Roxburgh, Perth, and St Andrews, reveals a pattern of relatively small towns in Scotland in terms of their size and population. Of course size is relative and it may be somewhat misleading to compare Welsh and Scottish towns with English ones, when what is perhaps more important is to view them in the context of their local and regional functions and status. It has been observed, for example, that in medieval Wales, for the twelfth and thirteenth centuries, there is a relatively 'flat' hierarchy of towns, with a larger number of small towns and market centres performing important localized urban functions, lacking overall the more ordered hierarchical structure evident in later medieval England, where settlement rank-size rule seems to have greater validity as an urban model (Carter 1988).

However the Gough Map is interpreted as a source of information about relative urban size and distribution across Britain, it nevertheless shows, on the whole, the more important urban centres. Yet as Dyer (2002) has observed, by far the most widespread and numerous types of medieval town to be found across the island as a whole were those of the smallest size, the local market towns. While many such places today might not even be reckoned 'urban', in the Middle Ages these settlements nevertheless had a palpable 'urban' status, either through performing commercial and trading functions—ostensibly by acting as markets—or through having particular legal status, as chartered boroughs, enfranchized with particular privileges that gave their inhabitants—or at least some of them—burgess status, for a fixed annual fee (Reynolds 1977).

Historians have argued for decades about how to define towns of the Middle Ages, some favouring constitutional definitions, others arguing more for economic and institutional definitions. It is a matter made complex by the fact that not all medieval boroughs functioned as towns, and not all towns were constitutionally boroughs! Take, for example, the borough chartered under King Edward I at Bere (Gwynedd, Wales), a place that certainly had burgesses living there soon after its charter was bestowed (in 1284) but a place that subsequently never thrived commercially as a town (Soulsby 1983). Indeed, only half a century later Bere was largely abandoned as a settlement and today is only a field. On the other hand, there were also settlements with wealth that clearly were sizeable in population, with a market and trade and craft specialization, all factors which marked urban status, yet they did not acquire charters conferring borough status. Examples of this un-chartered type of town include Halesowen in the West Midlands and Castle Combe in Wiltshire (Hare 2012; Hilton 1995). Of course, the former urban functions of a place can also be substantiated archaeologically, through structural and material remains. Past urban status in the absence of contemporary written accounts has been proven archaeologically in the case of Trellech in Monmouthshire (Wales), for example (Howell 2000).

Towns through Time

The waxing and waning fortunes of towns across Great Britain during the later Middle Ages, particularly pre- and post-Black Death (1348–9), is another contentious topic where archaeology provides new insights into changing and fluid patterns of urbanism. Rather than seeing urban decline and decay of the later Middle Ages as an all-encompassing process affecting whole towns and cities, the excavation of individual properties or groups of properties can reveal more subtle patterns of intra-urban change during the Middle Ages, with some areas prospering, even in times of overall economic decline or demographic collapse, as in England at the time of the Black Death (Lilley 2015; Slater 1999). For example, behind the built-up street frontages along streets, the plots and property parcels typically stretched back some distance, sometimes offering the property-holder a significant piece of land, perhaps up to an acre in area depending on the location and age of the site. Archaeology within these plots—coupled with documentary analysis—presents a picture of townscape change as well as continuity. The process of plot sub-division and what the geographer M. R. G. Conzen (1960) called 'plot repletion', can be traced archaeologically and morphologically through the Middle Ages. A case in point is the development of properties in two east coast towns, Kingston upon Hull and Hartlepool, which both have yielded clear evidence of the building up of the interior spaces of plots in the twelfth and thirteenth centuries, but then also continuing into the fourteenth and fifteenth centuries (Schofield and Vince 2003, 92–101). A sub-division of plots with the addition of more and more buildings often went hand in hand with the tenurial sub-letting of urban properties, a process that is reflected also in the built fabric of the domestic townscape with a general transition towards higher and larger buildings. Patrick Ottaway (1992, 181) notes also a transition towards 'increasing sophistication' in timber-construction for buildings in medieval towns in Britain, for example, and a move towards the use of stone for building footings and lower parts of walls in the twelfth and thirteenth centuries, creating a greater degree of permanence in the built fabric of medieval townscapes in the fourteenth and fifteenth centuries (see Grenville 1997; Milne 1992).

The inner cores of towns and cities reveal a denser pattern of urban occupation, with small parcels of property and complex tenurial arrangements. Towards the edges of a town, in the outskirts or suburbs, plots and properties were generally more spacious (Keene 1976). Here, pressures for land for building was less and rents lower, while conversely the central areas of medieval towns, as today, saw higher rents and more dense occupation of the land (Lilley 2002, 200–4). Consequently, smaller properties and plots characterized the inner areas of towns which could be almost completely built-up with various buildings, though lower density blocks of land in urban cores were retained through the presence of institutional landholders, such as the Church and Crown, with walled precincts for religious houses, palaces, and castles occupying sometimes considerable areas of the centre of towns and cities (Keene 1985b;

Ward 1990). The extent of these higher-status institutions, and their physical dominance in the medieval townscape, is evident especially when it is mapped out, as in the case of medieval London and York, with the generally more spacious precincts contrasting with the built-up street-frontages that existed outside their walls (Barron 2004; Rees Jones 2013).

Within the built-up areas of the town, plots with industrial as well as residential and commercial functions combined were the norm and this multifunctional nature of medieval properties can be seen archaeologically. In particular areas of plots, certain functions were performed in close spatial proximity to each other, with metal-working and smithying, baking and food-processing all occurring within a matter of a few metres from one another (Schofield and Vince 2003, 121–50). From Hartlepool in the northeast of England, to Coventry in the Midlands, and Bristol in the south-west, numerous excavations over the past forty years have revealed such multifunctional occupation of urban sites as a widespread phenomenon. That is not to say that a certain degree of occupational and functional 'zoning' is lacking in later medieval townscapes; for there is evidence too for areas of a town having particular characteristics based upon the kinds of localized activities that dominated there, the most obvious example of this being market places, a core component of every medieval town (see Chapter 20). Markets were highly regulated spaces and often spatially separated into discrete areas specializing in the sale of particular kinds of goods and services, a fish market being separate from the bread market, for example, and livestock sold in one area while ironmongery was to be found in another—a pattern of differentiation seen in Norwich (Ayers 1994). Here the large market place which still exists there dates back to the time the town was reshaped in the 1070s, soon after the Norman Conquest. By the later Middle Ages, the large expanses of market places, such as Norwich's, and their functional segregation, had become 'hardened' physically through the construction of new buildings with specific commercial roles, not least market halls but also rows and shops, as well as by being used as the location for market crosses, gild halls and toll houses, and other such structures symbolizing rising local civic and municipal authority of the fourteenth and fifteenth centuries (Giles 2000; Keene 1990).

The medieval townscape is therefore best seen as dynamic and fluid, not static and unchanging. Thus at the scale of a town as a whole again differentiation in activity is evident from the archaeological record when examined in combination with written accounts, and here occupational surnames in property deeds and local street-names too can provide some indication of how particular areas were characterized by certain craft or industrial processes, whether metal-working or textiles (Biddle 1990; Blair and Ramsay 1991; Miller and Hatcher 1995). A recent analysis of the material culture of medieval York using GIS has identified what Gareth Dean (2012) describes as 'neighbourhoods', not necessarily as homogenous socio-economic units but as areas of similar or common forms of consumption and production. As well as revealing new insights into intra-urban changes, archaeological evidence from within medieval towns has revealed the intricacy and complexity of trading networks and patterns of production and consumption.

The mobilities of objects and artefacts include not just obvious commercial items, such as coinage, from urban contexts but particularly significant volumes of pottery, as well as animal and plant-based products such as bone and textiles (Ottaway 1992, 188–99; Schofield and Vince 2003, 165–74). Analysis of the characteristics of these items and expanding bodies of detailed data on them, are yielding a greater understanding of the movement of goods and people around the country between urban markets and their rural hinterlands throughout the Middle Ages (see Chapter 13). Indeed mapping the local hinterlands of medieval towns reveals how integral their immediate surroundings were to urban life in the Middle Ages, through providing areas of pasture, for example, as well as mills and fields (Figure 18.7). The rural–urban divide was not a stark one but more a gradual differentiation, and characterized by linkages between urban and rural populations. Both longer distance and local/regional trading networks and patterns reveal geographical and cultural connections and linkages that bound medieval Britain together, as well as connecting the island to wider, overseas circuits of trade and movement both through major seaports, such as Bristol and London, and also smaller ones too, such as Grimsby and Tenby (Platt 1973; Rigby 1993). As a result of this huge volume of detailed information on medieval craft production it is now possible to see how certain places in the urban network were closely connected through the consumption of specialized products, generally traded over longer distances than more utilitarian wares, and with the flow of such goods there came of course a flow of people and ideas too. The medieval town was a cosmopolitan place therefore, interconnected and networked to a wider world.

Conclusions

Over the past fifty years or so—since medieval urban archaeology in the UK became a defined area of study in its own right—the volume of material gained through excavations, survey, and desk-top analysis has grown significantly. What has chararacterized the subject over the decades is the case-study, where either for a particular site or urban area archaeological reports are compiled and written, sometimes published, sometimes not. There is now a huge corpus of material awaiting analysis and synthesis therefore. While some have attempted such an overview (e.g. Ottaway 1992; Schofield and Vince 2003), the scope for a thematic or period-based study remains. Such thematic studies might valuably focus on particular types of medieval town, such as ports, or market towns, studying aspects of their morphology, evolution as well as structure and material culture. Processes of urban evolution too would benefit from a comparative study, such as the role of lords in urbanization, as well as in landholding and settlement, linking the urban and the rural. The links between medieval town and countryside has received attention (Giles and Dyer 2005), and more on patterns of production and consumption, and mobility, between rural and urban populations and markets would provide an interesting topic for a regional or cross-regional study.

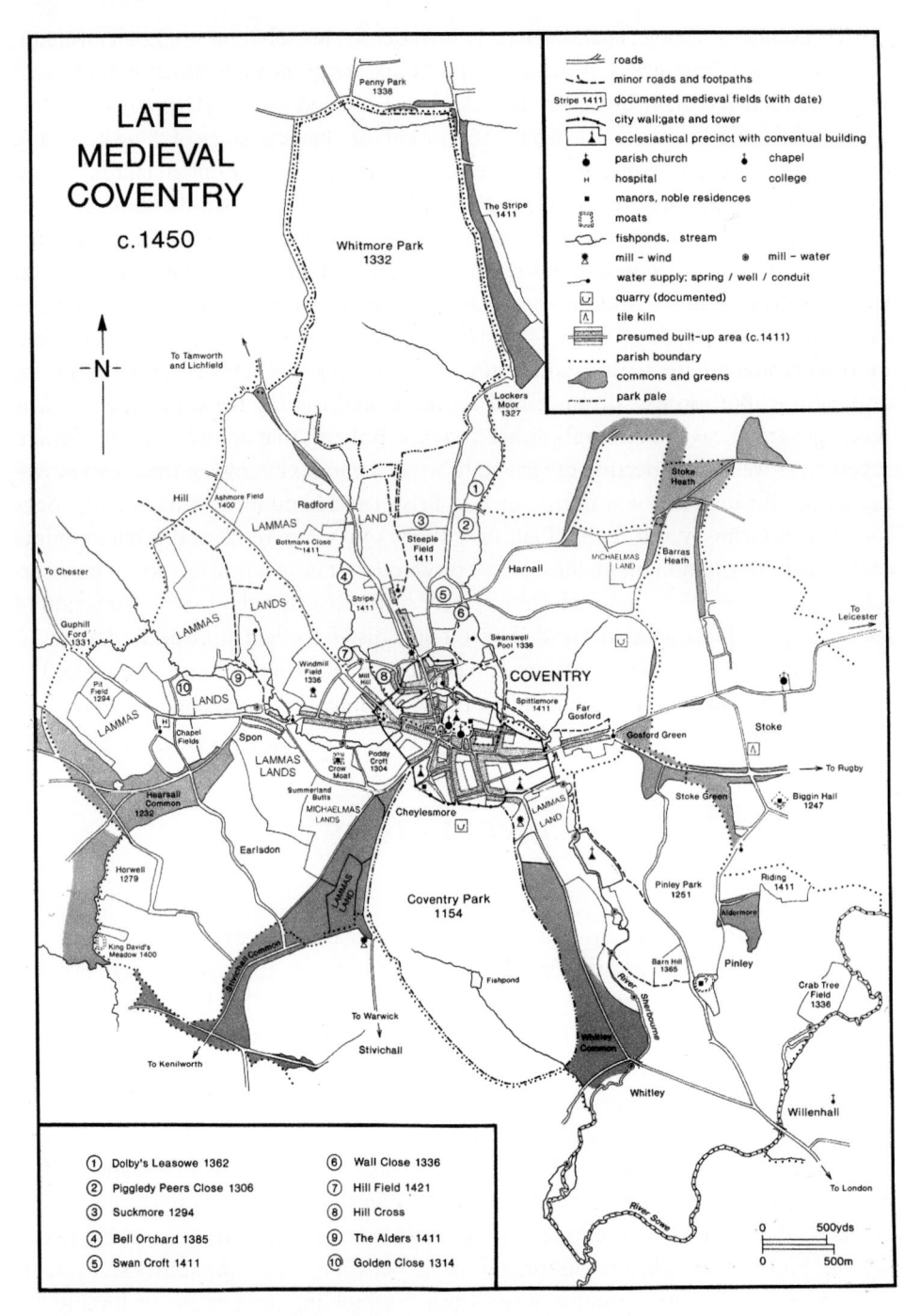

FIGURE 18.7 The hinterland of medieval Coventry, c.1450

(© Keith Lilley)

There is also methodological progress to be made, especially with the use of maps and mapping, and morphological analysis, in the study of medieval towns and cities, especially with the widespread use of Geographical Information Systems (GIS) in urban archaeology, which lends itself to geographical and spatial analysis of archaeological datasets and visualization in 2D and 3D. This would also help in analysing the significant quantities of 'grey literature' that exists for towns and cities across Britain, with so many site reports from commercial excavations awaiting critical study and assessment, and in many cases requiring digitization as a first step. The value of digital repositories of archaeological data, such as the Archaeological Data Service (ADS) at the University of York, is ever more apparent; but while these datasets continue to pile up, year in year, the time available to sift through these large datasets seems to diminish, yet should be a priority for archaeologists now, if only to take stock and begin to make sense generally of all the localized material that has built up over the decades. In so doing, not only will medieval urban archaeology be able to make a substantive contribution to scholarship and knowledge of medieval urbanism in Britain, it will help provide a much needed new agenda, going forward into the twenty-first century, for urban archaeology in the future.

References Cited

Addyman, P. 2015 *Historic Towns Atlas Vol. 5: the City of York*, Oxbow, Oxford

Aldsworth, F. and Freke, D. 1976 *Historic towns in Sussex: an archaeological survey*, Institute of Archaeology, London

Astill, G. 1985 'Archaeology and the smaller medieval town', *Urban History Yearbook* 1985, 46–53

Astill, G. 2009 'Medieval towns and urbanization', in R. Gilchrist and A. Reynolds (eds), *Reflections: 50 years of Medieval Archaeology 1957–2007*, The Society for Medieval Archaeology Monograph 30, Leeds, 255–70

Ayers, B. 1994 *Norwich*, Batsford, London

Baker, N. J., Dalwood, H., Holt, R. A., Mundy, C. F., and Taylor, G. 1992 'From Roman to medieval Worcester: development and planning in the Anglo-Saxon city', *Antiquity* 66, 65–74

Barley, M. W. (ed.) 1976 *The plans and topography of medieval towns in England and Wales*, Council for British Archaeology Research Report 14, London

Barron, C. 2004 *London in the Later Middle Ages: government and people 1200–1500*, Oxford University Press, Oxford

Beresford, M. W. 1967 *New towns of the Middle Ages*, Lutterworth Press, London

Biddle, M. 1990 *Object and economy in medieval Winchester*, Winchester Studies 7ii, Clarendon Press, Oxford

Blair, J. 2005 *The Church in Anglo-Saxon society*, Oxford University Press, Oxford

Blair, J. and Ramsay, N. (eds) 1991 *English medieval industries: craftsmen, techniques, products*, The Hambledon Press, London

Bond, C. J. 1990 'Central place and medieval new town: the origins of Thame, Oxfordshire', in T. R. Slater (ed.), *The built form of western cities*, Leicester University Press, Leicester, 83–106

Britnell, R. H. 1993 *The commercialisation of English society 1000–1500*, Cambridge University Press, Cambridge

Brooks, N. P. and Whittington, G. 1977 'Planning and growth in the medieval Scottish burgh: the example of St Andrews', *Transactions of the Institute of British Geographers* new series 2(3), 278–95

Cameron, A. S. and Stones, J. A. (eds) 2001 *Aberdeen: an in-depth view of the city's past*, The Society of Antiquaries of Scotland, Edinburgh

Carter, H. 1988 'The development of urban centrality in England and Wales', in D. Denecke and G. Shaw (eds), *Urban historical geography: recent progress in Britain and Germany*, Cambridge University Press, Cambridge, 191–210

Carver, M. O. H. 1980 *Medieval Worcester: an archaeological framework*, Worcester Archaeological Society, Worcester

Christie, N. and Creighton, O. H. (eds) 2013 *Transforming townscapes. From burh to borough: the archaeology of Wallingford, AD 800–1400*, The Society for Medieval Archaeology Monograph 35, London

Conzen, M. R. G. 1960 *Alnwick, Northumberland: a study in town plan analysis*, Institute of British Geographers Publication 27, London (2nd revised edn, 1969)

Conzen, M. R. G. 1968 'The use of town plans in the study of urban history', in H. J. Dyos (ed.), *The study of urban history*, Arnold, London, 113–30

Conzen, M. R. G. 1988 'Morphogenesis, morphological regions and secular human agency in the historic townscape, as exemplified by Ludlow', in D. Denecke and G. Shaw (eds), *Urban historical geography: recent progress in Britain and Germany*, Cambridge University Press, Cambridge, 252–72

Dean, G. 2012 'GIS, archaeology and neighbourhood assemblages in medieval York', *Post-Classical Archaeologies* 2, 7–30

Dyer, A. 2000 'Appendix: ranking lists of English medieval towns', in D. M. Palliser (ed.), *The Cambridge urban history of Britain. Vol. I: 600–1540*, Cambridge University Press, Cambridge, 747–55

Dyer, C. 2002 'Small places with large consequences: the importance of small towns in England, 1000–1540', *Historical Research* 75(187), 1–24

Gilchrist, R. 1999 *Gender and archaeology: contesting the past*, Routledge, London

Giles, K. 2000 *An archaeology of social identity: guild halls in York*, British Archaeological Reports British Series 315, Oxford

Giles, K. and Dyer, C. (eds) 2005 *Town and country in the Middle Ages: contrasts, contacts and interconnections, 1100–1500*, The Society for Medieval Archaeology Monograph 22, Leeds

Good, G. L., Jones, R. H., and Ponsford, M. W. (eds) 1988 *Waterfront archaeology: proceedings of the Third International Conference on Waterfront Archaeology*, Council for British Archaeology Research Report 74, London

Grenville, J. 1997 *Medieval housing*, Leicester University Press, London

Hare, J. 2012 *A prospering society: Wiltshire in the later Middle Ages*, University of Hertfordshire Press, Hatfield

Haslam, J. 1976 *Wiltshire towns: the archaeological potential*, Wiltshire Archaeological and Natural History Society, Devizes

Hilton, R. H. 1995 *English and French towns in feudal society: a comparative study*, Cambridge University Press, Cambridge

Howell, R. 2000 'Development by design: an investigation of thirteenth century industrialization and urban growth at Trelech, Gwent', *Studia Celtica* 34, 211–22

Jones, M. J., Stocker, D., and Vince, A. 2003 *The city by the pool: assessing the archaeology of the City of Lincoln*, Oxbow, Oxford

Jones, R. H. 1988 'Industry and environment in medieval Bristol', in G. L. Good, R. H. Jones, and M. W. Ponsford (eds), *Waterfront archaeology: proceedings of the Third International Conference on Waterfront Archaeology*, Council for British Archaeology Research Report 74, London, 19–26

Keene, D. 1976 'Suburban growth', in M. W. Barley (ed.), *Plans and topography of medieval towns in England and Wales*, Council for British Archaeology Research Report 14, London, 71–82

Keene, D. 1985a *Cheapside before the Great Fire*, Economic and Social Research Council, London

Keene, D. 1985b *Survey of medieval Winchester*, Winchester Studies 2, Clarendon Press, Oxford

Keene, D. 1990 'Shops and shopping in medieval London', in L. Grant (ed.), *Medieval art, architecture and archaeology in London*, Maney, Leeds, 29–46

Lilley, K. D. 1998 'Trading places: monastic initiative and the development of high medieval Coventry', in T. R. Slater and G. Rosser (eds), *The Church in the medieval town*, Ashgate, Aldershot, 177–208

Lilley, K. D. 1999 'Urban landscapes and the cultural politics of territorial control in Anglo-Norman England', *Landscape Research* 24, 5–23

Lilley, K. D. 2000 'Mapping the medieval city: plan analysis and urban history', *Urban History* 27(1), 5–30

Lilley, K. D. 2001 'Urban planning and the design of towns in the Middle Ages: the Earls of Devon and their "new towns"', *Planning Perspectives* 16, 1–24

Lilley, K. D. 2002 *Urban life in the Middle Ages, 1000–1450*, Palgrave Macmillan, London

Lilley, K. D. 2012 'Mapping futures? Spatial technologies and the medieval city: a critical cartography', *Post-Classical Archaeologies* 2, 227–54

Lilley, K. D. 2015 'Urban planning after the Black Death: townscape transformations in later-medieval England (1350–1530)', *Urban History* 42(1), 22–42

Lilley, K. D. 2017 'The Norman Conquest and its influences on urban landscapes', in D. M. Hadley and C. Dyer (eds), *The archaeology of the 11th century: continuities and transformations*, The Society for Medieval Archaeology Monograph 38, London, 41–63

Lilley, K. D. and Dean, G. 2015 'A silent witness? Medieval urban landscapes and unfolding their mapping histories', *Journal of Medieval History* 41(3), 273–91

Lilley, K. D. and Lloyd, C. D. 2009 'Mapping the realm: a new look at the Gough Map of Britain (c.1360)', *Imago Mundi* 61(1), 1–28

Lilley, K. D., Lloyd, C., and Trick, S. 2007 'Designs and designers of medieval "new towns" in Wales', *Antiquity* 81, 279–93

Lobel, M. D. (ed.) 1969 *Historic towns: maps and plans of towns and cities in the British Isles, Vol. 1*, Lovell-Johns Cook, London

Lobel, M. D. (ed.) 1975 *The atlas of historic towns, Vol. 2*, Scolar Press, Oxford

Lynch, J., Spearman, M., and Stell, G. 1988 *The Scottish medieval town*, J. Donald, Edinburgh

Martin, C. and Oram, R. 2007 'Medieval Roxburgh: a preliminary assessment of the burgh and its locality', *Proceedings of the Society of Antiquaries of Scotland* 137, 357–404

Martin, D. and Martin, B. 2004 *New Winchelsea, Sussex: a medieval port town*, Heritage Marketing and Publications, King's Lynn

Millea, N. 2007 *The Gough Map: the earliest road map of Great Britain*, Bodleian Library, Oxford

Miller, E. and Hatcher, J. 1995 *Medieval England: towns, commerce and craft, 1086–1348*, Longman, Harlow

Milne, G. 1992 *Timber building techniques in London c.900–c.1400*, London and Middlesex Archaeological Society, London

Milne, G. and Goodburn, D. 1990 'The early medieval port of London, 700–1200', *Antiquity* 64, 629–36

Morris, A. E. J. 1994 *History of urban form: before the Industrial Revolutions*, Wiley, London

Nicholas, D. 2003 *Urban Europe 1100–1700*, Houndmills, Basingstoke

Ottaway, P. 1992 *Archaeology in British towns*, Routledge, London

Platt, C. 1973 *Medieval Southampton: the port and trading community*, Routledge and K. Paul, London

Platt, C. 1976 *The English medieval town*, Secker and Warburg, London

Rees Jones, S. 2013 *York: the making of a city 1068–1350*, Oxford University Press, Oxford

Reynolds, S. 1977 *An introduction to the history of English medieval towns*, Clarendon Press, Oxford

Rigby, S. H. 1993 *Medieval Grimsby: growth and decline*, University of Hull Press, Hull

Rodwell, K. A. (ed.) 1975 *Historic towns in Oxfordshire: a survey of the new county*, Oxford Archaeological Unit, Oxford

Schofield, J. and Leech, R. (eds) 1987 *Urban archaeology in Britain*, Council for British Archaeology Research Report 61, London

Schofield, J. and Vince, A. 2003 *Medieval towns*, Continuun, London (2nd edn)

Schofield, J., Allen, P., and Taylor, C. 1990 'Medieval buildings and property development in the area of Cheapside', *Transactions of the London and Middlesex Archaeological Society* 41, 39–238

Schofield, J., Palliser, D., and Harding, C. 1981 *Recent archaeological research in English towns*, Council for British Archaeology Occasional Paper 12, London

Schofield, J. and Leech, R. (eds) 1987 *Urban archaeology in Britain*, Council for British Archaeology Research Report 61, London

Slater, T. R. 1985 'Medieval new town and port: a plan analysis of Hedon, East Yorkshire', *Yorkshire Archaeological Journal* 57, 23–51

Slater, T. R. 1990 'English medieval new towns with composite plans: evidence from the midlands', in T. R. Slater (ed.), *The built form of western cities*, Leicester University Press, Leicester, 60–82

Slater, T. R. 1999 'Geometry and medieval town planning', *Urban Morphology* 3, 107–16

Soulsby, I. 1983 *The towns of medieval Wales*, Phillimore, Chichester

Thomas, R. M. 2006 'Mapping the towns: English Heritage's urban survey and characterisation programme', *Landscapes* 7(1), 68–93

Ward, S. W. 1990 *Excavations at Chester: the lesser medieval religious houses*, Chester City Council, Chester

CHAPTER 19

URBAN HOUSING

JOHN SCHOFIELD

SINCE the 1970s there have been hundreds of excavations of domestic sites in medieval British towns. In larger, presently prosperous, cities the strata are much damaged by building in later periods, so that in most of the City of London, for instance, the evidence is quite rich until the fourteenth century, and then it becomes fragmentary (only foundations and cess pits, with few floors or external surfaces); this is however compensated for by deep deposits with complete buildings on the waterfront. Small towns have many standing buildings, but shorter sequences with much less artefactual evidence (for their merits, Dyer 2003). Archaeology provides measured surveys of parts of buildings, but usually only the ground floor or cellars, along with some evidence for fixed and mobile apparatus. Buildings destroyed by fire are exceptionally useful as their fire layers trap artefacts in their original settings (up to 2 m high in Norwich; Atkin et al. 1985).

Surviving buildings allow understanding of upper floors and roofs (the part which most often survives intact), but they have always been changed internally, sometimes completely. There are large groups of medieval houses in several English towns, such as Rye in East Sussex, Salisbury in Wiltshire (eighteen from the fourteenth century), Sandwich in Kent (sixty-seven from the fourteenth century to 1520), or Shrewsbury in Shropshire; and in smaller groups in many other towns (or were until the twentieth century, as in Bristol and Exeter). Medieval Welsh towns were small and relatively poor. The only complete town house here is Aberconwy House, Conwy, with remains of other stone houses incorporated into later buildings in Kidwelly in Carmarthenshire and Tenby in Pembrokeshire. In Scotland very few houses pre-date the Reformation (Stell 1988).

Dendrochronology has been of great assistance in dating and understanding urban and rural houses, both standing structures and excavated examples; for instance in Shropshire, over one hundred buildings from the 1190s to the middle of the sixteenth century were successfully sampled up to 2002 (Moran 2003, 351–4). Timbers found in several Scottish burghs in the 1970s and 1980s were saved for future analysis, and have now produced a chronology from the mid-tenth century to the late thirteenth (Crone 2000). Dendrochronology has been important in studies of continental European towns, such as Lübeck (Germany), where forty timber buildings have been dated to the period 1175–1210 when the town was being established (Gläser 2001), and in towns all over France from the second half of the thirteenth century onwards (Alix and Épaud 2013). But some timbers have too few rings: in Essex, Coggeshall has produced seventeen dates from 1353 to 1555, but nearby Maldon and Colchester, none at all (Andrews 2013). Timbers sampled from later medieval houses are sometimes fast-grown, which does not help.

This paper surveys the period in three arbitrary chronological stages, in each case noting plans of buildings, their fittings, and infrastructure, materials, and construction. At the end are some conclusions about developments, the idea of types of building plans, development of facilities and use of spaces, and regional and national trends. Each section includes brief notes on parallels in other European countries, but cultural links or comparisons are largely left to the other chapters in this volume (Part X, this *Handbook*).

From 1100 to about 1250

Excavations in several towns have produced a corpus of buildings from the late ninth to the twelfth century; evidence of carpentry techniques and some pieces of buildings have been found in waterlogged contexts in London (Goodburn 1997; Horsman et al. 1988; Milne 1992). The majority of buildings were single-storeyed, but some in larger towns (London, Oxford) had timber-lined cellars which could be of considerable size; most often dated to the eleventh century, these usually lay at right-angles or parallel to the streets but set back from them. The cellared buildings were parts of wide properties with yards or courtyards, divided from the street by a row of smaller dwellings (Schofield and Vince 2005, 80–3). Initially, large enclosures in towns were gradually subdivided into the narrow properties which mostly stayed fixed from the twelfth century. By 1200 many properties in towns were long and thin, but only in unpressurized or suburban settings or over time along the waterfront (reclamation in stages produced elongated properties), and not usually in the centres of larger towns. Private alleys through a property developed to give access to buildings, sometimes separately let, towards the rear. This is not only a feature of larger towns: in thirteenth-century Hartlepool (Co. Durham), for instance, buildings with stone foundations showed that the medieval shopping experience extended down the lanes as well as being along the frontage (Daniels 2010, 110; see Chapter 20 in this *Handbook*). Thus one theme of the period is the gradual development of buildings on the plot, from the front to the back, where space allowed.

Behind major streets and in peripheral areas within towns, development was equally intense but apparently far more haphazard and jumbled in appearance. A mid-twelfth-century alley in London which led to the new stone Guildhall comprised buildings of several sizes, some ranged along the frontage and some at right angles, not arranged formally and with one oven in the lane itself (Figure 19.1). These buildings were occupied by people and their animals, and also functioned as workshops (see Chapter 30). They

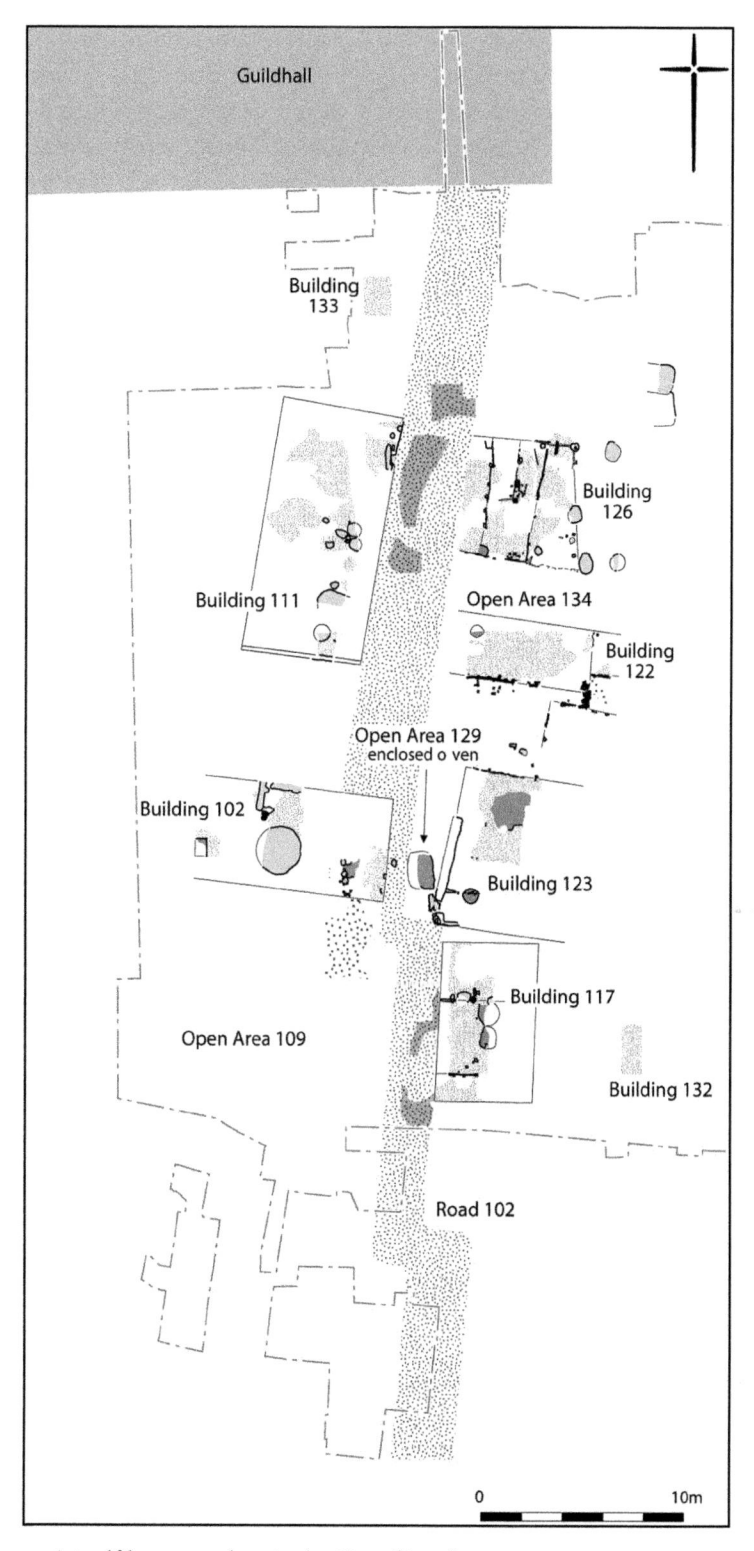

FIGURE 19.1 A twelfth-century lane in the City of London

(drawn by Carlos Lemos, © MOLA)

changed rapidly over time. Excavations at Eastgate, Beverley (East Yorkshire), uncovered twelve phases of building on the same property or properties during the period from the late eleventh to the fifteenth centuries, so an average of one episode of radical change every thirty years (Evans and Tomlinson 1992). Such buildings had simple plans, and at this period functions of excavated rooms cannot be related to those commonly proposed for standing houses of the fourteenth century and later (hall, parlour, and so on), except where (as at Beverley) they incorporated industrial-sized ovens and dyeing vats.

Although shops are considered in another chapter (see Chapter 20), they are also of importance for the development of the urban house. Many smaller dwellings were just houses, but others were distinctively urban: the domestic accommodation was attached to a commercial front (Clark 2000). Along streets given to retail trading or manufacturing, the structure of the building would be governed by the need to use the ground floor for trading purposes, with domestic accommodation fitted around and above that overarching and essential requirement. Sometimes a property was wide enough to accommodate a small row of shops of timber or stone, perhaps with cellars too, which would form a frontage on the street with a large stone building, probably a related hall, to the rear; this was the arrangement at Poultry in the City of London, dating from around 1220 (Burch and Treveil 2011, 118–21).

A further influence on the form of buildings were local regulations to guard against fire, bad construction, and to control sewage. Building regulations were in force in London by 1200, and observation of them can be traced on archaeological sites, with an increased availability of ceramic roof tiles, fire-break stone walls between properties, and the increasing use of latrine pits of stone. The demand for stone party-walls, in particular, greatly influenced the topography and development of house-forms for the next three centuries (Schofield 2003; 2011, 74–7). As these walls had to be 16 feet (4.9 m) high, they indicate that two-storey buildings were to be expected by 1200, whether or not the intervening frontage between the party walls was of stone or (more likely) of timber infilled with other materials. Urban regulations were however not widespread: Nottingham and Worcester only forbade chimneys of wood in the 1490s.

Fragments of thirteenth-century furniture are found in waterlogged contexts (e.g. at Perth; Yeoman 1995, 59). No doubt rooms were decorated with wall paintings, such as that of the thirteenth century recovered from a house in Salisbury (RCHME 1980, 73). At this earliest period there is little information yet on arrangements for water supply and sanitation. In the larger towns, provision of water was a public matter, either from conduits in the streets (in London, from 1237) and/or human water-carriers, so there would be few relevant archaeological fittings to excavate within houses; but wells of superimposed casks, and later ones of more enduring stone, are found on house sites. Sometimes the well's situation suggests it was inside the building rather than in a yard, but both were no doubt possible. Many of the timber-lined and later stone-lined pits recorded behind buildings would have been cess pits, and their use must have started with the houses. Where stone walls survive, privies are found on the first floor in houses throughout the medieval period in French towns, and were probably located there in British towns also.

Although buildings of timber were always in the majority, they were interspersed with both religious and secular residential buildings of stone, which generally shared an architecture of features such as doors, windows, and decoration. They may not be visible; at Canterbury there are records of at least thirty stone houses of the twelfth and thirteenth century, and most survive below ground (Urry 1967). Stone buildings could lie on the street (as at Chester, Lincoln, and Southampton) or set back from the street, either in alignment with it or at right angles, as from the twelfth century in Winchester (Ford and Teague 2011) and at Bristol (Leech 2014, 81–2). The stone-vaulted undercrofts around Haverfordwest's market place and on Main Street, Pembroke, are evidence for a prosperous merchant class in Welsh towns, where otherwise evidence has only been found of short-lived earth and timber houses (Murphy 1997; Smith 1988, 372–4). There were probably fewer stone houses of note in British towns than there were across mainland Europe. Stone buildings of the twelfth and early thirteenth century have survived in quantity at Cluny, Regensburg, and within later buildings at Prague. In France, where very few houses with timber-framed storeys dating to before 1400 have survived in towns, this apparent preference for stone may be misleading; the timber buildings have vanished (Esquieu and Pesez 1998; Garrigou Grandchamp 2006). From the eleventh century stone towers were added in courts behind timber buildings which fronted the streets, as at Zürich, Basel, Lübeck, and Riga (Fehring 1991, 204); stone cellars are often found towards the back of houses, beneath ground-level timber structures. At Nijmegen (Holland), stone houses of the thirteenth century had the same plans as their timber predecessors (Sarfatij 1990, 190); all these are useful analogies.

Construction of walls in early British timber buildings could involve staves, wattles, horizontal planking, or cob (for London, Bowsher et al. 2007; Horsman et al. 1988). Walls of clay were common in Norwich from the twelfth century to the sixteenth century (Ayers 2001); or of wattle around posts in several northern towns, from Beverley to Aberdeen in the eleventh to fourteenth centuries, for instance at Durham (Carver 1979; Ewan 1990, 16–24). From around 1200 timber-framed buildings in English towns also became taller. Many of the joints used by medieval carpenters were known to their Romano-British predecessors, and perhaps some Roman examples remained to be studied. Dendrochronological analysis of timbers from waterfront contexts suggests that medieval carpenters were working out how to do it, along with the invention of box framing (Milne 1992). Buildings with overhanging upper storeys or jetties are criticized in London streets in 1246, and must have been a widespread nuisance by then. Precisely dated surviving jettied buildings in Europe start in the decades after 1250, so the earliest examples are lost. Thereafter jettied houses are an urban feature (and perhaps first in towns, only later in the countryside), not only in England but also known or presumed in Wales (Conwy) and Scotland (a fifteenth-century drawing of the Battle of Bannockburn shows jettied houses in Stirling; Stell 1988, 74; Yeoman 1995, 61–2).

The technology of the bay division, in which many pairs of generally thin rafters are replaced by single pairs of larger size at set intervals held together by a tie-beam, may have been developed first in towns in the twelfth and thirteenth centuries, arising from the number of large construction sites there and the necessary organization of building trades, as has been suggested for France (Esquieu and Pesez 1998, 73, 77). Sometimes bay divisions were emphasized with larger posts in the ground, as at Hartlepool; soon after the posts were set on large stones at intervals, as at Beverley. The development of low stone walls to support frames comes in the next period, after 1250. Roof coverings started by being of thatch or wooden shingles, and in large towns such as Norwich, thatch was still widespread in 1570 (and even later in smaller towns). Shingles were still the norm in Winchester until the fourteenth century, when blue slates were much used. London had insisted on clay tiles from 1212, and after some experimentation with designs, the pegtile was adopted; even so, the authorities had to demand tile roofs for smaller buildings down alleys as late as 1422 (Schofield 2003, 96–8).

FROM 1250 TO 1400

For the religious and secular elite, especially in London, the preferred form during this period was a courtyard house with a masonry hall stretching across the wide property, and an extensive private garden behind. In the early fourteenth century, magnates could build imposing platforms into the Thames for their houses, or otherwise manipulate the river bank by creating moated sites. But these mansions, which are also occasionally found in towns outside the capital, were the exception and are not considered urban in the sense explored here. They did not respond much to the constraints of town space.

There are medieval buildings still-standing from this period. A surviving example, 39 Strand Street, Sandwich (Kent), provides a general model for a medium-sized house (Figure 19.2). The ground-floor rooms at the front probably contained shops (that is, workshops). Behind was an open hall, entered only from the yard at the side, and at the back was another building of two and a half storeys over an undercroft. No documentary history can yet be associated with it.

Open halls may have been more common in the centres of medieval towns than the number of survivals suggest; extant examples are mainly of the fourteenth and fifteenth centuries (Pearson 2009, 5–7). A plan of a hall and two chambers is common in Winchester (Keene 1985, 158). But pressure on urban space, and the small size of many central properties, led to innovation and the creation by the end of the fourteenth century of a simple plan of two rooms on two or three floors and usually at right-angles to the street, a self-contained unit without an open hall. This is known from documentary and plan sources in London, and from surviving examples such as 52–54 High Street, Salisbury, and perhaps later in Exeter and York; examples with a long side to the street are found in Norwich. In the fourteenth century, when buildings of three storeys are found in York, there was also development of the rear parts of properties to generate income from rents (Rees Jones 2008, 71). Division into smaller units forced buildings

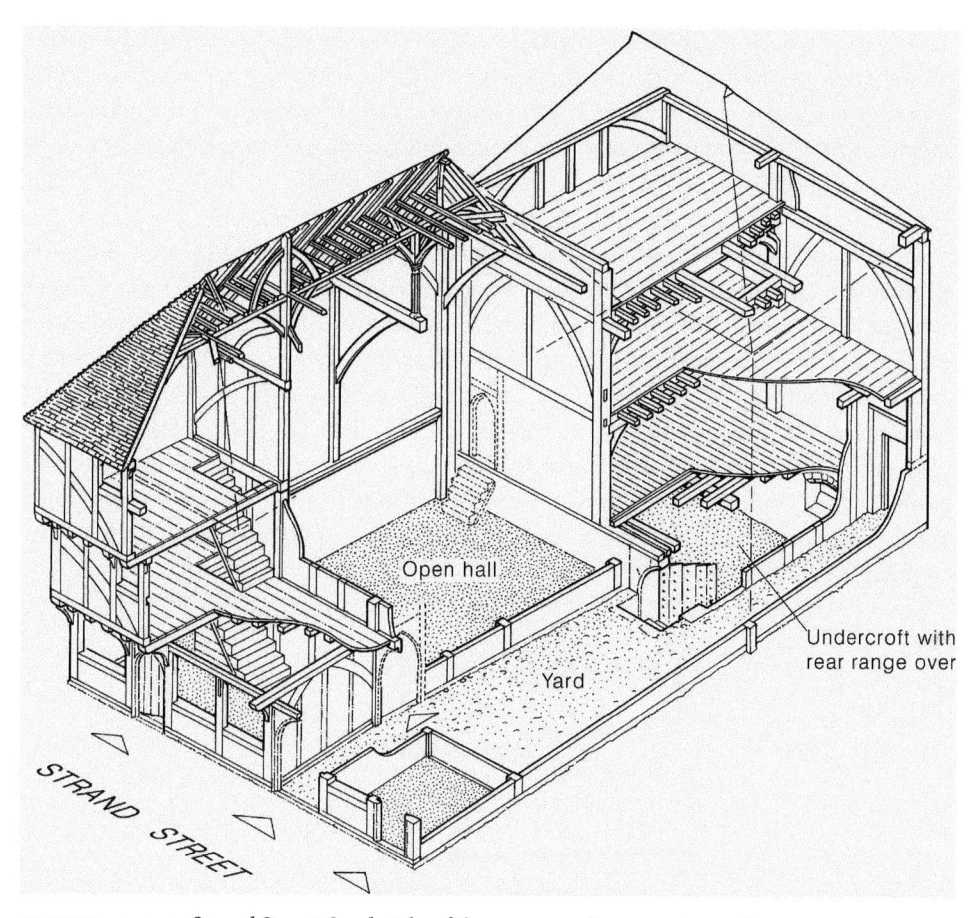

FIGURE 19.2 39 Strand Street, Sandwich, of the 1330s, partly reconstructed

(© Alan T. Adams, by permission of Sarah Pearson)

to become taller and to extend backwards from the street, as shown in the middle of Sandwich (Clarke et al. 2010, 267). At Salisbury in the next century, some prosperous traders avoided courtyard houses but instead built a compact gabled house two bays wide and two or three bays deep, with a passage at the side, which is similarly a move towards compaction (RCHME 1980, xlvi).

The house at Strand Street in Sandwich had a cellar or undercroft simply ceiled with beams. A feature of this period is the stone undercroft with vaulting, either groined (the vaulting unemphasized) or exceptionally with stone arches, sometimes further embellished with carved corbels, occasionally painted. These are considered in detail by Antrobus (Chapter 20) and suffice it to reiterate here that good examples have been recorded in Chester and New Winchelsea (Brown 1999, 22, 34; Martin and Martin 2004). A later large group of about eighty brick undercrofts at Norwich, of fourteenth- and especially fifteenth-century date, provided fire-proof storage and a platform for building in timber above, which is what their stone predecessors had done.

A probably quite usual mix of urban forms is shown by excavation at Brook Street, Winchester, of several contiguous properties from the tenth century onwards. By the fourteenth century the block comprised several kinds of houses and a small church (Figure 19.3). Documents suggest that three buildings (Figure 19.3, I, IX, and X) were on separate properties by the late fourteenth century, but in the twelfth century their ground was a single holding. In 1304 House I was in the possession of a dyer; much of the street, interlaced with drains and small streams, was occupied by cloth-finishing premises. At the north end of the site was a lane of timber-framed cottages (Houses XI and XII) (Keene 1985, 758–66). Though cottages had been built as speculation in twelfth-century Winchester, the fourteenth century is a time of development of whole blocks of building. At York, the Lady Row of 1316 survives, a parish speculation along the street frontage of its churchyard; also in York, a contract of 1335 for a row in Coney Street specifies that it should be a hundred feet long, divided into six houses (Salzman 1967, 430–2). In Coventry (West Midlands), Sandwich (Kent), and Tewkesbury (Gloucestershire) there are rows or pairs of small houses with open halls, perhaps also speculative developments.

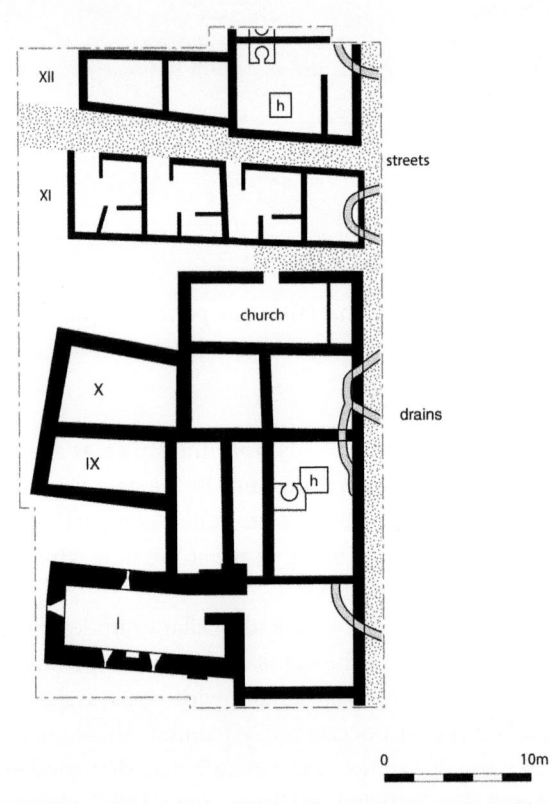

FIGURE 19.3 Brook Street, Winchester, in the fourteenth century. The street comprised a church, stone houses of thirteenth- and fourteenth-century dates, and an alley of cottages (h = hearth)

(© Carlos Lemos, with permission of Derek Keene and OUP)

This second period has intentionally bridged the time of the Black Death in 1348–50, which might have brought about changes to domestic building history. At Winchester, a change is noticed 'from grand timber houses and impressive stone architecture to less imposing and cheaper alternatives and alterations' (Beaumont James and Roberts 2000, 199). In Sandwich, large storage cellars and domestic buildings of the fourteenth century and earlier gave way to smaller houses, many of which remain, though their building dates are after 1380. But the effect of the Black Death on housing has not yet been studied nationally.

There are more excavated examples of household fittings, for instance from London waterfront contexts, which are dated by dendrochronology, ceramics, and coins (Egan 1998). Though they are displaced from their original settings in buildings, these form an important corpus of hinges, locks and keys, candlesticks, kitchen ware, and pieces of louvres from roofs or window furniture (Figure 19.4). Overall, the increased range and number of artefacts from this period suggest that people now had more possessions,

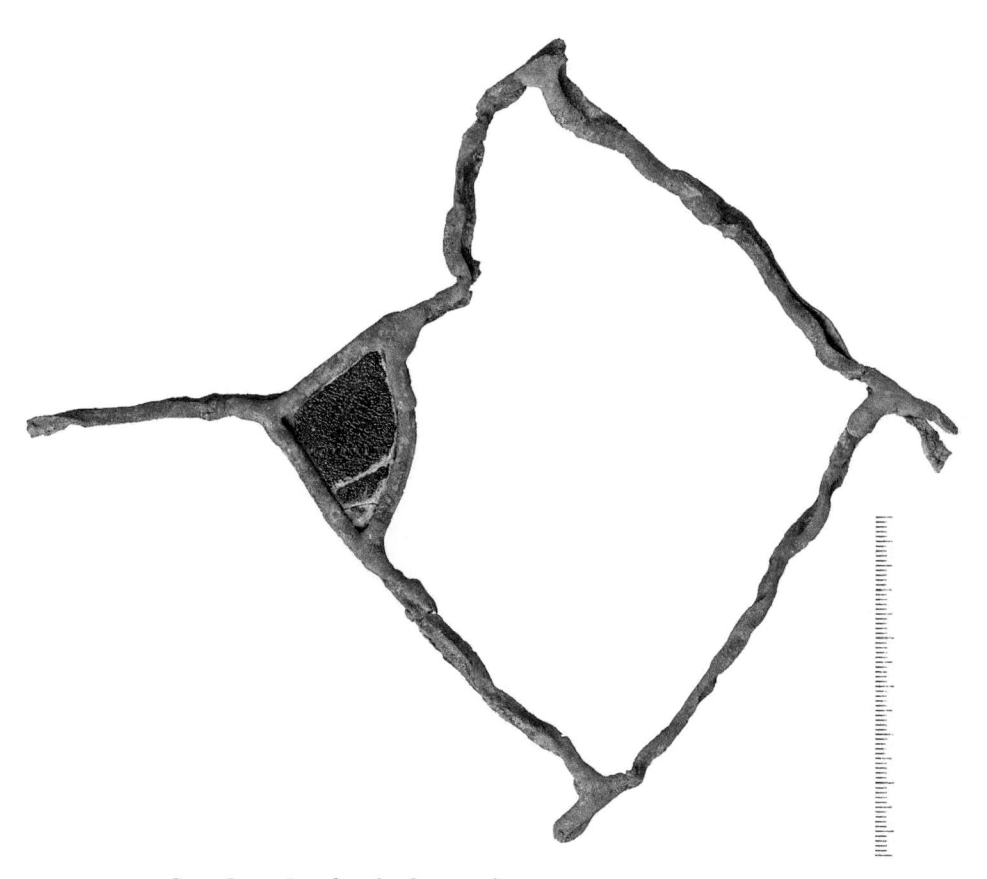

FIGURE 19.4 Swan Lane, London: lead cames forming a pane or quarry from a window, with a fragment of blue glass, from a waterfront dump of 1270–1350. Though this could be from a church, it is probably evidence of glazed windows in fourteenth-century London houses

(photo by Andy Chopping © MOLA)

and consequently discarded more than in previous generations. The fourteenth century was a time when urban people increasingly indulged in new fashions in dress and shoes; possibly this century gave birth to 'fashion' in the sense of novelty dominating taste (Kowaleski 2006, 247–9). New well-built houses followed in numbers in the fifteenth century. Goldberg (2008) calls this 'a different system of values' in urban as compared with rural houses. Perhaps urban houses looked and felt different.

In some areas, materials for building houses did not change much. Houses in Scottish towns continued to be built in a mixture of wood, clay, and stone, as for instance at Rattray (Aberdeenshire) (Murray and Murray 1993).

From 1400 to 1540

There are more surviving buildings (or recorded ones, sometimes before demolition) dating to this period, especially in smaller and medium-sized towns, for instance at least twenty-nine in Ludlow (Shropshire) and at least forty known buildings at Shrewsbury (Carver 1983; Moran 2003). In Scotland, stone houses of 1500 and later decades form the cores of buildings in Edinburgh, Dunfermline, Kirkcaldy, and St Andrews; by this date the tenement tradition of different families living on different floors was probably established in Scottish towns, and would lead to the high stone buildings of the sixteenth century.

During the fifteenth century, houses on major market streets, including shops, could reach three storeys with garrets (in Ludlow, from 1405) or even four or five storeys on cellars, such as at Abingdon in Oxfordshire (Steane and Ayres 2013, 186–9). Larger complexes incorporated simple buildings which were warehouses, often on the bank of a river, but also elsewhere in the town. The commercial face of a property could expand above shops on the ground floor; at Norwich, different sources (excavation, standing building recording, dendrochronology, and documents) combine to illuminate the history of Dragon Hall in King Street, where in 1427 a merchant rebuilt a street-range to form a first-floor showroom (see Figure 28.5); but being principally a commercial venture, the carpentry and decoration have been called shoddily meretricious (Shelley 2005). The general rule was adaptation, not wholesale clearance and new buildings. At King's Lynn (Norfolk), houses were modernized or extended, but not radically rebuilt. This led to conservatism. At Chester and Bristol, open halls continued in vogue in the sixteenth and even seventeenth centuries, in many cases as conscious statements of participation in a noble civic past, being decorated with arms and heraldry (Leech 2014, 98–111). At the humbler level of single-storey buildings, there were now more rooms and their functions can sometimes be suggested for excavated buildings such as for the hall at Lurk Lane, Beverley (Evans 2001).

Framing was also changing. After about 1440, the fronts of houses were sometimes embellished with structurally superfluous designs in timber, especially rows of vertical braces called close studding; this seems to have been most popular in towns, an urban fashion or social requirement. By 1540, on the other hand, jetties on the sides of houses were already becoming much smaller than in preceding generations (that is, protruding less), and jetties would be increasingly banned by civic authorities from the late sixteenth century. It was the same abroad: jetties were banned at Rouen in 1523 and at Angers in 1541. By this time some houses in French towns rose four and a half storeys with hardly any jetties at all (Alix and Épaud 2013).

The interiors of medieval urban houses become clearer to us due to the survival of an increasing number of inventories, that is, lists of moveable household contents made at the death of the occupier. Standing buildings provide many examples of fittings (Hall 2005). An influential catalogue of excavated household artefacts from Norwich published in 1993 led the way in dealing with objects by their use and function, not their component material: metal fittings from furniture, lighting and heating equipment, structural ironwork, locks, and painted window glass were recovered from a group of small houses destroyed by fire in 1507 (Margeson 1993). This was followed by corpora of finds from London (Egan 1998) and York (Ottaway and Rogers 2002). In London, landfill deposits dating to the century after 1450 have produced pieces of lead window cames, hinges, pintles, gilded lead mounts from ceilings, and fragments of wooden furniture (Egan 2005). Fireplaces and chimneys were now more widely attached to walls, replacing the former central hearth. Stone fireplaces are found in twelfth-century buildings, but during the fifteenth century they appear in timber-framed and brick houses, and could be bought from a local mason rather like today. Glazed windows and chimneys may have developed simultaneously because of the way smoke escaped from the fire (as it now went up an enclosed chimney, the windows could be glazed). Accounts of 1461–2 for properties in the City of London owned by London Bridge mention white glass, 'blood-red glass', and images in glass (Harding and Wright 1995, 138).

Conclusions

Research on many sites, for instance in Norwich, suggests that medieval houses were usually growing entities with different parts of their structures dating from the fourteenth to the seventeenth centuries, as their functions and the needs of their owners and occupiers changed. Surviving houses reveal up to five different periods of rebuilding in their timber framing: eighteenth-century houses in Bristol incorporate thirteenth- and fourteenth-century masonry. Thus, the very idea of standard or common plan forms, in other words, types of houses at specified periods, must be called into question. It is far more likely that houses were constantly brought up to date, retaining much of their older structure, just like the later re-facing of medieval houses in towns in order to appear Georgian. On that basis the rigid typological classification of house plans, for instance those developed by Pantin fifty years ago (1962–3) and from 1987 by the present writer (Schofield 1987; Schofield and Vince 2005) should be laid aside. Nevertheless, the identification of house plans is not time wasted, and the larger cities (Bristol, London, York) should be studied for the wide range of forms they present, from courtyard mansions to single-room, unheated houses. There is also surprising diversity within medium-sized and smaller towns; houses were narrow and tall in the centre, and low and sideways to the street on the outskirts (Pearson 2009).

At present we are largely ignorant of poorer housing. The fourteenth-century cottages excavated at Brook Street in Winchester were the same size in area as surviving fifteenth-century small houses in Sandwich. The houses of the poor from the twelfth to the sixteenth centuries will have their own history, and they may have evolved more slowly than their more prosperous neighbours. Thus groups of houses at different social and economic levels probably developed at different rates over time.

Finally, London house-plans of the early seventeenth century suggest how large houses were ordered internally by functional area, that is, into groups of ground-floor rooms concerned with commercial, domestic, storage, and service activities, and to have these separate parts in a large urban house was probably a well-established practice by 1540 (Schofield 1994; Schofield and Vince 2005, 113). In Britain and across mainland Europe, archaeologists have been noticeably reluctant to assign proposed functions to individual rooms, such as hall, parlour, or bedchamber, because complete plans and access routes are rarely defined. For medieval houses it may be wise to conclude that men and women, servants and children usually used all the rooms of the house; few spaces were strictly gender-specific (Flather 2007). The further study of commercial activity, however, and in particular the fitting together of a workplace (most often a shop) with residential accommodation would be very worthwhile. Most urban medieval houses were designed around their commercial function and parts; the domestic spaces were always behind or above the commercial, the workspace, which comprised the front face of the property.

Now that we have a body of information from both excavations and standing buildings for a number of towns, it is time to consider whether urban buildings were different from rural buildings, and whether one town looked much like another. Pearson (2005) argues against the traditional view presented by Pantin that urban houses were adaptations of rural ones, suggesting instead that influences may instead have moved from town to country (from the twelfth century for standing buildings, and perhaps earlier from excavated examples). It is also now suggested that rural peasant houses had a distinct character of their own, and were not imitations of urban buildings (Dyer 2013, 112).

Houses in the most compressed parts of towns displayed a peculiar urban characteristic. The trade of the householder was presented at the front, with domestic accommodation to the rear or increasingly above where space was restricted. This need to differentiate work from the home resulted in higher buildings aided by the development of more sophisticated carpentry but constrained by urban regulations and, in consequence, in larger houses and some differentiation of functions between individual rooms. These larger, higher houses had assertive displays, first with jetties and later with exuberant framing, nearly always on the front and more public façade. The house made a face to the town, but inside it was adapted for personal uses, a utensil for family life.

Acknowledgements

I am grateful to Sarah Pearson and Amanda Richardson for criticism of this paper in draft, and to Richard Turner for information on Welsh houses. Thanks are also due to: Alan T. Adams, Andy Chopping, Derek Keene, Carlos Lemos, Museum of London Archaeology, Oxford University Press, and Sarah Pearson for permission to use their illustrations.

References cited

Alix, C. and Épaud, F. (eds) 2013 *La construction en pan de bois au Moyen Âge et à la Renaissance*, Presses universitaires de Rennes, Rennes

Andrews, D. (ed.) 2013 *Discovering Coggeshall 2: the 1575 rental survey and the dated buildings*, John Lewis, Coggeshall

Atkin, M., Carter, A., and Evans, D. H. 1985 *Excavations in Norwich 1971–1978. Part II*, East Anglian Archaeol 26, Norwich

Ayers, B. 2001 'Domestic architecture in Norwich from the twelfth to the seventeenth century', in M. Gläser (ed.), *Der hausbau*, Lübecker Kolloquium zur Stadtarchäologie im Hanseraum III, Verlag Schmidt-Römhild, Lübeck, 35–48

Beaumont James, T. and Roberts, E. 2000 'Winchester and late medieval urban development: from palace to pentice', *Medieval Archaeology* 44, 181–200

Bowsher, D., Dyson, T., Holder, N., and Howell, I. 2007 *The London Guildhall: an archaeological history of a neighbourhood from early medieval to modern times, Part 1*, Museum of London Archaeology Service Monograph 36, London

Brown, A. B. (ed.) 1999 *The Rows of Chester: the Chester Rows Project*, English Heritage Archaeological Report 16, London

Burch, M. and Treveil, P. 2011 *The development of early medieval and later Poultry and Cheapside*, Museum of London Archaeology Monograph 38, London

Carver, M. O. H. 1979 'Three Saxo-Norman tenements in Durham City', *Medieval Archaeology* 23, 1–80

Carver, M. O. H. 1983 *Two town houses in medieval Shrewsbury*, Transactions of Shropshire Archaeological Society 61, Shrewsbury

Clark, D. 2000 'The shop within? An analysis of the architectural evidence for medieval shops', *Architectural History* 43, 58–87

Clarke, H., Pearson, S., Mate, M., and Parfitt, K. 2010 *Sandwich, the 'completest medieval town in England': a study of the town and port from its origins to 1600*, Oxbow Books, Oxford

Crone, A. 2000 'Native tree-ring chronologies from some Scottish medieval burghs', *Medieval Archaeology* 44, 201–16

Daniels, R. 2010 *Hartlepool: an archaeology of the medieval town*, Tees Archaeology Monograph Series 4, Hartlepool

Dyer, C. 2003 'The archaeology of medieval small towns', *Medieval Archaeology* 47, 85–114

Dyer, C. 2013 'Medieval peasant buildings 1250–1550: document and historical significance', in N. Alcock and D. Miles (eds), *The medieval peasant house in Midland England*, Oxbow Books, Oxford, 105–18

Egan, G. 1998 *The medieval household: daily living c.1150–c.1450*, Medieval Finds from Excavations in London 6, Her Majesty's Stationery Office, London

Egan, G. 2005 *Material culture in London in an age of transition*, Museum of London Archaeology Service Monograph 19, London

Esquieu, Y. and Pesez, J.-M. (eds) 1998 *Cent maisons médiévales en France*, CNRS Monographie du CRA 20, Paris

Evans, D. H. 2001 'Urban domestic architecture in the Lower Hull Valley in the medieval and early post-medieval periods', in M. Gläser (ed.), *Der hausbau*, Lübecker Kolloquium zur Stadtarchäologie im Hanseraum III, Verlag Schmidt-Römhild, Lübeck, 49–76

Evans, D. H. and Tomlinson, D. G. 1992 *Excavations at 33–35 Eastgate, Beverley, 1983–86*, Sheffield Excavation Reports 3, Sheffield

Ewan, E. 1990 *Townlife in fourteenth-century Scotland*, Edinburgh University Press, Edinburgh

Fehring, G. P. 1991 *The archaeology of medieval Germany: an introduction*, Routledge, London

Flather, A. 2007 *Gender and space in early modern England*, Boydell Press, Woodbridge

Ford, B. M. and Teague, S. 2011 *Winchester, a city in the making: archaeological excavations between 2002 and 2007 on the sites of Northgate House, Staple Gardens and the former Winchester Library, Jewry St*, Oxford Archaeology Monograph 12, Oxford

Garrigou Grandchamp, P. (ed.) 2006 *La maison au Moyen Âge*, Société Archéologique et Historique de la Charente, Angoulême

Gläser, M. (ed.) 2001 *Der hausbau*, Lübecker Kolloquium zur Stadtarchäologie im Hanseraum III, Verlag Schmidt-Römhild, Lübeck

Goldberg, P. J. P. 2008 'The fashioning of bourgeois domesticity in later medieval England: a material culture perspective', in M. Kowaleski and P. J. P. Goldberg (eds), *Medieval domesticity: home, housing and household in medieval England*, Cambridge University Press, Cambridge, 124–44

Goodburn, D. 1997 'London's early medieval timber buildings: little known traditions of construction'. *Urbanism in Medieval Europe, preprinted papers of Medieval Europe Conference Bruges (1997)* 1, 249–57

Hall, L. 2005 *Period house fixtures & fittings 1300–1900*, Countryside Books, Newbury

Harding, V. and Wright, L. (eds) 1995 *London Bridge: selected accounts and rentals, 1381–1538*, London Record Society 31, London

Horsman, V., Milne, C., and Milne, G. 1988 *Aspects of Saxo-Norman London I: building and street development*, London and Middlesex Archaeological Society Special Paper 11, London

Keene, D. 1985 *Survey of medieval Winchester, Winchester Studies II*, Oxford University Press, Oxford

Kowaleski, M. 2006 'A consumer economy', in R. Horrox and W. M. Ormrod (eds), *A social history of England, 1200–1500*, Cambridge University Press, Cambridge, 238–59

Leech, R. H. 2014 *The town house in medieval and early modern Bristol*, English Heritage, Swindon

Margeson, S. 1993 *Norwich households: the medieval and post-medieval finds from Norwich Survey excavations, 1971–1978*, Norwich Survey/Norfolk Museums Service East Anglian Archaeology Report 58, Norwich

Martin, D. and Martin, B. 2004 *New Winchelsea Sussex: a medieval port town*, Institute of Archaeology, University College London Field Archaeology Unit Monograph 2, London

Milne, G. 1992 *Timber building techniques in London c.900–c.1400*, London and Middlesex Archaeological Society Special Paper 15, London

Moran, M. 2003 *Vernacular building in Shropshire*, Logaston Press, Almeley

Murphy, K. 1997 'Small boroughs in south-west Wales: their planning, early development and defences', in N. Edwards (ed.), *Landscape and settlement in medieval Wales*, Oxbow Books, Oxford, 139–56

Murray, H. K. and Murray, C. 1993 'Excavations at Rattray, Aberdeenshire, a Scottish deserted burgh', *Medieval Archaeology* 37, 108–218

Ottoway, P. and Rogers, N. 2002 *Craft, industry and everyday life: finds from medieval York*, York Archaeological Trust and Council for British Archaeology, The Archaeology of York 17/15, York

Pantin, W. A. 1962–3 'Medieval English town-house plans', *Medieval Archaeology* 6–7, 202–39

Pearson, S. 2005 'Rural and urban houses 1100–1500: "urban adaptation" reconsidered', in K. Giles and C. Dyer (eds), *Town and country in the Middle Ages: contacts and interconnections*, The Society for Medieval Archaeology Monograph 22, Leeds, 43–63

Pearson, S. 2009 'Medieval houses in English towns: form and location', *Vernacular Architecture* 40, 1–22

RCHME 1980: Royal Commission on Historical Monuments England, 1980 *City of Salisbury: I*, Her Majesty's Stationery Office, London

Rees Jones, S. 2008 'Building domesticity in the city: English urban housing before the Black Death', in M. Kowaleski, and P. J. P. Goldberg (eds), *Medieval domesticity: home, housing and household in medieval England*, Cambridge University Press, Cambridge, 66–91

Salzman, L. F. 1967 *Building in England down to 1540*, Clarendon Press, Oxford (revised edn)

Sarfatij, H. 1990 'Dutch towns in the formative period (AD 1000–1400): the archaeology of settlement and building', in J. C. Besteman, J. M. Bos, and H. A. Heidingam (eds), *Medieval archaeology in the Netherlands*, Van Gorcum, Assen/Maastricht, 183–98

Schofield, J. 1987 *The London surveys of Ralph Treswell*, London Topographical Society Publication 135, London

Schofield, J. 1994 'Social perceptions of space in medieval and Tudor London houses', in M. Locock (ed.), *Meaningful architecture: social interpretations of buildings*, Ashgate, Avebury, 188–206

Schofield, J. 2003 *Medieval London houses*, Yale University Press, London (revised edn)

Schofield, J. 2011 *London 1100–1600: the archaeology of a capital city*, Equinox, Sheffield

Schofield, J. and Vince, A. 2005 *Medieval towns: the archaeology of British towns in their European setting*, Equinox, London (revised edn)

Shelley, A. 2005 *Dragon Hall, King Street, Norwich: excavation and survey of a late medieval merchant's trading complex*, East Anglian Archaeology 112, Norwich

Smith, P. 1988 *Houses of the Welsh countryside*, Her Majesty's Stationery Office, London (2nd edn)

Steane, J. and Ayres, J. 2013 *Traditional buildings in the Oxford region c.1300–1840*, Oxbow Books, Oxford

Stell, G. 1988 'Urban buildings', in M. Lynch, M. Spearman, and G. Stell (eds), *The Scottish medieval town*, John Donald, Edinburgh, 60–80

Urry, W. 1967 *Canterbury under the Angevin Kings*, University of London, Athlone Press, London

Yeoman, P. 1995 *Medieval Scotland*, Batsford, London

CHAPTER 20

MEDIEVAL SHOPS

ABBY ANTROBUS

SHOPS and commercial premises formed a fundamental and varied element of the medieval urban landscape, and would have lined many a street. Much as today, they supplied provisions, services, necessities, and luxury goods, once-in-a-lifetime acquisitions, hot pies, hair-cuts, and shoe-mending (e.g. Britnell 2006, 117–18). This chapter reviews the evidence for and recent current debates on the types and character of medieval shops, *shophouses*, stalls, *selds*, and undercrofts, revealing in the process some of the environs experienced by the medieval shopper and the types of structure students of towns should consider when reconstructing medieval towns. It also draws out geographical and chronological trends in commercial building stock (1050–1550) and, in doing so, frames the street as an arena where consumer choices and the businesses and identity of sectors of urban society were made.

The study of medieval shops is not new. Building accounts and contracts, rentals, charters and deeds, judicial records, and guild and civic regulations, all these provide insights into the vibrancy of medieval streets and market practices across Britain (e.g. Kowaleski 2007 for a selection; Salzmann 1952). Further, the gradual recognition of the significance, survival, diversity, development, and, above all, antiquity of urban buildings was particularly engendered by the post-war redevelopment of historic towns, with which the pioneering research of W. A. Pantin is closely associated (Pantin 1962–3; 1963). Despite this, there has been a tendency to perceive the medieval shopping scene as locally organized, primitive, and as an undifferentiated backdrop to a later early modern watershed in retail practice as it moved towards the mass consumerism of the nineteenth century. More recent critical studies in history, archaeology, and architectural history, however, have reached a more nuanced understanding of a widespread and well-developed shopping culture, and the specialized buildings needed for it and commerce generally, by at least 1300, if not at least two centuries before (Keene 1990, 29–30; Benson and Shaw 1999; Blondé et al. 2006; Cox 2000; Howell 2010; Welch 2005; for buildings see Grenville 1997, 165–75; Harris 2002, 47; Pearson 2003; 2005; 2009).

Architectural Detailing

Identifying physical traces of shops is not always easy, particularly where buildings have been continuously modified and traces of fixtures, fittings, and architectural detailing swept away. Medieval shop fronts are characterized by wide arched openings, often paired (Figure 20.1). East Anglia, where the regional rise and decline of the cloth trade has left behind a legacy of late medieval timber-framed buildings, has a particular concentration of surviving examples, comprising four-centred arched window heads, or, for earlier examples, two-centred arches or straight lintels laid onto brackets (Alston 2003, 42; Morrison 2003, 19, 24). The distribution of these window forms is predominantly urban, apart from occasional examples on major roads (Alston 2003, 42). An absence of mortices for glazing bars usually indicates that windows were unglazed, and contemporary images depict a general practice, albeit not necessarily universal, whereby

FIGURE 20.1 The restored early sixteenth-century shop adjacent to St Mary's Guildhall in Lavenham Market Place, owned by the National Trust. Other places to visit include reconstructed shops from Horsham at the Weald and Downland Museum, Singleton (West Sussex); 58 French Street, Southampton (Hampshire); and Abbey Row, 30–50 Church Street, Tewkesbury (Gloucestershire), one of which is set up as a merchant's house

(© Abby Antrobus)

customers made their purchases through the windows from outside the shop (Alexander 2001; Basing 1990; Frugoni 2005; Welch 2005) (Figure 20.2). The importance of windows is reinforced by the occasional let of spaces in them to traders, particularly perhaps to widows (e.g. Keene 1990, 34), and at Bury St Edmunds, twelfth- and thirteenth-century charters often included a clause that allowed the monastic landlords the right to retain or let to foreign merchants the commercial ground floor or windows of properties during fairs (Antrobus 2009, 218–19). Other buildings may have had arcaded or open fronts: an older, stone example is the twelfth-century Jew's House in Lincoln (Harris 2002, 50).

Shop windows would have been shut with internal or external shutters, often indicated by rebates (Stenning 1985, 35). Top shutters, when opened, often formed a canopy to shelter goods and customers, and at No. 2, St Ann's Street, King's Lynn (Norfolk), pulleys were attached to the lintel to facilitate opening (Morrison 2003, 24). Documents mention forelocks and iron hooks to hold the shutters in place, as well as locks and fastenings (Bennell 1989, 199; Leech 2014, 64). Downward- and outward-opening shutters may have been held by chains or rested on legs to provide an external counter or stall board to maximize display or selling space (Keene 1990, 34–6). Saffron Walden Youth Hostel (Essex) has mortices under the window which suggest that a counter was fixed there (Alston 2003, 40), whilst at Blackfriar's Barn and other examples in New Winchelsea (East Sussex), evidence for low walls in front of the walls of halls are

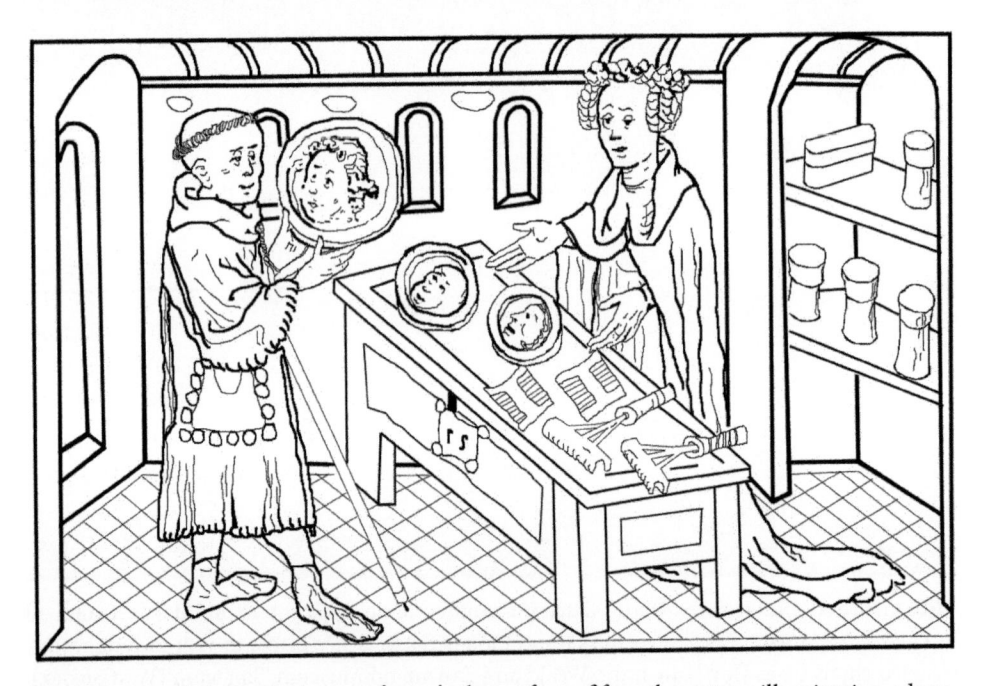

FIGURE 20.2 A customer in a perfumer's shop, after a fifteenth-century illumination adorning John Lydgate's *The pilgrimage of the life of man*, showing the shopkeeper, counter, and storage shelves (British Library Cotton MS Tiberius A VII f. 93), redrawn by the author. Basing discusses the imagery of the mirror and curry combs (1990, 47 and plate III)

(© Abby Antrobus)

interpreted as supporting benches for sitting on or for the display of goods (Martin and Martin 2004, 148).

Pentices or half roofs also gave protection to shop fronts. These are evidenced by contemporary depictions as well as empty sockets in timber framing, for example, mortice holes at Nos 30–32, King Street, King's Lynn (Parker 1971, 125). At The Court Hall, New Winchelsea, a corbel table running along the street façade of a house of *c.*1300 suggests a pentice roof over a likely commercial façade (Martin and Martin 2004, 136). Provision of shelter may have encouraged trade and ensured the comfort of customers. Jetties, whereby joists of a floor projected out to give a stable, cantilevered structure above, also offered shelter to shop fronts below, as well as providing a display space for hanging goods. In some towns, covered walks were created, as at Denbigh (Denbighshire) (Suggett 2012, 77).

There is also a type of doorway which is particularly associated with the medieval shop. These are narrow 'coffin' doors, interpreted variously as a way to control access to rooms and hence stock, and/or as a way to maximize shop space and allow room for display or manufacture. With shops in Cheapside in London at less than 2 m wide, these doors were less than 0.5 m wide. It may be that a form first developed of necessity took on a symbolism of 'the shop', serving to differentiate between doors into commercial and domestic parts of an urban property (Alston 2003, 43–4, 52; Stenning 1985, 35).

Furnishings and Fittings

Shops could be of varying sizes depending on the buildings and plots on which they were built. The King's Lynn Red Register records a shop in 1321 that measured 0.68 x 0.99 m (2¼ by 3¼ ft) (Parker 1971, 125): every space was useful. Shops in Cheapside included small lockable units at 1.82 m (6 ft) wide. In contrast, a 'great shop' in Bucklersbury, also in London, measured 5.5 x 6.7 m (18 by 22¼ ft), and had a probable store house behind (Bennell 1989, 194). It is relatively rare to find direct documentary, architectural, or archaeological evidence for the furnishings of shops prior to the proliferation of probate inventories in the sixteenth century. One unusual reference gives an insight into the interior of the shop of John Welys, cutler, and Johan, his wife, on London Bridge in 1410: their premises had glazed windows, benches in the hall, a wooden wall and lattice, shelves, partitions, and chests (Kowaleski 2007, 142). Among other features noted in documents, 'shewyng bordes' were probably for display (Clarke 2000, 59); coffers or chests for storage could have doubled up as counters, while weigh beams and weights would have included hand balances for coins and goods (e.g. Leech 2014, 402). Detailed study of surviving timber frames can be repaid by traces of large pegs in horizontal rows, which could have supported shelves and benches (Alston 2003, 40), while a linenfold benchback in the gable end of the end shop at No. 7, Town Hill, Wrexham (Clwyd), is a rare survival of original décor (Suggett 2012, 75). As Figure 20.2 shows, contemporary depictions (mostly from mainland Europe) portray shelves, cupboards, benches, counters, trestles, jars, sacks, barrels, and goods on hooks and, perhaps for the more luxurious, fabric drapes. Buckets of fish, casks, and poles strung with sausages, stockings, and shoes are all on show (Alexander 2001; Basing 1990; Bennell 1989, 199; Frugoni 2005; Welch 2005).

Shops of Different Kinds

Documentary and archaeological evidence identifies shops on main streets, side streets, courtyards, market places, in buildings of varying size and status, and accessed from the street or passages in houses, and these have been the subject of typological research (Clarke 2000; Pantin 1963; Stenning 1985). They may have been purpose-built units, with or without ancillary accommodation, or more intimately connected to the more private space of larger complexes such as merchant houses. Hampton Court, a merchant's house at King's Lynn, had a range of shops on the frontage with an archway to a courtyard that led to a fourteenth-century hall, service rooms, and counting house (Parker 1971, 40). Nos 38–42, Watergate, Chester, c.1325, had a stone hall parallel to the street spanning three burgage plots, with a door from the hall for direct access to the commercial frontage of one shop. The hall was open to the roof, and so the shops on the frontage must have had the only access to rooms over them. Jane Grenville compares this to Nos 48–52, Bridge Street, York, a hall had which doors into at least three shops (Grenville 1997, 181–3). The architectural spaces for the conducting of merchant business, which may have involved more intimate sale, personal credit, and bulk exchange, prompts questions about the function of the shops as part of the main household, while the relationship to workshops and tenements generally is another challenge (e.g. Clarke 2000, 74).

Lock-up shops were often under public buildings. For example, shops are recorded under the Tolbooth in Northallerton, North Yorkshire (Newman 1999, 105), and shop windows survive below the Moot Hall at Aldeburgh in Suffolk. At Felsted (Essex), there are four lock-up shops with windows and shutters on the ground floor of the fourteenth-century Trinity Guildhall, flanking a passage to the churchyard (Morrison 2003, 20). Chester's Pentice, which abutted St Peter's Church and housed the sheriff's court from the late thirteenth century, had at least seven shops under it in 1463 (Laughton 2008, 77). Where two or three shops were built under a solar, some were probably live-in units, whilst others were rented out as small commercial premises (Grenville 1997, 174).

Rows or multiple units of timber-framed shops (from symmetrical pairs upwards) were often speculative developments by individuals and institutions, intended to maximize use of commercial frontages and generate revenue. 'Renters' were ubiquitous by 1300 and are often found on plots with limited ground space, for example in market places and shambles, or on the edges of religious precincts (e.g. Bennell 1989, 191, 194). Pantin cites as examples Stranger's Hall in Norwich, or Marshall's Inn in Oxford (1962–3, 175). Archaeologically, the practice of building speculative row shops in the twelfth century is suggested by excavated examples of stone chamber blocks set back from the frontage, with runs of smaller timber buildings that may have been shops or other sublet properties on street frontages (Harris 2002, 49). In corroboration, there are documentary references to *eschopes* in the early twelfth century which ran along the High Street in front of a larger house in Winchester (Keene 1990, 31). Urban manor or merchant houses set back from streets frequently lay behind shop buildings that flanked ostentatious gateways (Brown 1999, 15; Schofield 2003, 61): this was an arrangement that maximized use of a commercial frontage whilst maintaining a presence on the street. Stone doorways of twelfth- to thirteenth-century date are recorded in Bristol (Leech 2014, 67). A thirteenth-century charter from Bury St Edmunds relating to the estate of Richard Fitz Drogo describes 'rents' on the street front of what is now Abbeygate Street, flanking the gateway to his stone house. A complex of buildings on that street (Nos 46–7) was recorded during restoration in 1988 and, if not the properties mentioned, it certainly provides a good parallel: a Norman stone building stood to the rear of the plot and, on the frontage, timber framing of *c*.1300 was identified, with holes that may have held pegs for shelving or a counter. Stone party walls and the cellar survived, with evidence for access through to the rear. The timber framing was sparse, including some pine, which was interpreted by architectural historian Philip Aitkens to be evidence of an economic approach to construction (Antrobus 2009, 217, 242).

Often-cited examples of rows are Butcher's Row in Shrewsbury (Shropshire), which was built by the Abbot of Lilleshall *c*.1459; Spon Street in Coventry (West Midlands); Abbey Row in Tewkesbury (Gloucestershire), which had small halls to the rear of shops and chambers on the street front (Martin and Martin 2004, 135); and the Rows of York, including Lady Row on Goodramgate constructed in 1315 against the churchyard of Holy Trinity, which had rooms over (Grenville 1997, 190). The form and provision of other spaces varies. Some shops were built with multiple rooms—perhaps studies, offices or domestic provision (Clarke 2000, 74); by 1400, London examples often had an upstairs hall and kitchen (Bennell 1989, 194), in other places these were to the rear. A contract of 1410 for building three houses in London on Friday Street required a shop each on the ground floor with a sale room and office; first-floor hall, larder, and kitchen, second-floor principal chamber, privy, and bedroom (Salzmann 1952, 483–5)—different accommodation to the more modest Lady Row, for example.

A particular question in current debate is whether these units were intended to be lived in or whether they were intended more for use as workshops and storage, and indeed whether, if more commercial, there are larger scale patterns to be discerned in the trading organization of urban trade and industry. Nos 12–15, Newgate in York, lining the south side of St Sampson's Church, are not adorned, with scarce chamfering and un-jowled crown posts, and were perhaps built with economy in mind (Short 1979, 120). Similarly, Lady Row has simple jettied framing which may either reflect the date or function of the buildings (Grenville 1997, 190). Quoting Jayne Rimmer's work on smaller houses in York, Sarah Pearson (2009, 7) has pointed out that not all smaller houses (without halls) were 'poor': some were in the hands of wealthier tenants and freemen, whose interests may have been spread across the city, and some were of high quality and commanded high rents, which may indicate that buildings were used for craft, trade, or storage, as has also been noted for Sandwich (Clarke et al. 2010, 191). Merchants might have several shops operating for distribution; for example, Richard de Elsyng, a London mercer, in 1332 had shops in Soper Lane with goods looked after by three apprentices (Keene 2006, 132). Unfortunately, contemporary terminology does not provide elucidation on the domestic versus commercial question. For Bristol, a rental of 1412 records buildings as shop, hall, or 'hall and shop', with halls commanding two to three times the rent, and in 1473 a clerk recording endowments in the same city made a distinction between *hallhouses* and *shophouses*. Roger Leech's study explores them in relation to building types, suggesting that generally the latter may refer to one or more rooms for living over a shop, and the former usually larger complexes associated with a hall (Leech 2014, 117–23).

Another kind of fundamentally commercial structure in the urban context was the undercroft and these are often the earliest surviving elements of buildings. Undercrofts provided cool, dark, constant environments well protected from fire, ideal for the storage of wine and also, being slightly damp, for the storage of other goods such as woollen cloth and furs. The presence of undercrofts is to some extent related to local topography and geology, but also to particular activities and regional architectural styles; their role and purpose as primarily for storage, retail, or as taverns has been a subject of debate, particularly in relation to the wine trade (e.g. Grenville 1997, 180; Pearson 2003, 417; Schofield 2003, 76). In some cases, cellars or undercrofts may have served as a storage area for premises above them or elsewhere but frequently they had their own access from the street and may have served as semi-public accessible spaces that could have been let separately as spaces for a workshop, sale, or display. Many of the fourteenth-century cellars from New Winchelsea had wide street entries and stairs, one of which, the Salutation, had carved corbels and handrails. Some were lit with light wells and bore traces of plaster finish, and were equipped with cupboards (Martin and Martin 2004, 111, and ch. 9). The undercroft on Simnel Street, Southampton, had corbels carved with heads, carved bosses, moulded ribs, hooded fireplaces, and lamp brackets with ball flower ornaments and Patrick Faulkner imagined a scene where this space was used as a sales room for luxury goods, perhaps with customers looking at silks before a fire (Faulkner 1966, 131). The vaulting at a fourteenth-century example from Chepstow (Monmouthshire) has a boss carved with vines, and another with a foliate head with a protruding tongue. This possibly represents Bacchus and may therefore indicate a function as an inn and/or for the storage and sale of wine (Suggett 2012, 67).

Undercrofts introduce split-level retailing as a method by which street frontages could be maximized through the provision of multi-storey commercial fronts accessed from the street. The prime example is the celebrated Chester Rows, where shops over semi-subterranean undercrofts were joined by galleried and continuous first-floor walkways, with provision for stall boards opposite shops in what were probably originally porch extensions over the undercrofts. The use of communal galleried walkways maximizes undisturbed frontage at first-floor level by minimizing the number of required sets of steps. Chester flourished as a garrison centre for Edward I's campaigns in Wales and at least twenty-five of the undercrofts date to the thirteenth century. The

Chester Rows may represent deliberate design, or communal planning and a degree of individual subscription to a building scheme, and nuanced research on their origins sets them as a local response to a more widespread practice of split-level retailing (Brown 1999; Faulkner 1966; Harris 2000).

EVOLUTION FROM MARKET STALLS

Some commercial premises may have their origins as market infill, fossilized stalls, or booths. At their most basic, these would have been shelters to which boards could be fixed, with cloth awnings and timber cross beams from which to show wares. By the fourteenth century, Gallowgate and Broad Streets in Aberdeen were populated by semi-permanent stalls, for example (Cameron and Stones 2002, 146), and Denbigh Shop Row is based on such units (Suggett 2012, 57). Elsewhere, traders could rent spaces and sell from chests, tables booths, or cupboards—effectively covered bazaars—to which the word *seld* or *seuda* was applied into the sixteenth century. Usually perpendicular to and entered from main shopping streets, the *seld* might be located in a hall or undercroft: some were single-storey buildings—at least one London example had a louvre in the roof—while others had buildings over them (Keene 2006, 38; Morrison 2003, 24; Schofield 2003, 55). In Bristol, there were *selds* on some of the more central streets, including *Ropeseld* at Nos 11–13, High Street (1309), which was 30 ft wide (9.1 m), and a *seld* at No. 47, Corn Street (1290), which was on the lands of St Augustine's Abbey (Leech 2014, 23). Around 1300, there were an estimated four hundred shops in Cheapside, London, with a further four thousand units in *selds* (Keene 2006, 135). Examples here extended back up to 30 m from the street frontage, and could have been up to 7 m wide, with three or four shops at their front (Keene 2006, 133). Records suggest that St Martin's Seld, off Soper Lane, was furnished with stalls, benches, and chests on either side of a central passage. In 1250, there were twenty-one plots and thirty chests within it, with traders specializing in the sale of gloves and leather; by 1300 it was associated with trade in girdles and other wares of mercers (Keene 1990, 38).

CHRONOLOGICAL COMMENT

The 'long thirteenth century' saw a growth in the size and number of towns, together with an increasing reliance on cash and credit transactions; intensification in buying, selling, and transporting goods; greater movement of bulk commodities, changes in production, consumption, and purchasing patterns; rising population growth; and innovation and specialization in industry (Britnell 1996; Miller and Hatcher 1995). This is the context for the development of the shops, undercrofts, and *selds* described above (Harris 2002, 47). Many towns were laid out, initially with spacious plots, but frontages became heavily developed and subdivided; *selds*, for example, are an interesting marker of the pressure on space and the proliferation of smaller-scale traders. Investment in shops and properties was common during this period, as was speculative development. Detailed study of Bury St Edmunds, for example, shows investments by individuals which, within the context of monastic planning and lordship, were formative of a clustering of stone houses and the trade of goldsmiths at the Great Gate of the abbey in the twelfth century, as well as deliberate concentrations of suburban estates by the town's hospitals which must have related to the ribbon development of suburbs from the twelfth century and the economic benefit of building on routes into a busy town (Antrobus 2009, 47, 201–8).

After the fourteenth century, however, rows and *selds*, split-level retailing, and undercrofts seem to become less fashionable (see Harris 2000; Leech 2014, 146 for changes in Bristol), and social and economic changes associated with the Black Death may be significant. The most ornate of the London cellars, for example, date to the period 1270–1400, which is comparable to those in Chester, Southampton, Stamford, and Canterbury (again, connection is made to the wine trade) (Schofield 2003, 81). Perhaps with decreasing pressure and land value, from the fourteenth century, reduced urban property values meant that the attraction of using cellars as public space rather than storage had lessened. More generally, for York, Short has considered factors such as a decreased demand for smaller houses when people could now afford larger ones (Short 1979, 131). The prevalence of smaller shops on Cheapside's frontage was also decreasing in the mid-fourteenth century and, by the fifteenth century, many of the tiniest had disappeared, with more residential properties, warehouses and larger premises (Schofield 2003, 73, 116). Records from Chester in the 1350s show shops empty and in danger of collapse, with ruined buildings through the city (Brown 1999, 63). On a macroscale, as well as responses to economic factors, these changes have been considered in the context of changing organization of trade and commerce (e.g. Keene 2006).

Shops in the Townscape

Street and row names which indicate grouping of trades at formative times are a legacy of many medieval towns (e.g. Lilley 2002). The organization of towns in this manner may have resulted both from top–down imposition, and an individual or communal subscription to urban order. Grouped trades would have encouraged competition and facilitated purchases for the seller, and encouraged self or communal regulation (Davis 2012). At the same time, there is a general coincidence between prime commercial spaces and the shops of purveyors of high value and luxury goods such as gold, spices, gloves, and textiles. In Cheapside around 1500, there were fifty-two goldsmith's shops concentrated on La Strada leading to St Paul's (Britnell 2006, 116). Bridges and routes to gates also funnelled passing trade. In York, some of the wealthiest medieval parishes with highest rents and taxes were adjacent to the river and especially clustered round

Ouse Bridge. The bridge itself, which was built with shops from the early fourteenth century, has been likened to the 'Bond Street of Medieval York' by Sarah Rees Jones (quoted in Wilson and Mee 2002, 41). In 1440–1, it was occupied by barbers, glovers, cutlers, furbishers, and merchants, with buildings cantilevered out over edge (Wilson and Mee 2002, 26). London Bridge was similarly populated, with approximately 138 shops in 1358 (Kowaleski 2007, 142).

Important though it is to contemplate the development of the plan of the medieval town, consideration of the street scene as a three-dimensional space is also very worthwhile. While the location of buildings was important so is how they were presented and, where we have information from patrons or standing buildings, it is evident that some thought went into design details. In the context of commercial enterprise, the shop front is an active medium for garnering business. Spandrels in window arches were often richly decorated, and a corpus of corner properties from Ludlow, Lincoln, Shrewsbury, Salisbury, have fine carpentry on jetties, bracing, dragon beams, and posts (Grenville 1997, 183). A unique architect's drawing dating to 1520–30, bound into a register of the Bishop of Worcester, depicts a row of four shops, with spandrels in the four centred arched head and decoration on the street frontage (Charles and Down 1972). Other written orders imply imitation and emulation: for Southwark in 1373 the Prior of Lewes was to have two rows of shops at the gatehouse '12 feet front to back with a jutting upper storey, on the lines of Adam Frauncey's range of shops at the Friar's Austin' (Salzmann 1952, 446). Buildings represented investment, and effort was put in to creating inviting environments.

Michael Camille's portrayal of streets as a canvass on which signs and images put up by different people in late medieval French streets is evocative (2001, 92–3). Ale sellers hung up poles or wreaths, bakers bread, potters pots but other signs may have been more symbolic or quasi-religious, for example, the icon of St Lawrence's grill for a meat seller (Camille 2001, 102–3). Signs got to be so large that a London act of 1375 set out fines for poles hung with signs more than 7 ft out as they impeded riders and, if too heavy, damaged buildings (Camille 2000, 22). Buildings became known by their sign; for example, the *seld* of 'The Leg' (1408) had its origins as 'Seld of the Huse' 1321–2 (Keene 1990, 39). The Painted Seld 1220 (later Broad Seld) on London's Cheapside may have been brightly coloured (Keene 2006, 135). With goods on display too, the street presented a multisensory experience for the shopper (see Chapter 45). There is more scope to explore this field by tracing British evidence.

Narratives give some insight into a walk down a medieval street, ranging from Alexander Neckham's twelfth-century descriptions of Paris in *De naturis rerum* (Holmes 1966, 60–2); William FitzStephen's *Description of London* c.1173, which particularly describes fast food ('there is in London on the river bank a public cook shop. There, eatables are to be found every day, dishes of meat; roast, fried and boiled... coarser for the poor, more delicate for the rich'; Douglas and Greenaway 1953, 958); and John Lydgate's later medieval *London Lykpeny*, which portrays varied sellers and hustlers down London streets (Kowaleski 2007, 131–2). Shop-keeping was also a skill, and Derek Keene has suggested that in 1350 as for 1650, the interplay between retailed and purchaser was 'carefully and theatrically managed ... to encourage the shopper to indulge in the delights of choice and acquisition' (Keene 2006, 136): much as it is in many contemporary situations. There is not scope to offer more than a passing reference to the identity of shop-keepers here, although it is worth noting that trade was subject to regulation, and the freedom of a town was often a passport to free trade. Women were prominent as shop-keepers, particularly widows: Margary of the Buttershops in Chester 1322–3 is recorded for posterity for her crime of forestalling cheese and butter (selling before permitted hours) (Laughton 2008, 43).

Conclusion

Future opportunities lie in detailed research and the multidisciplinary combination of historical, architectural, and archaeological evidence, particularly, for example, into evolving urban streets. This is not without challenges: it is rare to find exact correlations between documentary sources and physical remains, although detailed study may reap dividends. Fieldwork is required to record and understand features, particularly as buildings are restored or altered. This evidence may be as subtle and difficult to date as empty mortices in timber framing relating to openings, shelves, and partitions: often all that remains of buildings formerly subdivided into shops, *selds*, booths, and lock-ups are the stone party walls (Harris 2002, 55). In excavated sites, shops as discussed here, with their ephemeral traces (rather than workshops in particular), are often evidenced by 'gaps'. More generally, medieval perceptions of shops as semi-public spaces would be rewarding, increasing commercialization did not go unnoticed to contemporary moral, ideological, or social comment and drinking, perfidy, fraud, injustice, and avarice are all themes to be found in literature (Davis 2012, 2). As a closing comment, the openness of shops and display of goods available must on some level be related to the propagation of desires for goods, changing fashions, consumer choices, and emulation. Shops therefore framed social and cultural encounters in addition to commercial ones. Many objects and ecofacts in the archaeological record, which engender their own questions of fashion, manufacture, distribution networks, and consumption, will have passed through their doors and windows.

References cited

Alexander, J. J. G. 2001 '"The butcher, the baker and the candlestick maker": images of urban labor, manufacture and shopkeeping from the Middle Ages', in C. Perry (ed.), *Material culture and cultural materialisms in the Middle Ages and the Renaissance*, Arizona Studies in the Middle Ages and Renaissance 5, Brepols, Turnhout, 89–110

Alston, L. 2003 'Late medieval workshops in East Anglia', in P. S. Barnwell and M. Airs (eds), *The vernacular workshop: from craft to industry 1400–1900*, Council for British Archaeology Research Report 140, 38–59

Antrobus, A. 2009 *Urbanisation and the urban landscape: building medieval Bury St Edmunds*, unpublished PhD thesis, University of Durham

Basing, P. 1990 *Trades and crafts in medieval manuscripts*, The British Library, London

Bennell, J. 1989 'Shop and office in medieval and Tudor London', *Transactions of the London and Middlesex Archaeological Society* 40, 189–206

Benson, J. and Shaw, G. (eds) 1999 *The retailing industry vol. I: perspectives and the Early Modern period*, Taurus, London

Blondé, B., Stabel, P., Stobart, J., and Van Damme, I. (eds) 2006 *Buyers and sellers: retail circuits and practices in medieval and early modern Europe*, Brepols, Turnhout

Britnell, R. H. 1996 *The commercialisation of English society*, Manchester University Press, Manchester (2nd edn)

Britnell, R. H. 2006 'Markets, shops, inns, taverns and private houses in medieval English trade', in B. Blondé, P. Stabel, J. Stobart, and I. Van Damme (eds), *Buyers and sellers: retail circuits and practices in medieval and early modern Europe*, Brepols, Turnhout, 109–23

Brown, A. 1999 *The Rows of Chester: the Chester Rows Research Project*, English Heritage, London

Cameron, A. S. and Stones, J. A. (eds) 2001 *Aberdeen: an in depth view of the city's past*, The Society of Antiquaries of Scotland Monograph 19, Edinburgh

Camille, M. 2000 'Signs of the city: place, power and public fantasy in medieval Paris', in B. Hanawalt and M. Kobialka (ed.), *Medieval practices of space*, University of Minnesota Press, London, 1–36

Camille, M. 2001 'Signs on medieval street corners', in G. Jaritz (ed.), *Die Strasse: zur funktion und perzeption öffentlichen Raums in späte Mittelalter*, Verlag/Die Österriechischen Akademie der Wissenschaften, Vienna, 91–118

Charles, F. W. B. and Down, K. 1972 'A sixteenth century drawing of a timber-framed town house', *Transactions of the Worcestershire Archaeological Society Series* 3, vol. 3, 67–73

Clarke, D. 2000 'The shop within? An analysis of the architectural evidence for medieval shops', *Architectural History* 43, 58–87

Clarke, H., Mate, M., Parfitt, K., and Pearson, S. 2010 *Sandwich, the completest medieval town in England: a study of the town and port from its origins to 1600*, Oxbow, Oxford

Cox, N. 2000 *The complete tradesman: a study of retailing*, Ashgate, Aldershot

Davis, J. 2012 *Life, law and ethics in the English marketplace, 1200–1500*, Cambridge University Press, Cambridge

Douglas, D. and Greenaway, G. (eds) *English historical documents 1042–1189*, Eyre and Spottiswoode, London

Faulkner, P. A. 1966 'Medieval undercrofts and town houses', *The Archaeological Journal* 123, 120–35

Frugoni, C. 2005 *A day in a medieval city*, The University of Chicago Press, London

Grenville, J. 1997 *Medieval housing*, Leicester University Press, Leicester

Harris, R. B. 2000 'The origins of the Chester Rows', in A. Thacker (ed.), *Medieval art, archaeology and architecture at Chester*, BAA Conference Transactions XXII, Leeds, 132–51

Harris, R. B. 2002 'The English medieval townhouse as evidence for the property market', in D. Pitte and B. Ayers (eds), *The medieval house in Normandy and England: Proceedings of seminars in Rouen and Norwich (1998–1999)*, Société Libre d'Émulation de la Seine Maritime, Rouen, 47–56

Holmes, U. T. 1966 *Daily living in the twelfth century, based on the observations of Alexander Neckham in London and Paris*, University of Wisconsin Press, London

Howell, M. C. 2010 *Commerce before Capitalism in Europe 1300–1600*, Cambridge University Press, Cambridge

Keene, D. 1990 'Shops and shopping in medieval London', in L. Grant (ed.), *Medieval art, architecture and archaeology in London*, British Archaeological Association Conference Transactions 10, London, 29–46

Keene, D. 2006 'Sites of desire: shops, selds and wardrobes in London and other English cities, 1100–1550', in B. Blondé, P. Stabel, I. Van Damme, and J. Stobart (eds), *Retail circuits and practices in medieval and early modern Europe*, Brepols, Turnhout, 125–53

Kowaleski, M. (ed.) 2007 *Medieval towns: a reader*, Broadview Press, Peterborough, Canada

Laughton, J. 2008 *Life in a late medieval city: Chester, 1275–1520*, Windgather Press, Oxford

Leech, R. 2014 *The town house in medieval and early modern Bristol*, English Heritage, Swindon

Lilley, K. 2002 *Urban life in the Middle Ages*, Palgrave Macmillan, London

Martin, D. and Martin, B. 2004 *New Winchelsea, Sussex: a medieval port town*, English Heritage, King's Lynn

Miller, E. and Hatcher, J. 1995 *Medieval England; towns, commerce and crafts 1086–1348*, Longman, London

Newman, C. M. 1999 *Late medieval Northallerton*, Shaun Tyas, Stamford

Morrison, K. A. 2003 *English shops and shopping*, Yale University Press/English Heritage, London

Pantin, W. A. 1963 'Some medieval English town houses: a study in adaption', in I. L. Foster and L. Alcock (eds), *Culture and environment: essays in honour of Cyril Fox*, Routledge and Keegan Paul, London, 445–78

Pantin, W. A. 1962–3 'The merchant's houses and warehouses of King's Lynn', *Medieval Archaeology* 6–7, 173–81

Parker, V. 1971 *The making of King's Lynn: secular buildings from the 11th to the 17th centuries*, Oxford University Press, London

Pearson, S. 2003 'Houses, shops and storage: building evidence from two Kentish ports', in C. Beattie, A. Maslakovic, and S. Rees Jones (eds), *The medieval household in Christian Europe*, Brepols, Turnhout, 409–31

Pearson, S. 2005 'Rural and urban houses 1100–1500: "urban adaptation" reconsidered', in K. Giles and C. Dyer (eds), *Town and country in the Middle Ages: contacts and interconnections*, The Society for Medieval Archaeology Monograph 22, Leeds, 43–63

Pearson, S. 2009 'Medieval houses in English towns: form and location', *Vernacular Architecture* 40, 1–23

Salzmann, L. F. 1952 *Building in England down to 1540*, Clarendon Press, Oxford

Schofield, J. 2003 *Medieval London houses*, Yale University Press, London

Short, P. 1979 'The fourteenth-century rows of York', *The Archaeological Journal* 137, 86–136

Stenning, D. 1985 'Timber framed shops 1300–1600: comparative plans', *Vernacular Architecture* 16, 35–9

Suggett, R. 2012 'Townscape 1400–1600', in H. Fulton (ed.), *Urban culture in medieval Wales*, University of Wales Press, Cardiff, 51–94

Welch, E. 2005 *Shopping in the Renaissance: consumer cultures in Italy 1400–1600*, Yale University Press, London

Wilson, B. and Mee, F. 2002 *The fairest arch in England: old Ouse Bridge, York, and its buildings: the pictorial evidence*, Archaeology of York Supplementary Series VI 2, York

CHAPTER 21

TOWN AND COUNTRYSIDE

CHRISTOPHER DYER

In the twelfth and thirteenth centuries towns were a dynamic force in most of medieval Europe, and British towns advanced like those on the Continent, though with two distinct chronologies. England's existing urban base in 1100 was near to a hundred towns, which then increased sixfold by 1300. Towns in Scotland and Wales were still at an early stage in 1100, with more small-scale trade centres than well-established towns, but between them they could count more than 150 towns by 1300. Not just in most of Scotland and Wales, but also in some English regions, especially in the north, towns were appearing for the first time in the twelfth and thirteenth centuries. Between 1100 and 1300 the more important centres, mainly confined to eastern, southern, and midland England with outliers at Chester and Exeter, grew in size: thirty-three may have had more than one thousand inhabitants in 1100, but by 1300 sixty or so had greater than two thousand (Dyer 2000). The walled area of the larger towns, often in the region of 40–50 ha, was usually surrounded by suburbs which added at least another 20 ha to the built-up area (Kermode 2000). Space within the towns was more densely occupied, as the plots behind houses filled with cottages and workshops.

Towns were still dynamic in 1300–1540. They lost population and their housing stock diminished, so that many urban excavations (at Leicester and Ely for example) show that the houses which had taken over former agricultural land in earlier centuries were vacated and their sites reverted to farming in the fourteenth century (Finn 2004, 22–30; Mortimer et al. 2005). A few towns like Roxburgh in Scotland and Caus in Shropshire were abandoned. Within towns throughout Britain which were in no danger of depopulation, the density of buildings was reduced, and the area devoted to gardens and orchards increased. However, in a remarkable tribute to the resilience and stability of the earlier urban growth, despite the Great Famine of 1315–17, the Black Death of 1348–50, the halving of the whole population, and all of the problems of disruptive war and trade depressions, the great majority of towns survived and continued to perform the functions that had enabled them to grow in earlier centuries. They were smaller, but could still serve as market centres in their locality. A few even managed to expand against the trend, Colchester and Coventry for example, and a handful of new towns appeared like Pensford in the clothing country on the Somerset/Wiltshire border.

The countryside was sharing in the dynamism. Rural settlements, which had been abundant before the urban growth that began in the late ninth century, went through important processes of reorganization such as village nucleation while the towns were surging forwards. Whenever a hamlet or farmstead is excavated in the Sussex Weald or on the edge of the Essex marshes or on Dartmoor the first phase is often dated to the twelfth or thirteenth centuries which helps to date a process of internal colonization. After 1300 villages shrank in size, and in the long run hundreds of villages and thousands of smaller settlements were abandoned. In that respect the rural settlements seem less durable than the towns but, as with the towns, they did not all run downhill, as new farms and cottages were founded in the fifteenth century reflecting new forms of landholding and the spread of rural industry.

Comparing the ups and downs of town and country, one might be glibly tempted to say that they existed in parallel and had similar experiences. But a deeper probing sees some complex interconnections. Was town growth driven by the engine of rural expansion, which could populate the towns with immigrants, and fill the markets with surplus produce? Or were the towns the motor which powered the country dwellers into expansion and new ventures? Rural and urban societies were intertwined and encouraged each other, and their mutual stimulus had profound effects on the outlook of everyone, both rich and poor. The population in the fourteenth and fifteenth centuries reverted to a level similar to that of the eleventh century, but the economy did not go back to its underdeveloped state of 1086, as it had been transformed by the connections and exchanges that came from a pervasive urban presence.

How do we draw the line between town and country? We cannot do this with any certainty, especially after historians abandoned legal and tenurial definitions based on the 'borough' and instead favoured the idea that in a town the inhabitants pursued a variety of occupations (Reynolds 1977, 87–90). Full lists of trades and crafts are scarce in the documents, but excavation often produces evidence from crafts in the form of slag, crucibles, pieces of worked bone, leather offcuts, spindle-whorls, and manufacturing detritus (see Chapter 30). These are often found in accumulations of rubbish in middens or pits which figure prominently in larger towns. Urban sites also produce abundant traces of consumption, the result of large numbers of people living in a confined space, and leaving behind heaps of animal bones, shells, potsherds, and much else. When preservation conditions are right, the botanical remains of food plants are found, together with vegetation used for animal fodder, litter, thatch, and strewing on floors (see Chapter 8). Towns contained large ovens and other structures for preparing food, and storage facilities for food and drink, such as undercrofts or cellars for barrels of wine (see Chapter 20). London even had an impressive public granary built around 1440, though it was soon converted into a market (Samuel 1989). No excavation is needed to recognize the distinctive features of the town plan which are still visible in the modern town centres, with market place, encroachments from permanent market stalls, streets with rows of houses, long narrow burgage plots, and an infrastructure of bridges, mills, and quays (Slater 2000) (Figure 21.1). Many towns expressed their sense of confidence and civic unity through churches and chapels, guildhalls, schools, almshouses, and hospitals (see Chapter 52). Some of these assets were

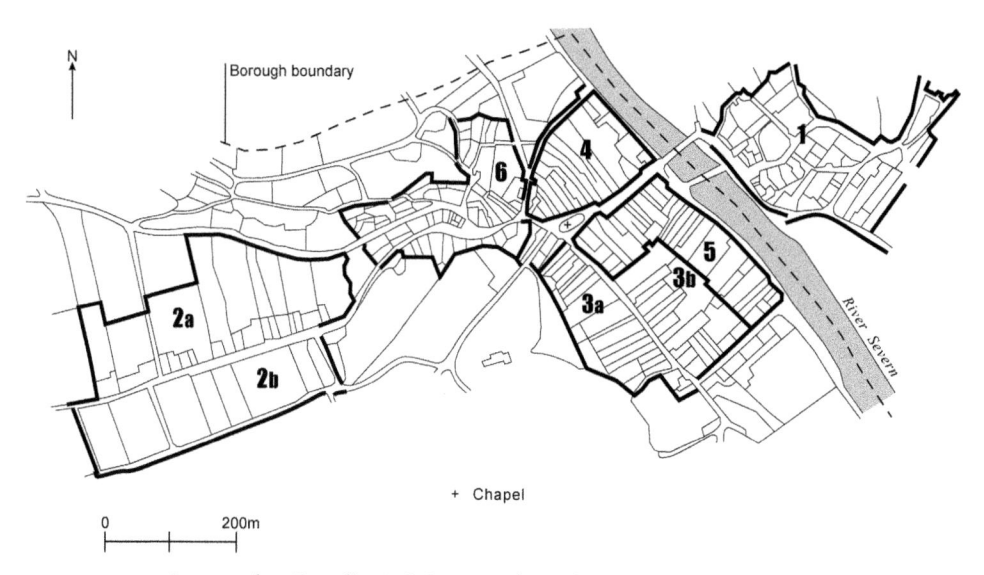

FIGURE 21.1 A town plan: Bewdley in Worcestershire, showing streets and property boundaries in successive phases of growth, beginning in the thirteenth century (after Slater 1990, fig. 4.1)

(© Alejandra Gutiérrez)

provided by the lord of the town, but many public buildings were funded either by wealthy townsmen or more often by collective efforts by many townspeople.

Houses present the most striking contrast between town and country. There are some similarities in the domestic plan, as the hall could have been the principal room in both rural and urban houses, though in towns one was more likely to encounter halls on the first floor, or even houses without an easily recognized hall (Pearson 2005; 2009; see Chapter 19 in this *Handbook*). Outside the south-east, rural houses only gradually acquired wings with two storeys, whereas from the late twelfth century two storeys or more were normal in towns. Townspeople's houses were short of space, which led to the jettying of upper floors. Urban houses were more likely to be supplied with a garderobe and cesspit. In both town and country houses were places where work was done, so the peasants' houses were accompanied by a barn and other outbuildings around a yard. Town houses in more cramped conditions incorporated shops for selling goods, workshops for making them, and stores for raw materials or finished goods (Figure 21.2). Beneath the house, especially but not exclusively in larger towns, an undercroft or cellar might be used as a retail or storage space. Our view of these buildings tends to be coloured by the impressive surviving examples with three storeys, six or more rooms or chambers where family, servants, and apprentices slept and from which business was conducted. The grandest town centre houses might be ranged round a courtyard, with a row of shops on the street frontage which were rented out to a number of tenants. From a few houses still standing, and even more often from excavated buildings, we know of small houses with only one or two rooms and no obvious means of heating. Those found in the Scottish towns like Perth had only one storey and were built rather flimsily

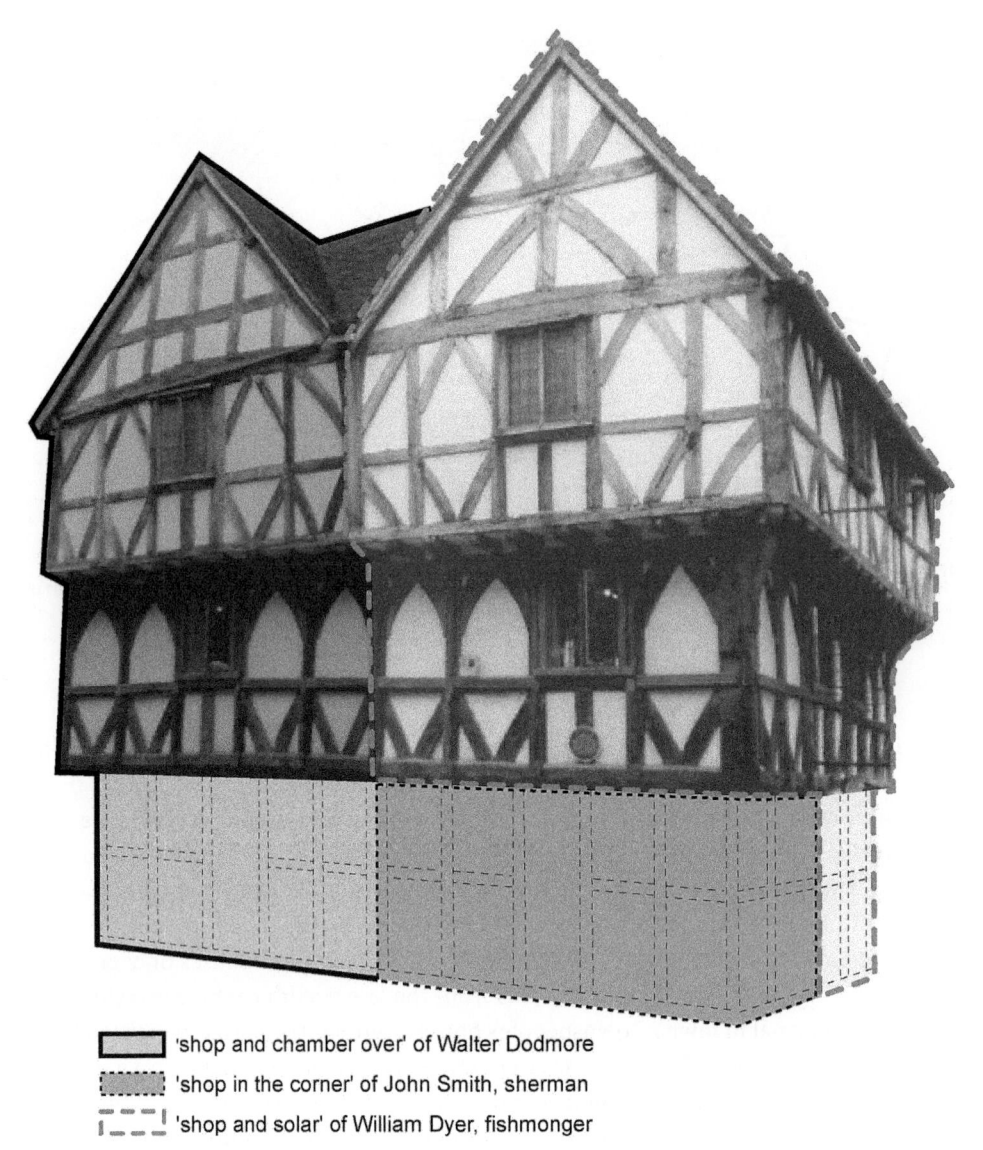

▬▬▬ 'shop and chamber over' of Walter Dodmore
▭▭▭ 'shop in the corner' of John Smith, sherman
┌╴╴╴┐ 'shop and solar' of William Dyer, fishmonger

FIGURE 21.2 A town house: a three-storey corner shop at Ludlow (Shropshire) showing a combination of residential and commercial use in the 1430s (after Pearson 2009, fig. 7)

(© Alejandra Gutiérrez)

of stakes and wattle, though more substantial building techniques were adopted in the late thirteenth century (Perry et al. 2010, 112–13, 127–47). Everyone agrees that houses in towns differed from those in the country. The technology for building stable two-storey or multi-storey structures was devised in towns around 1200, and houses with two or more storeys could accommodate high densities of people in compact urban settlements. But the idea persists that town houses developed from rural originals, and we can debate whether the urban family or household was based on different principles from those found in the country (Grenville 2008).

Sometimes the impression is given that towns represented opulence in contrast with rural poverty, hence the flow of migrants to build up urban populations and sustain them. Small houses indicate one dimension of poverty within the urban community, and another comes from human bones found in urban churchyards, of which the most striking example was that of the deprived York parish of St Helen-on-the-Walls. The bones revealed, when compared with the rural burials at nearby Wharram Percy, a short life span, a high incidence of episodes of infectious disease or malnutrition, and vulnerability to atmospheric pollution (Dawes and Magilton 1980; see Chapter 51 in this Handbook).

At the other end of society, kings and aristocrats clearly perceived towns as important centres for the visible exercise of their power. Within a generation or two of the Norman Conquest the larger towns had a castle imposed on them, and cities with cathedrals saw these structures rebuilt in a new style and a larger scale. Monasteries, which often lay in towns, were also transformed. The aristocracy in later centuries continued to regard towns as backdrops for their displays of grandeur and wealth, with the rebuilding of some urban castles, and the construction of the town houses of gentry as well as greater families. Towns were founded next to castles such as Dunster (Somerset) or Tutbury (Staffordshire) because a dependent town was as much a status symbol as a deer park, a monastic house, or collegiate church. Some religious houses were added to larger towns in order to cater for the extra needs of a large and potentially heretical population. In the twelfth century Augustinian canons settled near towns, and in the thirteenth friaries were founded, specifically in larger towns (see Chapter 35).

Town communities had an internal life, in which employment, manufacture, and religious worship could all be sustained from within the resources of the settlement. The larger the town, the more it depended also on networks binding towns together, so that, for example, pottery from distant rural centres of manufacture would have been trafficked from town to town. The grave slabs carved with crosses at Barnack in Northamptonshire which are found in south Lincolnshire and east Leicestershire could have passed through the hands of traders in Stamford (Butler 1964, 118–25). Towns also can be arranged in hierarchies, in which smaller towns gathered produce, such as wool or grain, for transmission up to the larger and more complex centres, and in the reverse direction manufactured and imported goods would be distributed from the large towns and ports to the market towns. Travel between towns and through towns depended mainly on roads, and journeys were made easier by bridge building, and by the inns which provided accommodation, especially in the so-called 'thoroughfare towns' (see Chapter 22).

The most important function of any town, especially the numerous smaller market towns, was to serve the surrounding rural population (Figure 21.3). Some towns claimed that they had a privilege of trade within their vicinity, and a lord might seek to compel rural tenants to use his town's market. Such claims were not sustained in England, though the monopolies granted to Scottish and Welsh towns (such as the grant in 1285

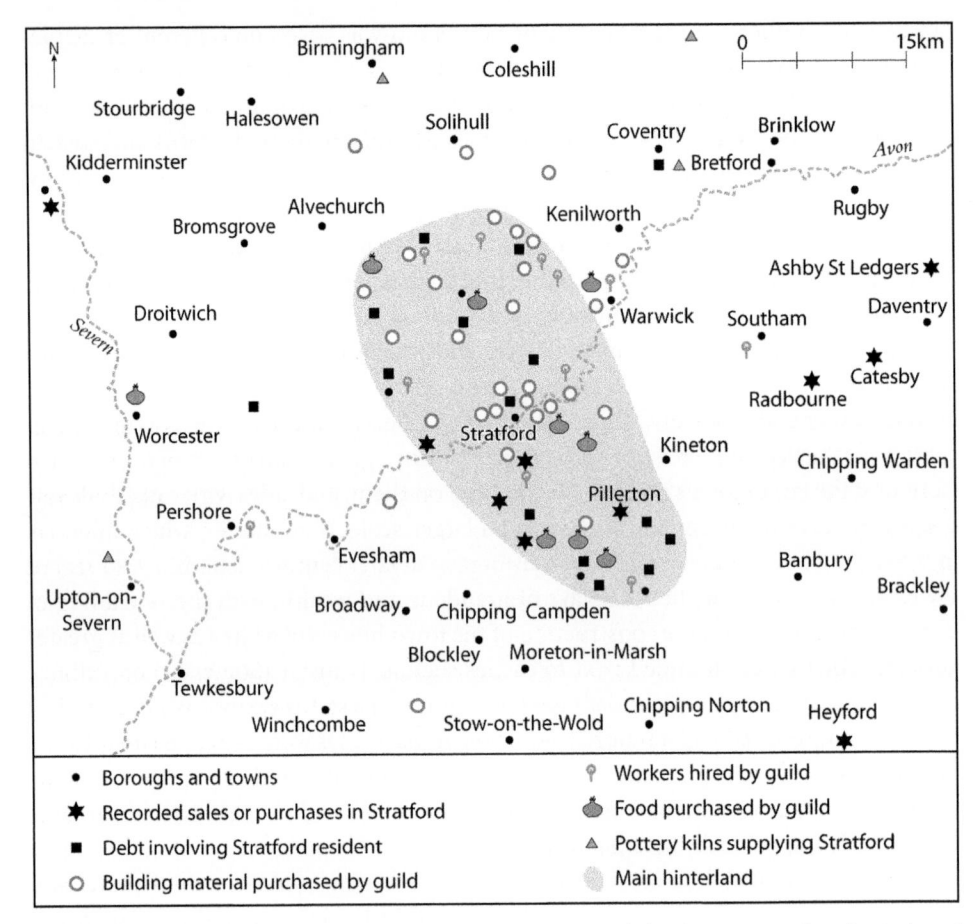

FIGURE 21.3 A hinterland: Stratford-upon-Avon (Warwickshire), using archaeological and documentary evidence, c.1200–1520 (after Dyer 2002, fig. 1)

(© Alejandra Gutiérrez)

to Lanark of trade in Lanarkshire) were taken more seriously, even if they may not have been rigorously enforced (Ballard and Tait 1923). Most country dwellers had some choice as to the centre to which they would take their produce for sale, and where they would make their purchases. Their decision would be heavily influenced by the time and expense of travelling to the town, but there would be other considerations. The area within which town and country connected is often known as the *hinterland*, but in Germany where the term and various theories about it were developed, a distinction is made between an inner zone, the *umland*, where numerous everyday contacts were made, for example for the supply of food and fuel, and a wider sphere of influence, where trade was occasional and more specialized. So, for example, a town like Gloucester had frequent and intense interaction with villages within 12 km, but obtained its iron from the Forest of Dean, its wine from Bristol, and dyestuffs from Southampton (Holt 1985). Exchange of mundane or high-value goods was only one way in which country people engaged with Gloucester. Country people went there for work, and many migrated permanently; villagers expected to find specialist services in the town, provided by money lenders, lawyers, preachers, and medical experts. They could hear music, attend dramatic performances, watch a bull baiting, and see a dancing bear.

The *umland* and *hinterland* distinction has not been absorbed into British terminology, and the term hinterland is used to mean 'the zone around the town incorporated into and reliant upon its economic system', though researchers are aware that the town's influence extended into non-economic spheres (Perring 2002, 11). One approach to defining hinterlands, or rather the 'sphere of influence' of each town, is to apply another German theory, that of central places, which sees a network and hierarchy of towns, and allows the drawing of boundaries between urban territories based on a mathematical model. Using more empirical methods, the extent of the rural area with connections to a town can be plotted from written sources, such as debts settled by courts, surnames deriving from a village of origin, appearances before church courts, lists of fraternity members, and business accounts. Such urban documents show that a majority of country people who had contacts with a town lived within 10 km (6.2 miles), and almost all of them within 25 km (Dyer 1996). Towns were often situated only 15–20 km apart, so their spheres of influence were overlapping, and they were drawn into competition with one another. This introduced some instability or dynamism into the system, leading to neighbouring towns experiencing changes in fortune.

Archaeological evidence from towns gives abundant evidence of contacts with the country, some of which can be precisely located. Most of the pottery recovered from urban excavations was produced at a number of manufacturing centres, most of them rural. At late medieval Peterborough (Cambridgeshire), for example, the urban kilns of Stamford (Lincolnshire) and Ely (Cambridgeshire) supplied some pottery, but the bulk came from Lyveden and Stanion (Northamptonshire), 20 km to the south-west, and from Bourne in Lincolnshire at a similar distance to the north. Other sources included Sible Hedingham in Essex and Grimston in Norfolk, which might seem remote but were connected with Peterborough by boat on the fenland waterways (Spoerry and Hinman 1998, 50–82). The indirect route between the rural potter and the urban consumer no doubt depended on middlemen, of whom we have no direct evidence. Perhaps traders in nearby Oundle played a part in the distribution of the Lyveden wares, and Grimston pottery was carried by boat from King's Lynn. Towards the end of the period the number of centres of manufacture was reduced and a pattern emerges of large rural potting centres being located near more important towns, such as Brill and Boarstall near Oxford, or Chilvers Coton next to Coventry (Astill 1983, 226–8, 245). Distribution by well-placed traders must explain the cargoes of pots carried by boats and long-distance carts into Southampton from Dorset, Surrey, and Scarborough, as well as wares made in the immediate locality. As a major port, Southampton also received pottery from France, the Low Countries, the Rhineland, Spain, Portugal, and Italy (Brown 2002; Gutiérrez 2000).

Some pottery was made in towns, and finds on rural sites give another means of tracing the connections of town crafts and traders. A well-studied example is that of

Stamford ware, a distinctive pottery which began in the newly founded borough in the late ninth century, and continued to be made in the twelfth and thirteenth centuries. The later Stamford ware cooking pots attracted purchasers as far afield as Norfolk, Bedfordshire, and even Gloucester and Oxford, and help to define an unusually large specialized urban hinterland (Kilmurry 1980, 166–8).

Identifying the place of manufacture for pottery depends in most cases on geological analysis of the clay and its inclusions. In the same way the source of stone objects found on urban sites can be traced. Many towns could obtain building stone from nearby quarries, with different types appropriate to particular purposes (see Chapter 29). A town house in Windsor, on the Thames and so well served by water transport, used sandstone from the Reigate district in Surrey, chalk from the Reading area, and Oxfordshire oolite (Hawkes and Heaton 1993, 55–7). Longer-distance journeys by boat were needed in East Anglia where local stone was absent, so the Northamptonshire quarries such as those at Barnack provided the materials for Ely, Cambridge, and Bury St Edmunds. Quarries with suitable stone made roofing slates which were carried very long distances, such as the Devon slates that were used along the south coast and in London. More specialized stone objects were again transported for many kilometres, with native millstones from the Peak district or the Forest of Dean, or superior millstones from the Rhineland, schist whetstones from Norway, and mortars from a number of centres. Mortars were pieces of quite routine kitchen equipment, necessary for grinding ingredients into a paste. The external connections of a busy port like King's Lynn are vividly displayed by the sources of its mortars (Figure 21.4), from Purbeck (Dorset) and Quarr (Isle of Wight), Caen (Normandy), which also supplied much of south-east England with high-quality building stone, and Weldon (Northamptonshire). Precise locations cannot be given for the quarries which produced mortars found at Lynn made of fine limestones, one from Lincolnshire, and another from northern France (Clarke and Carter 1977, 320–47).

This useful evidence for the contacts between towns and places both near and far does not define precisely their rural hinterlands, that is, the area from which they obtained foodstuffs, fuel, and mundane raw materials. From the assemblages of bone likely sources can sometimes be identified, such as the bones of water fowl and freshwater fish found at Ely, which almost certainly came from the fenland adjacent to the town (Alexander 2003, 168–72, 175–6). In most towns the abundance of bones of domesticated animals, cattle, sheep, and pig cannot be shown to have come from a particular place or region, though the identification of differences between the breeds of cattle found at Norwich and Thetford has suggested that the two towns drew on different rural catchment areas (Albarella 2005, 143–4). Stable isotope analysis can provide in the future an indication of the different environments in which animals have fed, as the skeletons of sheep that have grazed on chalk hills will have a different chemical signature from those reared on granite moorlands (see Chapter 7). The way forward is suggested by the isotope signature of cod bones found in London and other towns, which in many cases derive from fish preserved by drying. Fish can be shown to have lived in the North Sea, but in the fourteenth and fifteenth centuries they came from the northern Arctic waters and are likely to have reached English consumers from the major fishmongers

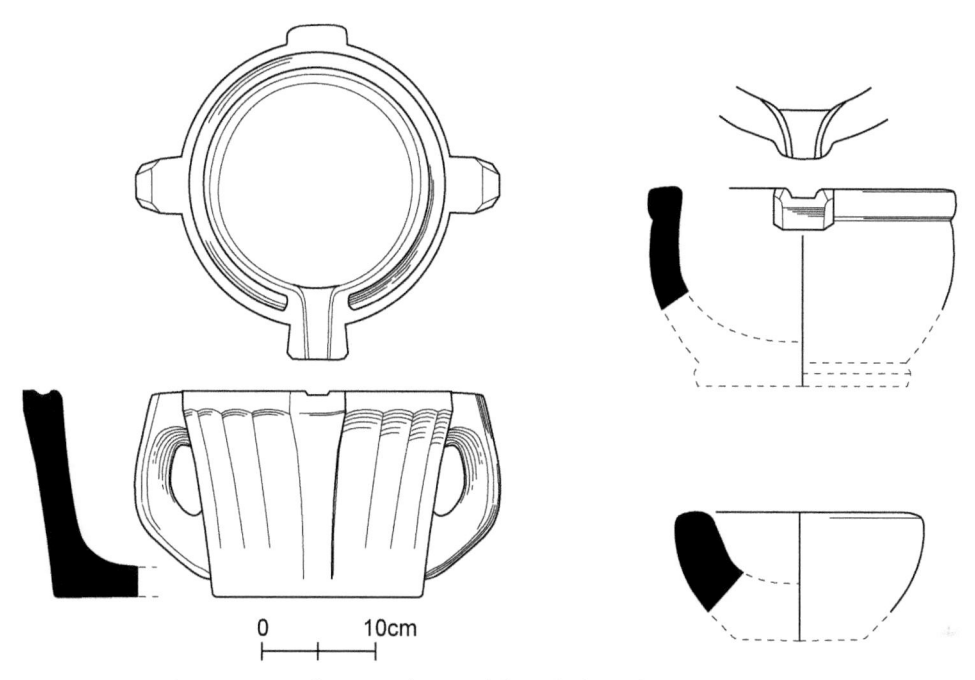

FIGURE 21.4 Stone mortars from King's Lynn (after Clarke and Carter 1977, 326–330)

of London and other east coast ports trading with Norway and the merchants of the Hanseatic League (Barrett et al. 2011; see Chapter 9 in this *Handbook*).

A theoretical approach to the rural zones supplying towns come from von Thunen, who analysed the specialisms of the countryside surrounding towns, which he saw as depending on such factors as the ease and cost of transport (Hall 1966). He saw the land nearest to the town as well suited to horticulture, and there is good archaeological evidence for garden soils both in and very near to the built-up area. 'Black earth' is found in the northern part of Leicester when that part of the town lost its housing in the later Middle Ages and the waste land was cultivated for vegetables and fruit. Urban rubbish pits which have preserved organic materials in damp conditions contain a mass of evidence for the consumption of fruits and berries, some of which were perishable and were likely to have been cultivated within easy reach of the town. Von Thunen also saw an opportunity for some use of land very near the town for pastoral purposes, including dairying and the grazing of animals before slaughter. This has left its traces in the form of bones from neonates (very young calves in particular) from even the large town of Norwich which seem out of place in a place devoted to consumption rather than agricultural production. The theory's prediction of zones further removed from the town being devoted to arable crops and woodland producing fuel and larger timber trees for building cannot be reflected precisely in deposits within the town, though grain, brushwood, and timber of unknown origin are found. Pastures lay far from the town, and many of the bones of adult animals may well have been brought by droving from a considerable distance. Historical evidence tells us that Welsh cattle were consumed in London and that drovers often sold their beasts in midland markets, near which they were fattened and sold in prime condition to the London butchers (Watkins 1989).

The analysis of the supply of foodstuffs to towns reminds us that the country was not the only source of food, as the townspeople were also producers of at least some of their own requirements. The archaeological evidence for cattle breeding, deposits of dung, and buildings in which animals could be kept is entirely in accordance with the testimony of documents. Large arable fields were attached to such towns as Cambridge, Colchester, Leicester, and Nottingham, and common pastures were often available to townspeople. Wandering, badly behaved pigs posed a threat to good order and cleanliness.

From the rural perspective, urban demand exerted a strong influence on the routines of production. Combining the documents for the grain trade in London with the records of the use of land and choice of crops in a large area extending as far as Oxfordshire and Northamptonshire shows that cultivators were reacting in the thirteenth century to the needs of urban consumers, as London's population rose to at least eighty thousand (Campbell at al. 1993). About 140 towns in the same area, with populations varying from three hundred to six thousand, all had to be fed from agricultural surpluses. The environmental evidence for the predominant crops shows a marked preference for wheat in some settlements producing grain near to the capital, in Essex for example, and the choice in other counties of varieties of cereals, not just wheat but also barley, may reflect demand from urban consumers (Rippon et al. 2014). The drinking of ale in towns encouraged the large-scale malting of barley in such settlements as West Cotton (Northamptonshire), where well-built and large malting kilns were found (Chapman 2010).

The early stages of urbanization encouraged the adoption of open fields in the Midlands, which was accompanied by two- and three-course rotations (see Chapter 6). Occasional documentary references to open fields do not enable the expansion of their use to be traced with any certainty. A marked shift in the balance of animal species from cattle to sheep in the midland region found in bone assemblages in the tenth and eleventh centuries, which persisted in subsequent centuries, comes from towns as well as rural settlements. This was linked to the crop rotations found in open fields, in which sheep played a valuable part in grazing on the fallow and manuring the land to maintain fertility (Sykes 2007). Sheep had the added advantage that their wool was in demand from urban textile industries, both in the towns of England and Flanders. The swing from cattle could not be taken too far, as they had many useful functions in the country as dairy and draught animals, and they were also in demand because townspeople had a liking for beef. Developments in agricultural techniques were influenced by market demand as well as the subsistence requirements of the rural population, with more intensive cultivation in some regions. In the less densely populated woodlands and uplands pastoral farming expanded, again in response to the better opportunity to sell produce. Towns did not just encourage the extension of cereal cultivation, because as von Thunen's theory shows, towns needed a rural environment of varied land use. Fuel supply in particular insisted that, unless like Cambridge and Norwich there were local sources of peat, large towns should have a conveniently located area of woodland, which would be managed and protected from encroachment for agriculture.

Woodlands and pastoral uplands attracted rural industries, and these contributed to the interaction between town and country. The woods were sometimes producing nothing more complex than bundles of firewood, or bark for tanning. The rural metal industries mined the ore and smelted it to produce pieces of iron (blooms), or in the case of lead, ingots of the metal, which would be acquired by urban traders and worked into finished articles (see Chapter 29). Pewter plates and saucers, for example, were made from tin from the south-west and lead from the Mendips and Pennines. The manufacture and distribution of the pewter ware was in the hands of urban artisans and traders, the pewterers, who were concentrated on London. This gives the impression that a division of labour gave rural people an extractive role, and the more complex manufactures belonged to the town.

The rural contribution to the alabaster industry, which was to quarry the stone in north Staffordshire, seems to contrast with the sophisticated artistry of the urban craftsmen of Burton on Trent (Staffordshire) and Nottingham who carved and painted exquisite religious images for sale in Britain and the Continent (see Chapters 29 and 59). In fact, rural craftsmen also worked this material to produce incised slabs, and ambitious three-dimensional effigies, mainly from the Derbyshire village of Chellaston (Badham 2005). The raw materials and fuel of the woodlands enabled craftsmen to make not just pottery but also glass, barrels and tubs, ropes (of lime bark, called bast), whips, and other artefacts which would be used in towns or sold by urban traders. A complicated and dynamic relationship between town and country emerges from examining the cloth-making industry. Finds of the teeth of combs for separating fibres, and spindle-whorls to weight distaffs used in hand spinning show that converting raw wool and flax into yarn was a widespread rural activity. In the twelfth and thirteenth centuries this was likely to have been to supply town-based weavers. There was always a rural cloth industry, and many fulling mills were built in the thirteenth century in rural locations. In the fourteenth and fifteenth centuries cloth-making developed in the country, with marked concentrations in specialist centres such as the Stroud valley in Gloucestershire, the Stour valley on the border of Essex and Suffolk, or in West Yorkshire. Towns were drawn into this activity, and at Lavenham and Long Melford (Suffolk) in particular the architectural heritage of timber-framed houses for textile workers and clothiers is still visible. The grandest houses belonged to the clothiers, who were based both in towns and villages, and who coordinated the supply of materials, the stages of manufacture, and the eventual sale of the products, mainly through the dominant port of London. The reason for the shifts between urban and rural cloth-making can be debated, but no easy distinction can be drawn between the simple and basic skills of the countryside and the sophistication of the towns.

Towns were full of consumers, which attracted country people with foodstuffs or craft products to sell. But the consumers in the country would also look to the towns to supply their needs. They bought foodstuffs some of which like bread, ale, and pies could be obtained in their villages, but not of the same quality. Marine fish, often in preserved form, came from afar to rural populations living inland, and was sold by the ubiquitous town 'fishers'.

The most plentiful finds from rural excavations which clearly came from urban suppliers are the objects made from copper alloy. The casting of cooking pots was in the hands of founders or bellyeters who plied their trade in larger towns, and they and other urban craftsmen working on a smaller scale made the buckles, belt-ends, and other dress accessories and ornaments which country people bought (Goodall 1981; see Chapter 49 in this *Handbook*). Perhaps their presence on rural sites shows that clothing, to which these artefacts were attached, also came from the towns, but of course little survives of these perishable materials. Villagers were brought together in fund-raising for the fabric, fixtures, and fittings of parish churches, which included such expensive items as incense and wainscots which were bought in towns, and bells, bearing the names of their urban makers, still hang in country church towers.

Rural dwellings, on the basis of both standing and excavated buildings, might seem to embody a rural ideal of sustainability, as they were built with local materials by local craftsmen. However, documents make it clear that timber often came from town markets, as did the ironwork for doors and shutters; the carpenters may well have been based in a town; and the contents of the houses, such as textiles and kitchen utensils would have been bought from urban retailers. The cost of the building was affordable because the householder made a profit from the sale of produce, and could obtain credit from urban traders.

The rural population practised a limited degree of self-sufficiency, and expected to buy goods in their local market town. They also relied on the town traders to provide commercial links with other parts of the countryside, such as pottery and cloth made by rural craftsmen and sold on urban market stalls (Moorhouse 1981; Walton 1991). And country people through the towns were tapping into complex trade networks which gave them access to long-distance imported goods, such as German millstones and Norwegian whetstones, and they were indirectly consuming foreign products because the raw materials for dyeing cloth and making copper-alloy cooking pots often came from overseas (Dyer 2012; and see Chapter 55 in this *Handbook*).

Town–country relations give us an insight into regional difference across Britain. East Anglia and Essex had a high level of urbanization, with three, four, or five towns in the top fifteen in the various league tables compiled for the eleventh, twelfth, and fourteenth centuries. Four major ports connected the region to especially lively sections of the Continental economy in the Low Countries, Rhineland, and the Baltic. The addition of a concentration of smaller towns means that in parts of the region at least a quarter of the population were town dwellers. The surviving late medieval buildings in towns such as Thaxted (Essex), Sudbury, and Hadleigh (Suffolk) suggest a peak of prosperity, as do the variety and quantity of ceramics and small finds from urban excavations. We can glimpse the full range of utensils and possessions of urban households in Norwich in 1507 when a fire overwhelmed a city street and the goods were left in the ruins: candlesticks, parts of spits, pot hooks, skillets, ewers, and a glass beaker or bowl for drinking (Margeson 1993, 83–155). In the East Anglian countryside, which benefited from the fertility of the soil, the resources of the Fens, and cloth-making, an index of material well-being comes from the high density of metal objects, such as dress accessories and harness fittings, reported to the Portable Antiquities Scheme from the fields of the region.

By contrast, in the north-west of England and the adjacent south-western parts of Scotland no town's population rose above the bench mark of two thousand, not even the regional centre of Carlisle, so all towns count as 'small'. Towns were also widely scattered. Excavations at Penrith, one of the more important urban centres in Cumberland, encountered timber buildings without stone foundations, an absence of small finds, and a sparse pottery assemblage (Newman et al. 2000). In the adjoining countryside rural buildings likewise lacked architectural refinement and finds are also limited in quantity. The contrasts between regions should not lead to disparagement of the pastoral uplands. Towns were needed just as much as in East Anglia, because cattle and sheep rearing depended on markets, and the rural population probably sold a higher proportion of their produce than did the husbandmen of the lowlands. In a thinly populated countryside the towns were as large and numerous as was necessary.

REFERENCES CITED

Albarella, U. 2005 'Meat production and consumption in town and country', in K. Giles and C. Dyer (eds), *Town and country in the Middle Ages: contrasts, contacts and interconnections*, The Society for Medieval Archaeology Monograph 22, Leeds, 131–48

Alexander, M. 2003 'A medieval and post-medieval street frontage: investigations at Forehill, Ely', *Proceedings of the Cambridge Antiquarian Society* 97, 135–82

Astill, G. 1983 'Economic changes in later medieval England: an archaeological review, in T. Aston, P. Coss, C. Dyer, and J. Thirsk (eds), *Social relations and ideas. Essays in honour of R. H. Hilton*, Cambridge University Press, Cambridge, 217–47

Badham, S. 2005 'Evidence for the minor funerary monument industry, 1100 1500', in K. Giles and C. Dyer (eds), *Town and country in the Middle Ages: contrasts, contacts and interconnections*, The Society for Medieval Archaeology Monograph 22, Leeds, 165–95

Ballard, A. and Tait, J. 1923 *British borough charters 1216–1307*, Cambridge University Press, Cambridge

Barrett, J. H., Orton, D., Johnstone, C., Harland, J., Van Neer, W., Ervynck, A., Roberts, C., Locker, A., Amundsen, C., Bødker Enghoff, I., Hamilton-Dyer, S., Heinrich, D., Hufthammer, A. K., Jones, A. K. G., Jonsson, L., Makowiecki, D., Pope, P., O'Connell, T. C., de Roo, T., and Richards, M. 2011 'Interpreting the expansion of sea fishing in medieval Europe using stable isotope analysis of archaeological cod bones', *Journal of Archaeological Science* 38(7), 1516–24

Brown, D. H. 2002 *Pottery in medieval Southampton, c.1066–1510*, Council for British Archaeology Research Report 133, York

Butler, L. 1964 'Minor medieval monumental sculpture in the East Midlands', *The Archaeological Journal* 121, 111–53

Campbell, B., Galloway, J., Keene, D., and Murphy, M. 1993 *A medieval capital and its grain supply: agrarian production and distribution in the London region c.1300*, Historical Geography Research Paper Series 31, London

Chapman, A. 2010 *West Cotton, Raunds: a study of medieval settlement dynamics AD 450–1450*, Oxbow, Oxford
Clarke, H. and Carter, A. 1977 *Excavations in King's Lynn 1963–1970*, The Society for Medieval Archaeology Monograph 7, London
Dawes, J. D. and Magilton, J. R. 1980 *The cemetery of St Helen-on-the-Walls, Aldwark*, Archaeology of York 12/1, Council for British Archaeology, London
Dyer, A. 2000 'Ranking lists of English medieval towns', in D. Palliser (ed.), *The Cambridge urban history of Britain, vol. 1, 600–1540*, Cambridge University Press, Cambridge, 747–68
Dyer, C. 1996 'Market towns and the countryside in late medieval England', *Canadian Journal of History/Annales Canadiennes d'Histoire* 31, 17–35
Dyer, C. 2002 'Small places with large consequences', *Historical Research*, 75 no. 187, 1–24
Dyer, C. 2012 'Did peasants need markets and towns? The experience of late medieval England', in M. Davies and J. Galloway (eds), *London and beyond: essays in honour of Derek Keene*, Institute of Historical Research, London, 25–47
Finn, N. 2004 *The origins of a Leicester suburb: Roman, Anglo-Saxon, medieval and post-medieval occupation on Bonner's Lane*, British Archaeological Reports British Series 372, Oxford
Goodall, A. 1981 'The medieval bronzesmith and his products', in D. W. Crossley (ed.), *Medieval industry*, Council for British Archaeology Research Report 40, 63–71
Grenville, J. 2008 'Urban and rural houses and households in the late Middle Ages: a case study from Yorkshire', in M. Kowaleski and P. Goldberg (eds), *Medieval domesticity: home, housing and household in medieval England*, Cambridge University Press, Cambridge, 92–123
Gutiérrez, A. 2000 *Mediterranean pottery in Wessex households (12th to 17th centuries)*, British Archaeological Reports British Series 306, Oxford
Hall, P. 1966 *Von Thunen's isolated state*, Pergamon Press, Oxford
Hawkes, J. W. and Heaton, M. J. 1993 *Jennings Yard, Windsor: a closed-shaft garderobe and associated medieval structures*, Wessex Archaeology Report 3, Salisbury
Holt, R. 1985 'Gloucester in the century after the Black Death', *Transactions of the Bristol and Gloucestershire Archaeological Society* 103, 149–61
Kermode, J. 2000 'The greater towns 1300–1540', in D. Palliser (ed.), *The Cambridge urban history of Britain, vol. 1, 600–1540*, Cambridge University Press, Cambridge, 441–65
Kilmurry, K. 1980 *The pottery industry of Stamford, Lincolnshire, c. AD 850–1250*, British Archaeological Reports British Series 84, London
Margeson, S. 1993 *Norwich households: the medieval and post-medieval finds from Norwich survey excavations 1971–1978*, East Anglian Archaeology 58, Norwich
Moorhouse, S. 1981 'The medieval pottery industry and its markets', in D. W. Crossley (ed.), *Medieval industry*, Council for British Archaeology Research Report 40, London, 96–125
Mortimer, R., Regan, R., and Lucy, S. 2005 *The Saxon and medieval settlement at West Fen Road, Ely: the Ashwell site*, East Anglian Archaeology 110, Cambridge
Newman, R. M., Hair, N. S., Howard-Davis, C. L. E., Brooks, C., and White, A. 2000 'Excavations at Penrith Market, 1990', *Transactions of the Cumberland and Westmorland Antiquarian and Archaeological Society* 100, 105–30
Pearson, S. 2005 'Rural and urban houses 1100–1500: "urban adaptation" reconsidered', in K. Giles and C. Dyer (eds), *Town and country in the Middle Ages: contrasts, contacts and interconnections*, The Society for Medieval Archaeology Monograph 22, Leeds, 43–63
Pearson, S. 2009 'Medieval houses in English towns: form and location', *Vernacular Architecture* 40, 1–22

Perring, D. 2002 *Town and country in England: frameworks for archaeological research*, Council for British Archaeology Research Report 134, York

Perry, D., Murray, H., Beaumont-James, T., and Bogdan, N. 2010 *Perth High Street archaeological excavation 1975-1977, vol. 1: the excavations*, Tayside and Fife Archaeological Committee, Perth

Reynolds, S. 1977 *An introduction to the history of English medieval towns*, Clarendon Press, Oxford

Rippon, S., Wainwright, A., and Smart, C. 2014 'Farming regions in medieval England: the archaeobotanical and zooarchaeological evidence', *Medieval Archaeology* 58, 195–255

Samuel, M. 1989 'The fifteenth-century garner at Leadenhall, London', *The Antiquaries Journal* 69, 119–53

Slater, T. 1990 'English medieval new towns with composite plans: evidence from the Midlands', in T. Slater, (ed.), *The built form of western cities: essays for M. R. G. Conzen on the occasion of his eightieth birthday*, Leicester, 60–82

Slater, T. 2000 'Understanding the landscape of towns', in D. Hooke (ed.), *Landscape: the richest historical record*, Society for Landscape Studies, supplementary series, 97–108

Spoerry, P. and Hinman, M. 1998 *The Still, Peterborough: medieval remains between Cumbergate and Westgate*, Cambridgeshire County Council Archaeology Field Unit Monograph 1, Fulbourn, Cambridgeshire

Sykes, N. J. 2007 *The Norman Conquest: a zoological perspective*, British Archaeological Reports International Series 1656, Oxford

Walton, P. 1991 'Textiles', in J. Blair and N. Ramsay (eds), *English medieval industries: craftsmen, techniques, products*, The Hambledon Press, London, 319–54

Watkins, A. 1989 'Cattle grazing in the Forest of Arden in the later middle ages', *Agricultural History Review* 37, 12–25

CHAPTER 22

URBAN INFRASTRUCTURE

GARETH DEAN

This chapter discusses the various elements that comprise the primary infrastructure of the urban environment: roads, bridges, waterways, and their associated structures. An interdisciplinary approach is adopted here, one which draws on documentary, cartographic, pictorial, and archaeological evidence. While previous studies have stressed the role of infrastructure in the economy or developing morphology of a place, there is now a growing awareness of its importance as an expression of civic pride (e.g. Dean 2016; Gardiner and Rippon 2007, 3–4; Harrison 2010; Hinton 2000; Rees Jones 2016) and as spaces where we can explore, in Edgeworth's phrase (2011), the 'dynamic entanglements' between people and concepts of flow and movement.

Streets

In all pre-modern cities, streets marked the daily comings and goings of the residents, and were a place for communication and interaction whether on foot or in wagons (Mumford 1989, 308). Alongside the principal thoroughfares a more fluid pattern of lanes and alleys existed, some of which defined property boundaries, gave access to shops and yards, or developed into common routes linking the main streets. They were not a submerged morass of rubbish and excrement, as Victorian sanitary reformers would have us believe, instead there were regulations relating to the disposal of rubbish, the upkeep of streets, perceptions of appropriate behaviour in public spaces, and a growing commitment to matters of communal welfare by civic authorities and mercantile elites (Rawcliffe 2013, 3–4, 140; Rees Jones 2016) (see Chapter 45).

Not only did the majority of streets belong to the Crown and were subject to royal jurisdiction, it was also an obligation for citizens to pave and maintain roads. The funding for this probably began as a collaborative effort, perhaps as part of labour service, but by the later medieval period contributions for repairs was sought directly from tenement owners and through bequests (Allen 2016, 85–7; Vince 2003, 261). Pavage, a toll imposed on commodities passing into and out of towns, was another source of revenue, as were bequests such as that left by William de Wollechirchehawe in 1304 who left £19 to the mayor, alderman, and commonality to repairs for the pavement in Bishopsgate in London (Harvey 2010, 151–4). The growing number of craftsmen who specialized in paving reflects increasing civic pride. In Hull (Yorkshire), funds were used in 1321–4 for sand, limestone, carriage for transport, and the wages of 'paviors' and their servants (Harvey 2010, 154–5). In Chester (Cheshire), Miles Paver received 6s 8d for paving Eastgate Street, and in the 1480s John Paver repaired pavement in Cuppin Lane at a rate of one penny a foot (Laughton 2008, 23, 61–2). In London, four and then six pavers were maintained on a permanent basis by the fourteenth and fifteenth century (Rawcliffe 2013, 131). Paving was often linked to other initiatives such as schemes for refuse collection and the provision of communal dumps set apart from residential areas (Harvey 2010, 158; Rawcliffe 2013, 126–8, 134–7).

Opportunities for archaeologists to examine the street surfaces of the medieval town are surprisingly rare. The evidence suggests that the materials used were usually local and that paving varied not only from town to town but also within towns. Excavations in Oxford have recorded late eleventh-century street surfaces of gravel, pebbles, and cobbles, while Winchester's streets were of flints over chalk (Dodd 2003, 59, 262–3; Platt 1976, 48). In York, cobbles were used for streets, alleys, and yards from the twelfth century, while Norwich (East Anglia) used locally sourced gravel, and combinations of cobble and gravels were used in London (Rawcliffe 2013, 131). In Exeter (Devon) a reference to raking of gravel indicates its use in paving, quite possibly as a bedding medium (Harrison 2010, 158). The presence of rubbish layers has been interpreted as suggesting that refuse was allowed to accumulate (Keene 1982), however historical sources indicate this material may be associated with levelling and make-up prior to resurfacing (Jørgensen 2008; Rawcliffe 2013, 126–8). Rubbish layers may therefore pinpoint episodes of refurbishment rather than neglect. This, however, does not mean that the medieval city was entirely clean and sanitary; environmental evidence from cities such as York indicates the presence of refuse and the associated health risks although there was a gradual trend towards greater urban cleanliness following the Norman Conquest, reflecting the tighter controls imposed by the civic authorities (King and Henderson 2014, 134–5, 139).

Medieval streets were provided with gutters and drains and these were often a cause for concern for the town officials (e.g. Barron 2005, 261–3). They often ran down the middle of the street, a feature which is documented for Cheapside in London, while excavations in Oxford identified a central drain at Queen Street/Castle Street and the High Street which had been re-cut in the twelfth century (Dodd 2003, 59; Keene 1990, 33; Nicholas 1997, 331). Significant engineering was sometimes implied, including hydraulic projects to create and realign the streams and rivers used to flush away industrial waste, butchers offal, power town mills, and service public latrines (Keene 2000, 74–5, 85). At Salisbury (Wiltshire) some of the streets of the new city were made wider to accommodate watercourses running down their centres, and the diverted watercourses sometimes required small bridges to facilitate access across the street. Their upkeep is mentioned as early as 1310 (Frost 2009, 59, 61).

Medieval streets were more than a means of connection, they were dynamic spaces in their own right for buying, selling, talking, fighting, being entertained; above all, they encouraged social exchange and engagement (Dean 2016; Keene 2000, 91; Kostof 192, 189; Nicholas 1997, 335; Rees Jones 2016). In towns, streets often converged on the market places which were integral to the urban economy and a preferred location for civic buildings (Lilley 2002, 146–8, 230). At Bury St Edmunds (Suffolk), for example, a new town was planned outside the monastery gate with a grid of streets, one of which was devoted to a market, and the new town of Salisbury also had an area laid out in the 1220s for the same purpose (Keene 2000, 85). Street names can indicate the clustering of trades, although they were rarely if ever exclusive, and while goldsmiths, spice sellers, or saddlers tended to occupy prime sites near markets, other trades could be found in marginal areas at the edges of towns and some medieval towns were reliant on the road network for their passing trade (Keene 2000, 93; see Chapters 20 and 30 in this *Handbook*). Coventry (West Midlands), for example, was dependent on transport to ports at Bristol, Boston (Lincolnshire), Chester, London, and Southampton (Kermode 2000, 446). Elsewhere, the streets also took on a ritual and ceremonial role at certain times of the year that displaced everyday functions altogether (Phythian-Adams 1979, 121–2; Rees Jones 2016, 116).

Waterways and Waterfronts

Watery landscapes deserve detailed consideration for their influence in shaping the urban environment though they have not always received the attention they deserve (Blair 2007a; Edgeworth 2011, 18–21, 42, 45). Water was important for a number of different activities within medieval towns, ranging from the washing of clothes to craft and industrial purposes, transport of materials, mills, river crossings, and improvements to navigation, drainage, boundaries, and aesthetics (Harrison 2004, 80–1; King and Henderson 2014; Nicholas 1997, 338). Place-names for settlements, incorporating terms such as port, hythe, landing, and haven, directly reflect this significance while the accessibility of waterways and the types of river crafts that served them had a bearing on the development of the urban area; by the thirteenth century ports were generally larger urban centres (Gardiner 2007, 85–6).

The waterfront itself often developed as a strip of reclaimed land along the river bank or shore, afterwards modified to suit the needs both of landing and exporting goods, and later for warehousing and other structures including housing and churches (Schofield and Stell 2000, 375). The understanding of the process of waterfront construction has been greatly enhanced through archaeology, particularly from excavations carried out in the 1970s and 1980s which provided a wealth of information about the development and the technology involved in their management and development (Gerrard 2003, 98).

Drawing on the evidence for London, Gustav Milne (1981, 33–6) identified four main motives for the reclamation of land: firstly, to extend and improve properties, and provide space for buildings and open areas for working, loading, and unloading vessels; secondly, to provide deeper berths for shipping; thirdly, to counteract the problem of silting; and finally, as protection from erosion by the river. Much of the analysis and study of the development of waterfronts has unsurprisingly been related to chronology, motivation, and reaction to changing water levels (Schofield and Vince 2005, 68); much less has been written about the development of waterfronts as expressions of civic pride.

Anglo-Saxon waterfronts were generally reinforced beaching positions, but by the late eleventh to early thirteenth century the introduction of timber revetments shows increasing sophistication in carpentry techniques as well as evidence for the re-use of timbers. River frontages begin to stabilize their expansion through the thirteenth century with stone jetties or quays (Ottaway 1992, 189–90; Schofield and Vince 2005, 71). Initially, the process of reclamation involved trapping river silts, usually in combination with the dumping of rubbish produced by the town. At Newcastle the process of consolidating and developing the river front along the Tyne began in the twelfth century with stone revetments built to retain dumps of stones, cobbles, and flood material. From the thirteenth to sixteenth centuries more substantial waterfronts were created and, while much of the material dumped behind the successive waterfronts was found locally, there was also imported material such as Thames gravel probably derived from ship ballast. Piers were built out into the river with docking spaces between them which were later packed with material to create a continuous raised waterfront (Harbottle 2009, 29–31). This process of reclamation is a characteristic signature in the archaeological record of medieval cities such as London, Hull, King's Lynn, Norwich, and Doncaster (Ayre and Wroe-Brown 2015; Clarke 1973; Good et al. 1991; McComish et al. 2010; Milne 1981; 2003; Sheeran 1999, 116).

Reclamation was not necessarily a centrally organized activity, and could reflect the activities of individuals who held riverside properties, and developed and adapted their stretch of the waterfront. An example of combined civic enterprise to develop the waterfront comes from Bristol, where trade expansion put pressure on the existing quayside. In the 1240s it was the citizens' own initiative which led to the purchase of a marsh from the Augustinian friary through which a new channel was dug for the River Frome to improve access to the River Avon. Associated with these works was the construction of a new bridge and, in the thirteenth century, an expansion of the defences referred to as the Port Wall. Excavations suggest it was the Redcliffe bank of the Avon which saw the most intensive development (Bond 2007, 199–200; Hinton 2000, 240; Keene 2000, 85; Ottaway 1992, 196–7). Once towns had established their waterfront there was the issue of repair and maintenance to consider, and this was a civic responsibility supported from early in the reign Henry II by new taxes on goods entering towns with responsibility for collection being ceded to burgesses (Rees Jones 2010, 261–2).

The fortunes of many towns depended upon their ability to capitalize on waterfront trade. The development and expansion of King's Lynn (Norfolk), for example, were closely related to modifications to the course of the Great Ouse, which formerly fed into the Wash at Wisbech but had silted up in the thirteenth century. The new route of the Great Ouse through Lynn saw it develop from a small port to a centre for loading or unloading and trading, changes which were reflected in the development of waterfronts and a new area of the town set out on a grid of streets with a new market place (Clarke 1973; Gardiner 2007, 107). Similarly, at Bawtry (South Yorkshire) on the River Idle, a tributary of the Trent, the town's prosperity derived from its position close to the Great North Road and to a navigable river that allowed its market to thrive as a centre of transhipment for Derbyshire lead and Nottinghamshire wool (Hey 1980, 108–9).

There is less archaeological evidence for the structures that would have lined the waterfronts and which are recorded in documentary sources. Few medieval harbours have been thoroughly investigated, and much of the focus has been on larger urban centres. There were many smaller ports and, although they did not have the facilities of larger centres, they were an important part of the trade network for the movement of goods (Gardiner 2007, 109). Port structures included warehouses and cranes which appeared on the quays of London, Southampton, Bristol, Poole, and elsewhere (Childs 2006, 265). These structures were used for the unloading and storage of goods and the upkeep of the waterfront (Lilley 2002, 225–6). At York, the mayor and commonality were building river walls in 1305 in Skeldergate that might coincide with the construction of the site for the crane, called the *cranegarth* and first recorded in 1403, which was used for weighing and the tax collection of tolls on goods entering the city by river (Rees Jones 2010, 261–2; Wilson and Mee 2002, 20). Similarly, the town crane at the quay in Sandwich (Kent) is first recorded in 1432, although it may have existed earlier (Clarke et al. 2010, 135). Hull had a wool house built around 1389, which included the Custom House, as well as warehousing for foreigners, a weigh beam, and a common crane. Most of the warehouses were private although some were owned by institutions such as Selby Abbey's quay and timber yard, known from the fifteenth century as the Abbot's Staith. This warehouse still stands on the north-east bank of the Ouse (Sheeran 1999, 116).

The management and manipulation of water was a specialist task. One particular concern was the growth of vegetation and the build-up of silt inside drains and channels. The responsibility for clearing this obstruction fell to householders, who faced fines or public censure for failure to comply (Rawcliffe 2013, 187). Other frustrations included the many fish traps, weirs, and fords which hindered water traffic (Childs 2006, 265). Monastic houses, in particular, developed the technical competencies needed to design and maintain water systems, including the building of dams, diversion of water courses, construction of embankments, and systems of balancing water levels through systems of locks (Bond 2007, 202–3). Many examples of their considerable water management skills could be cited, among them the development of new waterfronts along the Great Ouse in Ely, Cambridgeshire (Blair 2007b, 266–7; Bond 2007, 177, 185–6).

By the twelfth century it was recognized in law that waterways had to be kept clear and free flowing, but ongoing disputes show how town authorities extended their control beyond the urban confines (Blair 2007a, 9). For example, York jurors declared in 1394 that the king's highway of the Ouse used for ships for the transport of various merchandise was being jeopardized by fish weirs and fish nets (Childs 2006, 265). Gloucester meanwhile developed as a regional inland port through long-distance trade along the length of the Severn and, to ensure that the passage of ships was not impeded, it became accepted practice by the 1380s for weirs below the town to leave a certain width of gap for the passage of ships (Blair 2007b, 279; Britnell 2006, 144). New channels were sometimes cut to ease navigation. The antiquary John Leland recorded canals or cuts in the sixteenth century on the Thames at Abingdon (Oxfordshire), on the River Brue near Glastonbury (Somerset), and along the Foss Dyke in Lincolnshire (Bond 2007, 154). At Oxford, improvements to navigation on the Thames were made in the eleventh and twelfth centuries when a channel was cut across Osney Island (Blair 2007b, 267; Bond 2007, 157). Rivers were also used for the disposal of rubbish. At York there is environmental evidence for the pollution of the Rivers Ouse and Foss from the eleventh century with a decline in the diversity of fish, and a concern over the disposal of refuse is reflected in the council decreeing it illegal to throw manure, household sweepings, or other filth into the rivers and eventually appointing in 1540 a water bailiff to enforce the restrictions (King and Henderson 2014, 135).

The management of waterways could be integral to a town's survival. Dunwich's harbour in Suffolk was kept open through the cutting of channels to improve access to the port and River Blythe until silting became too heavy (Comfort 1994; Sear et al. 2011, 3). Lincoln's urban success meanwhile depended on water transport; the city was connected to the Trent by the Foss Dyke, and the North Sea and the Wash via the Witham and an outport at Boston. The Brayford Pool at Lincoln was where the water courses joined, and excavation around the waterfront area has provided evidence for its development (Vince 2003, 237). The Foss Dyke, probably itself a Roman canal (Chitwood 1991, 169), was kept navigable until the fourteenth century until it became too much of a financial strain. Commissions in 1365, 1376, and 1395 make reference to the Foss Dyke's condition and obstructions to shipping but also to the process of scouring which secured the ships' passage. The River Witham, on the other hand, was managed by dams and weirs which controlled water levels in the river and permitted the development of quaysides along the north bank of the Brayford Pool (Vince 2003, 238–42). The ability to maintain these links by water allowed Lincoln to become a staple town for wool from the English Midlands on the strength of its transport facilities (Bond 2007, 175–6).

Bridges and River Crossings

Bridges and river crossings mark the point at which the urban infrastructure of streets and rivers meets, and recent studies have sought to consider bridges not only within the broader context of road and trade networks, but also as expressions of civic pride and identity (Cooper 2006; Harrison 2004). Rivers had to be crossed, or made accessible, and the construction of a bridge could be a stimulus to urban growth. In Scotland, towns developed around bridges at Dumfries, Glasgow, Perth, and Stirling. For some towns the construction of a bridge could have a negative impact. The development of Salisbury and its new bridges over the Avon in the thirteenth century took traffic away from the historic county town of Wilton, and the new bridge over the upper Thames at Abingdon in the fifteenth century had an impact on Wallingford (Frost 2009, 67; Harrison 2004, 58; Schofield and Stell 2000, 376). Many urban centres also had ferries. At York, two ferries are recorded in the accounts of the Bridge Masters, crossing the Ouse between the Lendal Tower and Barker Tower (Wilson and Mee 2002, 7–8).

The period after the Norman Conquest saw an increase in the records for bridges, although many existed earlier and it is likely they were built of timber, or had timber roadways on stone piers. The transition from fords and timber bridges to stone bridges and causeways between the tenth and twelfth centuries was partly due to changing demands in road traffic, but the embanking of rivers and construction of mill leats, mill dams, and weirs must also have deepened river channels (Cooper 2006, 15–18; Harrison 2004, 44). Many place-names ending in 'ford' (Chelmsford, Rochford, Romford) had bridges by the thirteenth century (Britnell 2006, 137). The Grand Pont, Oxford, replaced an earlier timber trestle bridge and cobbled ford, but also narrowed the river channel leading to a build-up of ground levels through the twelfth and thirteenth centuries. Associated with the new bridge was a stone causeway with intermittent flood arches across the marshy ground which ran south of the town carrying the roadway (Dodd 2003, 13–16, 32–5, 53–6, 65–82). Exeter Bridge was rebuilt in stone, and excavations in 1968–72 exposed eight of the arches and showed that it had replaced a ford. Exactly when work on the bridge commenced is unclear, but in 1196 a chaplain of the bridge is recorded as a witness, and by 1214 there is reference to two chapels on the bridge (Henderson 1981). At Wallingford (Oxfordshire), the replacement of the timber bridge in stone probably played a part in the replacement of the ford; the earlier and less substantial bridge may have coexisted with the ford, with heavier traffic passing through, rather than over, the water (Christie et al. 2013, 221–30).

Stone bridges shared the same technology as the new cathedrals, and sometimes the Church paid for both; Bishop Flambard ordered the construction of Framwellgate (or 'Old') Bridge in Durham at the same time as the vaulted nave of the cathedral. His successor Hugh de Puiset (1153–95) commissioned the stone Elvet Bridge (largely intact, central arches replaced after eighteenth-century floods). The Framwellgate bridge was brought down by floods in 1400 and the structure which survives today is fifteenth century with a nineteenth-century widening; the original bridge was an important stimulus to urban development and led to the creation of a new borough adjacent to the castle (Britnell 2006, 137). The same craftsmen were sometimes employed for both kinds of construction project; the mason Henry of Yevele was involved in the construction of the bridge at Rochester as well as the nave of Canterbury Cathedral in Kent (Harrison 2004, 112).

Bridges could be an integral part of urban defences and historical records identify fortified examples at many medieval towns including Bath, Bedford, Bristol, Durham (Elvet Bridge), Newcastle upon Tyne, Norwich, Shrewsbury, York (Layerthorpe Bridge), and Oxford (Harbottle 2009, 24; Harrison et al. 2010, 48). At London the defences were part of construction design (Watson et al. 2001, 83, 105–7), and in 1347–8 Sir Thomas de Ferrers, the justiciar, paid £150 to complete the Dee Bridge, Chester, and to build a tower at the Flintshire end (Harrison 2004, 112, 178). Two surviving bridge gatehouses are Warkworth Bridge (Northumberland) and Monnow Bridge, Monmouth, in Wales which is unusually located in the middle of the bridge (Harrison et al. 2010, 48; Rowlands 1994). At Shrewsbury (Shropshire), there is limited documentary evidence for the Welsh Bridge, demolished in 1795, but archaeology has shown the sequence of masonry defences from the twelfth century and their successive rebuilding and enlargement up to the fourteenth century (Watson 2011). The other bridge in Shrewsbury, the English Bridge which was demolished in 1770, made use of a river island, Coleham Island, as the mid-point and had gate towers with a drawbridge at its eastern end (Baker 2010, 109–11).

Another feature of medieval bridges was their buildings. John Stow's description of London Bridge in 1598 mentions 'upon both sides be houses built, so that it seemeth rather a continual street rather than a bridge' (Wilson and Mee 2002, 33). On London Bridge in 1358 there was a tavern at each end, a chapel dedicated to Thomas Becket in the centre, as well as 138 shops, while the Ouse Bridge at York (Figure 22.1) was lined with houses and shops as well as important civic and religious buildings such as St William's chapel, Council Chamber, and Exchequer as well as a hospital, toll booth and public latrines after it was rebuilt in stone between 1189 and 1200 (Nicholas 1997, 34; Rawcliffe 2013, 142; see Chapter 45 in this *Handbook*). Documentary sources also show that many other bridges were similarly covered with structures such as Bristol, Exe Bridge (Exeter),

FIGURE 22.1 Old Ouse Bridge in York packed with buildings, including St William's chapel (on the left), houses and shops, as depicted by William Marlow in 1758

(Image courtesy of York Museums Trust, https://yorkmuseumstrust.org.uk, public domain)

Elvet Bridge (Durham), the English and Welsh Bridges (Shrewsbury), and Tyne Bridge (Newcastle). High Bridge, Lincoln, is still lined with buildings today (Harrison et al. 2010, 49).

Medieval bridges also housed chapels for priests to say Mass, and to collect funds for the upkeep of the bridge (Wilson and Mee 2002, 35). This may be associated with the rise from the twelfth century of bridge-building as an act of piety, as much as for the protection for travellers. Some medieval chapels still survive at Derby, St Ives, Rotherham, Wakefield, and Elvet Bridge (Durham, part only) (Harrison 2004, 199–201). That on the High Bridge, Lincoln, was removed in the eighteenth century. These chapels were usually situated on piers or at the ends of the bridge, and there are several published accounts that discuss bridge chapels, their maintenance, and upkeep (Harrison 2010; Harrison et al. 2010; Stell 2003; Wilson and Mee 2002). A cross often stood at the midpoint of the bridge, although many of these were destroyed in the sixteenth and seventeenth centuries (Harrison 2004, 199–201; Wilson and Mee 2002, 35).

Three methods evolved for the maintenance of bridges: obligation, charity, and royal grants of pontage (Cooper 2006). The Church could itself source funds for the maintenance of bridges as when the chaplain Hugh de Hemeleseye collected alms for the maintenance of the bridge over the River Eden in Carlisle in 1280 (Summerson 1993, 164–5). Similarly, when Elvet Bridge, Durham, was damaged in flooding in 1400, Bishop Richard Fox issued indulgencies to those contributing to the repair (Bonney 1992, 53–4). Some religious institutions also funded repairs themselves if they were responsible through ancient liability or endowment and, during the fourteenth century, secular institutions became increasingly involved, perhaps following the example of London where in 1179–80 five London Bridge guilds are mentioned (Harrison 2004, 159, 202–6, 211). Secular estates were managed by a bridge warden chosen by the town to collect of tolls and rents from property and, by the fifteenth century, 'bridge estates' were common. The creation of these estates could be associated with a town's incorporation. York's charter in 1393 from Richard II authorized the citizens to purchase land to the value of £100 to provide for the upkeep of bridges as well as rents from properties on the bridges themselves (Rees Jones 2010, 224). Funding also came through charitable donations and bequests of money, property, or land from benefactors. The motives for donations were a mix of piety, civic pride, and the desire to be well thought of by contemporaries (Harrison 2004, 184–5, 193–7).

Conclusion

Although Christianity favoured pious works such as the upkeep of roads and bridges (Rawcliffe 2013, 223), the upkeep and maintenance of the urban infrastructure generally required a combination of royal support and local interests which were woven into the fabric of civic identity. Archaeology, as we have seen, has much to contribute in understanding the dating and sequence of construction, modification, and the detail of the urban environment. More work is needed on many aspects, particularly the role of minor watercourses and hydraulic technology, such as locks and dams, and the symbolic importance of water in shaping urban identity. Streets, rivers, and associated infrastructure are all interconnected, and form far more than a backdrop to medieval urban life; they were an active expression of daily life and a statement of civic pride and ambition and provided an essential link between urban centres and their immediate hinterland and the wider world.

REFERENCES CITED

Allen, V. 2016 'When things break: mending roads, being social', in V. Allen and R. Evans (eds), *Roadworks: medieval Britain, medieval roads*, Manchester University Press, Manchester, 97–126

Ayre, J. and Wroe-Brown, R. 2015 'The eleventh- and twelfth-century waterfront and settlement at Queenhithe: excavations at Bull Wharf, City of London', *The Archaeological Journal* 172(2), 195–272

Baker, N. 2010 *Shrewsbury: an archaeological assessment of an English border town*, Oxbow, Oxford

Barron, C. M. 2005 *London in the later Middle Ages. Government and people 1200–1500*, Oxford University Press, Oxford

Blair, J. 2007a 'Introduction', in J. Blair (ed.), *Waterways and canal building in medieval England*, Oxford University Press, Oxford, 1–18

Blair, J. 2007b 'Transport and canal-building on the Upper Thames, 1000–1300', in J. Blair (ed.), *Waterways and canal building in medieval England*, Oxford University Press, Oxford, 254–94

Bond, J. 2007 'Canal construction in the early Middle Ages: an introductory review', in J. Blair (ed.), *Waterways and canal building in medieval England*, Oxford University Press, Oxford, 153–206

Bonney, M. 1992 *Lordship and the urban community: Durham and its overlords 1250–1540*, Cambridge University Press, Cambridge

Britnell, R. 2006 'Town life', in R. Horrox and W. M. Ormrod (eds), *A social history of England, 1200–1500*, Cambridge University Press, Cambridge, 134–78

Childs, W. R. 2006 'Moving around', in R. Horrox and W. M. Ormrod (eds), *A social history of England, 1200–1500*, Cambridge University Press, Cambridge, 260–75

Chitwood, P. 1991 'Lincoln's ancient docklands: the search continues', in G. L. Good, R. H. Jones, and M. W. Ponsford (eds), *Waterfront archaeology: proceedings of the Third International Conference on Waterfront Archaeology*, Council for British Archaeology, London, 169–76

Christie, N. and Creighton, O. H., with Edgeworth, M. and Hamerow, H. 2013 *Transforming townscapes. From burh to borough: the archaeology of Wallingford AD 800–1400*, The Society for Medieval Archaeology Monograph 35, London

Clarke, H. 1973 'The changing riverline of King's Lynn, Norfolk, in the Middle Ages', *The International Journal of Nautical Archaeology and Underwater Exploration* 2(1), 95–106

Clarke, H., Pearson, S., Mate, M., and Parfitt, K. 2010 *Sandwich: the 'completest medieval town in England'*, Oxbow, Oxford

Comfort, N. 1994 *The lost city of Dunwich*, Terence Dalton, London

Cooper, A. 2006 *Bridges, law and power in medieval England 700–1400*, Boydell, Woodbridge

Dean, G. 2016 'Space for neighbourhood: social identity and the built environment in medieval York', in S. Griffiths and A. von Lünen (eds), *Spatial cultures: towards a new social morphology of cities past and present*, Routledge, London, 54–64

Dodd, A. (ed.) 2003 *Oxford before the university: the late Saxon and Norman archaeology of the Thames crossing, the defences and the town*, Oxford Archaeology, Oxford

Edgeworth, M. 2011 *Fluid pasts: archaeology of flow*, Bristol Classical Press, London

Frost, C. 2009 *Time, space and order: the making of medieval Salisbury*, Peter Lang, Oxford

Gardiner, M. 2007 'Hythes, small ports, and other landing places in late medieval England', in J. Blair (ed.), *Waterways and canal building in medieval England*, Oxford University Press, Oxford, 85–109

Gardiner, M. and Rippon, S. 2007 'Introduction: the medieval landscapes of Britain', in M. Gardiner and S. Rippon (eds), *Medieval landscapes*, Windgather, Macclesfield, 1–10

Gerrard, C. M. 2003 *Medieval archaeology: understanding traditions and contemporary approaches*, Routledge, London

Good, G. L., Jones, R. H., and Ponsford, M. W. (eds) 1991 *Waterfront archaeology: Proceedings of the Third International Conference on waterfront archaeology*, Council for British Archaeology Research Report 74, London

Harbottle, B. 2009 'The medieval archaeology of Newcastle', in A. J. Pollard and D. Newton (eds), *Newcastle and Gateshead before 1700*, Philimore & Co Ltd, Chichester

Harrison, D. 2004 *The bridges of medieval England*, Clarendon Press, Oxford

Harrison, D. 2010 'Bridges: past and future. The current state of knowledge and proposals for future research', *Medieval Settlement Research* 25, 32–9

Harrison, D., McKeague, P., and Watson, B. 2010 'England's fortified medieval bridges and bridge chapels: a new survey', *Medieval Settlement Research* 25, 45–72

Harvey, E. 2010 'Pavage grants and urban street paving in medieval England, 1249–1462', *The Journal for Transport History* 31(2), 151–63

Henderson, C. G. 1981 'Exeter', in G. Milne and B. Hobley (eds), *Waterfront archaeology in Britain and Northern Europe*, Council for British Archaeology Research Report 41, London, 119–22

Hey, D. 1980 *Packmen, carriers and packhorse roads*, Leicester University Press, Leicester

Hinton, D. 2000 'The large towns 600–1300', in D. Palliser (ed.), *The Cambridge urban history of Britain, 600–1540*, Cambridge University Press, Cambridge, 217–43

Milne, G. and Hobley, B. (eds) *Waterfront archaeology in Britain and Northern Europe*, Council for British Archaeology Research Report 41, London

Jørgensen, D. 2008 'Cooperative sanitation: managing streets and gutters in late medieval England and Scandinavia', *Technology and Culture* 49(3), 547–67

Keene, D. 1982 'Rubbish in medieval towns', in A. Hall and H. Kenward (eds), *Environmental archaeology in the urban context*, Council for British Archaeology Research Report 43, York, 26–30

Keene, D. 1990 'Shops and shopping in medieval London', in L. Grant (ed.), *Medieval art, architecture and archaeology in London*, British Archaeological Association, Oxford, 29–46

Keene, D. 2000 'The medieval urban landscape, AD 900–1540', in P. Waller (ed.), *The English urban landscape*, Oxford University Press, Oxford, 74–98

Kermode, J. 2000 'The greater towns 1300–1540', in D. Palliser (ed.), *The Cambridge urban history of Britain vol. 1: 600–1540*, Cambridge University Press, Cambridge, 441–66

King, G. and Henderson, C. 2014 'Living cheek by jowl: the pathoecology of medieval York', *Quaternary International* 314, 131–42

Kostoff, S. 1991 *The city shaped*, Thames and Hudson, London

Laughton, J. 2008 *Life in late medieval Chester*, Oxbow, Oxford

Lilley, K. 2002 *Urban life in the Middle Ages: 1000–1450*, Palgrave Macmillan, London

McComish, J. M., Mainman, A. J., Jenner, A., and Rogers, N. 2010 'Excavations at Low Fisher Gate, Doncaster, South Yorkshire', *Yorkshire Archaeological Journal* 82(1), 73–230

Milne, G. 1981 'Medieval riverfront reclamation in London', in G. Milne and B. Hobley (eds), *Waterfront archaeology in Britain and northern Europe*, Council for British Archaeology Research Report 41, London, 32–6

Milne, G. 2003 *The port of medieval London*, Tempus, Stroud

Mumford, L. 1989 *The city in history: its origins, its transformations, and its prospects*, Harcourt, New York, Brace and World

Nicholas, D. 1997 *The later medieval city*, Longman, Harlow

Ottaway, P. 1992 *Archaeology in British towns*, Routledge, London

Phythian-Adams, C. 1979 *Desolation of a city: Coventry and the urban crisis of the late Middle Ages*, Cambridge University Press, Cambridge

Platt, C. 1976 *The English medieval town*, Martin Secker and Warburg, London

Rawcliffe, C. 2013 *Urban bodies: communal health in late medieval English towns and cities*, Boydell, Woodbridge

Rees Jones, S. 2010 *York: the making of a city 1068–1350*, Oxford University Press, Oxford

Rees Jones, S. 2016 'The word on the street: Chaucer and the regulation of nuisance in post-plague London', in V. Allen and R. Evans (eds), *Roadworks: medieval Britain, medieval roads*, Manchester University Press, Manchester, 97–126

Rowlands, M. L. J. 1994 *Monnow Bridge and Gate*, Alan Sutton, Stroud

Schofield, J. and Stell, G. 2000 'The built environment 1300–1540', in D. M. Palliser (ed.), *The Cambridge urban history of Britain, 600–1540*, Vol. 1, Cambridge University Press, Cambridge, 371–93

Schofield, J. and Vince, A. 2005 *Medieval towns*, Equinox, London

Sear, D. A., Bacon, S. R., Murdock, A., Doneghan, G., Baggaley, P., Serra, C., and LeBas, T. P. 2011 'Cartographic, geophysical and diver surveys of the medieval town site at Dunwich, Suffolk, England', *International Journal of Nautical Archaeology* 40(1), 113–32

Sheeran, G. 1999 *Medieval Yorkshire towns: people, buildings and spaces*, Edinburgh University Press, Edinburgh

Stell, P. M. 2003 *York bridgemasters' accounts*, York Archaeological Trust, York

Summerson, H. 1993 *Medieval Carlisle: the city and the border from the late eleventh to the mid-sixteenth centuries*, Vol. 1, Cumberland and Westmorland Antiquarian and Archaeological Society, Kendal

Vince, A. 2003 'The new town: Lincoln in the high medieval era (*c*.900–*c*.1350): archaeological account', in M. J. Jones, D. Stocker, and A. Vince (eds), *The city by the pool: assessing the archaeology of the city of Lincoln*, Oxbow, Oxford, 159–296

Watson, B., Brigham, T., and Dyson, T. 2001 *London Bridge: 2000 years of a river crossing*, Museum of London Archaeology, London

Watson, B. 2011 'The Old Welsh Bridge, Shrewsbury, England: a rediscovered fortified medieval bridge', in M. Prell (ed.), *Archäologie der Brücken*, Verlag Friedrich Pustet, Regensburg, 221–5

Wilson, D. and Mee, F. 2002 *'The fairest arch in England': Old Ouse Bridge, York and its buildings*, York Archaeological Trust, York

PART V

POWER AND DISPLAY

CHAPTER 23

OVERVIEW

Castles and Elite Landscapes

OLIVER H. CREIGHTON

The academic field of castle studies—or *castellology*—developed rapidly and in new directions in the latter part of the twentieth century, building on an already formidable body of work by documentary historians, archaeologists, and scholars of medieval architecture. The archaeological contribution is only one component part of the study of medieval castles, of course, and future research successes will hinge on the willingness and ability of scholars to work at the interface between overlapping areas of specialism. The foundation statement of the Castle Studies Group (1987) underlined the need to study castles not as an isolated phenomenon, but in a holistic manner that explores their wider inter-relationships with medieval economy, society, and environment. These observations skirt around the fundamental question of whether castle studies should continue to exist at all as a discrete field of academic research in the future, or whether castles can and should most meaningfully be studied as one element within the wider repertoire of lordship and within the total medieval settlement pattern. Accordingly, this overview assesses key achievements, areas of debate, and research priorities not only for the archaeology of medieval castles, but also their surrounding landscapes.

DEBATES

In works of synthesis, individual castles have often slotted neatly into a familiar narrative sequence reflecting received historical interpretations and 'facts' about how castle-building evolved from the eleventh to the sixteenth century. Key drivers behind changing castle design and planning were seen as the increasing sophistication of medieval siege warfare and building technologies, with social change often taking a back seat in explanatory frameworks. Castle studies probably saw too little debate for too long. Emphasis on sites with major upstanding masonry remains, especially those that are well documented and built by the Crown or by major magnates, has been another consistent theme. For too long, scholarship was skewed towards structures at the 'sharp end' of medieval building, with the 'background noise' of supposedly lesser sites, including earth-and-timber castles, receiving more limited attention, while site-centric approaches ensured that the place of the castle within its contemporary environment remained neglected. Against this background, two important debates have cast a long shadow over the ways in which archaeologists have approached and interpreted medieval castles.

First, the 'origins of the castle' debate, crystallizing in the late 1960s but rooted in late nineteenth-century scholarship, concerned the introduction of the castle into England by the Normans. Received historical wisdom saw the castle as an entirely new species of fortification whose introduction accompanied a distinctive mode of (cavalry-based) warfare and a new social system (Allen Brown 1969). Scholars have since come to understand the genesis of the castle much more flexibly. Davison (1967) highlighted that many of the earliest castles of the Norman Conquest built during the initial subjugation of urban centres were not in fact motte and baileys, which were also arguably uncommon in Normandy before this point, but ringworks (examples include the fortification in the south-east corner of London's city walls later occupied by the Tower of London, and Exeter Castle, Devon), and also suggested that traditions of private ringwork-building had an Anglo-Saxon ancestry. A programme of excavation on a careful selection of castles including Hen Domen (Powys), the Old Baile, York, and Sulgrave (Northamptonshire), funded by the Royal Archaeological Institute, amounted to an early archaeological research strategy intended to address this 'origins of the castle' question. The project also, however, brought into sharp focus the varying conditions of preservation which might be encountered and the limitations of available dating techniques and arrived at the inevitable conclusion that excavation on early castle sites could not hope to answer such narrow historical questions (Saunders 1977). The investigation of Sulgrave and other sites excavated subsequently, most notably 'Goltho' (Lincolnshire),[1] revealed sequences where the appearance and defences of aristocratic seats evolved across and beyond the Saxo-Norman divide. Crucially, the point at which a castle existed as opposed to some other supposed category of lordly site or fortification becomes a matter of interpretation. The presence of other late Anglo-Saxon thegnly fortifications (problematically termed 'proto-castles') might be indicated by turriform churches (Baker and Brookes 2013, 106–17), while many others are doubtless sealed beneath Norman castles. It seems clear that private fortification was not an entirely new phenomenon in the late eleventh century; rather, castles represented a different face for lordship which often operated from traditional locations. The situation is not the same in all parts of Britain, however: in Scotland, the question of pre-castle defended residences has been bypassed by the English debate, and although understanding of

---

[1] The site name 'Goltho' is given with inverted commas as the identification of the site has been challenged; this is very likely to have been the manor and castle/manor house of Bullington (Everson 1988).

pre-*c*.1250 'native' high-status sites is poorly developed it is clear that here too models of castles as an entirely alien form of imposition are probably misleading (Oram 2008b).

A second area of debate, referred to in shorthand as the 'military *v.* symbolism' debate, has seen revisionist scholars question the supposed primacy of military motivations in the minds of castle builders (compare, for example, Stocker 1992 and Thompson 1994; Platt 2007 and Creighton and Liddiard 2008; for overviews and synthesis, see Johnson 2002; Liddiard 2005). The late fourteenth-century site of Bodiam Castle (East Sussex) has been a touchstone for the argument, attracting a considerable historiography in its own right, but this scholarly 'Battle for Bodiam' is now a cliché. The argument represents a false dichotomy: to reduce understanding of the functions and meanings of such complex buildings and institutions to a spectrum of militarism at one extreme and social display at the other misrepresents medieval society's own views of castles. It is possible to locate in many contexts evidence of, on the one hand, castles that were built as vehicles for social display with 'military' architecture that was showy as much as utilitarian and, on the other, castles intended as fighting machines. Any playoff between 'military' and 'social/symbolic' purposes depended heavily on social context and, of course, geographical setting and period. An arbitrary date such as *c*.1200 or *c*.1300 might mark a shift in emphasis away from militarism towards domesticity in certain regions but not in others. Critically, the debate also highlights how we have also probably laid far too much emphasis on trying to understand the functions and significance of castles at their supposed points of origin rather than their lived-in meanings over the longer term.

Both areas of debate oblige us to confront the eternal question of defining the medieval castle. As physical entities castles were a heterogeneous bunch, ranging from earth-and-timber strongholds of lords of the manor and impermanent siege castles (see Chapter 26), to monumental edifices of stone built for the Crown. Crucially, all the essential aspects of medieval lordly identity coalesced in the physical form of the castle which was at once a display of martial prowess and a symbol of social distinction that marked territorial power (for other forms of elite symbolism see Chapter 27). While a unifying 'castle idea' ensured that these sites were central to the creation and perpetuation of a culture of nobility, medieval chroniclers and literary sources applied terms such as *castrum* and *castellum* quite widely to embrace walled towns, palaces, and even monastic sites, as well as castles and sometimes their territories (Wheatley 2004). Definitions of castles were mutable and negotiated rather than fixed; medieval understandings of the castle changed through time; and these structures were perceived and experienced differently depending on rank. Archaeologists, on the other hand, have shown an enduring tendency to sub-divide castles into categories and sub-categories. While some such categories are meaningful and authentically medieval, others, such as 'ringwork' and 'tower-house' are modern jargon and need to be treated with care. No matter how the definition of castle is framed, it is quite clear that there were many more sites than most students and researchers assume. In a magisterial gazetteer King (1983) counted 2413 'castles' in England and 688 in Wales, and entries in National Monument Records and Historic Environment Records suggest that these are underestimates; the figure in Scotland has not been reliably calculated, but given the proliferation of late medieval towers and minor defensive buildings it is not fanciful to think that the total there approaches or even exceeds the number in the rest of Britain.

THE EVIDENCE BASE

The most important long-term trends in the nature and direction of castle archaeology are the virtual extinction of excavations of sites under State care, partnered with a sharp decrease in castle-focused research excavation. Large-scale investigations of important masonry castles, driven in part by the desire to expose, display, and conserve remains for the public benefit, were critical in the development of castle studies in the 1960s, 1970s, and 1980s; this body of work furnishes us with many key case studies, including publications on (in England) Barnard Castle (Co. Durham), Castle Acre (Norfolk), Launceston (Cornwall), Ludgershall (Wiltshire), Okehampton (Devon), Portchester (Hampshire), and Sandal (West Yorkshire); (in Wales) Dolforwyn (Powys) and Dryslwyn (Carmarthenshire); and (in Scotland) Dundonald (Ayrshire), Threave (Dumfries and Galloway), and Spynie (Moray). Other important excavations remain to be written up, while delays in publication can prompt re-assessment of earlier findings due to advances in the state of the art. The published report on Ludgershall (Ellis 2000) is a clear case in point: excavation from the mid-1960s exposed and sequenced this structurally modest but well-documented royal castle and hunting lodge, but these findings were later set within the context of, and in part re-appraised in the light of, a landscape survey. This showed the site to be embedded within a park-land setting with garden-like qualities, with lodgings linked to a walkway previously interpreted as a purely defensive feature. In terms of research-driven excavations, work on the borderland motte and bailey of Hen Domen (Powys) (Figure 23.1) was to castle studies what Wharram Percy was to rural settlement studies: an evolving long-term venture whose research aims broadened so that the project illuminated not only the defences and social environment of the site but also its place within the wider Marcher landscape (Barker and Higham 1982; Higham and Barker 2000).

These trends, partnered by a rise in developer-funded investigation, mean that the scale of castle excavations has tended to diminish, with prominent exceptions such as Norwich (see below). Where research projects since 1990 have included castle excavation this has often been part and parcel of broader landscape-scale work, while community-focused archaeological ventures have also grown in importance in the twenty-first century. Much valuable information remains as 'grey literature', however, and synthesis is a challenge; many larger castle sites are pockmarked with multiple widely spaced interventions that provide small windows into inordinately complex and deeply stratified records. Many of these points are exemplified by work at Wallingford (Oxfordshire), where excavation, survey, and documentary analysis of the castle were embedded within a project focused on the evolving Saxo-Norman townscape, including

FIGURE 23.1 Hen Domen: excavations within the bailey, showing the granary to the left and the lesser hall to the right

(© Robert Higham)

re-appraisal and writing-up of unpublished excavations and synthesis of developer-funded interventions (Christie and Creighton 2013).

Urban castles comprise some of the best surviving islands of stratigraphy in English towns, and archaeological investigation can reveal the place of the castle in longer-term sequences of continuity and change. At scale, developer-funded work can produce spectacular results. At Norwich, large-scale excavations carried out by the Norfolk Archaeological Unit in the Castle Mall and Golden Ball Street areas between 1987 and 1998, investigating some 21 per cent (2 ha) of the 9.3 ha castle fee and amounting to one of the largest urban excavations anywhere in Europe (Figure 23.2), illuminate much more than the development of a castle (Shepherd Popescu 2009). The scale of the work was such that excavation revealed no less than an entire fossilized late Saxon townscape sealed beneath the castle fee, highlighting the extent to which the Norman Conquest had transformed the townscape (with the imposition of the castle fee and a new French borough) and the complexity of change which can lie behind the most basic of Domesday Book references, in this case to 'waste' on account of castle-building. To understand the castle as a discrete fortified site is probably misleading: such is the scale and complexity of the motte and multiple bailey that it is, in archaeological terms at least, a settlement in its own right with its own distinctive activity areas—industrial, military, residential, and religious—and its own internal social hierarchy too.

A striking array of different elements of masonry castles have been excavated: defensive (towers, curtain walls, donjons/keeps); residential, religious, and domestic (kitchens,

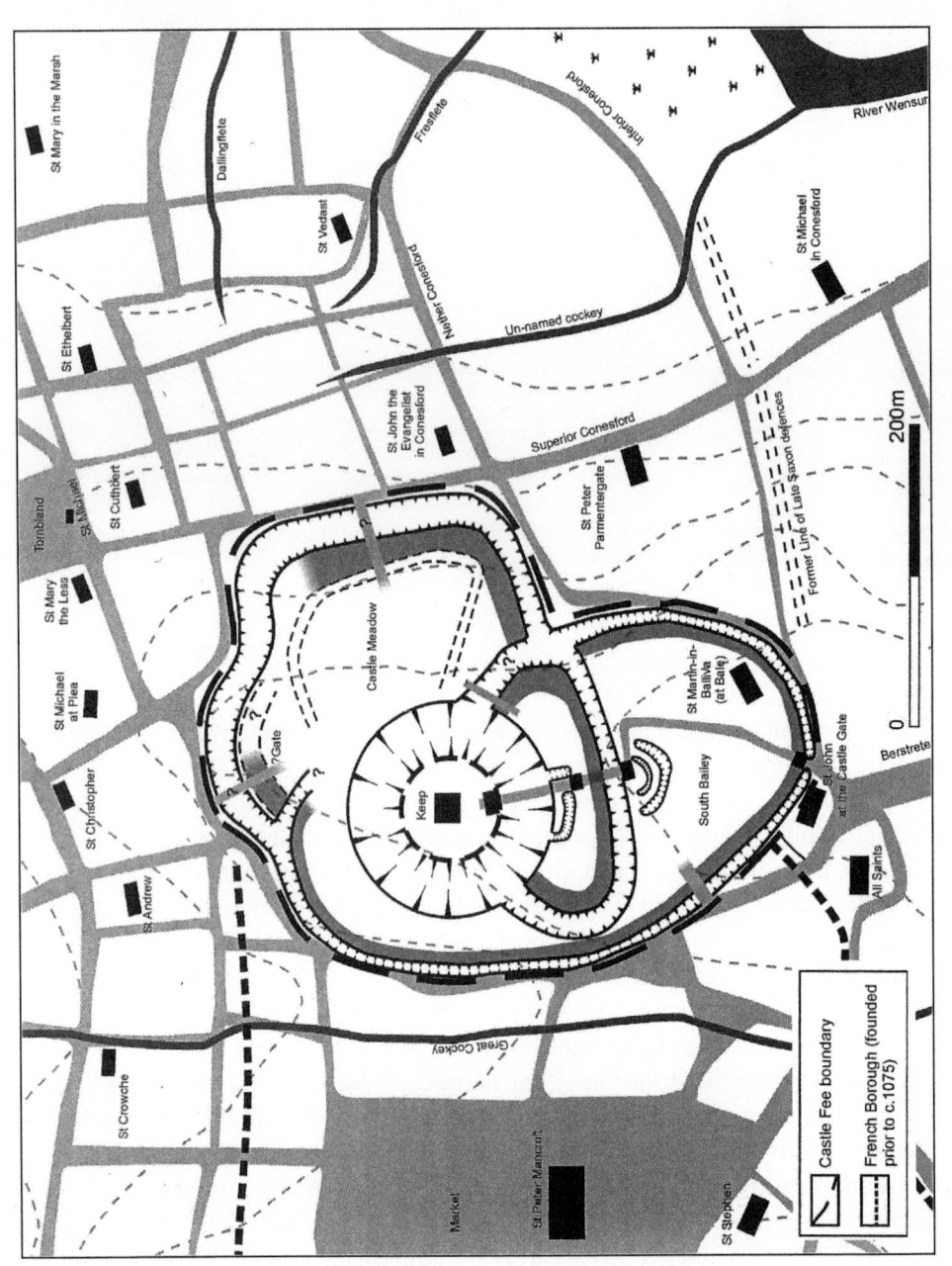

FIGURE 23.2 Norwich Castle, showing the positioning of the Norman castle within the Anglo-Saxon townscape (from Shepherd Popescu 2009)

(© reproduced with the kind permission of Norfolk Historic Environment Service)

halls, chapels, lodgings); and others associated with access (bridges, barbicans, and gatehouses) (for overview, see Kenyon 1990, 39–162). The propensity of archaeologists to focus on defensive and higher-status elements of the castle means that more mundane structures typically located in baileys or outer wards are rather less well represented, among them agricultural or industrial buildings or activity areas, or those associated with building works, such as lime kilns or tile kilns. The startling discovery, during excavations in 1972 in advance of proposed development, of a cob-built complex of thirteenth-century kitchens within the middle bailey of Wallingford castle (Figure 23.3) demonstrates that even a fortress near the summit of the social scale could contain working buildings of essentially vernacular form (see Christie and Creighton 2013, 183–202).

Investigations of earth-and-timber castles have done much to illuminate castle-building practices and lifestyle within sites distributed towards the lower end of the castle-building spectrum—including the castles of knights, lords of the manor, and in some cases under-tenants. An under-represented type of the site is the siege castle, military in purpose and short-term in nature but not without a symbolism of its own, as indicated by the Anarchy-period royal siege castle investigated in advance of housing development at Crowmarsh Gifford (Berkshire) (Laban 2013; and see Chapter 26 in this *Handbook*). Scholarship on earth-and-timber castles (there was no such thing as an 'earthwork castle') has displayed an enduring tendency to categorize the often vestigial physical remains of these sites into different types of mottes and ringworks, with or without baileys. Earthwork forms represent a 'catena'—or continuum of interlinked forms—rather than watertight morphological categories, however, and excavation highlights how the final forms of castle earthworks usually conceal considerable time-depth. The field archaeology of such sites is bedevilled by the host of 'possible', 'probable', and 'doubtful' castle earthworks, some confused with other features such as mill mounds, barrows, and prospect mounds, and others where fleeting and problematic documentary references are equated with dubious evidence on the ground.

A key achievement has been the general acceptance, based on archaeological evidence, that the timber castles which comprised such an important part of the total number of castles in the British landscape were not necessarily humble equivalents to their masonry counterparts, but could be sophisticated and visually impressive lordly residences (Higham and Barker 1992). It is deeply misleading to think of castles of stone as the superior successors to 'humble' castles of earth and timber: some of the earliest Norman castle-building in England involved stone (as with the late eleventh-century gatehouses at Exeter, Devon, and Ludlow, Shropshire); technologies were often mixed, with masonry castles containing timber buildings and components; and different sequences are apparent dependent upon region and upon the status of sites.

Archaeology documents the individuality and sometimes idiosyncrasy of timber castle-building; lords did not build to a blueprint. This reminds us once again that the castellologist's tendency to categorize sites has conceptual flaws: early castles were not intended as 'types' of motte and baileys, ringworks, and so on, but individualized creations that exhibited the character and coercive power of elite members of society. A key example is the Anarchy-period castle at South Mimms (Hertfordshire), where the motte would have actually been invisible to observers behind a palisade within which stood a timber

FIGURE 23.3 Wallingford: castle kitchens under excavation in 1972 (photograph by Robert Carr)

(© Oliver Creighton)

tower on a base of Roman *spolia*, accessible via a tunnel-style entrance cut through the earthwork; despite its modest scale the impression would still have been of a multi-tiered edifice looming above its hunting landscape (Kent et al. 2013). Other representative excavated earth-and-timber castles are (in Wales) Penmaen (Glamorgan) and Nevern (Pembrokeshire), and (in Scotland) Cruggleton and Mote of Urr (both Dumfries and Galloway), and Rattray and Castle Hill of Strachan (both Aberdeenshire). Other, less complete data on timber castles derive from investigations of early phases sealed beneath masonry fortifications.

Archaeological investigation of baileys provides the best means of exploring the everyday social and economic lives of castles and their interactions with outlying settlements, communities, estates, and hinterlands. Large-scale geophysics is under-used in castle archaeology but resistivity survey of Stafford Castle shows its potential, highlighting a multi-phase suite of buried settlement, garden, and other features within and beyond the defences (Darlington 2001, 88–99, 129–34). LiDAR data hold further potential to elucidate the more ephemeral and subtle castle earthworks (such as internal structures within baileys) and to map features in the environs such as field systems, gardens, water features, settlements, and pleasure grounds.

Integration of the evidence of often sizeable artefact and environmental assemblages with structural data has not always been realized, especially due to the challenges of post-excavation work, so that voluminous appendices of animal bone, pottery, and small finds do not always feed into analysis as fully as might be expected. Analysis of the huge assemblage of pottery from Barnard Castle (Co. Durham) highlights some important caveats in making inferences about castle life from such data. Detailed spatial plotting of sherds from individual vessels highlights the complexity of post-depositional processes: the conclusion being that while pottery deposits have little to tell us about the functions of rooms and 'micro-spaces', there was very little movement of pottery between the castle's larger units (its wards), so at this scale any social differences distinguishable within the pottery assemblages might be more 'real' (Austin 2007, 357–87). The sheer size of this overall assemblage, at some forty thousand sherds, many from previously unidentified types, tells us of the massive consumption and deposition of 'ordinary pottery' within an elite site; many of the finer wares did not find their way into the archaeological assemblage.

Techniques of spatial analysis, in particular planning diagrams and access analysis, have been employed with telling effect to the study of masonry castles (e.g. Fairclough 1992). They have also been adopted in the study of Irish tower-houses (Sherlock 2011). This mode of enquiry has much to tell us about the changing dynamic between castle planning and social changes, but only where structural survival is good. Through the configuration of residential, service, and other components we can engage critically with concepts such as the progressive privatization of space and the segregation of lords, the changing place of noblewomen, and the growth of households, for example. Such trends within castles studies can and must be related to changes in palaces and other elite structures and not viewed in isolation, however (see also Chapter 24). Detailed studies of architecture, chronology, and distribution still have prominent roles to play and traditional interpretations of even the supposedly best-known buildings can be treated critically and revised. A prime example is a re-interpretation of the Great Tower of Chepstow Castle

FIGURE 23.4 Chepstow Castle: the Great Tower

(© Oliver Creighton)

(Monmouthshire) (Figure 23.4), based on detailed fabric analysis (including geological analysis of the building stone) and fresh scrutiny of the documentary material (Turner 2004). This re-interpretation highlights the ceremonial function of the tower through its three phases, with the form, size, and decoration of its first-floor space indicating that this was no traditional great hall, and raises the likelihood that it was built for one of the Norman kings rather than Earl William fitz Osbern, as had been assumed from a problematical entry in Domesday Book. Even the internationally renowned Edwardian castles in Wales of the late thirteenth century can be re-appraised and new truths gained from integrated archaeological, historical, and architectural study (Williams and Kenyon 2010). In terms of archaeological science, radiocarbon dating of lime mortars holds great potential for studies of masonry castles. Dendrochronology, meanwhile, can be applied not only to roof timbers but also to the remains of joists, as it has with spectacular effect at Loches (Indre et Loire, France) where an unexpected early eleventh-century date was confirmed together with later phases of construction (Dormoy 1997).

Late medieval tower-houses are a renewed focus of debate, meaning that they are not necessarily regarded as a 'second-division sub-category of a superior genus labelled "castles"' (Oram 2015, ix). The label 'tower-house' is artificial and inadequate; new research is showing how they were not necessarily symptomatic of poverty and instability, but social arenas in their own right. A key question is to which extent towers were self-contained or set within larger units such as barmkins (courtyards) and accompanied by other structures. The case of Smailholm (Roxburghshire) is instructive. Here excavation next to the fifteenth-century tower-house showed that this cramped defensive unit was supplemented with an adjoining domestic building, kitchens, and a garden space (Good and Tabraham 1988). Bastles (thick-walled defensible upper-floor houses, typically of the sixteenth and seventeenth centuries and characteristic of the Anglo-Scottish borderlands) have been neglected but studies reveal denser distributions than previously envisaged for a type of structure closely related to farming and, chronologically, constructed on the cusp of the post-medieval world (see, for example, Ryder 1992).

Research Directions

The need to look beyond the castle walls and appreciate not only the place of fortification in the landscape, but also the active role of their lords in transforming contemporary environments has emerged as a key theme in research (Austin 1984; Creighton 2005). The landscape of any given castle was not just a 'setting' and a collection of resources and geographical features that can help us understand why a particular site was positioned where it was. Rather, castles were enmeshed within different sorts of landscape at different levels. As estate centres, castles were integrated within the workaday world of the manor; agricultural facilities such as mills and granaries could be found in close association and they were, in effect, working farms. But at the same time, most castles were also elevated above the vernacular landscape as centres of high-quality living, consumption, and display. Associations with estate churches that received patronage visually distinguished the seigneurial core within settlements, as did the frequent setting of castles within or on the edges of lordly landscapes of leisure that could include gardens, parks, and hunting grounds.

Important case studies such as 'Goltho' (Lincolnshire), Laxton (Nottinghamshire), and Middleton Stoney (Oxfordshire) tell us about the agency of seigneurial families at the scale of individual parishes. Park creation, settlement planning, the diversion of road systems, and the foundation and patronage of churches and sometimes monasteries are among the hallmarks of lordly influence in the countryside (Creighton 2005, 21–7, 175–222). Boteler's (or Oversley) Castle, near Alcester (Warwickshire), known from excavation in advance of road building in the early 1990s (Jones et al. 1997) is a key site. A small and entirely undocumented early twelfth- to thirteenth-century settlement was revealed, with a planned layout and hints of a non-agricultural economic base, all enclosed within bailey-like defences attached to this timber castle; this speaks of a specialist unit linked to the seigneurial core or even a nascent (but entirely undocumented) borough.

More holistic approaches to the settings of medieval castles have dovetailed with a wider upsurge in interest in 'designed medieval landscapes' (Creighton 2009), although the idea is not without its conceptual caveats as well as practical issues of dating (Liddiard and Williamson 2008). Features associated with lordly presence could be used for display as well as constituting features of seigneurial exploitation. These included features on the demesne, in the immediate setting of a castle, such as the dovecote, fishponds, and water mills that might be integrated with moated defences, and those further afield, such as rabbit warrens and deer parks (see also Chapter 25). Arrangements of such features, many with ostensibly economic-productive functions, not only take on added significance as emblems of lordship, but were arguably laid out to impress, overawe, or transmit social messages to contemporaries. Yet it is critical that models based on lowland England are not somehow seen as the 'norm'. Across great tracts of the British landscape castles were part and parcel of non-nucleated landscapes, and different environments saw lordship manifested and expressed in widely different ways. In parts of Scotland and Ireland with strongly Gaelic character, burgeoning research is revealing distinctive relationships between lordship and landscape where native dynasts expressed their power in fundamentally different ways to the 'Anglo-Norman' model (Duffy et al. 2001, 271–435; Oram 2008a, 355–6). Lordly command of seascapes, seaways, and lakes could be as strong as control of the terrestrial landscape, and the locations of tower-houses and crannogs could reference past ritual landscapes.

The multiple visual qualities of castles ensure that studies of 'projective' views (i.e. looking in on the castle from its surroundings) and 'reflective views' (looking outwards from the site, from windows or parapet tops) are further important dimensions to the elite landscape. Re-interpretation of the mid-thirteenth-century triple-tiered High Tower at Launceston Castle (Cornwall) as a both a viewing point to observe the surrounding deer park and a crown-like icon of the Earl of Cornwall's authority (Saunders 2006, 231–2, 457–8) highlights these two essential dimensions to the visual qualities of noble buildings. Geographic Information System (GIS) technologies hold unlocked potential for understanding not only the privileged lordly gaze, but the impact of these sites on populations (McManama-Kearin 2013). Medieval gardens are also being interpreted in new ways and understood at different scales. The King's Knot at Stirling, the site of a late medieval formal garden remodelled in the seventeenth and nineteenth centuries, was part of a complex landscape of leisure embedded within a deer park and clearly intended to be viewed from high-status apartments above (Figure 23.5);

FIGURE 23.5 The King's Knot, Stirling, looking south from the royal apartments and showing part of the area taken up by the deer park

(© Oliver Creighton)

geophysical survey has highlighted its time depth, with underlying early medieval or even prehistoric features (Digney and Jones 2013).

The notion that landscapes could be composed for 'structured viewing' and impact upon the senses before the Renaissance is contentious. Pre-modern ideas of space, visuality, and aesthetics are certainly complex, but how controversial can the 'medieval designed landscape' idea really be when the notion that landscapes were used to condition human experiences of ritual settings is such a mainstay of research in prehistory? Future research needs not merely to identify further examples of 'designed' castle landscapes, but also to devote attention to the origins and multiple meanings of these settings and to examine the spread of the phenomenon, for which contextual study within Europe is essential. Landscapes of the lesser nobility also require consideration (Hansson 2009). Another imperative in researching how lordly agency impacted upon the countryside is to move beyond polarized notions of 'power and domination' (Saunders 1990), to embrace themes such as peasant resistance in the face of seigneurial authority, and limitations on the growth and impact of lordship.

Lordship could have an ecological signature too; the living 'animalscape' was an extension of the material culture of aristocracy (Pluskowski 2007, 43–4; see Chapter 10 in this *Handbook*). It is for this reason that we find the first or very early instances of newly introduced animal species attested at castle sites: species such as fallow deer and rabbits, but also less obviously peacocks, for example, recorded in a late eleventh-/twelfth-century context from Carisbrooke Castle (Isle of Wight) (Serjeantson 2006, 142).

Zooarchaeological assemblages from castle sites tell us about changing environments, fashions, and tastes; one important trend is the increasing diversity of wild game found on aristocratic tables in the post-Black Death world where the lower classes were eating more and more meat and the aristocracy sought new ways to differentiate themselves.

The place of the castle in the medieval imagination and mind-set must be another key theme for future work; the motif of the castle in medieval poetry and literature (Wheatley 2004) has the potential to enrich archaeological understandings and make interpretations more authentically grounded in medieval society's own view of one of its most characteristic institutions. Such concerns will influence the evidence that we use but also the way we write: Barnwell's (2007) treatment of Peak, or Peveril Castle (Derbyshire), shows how 'hard' archaeological analysis can be enriched by cognisance of twelfth-century literature. This account explores the sensory experiences of those moving in and around the site—for example from the point of view of returning hunting parties whose participants, drawn from different social groups, had different sensory experiences of the castle. The spatial level of resolution for archaeological studies of castles is another important issue. The changing focus away from the archaeological study of elite components within castles towards baileys, castle communities, and inter-relationships with settlements has been highlighted, but archaeologies of lordships present another area with clear potential. Archaeology can illuminate how lordship was manifested and articulated over networks of estates containing multiple residences, exploring for example whether lordship sites operated within or outside 'normal' food procurement and the extent to which estate networks shaped pottery supply.

Internationalizing archaeological approaches must be another priority. In studying castles we are examining the products of a social elite whose cultural and landholding interests spanned national boundaries and it is only right that we should take account of this. Like other branches of later medieval archaeology castle studies remains compartmentalized on national grounds and this must change. The notion of an aristocratic mind-set with common pan-European currency has appeal (Creighton 2012; Hansson 2006; 2009), and we can better explore commonalities that move us away from nationally focused research agendas.

References cited

Allen Brown, R. 1969 'An historian's approach to the origins of the castle in England', *The Archaeological Journal* 126, 131–48

Austin, D. 1984 'The castle and the landscape', *Landscape History* 6, 70–81

Austin, D. 2007 *Acts of perception: a study of Barnard Castle in Teesdale*, Architectural and Archaeological Society of Durham and Northumberland, Durham (2 vols)

Baker, J. and Brookes, S. 2013 *Beyond the Burghal Hidage: Anglo-Saxon civil defence in the Viking Age*, Brill, Leiden and Boston

Barker, P. and Higham, R. 1982 *Hen Domen, Montgomery: a timber castle on the Welsh border*, Royal Archaeological Institute, London

Barnwell, P. S. 2007 'The power of Peak Castle: cultural contexts and changing perceptions', *Journal of the British Archaeological Association* 160, 20–38

Castle Studies Group 1987 'Statement of intent', *Castle Studies Group Newsletter* 1, 2
Christie, N. and Creighton, O. H., with Edgeworth, M. and Hamerow, H. 2013 *Transforming townscapes. From burh to borough: the archaeology of Wallingford, AD 800–1400*, The Society for Medieval Archaeology Monograph 35, London
Creighton, O. H. 2005 *Castles and landscapes: power, community and fortification in medieval England*, Equinox, London
Creighton, O. H. 2009 *Designs upon the land: elite landscapes of the Middle Ages*, Boydell Press, Woodbridge
Creighton, O. H. 2012 *Early European Castles: aristocracy and authority, AD 800–1200*, Duckworth, London
Creighton, O. H. and Liddiard, R. 2008 'Fighting yesterday's battle: beyond war or status in castle studies', *Medieval Archaeology* 52, 161–9
Darlington, J. (ed.) 2001 *Stafford Castle: survey, excavation and research 1978–1998, Vol. I: the surveys*, Stafford Borough Council, Stafford
Davison, B. K. 1967 'The origins of the castle in England: the Institute's research project', *The Archaeological Journal* 124, 202–11
Digney, S. and Jones, R. E. 2013 'Recent investigations at the King's Knot Stirling', *Forth Naturalist and Historian* 36, 129–48
Dormoy, C. 1997 'L'expertise dendrochronologique du donjon de Loches (Indre-et-Loire): des donnés fondamentales pour sa datation', *Archéologie Médiévale* 27, 73–87
Duffy, P. J., Edwards, D., and FitzPatrick, E. (eds) 2001 *Gaelic Ireland c.1250–c.1650: land, lordship and settlement*, Four Courts Press, Dublin
Ellis, P. 2000 *Ludgershall Castle, Wiltshire: a report on the excavations by Peter Addyman, 1964–1972*, Wiltshire Archaeological and Natural History Society, Devizes
Everson, P. 1988 'What's in a name? "Goltho", Goltho and Bullington', *Lincolnshire History and Archaeology* 23, 93–9
Fairclough, G. 1992 'Meaningful constructions: spatial and functional analysis of medieval buildings', *Antiquity* 66, 348–66
Good, G. L. and Tabraham, C. J. 1988 'Excavations at Smailholm Tower, Roxburghshire', *Proceedings of the Society of Antiquaries of Scotland* 118, 231–66
Hansson, M. 2006 *Aristocratic landscape: the spatial ideology of the medieval aristocracy*, Almqvist and Wiksell International, Stockholm
Hansson, M. 2009 'The medieval aristocracy and the social use of space', in R. Gilchrist and A. Reynolds (eds), *Reflections: 50 years of medieval archaeology 1957–2007*, The Society for Medieval Archaeology Monograph 30, Leeds, 435–52
Higham, R. and Barker, P. 2000 *Hen Domen, Montgomery. A timber castle on the English-Welsh Border: a final report*, Exeter University Press, Exeter
Higham, R. and Barker, P. 1992 *Timber castles*, Batsford, London
Johnson, M. 2002 *Behind the castle gate: from medieval to Renaissance*, Routledge, London
Jones, C., Eyre-Morgan, G., Palmer, S., and Palmer, N. 1997 'Excavations in the outer enclosure of Boteler's Castle, Oversley, Alcester, 1992–3', *Transactions of the Birmingham and Warwickshire Archaeological Society* 101, 1–98
Kent, J., Renn, D., and Streeten, A. 2013 *Excavations at South Mimms Castle, Hertfordshire 1960–91*, London and Middlesex Archaeological Society Special Paper 16, Lavenham Press, Lavenham
Kenyon, J. R. 1990 *Medieval fortifications*, Leicester University Press, Leicester
King, D. J. C. 1983 *Castellarium anglicanum* (2 vols), Kraus, London
Laban, G. 2013 'Evidence for a Stephanic siege castle at the Lister Wilder Site, The Street, Crowmarsh Gifford', *Oxoniensia* 78, 189–212

Liddiard, R. 2005 *Castles in context: power, symbolism and landscape, 1066 to 1500*, Windgather, Bollington

Liddiard, R. and Williamson, T. 2008 'There by design? Some reflections on medieval elite landscapes', *The Archaeological Journal* 165, 520–35

McManama-Kearin, L. K. 2013 *The use of GIS in determining the role of visibility in the siting of early Anglo-Norman stone castles in Ireland*, British Archaeological Reports British Series 575, Archaeopress, Oxford

Oram, R. 2008a 'Castles, concepts and contexts: castle studies in Scotland in retrospect and prospect', *Château Gaillard* 23, 349–58

Oram, R. 2008b 'Royal and lordly residence in Scotland c.1050 to c.1250: an historiographical review and critical revision', *The Antiquaries Journal* 88, 165–89

Oram, R. (ed.) 2015 *A house that thieves might knock at: proceedings of the 2010 Stirling and 2011 Dundee conferences*, Paul Watkins Publishing, Donington

Platt, C. 2007 'Revisionism in castle studies: a caution', *Medieval Archaeology* 51, 83–102

Pluskowski, A. 2007 'Communicating through skin and bone: appropriating animal bodies in medieval Western European seigneurial culture', in A. Pluskowski (ed.), *Breaking and shaping beastly bodies: animals as material culture in the Middle Ages*, Oxbow, Oxford, 32–51

Ryder, P. F. 1992 'Bastles and bastle-like buildings in Allendale, Northumberland', *The Archaeological Journal* 149, 351–79

Saunders, A. D. 1977 'Five castle excavations: reports on the Institute's research project into the origins of the castle in England', *The Archaeological Journal* 134, 1–156

Saunders, A. D. 2006 *Excavations at Launceston Castle, Cornwall*, The Society for Medieval Archaeology Monograph 24, Leeds

Saunders, T. 1990 'The feudal construction of space: power and domination in the nucleated village', in R. Samson (ed.), *The social archaeology of houses*, Edinburgh University Press, Edinburgh, 181–96

Serjeantson, D. 2006 'Birds: food and a mark of status', in C. M. Woolgar, D. Serjeantson and T. Waldron (eds), *Food in medieval England: diet and nutrition*, Oxford University Press Oxford, 131–47

Shepherd Popescu, E. 2009 *Norwich Castle: excavations and historical survey 1987–98. Part I: Anglo-Saxon to c.1345; Part II: c.1345 to modern*, Norfolk Archaeological Unit/Historic Environment, Norfolk Museums and Archaeology Service, Dereham

Sherlock, R. 2011 'The evolution of the Irish tower house as a domestic space', *Proceedings of the Royal Irish Academy* 111C, 115–40

Stocker, D. 1992 'The shadow of the general's armchair', *The Archaeological Journal* 149, 415–20

Thompson, M. W. 1994 'The military interpretation of castles', *The Archaeological Journal* 151, 439–45

Turner, R. C. 2004 'The Great Tower, Chepstow Castle, Wales', *The Antiquaries Journal* 84, 223–318

Wheatley, A. 2004 *The idea of the castle in medieval England*, Boydell Press, Woodbridge

Williams, D. M. and Kenyon, J. R. 2010 *The impact of the Edwardian castles in Wales: the proceedings of a conference held at Bangor University, 7–9 September 2007*, Oxbow, Oxford

CHAPTER 24

MEDIEVAL PALACES AND ROYAL HOUSES

TOM BEAUMONT JAMES

THE concept of the palace in later medieval Britain derived from various origins: the houses on the Palatine Hill in Rome, Anglo-Saxon royal houses such as Cheddar in Somerset (excavated by Philip Rahtz in the 1960s; Rahtz 1979), and Yeavering in Northumberland (excavated by Brian Hope-Taylor in the 1950s; Hope-Taylor 1977). These last two were royal sites for pre-Conquest dynasties in different parts of Britain. By the time these kingdoms were united under the Normans, the royal family had a base at Westminster, outside the walls of the city of London, squeezed between the abbey and the Thames on a rather indifferent site. In order to control its large and diverse population, the Tower of London was built before 1100 and its orientation leaves no doubt as to its purpose: it occupies the south-east corner of the walled area and confronts the city. Apart from its exceptional size, the arrangement of the Tower, with its main royal accommodation on the upper storey, speaks volumes not only for the vigour of the Norman kings, but also their skill with fortifications, their ambition in controlling the London metropolis, and their forward-looking architecture with its wall-fireplaces for added comfort (Ashbee 2006; Harris 2016; Hiller and Keevill 1995; Impey 2008; Keevill 2004; Parnell 1977; 2013; Thurley 1995; 1993).

These two structures, the palace of Westminster and the Tower of London, epitomize the two types of palatial residence occupied by royalty by 1100: the undefended palace and the castle-palace. Other royal palaces and castle-palaces included more rural retreats such as Clarendon in Wiltshire and Woodstock in Oxfordshire, both undefended residences in the grand *villa rustica* style. The other great castle-palace which developed in the period 1100–1540 was Windsor in Berkshire (Thurley 1993).

In addition there were episcopal palaces. The collapse of the western Roman Empire from the early fifth century, and the subsequent colonization by Islam from the seventh century of most of the Christian centres of the eastern Mediterranean and north Africa heightened the focus on Rome, the centre of the western church. This political weakness in western Europe propelled bishops into the role of managing large areas of the Christian west in collaboration with local leaders. For this reason, and in contrast to the episcopate in the eastern Church, western bishops found themselves working closely with local rulers. In the Winchester diocese, for example, the kings of Wessex endowed the bishopric with sufficient land to render it the wealthiest seen north of the Alps long before 1100. Church and state at the highest level of society were very closely connected. In turn, such enormous landholdings enabled bishops to create luxurious residences funded by the income from their many manors (Rollason 2017). Their principal Winchester residence, the mighty Romanesque structure called Wolvesey, was described in the twelfth century variously as a *domus quasi palatium*, an element within de Blois's wider scheme of *palatia sumptuosissima*. Wolvesey was extensively, if partially, excavated and recorded by Martin Biddle in the 1960s but remains unpublished (see, for example, Biddle 1970). Lyddington Bede House (Figure 24.1) was originally a medieval wing of a palace of the bishops of Lincoln. Like many palaces it later changed its use and was converted into an almshouse by the end of the sixteenth century.

Royal houses were associated with specialized landscapes which were in place by 1100. In France for example, the Capetian kings settled on Paris as their capital because of the quality of the hunting grounds nearby; at a later date kings of Scotland were to select Falkland (Fife) for similar reasons. William the Conqueror had been described as loving deer as if they were his children (in any case the deer were more pleasant than his children). His son Henry I (1100–35) was a keen hunter, creator of parks, and a keeper

FIGURE 24.1 Lyddington Bede House in Leicestershire, part of a medieval bishop's palace, probably private chambers with extensive buried remains which would once have enclosed an open courtyard

(© Paul Stamper)

of wild animals including camels, lynx, and porcupine in his park at Woodstock (Bond 1987; for buildings here and elsewhere, see Brown et al. 1963; for lions at the Tower of London, see Keevill 2000 and O'Regan et al. 2006). Deerparks were associated both with royal houses and palaces and also with episcopal houses and palaces. Some residences were moated, such as Writtle, a hunting lodge in Essex associated with King John (Rahtz 1969) and equipped with fashionable and labour-intensive fishponds, or Wells, the episcopal residence in Somerset constructed for the bishops of the diocese of Bath and Wells (Dunning 2010).

The use of palaces by royalty, and to a lesser extent by the archiepiscopate and episcopate, was intermittent (Figure 24.2). Some kings were more mobile than others. The early Norman kings of England, William I (1066–89) and William II (1089–1100), began oversize, 'colonial' building schemes such as the Tower of London, Winchester Cathedral with its giant nave and westworks designed to be used for crown-wearing ceremony, and Westminster great hall, the largest of its kind in Europe (Courtney and Mark 1987). It may be argued that similar grand landscape schemes, such as the walled park at Woodstock, where the buildings were lost in the early eighteenth century and thus are recorded now only in antiquarian accounts, and the exceptionally sized park at Clarendon, were products of the same, 'colonial' regimes (Richardson 2005). Keen to impress and overawe the local population, schemes such as these were created with funds seized from the previous regime.

Norman rulers controlled large parts of Europe from Sicily to northern Europe to England in the eleventh to thirteenth centuries. This produced cross-fertilization of design—for example the introduction of the donjon keep into England from Normandy, while the introduction of fallow deer and park culture flowed northwards from Sicily to England, whence fallow deer culture was exported to Normandy, for example (Sykes 2004). Occasionally elements of southern European palace design, e.g. interconnecting pools such as those found at Palermo (Sicily) and later at the Alhambra (Granada, Spain), found their way into England, for example into Everswell in Woodstock Park, the bijou residence created in the royal park by Henry II for his young mistress Rosamund Clifford in the late twelfth century (Bond 1987, 46). This structure echoed contemporary literature, the tale of Tristan and Isolde, popular at that time, where an enclosed residence for Isolde necessitated the passing of notes via waterways. There was, no doubt, a pan-European interest among elites in aspects of these structures. Henry of Blois, brother of King Stephen (1135–54) and the most likely candidate for extensive building work at Guildford Castle, Surrey, was well known for his use of imported ancient Classical *spolia* to his episcopal palace at Wolvesey in Winchester, while his dazzling Winchester Bible of *c*.1160 illustrates Romanesque interiors, roofs, decorative schemes, palace life, and furnishings (Donovan 1993).

By 1200 much Romanesque palace building was completed under the Norman and Angevin kings, especially during the long reigns of Henry I (1100–35, the remains of his Romanesque Great Hall at Woodstock being recorded by John Aubrey before 1700) and Henry II (1154–89). John's busy itineraries led to the creation of many facilities appropriate for the arrival of royal retinues at short notice, such as the kitchen arrangements at

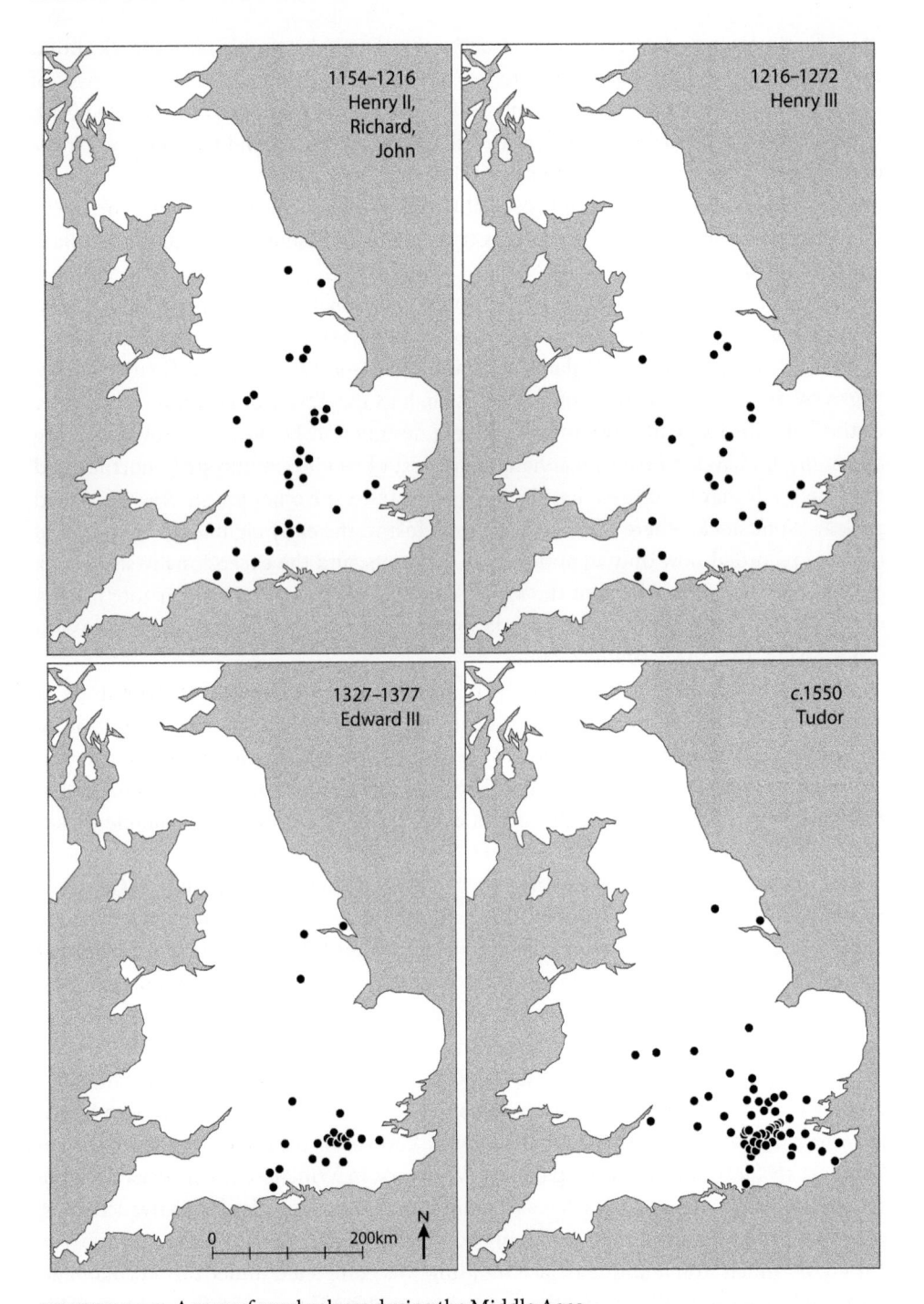

FIGURE 24.2 A map of royal palaces during the Middle Ages

(© Alejandra Gutiérrez)

the royal castle of Marlborough in Wiltshire (not excavated but for a plan, see Brentnall 1938), where hearths were capable of roasting two oxen at once. However costly these building works might be, they were dwarfed by other expenses such as the furnishings recorded in the Exchequer Rolls which begin in regular series from 1154. The earliest English royal household account of 1207 shows that the greatest expense in royal travel was the fodder for the horses rather than the food and drink for the court travellers (Woolgar 1999). Hunting parks such as Clarendon, Woodstock, and elsewhere were used seasonally by the kings according to set patterns of the hunting year, supply and availability of sport, and so on. In the thirteenth century some evidence shows that kings such as Henry III visited the park at Clarendon during the doe hunting season (today 1 November to 29 April), the buck hunting season was earlier, more of a summer activity and that is when we find Edward II—who is documented engaged in hunting there in 1326—and Edward III at Clarendon (Richardson 2005). These palaces within their parks were undefended sites in rural areas, the rural counterparts of Westminster, and with their extensive paling fences and embankments have been described as 'castles for deer'.

One of the reasons for King John's (1199–1216) unpopularity in England was that he was exceptionally mobile. He was never in the same place for more than a month in his seventeen-and-a-half year reign. This has resulted in a plethora of sites being dubbed 'King John's' house or palace and he no doubt visited many of them (e.g. Rahtz 1969). Many of his subjects' communities had not been visited by royalty for generations, if ever, although it remains a moot point as to whether the king was welcomed by all, as the debacle of Magna Carta and the civil war of 1215–16 was to demonstrate. The lifestyle of John was mirrored by his Welsh counterparts, who were likewise itinerant and who also travelled to royal and other sites during progresses, stopping for example at Rhuddlan or Degannwy, Gwynedd, to do business, justice, and 'to eat [their] way through' taxes (Pound 1994). This was a lifestyle readily recognizable in England and Scotland in the Middle Ages among royalty, prelates, and nobility, but which in Wales came to an end for their kings with the conquest of Wales in 1283 and subsequent attempts from a string of comfortable royal castles in North Wales to pacify the principality. Geophysical work at the end of the last century identified some of these *llys* or royal complexes of the Welsh kings (Smith 2014).

Then as now, fashions changed, and royalty often led the way, or at least picked the best of what they saw others doing. Thus, when Romanesque architecture with its solid, rounded arches, gave way to the pointed architecture of the Gothic, royalty were among the leaders of this fashion. Louis IX of France (1226–70) inspired his brother-in-law Henry III of England (1216–72) to become a 'champion of the Gothic'. Various claims have been made and disputed about the influence of Arab architecture on the transition from Romanesque to Gothic arising from contacts made during the crusades which began in 1095. What is more certain is the spread of Christian material culture from Byzantium after the fourth crusade of 1207 when many relics were looted by the western European crusaders who sacked the ancient capital of the eastern church. Of these relics, the Crown of Thorns from Christ's passion was the most prized. This led to the establishment of a series of chapels of *l'epine* across France as individual thorns were disposed of by the king. The most significant of these repositories in the Gothic style was the Sainte-Chapelle in Paris, with is full-size reliquary design both exterior and interior (Cohen 2008). Chapels similar in design, tall and narrow, were built across Europe from the middle of the thirteenth century, for example in London and at Clarendon in Wiltshire. Among the European building stock, three from France might be highlighted. The first, at Perpignan, was begun c.1270 for the kings of Majorca and incorporated Islamic influences (Passarius and Catafau 2014). The second, at Hesdin (Artois), was created c.1295 as a palatial pleasure garden over 940 hectares enclosed by a wall 13 km in length; it was intended as a Garden of Eden complete with various machines which dispensed water, feathers, and soot and further amused (or confused) visitors with mirrors (Van Buren 1986). Hesdin may have been the inspiration, after a visit in 1313, for Edward II to lavish attention on enlarging his own parks. But if Hesdin was an inspirational garden, the greatest palace in the early fourteenth century was the massive Palace of the Popes at Avignon, built during the exile of the papacy from Rome between the early and mid-fourteenth century (Renoux 1994). Claimed as the largest Gothic building in Europe, the campaigns of Benedict XII (1334–42) and subsequently Clement VI (1346–56) were outstanding, the buildings combining the grandeur of French Gothic with decorative schemes by Italian craftsmen.

During the fourteenth century, war between France and England, insecurities of succession in the Capetian family, and dispossession of monarchs in England such as Edward II (1327) and Richard II (1399) all inhibited grand palace development, although Richard did create small-scale building-jewels, such as his palatial accommodation on the south coast at Portchester, Hampshire (Cunliffe 1977; 1985), and his island retreat (now entirely lost) at 'La Nayght' on the Thames at Surbiton, Surrey. He is recorded as adding 'dancing rooms' at various palaces across England. Notably, he razed the palace at Sheen, Surrey, to the ground following the death there of his wife Anne of Bohemia in 1392. However, by far the greatest achievements in palace building in England were a result of the coming together of the necessary leadership (for example by William of Wykeham and William Wynford) and the required financial resources which arose from the capture and ransom of John II of France at the Battle of Poitiers in 1356. This enabled the completion of outstanding works such as the chapel of St Stephen at Westminster (traditionally begun in the reign of King Stephen, d. 1154) which was achieved despite the shortage of labour and skills following the Black Death of 1348–50. Greater still was the work carried through after 1356 at Windsor castle-palace where the Norman keep was upgraded and rerofed, and the unusual 'Round Table' building of 1344, based on a Mediterranean prototype, was dismantled and replaced by a major building scheme in the upper bailey consisting of an end-on hall and chapel under a single roof-ridge, accommodation for retainers, upgraded kitchens etc., all of this on a grand scale (Tatton-Brown 2010).

Agency of popes, royalty, their relations, and leading staff, such as Wykeham (in the 1350s) and other prelates, is key in these works. As Edward III declined militarily, physically, and financially (ransom monies stopped with the death of King John II in 1364), royal building slowed although the heir to the throne, Edward the Black Prince, upgraded and modernized his palatial residence at Kennington, in London south of the Thames. Both Edwards were dead by the end of 1377. The significant decline in royal and episcopal incomes following the Black Death put a brake on the more grandiose schemes. In England the change from richly carved, labour-intensive, decorated architecture to the regional mass-produced conformity of the Perpendicular style illustrates the changing circumstances very well. Continuing international and civil wars in Europe drained resources, with a kaleidoscope of changing fortunes and monarchs, as France recovered towards the mid-fifteenth century, so England fell into disarray.

In common with his predecessor Richard II, Henry V (1412–22) took special delight in small private and secluded sites, such as the moated 'Pleasaunce' at Kenilworth Castle in Warwickshire, across the lake from the main magnate residence (Jamieson and Lane 2015). But he also drove forward grand schemes such as the reconstruction of a residence at Sheen adorned with antelope images on the roof. All this was in stark contrast to Henry VI, who was not renowned as a builder of palaces (although his colleges at Eton, Berkshire, and at King's in Cambridge were, so far as they went, significant architectural achievements, left incomplete at his death). Meanwhile in Scotland, James I (1406–37), after eighteen years of captivity in England, returned to Scotland in 1424 to a small group of residences or palaces, notably Edinburgh and Stirling castles and Linlithgow palace. Kings of an earlier era had been crowned at Scone Palace, Perthshire, an abbey and abbatial palace adjacent to Perth on the Tay. Scone had long been a key site in Scottish royal ceremony and remained so until dissolved as a monastery in 1559, analogous arguably to Westminster Abbey and Palace near London (Dunbar 1999). Perhaps the greatest extent of Scottish royal residences developed under James V (1514–42) with the capable assistance of his advisers for he came to the throne aged only 1 year old. The royal property portfolio of residences expanded into Angus and the lordship of Glamis at which point in the mid-sixteenth century he laid claim to some thirty-six properties which could be drawn upon during his itineraries.

With the deposition of Henry VI and his untimely death in 1471, the Yorkist kings drew in their ambitions for widespread travel and reduced use of the more remote residences such as the most westerly at Clarendon, where Henry VI had suffered the first onset of his mental collapse in 1453. So although ovens there were kept up as late as 1485 against the visit of the 'northern' King Richard III, there is no evidence that he or his Tudor successors visited the palace as a residence although Henry VII, Henry VIII, and Elizabeth used the park (Beaumont James and Gerrard 2007). Under Henry VIII (1509–47), however, matters were to alter substantially so far as palaces were concerned. What first changed the scene was the king's falling out with his senior churchmen which brought new palaces into royal hands. Among these were Cardinal Wolsey's Hampton Court in 1529 and York Palace (Whitehall), as well as a range of other episcopal and archiepiscopal residences such as Mayfield in Sussex and Oatlands in Kent. Second, when this king entered into his dispute with the monasteries, their dissolution provided further opportunities for palatial royal endeavours, for example the conversion of part of the enormous St Augustine's Abbey in Canterbury, Kent, dissolved in 1538, to a royal residence used for example by the new Queen Anne of Cleves as she made her way to London in 1540.

Undoubtedly the major achievement in palace building in the final phase of the period to 1540 was the creation of the eponymous Nonsuch Palace, Surrey (Biddle 2005), following the birth of Prince Edward in 1537. Here the king drew on French and Italian craftsmen; the materials, moulded plaster with gilded slate covering over an oak frame, were unique in England, and not well suited to the climate. What is apparent from the layout and the plans of Nonsuch, and other royal residences of the same period, is that in many respects they followed the ancient gendered plans of apartments for the king, apartments for the queen. When compared to the Tower of London of the Normans, Angevin, or Plantagenet palaces—or indeed to palaces in use today for that matter—the royal apartments and persons were deeply hidden (Richardson 2003; see Chapter 50 in this *Handbook*). Work on queens' accommodation, palaces, and landholdings is one area awaiting closer scrutiny.

Archaeology and Complementary Sources for Palaces

For England the greatest royal palace was undoubtedly Westminster which lies beyond the walled area of the City of London. The Westminster complex of buildings, which includes the royal abbey, is most certainly the most significant source of evidence for the medieval palace and for royal-ecclesiastical links, the abbey being the coronation church of the kings with its late medieval coronation chair and its unique survivals of architectural style and decorative schemes including the late thirteenth-century Cosmati pavements (see cover), polychromy, and sculpture. Westminster boasts fossilized fragments of decor which have vanished almost everywhere else. Although St Stephen's chapel at the palace has gone, the Chapel of the Pew in the Abbey contains in microcosm much detail which matches records of what was once to be seen at St Stephen's, from doorway to vaulting and architectural detail of the 1370s (Spooner 2015).

Much of the medieval palace at Westminster was destroyed in the fire of 1834 but the great hall of William II (Rufus) survives (Figure 24.3). Recent work argues for a remarkable panelled ceiling to the eleventh-century hall, so that it was never an aisled hall (Harris and Miles 2015). The 600-tonne hammer beam roof of the 1390s stands today as a monument to the technical, lapidary, engineering, and craft skills of that era (Munby 2015). While archaeology is of great value, much of the historic palace has disappeared over the centuries, not least in the fire of 1263. Changes, upgradings, and demolitions in the early nineteenth century (for example of the queen's apartments and her chapel) were recorded by antiquarians and others, and they have provided, for example, a record of the thirteenth-century Painted Chamber before its murals were wallpapered over. These remarkable watercolour records by artists such as Capon and Stothard are

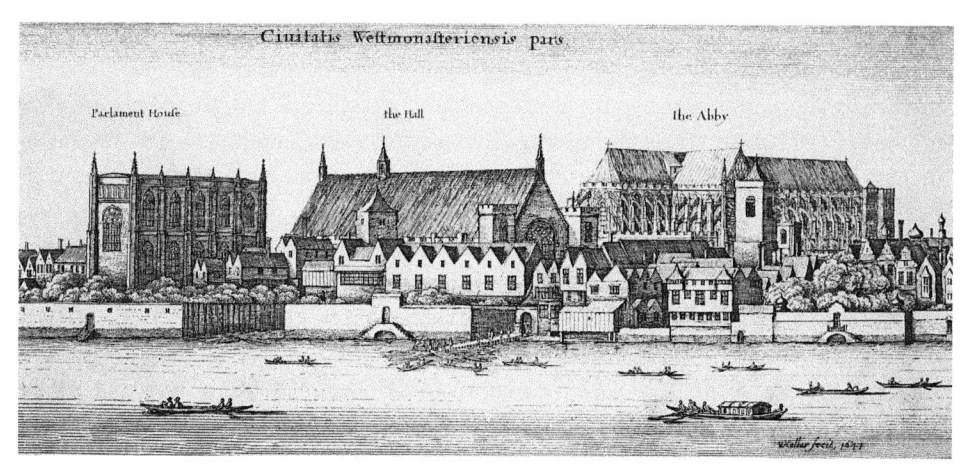

FIGURE 24.3 Westminster palace and abbey, as depicted by Wenceslaus Hollar in 1647 (Thomas Fisher Rare Book Library, University of Toronto, public domain)

invaluable for understanding the later medieval structures and their décor (Emery 2006, 258). The fire of 1834 also cleared accretions to some buildings leaving, for example, the outer walls of St Stephen's Chapel, which had been used since the Reformation as the parliament chamber (medieval parliaments having met in such spaces as the Chapter House of the adjacent abbey). The reconstruction of the parliament debating space by Barry post-1834 as a reproduction of the north and south confronting medieval canons' stalls has been argued to have continued the tradition of adversarial English politics encouraged by the re-use of the facing stalls of the former canons, established by Edward III (d. 1377) (Rodwell 2015).

Because of its scale, the ongoing use of Westminster as a centre of national government, the needs for security, and the challenge of making the medieval abbey partly available to interested members of the public through use of a 'trail', the detailed study of the structure is currently very difficult. In addition, there were many later changes when the major medieval structures continued to be used not only for parliaments and royal religious observance but also for key political events, such as the trial and condemnation of Charles I (d. 1649) and also as the home for many centuries to the courts of Common Pleas and King's Bench, both sited also within the Great Hall. All this contributes to an explanation as to why this supremely important complex has not been studied in its medieval incarnations as it should have been. Nevertheless, of particular interest at Westminster is the wide range of pigments and paintings which have survived from the period c.1250 to 1350. Reds (including lac lake and vermilion), copper greens (verdigris and malachite), yellows (e.g. orpiment in imitation of gold leaf), indigo, and many combinations of these pigments with white, black, and other colourings and drawing media all survive in the decoration at the Abbey (Howard and Sauerberg 2015). For example, the scheme of vices and virtues in the window reveals of the Painted Chamber and recorded in watercolour before their destruction would, like the furnishings in the abbey, have been decorated with inlaid stones or jewels and with raised tinwork decorative schemes. These echo royal commissions elsewhere such as at Clarendon palace where fragments of azurite and ultramarine (lapis lazuli) have been recovered, as has minium (red lead) foundation painting on stone fragments together with evidence for the gilding of stonework and statuary (Beaumont James and Gerrard 2007, 78). Surviving pieces of furniture, royally embellished such as the coronation chair of the late thirteenth century and the altar retable both also in Westminster Abbey, illustrate just how lavish such furnishing could be. The so-called Wilton Diptych of the late fourteenth century also once stood in the Chapel of our Lady of the Pew while Richard II (d. 1399) revered it (Spooner 2015). This astonishing survival would have travelled with the king and have been set up in the now lost palaces round the country, such as Woodstock and Clarendon, where the kings had a special shelf for their travelling relics.

Archaeology shows on the one hand how little royal material culture remained in palaces unless it was broken on site and dumped. Among the fragments which survive is a remarkable travelling chest from Knaresborough Castle in Yorkshire, once the possession of Queen Philippa of Hainault (d. 1369). Muniment chests found today at the Public Record Office also date from the medieval period (Steane 1993, 127); *in situ* storage arrangements for records can be found in William of Wykeham's colleges in Oxford and in Winchester. Elsewhere, surviving decorative schemes include tiles from Chertsey, Surrey, which probably started out in Westminster before being passed on to the abbey and the fine thirteenth-century palace floors from Clarendon which are now on display in the British Museum (Figure 24.4), while part of the tile kiln in which they were made can be seen at the Victoria and Albert Museum in London. The pre-1250 circular pavement from Clarendon is exceptional both in survival and more significantly in the apparently exceptional skill of the English tilers who made it (Beaumont James and Gerrard 2007, 82–3). Also from Clarendon are a handful of lead stars, linked to documentary references to *scintillis* noted in documentation of Henry III's reign.

Royalty, bishops, and nobility were peripatetic and carried all kinds of supplies from site to site. Bishop Swinfield of Hereford, travelling from his westerly diocese to his London house, suffered a disaster when a cart capsized and severely damaged the ceramics he was transporting to the capital for his use. When the wagon train halted, potters were found then and there to replace the damaged items. Foodstuffs too were required in quantity. Food remains such as crab-carapaces were recovered from Kings Langley in Hertfordshire, and from Clarendon there was a wide range of deer, as well as cod, conger eel, ray, and wrasse from deep sea fishing and coastal-raised oysters. Documentary sources show how fresh-water fish were transported to royal and episcopal sites (Dyer 2000, 107), in the case of the bishops of Winchester's palace at Wolvesey for example, all the way from Somerset in damp sacks for a feast attended by Richard II in 1393. Several kitchens and their waste have been investigated archaeologically, including those at Windsor Castle and Clarendon, while a standing medieval episcopal kitchen complete with its roof is to be found at the bishop's palace at Chichester (Sussex), with remains of a

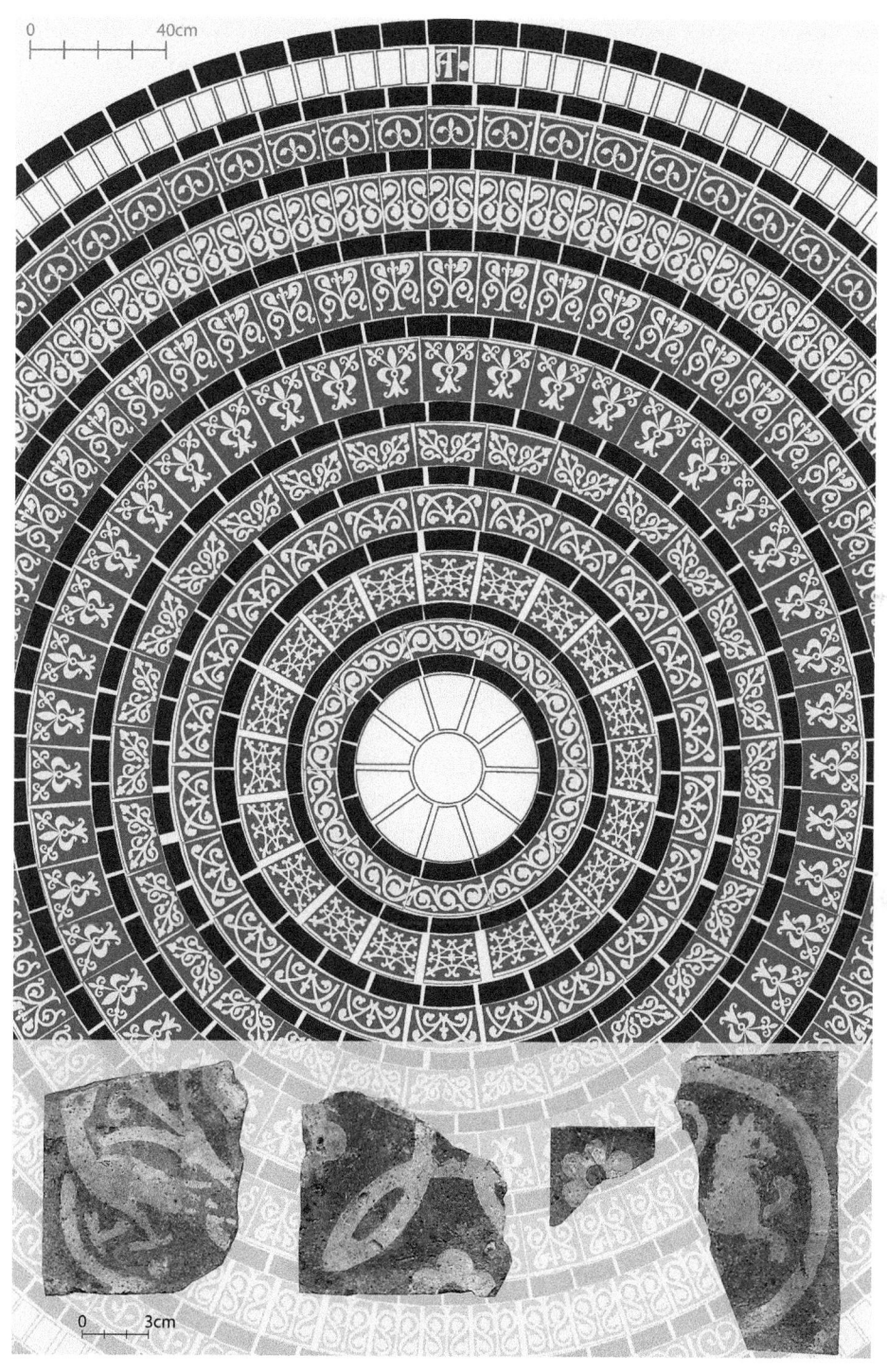

FIGURE 24.4 A reconstruction of the thirteenth-century palace floor from the king's apartments at Clarendon Palace, Wiltshire, together with other floor tiles from other areas of the same site

(© Alejandra Gutiérrez)

later structure in the adjoining diocese of Winchester at Bishops Waltham, although no below ground archaeology has been undertaken at either location (Hare 1988).

Current Work

As a result of work by John Steane (1993; 2001) on the archaeology of the monarchy and symbols of power, recent national syntheses (Dunbar 1999; James 1990; Keevill 2000; Thurley 1993) and case studies (e.g. Beaumont James and Gerrard 2007 for Clarendon; Gilchrist 2005 for Norwich Cathedral close; Payne 2003 for the palaces of the Bishops of Bath and Wells; White and Cook 2015 for Sherborne Old Castle and the Bishops of Salisbury), medieval palaces are now emerging once again as a field of study and there is much to look forward to. The themes outlined by Creighton (Chapter 23) stand equally well for palaces. A selection of projects underway might include a major scheme to recover a detailed plan of the palace of Westminster (under preparation at the University of York) or landscape research at King's Norton in Leicestershire, led by James Wright of the Museum of London. A final report of the 'spoilheap' archaeology at Clarendon Palace undertaken while the site was being rescued from the overgrowth and undergoing emergency consolidation, is also in preparation. In Scotland a survey of deerparks is being carried out by Derek Hall at Buzzart Dykes, Perthshire, and elsewhere while Penny Dransart has run a long series of excavations at the bishop's palace at Fetternear, Aberdeenshire. Medieval palace studies are in search of champions for the new millennium and a major international conference on medieval palaces at Bishop Auckland (Co. Durham) in 2015, where excavations are underway in advance of a new museum within the episcopal palace complex, sets a new agenda (Rollason 2017).

Threats continue. In 1972 the disastrous creation of the underground carpark at Westminster destroyed much archaeology there without any recording (Gerrard 2003, 134). Fragile structures such as the remains at Clarendon are once again heading towards Heritage England's Buildings at Risk Register. However, new ideas are being posited about the arrangement and sequencing of palace buildings nationally, heavily but almost entirely unscientifically excavated at different periods from the eighteenth to the twentieth centuries. Keyhole sites at Tudor palaces in London have brought much to light in recent years, but are of necessity small-scale. So far as rural palace sites are concerned, new sites are under investigation. Current work at Kings Clipstone (Nottinghamshire) led by Andy Gaunt (Mercian Archaeological Services) and James Wright (Museum of London Archaeology) have involved standing remains survey, landscape work, and geophysical survey, similarly to community excavations at Woking Palace, Surrey (ongoing Heritage Lottery Fund project). A plan of 'John of Gaunt's' palace at King's Somborne (Hampshire) was recovered some years ago while outlines of what appears to be a Romanesque palace hall and other buildings have likewise shown up dramatically in recent work at Old Sarum by the University of Southampton. There is much to be done, not least considered excavation using modern methods at sites where the surface has only been scraped, at such sites as Clarendon, Kings Clipstone, and Woodstock. Such work promises to transform our understanding of the archaeology, architecture, and ecology through properly dated sequences. The combination of detailed documentary study in close relation to physical archaeology and architectural study of these uniquely recorded sites is essential. Among recent developments have been reconstructions of medieval décor of the twelfth century (Dover Castle, Kent), thirteenth century (Tower of London, now largely replaced), and the thirty-five-year programme of reconstruction on the Great Hall of Stirling Castle including the manufacture of a medieval-style roof of c.1500 to recreate the hall of James IV of 1503 with some furnishings. Such schemes are sometimes problematic and controversial, but they are intended to breathe life back into buildings which have not seen royal residents for many centuries.

References cited

Ashbee, J. A. 2006 *The Tower of London as a royal residence: 1066–1400*, unpublished PhD thesis, University of London

Beaumont James, T. and Gerrard, C. M. 2007 *Clarendon: landscape of kings*, Windgather, Macclesfield

Biddle, M. 1970 'Excavations at Winchester, 1969: eighth interim report', *The Antiquaries Journal* 50, 277–326

Biddle, M. 2005 *Nonsuch Palace*, Oxbow, Oxford

Bond, C. J. 1987 'Woodstock Park in the Middle Ages', in J. Bond and K. Tiller (eds), *Blenheim: landscape for a palace*, Sutton, Gloucester, 22–54

Brentnall, H. C. 1938 'Marlborough Castle', *Wiltshire Archaeological and Natural History Magazine* 48, 133–43

Brown, R. A., Colvin, H. M., and Taylor, A. J. 1963 *The history of the King's works, vol. 2: the Middle Ages*, Her Majesty's Stationery Office, London

Cohen, M. 2008 'An indulgence for the visitor: the public at the Sainte-Chapelle of Paris', *Speculum* 83, 840–83

Courtney, L. T. and Mark, R. 1987 'The Westminster Hall roof: a historiographical and structural study', *The Journal of the Society of Architectural Historians* 30, 374–93

Cunliffe, B. W. 1977 *Excavations at Portchester Castle vol. 3: medieval, the outer bailey and its defenses*, The Society of Antiquaries of London, London

Cunliffe, B. W. 1985 *Excavations at Portchester Castle vol. 4: medieval and inner bailey*, The Society of Antiquaries of London, London

Donovan, C. 1993 *The Winchester Bible*, The British Library, London

Dunbar, J. G. 1999 *Scottish Royal Palaces: the architecture of the royal residences during the late Medieval and early modern periods*, Tuckwell Press, East Linton

Dunning, R. 2010 *Jocelin of Wells: bishop, builder, courtier*, Boydell Press, Woodbridge

Dyer, C. 2000 *Everyday life in medieval England*, Hambledon and London, London

Emery, A. 2006 *Greater medieval houses of England and Wales, 1300–1500: Vol. 3, southern England*, Cambridge University Press, Cambridge

Gerrard, C. M. 2003 *Medieval archaeology: understanding traditions and contemporary approaches*, Routledge, London

Gilchrist, R. 2005 *Norwich Cathedral Close: the evolution of the English cathedral landscape*, Boydell, Woodbridge

Hare, J. N. 1988 'Bishop's Waltham Palace, Hampshire: William of Wykeham, Henry Beaufort and the transformation of a medieval episcopal palace', *The Archaeological Journal* 145, 222–54

Harris, R. B. 2016 'Recent research on the White Tower: reconstructing and dating the Norman building', in J. A. Davies, A. Riley, J.-M. Levesque, and C. Lapiche (eds), *Castles and the Anglo-Norman World*, Oxbow Books, Oxford, 177–89

Harris, S. and Miles, D. 2015 'Romanesque Westminster Hall and its roof', in W. Rodwell and T. W. T. Tatton-Brown (eds), *Westminster: the art, architecture and archaeology of the royal palace and abbey, Part 2*, British Archaeological Association Conference Transactions volume 39, Leeds, 22–71

Hiller, J. and Keevill, G. D. 1995 'Recent archaeological work at the Tower of London', *Transactions of the London and Middlesex Archaeological Society* 45, 147–81

Hope-Taylor, B. 1977 *Yeavering: an Anglo-British centre of early Northmbria*, Her Majesty's Stationery Office, London

Howard, H. and Sauerberg, M. L. 2015 'The polychromy at Westminster Abbey, 1250–1350', in W. Rodwell and T. W. T. Tatton-Brown (eds), *Westminster: the art, architecture and archaeology of the royal palace and abbey, Part 1*, British Archaeological Association Conference Transactions volume 39, Leeds, 205–61

Impey, E. (ed.) 2008 *The White Tower*, Yale University Press, London and New Haven

Jansen, V. 2015 'Henry III's palace at Westminster', in W. Rodwell and T. W. T. Tatton-Brown (eds), *Westminster: the art, architecture and archaeology of the royal palace and abbey, Part 2*, British Archaeological Association Conference Transactions volume 39, Leeds, 89–110

James, T. B. 1990 *The palaces of medieval England, c.1050–1550: royalty, nobility, the episcopate and their residences from Edward the Confessor to Henry VIII*, Seaby, London

Jamieson, E. and Lane, R. 2015 'Monuments, mobility and medieval perceptions of designed landscapes: the Pleasance, Kenilworth', *Medieval Archaeology* 59(1), 255–71

Keevill, G. D. 2000 *Medieval palaces: an archaeology*, Tempus, Stroud

Keevill, G. D. 2004 *The Tower of London moat: archaeological excavations 1995–9*, Oxford Archaeology, Historic Royal Palaces Monograph 1, Oxford

Munby, J. 2015 'Late-14th-century reconstruction of Westminster Hall', in W. Rodwell and T. W. T. Tatton-Brown (eds), *Westminster: the art, architecture and archaeology of the royal palace and abbey, Part 2*, British Archaeological Association Conference Transactions volume 39, Leeds, 120–32

O'Regan, H., Turner, A., and Sabin, R. 2006 'Medieval big cat remains from the Royal Menagerie at the Tower of London', *International Journal of Osteoarchaeology* 16, 385–94

Parnell, G. 1977 'Excavations at the Tower of London', *London Archaeologist* 3(4), 97–9

Parnell, G. 2013 'The Great Hall in the inmost ward, Tower of London', *London Archaeologist* 13(8), 211–14

Payne, N. 2003 *The medieval residences of the bishops of Bath and Wells, and Salisbury*, unpublished PhD, University of Bristol

Passarius, O. and Catafau, A. (eds) 2014 *Un palais dans le ville, vol. 1. Les Palais des Rois de Majorque à Perpignan*, Trabucaire, Canet en Roussillon

Pound, N. J. G. 1994 *The medieval castle in England and Wales: a political and social history*, Cambridge University Press, Cambridge

Rahtz, P. A. 1969 *Excavations at King John's hunting lodge, Writtle, Essex, 1955-57*, The Society for Medieval Archaeology Monograph 3, London

Rahtz, P. A. 1979 *The Saxon and Medieval Palaces at Cheddar*, British Archaeological Reports British Series 65, Oxford

Renoux, A. (ed.) 1994 *Palais médiévaux (France-Belgique): 25 ans d'archéologie*, Université du Maine, Le Mans

Richardson, A. 2003 'Gender and space in English royal palaces c.1160–c.1547: a study in access analysis and imagery', *Medieval Archaeology* 47, 131–65

Richardson, A. 2005 *The forest, park and palace of Clarendon, c.1200–c.1650: reconstructing an actual, conceptual and documented Wiltshire landscape*, British Archaeological Reports British Series 387, Oxford

Rodwell, W. 2015 'The archaeology of Westminster Abbey: and historiographical overview', in W. Rodwell and T. W. T. Tatton-Brown (eds), *Westminster: the art, architecture and archaeology of the royal palace and abbey, Part 1*, British Archaeological Association Conference Transactions volume 39, Leeds, 34–60

Rollason, D. (ed.) 2017 Princes of the Church: bishops and their palaces, The Society for Medieval Archaeology Monograph 39, Abingdon

Smith, S. G. 2014 'Parks and designed landscapes in medieval Wales', in K. Baker, R. Carden, and R. Madgwick (eds), *Deer and people*, Oxbow, Oxford, 231–9

Spooner, J. 2015 'The Virgin Mary and white harts great and small: the 14th-century wall-paintings in the Chapel of Our Lady of the Pew and the muniment room', in W. Rodwell and T. W. T. Tatton-Brown (eds), *Westminster: the art, architecture and archaeology of the royal palace and abbey, Part 1*, British Archaeological Association Conference Transactions volume 39, Leeds, 262–90

Steane, J. M. 1993 *The archaeology of the medieval English monarchy*, Batsford, London

Steane, J. M. 2001 *The Archaeology of power: England and Northern Europe AD 800–1600*, Tempus Publishing, Stroud

Sykes, N. J. 2004 'The introduction of fallow deer to Britain: a zooarchaeological perspective', *Environmental Archaeology* 9, 75–83

Tatton-Brown, T. W. T. 2010 *St George's Chapel, Windsor: history and heritage*, Dovecote Press, Dorset

Thompson, M. 1998 *Medieval bishops' houses in England and Wales*, Ashgate, Aldershot

Thurley, S. 1993 *The royal palaces of Tudor England: architecture and court life, 1460-1547*, Paul Mellon Centre for Studies in British Art, Yale University, New Haven

Thurley, S. 1995 'The Royal Lodgings at the Tower of London 1240–1320', *Architectural History* 38, 36–7

Van Buren, A. H. 1986 'Reality and literary romance in the park of Hesdin', *Medieval Gardens* 127, 115–34

White, P. and Cook, A. 2015 *Sherborne Old Castle, Dorset: archaeological investigations 1930-90*, The Society of Antiquaries of London, London

Woolgar, C. M. 1999 *The great household in late medieval England*, Yale University Press, New Haven

CHAPTER 25

ROYAL AND ARISTOCRATIC LANDSCAPES OF PLEASURE

STEPHEN MILESON

SINCE the late 1980s there has been growing interest amongst archaeologists in the landscapes used by kings and aristocrats for recreation, socializing, and what seems to have been a conscious display of power, prowess, and refinement. Modern scholars commonly understand such places to include the immediate setting of castles, palaces, and manor houses, notably ornamental gardens, orchards, and ponds, as well as surrounding and more distant hunting reserves—forests, chases, parks, and warrens—and land used from time to time as tournament fields. All of these landscapes have long been studied, but largely separately. In recent times they have been linked under a range of terms, including 'elite landscapes', 'landscapes of lordship', 'designed landscapes', and 'ornamental landscapes' (e.g. Creighton 2009, 1–7; Liddiard 2005, 97, 100). Each term has slightly different connotations and debate continues about the nature of the individual elements just as it does about any proposed collective function. What is more, almost everyone acknowledges the existence of considerable geographical and temporal variation.

Such complexity invites careful thinking about categorization and meaning. Quite reasonably, these features have been grouped together to make sense of landscapes and the activities that went on within them in a broad social context. In particular, there has been a desire to integrate gardens, parks, and apparently related places into more substantial narratives around power and social change. Hunting and landscaping have been linked with efforts to assert social authority in specific situations and attention has also been paid to the responses of ordinary inhabitants. This is an essential part of the engagement of landscape archaeology with culturally focused questions about perceptions. Nevertheless, divergent interpretations and sometimes inadequate definitions force us to ask what is really meant by concepts such as 'designed landscapes', given that almost all medieval British landscapes were closely managed and exploited and that a whole host of venues, some of strikingly different character, were used for the public demonstration of authority, including churches, civic buildings, and market squares.

Traditions and Debates

Hunting Reserves

The study of forests, parks, and warrens has antiquarian roots stretching back to the early modern period (Turner 1901; Young 1979). Historians, geographers, and archaeologists have all made major contributions although much more work has been done on England than Wales or Scotland, a limitation which is beginning to be remedied. Until the 1980s, research on hunting grounds was predominantly concerned with legal definitions and collecting information on a local and regional basis (e.g. Cantor and Wilson 1961–9). As a result, and despite recognition of the political importance of royal forests, discussion of hunting was largely restricted to specialist literature. In the last twenty years, the profile of the subject has been raised somewhat by its inclusion in wider discussions in medieval archaeology and history concerning the role of material culture in the expression and contestation of power. In part this has been through the broadening of castle studies to include consideration of wider landscapes (see Chapter 23), but it is also a result of the emergence of focused analysis of parks (e.g. Mileson 2009).

Hunting was a key facet of aristocratic recreation in the Middle Ages. It is often portrayed as mainly an activity for men because it was physically demanding and dangerous. The sport was seemingly associated closely with the authority of male group leaders and the skills acquired by the hunter were a useful preparation for war. Hunting deer on horseback using bows and other weapons was particularly risky and prestigious and led to a number of royal deaths. Women, it seems, were most often involved as spectators or took part in the safer pursuit of hawking. The origins of hunting were ancient, but the period after the Conquest is usually regarded as one of fundamental change in organization, first in England and then elsewhere in Britain.

From William I onwards, English kings claimed wide-ranging control over hunting and hunting territory in a way which appears to have been unknown in the Anglo-Saxon period (Rackham 1986, 130–1). Later Anglo-Saxon kings and lords were also keen huntsmen and made efforts to improve their sport by managing woodlands and creating hedged barriers (or 'hays') in which to trap deer, but the concept of royal forests extending over large areas seems to have been an innovation of the Normans. Within the medieval forest the right to hunt deer was in the gift of the king, and in its wooded or moorland core land was managed to promote the welfare of game animals. Forest jurisdiction expanded greatly during much of the twelfth century. By the reign of Henry II (1154–89) forest law was in operation over as much as a third of the kingdom, including settlements and fields as well as woods and wastes, and over land in the hands of subjects as well as royal manors (Grant 1991; Young 1979).

Forests can be difficult to detect on the ground. Some forest bounds were marked by natural features or signs carved into trees; other stretches were fenced and gated. The interior of the forest was divided administratively into bailiwicks, each served by its own officials and often with a house or lodge as its headquarters, some of which were located inside parks. King John's moated forest residence at Writtle (Essex) was excavated in the 1950s, and fragments of some medieval lodges survive as part of standing structures, including one in Odiham Park in Hampshire (Rahtz 1969; Roberts 1995). Recent research emphasizes the complex character of forest demarcation, which included temporary and seasonal barriers as well as permanent ones. Many once-distinctive features have been lost through post-medieval landscape changes, but others (such as extra-wide ditches) may still be identifiable through careful fieldwork (Langton 2014).

Forests were not only hunting reserves and manifestations of royal authority, but also an important source of income and materials. Forest jurisdiction brought in money from fines against those who poached deer or felled trees and from charges on grazing and other activities which were managed by forest officers. The area covered by forest law was reduced after 1200, largely due to protests by subjects, and management declined from the fourteenth century as the regularization of taxation made forests an unimportant source of revenue. Nonetheless, forests remained a significant form of land-management long after, providing timber, firewood, and venison for use by kings and favoured subjects.

Forests in non-royal possession also existed from an early period, though many of these are poorly documented (Langton and Jones 2010; Turner 1901, cix–cxv). Owned by great lords and claimed by prescriptive right or royal licence, they were run on similar lines to their royal counterparts and concentrated in areas of low population and limited interference from the crown, including the north of England, the Welsh Marches, and Sussex rapes. By the thirteenth century these deer-filled reserves were increasingly called 'chases' (Crouch 1992, 306), presumably because kings and their officials made greater efforts to designate the forest proper as a royal prerogative. Some chases were short-lived and many shrank due to growing agrarian land-use after 1200.

Deer were also kept in parks, which by the fourteenth century had become the predominant hunting grounds (Figure 25.1). Medieval parks encompassed large areas of land enclosed by wooden pales erected on banks or less often by walls. These reserves were owned first by kings and great lay and ecclesiastical lords and later by the greater gentry. Parks usually incorporated a variety of woodland and open ground and were typically between 100 and 300 acres in extent. A minority were considerably larger, including some in forests and chases. It has been argued that Anglo-Saxon 'hays' were the same as later parks (Liddiard 2003, 7), but this is unlikely since roe deer, with which hays were associated, are intolerant of confined spaces (Fletcher 2011, 97; Sykes 2007, 60–1). In fact, parks are likely to have developed only after the large-scale introduction of fallow deer in the twelfth century, a species of deer which was well suited to life in confinement and easier to hunt and manage within a park environment than the larger native red deer (Fletcher 2011, 100, 103). Parks also housed other game animals for hunting and game birds for hawking while their fish-filled ponds were an ideal habitat for waterfowl, including swans and herons, as well as a source of drinking water for deer (Pluskowski 2007, 67–8; Sykes 2007, 58–9).

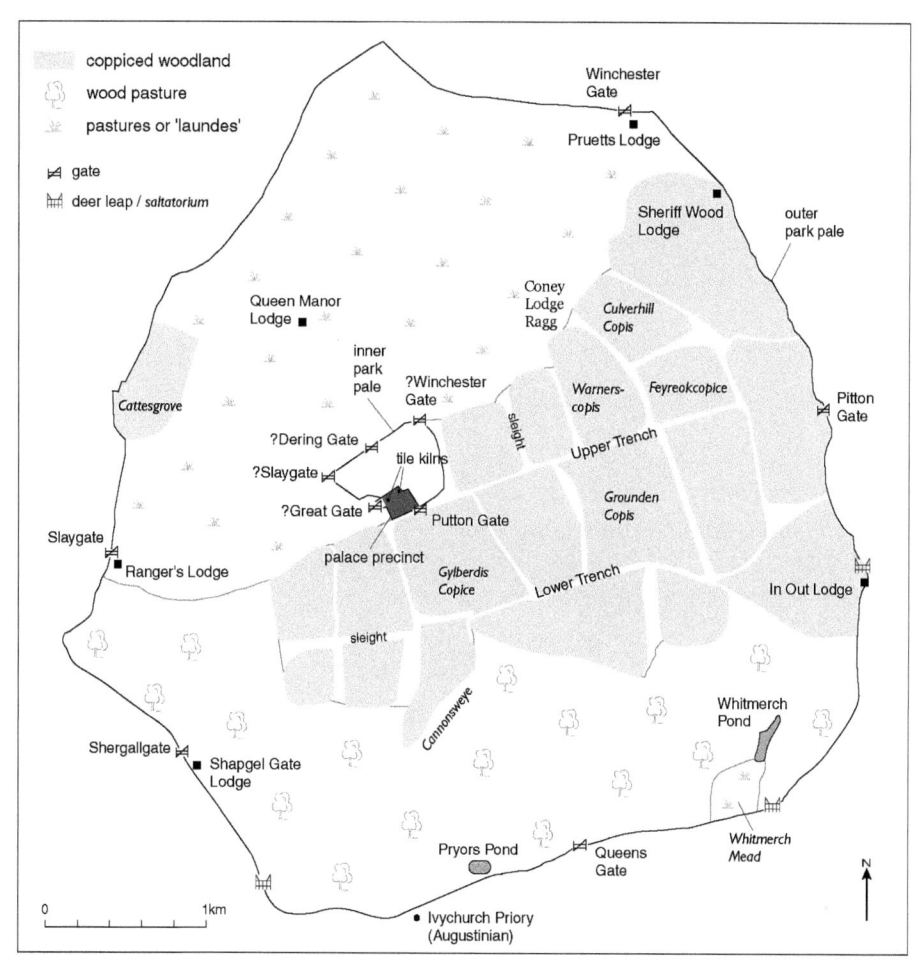

FIGURE 25.1 The great royal park of Clarendon (Wiltshire) with its palace, inner park, multiple compartments, and several gates (from Beaumont James and Gerrard 2007, 46)

(© Alejandra Gutiérrez)

Individual parks can be detected through their distinctive curving perimeters but they are almost impossible to date archaeologically (e.g. Hall et al. 2011). Some park-makers obtained royal permission for their parks, especially when their lands were within or close to a royal forest, nevertheless the resulting licences were quite often retrospective. Parks are poorly documented before 1200, but it seems that their numbers expanded greatly in the thirteenth and early fourteenth century, mainly in wood-pasture landscapes (Cantor 1983; Cantor and Hatherly 1979, 79) (Figure 25.2). Most likely this was because population growth and the spread of farming placed increasing pressure on the availability of open land for hunting, including within forests. Lesser aristocrats, whose income was rising but who could not aspire to possessing forests, were keen to claim their own hunting grounds in emulation of their superiors. In England, by the fourteenth century, perhaps one in five of the richer gentry owned a park, and possibly as

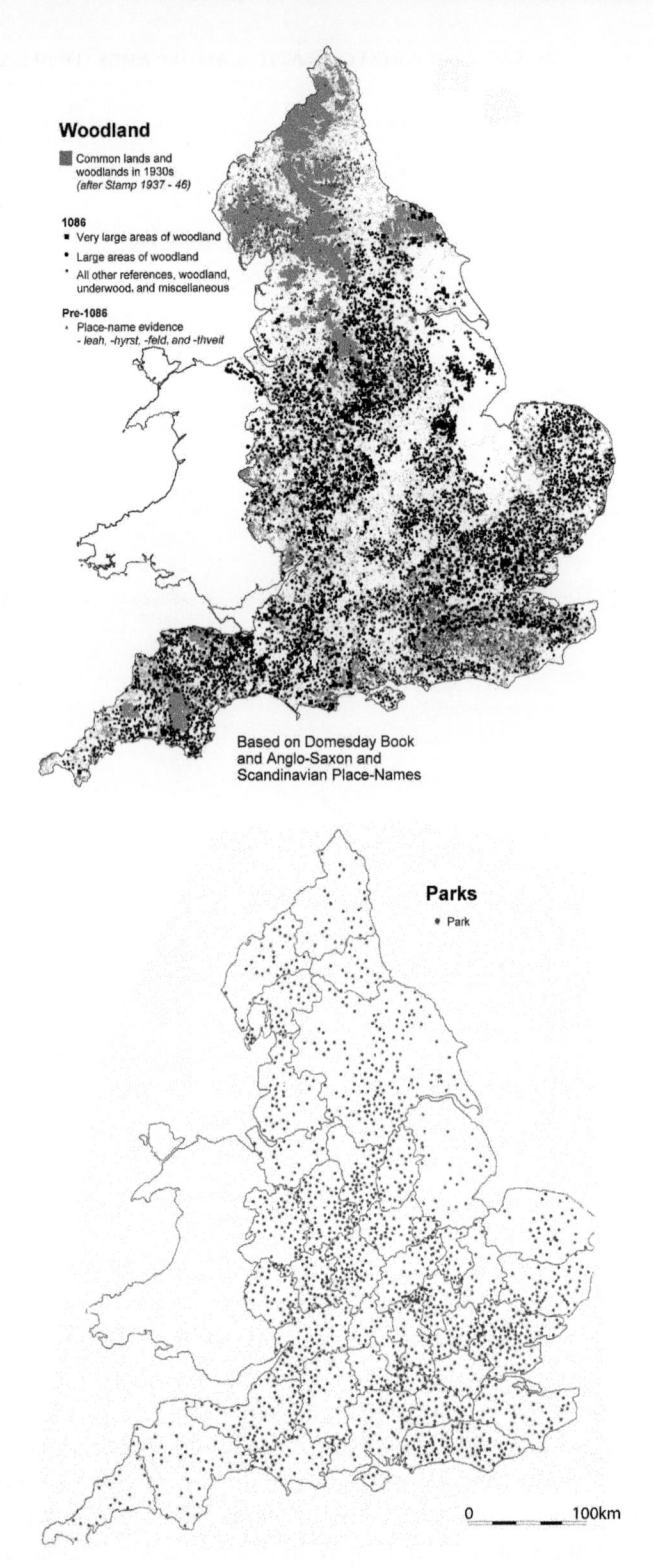

FIGURE 25.2 The distribution of woodland and parks in medieval England (for Scottish and Welsh hunting grounds, see Gilbert 1979; Langton and Jones 2010; Linnard 2000). About 1900 parks are shown, which is considerably fewer than existed during the Middle Ages as a whole, but the geographical spread indicated is broadly accurate (from Mileson 2009, 50)

(© Stephen Mileson)

many as three thousand parks existed at one time or another during the Middle Ages (Cantor 1983; Mileson 2007, 20; 2009, 109; Rackham 1986, 123). No other country in Europe had so many. Many parks were disparked in the challenging economic conditions of the late fourteenth and fifteenth century, but others were created, notably in the south-east, where there was a spate of park-making by royal courtiers and newly landed merchants (Mileson 2005, 31–2). Parks long outlived the Middle Ages, although like forests their function continued to evolve and by the eighteenth century few parks were used for deer hunting.

Parks are usually understood to have been hunting reserves, but some authors have questioned this or highlighted other uses. Certainly, parkland was multi-functional (Figure 25.3). Like forests, parks were used for grazing livestock and for the production of timber and firewood. However, a strong case can be made that parks were set up primarily with deer breeding and hunting in mind (Pluskowski 2007, 64–6), rather than for economic exploitation, which was hampered by the presence of game animals. Most parks ran at a net financial loss because of the costs of enclosure and of employing a park keeper to look after the deer (Mileson 2009, ch. 2; Rowe 2009). At Crondon park in Stock (Essex) ceramic finds from field-walking indicate that manuring went on around the park but not within it, reinforcing the documentary evidence for the generally limited exploitation of parkland for arable farming (Germany 2001).Venison was seldom sold, except by poachers, and was mainly eaten by the lord's household or given away as a prestigious gift. Nor were parks mere 'deer larders' as some have suggested: recreational hunting by lords was important even if it was less frequent than culling by servants to supply the lord's table.

The final and most widespread hunting ground was the warren, an area where the lord of the manor had an exclusive right to hunt lesser game such as hares, foxes, wild cats, badgers, pheasants, and partridges. Rights of warren were acquired initially by great ecclesiastics and lay lords, but from the 1250s the crown sold many charters of 'free warren' to lesser land-owners eager to secure privileged access to game animals on their estates outside royal forests (Crook 2001, 36–7). Warrens were in some cases marked out on the ground, but on the whole they left no distinctive archaeological traces. The exception to this is where warren rights were used to give protection to artificial rabbit warrens called 'coneygarths', which were created in large numbers especially on the sandy soils of eastern England, and which after 1350 produced meat and fur in significant quantities for sale as well as for consumption by the household (Bailey 1988; Gilbert 1979, 213). Coneygarths can sometimes be identified by the presence of relict pillow mounds or lodges used to house rabbit-keepers (Williamson 2007).

The creation of so many hunting reserves was a lengthy and contentious process which was of significance beyond the creation of a common aristocratic hunting culture. Assertion of exclusive hunting rights and above all enclosure disrupted established hunting practices and land uses, for lords and ordinary inhabitants alike (Mileson 2009, ch. 6 and 7). Kings may have been concerned that their subjects' chases, parks, and warrens encroached upon the forests, but this was a greater worry for magnates with their smaller and less numerous reserves. Townsmen and peasants were aggrieved at the

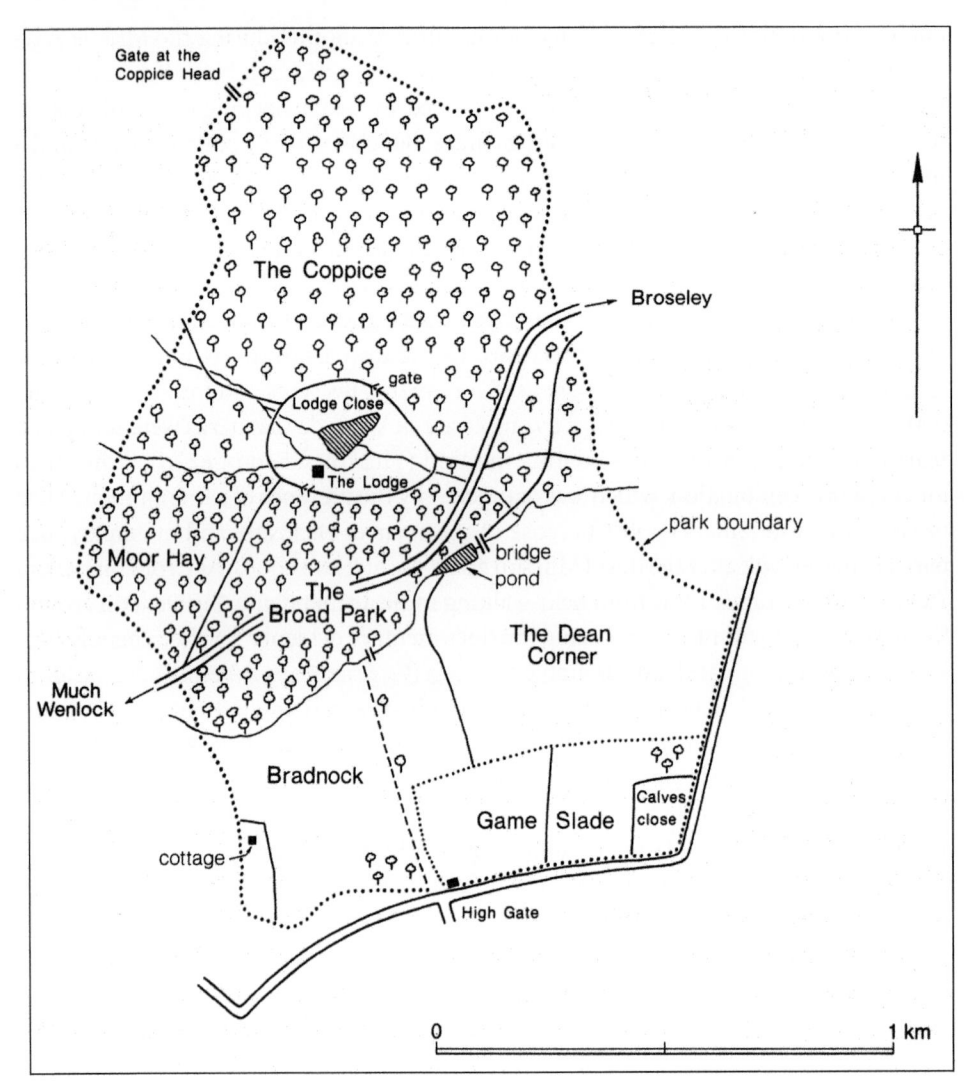

FIGURE 25.3 The park at Willey (Shropshire), first documented in the late thirteenth century, was located at some distance from the manor house. The medieval park was divided into compartments and, unusually, was bisected by a highway, which would have made it more freely accessible than many parks (from Stamper 1988, 142)

(© Paul Stamper)

restriction or loss of customary rights to hunt, graze animals, and gather wood, and at the obstruction of roads by park fences. Disputes over hunting reserves became part of national politics, notably in the crisis of John's reign, during the baronial revolt of the 1250s, in the Peasants' Revolt of 1381, and in the disorder of the 1450s. Aristocrats traded blows with their superiors and rivals by destroying park fences, slaughtering deer, and killing park keepers (Marvin 1999). Policing was very inadequate and lesser landowners and peasants often made illicit use of hunting grounds, especially when the owners were absent. Deer bones recovered archaeologically from village wells were probably deposited by peasant poachers.

Hunting reserves were also important features of the landscape in Scotland and Wales, although here they are less well documented and have been much less studied until recently (Hall et al. 2011, 59). In Scotland there were numerous royal and baronial forests and at least seventy-five parks are known, the earliest being mentioned in 1165 (Gilbert 1979, 183–203, 222, 356–9). Forests were located in both highlands and lowlands, but parks were almost entirely restricted to the lowlands. In Wales there were many small forests, especially in the uplands, and at least fifty parks, concentrated in the south and east (Cantor 1983; Linnard 2000, 38; Rackham 1986, 124–5, 131; Silvester 2010). In both countries, forests, parks, and warrens were a foreign, English, idea. In Scotland the native elite quickly absorbed and adopted the fashionable new hunting culture, while retaining some long-established practices (Gilbert 1979, esp. ch. 4). In Wales, and on a smaller scale in Ireland (Beglane 2015), hunting reserves were imposed by often harshly exploitative non-native rulers as part of a package of new laws and controls. The alien character of these reserves and the sense that they overrode established communal forms of resource management made them doubly contentious (Davies 1978, 123–7). Native elites began to adopt hunting reserves in north Wales before the Edwardian conquest, but on a small scale (Smith 2014).

Gardens and Tournament Grounds

Medieval gardens have traditionally been seen as small, distinctive enclosures which ranged in function from workaday plots for producing fruit and vegetables to sophisticated pleasure grounds (Dyer 1994, 113–31; Harvey 1981; Landsberg 1995; Taylor 1983, 33–40). The aristocratic pleasure garden occupied an ambiguous position in literature and reality, associated as it was with both sanctity and lust (Gilchrist 1999; McLean 1981, ch. 4). The garden, often located next to a bedchamber, was a place for contemplation and suitably restricted leisure for ladies, but it was also a place where men and women might make love. Beaumont James (see Chapter 24) highlights Everswell at Woodstock (Oxfordshire) where Henry II created a leafy garden retreat resembling the bower and orchard described in the popular Tristan story (Crossley 1990, 438; McLean 1981, 99–101).

Yet there are strong reasons for questioning whether the difference between garden and park or forest was actually so clear cut. The recent study of landscapes around great houses has underscored their integration rather than their separation. Not only were these features often found in close proximity, but there seems to have been no hard and fast distinction in terms of their function. Aesthetic response was not restricted to gardens: medieval writers often described parks as 'beautiful', and their bucolic appeal is suggested by their use as venues for walking, picnicking, and other forms of entertainment besides hunting (Mileson 2009, 83–4). Some parks incorporated ornamental features to enhance their visual appeal, such as pools and fountains; these landscapes appear to have been closely inspired by romance literature and occasionally became the subjects of poetry themselves (e.g. Hagopian van Buren 1986). The distinction between park and garden is further troubled by the garden-like character of certain little parks located next to castles, and by the establishment of pleasure gardens within the bounds of parks, notably by Edward III in the later fourteenth century (Harvey 1981, 73, 87–8; Landsberg 1995, 21–5; Richardson 2007, 38). What is more, lust was hardly confined to the garden: both hunts and tournaments brought the sexes together in isolated or enclosed settings and had amorous potential (Harvey 1981, 106; Sykes 2007, 55).

Physical evidence for what have been interpreted as walkways and viewing platforms has encouraged some archaeologists to focus on the aesthetic appeal of landscapes around royal and aristocratic residences, especially after 1300 (Figure 25.4) (e.g. Bond 1994, 144; Cooper 1999; Creighton 2009; Leslie 1993; Taylor 2000). More recently, there has been a backlash against such views: Colin Platt, for example, has argued that they underplay the military role of the castle and treat medieval landscapes as mere forerunners of the Renaissance rather than representing medieval culture in its own right (Platt 2007). In particular, some have found the term 'designed landscape' to be unhelpful, not least for its overtones of seventeenth-century planning and surveying, in which elaborate views and approaches were created mainly for aesthetic effect (Everson 1998, 38; Liddiard and Williamson 2008). Detailed archaeological surveys certainly reveal the need for caution in assuming conscious planning of views between castle and garden (Richardson and Dennison 2014, 34). This raises the possibility that in some places, perhaps many, walking through a garden was more important than looking at it from afar (Howes 2002, 193–4). Opinions remain divided, but a balanced view may be to recognize the influence of romance literature, the capacity for appreciation of beauty and manipulation of the landscape, while retaining an emphasis on the medieval values of lordship and largesse, expressed through the control over land, resources, and activities, including hunting.

The study of tournaments has been poorly integrated with the landscapes discussed so far, but it appears to indicate a similar spatial evolution to the hunting ground, from large and open to smaller and enclosed. Tournaments developed from rather disorderly mêlées ranging over extensive areas and sometimes attracting large numbers of spectators to more contained and controlled events (Crouch 2005; Steane 1993, 155–7). In their early phase before 1300 they took place on land outside city walls or close to main roads, but in the first half of the fourteenth century large-scale mêlées were replaced by jousts and other events taking place in the grounds of castles or in city palaces. The influence of literature can be detected from the beginning, but refinement and exclusivity increased with the rising costs of participation (Creighton 2009, 72–3). For kings, a real and threatened link with rebellion was balanced by the potential for strengthening relations with the nobility through participation and, eventually, leadership, the first seen in Edward I's establishment of an Arthurian 'Round Table' of knights, the second encapsulated by Edward III's splendid patronage. In Scotland the high-point of royal involvement in tournaments seems to have happened rather later (Stevenson 2006, ch. 4).

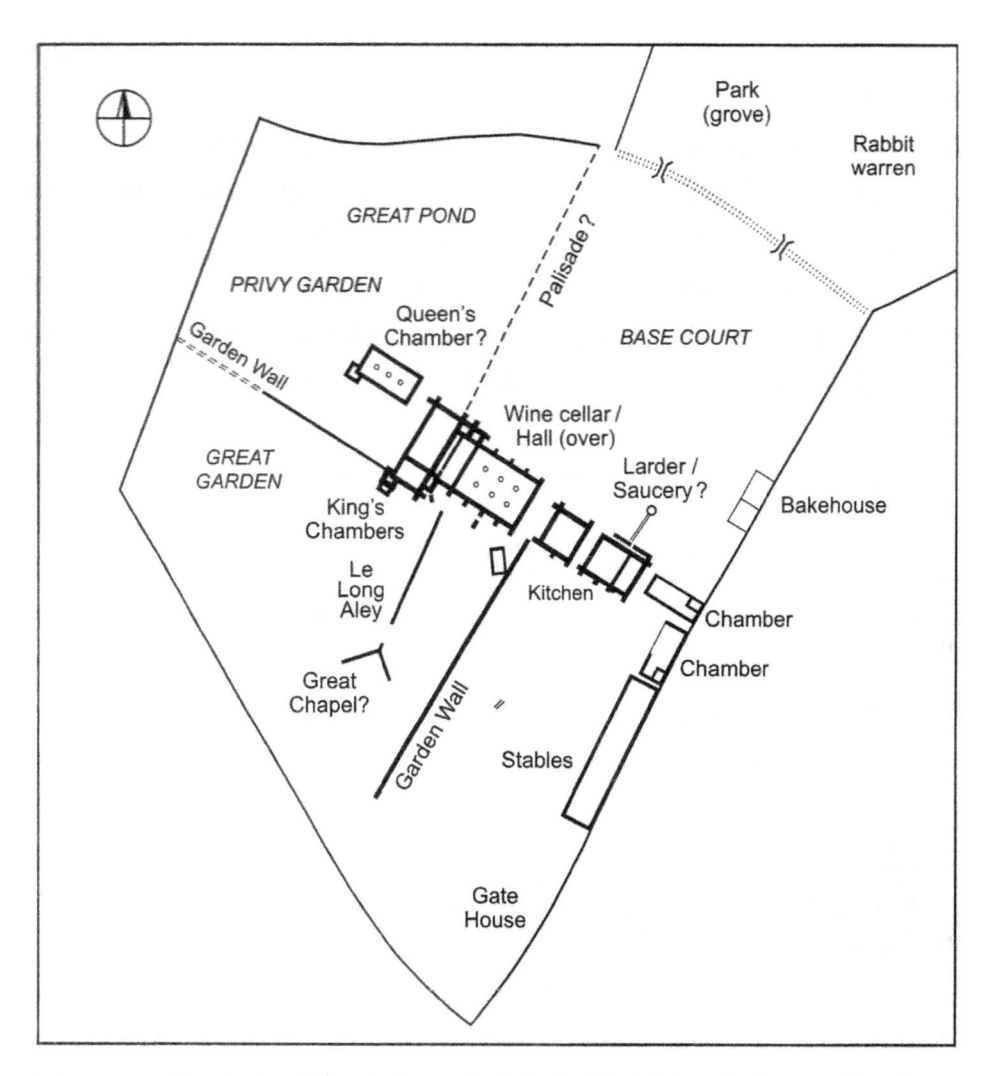

FIGURE 25.4 Kennington Palace in Surrey. Built for the Black Prince in the 1340s, Kennington was much used by Richard II. In the 1440s a stone wall was built between the privy garden and the more accessible great garden to the south (from Creighton 2009, 177)

(© Oliver Creighton)

Prospects for Future Research

This potted account of generations of scholarship underlines the benefits of conceptual ambition and multi-disciplinarity. It also highlights uncertainties and contested interpretations. So what does the future hold for the study of medieval elite landscapes in the twenty-first century? Knowledge continues to grow through ongoing research. Some work showcases the special contribution of archaeological science, such as the dating of park features through radiocarbon determination, as recently achieved at Earlspark,

Co. Galway by dating of charcoal preserved in the mortar of a perimeter wall (Beglane 2015, 15). Careful examination of parkland morphology in relation to neighbouring settlements and field-systems and the dating of pottery finds yields fresh insights into the disruption caused by emparkment and the results of temporary or permanent disparkment (e.g. Demidowicz 2012; Henderson and Weddell 1994, 129–31). Yet there may be diminishing returns from building an ever larger corpus of examples, even a risk of circularity. For example, those convinced of the economic importance of parks can produce more documented cases or point to the material evidence for livestock grazing (Moorhouse 2007, 112–15). Others focused on hunting can draw upon field survey and place-name evidence for the use and enhancement of natural features such as narrow valleys and mounds for deer management and hunting, including the creation of deer courses (Gilbert 2013–14, 92–3; Moorhouse 2007, 118; Taylor 2004). As the fruitful debate about designed landscapes shows, real advances in understanding require new thinking as well as new facts. It may well be advantageous for future work to analyse the meaning of these places more firmly in the context of wider social and institutional changes.

Throughout the Middle Ages, lordly power required some measure of demonstration and performance. Thirteenth-century kings and lords used their fine residences and their attractive and well-ordered surroundings to impress and entertain their fellows. Visiting nobles might be taken on tours (Mileson 2009, 106), and at some houses guests would have joined lords in upper rooms with large windows facing out over the estate (Creighton 2009, ch. 6; Liddiard 2005, 111–15). Lords, or their officials, also used these landscapes to communicate with local inhabitants, as at Huntington in the Welsh Marches, where in 1302 royal officers signalled the king's formal possession of the castle by hunting. Non-aristocrats could evidently be impressed by grand residences and the lifestyle with which they were linked. So much is occasionally made clear by even the most bureaucratic documents, such as the report of the Somerset jurors for the inquisition *post mortem* of John Tiptoft, first Baron Tiptoft (*c.*1378–1443), which mentioned the 'large and attractive buildings' (*grande et pulchr' edificat'*) at Stoke-sub-Hamdon, near Yeovil (*Cal IPM* 26, no. 93, p. 49).

Nonetheless, the way the lordly lifestyle was projected and the nature of the audience did change over time. In the twelfth and thirteenth century lords moved regularly between numerous manors and were highly visible; great lords called on large numbers of tenants to assist in hunting forays. Later there was less itineration and greater investment in fewer properties and the physical link between aristocratic houses and parks was a particular feature of the fourteenth and especially the fifteenth century (Mileson 2005; Rowe 2009, 12); almost every new park was created next to or especially around a house so that, in a real sense, the park had become part of an inward-looking stage for courtly living. The castle as a physically and socially liminal place between closed park and open settlement gave way to the great house within its island of parkland; the fashionable houses of the period were towers tantalizingly visible from afar, rather than core elements of the town or village street like so many of their predecessors (Dyer 2014; Mileson 2009, 88–9). It might be argued that lords were less visibly dominant in the landscape of the period after 1350 than they had been in the twelfth and thirteenth century, and that this signalled a real and permanent shift in local power rather than a temporary realignment resulting from demographic change.

Nevertheless, in no part of the period was aristocratic power founded simply on display, nor were these landscapes purely expressions of conspicuous consumption and domination. Great men and women used fine residences not just to show off, but also to relax and escape from the pressures of their public roles, especially as they grew older (Mileson 2009, 95; Richardson 2012a). The well-ordered garden was a pleasant place for men as well as women to talk to their companions or to engage in personal devotions (Harvey 1981, 87; Noble 2000, 197). For some, gardening appears to have been a hobby and especially for women the exchange of herbs and plant-based perfumes was important in social networks and friendships. Plants, animals, and water, all these were rich in religious symbolism (Pluskowski 2007, 69–71; Sykes 2007, 57–8).

Layers of meaning may be better appreciated by more careful consideration of who used the landscapes of the powerful and in what circumstances. This applies to female participation in hunting, which has recently been reappraised (e.g. Richardson 2012b). According to one view, aristocratic women did not hunt much when hunting mainly took the form of dangerous horseback chases through forests but they did so more frequently when hunts were transferred to parks and took the more sedate form of 'bow and stable', in which deer were driven towards waiting archers standing on wooden platforms (Sykes 2007, 54–5). In other words, they were transformed from spectators to participants in the later thirteenth and early fourteenth century. This idea requires further investigation, but it is part of an important effort to join activities to places and identify the implications for contemporary resonance, which may have differed according to gender as well as class. Historians might see female hunting in parks as a positive opportunity for active involvement in a previously male-dominated activity, or as a continuing restriction along gender lines expressed through enclosure. How contemporaries saw it may be recoverable through research on the way landscapes associated with high-status women were used, especially those landscapes known to have been created or enhanced by particular individuals.

In broader terms, future research on the creation of hunting reserves might profitably investigate how local conditions affected the experiences of those living near them. Factors include population density, resource availability, market opportunities, lordship, social structure, and settlement character. In some places manorial documents can highlight how tenants used parks and the role of parkers and leading inhabitants in organizing grazing, as well as the temporality of access—for instance the closure of parks during deer fawning and rutting. Everywhere zooarchaeology has a particular potential to reveal more about human–animal relations and the consumption of particular species. Finally, we should be alert to differences in lordly landscapes in England, Scotland, and Wales as well as further afield (Buylaert et al. 2011; Harvey 1981, 92). For this reason, royal and aristocratic landscapes of pleasure deserve investigation in a pan-European context.

Acknowledgements

I am very grateful to Oliver Creighton, Rachel Delman, Chris Dyer, Amanda Richardson, and John Watts for comments on draft versions of this chapter. John Gilbert kindly alerted me to current work on Scottish parks.

References Cited

Bailey, M. 1988 'The rabbit and the medieval East Anglian economy', *Agricultural History Review* 36(1), 1–20

Beaumont James, T. and Gerrard, C. M. 2007 *Clarendon: landscape of kings*, Windgather, Bollington

Beglane, F. 2015 *Anglo-Norman parks in medieval Ireland*, Four Courts Press, Dublin

Bond, C. J. 1994 'Forests, chases, warrens and parks in medieval Wessex', in M. Aston and C. Lewis (eds), *The medieval landscape of Wessex*, Oxbow Monograph 46, Oxford, 115–58

Buylaert, F., De Clercq, W., and Dumolyn, J. 2011 'Sumptuary legislation, material culture and the semiotics of *"vivre noblement"* in the county of Flanders (fourteenth–sixteenth centuries)', *Social History* 36(4), 393–417

Cal IPM 26: *Calendar of inquisitions post mortem and other analogous documents preserved in the Public Record Office, Vol. 26: Henry VI (1442–1447)*, edited by M. L. Holford, Boydell, London

Cantor, L. M. 1983 *The medieval parks of England: a gazetteer*, Loughborough University of Technology, Loughborough

Cantor, L. M. and Hatherly, J. M. 1979 'The medieval parks of England', *Geography* 64, 71–85

Cantor, L. M. and Wilson, J. D. 1961–9 'The mediaeval deer-parks of Dorset', *Proceedings of the Dorset Archaeological and Natural History Society* 83–91 [continued by Wilson in vols 92–6 (1970–4)]

Cooper, S. 1999 'Ornamental structures in the medieval gardens of Scotland', *Proceedings of the Society of Antiquaries of Scotland* 129, 817–39

Creighton, O. H. 2009 *Designs upon the land: elite landscapes of the Middle Ages*, Boydell and Brewer, Woodbridge

Crook, D. 2001 'The "Petition of the Barons" and charters of free warren, 1227–58', in P. R. Coss and M. Prestwich (eds), *Thirteenth century England VIII*, Boydell and Brewer, Woodbridge, 33–48

Crossley, A. (ed.) 1990 *The Victoria history of the counties of England. A history of the county of Oxford, vol. 12: Wootton hundred (South) including Woodstock*, Oxford University Press, Oxford

Crouch, D. 1992 *The image of aristocracy in Britain, 1000–1300*, Routledge, London

Crouch, D. 2005 *Tournament*, Hambledon, London

Davies, R. R. 1978 *Lordship and society in the March of Wales, 1282–1400*, Oxford University Press, Oxford

Demidowicz, G. 2012 'From Queen Street to Little Park, Coventry: the failure of the medieval suburb in Cheylesmore Park and its transformation into the Little Park', *Midland History* 37(1), 106–15

Dyer, C. 1994 *Everyday life in medieval England*, Hambledon Press, London

Dyer, C. 2014 'A landscape for pleasure: Fulbrook, Warwickshire and John Duke of Bedford in the fifteenth century', *Warwickshire History* 15(6), 239–50

Everson, P. 1998 '"Delightfully surrounded with woods and ponds": field evidence for medieval gardens in England', in P. Patterson (ed.), *There by design: field archaeology in parks and gardens*, Archaeopress, Oxford, 32–8

Fletcher, J. 2011 *Gardens of earthly delight: the history of deer parks*, Windgather, Bollington

Germany, M. 2001 'Fieldwalking at Crondon Park, Stock', *Essex Archaeology and History* 32, 178–88

Gilbert, J. M. 1979 *Hunting and hunting reserves in medieval Scotland*, John Donald, Edinburgh

Gilbert, J. M. 2013–14 'Falkland Park to c.1603', *Tayside and Fife Archaeological Journal* 19–20, 78–102

Gilchrist, R. 1999 *Gender and archaeology: contesting the past*, Routledge, London

Grant, R. 1991 *The royal forests of England*, Sutton, Stroud

Hagopian van Buren, A. 1986 'Reality and literary romance in the park of Hesdin', in E. B. Macdougall (ed.), *Medieval gardens*, Dumbarton Oaks Research Library, Washington, DC, 115–34

Hall, D., Malloy, K., and Oram, R. 2011 '"A hunting we will go"? Stirling University's medieval deer parks project', *Tayside and Fife Archaeological Journal* 17, 58–67

Harvey, J. 1981 *Mediaeval gardens*, Batsford, London

Henderson, C. G. and Weddell P. J. 1994 'Medieval settlements on Dartmoor and in west Devon: the evidence from excavations', *The archaeology of Dartmoor: perspectives from the 1990s*, Devon Archaeological Society Proceedings 52, 119–40

Howes, L. L. 2002 'Narrative time and literary landscapes in Middle English poetry', in J. Howe and M. Wolfe (eds), *Inventing medieval landscapes: senses of place in western Europe*, University Press of Florida, Gainesville, 192–207

Landsberg, S. 1995 *The medieval garden*, British Museum Press, London

Langton, J. 2014 'Forest fences: enclosures in a pre-enclosure landscape', *Landscape History* 35(1), 5–30

Langton, J. and Jones, G. 2010 *Forests and chases of medieval England and Wales c.1000–c.1500: towards a survey and analysis*, St John's College Research Centre, Oxford

Leslie, M. 1993 'An English landscape garden before the English landscape garden', *Journal of Garden History* 13, 3–15

Liddiard, R. 2003 'The deer parks of Domesday Book', *Landscapes* 4, 4–23

Liddiard, R. 2005 *Castles in context: power, symbolism and landscape, 1066 to 1500*, Windgather, Bollington

Liddiard, R. and Williamson, T. 2008 'There by design? Some reflections on medieval elite landscapes', *The Archaeological Journal* 165(1), 520–35

Linnard, W. 2000 *Welsh woods and forests: a history*, Gomer, Llandysul (2nd edn)

Marvin, W. P. 1999 'Slaughter and romance: hunting reserves in late medieval England', in B. Hanawalt and D. Wallace (eds), *Medieval crime and social control*, University of Minnesota Press, Minneapolis, 224–52

McLean, T. 1981 *Medieval English gardens*, Collins, London

Mileson, S. A. 2005 'The importance of parks in fifteenth-century society', in L. Clark (ed.), *The fifteenth century 5: image, belief and regulation in late medieval England*, Boydell and Brewer, Woodbridge, 19–37

Mileson, S. A. 2007 'The sociology of park creation in medieval England', in R. Liddiard (ed.), *The medieval park: new perspectives*, Windgather Press, Macclesfield, 11–26

Mileson, S. A. 2009 *Parks in medieval England*, Oxford University Press, Oxford

Moorhouse, S. 2007 'The medieval parks of Yorkshire: function, contents and chronology', in R. Liddiard (ed.), *The medieval park: new perspectives*, Windgather Press, Macclesfield, 99–127

Noble, C. 2000 'Spiritual practice and the designed landscape: monastic precinct gardens', *Studies in the History of Gardens and Designed Landscapes: An International Quarterly* 20(3), 197–205

Platt, C. 2007 'Revisionism in castle studies: a caution', *Medieval Archaeology* 51, 83–102

Pluskowski, A. 2007 'The social construction of medieval park ecosystems: an interdisciplinary perspective', in R. Liddiard (ed.), *The medieval park: new perspectives*, Windgather Press, Macclesfield, 63–78

Rackham, O. 1986 *The history of the countryside*, Dent, London

Rahtz, P. A. 1969 *Excavations at King John's hunting lodge, Writtle, Essex, 1955–57*, The Society for Medieval Archaeology Monograph 3, London

Richardson, A. 2007 '"The king's chief delights": a landscape approach to the royal parks of post-Conquest England', in R. Liddiard (ed.), *The medieval park: new perspectives*, Windgather Press, Macclesfield, 27–48

Richardson, A. 2012a 'Greenwich's first royal landscape: the lost palace and park of Humphrey of Gloucester', *Southern History* 34, 50–71

Richardson, A. 2012b '"Riding like Alexander, hunting like Diana": gendered aspects of the medieval hunt and its landscape settings', *Gender and History* 24(2), 253–70

Richardson, S. and Dennison E. 2014 'A wall with a view? The gardens at Ravensworth Castle, North Yorkshire', *Landscape History* 35(2), 21–38

Roberts, E. 1995 'Edward III's lodge at Odiham, Hampshire', *Medieval Archaeology* 39, 91–106

Rowe, A. 2009 *Medieval parks of Hertfordshire*, Hertfordshire Publications, Hatfield

Silvester, R. 2010 'Historical concept to physical reality: forests in the landscape of Welsh borderlands', in J. Langton and G. Jones (eds), *Forests and chases of medieval England and Wales c.1000 to c.1500*, St John's College, Oxford, 163–78

Smith, S. G. 2014 'Parks and designed landscapes in medieval Wales', in K. Baker, R. Carden, and R. Madgwick (eds), *Deer and people*, Oxbow, Oxford, 231–9

Stamper, P. 1988 'Woods and parks', in G. Astill and A. Grant (eds), *The countryside of medieval England*, Blackwell, Oxford, 128–48

Steane, J. 1993 *The archaeology of the medieval English monarchy*, Batsford, London

Stevenson, K. 2006 *Chivalry and knighthood in Scotland, 1424–1513*, Boydell and Brewer, Woodbridge

Sykes, N. J. 2007 'Animal bones and animal parks', in R. Liddiard (ed.), *The medieval park: new perspectives*, Windgather Press, Macclesfield, 49–62

Taylor, C. 1983 *The archaeology of gardens*, Shire, Princes Risborough

Taylor, C. 2000 'Medieval ornamental landscapes', *Landscapes* 1, 38–55

Taylor, C. 2004 'Ravensdale park, Derbyshire, and medieval deer coursing', *Landscape History* 26, 36–57

Turner, G. J. 1901 *Select pleas of the forest*, Selden Society 13, London

Williamson, T. 2007 *Rabbits, warrens and archaeology*, Tempus, Stroud

Young, C. R. 1979 *The royal forests of medieval England*, Leicester University Press, Leicester

CHAPTER 26

MEDIEVAL BATTLEFIELD ARCHAEOLOGY

GLENN FOARD

BATTLEFIELD archaeology, the archaeologically-led interdisciplinary study of military action, is one component of the archaeology of conflict. Its methodology is most applicable to medieval and early modern sites and the principal focus is on battles, that is, large-scale military action in the field. However, the same techniques may also be appropriate for skirmishes, defined here as smaller scale and usually disbanded action in open ground, as well as some aspects of sieges. The other main strands of conflict archaeology, the study of prehistoric and modern warfare, have separate origins and methodologies that reflect the varying scale and character of the evidence (Carman 2013).

Modern archaeological investigation of battlefields originated in the USA in the mid-1980s, first appearing in Britain in the mid-1990s, although some aspects were explored here during the nineteenth and twentieth centuries by antiquaries, local historians, and military historians (Foard 2012, 1–7; Scott and McFeaters 2011). Since 1995 it has spread across Europe, though not all countries have seen significant work and none have more than a handful of practitioners (Carman 2013, 5–9). Britain has seen the most extensive investigations, including battlefield-wide projects for Bosworth in Leicestershire [1485] and Towton in Yorkshire [1461] (Foard and Curry 2013; Sutherland and Holst 2014, and other works listed there), as well as conservation management projects. Since 2000 this interest has been encouraged by biennial international Fields of Conflict (FOC) conferences, publication of the *Journal of Conflict Archaeology*, and networking through the Conflict Archaeology International Research Network (CAIRN). The published papers from FOC conferences in 2000 and 2004, and conferences in Germany in 2008 on battlefield archaeology and 2011 on mass graves, provide insights into recent advances (Eickhoff and Schopper 2014; Freeman and Pollard 2001; Meller et al. 2009; Scott et al. 2007).

The period covered here is 1066 to 1550, Hastings in 1066 being the first well-documented battle and the final date reflecting a fundamental transition in medieval warfare involving large-scale application of pike and hand-gun to the British battlefield, more than fifty years after leading Continental armies. Because the evidence tends to be better later in the medieval period, our best data so far come from the battles of the Wars of the Roses [1455–87] in England. However, other key studies are now approaching publication, notably Bannockburn [1314] in Stirling, Scotland, and Masterby [1361] in Sweden.

The Resource

Figure 26.1 is a map of medieval battles in Britain, based on the Fields of Conflict database first created for England in 2002 to underpin the Battlefields Trust's online Resource Centre[1] and then enhanced with assessments for Scotland and England. A wide range of secondary works on military history has been incorporated here, together with SMR/HER data and national records using the on-line systems Canmore and Pastscape (Foard and Morris 2012; Foard and Partida 2006; Pollard and Banks 2010). In 2015 Wales was added using data from each HER, the RCAHMW gazetteer of fields of conflict and their online database Coflein.

This exercise demonstrates some major problems of terminology. While the boundary between lesser battles and skirmishes is always difficult to define, in Wales the term 'battle' has been used for any type of conflict, from armies deployed in battle array, through skirmishes, ambush, and raids. In part, this reflects the different character of medieval warfare in Wales but it is not helpful for wider comparative study. In Wales, the Scottish Highlands, and to some degree the Anglo-Scottish border, a high proportion of records also relate to traditional battle sites, perhaps due to a stronger oral history and a heightened degree of instability there during the Middle Ages. These sites, often associated with a place-name or features such as cairns or standing stones, sometimes do represent genuine folk memory of military events but many are spurious. Sieges prove even more problematic because there is no standard monument classification in any of the three nations. It is clear that there will need to be greater consistency in the classification of data for conflict sites in Britain as a whole.

A graph of battles by half century (Figure 26.2) demonstrates the potential for archaeological investigation at different periods. While individual battles may provide singular opportunities for study, several phases of warfare offer potential for comparative study between battles, for example the Scottish Wars of Independence in the later thirteenth and earlier fourteenth centuries. These span the period of the ascendancy of infantry over cavalry, achieved in Bruce's devastating defeat of the English at Bannockburn but presaged by his success at Loudon Hill [East Ayrshire, 1307] and followed by an English response which deployed the longbow, beginning with Dupplin Moor [Perth and Kinross, 1332] and leading to the weapon's decisive role on the European stage during the

---

[1] http://www.battlefieldstrust.com/resource-centre/.

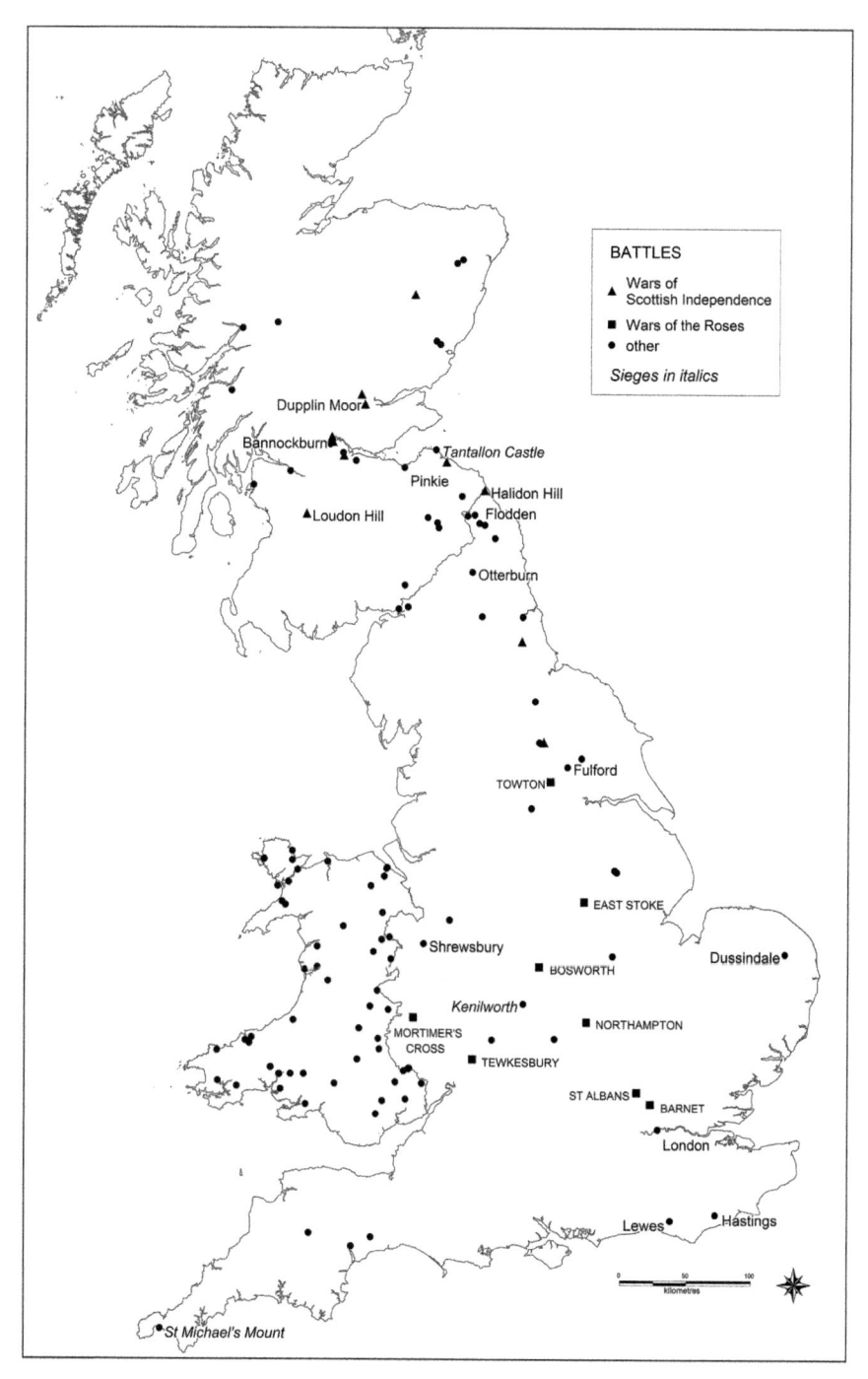

FIGURE 26.1 Map of all medieval battles, distinguishing battles of the Wars of the Roses and identifying battles and sieges named in the text. The higher density in Wales reflects biases in classification

(© Glenn Foard)

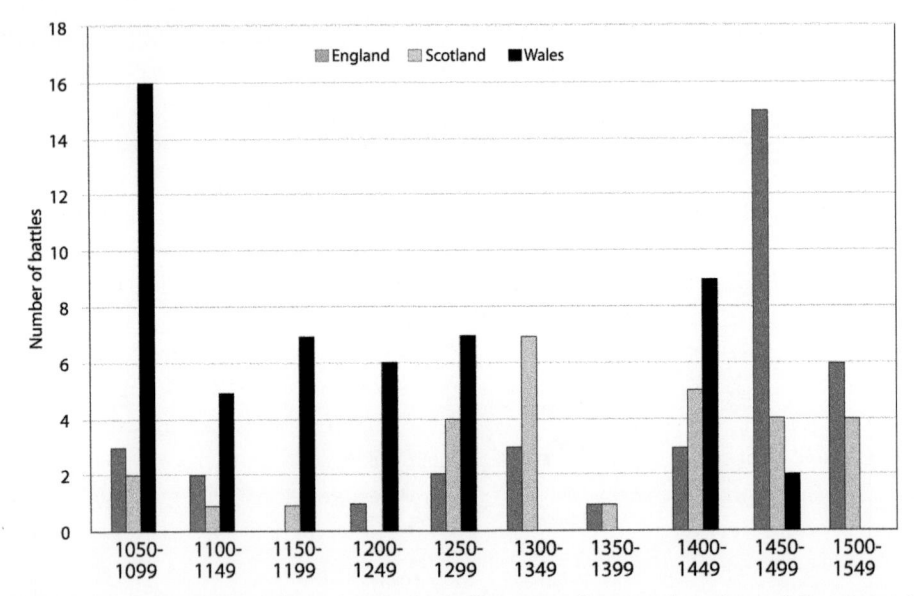

FIGURE 26.2 Graph of battles in Britain by half century, showing the substantial variation in potential for study at different times, though the data are confused by the bias in the Welsh data

Hundred Years' War, from Crecy [1346] to Agincourt [1415] (Strickland and Hardy 2005, 167–89). Recent work at Bannockburn shows the difficulty in recovering sufficient physical evidence on these early battlefields which might allow archaeology to make a more significant contribution to the study of these important tactical advances. For the next major transition, the rise to dominance of gunpowder weapons, the battlefields of 1450–1550 certainly do provide such an opportunity, in particular the series of battles during the Wars of the Roses in England and those in the 1540s on the Anglo-Scottish border and during the English rebellions (Foard and Curry 2013, 196–7).

The Evidence and Its Investigation

Battlefield archaeology draws upon three main strands of evidence. First, documentary records are important for understanding military action and the armies that fought, including equipment and the tactics of the period. This must include sufficient evidence for the general location of a battle to allow meaningful investigation, although there is rarely much topographical detail for medieval battles. Some battles have candidate sites miles apart, while reassessment regularly casts doubt on the location of others (Foard and Morris 2012, 56, 83–5); Bannockburn formerly had nine alternatives, though Pollard's as yet unpublished archaeological investigation may now have resolved the issue. Knowledge of medieval battlefield tactics is also limited: the only manual of military practice is a late classical volume by Publius Flavius Vegetius Renatus, known as Vegetius, and its various medieval reworkings (Allmand 2011). The first tactical manual in Britain is by Thomas Audley in the 1540s, which can be viewed alongside the first contemporary plans of a British battle, those for Pinkie in 1547 (Audley 1540; Foard and Morris 2012, 99; Hodgkins 2013). Prior to the mid-sixteenth century, certain knowledge of depths and forms of battle array is generally lacking and, coupled with uncertainty over the size of armies, this means that we have a poor understanding of their frontage in battle array and hence the scale of medieval battlefields.

Second, there is documentary and archaeological evidence for the landscape as it was at the time of the action, from relief and drainage through communications to land use, including what was wooded, enclosed, or open. Reconstructing this landscape provides a framework to build a hypothesis as to how the events played out across the terrain, and why. Detailed studies of this type are available for Bosworth, Northampton, and forthcoming for Bannockburn, while others with only documentary-based reconstruction include London (1554) and Dussindale (Norfolk, 1549) (Foard and Curry 2013, 73–98; Foard and Partida 2013; Hodgkins 2013; 2014).

The final, crucial step is to test the hypotheses through investigation of physical evidence left by the action or its aftermath. Typically, the most substantial physical evidence relates to later commemoration, including chantry chapels or, as at Hastings (East Sussex), a monastery where prayers could be said for the souls of the dead (Foard and Morris 2012, 10–17). These are not necessarily reliable guides to events on the ground, however, as chantries were sometimes established off-site, as at Bosworth and Towton (Foard and Curry 2013, 60–1; Sutherland and Holst 2014). Thus, despite their chantries being located, several alternative sites for the battles of Hastings and Barnet [Hertfordshire, 1471] have been proposed (Bradbury 1998; Foard and Morris 2012, 83–5; Warren 2009). As for the action itself, few battles saw the preparation of fixed defences that would leave substantial cut features amenable to their recognition through geophysical survey or excavation. Exceptions might include the bank and ditch defending the Lancastrian camp assaulted at Northampton [1460] or the rows of small shallow pits which protected Scottish infantry against English cavalry at Bannockburn (English Heritage 1995; Strickland and Hardy 2005, 168), though neither have been identified. The only excavated example comprises hollows where Scottish artillery may have dug-in before the battle of Flodden [Northumberland, 1513] (Pollard and Oliver 2002, 118–82).

The only archaeological feature left by most battles is the mass grave. Many of the skeletons recovered will show weapon trauma but rarely are they accompanied by objects because of the practice of stripping the dead, as the Bayeux Tapestry shows for Hastings. However, there are many variations in the disposal of the dead (Curry and Foard 2017). High-status individuals might be removed for burial, as Richard III was when he was carried 15 miles (24 km) from Bosworth battlefield to Leicester so as to demonstrate his death publically (Pitts 2014). More typical is the battle of Northampton after which the Duke of Buckingham was buried in Greyfriars and other high-status individuals in St John's Hospital, both less than a mile away (1.5 km) in the town itself. When bodies were widely scattered and were brought together by cart for burial it was more practical to use consecrated ground, as at Pinkie in East Lothian (Fergusson 1963, quoting the Treasurers Accounts; Patten 1548; Strickland and Hardy 2005, 279–83). More often, especially with densely distributed bodies, mass graves were dug in unconsecrated ground near where they fell. At Towton there are mass graves in the centre of the battlefield and another in the village 1.5 km away, close to a pre-existing chapel (Sutherland and Holst 2014, 90–1) (Figure 26.3). The battlefield graves are just 800 m from the parish church at Saxton and 900 m from the chapel in Towton. The only other excavated example, at East Stoke [Nottinghamshire, 1487], is probably just one of a series of graves dug at the spot where troops fell in the rout, and lies equally close to a parish church (Peter Masters pers. comm.; Foard and Morris 2012, 33).

The Towton chapel mass grave was also accompanied by several individual burials which exhibit weapon trauma on their skeletons (Holst and Sutherland 2014). These may be men of higher status, but equally they could be common soldiers who died of their wounds days or weeks later. After early modern battles, severely wounded men could be treated for days or weeks in settlements nearby, others might be cared for many miles away. When they died they were buried with the same respect as any other dead, though if several died on the same day then they might be grouped together for burial (Foard 1995, 309–14). The grave containing three bodies adjacent to the Towton chapel mass grave may be explained in this way, whereas treatment in distant settlements may explain the confusing presence of a burial showing weapon trauma in the hospital at the west end of Lewes. This is on the edge of the 1264 battlefield, so the body was initially thought to be from that battle until it produced a C^{14} date compatible with the 1066 campaign (Livesey 2014). Clearly, the size and location of mass graves varies dramatically between battlefields and when we add to this the difficulty of applying geophysics to sites which might cover several square kilometres, it is no wonder that so few mass graves have been securely located.

The Towton chapel mass grave had skeletons intermingled in a complex way resulting from the typical practice of packing the bodies tightly in order to limit the labour in digging the grave. This makes archaeological investigation difficult, although the application of 3D digital imaging should enable recovery of the maximum possible data in the future. Once excavated, osteology can provide a wealth of information. The study of the Towton remains revealed patterns of trauma associated with different weapon types and techniques of fighting, while serious wounds long healed indicated experienced soldiers injured in previous battles. The study of the human bone also cast light on the age, physical character, and the health history of the soldiers. A case has even been made for certain asymmetrical strengthening of the upper body enabling the identification of archers, though this has been disputed (Fiorato et al. 2000; Holst and Sutherland 2014). Future application of techniques such as isotope and DNA analysis promises further possibilities, perhaps even the ability to distinguish between combatants from different armies.

Inevitably, there are caveats. Just forty-four individuals were available for analysis at Towton compared to the 1185 excavated in the early twentieth century at Visby, Sweden [1361]. There is also uncertainty as to which phase of the battle the graves relate to, as they may have been brought in from a wide area of the rout. Nor is osteological study always

MEDIEVAL BATTLEFIELD ARCHAEOLOGY 407

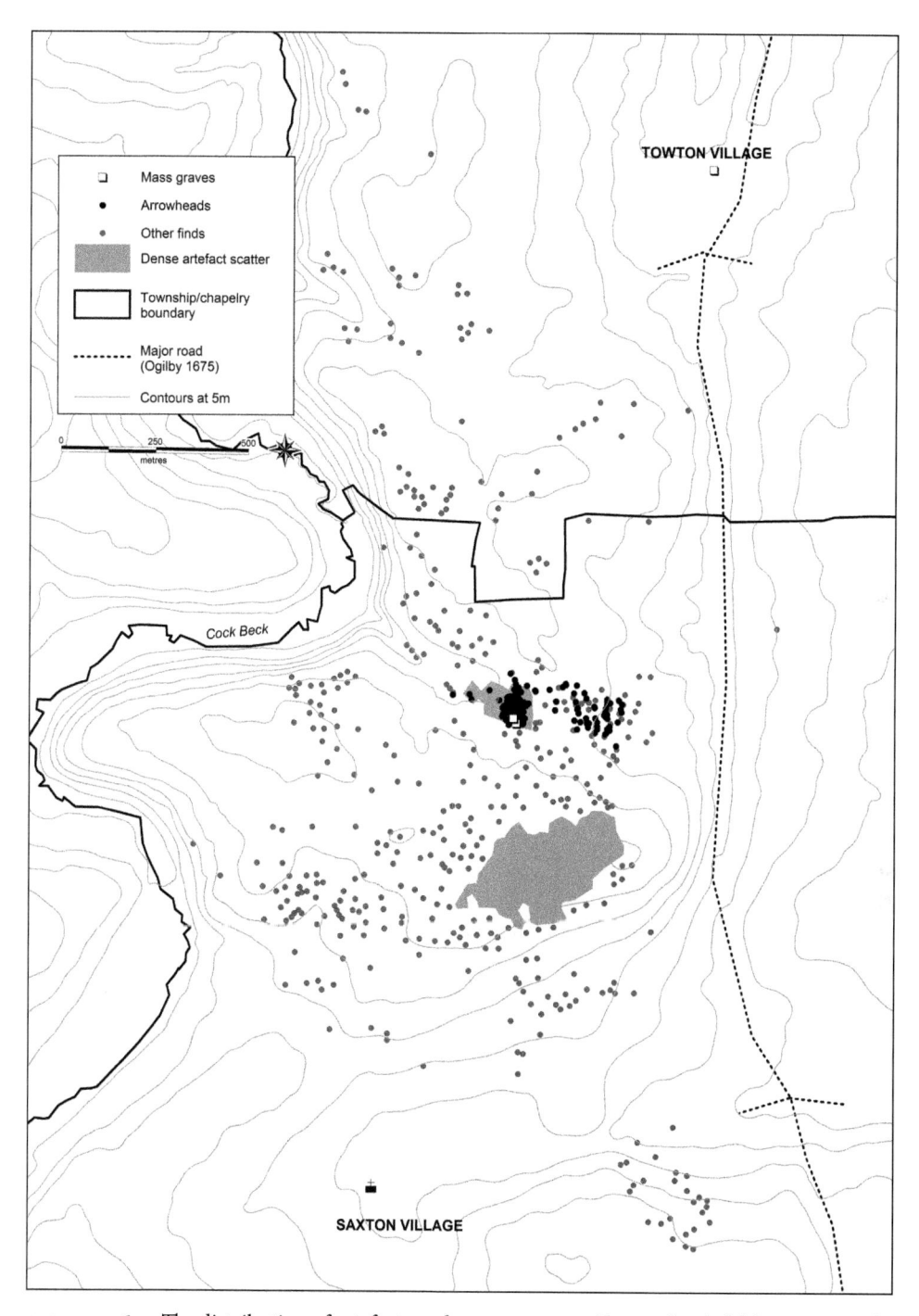

FIGURE 26.3 The distribution of artefacts and mass graves on Towton battlefield, set against the historic terrain

(© Glenn Foard)

possible, because the medieval concern for the souls of the dead led to some graves being cleared in later decades and the remains removed to consecrated ground where a chantry might be established. Thus the mass grave on the battlefield at Towton now contains only the small bones which were missed during the clearance (Sutherland 2009).

Finally, there may be archaeological evidence for the logistical support needed by medieval armies, including a large baggage train carrying food and equipment and supported by a wide range of specialists and camp followers. Camps were established each night on campaign, with troops often distributed between several villages. The archaeological evidence they left is likely to be ephemeral and, where it is within or adjacent to existing settlements, it will be difficult to separate from centuries of domestic occupation. However, if the camp was plundered then there may be a distinctive archaeological signature. While substantial evidence has yet to be recovered from any site of this type, the discovery of a processional cross and two Burgundian coins on Ambion Hill may hint at the location of Richard III's camp before Bosworth (Foard and Curry 2013, 129).

Artefact Scatters

The key dataset from battlefields is usually the distribution of metal artefacts in the topsoil, deposited during the action and its aftermath. Sampled in a systematic archaeological survey, using metal detectors accompanied by GPS recording at sub-metre accuracy, this can provide a unique battlefield-wide perspective. The identification of weapons and equipment is greatly assisted by collections in armouries and elsewhere as well as graphic or sculptural representation (e.g. Foard and Curry 2013, 124–5). In some cases the preserved equipment represents booty captured from defeated armies and retained as trophies by future generations. For example, artillery captured by the Swiss from the Burgundians at Grandson and Murten [1476]—battles with similar cultural significance for the Swiss as Bannockburn has for Scots—has been invaluable in interpreting late medieval lead projectiles from British battlefields. While there are occasional survivals of equipment from British battles, such as the Douglas standard carried at the battle of Otterburn [Northumberland, 1387], they have yet to impact greatly on archaeological interpretation (Foard and Curry 2013, 135–77; Prestwich 1996, 108).

On early modern sites, lead projectiles from gunpowder weapons represent the vast majority of finds. However, guns were not introduced to the battlefield until the later fourteenth century, while armies in Britain appear not to have adopted artillery for field action until the mid-fifteenth century. Even then, the numbers of lead projectiles are very low, because hand-guns did not begin to displace the longbow on British battlefields until the sixteenth century. There were just two earlier battles, St Albans II [Hertfordshire, 1461] and Barnet where large numbers of Continental hand-gunners are documented. This is why by far the largest assemblage of gunpowder projectiles from a medieval battlefield, at Bosworth, numbers just thirty-four, almost all of them fired from artillery. Likewise, the density of other battle-related artefacts at Bosworth, including weapon parts and fitments from personal equipment, is low (Foard and Curry 2013, 118–90) (Figure 26.4). This is

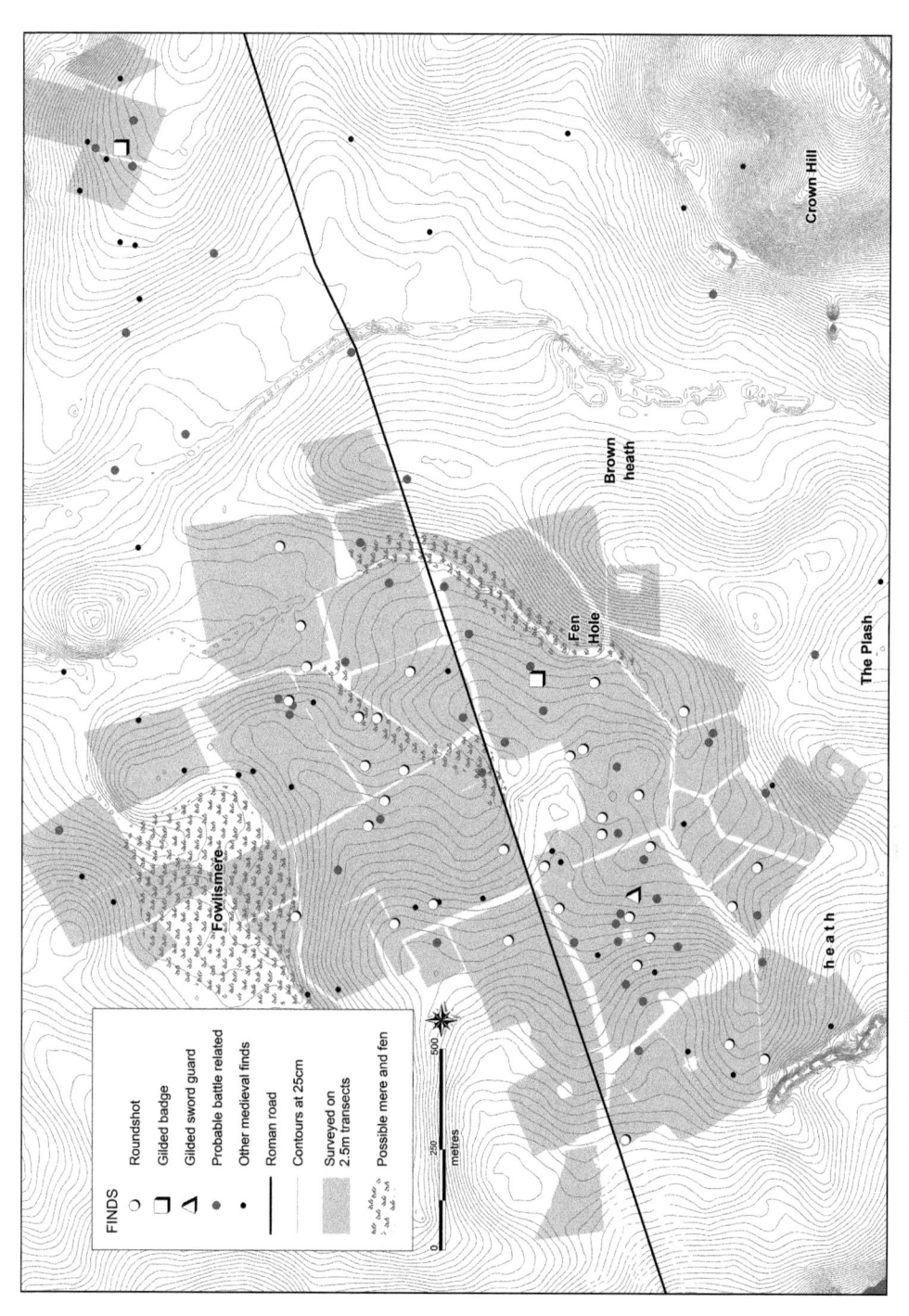

FIGURE 26.4 Distribution of battle archaeology on Bosworth battlefield

also the case at Bannockburn, Flodden, and Pinkie and may explain the failure of smaller-scale work on other battlefields to produce any battle-related archaeology, including Shrewsbury [1403], Agincourt [1415], Lewes [1264], and Hastings (Livesey 2013; Pollard and Oliver 2002, 12–73; Sutherland 2009). Towton battlefield, which has produced several thousand non-ferrous objects, thus appears exceptional, though a full catalogue has yet to be published (Fiorato et al. 2000; Sutherland and Holst 2014).

Most artefacts lost during medieval battles were probably ferrous, the most common metal for fitments on military and personal equipment; non-ferrous items tend to represent the equipment of higher-status individuals. Unfortunately, ferrous objects normally decay rapidly in topsoil, even in the least aggressive soil chemistry, so special conditions are needed for their survival. Where such conditions exist, as at Masterby in Sweden and Hartzhorn (Roman) in Germany, almost all battle-related objects are ferrous, with non-ferrous artefacts representing just a tiny percentage of the assemblage. At Towton the presence of large numbers of non-ferrous artefacts has several possible explanations, including ground conditions on the day which enabled many items to be trodden-in so they were not recovered in subsequent days; the scale and intensity of the action; and, most crucially, the exceptional number of high-status individuals killed, which led to unusually large numbers of non-ferrous items being lost. The recovery of more than three hundred ferrous arrowheads at Towton is also unique and yet to be adequately explained. Likely factors include high soil pH plus burial by colluviation, but their very restricted spatial distribution also suggests mass graves and/or remnant furrows from medieval cultivation which may provide reservoirs below the topsoil from where ploughing has progressively introduced them into the ploughsoil. Significantly, almost no other ferrous artefacts have come from the survey, yet the one buckle found in the more stable context of the chapel mass grave was ferrous (Simon Richardson, pers. comm.; Holst and Sutherland 2014). Thus, even at Towton it appears that the surviving assemblage is highly distorted by the loss through decay of ferrous objects.

The low density of finds on most medieval battlefields requires intensive survey both to locate the site and reveal artefact distributions. For the early gunpowder era, the experience of the Bosworth project suggests a minimum of systematic metal-detecting survey, directed by an experienced battlefield archaeologist using skilled detectorists with high specification detectors, sampling on 2.5 m spaced transects (Foard and Curry 2013, 101–18). The lack of agreed international standards for battlefield survey impedes comparison, however, and in some cases even the highest-intensity survey could fail to recover definitive evidence; the lack of any battle archaeology in a survey of a medieval battlefield cannot be used as negative evidence to prove that a site lies elsewhere. It should also be remembered that most battlefield surveys produce a wide range of artefacts which are not battle-related, a good example being at Fulford [Yorkshire, 1066] (Jones 2011), where a detecting survey at the most likely location failed to find battle-related artefacts but did recover extensive evidence of ferrous metal-working. This was interpreted as the reworking of large numbers of ferrous artefacts retrieved after the action, even though nothing comparable is known elsewhere and there is no documentary evidence for this practice. A more logical conclusion, perhaps, is the superimposition of unrelated activities at different times, as with Roman weights and medieval round shot at Bosworth (e.g. Foard and Curry 2013, fig. 6.1a).

Even when artefact distributions can be analysed and mapped, questions remain as to how representative this is of the total population surviving in the ground and how representative that might be of the assemblage originally deposited. Factors requiring further research include the decay of artefacts in the topsoil, removal by collectors, biases introduced by sampling methods, and the distortion of distributions by horizontal displacement caused by cultivation. For the latter, data already collected for other types of artefact scatter can assist, although the shape and mass of metal objects may cause them to move differently. Moreover, most battle archaeology has remained in the topsoil since deposition. Initial experiments over one season of ploughing and harrowing suggest maximum movement of musket calibre lead ball of around 1 m. However, another experiment shows metal artefacts, especially the large calibre (30–60 mm) round shot present on later fifteenth- and sixteenth-century battlefields, to be far more vulnerable to modern cultivation techniques for potatoes. De-stoning and potato harvesting machinery in a single season moved these large calibre rounds by as much as 10 m, apparently shifting a small percentage beyond the 30 m wide survey area, and removing one entirely from the potato field; even small calibre rounds for hand-guns suffered unusually long distance movement (Foard, in preparation). At least two Wars of the Roses battlefields, Towton and Mortimer's Cross [Herefordshire, 1461], have seen decades of potato cultivation so their artefact patterns may have been significantly distorted.

Where sufficient artefacts are recovered they may allow archaeology to contribute to the wider study of warfare, especially when accompanied by scientific analysis. Thus arrowheads from Towton have led to reconsideration of the method and significance of military arrowhead manufacture. The recovery of heraldic badges from Bosworth, Towton, and recently Flodden suggests they may indeed have been worn in action by high-status individuals for practical purposes. Perhaps most significant has been the recovery of round shot from Bosworth, Northampton, Towton, St Albans II, Barnet, Flodden, and Pinkie, together with the cast gun fragments from Towton. Such data offer a new approach to the use of gunpowder weapons on the battlefield during a key period in the evolution of European warfare between 1450 and 1550 (de Crouy-Chanel 2014; Foard and Curry 2013, 135–77; Sutherland 2012). Of particular importance in Britain will be the fifteen battlefields of the Wars of the Roses [1455–87] and their comparison with sites of the 1540s for the insights this might provide into Britain's unique trajectory in this transitional period for weaponry.

SIEGES

While there have been many excavations on medieval siege sites, nowhere do the techniques of battlefield archaeology seem to have been applied to investigate artefact scatters. Some pre-fifteenth-century sites do contain such material, such as the large stone projectiles at Kenilworth Castle (Warwickshire), although it may only be with the application of gunpowder weapons that sufficient evidence exists to allow meaningful investigation. Armies attacking and defending fortified sites did employ both large and small artillery and hand-guns earlier and in larger number than in field actions (e.g. Grummit 2000) and finds have been recovered, albeit unsystematically, from several sites. Among these is Tantallon Castle (East Lothian), where lead-stone and lead-iron composite round shot has been found (Caldwell and O'Neil 1991), and St Michael's Mount (Cornwall) where there are similar finds in the private collection. While artefacts from within the garrison are only recoverable through excavation, similar material representing outgoing fire, or action during sallies beyond the defences, is to be expected close to besieged garrisons.

FIGURE 26.5 A lead-iron composite round shot of *c.*39 mm diameter with an area of lead lost, either from an impact or due to expansion as the iron core corroded, revealing the corroding iron die. Said to have been found above Marazion near St Michael's Mount, Cornwall (collection of Adam Dolling)

(© Glenn Foard)

For example, at least three lead-iron composite round shot (of $c.48$, 39, and 35 mm) were found by a detectorist immediately above Marazion on the slope facing St Michael's Mount (Adam Dolling pers. comm.) (Figure 26.5). In the same area other detectorists are said to have found 'lots of lead musket balls', a catch-all term for small-calibre lead bullets intended for hand-guns. They could actually have been fired from fifteenth-century hand-cannon, fifteenth- or sixteenth-century arquebus, or early modern muskets, carbines, and pistols. Lying about 900 m from the defences, the artillery rounds are probably within the final range of the guns on the Mount, but the small arms rounds would not be. The composite round shot must surely be from the brief siege of 1473–4 or the much longer siege of 1549, as this type of projectile had already gone out of use by 1600. The small arms rounds could represent action beyond the defences in either of the late medieval sieges or even that of 1646. Detailed study of calibre, manufacture, firing evidence, and distribution would be needed for a more accurate assessment, but the opportunity for any meaningful study of these objects and their individual locations is now lost.

St Michael's Mount demonstrates the error in claiming that the scheduling of a fortified site will effectively protect the archaeology of a siege (English Heritage 1995). This is a resource that needs to be managed, both through the integration of systematic detecting within excavation programmes and the protection of unstratified artefact scatters which may lie beyond scheduled areas. At present, sieges are not even recorded in local and national records. Without that, their archaeology will never be adequately managed. 'Siege site' needs to be added as a distinct class of monument on archaeological record systems and their boundaries extended well beyond the fortifications to include potential artefact scatters as well as any siege works, taking into account the range of artillery pieces and the potential for action beyond the defences. Exemplar studies are also needed to determine exactly what can be achieved through survey, because investigation of a siege site is likely to be more complex than a battle. Many garrisons saw more than one siege, as at St Michael's Mount, with action sometimes lasting for months, resulting in overlapping patterns of unstratified artefacts. Thorough national resource assessments are required, and without them many of our best preserved siege sites are likely to suffer the same fate as St Michael's Mount.

Conservation Management

Conservation management of battlefields was initiated in England with the Battlefields Register in 1995 and at the time of writing includes twenty-one medieval sites; in Scotland the Battlefields Inventory established in 2014 included fourteen medieval sites, with work now underway towards a Welsh equivalent.[2] However, these measures

---

[2] http://historicengland.org.uk/listing/the-list/advanced-search; http://www.historic-scotland.gov.uk/index/heritage/battlefields/inventorybattlefields.htm.

are non-statutory and no battle archaeology has yet been protected in its own right through scheduling. The Battlefields Register has proven effective against development and related threats through the planning process, but only where supported by well-informed local action. Other avenues for protection include influencing agricultural practices through agri-environment grant schemes. The assessment of battlefields for the At Risk Register in England has been another important advance, as is the current drafting of general guidance on their management in Scotland, and the heritage crime initiative which is tackling illicit detecting at Towton. Management of individual sites is best guided through specific conservation statements of which the first have been prepared for Northampton and Bosworth battlefields. The effectiveness of these documents needs to be critically assessed then others produced, starting with those sites most under threat. But effective implementation requires further research on the character of the resource and the processes leading to its degradation, with the first steps currently being taken to advance understanding of decay of metal objects in ploughsoil through PhD research funded by the Arts and Humanities Research Council and Historic England.

Unfortunately, the greatest single threat has largely been ignored: the removal of artefacts from both registered and unregistered battlefields. Although Fergusson has reasonably argued that much can be achieved by collaboration with detectorists, this is not enough on nationally important sites, because even the most conscientious detectorist will cause greater loss of evidence than a team working to a well-designed archaeological scheme (Fergusson 2013a; 2013b). Indeed, it is essential that the artefacts are left in the ground on most sites until we understand better how to sample that evidence more effectively. A current initiative in Flanders, which is examining the potential for the control of detecting through a programme of licensing, may provide a model for Britain (Foard and Partida forthcoming). In Ireland the banning of non-archaeological metal-detecting is an example of the effective implementation of a complete ban (Shiels 2015).

One final threat comes from an unexpected direction. We must take care that interpretative initiatives do not compromise the archaeological potential of medieval battlefields. Now we have begun to understand the battle archaeology on medieval sites, and its vulnerability, there is no excuse for continuing public events on nationally important battlefields. As work at Hastings has shown, the result is contamination with thousands of modern items, like ring pulls, foil, and coins, which make normal battlefield survey impossible, while some reproduction artefacts from re-enactment, once corroded, may be indistinguishable from the originals (Foard, in preparation). It is likely that similar if not greater damage has been done at Tewkesbury (Gloucestershire, 1471) by decades of large-scale re-enactment events, which have migrated across almost the whole battlefield. The Hastings work has shown that, as modern material migrates down the soil column, pre-modern finds still remain uncontaminated for decades at the base of the topsoil, but only where land has not been cultivated. Theoretically, it is possible to retrieve these finds by machining off the contaminated upper level of topsoil and detecting the lower level, but this is prohibitively expensive on all but the most important of sites and only practical when a few hectares need to be examined, as at Hastings.

Conclusion

The first role of battlefield archaeology must be to test current interpretations of medieval battle locations. Once located, we must add to the tiny corpus of existing battlefield-wide studies. These can then be used to explore the way in which the action, as understood from a combination of documentary evidence and battle archaeology, played out in relation to the contemporary terrain. Only then can we begin a more sophisticated comparative analysis between battlefields than Carman and Carman were able to achieve a decade ago (Carman and Carman 2006). While this should certainly test the more intangible factors favoured by the Carmans, it is essential first to explore more prosaic explanations. Can changes seen over time in the use of terrain be explained as tactical responses to evolving weapons technology, the increasing size of armies, and other practical military considerations described in military manuals? If sufficient physical evidence can be retrieved from key sites then it may be possible to tackle more challenging questions about the character and evolution of European warfare. For the medieval period, documents can only take us so far in addressing such issues. Finally, we must consider the wider cultural significance of battlefields. While we, as archaeologists, approach fields of conflict in a scientific manner to advance understanding of the events and of warfare in general, it must be remembered that these sites also have commemorative value. In the decades after the event they were important to individuals who fought there or had connections with those who fought. As those working on twentieth-century warfare know, archaeological investigation of fields of conflict becomes increasingly acceptable as the events pass out of living memory and individual personal connections are lost. However, some battles resonate down the centuries and can be used, and abused, in the reinforcing or creation of cultural identities. Conservation management of battlefields must take account of this, as well as their value as historic and archaeological sites. These wider concerns can also impact on the treatment of the archaeological evidence itself, especially for human remains, as revealed by the recent dispute over where the body of Richard III should finally be laid to rest. In all such situations the objective presentation of the historical and archaeological evidence is an important corrective.

Acknowledgements

The author would like to thank Tracey Partida for enhancing the database and preparing the maps, HERs in Wales for providing data, staff at Clywd-Powys Archaeological Trust for their extensive assistance and advice, and Brian Mallaws for information and guidance over many years on Welsh battlefields.

References cited

Allmand, C. 2011 *The De re militari of Vegetius: the reception, transmission and legacy of a Roman text in the Middle Ages*, Cambridge University Press, Cambridge

Audley, T. 1540 *Arte of warre*, The Pike and Shot Society, Farnham (reprinted 2002)

Bradbury, J. 1998 *The battle of Hastings*, Sutton, Stroud

Caldwell, D. and O'Neil, M. 1991 'Tantallon Castle, East Lothian: a catalogue of the finds', *Proceedings of the Society of Antiquaries Scotland* 121, 335–57

Carman, J. 2013 *Archaeologies of conflict*, Bloomsbury Academic, London

Carman, J. and Carman, P. 2006 *Bloody meadows: investigating landscapes of battle*, Sutton Publishing, Stroud

Curry, A. and Foard, G. 2017 'Where are the dead of medieval battles? A preliminary survey', *Journal of Conflict Archaeology* 12, 1–17

de Crouy-Chanel, E. 2014 *D'Histoire le canon jusqu'au milieu du XVIe siècle, France, Bretagne et Pays-Bas bourguignons*, PhD thesis, Sorbonne University, Paris

English Heritage, 1995 *Register of historic battlefields*, English Heritage, London

Eickhoff, S. and Schopper, F. (eds) 2014 *Schlachtfeld und Massengrab: Spektren interdisziplinärer Auswertung von Orten der Gewalt*, Forschungen zur Archäologie im Land Brandenburg, Zossen

Fergusson, N. 2013a *An assessment of the positive contribution and negative impact of hobbyist metal detecting to sites of conflict in the UK*, unpublished PhD thesis, University of Glasgow

Fergusson, N. 2013b *Biting the bullet: the role of hobbyist metal detecting within battlefield archaeology*, Internet Archaeology 33, https://doi.org/10.11141/ia.33.3

Fergusson, S. J. 1963 *The white hind and other discoveries*, Faber and Faber, London

Fiorato, V., Boylston, A., and Knüsel, C. 2000 *Blood red roses: the archaeology of a mass grave from the battle of Towton AD 1461*, Oxbow, Oxford

Foard, G. 1995 *Naseby: the decisive campaign*, Pryor Publications, Whitstable

Foard, G. 2012 *Battlefield archaeology of the English Civil War*, Archaeopress, Oxford

Foard, G., in preparation 'Artefacts don't lie?', paper to the Fields of Conflict Conference, Dublin 2016

Foard, G. and Curry, A. 2013 *Bosworth 1485: a battlefield rediscovered*, Oxbow, Oxford

Foard, G. and Morris, R. 2012 *The archaeology of English battlefields*, Council for British Archaeology, York

Foard, G. and Partida, T. 2006 *Scotland's Historic Fields of Conflict: An Assessment for Historic Scotland*, The Battlefields Trust.

Foard, G. and Partida, T. 2013 *Northampton battlefield 1460: an assessment*, unpublished report for Northampton Borough Council

Foard, G. and Partida, T. forthcoming, 'The archaeology of medieval and early modern battlefields in Flanders', *Monumenten, Lanschappen & Archeologie (Journal of the Flemish Heritage Agency)*

Freeman, P. and Pollard, T. 2001 *Fields of conflict: progress and prospect in battlefield archaeology*, Archaeopress, Oxford

Grummitt, D. 2000 'The defence of Calais and the development of gunpowder weaponry in England in the late fifteenth century', *War in History* 7, 253–72

Hodgkins, A. J. 2013 *Rebellion and warfare in the Tudor state: military organisation, weaponry, and field tactics in mid-sixteenth century England*, unpublished PhD thesis, University of Leeds

Hodgkins, A. J. 2014 'Reconstructing rebellion: digital terrain analysis of the battle of Dussindale (1549)', *Internet Archaeology* 38, 1 January 2015

Holst, M. and Sutherland, T. 2014 'Towton revisited: analysis of the human remains from the Battle of Towton 1461', in S. Eickhoff and F. Schopper (eds), *Schlachtfeld und Massengrab: Spektren interdisziplinärer Auswertung von Orten der Gewalt*, Forschungen zur Archäologie im Land Brandenburg, Zossen, 97–127

Jones, C. 2011 *Finding Fulford: the search for the first battle of 1066*, WPS, York

Livesey, E. 2013 'Solving Lewes battle riddles? Skeleton 180 sent for further analysis', *Sussex Past and Present* 130, 10

Livesey, E. 2014 'Shock dating result: a victim of the Norman invasion?', *Sussex Past and Present* 133, 6

Meller, H., Reichel, C., Jung, R., and Luik, M. (eds) 2009 *Schlachtfeldarchäologie: Battlefield Archaeology 1*, Landesmuseums für Vorgeschichte, Halle

Patten, W. 1548 *The expedicion into Scotlande of the most woorthely fortunate prince Edward*, Richard Grafton, London

Pitts, M. 2014 *Digging for Richard III*, Thames and Hudson, London

Pollard, T. and Banks, I. 2010 'Now the wars are over: the past, present and future of Scottish battlefields', *International Journal of Historical Archaeology* 14(3), 414–41

Pollard, T. and Oliver, N. 2002 *Two men in a trench: battlefield archaeology, the key to unlocking the past*, Michael Joseph, London

Prestwich, M. 1996 *Armies and warfare in the Middle Ages: the English experience*, Yale University Press, New Haven and London

Scott, D., Babits, L., and Haecker, C. (eds) 2007 *Fields of conflict: battlefield archaeology from the Roman Empire to the Korean War*, Praeger Security International, Westport

Scott, D. and McFeaters, A. 2011 'The archaeology of historic battlefields: a history and theoretical development in conflict archaeology', *Journal of Archaeological Research* 19, 103–32

Shiels, D. 2015 'Reconstructing battlefield landscapes', in T. Barry and V. McAlister (eds), *Space and settlement in medieval Ireland*, Four Courts, Dublin, 186–202

Strickland, M. and Hardy, R. 2005 *The great warbow: from Hastings to the Mary Rose*, Sutton Publishing, Stroud

Sutherland, T. 2009 'Archaeological evidence of medieval conflict: case studies from Towton, Yorkshire, England (1461) and Agincourt, Pas de Calais, France (1415)', in H. Meller, C. Reichel, R. Jung, and M. Luik (eds), *Schlachtfeldarchäologie: Battlefield Archaeology 1*, Landesmuseums für Vorgeschichte, Halle, 109–15

Sutherland, T. 2012 'Conflicts and allies: historic battlefields as multidisciplinary hubs: a case study from Towton AD 1461', *Arms & Armour* 9(1), 40–53

Sutherland, T. and Holst, M. 2014 'Demonstrating the value of battlefield archaeology: war graves on Towton field, their location and excavation', in S. Eickhoff and F. Schopper (eds), *Schlachtfeld und Massegrab*, Zossen, 87–95

Warren, B. 2009 *Reappraisal of the battle of Barnet, 1471*, Potters Bar & District Historical Society, Potters Bar

CHAPTER 27

SYMBOLS OF POWER

DAVID A. HINTON

The Bayeux Tapestry, embroidered in the 1070s/1080s, provides an apt starting-point for consideration of the later Middle Ages in Britain, and its opening image is particularly appropriate for observing the symbols of power, as it shows a king, Edward the Confessor, wearing a crown such as that which had been bestowed on him at his coronation, and carrying his staff of office, also a coronation item, symbolic of Aaron's rod in the Old Testament (Nelson 2012). He is wearing expensive, embroidered clothes that expressed his special position (Tyler 1999), and is seated on a throne on a dais, raised as was suitable for one who had been blessed by God through his anointing at the coronation. His gesture emphasizes his authority over the other two figures in the scene, who are smaller than the king, a trope of medieval art to show importance.

If the Bayeux Tapestry can begin the period, then its end can be taken as the Battle of Bosworth in 1485, and the demise of another king, Richard III. The words that Shakespeare put into Richard's mouth, 'A horse, a horse …' are no less symbolic of medieval power than the image of the Confessor: a mounted warrior was a fearsome implement of war, the size of his horse making him tower over those around him, physically expressing his dominance. The cost of the specially bred horse, of the armour that became increasingly sophisticated, of the training that he needed, of his supporting entourage and of the weapons that he carried all put knighthood beyond the reach of most, even if social convention had not precluded it.

There is little between a status symbol and a symbol of power in societies like those of the Middle Ages, where power derived from the ability to manipulate affairs through control of land or of money. The balance in Britain favoured the former, as through it came not only resources, but a power-base, usually a castle (see Chapter 23), and traditional rights to serve and be served. Merchants like William Cade of London might be able to amass fortunes, and through the loans that they made to kings and barons were not without influence, but their power was indirect. Of the twenty-five men who forced Magna Carta upon King John in 1215, the only one who was not a landed baron was the Mayor of London, testimony to the City's importance, but only a token gesture to the power of capital.

Regalia, Royal Wealth, and Royal Images

Little survives physically of the trappings of medieval royal power; a large 'ruby', actually a spinel and originally a pendant, on the front of the present-day Imperial State Crown may have been acquired by the Black Prince in the fourteenth century, and could be one of the few things that Charles I was able to re-acquire in 1661 after most of the royal treasure had been dispersed during the Commonwealth interregnum (Bury 1998, 27). A silver-gilt spoon is the only other precious-metal item to survive, though how much of it is of the later twelfth century and how much is later replacement or embellishment is disputable; it is not recorded until 1349, so may not even have been intended originally for use in the anointing ceremony (Bury 1998, 87–9). Despite the appeals to ancient traditions made at coronations, and the stress that items had descended from the sainted Edward, the ceremonies were manipulated. To return to the Bayeux Tapestry, the crux of its story is Harold's acceptance of the crown, and he is shown enthroned and supported on one side by the Church in the dubious figure of Archbishop Stigand, and on the other by the laity of the 'witan', who are offering him a sword as a token of their acceptance that he should protect the kingdom on their behalf (Figure 27.1). By the end of the twelfth century, this had become three swords, taken from the royal treasury, their number because King Arthur had had three swords in the legendary story that was becoming the *Roman* with which every king wanted to be associated. They were to become emblematic of the English kings' claims to rule England, Normandy, and Anjou in the first half of the thirteenth century, just as the surrender of Arthur's crown in the 1280s meant that 'the glory of Wales passed to the English' (Lightbown 1998, 93). Relations with Scotland were expressed by the removal in 1296 of the Stone of Scone to Westminster to be placed within the Coronation Chair, although its ritual antiquity is questionable—it was not recorded until 1249 (Lightbown 1998, 144), though use of other stones for inauguration rites is deduced from carved footprints such as that at Dunadd (Argyll and Bute), a person's suitability for kingship involving fitting his foot into the impression (Nieke and Duncan 1988, 16). It was chivalric notions not vague memories of antiquity that led to the inclusion of spurs being fitted on to the royal feet.

Crowns, staffs, orbs, and sceptres are 'signifiers', emblems of power that are not symbolic of instruments through which it was wielded, such as swords. Knowledge of them depends upon documentary records and images. Coin and seal designs show Edward the Confessor wearing a new sort of crown, modelled on Byzantine styles, and with dangling pendants, twelve stones symbolizing the twelve gates of Jerusalem. It all became too much for the goldsmith-bishop Spearhavoc, who absconded with what he had been entrusted with to make Edward's crown. The coins were silver pennies, on which the royal image became more and more degraded as they became more and more familiar in everyday use, until gold coins were introduced, at first briefly in the 1250s and then more permanently in the fourteenth century; great care went into the designs of those much

FIGURE 27.1 Harold's coronation depicted on the Bayeux Tapestry. The king can be easily identified because of the crown, orb, and sceptre (photo by Myrabella, public domain)

more valuable and prestigious items, with kings wielding swords above ships and war-like angels (see Chapter 32). Great care always went into the designs on the Great Seal and others, with images of kings on one side as sword-wielding mounted knights and on the other as enthroned icons, the details changing according to political aspirations. An extreme use of an image was Richard II's portrait placed on his seat at Westminster Abbey as a reminder of him in his absences, though whether courtiers were expected to bow to it as to the monarch in person is not recorded (Alexander and Binski 1987, no. 713; Binski 1999, 80–3).

Early medieval kings wore their crowns regularly on certain feast-days, at royal centres such as Winchester, Gloucester, and Westminster, demonstrating their understanding of the importance of 'presence culture' (Hare 1999; Nelson 2012, 119; cf. 'presence chambers' in buildings, Chapter 23 in this *Handbook*). The recent recognition of an inventory of Richard II's portable wealth in 1398–9 reveals that he owned eleven different crowns and coronets, excluding the coronation crown traditionally kept at Westminster Abbey. They were set with rubies, diamonds, sapphires, emeralds, and pearls; one of these probably survives as Blanche's Crown, taken overseas when she married in 1401, and therefore one of the few things to escape the next three hundred years unscathed. Its gems and pearls are set off by blue, white, and red enamelling, a medium used to create an inscription on the only other crown to survive from medieval Britain, its owner's name, Margaret of York—sister of King Edward IV—datable to the 1460s (Alexander and Binski 1987, no. 13; Marks and Williamson 2003, no. 11; Stratford 2010).

Feasts and entertaining were an essential part of kingship, the foods and wine offered being a statement of the royal ability to acquire resources and to spend conspicuously beyond the reach of others. Venison from forests and parks, fresh fish from ponds, and squabs from dovecotes (see Chapter 25) were all 'reserved foods', only available to the less well-off if they were prepared to poach and steal. Wine became increasingly affordable, sold in urban taverns, but sweet wines from Italy retained the cost advantage that gave status. Feasts were also an opportunity to show off gold and silver plate; Richard II's inventory has long lists of what he could display on his table—or on his cupboard if he chose. A few beakers, salts, bowls, and basins survive, which, although not from the royal household, are enough to show the reality of the records not only of Richard's property, but also of aristocrats such as the Earl of Arundel. The latter's goods were inventoried because he had fallen from the king's favour, however, and his property had been confiscated. In politically dangerous times, a stock of valuables of all sorts was useful; hoards of coins and jewels such as those from Fishpool (Nottinghamshire) and Thame (Oxfordshire) show that portable wealth could be hidden, hopefully to be recovered.

Including all its individual items such as separately recorded gemstones, Richard's inventory is 28 m long, perhaps a better measure of value than any attempt to turn the financial estimates given into modern currency. Another reason why kings needed to know what they owned was that the objects could be used as pledges against loans, often essential for high-spending kings who could not get enough from taxes and customs levies to maintain their state and conduct their wars.

Badges, Seals, and Other Insignia

Some jewels were badges, to show loyalties and affiliations. The extreme case was the Order of the Garter, created from the ransoms won from the French by Edward III, and given to those who had served with him at the Battle of Crécy, soon extended to others whose particular loyalty was required. They were associated with Windsor Castle, where the great chapel is a fifteenth-century testimony to the Order's enduring role. At other royal places, knighthoods were bestowed with great ceremony, and Edward I with his Arthurian bent created Round Table events, where knights role-played those of the legends—but the apparent democracy of a round table where none has a special place in the hierarchy of seating was probably undermined by the reservation of a special place for the king, if the Tudor enhancement of the table hanging in the great hall at Winchester Castle (Hampshire) shows medieval practice (Biddle 2000).

Richard II's inventory reveals that he had two garter brooches ready for his specially favoured knights, and a larger stock of collars of SS, originally a badge of office showing service to the king. Among several other designs, he had hart brooches that played on his name, 'Rich hart'. On the Wilton Diptych, they are shown being worn even by the Virgin Mary and her supporting angels, to show Heaven's blessing on the king, who on the opposite panel has them sewn into his robes, as well as on a pendant. He is also wearing a collar made to resemble broom-pods, a badge of his father-in-law that played on the dynasty's name 'plante à genet', though used earlier by Henry II. Such items were given and received on occasions such as New Year's Eve. They added to the insecurity of the times, as not to be given one would be a mark of the king's disfavour, and factions would be fostered. Richard, despite his treasury, was ousted and killed by Henry of Lancaster whom he had sought to exile, an annexation which was eventually to cause the civil war that came to be known as the Wars of the Roses, alluding to the two different colours of the York and Lancaster badges, although the white was not adopted until Henry VII's reign (Hepburn 2008). To modern eyes the most beautiful survival from the period is the enamelled gold swan-brooch, made *c.*1400 and now on display in the British Museum; the coronet and chain round the bird's neck show that it was more than just an ornament, but a Lancastrian badge, possibly a token for a supporter of someone jousting at Dunstable, a well-known venue and close to where the brooch was found (Cherry 1969). It probably also alluded to the story of the swan-knight, which the Bohun family associated itself with, so that their Lancastrian connection took the badge to Henry V.

Recognition of badges was essential—riots occurred when supporters of different factions encountered each other, and there were occasions when failure to identify a badge correctly led to parties of the same faction fighting. This was supposedly countered by the 'mystery' of heraldry developed from the second half of the twelfth century. The royal creatures of choice vired between leopards and lions, beasts of great courage and strength, obvious royal virtues; other families might appropriate a creature that was a play on its name—the Vere family took a boar because of the Latin *verres* (cf. Figure 27.2).

FIGURE 27.2 Gilt copper-alloy badge from London, fourteenth–fifteenth centuries, depicting a standing boar on a twisted rope. The boar has a crown around its neck, a crescent on its shoulder, and a chain along its back. The symbol of the boar was already used by Edward III but Richard, Duke of Gloucester, took the white boar as his symbol and at his coronation in 1483 thousands of boar badges were produced

(© Portable Antiquities Scheme Object ID: LON-A33FF5, CC BY)

Most designs were geometric, more easily rendered and supposedly recognizable to initiates. Colour became an essential discriminator, emphasizing the power of sight (Woolgar 2006, 181). Legal protection was applied to the coats of arms, and arcane disputes reflected anxiety to be seen to be associated with great and ancient families. Benefactions and patronage could be shown by a family badge in a church carving, on a stained-glass window, or on floor-tiles, or on the gate of a town which sought the support of its local land-owners. In thanks for benefactions received and hoped for, the fifteenth-century roof of the Oxford University Divinity School looks as if badges and devices are raining down from its elaborate vaulting (Marks and Williamson 2003, no. 246). Badges were produced in large numbers in base metal, to be worn by a family's retainers and other supporters, and were an obvious way of showing the power of numbers, despite intermittent attempts to control such displays. Even royal ships were given names of the king's badges: Henry V's *Swan*, Henry VIII's *Peter Pomegranate* (Siddons 2009).

The Great Seal became one of several used by medieval kings and their various officers, but they were not the only ones to need seals to authenticate documents. Even before the Norman Conquest a few seal-dies in metal and ivory are known, the property of church people and secular aristocrats. The former usually showed robed ecclesiastics or the dedicatory saint, increasingly in the thirteenth century in architectural settings. As communality spread from the Church to lay institutions such as guilds and urban corporations, so seals were needed for their businesses, with designs that reflected their claims and aspirations. An early example is the image created for the 'barons of London' in *c*.1220; the walls and magnificent gates and towers of the city are shown enclosing a multitude of church spires, presided over on one side by the best-known of all Londoners, Archbishop Thomas Becket, and on the other by St Paul but with a banner alongside him sporting the three leopards emblematic of the English kings, and with a raised sword to hint at royal justice lest claiming the help of the man who had defied royal authority should be thought a sign of disloyalty (Alexander and Binski 1987, no. 193; Cherry 2015, 284–5). London was followed by others; ports with images of ships, or appropriation of stories, such as Grimsby's depiction of a giant figure identified as the legendary Scandinavian Grim which the town wanted to be thought an eponym (Pedrick 1904, 68–9).

Individuals' seals increasingly bore heraldic coats of arms, but even those who were not armigerous needed seals, such as merchants and even rural peasants (Schofield 2015). Those who could afford them might set a Roman gemstone into a ring or pendant, though whether they would have understood the original meaning of the device is questionable. Purpose-made seals at the lower social levels were usually small but still well cut, often just with a name, often impersonal and even carrying sexual innuendo, such as a squirrel with the legend 'I crack nuts' (Harvey and McGuiness 1996; this may not have had the same message when first introduced). Merchants used the geometrical devices that they used in their other business transactions, which probably could have been found cut into tally-sticks and the like. One or two are even to be seen on medieval jugs, not to guarantee the quality of the contents, but to show ownership (Robinson 2015; 'Thomas me fecit' on one that might refer to the patron who had commissioned the jug, not to the potter). On death, or loss of authority, a seal might be broken or scored across to make it unusable (Cherry 1992; Gilchrist and Sloane 2005, 176–7).

Some favoured officials had symbolic objects that originally had had a practical function, such as the hunting-horn needed by a royal servant who had charge of the king's forest where he had to ensure the protection of the deer. This was an office that became increasingly one of high status, implying as it did that the huntsman was special to the king. Consequently the horns became badges of office, elaborately decorated; a notable survival is made of elephant ivory, not horn from a mere ox, and is embellished with silver bands elaborately enamelled with images of deer and other forest creatures, as well as of a king, a bishop, a huntsman, and mythical animals. It was a 'horn of tenure' and the property of the Warden of Savernake Forest in Wiltshire, which came to be valued as a token of the Seymour family's right to the office since the twelfth century (Alexander and Binski 1987, no. 544; Bathe 2012). By coincidence, another surviving medieval horn is also from Wiltshire; it is an ox-horn with silver-gilt mounts, including two legs so that it can stand upright (Figure 27.3). An inscription records its ownership by William Pusey, whose family held their land for as long as they could produce the horn (Marks and Williamson 2003, no. 182). Less up-market but more than a simple ox-horn was one in gunmetal that belongs to the City of Winchester, cast probably in the late twelfth

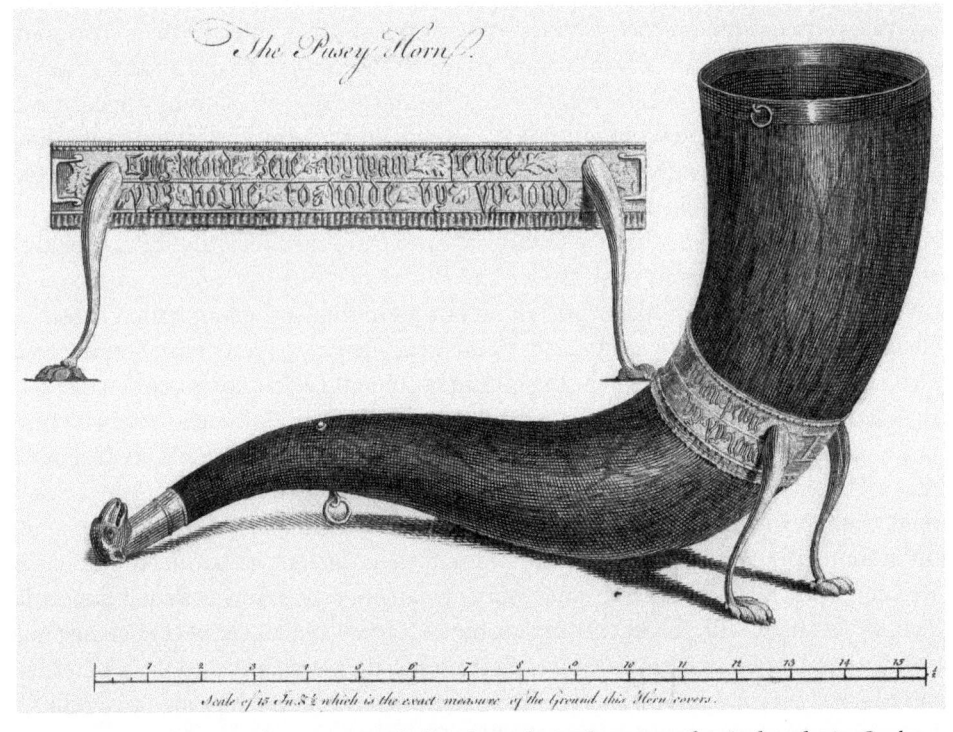

FIGURE 27.3 The Pusey horn as recorded in the eighteenth century for *Archaeologia*. Ox-horn with silver-gilt mounts, *c*.1400, inscribed 'I kynge knowde [Cnut] gave Wyllyam Pecote [Pusey] thys horne to holde by thy land' (from Pegge 1775, 13)

century and with figures in relief: a bishop because of the city's ecclesiastical connection, a king, and four lions to show where power lay (Crummy et al. 2008).

The Pusey horn is a reminder that customs still held in medieval England that were more powerful than written law. Nevertheless, statute and Parliament increasingly controlled lives and behaviour, and the role of lawyers increased accordingly. Theirs was the power of interpretation, their status symbolized then as now by peculiar dress codes and by inns of court (Steane 2001, 178–87).

Warfare and Commemoration

Medieval kings were expected to be fighters, to protect and to enlarge their kingdoms, the latter increasingly under dubious legal pretexts rather than by naked annexation. The reality of war was the disfigurement and slaughter that shows on some medieval bodies; the image was of the glorious knight on his splendid horse, or the finely dressed and equipped infantryman. There is therefore a very fine line between what was practicable and effective and what was worn for display; jousting equipment was adapted to restrict injury, but could still cause fatality.

The extent to which weapons were chosen for their ability to display their owners' right to fight rather than solely because of their ability to kill an enemy was a facet of social expectation; to suggest that a mounted knight should descend to fight on foot would have been to demean him, even though there were occasions when cavalry were ineffective, and later medieval tournaments included unmounted pole-axe combats. Anglo-Saxon swords had once been embellished with gold and silver, but that form of display had given way to an emphasis on better blades and balanced pommels; nevertheless, some swords became named, particularly those like 'Curtana' which featured in the coronation ritual and had Arthurian overtones. It was increasingly a knight's armour, and especially his helmet and crest, that marked him out, as did his horse with its saddle-cloth embroidered with his coat of arms. This may have featured more in the tournament than on the battlefield, the pretence rather than the actuality of power, but was potent nevertheless; the painting in the Luttrell Psalter of the knight having his helmet held up to him by his wife provides a model, even if the metal harness fitting with his coat of arms enamelled on it is grossly exaggerated in its size (Backhouse 1989, ill. 1).

Gunpowder and artillery show the ambivalence of the use of weaponry in the later Middle Ages (see Chapter 26). Flask-shaped weapons firing arrows were soon replaced by stave-bound wrought iron, cast-bronze and then cast-iron cannons during the fourteenth century. Such weapons were expensive to acquire and equip, and the noise of their discharge struck an enemy with awe. Cast into some were badges and inscriptions (e.g. Marks and Williamson 2003, no. 66). Firing them was a dangerous job, however, and the operation of the guns was therefore not carried out by the gentry, who continued to fight on horseback as was traditional, and indeed remained effective for centuries to come. It was not until well into the sixteenth century, however, that manuals began to appear instructing such fighters how to handle pistols.

Death in warfare, bravely facing a foe, was regarded as meritorious, particularly if the enemy was an infidel. Tombs with knights in armour did not indicate death in battle, however, but commemorated the right to bear arms and symbolized power over the community in which the tomb was sited (Figure 27.4): land-ownership in a parish church, family patronage in a monastery. As belief in Purgatory formalized during the later Middle Ages, so burial within the church building rather than in its extra-mural graveyard became increasingly important (Bertram 2007; Horrox 1999, 103–10), especially proximity to the high altar where the Almighty might expect to find the most salvation-worthy; an archbishop of Canterbury even sought to have the graves of three of the cathedral deans disinterred to create space in front of the 'great cross' for himself (Gilchrist and Sloane 2005, 194). Archbishop Chichele was able to create a whole 'memorial landscape' for himself at Higham Ferrers (Northamptonshire), his birth-place, endowing a school, a college, and an almshouse there, although he chose to have his 'cadaver' tomb within the monks' choir of Canterbury Cathedral (see Figure 41.3 in this *Handbook*), and had it inscribed long before his death as a reminder to himself and to everyone else then and thereafter that he 'was pauper-born' and would be 'cut down and served up for worms' (Marks and Williamson 2003, ill. 105; Morgan 1999, 136–9). Other senior ecclesiastics chose to have their power over their buildings symbolized by encroaching on the even more public space, the nave, like Bishop William Wykeham of Winchester. Few could afford such elaborate chantry tombs, let alone to emulate King Edward I who erected crosses where his queen's body had rested on its final journey to Westminster, each showing her elevated above their subjects below, and gazing out at the land over which her husband exercised his power (Alexander and Binski 1987, nos 368–76; Binski 1999, 76; see Chapter 53 in this *Handbook*).

Land-owners might express their authority over a manor by what they did to its church, adding a chapel for family tombs, as Sir Thomas Tropenell did at Great Chalfield

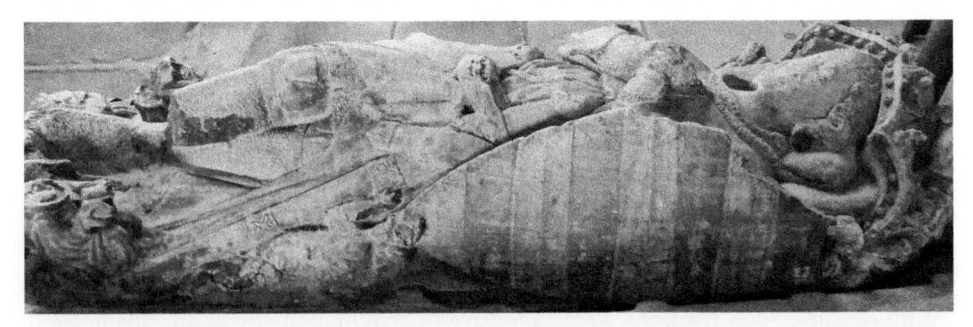

FIGURE 27.4 Effigy of Brian Fitzalan, Lord of Bedale, in St Gregory's church, Bedale, North Yorkshire, early fourteenth century. Fitzalan died in 1306 after campaigns in Wales and Scotland. Here he is dressed as a knight in chain mail, cross-legged, with a sword and pointed shield depicting his coat of arms. The effigy would originally have been richly painted

(© Alejandra Gutiérrez)

(Wiltshire), or making similar provision by rebuilding its chancel, as the Barentins did at Chalgrove (Oxfordshire) (Driver 2000, 86; Page et al. 2005, 19). Donation of a glass window, or of a vestment for use by the priest, or of a pall for use at funerals, was another way of ensuring visibility and memory for those not only rich enough to pay for the gift but also powerful enough to expect its perpetuity (Duffy 2003, 56–7). Even having a prescribed seat inside a church became a sign of power over the space within the building (Steane 2001, 141).

Symbols of Resistance to Power

Objects might be used to symbolize the resentment of peasants and artisans towards their social superiors. The most common artefacts to survive are clay pots, undoubtedly produced by artisans for a wide market, but to see status hostility in glazed jugs is difficult. Although not valuable enough to appear in more than a handful of inventories, one exception could be the pottery aquamaniles imitating the form of copper-alloy vessels; but the latter were finely made knights on horseback and heraldic beasts; the knights of clay look suspiciously tumble-down, and the animals are rams not lions (Alexander and Binski 1987, no. 548). Probably deliberate mockery, if not actual sedition, is the puzzle-jug found in Exeter: a late thirteenth-century import from the south-west of France, it looks at first glance like a harmless procession of musicians, watched from a building by women leaning out of windows; a closer look, however, reveals that inside is the figure of a bishop, with mitre and crozier, but apparently unrobed. As the citizens of Exeter were frequently in dispute, sometimes fatally, with the ecclesiastical authority that too closely controlled their town, it seems that the jug was a special commission to mock a bishop in a bawdy house (Hinton 2005, 216 and col. Pl. G).

The Luttrell Psalter has images of both a watermill and a windmill, symbols of a lord's control over his estate, its resources, and the income derived from them. The lord could force his servile tenants to have their grain ground into the bread that was the 'staff of life' (Camille 1998, 212–16). Evidence of resistance to this 'multure' imposition is slight, however, and free tenants usually chose to pay to have their corn ground, as it was so labour-saving (Holt 1988, 39–53). At St Albans, the abbot symbolized his control over his peasantry by breaking up their hand-mills and laying them in a pavement so that his tenants had to walk over them when they came to pay their rent. Although the abbot used their material culture against his peasantry in an interesting way, it was not typical behaviour, any more than was the peasants' action in taking up the fragments and passing them round as though they were Eucharistic bread, as well as symbols of servitude—they well understood such symbolism, as their stringing-up of a live rabbit on a pillory to show their feelings about the lord's right of free warren shows. More practically, they had broken into the Muniments to destroy the written records of their condition. In general, however, grudging acceptance and co-operation were the norm (Campbell 2006, 222–30); the riots in 1381 were against the general trend. How, then, to interpret the large numbers of fragments of hand-mills and querns found on peasant sites? They were purchased items, difficult to smuggle in from the market without the steward seeing. Acquiring and using them was not an act of defiance, although breaking them up would have been a reminder of manorial control (Hinton 2010, 106; Smith 2009, 408–9). Putting broken stones from a seigneurial building into house foundations can only be taken as illicit pillaging if there is evidence that provident recycling was not permitted—unfortunately court rolls for Wharram Percy (North Yorkshire), the site where the frequency of the broken stones was first observed, do not survive, so whether fines were paid is unknown.

Hand-mills were not cheap items, and their numbers show peasants' purchasing ability. Similarly, the large numbers of gold and silver finger-rings now being reported to the Portable Antiquities Scheme must represent purchases, and are too many all to have belonged to the landed and the mercantile. Peasants who owned and wore such things might be viewed as expressing their reluctance to be cowed; sumptuary legislation sought to ensure that what people owned and wore was appropriate to their station in life, but was very rarely enacted, and evidence of fines being paid for the wrong attire would be needed to prove that authorities noticed (Hinton 1999). This may smack of late medieval archaeology being subjected to 'the constraining paradigms of history' (McClain 2012, 143), but interpretations of objects as symbols of resistance can be too easily made, and reported cases of riots, trespass, and refusal of service do not mention them (e.g. Birrell 2010; Kilby 2015). Very few base-metal objects do not copy those in gold and silver. A buckle with a cast king's head on it is not a flattering image, but its very presence may have been a token of loyalty—or, given its context in a preceptory of one of the military orders, it may have alluded to the King of Heaven (Mayes 2002, fig. 7.9, no. 102). A few base-metal badges were neither religious nor livery, but seem mocking: monkeys pissing into bowls might have been imagery used to jeer at apothecaries and alchemists, mixing potions that they did not understand, but the presence of a fish means that they were probably mere sexual innuendo; none is evidently subversive (Spencer 1990, 115–16).

Another issue is the extent to which 'resistance' to the Church and its teaching might be expressed. Personal prayers and devotions could slide into 'magic', but accepted belief in the 'properties' of objects, particularly gemstones, meant that their use as amulets was not sacrilegious. Few things survive that can be certainly associated with 'magic', but bent coins are not infrequent, and do not show deliberate damaging of the royal image and thus resistance to authority, but that a vow had been taken, for instance to go on a pilgrimage (see Chapter 32). Subsequent fixing to a gatepost to act as protection of livestock transformed them into amulets, as did ascribing healing powers to them and wearing them in a bag round the neck; these were acceptable practices, as was using them to invoke divine aid in a law-suit, but not to seek revenge (Flint 2006, 346, 350; Gilchrist 2008). The Church's wealth and aspects of its priesthood were challenged by Lollardy, but only a few went as far as to challenge its doctrines.

Conclusion

Medieval people were so familiar with imagery that teasing out symbols that were specifically viewed as emblematic either of power or of resistance to it is problematic; besides, a maker may have had one intention, the owner another, and a viewer another. Only the literate would have understood the range of meanings of gemstones, and therefore of the power that they had to perform supernatural functions. The ability to read and to write, in whatever language was spoken at the time by the dominant authority, gave a degree of power to the literate, who could manipulate the record either in creating it or transmitting it orally. The power of the Church was symbolized in its images and cult objects, as also in its control of teaching and learning, producing the clerks who produced the documents. Symbolic of power also was control of the environment; not only of the landscape, but of the sensations experienced in living conditions that the wealthy could control through access to perfumes, soap, wax candles, and music (Woolgar 2006; see Chapter 42 in this *Handbook*); all these were more than merely symptomatic of the ability to spend money for the sake of acquisition.

References cited

Alexander, J. and Binski, P. (eds) 1987 *Age of Chivalry: art in Plantagenet England 1200–1400*, Royal Academy of Arts/Weidenfeld and Nicolson, London

Backhouse, J. 1989 *The Luttrell Psalter*, The British Library, London

Bathe, G. 2012 'The Savernake horn', *Wiltshire Archaeological and Natural History Society Magazine* 105, 168–81

Bertram, J. 2007 'From Duccius to Daubernoun: ancient antecedents of monumental brass design', in L. Gilmour (ed.), *Pagans and Christians: from Antiquity to the Middle Ages. Papers in honour of Martin Henig, presented on the occasion of his 65th birthday*, British Archaeological Reports International Series 1610, Oxford, 219–28

Biddle, M. 2000 *King Arthur's Round Table*, Boydell, Woodbridge

Binski, P. 1999 'Hierarchies and orders in English royal images of power', in J. Denton (ed.), *Orders and hierarchies in late medieval and Renaissance Europe*, Macmillan, Basingstoke, 74–93

Birrell, J. 2010 'Confrontation and negotiation in a medieval village: Alrewas before the Black Death', in R. Goddard, J. Langdon, and M. Müller (eds), *Survival and discord in medieval society: essays in honour of Christopher Dyer*, Brepols, Turnhout, 197–212

Bury, S. 1998 'The Regalia catalogue', in C. Blair (general ed.), *The Crown Jewels: the history of the Coronation Regalia in the Jewel House of the Tower of London*, vol. 2, The Stationery Office, London, 1–274

Camille, M. 1998 *Mirror in parchment: the Luttrell Psalter and the making of medieval England*, Reaktion Books, London

Campbell, B. M. S. 2006 'The land', in R. Horrox and W. M. Ormrod (eds), *A social history of England 1200–1500*, Cambridge University Press, Cambridge, 179–237

Cherry, J. 1969 'The Dunstable swan jewel', *Journal of the British Archaeological Association* 32, 38–53

Cherry, J. 1992 'The breaking of seals', *Art and symbolism: preprinted papers volume 7*, Medieval Europe 1992, York

Cherry, J. 2015 'Seals of cities and towns; concepts of choice?', in S. Solway (ed.), *Medieval coins and seals: constructing identity, signifying power*, Brepols, Turnhout, 283–95

Crummy, N., Cherry, J., and Northover, P. 2008 'The Winchester Moot horn', *Medieval Archaeology* 52, 211–30

Driver, J. T. 2000 'A "perillous, covetous man": the career of Thomas Tropenell Esq. (*c*.1405–88), a Wiltshire lawyer, Parliamentary burgess and builder of Great Chalfield', *Wiltshire Archaeological and Natural History Society Magazine* 93, 83–9

Duffy, E. 2003 'Late medieval religion', in R. Marks and P. Williamson (eds), *Gothic art for England 1400–1547*, Victoria and Albert Museum Publications, London, 56–67

Flint, V. I. J. 2006 'A magic universe?', in R. Horrox and W. M. Ormrod (eds), *A social history of England 1200–1500*, Cambridge University Press, Cambridge, 340–55

Gilchrist, R. 2008 'Magic for the dead? The archaeology of magic in later medieval burials', *Medieval Archaeology* 52, 119–60

Gilchrist, R. and Sloane, B. 2005 *Requiem: the medieval monastic cemetery in Britain*, Museum of London Archaeology Service, London

Hare, M. 1999 'Kings, crowns and festivals: the origins of Gloucester as a royal ceremonial centre', *Transactions of the Bristol and Gloucestershire Archaeological Society* 115, 41–78

Harvey, P. D. A. and McGuiness, A. 1996 *A guide to British medieval seals*, The British Library and Public Record Office, London

Hepburn, F. 2008 'The 1505 portrait of Henry VII', *The Antiquaries Journal* 88, 222–57

Hinton, D. A. 1999 '"Closing" and the later Middle Ages', *Medieval Archaeology* 43, 172–82

Hinton, D. A. 2005 *Gold and gilt, pots and pins: possessions and people in medieval Britain*, Oxford University Press, Oxford

Hinton, D. A. 2010 'Deserted medieval villages and the objects from them', in C. Dyer and R. Jones (eds), *Deserted villages revisited*, University of Hertfordshire Press, Hatfield, 85–108

Holt, R. 1988 *The mills of medieval England*, Oxford University Press, Oxford

Horrox, R. 1999 'Purgatory, prayer and plague: 1150–1380', in P. C. Jupp and C. Gittings (eds), *Death in England: an illustrated history*, Manchester University Press, Manchester, 90–118

Kilby, S. 2015 'Mapping peasant discontent: trespassing on manorial land in fourteenth-century Walsham-le-Willows', *Landscape History* 36, 69–88

Lightbown, R. 1998 'The English Coronation before the Commonwealth', in C. Blair (general ed.), *The Crown Jewels: the history of the Coronation Regalia in the Jewel House of the Tower of London, vol. 1*, The Stationery Office, London, 53–256

Marks, R. and Williamson, P. 2003 *Gothic art for England 1400–1547*, Victoria and Albert Museum Publications, London

Mayes, P. 2002 *Excavations at a Templar preceptory: South Witham, Lincolnshire, 1965–67*, The Society for Medieval Archaeology Monograph 19, Leeds

McClain, A. 2012 'Theory, disciplinary perspectives and the archaeology of later medieval England', *Medieval Archaeology* 56, 131–70

Morgan, P. 1999 'Of worms and war: 1380–1555', in P. C. Jupp and C. Gittings (eds), *Death in England: an illustrated history*, Manchester University Press, Manchester, 119–46

Nelson, J. 2012 'Coronation rituals and related materials', in J. T. Rosenthal (ed.), *Understanding medieval primary sources: using historical sources to discover medieval Europe*, Routledge, London/New York, 114–30

Nieke, M. R. and Duncan, H. B. 1988 'Dalriada: the establishment and maintenance of an Early Historic kingdom in northern Britain', in S. T. Driscoll and M. R. Nieke (eds), *Power and politics in early medieval Britain and Ireland*, Edinburgh University Press, Edinburgh, 6–21

Page, P., Atherton, K., and Hardy, A. 2005 *Barentin's manor: excavations of the moated manor at Harding's Field, Chalgrove, Oxfordshire, 1976–9*, Oxford University School of Archaeology, Oxford

Pedrick, G. 1904 *Borough seals of the Gothic period*, J. M. Dent, London

Pegge, S. 1775 'Of the Pusey horn', *Archaeologia or Miscellaneous tracts relating to Antiquity* 3, 13–14

Robinson, J. 2015 'Medieval seals: images and truth', in S. Solway (ed.), *Medieval coins and seals: constructing identity, signifying power*, Brepols, Turnhout, 361–76

Schofield, P. R. 2015 'Seals and the peasant economy in England and Marcher Wales', in S. Solway (ed.), *Medieval coins and seals: constructing identity, signifying power*, Brepols, Turnhout, 347–58

Siddons, M. P. 2009 *Heraldic badges in England and Wales*, The Boydell Press, Woodbridge

Spencer, B. 1990 *Salisbury and South Wiltshire Museum medieval catalogue, part 2. Pilgrim souvenirs and secular badges*, Salisbury and South Wiltshire Museum, Salisbury

Smith, S. 2009 'Towards a social archaeology of the late medieval English peasantry', *Journal of Social Archaeology* 9, 391–416

Steane, J. M. 2001 *The archaeology of power: England and northern Europe AD 800–1600*, Tempus, Stroud

Stratford, J. 2010 *Richard II and the English royal treasure*, Boydell, Woodbridge

Tyler, E. 1999 ' "The eyes of the beholder were dazzled": treasure and artifice in *Encomium Emmae Reginae*', *Early Medieval Europe* 8, 247–70

Woolgar, C. M. 2006 *The senses in late medieval England*, Yale University Press, New Haven

PART VI

CRAFTS, INDUSTRY, AND OBJECTS

CHAPTER 28

OVERVIEW

Medieval Industry and Commerce

MAUREEN MELLOR

This section of the *Handbook* explores different aspects of later medieval industry and includes articles on quarrying and materials extraction, the medieval wind and water power, domestic objects, coins, and pastimes. These papers complement and update the essential 1991 *English medieval industries* volume (Blair and Ramsay 1991) which drew together so much important evidence for this topic and was in turn inspired by L. F. Salzman's *English industries of the Middle Ages*, first published more than a hundred years ago (Salzman 1913). In between these two, David Crossley's edited *Medieval industry* contained important reflections on the large quantities of data freshly emerging from post-excavation projects on rescue archaeology sites. With the exception of Crossley's volume, the English evidence (particularly southern English) seems to have taken the lead but this bias is now being corrected and is reflected in a better balance of evidence considered in the chapters here. Further synthetic writing is also available on, for example, extractive and manufacturing industry on monastic estates (Bond 2004), but most articles tend to pick out excavated case studies highlighting particular industries and their products such as pottery kilns (e.g. Cumberpatch and Roberts 2013 for a Stamford ware pottery kiln in Pontefract) or brass-engraving (Badham 1990) or else provide detailed analyses of artefact assemblages either individually (e.g. Anderson 2013 for floor and roof tiles from Melrose Abbey) or as one of a series of specialist reports wrapped into a single monograph or excavation report. As elsewhere in medieval archaeology, 'grey literature' produced by developer-led projects carries the bulk of the analyses now being undertaken.

Evidence for medieval industry can be expected almost anywhere. In the towns, villages, hamlets, and forests of medieval Britain, people could learn a skilled craft (Birrel 1969), and peasant craftsmen combined theirs with agriculture. Archaeology has the potential to investigate their trades and the consumption of different products from the waste found in middens, pits, and ditches (Ford and Teague 2011; Ivens et al. 1995; Mynard and Zeepvat 1992). Some of these industrial products are humble. Charcoal, for example, was a rural commodity which was vital for domestic life, a seasonal product of the forest which was used in cooking, for warmth, and widely in industrial processes such as iron smelting and blacksmithing (Bond 2007; Tringham 2013; and see Chapter 29 in this *Handbook*). The demand for charcoal must have necessitated very considerable production in any one year: it was available in the market place in Oxford by at least AD 1370 (Crossley 1979, 306). Other products and industrial processes may be harder to detect in the historical and archaeological record. Candles made from beeswax or tallow rendered from beef or mutton fat were required in very considerable numbers, for example. More visible to the archaeologist are the diverse hand-made crafts, the leather shoes, leather belts and scabbards, textiles, and earthenware pots that were for sale in the market place where exchanges were often negotiated (McClain 2012). A variety of containers were available here in different materials to convey the products to market or fairs. Medicines and spices, for example, were transported inland to the Coventry area for example, where excavations have provided useful chronological sequences for ceramics and other material culture for the late medieval and early post-medieval periods (Colls and Mitchell 2013; Rátkai 2005). In this introductory chapter, rather than consider medieval industries in turn, we explore some emerging themes. These are: the landscape archaeology of medieval industry and commerce; the archaeology of medieval production; the archaeology of craftworkers and artisans; and the archaeology of consumption. Finally, some new directions for research are identified.

The Landscape Archaeology of Medieval Industry and Commerce

Several pan-European conferences and publications have stressed the need to place industrial sites into a wider historical and cultural context but retaining a strong appreciation of regionality (Arnoux and Flambard Héricher 2010; Astill and Davies 1997; de Groote 2008; Gaimster 2014; Klápště and Sommer 2009). Surveys of geological potential which focus on mineral resources to identify sites and regions with specialized production (Figure 28.1) are therefore valuable (Rippon et al. 2009). Environmental sampling in Northumberland, for example, has identified coal and tarred material from surface or near-surface exposures (Gaimster and O'Conor 2005, 397; for coal, see Chapter 29 in this *Handbook*). The exploitation and extraction of raw materials could be on a near-industrial scale, as is illustrated by the application of lime as a fertilizing agent from the thirteenth century onwards. Limestone was sometimes transported over considerable distances before firing in a kiln, coal-fired where available (Johnson 2010). The archaeological aim should be to understand the practices of extraction and processing as experienced by the medieval quarryman, miner, or agriculturalist and the associated infrastructure required to support and transport goods, heavy equipment, and weighty loads. Communities routinely modified their environment to improve and

FIGURE 28.1 The leat tunnel in Shillamill Wood, near Tavistock, Devon, part of an extensive system constructed in the 1470s to supply water to a wheel powering 'suction lift' pumps used to drain a silver mine at Bere Ferrers

(© Peter Claughton)

enhance their lifestyles, but medieval landlords were quick to recognize the potential of the earth's raw materials and controlled their extraction through taxes. Their tenants, even those whose skills were regarded as at the low end of the craft hierarchy such as peasant potters, did not escape payment.

Recent research into the industrial landscapes of monasteries shows how communities with well-organized manors supported themselves through agricultural and industrial granges, sometimes located at a great distance from the mother house (Bond 2004, 327–53; Robinson 2006). Industrial activities included mining, smelting, and forging at Tintern Abbey, Wales, and at Bordesley Abbey in the West Midlands (Allen 1996; Astill 1993; for mills see Chapter 31 in this *Handbook*), stone quarries for rough walling and ashlar at Rievaulx (North Yorkshire), rights to obtain millstones at Furness Abbey (Lancashire), brick kilns at Coggeshall (Essex), tile kilns at Norton Priory (Cheshire), coal mines, and glass-making. Scottish monasteries too were involved in mining for coal, gold, lead, and silver as well as working iron, quarrying stone, and digging clay for the ceramic industries which made pottery and paving tiles. Monastic institutions were also engaged with the production of salt, which was vital at this period for the preservation of foodstuffs, and they owned numerous salt pans on the coast (Hall 2006). As the recently published detail of the provisioning of Norwich Cathedral Priory and its associated agricultural regime 1260–1536 suggests, the role of the monastic orders in medieval industry still offers much potential (Slavin 2012).

The Benedictine abbey at Ramsey, Cambridgeshire, offers an interesting case study. In the eleventh century the abbey bought a stone quarry at Barnack from nearby Peterborough Abbey and used it to rebuild the monastery, refashioning its church during the twelfth century. The abbey continued to import building stone during the late thirteenth and fourteenth centuries for expensive building programmes and there is evidence for a later medieval artificial waterway (or 'lode'), a wharf with facilities for the loading/unloading and storage of goods, and a medieval 'wippe' crane. This 'see-saw' or hoisting crane, dating to the thirteenth to the fifteenth century, is unique in Britain, though a larger crane of the same type is on display in the museum in Bergen, Norway. Historical documents help to reconstruct a marshy landscape of ditches, gullies, waterways, and causeways; sluice gates were required to hold back the water with disputes arising between various landowners. Lock technology was known in the Netherlands in the late twelfth century and a flash lock system is also implied at Ramsey (Spoerry et al. 2008, 201). The monastic records also make mention of a corn mill and a malt mill in the fourteenth century, as well as the repair of many buildings including three storehouses and various barns. Clearly, the abbey was sending produce down the river Nene to King's Lynn, where a significant corn and wool market was held. Grain transport *to* Ramsey is also well documented; other Fenland manors transported grain to the monks and there is evidence for river trade in fodder, lumber, and wine.

An Archaeology of Medieval Production

The study of crafts and industry is not merely about finished objects, industry also has a wider impact on townscapes (Grenville 2004) like medieval Birmingham (Forster and Rátkai 2009; Patrick and Rátkai 2008), as well as on rural estates and their surrounding landscapes (Gardiner 2011). Workshops, including one belonging to a thirteenth- to sixteenth-century apothecary, have been published or excavated in different parts of mainland Europe (France: Alexander-Bidon 2013; Ravoire 2011, 11–24; Rhineland, Germany: Gaimster 1997, 122–7; and Hungary: Klápště and Sommer 2007). From the first half of the eleventh century at Viborg Søndersø in Denmark, a waterlogged workshop preserves evidence of a smithy with hearth, bellows, and anvil all still *in situ*. The metalworker had used crucibles to melt silver, copper alloys, and iron. Waste from antler comb-working was also found nearby (Iversen et al. 2005; Linaa 2015) and this raises the question as to whether this was a seasonal workshop, one craft-worker who had learnt a variety of skills or some sort of shared space. Excavations at Trondheim Palace, Norway, also discovered a workshop complex, but ethnographers remind us that a skilled artisan attached to an aristocratic environment (whether castle, monastic house, or palace) need not be subject to the same conditions or organizational structures as one producing tools for the general population (Ashby 2015). Site formation processes must be understood if the scale, intensity of production, craft competency, and organization are to be fully assessed (Costin 1991, 19).

Whatever the case, it is important to grasp the chain of processes involved from raw material to finished product as well as the disposal of debris and waste (e.g. leather offcuts or pottery wasters). In particular, the question of storage is often excluded from this 'artefact biography', whether that be domestic spaces (Clarke et al. 2010, 193–4) or guildhalls, a new form of public building which developed in the late fourteenth century and which on occasions may have been used for storage (Giles 2000; Giles and Clark 2011; Moran 2011; see Chapter 30 in this *Handbook*). Keys are common in the archaeological record suggesting that portable goods were locked up (Goodall 2011, 231–95) and, as the Ramsey Abbey case study above indicates, barns, granaries, and storehouses were necessary to house and protect the many different foodstuffs and goods imported and exported to and from the site. Storage facilities might be expected for bake-houses, bale-houses, brew houses, cold larders (e.g. St Mary of Merton Priory, Surrey), grain dryers, kiln houses, malt houses, ovens, silos, wool houses (Fountains Abbey, North Yorkshire). These were the staple buildings of manors and monastic houses (e.g. Coppack 2009; Horsey 1992; Slavin 2012) and functioned on a near-industrial scale to serve their inhabitants, local communities, visiting clerics, and pilgrims.

Overall, there is now a significant volume of archaeological evidence for medieval industrial production (see Chapter 29) and there are several excellent corpora of artefacts (e.g. Egan 1998; Goodall 2011). For the stone industries even a preliminary list (McClain 2010) would have to include quarrying as well as slab monuments and domestic items, such as soapstone (Figure 28.2). Poole acted as the main distribution centre for stone from the Isle of Purbeck, including mortars for domestic use (Dunning 1965–6, 205–7; Horsey 1992), but workshops sometimes developed at a distance so that 'marble' from Dorset was also transported to London, mainly to Westminster (Badham 2010). Alabaster was fashioned for altar pieces and exported widely (see Chapters 29 and 59); jet was used to make jewellery, and an industry in jet items flourished in Coventry in central England and at the east coast town of Whitby (Forster 2013, 63–6). Stone moulds for casting lead or tin accessories have also been found in Coventry (Colls and Mitchell 2013, 348). Metal-working meanwhile is evident in many towns (e.g. Birmingham, Coventry, Doncaster, Hartlepool, Lincoln, and York), but mainly on smaller tenements as well as in rural settings associated with monastic houses (e.g. Newington, Oxfordshire; Williams 2012) and Shapwick, Somerset (Gerrard with Aston 2007). Bell foundries are also known, for example at York and Exeter, with their moulds, casting pits, and debris (Richards 1993). Exeter's foundry included a reverberatory furnace, bronze cauldrons, and skillets for domestic use (Blaylock 2000). Iron-smelting furnaces are rare finds (Spoerry et al. 2008) with important centres in the Weald. This same area also saw the re-emergence of the glass industry, but towns such as Coventry may have been a centre for the painted glass which was recovered from the debris of the Carmelite friary

FIGURE 28.2 Quarry for steatite, or soapstone, at Catpund near Cunningsburgh in Shetland, Scotland. Vessels were carved out of the rock and are known from twelfth- and thirteenth-century archaeological contexts on Shetland and as far as Iceland

(© Alejandra Gutiérrez)

(Willmott 2005). The greatest progress in understanding medieval industry has perhaps been made for the ceramic industries. Many new production sites and centres have been located since the synthesis published in 1994 (Irving 2011; Marter 2005; Mellor 1994), though none with workshops identified. A possible potting village with a community of potters and fourteen production-site centres has been identified on Sible Hedingham, north Essex (Walker 2012). In Dublin a crocker's (potter's) district was apparently established just outside the city walls within a generation of the Norman invasion in AD 1169. Potters from Nottingham and London are recorded in the Dublin guild merchants' roll in the thirteenth century (McCutcheon 2006). The adoption of scientific techniques to interrogate the raw material—clay—has led to a far clearer picture of ceramic traditions, their distributions, and the range of marketing networks (Lewis 1999; Peacock 1977; Vince 2005). The exploitation of this natural resource for bricks was on a near-industrial scale, and some potteries and tileries were voracious consumers of clay with ready markets among the monasteries and merchant classes. Ramsey Abbey, Cambridgeshire, was making and selling high-relief decorated tiles from at least the middle of the fourteenth century and brick from the early fifteenth century. Their intricate designs link the tiles to St Albans Abbey and to mainland Europe. Fabric analysis has shown that there are links between the production of pottery, flat roof tiles, ridge tiles, bricks, and floor tiles, but that artisans mainly concentrated on a single category of material (Freestone 1993; see Chapter 30 in this *Handbook*). Industrial ceramics including mould and crucible fragments are common finds on later medieval sites; specialist vessels were used for melting lead glass for trinkets and settings for jewellery (Vince 2005).

The best wool in medieval England was reputed to be from the Cotswolds, but archaeologically it has proved difficult to identify the wool and cloth trade (Patrick and Rátkai 2008; see Chapter 30 in this *Handbook*). The evidence from lead cloth seals (Egan 1994) and spindle-whorls in bone, stone, and lead is more robust (Standley 2016); iron teeth from heckle combs for preparing wool and flax fibres for spinning, tenter hooks, needles, and blades from small shears can all be found in the archaeological record. Other cloth-working tools include bone needles or bodkins, pin beaters, thread twisters, and numerous points (e.g. Biddle 1990). More unusual evidence for the textile industry comes from the inland port of Doncaster and medieval waterfronts along the eastern seaboard at Newcastle upon Tyne, Hartlepool, Hull, Grimsby, and York. Together with wads of cattle hair, waste from the textile industry, some dyed blue, was rolled up to line the horizontal overlap between the lengthways strakes in clinker-built ships. At Doncaster felt offcuts were used to line the scarf-joints, while in Newcastle they were associated with tarred fibre rolls at the quayside (Allen et al. 2005). This tarred fibre has parallels in Bergen, Norway, and may also occur in London.

Finally, the mass of leather offcuts found shows that many towns had a medieval tanning industry (Mould et al. 2003; Thomson and Mould 2011). In some cities preservation is exceptional, as at Perth High Street, the first major urban excavation in Scotland. Here a depth of two metres of dense occupation in a flood-prone area near to the River Tay was revealed and contained twenty-seven timber buildings along with wattle pathways and fences. A large corpus of textiles and a collection of leather were recovered (Dransaart et al. 2012; Perry et al. 2011; Thomas 2012).

The Archaeology of Craftworkers and Artisans

Tracing the identities of individual craftworkers is a challenge and craftsmen in Britain have been overlooked by comparison with studies in Baltic countries and Scandinavia (Hansen et al. 2015). The Portable Antiquities Scheme is collecting new data on seal matrices that may allow us to grow closer to people and families in the future; craftsmen occasionally signed their work on seals in the first decade of the thirteenth century; LUCAS FECIT (Figure 28.3) may possibly be Exeter-based (Elizabeth New pers. comm.). In one Oxford tenement that had (previously?) housed a manuscript illuminator, in AD 1453 Thomas Brikar 'harpemaker' left carpentry tools, unfinished tuning pegs of more than one type of instrument, and the wire for stringing the instruments. But the same name also appears for a different address and a less-elevated craft, forging the king's money (Durham 1977, fig. 43, 196)! What we can say is that crafts were embraced by all levels of society from peasants to townspeople and aristocrats (silk embroidery), from high-grade specialists to small-scale itinerant workers rooted in the local community (White 2012, 19). They included women, widows, and daughters who worked alongside their husbands

FIGURE 28.3 Silver matrix seal of the city of Exeter (obv. on the left) with the craftman's signature LUCAS ME FECIT on the reverse (right), c.1200–1208 (6.5 cm diameter)

(© Marian Campbell, Devon Record Office)

without pay and sometimes took over the running of their affairs when they were absent (McIntosh 2005; Mellor 2013, 135–43; 2014, 75–94). For example, Agnes, a marbler, took over her father's business while Alice de Keles, a seal maker, took over her husband's workshop (McEwan 2015, fig. 5.1, 79; New 2015). In other cases we know that women brewed at home: in Aberdeen it was a well-regulated craft where the town authorities bought in malt from the hinterland. Ale tasters were appointed and the quality of the ale was checked on Sundays, then a price was proposed and the house became a space for public drinking (Gemmill 2001; Mayhew 1996). When the brewing industry moved from a part-time household occupation to large-scale production, with the introduction of hops, women largely withdrew from the new industry (Clarke et al. 2010, 236–7). Women in towns were particularly associated with trades with small capital outlay. At home, they washed wool, carded it, and spun on a small scale. They were petty traders in towns (hucksters or regrators), and often found themselves in court for 'forestalling', as recounted in *Piers Plowman* (Langland 2009). Other occupations included making candles, lace-making, and embroidery and it is clear that there were more opportunities for women in London. Some apprenticeships here were available to women, such as for embroiderers, and when labour was short they were employed to fill the vacancies in the building trades (Langdon 2011).

The demographic profile in workshops probably showed a range of different ages. In Denmark children as young as six contributed to professional crafts (lace-making, knitting); children were apprenticed and gradually learnt all aspects of the trade, including how to travel and possible trade routes (Hansen 2015, 29; and see Chapter 48 in this *Handbook*). An apprentice, journeyman and master system was a component of the education of northern German potters (Gaimster 1997, 122–7). There is some indication of 'craft families' too. Pictorial evidence suggests that Bohemian glass-making was a family enterprise with the young and the old involved at various stages of production (cover illustration of Blair and Ramsay 1991: medieval glass-making from a manuscript of 'Sir John Mandeville's Travels', probably Bohemian, c.1420, British Library MS Add. 24189). Flemish brickmakers are also depicted as embracing a variety of ages, but not necessarily families (Mellor 2014, 79, fig. 5.3, illustrating a medieval tile workshop; Binding 2004, No. 9, 19). It is also true that craftsmen collaborated to handle particularly large commissions: a thousand pots ordered for the court at Westminster from the Kingston potteries must have been supplied by a number of potters. The same may be true of potters centred on Laverstock, who dispatched a thousand vessels for a Christmas feast in 1268 at a price of 20s with a charge of 5s 10d for their carriage (see Chapter 30). The late medieval period saw individuals employed to find new raw materials for new technologies, combining their first-hand knowledge of a craft with the ability to manage scale. William de Vesey 'brikemaker', a northern European, was not only skilled in the making of bricks, but was also employed by the king to find large deposits of suitable clay to build Windsor Castle in 1430, where two million bricks were fired. He received another commission in 1441 in connection with Eton College and his considerable ability led to his becoming controller in England of ale and beer-making, presumably the new hopped 'beer', introduced from the Low Countries with immigrants in the fifteenth century (*CPR* 1429–36, 537–9, 541–88). Some paving tilers and paviours may have become entrepreneurs, but few names come down to us. Elias of Dereham, a master stone mason, and Henry Yevele, in the service of the court, are both documented. The former oversaw the building of Salisbury Cathedral and the magnificent tiled pavement, the latter the nave of Westminster Abbey.

The Archaeology of Consumption: Local, Regional, Interregional Trade, and International Commerce

Medieval commerce can be considered at three levels: local, regional, and international. Research into towns and their economic hinterlands has long been considered important, particularly the distinction between local and regional trade systems (Carver 1993, 100), and there have been some recent valuable contributions on this theme, both in the form of synthesis (Giles and Dyer 2005) and the analysis of local exchange networks (Daniels 2010; Rátkai 1990). Many products would have been distributed locally using packhorses or carts which required the maintenance of the roads and bridges that underpin communication (Chapter 22): the long distance droving of cattle, sheep, and horses on the hoof from Welsh to English markets is already evident by the end of the thirteenth century (Dodds and Liddy 2011, 113). Bulkier goods were more easily moved by water and demanded facilities and lifting gear which required the modification of water channels and landing places as well as transhipment sites where, for example, commodities such as quarried stone could be loaded onto river craft (Alexander 1995).

Potsherds, in particular, are a priceless indicator for the archaeologist of how other commodities might be travelling and sometimes reveal unexpected connections (Figure 28.4). London-type ware made at Woolwich, for example, travelled in small quantities to Scotland (imports are rarely found on Scottish rural sites), across the North Sea to Norway, and into the Baltic at Schleswig, and so to Sweden (Blackmore and Pearce 2010, figs 3, 8). Many different kinds of objects were collected at ports as ships moved along the coastline. Goods were bought and sold for a little profit by the ship's crew (for example, small items made of jet, such as finger rings), as well as being brought aboard in a more official capacity to fill spaces left in the cargo and thereby maintain the correct ballast for the boat. Many pots are in this latter category perhaps, and small, heavy objects such as stone mortars for food processing such as those fashioned from Dundry and Purbeck stone (UK) and found on excavations in Cork and Waterford in Ireland would also have fulfilled this role. All these, however, were incidental to the principal cargoes which have generally not survived in the archaeological record (such as wool, iron, salt, and wine) but which were transported in bulk by water (Hutchinson 1994). In Ireland, for example, the principal pottery in use in the twelfth to fourteenth centuries was manufactured either in Bristol, Bordeaux, or locally (Murphy and Potterton 2010, 456); Ham Green pottery from near Bristol is a routine find in Dublin (McCutcheon 2006). Floor tiles were exported from England into SW Ireland in the thirteenth century,

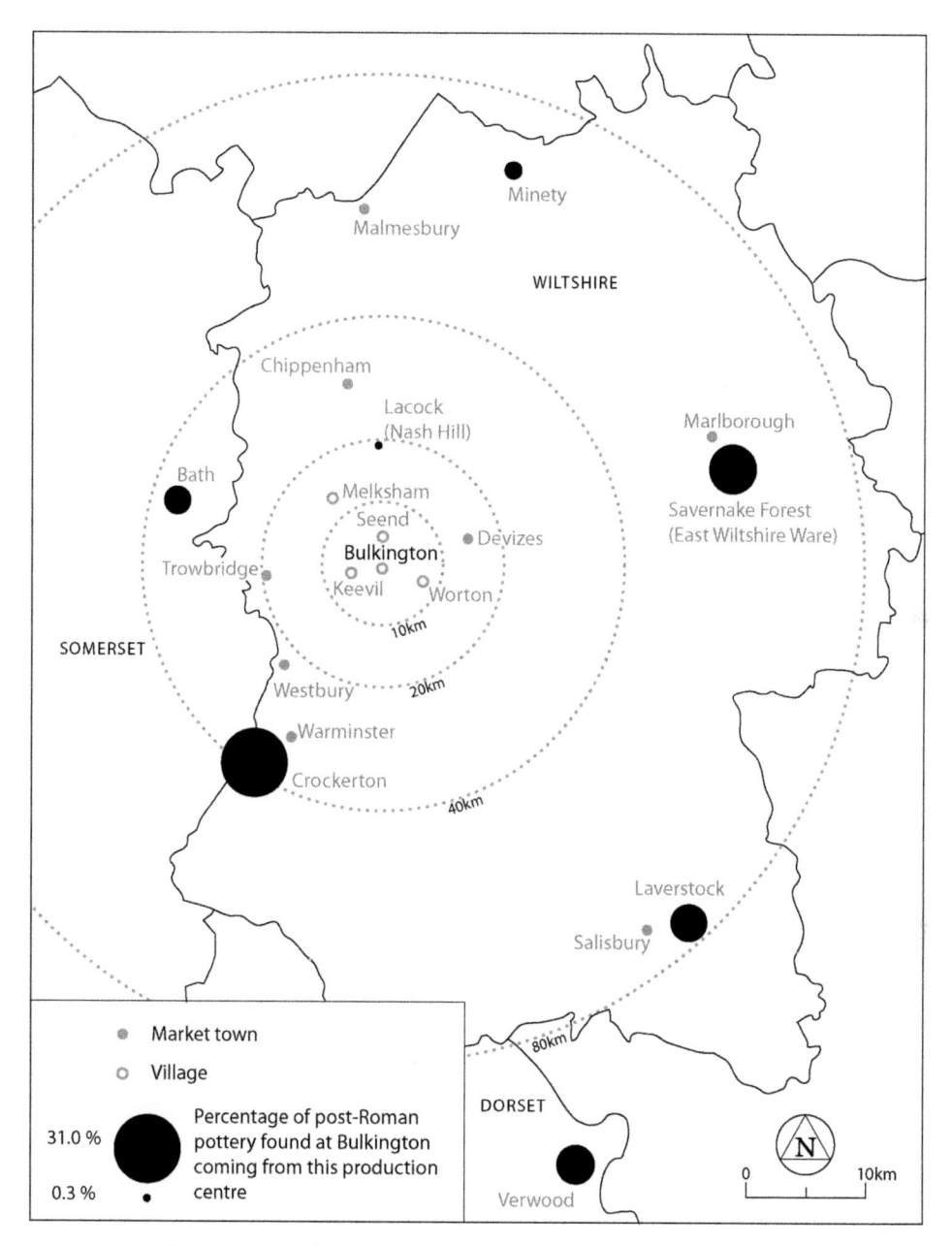

FIGURE 28.4 Bulkington, Wiltshire, tiny hamlet drawing on pottery from a variety of production centres in the medieval period (based on Durham 1997, fig. 6)

(© Alejandra Gutiérrez)

window glass from northern France found its way to Cashel Cathedral (Ireland), possibly transhipped from West Country ports, and ironwork repairs at Holy Trinity, Dublin, were made with Spanish iron in the fourteenth century (Childs and O'Neill 1993). Among the most interesting of these seafaring commodities, Caen stone can be seen at Mellifont Abbey (Louth, Ireland) (Waterman 1970) and is associated with the Anglo-Norman invasion and the subsequent construction of cathedrals and castles in the twelfth and thirteenth centuries as a symbol of Norman supremacy. The import of Caen stone to Ireland was much reduced after the mid-fifteenth century, but it is not well understood why this was the case (Hourihane 2000). Along the eastern seaboard, archaeological interventions have also repeatedly confirmed the extent to which small ports and inland ports participated in the movement of goods. Grain and pottery travelled to Trondheim and Bergen in Norway (Leah 1994; Reed 1990); stone ballast used to steady under-laden ships was incorporated into the town wall at the port of King's Lynn and includes pebbles originating in Estonia (Hoare et al. 2002).

London, the Cinque Ports, Southampton, and Poole have all benefited from recent archaeological research and publication (Brown and Hardy 2011; Clarke et al. 2010; Cotter 2006; Draper and Martin 2009; Horsey 1992; Mackinder with Egan 2009). It is clear that political stability was all important for buoyant trading conditions between Britain and north-west Europe and the Mediterranean, so that dynamic commercial activity coincided with periods of general economic expansion: treaties between the English and Portuguese in the late fourteenth century, for example, boosted commercial trade and brought Portuguese wines to English tables. By contrast, earlier in the same century the Gascony wine trade had suffered following political disruptions. War with the English in 1337 made carriage more dangerous and doubled prices, leading to a halving of the five million gallons of wine a year previously imported into English ports such as London, Bristol, and Southampton (Bolton 1985, 290). Medieval merchants reacted by seeking preferential trading privileges elsewhere and by moving their goods through 'neutral' nationalities, such as the Genoese, or using 'neutral' ports. The Spanish merchant visiting an English port such as Sandwich or Plymouth expected to sell his goods wholesale through a network of brokers and agents who often specialized in one commodity, so the distribution of products was left to the local retail trade. But in cases where trading was routine, as was the case in Southampton, foreign merchants lived in semi-permanent communities and maintained a high degree of independence (Childs 1978, 182). These arrangements varied depending upon the frequency of trade and the quantities involved, and, in spite of endemic warfare, there was usually sufficient stability for trade to continue in some form (see Chapter 55). The introduction of credit in the thirteenth century must have greatly facilitated exchange of goods and trade amongst many sectors of society (Courtney 1997).

Conclusion and Future Directions

Various themes emerge from the papers which follow this overview. They include:

- the need for greater standardization in terminology and definitions so that comparisons can be made more easily between crafts and industries (Costin 1991; Hansen et al. 2015);

- deeper collaboration and joint projects with numismatists who are now adding to their databases with the help of the Portable Antiquities Scheme and whose work is central to an understanding of the medieval economy;
- the need for regional surveys of raw materials, including agricultural production, food processing, and storage facilities, these would in turn feed into a national overview; such synthetic studies would fall to universities to implement, but the reality may be harder to achieve as academics do not always have first-hand experience of working in complex urban excavation environments, while fieldworkers responding to planning requirements are seldom able to address wider networks of trade and consumption;
- studies of specific materials to establish local and regional characteristics; only very few towns and their hinterlands already have such datasets (Symonds 2003) but this may be achievable within the current framework of developer-funded interventions and PPG16;
- correcting some chronological gaps, in particular trade patterns of the late eleventh to twelfth century are less well understood;
- understanding the infrastructure: warehouses, for example, deserve greater archaeological attention; a rare reference to a warehouse built by mercer Robert Toppe (Figure 28.5), sheriff of Norwich in 1430, indicates that he displayed his wares of

FIGURE 28.5 Dragon Hall, Norwich, a warehouse built by Robert Toppe, a mercer and sheriff of Norwich 1430

(© Brian Durham)

coal, salt, iron, and fish and along with fine fabrics, though perhaps not at the same time! (Shelley 2005);
- the role of monastic houses in stimulating innovation, industry, and commerce;
- the possible role of secular manorial systems in inhibiting enterprise; for instance in central southern Britain, where the manorial system was already well established, the potter's wheel disappeared from use in the mid- to late eleventh century, while in the late fourteenth century agricultural workers were effectively prevented from leaving their residence to improve their prospects elsewhere (Cambridge statute AD 1388); life in the towns may have been harsher, but there were fewer constraints on individual enterprise;
- a lack of engagement among those studying the industry of mechanics of trade and commerce with concepts of agency, gender, identity, individuality, mentality, social action, and negotiation (Gilchrist 2009, 385–408);
- the continued need for scientific analysis for all archaeological materials, just as Peacock encouraged for economic aspects of pottery production and marketing some forty years ago (Peacock 1977, vii);
- the application of multi-disciplinary approaches, including historic geopolitics and economics;
- a wider European economic and cultural perspective such as that fostered by the long-running conferences at Lübeck and organizations such as the Medieval European Research Council (MERC), now integrated within The Association of European Archaeologists.

As the papers in this part of the *Handbook* make clear, if some of the gaps listed above could be addressed through a combination of local research agendas (such as those currently being revised by Historic England for all regions) and European initiatives and if historians and economists could be encouraged to integrate the physical record with their documentary and topographical sources then the future is indeed bright for the medieval archaeology of industry and crafts.

Acknowledgements

This paper benefited greatly from a day school on medieval craftsmen, held in 2015 at the Department for Continuing Education, University of Oxford, organized by Dr Elizabeth Gemmill, where James Bond, Elizabeth New, Christian Steer, and the author contributed. My thanks also to John Cotter, Oxford Archaeology, for sharing his knowledge on south-east England; to Peter Claughton, Alejandra Gutiérrez, Marian Campbell, and Brian Durham for kind permission to use their images.

References Cited

Alexander, J. S. 1995 'Building stone from the East Midlands quarries: sources, transportation and usage', *Medieval Archaeology* 39, 107–35

Alexandre-Bidon, D. 2013 *Dans l'atelier de l'apothicaire: histoire et archeologie des pots de pharmacie du XIII au XVI siècle*, Editions Picard, Paris

Allen, J. R. L. 1996 'A possible medieval trade in iron ores in the Severn estuary of south-west Britain', *Medieval Archaeology*, 40, 226–9

Allen, S. J., Goodburn, D. M., McCornish, J. M., and Walton Rogers, P. 2005 'Re-used boat planking from a 13th-century revetment in Doncaster, South Yorkshire', *Medieval Archaeology* 49, 281–304

Anderson, S. 2013 'Medieval floor and roof tiles from Melrose Abbey, Scottish Borders, and the "Westminster tilers"', *Medieval Archaeology* 57, 238–50

Arnoux, M. and Flambard Héricher, A.-M. 2010 *La Normandie dans l'économie européenne (XIe–XVIIIe siècle)*, CRAHM, Caen

Ashby, S. P. 2015 'With staff in hand, and dog at heel? What did it mean to be an "itinerant" artisan?', in G. Hansen, S. P. Ashby, and I. Baug (eds), *Everyday products in the Middle Ages: crafts, consumption and the individual in Northern Europe c. AD 800–1600*, Oxbow Books, Oxford, 11–27

Astill, G. G. 1993 *A medieval industrial complex and its landscape: the metalworking watermills and workshops of Bordesley Abbey*, Council for British Archaeology Research Report 92, York

Astill, G. and Davies, W. 1997 *A Breton landscape*, UCL Press, London

Badham, S. 1990 'London standardisation and provincial idiosyncrasy: the organisation and working practices of brass-engraving workshops in the pre-Reformation period', *Church Monuments* 5, 3–25

Badham, S. (ed.) 2010 'What constituted a "workshop" and how did workshops operate? Some problems and questions', in S. Badham and S. Oosterwijk (eds), *Monumental industry: the production of tomb monuments in England and Wales in the long fourteenth century*, Shaun Tyas, Donington, 12–36

Biddle, M. 1990 *Object and economy in medieval Winchester*, Winchester Studies 7ii, Clarendon Press, Oxford

Binding, G. 2004 *Medieval building techniques*, Tempus, Stroud

Birrell, J. 1969 'The peasant craftsman in the medieval forest', *Agricultural History Review* 17(2), 91–107

Blackmore, L. and Pearce, J. 2010 *Dated type series of London medieval pottery Part 5: shelly-sandy ware and the greyware industries*, Museum of London Archaeology, London

Blair, J. and Ramsay, N. (eds) 1991 *English medieval industries: craftsmen, techniques, products*, The Hambledon Press, London

Blaylock, S. R. 2000 'Excavation on an early post-medieval bronze foundry at Cowick Street, Exeter, 1999–2000', *Devon Archaeological Society Proceedings* 58, 1–92

Bolton, J. L. 1985 *The medieval English economy 1150–1500*, Dent, London

Bond, J. 2004 *Monastic landscapes*, Tempus, Stroud

Bond, J. 2007 'Medieval charcoal-burning in England', in J. Klápště and P. Sommer (eds), *Arts and crafts in medieval rural environment*, Ruralia 6, Brepols, Turnhout, 27–294

Brown, R. and Hardy, A. 2011 *Southampton trade and prosperity war and poverty: an archaeological and historical investigation into Southampton's French Quarter*, Oxford Archaeology, Oxford

Carver, M. O. H. 1993 *Arguments in stone*, Oxbow Monograph 29, Oxford

Childs, W. 1978 *Anglo-Castilian trade in the later Middle Ages*, Manchester University Press, Manchester

Childs, W. and O'Neill, T. 1993 'Overseas trade', in A. Cosgrove (ed.), *A new history of Ireland: II, (1169–1534)*, Oxford University Press, Oxford, 492–524

Clarke, H., Pearson, S., Mate, M., and Parfit, K. 2010 *Sandwich: the 'completest medieval town in England'. A study of the town and port from its origins to 1600*, Oxbow, Oxford

Colls, K. and Mitchell, W. 2013 *A cycle of recession and recovery AD 1200-1900: archaeological investigations at Much Park Street, Coventry 2007 to 2010*, British Archaeological Reports British Series 582, Oxford

Coppack, G. 2009 *Fountains Abbey*, Amberley, Stroud

Costin, C. L. 1991 'Craft specialization: issues in defining, documenting and explaining the organization of production', *Archaeological Method and Theory* 3, 1-56

Cotter, J. P. 2006 'The pottery', in K. Parfitt, B. Corke, and J. Cotter, 'Townwall Street, Dover Excavations 1996', *The Archaeology of Canterbury New Series* III, 121-254 and 407-16

Courtney, P. 1997 'Ceramics and consumption: pitfalls and prospects', *Medieval Ceramics* 21, 95-108

CPR 1429-1436: Calendar of Patent Rolls preserved in the Public Record office: Henry VI (vol. II) AD 1429-1436, Her Majesty's Stationery Office, London

Crossley, A. (ed.) 1979 *A history of the county of Oxford, Vol. 4: the city of Oxford*, Oxford University Press, London

Crossley, D. W. 1981 *Medieval industry*, Council for British Archaeology Research Report 40, London

Cumberpatch, C. and Roberts, I. 2013 'A Stamford ware pottery kiln in Pontefract: a geographical enigma and a dating dilemma', *Medieval Archaeology* 57, 111-50

Daniels, R. 2010 *Hartlepool: an archaeology of the medieval town*, Tees Archaeology Monograph Series 4, Hartlepool

de Groote, K. 2008 *Middeleeuws aardewerk in Vlaanderen*, Relicta Monografieën 1, Brussels

Dodds, B. and Liddy, C. 2011 *Commercial activity, markets and entrepeneurs in the Middle Ages*, Boydell Press, Woodbridge

Dransaart, P. Z., Bennett, H., and Bodgan, N. Q. with Ryder, M. L. 2012 *The textiles and leather in Perth High Street archaeological excavation 1975-1977: excavations at 75-95 High Street and 5-10 Mill Street, Perth*, Fascicule 3, Perth

Draper, G. and Martin, D. 2009 *Rye: a history of a Sussex Cinque Port to 1660*, Phillimore, Chichester

Dunning, G. C. 1965-6 'Medieval pottery and stone mortars imported to Aardenburg from England and France', *Berichten Van de Rijksdienst voor het Oudeidkundig Bodeemonderzoek Jaargand*, 15-16

Durham, B. G. 1977 'Archaeological investigations in St Aldates Oxford', *Oxoniensia* 42, 83-203

Egan, G. 1994 *Lead cloth seals and related items in the British Museum*, British Museum, London

Egan, G. 1998 *The medieval household: daily living c.1150-c.1450*, Medieval Finds from Excavations in London 6, Her Majesty's Stationery Office, London

Ford, B. M. and Teague, S. with Biddulph, E., Hardy, A. and Brown, L. 2011 *Winchester, a city in the making: archaeological excavations between 2002 and 2007 on the sites of Northgate House, Staple Gardens and the former Winchester Library, Jewry St.*, Oxford Archaeology Monograph 12, Oxford

Forster, A. 2013 'Jet', in K. Colls and W. Mitchell (eds), *A cycle of recession and recovery AD 1200-1900: archaeological investigations at Much Park Street, Coventry 2007 to 2010*, British Archaeological Reports British Series 582, Oxford, 63-6

Forster, A. and Rátkai, S. 2009 'West Midlands life, work and death in Birmingham City centre', *Medieval Archaeology* 53, 363-71

Freestone, I. 1993 'Petrological examination of roof tile', in G. G. Astill (ed.), *A medieval industrial complex and its landscape: the metalworking watermills and workshops of Bordesley Abbey*, Council for British Archaeology Research Report 92, York, 137–8

Gaimster, D. 1997 *German stoneware 1200-1900: archaeology and cultural history*, The British Museum Press, London

Gaimster, D. 2014 'The Hanseatic cultural signature: exploring globalization on the microscale in late medieval Europe', *European Journal of Archaeology* 17(1), 60–81

Gaimster, M. and O'Conor, K. 2005 'Medieval Britain and Ireland in 2004', *Medieval Archaeology* 49, 349–473

Gardiner, M. 2011 'Stacks, barns and granaries in early and high medieval England: crop storage and its implications', *Arqueología Medieval* 5, 23–38

Gemmill, E. 2001 'Signs and symbols in medieval Scottish trade', *Review of Scottish Culture* 13, 7–16

Gerrard, C. M. with Aston, M. 2007 *The Shapwick Project, Somerset: a rural landscape explored*, The Society for Medieval Archaeology Monograph 25, Leeds

Gilchrist, R. 2009 'Medieval archaeology and theory: a disciplinary leap of faith', in R. Gilchrist and A. Reynolds (eds), *Reflections: 50 years of Medieval Archaeology 1957-2007*, The Society for Medieval Archaeology Monograph 30, Leeds, 385–408

Giles, K. 2000 *An archaeology of social identity: guildhalls in York, c.1350-1630*, British Archaeological Reports British Series 315, Oxford

Giles, K. and Clark, J. 2011 'St Mary's Guildhall, Boston, Lincolnshire: the archaeology of a medieval "public" building', *Medieval Archaeology* 55, 226–56

Giles, K. and Dyer, C. (eds) 2005 *Town and country in the Middle Ages: contrasts, contacts and interconnections, 1100-1500*, The Society for Medieval Archaeology Monograph 22, Leeds

Goodall, I. H. 2011 *Ironwork in medieval Britain: an archaeological study*, The Society for Medieval Archaeology Monograph 31, Leeds

Grenville, J. 2004 'The archaeology of the late and post-medieval workshop: a review and proposal for a research agenda', in P. S. Barnwell, M. Palmer, and M. Airs (eds), *The vernacular workshop: from craft to industry 1400-1900*, Council for British Archaeology Research Report 140, York, 28–37

Hall, D. 2006 *Scottish monastic landscapes*, Tempus, Stroud

Hansen, G. 2015 'Itinerant craftspeople in 12th century Bergen, Norway: aspects of their social identities', in G. Hansen, S. P. Ashby, and I. Baug (eds), *Everyday products in the Middle Ages crafts, consumption and the individual in Northern Europe c. AD 800-1600*, Oxbow Books, Oxford, 28–50

Hansen, G., Ashby, S. P., and Baug I. (eds) 2015 *Everyday products in the Middle Ages: crafts, consumption and the individual in Northern Europe c. AD 800-1600*, Oxbow Books, Oxford

Hoare, P. G., Vinx, C. R., Stevenson, C. R., and Ehlers, J. 2002 'Re-used bedrock ballast in King's Lynn "town wall" and the Norfolk's medieval trading links', *Medieval Archaeology* 46, 91–105

Horsey, I. P. 1992 *Excavations in Poole, 1973-1983*, Dorset Natural History and Archaeological Society, Dorchester

Hourihane, C. 2000 *The mason and his mark: masons marks in the medieval Irish archbishoprics of Cashel and Dublin*, British Archaeological Reports British Series 294, Oxford

Hutchinson, G. 1994 *Medieval ships and shipping*, Leicester University Press, London

Irving, A. 2011 *A research framework for post-Roman ceramic studies in Britain*, Medieval Pottery Research Group Occasional Paper 6, London

Ivens, R., Busby, P., and Shepherd, N. 1995 *Tattenhoe and Westbury: two deserted medieval settlements in Milton Keynes*, Buckinghamshire Archaeological Society Monograph 8, Milton Keynes

Iversen, M., Earle Robinson, D., and Hjermind, J. C. C. (eds) 2005 *Viborg Søndersø 1018–1030*, Jysk Arkaeologisk Selskab/Aarhus University Press, Moesgard

Johnson, D. S. 2010 *Liming and agriculture in the Central Pennines: the use of lime in land improvement from the late thirteenth century to c.1900*, British Archaeological Reports British Series 525, Oxford

Klápště, J. and Sommer, P. (eds) 2007 *Arts and crafts in medieval rural environment*, Ruralia 6, Brepols, Turnhout

Klápště, J. and Sommer, P. (eds) 2009 *Medieval rural settlement in marginal landscapes*, Ruralia 7, Brepols, Turnhout

Langdon, J. 2011 'Minimum wages and unemployment rates in medieval England', in B. Dodds and C. Liddy (eds), *Commercial activity, markets and entrepreneurs in the Middle Ages: essays in honour of Richard Britnell*, Boydell, Woodbridge, 25–44

Langland, W. 2009 *Piers Plowman: a new translation of the B-text*, Oxford University Press, Oxford

Leah, M. 1994 *Grimston Norfolk: the Late Saxon and medieval pottery industry, excavations 1962–92*, Norfolk Museum Service, Dereham

Lewis, J. M. 1999 *Medieval tiles of Wales: census of medieval tiles in Britain*, National Museum of Wales, Cardiff

Linaa, J. 2015 'Crafts in the landscape of the powerless: a combmaker's workshop at Viborg Søndersø, AD 1020–1024', in G. Hansen, S. Ashby, and I. Baug (eds), *Everyday products in the Middle Ages: crafts, consumption and the individual in Northern Europe c. AD 800–1600*, Oxbow, Oxford, 69–90

Mackinder, T. with Egan, G. 2009 'The Thames waterfront revisited', *Medieval Archaeology* 53, 350–5

Marter, P. 2005 *Medieval pottery production centres in England AD 850–1600*, unpublished PhD thesis, University of Winchester

Mayhew, N. J. 1996 'The status of women and the brewing of ale in medieval Aberdeen', *Review of Scottish Culture* 10, 16–21

McClain, A. 2010 'Cross slab monuments in the late Middle Ages: patronage, production, and locality in northern England', in S. Badham and S. Oosterwijk (eds), *Monumental industry in fourteenth century England*, Shaun Tyas, Donnington, 37–65

McClain, A. 2012 'Theory, disciplinary perspectives and the archaeology of later medieval England', *Medieval Archaeology* 56, 131–70

McCutcheon, C. 2006 *Medieval pottery from Wood Quay, Dublin: the 1974–6 waterfront excavations*, Royal Irish Academy, Dublin

McEwan, J. 2015 'Making a mark in medieval London: the social and economic status of sealmakers', in P. Schofield (ed.), *Seals and their context in the Middle Ages*, Oxbow, Oxford, 77–88

McIntosh, M. K. 2005 *Working women in English society 1300–1620*, Cambridge University Press, Cambridge

Mellor, M. 1994 *Medieval ceramic studies in England: a review for English Heritage*, English Heritage, London

Mellor, M. 2013 'Drink, women and song: exploring ale-wives and related folklore', in M. Henig and C. Paine (eds), *Preserving and presenting the past in Oxfordshire and beyond: essays in memory of John Rhodes*, British Archaeological Reports British Series 586, Oxford, 135–45

Mellor, M. 2014 'Seeing the medieval child: evidence from household and craft', in D. M. Hadley and K. A. Hamer (eds), *Medieval childhood: archaeological approaches*, The Society for the Study of Childhood in the Past Monograph 3, Oxford

Moran, M. 2011 *The Guildhall, Ludlow*, Historical Research Group, Ludlow

Mould, Q., Carlisle, I., and Cameron, E. 2003 *Leather and leatherworking in Anglo-Scandinavian and medieval York: craft, industry and everyday life*, Archaeology of York 17/16, Council for British Archaeology, York

Murphy, M. and Potterton, M. 2010 *The Dublin region in the Middle Ages*, Four Courts Press, Dublin

Mynard, D. C. and Zeepvat, R. J. 1992 *Excavations at Great Linford 1974-80*, Buckinghamshire Archaeological Society Monograph 3, Aylesbury

New, E. 2015 '(Un)conventional images: a case-study of radial motifs on personal seals', in P. Schofield (ed.), *Seals and their context in the Middle Ages*, Oxbow, Oxford, 151-60

Patrick, C. and Rátkai, S. 2008 *The Bull Ring uncovered: excavations at Edgbaston Street, Moor Street, Park Street and The Row, Birmingham city centre, 1997-2001*, Oxbow, Oxford

Peacock, D. P. S. (ed.) 1977 *Pottery and early commerce*, Academic Press, London

Perry, D., Murray, H., and Beaumont-James, T. 2011 *Perth High Street archaeological excavation 1975-1977: excavations at 75-95 High Street and 5-10 Mill Street*, Perth Fascicule 1, Tayside and Fife Archaeological Committee, Perth

Rátkai, S. 1990 'The medieval pottery', in S. Cracknel, 'Bridge End, Warwick: archaeological excavations of a medieval street frontage', *Transactions of the Birmingham and Warwickshire Society* 95, 33-72

Rátkai, S. 2005 'The medieval and later pottery and its implications for building sequences', in C. Woodfield (ed.), *The church of Our Lady of Mount Carmel and some conventual buildings at the Whitefriars, Coventry*, British Archaeological Reports British Series 389, Oxford, 315-31

Ravoire, F. 2011 'La céramique médiévale d'île-de-France (XIe–XVe siècle): Presentation du Project collectif de Recherche', in A. Bocquet-Liénard and B. Fajal (eds), *À prop[t]s de l'usage, de la production et de la circulation des terres cuites dans l'Europe du Nord-Ouest autour des XIVe–XVIe siècles*, Publications du CRAHM, Caen, 11–24

Reed, I. 1990 *1000 years of pottery: an analysis of pottery, trade and use*, Riksantikvaren Utgravningskontoret for Trondheim, Trondheim

Richards, J. D. 1993 *The medieval walled city north-east of the Ouse Part 3: the Bedern foundry*, The archaeology of York 10, Council for British Archaeology, York

Rippon, S., Claughton, P., and Smart, C. 2009 *Mining in a medieval landscape: the royal silver mines of the Tamar valley*, University of Exeter Press, Exeter

Robinson, D. M. 2006 *The Cistercians in Wales: architecture and archaeology 1130-1540*, The Society of Antiquaries of London, London

Salzman, L. F. 1913 *English industries in the Middle Ages*, Constable, London

Shelley, A. 2005 *Dragon Hall, King Street, Norwich: excavation and survey of a late medieval merchant's trading complex*, East Anglian Archaeology 112, Norwich

Slavin, P. 2012 *Bread and ale for the brethren: the provisioning of Norwich Cathedral Priory 1260-1536*, Studies in Regional and Local History 11, University of Hertfordshire Press, Hatfield

Spoerry, P., Atkins, R., Macaulay, S., and Shepherd Popescu, E. 2008 'Ramsey Abbey, Cambridgeshire: excavations at the site of a Fenland monastery', *Medieval Archaeology* 52, 171-209

Standley, E. R. 2016 'Spinning yarns: the archaeological evidence for hand spinning and its social implications, c.1200–1500', *Medieval Archaeology* 60, 266–99

Symonds, L. A. 2003 *Landscape and social practice: the production and consumption of pottery in 10th century Lincolnshire*, British Archaeological Report British Series 345, Oxford

Thomas, C. 2012 'The leather', in P. Z. Dransart, C. Thomas, et al., *Perth High Street archaeological excavation 1975–1977: the textiles and the leather*, Fascicule 3, Tayside and Fife Archaeological Committee, Perth

Thomson, R. and Mould, Q. 2011 *Leather tanneries: the archaeological evidence*, Archetype Publications, London

Tringham, N. J. (ed.) 2013 *A history of the county of Stafford, XI*, Keele and Trentham, Audley

Vince, A. 2005 'Ceramic petrology and the study of Anglo-Saxon and later medieval ceramics', *Medieval Archaeology* 49, 219–45

Walker, H. 2012 *Hedingham Ware: a medieval pottery industry in north Essex, its production and distribution*, Essex County Council, Chelmsford

Waterman, D. M. 1970 'Somersetshire and other foreign building stones in medieval Ireland c.1175–1400', *Ulster Journal of Archaeology* 33, 63–75

White, G. J. 2012 *The medieval English landscape, 1000–1540*, Bloomsbury, London

Williams, G. 2012 'Where are all the smiths? Some reflections on the excavation of rural blacksmithing', *Institute for Archaeologists Diggers' Forum Newsletter* 10, 20–4

Willmott, H. 2005 'The vessel glass', in C. Woodfield, *The church of Our Lady of Mount Carmel and some conventual buildings at the Whitefriars, Coventry*, British Archaeological Reports British Series 389, Oxford, 332–7

CHAPTER 29

QUARRYING AND EXTRACTIVE INDUSTRIES

DAVID PARSONS

PERCEPTIONS of industrial history and archaeology are heavily affected by the attention paid to the impact of the Industrial Revolution of the eighteenth and nineteenth centuries. It is commonly assumed, even by professionals in the field, that there was no industrial infrastructure in Britain before that. The specialist literature makes it clear, however, that this assumption is untenable, and that a different concept of 'industry' is called for. L. F. Salzman published in 1913 an overview in his *English industries in the Middle Ages* (revised edition Salzman 1923), followed in 1952 by a more detailed work on the construction industry, *Building in England down to 1540*, which presented a wealth of documentary evidence for stone quarrying, further extended in the corrected impression (Salzman 1967). The subtitle of this last publication (*A documentary history*) is revealing: archaeological evidence played little part in the otherwise exhaustive treatment of the subject. Meanwhile, however, medieval archaeology was developing rapidly (the journal of that name began publication in 1957) and the next general book on the subject, *English medieval industries*, expressly sought to include archaeological evidence (Blair and Ramsay 1991, xv–xvi). Nevertheless, a recent survey of mineral resources notes that the 'archaeological record is at best fragmentary' and continues to be heavily based on documentary evidence (Claughton 2011, 56).

These seminal publications are still reliable, indeed indispensible, sources of information. The historical evidence has been thoroughly worked over and the discovery of new documentary sources, while possible, is not likely to occur frequently nor to reveal unexpected evidence. On the archaeological side, however, the huge amount of fieldwork and excavation that has taken place since Blair and Ramsay (1991) was published has produced a mass of information. At the same time the scientific processing of materials, such as radiocarbon dating, isotope analysis, and the petrological examination of building stone, has become increasingly sophisticated and yields data that reflect on the sources of raw materials as well as on the artefacts themselves. From its inception the journal *Medieval Archaeology* has carried annually a substantial section recording fieldwork and excavation that took place in the previous year. Originally entitled 'Medieval Britain in [year]' (MB&I), it was expanded to include Ireland from Volume 27 (1983); from the previous volume the entries were numbered and an index provided. For the purposes of this chapter an attempt has been made to search *Medieval Archaeology* systematically for archaeological evidence to complement the well-established historical data for the extractive industries. The results of this search cannot be regarded as exhaustive, however; even important sites can slip through the net, for example the significant discoveries in the Leicestershire coalfield, which appear not to have reported in the journal (Hartley 1994). It is nevertheless an important source of information, since not all of the sites achieve full publication.

Many of the entries in 'Medieval Britain' are brief and the details of industrial processes slight. In the case of metal-working sites, for example, it is often not clear whether the evidence of furnaces and related materials indicates extraction or simply processing, or possibly both. More generally, features such as ditches and pits, dug to form boundaries or for storage, and later used as rubbish dumps, may equally have been excavated deliberately for the extraction of minerals. These difficulties of interpretation are inherent in the subject: extractive industries are by nature destructive, and it is rare that clear evidence, especially evidence of date, is left behind. The well-known Roman stone quarries in the vicinity of Hadrian's Wall, with their surviving working faces, some with inscriptions such as the famous MAXIMUS SCRIPSIT graffito, are the exception rather than the rule, and find no parallel in the medieval period. Most significant stone quarries exploited in the Middle Ages continued to be worked in the post-medieval period, with the consequent destruction of any evidence there might have been. Similarly, the continued working of metal ores and coal tended to obliterate the direct evidence for earlier extraction, though indirect evidence in the form of processing plants, slag which can be identified as the product of smelting, and ultimately long-distance channels supplying water-driven machinery can be recovered archaeologically and—in favourable circumstances—dated. What follows is therefore of necessity only a partial account, and one which is still heavily dependent on historical documents.

Quarrying for Stone, Sand and Gravel, Clay and Brickearth

The process of building construction is described briefly by Parsons (1991, 1–6). There are three basic requirements for the construction of a traditional stone building: dimension stone, which can range from large blocks of precisely cut sedimentary rock to relatively small, often unshaped, pieces of rubble of any rock type; limestone or chalk for burning to provide the active ingredient of lime mortar; and sand to act as aggregate in the mortar mix.

Of the wealth of documentary evidence available for the study of building materials, the building accounts for the construction of the chancel of Adderbury church, Oxfordshire, in 1408–19 provide a convenient conspectus of the payments for goods and transport services in the course of the project (Hobson 1926). The main source of dimension stone was the well-attested quarry at Taynton, near Burford, Oxfordshire, which also supplied the stone for prestigious building projects such as Eton College and St George's Chapel, Windsor. Identifying this stone in the fabric of the church is complicated by smaller quantities of stone brought from other quarries (Oxford, probably Headington, and Bloxham), and geological knowledge is required to distinguish between them. Stone was also dug in Adderbury itself, in or below the rectory garden, specifically for the building of the chancel rather than lime-burning (*contra* Parsons 1991, 24; the Marlstone Rock Bed is an iron-rich limestone unsuitable for this purpose), but it cannot be recognized in the fabric, having doubtless been used for foundations and wall core. The accounts indicate that lime, sometimes specified as quicklime, was brought in from Witney, Radcliffe, Woodstock, and Milton and bought from named merchants in unidentified places. There appears to be no mention of sand for the mortar, however, which is surprising given the detail of other purchases—timber, ironwork, even ropes for the crane.

Taynton is one of a number of major quarries that are well known from medieval documents, other examples spreading from Beer in Devon to Barnack in Cambridgeshire and to Hazlewood and neighbouring sites in Yorkshire (Salzman 1967, 119–39; Parsons 1990; 1991, 21–5). The source of Barnack stone, widely used from the Roman period to the early fourteenth century, has recently been investigated; the extent of the quarry has been shown by fieldwork to be much more extensive than the famous 'Hills and Holes' area (Everson and Stocker forthcoming), though it is not possible at present to identify archaeologically the location of the workings in the later medieval period. Archaeological evidence is gradually accumulating for other stone sources, especially where the lithology and petrology of the rocks are sufficiently distinctive to enable building stones *in situ* to be related to their place of origin. An early example of stone characteristics being used in this way was the investigation of Totternhoe stone in the late 1960s; this Chiltern stone is one of few chalks hard enough to be used as a building stone (Roberts 1974). A combination of fieldwork and documentary research led to the identification of the source of the stone, including flint nodules, used in churches in Hertfordshire and elsewhere. Subsequently another stone with a fairly local distribution was identified by its geological characteristics at Hildenley in North Yorkshire (Senior 1990). Its quality is described as 'fine' and it was used for artefacts as well as building stone in the Roman and medieval periods but its limited occurrence meant that it could not be exploited to the same extent as other, more famous, Yorkshire quarries. Another stone source of limited extent was the Upper Greensand at the base of the North Downs in Surrey, commonly known as Reigate stone. It was heavily used in the London area and Kent, beginning in the late Anglo-Saxon period but accelerating rapidly in the thirteenth century, first attested by documentary evidence at Waltham Abbey (Essex) in 1218, and continuing through the Middle Ages at major sites such as Westminster and Windsor Castle and more minor works in Surrey itself (Tatton-Brown 2001a). The characteristic green appearance of the stone means that it is easily recognizable when used in the fabric of a building. Tatton-Brown has investigated the use of several other types of building stone, for example Quarr stone from the Isle of Wight and Marquise oolite from the Boulogne area in northeast France (see below under 'Transport'); the former was used for the Romanesque cathedral in Winchester, as well as for several sites in Kent, and the latter can be seen in the cathedral priory and St Augustine's Abbey in Canterbury (Tatton-Brown 1990, 72–4). On the basis of the structural history of these buildings Tatton-Brown proposes that the use of both these stones had ceased by about AD 1120, though there is evidence for the use of Quarr stone at Norwich Cathedral in 1413–14 (Ayers 1990, 225). Meanwhile these and other major building projects had begun to use stone from the quarries in and around Caen (Normandy); the castle chapel at Bramber in West Sussex is proposed as the earliest datable example (1066–73) of the use of this stone, which continued throughout the Middle Ages in southern and eastern England (Figure 29.1) (Dugué et al. 2010; Dujardin 2009; Tatton-Brown 2001b; see Chapter 57 in this *Handbook*).

Other easily recognizable stone types include the so-called marbles, actually highly fossiliferous limestones which can be polished to resemble real marble. The best known of these is Purbeck marble, extensively employed from about AD 1170, most notably in the embellishment of Westminster Abbey church from 1245 onward; by *c*.1200 it had supplanted stone from Tournai (Belgium), previously imported in the form of finished artefacts, such as fonts (Blair 1991). Thereafter Purbeck was used for monuments and ledger slabs as well as for architectural components like shafts and capitals. It was widely distributed, appearing in the Galilee Chapel of Durham Cathedral *c*.1175; at the east end of the same cathedral, however, a local 'marble' from Frosterley was used in the Nine Altars Chapel in the following century. Another 'marble' from the same area was Egglestone stone from the Tees valley near Barnard Castle, which was not used architecturally but for tombs, ledger slabs, brass indents, and fonts, mainly in the period 1400–1550 (Badham and Blacker 2009). Similarly used for monuments and effigies was alabaster, quarried principally at Fauld near Hanbury (Staffordshire) and Chellaston (Derbyshire), and in regular use from *c*.1330 until the end of the Middle Ages (Ramsay 1991; and see Chapter 59 in this *Handbook*). Although the stone has a highly characteristic appearance, and its area of origin is attested by documents, it is considered 'not possible by petrological analysis or any other scientific means to determine the locality from which a piece of alabaster has been extracted' (Ramsay 1991, 30–1).

Many of the quarries mentioned above were in rural locations, often in river valleys as at Egglestone, but there is documentary as well as archaeological evidence for quarrying in towns: for example, flint was extracted in large quantities in Norwich to be used knapped as a building stone (Ayers 1990) and at Stamford limestone quarries are frequently revealed in excavation (MB&I 1996, no. 102; 2000, no. 232; 2005, no. 129). In these and many other cases the most locally available material was being exploited, as at Adderbury (above), where the likely site of the rectory garden quarry cannot be investigated because houses have been built there in recent times. Their foundations had to be reinforced because they were apparently built on the loose fill of an earlier excavation. Quarry pits are encountered as features in the course of routine excavations, rather than

QUARRYING AND EXTRACTIVE INDUSTRIES   459

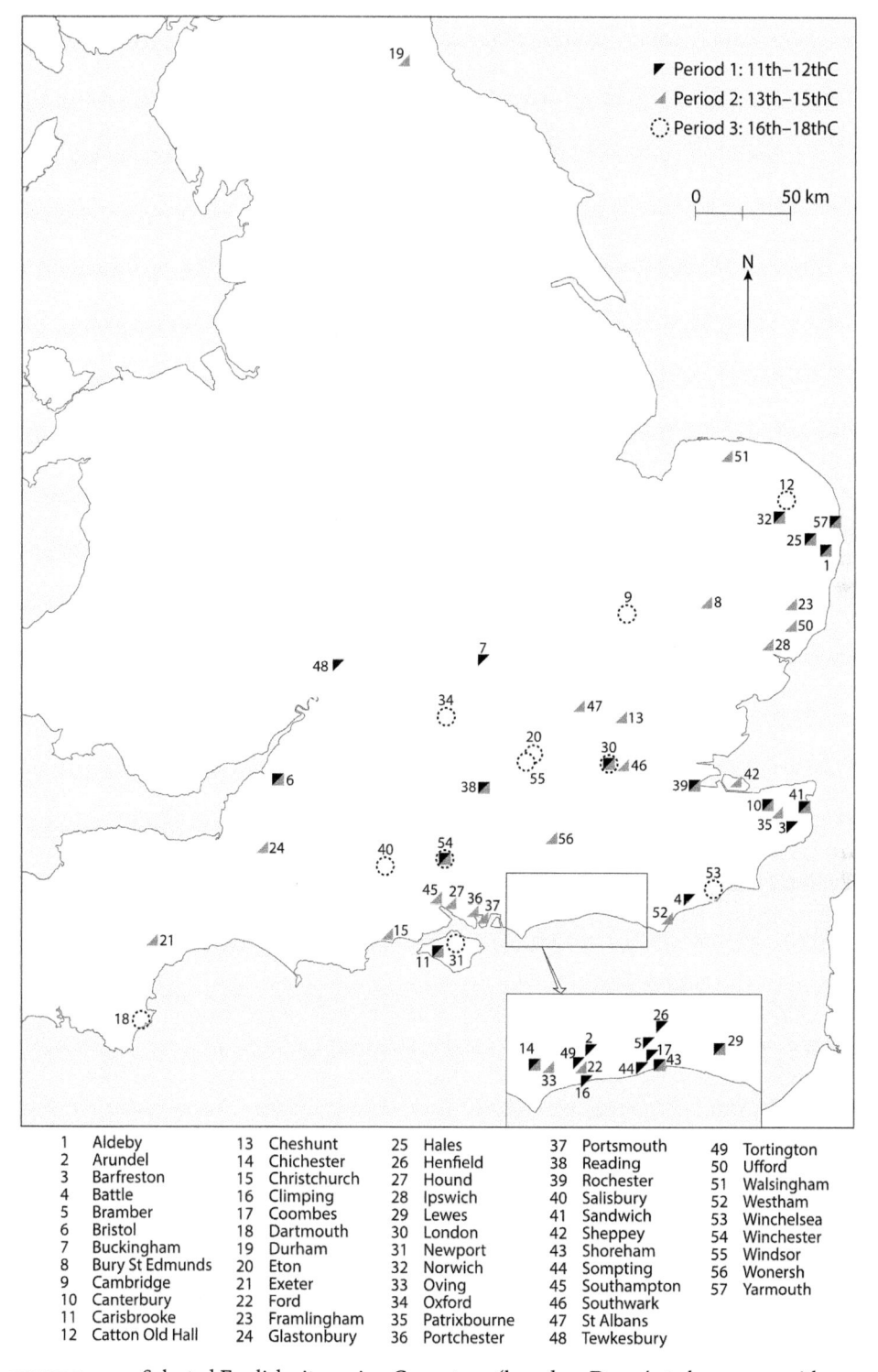

FIGURE 29.1 Selected English sites using Caen stone (based on Dugué et al. 2010, 73, with corrections and additions)

(© Alejandra Gutiérrez)

being targeted for their own sake; the classic site is North Raunds (Northamptonshire), investigated in a series of rescue excavations from 1977 to 1987, in an area of known historic and modern quarrying; the neighbouring village of Stanwick has a significant place-name (Cadman 1990). Cadman draws attention to the practical difficulties of excavating quarry sites and the paucity of evidence both for quarrying tools and for precise dating (1990, 191, 199). Subsequently many excavations have identified comparable evidence, which frequently features in MB&I entries; recent examples include Histon (Cambridgeshire; 2011, no. 40), Moulton (Northamptonshire; 2013, no. 115), Haddenham (Buckinghamshire; 2014, no. 12), Bilney and Postwick (Norfolk; 2014, nos 104, 107), Lincoln (2008, no. 127), Oxford (2006, no. 138; 2012, no. 100), and London (2012, nos 25, 41, 64, 102). Such sites are often of limited extent and not recognizable as landscape features independently of excavation: the account of shallow pits at Sutton Valence (Kent; 2011, no. 127) notes that they 'did not seem to have been deliberately backfilled but rather had silted up over a considerable period of time'—compare the late medieval quarrying at Alston Grange (Leicestershire), whose impact on the landscape is minimal (Parsons 1991, 17 and fig. 7). Equally insignificant are the many examples of the extraction of chalk and limestone for burning to quicklime; the purpose of such pits is sometimes confirmed by the discovery of lime kilns in the vicinity, as at Wharram Percy (North Yorkshire) in the early volumes of *Medieval Archaeology* (3 (1959), 318–19; 4 (1960), 164; 5 (1961), 337–8) or at Barrow upon Soar (Leicestershire), where the kilns yielded archaeomagnetic dates ranging from 1490 to 1570/1600 (MB&I 2007, no. 98). A pit used for the same purpose in thirteenth-century Oxford was identified by geochemical analysis (MB&I 2012, no. 100). The use of lime for agricultural purposes may also be noted (Johnson 2010; MB&I 2014, no. 16). Digging for sand, gravel, and brickearth are equally frequently reported, notably in the City of London and the Greater London Boroughs (e.g. MB&I 2000, nos 103, 111, 130; 2012, no. 57; 2013, no. 39; 2014, no. 67) as well as in the provinces (Chesterton, Cambridgeshire; Maldon, Essex; Yaxley, Cambridgeshire; Freeby, Leicestershire; Oxford: MB&I 2003, nos 12, 58; 2013, no. 29; 2000, no. 158; 2014, no. 124).

Mortar mixers, mechanical devices for combining quicklime, once it has been slaked, with aggregate (normally sand, but also crushed brick), have been excavated in increasing numbers in Britain and abroad. They consisted generally of a circular basin cut into the ground and typically between 2 m and 3 m in diameter, in which mortar was mixed by paddles suspended from a beam rotating around a central post. The summary paper by Hüglin (2011) lists some sixty-six instances, most with early medieval dates; a few appear to be later medieval, including a British example at Duxford (Cambridgeshire, fourteenth? to fifteenth century; Lyons 2011).

Precious Metals

Apart from its mining in Wales during the Roman period, the extraction of gold in Britain has been negligible. Campbell recounts an incident in the fourteenth century, when a London goldsmith prospected in Devon for a month, only to produce a quantity so small that its value was exceeded by the expenses of its discovery and retrieval (Campbell 1991, 108).

The extraction and processing of silver, mainly obtained from argentiferous lead ores, has been extensively studied by historians and numismatists, and much attention has been paid to the possible correlation of the silver output with the known or assumed quantity of coins minted at various times. The most comprehensive recent account is P. F. Claughton's doctoral thesis (2003). The sources most frequently referred to lie in Cumbria (the 'mine of Carlisle'), County Durham, and Somerset and Devon. The first and last of these were exploited on behalf of the Crown (the English kings in the case of the Tamar Valley sites and in the case of Carlisle the Scottish kings for a period in the twelfth century) and the Durham mines on behalf of the Prince Bishop. Other lead-mining areas also produced some silver: Derbyshire, Flintshire, and Glamorgan. The North Pennine mines in particular seem to have concentrated on lead production from about 1200; silver was then imported from central and eastern Europe, and German miners were brought in during the thirteenth century with a view to finding and working new sources. Towards the end of the century mines were opened in the Bere Ferrers area (Devon) and at Combe Martin on the north Devon coast (Figure 29.2). None of these sources has been subjected to intensive archaeological investigation, with the notable exception of the Tamar Valley Project, an important multi-disciplinary survey which included fieldwork and excavation, though the 'landscape impact of ... the actual extraction and processing of the ore, is ... surprisingly limited' (Rippon et al. 2009, 100). Figure 29.3 summarizes the evidence for medieval silver working on the Bere Ferrers peninsula. The lead/silver mines were located along a north–south line running north from the east bank of the River Tamar above the confluence with the

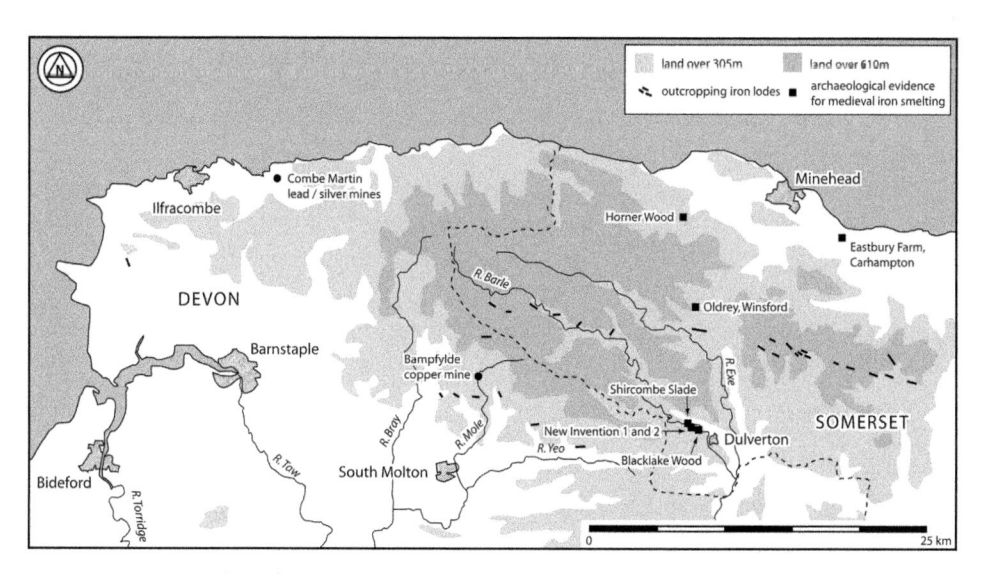

FIGURE 29.2 Metal-working sites on Exmoor

(from Rippon et al. 2009, fig. 2.06)

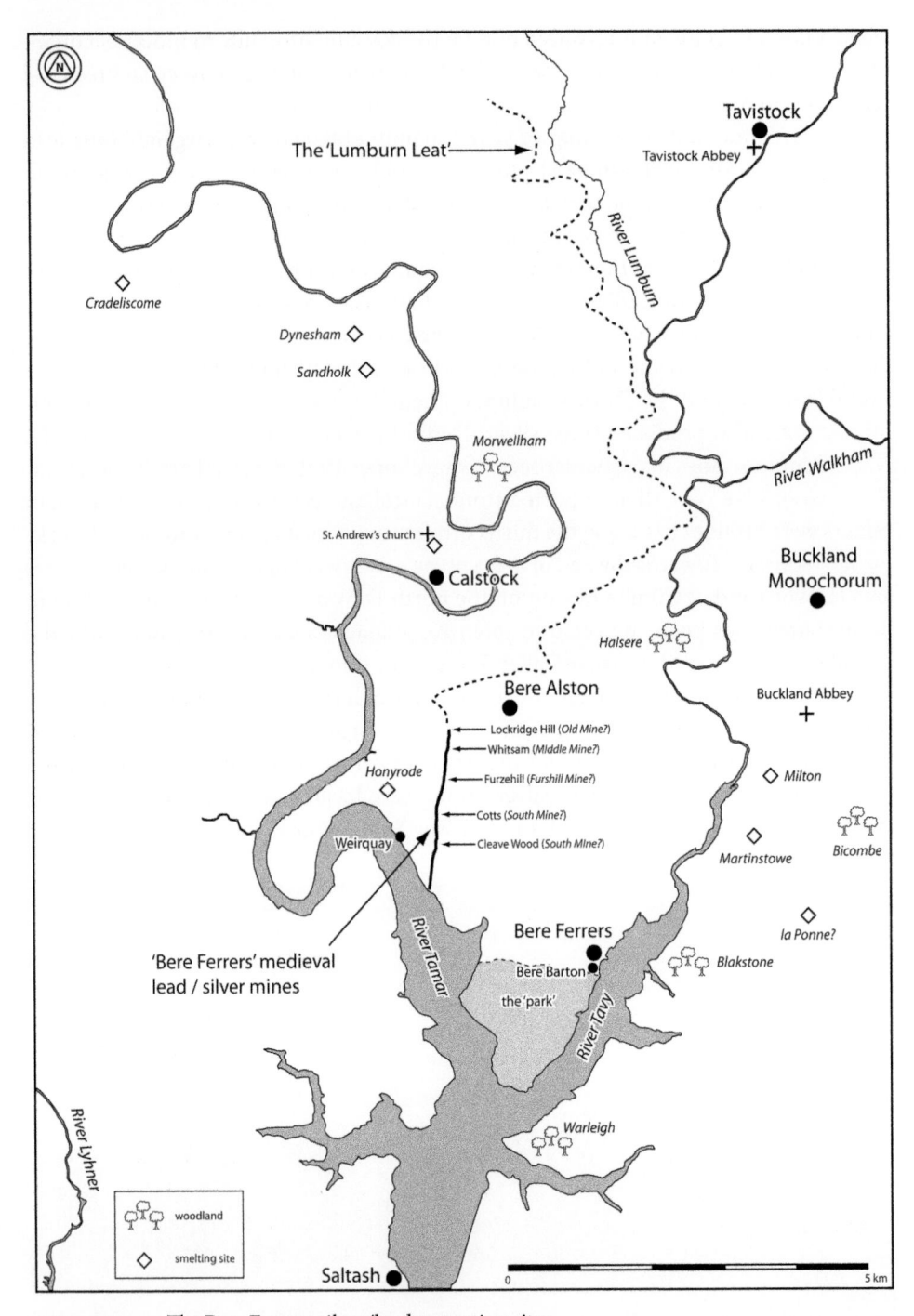

FIGURE 29.3 The Bere Ferrers silver/lead extraction sites

(from Rippon et al. 2009, fig. 3.05)

River Tavey in the general direction of Bere Alston. Smelting sites have been identified to the east of the Tavey, but the processing of the ore was moved to Calstock, further up the Tamar, in the early fourteenth century, with a ferry in operation between Calstock and 'Birland'. Smelting sites also existed to the north of Calstock. For the mines themselves the most visible physical evidence is the series of drainage adits; medieval features undisturbed by later mining are best represented at Furzehill. Most impressive, however, is the survival of the Lumburn Leat, an artificial water course supplying the Bere Alston mines, a remarkable example of late medieval technology. It is 16 km long, approximately 1 m wide and 0.5 m deep, and passes through two tunnels en route. It is tangible evidence for long-vanished waterwheels used to power lift pumps, which were introduced in the mid-fifteenth century to drain water from underground workings (Rippon et al. 2009, 109–17).

Base Metals

Since silver was primarily refined from lead ores in Britain, the history and archaeology of the *lead mining* industry are parallel to those of silver production. Lead mining is briefly summarized by Homer (1991, 62–4) and dealt with more extensively in papers by Blanchard to which he refers. Brook et al. 2004 discuss the sources of lead and its widespread recycling. More recent work includes the investigation of smelting slags in Wharfedale and Swaledale (North Yorkshire), where medieval dates have been returned from scientific analysis. In the Peak District of Derbyshire and the adjacent part of Staffordshire underground investigations have identified rock-cutting techniques and tool marks of probable medieval date. Various issues of the journals *Mining History* and *British Mining* carry site reports.

The extraction of *copper* hardly reached commercial proportions in medieval Britain. The limited amount of evidence is discussed by Blair and Blair (1991, 84–5), where there are references to entries in the respective Victoria County Histories for Cornwall, Cumberland, and Yorkshire in the thirteenth century and for the last two in the fifteenth. Since then, slag has been recovered from the site of the Bampfield mine at North Molton (Devon) in a late fifteenth-century context (Rippon et al. 2009, 24–7; see Figure 29.2).

The British *tin* industry is associated with the south-west peninsula of England: Devon and particularly Cornwall, where it was exploited in late Iron-Age and Roman times. General surveys tend to be document-based (e.g. Homer 1991, 58–62), but archaeological evidence has gradually accumulated. Tin-rich silts have been recognized, which are the result of redeposited gangue from streaming (the washing of ore); some have yielded radiocarbon dates in the thirteenth and late fifteenth–sixteenth centuries (Rippon et al. 2009, 28–35). The flooding of the West Colliford reservoir on Bodmin Moor (Cornwall) in the 1980s was preceded by fieldwork and excavation, which identified tin mills and associated buildings, as well as machinery platforms, leats, and tail races. The general date range appeared to be 1100–1700, but closer dating was rarely possible: for example the re-cutting of leats destroyed earlier evidence. The changeover from dry to wet stamping in the sixteenth century was recorded (Austin 1989; MB&I 1985, nos 21–2). In one instance, the eluvial streamwork at Beckamoor Combe, a medieval date was assured by its chronological relation to a field boundary with a medieval wall (Gerrard 2000, 142). At Dartmoor (Devon) two mills were recorded at Upper Merrivale, one earlier than the other, with a likely date range of c.1300 to c.1650 (MB&I 1990, no. 51).

The occurrence of *iron* ore is widespread; for an overview of its properties and methods of producing usable iron and steel from it, see Geddes 1991. Iron mining in the medieval period was surveyed by Salzman (1923, 21–40), but his account relied almost entirely on documentary evidence. More recent studies of particular iron-working areas have also been short of archaeological evidence, for example Cleere and Crossley, who note that despite discoveries of tap slag (important for the identification of smelting sites as opposed to smithies) very little excavation had taken place at that date, and only one investigation of a water-powered processing site at Chingley Forge (near Goudhurst, Kent). The introduction of water-driven bellows and the development of the blast furnace are described in the following chapter (Cleere and Crossley 1995, 104–8, 111–29). Rippon et al. report that field evidence for iron extraction is widespread in the south-west of England, but is archaeologically undatable (2009, 39), but in the Weald of Kent and Sussex excavated sites have yielded dating evidence. The investigation of minepits revealed in section by commercial clay digging at Sharpthorne (near West Hoathly, West Sussex) found possibly structural timbers in the fills of two pits, which yielded uncalibrated radiocarbon dates of AD 1120 ± 75 and 1220 ± 80, leading to a claim that this was the earliest medieval minepit in the Weald (Worssam and Swift 1987). More recently, excavation at various sites in and around Crawley (West Sussex) has shown this to have been a significant iron-working centre; at the ASDA site in 2002 two iron-working hearths were located. From one of them a charcoal sample gave a date of cal. AD 1040–1260 (Stevens 2008, 119–20, 131–2; see also MB&I 2014, nos 140, 141).

From the early 1960s the MB&I section of *Medieval Archaeology* carried frequent reports of iron-working sites, but it is often not clear whether hearths were used for smelting or simply for smithing. Even those which can be identified as smelting hearths are only indirect evidence for the source of the iron ore, since there is evidence for ore being transported from the mine for processing elsewhere (see below, 'Transport–Import–Export'). Excavations in East Sussex at both Jarvis Brook and Rotherfield in 1977 revealed evidence for bloomeries associated with medieval pottery (Webster and Cherry 1978, 187), while at Weldon (Northamptonshire) there was evidence for extensive quarrying, presumably for ironstone, and for smelting, with a general thirteenth/fifteenth-century date context (MB&I 2001, no. 246). Evidence for slag-tapping has recently been discovered in Worcester (MB&I 2014, no. 151). In Scotland, at Chapel Hill, Ballachly (Highland) iron ore and slag were found dating to the fourteenth to fifteenth centuries (MB&I 2008, no. 223), and at Tantallon Castle (East Lothian) there is evidence for smelting in the fifteenth–sixteenth centuries (MB&I 2014, no. 169); at Belmont on Unst (Shetland) 'the presence of iron bloom, slag and hammerscale … indicate that iron smelting and iron working could also have played an important role in the economy of Belmont. These finds ... raise ... questions about local sources of ore and fuel, given that iron refining is such a resource-intensive process'; the date range is eleventh to fourteenth century (MB&I 2009, no. 265). In Wales, Trelech (Monmouthshire) 'has produced evidence of substantial thirteenth-century iron-smelting activities at several locations'; at one of two sites investigated in 2000 there were 'significant amounts of iron slag, including tap slags, and furnace linings' (MB&I 2000, nos 555, 553).

Coal, Jet, and Related Substances

The medieval *coal mining* industry is relatively well documented (Hatcher 1993, ch. 2; Salzman 1923, 1–20). Most commentators point out that the word 'coal' in its various forms is ambiguous and can refer to charcoal as well as mineral coal. This is a serious problem only when trying to identify the earliest references to mineral coal in a particular locality; otherwise the context usually makes clear which material is being referred to. In addition there are more precise references to 'sea coal' and 'stone coal'. The first of these is taken to refer to coal obtained from the outcropping deposits on the sea coast, typically along the north-east coast of England from Yorkshire to Northumberland. Such outcrops are subject to erosion and limited quantities of coal can be simply gathered from the shore, though for exploitation on a commercial scale extraction from the cliff face is necessary. Like stone quarrying, this kind of extraction is not productive of archaeological evidence, since continued extraction or further erosion destroy the signs of earlier workings.

Underground workings are more likely to preserve archaeological information, but are usually inaccessible, so that little could be added to the documentary evidence. There was a significant breakthrough in 1985–93, when new opencast mining took place at the Lounge site at Coleorton (Leicestershire), and afforded the opportunity for extensive archaeological recording of the medieval and early modern shafts and galleries (Hartley 1994; 2007; 2015). Landscape evidence was also photographed from the air and was published by Hartley along with an earlier aerial photograph (2007, figs 11 and 12; here Figure 29.4). These show the location of a considerable number of shafts, though it is not possible to identify which of them are of medieval date.

The opencast excavations exposed a continuous series of pillar-and-stall workings over an area of some 0.5 km^2, which extended down to 30 m below the ground surface. Access to these galleries was by timber-lined vertical shafts with substantial remains of the original timber linings (Figure 29.5). There was further preserved timber in the form of pit props, which supplemented the pillars on unmined coal supporting the roof of the workings. Five of these were submitted for dendrochronological determination and returned felling dates between 1450 and 1463 (Hartley 2007, 26), so that there is no doubt that mining was taking place here in the mid-fifteenth century. Consistent with these dates are many of the artefacts recovered, some of which fall stylistically into the period

FIGURE 29.4 Leicestershire coalfield: aerial photograph showing landscape features

(© R. F. Hartley)

1450–1600. These include clothing and tools, and several pairs of runners from sleds, which have been plausibly reconstructed with basketwork upper parts—the 'corves' for transporting excavated coal to the foot of the mine shafts (Hartley 1994, 92–3, 96). Further dendrochronological determinations from a timber-lined roadway indicated a date in the 1620s for the development of longwall mining, which is conventionally thought to have been introduced in the late seventeenth century. These discoveries have recently been discussed in the historical context of mining in the Leicestershire–Derbyshire coalfield (Hartley 2015). In the quarter-century since these discoveries were made no comparable archaeological work has been carried out, and the Coleorton site remains the most important archaeological investigation in modern times of the medieval coal-mining industry.

Jet is a coal-like substance, similarly formed from organic material, and is related to shale, cannel coal, and lignite, with which it is commonly confused. 'The coastal cliffs in the vicinity of Whitby (North Yorkshire) are one of the primary sources of jet ... for much of Europe' (Pierce 2013, 198), and the pendant crosses she discusses appear to be genuine jet from this source. In another recent study, however, a range of artefacts subjected to scientific analysis proved to be diverse in material and in origin, with very little real jet (Hunter 2008). Although his study deals with Viking Scotland and is chronologically outside the scope of this *Handbook*, Hunter has an important section on analytical methods: the best method of identification is petrological examination, which is destructive and cannot usually be applied; non-destructive methods

QUARRYING AND EXTRACTIVE INDUSTRIES   467

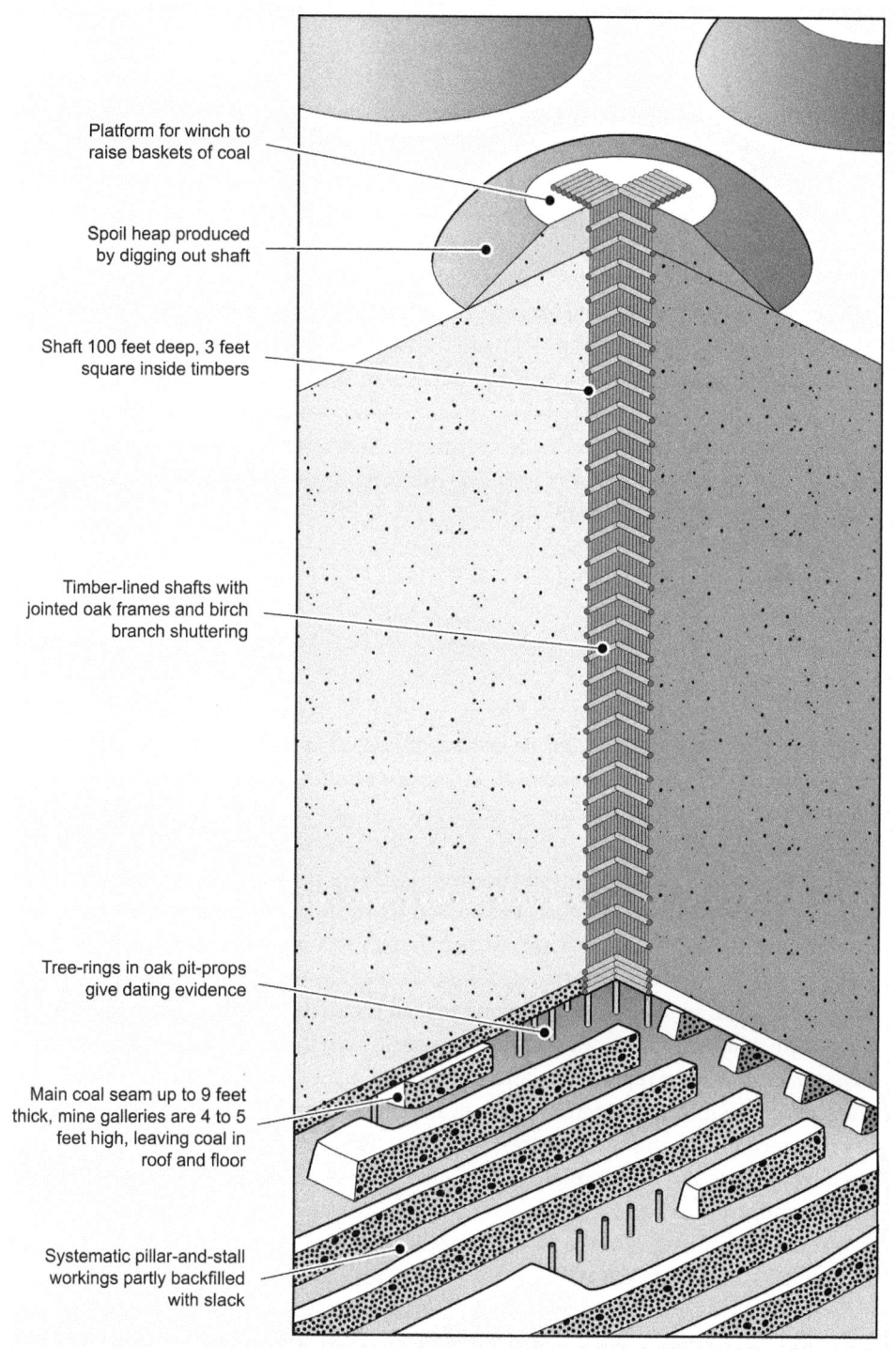

FIGURE 29.5 Leicestershire coalfield: reconstruction diagram of mineshaft and pillar-and-stall workings (from Hartley 2015, fig. 4)

(© R. F. Hartley and Leicestershire Fieldworkers)

are X-ray fluorescence (XRF), radiography, and visual inspection, which in combination are normally adequate for the identification of the material, but 'have not to date proved good at pinning down individual sources' (Hunter 2008, 108–9). Nevertheless, Hunter's fig. 1 shows that it is possible to indicate the general areas from which artefacts ultimately derive. Pierce (2013) is able to draw firmer conclusions on account of the homogeneity of her material and the limited number of possible sources for true jet. In addition to the Whitby area she mentions the north-west of Spain. Jet from this source is of finer quality than that from Whitby (Pierce 2013, 198) and is a possible factor in determining the origin of the material (see Chapter 59). But it is the distribution of the artefacts that makes clear the area from which it comes: there is a concentration of objects from Yorkshire, and those from the east of Scotland can easily be explained as the result of coastal traffic; while the outliers in Ireland and Winchester could in theory derive from Spain, the typology of the pendants makes it clear that they belong to the same group of artefacts (Pierce 2013, fig. 1). Apart from these recent publications the literature on jet and similar materials is minimal, and generally artefact-based (for example, Campbell 1991, 116, 138, 148).

Salt

The extraction of salt from inland brine springs or from seawater was an important medieval industry because of its use as a preservative. The economic status of salt in medieval society has been explored in various publications by Laurence Keen. His paper on coastal salt production is mainly document-based, and examines the evidence of Domesday Book, with lists of sites and maps, as the basis of our understanding of the industry in the Norman period (Keen 1988). There is an archaeological dimension to the evidence for the settlement areas of King's Lynn (Norfolk) and Bramber (West Sussex) encroaching on 'former salt works', though this is perhaps a slight over-interpretation of the wording of texts concerned, at least in the case of Bramber. There is nevertheless firm archaeological evidence for salt production in this general area, at the head of the tidal reach of the River Adur: as early as 1963 the Medieval Britain section of *Medieval Archaeology* reported saltern mounds on the opposite side of the river from Bramber at Botolphs [Annington] (Wilson and Hurst 1962–3, 348), while more recently trenches for cable-laying running west from Upper Beeding, adjacent to Bramber, have revealed hearths and other evidence for salt-working, some of it datable to the thirteenth to fifteenth centuries (MB&I 2007, no. 242; 2008, no. 170; 2009, no. 196). In Kent, on reclaimed saltmarshes in the Thames floodplain, a similar series of mounds has been interpreted as a possible salt-working site (MB&I 2013, no. 96).

In King's Lynn an investigation close to the medieval town defences uncovered dumped silts and clay-lined pits, though there was no clear dating evidence, but salt-making silts appear to have been incorporated in the medieval ramparts (MB&I 2002, no. 177). Some eight miles (13 km) from King's Lynn the village of Walpole St Peter has produced substantial evidence of salt extraction. The earliest evidence consisted of 'a large rectangular tank, associated with which were at least two phases of revetment. The latter took the form of a timber slot and a number of postholes, designed to stabilise the inner "working" bank of the channel. Following a possible period of abandonment further phases of revetment were constructed, which probably date from the mid-15th to ?17th centuries. Contemporary with these were several pits, tanks, troughs and channels that are likely to be associated with saltworking' (MB&I 2009, 156).

In neighbouring Lincolnshire the north-west coast of the Wash has produced evidence for salt-working, and at Wainfleet St Mary excavation took place in 1984 (McAvoy 1994). In addition to clay-lined pits and a mound of silt and waste, several alignments of filtration units were discovered. The detailed report discusses these in relation to the processing techniques recorded in the older literature. Some years earlier a saltern mound had been excavated at Bicker Haven, revealing a waste heap with stratified deposits of ash and silt, a hut, and a series of hearths; a fourteenth-century date was suggested by the associated pottery, the origins of which implied a distribution network in south Lincolnshire (Bell et al. 1999, 82–99).

The best-known inland salt-production sites are in northern Worcestershire and Cheshire. The brine springs of the Salwarpe valley have been exploited since the Iron Age, and a multi-period site at Upwich (Droitwich, Worcestershire) was excavated in 1983–4 (Hurst 1999). A timber-lined pit from the medieval period yielded a dendrochronological date of 1264, exactly matching documentary evidence for the construction of a large brine well in 1264–5. Another timber feature was interpreted as lifting gear, superseded by a pump framework in 1420–2, but there was no evidence for hearths during this period (Hurst 1999, 32–40). More recently, excavations in Nantwich (Cheshire) have revealed remains of salt-working preserved in waterlogged strata, including hollowed-out logs known as 'salt ships' used for the storage of brine (MB&I 2005, no. 29).

Transport–Import–Export

The location of the various extractive industries is geologically determined, and their products, whether the raw materials or finished artefacts, are not universally available and have to be transported to the point of use, or in some cases to a processing site. The widespread distribution of highly recognizable materials from a specific source, such as Purbeck marble (Blair 1991, 43), makes it apparent that distance was no object in the medieval period if the product was in sufficient demand; even iron travelled long distances (Geddes 1991, 168–9). In the case of building stone, the question of transport in the medieval period has been examined in some detail (Parsons 1991, 21–4; Salzman 1967, 349–54). A study of building accounts shows clearly that water transport was less expensive than carriage overland, reflected in the archaeological record by the recovery of wrecks such as the late fifteenth-century river barge at Blackfriars (ship no. 4), sunk with a load of Kentish ragstone on board (Marsden 1996, 105–6). Stone artefacts, being smaller than bulk consignments of building stone, could be more easily transported overland either by cart or by pack animals from a native source or from a port of entry. In the early medieval period there is abundant archaeological evidence for the importing of querns and whetstones from the Eifel region of Germany, but in the later Middle Ages finds of querns at least are considered residual rather than freshly imported (Ottaway and Rogers 2002, 2799). Millstones are a different matter: there is considerable documentary evidence for the acquisition and transporting of these specialist stones for use on medieval manors, including the importation of French material through the ports of Southampton and London (Farmer 1992). Smaller stone objects, such as mortars, where the composition of the stone was less critical, could often be produced in the immediate vicinity, but were also brought from farther afield. Of the many mortar fragments excavated in medieval York, most derived from the local Permian limestone (the nearest outcrop is in the Tadcaster–Wetherby area), but some had lithologies suggestive of an origin in Portland or Purbeck in Dorset (Ottaway and Rogers 2002, 2800).

Evidence for the transportation of iron is afforded by the Magor Pill wreck in the Severn Estuary, a broad-beamed vessel whose timbers were felled in 1239–40; its cargo consisted of 171 kg of iron ore, evidently being taken from its source to a smelting site (Nayling 1998). This evidence has to be seen in the context of a number of abandoned landing places along the estuary, two of which have produced quantities of iron ore; the raw material, both from the Forest of Dean (upstream of Magor Pill) and from the Mendips (downstream) appears to have been in transit along the Severn to an unidentified smelting site, possibly under the control of Tintern Abbey (Allen 1996).

Despite the abundance of native ores, iron was imported from Europe, notably from France, Sweden, and Germany, in the late thirteenth and early fourteenth centuries (Geddes 1991, 168). The much rarer copper was imported towards the end of the medieval period (Blair and Blair 1991, 84–5), and gemstones were always brought in from exotic locations (Campbell 1991). Particularly well documented is the importation of building stone from northern France. The instance of Caen stone is well known; Figure 29.1 shows the major building projects for which it was supplied. Less well known is the stone from Marquise, in the Boulogne area, which was used for example at St Augustine's Abbey, Canterbury. The transportation of these stones, and its hazards, are graphically described in the twelfth-century *Miracles of St Augustine*, which include an account of thirteen ships carrying stone from Caen, one of which was destined for St Augustine's. Twelve of the ships were sunk in a storm crossing the English Channel, but the thirteenth miraculously limped up the Adur as far as Bramber before it broke up; the stone was then taken round the coast to Canterbury in another vessel. Another story describes the acquisition of Marquise stone, mentioning specifically capitals, columns, and bases, so that finished items were available from the quarry as well as stone blocks (Gem 1987, 83–6).

The evidence for the exporting of mineral ores is unsurprisingly small. Tin was exported in quantity from Devon and Cornwall to France and Flanders in the twelfth century and to the Hanseatic League in the thirteenth (Homer 1991, 61); copper ore, which does not occur frequently in Britain, was nevertheless exported to Venice in the late fifteenth century (Blair and Blair 1991, 84). Stone was the commodity most commonly exported: alabaster carvings are easily recognizable and can be found in many places in Europe (Ramsay 1991, 38–9), while a small amount of Purbeck marble found its way to Normandy (Blair 1991, 44) and to Ireland (O Brien 2014, 127 and *passim*) as both building and artefact stone. The stone most frequently exported to Ireland, however, was Dundry stone from the Mendips, and the proximity of the quarry sites to Bristol suggests the route by which it was taken there (O Brien 2014, 125).

Research Directions

An archaeological approach to the study of the landscape of mineral extraction is demonstrated by the University of Exeter's Tamar Valley Project (Rippon et al. 2009). More generally, a research framework for extractive industries in England is being developed by the National Association of Mining History Organisations (NAMHO), supported by Historic England. Sections of this are in advanced draft at the time of writing.[1] The section on stone is less advanced, but is supplemented by another project being carried out by the British Geological Survey, also supported by Historic England. It aims to collate and map information on building stones, but is not concerned with artefact stone.[2] These are macro projects of national significance, but ultimately depend on—and are complemented by—regional initiatives and research projects at the micro level. In the building stone field several local publications have appeared in the recent past (Birch and Cordiner 2014; Stanier 2000; Sutherland 2003), but they are mainly descriptive and use historic buildings by way of illustration rather than taking a problem-based approach, and are not period-specific. As an example of local problem-solving, the stone quarries of West Sussex may be cited. Domesday Book of AD 1086 exceptionally records quarries at Iping, Stedham, Grittenham, and Bignor; the last is specifically defined as a millstone quarry (*molaria*), implying that the others were quarries for dimension or artefact stone. They were presumably the origin of late eleventh-century grave markers and covers surviving at Stedham and elsewhere, but could also have provided building stone; there is no reason to believe that they did not continue in production into the late medieval period as defined in this *Handbook*. The identification of the sites of these quarries, which may not have been very extensive, is an ongoing local project, in particular that of the millstone quarry. The lithology of the lower greensand stone at Bignor suggests that it would have been unsuitable for use as millstones, the source for which may have been a quarry in an outlier of Bignor parish, perhaps at Lodsworth, where there is evidence for quern stone production, or possibly at Easebourne (D. Bone pers. comm.). Investigations continue.

[1] These can be accessed at http://www.namho.org under Research.
[2] Its website is http://www.bgs.ac.uk/mineralsUK/buildingStones/StrategicStoneStudy/EH_project.html, with a database accessible at http://mapapps.bgs.ac.uk/buildingStone/BuildingStone.html.

Acknowledgements

I am grateful to many colleagues and friends for help and advice on various aspects of this chapter and for introducing me to other scholars in the field. Especial thanks are due to Professor Stephen Rippon, Dr Peter Claughton, NAMHO, Fred Hartley, D. A. J. Bone, Dr John Williams, and Dr Sally Foster. Steve Rippon and Fred Hartley kindly provided illustrations and Dr Alejandra Gutiérrez redrew Figure 29.1.

References Cited

Allen, J. R. L. 1996 'A possible medieval trade in iron ores in the Severn estuary of south-west Britain', *Medieval Archaeology* 40, 226–9

Austin, D. 1989 'Tin and agriculture in the Middle Ages and beyond: landscape archaeology in St Neot parish, Cornwall', *Cornish Archaeology* 28, 5–251

Ayers, B. S. 1990 'Building a fine city: the provision of flint, mortar and freestone in medieval Norwich', in D. Parsons (ed.), *Stone: quarrying and building in England AD 43–1525*, Phillimore, Chichester, 217–27

Badham, S. and Blacker, G. (eds) 2009 *Northern Rock: the use of Egglestone marble for monuments in medieval England*, British Archaeological Reports British Series 480, Archaeopress, Oxford

Bell, A., Gurney, D., and Healey, H. 1999 *Lincolnshire salterns: excavations at Helpringham, Holbeach St Johns and Bicker Haven*, East Anglian Archaeology 89, Hecklington

Birch, R. and Cordiner, R. 2014 *Building stones of West Sussex*, privately published

Blair, C. and Blair, J. 1991 'Copper alloys', in J. Blair and N. Ramsay (eds), *English medieval industries: craftsmen, techniques, products*, The Hambledon Press, London, 81–106

Blair, J. 1991 'Purbeck marble', in J. Blair and N. Ramsay (eds), *English medieval industries: craftsmen, techniques, products*, The Hambledon Press, London, 41–56

Blair, J. and Ramsay, N. (ed.) 1991 *English medieval industries: craftsmen, techniques, products*, The Hambledon Press, London

Brook, H., Crummy, N., and Archibald, M. M. 2004 'A medieval lead canister from Colchester High Street: hoard container, or floor safe?', *Medieval Archaeology* 48, 131–42

Cadman, G. 1990 'Recent excavations on Saxon and medieval quarries in Raunds, Northamptonshire', in D. Parsons (ed.), *Stone: quarrying and building in England AD 43–1525*, Phillimore, Chichester, 187–206

Campbell, M. 1991 'Gold, silver and precious stones', in J. Blair and N. Ramsay (eds), *English medieval industries: craftsmen, techniques, products*, The Hambledon Press, London, 107–66

Claughton, P. F. 2003 *Silver mining in England and Wales, 1066–1500*, unpublished PhD thesis, University of Exeter

Claughton, P. 2011 'Mineral resources', in J. Crick and E. van Houts (eds), *Social history of England, 900–1200*, Cambridge University Press, Cambridge, 56–65

Cleere, H. and Crossley, D. 1995 *The iron industry of the Weald*, Merton Priory Press, Cardiff (2nd edn)

Dugué, O., Dujardin, L., Leroux, P., and Savary, X. 2010 *La pierre de Caen: des dinosaurs aux cathédrales*, Musée de Normandie, Éditions Charles Corlet, Caen

Dujardin, L. 2009 'Le commerce de la pierre de Caen (XIe–XVIIIe siècle)', in M. Arnoux and A.-M. F. Héricher (eds), *La Normandie dans l'économie européenne (XIIe–XVIIe siècle): colloque de Cerisy-la-Salle (4–8 Octobre 2006)*, Publications du CRAHM, Caen, 139–54

Everson, P. E. and Stocker, D. forthcoming 'Potestas Petri: Barnack in the 10th and 11th centuries', in J. Hall et al. (eds), *Art, architecture and archaeology in Peterborough and the Soke*, British Archaeological Association Conference Proceedings 41

Farmer, D. L. 1992 'Millstones for medieval manors', *Agricultural History Review* 40(2), 97–111

Geddes, J. 1991 'Iron', in J. Blair and N. Ramsay (eds), *English medieval industries: craftsmen, techniques, products*, The Hambledon Press, London, 167–88

Gem, R. 1987 'Canterbury and the cushion capital ...', in N. Stratford (ed.), *Romanesque and Gothic: essays for George Zarnecki*, Boydell and Brewer, Woodbridge, 83–101

Gerrard, S. 2000 *Early British tin industry*, Tempus, Stroud

Hartley, R. F. 1994 'The Tudor miners of Coleorton, Leicestershire', *Bulletin of the Peak Mines Historical Society* 12(3), Matlock Bath, 91–101 (this volume also bears the title *Mining before powder*)

Hartley, R. F. 2007 'Lounge site revisited', in D. Poyner, A. Browning, and K. Lake (eds), *Mining in the landscape: NAMHO 2006 Conference Proceedings*, Shropshire Caving and Mining Club, 25–31

Hartley, R. F. 2015 'Coal mining in medieval Leicestershire', in K. Elkin (ed.), *Medieval Leicestershire: recent research on the medieval archaeology of Leicestershire*, Leicestershire Fieldworkers Monograph 3, Leicester, 195–204

Hatcher, J. 1993 *The history of the British coal industry, vol. 1: before 1700*, Clarendon Press, Oxford

Hobson, T. F. 1926 *Adderbury 'Rectoria'*, Oxfordshire Record Society, Oxford

Homer, R. F. 1991 'Tin, lead and pewter', in J. Blair and N. Ramsay (eds), *English medieval industries: craftsmen, techniques, products*, The Hambledon Press, London, 57–80

Hüglin, S. 2011 'Medieval mortar mixers revisited: Basle and beyond', *Zeitschrift für Archäologie des Mittelalters* 39, 189–212

Hunter, F. 2008 'Jet and related materials in Viking Scotland', *Medieval Archaeology* 52, 103–18

Hurst, J. D. (ed.) 1997 *A multi-period salt production site at Droitwich: excavations at Upwich*, Council for British Archaeology Research Report 107, York

Johnson, D. S. 2010 *Liming and agriculture in the central Pennines: the use of lime in land improvement from the late thirteenth century to c.1900*, British Archaeological Reports British series 525, Oxford

Keen, L. 1988 'Coastal salt production in Norman England', *Anglo-Norman Studies* 11, 133–79

Lyons, A. 2011 *Life and afterlife at Duxford, Cambridgeshire: archaeology and history in a chalkland community*, East Anglian Archaeology 141, Oxford Archaeology East, Oxford

Marsden, P. R. V. 1996 *Ships of the port of London, twelfth to seventeenth centuries AD*, English Heritage, London

McAvoy, F. 1994 'Marine extraction: the excavation of salterns at Wainfleet St Mary, Lincolnshire', *Medieval Archaeology* 38, 134–63

Nayling, N. 1998 *The Magor Pill medieval wreck*, Council for British Archaeology Research Report 115, York

O Brien, D. 2014 *The importation and use of building and other stone in Ireland c.1170–1400*, unpublished MPhil thesis, National University of Ireland, Cork

Ottaway, P. and Rogers, N. 2002 *Craft, industry and everyday life: finds from medieval York*, Archaeology of York 17/15, Council for British Archaeology/York Archaeological Trust, York

Parsons, D. (ed.) 1990 *Stone: quarrying and building in England AD 43–1525*, Phillimore, Chichester

Parsons, D. 1991 'Stone', in J. Blair and N. Ramsay (eds), *English medieval industries: craftsmen, techniques, products*, The Hambledon Press, London, 1–27

Pierce, E. 2013 'Jet cross pendants from the British Isles and beyond: forms, distribution and use', *Medieval Archaeology* 57, 198–211

Ramsay, N. 1991 'Alabaster', in J. Blair and N. Ramsay (eds), *English medieval industries: craftsmen, techniques, products*, The Hambledon Press, London, 29–40

Rippon, S., Claughton, P., and Smart, C. 2009 *Mining in a medieval landscape: the royal silver mines of the Tamar valley*, University of Exeter Press, Exeter

Roberts, E. 1974 'Totternhoe stone and flint in Hertfordshire churches', *Medieval Archaeology* 18, 66–89

Salzman, L. F. 1923 *English industries in the Middle Ages*, University of Oxford Press, Oxford (2nd edn)

Salzman, L. F. 1967 *Building in England down to 1540: a documentary history*, corrected impression, Clarendon Press, Oxford

Senior, J. R. 1990 'Hildenley limestone: a fine quality dimensional and artefact stone from Yorkshire', in D. Parsons (ed.), *Stone: quarrying and building in England AD 43–1525*, Phillimore, Chichester, 147–68

Stanier, P. 2000 *Stone quarry landscapes: the archaeology of quarrying in England*, Tempus, Stroud

Stevens, S. 2008 'Archaeological investigations at the ASDA site, Crawley, West Sussex', *Sussex Archaeological Collections* 146, 107–47

Sutherland, D. S. 2003 *Northamptonshire stone*, Dovecote Press, Wimborne

Tatton-Brown, T. W. T. 1990 'Building stone in Canterbury, c.1070–1525', in D. Parsons (ed.), *Stone: quarrying and building in England AD 43–1525*, Phillimore, Chichester, 70–82

Tatton-Brown, T. W. T. 2001a 'The quarrying and distribution of Reigate stone in the Middle Ages', *Medieval Archaeology* 45, 189–201

Tatton-Brown, T. W. T. 2001b 'La pierre de Caen en Angleterre', in M. Baylé (ed.), *L'architecture normande au Moyen Age*, Presses Universitaires de Caen, Caen, 305–14 (2nd enlarged edn)

Webster, L. E. and Cherry, J. 1978 'Medieval Britain in 1977', *Medieval Archaeology* 22, 142–88

Wilson, D. and Hurst, D. G. 1962–3 'Medieval Britain in 1961', *Medieval Archaeology* 22, 306–49

Worssam, B. and Swift, G. 1987 'Minepits at West Hoathly Brickworks, Sharpthorne, Sussex', *Wealden Iron: Bulletin of the Wealden Iron Research Group*, ser. 2, 7, 3–15

CHAPTER 30

THE MEDIEVAL WORKSHOP

DAVID A. HINTON

THE development of craft specialization is fundamental to Marxist approaches to the past, as it is seen as part of the process by which control of production moves from the individual responsible for his or her own labour to an employer dictating wages and output. Workshops in which individual crafts were practised are a physical manifestation of specialized production, and for many became the norm in the Middle Ages in Britain; factories with power-driven machinery, requiring investment capital for its installation, did not occur, though at the very end of the period a Wiltshire clothier, William Stumpe, set up a manufactory within the buildings of Malmesbury Abbey, Wiltshire, after its dissolution.

A nuanced approach to different scales of craft production was applied to Roman pottery by David Peacock (1982, 8–11) and is now finding a place in medieval studies (e.g. Unger 2004, 11–14). The basic level is 'household' or domestic, with each family unit meeting its own needs. Medieval families were nuclear, with all but the inheriting child normally leaving the parental tenement in adulthood, rather than having siblings and cousins grouped within a compound as in an extended family; the latter is more likely to foster craft production within it, as labour time is more easily pooled. With nearly all work therefore focused entirely on agriculture, most production was not at the domestic level, nor even in the more advanced 'specialized household' level, in which a few people acquire a reputation for having particular skills or knowledge, and exchange their work for whatever they need in compensation for the hours spent in their non-agricultural labour. At least after the eleventh century, most commodities were the work of 'individual workshop' specialists, who devoted nearly all their time to production, even if they also had small-holdings or the right to graze a few beasts on common land.

For some craftspeople, grouping around a resource—clay for potting, iron ore for smelting, stone for memorials and images—was determined by its availability rather than by any perceived benefit of working together, and whether any formalized co-operation took place is generally unknown but unlikely; 'partnerships' and trading companies developed in Italy, not northern Europe (Spufford 2002, 22–4). Occasional sharing of the expense of taking a cart to market probably happened, but casually and sporadically. Grouping themselves in towns close to markets was an advantage for most craftworkers, but although one or two journeymen, apprentices, or artisans might be employed, formalized 'nucleated workshops', with people working together, either with each making the whole product or with different people working on its different production stages, did not occur, except for coin-minting after 1180. Henry II 'centralized' the production of coins in specific buildings in a few towns, some specially built, though unfortunately none of them survives and there are no descriptions. Strict royal control of weights and dies had existed for a long time, and the long-established practice by which each moneyer stamped his own name on his coins so that any deficiencies of weight or alloy could be traced back to him was maintained, so each presumably remained responsible for his own output, despite the oversight of the master and wardens. This changed further after 1279, when individual names ceased to appear, except at the Bury St Edmunds mint, Suffolk. In London, the mint was moved into the Tower; expenditure on the castle's upkeep included '*schoppas* for the moneyers' in the barbican. Even then, the whole coin-making process may not have been confined within the Mint, since 'Sheremoiners Lane' elsewhere in the City seems likely to refer to shearmongers, who cut coin blanks from a cylinder of silver, a new technological process in the thirteenth century (Allen 2012, 41–53; Keene 1990a; North 1960, 8–9). Nevertheless, minting could be viewed as the only medieval equivalent of the 'official/military' mode of production in Peacock's classification, because the Crown otherwise placed contracts or temporarily conscripted a work-force. The final, 'estate', mode can be recognized on some of the great ecclesiastical estates, such as the tileries operated by the bishops of Winchester using service and waged labour (Hare 1991), but on nothing like the Classical scale with its slave economy.

Identifying 'workshops' through the physical record is not straightforward; disposal of unusable waste in rubbish-pits is usually the evidence that products were being made near-by, not recognition of the buildings in which they were made. Residues in late Saxon London attest blacksmithing and copper-alloy production, leather-working for shoes and knife sheaths, bone-working for handles, combs, and pins, textile dyeing, wood-turning for bowls, the finishing of imported stone quern 'blanks', and the minting of silver coins, but not the workshops in which the things were made (Vince 1991). Sometimes concentrations of waste show that a specific tenement was used for a particular craft, as in York's Coppergate, but there the evidence also shows that that use did not extend over several generations (MacGregor et al. 1999, 1919–22); although the name 'Coppergate' derives from 'cup-maker's street', there was no long-term or exclusive focus of that particular activity in it.

Written records relating to trade and commerce were usually concerned with taxation and did not need to do more than list people's names. As surnames did not become fixed until the later part of the thirteenth century, they can usefully reveal crafts by identifying an individual by their occupation rather than by their place of domicile or origin. No document needed to describe their working conditions, however, or even very often exactly where they lived. For only one town does late eleventh-century Domesday Book even give a list of trades—at Bury St Edmunds, Suffolk, were 'bakers, brewers, tailors, washers, shoe-makers, robe-makers, cooks, porters, agents'—a medium-sized town with a diversity of occupations, although the list is clearly incomplete without weavers, tanners, butchers, and others. Medieval London had 175 different trades, Norwich over 130, and Winchester 75 (Rutledge 2004, 157–8). To recognize their work-places is another matter; the cellars that ports in particular had in quantity were surely too dark and cold for much except storage and tavern use, and ground-level timber buildings rarely have evidence of their functions.

Agriculture: Processing and Production

Spaces in rural houses were not set aside for craftwork; farms needed dairies, threshing floors, and brew-houses, to turn milk into cheese and cereals into a product ready for milling into flour for bread or for malting into ale. Outputs could be sold for cash if they did not need to be consumed by the producer's family or used for payment of rent in kind. That money played a major part in rural affairs is testified by the vastly increased numbers of medieval coins now known (see Chapter 32) and peasants used any surplus they accrued to buy craft products in market places, at fairs, or from itinerant pedlars. By-employments included brewing and spinning, the latter attested by spindle-whorls found at excavated rural house sites, the former by occasional malting-ovens dug into the ground, but the hearths on which the pans were boiled are indistinguishable from any others, and indeed were probably multi-functional. Specialist tools may suggest an occasional craft, such as leather-working (Dyer 2012, 326), but no examples of specific rural work-spaces have been found. Personal names in the Lay Subsidy records also show that a few people were known for their non-agricultural work.

Frequent payments of fines recorded in manorial court proceedings reveal widespread ale-brewing. Brewing also took place in towns, and as hopped beer was increasingly preferred to ale from the late fourteenth century, brewing became more specialized; because the drink could be kept longer, more could be brewed at one time, and full-time, male, urban brewers supplanted many female rural part-timers. Many of the former were Dutch, leading to racial tensions and riots, but neither the tensions, nor the bigger barrels, nor the permanent brew-houses, have been found archaeologically, and hops can occur for other reasons (Unger 2004, 99–102).

Rural manor-houses with demesne farms attached had a wider range of out-buildings, such as dovecotes, but crafts other than blacksmithing were rarely practised in them after the eleventh century, although recognition of buildings' functions remains problematic (e.g. Gardiner 2006, 267; see also Chapter 16 in this *Handbook*); their owners, from kings downwards, relied on the market place. The restricted space within medieval castle baileys, as well as the need to control access to them, meant that those were not used by workers other than blacksmiths and occasionally armourers (Kenyon 1990, 157).

Evidence of the latter is, perhaps strangely, best seen at Bordesley Abbey, Worcestershire, where the products of the mill site suggest that the hammers and bellows attached to the wheels were used for production of armour and weapons (Astill 1993). Special-purpose monastic structures include the fulling-troughs at Fountains Abbey, North Yorkshire, but those were probably used, in 'estate production' mode, to produce cloth for the house's own use, not for sale into the wider market.

Grain and meat were of course the main outputs of the countryside, but timber was also very important, and carpenters were numerous and increasingly in demand as quite ordinary farm-houses from the middle of the thirteenth century onwards became more permanent, using joints that took skilled cutting. Also skilled was lathe-turning; some of the preliminary work took place near where the trees were cut down, and the blanks were then stored to dry before finishing. By 1100, the amount of end-waste and cones found in York shows that wood-turners made their bowls and other household items in urban tenements, although seasonal working remains a possibility in view of the quantities likely to have been in demand (Morris 2000, 2198–219). Barrel-coopering using staves was also skilled; the staves were bound with withies, so iron bands did not need to be put on by heat treating, although there are a few late medieval examples, in Lynn, Norfolk, for instance; the same process could be used on cart-wheels, but characteristically that practice is known only because it was banned for being too damaging to road surfaces.

Textiles

The driving force of the English medieval economy was woollen textiles, be it production of raw wool for export to Continental looms or for the internal market; growing flax for linen was more localized, though retting to remove the seeds is attested, with several pits identified (Geary et al. 2005). Processing involved outdoor activity such as washing, followed by carding which could be done indoors or outdoors using coarse combs, the teeth of which are often found, as at Westbury, Buckinghamshire (Ivens et al. 1995, 311), where spindle-whorls also attest spinning, an activity that could be done anywhere using a spindle, distaff, and whorls, also in the house or outside. The task could be put aside immediately if another demanded full attention. The many loom-weights and pin-beaters found on Anglo-Saxon sites show the importance of domestic weaving. Finding the spaces in which the looms were set up is more problematic, however; if many sunken-featured buildings were used as weaving-sheds, they cannot have had any particular advantages as they all but disappeared after the end of the eighth century, while loom-weights show that the vertical, warp-weighted loom remained in use, only slowly joined by the two-beam type (Hamerow 2012, 157–9; Walton Rogers 2007, 30–5).

By the eleventh century, the horizontal loom was coming into use; this piece of plant requires more space and is difficult for the weaver to leave for a few moments to do another task. Its operation therefore became a man's full-time work, though the possibility of earning more money from it would also have pressurized women away from it. That it supplanted the more basic loom is shown by the disappearance from the archaeological record of loom-weights, few even of the twelfth century being found—only a single certainly identifiable piece of one was found at Westbury (Ivens et al. 1995, 317). Spindle-whorls, however, seem not to have been totally displaced when the spinning-wheel appeared, probably towards the end of the thirteenth century in England (Buckland 2012). So engrained was the concept that this was women's work that spinning even with the wheel remained a domestic activity—but not one that demanded a separate household space, as it was portable (but see Standley 2016, 289). Whorls are also found in towns, though with a decrease in numbers, particularly of those made of bone (Walton Rogers 1999, 1964–6); more durable and also heavier stone and lead whorls may indicate that the wheel could not cope with all types of yarn (Woodland 1990).

Fibre washing may have taken place in a few towns; at any rate, wash-houses were to be found in a few large late medieval properties in London (Schofield 1995, 88). Although weaving was mainly an urban activity, its locales and qualities varied over time, but whereas much is known about regulations, and conflicts with merchants (Holt 2000, 89–92), much less is known about the physical conditions in which the weavers worked. Considering how important upper-floor chambers well-lit by glass windows became for post-medieval weavers, it is difficult to envisage how their predecessors coped, though as upper storeys became commoner in the thirteenth century, so presumably they were more likely to use an upstairs chamber with shuttered windows where the street traffic and buildings opposite would not have blocked out so much light. There seems to be no evidence of separate work buildings (Schofield and Vince 1994, 117).

Fulling involved water flows, so was mostly done in the open, in the twelfth century by the physical labour of 'walking' the greasy cloth, in troughs. Mills came into use in the thirteenth century (see Chapter 31) and although no longer seen as having caused a revolution in the industry, certainly changed not only the location of the work but also the status of the fullers themselves: no longer artisans, but by their control of the mills coming also to control the supply of cloth to dyers and merchants. Expensive dyes needed protection from the elements, and to be heated; dye-houses are therefore occasionally found, as in London (Schofield 1995, 213) or Winchester, where streams running along the streets in the low-lying part of the city were channelled into tenements, or Bristol (Figure 30.1). In outbuildings alongside the houses were stone hearths on which lead vats would have been heated so that the dyes could be fixed into the cloths by the heat. The capital investment in the plant involved, and in the purchase of the dyestuffs, explains why the dyers were the wealthiest of those involved in cloth production until supplanted by the fullers. When documents appear giving details of property ownership, it can be seen that some dyers were renting, not owning, their tenements, something which may also reflect their changing status and diminishing capital (Keene 1990b, 208–14). As urban pressures mounted, so extra-mural operations grew: emplacements for tenter racks for drying cloths have been found in the Redcliffe area of Bristol in the Temple fee, for instance, on the opposite side of the River Avon from the walled city.

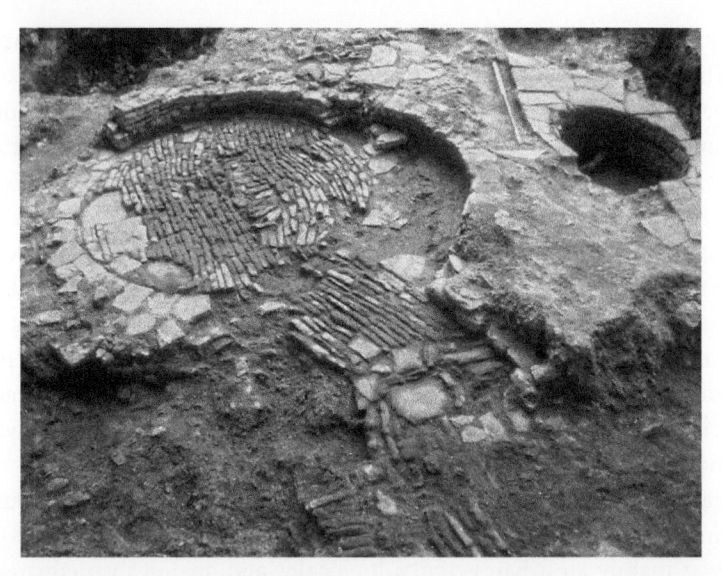

FIGURE 30.1 Excavations at 17, Redcliff Street, Bristol, revealed the remains of a hearth of fourteenth-century date with a pitched stone base and a stoking chamber. This hearth and others like it could have supported vats in which a dye bath was prepared. Cloth would have been dipped directly into the dye or the liquid poured into a separate vat into which the cloth was then added (Alexander 2016)

(© Cotswold Archaeology)

What were probably the bases of dye vats were found in the same area, as were traces of madder, greenweed, weld, and woad—alum was also imported (Jones 1991, 23–7).

One effect of trades grouping in particular centres is that skill levels build up; towns like Lincoln and Stamford, Lincolnshire, gained high reputations for their cloth, which served the upper end of the market. Coarser, cheaper cloths were also produced in towns, but producers could avoid high rents by working in suburbs or out in the countryside. Fulling-mills may not have caused this exodus, but made relocation more feasible, and in the late Middle Ages the Cotswolds, East Anglia, West Yorkshire, and Kent became best known for cloth, with small towns and large villages. Less manorialized economic and social structures facilitated these developments; well-built houses reflect their profitability, but also one of their limitations—profits went into improved living standards and into the purchase of land rather than into reinvestment. Wealthy clothier-middlemen usually bought the weavers' products by the piece, not by paying a wage, and had little incentive to bring workers together under one roof (Zell 1994); in Wiltshire, Stumpe tried and failed.

Metal-Working

Goldsmiths, silversmiths, and dealers in precious gems focused on London, though not exclusively. Again, it is one thing to know where they lived, another to know exactly how they used their premises. For security, they would have been amongst the first to want stone houses, and to work inside them rather than in flimsier outbuildings. The same problem of adequate light would have arisen as for weavers, but with the added need of fire and flame for alloying, annealing, casting, and soldering. Guild control meant that these smiths wanted premises near Goldsmiths' Hall, where from 1300 onwards precious metals were taken to have an assay mark stamped on them to guarantee the quality. Makers' marks followed, and other towns followed London's lead. But no other work was done within the guildhalls; individual premises were maintained, but direct evidence of workshops is lacking. Many were in London's Cheapside, where visitors marvelled at the goods displayed but did not find the buildings themselves worth describing, and inventories reveal tools and stock, but no more (Campbell 1991 for an informed summary).

The other metal trades were little different; copper-alloy workers and pewterers are known from documents, their waste, and occasionally their tools and products, but The Bedern in York can claim to be the only clearly identified foundry site, with wattle buildings and hearths in yards behind houses (Ottaway and Rogers 2002; Hatcher 1973 for the organization of tin and pewter production). Itinerant tinkers with portable equipment mended broken vessels, but also made small dress items, as a cache of unfinished castings found at Hambleden, Buckinghamshire, shows (Babb 1997). Because of the deep pits involved, bell-casting is very recognizable, but close to the church where the bells were to be installed, as presumably in Winchester where a thirteenth-century pit was close to the cathedral (Davies and Ovenden 1990, 110–12), not in permanent workshops. The founders also cast metal vessels, as mould fragments were found with bell-casting debris at Chichester and Worcester (Down 1978, 164–9; Taylor 1996). As both tin and lead are mined in England, pewter was a significant product, but its workshops have not been explored.

Blacksmiths and farriers must have been the most numerous of the metal-workers, in both villages and towns; in twelfth-century Wiltshire, for instance, there were at least three among the eighty-two tenants on Shaftesbury Abbey's large Tisbury estate, and there were probably four within Bradford-on-Avon, then emerging as a small town as well as a demesne and ecclesiastical centre (Hinton 2011, 196–7, and 186–96 for Anglo-Saxon smithing and smelting in general). Later medieval evidence in the archaeological record is surprisingly slight, augmented recently by the discovery of a smelting and smithing site in Melksham Forest, Wiltshire, where ore and fuel were readily available and perhaps beyond direct manorial control. A two-cell timber building, pits, and a platform of limestone slabs would probably not have allowed the operation to have been identified, but hearth bottoms and slags revealed its uses. Although no smelting furnaces were located, some of the slag derived from tapping outflow, a more complex system than the simple bowl type where the slag collects in the pit bottom (Hardy and Dungworth 2014). A different control system seems likely to have been behind the small smelting operation within the manorial complex at Alsted, Surrey, which seems an exception to the general rule that these enclosures were non-industrial: there, bowl furnaces seem to have sufficed (Ketteringham 1971), probably little different in appearance from the isolated works at Minepit Wood, Sussex. Here a low-temperature roasting furnace seemingly without a cover building prepared ore for the high-temperature smelting furnace a few yards away, which was protected by a rectangular post-built shed—as there was no roof-tile debris, thatch was used despite the fire risk, perhaps coated with clay for protection (Money 1971; the reconstruction drawing shows a polygonal structure over the furnace, which does not seem justified by the excavation plan; see Cleere and Crossley 1985 for a summary of Wealden production). Demand for iron for guns stimulated working in the late Middle Ages, and although the first blast furnace is known from documents not archaeology, Bordesley Abbey is not the only site to show that water-power was used (see Chapter 31).

Surprisingly little evidence of rural blacksmiths' forges has been found; accumulated slag was until recently the best clue to their presence, but slag gets spread as hardcore, and the actual sites of the smithing operation can now be detected by analysis in soil residues of hammerscale from the sparks flying off the iron. A late fourteenth- or early fifteenth-century example at Goltho, Lincolnshire, was a rectangular structure with timber posts resting on padstones that enclosed a hearth, the base on which the anvil stood, and a clay-lined water-pit necessary for cooling and annealing the iron (Beresford 1975, 46). Despite the problems of avoiding incorporation of sulphur into the iron, the smith there seems to have used coal; most would have used charcoal. A thirteenth-century forge at Newington, Oxfordshire, had good evidence that it was a three-sided building—not only improving the light but giving better access for horses to be shod. It too had a water-bosh, hearths, and an anvil setting (Williams 2012). Anvils in these smithies were probably stone rather than wrought iron or wooden blocks into which iron 'stakes' were driven—the last would have been all right for nails and finer work, but not for ploughshares and shoes.

Carcass Products

After butchery, animal parts provided raw materials for various workers—'secondary products' because the beasts' primary uses ceased after their meat had been taken. Of all medieval crafts, tanning of the skins is most likely to leave its traces in the archaeological record because it involved water-filled pits, and wide spaces where the hides could be stretched out or hung in preparation for preliminary de-fleshing and subsequent scraping down; for both those reasons, and because of the stench, it was usually a fringe, though not necessarily an extra-mural, activity. Tanning was carried out on at least one tenement in eleventh-century Winchester's Tanner Street, using the streams in that low-lying part of the city. Pits, two of them timber-lined, were fed by water channels so that hides could be soaked in them; one retained traces of cross-beams from which the skins would have hung. The area went up-market, however, and the tanners had to move out, leaving behind copious residues of animal hair and insect larvae from oak trees, the bark of which is used in the tanning process (Keene 1990b). Elsewhere, in the area of Bristol where much evidence of textile dyeing was found, tanning is suggested by lime deposits found at the bottom of well-preserved barrels sunk into the ground (Jones 1991, 23–7). Contraction of late medieval towns allowed a few tanners to move back inside the walls, though still in peripheral locations; this happened in Northampton in an area left derelict after a fire, allowing tanners to sink clay-lined pits (Shaw 1996: see also Thomson and Mould 2011). In Kent, more affected by the London market than most counties, tanning became rural (Semple 2006), a comparable process to its weaving. Winchester documents reveal that parchment-makers worked amongst the tanners, though their skins would have been washed and scraped, not put through the tanning-pits. Consequently they were less obnoxious and did not move out of the area, but instead took precedence over butchers in Flesmangere Street, which in the late thirteenth century became Parchment Street. The name survived despite the trade moving out only some fifty years later (Cameron and Mould 2011, 97; Keene 1985, 287–8).

The resulting leather went to shoe- and boot-makers, belt- and sheath-makers, saddlers, and makers of jugs and bottles, and of gloves (Cherry 1991); their offcuts survive in waterlogged deposits such as the lowest fills of pits, and some of their tools were specialized. York's Girdlergate Street, not recorded before the 1380s, shows the importance of strap-making; knife sheaths were important dress items, and elaborate and up-to-date designs were pressed into many (Mould et al. 2003). Untanned leather was also used, for gloves and other finer skin products, but no differences in workshop requirements resulted. A few skinned cats show furriers at work, with an occasional fox and other wild animals, and much larger quantities of rabbits in the later Middle Ages (see Chapters 8 and 10).

Bone and horns supplied a number of workers with the raw material for combs, knife-handles, and a wide range of products even including high-status caskets or chess pieces (Figure 30.2). Although in theory anyone can whittle a skate or a penny whistle, even a knife-handle requires a degree of craftsmanship, and some products, notably composite combs, required metal rivets to hold the pieces together, involving a further skill. Antler

FIGURE 30.2 Recent finds of twelfth-century antler carving found during excavation in Northampton include these unfinished chess pieces and large amounts of offcuts near a building that could represent the workshop itself

(© MOLA)

was also used, presumably brought into towns by country people who had foraged it, as the workers would not have had time to search it out for themselves. Ivory, whether walrus or elephant, was a much rarer commodity, for chess pieces and the like, and would not have been wasted on second-rate craftworkers; no offcuts have been found in York, for example (MacGregor et al. 1999, 1916). The twelfth century saw greater emphasis on products: general-purpose boneworkers became handle-makers, for instance, using wood as well as bone. They still did not need to work in specialized groups, however, nor to have anything but a small workshop within a house, and are never recognizable archaeologically. Nevertheless, Girdlergate shows that even in the fourteenth century some associations were made, and the name also shows how it was the product that caught the attention.

Stone, Mineral, and Clay Products

Much of the work of shaping stone for buildings and tombs was done in bankers' sheds at the quarries (see Chapter 29), with finishing at the building site—workshops were more or less permanent at the great monasteries and cathedrals. Domestic production of mortars and querns in nearby house plots in places like Corfe, Dorset, indicates a useful by-employment for the workers, indicated by discarded failures. Tombs were carved at the quarries, though brasses might be fitted to them later. Most masons worked away from home at the building sites; again, a few were employed by a master, but not on a permanent basis, and apart from a few tracing-floors in grand churches, their working conditions do not survive. Occasionally deep pits, needed for slaking lime to make mortar, are found, like a late thirteenth-century example at Southampton, Hampshire, which had three flues/rake-out shafts from ground level leading down to what in a late phase was an impressive stone-lined feature with three radiating stone flues on the bottom, ensuring a flow of air. Probably also concerned with construction were a number of pottery vessels in the upper fill; although no different in form from pots used for liquids and cooking, these contained traces of pitch that would have been used for tarring timbers, either inside the castle or for ships, as the sea was only a few yards away (Oxley 1986, 52–68, 103–6; also Kenyon 1990, 163–6). Ship-building and -repairing were shore-line activities, with boats raised on chocks and therefore leaving little evidence; a dry dock at Portsmouth, Hampshire, is a rare medieval exception (Fox and Barton 1986).

In a few places in the West Midlands in England, brine springs allow salt to be extracted, and in Nantwich, Cheshire, excavation found two solid late twelfth-century buildings that housed clay-lined or timber troughs in which the brine was stored after being brought in by a wooden aqueduct from the spring. Barrels sunk into the ground may have served the same purpose. After it had settled, some of the water could be drawn off before the rest was transferred to lead vats for boiling on large hearths until only salt remained, which was then transferred into large conical wicker baskets for transport on pack-horses—barrels were probably used for taking the salt by cart, but documents show both carriage systems being used (McNeil 1983). At Droitwich, Worcestershire, the hearths were stone-lined and elm pipes were used, with a pump to move the brine from the well-spring into the troughs; dendrochronology of the timbers lining the well-shaft gave a felling date of 1264, which fits with documentary records of the need to repair it. One of the fifteenth-century pump-shafts still had its iron piston inside (Hurst 1997). Sea-salt also involved large troughs and hearths; most medieval settling-ponds and the like have disappeared under later development and by erosion, though a filtration unit was excavated at Wainfleet St Mary, Lincolnshire, which used peat to filter out sand (McAvoy 1994). Mounds of filtered sand sometimes survive, with pits and ditches perhaps associated, as at Lymington, Hampshire (Powell 2009).

Britain had a few resources such as amber and jet, so the debris of bead-working is sometimes found; for the religious these were 'Paternosters' for counting off prayers. Small pendant crucifixes were also made, as were dice for the irreligious. The raw materials were also imported, so nowhere had a monopoly, although distribution suggests Whitby, North Yorkshire, as a production centre (Pierce 2013).

Glass had been made in Anglo-Saxon England, but apparently not in the Norman period. Its re-introduction depended on recognition of suitable sands, for their silica content, as well as plant ash for potash, although for some purposes marine ash is better. Iron oxide in sand gave a green tinge to the glass. Demand for church windows stimulated migrants to establish furnaces, the earliest recorded being in Surrey in 1226. Thereafter small-scale works were scattered through the Weald, opening and closing according to demand, and difficult to locate. Some vessels and lamps were produced, but British materials did not allow for Italian and other imports to be challenged (Hunter 1981; Tyson 2000).

In contrast to glass vessels marketed to the top end of society, pottery suffered from being made from a humble material considered inappropriate for religious use in chalices and therefore unlikely to be acceptable on top tables generally. A few eleventh-century kiln sites are known in the countryside, for instance at Michelmersh, Hampshire, and Domesday Book recorded three groups of potters paying to dig clay and take fuel; excavated urban kilns in Lincoln, Stamford, and other 'Danelaw' towns did not get entries in the Book, however. Stamford enjoyed high-quality refractory clay especially suitable for crucibles; it was naturally very white and eye-catchingly glossy with an external lead glaze, and production continued at least to the end of the twelfth century. Those pots were fired in kilns that had raised oven floors with flue-bars that gave good hot air circulation when the pots were stacked on them. High rents, fire risks, and the need for large amounts of fuel and water as well as for clay and tempers all militated against a low-value item being produced in towns, however. Instead, rural production was of cooking wares and a few glazed jugs, fired in earth-floored firing chambers that involved less time and effort to make than did updraught ovens. Occasionally, a potter attempted to establish a kiln within a town, closer to the market, but these enterprises were short-lived, like that of a potter from the large works at Laverstock, Wiltshire, who attempted to establish himself just inside the walls of Salisbury around 1300 (Algar and Saunders 2014). Against the general grain, potters established themselves in the thirteenth century in the small town of Kingston-on-Thames, well-placed to use the river to ship their products down to a seemingly ever-expanding London. Yet in the fourteenth century, when demand changed, they were ousted by rural producers around Cheam, Surrey, and by overseas imports.

Some roof-tiles and ridge-crests were produced in the same kilns as pots. Floor-tiles' appearance mattered, however, and raised oven floors were necessary to get the hot air circulation that was needed for even glazing. The general pattern seems to have been that overseas tilers were brought in to work on particular church or royal palace contracts, and that they trained native workers who spread their ideas. In the second half of the thirteenth century, growing demand for cheap floor-tiles in lesser churches and other buildings led to kiln complexes with longer lives being established, at Danbury, Essex, for instance, where small buildings were where the tiles were made, before stacking inside double-flue tile-lined chambers (Drury and Pratt 1975, 95–111). These involved investment of time to make, and large loads were needed for the work to be economic. A complex at Penn, Buckinghamshire, has not been excavated, but Lay Subsidy Rolls show that the tilers and paviours were independent workers, owning a few taxable items such as a horse, two cows, two pigs, and small amounts of grain as well as stocks of a few thousand tiles, and lime; they were not at the bottom of society, but were far from prosperous (Hohler 1941–6, 23). Their dependence on contracts at Windsor and in London contrasts with the paid and service workers on the Winchester estates, although the bishopric was also buying tiles on the open market (Hare 1991).

Conclusion

Recent excavations have not yielded much new direct evidence of workshops, and the main developments have been in analyses, distribution studies, and considerations of the financial values and personal meanings of medieval objects. Recognition of a site's function may be uncertain: 'one hearth or vat base looks very much like another' (Schofield and Vince 1994, 119). Pitched-tile hearth-bases might be for large-scale baking, for brewing, or for dyeing—and could be multi-functional. Even size is not necessarily a guide, as communal ovens in villages like Wharram Percy, documented though not excavated (Wrathmell 2012, 342), were presumably larger than domestic ovens, but were not commercial enterprises. Nor are documents necessarily entirely helpful; words such as *furna* are not used for specific types of ovens or furnaces.

Another terminological issue is that documents do not necessarily distinguish between a working and a retail space when using 'shop' (Grenville 1997, 172; Keene 1990a, 31–2; see Chapter 20 in this *Handbook*); fifteenth-century references in Bristol to 'shop-houses' were not to workshops, but to buildings with at least one upper storey and no open hall (Leech 2000). A study of Lavenham, Suffolk, where many fifteenth-century buildings survive to reflect the area's cloth prosperity, has suggested that window-sills were higher in workshops to maximize the amount of light reaching the work-space, whereas retailers' shops had lower sills so that goods could be seen from the outside. The former did not need external shutters that could be lowered to make a stall in front of the building during the day (Alston 2004). Slightly sloping fixed counters in the upper Rows in Chester, Cheshire, suggest that they were standard provision at least by the end of the thirteenth century. Ground-level terraced rows can still be seen in several towns, as in York's Goodramgate, or Tewkesbury, Gloucestershire, both of which fringe churchyards so have very limited rear space, but could house craftworkers as well as journeymen, and even better-off artisans, giving each a small room on the street frontages; inside the booths, however, tailors, cobblers, and others could ply their craft without leaving any archaeological trace (Quiney 2003, 245–50). Such rooms might even be let out separately.

Most workshops were 'individual', small scale, and often temporary in their use. Only the cloth industry had the capacity to raise the capital required for substantial investment, but although credit was available even to the less well-off, dogma discouraged the use of money for the creation of more wealth rather than for purchasing—of land, animal stock, and socially desirable commodities—despite the interaction of the Church with the market (Dyer 1998). Small producers operated within a money-using economy, but their limitations were one of the factors affecting the extent to which commerce could become a 'prime mover' in medieval systems (Rigby 2006). 'Proto-industrialization' might be seen in the specialization that some towns became known for, such as Walsall, West Midlands, for riding equipment, Thaxted, Essex, for knives, or Walden, Essex, for saffron, but these did not become centres for investment and the extinguishing of competition for their products (Britnell 2006; Zell 1994). Nor were the needs of equipment for warfare more than a temporary boost even for ship-building and ordnance towards the end of the period; although they were financed by a 'domain state' with wider geographical considerations that might have been more conducive to long-term entrepreneurial activity, the disruptions of wars were probably as damaging to trade as the Black Death and its concomitant population decline, limiting the size of the market. Sumptuary legislation in the fifteenth century began to express mercantilist views, seeking to protect home producers from foreign competition, a sign of changes to come, but not yet of any substantial movement towards the growth of capitalism.

REFERENCES CITED

Alexander, M. (ed.) 2016 *Medieval and post-medieval occupation and industry in the Redcliffe suburb of Bristol: excavations at 1–2 and 3 Redcliff Street, 2003–2010*, Cotswold Archaeology Monograph 8, Cirencester

Algar, D. and Saunders, P. 2014 'A medieval pottery kiln in Salisbury', *Wiltshire Archaeological and Natural History Society Magazine* 107, 148–55

Allen, M. 2012 *Mints and money in medieval England*, Cambridge University Press, Cambridge

Alston, L. 2004 'Late medieval workshops in East Anglia', in P. S. Barnwell, M. Palmer, and M. Airs (eds), *The vernacular workshop: from craft to industry 1400–1900*, Council for British Archaeology Research Report 140, York, 38–59

Astill, G. G. 1993 *A medieval industrial complex and its landscape: the metalworking watermills and workshops of Bordesley Abbey*, Council for British Archaeology Research Report 92, York

Babb, L. 1997 'A thirteenth-century brooch hoard from Hambledon, Buckinghamshire', *Medieval Archaeology* 41, 233–6

Beresford, G. 1975 *The medieval clay-land village: excavations at Goltho and Barton Blount*, The Society for Medieval Archaeology Monograph 6, London

Britnell, R. 2006 'Town life', in R. Horrox and W. M. Ormrod (eds), *A social history of England 1200–1500*, Cambridge University Press, Cambridge, 134–78

Buckland, K. 2012 'Spinning wheels', in G. Owen-Crocker, E. Coatsworth, and M. Hayward (eds), *Encyclopaedia of medieval dress and textiles of the British Isles, c.450–1450*, Brill, Leiden/Boston, 539–41

Cameron, E. A. and Mould, Q. 2011 'Devil's crafts and dragon's skins?', in M. Clegg Hyer and G. R. Owen-Crocker (eds), *The material culture of daily living in the Anglo-Saxon world*, Exeter University Press, Exeter, 93–115

Campbell, M. 1991 'Gold, silver and precious stones', in J. Blair and N. Ramsay (eds), *English medieval industries: craftsmen, techniques, products*, The Hambledon Press, London, 107–66

Cherry, J. 1991 'Leather', in J. Blair and N. Ramsay (eds), *English medieval industries: craftsmen, techniques, products*, The Hambledon Press, London, 295–318

Cleere, H. and Crossley, D. 1985 *The iron industry of the Weald*, Leicester University Press, Leicester

Davies, R. M. and Ovenden, P. J. 1990 'Bell-founding in Winchester in the tenth to thirteenth centuries', in M. Biddle, *Object and economy in medieval Winchester*, Winchester Studies 7ii, Clarendon Press, Oxford, 100–22

Down, A. 1978 *Chichester excavations III*, Phillimore, Chichester

Drury, P. J. and Pratt, G. D. 1975 'A late thirteenth- and early fourteenth-century tile factory at Danbury, Essex', *Medieval Archaeology* 19, 92–164

Dyer, C. 1998 'Trade, towns and the Church', in T. R. Slater and G. Rosser (eds), *The Church in the medieval town*, Ashgate, Aldershot, 55–75

Fox, R. and Barton, K. J. 1986 'Excavations at Oyster Street, Portsmouth, Hampshire, 1968–71', *Post-Medieval Archaeology* 20, 31–255

Dyer, C. 2012 'The late medieval village of Wharram Percy: farming the land', in S. Wrathmell (ed.), *A history of Wharram and its neighbours*, Wharram, a study of settlement on the Yorkshire Wolds 13, York University Archaeological Publications 15, York, 312–27

Gardiner, M. 2006 'Implements and utensils in *Gerefa* and the organisation of seigneurial farmsteads in the High Middle Ages', *Medieval Archaeology* 50, 260–7

Geary, B. R., Hall, A. R., Kenward, H., Bunting, M. J., Lillie, M. C., and Carrott, J. 2005 'Recent palaeoenvironmental evidence for the processing of hemp in eastern England during the medieval period', *Medieval Archaeology* 49, 317–22

Grenville, J. 1997 *Medieval housing*, Leicester University Press, London/Washington

Hamerow, H. 2012 *Rural settlements and society in Anglo-Saxon England*, Medieval History and Archaeology, Oxford University Press, Oxford

Hardy, A. and Dungworth, D. 2014 'Medieval iron production near Melksham', *Wiltshire Archaeological and Natural History Society* 107, 118–45

Hare, J. N. 1991 'The growth of the roof-tile industry in late medieval Wessex', *Medieval Archaeology* 35, 86–103

Hatcher, J. 1973 *English tin production and trade before 1550*, Clarendon Press, Oxford

Hinton, D. A. 2011 'Weland's work: metals and metalsmiths', in M. Clegg Hyer and G. R. Owen-Crocker (eds), *The material culture of daily living in the Anglo-Saxon world*, Exeter University Press, Exeter, 185–200

Hohler, C. 1941–6 'Medieval pavingtiles in Buckinghamshire', *Records of Buckinghamshire* 14, 1–49

Holt, R. 2000 'Society and population', in D. M. Palliser (ed.), *The Cambridge urban history of Britain. Vol. I: 600–1540*, Cambridge University Press, Cambridge, 79–104

Hunter, J. R. 1981 'The medieval glass industry', in D. Crossley (ed.), *Medieval industries*, Council for British Archaeology Research Report 40, York, 143–50

Hurst J. D. (ed.) 1997 *A multi-period salt production site at Droitwich: excavations at Upwich*, Council for British Archaeology Research Report 107, York

Ivens, R., Busby, P., and Shepherd, N. 1995 *Tattenhoe and Westbury: two deserted medieval settlements*, Buckinghamshire Archaeological Society Monograph Series 8, Aylesbury

Jones, R. H. 1991 'Industry and environment in medieval Bristol', in G. L. Good, R. H. Jones, and M. W. Ponsford (eds), *Waterfront archaeology: proceedings of the Third International Conference, Bristol, 1988*, Council for British Archaeology Research Report 74, York, 19–26

Keene, D. 1985 *Survey of medieval Winchester*, Winchester Studies 2, Clarendon Press, Oxford

Keene, D. 1990a 'Shops and shopping in medieval London', in L. Grant (ed.), *Medieval art, architecture and archaeology in London*, British Archaeological Association Conference Transactions, 29–46

Keene, D. 1990b 'The textile industry', in M. Biddle, *Object and economy in medieval Winchester*, Winchester Studies 7ii, Clarendon Press, Oxford, 200–14

Kenyon, J. R. 1990 *Medieval fortifications*, Leicester University Press, Leicester/London

Ketteringham, L. 1971 *Alsted: excavation of a thirteenth-/fourteenth-century sub-manor house with its ironworks in Netherne Wood, Merstham, Surrey*, Surrey Archaeological Society Research Volume 2, Guildford

Leech, R. H. 2000 'The symbolic hall: historical context and merchant culture in the early modern city', *Vernacular Architecture* 31, 1–10

MacGregor, A., Mainman, A. J., and Rogers, N. S. H. 1999 *Bone, antler, ivory and horn from Anglo-Scandinavian and medieval York*, The Archaeology of York 17/12, Council for British Archaeology, York

McAvoy, F. 1994 'Marine salt extraction; the excavation of salterns at Wainfleet St Mary, Lincolnshire', *Medieval Archaeology* 38, 134–63

McNeil, R. 1983 'Two twelfth-century wich houses in Nantwich, Cheshire', *Medieval Archaeology* 27, 40–88

Money, J. H. 1971 'Medieval iron-workings in Minepit Wood, Rotherfield, Sussex', *Medieval Archaeology* 15, 86–111

Morris, C. A. 2000 *Wood and woodworking in Anglo-Scandinavian and medieval York*, The Archaeology of York 17/5, Council for British Archaeology, York

Mould, Q., Carlisle, I., and Cameron, E. A. 2003 *Craft, industry and everyday life: leather and leatherworking in Anglo-Scandinavian and medieval York*, The Archaeology of York 17/16, Council for British Archaeology, York

North, J. J. 1960 *Medieval hammered coinage. Vol. 2, Edward I to Charles II 1272–1662*, Spink and Son, London

Ottaway, P. and Rogers, N. S. H. 2002 *Craft, industry and everyday life: finds from medieval York*, The Archaeology of York 17/15, Council for British Archaeology, York

Oxley, J. (ed.) 1988 *Excavations at Southampton Castle*, Southampton City Museums, Southampton

Peacock, D. P. S. 1982 *Pottery in the Roman world: an ethnoarchaeological approach*, Longman, London/New York

Pierce, E. 2013 'Jet cross pendants from the British Isles and beyond: forms, distribution and use', *Medieval Archaeology* 57, 198–211

Powell, A. B. 2009 'Two thousand years of salt making at Lymington, Hampshire', *Proceedings of the Hampshire Field Club and Archaeological Society* 64, 9–40

Quiney, A. 2003 *Town houses of medieval Britain*, Yale University Press, New Haven/London

Rigby, S. H. 2006 'Introduction: social structure and economic change in late medieval England', in R. Horrox and W. M. Ormrod (eds), *A social history of England 1200–1500*, Cambridge University Press, Cambridge, 1–30

Rutledge, E. 2004 'Economic life', in C. Rawcliffe and R. Wilson (eds), *Medieval Norwich*, Hambledon Press, London and New York, 157–88

Schofield, J. 1995 *Medieval London houses*, Yale University Press, New Haven/London

Schofield, J. and Vince, A. 1994 *Medieval towns*, Leicester University Press, London

Semple, J. 2006 'The tanners of Wrotham manor 1400–1600', *Archaeologia Cantiana* 126, 1–26

Shaw, M. 1996 'The excavation of a late fifteenth- to seventeenth-century tanning complex at The Green, Northampton', *Post-Medieval Archaeology* 30, 63–127

Spufford, P. 2002 *Power and profit: the merchant in medieval Europe*, Thames and Hudson, London

Standley, E. R. 2016 'Spinning yarns: the archaeological evidence for hand spinning and its social implications, c. AD 1200–1500', *Medieval Archaeology* 60(2), 266–99

Taylor, G. 1996 'Medieval bronze founding at Deansway, Worcester', *Journal of Historical Metallurgy* 30(2), 103–10

Thomson, R. and Mould, Q. (eds) 2011 *Leather tanneries: the archaeological evidence*, Archetype Publications, London

Tyson, R. 2000 *Medieval glass vessels found in England c. AD 1200–1500*, Council for British Archaeology Research Report 121, York

Unger, R. W. 2004 *Beer in the Middle Ages and the Renaissance*, University of Pennsylvania Press, Philadephia

Vince, A. (ed.) 1991 *Aspects of Saxo-Norman London: II. Finds and environmental evidence*, London and Middlesex Archaeological Society Special Paper 12, London

Walton Rogers, P. 1999 'Textile making equipment', in A. MacGregor, A. J. Mainman, and N. S. H. Rogers, *Bone, antler, ivory and horn from Anglo-Scandinavian and medieval York*, The Archaeology of York 17/12, Council for British Archaeology, York, 1964–71

Walton Rogers, P. 2007 *Cloth and clothing in early Anglo-Saxon England AD 450–700*, Council for British Archaeology, York

Williams, G. 2012 'Where are all the smiths? Some reflections on the excavation of rural blacksmithing', *Institute for Archaeologists Diggers' Forum Newsletter* 10, 20–4

Woodland, M. 1990 'Spindle-whorls', in M. Biddle, *Object and economy in medieval Winchester*, Winchester Studies 7ii, Clarendon Press, Oxford, 216–25

Wrathmell, S. 2012 *A history of Wharram Percy and its neighbours*, Wharram: a Study of Settlement on the Yorkshire Wolds 13, York University Archaeological Publications, York

Zell, M. 1994 *Industry in the countryside: Wealden society in the sixteenth century*, Cambridge University Press, Cambridge

CHAPTER 31

WATER AND WIND POWER

COLIN RYNNE

THE inhabitants of most urban and rural communities in both Britain and Ireland during the later medieval period would have lived a relatively short distance from either a watermill or windmill. Some 6082 watermills are recorded in the Domesday survey of 1086 (Darby 1977, 361) which, if anything, is an underestimate of the milling capacity of late eleventh-century England, as many mills in northern counties were not enumerated (Holt 1988; Langdon 2004, 9). In Ireland around 153 mill sites, mostly horizontal-wheeled mills, dated to AD 613–1124 (Rynne 2013), have been recorded to date and, based also on the documentary record, must surely have existed in their thousands before the advent of the Anglo-Normans in 1169. Between ten thousand and fifteen thousand watermills and windmills are estimated to have been operating in Britain by *c.*1300 (Langdon 2004, 171). Of these, upward of some four thousand mills are believed to have been windmills (Langdon 1992, 55) which only come into use from the 1180s onwards.

Even the most basic water-powered installation required expensive and often elaborate preparatory groundworks. The *mill system* was designed to abstract and direct a supply of water from an adjacent, natural water source to the mill-works. The source of water might include natural springs, small streams, and rivers and even, from at least the seventh century AD in Britain and Ireland, water impounded from tidal estuaries. In most cases, this entailed the construction of artificial impounding and diversion elements (dams and weirs), water-courses (head and tail-race channels), and storage reservoirs (millponds). In landscape terms, the creation of a hydraulic system for any variety of watermill could be spread over several acres, alternately draining or irrigating the areas through which the artificial feeder channel for the mill was led. From the early medieval period onwards the law codes of regions as far distant as early medieval Ireland and the Germanic kingdoms of post-Roman Europe were obliged to regulate the working environment of watermills (Rynne 2015b). Windmills, on the other hand, while a useful supplement to watermills where sources of hydraulic energy were either unavailable or unsuitable, suffered from the disadvantage of being unable to store their energy.

Watermill Types

Horizontal Mills

In *horizontal-wheeled* mills (Figure 31.1) the water wheel is set in the horizontal plane and turned the upper millstone, directly, without intermediate gearing via a vertical driveshaft. In most cases a small storage reservoir, or millpond, would be formed by impounding an adjacent natural watercourse, or springs, through the construction of a rudimentary dam with a core of earth and stone reveted with either timber planks or stone walling. From this latter the water was led in an open channel, or headrace, to the millworks. Before the water was allowed to strike the waterwheel it was directed into a large chute hollowed-out from a tree-trunk. As the drive to the rotating upper millstone was direct, one revolution of the waterwheel produced a corresponding revolution of the millstone. There are basically two different paddle types. In the first, the paddle has a complicated dished or spoon-shaped profile, which has been recorded throughout early medieval Ireland and at a number of pre-tenth century English sites

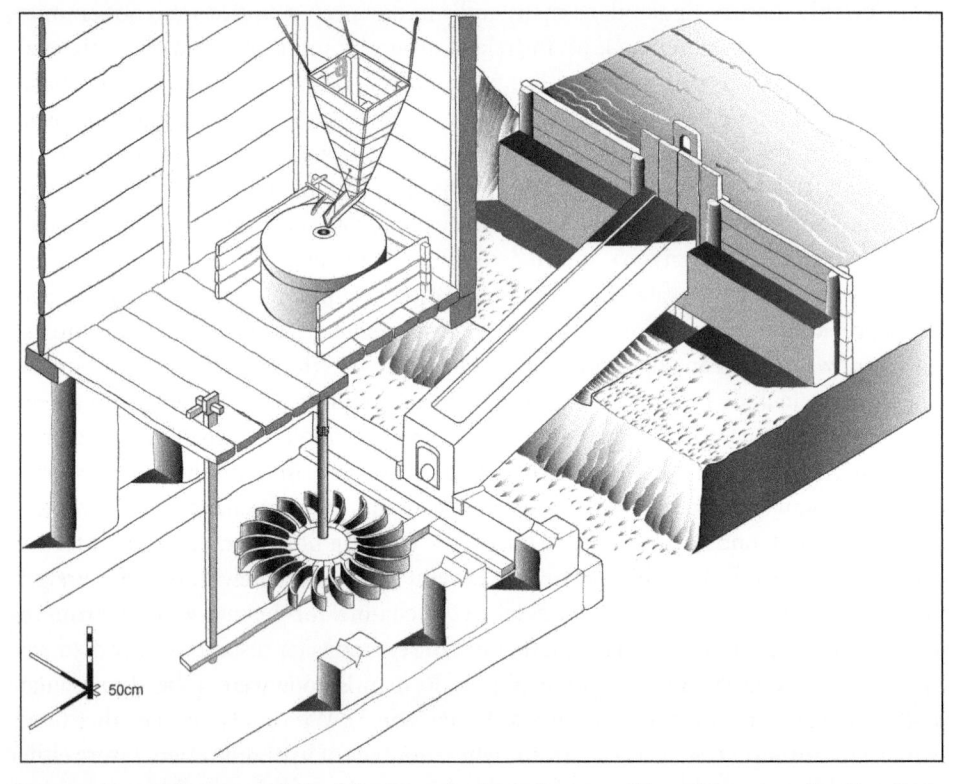

FIGURE 31.1 Reconstruction of horizontal-wheeled watermill at Cloontycarthy, Co. Cork, Ireland, dendro-dated to AD 833

(© Colin Rynne)

such as at Northfleet, Kent, and Tamworth, Staffordshire (Rahtz and Meeson 1992; Watts and Hardy 2011). However, the earliest recorded paddle form, from Nendrum Mill 1, in County Down, Ireland, is of a second variety, the inclined flat-vaned paddle. Both forms now appear to have existed contemporaneously (Rynne 2015a).

There can be little doubt that horizontal mills continued to be used in Gaelic and gaelicized areas of Ireland throughout the high medieval period, even though vertical-wheeled mills (see the following section) are likely to have been favoured within the Anglo-Norman colony (Rynne 1998; 2011). On mainland Britain, with the exception of Scotland and the northern isles of Orkney and Shetland, continuity of use has hitherto been difficult to prove (Fenton 1978). Indeed, many historians, based solely on the absence of references to them in the written sources, have been perhaps a little too quick to rule out continuity of use (Holt 1988; Langdon 2004). However, while the documentary evidence, as John Langdon has asserted, 'seems to be entirely unambiguous' in this regard (Langdon 2004: 72), this would also appear to be the case for the admittedly sparser manorial records from the Anglo-Norman lordship of Ireland. The discovery of a thirteenth-century horizontal-wheeled example at Corcannon, County Wexford (dendrochronology *c*. AD 1228), within a heavily feudalized area of the Anglo-Norman lordship of Ireland, on the other hand, tells a rather different story (Rynne 1998). There is also, indeed, a growing body of archaeological evidence for the continued use of horizontal-wheeled mills in northern England during the late Saxon and early Norman periods (Moorhouse 2003a; 2003b). The written sources have always been notoriously unreliable with regard to the types of waterwheel employed in early and later medieval Europe, even in regions where horizontal-wheeled forms became the seigneurial mill.

Vertical Watermills

In *vertical watermills* the axle is set horizontally (Figure 31.2), which required the use of intermediate gearing to transmit the motion of the axle, indirectly, to the millstones. The use of intermediate gear transmission provided it with the added advantage of being able to be either geared up or down to suit its water supply. It was, therefore, inherently more flexible than horizontal wheeled forms and could be used with a wider and more challenging range of water sources. The three basic types of vertical waterwheel (*undershot*, *breast shot*, and *overshot*) used during the later medieval period are all archaeologically attested in the Roman world (Wikander 2000; 2008). In medieval Europe as a whole, however, the overwhelming majority of the excavated early and later medieval vertical watermill sites employed undershot waterwheels.

Undershot wheels were generally found on sites in low-lying areas, where the fall of water was negligible, such as large rivers or tidal estuaries, or in mills built on bridges in urban areas. Based upon both surviving fragments of waterwheel rims and known paddle widths, most early and later medieval undershot waterwheels recorded in Europe consisted of a single rim, into which either single piece or composite paddle blades were morticed. Individual rim segments were usually assembled together using lap

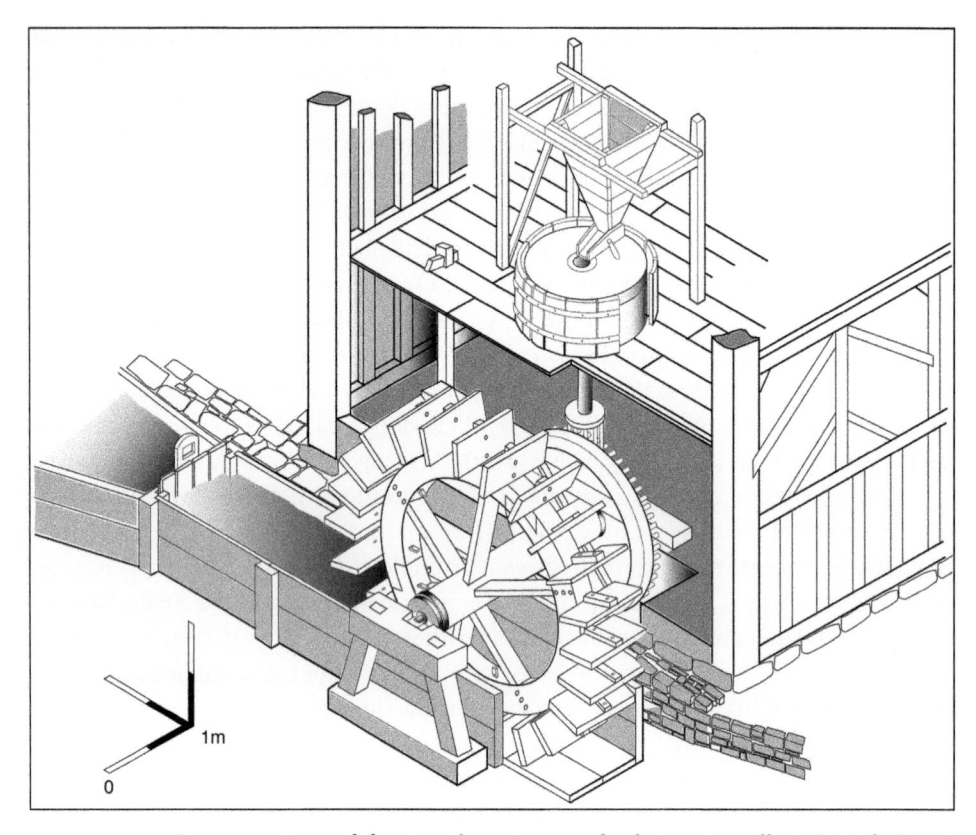

FIGURE 31.2 Reconstruction of fourteenth-century undershot watermill at Patrick Street, Dublin, Ireland

(© Colin Rynne)

joints. The only high medieval example to be recorded in either Britain or Ireland is that recently excavated at Greenwich, England, which has been dendro-dated to AD 1194 and has an estimated original diameter of *c*.5.1 m (Davis 2009). Not only is this the largest known vertical waterwheel, of any type, to have come to light from medieval Europe, it is also the earliest example of its type associated with a tidal mill. Its basic mode of assembly, however, while closely comparable to undershot wheels excavated at Thervay, France (AD 1160–1170; David and Mordefroid 2011) and Ahrensfelde, Germany (*c*.1330–1500; Issleib 1955), is also similar to those from Dasing, Germany (eighth century; Cyzsz 1998), and Audun-le-Tiche, France (AD 840–51; Rohmer 1996).

Between the seventh and the sixteenth centuries, two basic forms of undershot waterwheel paddle assembly have been identified (Figure 31.3). In the first, the float and paddle tenon (or 'start') is fashioned from one piece (e.g. Dasing, Audun-le-Tiche, Colomby, and Thervay). The second paddle form, of which there are a number of variants, is essentially a two-piece construction, in which the start is affixed by dowels to the float section. On present evidence, some four basic varieties of single- and two-piece paddles have been recorded throughout Europe (Fischer 2004, 43). A number of important recent discoveries, indeed, have demonstrated a degree of often startling similarity between paddle

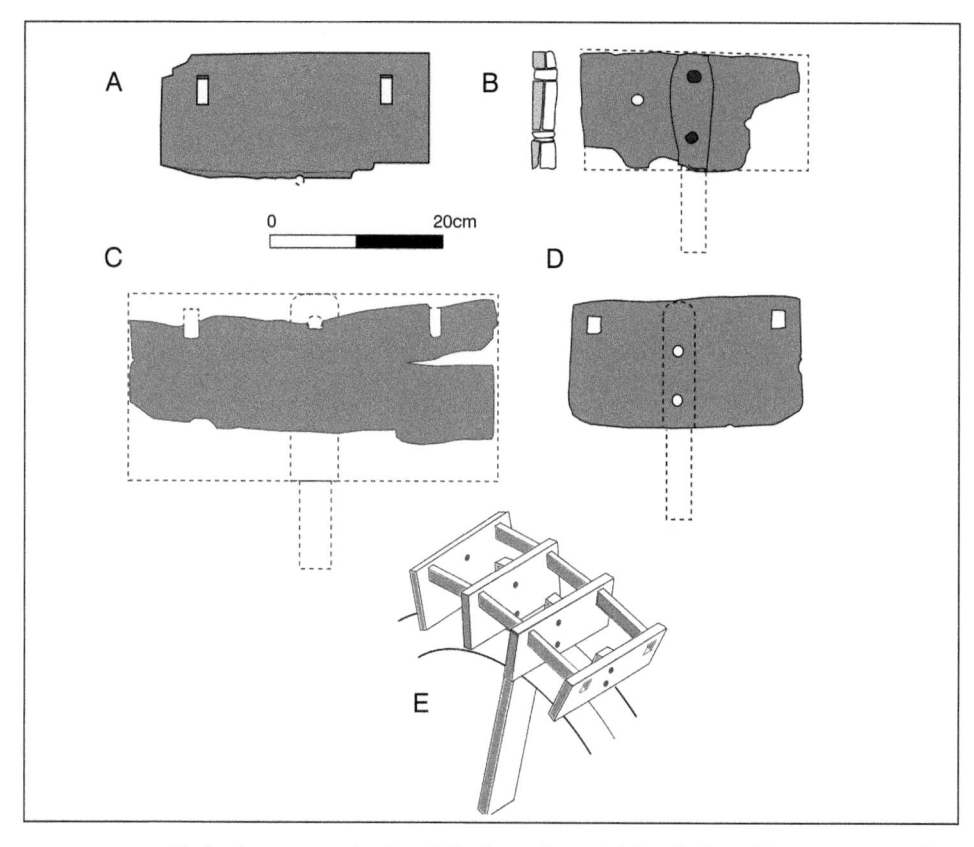

FIGURE 31.3 Undershot waterwheel paddle floats from (a) Bordesley Abbey, Worcestershire (twelfth century; after Astill 1993), (b) St Giles, Reading (after Ford et al. 2013), (c) Colomby, France (twelfth century; after Bernard 2011), (d) Tovstrup, Denmark (late-fifteenth/early sixteenth century; after Fischer 2004); (e) reconstruction of paddles struts

(© Colin Rynne)

forms recorded in Britain and Ireland and contemporary examples on the Continent. Furthermore, not only do these stylistic similarities, between what are essentially early medieval forms, continue to be employed not only throughout the later medieval period and into recent times, they also extend across a wide geographical area. Two excavated examples from Britain, from Bordesley Abbey (thirteenth century; Astill 1993) and Greenwich, have mortices parallel to their upper edges which were used to position props. By effectively wedging the rear face of one paddle to the front face of the paddle immediately behind it, these props (or stabilizers) provided further protection for what were, in most cases, relatively thin paddle tenons. The twelfth-century paddle floats from Bordesley Abbey (Astill 1993) and the St Giles Mill, Reading (Ford et al. 2013) were each 0.54 m wide, and are similar to an example from a mill at Colomby, France (Bernard 2011). A fourth example of this type of paddle float has been found at a mill site at Tovstrup, Denmark (AD 1407–1531), which was 0.44 m wide (Fischer 2004, 43–4).

In undershot waterwheels the incoming water strikes the vanes or floats at the lowest part of the wheel's circumference. Since the Roman period, the lowest section of such wheels have been provided with a single-piece or composite wooden trough, which carefully guided the water onto the floats, while at the same preventing it from escaping around their sides. To date, three main types of wheel trough have been identified in Britain, Ireland, and Europe during the high medieval period. These latter, again, demonstrate clear continuity with very similar forms recorded at early medieval undershot watermills. They include:

- Single piece wheel troughs, carved out of a large tree trunk, with the inlet side curved downwards to base of the interior and with its outlet end open; examples of this type include Galten (AD 1143), Tovstrup (AD 1155; Fischer 2004) and Hessel in Denmark (c. AD 1140–50; Oleson 2001), and Greenwich, England (AD 1194; Davis 2009);
- Composite forms, where the trough consists of separate sections but where an internal longitudinal curvature is imparted to individual sections, as recorded at Bourges, France (AD 1140–50), Castle Donington, England (early twelfth century; Clay and Salisbury 1990);
- Composite forms, where the trough is constructed with boards and is open at both ends (e.g. Bordesley Abbey, c. AD 1174–6; Astill 1993; Patrick Street, Dublin, fourteenth century; Rynne 1997).

Of the twenty-two recorded European examples of these wheel troughs, dating from the second century AD to the sixteenth century, there are close similarities, not only in their basic design but also in their overall dimensions, and over a wide geographical area (e.g. Morett, Co. Laois, Ireland; Rynne 2013; and Bordesley Abbey; Astill 1993). The dimensional similarity is suggestive of technological continuity in their construction.

In the *overshot* waterwheel the water is delivered into buckets, which are fed from directly above the upper section of the wheel's circumference. Of all the traditional varieties of waterwheel this was the most effective, being capable of providing from the same volume and fall of water almost twice as much power as an undershot wheel. However, while the latter and the breastshot variety (where water was directed into the buckets about midway up the circumference of the wheel) are illustrated in (mostly later) medieval manuscripts, only a very small number of examples have come to light. These include the overshot wheels, Chingley, Kent (thirteenth century; Crossley 1975, 14) and Batsford, Sussex (fourteenth century; Bedwin 1980). On present evidence, all varieties of early and later medieval waterwheels had four (or less frequently six) wooden *compass arms* or spokes with which to support the waterwheel's rim. In the most commonly recorded arrangement, the individual spokes were morticed at one extremity to the rim and at the other to the axle, as was evident on the Batsford overshot waterwheel. The waterwheels from Dasing (Cyzsz 1998), Audun-le-Tiche (Rohmer 1996), Colomby (Bernard 2011), and Thervay (David and Mordefroid 2011) each had four compass arms, set at right angles to each other. With the notable exception of the twelfth-century Greenwich undershot waterwheel, nearly all of the recorded early and later medieval examples do not exceed 3 m in overall diameter.

Mill Buildings and Components of the Mill Landscape (Dams, Weirs, Mill Ponds, and Millraces)

Although the medieval watermill is essentially a technology of timber, stone walling and earthfast posts along with combinations of the latter with sill beams have all been recorded in later medieval Britain and Ireland. The most common of all, however, involved the use of morticed sill beams with tenoned uprights which formed part of an interlocking framework of beams, incorporating the wheel pit (in which the pit-wheel rotated) and the structures housing the millstone assembly. These include the twelfth-century Greenwich tide mill (Davis 2009), Batsford, East Sussex (Figure 31.4a, fourteenth century), Chingley forge, Kent (Figure 31.4b, c. AD 1300), and the early fourteenth-century phase of the St Giles mill (Figure 31.4c; Ford et al. 2013, 89). Similar timber framing was also combined with stone mill house structures at two later medieval Irish sites, at Twomileborris, Co. Tipperary (AD 1199–1217) and that at Patrick Street, Dublin, built in the early thirteenth century (Figure 31.4d; Rynne 1997). The stone structure housing the grain mill at Fountains Abbey, begun in the 1140s, the earliest surviving mill at any Cistercian site, exhibited four main construction phases over the twelfth to the fourteenth centuries (Coppack 1998). In later periods it operated with two overshot wheels. The Abbey Mill at Abbotsbury, Dorset, was also a two-storey stone building, which accommodated two waterwheels, although in this instance operating side by side (Figure 31.4e; Graham 1986).

The surviving earthworks within the monastic precinct of Bordesley Abbey included a triangular millpond, a mill dam and a complex series of timber-lined mill-races, and mill buildings, operated through six main phases of use from the late twelfth to the early fifteenth centuries (Astill 1993, 3). The millpond was formed by two earthen banks, that at the south being formed with upcast material from an exterior ditch. The northern millpond bank was similarly constructed, although the sequence in which it was constructed was more complicated. At the base of this bank was laid a roughly square in cross section, timber pipe or drain, fashioned from an oak tree, the upper face of which was covered with a well-made, plank-lined lid (Figure 31.5). The southern extremity of the wooden drain was jointed to a transverse wooden baseplate with a series of braces, which held a pivoted post. When the mill was in operation, an upward movement of this post lifted a bung, which allowed water from the bed of the millpond into the pipe. This water could then exit via the wooden drain, pass underneath the millpond bank, and then discharge into an overflow channel in the adjacent field (Astill 1993, 89). This particular drain was dendro-dated to 1227, but seems to have replaced an earlier, similar device (Allen 1993a).

The Wharram Percy mill site (apparently derelict by the twelfth century) produced evidence for a series of clay dams faced with wattle hurdling, which were regularly

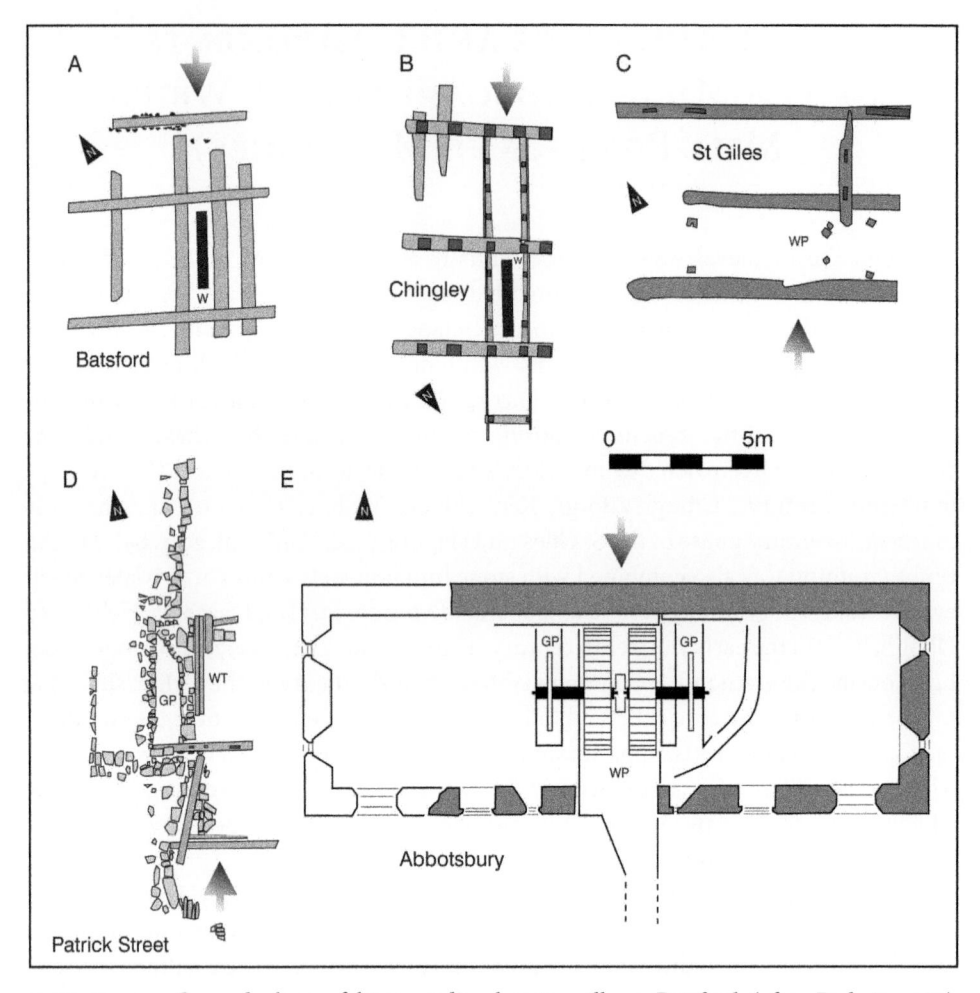

FIGURE 31.4 Ground plans of later medieval watermills at Batsford (after Bedwin 1980), Chingley (after Crossley 1975), St Giles (after Ford et al. 2013), Patrick Street (Walsh 1997) and Abbotsbury (after Graham 1986). Key: W = waterwheel *in situ*, WP = wheel pit, WT: wheel trough, GP = gear pit

(© Colin Rynne)

repaired and rebuilt (Beresford and Hurst 1990, 66–7; Hurst 1984, 101–2), while that at Castle Donington (first half of the twelfth century) consisted of two rows of vertical oak timbers, with a mixture of brushwood, gravel, silt, and stone packed in between (Clay and Salisbury 1990, 283). The documentary evidence for the construction of dams and related features in medieval Yorkshire indicates that mill dams were normally constructed by fixing vertical piles in the river bed, inserting horizontal planks, and filling the area enclosed by them with a mixture of stones, turves, faggots and clay (Faull and Moorhouse 1981, 713–15).

While for the most part the site on which a mill was to operate was carefully chosen, considerable effort and resources could often be expended on the opening up and

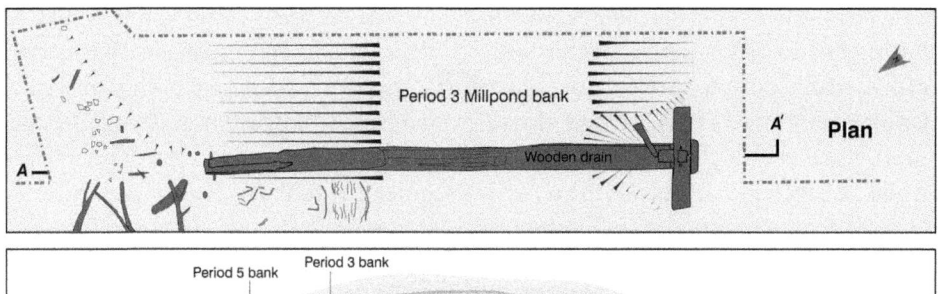

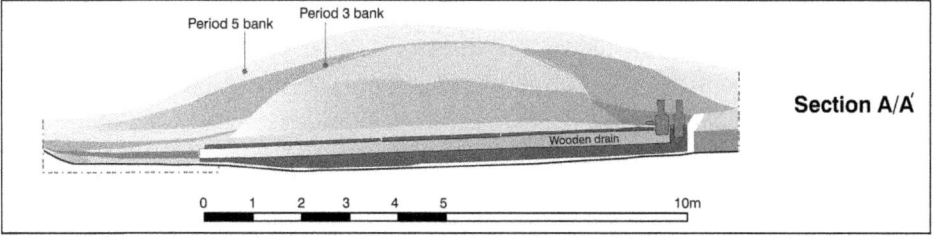

FIGURE 31.5 Mill-pond drain at Bordesley Abbey, dendro-dated to AD 1227 (after Astill 1993)

(© Colin Rynne)

maintenance of mill leats/races. One later medieval leat, which led from Kinewards Bridge to Baltonsborough Mill in Somerset, was around 6.4 km long (Hollinrake and Hollinrake 2007, 241).

The means by which mill channels were protected against erosion in the later medieval and post-medieval periods were exactly the same as those found in the early historic period (Rynne 2013). Timber-lined channels have been recorded at the fourteenth-century and later mills excavated at Chingley (Crossley 1975), at Batsford (Bedwin 1980), Bordesley Abbey (Astill 1993), Patrick Street, Dublin (Rynne 1997), Twomileborris, Co. Tipperary, the King's Mills, Leeds (Goodchild and Wrathmell 2002), and St Giles Mill, Reading (Ford et al. 2013). Indeed, the archaeological evidence from Europe would suggest that this practice was almost universal during the medieval period in Europe.

Mill Machinery

The vast majority of water-powered mills constructed during the later medieval period were used for grinding cereals. And although other industrial processes such as iron-processing (bloomeries and forges), fulling (in which woollen cloth was degraded and pre-shrunk), and the grinding of oak bark for tanning were also mechanized, thus far only the remains of water-powered bloomeries and forges have come to light in both Britain and Ireland. Recent discoveries, and in particular, the excavation of a complete, twelfth-century pit-wheel, at the St Giles mill in Reading, Berkshire, have greatly improved our knowledge of the working of the internal machinery of the medieval water-powered grain mill. The St Giles pitwheel (Figure 31.6, no. 1) was 1.38m in diameter and was formed with four 'felloe' sections cut from naturally curving oak branches. Each section was jointed to another with scarf (i.e. 'end to end') joints, with thirty-six evenly spaced holes to receive cogs (Allen 2013). A small section of a pit-wheel of a similar diameter to that at St Giles was also recovered from Chingley Forge, Kent (Crossley 1975), and at two further English sites at Beckside and Beverly (Allen 2013). Nonetheless, while archaeological evidence for pit-wheel segments is rare, the cogs or pegs inserted into them have become an increasingly more common find in recent years. Pit-wheel gear pegs have been excavated at early medieval mill sites such as Dasing, Germany (Cyzsz 1998), and at later medieval sites such as Verjeslev and Tovstrup in Denmark (Fischer 2004), and Ballyine, County Limerick (Figure 31.6) in Ireland (Rynne 2007, 24–6). Similar gear pegs have also been found at water-powered iron-working sites such as Bordesley Abbey, Chingley Forge, and Batsford, England (Figure 31.6). In all cases the

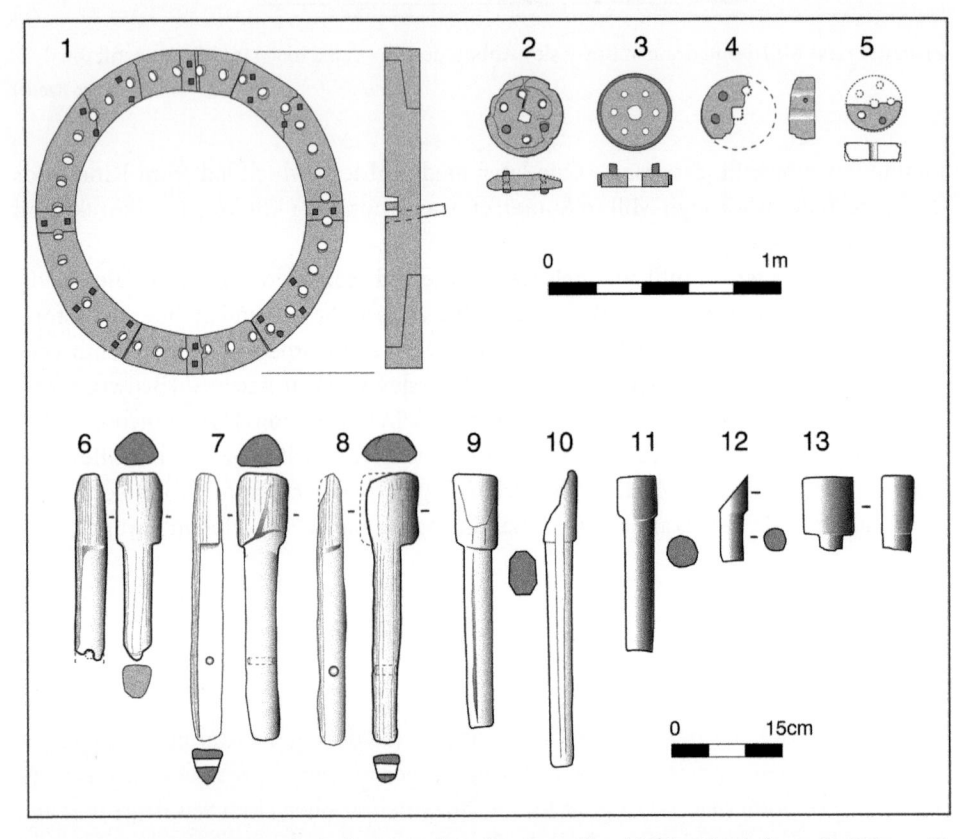

FIGURE 31.6 Machinery from later medieval watermills. (1) Pit-wheel from St Giles mill, Reading (twelfth century; after Allen 2013). Lantern pinion disks from (2) Colomby, France (after Bernard 2011), (3) Bardowick, Germany (after Kruger 1934), (4) St Giles, Reading (after Allen 2013), and (5) Thervay, France (after David and Mordefroid 2011). Gear pegs (6–8) from Ballyine, Co. Limerick, Ireland (after Rynne 2007), (9–10) Chingley, Kent (after Crossley 1975), and (11–13) Batsford, Sussex (after Bedwin 1980)

(© Colin Rynne)

gear pegs, whether from pit-wheels or cams, are generally made of oak (or *pomoideae* woods as at Bordesley Abbey), have a T-shaped profile, and share a distinctive wear pattern, in which one upper corner of the peg is worn down at an angle of about 45 degrees where it had meshed with either a pinion or a cam wheel (Allen 1993b, 215; Bedwin 1980, 199–200; Crossley 1975).

The pit-wheel meshed with a second gear wheel, the lantern pinion, constructed using two circular wooden disks with six concentric perforations into which were received the opposing ends of six wooden gear staves. The upper disk also had a central rectangular perforation, which held the vertical, iron mill *spindle*, whose upper section was tied to the mill rynd. The spindles-and-rynd combination formed the power take-off for the upper rotating millstone (see the following section), whose lower face usually had dovetail sockets to hold the rynd. Lantern pinions recorded from the Roman and succeeding early and later medieval periods are remarkably similar in size and construction (e.g. at Gimbscheim, on River Rhine; Höckmann 1994; and at Bardowick in northern Germany; Krüger 1934).

To date no medieval examples of rynd-and-spindle assemblies have come to light in either Britain or Ireland, and in nearly all cases it would appear that the high-quality iron and steel used in their manufacture would have ensured that most mill iron would have been recycled. From later medieval English mill accounts the spindle (*fusillum*) and rynd (*ynkum*) clearly required regular maintenance, with anything up to 28 lb of iron being used in the manufacture of a single spindle (Holt 1988, 123; Langdon 2004, 94). Both horizontal and vertical watermills also required bearings to support the ends of vertical and horizontal drive-shafts. The so-called 'pivot-stones', which acted as footstep (i.e. thrust) bearings for vertical shafts, are common to both horizontal and vertical-wheeled mills. Indeed, so close are the types of stone bearing employed, as the Irish and ethnographic evidence demonstrates, that in the case of stray finds it is impossible to determine whether the bearing stone was used in either a horizontal or vertical mill. The footstep bearings recovered from the eighth-century undershot vertical mill at Morett, Co. Laois (Lucas 1953), and from later medieval and Twomileborris, Co. Tipperary, and Ballyine, Co. Limerick, for example, are virtually indistinguishable (Rynne 2007).

Horizontal bearing blocks, used to support the journals of the axles of vertical water-wheels, have been recovered from at least three Roman sites. Several examples have also been excavated at two English monastic sites, Bordesley Abbey and Abbotsbury Abbey, Dorset. At Bordesley Abbey all of those recovered were manufactured from large pebbles, mostly quartz or quartzite, from which it was possible to estimate the diameter of the journals as being 170–236 mm (Astill and Wright 1993, 110). Of the nineteen bearing stones found at Abbotsbury Abbey, thirteen were for horizontal journals (Graham 1986, 123–4). Given that nearly all of the watermills with which these horizontal bearing stones were associated were timber structures, it seems likely that these were emplaced in wooden brackets. One such bracket was recorded at Mølleån, Denmark (C^{14}-dated to AD 1000), and exhibited abrasion marks, presumably caused by the jolting action of the journal (Friis-Hansen 1991, 107). A less-elaborate wooden bearing bracket, dated to *c.* AD 1150, was also recovered from the Castle Donington mill (Clay and Salisbury 1990, 293, fig. 16.4).

To date, water-powered iron-processing mills have been excavated at the Cistercian abbeys of Kirkstall Abbey (Lucas 2014), Bordesley Abbey (Astill 1993), and at Chingley, Kent (Crossley 1975). Yet only Bordesley Abbey, from which a section of a wooden cam wheel was recovered, has produced surviving evidence of the mill's mechanism. However, at two sites, the late thirteenth-century water-powered forge at North Gate Bridge, Cork, Ireland (Hurley 1997, 45–9), and at Chingley, the original wooden anvils were examined *in situ*. There is also a building at Beaulieu Abbey, Hampshire, which has been interpreted as a possible fourteenth-/fifteenth-century fulling mill (Watts 2002, 115).

Millstones

Querns of basalt lava stone had been imported into England from at least the first century AD, but by the third and fourth centuries these were somewhat less common. Until recently it was believed that the trade in Mayen quernstones from Germany was not revived until the seventh and eighth centuries, but it is now clear that lava querns can be dated to the earliest period of Anglo-Saxon settlement in Britain (Coulter 2011, 181–2; Parkhouse 1997). In Britain, therefore, this trade appears to have been largely uninterrupted. The absence of either imported lava querns, or millstones blanks, in northern England and Scotland has been interpreted as self-sufficiency in these regions in stone suitable for milling (Campbell 1987, 105–17). It seems likely that stone from the Mayen quarry was transported to Andernach on the Rhine (via the River Nette), and thence to Denmark, via Deventer, and to Britain via Utrecht (Pohl 2011, 171). Finds from early medieval wrecks indicate that blanks for quernstones, of 20–25 kg (50 kg for a full set), were being shipped to destinations throughout Europe (Mangartz 2008, 125; Parkhouse 1997, 102; Pohl 2011, 173). However, the tenth-century Mayen and Niedermendig millstones from West Cotton, Northamptonshire, which were, on average, 64 mm thick, weighed around 80–85 kg each, a millstone set weighing *c.*160–170 kg (Chapman 2010, 142; see also Chapter 29 in this *Handbook*). The persistence of this trade in early and later medieval Europe is quite striking: not only were slightly over 50 per cent of the known corpus of millstones sourced from distant locations, but also from quarries that had been exploited since the Roman period (Rynne 2017).

The native millstones employed in animal-, water-, and wind-powered mills included millstone grit from the Peak District of Derbyshire, granite from Dartmoor and Wales along with some sandstones from the West Midlands (Farmer 1992, 98). In Ireland, where both English and French millstones began to be imported into the Anglo-Norman colony from at least the beginning of the fourteenth century (Lydon 1981; O'Neill 1987, 92), locally manufactured stones were generally cut from sandstone, usually conglomerates (Carey 2007; Lynn 1982; Manning 2009). With very few exceptions, recorded examples of European, water-powered millstones from pre-1300 contexts, from both horizontal- and vertical-wheeled mills, rarely exceed 1 m in diameter (Rynne 2017). By way of contrast, the diameters of the millstones, described in 'hands' in fourteenth-century English documents, are the equivalent of 52–56 inches (c.1.32–1.42 m; Langdon 2004, 172). The wear and tear on the upper rotating millstone in later medieval Britain also required that it be replaced at least every five years (Langdon 2004, 171). As in the early medieval period, special iron mill picks were used for preparing grinding surfaces, and a number have been recovered from medieval vertical mill sites in England and on the Continent as, for example, at South Witham (late twelfth century), West Cotton (thirteenth-/fourteenth-century contexts), and King's Lynn (Mayes 2002, 15; Chapman 2010, 383; Goodall and Carter 1977).

The Archaeology of Windpower

In the year 1185 two references to the existence of windmills appear in the English written sources. The first of these was at Weedley in the East Riding of Yorkshire, the second is to another mill, already in existence since 1180, at Amberley, Sussex. By the 1190s at least twenty windmills were at work in England (Holt 1988, 20): in around 1300 it is estimated that upwards of four thousand windmills were in operation in Britain (Langdon 1992). The earliest documented windmill in Ireland was at work at Kilscanlan, near Old Ross, Co. Wexford, in AD 1281, but given the generally poor survival of records from the medieval lordship of Ireland, their introduction could have been much earlier (Rynne 1998). And, while there has been much debate, mostly of the naive diffusionist type (e.g. Hills 1994; Kealey 1987), about the European origins of the vertical windmill, there is really nothing to suggest that they may not have developed first in Britain (Holt 1988, 20).

There is a marked concentration of sites in eastern England, owing to a general lack of streams with sufficient volume to power watermills (Langdon and Watts 2005, 698). However, while generally a useful supplement to watermills where sources of hydraulic energy were either unavailable or unsuitable, windmills suffered from the disadvantage of being unable to store their energy. As is evident from the documentary and archaeological record, before the early 1290s, the vast majority of the windmills at work in Britain were *post-mills* (Figure 31.7) in which the actual mill building is rotated about a central wooden pivot in order that the wind sails can face into the prevailing wind (Zeepvat 1980). The entire structure could be rotated through 360 degrees by means of a *tail pole*, which enabled the miller to adjust the position of his sails to accommodate changes in wind direction, by the simple expedient of rotating the entire mill building. The mill machinery was contained within a wooden framework, and the entire structure was usually erected on high ground, often on a specially prepared mound.

Thus far around fifty post-mill sites, dating from the early thirteenth to the sixteenth centuries, have been identified in Britain (Watts 2013, 48), along with a further five probable windmill mounds recorded in Ireland, all in Co. Meath (Rynne 1998). In the main, these mounds tend to be around 11.5–24 m in overall diameter, and vary somewhat

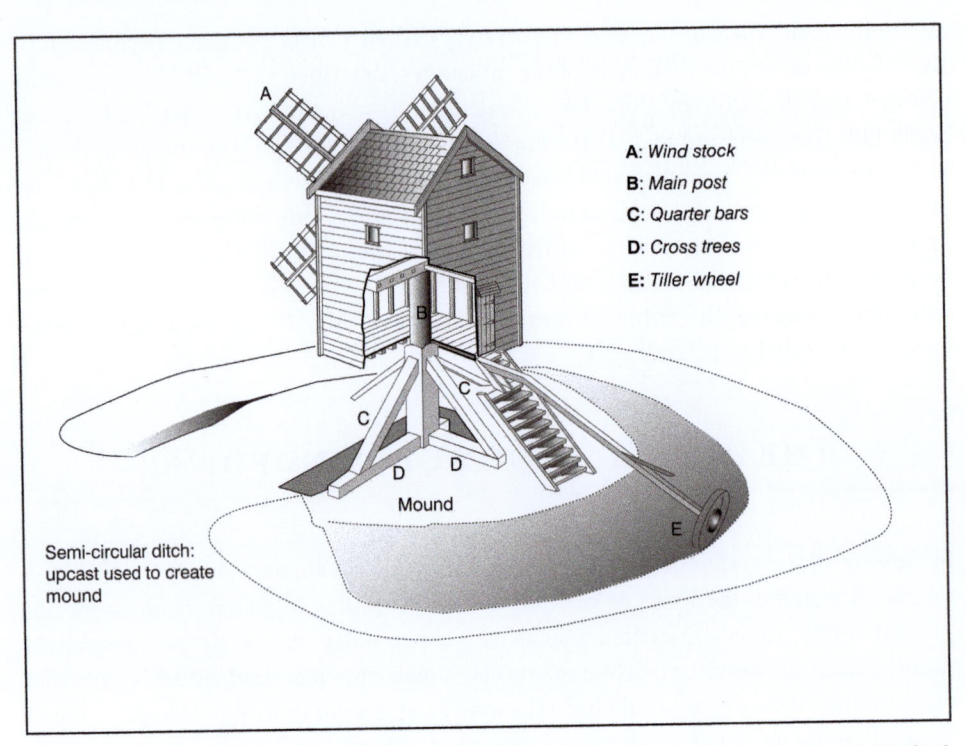

FIGURE 31.7 Reconstruction of the later medieval post windmill at Great Linford, Buckinghamshire (after Mynard and Zeepvat 1992)

(© Colin Rynne)

in height. They are commonly surrounded by C-shaped ditches, as at Manor Farm, Humberstone, Leicester (Thomas 2009), which are both wide and shallow, and the material upcast from them was used to construct the mound. One, and occasionally two causeways, extended across the ditch to facilitate access. When later medieval windmill mounds are excavated, as at Bridlington, Yorkshire (Earnshaw 1973), Tansor Crossroads, Northamptonshire (Chapman 1997), Great Linford, Buckinghamshire (Mynard and Zeepvat 1992), the foundation trenches in which the cross-trees or trestles were laid are commonly revealed. At Lamport, Northamptonshire, the cross-trees had been laid on stone cross walls (Posnasky 1956). Excavation at many sites has also demonstrated that the foundation trenches, in which the cross-trees were laid, were packed with clay and/or stones, to either counteract penetration of water from the surface or to assist in drainage (Watts 2013, 50). However, while a number of windmills mounds show modifications to their height over time, and were thus not operating over a single phase, many later medieval sites were not re-used by later mills (Watts 2013, 51–2).

During the excavation of the windmill mound at Manor Farm, two relatively well-preserved cross-trees of box heart oak were investigated *in situ*. The longest cross-tree was 5.4 m long and around 40 cm square, and the two cross-trees had joined at the centre by halving. Pottery recovered from the construction slots for these beams would indicate a twelfth- to thirteenth-century date for the mill's construction (Thomas 2009,

119). Excavation of a windmill mound at Bridgewater Without, Somerset (Webster and Cherry 1972, 212), also produced a large section of a cross-tree, along with near-complete section of a *quarter bar* (a raking strut morticed at an angle into the trestle, by which means it provided lateral support for the main pivot post of the mill). Surviving sections of the cross-trees from the Great Linford mill are C^{14}-dated to AD 1200 ± 70 (Mynard and Zeepvat 1992), while pottery from Tansor Crossroads suggests a date of *c.*1225–50 (Chapman 1997, 20). However, at many later medieval sites the timber substructure of the post-mill was often deliberately dismantled when the site went into disuse. The cross-trees of the Tansor Crossroads mill would have been 5.6–5.8 m long (Chapman 1997, 35) and their salvage and recycling for uses, structural or otherwise, would have saved the expense of the felling and carriage of new timbers of the same scantling. As many authorities have posited, one of the principal technical developments associated with later medieval post-mills is the gradual abandonment of the practice of burying the substructure of the mill (Crossley 1990; Watts 2013). This enabled both increased structural stability for the mill structure and considerably reduced the likelihood that the buried cross-tree would be susceptible to un-monitored decay (Figure 31.8). Furthermore,

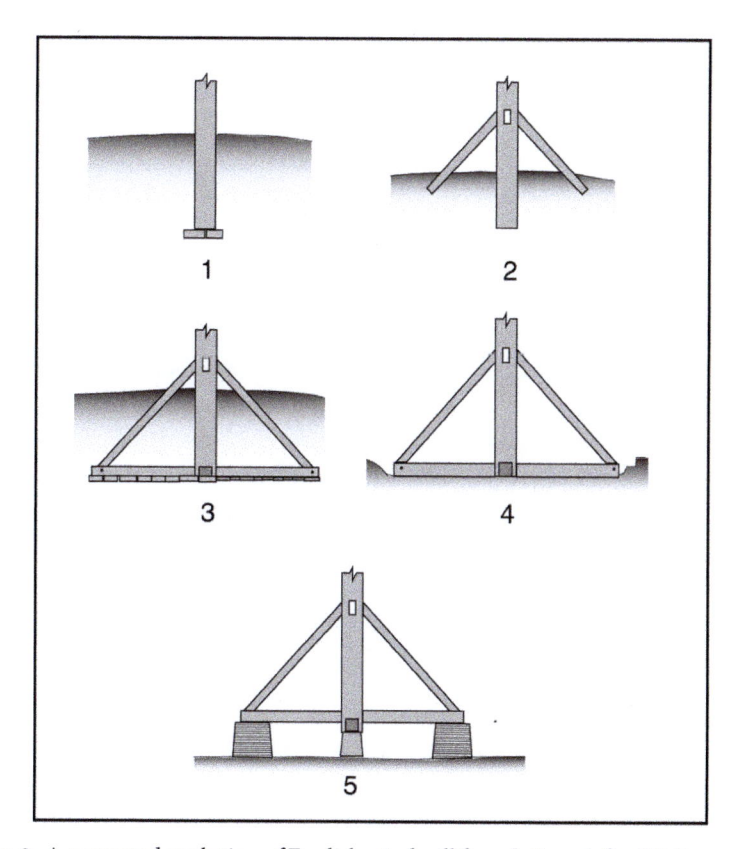

FIGURE 31.8 A suggested evolution of English windmill foundations (after Watts 2002)

(© Colin Rynne)

with the trestle frame now above ground, taller post-mills with longer sails (which could create greater power) could now be built, while the condition of the cross-trees could be more easily monitored (Watts 2013, 50–1). Very little is known about the machinery of the later medieval post-mill, save what can be gleaned from contemporary and frequently stylized representations in medieval manuscripts. Thus far a single piece of windmill machinery—a pivot stone for a vertical driveshaft—has been recovered at the Bridlington post-mill site (Earnshaw 1973).

A number of recorded sites, as one might expect, are located close to, and likely serviced, contemporary settlements. There is a possible windmill mound at Barton Blount, Derbyshire, close to the earthworks of a deserted medieval village (Watts 2013, 53). Aerial photography has also demonstrated that these mounds can also be sited either within or occasionally over ridge-and-furrow field systems, as was the case at the excavated thirteenth-century windmill mound at Great Linford (Mynard and Zeepvat 1992). Considerably less is known about the buildings associated with later medieval windmills in general. However, a number of excavated sites around Eastbourne, Sussex, have uncovered functionally related structures such as a bolting house (in which the flour and meal was sieved and dressed) and even a miller's dwelling (Stevens 1982, 91–3).

In the post-medieval period post-mills tended to become rarer and were gradually replaced by more powerful *tower-mills*, so-called because the mill machinery was contained within a typically cylindrical masonry tower. In the tower-mill the building is a fixed entity and the moving portion containing the sails and the driveshaft (or *windshaft*) are carried in a rotating *cap* section set on top of the tower. A *tailpole* with a tiller wheel at its lower end was connected to the cap portion, a movement of the pole in any direction enabling the miller to turn the cap and thence the sails into the prevailing wind. This indeed is the precursor of the multi-storeyed windmills with which most people today would be more familiar. However, from at least the late thirteenth century, a small number of these mills were beginning to be erected in England. The 'stone windmill' recorded at Dover castle in 1294–5 would appear to have been a tower-mill, while a further example was in existence at Turweston, Buckinghamshire, in 1303 (Langdon and Watts 2005, 701, 707). All told, there are around six recorded example of later-medieval tower-mills in Britain, three of which, Burton Dassett, Warwickshire, Fowey, Cornwall, and Tidenham, Buckinghamshire, have standing remains (Langdon and Watts 2005, 712; Watts 2002). The high cost of their construction, for the most part, would appear to have acted as a brake on their widespread adoption in Britain during this period, although other factors such as a reluctance from contemporary carpenters to build them may also have played a part (Langdon and Watts 2005, 717).

Conclusion

The archaeology of water power in Europe in general and in Britain and Ireland in particular exhibits marked continuity from the Roman period onwards. This applies to both the hydraulic systems employed to power individual mills (whether they used horizontal or vertical waterwheels) and the mechanisms actuated by them. Even the diameter of the millstones turned by them, it is now clear, changed little until the fourteenth century. The same continuity can be demonstrated for the long-distance trade in millstones made from German lava, which continued in most of Europe and in mainland Britain (with the exception of Scotland).

REFERENCES CITED

Allen, S. J. 1993a 'The mill (BAB) structural timber sequence', in G. G. Astill, *A medieval industrial complex and its landscape: the metalworking watermills and workshops of Bordesley Abbey*, Council for British Archaeology Research Report 92, York, 66–84

Allen, S. 2013 'Watermill machinery and fittings from excavations', in B. M. Ford, D. Poore, R. Shaffrey, and D. R. P. Wilkinson, *Under the oracle: excavations at the Oracle Shopping Centre site 1996–8; the medieval and post-medieval urban development of the Kennet floodplain in Reading*, Oxford University School of Archaeology, Oxford, 268–77

Astill, G. G. 1993 *A medieval industrial complex and its landscape: the metalworking watermills and workshops of Bordesley Abbey*, Council for British Archaeology Research Report 92, York

Astill, G. G. and Wright, S. M. 1993 'Stone bearings', in G. G. Astill, *A medieval industrial complex and its landscape: the metalworking watermills and workshops of Bordesley Abbey*, Council for British Archaeology Research Report 92, York, 110–17

Bedwin, O. 1980 'The excavation of Batsford mill, Warbelton, East Sussex, 1978', *Medieval Archaeology* 25, 187–201

Beresford, M. and Hurst, J. 1990 *English Heritage book of Wharram Percy deserted medieval village*, Batsford, London

Bernard, V. 2011 'Un moulin hydraulique en Normandie, récente découverte', *Les Dossiers d'Archéologie* 344, 34–5

Campbell, E. 1987 'A cross-marked quern from Dunadd', *Proceedings of the Society of Antiquaries of Scotland* 117, 105–17

Carey, A. 2007 'The grinding stones', in M. Clyne, *Kells priory, County Kilkenny: archaeological excavations by Tom Fanning and Miriam Clyne*, The Stationery Office, Dublin, 436–40

Chapman, A. 1997 'The excavation of Neolithic and medieval mounds at Tansor Crossroads, Northamptonshire 1995', *Northamptonshire Archaeology* 1996–7, 3–50

Chapman, A. 2010 *West Cotton, Raunds: a study of medieval settlement dynamics AD 450–1450. Excavations of a deserted medieval hamlet in Northamptonshire 1985–89*, Oxbow Books, Oxford

Clay, P. and Salisbury, C. R. 1990 'A Norman mill dam and other sites at Hemington Fields, Castle Donington, Leicestershire', *The Archaeological Journal* 147, 276–307

Coppack, G. 1998 'The water-driven corn mill at Fountains Abbey: a major Cistercian mill of the twelfth and thirteenth centuries', *Studies in Cistercian Art and Architecture* 5, no. 167, 271–96

Coulter, C. 2011 'Of cakes and kings: breadmaking in early medieval England', D. Williams and D. Peacock (eds), *Bread for the people: the archaeology of mills and milling*, British Archaeological Reorts International Series 2274, 179–91

Crossley, D. 1975 *The Bewl Valley ironworks, Kent, c.1300–1730*, Royal Archaeological Institute, London
Crossley, D. 1990 *Post-medieval archaeology in Britain*, Leicester University Press, Leicester
Czysz, W. 1998 *Die ältesten Wassermühlen: Archäologische Entdeckungen im Paartal bei Dasing*, Thierhaupten Klostermuhlenmuseum
Darby, H. C. 1977 *Domesday England*, Cambridge University Press, Cambridge
David, S. and Mordefroid, J. L. 2011 *Le château et la seigneurie dans le Jura, XIe–XVe siècles*, Musée d'Archéologie de Jura, Jura, np
Davis, S. 2009 'Water-power in medieval Greenwich', *Current Archaeology* XX(8) (November 2009), 230–5
Earnshaw, J. 1973 'The site of a medieval post mill and prehistoric site at Bridlington', *Yorkshire Archaeological Journal* 45, 19–40
Farmer, D. L. 1992 'Millstones for medieval manors', *Agricultural History Review* 40, II, 97–111
Faull, M. and Moorhouse, S. A. (eds) 1981 *West Yorkshire: an archaeological survey to AD 1500*, West Yorkshire Metropolitan County Council, Wakefield
Fenton, A. 1978 *The northern isles: Orkney and Shetland*, Tucknell Press, East Linton
Fischer, C. 2004 *Tidlige Danske Vandmøller: to middelalderlige vandmøller ved Tovstrup og Vejerslev*, Jysk Archælogisk Selskabs Schrifter 50, Højbjerg
Ford, B. M., Poore, D., Shaffrey, R., and Wilkinson, D. R. P. 2013 *Under the oracle: excavations at the Oracle Shopping Centre site 1996–8; the medieval and post-medieval urban development of the Kennet floodplain in Reading*, Oxford University School of Archaeology, Oxford
Friis-Hansen, J. 1991 'Vikingetidens vandmølle ved Mølleåen', *Lyngby-Boden*, 97–112
Goodall, I. H. and Carter, A. 1977 'Iron objects', in H. Clarke and A. Carter (eds), *Excavations in King's Lynn 1963–70*, The Society for Medieval Archaeology Monograph 7, London, 291–8
Goodchild, J. and Wrathmell, S. 2002 *The King's Mills, Leeds: the history and archaeology of the manorial water-powered mills*, Leeds Philosophical and Literary Society, Leeds
Graham, A. H. 1986 'The Old Matlhouse, Abbotsbury, Dorset: the medieval watermill of the Benedictine abbey', *Proceedings of the Dorset Natural History and Archaeological Society* 108, 103–25
Hills, R. L. 1994 *Power from wind: a history of windmill technology*, Cambridge University Press, Cambridge
Höckman, O. 1994 'Post-Roman boat timbers and a floating mill from the upper Rhine', in C. Westerdahl (ed.), *Crossroads in ancient shipbuilding: proceedings of the sixth international symposium on boat and ship archaeology, Roskilde 1991*, Oxbow, Oxford, 105–15
Hollinrake, C. and Hollinrake, N. 2007 'Glastonbury's Anglo-Saxon canal and Dunstan's dyke', in J. Blair (ed.), *Waterways and canal-building in medieval England*, Oxford University Press, Oxford, 228–43
Holt, R. 1988 *The mills of medieval England*, Blackwell, Oxford
Hurley, M. F. 1997 *Excavations at North Gate, Cork*, Cork Corporation, Cork
Hurst, J. G. 1984 'The Wharram research project: results to 1983', *Medieval Archaeology* 28, 77–111
Issleib, H. 1955 'Die Betriebsanlagen der alten Wassermühle im Ahrensfelder Teich', *Hammaburg* 4, 68–70
Kealey, E. J. 1987 *Harvesting the air: windmill pioneers in twelfth-century England*, Boydell, Woodbridge
Krüger, F. 1934 'Eine frühmittelalterliche Wassermühle in Bardowick', *Mannus* 26, 344–54.
Langdon, J. 1992 'The birth and demise of a medieval windmill', *History of Technology* 14, 54–76

Langdon, J. 2004 *Mills in the medieval economy: England 1300–1540*, Oxford University Press, Oxford

Langdon, J. and Watts, M. 2005 'Tower windmills in medieval England: a case of arrested development', *Technology and Culture* 46(4), 697–718

Lucas, A. 2014 *Ecclesiastical lordship, seigneurial power and the commercialization of milling in medieval England*, Ashgate, Farnham

Lucas, A. T. 1953 'The horizontal mill in Ireland', *Journal of the Royal Society of Antiquaries of Ireland* LXXXIII, 1–36

Lydon, J. 1981 'The mills at Ardee in 1304', *Journal of County Louth Archaeological and Historical Society* 4, 259–63

Lynn, C. 1982 'The excavation of Rathmullan, a raised rath and motte in County Down', *Ulster Journal of Archaeology* 44–5, 65–171

Mangartz, F. 2008 *Römischer Basaltlava-Abbau zwischen Eifel und Rhein*, Römisch-Germanisches Zentralmuseum, Mainz

Manning, C. 2009 *The history and archaeology of Glanworth Castle, County Cork*, The Stationery Office, Dublin

Mayes, P. 2002 *Excavations at a Templar preceptory: South Witham, Lincolnshire, 1965–67*, The Society for Medieval Archaeology Monograph 19, Leeds

Moorhouse, S. 2003a 'Medieval corn mills in the manor of Rothwell', in S. Wrathmel, *Rothwell: the medieval manor and manorial mills*, West Yorkshire Archaeology Service, Leeds, 18–28

Moorhouse, S. 2003b 'Medieval Yorkshire: a rural landscape for the future', in T. G. Manby, S. Moorhouse, and P. Ottaway (eds), *The archaeology of Yorkshire: an assessment at the beginning of the 21st century*, Yorkshire Archaeological Society, York, 181–214

Mynard, D. C. and Zeepvat, R. J. 1992 *Great Linford: excavations of the medieval village and church*, Buckinghamshire Archaeological Monograph 3, Milton Keynes

Oleson, L. H. 2001 'Vandmølle ved Hessel', *Holstbro Museum Årrskift*, 5–15

O'Neill, T. 1987 *Merchants and mariners in medieval Ireland*, Irish Academic Press, Dublin

Parkhouse, J. 1997 'The distribution and exchange of Mayen lava quernstones in early medieval Europe', in G. de Boc and F. Verhaege (eds), *Exchange and trade in medieval Europe: papers of the medieval Europe Brugge Conference 1997. Conference III*, Zellik, 97–106

Pohl, M. 2011 'Querns as markers for the determination of medieval European trade spheres', D. Williams and D. Peacock (eds), *Bread for the people: the archaeology of mills and milling*, British Archaeological Reorts International Series 2274, 169–77

Posnasky, M. 1956 'The Lamport post mill', *Journal of the Northamptonshire Natural History Society and Field Club* 33, 66–79

Rahtz, P. and Meeson, R. 1992 *An Anglo-Saxon watermill at Tamworth: excavations in the Boleridge Street area of Tamworth, Staffordshire in 1971 and 1978*, Council for British Archaeology Research Report 83, London

Rohmer, P. 1996 'Le Moulin carolingien d'Audun-le-Tiche', *L'archéologue*, 22, 6–8

Rynne, C. 1997 'The Patrick Street Watermills: their technological context and a note on the reconstruction', in C. Walsh, *Archaeological excavations at Patrick, Nicholas and Winetavern Streets Dublin*, Brandon, Dingle, 81–9

Rynne, C. 1998 *Technological change in Anglo-Norman Munster*, Barryscourt Trust, Kinsale

Rynne, C. 2007 'A medieval watermill at Ballyine, County Limerick', *Journal of the Cork Historical and Archaeological Society* 112, 23–8

Rynne, C. 2011 'Technological continuity, technological "survival": the use of horizontal mills in western Ireland, c.1632–1940', *Industrial Archaeology Review* XXXIII(2), 94–103

Rynne, C. 2013 'Mills and milling in early medieval Ireland', in N. Jackman, C. Moore, and C. Rynne, *The mill at Kilbegly: an archaeological investigation on the route of the M6 Ballinasloe to Athlone national road scheme*, The National Roads Authority, Dublin, 115–47

Rynne, C. 2015a 'The technical development of the horizontal water-wheel in the first millenium AD: some recent archaeological insights from Ireland', *International Journal for the History of Science and Technology* 85(1), 70–93

Rynne, C. 2015b 'Landscapes of hydraulic energy in medieval Europe', in A. Chavarría Arnau and A. Reynolds (eds), *Detecting and understanding historic landscapes*, SAP Società Archeologia, Mantua, 225–52

Rynne, C. 2017 *The archaeology of water-power in early medieval Ireland*, Brill, Leiden

Stevens, L. 1982 'Some windmill sites in Friston and Eastbourne, Sussex', *Sussex Archaeological Collections* 120, 93–138

Thomas, J. 2009 'Excavation of a medieval post-mill mound at Manor Farm, Humberstone, Leicester', *Transactions of the Leicestershire Archaeological and Historical Society* 83, 113–29

Walsh, C. 1997 *Archaeological excavations at Patrick, Nicholas and Winetavern Streets Dublin*, Brandon Press, Dingle

Watts, M. 2002 *The archaeology of mills and milling*, Tempus, Stroud

Watts, M. 2013 'The archaeological exploration of windmill sites in England', in J. Dufour and O. Bauchet, *Le moulin et la maison du meunier de Roissy-en-France: archéologie et histoire*, Paris, 48–53

Watts, M. and Hardy, A. 2011 'The design and operation of the Northfleet mill', in P. Andrews, E. Biddulph, A. Hardy, and R. Brown, *Settling the Ebbsfleet Valley. High Speed 1. Excavations at Springhead and Northfleet, Kent, the Late Iron Age, Roman, Saxon, and medieval landscape. Vol. 1: the sites*, Wessex Archaeology, Oxford, 325–38

Webster, L. E. and Cherry, J. 1972 'Medieval Britain in 1971', *Medieval Archaeology* 16, 147–212

Wikander, Ö. 2000 'The water-mill', in Ö. Wikander (ed.), *Handbook of ancient water technology*, Brill, Leiden, 371–400

Wikander, Ö. 2008 'Sources of energy and exploitation of power', in J. P. Oleson (ed.), *The Oxford handbook of engineering and technology in the classical world*, Oxford University Press, Oxford, 136–57

Zeepvat, R. J. 1980 'Post windmills and archaeology', *Current Archaeology* 71, 375–7

CHAPTER 32

OLD MONEY, NEW METHODS

Coins and Later Medieval Archaeology

RICHARD KELLEHER

COINS are among the most abundant objects to survive from the Middle Ages and many hundreds of millions of coins were struck in the British Isles over the five centuries covered in this chapter, first in silver, and from the mid-fourteenth century also in gold. The traditional strength of coinage as a form of evidence comes from its association with a known authority and the ability of the numismatist to situate the production of a coin in time and space; indeed coins were among the few mass-produced objects that enabled rulers to convey messages directly to their subjects. Numismatic study in Britain has refined internal chronologies to such an extent that there are usually relative dating schemes to within the space of a few years and these provide a valuable *terminus post quem*. This perceived precision in dating is also an attractive prospect to the archaeologist, although one not without its caveats. While it is possible to draw useful information from the production aspects of coinage, it is only through an appreciation of consumption that the economic and monetary conditions of a particular site, region, or nation can really begin to be understood (Kemmers and Myrberg 2011, 89) while at the same time enabling the study of iconography, metrology, and die-studies. Criticisms levelled at artefact-based studies in late medieval archaeology include their lack of engagement with theoretical approaches and an overtly skewed focus on the mundane objects of everyday life which fail to engage with elite material culture (McClain 2012, 132). While theoretical approaches are seldom applied in numismatics, coinage, more than any other artefact type, was 'consumed' by a broad cross-section of society and has much to offer.

Coins of the later medieval period are found annually in their thousands, and while some of these come from excavations, nowhere have finds numbers been more dramatically accelerated than through metal-detecting. So, while a single coin can provide useful chronological evidence for a particular archaeological feature, the true strength of coin evidence comes from aggregated assemblages which can tell us about the economic, social, and political landscape though which they circulated. Since the emergence of metal-detecting in the 1960s there has been an uneasy relationship between finders and archaeologists (Campbell and Thomas 2015; Thomas and Stone 2009). The establishment of the Portable Antiquities Scheme (PAS) in parts of England and Wales in 1997 and its national roll-out in 2003 provided a central mechanism through which to foster cooperation between parties and the new finds data made available on the Scheme's website[1] has begun to revolutionize how we think about metal artefact studies. The purpose of this chapter is to provide a conspectus of the role of numismatics within the broader discipline of later medieval archaeology and to illustrate the new directions that current research is taking. Other numismatic objects such as jettons, tokens, and coin weights are not considered.

COINS, COLLECTING, AND ARCHAEOLOGY

The first systematic coin collections were formed in Renaissance Italy when medieval coins were collected alongside their classical antecedents (Grierson 1992, 114–15). In Britain collecting was slower to emerge but the important collections of the sixteenth century became the foundations of the great museum collections in London, Oxford, and Cambridge. While strides were made in categorizing the ancient Greek and Roman series, English coins were woefully underserved. In 1736, at the behest of the Society of Antiquaries, the first volume on English medieval coins was published by Martin Folkes (1690–1754). His *Table of English silver coins from the Normans to the present time* (1745), reissued in 1748 with plates, established post-Conquest coinage as a serious subject for collectors and scholars.

As later medieval numismatics slowly emerged in the nineteenth century its focus was staunchly typological and directed towards classification, meaning that British and English medieval coinages are now arguably the best classified and studied in Europe, with obvious benefits for those working with British coins. Engagement with archaeological methods, however, was hindered by the meagre nature of coin finds from British excavations when compared with those of the Roman period (Archibald 1988, 264). Stuart Rigold's work on site finds from properties under the protection of the Ministry of Works was a major advancement, and his analysis of finds from one hundred sites was a resounding endorsement of the viability of medieval coins for interpreting patterns of chronology and site-function (Rigold 1977). At around the same time the proceedings of a conference on 'Coins and Archaeology' were published, although only one paper covered later medieval coins. These were republished in a revised edition in 1988 but there was little new scholarship on the subject in Britain (but see Blackburn 1989) compared with other parts of Europe.

The major medieval coin collections of the British, Fitzwilliam, and Ashmolean Museums were built upon hoard finds, a consequence of the superior condition and

---

[1] www.finds.org.uk/.

availability of such material, but single coins which have become numerous in recent years are now an increasingly important contributor to acquisition and scholarship (Figure 32.1a). Important public and private collections have been published in the British Academy's *Sylloge of coins of the British Isles* (*SCBI*) which provides the most up-to-date classification and chronology in some series. Initiated by Philip Grierson in the 1980s and based largely on his great collection bequeathed to the Fitzwilliam Museum in 2006, *Medieval European Coinage* (*MEC*) continues to publish the Museum's collection. Significant surveys of the coinage from organizational and economic (Allen 2012) and numismatic (Stewartby 2009) perspectives have appeared recently, while Jeffrey North's two volumes remain the standard practical catalogue (North 1991; 1994). A significant proportion of numismatic work is carried out by 'amateurs' and can be found as articles in the *British Numismatic Journal* (*BNJ*) and *Numismatic Chronicle* (*NC*). As digital technology has advanced so coins in public collections have started to appear online and are a powerful tool for study. The databases of the Portable Antiquities Scheme (PAS) and Early Medieval Corpus[2] (EMC), which make available records of single finds have unlocked the potential of single-find data for scholars. Away from purely numismatic publications, coins can be found in the pages of excavation monographs, journals, and grey literature.

THE COIN: DOCUMENT AND ARTEFACT

It is widely accepted that coins are both documents and artefacts (Blackburn 2011, 581; Haselgrove and Krymnicek 2012, 245; Kemmers and Myrberg 2011, 89) and as such the approaches to them can be wide-ranging. The coinages of England and Scotland were minted for the king and their texts and images reflect the intentions of the authority who commissioned them. Most coins tell us the name of the king and his titles and the place of minting and, until 1278, the moneyer responsible for producing the coin (Figure 32.1b). Compared to European coins, English coinage was stylistically conservative, especially once the frequent changes of type under the Norman kings ceased in 1158. From 1279 to 1489 there was little change in coin design, but the introduction of new gold coinages in 1344 and 1465 brought the English coinage in line with commercially motivated monetary innovations in other parts of Europe. Until the fourteenth century Scottish coinage largely mirrored that of England but adopted a profile bust instead of a facing one and mullets in place of pellets. In overseas territories under English sovereignty there was more diversity; in Ireland for example the king's bust was set in a triangular frame while the Anglo-Gallic series used a variety of imagery, often with military connotations (Figure 32.1c).

As a class of artefact there is much to be learnt from coins even if contextual information is absent. Manufacture was a labour-intensive process requiring the input of

---

[2] www-cm.fitzmuseum.cam.ac.uk/emc/.

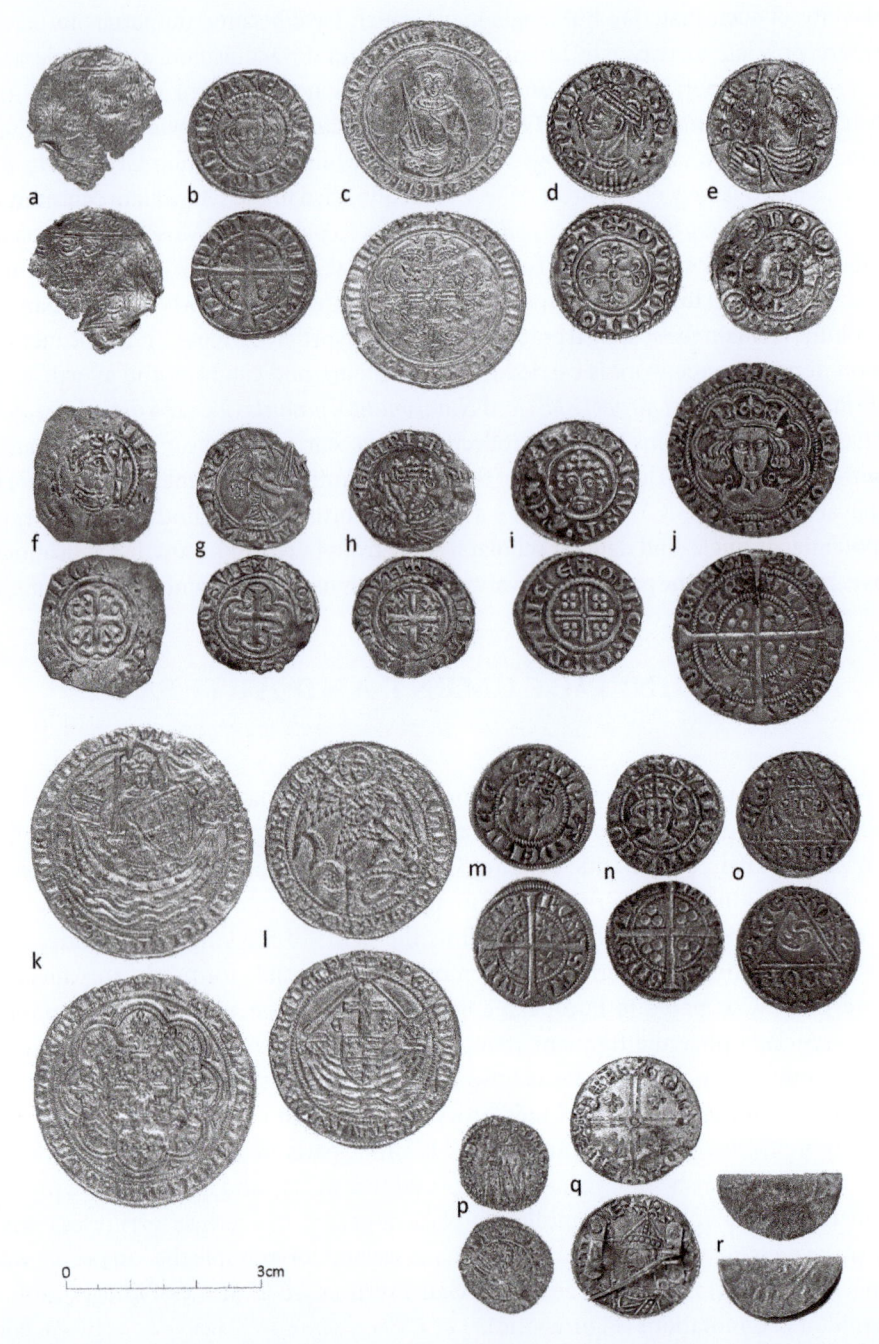

FIGURE 32.1 A range of medieval coins found in Britain: a) Almohad half dinar of Abu Ya'qub Yusuf I (AH 558-80/AD 1163-84), struck in North Africa (the mint is not named) 1168-84. Found at Wattisham, Suffolk. b) Edward I, silver penny, class 2b, London. c) Anglo-Gallic. Edward the Black Prince, gold hardi d'or, Bordeaux. d) William I, silver penny of the Profile/Cross Fleury type (1066-8?), Hastings, Duninc. e) Henry I, silver penny of the Double Inscription type (c.1115), Thetford, Burehard. The snick or cut is visible at about 8 o'clock,

different skilled workers; from the miners who extracted the silver and iron ores to the smiths who made and engraved the dies and the workmen and moneyers who prepared the blanks and struck them into coins. Numismatists have a long pedigree of studying the coins of a particular mint in order to identify the dies they were struck from (Harvey 2012; Mossop 1970). Despite the many thousands of dies that were used very few actually survive and this speaks to the strict level of supervision involved in their distribution and disposal. From the Thames Exchange site in London came reverse dies of William I, Henry I, and Stephen (Archibald et al. 1995), while an exceptional group of over three hundred dies, predominantly from the reign of Edward III, were preserved in the Pyx Chapel at Westminster Abbey until the nineteenth century, and these demonstrate the process of die recycling and refurbishment (Cook 2000, 228–9). Once minted, coins entered circulation and were subject to a dynamic system of use and re-use. They were used to pay wages and taxes, exchanged for goods at market, given as gifts, or offered in religious contexts; they were stored in groups and buried or hidden to later re-emerge and re-enter circulation; they were melted down and struck into new coins at the mint; they were mutilated or beautified to perform as non-monetary agents; and every coin we study today was lost or deposited and not recovered, either by design or accident, and it is these factors that dictate the methodologies we use to interpret such finds.

Digging and Dating: Excavation Coins

It is rare for European coinages to be structured in such a way that they can easily be broken down into circulation periods. Post-Conquest coinage can be divided into ten circulation periods within three broad phases and this helps in establishing when a coin was deposited as well as providing a structure for comparative analysis (Figure 32.2).

The coinage system after 1066 differed very little from that established by Eadgar in c.973 (Figure 32.1d). New designs, introduced at regular intervals at more than forty mints, refreshed the currency on a regular basis and prevented the accrual of worn, clipped, or bad money in the circulation pool. This *renovatio monetae* system is characteristic of most of Phase A. Eight types are conventionally attributed to the Conqueror,

---

some type 6 and all types 7–12 show this treatment. f) Stephen, silver penny of the 'Watford' type, Stamford, Lefsi. g) Eustace FitzJohn, silver penny depicting a knight with sword, York, Thomas Fitz Ulf. h) Henry II, class C1 silver penny of the Cross-and-Crosslets type, Bury St Edmunds, Willam. i) Henry II, Short Cross silver penny, class 1b1, Winchester, Osber. j) Henry VI, silver groat, annulet issue, Calais. k) Edward III, gold noble, pre-treaty, London. l) Edward IV (second reign), gold angel. m) Scotland. Alexander III, silver penny. n) Namur. William I (1337–91). Silver sterling imitation, Namur. o) Ireland. John, silver penny, third REX coinage, Dublin, Roberd. p) Venice. Michel Steno (1400–13). Silver soldino. q) Edward the Confessor silver penny, pointed helmet, Oxford, Heargod, coin jewellery. r) Henry III, Short Cross silver penny, class 6c1, folded

(© Fitzwilliam Museum, Cambridge; [r] © Richard Kelleher)

Phase	Period	Date range	Rulers and types
A	I	1066–1100	William I and II
	II	1100–1135	Henry I
	III	1135–1158	Stephen and the Baronial coinages
B	IV	1158–1180	Henry II's Cross-and-Crosslets coinage
	V	1180–1247	Short Cross coinage (Henry II, John, Richard I and Henry III)
	VI	1247–1279	Long Cross coinage (Henry III and late Edward I)
C	VII	1279–1351	Edward I and II to Edward III 'florin' coinage, penny weight 20.0 to 22.2 grains (1.30 to 1.44 g)
	VIII	1351–1412	Edward III's fourth coinage to Henry IV's heavy coinage, weight reduced to 18 grains (1.16 g)
	IX	1412–1464/5	Henry IV's light coinage to Edward IV's heavy coinage, weight reduced to 15 grains (0.97 g)
	X	1464/5–1544	Edward IV's light coinage to Henry VIII's second issue, weight reduced to 12 grains (0.78 g)

FIGURE 32.2 Periodization scheme for analysing medieval coins 1066–1544

five to William II, fifteen to Henry, and four to Stephen (for recent surveys of the Norman coinage see Allen 2014a for William I and II; Blackburn 1990 for Henry I; and Blackburn 1994 for Stephen). In Henry's reign problems began to emerge. A reform of about 1108 decreed that all pennies be 'snicked' in the edge prior to leaving the mint, evidently to prove they were not plated forgeries (Figure 32.1e) and at Christmas 1124 the *Anglo-Saxon Chronicle* reports a great purge of moneyers at Winchester, Hampshire, in which the guilty men each lost a hand and their testicles as punishment for 'false coining'. The coinage of Stephen's reign is iconographically the most interesting of the post-Conquest period (Figure 32.1f). In the 1140s, as Stephen lost control of those areas away from his power base in the south and east, irregular copies of the king's first type and coins of independent types were minted using local dies. The notion that individuals other than the king might strike coins, otherwise inconceivable in English currency, became a reality as Matilda and her Angevin supporters usurped the privilege. In the region of York a handsome and varied group of issues both for supporters and opponents of the king was issued (Figure 32.1g).

It was four years into his reign before Henry II turned his administrative zeal toward the coinage and when he did the results were revolutionary (Allen 2007). Henry's new 'Cross-and-Crosslets' coinage began a process of centralization, characteristic of Angevin-Plantagenet domestic policy generally (Figure 32.1h). Phase B is characterized by three 'closed' currency periods in which a rapid, comprehensive re-coinage completely replaced the previous issue. We can be confident that almost all period IV–VI losses occurred within their circulation period. The number of moneyers was severely reduced over Phase B as the mint network itself was reduced from forty-five or forty-six before 1158 to just four by the end of the Long Cross coinage (re-coinage periods notwithstanding). More fundamental was the abandonment of periodic changes of type, which meant that coins minted at the start of the Cross-and-Crosslet, Short Cross, and Long Cross were current until the next re-coinage (Figure 32.1i). New denominations were launched in this phase with experimental halfpennies and farthings in *c*.1222 and a gold penny struck in 1257, although none of these proved popular and were quickly abandoned.

Edward I's reform moved the coinage into a new phase. The new pennies were accompanied by round halfpence and farthings, but the characteristic element of this phase was the absence of any full re-coinage. This poses a number of problems for dating finds as a penny of 1279 could (and did) circulate into the sixteenth century. After 1351 groats, halfgroats, and gold coins became permanent fixtures in the currency (Figure 32.1j) creating a flexible suite of coins from the 6s 8d noble at the top (Figure 32.1k) down to the farthing. This denominational structure continued with little change up to 1544 other than the weight reductions of 1351, 1412, and 1464/5 and the introduction of a new gold coin, the ryal under Edward IV, and the angel as a replacement for the discontinued noble (Figure 32.1l). The debased money of Henry VIII's third coinage (1544–7) drove the good silver out of circulation and brought this phase to an end.

Hoarding in Medieval Britain

Der Schwedt ist komme, hat alz mitgenomme, hat auch wolle hawe, I habs vergrabe. 1634. Bozehartt (The Swedes came, took everything, also wanted [the coins], I buried [them]). So read the panicked handwritten note that accompanied a small hoard from the Thirty Years' War found at Bollingen (Württemberg) in Germany in 1910 (Grierson 1975, 132). Despite the existence of this unlikely, if evocative, tract rarely are the circumstances of a hoard's deposition so gratifyingly revealed. The only British parallel is an English Civil War hoard from Breckenborough (North Yorkshire) which was found in 1985 with two cheese receipts accompanying the coins (Besly 1987, 6). Coin hoards are the foundations upon which the numismatic discipline was built and remain a vital source of evidence. Since 1996 coin hoards from England and Wales have been legislated through the Treasure Act which superseded the old Treasure Trove laws. To qualify as Treasure a find must be at least 300 years old and comprise two or more silver or gold coins or ten or more base metal coins. In Scotland different statutory conditions obtain, with all finds subject to Treasure Trove law.

The hoard record is meagre until the mid-seventeenth century after which all but one decade, from the 1660s to the present day, has produced at least one recorded medieval hoard (Figure 32.3). Up to 2009 we have record of 534 English and Welsh hoards, which contained at least 536,404 coins. This impressive total is tempered by the poor recording and uncertain disposition of many antiquarian finds but the pattern is broadly one of growth in hoard numbers over time. The impact of major infrastructure works, such as canal and railway building, can be seen in the peaks in the 1850s and 1860s, while conversely the two World Wars are visible in the low numbers found in those decades. The rise from 1960 and particularly in the 1980s can be ascribed to the impact of

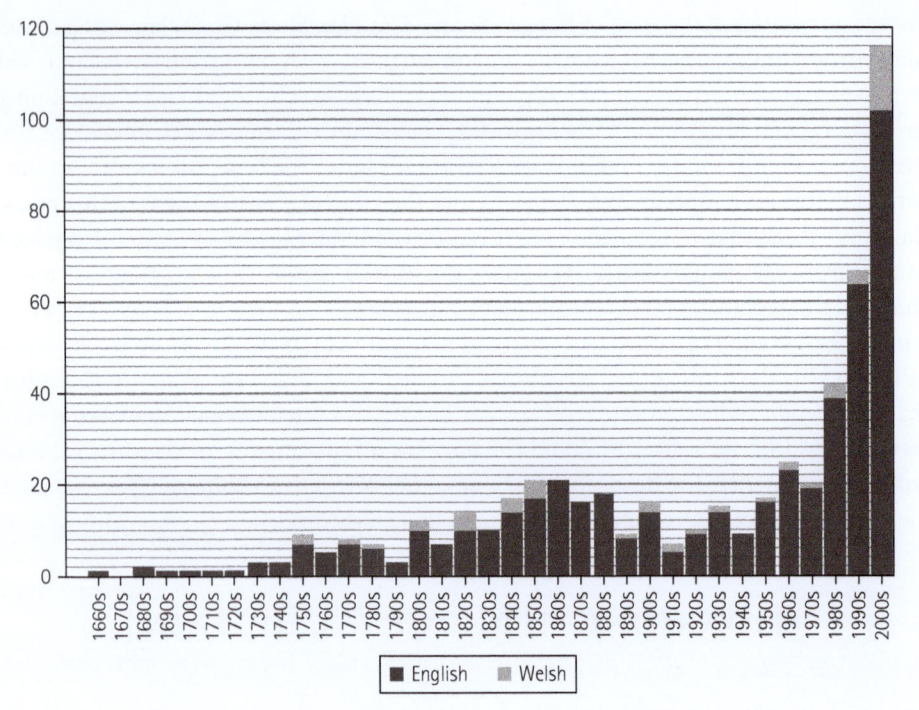

FIGURE 32.3 Finds of medieval coin hoards (1066–1544) made in England and Wales per decade (sources Allen 2012; 2015). Hoards without a definitive date of deposition are excluded; hoards with later addenda have been counted in the decade of the original find

metal-detecting, but it is no coincidence that the unprecedented leap in hoards in the 1990s and 2000s accords with the passing of the Treasure Act (Cook 2015, 159).

Hoard publication has been inconsistent. The first to provide a serious inventory of the British hoard evidence was J. D. A. Thompson's influential volume, which was followed by a less-detailed work covering hoards dated 1500–1967 (Brown and Dolley 1971; Thompson 1956). Individual hoards have traditionally found publication in the *British Numismatic Journal* (*BNJ*), *Numismatic Chronicle* (*NC*), and various local archaeological and historical journals (see Allen 2012, 446–514; 2015, 153–6). In the 1970s and 1980s, as hoard numbers were increasing, a series of seven *Coin Hoards* volumes was published by the Royal Numismatic Society, and between 1994 and 2011 the *NC* continued the format established in the *Coin Hoards* series. The first in a detailed series of volumes on medieval hoards recorded at the British Museum appeared in 2001 (Archibald and Cook 2001), the sequels on Norman and post-1279 hoards await publication. Between 1997 and 2007 details of all Treasure cases including medieval hoards were published in the *Treasure Annual Report*. In 2012 the British hoard element of the 'Coin Hoards' section published in the *NC* was reincarnated as 'Coin hoards of the British Isles' in the *BNJ*.

The hoard note cited above establishes unequivocally those details of deposition that usually remain ambiguous for most finds: namely the conditions under which it was assembled and concealed, the date of deposit, and something about its owner/depositor.

These are the strands of enquiry, coupled with the more tangible numismatic details of findspot, value, and class of hoard, which numismatists are keen to establish in order to build up a hoard corpus which informs our understanding of monetary conditions. In theory at least a coin hoard may represent a sample of the currency in circulation at the time it was assembled and buried, but the conditions under which the coins came together and were deposited make many finds unrepresentative of general currency and they are therefore to be interpreted with care (Blackburn 2011, 586; Grierson 1975, 130–6).

The hoard record represents the evidence of non-recovery rather than of deposition, so the question becomes not why the hoard was buried, but rather why it was not recovered. It is unwise to associate every hoard with turbulent historical events such as war or military movements as numismatists are often over-eager to do. It remains true, however, that in the period from *c.*1305/10 to the early/mid-1340s the previously barren county of Northumberland ranks first among all English counties for hoard finds (Cook 2015, 162), a clear correlation between the finds evidence and the disruption caused by the Scottish Wars. Hoard distributions have been used to good effect when compared with taxation and lay subsidy records to indicate patterns of wealth and population (Allen 2015, 148–9). New finds are capable of transforming our subject, particularly in those periods where the hoard record is weak, such as the twelfth century, the 1280s, 1400–25, and the early sixteenth century, but more often they tend to confirm existing interpretations.

This chapter began with the notion that coinage could provide evidence for the wealth of a range of social classes, and as hoards can comprise many thousands of coins or as few as two they are a particularly suitable source material for addressing such questions. One of the most astonishing hoards we know of was found in 1831 in the River Dove near Tutbury in Staffordshire. The hoard, probably comprising £1500, (as many as 360,000 silver pennies), was the war chest of Thomas, Earl of Lancaster, in his rebellion against Edward II and was buried or lost in the earl's flight from Tutbury Castle in 1322 (Kelleher and Williams 2011, 68). A find of 1237 gold coins (*c.*£400) and jewellery made at Fishpool, Nottinghamshire, in 1966 has similar elite links and has been interpreted as the property of a prominent member of one of the opposing factions in the Wars of the Roses (Archibald 1967, 140). Hoards comprising many thousands of coins have also been found in urban settings. The 1969 Colchester find of over 14,000 silver pennies (just over £58) of Henry III was possibly the property of two Jewish financiers (Archibald and Cook 2001, 95–6). Excavated medieval villages rarely yield coins but PAS finds suggest that coinage became a common element in rural communities in this period. A hoard of five silver pennies from the Northumberland village of West Whelpington is an indicator of pecuniary activity in such a context (Dyer 1997; Evans and Jarrett 1987; Kelleher 2018).

The Emergence of the Single Find

Metal-detected single finds are more representative of general currency than hoards and more abundant than excavated coins; they therefore provide a detailed and reliable statistical basis for gauging the volume of currency and patterns of circulation. The pioneering work of Michael Metcalf on Anglo-Saxon and Norman coins and Mark Blackburn on the so-called 'productive sites' established the potential applications of single-find evidence (Blackburn 2003; Metcalf 1998); and in recent years the explosion of new data made available through online databases has permitted interpretations of coin use that were previously impossible. The single-find evidence cannot be taken wholly at face value and its limitations require a considered methodology. Recovery levels are impacted by a number of variables, including the volume of coin in circulation at the time of loss, the extent (geographic and social) of participation in a monetary economy, how the coin was being used at the time of loss (whether in a transaction or as an offering), and the competence of the searcher and their equipment for locating small objects. The place of loss was important because a public space, such as a market place, provided more obstacles to recovery than a domestic setting (Blackburn 1989, 17), while itinerant or seasonal activities such as markets and fairs could be sited on pasture or meadow, where dropped objects might be difficult to see if they were trodden into the grass or soil. Interior flooring might be thought to aid recovery, for example on stone or clay surfaces coins could be more easily seen, but they also fall through the cracks between floorboards as did three fifteenth- to sixteenth-century coins excavated at Whitefriars, Coventry (Woodfield 2005). Moreover, floor coverings such as rushes, straw, or sand would impede recovery as would low levels of artificial light within buildings. Value is a subjective concept but the size and denomination of a coin were important considerations; smaller coins are more easily lost and less easily seen and the value of the coin and relative wealth of its loser would dictate the time spent in searching for it (Blackburn 1989, 17). Experiments have shown similar patterns among modern coin finds (Frazer and Van der Touw 2010; Newton 2006).

Single finds are assumed to be present in modern fields due to their accidental incorporation into manure or rubbish from local households. Thus a coin accidentally dropped in the home (or yard) might be swept up with floor-covering material and deposited on the manure heap and later ploughed into the owner's arable plot (Metcalf 1998, 14). Recent research has provided compelling evidence for the viability of metal-detected assemblages if collecting biases are understood (Bevan 2012; Robbins 2013) and the value of PAS data for looking at patterns of monetization and coin use in England and Wales has been demonstrated (Kelleher 2018). Using a sample of over 18,000 coins, chronological and denominational trends were observed between 1066 and 1544 (Figure 32.4). These provide a solid base for future studies.

The figures show growth in total coins and losses per year from Period I to VII. The massive increase visible in Period V is remarkable and is linked to increased output at English mints, fuelled by the availability of new bullion sources from central European mines (Spufford 1988) which greatly increased the currency pool. Loss levels continued to rise into Periods VI and VII after which there was a sharp downturn. The lack of a comprehensive re-coinage after 1279 meant coins of Periods VII–IX could circulate into later periods and scholars have used hoard evidence to estimate carry-overs from one period to the next (Allen 2005; Archibald 1988). Allen has estimated the length of

Period	Coins (PAS)	Losses/year	Value/loss (pence)	Hoards (per year)
I (1066–1100)	23	0.7	0.93	39 (1.5)
II (1100–1135)	40	1.1	0.87	17 (0.5)
III (1135–1158)	83	3.6	0.8	26 (1.13)
IV (1158–1180)	210	9.6	0.78	23 (1.1)
V (1180–1247)	3152	47	0.72	67 (1)
VI (1247–1279)	2593	81	0.65	21 (0.7)
VII (1279–1351)	5887	81.7	0.91	101 (1.4)
VIII (1351–1412)	1577	25.9	1.7	61 (1)
IX (1412–1464/5)	962	18.5	0.81	46 (0.9)
X (1464/5–1544)	1200	15	1.88	86 (1.1)

FIGURE 32.4 PAS single find evidence from England and Wales to 2008

circulation period as being contingent upon the type of coin; thus gold and groats were more likely to be lost within their period of issue than were the halfgroats and even more so the pence and fractions (2014b, 18–19). One of the more unexpected trends to come from the single-find evidence, and invisible in other sources, is the relative proportion of small denomination coins. This can be seen, in Phases A and B at least, in the value per loss diminishing from 0.93 pence in Period I to 0.65 pence in Period VI and is indicative of a developing diversification in denominational use, as coins came to be used in smaller transactions. The pattern after Period VII differs significantly as the minting of large denomination gold coins, silver groats, and halfgroats inflated the value of each loss; when combined with a reduction in population and inflation in the aftermath of the Black Death, this made a marked impact on the dynamics of the circulating coinage.

Imports

Imported foreign coins have been surveyed by Cook (1999a). England's south-east coast was the gateway through which monetary ideas and prototypes passed. From the eleventh century, and as national political networks became ever more international, ports of entry for foreign coins spread north and west. Foreign coins, at least in the eleventh to thirteenth centuries, tended to be actively excluded from hoards, and so the burden of evidence comes from single finds, both metal-detected and excavated. Figure 32.5 maps the sources of single finds found in England and Wales and between the eleventh and sixteenth century imported coin generally became more frequently encountered. These were the product of various mechanisms including political contacts, the movement of travellers and pilgrims, and trade links.

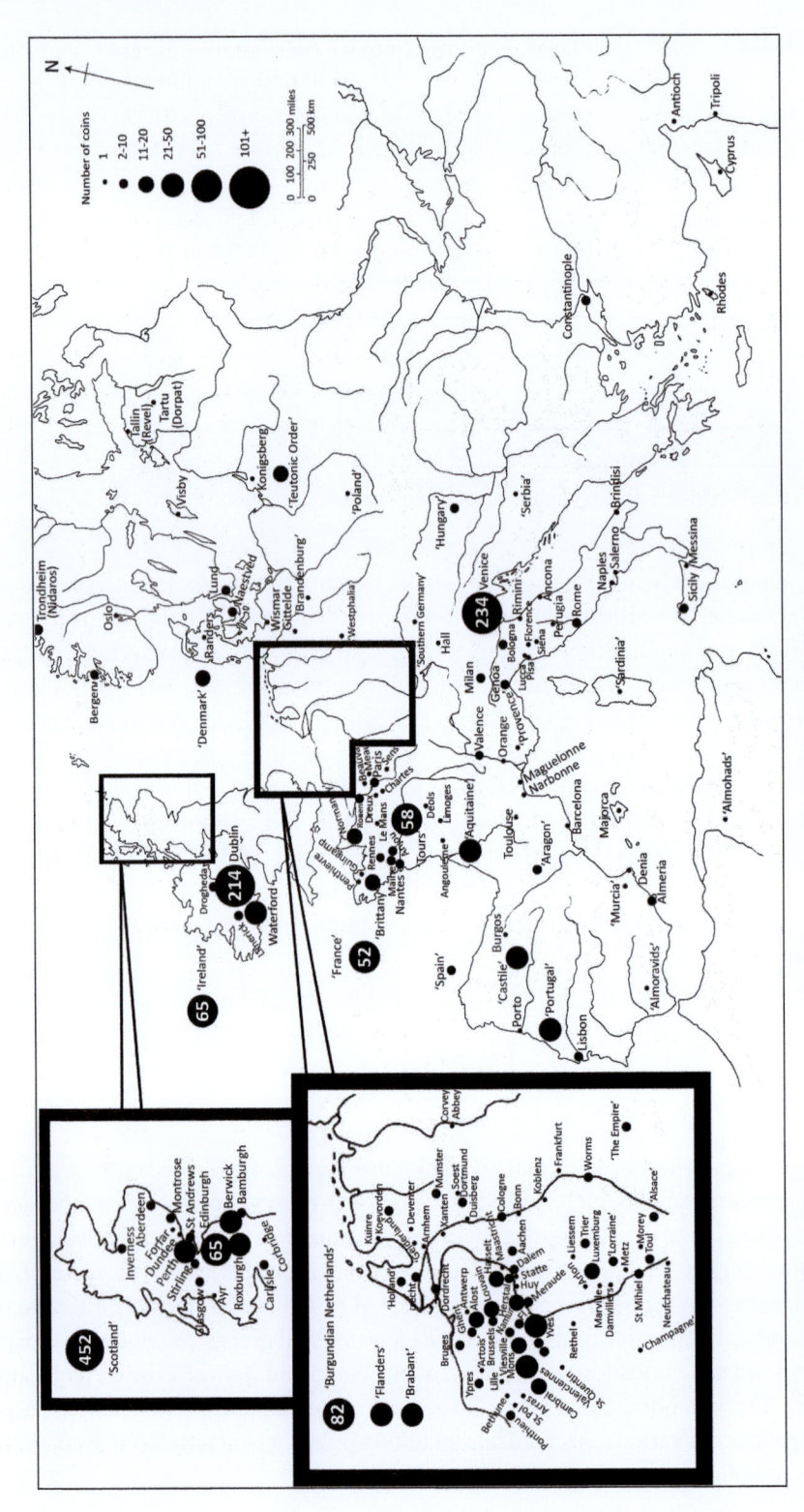

FIGURE 32.5 Map illustrating the sources of non-English coins found in England and Wales

(© Richard Kelleher)

Prior to the Norman Conquest England's primary political axis faced north-east to Scandinavia, but when the duke of Normandy became king mainland France became preeminent. This is reflected in Danish and Norwegian pennies giving way first to feudal deniers and thereafter to royal French coins as the resurgent monarchy of Philip II re-established control over the currency. The French gold ecu and silver gros tournois inspired English imitation, while the maintenance of English-held lands in France ensured that Anglo-Gallic coins continued to enter England in small numbers. The production of Scottish coins began with David I's capture of Carlisle, Cumbria, and its mint in 1136, and for the next two hundred years the Scottish coinage, struck at perhaps twenty-eight mints, was heavily influenced by the English (Figure 32.1m). In the Short and Long Cross periods (1180–1279), Scots coin accounts for 5–7 per cent of single finds and hoards, growing to a peak at the start of the Edwardian period (1279–1351), when Scottish coins average 8–12 per cent of hoards; this drops to 5 per cent between 1300–c.1315 and 2 per cent after 1320, as Scottish mint output shrunk. Debasement eventually led to legislation in the 1350s and 1370s prohibiting Scottish coins from circulating in England.

The coins from the commercially advanced Low Countries come from two main periods of activity. The tradition of imitating English pennies in mid-twelfth-century Westphalia and the Rhineland intensified in the thirteenth and early fourteenth century, threatening the integrity of English currency. Coins of the first phase (c.1280–99) include a bare headed bust ('pollard') or one wearing a chaplet of roses ('crockard'). Estimates suggest that more than seventy-two million of these were re-minted into English sterling in 1299 (Allen 2000, 43). From 1310 the imitative types, such as those struck for William of Namur (Figure 32.1n), adopted the crowned bust of the king and were again a cause for concern, even being referenced by contemporary writers such as Chaucer and the author of *Piers Plowman*. While documentary evidence is clear on the grand scale of the problem, the hoard evidence does not support such an interpretation and it has fallen to the single-find evidence to prove the veracity of the documentary evidence. The second period came in the late fifteenth century. Although never ratified, a monetary agreement of 1469 between Edward IV and Charles the Bold of the Burgundian Netherlands proposed that the Burgundian double patard should circulate at the value of the English groat, and these coins are found in some numbers as single finds and in hoards of the mid-1480s to 1544.

Anglo-Irish coinage was first struck by John as Lord of Ireland (from 1185), but it was his later pennies as king (1199–1216), with their distinctive triangular frame (Figure 32.1o), that were legalized as current in England in 1210. This led to large numbers of Irish pennies of John, Henry III, and Edward I entering English currency. These account for 2–4 per cent of English hoards and single finds. Irish minting ceased in 1302, after Edward's re-coinage, and was not revived until 1460, when silver coins of Henry VI and Edward IV were struck on a three-quarter weight standard to prevent them draining out of Ireland. Of this complex series, it is predominantly the pennies of the light cross and pellets coinage that are known as finds; their distribution patterns might indicate their entry via Scotland.

The large numbers of coins of Venice are the result of a specific phenomenon that plagued the English currency in 1400–15 and again in c.1500–20 (Daubney 2009). These small silver *soldini*, known as *galy hapens* in England, came annually with the Venetian trading fleet and, in a country lacking sufficient small coins, found use as halfpenny equivalents and are recovered across much of the country (Figure 32.1p). Spanish and Portuguese coins are scarce until the fifteenth century, when political and commercial links between England and Portugal in particular gave rise to an abundance of silver *chinfrões* (which were similar to the halfgroat) and copper *ceitils* as finds in London and also the south-west, which enjoyed substantial maritime trade with Portugal. Baltic coins are known in small numbers, and these are mostly *vierlings* of the Teutonic Order, which may possibly have circulated as halfpenny equivalents. Although it is tempting to link these with English participation in the Northern Crusade, Hanseatic trade is another possible source. Gold coins are generally rare finds but eight Islamic gold coins, mostly early twelfth-century Almoravid *dinars* minted in Spain, are known from England and support documentary evidence of the twelfth century showing payments being made in *oboli de musc* well before any indigenous gold coins were produced (Cook 1999b).

Secondary Use

Numismatic and archaeological approaches converge in those coins subject to secondary use. Coins were re-used in a variety of ways, either by physical adaption, such as beautification or mutilation, or by placement in a specific context, neither of which was mutually exclusive. Best known are Anglo-Saxon and Norman coins converted into 'brooches', but recent metal-detector finds reveal the presence of other styles. The coin badges which peaked in popularity c.1050–80 are typically gilded on the reverse side, thus displaying the cross design, while a pin and catchplate were soldered or riveted onto the obverse (Figure 32.1q). The thin pins on surviving examples suggest that their use was decorative or symbolic rather than functional to fasten clothing, and that they would be used to display the spiritual, political, or social allegiances of the wearer. These were followed in the twelfth century by a new type in which coins were transformed into open-frame annular brooches. The central roundel of the coin was neatly removed and a small hole added to allow the addition of a pin. A large group of converted coins comes from the late thirteenth and early fourteenth century. These conversions were dress-hooks made from English and Continental coins. Most involved the use of large *gros* or groat-sized coins, and have soldered on them either a single bar, looped at one end and hooked at the other, or a loop and hook separately affixed. In most cases the coin is gilded on one or both sides, with the face of the coin bearing the cross usually positioned for display. These were of a more permanent character than the previous types, as they would have been sewn onto a garment to enable fixing. The final type of coin jewellery comprises coin pendants. Surviving examples do not form a coherent chronological group and thus the meanings of each might be quite different, but they typically infer some devotional characteristic through the image of the Virgin Mary, as in a Byzantine example from Ware, Hertfordshire, or the cross. The addition of stone or glass embellishment speaks to the prophylactic use of some pendants (Kelleher 2012, 191–2). These adaptations extended the life span of the coin well beyond its circulation period. By 1350, however, there was a move away from adapting coins in this way perhaps as a response to changes in fashion or the wider availability of alternative and more affordable or desirable accessories. In recent years the number of gilded fifteenth-century low denomination coins has grown significantly although their purpose awaits scholarly consideration.

While the coins discussed above were adapted by the *addition* of fittings and gilding others were subject to *subtraction* by mutilation. This could involve bending, piercing, or cutting, as the physical embodiment of a religious vow or in being transformed into ceremonial paraphernalia. Finds of folded or bent coins are beginning to populate the landscape and change how we view a practice which has been historically linked to religious sites (Figure 32.1r) (Kelleher 2012). Despite the many miracle records which describe the practice of folding coins as a vow to a saint, just a handful of excavations have yielded folded coins (Merrifield 1987). Two Short Cross pennies found with the skeleton of a mature adult male in the cemetery of St James's Priory, Bristol, are rare examples of folded coins from a burial context (Gilchrist and Sloane 2005; Jackson 2006, 99).

Over 130 coins recorded on the PAS database show evidence of having been deliberately folded in antiquity. The question is why we find these objects in the ploughsoil. Some may perhaps have been intentionally deposited in the fields: there is some evidence for offerings of food and *ampullae* of holy water being placed to ensure a fruitful harvest (Anderson 2010). One recent PAS find provides compelling evidence. A silver-gilt groat of Henry VII (1485–1509) had within its fold a fragment of textile, which might be the remnant of a means of suspending the coin around the neck. We know that gilded coins were sometimes presented as offerings and also that folded coins were sometimes bound to the injured part of the pilgrim's body. This and other folded coins are an important source of evidence for the devotional behaviour of the medieval populations of Britain and merit further consideration alongside other pilgrim objects such as badges and *ampullae*.

Future Research

Numismatic scholarship continues to produce useful and thorough research and the traditional approaches and the forms they are disseminated in (catalogues, typological studies) are vital in underpinning the discipline. The sporadic nature of interdisciplinary collaboration, however, has led to limited dialogue between numismatists and archaeologists (especially so for the later medieval and early modern periods). It has been suggested that those working with coins could do more to engage with archaeological methodology (Kelleher and Leins 2011, 19-20) and vice versa and published articles from the last five years or so indicate this has begun to happen, but in Britain progress has been slow. In a survey of the condition of medieval archaeology in 2007, it was recognized that numismatics was a rare visitor to the pages of *Medieval Archaeology* (Gerrard 2009, 82), and the one exception in the Journal after 2007 was on Scandinavian coinage (Myrberg 2010a). To escape the impression that 'numismatics is only the handmaiden of history and archaeology' (Mayhew 2011, 11) it is vital that we engage numismatic material with methodological approaches and theoretical perspectives familiar in archaeology, anthropology, history, art history, and economics as some scholars have begun to do (Myrberg 2010b on colour).

There are some obvious areas where a holistic methodological approach would reap benefits and expand the questions we can ask of coin finds. As we have seen, hoards are a vital source for numismatics with interpretation focused on traditional questions about the money supply and composition of the circulating medium. Later medieval hoard analysis lags well behind Roman and prehistoric scholarship which has advanced theoretical ideas about the meanings behind the placement of the hoard within the landscape and the ritual or symbolic value its burial had for the community. Five coins excavated at Wanborough, Surrey, were found on the parish boundary and interpreted as a deliberate 'ritual' deposit (Williams 2007) but this type of interpretation is rare (but see van Vilsteren 2000 on hoards from wet contexts; and Myrberg 2009 on 'gendered' hoards). In order to fully realize the potential of hoards serious thought must be given to developing a pan-European database, which provides detailed records of the contents of each find (both coin and non-coin), the container, and full find-spot details. The application of methods to the growing material available through the PAS is in its early stages and must continue to develop as the corpus grows ever larger. Lost in these grand ideas is, however, the fact that without specialist numismatists to identify coins, all other research is compromised (Blackburn 2011, 596). Numismatists must be more proactive in leading initiatives and that in itself places the responsibility on an ever-shrinking group of professionals, most of whom work in museum departments. It will fall to these scholars to highlight the value of their work, and an integrated approach with other disciplines will be a vital tool in that endeavour.

Acknowledgements

I am grateful to Martin Allen, Barrie Cook, and Rory Naismith for comments on a draft of this chapter. Any errors remain the author's own.

References Cited

Allen, M. 2000 'The volume and composition of the English silver currency, 1279-1351', *British Numismatic Journal* 70, 38-44

Allen, M. 2005 'The interpretation of single-finds of English coins, 1279–1544', *British Numismatic Journal* 75, 50–62

Allen, M. 2007 'Henry II and the English coinage', in C. Harper-Bill and N. Vincent (eds), *Henry II: new interpretations*, Boydell, Woodbridge, 257–77

Allen, M. 2012 *Mints and money in medieval England*, Cambridge University Press, Cambridge

Allen, M. 2014a 'Coinage and currency under William I and William II', in R. Naismith, M. Allen, and E. Screen (eds), *Early medieval monetary history*, Ashgate, Farnham, 85–112

Allen, M. 2014b 'Coin finds and the English money supply, c.973–1544', in M. Allen and D. Coffman (eds), *Money, prices, and wages: essays in honour of Nicholas Mayhew*, Palgrave Macmillan, London, 7–23

Allen, M. 2015 'Coin hoards in England and Wales, c.973–1544', in R. Bland and J. Naylor (eds), *Hoarding and the deposition of metalwork from the Bronze Age to the 20th century: a British perspective*, British Archaeological Reports British Series 615, Oxford, 140–58

Anderson, W. 2010 'Blessing the fields? A study of late-medieval ampullae from England and Wales', *Medieval Archaeology* 54, 182–203

Archibald, M. M. 1967 'Fishpool, Blidworth (Notts.), 1966 hoard', *Numismatic Chronicle* 7th series, 7, 133–45

Archibald, M. M. 1988 'English medieval coins as dating evidence', in J. Casey and R. Reece (eds), *Coins and the archaeologist*, Seaby, London, 264–301 (2nd edn)

Archibald, M. M. and Cook, B. 2001 *English medieval coins hoards 1: Cross and Crosslets, Short Cross and Long Cross hoards*, British Museum, London

Archibald, M. M., Lang, J. R. S., and Milne, G. 1995 'Four early medieval coin dies from the London waterfront', *Numismatic Chronicle* 155, 165–200

Besly, E. 1987 *English Civil War coin hoards*, British Museum, London

Bevan, A. 2012 'Spatial methods for analysing large-scale artefact inventories', *Antiquity* 86, 492–506

Blackburn, M. 1989 'What factors govern the number of coins found on an archaeological site?', in H. Clarke and E. Schia (eds), *Coins and archaeology: Medieval Archaeology Research Group Proceedings of the first meeting at Isegran, Norway*, British Archaeological Reports International Series 556, Oxford, 15–24

Blackburn, M. 1990 'Coinage and currency under Henry I: a review', *Anglo-Norman Studies* 13, 49–81

Blackburn, M. 1994 'Coinage and currency', in E. King (ed.), *The anarchy of King Stephen's reign*, Clarendon Press, Oxford, 145–205

Blackburn, M. 2003 '"Productive" sites and the pattern of coin loss in England, 600–1180', in T. Pestell and K. Ulmschneider (eds), *Markets in early medieval Europe: trading and 'productive' sites, 650–850*, Windgather, Macclesfield, 20–36

Blackburn, M. 2011 'Coinage in its archaeological context', in H. Hamerow, D. A. Hinton, and S. Crawford (eds), *The Oxford handbook of Anglo-Saxon archaeology*, Oxford University Press, Oxford, 580–99

Brown, I. D. and Dolley, M. 1971 *Coin hoards of Great Britain and Ireland 1500–1967*, Spink, London

Campbell, S. and Thomas, S. (eds) 2013 *Portable Antiquities: archaeology, collecting, metal detecting*, Internet Archaeology Issue 33 (http://intarch.ac.uk/journal/issue33/index.html)

Cook, B. J. 1999a 'Foreign coins in medieval England', in L. Travaini (ed.), *Local coins, foreign coins: Italy and Europe 11th–15th centuries. The Second Cambridge Numismatic Symposium*, Società Numismatica Italiana Collana di Numismatica e Scienze Affini 2, Milan, 231–84

Cook, B. J. 1999b 'The bezant in Angevin England', *Numismatic Chronicle* 159, 255–75
Cook, B. J. 2000 'Coining dies in late medieval England with a catalogue of the British Museum collection', *Numismatic Chronicle* 160, 219–47
Cook, B. J. 2015 'England's silver age: new and old hoards from England under the three Edwards (c.1279–1351)', in R. Bland and J. Naylor (eds), *Hoarding and the deposition of metalwork from the Bronze Age to the 20th century: a British perspective*, British Archaeological Reports British Series 615, Oxford, 159–71
Daubney, A. 2009 'The circulation and prohibition of Venetian soldini in late medieval England', *British Numismatic Journal* 79, 186–98
Dyer, C. 1997 'Peasants and coins: the uses of money in the Middle Ages', *British Numismatic Journal* 57, 31–47
Evans, D. H. and Jarrett, M. G. 1987 'The deserted village of West Whelpington, Northumberland: third report part one', *Archaeologia Aeliana* 5th series, 15, 254–5
Folkes, M. 1745 *A table of English silver coins from the Normans to the present time*, The Society of Antiquaries, London
Frazer, E. and Van der Touw, J. 2010 'The random walk: a study of coins lost and found in an urban environment', *Numismatic Chronicle* 170, 375–405
Gerrard, C. M. 2009 'Tribes and territories, people and places: 50 years of medieval archaeology in Britain', in R. Gilchrist and A. Reynolds (eds), *Reflections: 50 years of medieval archaeology 1957–2007*, The Society for Medieval Archaeology Monograph 30, Leeds, 79–112
Gilchrist, R. and Sloane, B. 2005 *Requiem: the medieval monastic cemetery in Britain*, Museum of London Archaeological Service, London
Grierson, P. 1975 *Numismatics*, Oxford University Press, London
Grierson, P. 1992 'Numismatics', in J. M. Powell (ed.), *Medieval studies: an introduction*, Syracuse University Press, 114–61
Harvey, Y. 2012 'Catalogue and die-analysis of the Winchester mint-signed coins', in M. Biddle (ed.), *The Winchester mint and coins and related finds from the excavations of 1961–71*, Winchester Studies 8, Oxford
Haselgrove, C. and Krymnicek, S. 2012 'The archaeology of money', *Annual Review of Anthropology* 41, 235–50
Jackson, R. 2006 *Excavations at St James's Priory, Bristol*, Oxbow Books, Oxford
Kelleher, R. 2012 'The re-use of coins in medieval England and Wales c.1050–1550: an introductory survey', *Yorkshire Numismatist* 4, 183–200
Kelleher, R. 2018 *Money in the medieval town and countryside: coin finds from England and Wales 1066–1544*, British Numismatic Society Special Publication 14, London
Kelleher, R. and Leins, I. 2011 'Coins in context: archaeology, treasure and the Portable Antiquities Scheme', in B. J. Cook (ed.), *The British Museum and the future of UK numismatics: proceedings of a conference held to mark the 150th anniversary of the British Museum's Department of Coins and Medals*, British Museum Research Publication 183, London, 18–24
Kelleher, R. and Williams, G. 2011 'The Tutbury Hoard of 1831', in M. Hislop, M. Kincey, and G. Williams (eds), *Tutbury: 'A castle firmly built': archaeological and historical investigations at Tutbury Castle, Staffordshire*, British Archaeological Reports British Series 546/Birmingham Archaeology Monograph Series 11, 62–87
Kemmers, F. and Myrberg, N. 2011 'Rethinking numismatics: the archaeology of coins', *Archaeological Dialogues* 18(1), 87–108
Mayhew, N. 2011 'The British Museum and the UK numismatic community: past experience and future possibilities', in B. J. Cook (ed.), *The British Museum and the future of UK*

numismatics. Proceedings of a conference held to mark the 150th anniversary of the British Museum's Department of Coins and Medals, British Museum Research Publication 183, London, 11–13

McClain, A. 2012 'Theory, disciplinary perspectives and the archaeology of later medieval England', *Medieval Archaeology* 56, 131–70

Merrifield, R. 1987 *The archaeology of ritual and magic*, Batsford, London

Metcalf, D. M. 1998 *An atlas of Anglo-Saxon and Norman coin finds, c.973–1086*, Royal Numismatic Society Special Publication 32, London

Mossop, H. R. 1970 *The Lincoln mint, c.890–1279*, Corbitt and Hunter, Newcastle

Myrberg, N. 2009 'The hoarded dead: Late Iron Age silver hoards as graves', in I. M. Back Danielsson, I. Gustin, A. Larsson, N. Myberg, and S. Thedéen (eds), *On the threshold: burial archaeology in the twenty-first century*, Stockholm Studies in Archaeology, 47, 131–45

Myrberg, N. 2010a 'A worth of their own: on Gotland in the Baltic Sea, and its 12th-century coinage', *Medieval Archaeology* 54, 157–81

Myrberg, N. 2010b 'The colour of money: crusaders and coins in the thirteenth-century Baltic Sea', in F. Fahlander and A. Kjellström (eds), *Making sense of things: archaeologies of sensory perception*, Stockholm Studies in Archaeology 53, 83–102

Newton, D. P. 2006 'Found coins as indicators of coins in circulation: testing some assumptions', *European Journal of Archaeology* 9(2–3), 211–27

North, J. J. 1994 *English hammered coinage. Vol. 1: early Anglo-Saxon to Henry III, c.600–1272*, Spink, London

North, J. J. 1991 *English hammered coinage. Vol. 2: Edward I to Charles II, 1272–1662*, Spink & Son, London

Rigold, S. E. 1977 'Small change in the light of medieval site finds', in N. J. Mayhew (ed.), *Edwardian monetary affairs (1279–1344)*, British Archaeological Reports British Series 36, Oxford, 59–80

Robbins, K. J. 2013 'Balancing the scales: exploring the variable effects of collection bias on data collected by the Portable Antiquities Scheme', *Landscapes* 14(1), 54–72

Spufford, P. 1988 *Money and its use in medieval Europe*, Cambridge University Press, Cambridge

Stewartby, B. H. I. H. 2009 *English coins 1180–1551*, Spink, London

Thomas, S. and Stone, P. G. (eds) 2009 *Metal detecting and archaeology*, Boydell, Woodbridge

Thompson, J. D. A. 1956 *Inventory of British coin hoards, AD 600–1500*, Royal Numismatic Society, Oxford

Van Vilsteren, V. T. 2000 'Hidden and not intended to be recovered: an alternative approach to hoards of mediaeval coins', *Jaarboek voor Munt-en Penningkunde* 87, 51–63

Williams, D. 2007 'Green Lane, Wanborough: excavations at the Roman religious site 1999', *Surrey Archaeological Collections* 93, 149–265

Woodfield, C. 2005 *The church of Our Lady of Mount Carmel and some conventual buildings at the Whitefriars, Coventry*, British Archaeological Reports British Series 389, Oxford

CHAPTER 33

PLAY AND PLAYFULNESS IN LATE MEDIEVAL BRITAIN

Theory, Concept, Practice

MARK A. HALL

The English engraver and antiquary Joseph Strutt, in his seminal *The sports and pastimes of the people of England*, observed that: 'In order to form a just estimation of the character of any particular people, it is absolutely necessary to investigate the Sports and Pastimes most generally prevalent amongst them' (Strutt 1833, xvii–xviii). More than two hundred years later, 'play' is seen to be of fundamental importance not only to happiness and creativity but also to our understanding of past human behaviour (Harari 2014). In the context of the archaeology and material culture of later medieval Britain, there is still a conventional view of medieval play which sees it as light-hearted, inconsequential, ephemeral, and largely the province of children in spite of tremendous interest in theorizing play and playfulness across the social sciences, inspired in part by the huge popularity of computer and video games (Bateson and Martin 2013; Costikyan 2013; Sicart 2014). Here it is generally recognized that play and playfulness is a key element in enabling social performance and one that transcends ethnicity, time, and space across all social levels. Time devoted to leisure is time not devoted to one's occupation and survival needs and is therefore, in some senses, a measure of the strictures on time applied within any given part of society.

Games and play have a complex role in modern everyday life as they did in the past. Psychologist Sutton-Smith (1997) identifies seven key messages they might embody, namely: progress, fate, power, identity, the imaginary, self-absorption, and the frivolous. This is a useful starting point because it emphasizes the extent to which play is meant to enable an escape from the everyday but, at the same time, may mirror specific situations in life (as between competing ethnic and national groups, for example) and the broader struggles of human existence. Whether they were played by a child or an adult in the medieval period, board games were fundamental to an enjoyment of life, to a sense of identity, to rebellion and subversion, to an engagement with metaphor, and a desire to understand the future. This chapter focuses especially on board and dice games but complementary reading might include items such as musical instruments, balls, dolls, miniatures (such as Raeren stoneware figurines), rattles, puppets, and much else besides. There is now quite a range of literature on the topic from across Europe but key texts for Britain would feature *Medieval children* (Orme 2003), *Pleasures and pastimes in medieval England* (Reeves 1995), *Growing up in medieval London* (Hanawalt 1993), and *Toys, trifles and trinkets* (Forsyth with Egan 2004), together with the range of shorter articles which feature in the bibliography.

Performing the Social Sphere: Secular, Religious, and Gendered Play Networks

The many stories of miraculous aid recorded by Bernard of Angers in *The book of Sainte Foy* include that of the knight Raymond de Montpezat. Imprisoned by his enemies and heavily chained, St Foy intervenes, Raymond's chains fall away and his guards remain sleeping as he flees. Standing in the great hall of the castle, it occurs to Raymond that 'although he could not convey his chains to the holy virgin's basilica because of their great weight, at least he could carry off the chessboard hanging there, as evidence of his escape. After he had grabbed it and thrown himself headlong over the wall ... he sped away on bare feet.' Foy gives Raymond further aid—this time a pair of shoes—to speed his escape and on reaching Cahors he stops and takes refuge in St Stephen's Cathedral. He sends a large candle to St Foy's shrine and she appears once more, upbraiding him for not completing his vow, urging him to 'Throw off the bonds of delay, take up the chessboard that is the physical proof of your liberation, set out swiftly on the footpath to Conques and celebrate the joyous feast of Easter there'. He resumes his journey arriving 'at the oft-mentioned place carrying the chessboard with him and prostrated himself in prayer'. He then gives a public account of his imprisonment. By chance the son of his captor is in the crowd and as astonished as everyone else present to hear about Raymond's adventures. But he could not deny the escape because he saw in Raymond's hands 'his own chessboard which Raymond had carried off to Conques [and] offered to the lady virgin as evidence of the miracle' (Sheingorn 1995, 191–6). The gaming board reliquaries of St Rupertus and of Charlemagne are still to be seen, in the churches of Aschaffenburg, Germany, and Roncesvalles, Spain, respectively (Gauthier and Heredia 1982; Hüseler 1957, 620–2; Jenderko-Sichelscmidt et al. 1994 cat. 70). In this miracle story performance, mobility and play are all closely bound together and Raymond's escape opens up some key lines of investigation around the social context of board games.

Identity and Status

The story of Raymond makes it clear that the chessboard was a key piece of material culture associated with castles. Indeed, in France and the Rhine Valley they are tantamount to a signature find from early castle sites (Creighton 2012, 112–14; Grandet and Goret 2012). From Gloucester Castle a substantially complete, highly decorated, tables (or *tabula*) board with its pieces was recovered from a refuse deposit (Stewart 1988; Watkins 1985). Other examples (Figure 33.1) including graffiti gaming boards for *merels* (or Nine Men's Morris) and for *daldos*, and gaming pieces have been found, for example, at Launceston Castle, Cornwall (Riddler 2006, 365–71); Dryslwyn, Carmarthenshire (O'Connor et al. 2007, 264–5); Castle Acre, Norfolk (Coad and Streeten 1982, 253 and 260–3); Carrick, Argyll (Ewart and Baker 1998, 975); and Dundonald, Ayrshire (Caldwell 2006, 107–9). As Raymond's narrative indicates, chess and other games were often a matter of public display—the board he took had been left hanging in the great hall, and this is also reflected in the evidence gathered from medieval paintings. The illumination f. 265v from Royal MS 14.E.iv, a late fifteenth-century copy of Jean Froissart's *Chronicles*, shows a banquet attended by Richard II and the Dukes of York, Gloucester, and Ireland. To the king's left, hanging on the wall behind him, is a chessboard. In *c.*1530, a cycle of four murals, each covering three months in a 'labours of the months' cycle, was painted in the Imperial Free City of Augsburg, Bavaria. The painting for January–March depicts a feast being held in the Fuggerhäuser (itself only completed in 1515), the private residence and administrative centre of Jacob Fugger 'the rich', the wealthy head of the Fugger merchant and entrepreneurial family. Hanging on the wall of the house is

FIGURE 33.1 One of the Nine Men's Morris boards, with playing piece, from Nevern Castle, Wales. This board is clearly playable; excavations at Nevern have also revealed a range of graffiti boards, some of apotropaic significance (Caple and Davies 2008; Caple 2012)

(© Chris Caple)

a chessboard. As Jacob Fugger and his family enjoy the feast so other guests engage in cards and tables (or tric-trac). Chess and other board games were as much a social performance as they were an individual or family contest and in this case the interior scene is complemented by another, this time outside in the courtyard, in which two knights joust in a tournament. Although Fuggerhäuser was not a castle, Fugger's great wealth enabled him to display his acquired aristocratic status in various forms of ostentation, including games.

In late medieval Britain, as in the rest of Europe, board games and the tournament (along with hunting and other outdoor sports; see Chapters 10 and 25) were staples of court life. Invariably they were gambled upon, as the exchequer records for Edward II demonstrate (Vale 2001, 171–2). This was also true of chess, which was recognized as a skill that contributed to the very definition of a knight, and which also made it an integral element of the etiquette of chivalry and courtly love. These forms of play both enshrined and appealed to aristocratic values and were readily adaptable to the changing context of court life, chess being the pinnacle of all aristocratic pursuits (Eales 1985, 58; Hopkins 1994; Vale 2001, 175–9). Logically, descriptions were common in imaginative medieval romances, particularly the motif of the magical chessboard which appears, for example, in tales of the Arthurian cycle such as the *Roman van Walewein*, the Dutch version of Gawain (Hall 2016). In this way games were embedded within aristocratic values but not restricted to aristocratic circles and a key way in which aristocratic privilege, or sense of ownership over games, was maintained was through skill and proficiency achieved through the leisure time to play the games as well as through expenditure on finely crafted playing pieces and boards in gold, silver, precious stones, and rock crystal, together with books and works of art that depicted aristocratic play, and in the huge amounts of money spent in gambling. While losses could be written off, winnings might be given away, 'an aspect of upper-class social relations, a disguised form of patronage and largesse' (Eales 1985, 29). Both games and gambling were avidly engaged in across society and repeated attempts by church and state to prevent or control such behaviours generally failed (Dean 2001; Hall 2014b; McIntosh 1998). As well as the castle assemblages, therefore, many urban assemblages also include gaming equipment (Figure 33.2; and see also Figure 30.2), and there are examples from Norwich (Margeson 1993), York (MacGregor et al. 1999; Mainman and Rogers 2000; Morris 2000; Ottaway and Rogers 2002), Perth (Hall 2005), Beverley (Armstrong et al. 1991), and London (Egan 1998). European comparisons do exist (e.g. Øye 2013; Rybina 2007) and chess was already played in al-Andalus in the ninth century. As later Spanish archaeological finds and treatises on chess, dice, and *tablas* make clear, these games were popular pastimes (Valor and Gutiérrez-González 2014, 190; for artisanal activity see Farr 2000, 258–75).

Occasionally, archaeology also affords a rare insight into the taste for and role of board games in rural communities. From England the key example is West Cotton, Raunds, Northamptonshire. In the thirteenth and fourteenth centuries this hamlet comprised five tenements. The fifth of these was smaller than the others and understood to be a cottage converted from a former kitchen. Labelled Tenement D, it lacked yards and outbuildings and only had a croft of half an acre. The limited finds from the building

FIGURE 33.2 A selection of medieval dice from the High Street excavations, Perth, Scotland
(© Perth Museum and Art Gallery)

included three stone gaming boards for *merels*. This has led to the suggestion that the building had a special purpose such as a social meeting place and possibly retired peasants may have had more time for such pursuits (Chapman 2010, 157–61; Gilchrist 2012, 152–3). One of the boards was found in a pit alongside a stone carving of a person at prayer. The excavators saw the latter as a 'rare example of peasant or domestic art' (Chapman 2010, 359) and the association with the gaming board suggested 'religious or mystical associations' (Chapman 2010, 178). Developing this idea, Gilchrist (2012, 231) suggests it could have been a divination gaming board in line with Braekman's (1980) description of such practice in which casting dice, playing cards, or counting lots—the holes on a gaming board—served as the oracular answers to formulaic, future-orientated questions. This association is a long-established aspect of board and dice games and it has been suggested that the roots of board games may lie in divination and related rituals (Huizinga 1955; Lévi-Strauss 1972) as well as wider links between medieval play and religion (Bornet and Burger 2012).

At Castle Acre Castle, Norfolk, there is a striking parallel for the West Cotton 'games room'. Here, four chalk gaming boards (three for Nine Men's Morris, one for tables) plus three further fragments, along with two chalk chess pieces and two further probable gaming pieces were all recovered from a small, crudely built rectangular structure (Building A) that abutted the north wall of the early twelfth-century country house (itself later converted to a keep). The room had also been decorated with crudely carved human figures on chalk blocks (Coad and Streeten 1982, 157 and 260–3; a further fragment of a *merels* board was recovered from the upper ward ditch, Coad et al. 1987, 298). The structure seems unlikely to be the 'games room' of the castle's owners, the de Warenne earls of Surrey, but it would be consistent with use by the castle's household staff and craftsmen. We also know from textual evidence that gentry families used their homes as play spaces, 'where men and women came together to solve puzzles and play games, including fortune-telling by dice, chess, cards and backgammon' (Gilchrist 2012, 152; and see also MacDonald 2008). The majority of these examples are enclosed spaces within quite tightly defined social contexts but we should also remember that the openness of social life meant that much was done in the public view. The greater part of the evidence for board games excavated, for example, in Winchester (playing piece, dice, a *merels* board, etc.) was recovered from the open spaces around the cathedral (Brown 1990, 698). Some of this play could have involved pilgrims or the cathedral community (compare the dice and counters from the male college community of the Vicar's Choral, York; Rogers 2005).

Playful Pilgrims and Spirited Saints

In spite of the Church's dual stance of both condemnation and endorsement, games were played in monasteries and cathedrals. When the Franciscan house at Greyfriars Carmarthen, Wales, was excavated in the 1980s, the finds included two slate-incised *merels* boards recovered from a void beneath the choir stalls (Brennan 2001, 89). This may indicate illicit gaming activity in the choir but there were certainly other areas of monastic or cathedral precincts where such play was permitted, chiefly the cloisters. Graffiti boards have long been known from English cathedrals and abbeys including Norwich, Salisbury, Westminster, and Gloucester and were first recognized by Micklethwaite (1892). He assumed that all the graffiti he had identified were the work of medieval and later schoolboys but confirmation of the use of cloisters by monks for the playing of games comes in a ghost story by Caesarius of Heisterbach. In his *Dialogue on miracles* he records a ghostly apparition describing it as taking place 'after vespers ... [when] the scholars were playing in the twilight in the cloisters' (Joynes 2001, 49). As might be expected, recorded examples tend to concentrate in those areas of the cloister where the daylight lingers longest but they are also found elsewhere. Several games are represented including *merels* (probably the commonest), hare-tafl, daldos, alquerque, and variations of chess.

Graffiti gaming boards can also be found within the more publicly accessible parts of cathedrals (see Chapter 39). In Lincoln Cathedral the stone benches of the nave bear traces of boards. Their dating is challenging and some may well have been carved as a diversion from church services although other interpretations are possible. At Salisbury Cathedral, after a long campaign over several centuries, St Osmund was finally officially canonized in 1457. The shrine comprised a *foramina* of the twelfth century which, when it was finally completed, was placed in the Holy Trinity chapel (Figure 33.3). Following the Reformation, the shrine exists once more as only the *foramina* (Tatton-Brown 2009) located on an arcade bench on the south side of the Holy Trinity chapel. Built of fossil-rich Purbeck marble, its southern margin has been incised with two alquerque

FIGURE 33.3 The tomb of St Osmund, Salisbury Cathedral, Wiltshire, with detail of one of the gaming boards (for alquerque)

(© M. A. Hall, courtesy of Salisbury Cathedral)

boards and a chess-style board of 10 x 10 cells. The boards are impractically small to be played and too difficult to see clearly against the fossil background they were cut into. A likely explanation is that they were carved by pilgrims, not necessarily to pass the time but to leave a mark of their visit. The choice of gaming boards may reflect an unrecorded, orally transmitted gaming episode in Osmund's own life, an everyday pursuit which linked saint with believer, or they may represent a miracle story. The 1450 papal inquiry into Osmund's holiness recorded at least two stories of miracles which relate injuries from bat-and-ball and quoits games (Malden 1901; McLean 1984, 6). The Salisbury graffiti therefore might be seen as a form of self-determined engagement with the cult of saints by pilgrims who did not always distinguish them from heroic great men as a source of spiritual aid (for a wider analysis of the invocatory character of graffiti; see Owen 2010 and Plesch 2002). In many cathedrals and parish churches the tomb figures of the powerful, local nobility seem to have attracted invocations. The late sixteenth-century tomb of Sir William Wodehouse at St Mary's Church, Hickling (Norfolk) bears a rich palimpsest of graffiti including several gaming boards. Norfolk retained its Catholic sympathies for many years after the Reformation and this tomb graffiti are a vivid example of continuing practices into the post-medieval period.

In these examples, play is deliberately entangled into religious practice (Hall 2009; 2014b) and it continued to be so despite the Reformation and changes in social context. Such entanglements were contested, as had been recently demonstrated by the case study of a playing card re-purposed as an item of religious devotion and recusancy (Williams 2010). The card in question is a three of hearts, which, when it was removed from a prisoner (either Anthony Norton or Richard Lowther, both men of the Duke of Norfolk, all rescusants) in the Tower of London in 1571, had been adapted as a devotional aid. The blank reverse had been filled by the addition of a coloured drawing of a Crucifixion group arranged as a triptych and the card folded and cut to create the effect of triptych wings and a rounded arch effect. Folding the card made it easier to conceal and, because it was portable, it could function as a personal amulet. The card was confiscated because it was regarded as seditious; recognized as having a powerful agency in recalling the Old Religion and its practices. The particular playing card chosen, the three of hearts, could readily serve both as a Trinitarian symbol and as symbolic of devotion to the heart of Jesus. Other examples of playing cards with religious symbolism include a pack of cards printed in Rouen in the sixteenth century, its wrapper being printed with the Vernicle and the motto *Sauveur de Monde*.

Gender and Childhood

Gaming equipment was open to use by all, but specific contexts can be revealing. Reference has already been made to the male religious community of the Bedern or Vicar's Choral in York, where the evidence for gambling games and also drink, knife-carrying, and sexual innuendo indicates a certain moral laxity amongst its male members. A different community of men who also played is revealed by the excavation of the *Mary Rose* (sunk in 1545), where board games were clearly an essential, anti-boredom remedy in the kit of the navy's sailors (Redknap 2005). Within the various religious orders, nuns, monks, and friars all participated and there are several testaments and account records which show that royal and aristocratic women possessed board games (Vale 2001, 172, 176–7); these were sometimes passed on as heirlooms into church treasuries where they were accepted as donations and commemorated both family and saints. Several donated chess sets in church treasuries are said to have belonged to Charlemagne. What is clear is that no one game seems to have been the preserve of a single gender, at the same time the ambiguity of play means that it was amenable to being engendered in particular contexts. MacDonald's case study (2008) is an admirable example of the erotically charged word games of love which were aimed at a predominantly female audience who valued levity as much as piety. Gendered play in gentry households included amorous games between young men and women, many of them a playful form of dice-based divination (Gilchrist 2012, 152; MacDonald 2008, 239).

The link between play and children may seem obvious but medieval childhood has only recently emerged as a topic for study (see Chapter 47). It is not true that there was no concept of medieval childhood and archaeology has long demonstrated otherwise (e.g. Woodfield 1981: a case study of school life). In the wake of Orme's study of *Medieval children* (2003) and also the re-evaluation of the available evidence from material culture, several studies of medieval childhood and play have appeared, including Willemsen (2008), Gläser (2012), and Hall (2014a), which collectively demonstrate the ubiquity of play, often best evidenced from urban contexts. For children almost any object can become a toy and any space a playground (see Chapter 48; Lewis 2009) and in the medieval period children would almost certainly have availed themselves of board games. They were a mechanism for embedding a sense of gender in boys and girls, a tool of socialization or social reproduction (Smith 2014, 70–1), a means of informal education, and, within the family, they served to strengthen bonds. Late medieval texts confirm that children had access to and enjoyed what are often mistakenly assumed to be adult games: tables, chess, dice (Orme 2003, 178). Girls were not excluded from such play—indeed they contributed to the popularity of chess through its inclusion in strategies of courtly love, which permitted young women to pit themselves against young men. Women/girls could also compete against other women/girls as several illuminations in the thirteenth-century *Book of games* of Alphonso X of Castile show (Schädler and Calvo 2009; Yalom 2004). Humanist writers, Erasmus and Vives included, advocated play as being character-forming, in particular for boys, 'restoring the body for further intellectual study' (Hindman 1981, 459). Erasmus also wrote a colloquy entitled 'Knucklebones or the Game of Tali', tracing their history from ancient Greece (and its play by men and boys) down to his own time where it had become 'only' a girl's game (Hindman 1981, 452). Flemish artist Pieter Bruegel's mid-sixteenth-century oil-on-panel, *Children's games*, shows precisely this, as well as girls playing with dolls.

Final Score

Play is fundamental to the performance and negotiation of agency in a range of gendered settings both secular and religious. Board games, as we have seen, encourage interaction between people as well as a sense of shared identity but they can also be involved in the expression of religious belief and its subversion, as objects and graffiti can testify. For children and for adults, play was a means to perform, negotiate, and advocate their agency and the ambiguous, uncertain and metaphorical qualities of play are fundamental to the development and display of human behavioural traits across all contexts. Play delivers an escape from reality but, at the same time, it can define reality whilst being divorced from it. The material culture evidence (texts, objects, spaces) from medieval Britain is complex and varied, replete with biographical trajectories and ripe for further analysis.

Acknowledgements

I am grateful to the editors for inviting this contribution and to colleagues who contributed advice and information: David Caldwell, Katherine Forsyth, Roberta Gilchrist, Ulrich Schädler, Annemarieke Willemsen, and Howard Williams. All remaining errors are my own.

References cited

Armstrong, P., Tomlinson, D., and Evans, D. H. 1991 *Excavations at Lurk Lane Beverley 1979–82*, Sheffield Excavation Reports 1, J. R. Collis, Sheffield

Bateson, P. and Martin, P. 2013 *Play, playfulness, creativity and innovation*, Cambridge University Press, Cambridge

Bornet, P. and Burger, M. (eds) 2012 *Religions in play: games, rituals and virtual worlds*, Pano Verlag, Zurich

Braekman, W. L. 1980 'Fortune-telling by the casting of dice: a Middle English poem and its background', *Studia Neophilologica* 52, 3–29

Brennan, D. 2001 *The small finds and other artefacts from excavations at Camarthen Greyfriars 1983–90*, Dyfed Archaeological Report unpublished Topic Report 4, Camarthen

Brown, D. 1990 'Dice, a games-board, and playing pieces', in M. Biddle, *Object and economy in medieval Winchester*, Winchester Studies 7ii, Clarendon Press, Oxford, 692–706

Caldwell, D. 2006, 'Inscribed and engraved slates', in G. Ewart and D. Pringle, '"There is a castle in the west ...": Dundonald Castle Excavations 1986–93', *Scottish Archaeological Journal* 262, 107–10

Caple, C. 2012 'The apotropaic symbolled threshold to Nevern Castle–Castell Nanhyfer', *The Archaeological Journal* 169(1), 422–52

Caple, C. and Davies, W. 2008 'Surveys and excavations at Nevern Castle 2005–8', *Archaeology in Wales* 48, 39–46

Chapman, A. 2010 *West Cotton, Raunds: a study of medieval settlement dynamics AD 450–1450. Excavations of a deserted medieval hamlet in Northamptonshire 1985–89*, Oxbow Books, Oxford

Coad, J. G. and Streeten, A. D. F. 1982 'Excavations at Castle Acre Castle, Norfolk, 1972–77: country house and castle of the norman earls of Surrey', *The Archaeological Journal* 138, 138–301

Coad, J. G., Streeten, A. D. F., and Warmington, R. 1987 'Excavations at Castle Acre Castle, Norfolk, 1975–1982: the bridges, lime kilns and eastern gatehouse', *The Archaeological Journal* 144(1), 256–307

Costikyan, G. 2013 *Uncertainty in games*, MIT Press, Cambridge, MSS

Creighton, O. H. 2012 *Early European castles: aristocracy and authority, AD 800–1200*, Bristol Classical Press, London

Dean, T. 2001 *Crime in medieval Europe 1200–1500*, Longman, Harlow

Eales, R. 1985 *Chess: the history of a game*, Batsford, London

Egan, G. 1998 *The medieval household: daily living c.1150–c.1450*, Medieval Finds from Excavations in London 6, Her Majesty's Stationery Office, London

Ewart, G. and Baker, F. 1998 'Carrick Castle: symbol and source of Campbell power in South Argyll from the 14th to the 17th century', *Proceedings of the Society of Antiquaries of Scotland* 128, 937–1016

Farr, J. R. 2000 *Artisans in Europe 1300–1914*, Cambridge University Press, Cambridge

Forsyth, H. with Egan, G. 2004 *Toys, trifles and trinkets: base metal miniatures from London 1200–1800*, Unicorn, London

Gauthier, M.-M. and Heredia, M. C. 1982 *El retablo de Aralar y otros esmaltes navarros*, Institución Principe de Viana, Pamplona

Gilchrist, R. 2012 *Medieval life: archaeology and the life course*, The Boydell Press, Woodbridge

Gläser, M. (ed.) 2012 *Lübecker Kolloquium zur Stadtarchäologie im Hanseraum VIII: Kindheit und Jugend, Ausbildung und Freizeit*, Verlag Schmidt-Römhild, Lübeck

Grandet, M. and Goret, J.-F. (eds) 2012 *Échecs et Trictrac: fabrication et u des jeux de tables au Moyen Âge. Catalogue de l'exposition présentée du 23 juin au 18 novembre 2012 au Musée du château de Mayenne*, Editions Errance/Mayenne: Château de Mayenne, Paris

Hall, M. A. 2005 'Burgh mentalities: a town-in-the-country case study of Perth, Scotland', in K. Giles and C. Dyer (eds), *Town and country in the Middle Ages: contrasts, contacts and interconnections, 1100–1500*, The Society for Medieval Archaeology Monograph 22, Leeds, 211–28

Hall, M. A. 2009 'Where the abbot carries dice: gaming-board misericords in context', in E. C. Block (ed.), *Profane imagery in marginal arts of the Middle Ages*, Turnhout, 63–81

Hall, M. A. 2014a ' "Merely players …" Playtime, material culture and medieval childhood', in D. M. Hadley and K. A. Hemer (eds), *Medieval childhood: archaeological approaches*, The Society for the Study of Childhood in the Past Monograph 3, Oxford, 39–56

Hall, M. A. 2014b 'Board of the kings: the material culture of playtime in Scotland AD 1–1600', in M. Teichert (ed.), *Sport und Spiel bei den Germanen, Nordeuropa von der römischen Kaiserzeit bis zum Mittelalter*, De Gruyter, Berlin and Boston, 163–96

Hall, M. A. 2016 '*Jeux sans frontières*: play and performativity or questions of identity and social interaction across town and country', in B. Jervis, L. Broderick, and I. Grau-Sologestoa (eds), *Objects, environment, and everyday life in medieval Europe*, Brepols, Turnhout, 189–212

Hanawalt, B. A. 1993 *Growing up in medieval London: the experience of childhood in history*, Oxford University Press, London and New York

Harari, Y. N. 2014 *Sapiens: a brief history of humankind*, Harvill Secker, London

Hindman, S. 1981 'Pieter Bruegel's *Children's games*', *The Art Bulletin* LXIII.3 (Sept. 1981), 447–75

Hopkins, A. 1994 *The book of courtly love: a celebration of romance and passion*, Aquarian, London

Huizinga, J. 1955 *Homo Ludens: a study of the play-element in culture*, Beacon Books, Boston

Hüseler, K. 1957 'Das Aschaffenburger Brettspiel "Sanct Ruprechs-Bredtspiel und Schachspiel" ', *Aschaffenburger* 4, 593–623

Jenderko-Sichelscmidt, I., Marquart, M., and Ermischer, G. 1994 *Stiftsmuseum der Stadt Aschaffenburg*, Bayerische Museen, Munich

Joynes, A. 2001 *Medieval ghost stories*, Boydell and Brewer, Woodbridge

Lévi-Strauss, C. 1972 *The savage mind*, Weidenfeld and Nicolson, London

Lewis, C. 2009 'Children's play in the later medieval English countryside', *Childhood in the Past* 2, 86–108

MacDonald, N. 2008 'Fragments of *(Have Your) Desire*: Brome women at play', in M. Kowaleski and P. J. P. Goldberg (eds), *Medieval domesticity: home, housing and household in medieval England*, Cambridge University Press, Cambridge, 232–58

MacGregor, A., Mainman, A. J., and Rogers, N. S. H. 1999 *Bone, antler, ivory and horn from Anglo-Scandinavian and medieval York*, The Archaeology of York 17/12, Council for British Archaeology, York

Mainman, A. J. and Rogers, N. S. H. 2000 *Craft, industry and everyday life: finds from Anglo-Scandinavian York*, The Archaeology of York 17/14, Council for British Archaeology, York

Malden, A. R. (ed.) 1901 *The canonisation of St Osmund from the manuscript records in the Muniment Room of Salisbury Cathedral*, Wiltshire Records Society, Salisbury

Margeson, S. 1993 *Norwich households: medieval and post-medieval finds from Norwich Survey Excavations 1971–78*, East Anglian Archaeology 58, Norwich

McIntosh, M. K. 1998 *Controlling misbehaviour in England 1370–1600*, Cambridge University Press, Cambridge.

McLean, T. 1984 *The English at play*, Kensal Press, Windsor Forest

Micklethwaite, J. T. 1892 'On the indoor games of school boys in the Middle Ages', *The Archaeological Journal* 49, 319–28

Morris, C. A. 2000 *Craft, industry and everyday life: wood and woodworking in Anglo-Scandinavian and medieval York*, The Archaeology of York. The Small Finds 17/13, York

O'Connor, S., Spence, C., and Caple, C. 2007 'Bone, antler and ivory objects', in C. Caple (ed.), *Excavations at Dryslwyn Castle 1980-95*, The Society for Medieval Archaeology Monograph 26, Leeds, 264–72

Orme, N. 2003 *Medieval children*, Yale University Press, London

Ottaway, P. and Rogers, N. S. H. 2002 *Craft, industry and everyday life: finds from medieval York*, The Archaeology of York 17/15, Council for British Archaeology, York

Owen, K. 2010 'Traces of presence and pleading: approaches to the study of graffiti at Tewksbury Abbey', in J. Oliver and T. Neal (eds), *Wild signs: graffiti in archaeology and history*, British Archaeological Reports International Series 2074, Banbury, 35–46

Øye, I. (ed.) 2013 *'Small things forgotten': locks and keys and board games*, The Bryggen Papers Supplementary Series 9, Bergen

Plesch, V. 2002 'Memory on the wall: graffiti on religious wall paintings', *The Journal of Medieval and Early Modern Studies* 32(1), 167–98

Redknap, M. 2005 'Recreation: games and gaming', in J. Gardiner and M. J. Allen (eds), *Before the mast: life and death aboard the Mary Rose*, The Archaeology of the *Mary Rose* 4, Portsmouth, 133–40

Reeves, A. C. 1995 *Pleasures and pastimes in medieval England*, Alan Sutton Publishing, Stroud

Riddler, I. 2006 'Stone, bone, antler and ivory', in A. Saunders, *Excavations at Launceston Castle, Cornwall*, The Society for Medieval Archaeology Monograph 24, Leeds, 357–80

Rogers, N. 2005 ' "Wine, women and song": artefacts from the excavations at the College of Vicars Choral at the Bedern, York', in R. A. Hall and D. Stocker (eds), *Vicars choral at English Cathedrals. Cantate domino: history, architecture and archaeology*, Oxbow, Oxford, 164–87

Rybina, E. A. 2007 'Chess pieces and game boards', in M. Brisbane and J. Hather (eds), *Wood use in medieval Novgorod*, Oxbow Books, Oxford, 354–9

Schädler, U. and Calvo, R. (eds) 2009 *Alfons X. 'der Weise': Das Buch Der Spiele*, LIT, Vienna and Berlin

Sheingorn, P. (trans.) 1995 *The book of Sainte Foy*, University of Pennsylvania Press, Philadelphia

Sicart, M. 2014 *Play matters*, MIT Press, Cambridge, MSS

Smith, S. V. 2014 'The spaces of late medieval peasant childhood: children and social reproduction', in D. M. Hadley, and K. A. Hamer (eds), *Medieval childhood: archaeological approaches*, Oxbow Books, Oxford, 57–74

Stewart, I. J. 1988 'Note on the *Tabula*', in T. Darvill, 'Excavations on the site of the early Norman castle at Gloucester, 1983–84', *Medieval Archaeology* 32, 31–2 (1–49)

Strutt, J. 1833 *The sports and pastimes of the people of England including the rural and domestic recreations: May games, mummeries, shows, processions, pageants, and pompous spectacles from the earliest period to the present time*, new edition by William Hone, London

Sutton-Smith, B. 1997 *The ambiguity of play*, Cambridge University Press, Cambridge

Tatton-Brown, T. W. T. 2009 *Salisbury Cathedral: the making of a medieval masterpiece*, Scala, London

Vale, M. 2001 *The princely court medieval courts and culture in north-west Europe 1270–1380*, Oxford University Press, Oxford

Valor, M. and Gutiérrez-González, J. A. 2014 *The archaeology of medieval Spain 1100–1500*, Equinox, Sheffield

Watkins, M. 1985 *Gloucester, the Normans and Domesday; exhibition catalogue and guide*, Gloucester Museum, Gloucester

Willemsen, A. 2008 *Back to the schoolyard: the daily practice of medieval and Renaissance education*, Brepols, Turnhout

Williams, R. L. 2010 'Contesting the everyday: the cultural biography of a subversive playing card', in T. Hamling and C. Richardson (eds), *Everyday objects: medieval and early modern material culture and its meanings*, Ashgate, Farnham, 241–56

Woodfield, C. 1981 'Finds from the Free Grammar School at the Whitefriars, Coventry c.1545–1557/8', *Post-Medieval Archaeology* 15, 81–159

Yalom, M. 2004 *Birth of the chess queen: a history*, Pandora Press, London

PART VII

THE ARCHAEOLOGY OF RELIGION AND BELIEF

CHAPTER 34

OVERVIEW

Church and Landscape c.1100–1550

RICHARD MORRIS

By 1250 Britain was notionally covered by areas within which each household was allocated to a parish church containing an altar, and each household member knew where it was. The idea that this was all-embracing, or that parish churches lay at the centre of everyone's devotional life, is a simplification that has been attributed more to medieval legal imagination than to reality (Rosser 1991; 1996). But the parishes were real enough. There were about 11,725 of them, and they were overseen through sub-regional and regional groupings of archdeaconries and dioceses. Alongside the parishes were well over a thousand institutions of many kinds and sizes that included monastic houses, colleges, hospitals, and centres of pilgrimage (Burton 1994; Cowan and Easson 1976; Graham-Campbell 1994; Heale 2004). All these in turn co-existed with expressions of more or less informal devotion that included public and private chapels, oratories, hermitages, wayside monuments, wells, steles and crosses at river crossings, processional pathways, and offering places. Large tracts of the landscape itself were owned, managed, or exploited by religious bodies. The proportions varied according to the region of Britain and type of land, but roughly a quarter of recorded land value seems to have been booked to ecclesiastical owners at the end of the eleventh century, while four centuries later the suggested figure lies between one quarter and a third (Trim and Balderstone 2004, 17). Institutional and vernacular religion readily interacted with forms of ritual and behaviour like magic or witchcraft that we might now regard as their opposites (Gilchrist 2008; Houlbrooke 2004; Mitchell 2011; Rider 2012). Landscape is also a realm of legend, cultural memory, custom, and tradition, reflected, for example, at Glastonbury, or Strata Florida where many of the dominant texts of Welsh identity were worked on (Austin 2004; 2013; Gilchrist and Green 2015; Whyte 2009).

Economically and organizationally, then, the Church was not one agent but a swirl of interests. In terms of symbolism, on the other hand, it was a focused force, while through law it drew people and landscape into deep connection (Iogna-Prat 2008). This is thus a richly textured field, and as Part VII of this *Handbook* shows, elements of it have been attracting archaeological attention since the 1960s. However, archaeology's collecting processes are not like the suction of a Hoover, and even if they were it is often the habit of things in the Hoover's bag to mask their meanings. At any given point, moreover, the ways in which subjects are defined or examined will be influenced by traditions, personal enthusiasms, prevailing assumptions, and regional and national preoccupations (Oexle 1997, 79). More than this, 'the Church in the landscape' is not a single field of study across Britain. At the close of the period attitudes to sacred vernacular landscape and parish structure in Scotland differed markedly from those in England and Wales (Cowan 1961, 50–1; Spicer 2010, 266). Or again, many of the underlying affinities of churches and chapels in the coastal landscapes of north and north-west Britain (and that is a lot of landscape) belong more with Scandinavia and Ireland than with developments in southern Britain (Morris 2001, 71; cf. Fellows-Jensen 2001).

Intellectual influences in monastic and church archaeology over the last quarter century have been surveyed by Roberta Gilchrist (2014), who recognizes two broad phases. The first, to the mid-1990s, asked historical, economic, and technological questions, concentrated on particular sites and worked under the influence of landscape history and processualism. The second, from the mid-1990s, was informed by post-processual approaches and considered 'change and complexity in religious landscapes and perspectives on religious space, embodiment, and agency' (Gilchrist 2014, 235). Alongside Gilchrist's survey there have been others, such as the work of John Schofield and Alan Vince considering religion in British towns in a European context (2003, 175–211), and interdisciplinary studies of areas where spiritual and temporal spheres interacted around the time our period ends (Coster and Spicer 2005; Walsham 2011). What follows sets out very selectively to augment or annotate some of these rather than to repeat them, firstly by pointing to examples of genres within which different kinds of landscape topic have been or could be addressed, and latterly by taking up Gilchrist's challenge for a more expansive approach to the archaeological study of medieval belief through reflection on two themes that invite fuller attention than they have so far received.

At the start of our period the story of how Britain's landscape came to be churched had already been in progress for several hundred years. Picking the story up at the start of the twelfth century is thus a little arbitrary, not least because campaigns of monastic and local church building and founding were then in full swing (Wand and Wand 2010). It is no exaggeration to say that by the end of the twelfth century the face of Britain had been changed as a result. Looking at the parish churches first, their proliferation (eventually 1250-plus in Scotland, over 975 in early modern Wales, around 9500 in England) ran from the tenth century to the early twelfth in England and Wales (Blair 1988; 2005; Evans et al. 2000; Saul 2017, 19–37), sometimes a little later in Scotland (Cowan 1967), and the churches appeared before the full working out of the jurisdictions and responsibilities that they later came to acquire. Thereafter the nature and tempo of renewal varied from place to place. In some areas, the initial buildings were never much altered. In others, they evolved bit by bit, and in yet more, but less often, they were replaced wholesale. Degrees of prosperity have been adduced for such variability, with change at its fullest in wealthy areas like Suffolk, parts of Norfolk and fenland, and least in poorer districts such as the South Downs or uplands of the Welsh Marches. In between were areas like Warwickshire or Northamptonshire where churches evolved step by step, and so enable us to trace patterns of preference behind the forms that enlargement took (Barnwell 2004).

Wealth was far from being the only influence on change. Taking parish churches first, the relationship between historical demography and parish size, community feeling, family interests, and the influence of corporate rectors were all important (Lawrence 2003). For reasons to do with the character of lordship, social structure, and numbers of tithe-paying households, districts of concentrated population in the eleventh century tended to produce small, close-packed parishes. As a result, parishioners in such areas during the later Middle Ages could find themselves in competition for resources with neighbouring parishes and thus unable to expand or renew to the extent that they would like. Contrariwise, gentry in the fourteenth and fifteenth centuries 'started almost to overwhelm' some parish churches with their presence (Saul 2006, 247).

One turning point in the modern study of the social and landscape contexts in which local churches came into being—for instance whether through lordly initiative or neighbourly collaboration—is represented by the work of Paul Everson and David Stocker in Lincolnshire and Sarah Gibbon in Orkney (Everson and Stocker 2006; Gibbon 2012). A number of completed projects such as Wharram Percy (North Yorkshire), The Hirsel (Berwickshire), Auldhame (East Lothian), and Gogar (Edinburgh) offer new or confirmatory insights, although given the ways in which medieval Britain was regionalized, the extent to which results from one area may hold good in another call for more consideration (Cramp 2014; Crone et al. 2016; Mays et al. 2007; Morrison et al. 2009). A similar point applies in areas where places of worship feature in the results of interdisciplinary projects like Shapwick (Somerset) or Whittlewood (Northamptonshire) that have set out to characterize rural settlement at landscape scale (Barnwell 2008; Gerrard and Aston 2007; Jones and Page 2004; 2006). In this opening-up of discussion of the setting of the church, relationships between church interior and exterior, the relative influences of parishioners and lords, and location, enjoy widening exploration (Graves 2000; McClain 2011; Sánchez-Pardo and Shapland 2015; Saul 2017 12–15; Steele 2014). Alongside them runs continuing debate on fractional matters like church alignment (Hinton 2006; 2010; Hoare 2014).

Looking outward, there are rewarding themes that have been examined locally but await comparative exploration on a wider scale. Among them are the relationships between churches and communications. Both parish structure and monastic landholding had effects on the landscape by determining the existence and direction of rights of way. In areas where there was little or no correspondence between lay landholdings and parish boundaries the influence of the church was additional to the service needs of the manor. In areas where parishes and settlements were compact and churches were co-located with villages the effect on the road system could be small, but in areas of dispersed settlement new paths and roads were often created when churches and chapels were built. In places, of course, such routes could make use of lengths of existing ways, or lead to their realignment (Moorhouse 1981a, 626–7). However, where original stretches of such ways crossed or respected pre-existing elements in the human landscape, or where later features were superimposed, they provide indications of relative chronology and weight of use. Similarly, in regions where large blocks of land came into the hands of religious houses, new routes were often created or existing ones adjusted either to reach them or to connect dispersed parts of an estate. The presence of extensive monastic property could thus have a large effect on an area's road system (Moorhouse 1981a, 628–9).

Related themes include religious features that were associated with the roadside, such as hermitages and crosses. For a traveller, the customary duties of a hermit included those of 'host, guide, light bearer, labourer, alms gatherer, turnpike man and bridge warden' (Clay 1914, 57). The positions of hermitages at ends of bridges, by fords, in empty areas, tended to reflect these roles, and their insubstantial structure poses a corresponding challenge in the reconstruction of their geography (Gilchrist 1995, 157–208; Moorhouse 1981b, 650–1).

A similar challenge applies to wayside crosses. Place-names, judicial records, records of land transactions, and roadside stumps of stone reveal the frequency with which crosses were positioned in places of local significance. Examples are the township edge, at bridge ends, points where ways met, or where one jurisdiction began and another ended. This was an ancient monumental tradition: the corpora of stone sculpture in England and Wales reveal the extent to which places of crossing were accompanied by large monuments. Just how numerous and impressive they could be is revealed by the remarkable map that was produced around 1450 to inform a legal dispute between the Duchy of Lancaster and St Mary's Abbey, York, over rights to turbaries and pasturage in Inclesmoor, on the Lincolnshire-Yorkshire boundary (TNA MPC 1/56; Beresford 1986). The area corresponded with Thorne and Goole Moors, which even today forms a strange waterland of raised bogs bounded by the rivers Aire, Ouse, Humber, Trent, and (formerly) the old Don. In the fifteenth century, elaborate crosses stood beside village entrances, bridges, parks, and roads. Almost all traces of them have gone, here as elsewhere chiefly as a result of their systematic beheading in the sixteenth century.

Cross-heads, along with who knows how many parochial and monastic devotional objects, were among items sequestered during the early Reformation. As new examples of such bestowal come to attention, so older discoveries once explained in prosaic ways present themselves for reconsideration, as in the case of the gold rings and sumptuous reliquary ring that were sequestered in the River Thame (Oxfordshire) by members of Notley Abbey in the 1530s (Standley 2016; see Figure 49.3 in this *Handbook*). Following pioneering work in the Witham valley and East Anglia it no longer comes as a surprise to encounter such deposits in the context of long-term ritual continuities in later medieval places under ecclesiastical influence, or evidence for the structuring of monastic landscapes in symbolic as well as functionalist ways (Bezant 2013; Everson and Stocker 2011a; 2011b; Pestell 2004; Stocker and Everson 2003).

A related subject arises from patterns of metal *ampullae* finds which in England and Wales have begun to crystallize as a result of the Portable Antiquities Scheme. A reappraisal of these souvenirs suggests that towards the end of the Middle Ages they were being left on agricultural land as votive objects (Anderson 2010; see Chapters 40 and 49 in this *Handbook*). Pilgrimage was held to be a state of being as well as something one did, and there are kinds of locality to which pilgrimage was made—like remote Pennant Melangell (Powys) or Orkney—which invite questions to do with cultural memory and innovation (Britnell 1994; Britnell and Watson 1994; Buer 2004; Heaton and Britnell 1994). Patterns can also be discerned in the positions and dedications of churches in the vicinity of certain towns, as around Winchester where the hill-sited churches and chapels of St Catherine, St Helen, and St Giles, and the church of St Faith, evoked the harmonics of pilgrimage to Conques in southern France, routes to Compostela in northern Spain, and associations with Jerusalem (Keene 2015, 435–9).

This brings us to towns, which in the Middle Ages were places where interactions between different groups—religious houses, lay lords, churchmen, burgesses—shaped the physical and cultural fabric through a continuum of buying and selling property, campaigns of building and repair, and—sometimes—competing interests (Slater and Rosser 2016). The church in the urban landscape is thus ideally approached through contextualized study of these relative forces across the town as a whole, as it has for example in places like York and Coventry (Goddard 2004; Palliser 2014; Rees Jones 2013).

Relationships between urban space, parishes, and churches have been examined in provincial cities like Exeter, Winchester, and Lincoln (Jones et al. 2003, 159–295; Keene 1985; Orme 2014), thematically (for instance in relation to boundaries, clerical communities, and lordship; Baker and Holt 1998; Simms and Clarke 2015); in multi-church towns of middling size like Worcester and Gloucester (Baker and Holt 2004); and at smaller centres such as Ripon, Grantham, and early modern Birmingham (Brickley 2006; Start and Stocker 2011; Werronen 2013). A feature of churches in larger towns is the extent to which their sites were tightly circumscribed by other property, sometimes to the point at which boundaries were intricately described or indicated, or the same site was shared with different uses at different levels. Four or five London churches, for instance, were raised over vaulted spaces that were let out to secular interests (Schofield 1994, 79; 1997). Graveyard margins were dual-facing areas, suited for social or poor relief. Rows of well-carpentered small houses for rent by poorer townspeople were erected on the borders of at least five parish churches in York, for instance; they are dated by contract and tree-rings to dates in the first half of the fourteenth century, and by building them 'the parishes were able to combine meeting housing needs with raising income for church purposes' (Palliser 2014, 179).

City-wide studies are instructive for their contrasts. The ecclesiastical geographies of medieval towns were not cut from one bolt of cloth. Lincoln and Norwich, for instance, are less than 145 km apart and resemble one another to the extent that they each contained upwards of forty-five parish churches (in the case of Norwich, upwards of fifty-five) together with dozens of other religious institutions that in each case included all four principal orders of friars. In other respects, however, such as the tempo and scale of building, and their profiles of growth and decline, they differ sharply. Small towns have benefitted from the work of historians like Christopher Dyer and Gervase Rosser who have put records of the towns themselves into conversation with urban topography

(Dyer 2000; Laughton and Dyer 1999). Lesser towns often surprise for their intricacies: beyond Grantham's single parish church, for instance, stood a hospital, friary, oratory, and stational features that included the Apple Cross, Market, and Eleanor Crosses. Popular use of and responses to such features through civil and religious processions, drama, and events at special times invite discussions that could not be undertaken through study of the monuments one by one (Start and Stocker 2011).

The lords of many smaller towns were religious bodies who took a creative interest in their planning (Slater 1998). Well-known examples of such instigators are the bishop, dean, and canons of Salisbury, who in the 1220s were responsible for the new town laid out beside their close, and the Benedictine authors of the 'classic monastic town' of St Albans (Clark 2011; Rogers 1969, 3; Slater 1998). Plan analysis in the Conzenian tradition has centred on concepts such as plot pattern, building cycles, 'and the link between decision taking and the urban form' (Lilley 2000; Whitehand 2001, 103; and see Chapter 18 in this *Handbook*). In places, however, there are signs that symbolism played a part. Keith Lilley (2004; 2009) has argued the medieval city to represent a scaled-down model of the universe, and there were occasions when ecclesiastical seigniors embedded cultural references into urban layouts. A case has been made, for instance, that the plan of St Andrews was intentionally patterned on the Borgo of Rome, and that its cathedral (the largest in Scotland) was dimensionally linked to Old St Peter's and St John Lateran as part of a campaign for the recognition of St Andrews as an apostolic see like Compostela, the only other western European shrine outside Italy to claim the relics of an apostle (Brooks and Whittington 1977; Campbell 2013).

Like nesting dolls, towns contained subsidiary areas of particular identity. Alongside their parish churches were institutional liberties, grounds of private and castle chapels, colleges and precincts of urban monasteries (Burgess and Heale 2008; Butler 1987; Röhrkasten 2013). Prominent among the last were the mendicant houses which were often sited on the urban fringe as it was in the thirteenth or fourteenth century, partly because of their late arrival on the scene and partly because the preaching orders gravitated towards neighbourhoods of need (O'Sullivan 2013). Conversely, it is a question why some types of urban space familiar on the Continent do not occur in Britain: why was it, for example, that the Beguine movement did not develop more fully than it did in cities in close contact with the Low Countries (Simons 2001)?

In cathedral towns, closes and colleges of Vicars Choral were areas wherein clergy struggled to reconcile the 'various and often contradictory purposes' of a medieval cathedral, and to combine liturgical duties with private lives (Dobson 2005, 1; Richards 2001; Rogers 2005; Stocker 2005). Such restricted areas invite investigation of their relationship with and effect on urban layouts, and as landscapes in their own right. Some closes ghosted older spaces with long memories (Norton 1998; Rodwell 2001). An emerging challenge, exemplified by Gilchrist's study of the forty-acre (16.2 ha) cathedral close at Norwich, is to move beyond description and sequence towards interdisciplinary investigation of spatial purpose, meanings, and comparative context. The Norwich close is explored through a principle of graduated sanctity (rules of entry, segregation, hospitality, power, the influence of memory), with attention to the feeling of movement through and responses to different kinds of space (Gilchrist 2005). This method connects with others, such as the social history of sound and aurality (Boynton et al. 2016; Garrioch 2003; Smith 1999; Part VIII of this *Handbook*). Digital techniques can augment both kinds of approach through the simulation of ways in which places, spaces, and liturgical performances were experienced. Pioneering examples include the use of acoustic modelling to explore staging of the York Mystery Plays, and digital reconstructions of medieval church interiors and complexes (Giles et al. 2010; López 2013; Masinton 2006). Among the latter has been the re-visualization of the largely lost seven-acre (2.83 ha) precinct of the priory of Holy Trinity Micklegate, York.

Holy Trinity introduces another urban theme: the conceptual reinstatement of landscape features and relationships that have disappeared (cf. Warren 2013). Holy Trinity was founded after 1086 as successor to a pre-Conquest collegiate church of Christ Church (Stocker 1995). In the late eleventh century Christ Church was regarded as one of the five great Minsters of northern England (the others being Beverley, Ripon, Durham, and York). The community seems once to have been at the heart of an extensive and ancient ecclesiastical complex in the former Roman *colonia* that balanced the metropolitan cathedral on York's east bank (Blair 2005, 67, fig. 9, 68 n. 225, 126 n. 219). Sarah Rees Jones has pointed to close jurisdictional and territorial ties between the two and the implication of this 'strong association' for a common history (2013, 43). Rees Jones has further noted that Christ Church/Holy Trinity was the starting point of one of two major processional routes across medieval York which converged on the Minster, suggesting that this route 'reflected an ancient processional way linking York's two collegial churches from as early as the seventh century' (2013, 267). This same route seems to have been traced by Norman and Angevin kings, while the list of performance places of the Corpus Christi play cycle that survives from 1399 shows that it began outside the gate of Holy Trinity Micklegate and that ten out of the twelve playing stations lay along its path (A/Y Memorandum Book Y: E20, f. 19v, printed in Johnston and Rogerson 1979, 11; Dobson 1997; Meredith 2000; Rees Jones 2013, 267; 2007). The performances through the city spanned the history of the world, from Creation to Doomsday, in a sequence influenced by liturgical readings of the York Use that were heard in the city's churches between Epiphany and Palm Sunday (King 2006). It is a question how far this relationship was perceived by spectators or citizens, 'Yet, over a lifetime of hearing the liturgy and attending performances of the York cycle, connections would be made, ideas and narratives recognized, and the main theological background to popular worship understood and accepted' (Rastall 2008, 356). In effect, on performance days, and through their widely involving preparations (Palliser 2014, 211; Rogerson 2011), the city itself became a vernacular religious landscape.

Alongside the church in the landscape, then, are symbolic landscapes that were rendered holy at particular times through communal behaviour, and questions of how or in whose minds they found expression (Keene 2015; Rees Jones 2007). This brings us to two themes awaiting fuller exploration than they have so far received: the church and landscape aesthetics, and what have been described as 'the other parish churches'

(Orme 2006, 78): chapels and other sub-parochial institutions that abounded before the Reformation and largely vanished in its aftermath.

Taking the chapels first: although these places formed a 'huge class' until recently they have received little systematic little attention, save on the Atlantic fringe where they have been at the centre of a number of landscape studies (Gibbon 2007; Morris 2001; Thomas 2009). In England, Wales, and the borders the neglect may be partly because most of them generated few records of their own, while the resulting need to screen many different kinds of source to track them down is time-consuming (Orme 2006, 78–9). In most areas, therefore, apart from a number of county studies (surveyed by Orme 1996, 75) scholarly interest in their whereabouts and significance has been small. Luckily, there are exceptions. Among them is the Diocese of Exeter, where fourteenth- and fifteenth-century records for chapels were more fully kept and modern interest in their numbers has thus been encouraged. The results are instructive. A careful search in west Cornwall found 188 chapels in 95 parishes: a ratio of about 2:1 (Orme 2006, 79, n. 4). In Devon the matching figures are 1300 chapels in 409 parishes: more than 3:1 (James 1997). It may be, as Orme suggests, that Cornwall and Devon were unusual to the extent that they contain much upland, with scattered settlement in areas where travel was difficult. However, analogous conditions could be cited over most of Scotland and Wales and much of northern England. Records of the chantry commissioners for the West Riding of Yorkshire in 1549, for instance, contain references to many chapels recorded nowhere else, and some dozens of others that have since disappeared (TNA E315/123 ff. 151, 152).

Extrapolating from areas like Lancashire, Northamptonshire (Parsons 2000), and the south-west where chapel counts provide minimum orders of magnitude we can agree that in England, at least, chapels must numerically have formed the largest category of institutions in the medieval Church; they outstripped religious houses and parish churches combined, and by the early sixteenth century may have totalled twenty thousand or more (Orme 2006, 80). If the conservative formula of at least two chapels for every parish church is applied across Britain as a whole the baseline figure becomes around twenty-five thousand. As Orme suggests, the ubiquity of chapels reflected their versatility: they 'were recognisably religious buildings, yet they could be large or small, cheap or expensive, and sited by themselves or inside larger structures, at any location desired' (2006, 80).

Orme recognizes three broad categories of chapel: those for reserved use, mainly within gentry and elite households (Saul 2017, 105–34) but also serving groups with restricted membership like town councils or craft guilds; chapels of ease serving local communities (Saul 2017, 83–104); and chapels with specialized cultic functions, which could also be chapels of ease 'but sought to make wider social links than the other two kinds'. Distinctions between the three kinds were not always precise, with some chapels migrating from one category to another or sharing aspects of several (Orme 2006, 80). Nor are the three categories sufficient for Britain as a whole: in the Northern Isles, the Hebrides, south-west Scotland, parts of Ireland-facing Wales, and very likely Caithness and Sutherland there are different contexts and further classes to be reckoned with.

Looking more closely at the public chapels of southern Britain: aside from types of site which present strong symbolism (like bridge ends) or responses to difficulties of access to the 'real' parish church, their landscape contexts have not been much considered. Distance from the mother church and obstructions to churchgoing 'in winter and foul weather' were commonly mentioned by the commissioners who culled chapels in the mid-sixteenth century. However, the image of chapels as typically on the edge of things is not a valid path down which to approach them as a whole (Rosser 1991, 176). There were many prompts to chapel-founding. 'Ease' could have to do with time as well as distance (such as market-goers at unsocial hours or seasonal workers in temporary settlements), while factors such as divided lordship or collective agricultural interests could give latitude or context for lay-directed religious initiatives.

Improving record survival in the later Middle Ages can give the impression that chapels were always multiplying (Brown 2006, 286). In fact, as Orme points out, there may have been variations in the pace of chapel founding, or indeed episodes of contraction (references to ruined chapels in later medieval sources are not unusual), and regional differentials between both. Records of renovations of derelict chapels point to revivals of popular devotion in places with remembered associations. Where these centred on pre-parochial features that had been re-employed in later boundaries, it may sometimes have been this, 'rather than the chronology of settlement or variations of lordship' that explained the presence of liminal sites (Rosser 1991, 183). Another process that put chapels near boundaries was lay cooperation, for example through the creation of a chapelry across the border between two adjacent parishes (Moorhouse 1981a, 626–7), or where there were older reasons for cross-parish associations (Gibbon 2007, 243).

Excavation of parochial chapels like Burnham (Lincolnshire) and (currently) Malham (North Yorkshire) shows that some of them came into existence alongside or within settlements at or around the same time as neighbouring parish churches (Coppack 1986; Spence 2015). In such cases, it may be that the chapel either failed to progress to parish rank or did so and then lost it (cf. Cramp et al. 1996).

In areas where settlement was particularly thin, as it was in parts of Wales and Cornwall, it is possible that twelfth-century parochial organization sometimes promoted newer churches over those of longer standing (Rosser 1991, 178). On Atlantic margins in the north, chapels frequently ante-date the parish system that was put in place in the twelfth and thirteenth centuries. Landscape-scale survey in Shetland relates them to evolving organization: from pre-Scandinavian missionary or monastic sites, through a tier of later Norse private farm-churches ('perhaps reflected in the numerous small chapel-foundations and related to the land units of the *scattalds*'; Smith 1984), through to the adoption of parishes in which concentration on a few 'head churches' led to the abandonment of many of the older sites (Cant 1975; 1984; 1996; Morris 2001, 73). A cognate picture has been described in the Orkneys where survey reveals a seemingly loose pattern of pre-parochial chapels in a diversity of landscape contexts, succeeded by parish churches associated with elite landholders (the earl, bishop, chieftains). A number of the parish churches appear to be upgradings of pre-existing chapels (Gibbon 2007, 240–5; 2012; cf. Thomas 2009).

Returning south, a further factor arises from regional variation in what counted as a parish. Some parochial chapels became difficult to tell apart from parish churches, while in western English dioceses like Worcester and Lichfield the pre-Conquest relationship between *matrices ecclesiae* dominating large parishes locally served by parochial chapels survived into the early modern period. Similar two-tier or blurred relationships can be found in pockets elsewhere. An example is Richmondshire, a huge lordship in the northern Yorkshire Dales—larger, say, than today's Bedfordshire—wherein existed several gatherings of chapelries, and the role of the archdeacon was akin to that of a surrogate bishop.

While thousands of chapels arose in the interstices of well-settled landscapes, many others—as if in equal and opposite reaction—present a geography of extremes: crowning hilltops, at the feet and tops of cliffs, on headlands, peninsulas, offshore islands, islands in lakes, rivers, and fens, caves, woodlands, and forests (examples in Blair 2005 144–5, 216–20; Clay 1914, 1–48). A number of such sites were chosen by monastic pioneers in the sixth and seventh centuries, but interest in the genre remained keen. It may have strengthened in the later Middle Ages. Some were in places guaranteed to attract attention while others were apparently located to avoid it; both evoked the ambiguities of desert-wilderness (Le Goff 1985), and both acknowledged nature in tandem with social needs. If challenging sites were not locally available they could be created artificially, as at Pontefract in the 1380s where a subterranean hermitage and oratory were hewn out through 15 m of millstone grit. John Blair has suggested that hermits as a class in the earlier Middle Ages were widely admired for the way in which they formed a bridge between ecclesiastical high culture 'and the undisciplined, suspect world of charismatic popular religion' (2005, 145). Did later chapels in places evoking eremitical values reflect that?

Patterns of devotion found diverse expression in different parts of Britain. They did not always include chapels. In southern Scotland in the later fifteenth century, for instance, new foundations by both clerical and lay founders (Brown 2008), new dedications of chaplainries and altars in collegiate churches were 'marked by the inclusion of Scottish saints, auxiliary saints or saints with specialised interests ... and dedications to specific attributes or aspects of Our Lord and Our Lady' (Brown 2006, 283). While chapels reflecting growing enthusiasm for several saints of international standing (Katherine, Anthony, Nicholas of Myra) do occur, the new geography of pilgrimage here 'consisted of a cosmopolitan mix of shrines based around images, miraculous crosses, healing wells and only rarely the relics of saints' (Turpie 2011, 39).

Chapels are archaeologically under-researched, both as a class and as the largest single component of this chapter. Given the scale on which they existed, the intimacy and variety of their relationships with landscape, the wide range of social contexts in which they were founded, the deposit quality that often attends early abandonment, and the extent to which many of them are to all intents and purposes prehistoric, there is both need and scope for interdisciplinary research at landscape scale to address them.

This brings us, finally, to the church in the landscape as a source of aesthetic emotion. Muted or stock references to this subject can be traced at least as far back as the sixteenth century; it becomes very evident in writing and visual culture in the eighteenth century (Myers 2013) and intensely so in the Romantic Movement and Gothic revival that followed. The least understood stage in this course is its start: what was the audience of the later medieval church in the landscape, how did it react, and in what ways were its perceptions formed?

The churches give inklings of themes. Seen close to, there is sometimes a 'display face', an elevation more richly adorned than the others that was meant to be seen from the usual direction of approach. As time passed, more and more churches (but not all) were modified to impress from beyond the churchyard boundary: donors often liked to concentrate on 'those parts of the fabric that caught the eye' (Saul 2017, 217). Late medieval steeples can sometimes be seen across four or five parishes, and in the Great Limestone Belt that extends north-eastward from Somerset to the East Riding there are districts bedecked by inter-visible towers and spires. The limestone reminds us that the church as a landscape feature is partly also a function of natural resources, with side-paths branching off to subjects such as regionality of materials (e.g. Hart 2000; Johnson 2010; Palmer 2007; Potter 2001), aspects of historical ecology (e.g. Bridge 2012), and the effects of rural economic fluctuation (e.g. Batcock 1991; Hare 2007; Middleton-Stewart 2007).

Spires dominate imagination but were overall quite rare; a recent study finds that only one in fifteen or so English medieval towers now carries one (Flannery 2016). Steeples are frequently found in distinctive regional varieties. Pembrokeshire's lanky towers differ from those in the Vale of Glamorgan, for instance, while spire forms in Lincolnshire vary according to the parts of the county in which they stand (Morris 1989; cf. Hart 2003). Such differences gave visible embodiment to neighbourhood identity. More than this, the enlarged late medieval church was heard as well as seen. A taller and stronger tower enabled more and larger bells, whose voices (which spoke on all kinds of occasions for many symbolic reasons) were audible over longer distances (Arnold and Goodson 2012; Chapter 44 in this *Handbook*).

By the fifteenth century a cumulative effect of such aspects was the accentuation of difference between the church and other buildings in its vicinity. This said, not all churches were made to be conspicuous. Those sited in hollows, valleys, or other semi-enclosed surroundings often seem to form part of those settings, as if in harmony with nature rather than any sort of cultural repudiation of it. Or at least, this is how we see them today; how they impinged on the onlooker when they were new is another question.

If one dimension of the church in the landscape concerns attachment to place, another has to do with the attachment of certain landholders to churches. The personification of lordship in local churches goes back at least to the late-Saxon period (Blair 2005; Shapland 2012). From the later twelfth century the names, arms, and images of gentry were increasingly emblazoned across churches that had been enlarged with their donations, and in which their effigies and chantries were later displayed (Saul 2017). The positioning of monuments in or near the sanctuary led to the pervasion of community worship with awareness of the families concerned, and since chantry priests prayed for all Christian souls as well as their founders, the result was a cycle of reciprocity in which all prayed for all, and parish communities were centred as much on the remembrance of their gentry as devotion to God (James 2012, 168). One influential factor behind these relationships was the mechanism of landholding. Heads of families were loath to split their patrimony; if younger sons received lands from their fathers it was usually on condition that that the land would revert to the main heir when the beneficiary died (James 2012, 162–3). Churches associated with manors held on life terms or through entails were thus less likely to attract large or sustained investment than those on lands that were held in perpetuity. For the same reason, younger gentry who suddenly gained a heritable estate (for instance in reward for service) could react by embarking on the enlargement or embellishment of its church.

Returning to perception of churches in the landscape, something of the associated strength of popular feeling is revealed in the scale of the semi-connected revolts that occurred during the autumn and winter of 1536–7 in partial reaction to rumours about Crown intentions towards church property (Hoyle 2001, 293). It remains a question how far literary descriptions take us towards the mental surroundings in which such feelings were actually held. John Leland's impressions of places and buildings at the time were expressed in a vocabulary of routine terms ('poor', 'mean', 'goodly', 'fair') which were occasionally intensified with the addition of more stock words ('marvellous fair', 'meetly fair', and so on). The Reformation also took onlookers in new directions through reinvention of the medieval past and contemplation of old buildings as a form of storytelling (Myers 2013, 2; Parish 2005). Medieval descriptions of imaginary buildings (of which there are not that many) tend to work through the enumeration of features, sometimes coupled with an adjective to intensify some sensory aspect (Barber 2007; Whitehead 2003). The description of Sir Bertilak's castle in the late fourteenth-century *Sir Gawain and the Green Knight*, listed up-to-the-minute features which at that point had possibly never yet been brought together in a single building. It piles up detail ('fair embrasures' that were 'fairly long', 'lovely loop-holes') and describes walls and features in such terms as being 'full gay', 'full thick', 'full clean', 'full white' (Gollancz 1940, 29). What turns this banality into something exceptional is the surprise of a concluding simile: it was, wrote the poet, 'that pared out of paper purely it seemed' (l. 802). This points towards a kind of bedazzlement through contrasts, of beauty through the conjunction of different things (height, texture, material), and the ultimate contrast of something made by people in a landscape made by God (Binski 2014; Carruthers 2013). This in turn invites an association between the contemplation of devotional objects (images, statuary, painting, glass) and entire buildings in their surroundings. Images were linked in medieval thought with a theory of wonder (*admiratio*) in which the mind was freed from rational engagement and so enabled to enter a state of cloudy enchantment in the presence of mystery beyond reason (Barnum 2001, 50; Boldrick et al. 2002). It comes almost as a shock to realize that this life-enhancing presence in the late medieval landscape was almost entirely on behalf of the dead (Duffy 2006, 381), and that this must have affected the way in which it was perceived.

References cited

Anderson, W. 2010 'Blessing the fields? A study of late-medieval ampullae from England and Wales', *Medieval Archaeology* 54, 182–203

Arnold, J. H. and Goodson, C. 2012 'Resounding community: the history and meaning of medieval church bells', *Viator* 43(1), 99–130

Austin, D. 2004 'Strata Florida and its landscape', *Archaeologia Cambrensis* 153, 192–201

Austin, D. 2013 'The archaeology of monasteries in Wales and the Strata Florida Project', in J. Burton and K. Stober (eds), *Monastic Wales: new approaches*, University of Wales Press, Cardiff, 3–20

Baker, N. and Holt, R. 1998 'The origins of urban parish boundaries', in T. R. Slater and G. Rosser (eds), *The Church in the medieval town*, Ashgate, Aldershot, 209–35

Baker, N. and Holt, R. 2004 *Urban growth and the medieval Church: Gloucester and Worcester*, Routledge, London

Barber, R. 2007 'Imaginary buildings', in J. Munby, R. Barber, and R. Brown, *Edward III's round table at Windsor: the house of the round table and the Windsor festival of 1344*, Boydell Press, Woodbridge, 100–18

Barnum, C. W. 2001 *Metamorphosis and identity*, Mit Press, New York

Barnwell, P. S. 2004 'Churches built for priests? The evolution of parish churches in Northamptonshire from the Gregorian reform to the Fourth Lateran Council', *Ecclesiology Today* 32, 7–23

Barnwell, P. S. 2008 'The medieval churches of Whittlewood Forest', *Ecclesiology Today* 41, 3–28

Batcock, N. 1991 *The ruined and disused churches of Norfolk*, East Anglian Archaeology Report 51, University East Anglia, Norwich

Beresford, M. W. 1986 'Inclesmoor, West Riding of Yorkshire', in R. A. Skelton and P. D. A. Harvey, *Local maps and plans from medieval England*, Oxford University Press, Oxford, 147–61

Bezant, J. 2013 'The medieval grants to Strata Florida Abbey: mapping the agency of lordship', in J. Burton and K. Stober (eds), *Monastic Wales: new approaches*, University of Wales Press, Cardiff, 73–88

Binski, P. 2014 *Gothic wonder: art, artifice and the Decorated Style 1290–1350*, Yale University Press, New Haven

Blair, J. (ed.) 1988 *Ministers and parish churches: the local church in transition, 950–1200*, Oxford University Committee for Archaeology, Oxford

Blair, J. 2005 *The Church in Anglo-Saxon society*, Oxford University Press, Oxford

Boldrick, S., Park, D., and Williamson, P. 2002 *Wonder: painted sculpture from medieval England*, Henry Moore Institute, Leeds

Boynton, S., Kay, S., Cornish, A., and Albin A. 2016 'Sound matters', *Speculum* 91(4), 998–1039

Brickley, M. 2006 *St Martin's uncovered: investigations in the churchyard of St Martin's-in-the-Bullring, Birmingham, 2001*, Oxbow, Oxford

Bridge, M. 2012 'Locating the origins of wood resources: a review of dendroprovenancing', *Journal of Archaeological Science* 39(8), 2828–34

Britnell, W. J. 1994 'Excavation and recording at Pennant Melangell church', *Montgomeryshire Collections* 82, 41–102

Britnell, W. J. and Watson, K. 1994 'Saint Melangell's shrine, Pennant Melangell', *Montgomeryshire Collections* 82, 147–66

Brooks, N. P. and Whittington, G. 1977 'Planning and growth in the medieval Scottish burgh: the example of St Andrews', *Transactions of the Institute of British Geographers*, new series 2, 278–95

Brown, H. S. 2006 *Lay piety in later medieval Lothian, c.1306–c.1513*, unpublished PhD thesis, University of Edinburgh

Brown, H. 2008 'Secular colleges in late medieval Scotland', in C. Burgess and M. Heale (eds), *The late medieval college and its context*, York Medieval Press/Boydell and Brewer, Woodbridge, 44–66

Buer, M. 2004 *Orkney pilgrimage: perspectives of the cult of St Magnus*, unpublished PhD thesis, University of Glasgow

Burgess, C. and Heale, M. (eds) 2008 *The late medieval college and its context*, York Medieval Press/Boydell and Brewer, Woodbridge

Burton, J. 1994 *Monastic and religious orders in Britain, 1000–1300*, Cambridge University Press, Cambridge

Butler, L. A. S. 1987 'Medieval urban religious houses', in J. Schofield and R. Leech (eds), *Urban archaeology in Britain*, Council for British Archaeology Research Report 61, London, 167–76

Campbell, I. 2013, 'Planning for pilgrims: St Andrews as the second Rome', *The Innes Review* 64(1), 1–22

Cant, R. 1975 *The medieval churches and chapels of Shetland*, Shetland Archaeological and Historical Society, Lerwick

Cant, R. G. 1984 'Settlement and society in the Northern Isles', in A. Fenton and H. Pálsson (eds), *The Northern and Western Isles in the Western World*, Edinburgh, 168–79

Cant, R. G. 1996 'The medieval Church in Shetland: organisation and buildings', in D. J. Waugh (ed.), *Shetland's northern links: language and history*, Scottish Society for Northern Studies, Edinburgh, 159–73

Carruthers, M. 2013 *The experience of beauty in the Middle Ages*, Oxford University Press, Oxford

Clark, J. G. 2011 *The Benedictines in the Middle Ages*, Boydell Press, Woodbridge

Clay, R. M. 1914 *Hermits and anchorites of England*, Methuen, London

Coppack, G. 1986 'St Lawrence Church, Burnham, South Humberside: the excavation of a parochial chapel', *Lincolnshire History and Archaeology* 21, 39–60

Coster, W. and Spicer, A. (eds) 2005 *Sacred space in Early Modern Europe*, Cambridge University Press, Cambridge

Cowan, I. B. 1961 'The development of the parochial system in medieval Scotland', *Scottish Historical Review* 40, 43–55

Cowan, I. B. 1967 *The parishes of medieval Scotland*, Scottish Record Society, Edinburgh

Cowan, I. B. and Easson, D. E. 1976 *Medieval religious houses in Scotland with an appendix on the houses in the Isle of Man*, Longman, London (2nd edn)

Cramp, R., Boddington, A., and Cadman, A. 1996 *Raunds Furnells: the Anglo-Saxon church and churchyard*, English Heritage, Swindon

Cramp, R. 2014 *The Hirsel excavations*, The Society for Medieval Archaeology Monograph 36, London

Crone, A., Hindmarch, E., and Woolf, A. 2016 *Living and dying at Auldhame: the excavation of an Anglian monastic settlement and medieval parish church*, The Society of Antiquaries of Scotland, Edinburgh

Dobson, R. B. 1997 'Craft guilds and city: the historical origins of the York Mysteries reassessed', in A. Knight (ed.), *The stage as mirror*, Cambridge University Press, Cambridge, 91–105

Dobson, R. B. 2005 'The English vicars choral: an introduction', in R. Hall and D. A. Stocker (eds), *Vicars choral at English cathedrals, Cantate Domino: history, architecture and archaeology*, Oxbow, Oxford, 1–10

Duffy, E. 2006 'The end of it all: the material culture of the medieval english parish and the 1552 inventories of Church goods', in C. Burgess and E. Duffy (eds), *The parish in Late Medieval England*, Shaun Tyas, Donington, 381–99

Dyer, C. 2000 'Small towns, 1270–1540', in D. M. Palliser (ed.), *Cambridge Urban History of Britain, Vol. 1*, Cambridge University Press, Cambridge, 505–37

Evans, E. with Davidson, A., Ludlow, N., and Silvester, B. 2000 'Medieval churches in Wales: the Welsh Historic Churches Project and its results', *Church Archaeology* 4, 5–26

Everson, P. L. and Stocker, D. 2006 *Summoning St Michael: early Romanesque towers in Lincolnshire*, Oxbow, Oxford

Everson, P. L. and Stocker, D. 2011a 'The Witham Valley: a landscape with monasteries?', *Church Archaeology* 13, 1–15

Everson, P. L. and Stocker, D. 2011b *Custodians of continuity: the Premonstratensian Abbey at Barlings and the landscape of ritual*, Lincolnshire Archaeology and Heritage Reports 11, Heritage Trust of Lincolnshire, Sleaford

Fellows-Jensen, G. (ed.) 2001 *Denmark and Scotland: the cultural and environmental resources of small nations*, Royal Danish Academy of Sciences and Letters, Copenhagen

Flannery, J. 2016 *Fifty English steeples: the finest medieval parish church towers and spires in England*, Thames and Hudson, London

Garrioch, D. 2003 'Sounds of the city: the soundscape of early modern towns', *Urban History* 30, 5–25

Gerrard, C. M. with Aston, M. 2007 *The Shapwick Project, Somerset: a rural landscape explored*, The Society for Medieval Archaeology Monograph 25, Leeds

Gibbon, S. J. 2007 'Medieval parish formation in Orkney', in B. B. Smith, S. Taylor, and G. Williamson (eds), *West over sea: studies in Scandinavian sea-borne expansion and settlement before 1350*, Brill, Leiden, 235–50

Gibbon, S. J. 2012 'The Church in the Orkney Earldom', in H. Þorláksson and Þ. B. Sigurðardóttir (eds), *From nature to script: Reykholt, environment, centre, and manuscript making*, Reykholt, Snorrastofa, 65–184

Gilchrist, R. 1995 *Contemplation and action: the other monasticism*, Leicester University Press, London

Gilchrist, R. 2005 *Norwich Cathedral Close: the evolution of the English cathedral landscape*, Boydell and Brewer, Woodbridge

Gilchrist, R. 2008 'Magic for the dead? The archaeology of magic in later medieval burials', *Medieval Archaeology* 52, 119–59

Gilchrist, R. 2014 'Monastic and church archaeology', *Annual Review of Anthropology* 43, 235–50

Gilchrist, R. and Green, C. 2015 *Glastonbury Abbey: archaeological investigations 1904–79*, The Society of Antiquaries of London, London

Giles, K., Masinton, A., and Arnott, G. 2010 'Seeing and believing: the use of virtual models of historic churches', *Historic Churches* 17, 27–31

Goddard, R. 2004 *Lordship and medieval urbanisation: Coventry 1043–1355*, Royal Historical Society/Boydell, Woodbridge

Gollancz, I. (ed.) 1940 *Sir Gawain and the Green Knight*, Early English Text Society original series 210, Oxford University Press, London

Graham-Campbell, J. (ed.) 1994 *Archaeology of pilgrimage*, World Archaeology 26(1), Routledge, London

Graves, C. P. 2000 *The form and fabric of belief: an archaeology of the lay experience of religion in medieval Norfolk and Devon*, British Archaeological Reports British Series 311, Oxford

Hare, M. 2007 'Church-building and urban prosperity on the eve of the Reformation: Basingstoke and its parish church', *Proceedings of the Hampshire Field Club and Archaeological Society* 62, 181–92

Hart, G. 2000 *Flint architecture of East Anglia*, Giles de La Mare, London

Hart, S. 2003 *The round tower churches of England*, Lucas Books, Thorndon

Heale, M. 2004 *The dependent priories of medieval English monasteries*, Boydell Press, Woodbridge

Heaton, R. B. and Britnell, W. J. 1994 'A structural history of Pennant Melangell Church', *Montgomeryshire Collections* 82, 103–26

Hinton, I. 2006 'Church alignment and patronal saints' days', *The Antiquaries Journal* 86, 206–26

Hinton, I. 2010 *Aspects of the alignment and location of medieval rural churches*, unpublished PhD thesis, University of East Anglia

Hoare, P. G. 2014 'Orientation of English medieval parish churches', in C. L. N. Ruggles (ed), *Handbook of Archaeastronomy and Ethnoastronomy*, Springer, New York, 1711–18

Houlbrooke, R. A. 2004 'Magic and witchcraft in the diocese of Winchester, 1491–1570', in D. J. B. Trim and P. Balderstone (eds), *Cross, crown and community: religion, government and culture in early modern England 1400–1800*, Peter Lang, Oxford, 113–42

Hoyle, R. W. 2001 *The pilgrimage of grace and the politics of the 1530s*, Oxford University Press, Oxford

Iogna-Prat, D. 2008 'Churches in the landscape', in T. F. X. Noble and J. M. H. Smith (eds), *The Cambridge history of Christianity, Vol. 3*, Cambridge University Press, Cambridge, 363–80

James, A. 2012 'To knowe a gentilman': men and gentry culture in fifteenth-century Yorkshire, unpublished PhD thesis, University of York

James, J. 1997 *Medieval chapels in Devon*, MPhil thesis, University of Exeter

Johnson, D. 2010 'Hushes, delfs and river stonary: alternative methods of obtaining lime in the gritstone Pennines in the early modern period', *Landscape History* 31(1), 37–52

Johnston, A. F. and Rogerson, M. (eds) 1979 *York: 1 Introduction, The Records*, Records of Early English Drama, University of Toronto Press, Toronto

Jones, M. J., Stocker, D., and Vince, A. 2003 *The city by the pool: assessing the archaeology of the city of Lincoln*, Lincoln Archaeological Studies 10, Oxbow, Oxford

Jones, R. and Page, M. 2004, 'Characterising rural settlement and landscape: Whittlewood Forest in the Middle Ages', *Medieval Archaeology* 47, 55–83

Jones, R. and Page, M. 2006 *Medieval villages in an English landscape*, Windgather Press, Macclesfield

Keene, D. J. 1985 *Survey of medieval Winchester*, Clarendon Press, Oxford

Keene, D. J. 2015 'Early medieval Winchester: symbolic landscapes', in A. Simms and H. B. Clarke (eds), *Lords and towns in medieval Europe: the European Historic Towns Atlas Project*, Ashgate, Farnham, 419–46

King, P. M. 2006 *The York Mystery Cycle and the worship of the city*, D. S. Brewer, Rochester and New York

Laughton, J. and Dyer, C. 1999 'Small towns in the east and west Midlands in the later Middle Ages', *Midland History* 24, 24–52

Lawrence, C. H. 2003 'The English parish and its clergy in the thirteenth century', in P. Linehan and J. Nelson (eds), *The medieval world*, Routledge, Abingdon, 648–70

Le Goff, J. 1985 'The wilderness in the medieval West', in J. Le Goff (ed.), *The medieval imagination*, University of Chicago Press, Chicago, 47–59

Lilley, K. D. 2000 'Mapping the medieval city: plan analysis and urban history', *Urban History* 27(1), 5–30

Lilley, K. D. 2004 'Cities of God? Medieval urban forms and their Christian symbolism', *Transactions of the Institute of British Geographers* new series 29, 296–313

Lilley, K. D. 2009 *City and Cosmos: the medieval world in urban form*, Reaktion Books, London

López, M. J. 2013 *Hearing the York Mystery Plays: acoustics, staging and performance*, unpublished PhD thesis, University of York

Masinton, A. W. 2006 *Sacred space: priorities, perception and the presence of God in late medieval Yorkshire parish churches*, unpublished PhD thesis, University of York

Mays, P., Harding C., and Heighway, C. 2007 *Wharram. A study of settlement on the Yorkshire Wolds XI: the churchyard*, University of York Archaeological Publications 13, York

McClain, A. 2011 'The archaeology of parish churches in late medieval England', in M. O. H. Carver and J. Klápště (eds), *The archaeology of medieval Europe, Vol. 2: twelfth to sixteenth centuries*, Aarhus University Press, Aarhus, 468–78

Meredith, P. 2000 'The city of York and its "Play of Pageants"', *Early Theatre* 3, 23–47

Middleton-Stewart, J. 2007 'Change and decay in east Suffolk: the vicissitudes of parish fortunes', *Proceedings of the Suffolk Institute of Archaeology and History* 41(3), 323–34

Mitchell, L. 2011 *Cultural uses of magic in fifteenth-century England*, unpublished PhD thesis, University of Toronto

Moorhouse, S. A. 1981a 'Communications', in M. L. Faull and S. A. Moorhouse, *West Yorkshire: an archaeological survey to AD 1500, Vol. 3: the rural medieval landscape*, West Yorkshire Metropolitan County Council, Wakefield, 614–37

Moorhouse, S. A. 1981b 'Features associated with communications', in M. L. Faull and S. A. Moorhouse, *West Yorkshire: an archaeological survey to AD 1500, Vol. 3: the rural medieval landscape*, West Yorkshire Metropolitan County Council, Wakefield, 638–55

Morris, C. D. 2001 'Norse settlement in Shetland: the Shetland chapel-sites project', in G. Fellows-Jensen (ed.), *Denmark and Scotland: the cultural and environmental resources of small nations*, Royal Danish Academy of Sciences and Letters, Copenhagen, 58–78

Morris, R. 1989 *Churches in the landscape*, Orion, London

Morrison, J., Oram, R. D., and Ross, A. 2009 'Gogar archaeological and historical evidence for a lost medieval parish near Edinburgh', *Proceedings of the Society of Antiquaries of Scotland* 139, 229–56

Myers, A. M. 2013 *Literature and architecture in Early Modern England*, John Hopkins University Press, Baltimore

Norton, C. 1998 'The Anglo-Saxon cathedral at York and the topography of the Anglian city', *Journal of the British Archaeological Association* 151, 1–42

Oexle, O. G. 1997 'Jacques Le Goff in Germany', in M. Rubin (ed.), *The work of Jacques Le Goff and the challenges of medieval history*, Boydell Press, Woodbridge, 79–84

Orme, N. 1996 'Church and chapel in medieval England', *Transactions of the Royal Historical Society*, 6 series, 6, 75–102

Orme, N. 2006 'The other parish churches: chapels in late medieval England', in C. Burgess and E. Duffy (eds), *The parish in late medieval England*, Shaun Tyas/Paul Watkins, Donington, 78–94

Orme, N. 2014 *The churches of medieval Exeter*, Impress Books, Exeter
O'Sullivan, D. 2013 *In the company of preachers: the archaeology of medieval friaries*, Leicester University Press, Leicester
Palliser, D. M. 2014 *Medieval York 600–1540*, Oxford University Press, Oxford
Palmer, T. 2007 'Ergyn stone: a forgotten Welsh freestone', *Archaeologia Cambrensis* 156, 149–60
Parish, H. 2005 *Monks, miracles and magic: Reformation representations of the medieval Church*, Routledge, London
Parsons, D. 2000 *Lost chantries and chapels of medieval Northamptonshire*, The Brixworth Lectures, 2 series, 3, University of Leicester, Leicester
Pestell, T. 2004 *Landscapes of monastic foundation: the establishment of religious houses in East Anglia c.650–1200*, Boydell and Brewer, Woodbridge
Potter, J. F. 2001 'The London Basin's gravel churches: indications of geology, medieval history and geographical distribution' *Landscape History* 23, 5–26
Rastall, R. 2008 Review of King (2006), *Catholic Historical Review* 94(2), 355–6
Rees Jones, S. 2007 'Richard Scrope, the Bolton Hours and the church of St Martin in Micklegate: reconstructing a holy neighbourhood in later medieval York', in P. J. P. Goldberg (ed.), *Richard Scrope: archbishop, rebel martyr*, Shaun Tyas, Donington, 214–36
Rees Jones, S. 2013 *York: the making of a city 1068–1350*, Oxford University Press, Oxford, 42–3
Richards, J. D. 2001 *The Vicars Choral of York Minster: the college at Bedern*, Council for British Archaeology, York
Rider, C. 2012 *Magic and religion in medieval England*, Reaktion Books, London
Rodwell, W. 2001 *Wells Cathedral: excavations and structural studies, 1978–93*, 2 vols, English Heritage, Swindon
Rogers, K. H. 1969 'Salisbury', in M. D. Lobel (ed.), *Historic towns: maps and plans of towns and cities of the British Isles, Vol. 1*, Historic Towns Trust, London, 1–9
Rogers, N. 2005 '"Wine, women and song": artefacts from the Excavations at the College of Vicars Choral at The Bedern, York', in R. Hall and D. Stocker (eds), *Vicars choral at English cathedrals, Cantate Domino: history, architecture and archaeology*, Oxbow, Oxford, 164–87
Rogerson, M. (ed.) 2011 *The York Mystery plays: performance in the city*, York Medieval Press/Boydell Press, Wodbridge
Röhrkasten, J. 2013 'Monasteries and urban space in medieval Welsh towns', in J. Burton and K. Stober (eds), *Monastic Wales: new approaches*, University of Wales Press, Cardiff, 55–70
Rosser, G. 1991 'Parochial conformity and voluntary religion in late-medieval England', *Transactions of the Royal Historical Society* 1, 173–89
Rosser, G. 1996 'Religious practice on the margins', in J. Blair and C. Pyrah (eds), *Church archaeology: research directions for the future*, Council for British Archaeology Research Report 104, York, 75–84
Sánchez-Pardo, J. and Shapland, M. (eds) 2015 *Churches and social power in early medieval Europe: integrating archaeological and historical approaches*, Brepols, Turnhout
Saul, N. 2006 'The gentry and the parish', in C. Burgess and E. Duffy (eds), *The parish in late medieval England*, ShaunTyas/Paul Watkins, Donington, 243–60
Saul, N. 2017 *Lordship and faith: the English gentry and the parish church in the Middle Ages*, Oxford University Press, Oxford
Schofield, J. 1994 'Saxon and medieval parish churches in the City of London: a review', *Transactions of the London and Middlesex Archaeological Society* 45, 23–145

Schofield, J. 1997 'Medieval parish churches in the City of London: the archaeological evidence', in K. L. French, G. C. Gibbs, and B. Kümin (eds), *The parish in English life*, Manchester University Press, Manchester, 35–55

Schofield, J. and Vince, A. 2003 *The archaeology of British towns in their European setting*, Continuum, London (2nd edn)

Shapland, M. G. 2012 *Buildings of secular and religious lordship: Anglo-Saxon tower-nave churches*, unpublished PhD thesis, University College London

Simms, H. B. and Clarke, A. 2015 *Lords and towns in medieval Europe: the European Historic Towns Atlas Project*, Routledge, London

Simons, W. 2001 *Cities of ladies: Beguine communities in the medieval Low Countries, 1200–1565*, University of Pennsylvania Press, Philadelphia

Slater, T. R. 1998 'Benedictine town planning in medieval England: the evidence from St Albans', in T. R. Slater and G. Rosser (eds), *The Church in the medieval town*, Ashgate, Aldershot, 155–76

Slater, T. R. and Rosser, G. (eds) 2016 *The Church in the medieval town*, Ashgate, Aldershot

Smith, B. 1984 'What is a Scattald? Rural communities in Shetland, 1400–1900', in B. E. Crawford (ed.), *Essays in Shetland history*, Shetland Times, Lerwick, 99–124

Smith, B. R. 1999 *The acoustic world of early modern England: attending to the O-factor*, University of Chicago Press, Chicago

Spence, V. 2015 'The ancient chapel of St Helen, Malham in Craven: dissolution and discovery', *Northern History* 52(1), 52–67

Spicer, A. 2010 '"God hath put such secretes in Nature": the reformed kirk, church-building and the religious landscape in early modern Scotland', *Studies in Church History* 46, 260–75

Standley, E. R. 2016 'Hid in the earth and secret places: a reassessment of a hoard of later medieval gold rings and silver coins found near the River Thame', *The Antiquaries Journal* 96, 117–42

Start, D. and Stocker, D. (eds) 2011 *The making of Grantham*, Heritage Trust of Lincolnshire, Heckington

Steele, J. 2014 *Seeking patterns of lordship, justice and worship in the Scottish landscape*, unpublished PhD thesis, University of Glasgow

Stocker, D. 1995 'The priory of the Holy Trinity, York: antiquarians and architectural history', in L. Hoey (ed.), *Yorkshire monasticism: archaeology, art and architecture from the 7th to the 16th centuries*, British Archaeological Association Conference Transactions 16, Leeds

Stocker, D. 2005 'The quest for one's own front door: housing the vicars choral at the English cathedrals', *Vernacular Architecture* 36, 15–31

Stocker, D. and Everson, P. 2003 'The straight and narrow way: fenland causeways and the conversion of the landscape in the Witham valley, Lincolnshire', in M. O. H. Carver (ed.), *The cross goes north: processes of conversion in Northern Europe, AD 300–1300*, Boydell, Woodbridge, 271–88

Thomas, S. E. 2009 *'From Rome to the ends of the habitable world': the provision of clergy and church buildings in the Hebrides, circa 1266 to circa 1472*, unpublished PhD thesis, University of Glasgow

Trim, D. J. B. and Balderstone, P. J. (eds) 2004 *Cross, crown and community: religion, government and culture in early modern England 1400–1800*, Peter Lang, Oxford

Turpie, T. J. M. 2011 *Scottish saints' cults and pilgrimage from the Black Death to the Reformation, c.1349–1560*, unpublished PhD thesis, University of Edinburgh

Walsham, A. 2011 *The Reformation of the landscape: religion, identity and memory in early modern Britain and Ireland*, Oxford University Press, Oxford

Wand, J. and Wand, K. 2010 'Norman churches, Domesday population and parish formation', *Church Archaeology* 14, 43–61

Warren, E. 2013 *Community and identity in the shadow of York Minster: the chapel of St Mary and the Holy Angels*, unpublished PhD thesis, University of Leeds

Werronen, S. 2013 *Ripon Minster in its social context, c.1350–1530*, unpublished PhD thesis, University of Leeds

Whitehand, J. W. R. 2001 'British urban morphology: the Conzenian tradition', *Urban Morphology* 5(2), 103–9

Whitehead, C. 2003 *Castles of the mind: a study of medieval architectural allegory*, University of Wales Press, Cardiff

Whyte, N. 2009 *Inhabiting the landscape: place, custom and memory, 1500–1800*, Windgather, Oxford

CHAPTER 35

THE MEDIEVAL MONASTERY AND ITS LANDSCAPE

JAMES BOND

THERE is an extensive, ever-expanding literature on the history, geography, architecture, and archaeology of medieval monasticism. Introductions to the material evidence in Britain include works by Platt (1984), Coppack (1990), Greene (1992) and Aston (2009); Scotland is covered by Fawcett (1994), Wales by Burton and Stöber (2015). The progress of historical and archaeological studies before 1990 is summarized by Coppack (1990, 12–31), while the evolving application of theoretical principles in relation to a specific project is considered by Everson and Stocker (2011).

The Benedictine rule remained the dominant regulation for monks after the Norman Conquest, but new interpretations developed in Continental Europe led to the introduction of reformed orders, notably the Cistercians. Alternative forms of communal religious life, including orders of hermits, regular canons, and friars, were also established, their differing customs and levels of engagement with lay society expressed in distinctive siting requirements and building plans (Aston 2001). Between 1100 and 1540 there were about 420 houses of monks, 360 of regular canons, 315 of friars, 205 of nuns, 115 of the military orders, and eleven of the hermit orders in Britain (Cowan and Easson 1976; Knowles and Hadcock 1971). They varied considerably in character and size, from large autonomous abbeys containing several hundred personnel down to small cells with just a few.

Thirteen English monastic churches were also episcopal sees, eight of them continuing to serve as cathedrals today (see Chapter 36). Eight more former monastic churches have become cathedrals since the Reformation while nearly two hundred others remain partly or wholly in ecclesiastical use. Some retain considerable portions of their attached claustral buildings and precincts but many others now in parochial use stand alone. Portions of monastic buildings were often subsequently converted for domestic occupation or retained as picturesque amenities. Many rural monasteries are now represented only by earthworks.

The Contribution of Archaeology

Archaeological approaches to monasteries and their landscapes include the study of architectural evidence and building materials; aerial photography and topographical survey; and excavation. Notable recent studies of building fabric include analysis at Cleeve Abbey, Somerset, which clarified the phasing of the church, claustral buildings, and gatehouse (Parker et al. 2007) (Figure 35.1) and the detailed recording of a surviving fragment of the nave at Barlings Abbey, Lincolnshire, which enabled reconstructions of its complete elevation (Everson and Stocker 2011, 64–7). Examination of lapidary collections has added significantly to our knowledge of otherwise largely destroyed buildings at Keynsham Abbey, Somerset (Lowe et al. 2005). Cecil Hewett's innovatory studies of monastic carpentry, undertaken over several decades, remain of fundamental importance (Hewett 1985). Dendrochronology offers the potential for more precise dating of timber structures, and at Combermere Abbey, Cheshire, and Chicksands Priory,

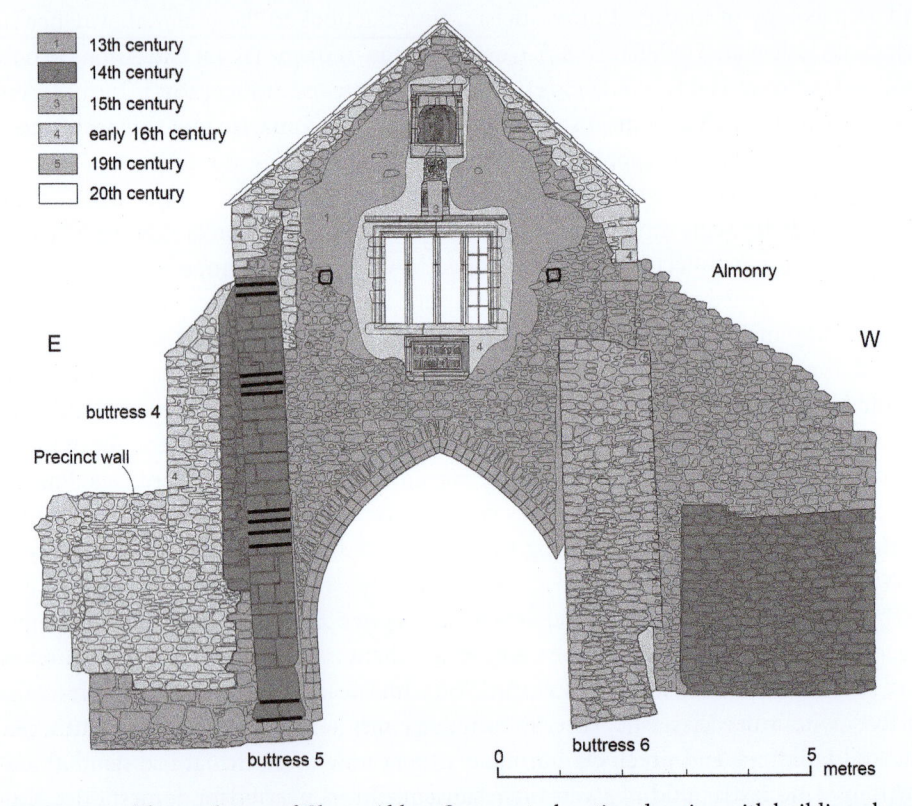

FIGURE 35.1 The gatehouse of Cleeve Abbey, Somerset: elevation drawing with building phases interpreted

(From Parker et al. 2007, 122 © Exeter Archaeology, image from a photogrammetric survey supplied by English Heritage, corrected and phased by R. W. Parker and digitised by the late Andrew Sage)

Bedfordshire, has identified surviving monastic roofs within drastically altered buildings (Arnold et al. 2004, 90; Howard et al. 1999, 91–2). Six medieval doors at Westminster Abbey have been sampled, one of which was found to date back to the original construction of 1050–65 (Miles et al. 2005, 91–2). Dendrochronology may also reveal sources of timber, showing, for example, that mid-thirteenth-century ceiling boards in Peterborough Abbey's nave came from north Germany (Tyers and Groves 2000, 119; 2001, 87–8; 2002, 115).

The value of aerial photographic coverage of monastic sites was first demonstrated by Knowles and St Joseph (1952). The Cambridge University aerial photograph collections contain many views of extensive earthwork sites revealed with dramatic clarity, and outlines of levelled buildings visible as parch-marks. Techniques of interpretative ground-level survey, developed by the three Royal Commissions in their county volumes, continue to feature in English Heritage's more recent Research Department Report Series. Precincts remaining under permanent pasture may preserve the earthworks remains of collapsed or robbed buildings, banks, or ditches outlining garden and orchard enclosures, and engineered water features such as leats, drains, canals, fishponds, and millponds, as well as later elements (e.g. Brown and Jones 2009, 44–5). Recent survey at Byland Abbey, North Riding of Yorkshire, has produced a major reassessment of its earthworks (Jecock et al. 2011). Geophysical survey has further enhanced our understanding, as at Thornton Abbey, Lincolnshire, where resistance and magnetometer surveys west of the claustral buildings located the probable boundary between the inner and outer courts and identified buildings, subsidiary enclosures, water management features, and probable ovens, hearths, or furnaces (Oswald et al. 2010, 58–66).

The early history of archaeological excavation on monastic sites has been summarized by Coppack (1990, 18–30), with more recent assessments by Gilchrist and Mytum (1993) and Keevill et al. (2001). Not all early excavations were adequately reported at the time: work at Glastonbury Abbey, Somerset, between 1904 and 1979 reached final publication only recently (Gilchrist and Green 2015). Since the 1950s large-scale redevelopment has provided particular opportunities for archaeological examination of monastic remains in towns, especially in London (Barber and Thomas 2002; Barker et al. 2004; Bull et al. 2011; Dyson et al. 2011; Grainger and Phillpotts 2011; Miller and Saxby 2007; Sloane and Malcolm 2004; Thomas et al. 1977). Research excavations have been undertaken within projected 'new town' developments at Bordesley Abbey near Redditch, Worcestershire (Astill et al. 2004), Sandwell Priory in the Black Country (Hodder 1991), and Norton Priory near Runcorn, Cheshire (Greene 1989). Elsewhere, targeted excavations to improve interpretation and presentation have also yielded new information, as have excavations in advance of service provisions and structural repairs. An extensive excavation at Eynsham Abbey, Oxfordshire, was necessitated by cemetery enlargement (Hardy et al. 2003). These opportunities must be matched against emerging academic agendas, which have included elucidation of the plan characteristics of less-familiar religious groups (Gilchrist 1995; Gray 1993); agricultural and industrial structures within the precincts (Astill 1993; Coppack 1986) (Figure 35.2); the contribution of environmental archaeology to the study of diet, health, plant cultivation, and livestock rearing; and the interface between the religious community and its hinterland. Interdisciplinary

FIGURE 35.2 The water-powered iron mill within the precinct of the Cistercian abbey of Bordesley, Worcestershire: excavation revealed that the mill had been reconstructed several times between the 1170s and the late fourteenth century, with a sequence of timber-lined races

(© Bordesley Abbey Project)

approaches have become accepted as normal procedure, although only rarely, as at Bordesley Abbey, has the ideal of a long-term research programme been achieved.

In the following text, several themes have been chosen to illustrate recent scholarship and to provide the reader with links to a wider bibliography. Other chapters in this *Handbook* deal with aspects of architectural evolution (see Chapters 36 and 37), construction (Chapter 29), pilgrimage (Chapter 40), and sensory perception (Chapter 42).

Siting

The foundation of a new religious house depended primarily upon patronage and grants of land. The selection of a suitable site then rested on a variety of practical considerations. Sufficient space was needed for buildings, courts, and gardens and most monasteries were close to rivers or streams. A reliable supply of water was required for cooking, brewing, washing, laundry, irrigating gardens, flushing latrines, filling fishponds and millponds, and other industrial uses. Some of these needs were met by diverting and canalizing natural watercourses. Fresh water was also brought in by conduits from springs, commonly up to 2–3 km away, and distributed by means of lead, ceramic, or timber pipes (Bond 2001). Water transport was sometimes used to bring in building stone and timber, and several monastic quays have been recognized, for example at Waltham Abbey, Essex (Huggins 1972, 81–8).

There was an inherent conflict between the seclusion required by the more contemplative forms of religious life and the practical need for agricultural labour and artisan support which could be supplied by nearby secular settlements. Cistercian regulations insisted on sites 'removed from the concourse of men', but in practice, by the twelfth century, little cultivable land in Britain remained unutilized; so most Cistercian foundations took place, not in the wilderness, but towards the margins of settled areas. Walter Map's contemporary complaint that the Cistercians were prepared to create their own solitude by destroying villages and removing their inhabitants elsewhere receives some support from both documentary and archaeological evidence (Bond 2010, 177–8, 243–50). The earlier Carthusian foundations and other communities with eremitic predecessors also generally succeeded in finding secluded locations. Other new monastic settlements achieved an illusion of isolation by selecting sites which were near yet visibly detached from local villages (Pestell 2004, 201–17). A high proportion of nunneries were perched just above flood meadows or marshland, which also limited their accessibility (Gilchrist 1994, 66).

Most Benedictine, Cluniac, and Augustinian houses founded after 1100 were located in anciently settled, well-populated countryside, insulated within precinct walls rather than deliberately seeking remote places. Early predecessors of Benedictine monasteries in Canterbury, Winchester, Bath, Gloucester, and Chester had consciously settled in former Roman towns. Subsequent Benedictine communities recognized the benefits of having artisans and tradesmen dwelling outside their gates, and not only tolerated, but actively encouraged, town development (e.g. St Albans in Hertfordshire, and Burton-upon-Trent in Staffordshire; Bond 2010, 279–85; Slater 1996; 1998). By the thirteenth century England had become a well-urbanized country, and the friars, pursuing their mission towards the literate bourgeoisie and disadvantaged urban poor, settled in large established towns, often initially in makeshift premises, later taking up permanent quarters and expanding their precincts by acquiring neighbouring properties and blocking and diverting pre-existing streets (O'Sullivan 2013).

Associations of ancient sanctity could be another factor in site selection. The new Norman Benedictine abbeys and priories at Bardney (Lincolnshire), Chester (Cheshire), Dover (Kent), Folkestone (Kent), Great Malvern (Worcestershire), Hackness (North Riding of Yorkshire), Jarrow (Northumberland), Lastingham (North Riding of Yorkshire), Leominster (Herefordshire), Lindisfarne (Northumberland), Monkwearmouth (Co. Durham), Stamford (Lincolnshire), Tewkesbury (Gloucestershire), and Tynemouth (Northumberland) were among those drawn by traditions of an early hermit colony or minster. In Scotland, Benedictine Coldingham (Berwickshire) and Iona (Argyll), Cistercian Melrose (Roxburghshire) and Premonstratensian Whithorn (Wigtownshire) all succeeded more ancient foundations. Some Cistercian houses in Wales and the Marches, including Dore (Herefordshire), Neath (Glamorgan), Strata Marcella (Montgomeryshire), Tintern (Monmouthshire), and Valle Crucis (Denbighshire), had associations with earlier Celtic *clas* churches or hermitages, though here there may be divergent motives, Welsh founders being drawn to such sites out of respect for ancient traditions, Norman founders from a wish to extinguish them (Bond 2005, 60). Aesthetic and symbolic aspects of landscape settings are reflected in names given to sites such as Strata Florida (Cardinganshire) and Valle Crucis (Robinson 2006, 268, 288).

Sometimes experience of occupation revealed unanticipated disadvantages to the chosen site. In 1292 the monks of Stanlaw on the Mersey, Cheshire, complained that their land was suffering erosion by spring tides and their buildings were regularly under several feet of floodwater, so they were permitted to move to a new site on their Lancashire estates at Whalley. Border conflict prompted the resettlement of the monks of Poulton, Cheshire, over 60 km further east at Dieulacres, Staffordshire, after complaints of prolonged harassment by the Welsh. Changes of patronage might also initiate a move: when Rhys ap Gruffudd took the Strata Florida community under his wing twenty years after its first settlement, he transferred it to a new site 3.2 km away, perhaps wishing to disassociate it from its Anglo-Norman beginnings. Moves were especially likely when a new patron provided additional lands offering superior resources to the original endowments: this prompted the moves from Rhedynog-felen (Caernarvonshire) to Aberconwy (Clwyd), from Little Trefgarn (Pembrokeshire) to Whitland (Camarthenshire), and from Darnhall to Vale Royal (Cheshire) (Bond 2005, 70–2; Robinson 2006, 223–4, 267–8, 294). Undisturbed original sites which became superseded at an early date have significant archaeological potential, but as yet few have received serious investigation.

Precinct Plans

The basic plan of most religious houses in Britain founded or reconstructed since 1066 was derived from a template developed by the early ninth century for Benedictine monasteries within the Carolingian empire. Space within the precinct was organized to minimize conflict between different activities. In particular there was a fundamental division between that part of the enclosure where contact with the outside world generated traffic, and a certain amount of disturbance had to be tolerated, and that part where quiet and seclusion were required. There were also distinctions between relatively public areas accessible to all who had business within the monastery, areas reserved for the monastic community itself, areas used by particular monastic officials, and private areas. Regular patterns of movement around and within the buildings, imposed by monastic rules and customs, affected both the juxtaposition of buildings and the position of doorways.

The main entrance to the precinct was normally from the west. A porter's lodge controlled access through a gatehouse, which included an entry wide enough to admit loaded carts, sometimes also a separate pedestrian entry. Augustinian houses constructed some particularly ostentatious gatehouses, including the late fourteenth-century brick example at Thornton, Lincolnshire, equipped with portcullis and arrow embrasures, and the late fifteenth-century gatehouse at St Osyth's, Essex, which was decorated with elaborate flint and clunch flushwork (Platt 1984, 190–2, 200–1, 212–14). Within the gate, buildings were arranged around one or more courtyards. Some, including the guesthouse and almonry, served the external lay community; others, such as barns, granaries, workshops, mills, bakehouses, and brewhouses, were connected with the storage and processing of commodities produced on the estates or purchased through the market. The eastern side of the precinct was normally the most secluded area, containing the infirmary, cemetery, and gardens designed for contemplation. There was often a pentice connecting the infirmary with the church or main cloister, and sometimes a separate infirmary cloister. The infirmary was usually a large aisled hall with a chapel at the east end: ruined examples survive at Canterbury Cathedral Priory, Kent, and at Gloucester (Coppack 1990, 76–8; Greene 1992, 158–9). The Benedictine Rule permitted a meat-enriched diet for sick and elderly monks, requiring a separate meat-kitchen. Every monk was expected to visit the infirmary up to seven times a year for blood-letting, which was believed to maintain good health.

Gardens, orchards, and fishponds would be accommodated into other available spaces. Only a few monastic gardens have been investigated archaeologically. Excavations at Haverfordwest Priory, Pembrokeshire, at the Austin Friars in Hull, East Riding of Yorkshire, and in a couple of the cells of Mount Grace Charterhouse, North Riding of Yorkshire, have revealed something of the rectilinear layout of vegetable and herb gardens (Coppack 1990, 78–80); regularly spaced tree pits at Dunstable Priory, Bedfordshire, suggest an orchard, while a possible bedding-trench for vines has been identified at

Merton Priory, Surrey (Miller and Saxby 2007, 31; Moorhouse 1991, 115). Medieval herbals and monastic gardeners' accounts indicate knowledge and cultivation of a much wider range of plants than can currently be authenticated from archaeological evidence. Nevertheless, drain sediments from the Oxford Blackfriars produced remains of various fruits and nuts probably from the gardens, indicating that the friars' diet was significantly more varied than that of most of the townsfolk, along with culinary and medicinal herbs, including marigold, opium poppy, greater celandine, and henbane (Lambrick 1985, 196–201). Box leaves suggest an ornamental component within this garden but figs, grapes, and almonds may have been imported (see Chapter 8). Merton Priory has yielded pollen from walnut, yew, juniper, borage, buckwheat, and hemp (Miller and Saxby 2007, 142, 245). Fishponds became much more common within monastic precincts after the mid-twelfth century, often leaving substantial and extensive earthworks, but archaeological examinations have been rare. Environmental sampling of Owston Abbey's fishponds, Leicestershire, produced scales and bones of pike, bream, roach, perch, rudd, and chub (Shackley et al. 1988). Despite the efforts put into fishpond construction, most of the fish routinely consumed in monasteries were marine species; freshwater pond fish seem to have been kept primarily for feast days and important visitors. The entire precinct was usually surrounded by a wall, sometimes reinforced by an outer ditch or moat, with one or more subsidiary gates.

Claustral Buildings

The daily routine of the religious community revolved around the claustral ranges, normally centrally located within the precinct. The church was usually the largest and most impressive building, with the cloister garth to the south to take advantage of light and warmth from the sun, the principal communal rooms being arranged around it. Cloisters vary considerably in size, to some extent reflecting the size of the monastic community, and on some sites there is evidence for their enlargement, as at Norton Priory, Cheshire, in the late twelfth century (Greene 1989, 94–109). The largest Benedictine cloister is at Norwich, Norfolk, rebuilt between 1297 and 1430, and about 55 m square (Woodman 1996, 165–78). Seven times each day the cycle of services required access to the church, normally through a door from the east walk of the cloister, and a standardized arrangement of communal domestic buildings around the cloister developed as a matter of convenience, those ranges requiring direct access to the church or to other buildings or courts being positioned accordingly.

The two-storey eastern range contained a large communal dormitory on the upper floor. Direct access from the dormitory to the church, required for the midnight service, was provided through a door to the night stairs. A second door in the west wall gave access by the day stairs to the cloister, and a third in the east or south wall entered a communal upper-floor latrine or reredorter. The later twelfth-century reredorter at Lewes, East Sussex, was nearly 48 m long internally, accommodating up to 59 cubicles (Lyne

1997, 55–68). The southern part of the ground floor normally included a parlour and a slype (passageway) giving access from the cloister to the infirmary and eastern precinct. The most important ground-floor room was the chapter house, which provided a dignified setting for daily assemblies, at which corporate business, matters of routine work, and prayer would be discussed, instruction and advice dispensed, complaints heard, faults confessed, judgements passed, and punishments administered. Here each day a chapter of the Benedictine Rule would be read aloud to ensure the monks' familiarity with its requirements. Episcopal visitations were also conducted there, while chapter houses were also occasionally commandeered for purely secular purposes, such as the Parliaments held at St Albans in 1215 and at Gloucester in 1378, the latter occasion causing much annoyance because of games of football taking place in the cloister garth (Welander 1991, 226–7). Chapter houses, commonly entered through an imposing vestibule with an ornate central doorway flanked by openings giving light, occasionally took a circular or polygonal form. The majority, however, were rectangular, with or without aisles. While some were entirely contained within the width of the range, most extended eastwards beyond it. Some terminated in a semicircular or three-sided apse, but the Cistercian preference was for rectangular square-ended plans.

The main room in the south claustral range was the refectory where communal meals were taken two or three times each day. For most orders of monks this was normally at ground level, but regular canons and nuns preferred a first-floor refectory with access by stairs, an allusion to the upper room in which the Last Supper took place. Meals were eaten in silence while listening to a reading; the pulpit for the reading survives intact at Chester (Cheshire) and Beaulieu (Hampshire). Storage recesses for table utensils were often located just within the entrance, while the floor may retain evidence of a dais for the high table and raised foot-paces along the side walls. Outside the refectory entrance were facilities for hand-washing, either in a round or polygonal building extending into the cloister-garth, or in a long arched recess within the cloister walk. The refectory was also linked to a detached kitchen with large fireplaces and ovens and a roof equipped with smoke louvres. Several monastic kitchens were of polygonal plan, including those at St Augustine's Canterbury (1287–91) and Durham Priory (mid-fourteenth century). The lower floor of the west range contained large storage rooms used by the cellarer, the upper floor often initially accommodating the abbot or prior.

The main cloister garth was surrounded by a covered passage (Henig and McNeill 2006). Many cloister walks were initially sheltered by lean-to timber structures, indicated today, where they were not later replaced, by sockets and corbels. Stone-built Romanesque open arcades, often supported on twin shafts, were developed during the twelfth century; these are known mostly from loose or re-used fragments or reconstructed portions, but six bays of Canterbury Cathedral Priory's original infirmary cloister survive *in situ* (Tatton-Brown 2006, 93–7). Syncopated cloister arcading appeared in the thirteenth century; the only surviving example is at Mont St Michel in Normandy, completed by 1228, although there is evidence for similar arrangements at Monk Bretton Priory, West Riding of Yorkshire (*c.*1230–50), and Tintern Abbey (*c.*1250–60) (Harrison 2006, 109, 111). During the fourteenth and fifteenth centuries many earlier arcades were replaced by fan-vaulted walks with glazed traceried lights, a type represented most completely at Gloucester, begun in 1351. Gloucester's cloisters also contain one of the few remaining examples of study carrels (Welander 1991, 215–35).

The ideal standard plan was often modified to suit local circumstances. At Worcester Cathedral Priory the preferred arrangement was negated by local topography, since the River Severn flowed below the west front of the church, so the main entrance with the almonry and guest-hall were placed to the south-east, the cellarage accommodated beneath the refectory, and the dormitory and reredorter extended westwards towards the river. At Easby, North Riding of Yorkshire, and at Durham the dormitory was placed in the west range of the cloister rather than the east, also due to drainage considerations (Coppack 1990, 72–3, 97). In a substantial minority of cases, including Gloucester, Malmesbury (Wiltshire), Tintern, and Melrose, the cloister garth was placed north of the church, often because the natural contour of the ground made it easier to channel water in that direction to flush the latrines. However, the higher proportion of north cloisters among nunneries may reflect a traditional association of women with the north side of the church, facing the figure of the Virgin Mary alongside the rood, while the preference for shade may be connected with penitence (Gilchrist 1994, 128–43).

Other variations arose out of the distinctive requirements of particular orders. The Cistercians provided their lay brothers with a separate refectory and dormitory on the upper floor of the west range, often resulting in its elongation well beyond the south side of the cloister, as at Fountains (West Riding of Yorkshire). From the ground level of the west range the lay brothers then had their own access into the nave of the church, occasionally, as at Byland, along a narrow passageway segregated by a high wall from the west walk of the monks' cloister. By contrast, in some Premonstratensian houses there were no resident lay-brothers, so the western side of the cloister was closed by a simple screen wall (as at Alnwick in Northumberland) and the cellarer's storage transferred to an undercroft below the refectory. Other distinctive, though not universal, Cistercian characteristics included a north–south alignment for the refectory, which was flanked by the kitchen and warming-house, a collation seat for the abbot in the cloister walk backed against the church, and a chapel for the use of lay people adjoining the gatehouse. Special arrangements were required by orders which accommodated both men and women within the same house, this segregation being best exemplified by the Gilbertine priory of Watton, East Riding of Yorkshire, where two completely separate cloisters had access to a shared church, divided along its length by a high spine wall (Hope 1901). Urban friary churches commonly had a large nave separated from the chancel by a through passage beneath a central tower. A yard often separated the cloisters from the church, allowing more light into the nave. To save space, the upper floors of the surrounding domestic ranges often oversailed the cloister walks (O'Sullivan 2013). A radically different plan was adopted by the Carthusians, using a very large cloister surrounded by two-storey cells with individual gardens and latrines. Adhering firmly to their original eremitic practices, the hermit-monks spent most of their time in silence inside their own cell, gathering in their church for only three of the daily offices and eating one communal meal a week in their refectory (Coppack and Aston 2002).

The preceptories and commanderies of the military orders more closely resembled Cistercian granges or estate farms, dominated by barns and other agricultural buildings, with a smaller enclosure for a hall, kitchen, and chapel (e.g. at South Witham, Lincolnshire; Mayes 2002).

Burials were accommodated in several areas. The chancel was generally reserved for abbots or priors, founders, and major benefactors. Memorial chapels could be added to provide mausolea for prominent local families. Ordinary monks were sometimes buried within the nave. Up to the fourteenth century the chapter house was often the chosen location for burials of abbots, priors, and other prominent members of the community: between 1170 and 1345 sixteen abbots were interred within the chapter house at Fountains, while in cathedral priories such as Durham they were often the burial-place of bishops. Burials also commonly took place within the cloister walks, and in friaries distinctive locations relating to gender and age have been detected. The main monastic cemetery usually lay to the east of the cloisters, while lay cemeteries including female and child burials were usually on the opposite side of the church to the claustral buildings. Cemetery excavations have provided much evidence for changing mortuary practices, the significance of grave goods, and distinctive medical conditions. Diffuse idiopathic skeletal hyperostosis (DISH) has been proposed as an 'occupational disease' of Benedictine monasticism, being linked with sedentary lifestyles and consumption of high levels of protein and alcohol with limited fresh fruit or vegetables (Gilchrist and Sloane 2005; but see Chapter 51 in this *Handbook*).

Monastic Estates

Many monasteries were endowed at their foundation with extensive lands, designed to provide sustenance and income to support the community. Initial endowments were commonly later enlarged through grants, exchanges, or purchases, and religious houses eventually held perhaps a quarter of all the land in England. There was significant investment in these estates, particularly after the late twelfth century when a growing population was pushing up prices for agricultural produce and many enterprising abbots took their demesnes back in hand to manage the land directly. The construction of new domestic, agricultural, and industrial buildings, including barns, granaries, livestock housing, dovecotes, and numerous watermills and windmills, all left a significant impact on the landscape. In particular, the huge scale and architectural magnificence of some monastic barns combined practical requirements with ostentation (Bond 2010, 101–52). At the same time, productivity was increased by clearing woodland, reclaiming marshland, and by adopting more intensive and specialized systems of farming. Meadows were irrigated, pastures enclosed, orchards and vineyards planted. As farming become increasingly diversified, some land was given over to prestigious uses as deer parks and rabbit warrens (Bond 2010, 43–86, 162–70, 171–82).

There were significant differences between the holdings of old-established Benedictine houses and those of the new monastic orders introduced after 1100. Those differences arose partly through differing ideological stances on the permissibility of various forms of income, partly through the variable resources of patrons, and partly through the circumstances and locations of their settlement. Benedictine income came mainly from *temporalities*, which included demesne lands, crops, livestock, rents, and mills; but *spiritualities*, which included churches, rectories, vicarages, tithes, glebe lands, oblations, mortuary fees, and offerings at shrines could also provide significant income. The key component of Benedictine estates was normally a group of manors containing both demesne land worked for the abbey by peasant labour, and land worked by peasant tenants on their own behalf. More distant pastoral and woodland properties could be managed more flexibly, and a wide range of other income came from urban rents, markets, and churches. In general the later arrivals were less able to acquire many complete manors, had more limited access to the best-quality land, and were less successful in establishing new boroughs and markets. Augustinian demesnes were often relatively small, formed around nuclei of glebe-land belonging to appropriated churches, supplemented by piecemeal gifts and purchases of land; over a third of Augustinian income in England in 1535 came from *spiritualities* (Robinson 1980). Early Cistercian regulations, insisting on avoidance of proximity to lay settlements, also forbade income from possession of churches, mills, courts, or fairs. Despite this, the Cistercians rarely settled in a wilderness; they still needed sufficient arable land for their own support, and usually compromised by seeking relative seclusion on the margins of old-settled countryside. Nevertheless, they did acquire extensive upland, marshland, and woodland endowments, developing a distinctive style of land management based upon *granges*, consolidated estate farms which lay outside the manorial system and were initially worked by lay brothers. Some Cistercian houses developed specialities in sheep- and cattle-farming (Donkin 1978, 68–102). Other reformed orders such as the Premonstratensians also adopted the grange system, and the preceptories and commanderies of the military orders, though designed primarily to raise cash which could be relayed on to their main theatre of operations in the east, operated in a rather similar fashion. By contrast the friars who arrived during the thirteenth century acquired no communal property outside their own urban precincts, though these often included extensive gardens and orchards.

After the fourteenth century profits from demesne farming declined, and it became more advantageous to lease out land to lay tenants for cash rents. By the Dissolution many abbeys kept in hand only a home farm, with a few former manor-houses, separated from their agricultural land, serving as country residences for high monastic officials.

The Suppression

Long before the Protestant Reformation some religious houses had failed through adversity, poverty, or mismanagement. A few succumbed during the Black Death. Recruitment to the Friars of the Sack and Pied Friars was forbidden after 1274, ending the existence of twenty friaries. When the Knights Templars were suppressed in 1312 only sixteen of their fifty preceptories passed to the Hospitallers. Between 1370 and 1440 most of the alien Benedictine and Augustinian priories, along with four Tironensian and two Grandmontine priories, all dependencies of abbeys in France, were terminated when the Crown confiscated their possessions.

Wolsey suppressed twenty-nine houses of monks, canons, and nuns between 1524 and 1529, using their endowments to found Cardinal College in Oxford. The first stage of the final Dissolution in England and Wales came in 1536 when closure of all houses with an annual income of less than £200 was proposed. Although 243 houses were then suppressed, another 176 were temporarily reprieved by special pleading. All remaining religious houses, including 187 friaries previously exempted, were extinguished between 1537 and 1540, though half a dozen houses were briefly revived under Mary Tudor in 1555–9. In Scotland events took a different course, and even after the Scottish Parliament rejected papal authority in 1560 the secularization of monastic sites was a protracted process. The Dissolution produced the greatest landownership disruption since the Norman Conquest, reflected in the archaeological record by complex processes of adaptation and replacement.

Conclusion

While the aims of monastic life, its rules, customs, and liturgical practices, the ambitions of patrons, the activities of monastic officials, the internal life of communities, and many aspects of monastic administration and economy are all illuminated by documents, scientific archaeology offers an essential complementary insight into the practicalities of servicing the needs of religious communities, constructing and maintaining buildings, managing water resources, the production, processing, and consumption of food, and dealing with sickness and death.

References cited

Arnold, A., Howard, R., and Litton, C. 2004 'List 151: dendrochronological dates from Nottingham University Tree-Ring Dating Laboratory', *Vernacular Architecture* 35, 89–94

Astill, G. G. 1993 *A medieval industrial complex and its landscape: the metalworking watermills and workshops of Bordesley Abbey*, Council for British Archaeology Research Report 92, York

Astill, G., Hirst, S., and Wright, S. M. 2004 'The Bordesley Abbey project reviewed', *The Archaeological Journal* 161, 106–58

Aston, M. 2001 'The expansion of the monastic and religious orders in Europe from the eleventh century', in G. Keevill, M. Aston, and T. Hall (eds), *Monastic Archaeology*, Oxbow, Oxford, 9–36

Aston, M. 2009 *Monasteries in the landscape*, Amberley, Stroud

Barber, B. and Thomas, C. 2002 *The London Charterhouse*, Museum of London Archaeological Services Monograph 10, London

Barker, B., Chew, S., Dyson, T., and White, B. 2004 *The Cistercian abbey of St Mary, Stratford Langthorne, Essex: archaeological excavations for the London Underground Limited Jubilee Line Extension Project*, Museum of London Archaeological Services Monograph 18, London

Bond, J. 2001 'Monastic water management in Great Britain', in G. Keevill, M. Aston, and T. Hall (eds), *Monastic Archaeology*, Oxbow, Oxford, 88–136

Bond, J. 2005 'The location and siting of Cistercian houses in Wales and the west', *Archaeologia Cambrensis* 154, 51–79

Bond, J. 2010 *Monastic landscapes*, The History Press, Stroud

Brown, G. and Jones, B. 2009 *Croxden Abbey and its environs: an analytical earthwork survey*, English Heritage Research Department Report 94/2009, London

Bull, R., Davis, S., Lewis, H., and Phillpotts, C. 2011 *Holywell Priory and the development of Shoreditch to c.1600*, Museum of London Archaeology Monograph 53, London

Burton, J. and Stöber, K. 2015 *Abbeys and priories of medieval Wales*, University of Wales Press, Cardiff

Coppack, G. 1986 'The excavation of an outer court building, perhaps the woolhouse, at Fountains Abbey, North Yorkshire', *Medieval Archaeology* 30, 46–87

Coppack, G. 1990 *Abbeys and priories*, Batsford, London

Coppack, G. and Aston, M. 2002 *Christ's Poor Men: the Carthusians in England*, Tempus, Stroud

Cowan, I. B. and Easson, D. E. 1976 *Medieval religious houses: Scotland*, Longman, London

Donkin, R. A. 1978 *The Cistercians: studies in the geography of medieval England and Wales*, Pontifical Institute of Mediaeval Studies, Studies and Texts 38, Toronto

Dyson, T., Samuel, M., Steele, A., and Wright, S. M. 2011 *The Cluniac priory and abbey of St Saviour, Bermondsey, Surrey: excavations, 1984–95*, Museum of London Archaeological Services Monograph 50, London

Everson, P. and Stocker, D. 2011 *Custodians of continuity? The Premonstratensian abbey at Barlings and the landscape of ritual*, Lincolnshire Archaeology and Heritage Reports Series 11, Sleaford

Fawcett, R. 1994 *Scottish abbeys and priories*, Batsford, London

Gilchrist, R. 1994 *Gender and material culture: the archaeology of religious women*, Routledge, London

Gilchrist, R. 1995 *Contemplation and action: the other monasticism*, Leicester University Press, Leicester

Gilchrist, R. and Green, C. 2015 *Glastonbury Abbey: archaeological excavations 1904–1979*, The Society of Antiquaries of London, London

Gilchrist, R. and Mytum, H. (eds) 1993 *Advances in monastic archaeology*, British Archaeological Reports British Series 227, Oxford

Gilchrist, R. and Sloane, B. 2005 *Requiem: the monastic cemetery in Britain*, Museum of London Archaeology Service, London

Grainger, I. and Phillpotts, C. 2011 *The Cistercian abbey of St Mary Graces, East Smithfield, London*, Museum of London Archaeology Monograph 44, London

Gray, M. 1993 *The Trinitarian Order in England: excavations at Thelsford Priory*, British Archaeological Reports British Series 226, Oxford

Greene, J. P. 1989 *Norton Priory: the archaeology of a medieval religious house*, Cambridge University Press, Cambridge

Greene, J. P. 1992 *Medieval monasteries*, Leicester University Press, Leicester

Hardy, A., Dodd, A., and Keevill, G. D. 2003 *Ælfric's Abbey: excavations at Eynsham Abbey, Oxfordshire, 1989-92*, Thames Valley Landscapes 16, Oxford

Harrison, S. 2006 'Benedictine and Augustinian cloister arcades of the twelfth and thirteenth centuries in England, Wales and Scotland', in M. Henig and J. McNeill (eds), *The medieval cloister in England and Wales*, Journal of the British Archaeological Association 159, Leeds, 105-30

Henig, M. and McNeill, J. (eds) 2006 *The medieval cloister in England and Wales*, Journal of the British Archaeological Association 159, Leeds

Hewett, C. A. 1985 *English cathedral and monastic carpentry*, Phillimore, Chichester

Hodder, M. A. 1991 *Excavations at Sandwell Priory and Hall, 1982-88*, Sandwell Metropolitan Borough Council and South Staffordshire Archaeological and Historical Society, West Bromwich

Hope, W. St J. 1901 'The Gilbertine priory of Watton in the East Riding of Yorkshire', *The Archaeological Journal* 58, 1-34

Howard, R. E., Laxton, R. R., and Litton, C. D. 1999 'List 98: Nottingham University Tree-Ring Dating Laboratory: dendrochronological dating for English Heritage', *Vernacular Architecture* 30, 91-6

Huggins, P. J. 1972 'Monastic grange and outer close excavations, Waltham Abbey, Essex, 1970-1972', *Transactions of the Essex Archaeological Society* 4, 30-127

Jecock, M., Burn, A., Brown, G., and Oswald, A. 2011 *Byland Abbey, Ryedale, North Yorkshire: archaeological survey and investigation of part of the precinct and extra-mural area*, English Heritage Research Department Report 4/2011, London

Keevill, G., Aston, M., and Hall, T. (eds) 2001 *Monastic archaeology*, Oxbow, Oxford

Knowles, D. and Hadcock, R. N. 1971 *Medieval religious houses: England and Wales*, Longman, London

Knowles, D. and St Joseph, J. K. S. 1952 *Monastic sites from the air*, Cambridge University Press, Cambridge

Lambrick, G. 1985 'Further excavations on the second site of the Dominican Priory, Oxford', *Oxoniensia* 50, 131-208

Lowe, B. J., Harrison, S. A., and Thurlby, M. 2005 'Keynsham Abbey excavations, 1961-1985. Final report, part 1: the architecture', *Somerset Archaeology and Natural History* 148, 53-102

Lyne, M. 1997 *Lewes Priory: excavations by Richard Lewis, 1969-82*, Lewes Priory Trust, Lewes

Mayes, P. 2002 *Excavations at a Templar preceptory: South Witham, Lincolnshire, 1965-67*, The Society for Medieval Archaeology Monograph 19, London

Miles, D., Worthington, M., and Bridge, M. 2005 'List 166: tree-ring dates from the Oxford Dendrochronological Laboratory', *Vernacular Architecture* 36, 88-96

Miller, P. and Saxby, D. 2007 *The Augustinian priory of St Mary Merton, Surrey: excavations, 1976-90*, Museum of London Archaeological Services Monograph 34, London

Moorhouse, S. 1991 'Ceramics in the medieval garden', in A. E. Brown (ed.), *Garden archaeology*, Council for British Archaeology Research Report 78, 100-17

O'Sullivan, D. 2013 *In the company of the preachers: the archaeology of medieval friaries in England and Wales*, Leicester Archaeology Monograph 23, Leicester

Oswald, A., Goodall, J., Payne, A., and Sutcliffe, T.-J. 2010 *Thornton Abbey, North Lincolnshire: historical, archaeological and architectural investigations*, English Heritage Research Department Report 100/2010, London

Parker, R., Ives, T., and Allan, J. 2007 'Excavation and building study at Cleeve Abbey, 1995–2003', *Somerset Archaeology and Natural History* 150, 73–167

Pestell, T. 2004 *Landscapes of monastic foundation: the establishment of religious houses in East Anglia, c.650–1200*, Boydell Press, Woodbridge

Platt, C. 1984 *The abbeys and priories of medieval England*, Secker and Warburg, London

Robinson, D. M. 1980 *The geography of Augustinian settlement in medieval England and Wales*, British Archaeological Reports British Series 80, Oxford

Robinson, D. M. 2006 *The Cistercians in Wales: architecture and archaeology, 1130–1540*, The Society of Antiquaries, London

Shackley, M., Hayne, J., and Wainwright, N. 1988 'Environmental analysis of medieval fishpond deposits at Owston Abbey, Leicestershire', in M. Aston (ed.), *Medieval fish, fisheries and fishponds in England*, British Archaeological Reports British Series 182, 301–8

Sloane, B. and Malcolm, G. 2004 *Excavations at the priory of the Order of the Hospital of St John of Jerusalem, Clerkenwell, London*, Museum of London Archaeological Services Monograph 20, London

Slater, T. R. 1996 'Medieval town-founding on the estates of the Benedictine order in England', in F.-E. Eliassen and G. A. Ersland (eds), *Power, profit and urban land: landownership in medieval and early-modern northern European towns*, Scolar Press, Aldershot, 70–93

Slater, T. R. 1998 'Benedictine town planning in medieval England: evidence from St Albans', in T. R. Slater and G. Rosser (eds), *The Church in the medieval town*, Ashgate, Aldershot, 155–76

Tatton-Brown, T. W. T. 2006 'The two mid-twelfth-century cloister arcades at Canterbury Cathedral Priory', in M. Henig and J. McNeill (eds), *The medieval cloister in England and Wales*, Journal of the British Archaeological Association 159, Leeds, 91–104

Thomas, C., Sloane, B., and Phillpotts, C. 1997 *Excavations at the priory and hospital of St Mary Spital*, Museum of London Archaeological Service Monograph 1, London

Tyers, I. and Groves, C. 2000 'List 114: tree-ring dates from the University of Sheffield Dendrochronology Laboratory', *Vernacular Architecture* 31, 118–28

Tyers, I. and Groves, C. 2001 'List 122: tree-ring dates from the University of Sheffield Dendrochronology Laboratory', *Vernacular Architecture* 32, 87–92

Tyers, I. and Groves, C. 2002 'List 133: tree-ring dates from the University of Sheffield Dendrochronology Laboratory', *Vernacular Architecture* 33, 115–18

Welander, D. 1991 *The history, art and architecture of Gloucester Cathedral*, Alan Sutton, Stroud

Woodman, F. 1996 'The Gothic campaigns', in A. Atherton, E. Fernie, C. Harper-Bill, and H. Smith (eds), *Norwich Cathedral: church, city and diocese, 1096–1996*, Hambledon Press, London, 158–96

CHAPTER 36

THE CATHEDRAL

RICHARD FAWCETT

WESTERN Christendom was administered through a network of territorial units known as dioceses, each governed by a senior prelate with the title of bishop. Groups of dioceses within provinces were governed by archbishops, who were also bishops of a diocese within their province. The church within which the bishop or archbishop chose to locate his *cathedra* (throne or seat of authority) was known as his cathedral or see and was generally a building of greater than usual size to reflect its importance.

In a majority of dioceses in the British Isles, as across the rest of Europe, cathedrals were staffed by chapters of secular (non-monastic) canons. At Salisbury, in England, there were eventually as many as fifty-four members of chapter, but at one of the smaller Scottish cathedrals, Dornoch, only thirteen. Led by a dean, and with other dignitaries that included a precentor and chancellor, the canons were also usually known as prebendaries because of the prebend or benefice which funded their office. That funding might include the income from estates owned by the chapter and the appropriated tithes of parish churches (Edwards 1967; Lepine 1995). Since many canons were unable, or chose not to be, resident at their cathedrals for much of the year, most of them had deputies known as vicars, who carried much of the burden of the daily worship. Several cathedrals, however, were staffed by priories of monks or of regular canons (communities of priests living a communal life), with a prior in the place of the dean, and the monks or regular canons and obedientiaries (office holders) in the place of the secular canons and dignitaries (Knowles 1963, 129–34). These monastic cathedrals included Ely in Cambridgeshire and Worcester in Worcestershire (both attached to Benedictine priories), Carlisle in Cumbria (Augustinian), and Whithorn in Dumfries and Galloway (Premonstratensian). Two dioceses had twin cathedrals, one secular and the other monastic: thus, the secular cathedral of Wells had a Benedictine counterpart at Bath (both in Somerset), while Lichfield (Staffordshire) had its Benedictine counterpart at Coventry (West Midlands), an arrangement that could result in friction.

The principal liturgical function of the cathedrals was the *opus dei* (the work of God), a daily round of prayer offered by the clergy, seated in ranks of choir stalls to the west of the presbytery where the high altar was located. The pattern of the services, consisting of psalms, anthems, prayers, and readings, was broadly similar in both the monastic and the secular cathedrals, taking its lead from the psalmist's vow to offer prayers seven times daily (Harper 1991). One or more principal Masses would also be celebrated each day. A number of cathedrals housed parochial congregations, among them the secular cathedrals of Chichester (West Sussex) and Hereford (Herefordshire) (Heale 2006; Lepine 2006). In Scotland, with the exceptions of Aberdeen (Aberdeenshire), Elgin (Moray), and St Andrews (Fife), all of the cathedrals served parishes.

Designing and Building

Cathedrals were the most complex structures to be built in the Middle Ages, and something of the processes involved in their construction can be pieced together through close study of documentation and physical evidence (Coldstream 1991; Hislop 2000; Salzman 1952). Partial professional biographies of many master masons have been assembled (Harvey 1987), and we have a uniquely full account of the rebuilding of Canterbury after 1174 by the masons William of Sens and William the Englishman as recorded by a monk named Gervase (Cragoe 2001). The conditions under which many journeyman masons might expect to work can be understood from ordinances drawn up by the chapter of York in 1370 (Knoop and Jones 1967, 223–4). In the design process it must be remembered that the only tools available to master masons were the ruler, the compass, and the set square, though drawings surviving on the Continent such as at Strasbourg in France and Vienna in Austria show that astonishingly complex designs could be drawn up within the limitations of those tools. Systems of proportions depending on the ratio of the diagonal of a square to its side have been identified in the planning of a number of cathedrals, including Norwich (Norfolk), Winchester (Hampshire), and Ely (Fernie 1983). There may also have been some reliance on the Golden Section, in which the diagonal of a halved square is rotated to give the length of the longer side of a rectangle. Details worked out at full scale on plaster tracing floors have survived over the vestibule to the chapter house at York and over the north porch at Wells (Pacey 2007), while a number of thirteenth-century tracery designs were inscribed on the internal walls of the west porch at Ely (Maddison 2000).

The individual stones could be worked with either a mell and chisel or an axe. Changes in the striations left on the stone by those tools can be helpful indicators of the phases of construction of building, as has been argued at Wells on the basis of a change from diagonal to vertical tooling (Robinson 1931, 162). Lifting the worked stones to the upper construction levels required cranes, which were usually of windlass type, examples of which remain in place in the thirteenth-century north-west tower at Peterborough (Cambridgeshire) and in the early fourteenth-century spire of Salisbury (Wiltshire). Occasionally small dimples at the centre of the face of individual stones may indicate where callipers were located to secure the stones during lifting, as along the internal wall above the west door at Elgin. Care was generally taken to tidy away visually intrusive evidence for the processes of building, but occasionally some was left in place. In the lobby of the stair at the west angle of the north-east transept at Lincoln, of soon after 1192, for example, some of the boarding that supported the webbing of the vault during construction was never removed (Bond 1913, 287).

Planning

A remarkable feature of many of the English cathedrals that replaced their Anglo-Saxon predecessors after the Norman Conquest is their great length (Figure 36.1). Winchester, started in 1079, eventually had a total length of about 157 metres (Fernie 2000, 304–7), for example. A cruciform plan was preferred, giving the building a symbolically significant form whilst providing space for additional altars in transepts that often had a single apsidal chapel on their east side when first built. The preferred eastern terminations for Anglo-Norman cathedrals were either a triplet of apses at the ends of the central vessel and aisles, as originally at Durham, or an ambulatory around a central apse with radiating chapels, as at Norwich. These radiating chapels could take many different forms, from semi-circular or figure-of-eight to polygonal. Several cathedrals were given additional external prominence by three towers, one over the crossing and a pair at the west

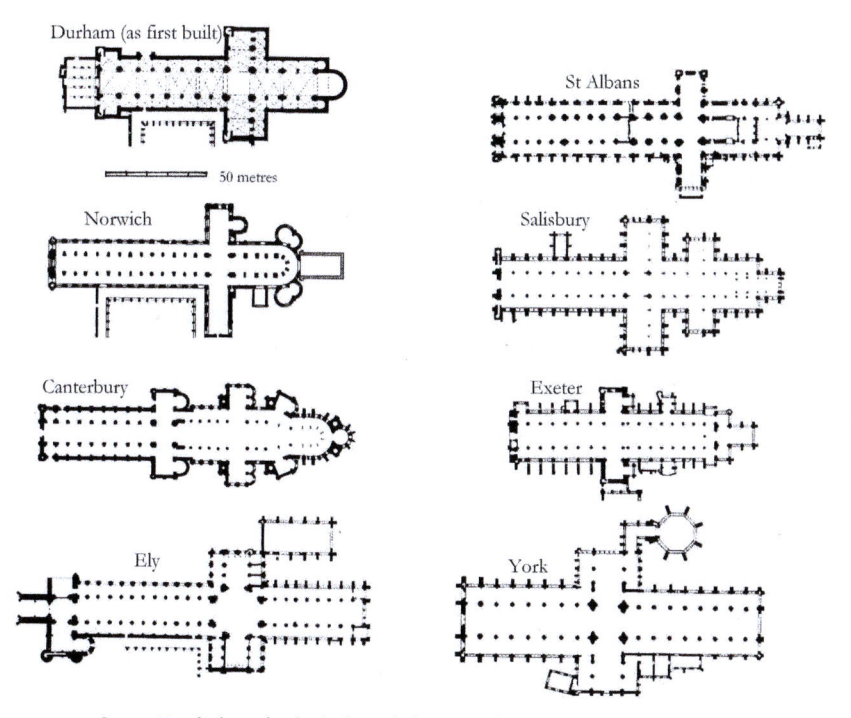

FIGURE 36.1 Some English cathedral plans (after Bond 1905)

end; but some cathedrals had more, Winchester perhaps being planned to have as many as nine (Crook 1996). Some also had free-standing bell towers, as at Chichester and Salisbury (McAleer 2001).

Internally, the principal focus of worship was the high altar, usually located a short distance within the east end of the central vessel, and there might also be a separate choir altar to its west, as originally at Ely. At Norwich the bishop's throne was positioned behind the high altar, elevated at the centre of the apse, while at Durham St Cuthbert's shrine was within the apse. The presbytery, or sanctuary, the ceremonial area around the high altar, occupied much of the east limb of many Anglo-Norman cathedrals, with the choir stalls of the canons or monks extending below the crossing and into the east bays of the nave, as is still the case at Norwich. The rest of the nave was essentially a processional space, but was also accessible to the laity; at cathedrals that were parochial it may have served as their parish church, as was the case at the majority of Scottish cathedrals. Elsewhere parochial congregations could be housed in various ways, including offshoots flanking the nave, as at Ely and London.

In addition to the high altar, cathedrals came to house large numbers of secondary altars. Chief amongst these would be one dedicated to the Virgin Mary, which was most often either at the far east end, as at Lichfield, or on the north side of the east limb, as at Ely. Another important altar would be associated with the great rood (crucifix) at the screen which separated the parts of the church accessible to the laity from the choir of the clergy. Many cathedrals housed the shrine of an important saint, with an associated altar, among them St Thomas at Canterbury and St Cuthbert at Durham (see Chapter 40). There would also have been altars dedicated to saints or aspects of the Divinity, and several associated with chantries at which Masses were offered for the salvation of the souls of their founders (Luxford and McNeill 2011).

The earlier generations of cathedrals in Wales and Scotland were planned on a less ambitious scale than those in England. The Welsh cathedrals of Llandaff (Glamorgan) and Bangor (Gwynedd) evidently had unaisled east limbs terminating in apses (Thurlby 2006, 75–84, 193–6). In Scotland the scale of cathedral building in the early twelfth century is seen in the church known as St Rule's at St Andrews, which is small and unaisled, but given architectural emphasis by an unusually tall tower. An exception to this picture of small scale, however, is Kirkwall in Orkney, which was started in 1137 when the islands were still under Scandinavian control, though it remained unfinished at the Reformation, perhaps because its scale was too great to be afforded. Although only half the size of Durham, many details of Kirkwall's initially tri-apsidal, cruciform, and fully aisled plan appear to have been derived from there.

From the later twelfth century onwards most cathedrals were greatly extended. The east limb was frequently the chief focus of attention, and it often came to be as long as the nave, or even longer; this permitted the liturgically more important presbytery and choir to be given greater emphasis by being housed within an architecturally distinct part of the structure. The thirteenth-century ideal of a cathedral is probably represented by Salisbury, which was started on a fresh site in 1220, and was substantially complete by 1266 (Cocke and Kidson 1993). Following the example of Canterbury, it has two sets of transepts, with the canons' choir in the three bays between those transepts. The full-height main body of the east limb is seven bays long; beyond that the aisles are returned as a straight ambulatory, and east of the ambulatory is a three-bay Lady Chapel which, although only the width of the central vessel, has narrow aisles. The east limb thus has a total length of eleven bays, whereas the nave has ten. In northern England, a flat end to the east limb came to be preferred, with the central vessel extending at the same height to terminate in a tall gable. The most unusual east end was the hammer-headed nine-altars transeptal east end at Durham of 1242–74, inspired by the east transept at Fountains Abbey in North Yorkshire; this allowed a more spacious setting for the shrine of St Cuthbert beyond the high altar and also accommodated more altars (Draper 1980).

Burial within cathedrals was reserved for the most favoured members of clerical and lay society, and was often associated with provisions for chantry Masses to be celebrated at a dedicated altar within a stone or timber enclosure. In some cases chantry chapels were added against the flanks of a cathedral, with care usually being taken to ensure that the architectural forms were in harmony with those of the cathedral itself. At Lincoln chapels were built on each side of the Last Judgement portal, on the south side of the east limb, for Bishops Russell and Longland, and although they died as far apart as 1494 and 1548 the architecture of the two chapels is carefully matched.

Of the ancillary buildings required, the most important was the chapter house, the clergy's meeting room. In monastic cathedrals this was part of the conventual buildings, within or attached to the range on the east side of the cloister. In secular cathedrals it was usually given architecturally distinct expression, and a centralized polygonal plan was often preferred, as at Lincoln and Wells. Other buildings within the complex probably included an episcopal palace (Thompson 1998), as well as individual residences for the canons and some form of communal accommodation for the vicars (Hall and Stocker 2005). At monastic cathedrals there was the usual arrangement of conventual buildings around a cloister, at the core of the gamut of domestic, industrial, and agricultural structures required for the smooth functioning of an enclosed community. The cloister was usually on the south side of the nave, but at Canterbury it was on the north side, and at Rochester it was on the south side of the east limb. A number of secular cathedrals also had cloisters, as at Lincoln and Wells, albeit without conventual buildings around the sides of the walks.

Architecture

The first generation of the cathedrals built or rebuilt in England after the Norman Conquest were massively constructed, with tiers of round-arched openings (Fernie 1983). Internally these Romanesque structures are most often of three stages: an arcade opens into the flanking aisles, above which is a gallery, tribune, or triforium over the aisle vaults, and at the top is the upper tier of windows known as the clearstorey, where a passage usually runs through the wall thickness. The characteristic articulation of component elements is achieved through the repeated unit of bays; the vertical divisions are defined by pilaster buttresses externally and by wall shafts internally, while internal horizontal divisions are marked by string courses. The earliest cathedrals were probably at least partly the work of masons from Normandy, albeit the sources of some of the architectural ideas are to be traced to Burgundy, north Italy, and the German Empire. Aisles are generally stone-vaulted, initially with groined vaults, as in the nave aisles of Ely started after 1082, but later with ribbed vaults, as at Peterborough after 1116. There was less inclination to construct vaults over the high central spaces, though the case for such a high vault has been made at St Albans (Hertfordshire), started in 1077. But it is at Durham as rebuilt from 1093 that the evidence is most certain, and, although the first vault over the east limb failed, ribbed vaults were eventually constructed throughout the whole building (Figure 36.2).

A change in architectural tastes began to take shape in the third quarter of the twelfth century, as patrons and masons increasingly drew inspiration from the Gothic architecture under construction in the Ile-de-France (Brieger 1957; Draper 2006). In northern England receptivity to these ideas was possibly increased by the churches being built across the area by the Cistercians. Fragments surviving from Archbishop Roger of Pont-l'Évêque's York, started soon after his election in 1154, include several that show awareness of the new Cistercian churches. York was in turn to be a major source of inspiration for others, including St Andrews in Scotland, started in 1160–2. The building that was to exert the greatest influence across southern and midland England for some decades was the east limb of Canterbury (Kent) as rebuilt and extended after a fire in 1174. The first master mason was William of Sens, whose name suggests a knowledge of, and perhaps even an origin in, that French archiepiscopal city, whose cathedral was an important contributor to the development of Gothic architecture. Within Canterbury's choir, the tall arcade piers of coloured marbles with their classicizing Corinthian-esque capitals, together with the compressed gallery stage composed of two paired openings in each bay, and the sexpartite rib vaulting, may all be at least partly indebted to Sens, albeit other features are essentially English. This approach to design, generally termed 'Early English', is taken further in the rebuilding of Lincoln, begun in 1192, and at Salisbury, built between 1220 and 1266 to a chastely uniform design. Salisbury's groupings of single pointed windows in each bay allowed unprecedented amounts of light into the building, and the continuing taste for structural colour is seen in the contrast between the Chilmark limestone of the walls and the Purbeck 'marble' of the *en-délit* shafts and capitals (Figure 36.3).

The impact of the design of Lincoln, perhaps through the medium of such as the east limb of Rievaulx Abbey (North Yorkshire), was felt as late as the 1240s in the three-storeyed east limb of Glasgow. However, in both Scotland and Wales there was a preference for reducing the dark area of the middle storey, or for eliminating it altogether. In the nave of St David's (Pembrokeshire), started in 1182, the twin arches of the gallery were slotted into the lower part of the clearstorey window openings, while in the east limb the middle storey was simply abandoned. At Elgin after 1224 and Dunblane (Stirling) after 1237, a two-storey design was also adopted.

FIGURE 36.2 Durham Cathedral, nave interior built between 1093 and 1133, showing the pointed rib arches used to cover the nave vault, the oldest in the country and one of the first in Europe. Previously, semi-circular arches had been used. Below, massive masonry drum columns with incised ornament support the upper walls

(© Richard Fawcett)

FIGURE 36.3 Nave of Salisbury Cathedral, showing the slender columns and capitals of black Purbeck marble abutting the Chilmark limestone, windows, and pointed arches that accentuate the sense of verticality

(© Richard Fawcett)

As the thirteenth century progressed, cathedrals tended to become ever more light-filled. This was made possible by the development of window tracery, initially with shapes cut through plates of stone, as in the triforium openings, and probably originally in the west window, of Lincoln's nave, and as is still seen in the choir aisles of Glasgow. From the central decades of the century, however, tracery forms were increasingly defined by curved bars of stone, in a way probably first seen at Reims in France from 1211. The magnificent culmination of this first phase of bar tracery was the eight-light east window of Lincoln, in the Angel Choir completed in 1280, in which there are four groupings of a basic unit of two lights with a circlet between their heads embraced within an arch.

The turn of the thirteenth century and the early decades of the fourteenth witnessed the emergence of two radically differing approaches to design, which are generally characterized as the 'Decorated' and 'Perpendicular' styles (Binski 2014; Bony 1979; Harvey 1978). For several decades there had been a tendency towards greater enrichment of the mouldings and carved details, as seen in the Angel Choir of Lincoln built between 1256 and 1280. There had also been a fascination with spatial complexity, as exemplified by the octagon that replaced the central tower of Ely in 1322–34, or the interpenetrating spaces of the ambulatory and Lady Chapel at the east end of Wells from around 1320. The love of two-dimensional complexity is perhaps most obvious in window tracery and an especially significant development was the introduction of the double curved ogee, which permitted richly curvilinear forms to be deployed, as in the wonderfully inventive nine-light east window of Carlisle that may only have been completed as late as the 1360s.

At the same time that these ideas were taking shape, however, an approach that drew much of its inspiration from the cool rationality of French Rayonnant architecture was also gaining favour. As started in 1291, the nave of York displayed a fresh concern for the planes rather than the depth and mass of the walls, with a carefully articulated inter-relationship between the supporting elements and the features they supported, as seen in the way the wall shafts emerging from the arcade piers separate to support either the vault springing or the wall ribs. A particularly significant feature at York is the way the shafts of the triforium openings are downward extensions of the clearstorey mullions, in a way that reflects the design of the east limb of Clermont-Ferrand, completed eleven years earlier. The resultant grid-like treatment of those two upper storeys was to be taken further in London, on the exteriors of the chapel of St Stephen in the Palace of Westminster, started in 1292, and the chapter house of St Paul's Cathedral, started in 1332 (Wilson 1990, 191–3 and 204–8). The fullest early expression of this new development is seen in the internal refacing of the east parts of Gloucester after the murdered Edward II was buried there in 1327.

The rectilinearity demonstrated in these buildings found little favour in Scotland. After a long period of warfare between England and Scotland from the 1290s, once major building again became possible around the 1370s guidance was increasingly sought beyond the southern neighbour. An inscription at Melrose Abbey (Roxburghshire) records that John Morow, a mason born in Paris, worked at both St Andrews and

Glasgow, amongst other buildings (Fawcett 2011, 236–51). So far as other fresh sources of architectural inspiration are concerned, in the cylindrical arcade piers of Aberdeen's nave, of around the third quarter of the fourteenth century, and in Dunkeld's (Perth and Kinross) nave started in 1406, there was probably awareness of the revived vogue for such piers in the Brabant region of the Low Countries.

Furnishings

The foretaste of heaven offered to the faithful by the architecture and furnishings of the cathedrals remains enormously powerful, though it is incomplete without the rich polychromy that would once have been all pervading (Rosewell 2008; see Chapter 42 in this *Handbook*). So far as furnishings are concerned, the most important liturgical foci of any church were the altars, where the mystery of transubstantiation was enacted at Mass, by which bread and wine were believed to be transformed into the body and blood of Christ. Most of the altars were removed or desecrated at the Reformation, though a number of reredoses have survived (Bond 1916, 1–100). At Durham (1376–80), the stone reredos known as the Neville Screen consists of an exquisite display of micro-architectural open tabernacle work topped by soaring spirelets that seems almost to defy the nature of the material (Wilson 1980). Other features close to the altar might include sedilia, piscinae, and the Easter Sepulchre or Tomb of Christ (see Chapter 41 for definitions). A late thirteenth-century example of the latter survives at Lincoln (Sekules 1986).

West of the presbytery, in the choir, were the timber stalls occupied by the clergy during their performance of the *opus dei* (Tracy 1987; 1990). They extended down the flanks of the choir and returned against a screen at its west end, with a central processional entrance between the latter. The senior clergy had their place in the upper rank of stalls, and from the fourteenth century their prominence was enhanced through the addition of openwork gabled canopies, as at Winchester or Ely; later there might be lavishly inventive tabernacle work at such as Lincoln, Chester, and Carlisle (Allen 2008). Particular prominence was given to the stall of the bishop, at the east end of the south rank of stalls. The largest and most lavishly detailed of these was the timber throne of Bishop Stapeldon at Exeter, of the second decade of the fourteenth century; its superstructure soared through three stages to a finial at mid-height of the clearstorey (Tracy and Budge 2015).

Medieval cathedrals were more subdivided than might appear today. Screens of stone, timber, or metal were constructed around the presbytery and choir, and would have restricted access to many of the chapels. The most prominent screen was usually placed at the west end of the choir, through the central door of which the clergy processed to their stalls and the high altar (e.g. Vallance 1947). This was frequently of stone and might have finely detailed image niches on the face towards the nave, as at Canterbury and York; there might also be recesses for altars, as at St David's. There was usually a platform on its top where the great rood or crucifix was located, and there might also be what was known as 'a pair' of organs to accompany the music. In some cathedrals, and especially monastic foundations, there was a second screen to the west. Screened-off chantry chapels were often a prominent feature, a favoured form being a cage-like structure set within an arcade arch, one of the earliest perhaps being that constructed for Bishop Edington (died 1366) in the nave of Winchester (Luxford 2011; see Chapter 54 in this *Handbook*). Rare survivals of other fixtures include the windlass attached to the north-east pier of the east crossing at Salisbury that allowed a veil to be drawn across the presbytery during Lent (Brown 1999, 13). A square slot in the steps leading up to the high altar platform at St Andrews was perhaps the seating for the Paschal Candle set up on Maundy Thursday during the build-up to Easter; at Durham we know the Paschal Candle reached up almost to the high vault. Several lecterns survive, including a late fifteenth-century Flemish example at Norwich, and pulpits are found in a number of cathedrals. The timber pulpit presented to Aberdeen by Bishop Stewart in about 1540, now in King's College Chapel there, had a backboard designed to fit the north-west crossing pier. Of fonts, amongst the earliest are examples at Winchester and Lincoln carved from marble quarried and carved at Tournai in Belgium around the third quarter of the twelfth century (Zarnecki 1953, 56).

The Study of Cathedrals

With the notable exception of Salisbury, which was set out on a virgin site in the earlier thirteenth century and subsequently only minimally expanded, most cathedrals in the British Isles occupy sites of considerable antiquity, and they only achieved their final medieval state as the result of many augmentations and adaptations. York overlays the buildings of a Roman legionary fortress, for example, while many others are on the sites of pre-Conquest predecessors. At most cathedrals much of the evidence for the earlier history of the site, and for superseded phases of the building, was concealed from view in the later phases of construction, in order to achieve an architecturally homogeneous appearance. At a number of cathedrals where rebuilding was never completed, however, that homogeneity was never achieved, as at St Albans, where there are striking differences along the length of the nave.

Any attempt to reach an understanding of the evidence for the earlier states of cathedrals requires painstaking specialist examination of both the structural and sub-soil archaeology whenever the opportunity arises (Rodwell 2012; Tatton Brown and Munby 1996). An essential pre-requisite for such examination was the development of techniques of taxonomic analysis of details as a basis for assessing relative chronology, and as early as the 1670s John Aubrey was studying window tracery as one way of doing so (Turner 2011). But it was the nineteenth century that saw the earliest systematic application of analytical approaches, with the first edition of Thomas Rickman's *Attempt to establish the styles of English architecture* of 1817 a landmark in this process. Scrupulously applied analysis of the structural archaeology found its first great master in Robert Willis

FIGURE 36.4 Glasgow Cathedral during excavation

(© Stephen Driscoll)

(1800–75) (Buchanan 2013). His 1845 account of the architectural evidence embodied within the fabric of Canterbury in the light of the documentation, and particularly of the account of rebuilding after 1174 by Brother Gervase, remains an invaluable starting point for all later studies of that cathedral. His approach was further developed by later scholars, including William St John Hope (1854–1919) and John Bilson (1856–1943), and was in due course reflected in the *Inventories* of the Royal Commissions on Ancient Monuments of England, Scotland, and Wales, as well as in the *Buildings of England, Scotland*, and

Wales series initiated by Nikolaus Pevsner. Since 1978, the conference *Transactions* of the British Archaeological Association have offered exemplary analytical accounts.

An important aid in the structural analysis of buildings over recent decades has been the development of increasingly sophisticated recording and analytical techniques. Rectified photography, photogrammetry, and laser scanning, for example, have made it possible to produce minutely detailed records of wall and floor surfaces as bases for study that are more accurate than measured drawing could be, though expert input remains essential in interpreting those records (Swallow et al. 2004). A valuable aid to the dating of timbers and the structures associated with them has been dendrochronological analysis, which has been brought to a high level of accuracy, as seen in studies of the timbers at Ely and Lincoln (Simpson and Litton 1996).

Amongst recent sub-surface archaeological investigations, excavation at Winchester in the 1960s exposed the plan of the predecessor of the Romanesque building, while investigations at Glasgow between 1988 and 1997 (Figure 36.4) revealed the western extent of the building started in the second decade of the twelfth century, together with evidence for its successor dedicated in 1197 (Driscoll 2002). There should be no doubt that works requiring the penetration of ground surfaces or disturbance to standing fabric must be undertaken under archaeological supervision if the risk of losing information critical to the understanding of cathedrals is to be averted, and if informed decisions on conservation or modified uses are to be reached. It is for this reason that the Care of Cathedrals Measure of 1990 requires all cathedrals to appoint a properly qualified archaeologist to oversee such works.

Conclusion

When structurally complete, fully furnished, and alive with colour, and as the setting for an unbroken round of worship in which glorious music and the scent of incense filled the air, at their best medieval cathedrals must have offered an incomparable feast for all the senses that was understood as anticipating the heavenly kingdom for those who merited a place there. Their fate at the Reformation varied according to their location. In England, where bishops continued to rule the Church except for a period under the Commonwealth, they generally survived structurally complete; it was the furnishings associated with the 'superstitious' Mass, and most notably the altars, together with 'idolatrous' images, that suffered most severely from successive waves of iconoclasm. Indeed, the number of cathedrals was increased following the Reformation, with several abbeys being raised to cathedral status, including Gloucester and Peterborough. The picture was very different in Scotland where, although bishops remained intermittently in authority until they were finally removed from the state Church in 1689, forms of worship became increasingly simple, and complex buildings were no longer required. At St Andrews and Elgin, for example, the bishops simply abandoned their cathedral in favour of the nearby parish church, while elsewhere it was usually no more than one limb of the building that continued in use, with the other parts being abandoned. The only cathedrals to survive largely complete were Glasgow and Kirkwall, the former because it was progressively subdivided to serve three congregations.

References cited

Allen, J. 2008 'The choir stalls of Lincoln Cathedral, Chester Cathedral and St Mary's Church, Nantwich', *Journal of the British Archaeological Association* 161, 104–30

Binski, P. 2014 *Gothic wonder, art, artifice and the Decorated Style 1290–1350*, Yale University Press, London

Bond, F. 1905 *Gothic architecture in England*, Batsford, London

Bond, F. 1913 *An introduction to English church architecture*, Oxford University Press, London

Bond, F. 1916 *The chancel of English churches*, Oxford University Press, London

Bony, J. 1979 *The English Decorated Style*, Phaidon, Oxford

Brieger, P. 1957 *English art 1216–1307*, Oxford University Press, Oxford

Brown, S. 1999 *Sumptuous and richly adorned: the decoration of Salisbury Cathedral*, Her Majesty's Stationery Office, London

Buchanan, A. 2013 *Robert Willis and the foundation of architectural history*, Boydell, Woodbridge

Cocke, T. and Kidson, P. 1993 *Salisbury Cathedral: perspectives on the architectural history*, Her Majesty's Stationery Office, London

Coldstream, N. 1991 *Medieval craftsmen, masons and sculptors*, British Museum Press, London

Cragoe, C. D. 2001 'Reading and rereading Gervase of Canterbury', *Journal of the British Archaeological Association* 154, 40–53

Crook, J. 1996 'Recent archaeology in Winchester Cathedral', in T. W. T. Tatton-Brown and J. Munby (eds), *The archaeology of cathedrals*, Oxford University Committee for Archaeology, Oxford, 135–51

Draper, P. 1980 'The Nine Altars at Durham and Fountains', in N. Coldstream and P. Draper (eds), *Medieval art and architecture at Durham Cathedral*, British Archaeological Association Conference Transactions for the Year 1977, Leeds, 74–86

Draper, P. 2006 *The formation of English Gothic, architecture and identity*, Yale University Press, London

Driscoll, S. 2002 *Excavations at Glasgow Cathedral 1988–1997*, The Society for Medieval Archaeology Monograph 18, London

Edwards, K. 1967 *The English secular cathedral in the Middle Ages*, Manchester University Press, Manchester (2nd edn)

Fawcett, R. 2011 *The architecture of the Scottish medieval church, 1100–1560*, Yale University Press, New Haven and London

Fernie, E. 1983 'The grid system and the design of the Norman cathedral', in T. A. Heslop and V. A. Sekules (eds), *Medieval art and architecture at Winchester Cathedral*, British Archaeological Association Conference Transactions for the year 1983, Leeds, 13–19

Fernie, E. 2000 *The architecture of Norman England*, Oxford University Press, Oxford

Hall, R. and Stocker, D. (eds) *Vicars choral at English Cathedrals: history, architecture and archaeology*, Oxbow, Oxford

Harper, J. 1991 *The forms and orders of western liturgy*, Clarendon Press, Oxford

Harvey, J. 1978 *The Perpendicular Style, 1330–1485*, Batsford, London

Harvey, J. 1987 *English medieval architects: a biographical dictionary down to 1550*, Alan Sutton Publishing, Gloucester (rev. edn)

Heale, M. 2006 'Monastic-parochial churches in late medieval England', in C. Burgess and E. Duffy (eds), *The parish in late medieval England*, Shaun Tyas, Donington, 54–77.

Hislop, M. 2000 *Medieval masons*, Shire Publications, Princes Risborough

Knoop, D. and Jones, G. P. 1967 *The medieval mason*, Manchester University Press, Manchester (3rd edn)

Knowles, D. 1963 *The monastic order in England*, Cambridge University Press, Cambridge (2nd edn)

Lepine, D. 1995 *A brotherhood of canons serving God: English secular cathedrals in the later Middle Ages*, Boydell Press, Woodbridge

Lepine, D. 2006 '"Ande alle oure paresshens": secular cathedrals and parish churches in late medieval England', in C. Burgess and E. Duffy (eds), *The parish in late medieval England*, Shaun Tyas, Donington, 29–53

Luxford, J. M. 2011 'The origins and development of the English "stone-cage chantry chapel"', in J. M. Luxford and J. McNeill (eds), *The medieval chantry in England*, British Archaeological Association, Leeds, 16–23

Luxford, J. M. and McNeill, J. (eds) 2011 *The medieval chantry in England*, British Archaeological Association, Leeds

Maddison, J. 2000 *Ely Cathedral: design and meaning*, Ely Cathedral Publications, Ely

McAleer, J. P. 2001 'The tradition of detached bell towers at cathedral and monastic churches in medieval England and Scotland (1066–1539)', *Journal of the British Archaeological Association* 154, 54–83

Pacey, A. 2007 *Medieval architectural drawing*, Tempus, Stroud

Robinson, J. A. 1931 'On the date of the Lady Chapel at Wells', *The Archaeological Journal* 88, 159–74

Rodwell, W. 2012 *The archaeology of churches*, Amberley, Stroud

Rosewell, R. 2008 *Medieval wall paintings*, Boydell, Woodbridge

Salzman, L. F. 1952 *Building in England down to 1540*, Oxford University Press, Oxford

Sekules, V. 1986 'The Tomb of Christ at Lincoln and the development of the sacrament shrine: Easter sepulchres reconsidered', in T. A. Heslop and V. A. Sekules (eds), *Medieval art and architecture at Lincoln Cathedral*, British Archaeological Association Conference Transactions VIII, Leeds, 118–31

Simpson, W. G. and Litton, C. D. 1996 'Dendrochronology in cathedrals', in T. W. T. Tatton-Brown and J. Munby (eds), *The archaeology of cathedrals*, Oxford University Committee for Archaeology, Oxford, 183–209

Swallow, P., Dallas, R., Jackson, S., and Watt, D. 2004 *Measurement and recording of historic buildings*, Donhead, Shaftesbury (2nd edn)

Tatton-Brown, T. W. T. and Munby, J. 1996 *The archaeology of cathedrals*, Oxford University Committee for Archaeology, Oxford

Thompson, M. 1998 *Medieval Bishops' houses in England and Wales*, Ashgate, Aldershot

Thurlby, M. 2006 *Romanesque architecture and sculpture in Wales*, Logaston Press, Woonton Almeley

Tracy, C. 1987 *English Gothic choir stalls, 1200–1400*, Boydell Press, Woodbridge

Tracy, C. 1990 *English Gothic choir stalls, 1400–1540*, Boydell Press, Woodbridge

Tracy, C. and Budge, A. 2015 *Britain's medieval Episcopal thrones*, Oxbow, Oxford

Turner, O. H. 2011 '"The windows of the church are of several fashions": architectural form and historical method in John Aubrey's *Chronologia Architectonica*', *Architectural History* 54, 171–93

Vallance, A. 1947 *Greater English church screens*, Batsford, London

Wilson, C. 1980 'The Neville Screen', in N. Coldstream and P. Draper (eds), *Medieval art and architecture at Durham Cathedral*, British Archaeological Association Conference Transactions for the Year 1977, Leeds, 90–104

Wilson, C. 1990 *The Gothic cathedral*, Thames and Hudson, London

Zarnecki, G. 1953 *English Romanesque sculpture, 1140–1210*, Alex Tiranti, London

CHAPTER 37

THE MEDIEVAL PARISH CHURCH

Architecture, Furnishings, and Fittings

RICHARD FAWCETT

THE experience that most people had of religion and the exercise of their faith was at the level of the parish, where a locally based priest was responsible for administering the sacraments and providing pastoral care (Burgess and Duffy 2006; French et al. 1997). By the time of the *Valor Ecclesiasticus* of 1535 there were about 8838 parishes within Henry VIII's kingdom, while in Scotland there were about 1136 (Cowan 1967). Within many parishes there would also have been chapels of various kinds (see Chapter 34). Some were chapels of ease serving populous suburbs, or were in outlying rural areas from where regular access to the parish church might have been difficult. Some may have been founded because of the site's association with a particular function, such as the existence of a miracle-working well or an event associated with the life of a saint, and they might be of specialized design. Others would have been private chapels within the residences of landholders, where the bishop of the diocese had granted license for worship to take place, and might be either free-standing structures or incorporated within the main body of the residence. But rights of baptism and burial were generally reserved to the mother church of the parish, at least partly because of the income that those functions generated.

Parishes originated in a number of ways. Some were centred on what had been early minster or monastic churches, while many others had their origins in foundations by the local landholder, to provide for the spiritual welfare of his family, household, and tenants. Those landholders would have initially exercised the advowson, or right of patronage, over the parish priest, who was known as a rector or parson, and who was supported by a tithe (in Scotland a *teind*), a tenth of the produce of the parish. However, as lay patronage of the church came to be seen as less acceptable, it was increasingly transferred to a religious corporation or individual, such as a monastery, a cathedral, or a bishop (Blair and Sharpe 1992). A common further stage was that the rectory was itself appropriated to that corporation or individual, which would then retain the greater part of the tithes, and a substitute priest, in the person of a vicar, curate, or chaplain, was appointed to exercise the day-to-day parochial cure of souls.

The Component Elements of a Church

The two main architectural requirements in a parish church were for an area to house the principal altar and the priest celebrating Mass there, usually known as the chancel or choir, which was located at the east end of the building, and a larger area west of the chancel to shelter the layfolk of the parish when attending worship, known as the nave. Financial responsibility for the chancel rested with the rector, whether that was a resident priest or the appropriator of the rectory, while the nave was the responsibility of the parishioners. These two parts of the church were usually architecturally distinct, and might eventually be of very different scale and architectural form because of the divided financial responsibility, though in Scotland a high proportion of smaller rural parish churches were simple rectangular structures with only a screen to demarcate the two areas.

Amongst possible augmentations of the two-compartment plan, in the earlier twelfth century there might be a semi-circular apse at the east end of the chancel as a backdrop to the principal altar (Figure 37.1). Apses went out of fashion in the later twelfth century and were often suppressed, though in the fourteenth and fifteenth centuries there was to be a limited vogue for polygonal apses, a vogue that took greater hold in Scotland than in England. There might also be a tower to house bells and to give architectural prominence to the building, most frequently either at the west end or at the junction of the chancel and nave. But in some cases towers were placed against the flank of the building, possibly also serving as a porch, as at Norbury (Derbyshire); more rarely they might be free-standing, as at West Walton (Norfolk). In the most ambitious churches there could be more than one tower, as at Ottery St Mary (Devon) where a pair of towers over the transepts emulated those of the cathedral at Exeter. One or more porches might be provided to shelter those entering the church and to accommodate functions associated with the point at which the outside world gave place to the sacred space of the church. In many cases porches also accommodated additional functions in an upper storey; exceptionally, at Cirencester (Gloucestershire), where the porch also housed the guild hall, there are two upper storeys. Another frequently provided offshoot was a sacristy, where the priests prepared themselves for the celebration of Mass and where the sacred vessels and vestments were stored; this was usually off the north side of the chancel. Aisles

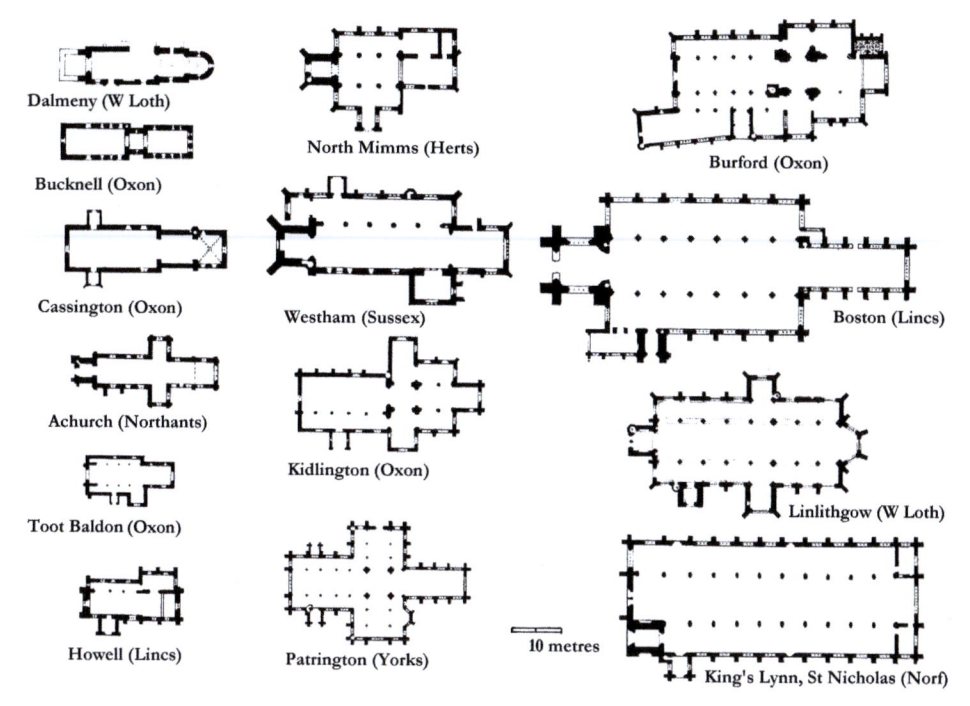

FIGURE 37.1 Parish church plans (after Bond 1905)

might be added either singly or symmetrically alongside one or both parts of the church in order to provide additional space, to house additional altars, and perhaps to serve as processional spaces; in the twelfth and thirteenth centuries these were usually relatively narrow, though later they were often much wider. Since the addition of aisles could darken the main part of the church, their construction was frequently accompanied by the heightening of the walls of the central vessel to provide an upper tier of windows known as a clearstorey.

In addition to the principal altar and those at any aisle ends, in larger churches space for other altars was occasionally provided in transepts that projected on one or both sides at the junction of chancel and nave, especially when there was a central tower. There might also be altars in front of the screen that separated chancel and nave, and possibly also on the loft above that screen. The need to provide space for additional altars became increasingly pressing in the later Middle Ages, whether to accommodate devotion to particular saints and cults, or as individuals, families, or guilds made provision for Masses to be offered for their welfare in life and to further the cause of their salvation in death. Depending on the funds available, those Masses could be in specified numbers, perhaps at an existing altar where they were celebrated by a priest who was already serving the church. More ambitiously, endowment could be provided for Masses to be celebrated for all time to come by a succession of priests at a specially provided altar. Such endowments were known as chantries. The altars at which those Masses were offered might be housed in screened-off areas within the body of the church, or in purpose-built chapels that could be added at almost any point around the periphery. The wish to attract the prayers of the faithful meant that the chapels were often given architectural prominence and were especially richly decorated (Burgess 2011; Roffey 2007, and see Chapter 54 in this *Handbook*; Saul 2009). The chapels might house the tombs of those for whom expiatory prayers were being offered, so that those commemorated were in the closest possible relationship with the holy mysteries (Badham and Oosterwijk 2010; Penman 2013). At the most ambitious scale of provision, a college of priests could be established within the church, a process often associated with rebuilding of the chancel or even the whole of the building, in order to provide a seemly setting for the expanded daily round of worship (Burgess and Heale 2008).

Design and Construction

Building parish churches of any complexity required an extended design process, calling for a high level of expertise from the master mason. Discussions with the patrons might be followed by drawing up a contract in which the form of the new work was specified, models cited, and penalties stated in case either party defaulted (Salzman 1952, 413–602). This would be followed by a period in the masons' lodge or tracing house, in which, amongst much else, full-size templates were drawn and cut to ensure that all of the moulded elements were worked to the correct profile (Hislop 2000; Pacey 2007). At Roslin (Midlothian) it was said that the master mason had his profiles drawn on boards that were cut out by the carpenters before being given to the masons (Salzman 1952, 20–1); Roslin also has a number of what appear to be working drawings on the walls of a chamber to the east of the chapel itself. Much of the medieval design process was based on the accumulated empirical experience of generations of master masons. The names of many masons have been found in the records of major church building operations (Harvey 1984), though relatively few parish churches can be ascribed to named individuals. Nevertheless, in the minor details that were outside the interest of the patrons the masons' creative personalities may sometimes be detected (Figure 37.2). A strikingly individual approach to the design of a group of moulding profiles, for example, has suggested that one East Anglian master mason worked on a number of projects (Fawcett 1982). So-called 'masons' marks', which are found on the dressed masonry at many buildings, were probably incised by subordinate masons as a way of ensuring they were producing work in sufficient quantity and of adequate quality (Alexander 2001).

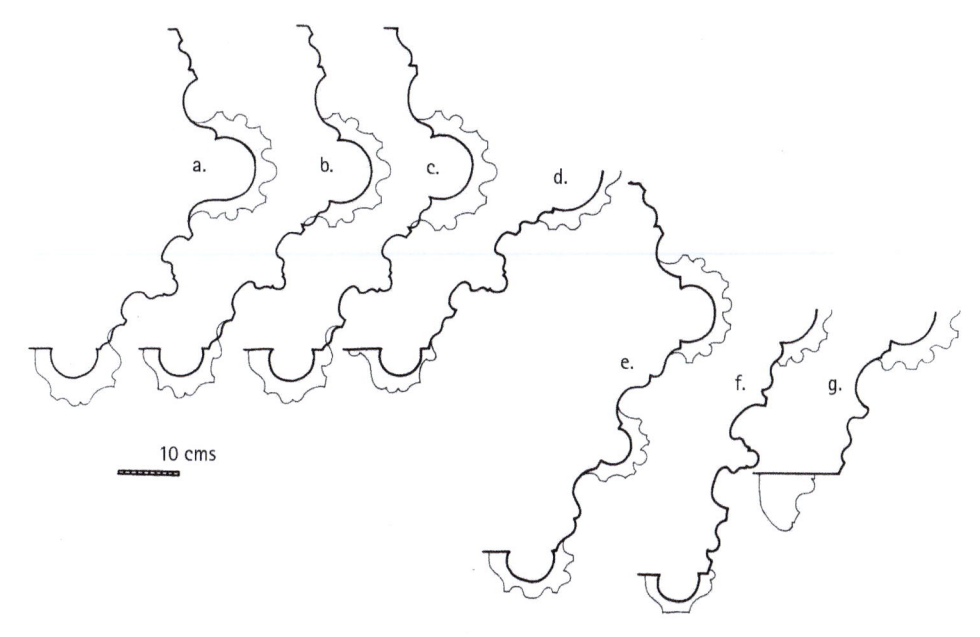

FIGURE 37.2 Moulding profiles attributable to a single master mason: a) Wiveton (north porch archway), b) Great Gressingham (south porch archway), c) Hilborough (south porch archway), d) Norwich St Mary Coslany (south porch archway), e) Blakeney (north porch archway), f) Walpole St Peter (north porch archway), g) Norwich St Margaret Westwick (south porch archway)

(© Richard Fawcett)

Changes in Architectural Fashions and Regional Differences

From the later eleventh century into the middle years of the twelfth, in the architectural phase characterized as 'Romanesque' (Fernie 2000), walls tended to be heavily constructed with openings of relatively small scale that were spanned by round arches. A sense of articulation of the component elements of the building might be established by regular rhythms of fenestration and pilaster buttresses. Special emphasis was often given to points of transition such as doorways and chancel arches by rich sculptural decoration, with some parts of the country, including Herefordshire, Kent, and Yorkshire, having particularly inventive teams of masons (Thurlby 1999; Zarnecki 1951). Repetitive mouldings including chevron or billet were especially favoured, and the most common types of capitals were of cushion, scalloped, or volute form. In large-scale churches with aisles, cylindrical or octagonal piers were favoured for the arcades.

In the later twelfth and earlier thirteenth centuries, in the phase of transition from Romanesque to Gothic, masonry construction became relatively lighter as empirically attained understanding of structural dynamics evolved, and there was an increasingly pronounced sense of articulation of the components. Buttressing was of greater projection, windows became larger, and mouldings around doors, windows, and arches became more slender and deeply undercut. Favoured repetitive mouldings included chevron of deeply undercut tubular profile, and nail-head or dogtooth. There was a growing preference for capitals of simply moulded or of foliate types; initially favoured waterleaf and crocket forms later gave way to stiff-leaf foliage composed of trifid-like leaves of increasing complexity. Aisles became more common, with arcades carried on slender cylindrical, octagonal, or clustered-shaft piers. Towers were often capped by spires, sometimes of broached form and with one or more levels of lucarne windows.

In the course of the earlier thirteenth century, in the phase traditionally known as 'Early English', interiors gained an increased sense of spaciousness and structural lightness (Draper 2006). Windows were frequently an important point of display, with groupings of individual lights within embracing arches sometimes having additional piercings through the plate of stone at their heads. But from the mid-century, tracery came into favour that was composed of curved bars of stone set out in geometric patterns, with foiled figures generally formed by cusped circlets and set within a hierarchy of sub-arches. In the later years of the century those containing circlets were increasingly removed, resulting in greater freedom in the interaction between the individual forms, and leading to the complexity made possible by the double curved ogee. Also in the later years of the century there was a short-lived taste for foliage carving based on minutely observed naturalism.

The first half of the fourteenth century has been characterized as the 'Decorated' period in England because of the love of enrichment found in many churches (Binski 2014). This is seen especially in window tracery, in which the full exploitation of the possibilities of the ogee curve resulted in some of the most complex combinations of flowing forms ever contrived, as seen especially in East Yorkshire, Lincolnshire, and Nottinghamshire. Despite the love of enrichment, mouldings tended to be less deeply undercut, and foliage carving became more formalized, with a taste for thickly carved seaweed-like forms. Towers could be given great prominence, many with spires rising from behind elaborately pinnacled and crenellated parapets and with multiple levels of lucarnes to their faces, while some towers had octagonal superstructures (Figure 37.3).

A marked change can be discerned in the architecture of the later fourteenth and earlier fifteenth centuries, which is again seen most obviously in window tracery. Instead of the curvilinear complexity previously favoured, English tracery was increasingly set out on rigidly rectilinear patterns with the strongly marked vertical and horizontal lines that have led to this phase being characterized as the 'Perpendicular' period (Harvey 1978). In major churches windows were both widened and heightened to their greatest extent, sometimes occupying the whole space available between the buttresses, while in some clearstoreys there were pairs of windows to each bay, leaving no more than slender piers of masonry between. There was a taste for arches of four-centred form, proportions

THE MEDIEVAL PARISH CHURCH 603

Single-light windows and plate tracery

Geometric tracery

Decorated/curvilinear tracery

Perpendicular/rectilinear tracery

FIGURE 37.3 Examples of window designs found in parish churches (from Parker 1850)

were often more vertically attenuated than ever and mouldings more streamlined. Open-timber roofs of a strikingly inventive range of types were becoming more important foci, with finely engineered hammer-beam roofs perhaps representing an apogee. Many of England's most ambitious towers were built in these years, some having soaring spires which might be connected to the wall-head pinnacles by flyers, or which might rise from octagonal cage-like bases (Figure 37.4).

Changes of fashion were generally more subtle from the mid-fifteenth century until the Reformation, and much of what has been said about the previous phase remains true. In some churches there is an increased preference for extreme simplicity of mouldings and of window tracery. Conversely, in others there is a taste for enhanced enrichment of surfaces, with more churches having blind tracery to the spandrels of the arcades and many East Anglian churches having particularly lavish external flushwork decoration. In a number of larger churches, aisles, chapels, and porches are covered by

FIGURE 37.4 Fotheringhay Church, Northamptonshire, an example of the 'Perpendicular' style
(© Richard Fawcett)

complex vaults, with fan and lierne forms being favoured, as seen in the fan vault of 1508 over the north chancel aisle of Cirencester (Gloucestershire).

The stylistic developments sketched out above might be modified in varying degrees by regional preferences, as seen in the family resemblance between several churches in Kent, such as Westerham and Sandwich, which have three parallel aisles of equal width and similar height, but no clearstorey. A particularly important factor in regional differences was the nature of the available building materials. In much of Cornwall, for example, the main material was granite, which could be cut in large blocks but could be carved only with the greatest difficulty, whereas in much of Kent reliance had to be placed on various forms of rubble, including flint. The correlation between wealth and architectural ambition is also evident in regions such as the West Country and East Anglia where the later medieval wool trade brought great prosperity. Soaring towers are a notable feature of many Somerset churches, with multiple tiers of windows set within a richly articulated framework of buttressing and string courses, and with traceried wallhead parapets framed and punctuated by tall pinnacles, as seen at Taunton St Mary.

The part of mainland Britain that showed the greatest architectural independence in the later Middle Ages was Scotland. During the twelfth and thirteenth centuries lowland Scotland's closest architectural relationships were with England; but after many decades of warfare, from the later fourteenth century onwards Scottish patrons and their masons increasingly chose to look elsewhere for their inspiration. Although a majority of rural parish churches were to be relatively simple buildings, where there was a wealthy patron, and in the great trading burghs, the churches were often rebuilt on an ambitious scale. In the burghs of Aberdeen, Dundee, Edinburgh, Haddington (East Lothian), Linlithgow (West Lothian), Perth, and Stirling magnificent cruciform structures eventually took shape, with several showing the impact of ideas absorbed in the course of the trading or diplomatic contacts with the Netherlands and France. The growing numbers of rural collegiate churches were smaller in scale, though the apsidal choirs of such as Seton (East Lothian), Dalkeith (Midlothian), and Biggar (Lanarkshire) also showed the impact of Continental contacts (Fawcett 2011).

Decoration, Fixtures, and Furnishings

Even the most structurally complete churches now give only a partial impression of their medieval appearance, to which colour must have been a particularly important contributor. Internal walls would have been initially plastered and lime-washed, with lines imitating masonry joints then painted in many areas. In the most sacred parts, and especially around altars, there may have been painting illustrating the life of Christ or the commemorated saints, some sense of which can be gained from the twelfth-century scheme in the chancel of Kempley (Gloucestershire) (Rosewell 2008). Moral themes encouraging the Christian life are seen in fifteenth-century scenes such as the Three Living meeting the Three Dead, as at Raunds (Northamptonshire), or in depictions of the demon

Tutivillus, who tempted women to gossip in church, as at Peakirk (Cambridgeshire). In many churches there would be a prominent painting of the Last Judgement, possibly above the chancel arch, as at Coventry Holy Trinity. The most vibrant source of colour was from stained glass windows, which tends to survive only in fragmentary state (Marks 1993); amongst rare exceptions is the wonderful early sixteenth-century group of windows at Fairford (Gloucestershire). Colour might also be found on the floor in important parts of the church, in the form of glazed tiles (Eames 1992). Most of these were plain but they could be decorated with formalized foliage or heraldry, as at Fordington (Dorset), or with figurative scenes, like examples at Tring (Hertfordshire).

The most important liturgical fixture in any parish church or chapel was the principal altar, located in the sanctuary area at the east end of the chancel, followed in importance by side altars elsewhere within the building in all but the humblest of churches. Unfortunately, as the place where the mystery of transubstantiation took place during Mass, whereby bread and wine were believed to be transformed into the body and blood of Christ, and as a fixture that was expected to contain sacred relics from at least the early fifth century, altars were prime targets of reforming zeal. Consequently, they have not survived well. The most important element was the mensa, a flat stone slab supported by a solid base or by legs, the upper surface of which was usually incised with five crosses commemorating the wounds of Christ, and which sometimes had a recess for relics, set below a seal stone. The mensa would normally be covered by one or more linen cloths, and hanging in front of the altar base, except in the penitential season of Lent when the church was stripped of much of its colour, would usually be a frontal in as fine fabric as could be afforded. Placed on the altar there would usually be no more than two candlesticks, perhaps with a crucifix between, and with a cushion on which the service books could be placed. Hanging on each side of the altar there could be curtains to emphasize its sacredness and to reduce draughts.

Rising behind many altars would be a reredos or retable, which could be of freestone, alabaster, timber, or metal, on which scenes from the life of Christ or from that of the saint commemorated at the altar could be carved or painted. Most of the reredoses that have survived in place have done so because they were part of the masonry fabric of the building and could not easily be removed; a fine example is at Llantwit Major (Glamorgan). Reredoses carved from the more tractable material of alabaster were perhaps more affordable than those of freestone, and a number are preserved in museums, including that depicting the joys of the Virgin known as the Swansea altarpiece in the Victoria and Albert Museum (Cheetham 1984, and see Chapter 59 in this *Handbook* for exports). Painted retables were probably the most common form of altarpiece; two are embodied in the rood screen at Ranworth (Norfolk), to each side of the door to the chancel, on which a number of full-length saints are depicted.

The fourth Lateran Council of 1215 required churches to reserve a consecrated host, which was believed to be the body of Christ, as an object for veneration and so that it could be administered to the sick in their own homes. The host was usually reserved in a vessel such as a monstrance, with a crystal pane through which it could be seen, or in a pyx, like the cup-shaped vessel found in the churchyard at Exning (Suffolk) and now in the British Museum (Marks and Williamson 2003, 414). In Scotland, as also in parts of Continental Europe, it was more common to place the host and its vessel in a lockable aumbry known as a Sacrament House, to the north or east of the principal altar (Timmermann 2009). That at Fowlis Easter (Perthshire) bears a depiction of Christ as *Salvator Mundi* flanked by angels holding the instruments of the Passion.

Against the north wall of the sanctuary area would have been an Easter Sepulchre, or Tomb of Christ, where a consecrated host and image of Christ were symbolically entombed on Good Friday and brought out on Easter Sunday to symbolize the death, entombment, and resurrection of Christ (Sheingorn 1987). In most churches this probably took the form of a portable timber structure, like the gabled hutch-shaped example at Cowthorpe (North Yorkshire). But in a number of cases a permanent masonry Sepulchre was provided, sometimes carved with iconography relating to the story of the Passion, as at Northwold (Norfolk).

On the south side of the sanctuary the three most common furnishings were the aumbry, piscina, and sedilia; like the Easter Sepulchre, the latter two could be either permanent stone structures or portable and possibly made of timber. The aumbry was a mural cupboard where the chalice, patten, and cruets might be stored for use at the adjacent altar. The piscina was a basin in which the ablutions of the vessels and the celebrant's hands took place; since the vessels had been in contact with what was believed to be the body and blood of Christ, and might have retained some particles of them, it was important for the water to be disposed of in consecrated ground. In many cases a simple bowl on a timber stand probably served this purpose; but, where it could be afforded, a permanent fixture was preferred in the form of a stone basin that drained down through the church walls, and was set within an arched recess enriched with micro-architectural forms. The sedilia were the seats where the celebrant and his assistants were able to sit at certain points of the Mass. Often no more than a timber bench, more richly carved examples include those at Hawton (Nottinghamshire) and Heckington (Lincolnshire) where their design reflects that of the Easter Sepulchre opposite.

Reading desks or lecterns were also required, and a major church might have as many as three of these: one for the epistles, to the south of the altar; one for the gospels, to the north of the altar; and one for any singers. The simplest lecterns have one or more sloping book rests on a stem that allowed the books to be supported near eye-height; an example with two book rests at Ranworth (Norfolk) has the music and words of an antiphon on one side, and a text from the gospel of St John on the other. A favoured form for lecterns had the outspread wings of either the eagle of St John or the Pelican in her Piety for the book rest. An eagle lectern at Redenhall (Norfolk) is of timber, but more lecterns of brass or other base metals have survived, with a good example at Croft (Lincolnshire). Other furniture within the chancel might include ranks of stalls down the flanks of the western part, which generally returned against the east side of the chancel screen (Tracy 1990). These might be occupied by landowners and by choirs; in cases where churches achieved collegiate status, as at Ludlow (Shropshire) and Manchester, those stalls could be richly embellished.

By as early as the thirteenth century, the chancel was usually separated from the nave by a screen that is sometimes known as the rood screen, because of its association with the church's principal representation of the crucified Christ. When there was a chancel arch the screen was generally within that arch; but when there were aisles alongside both chancel and nave it usually crossed both central vessel and aisles. Some screens are of stone: Bramford (Suffolk) and Bottisham (Cambridgeshire) have triplets of elegantly simple arches, while others were more complex, rising the full height of the chancel arch and having tracery at their heads, as at Great Bardfield and Stebbing (both in Essex). But it was more usual for screens to be of timber and of framed construction, with a solid boarded dado in the lower part and an openwork upper part. They remain in considerable numbers in the West Country and East Anglia (Cotton et al. 2014). Above the screen there was frequently a platform or loft, which might be projected out on timber vaulting, as at Marwood (Devon) and Attleborough (Norfolk). The loft usually had a panelled parapet towards the nave, several examples of which have survived in the West Country and Wales, as at Llanrwst (Denbighshire) and Patrishow (Brecknockshire). Associated with the loft there would generally have been the great rood, a carved or painted representation of the crucifixion, and there may also have been a rood altar on the loft. In addition, if the church had an organ it is likely to have been located here. At some churches there was a spiral stone stair at one end of the screen to give access to the loft, though in other cases there was perhaps only a timber ladder. Some priests may have addressed their congregations from the rood loft, but growing numbers of churches equipped themselves with a purpose-built pulpit, sometimes in stone as at Loxton (Somerset) but mostly of timber as Harberton and Bovey Tracey (both Devon). The most usual form was a small polygonal enclosure raised on a stem, with blind tracery or tabernacle work around the enclosure.

Seating appears not to have been provided as a matter of course for the laity worshipping in the nave. Stone benches were occasionally constructed along the walls, as at Burton (Wiltshire), or around the bases of arcade piers, as at Snettisham (Norfolk); but in general it seems that those who wished to sit would bring their own stools or chairs. Nevertheless, many churches did eventually provide rows of benches or pews, and these could be a notable feature (Cooper and Brown 2011). The most common form had plank seats, with or without backs, supported by pew ends terminating in a finial usually known as a poppy-head; the latter was commonly of formalized foliage, but might be figurative. Lavish enrichment to bench ends was found in some West Country churches, where a rectangular profile was often favoured, sometimes having blind tracery within foliate borders, as at Frithelstock (Devon), or biblical scenes, such as the Resurrection at Hatch Beauchamp (Somerset).

Entry to the Christian life was by way of baptism, and the font, where infants received that sacrament, was appropriately one of the first things to be seen on entering a church, being generally located at the west end of the nave (Bond 1908). The main element of twelfth-century fonts might be a tub-like stone cylinder, perhaps with scenes set within arcading around its perimeter: those scenes at Darenth (Kent) include a representation of baptism. Another favoured form for early fonts was a square basin carried on five columns: a large one at the centre and smaller ones at the angles, as at Isle Abbots (Somerset), though five supports were sometimes also provided beneath basically circular basins, as at Buckfastleigh (Devon). There was also a vogue for fonts with basins cast in lead, as at Siston (Gloucestershire), which has figures and formalized foliage set within arcading around the circular basin (Zarnecki

FIGURE 37.5 St Mary, Happisburgh, Norfolk. Octagonal baptismal font of the fifteenth century. The font is supported by a stem carved with lions and a 'woodhouse', a hirsute man bearing a wooden club, below a traceried frieze

(© Paul Stamper)

1957). By the later Middle Ages the most favoured form for fonts was octagonal, perhaps because the number eight was deemed to symbolize resurrection, after the seventh and final day of creation. The bowls, the supporting stems, and the stepped platforms on which they were sometimes set could be finely carved with tracery designs, heraldry, or figures (Figure 37.5). East Anglia was an area that showed great inventiveness in font design. That at Hoxne (Suffolk) is of the type with the four evangelists alternating with four angels around its bowl, while a type that can be particularly impressive has depictions of the seven sacraments around the bowl; that at East Dereham (Norfolk), datable to 1468, has the Crucifixion on its eighth side. The water within the font had to be protected from sacrilegious uses, usually by a lockable cover. In most cases this was probably relatively simple, but sometimes the complexity of its tabernacle work could rival that found in monastic and cathedral choir stall canopies. At Ufford (Suffolk) the cover rises through four stages and is capped by a finial with the Pelican in her Piety. In a small number of cases the font was set within an enclosure: that at Luton (Bedfordshire) is a fourteenth-century stone structure with gabled sides and pinnacled buttresses; the later timber examples at Norwich St Peter Mancroft and Trunch (both Norfolk) are square and hexagonal respectively, each capped by complex tabernacle work.

Conclusion

The dictates of architectural fashion and the need to respond to changing liturgical and funerary requirements, possibly together with varying degrees of inter-parochial rivalry, meant that very few churches continued in their primary state throughout their medieval history. Even where a church presents an appearance of architectural homogeneity, that appearance may be a consequence of nineteenth-century restoration to a supposed ideal state. Where archaeological excavation has been possible within churches, it has generally revealed that the stages by which even quite modest churches achieved their late medieval state could be remarkably complex (Blair and Pyrah 1996; Rodwell 2012). At the small rural church of Wharram Percy (North Yorkshire), for example, excavation revealed at least seven phases of medieval building, with further phases after the Reformation (Bell and Beresford 1987). At Pennant Melangell (Montgomeryshire), excavation outside the present church exposed the apse that had originally been its eastern termination (Figure 37.6).

The expense of excavation, together with the disturbance inevitably entailed, means it is only seldom an option within churches that remain in use; nevertheless, although no other form of investigation is likely to be so informative, much can be learned about the developmental history of the buildings by other means. As a first stage in any attempt to reach an understanding of a church, expert examination of the upstanding fabric, in the light of whatever documentary records may have survived, will usually offer invaluable first clues to some of the changes that have taken place (Figure 37.7). This is especially the

FIGURE 37.6 The footings of the twelfth-century apse at Pennant Melangell, Montgomeryshire (now Powys), revealed after the removal of a post-medieval cell-y-bedd in 1989

(© Clwyd-Powys Archaeological Trust, photo cs89-036-0232)

FIGURE 37.7 St Mary, North Shoebury in Essex. The structural phasing of this church can be read in its external fabric. The church was built in the thirteenth century, a top stage of the tower added in the fourteenth or fifteenth centuries. The south aisle was demolished and the arcade filled probably in two phases, the middle arch being blocked in the fifteenth century, possibly when a new roof was added

(© Steve Rippon)

case when accompanied by analytical surveying techniques such as photogrammetry (Swallow et al. 2004). Further pointers to the ways in which the component parts of a church were perceived and used by parishioners are being provided by increasingly sophisticated approaches to spatial analysis (Graves 2000). Where excavation is not possible, techniques of non-invasive geophysical investigation, such as ground-penetrating radar, have the potential to be highly informative about lost structural elements, albeit the presence of intramural burials can make the interpretation of such evidence problematic. With those caveats, it is certainly true to say that, with appropriate expert and technical input, the potential for reaching an understanding of church buildings has never been greater.

References cited

Alexander, J. 2001 'The use of masons' marks and construction instructions in medieval buildings', in J. Higgitt, K. Forsyth, and D. N. Parsons (eds), *Roman, Runes and Ogham, medieval inscriptions in the insular world and on the Continent*, Shaun Tyas, Donington, 211–22

Badham, S. and Oosterwijk, S. (eds) 2010 *Monumental industry: the production of tomb monuments in England and Wales in the long fourteenth century*, Shaun Tyas, Donington

Bell, R. D. and Beresford, M. W. 1987 *Wharram Percy: the church of St Martin*, The Society for Medieval Archaeology Monograph 11, London

Binski, P. 2014 *Gothic wonder, art, artifice and the Decorated Style 1290–1350*, Yale University Press, London

Blair, J. and Pyrah, C. 1996 *Church archaeology: research directions for the future*, Council for British Archaeology Research Report 104, London

Blair, J. and Sharpe, R. (eds) 1992 *Pastoral care before the parish*, Leicester University Press, Leicester

Bond, F. 1905 *Gothic architecture in England: an analysis of the origin and development of English Church architecture from the Norman Conquest to the dissolution of the monasteries*, Batsford, London

Bond, F. 1908 *Screens and galleries in English churches*, Oxford University Press, London

Burgess, C. 2011 'Chantries in the parish or "Through the Looking-Glass"', in J. M. Luxford and J. McNeill (eds), *The medieval chantry in England*, British Archaeological Association, Leeds, 100–29

Burgess, C. and Duffy, E. (eds) 2006 *The parish in late medieval England*, Shaun Tyas, Donington

Burgess, C. and Heale, M. (eds) 2008 *The late medieval English college and its context*, York Medieval Press, York

Cheetham, F. 1984 *English medieval alabasters*, Phaidon, Oxford

Cooper, T. and Brown, S. 2011 *Pews, benches and chairs: church seating in English parish churches from the fourteenth century to the present*, The Ecclesiological Society, London

Cotton, S., Helen, A., Lunnon, E., and Wrapson, L. J. 2014 'Medieval rood screens in Suffolk: their construction and painting dates', *Proceedings of the Suffolk Institute of Archaeology* 43(2), 219–34

Cowan, I. B. 1967 *The parishes of medieval Scotland*, Scottish Record Society, Edinburgh

Draper, P. 2006 *The formation of English Gothic: architecture and identity*, Yale University Press, London
Eames, E. 1992 *Medieval craftsmen, English tilers*, British Museum Press, London
Fawcett, R. 1982 'St Mary at Wiveton in Norfolk, and a group of churches attributed to its mason', *The Antiquaries Journal* 62(1), 35–56
Fawcett, R. 2011 *The architecture of the Scottish medieval church 1100–1560*, Yale University Press, London
Fernie, E. 2000 *The architecture of Norman England*, Oxford University Press, Oxford
Fletcher, B. 1901 *A history of architecture on the comparative method*, London
French, K. L., Gibbs, G. G., and Kümin, B. A. (eds) 1997 *The parish in English life, 1400–1600*, Manchester University Press, Manchester
Graves, C. P. 2000 *The form and fabric of belief: an archaeology of the lay experience of religion in medieval Norfolk and Devon*, British Archaeological Reports British Series 311, Oxford
Harvey, J. H. 1978 *The Perpendicular Style*, Batsford, London
Harvey, J. H. 1984 *English medieval architects: a biographical dictionary down to 1550*, Alan Sutton, Gloucester
Hislop, M. 2000 *Medieval masons*, Shire Publications, Princes Risborough
Marks, R. 1993 *Stained glass in England during the Middle Ages*, Routledge, London
Marks, R. and Williamson, P. (eds) 2003 *Gothic, art for England 1400–1547*, Victoria and Albert Museum Publications, London
Pacey, A. 2007 *Medieval architectural drawing*, Tempus, Stroud
Parker, J. H. 1850 *A glossary of terms used in Grecian, Roman, Italian and Gothic architecture*, David Bogue, London (5th edn)
Penman, M. (ed.) 2013 *Monuments and monumentality across medieval and early modern Europe*, Shaun Tyas, Donington
Rodwell, W. 2012 *The archaeology of churches*, Amberley, Stroud
Roffey, S. 2007 *The medieval chantry chapel: an archaeology*, Boydell, Woodbridge
Rosewell, R. 2008 *Medieval wall paintings*, Boydell, Woodbridge
Salzman, L. F. 1952 *Building in England down to 1540*, Oxford University Press, Oxford
Saul, N. 2009 *English church monuments in the Middle Ages: history and representation*, Oxford University Press, Oxford
Sheingorn, P. 1987 *The Easter Sepulchre in England*, Medieval Institute Publications, Kalamazoo
Swallow, P., Dallas, R., Jackson, S., and Watt, D. 2004 *Measurement and recording of historic buildings*, Donhead, Shaftesbury (2nd edn)
Thurlby, M. 1999 *The Herefordshire school of Romanesque sculpture*, Logaston Press, Little Logaston
Timmermann, A. 2009 *Real presence: Sacrament Houses and the body of Christ, c.1270–1600*, Brepols, Turnhout
Tracy, C. 1990 *English Gothic choir stalls 1400–1540*, Boydell, Woodbridge
Zarnecki, G. 1951 *English Romanesque sculpture, 1066–1140*, Alex Tiranti, London
Zarnecki, G. 1957 *English Romanesque lead sculpture: lead fonts of the twelfth century*, Alec Tiranti, London

CHAPTER 38

APPROACHING MEDIEVAL SACRALITY

MARK A. HALL

CREATING, inviting, and repurposing sacrality was a fundamental pursuit of social behaviour in the medieval period. From the major shrines of cathedrals down to the portable sanctity of amulets, the pursuit of sacredness affected the everyday lives of Christian believers. Drawing on history, art history, anthropology, and folklore under the broad umbrella of material culture, this contribution takes a socially informed and trans-disciplinary approach to archaeology and seeks a holistic interpretation of the medieval past, one that does not neglect the intangible. This can often seem out of reach for the archaeologist but medieval sacrality is a key exception because of the beliefs of medieval people in immanence, that is to say, the divine manifest in the material and the mundane. Until more recent theoretical turns (e.g. Bourdieu 1977; Hahn and Weiss 2013; Hodder 2012) this aspect of medieval life had been neglected in favour of harder economic explanations with a focus on the making and exchange of objects. Now, however, the challenge has been taken up by those studying later medieval archaeology (e.g. Gilchrist 2008; 2014; Spencer 1998; Stocker and Everson 2003; 2006) and this contribution seeks to underline the value of these new perspectives and broaden their application. Three overlapping themes are considered: relics, places, and mobility.

RELICS: SACRED BODIES, BODILY CONTACT, AND ANIMATE THINGS

Relics, the material manifestation of the cult of saints, were a key means through which medieval Christianity was articulated and performed (Bagnoli et al. 2011; Smith 2012; Spencer 1998). The prime relic category was the body of a saint and saintliness was central to the medieval concept of sacrality. 'Saint' derives from the Latin *sanctus*, meaning 'holy' or 'consecrated', and ultimately from an Indo-European root word meaning 'custom' or 'law'. The word *sanciō*, 'consecrate', 'appoint as sacred', 'made holy', 'blessed', 'saintly' is particularly applied to a person who lives a holy (heroically) virtuous life. There is then a sense that holiness is something that resides in the body and this bodily dimension of holiness justified and facilitated the circulation of holy relics including bodies, body parts, and body liquids such as Christ's blood and sweat, and the Virgin's breast-milk, and the 'touch relics' that had once been in contact with holy bodies during life or held up against them at their shrines. In Britain many of these relics were lost during the Reformation and its aftermath but their volume and variety can be gauged from surviving lists such as those to be found in the cartulary of Christchurch Priory, Twynham, Hampshire, which records the dedications of altars and the relics deposited within them by three Scottish bishops at an as-yet unrecognized North British church in the early thirteenth century (Marritt 2014).

The huge investment of wealth that was made in creating and refashioning reliquaries demonstrates the power of patrons and the dynamics of institutional and individual relationships. Such investment was not primarily carried out as a vulgar display of wealth but as an act of fragmentation and enshrinement that demonstrated the significance and power of the relics within (Smith 2012). At the same time, reliquaries also created commemorative episodes—catalysts for the memory of families and individuals who recalled their engagement with a particular saint (van Houts 1999, 90–120; for the monastic context, see Carruthers 1998). The application of this 'imaginative memory', as it is sometimes called, established traditions about the origins of many reliquaries that served to give families and institutions a foundational history with a sacral endorsement. When Charlemagne was canonized in 1172, for example, there was an upsurge of monasteries and cathedrals in mainland Europe who wished to associate their relics with a specifically Carolingian past (van Houts 1999, 119).

The great majority of relics were only fragmentary and therefore highly portable. The large gilt-silver and gem-encrusted brooch known as the Glenlyon brooch—an heirloom of the Campbells of Glenlyon (Perthshire, Scotland)—was made in c.1500 (for a comprehensive set of images see the British Museum online catalogue).[1] Its gemstones and crystals were perceived to have magical properties in the medieval period while two hollow cells either side of the central setting accessed a relic chamber. The reverse of the brooch carries Marian iconography, the names of the Three Magi (Jaspar, Melchior, and Balthazar) and the word 'consumatum' (from the last words spoken by Christ on the Cross, *consumatum est* ('it is finished'). Both phrases were powerful charms and the inclusion of the Three Magi may indicate the brooch was intended to commemorate a pilgrimage to their shrine at Cologne Cathedral (Spencer 1998, 261–6). According to this interpretation, the object might represent a recalling and a re-presencing of the religious ceremony witnessed in Cologne. Curiously, it is one of a clutch of distinctively

---

[1] http://www.britishmuseum.org/research/collection_online/collection_object_details.aspx?objectId=63346&partId=1.

large brooches (Ugadale and Lorne are still in private possession, Lochbuie is in the British Museum) which are linked with the powerful families of the West Highlands (Caldwell 1982, 58–9, 90), all of them devised around a central setting of a rock crystal charm-stone with small chambers for relics. They all have traditional links back to King Robert Bruce; or, more accurately, they have invented traditions as they were all made nearly two hundred years after Bruce's death. In the case of the Glenlyon brooch, the oral association of a heroic Scottish king with the Three Magi dedication probably added to the brooch's supernatural efficacy.

Sacred objects were not restricted to elite and Church patronage. Women parishioners are recorded as donating a range of personal and domestic objects which were used to dress the images of saints in the parish church (Gilchrist 2103, 176). Heirlooms were also sometimes interred as special deposits in churches, including the two examples of four silver spoons and a gold headdress fillet and a gold finger-ring and a second fillet, both buried at the nunnery on Iona (Gilchrist 2012, 234–6; 2013, 177–8). As heirlooms and objects intimately associated with life-course transitions, they may have possessed a kind of secular sacrality which was only fully sacralized when they entered the Church domain; as inalienable objects, heirlooms were also believed to absorb the essence of the giver when they changed hands. Other more mundane objects were involved in the heterodox practices that hybridized Christianity and magic to varying degrees. A typical example from Perth in Scotland is the Bronze Age barbed-and-tanged arrowhead found in the post-hole of a timber hall building. Popular belief regarded such objects (and similarly Neolithic stone axe-heads) as thunder and lightning bolts but also as elfshot that spread disease (especially when fired at animals). In terms of sympathetic magic the Perth arrowhead was regarded as a charm, averting the threat of fire from lightning strikes or disease from elfshot (Hall 2005b, 213–14; 2011, 94). This practice has also been recognized in pre- and post-medieval times (e.g. Ferris 2012, 75–93 for Roman and seventeenth-century examples) where the objects have been linked with the expression of 'otherness', as a link to a pre-Roman past and also with the ancestors.

The most prolific offering at medieval pilgrimage shrines was the bent coin or token, either intended as the completion of a pilgrimage vow or, if the bending was completed over the body of a sick person or animal, calculated to avert further illness; both represent bargains struck with the saints (Duffy 1992, 183–6; Hall 2012, 81; Merrifield 1987, 90–2; see Chapter 32 in this *Handbook*). Examples of bent silver pennies from Finlaggan in Islay (Inner Hebrides), Chalgrove (Oxfordshire), and St Aldates in Oxford, all of them embedded in the mortar of wall constructions, demonstrate that coins could be used not only as an invocation of supernatural protection as a physical form of prayer but also, following Italian and French examples, as a commemorative act linking the construction process to personal and communal memory (Hall 2012, 79–81; Travaini 2004, 170–1). It should be noted that the vast majority of medieval British coins combine the portrait of the issuing king with a cross on the reverse. The symbol of the cross firmly links them to the cult of the Holy Rood (and in some instances to specific saints such as Andrew) and, as a consequence, coins and copies of coins (with the same apotropaic agency) were frequently worn as jewellery (Hall 2012, 76–8; 2016; Koldeweij 2006). This same agency also made coins suitable protective amulets to place into the graves of the Christian dead (Hall 2012, 83–7).

Places: Sacred Sites

Later medieval Britain and Europe had a profusion of holy places: spaces that were made holy by events that had happened there in the past and by the presence of sacred objects or remains brought to that spot or buildings constructed to house them. Memory and the re-vitalization of memory is therefore a key ingredient in this recipe for making places holy and the Church's desire to control and direct belief as an orthodox practice was principally achieved through the creation of sacred sites: churches, monasteries, and cathedrals (for example, see Crook 2011; Nilson 1998), through which access to the authorized view of Christianity was maintained. These structures demonstrated the power and authority of Church and secular/royal authority acting together or in tension and also housed the liturgy, the set of practices (worship) used to enact the shared belief system of priests and congregation, which was shaped by and shaped its architectural and socio-political context (Doig 2008, xxi). This process was not always consensual and there was frequent social engineering by patrons and clergy (e.g. Durham and the cult of St Cuthbert; Abou-El-Haj 1991, 4–7) and violent rejection by townspeople who were forced to accept the burden of large numbers of pilgrims and the taxes for building work which made the shrines accessible (with particularly violent responses in Vézelay in France and Santiago de Compostela in Spain; Abou-El-Haj 1991, 7–10).

For the wider landscape, in England the focal point was the parish church, the connective tissue for the nodal network points of cathedrals and monasteries that drew the wider community into shared but not homogenous practices (for an overview see Morris 1989). There is, however, a growing recognition that other arenas of medieval life might be fruitfully investigated for what they can tell us about how people created a sense of sacredness in their everyday lives. A start has been made with the material excavated from the medieval burgh of Perth where several case studies have been identified and discussed (Hall 2005b; 2011; 2012; Hall and Spencer 2012), but in this paper the focus is on the role of watery places. The practice of making votive offerings by placing or throwing objects into water has a long pre-Christian history (Bradley 2000; Edgeworth 2011) and this custom continued into the medieval period, particularly for pilgrimage and secular badges, many of which have been recovered from rivers including the Avon in Salisbury, Wiltshire, and the Thames in London, and from other wet places across Europe (notably in the Low Countries). The magical flow of rivers finds its way into the orthodox liturgy of the Church (Underwood 1950) and of particular interest are the holy wells which carry a dedication to a particular saint, whether as an aspect of their conversion from pagan usage or whether perceived to be created *ab initio* by the actions of a saint (Rattue 1995). For example, a healing spring at Holywell in Flintshire, Wales, appeared at the site of the murder of St Gwenfrewi (Winefride) who was restored to life by her uncle, St Bueno, and an elaborate shrine and chapel developed there from the twelfth century (Figure 38.1). Pilgrims to the site included English royalty and nobility (Bourke 2009; Jones 1992, 49–50; Scully 2007, 202–3). Generally speaking, however, holy wells lacked elaborate superstructures and their use is understood primarily from the

FIGURE 38.1 The holy well or healing spring and chapel of St Gwenfrewi (Winefride) at Holywell, Flintshire, Wales

(Eurapart, public domain)

documentary record; many have still to fulfil their archaeological potential (Edwards 1996, 50-1) where they have not been cleaned out previously to retrieve votive objects to support church funds. A wide range of coins, tokens and medals of sixteenth- to nineteenth-century date were recovered from St Queran's Well, Cargen, Dumfriesshire (Dudgeon 1892) and coins, pins, a glass bead, buttons, a stone cup, and a cross-marked slab were recovered from Inchadney Well, Perthshire (Gillies 1925, 76-7). Nor were all offerings placed in the waters of the well. A common alternative was to tie strips of clothing and material onto the branches of surrounding trees or to hammer coins and nails into them. These aspects of Christian practice were part of a wider materiality that sought to make the invisible visible (Belting 1996; Bynum 2011, 125-76).

Sacred Mobility

The scale and parameters of international medieval pilgrimage have been scoped in some detail, including the most frequented British site, that of St Thomas Becket at Canterbury Cathedral, Kent (Bagnoli et al. 2011; Birch 1998; Finucane 1995; Husband 2001; Kessler and Zacharias 2000; Spencer 1998; Stopford 1999; Webb 2000; Yeoman 1999; and see Chapter 40 in this *Handbook*). There were also, however, many unofficial saints. The legend of St William of Perth (Scotland) casts him as a baker who undertakes a pilgrimage in the early thirteenth century. Leaving Rochester, Kent, for the final leg of his journey to Canterbury (and Becket's shrine), William was murdered by an orphan boy he had taken under his wing. Made a saint by popular acclaim, a chapel was built on the site of his murder, and a shrine was established in Rochester Cathedral. Although never given Papal approval, William was nevertheless entered into the cathedral's own calendar of saints. Oddly, there is no evidence of any dedications to William anywhere in Scotland, but this did not stop Scottish pilgrims flocking to his shrine in Rochester, and their offerings, along with those from elite patrons such as Edward I, were plentiful enough to allow the cathedral to undertake major restorations (Hall 2005a, 80-1 and references therein). Whether real or invented by Rochester, William's sacrality certainly seems to have accommodated all needs—of (Scottish) pilgrims en route to Canterbury and of the cathedral's requirement to generate income.

William is amongst the earliest of England's penchant for unofficial saints, of which there were several others with flourishing pilgrimage cults. They included the royal saint Henry VI, whose execution in the tower of London in 1471 led to his popular acclaim as a martyr and a flourishing cult across the country despite royal attempts to suppress it. These attempts could not compete with persistent reports of miracle-working, however, as the quantity of pilgrim badges (nearly four hundred from across England) testifies (Spencer 1998, 189-92). Social status was no bar to becoming sacred. John Schorn, rector of North Marston (Buckinghamshire) *c.*1282-1315, remained a popular saint until the Reformation. Perhaps because he was not canonized, we know very little about him but there are a significant number of pilgrim badges which usually depict one of two miracles: his calling forth a healing spring with his staff or his conjuring of the devil into a leather boot. Schorn was widely recognized as a skilled exorcist, a skill that would give him a strong appeal. His main cult centre was at North Marston parish church, Buckinghamshire, but his popularity was such that in 1478 the Bishop of Salisbury and Dean of Windsor (Richard Beauchamp) obtained Papal approval to remove Schorn's bones from North Marston and establish a new shrine in St George's Chapel, Windsor Castle, Berkshire. The official control of the cult was completed by Beauchamp's acquisition of the living of North Marston from Dunstable Priory. This gave him control of the image of Schorn in the church and of the holy well he had called forth, both valuable sources of potential income needed to help establish the Windsor shrine (Spencer 1998, 192–5).

One of the most surprising examples of popular saintliness is that of St Guinefort, in the Dombres region, France. This cult shows that not being human was also no bar to becoming sacred, for Guinefort was a dog (Schmitt 1983). Guinefort was slain by his master, who mistakenly thought the dog had killed his infant son (a widespread folklore trope) and on realizing his error elaborately buried the hound in a mound-topped well. Immediately the local peasants declared the hound a martyr and proceeded to bring their sick children to his cairn, enacting an elaborate ritual which saw the child being left for three days with the expectation that on their parents' return the child would be restored to health. Guinefort's cult flourished into a regional centre of pilgrimage in spite of being condemned as demonic by the Church. As an example of heterodox peasant practice, however, the key factor in its durability and resistance to clerical orthodoxy lay not so much in its unusual liturgical context as 'in the logic of its functioning ... for the peasants there was no contradiction between the notion of sanctity and the memory of a dog' (Schmitt 1983, 177).

The whole process of pilgrimage is one of ritualized movement, performances, and perceptions and part of a wider medieval culture of ritualized processions invoking the sacred. The understandable emphasis on medieval visual culture as a route to engaging with the supernatural (Giles 2007; Marks 2004) is increasingly being balanced by an understanding of other sensory perceptions (Day 2013; Jørgensen et al. 2015; Woolgar 2006) especially hearing (e.g. Williams 2013; see Chapter 44 in this *Handbook*). The intangible sound made by tangible instruments was one means of defining a sacral territory and an important aspect of both pilgrimage and processional activities. Indeed, the use of instruments to make music and noise was a fundamental tool of engagement with the supernatural and pivotal in averting the actions of demons and ill-luck. That most famous of English medieval manuscripts, the Luttrell Psalter, depicts a medieval city (f. 184v) out of which flow dancers and musicians (Figure 38.2). Camille (1998, 273–4 and developing the work of Alexander 1996) interprets this as a May time festival, specifically a Rogationtide procession. Rogation Days were the Christian appropriation of pagan spring cults timed to coincide with the feast of the Ascension; they served to exclude evil spirits and protect crops and cattle and by the fourteenth century had grown into a semi-ecclesiastical civic ritual. Rogation processions were but one of many variations on the processional form, including Sunday Mass, Feast Days (especially Christmas, Easter, and Corpus Christi) and relic processions (Ashley and Hüsken 2001;

FIGURE 38.2 A Rogationtide procession in the conceptualized city of Constantinople as depicted in the Luttrell Psalter c.1320–40 (f. 184v)

(© Alejandra Gutiérrez)

Hourihane 2005). At times this liturgical orthodoxy could also be fused with heterodoxy. This was true of Corpus Christi processions, where the drama enacted was often controlled as well as enacted by the townsfolk (through the guilds) as opposed to the clergy (Hall 2005b, 220–4; Lerud 2001) and it was also true of the Christmas season festivities which 'ritually inverted the ecclesiastical power structures to give dominance temporarily to the young and to minor clerics' (Ashley 2001, 8), especially Feast of Fools on the 1st of January.

Envoi: Reforming Sacrality

The Reformation was a process of both renewal and reduction: it diminished the sense of what was sacred and its enshrinement in bodies and their associated material culture, and at the same time placed a new emphasis on the sacredness of the word of God as enshrined by the Bible. Before the Reformation these were 'mere words' (Bynum 2011, 127–8) but afterwards they were read, preached, sung, and recited (Todd 2002, 24–176) and symbolic representations were no substitute for the spoken word. Thus the cult of the Holy Name of Jesus—often represented symbolically as the three letters 'ths/ihs'—found no more favour with Protestant Reformers than any other Catholic cult (Blake et al. 2003). The Bible and religious texts were no less valued before the Reformation, when many Gospel books were enshrined as relics and the making of relics was underpinned by the words of St John's gospel (1:1–14), but the difference now lay less in reverence for the word than in direct access to it.

The changes labelled today as the Reformation were neither instant nor uniform, varying in their take-up across Europe. Even in countries that became Protestant, there was often deep and persistent resistance and in many parts of Scotland the Reformation was still being played out in the eighteenth century (Duffy 2001; Hall 2005a, 87). Gaimster and Gilchrist (2003, 2) note how Protestants continued to create a sacralized religious environment, manifest in its buildings and in its material culture of bibles, hymnals, and catechisms. In later centuries relics did re-surface to some extent, though now more to commemorate than sacralize the great Protestant leaders: the family heirloom of a reputed walking stick of John Knox and the brass candlestick that deflected the shot from the assassination attempt on Knox in Edinburgh are both in the collections of Perth Museum. These objects of historical memory circulated at the same time as salvaged, sacred relics such as the stab-holed doublet of King James I, assassinated in Perth in 1437. The doublet had been a relic in the Carthusian monastery of Perth, rescued when Reformation destruction flared up in 1560 and was still available to view privately in the early seventeenth century (Adamson 1638, 37–8; Fittis 1885, 224–7). The Reformation changed much but it did not de-sacralize religion and the new Church was successful because it maintained a sense of sacredness built around words, time, and space, and communicated this through a material culture of the church and churchyard, along with the performance of ceremonial actions including the Sabbath and fasting rituals, the new Communion rite, and the proclamation of vows and oaths (Todd 2002, 360).

Acknowledgements

I am grateful to the editors for inviting this contribution (and to Chris Gerrard for his wise editing and to Alejandra Gutiérrez for her drawing of Figure 38.2) and to Roberta Gilchrist for her invaluable comments on an earlier draft. Advice and information was gratefully received from David Caldwell, Sally Foster, David Gaimster, and Estella Weiss-Krejci. All remaining errors are my own.

References Cited

Abou-El-Haj, B. 1991 'The audiences for the medieval cult of saints', *Gesta* 30(1), 3–15

Adamson, H. 1638 *The muses threnodie or mirthful mournings on the death of Mr Gall*, George Anderson, Edinburgh

Alexander, J. J. G. 1996 'Dancing in the streets', *The Journal of the Walters Art Gallery* LIV, 147–62

Ashley, K. 2001 'Introduction: the moving subjects of processional performance', in K. Ashley and W. Hüsken (eds), *Moving subjects: processional performance in the Middle Ages and the Renaissance*, Rodopi, Amsterdam, 7–34

Ashley, K. and Hüsken, W. (eds) 2001 *Moving subjects: processional performance in the Middle Ages and the Renaissance*, Rodopi, Amsterdam

Bagnoli, M., Klein, H. A., Mann, C. G., and Robinson, J. (eds) 2011 *Treasures of heaven: saints, relics and devotion in medieval Europe*, British Museum Press, London

Belting, H. 1996 *Likeness and presence: a history of the image before the era of Art*, University of Chicago Press, Chicago

Birch, D. J. 1998 *Pilgrimage to Rome in the Middle Ages: continuity and change*, Boydell Press, Woodbridge

Blake, H., Egan, G., Hurst, J., and New, E. 2003 'From popular devotion to resistance and revival in England: the cult of the Holy Name of Jesus and the Reformation', in D. Gaimster and R. Gilchrist (eds), *The Archaeology of Reformation 1480–1580*, The Society for Post-Medieval Archaeology Monograph 1, Leeds, 175–203

Bourdieu, P. 1977 *An outline theory of practice*, Cambridge University Press, Cambridge

Bourke, C. 2009 'The shrine of St Gwenfrewi from Gwytherin, Denbighshire: an alternative interpretation', in N. Edwards (ed.), *The archaeology of the early medieval Celtic churches*, The Society for Medieval Archaeology Monograph 29/Society for Church Archaeology Monograph 1, Leeds, 375–88

Bradley, R. 2000 *An archaeology of natural places*, Routledge, London

Bynum, C. W. 2011 *Christian materiality: an essay in religion in late medieval Europe*, Zone Books, New York

Caldwell, D. 1982 *Angels, nobles and unicorns: art and patronage in medieval Scotland*, National Museum of Scotland, Edinburgh

Camille, M. 1998 *Mirror in parchment: the Luttrell Psalter and the making of medieval England*, Reaktion Books Ltd, London

Carruthers, M. 1998 *The craft of thought meditation, rhetoric and the making of images, 400–1200*, Cambridge University Press, Cambridge

Crook, J. 2011 *English medieval shrines*, Boydell Press, Woodbridge

Day, J. (ed.) 2013 *Making sense of the past: toward a sensory archaeology*, South Illinois University Press, Carbondale

Doig, A. 2008 *Liturgy and architecture from the early Church to the Middle Ages*, Ashgate, Aldershot

Dudgeon, P. 1892 'Notice of St Querans well at Cargen and offerings recently made to it', *Proceedings of the Society of Antiquaries of Scotland* 26, 63–5

Duffy, E. 1992 *The stripping of the altars: traditional religion in England 1400–1580*, Yale University Press, New Haven and London

Duffy, E. 2001 *The voices of Morebath Reformation and rebellion in an English village*, Yale University Press, New Haven and London

Edgeworth, M. 2011 *Fluid pasts: archaeology of flow*, Bloomsbury Academic, London

Edwards, N. 1996 'Identifying the archaeology of the early Church in Wales and Cornwall', in J. Blair and C. Pyrah (eds), *Church archaeology: research directions for the future*, Council for British Archaeology Research Report 104, York, 49–62

Ferris, I. 2012 *Roman Britain through its objects*, Amberley, Stroud

Finucane, R. C. 1995 *Miracles and pilgrims: popular beliefs in medieval England*, Macmillan, London

Fittis, R. S. 1885 *Ecclesiastical annals of Perth, to the period of the Reformation*, J. Gemmell and S. Cowan & Co., Edinburgh and Perth

Gaimster, D. and Gilchrist, R. 2003 'Introduction', in D. Gaimster and R. Gilchrist (eds), *The Archaeology of Reformation 1480–1580*, The Society for Post-Medieval Archaeology Monograph 1, Leeds, 1–8

Gilchrist, R. 2008 'Magic for the dead? The archaeology of magic in late medieval burials', *Medieval Archaeology* 52, 119–59

Gilchrist, R. 2012 *Medieval life: archaeology and the life course*, The Boydell Press, Woodbridge

Gilchrist, R. 2013 'The materiality of medieval heirlooms. From biographical to sacred objects', in H. P. Hahn and H. Weiss (eds), *Mobility, meaning and transformations of things*, Oxbow Books, Oxford, 170–82

Gilchrist, R. 2014 'Monastic and church archaeology', *Annual Review of Anthropology* 43, 235–50

Giles, K. 2007 'Seeing and believing: visuality and space in pre-modern England', *World Archaeology* 39(1), 105–21

Gillies, W. A. 1925 'Notes on old wells and a stone circle at Kenmore', *Proceedings of the Society of Antiquaries of Scotland* 109, 75–8

Hall, M. A. 2005a 'Of holy men and heroes: the cult of saints in medieval Perthshire', *Innes Review* 56(1), 60–87

Hall, M. A. 2005b 'Burgh mentalities: a town-in-the-country case study of Perth, Scotland', in K. Giles and C. Dyer (eds), *Town and country in the Middle Ages: contrasts and interconnections 1100-1500*, The Society for Medieval Archaeology Monograph 22, Leeds, 211–28

Hall, M. A. 2011 'The cult of saints in medieval Perth: everyday ritual and the materiality of belief', *Journal of Material Culture* 16(1), 80–104

Hall, M. A. 2012 'Money isn't everything: the cultural life of coins in the medieval European town of Perth, Scotland', *Journal of Social Archaeology* 12(1), 72–91

Hall, M. A. 2016 ' "Pennies from heaven": money in ritual in medieval Europe', in C. Haselgrove and S. Krmnicek (eds), *The archaeology of money*, Leicester Archaeology Monograph 24, Leicester, 137–59

Hall, M. A. and Spencer, B. 2012 'Devotion and belief on the Perth High Street', in D. W. Hall, G. Haggarty, A. Vince, J. di Folco, C. Martin, A. Goodall, V. Smart, M. A. Hall, J. Franklin, I. Goodall, D. Caldwell, B. Ellis, N. Q. Bogdan, J. Cherry, J. D. Bateson, A. Curteis, C. A. Morris, and D. Wright, *Perth High Street archaeological excavation 1975-77, fascicule 2: ceramics, metalwork, religious and wooden objects*, Tayside and Fife Archaeological Committee, Perth, 203–20

Hahn, H. P. and Weiss, H. (eds) 2013 *Mobility, meaning and transformations of things*, Oxbow Books, Oxford

Hodder, I. 2012 *Entangled: an archaeology of the relationships between humans and things*, Wiley and Sons, Chichester

Hourihane, C. 2005 *The processional cross in late medieval England: the 'Dallye Cross'*, The Society of Antiquaries, London

Husband, T. 2001 *The treasury of Basel Cathedral*, Metropolitan Museum of Art, New York

Jones, F. 1992 *The holy wells of Wales*, University of Wales Press, Cardiff

Jørgensen, H. H. L., Laugerud, H., and Skinnebach, L. K. (eds) 2015 *The saturated sensorium principles of perception in the Middle Ages*, Aarhus university Press, Aarhus

Kessler, H. L. and Zacharias, J. 2000 *Rome 1300: on the path of the pilgrims*, Yale University Press, New Haven and London

Koldeweij, A. M. 2006 *Foi et bonne fortune. Parure et dévotion en Flandre médiévale*, Terra Lannoo, Arnhem

Lerud, T. K. 2001 'Quick images: memory and the English Corpus Christi drama', in K. Ashley and W. Hüsken (eds), *Moving subjects: processional performance in the Middle Ages and the Renaissance*, Rodopi, Amsterdam, 213–38

Marks, R. 2004 *Image and devotion in late medieval England*, Sutton, Stroud

Marritt, S. 2014 'Scottish bishops and the relic-lists of the cartulary of Christchurch Priory, Twynham, Hampshire 1220–1221 (with an edition and translation of the text by John Reuben Davies)', *Innes Review* 65(2), 128–52

Merrifield, R. 1987 *The archaeology of ritual and magic*, Batsford, London

Morris, R. 1989 *Churches in the landscape*, J. M. Dent and Sons, London

Nilson, B. 1998 *Cathedral shrines of medieval England*, Boydell and Brewer, Woodbridge

Rattue, J. 1995 *The living stream: holy wells in historical context*, Boydell Press, Woodbridge

Schmitt, J.-C. 1983 *The holy greyhound Guinefort, healer of children since the thirteenth century*, Cambridge University Press, Cambridge

Scully, R. E. 2007 'St Winefride's well: the significance and survival of a Welsh Catholic shrine from the early Middle Ages to the present day', in M. Cormack (ed.), *Saints and their cults in the Atlantic world*, University of South Carolina Press, Columbia, 202–28

Smith, J. H. 2012 'Portable Christianity: relics in the medieval West (c.700–1200)', *Proceedings of the British Academy* 181, 143–67

Spencer, B. 1998 *Pilgrim souvenirs and secular badges*, Medieval Finds from Excavations in London 7, London

Stocker, D. and Everson, P. 2003 'The straight and narrow way: fenland causeways and the conversion of the landscape in the Witham Valley, Lincolnshire', in M. O. H. Carver (ed.), *The cross goes north: processes of conversion in northern Europe AD 300–1300*, Boydell Press, Woodbridge, 271–88

Stocker, D. and Everson, P. 2006 *Summoning St Michael: early Romanesque towers in Lincolnshire*, Oxbow, Oxford

Stopford, J. (ed.) 1999 *Pilgrimage explored*, York Medieval Press, York

Todd, M. 2002 *The culture of Protestantism in early modern Scotland*, Yale University Press, New Haven and London

Travaini, L. 2004 'Saints and sinners: coins in medieval Italian graves', *Numismatic Chronicle* 164, 159–81

Underwood, P. A. 1950 'The fountain of life in manuscripts of the Gospels', *Dumbarton Oaks Papers* 5, 41–138

Van Houts, E. 1999 *Memory and gender in medieval Europe 900–1200*, Cambridge University Press, Cambridge

Webb, D. 2000 *Pilgrimage in medieval England*, Hambledon Press, London and New York

Williams, D. 2013 'Musical space and quiet space in medieval monastic Canterbury', in J. Day (ed.), *Making sense of the past: toward a sensory archaeology*, South Illinois University Press, Carbondale, 196–220

Woolgar, C. M. 2006 *The senses in late medieval England*, Yale University Press, New Haven and London

Yeoman, P. 1999 *Pilgrimage in medieval Scotland*, Historic Scotland, Edinburgh

CHAPTER 39

MEDIEVAL GRAFFITI INSCRIPTIONS

MATTHEW CHAMPION

On the 2 September 1486 an accusation was made in front of a senior cleric on the Maltese island of Gozo that fellow cleric Andreas de Bisconis had sexually harassed Jacoba Saliba whilst she was at prayer in the church of St James. The charge was brought by the husband and the father of the woman. Bisconis, they claimed, waited until Jacoba was alone in the church, and then approached and declared his love for her, stating that he had propositioned her to have sex with him. In the court case that followed Bisconis stated that it was a case of mistaken identity, and that, in the darkness of the church, he had believed he was actually addressing a local prostitute with whom he was acquainted. However, further evidence was presented against him by the family. It was claimed that some months earlier Bisconis had inscribed a slanderous statement about Jacoba Saliba into the walls of a local church. Although the witnesses differed as to the details of what the inscription actually said, it was claimed that the defamatory words were written clearly in Bisconis's handwriting. Despite a vigorous defence, and the calling of many character witnesses, Bisconis was found guilty of both the charges of sexual harassment and the slander, being sentenced to a year in prison confined in irons (Wettinger 2015).

Whilst the case itself is of interest, not least the cleric's defence that he thought he was speaking to a prostitute of his acquaintance, the use of church graffiti as evidence is one of the very few documentary references we have to the act of creating informal inscriptions in a church. As with the cleric's association with the prostitute, the fact that he created the graffiti on the church wall was not the subject of disapprobation, just the content of the message itself. It is also clear from the evidence presented during the court case that Bisconis had not just written one piece of graffiti, but was known to have created multiple inscriptions on the walls of several different churches. The act of creating the inscriptions appears to have been wholly acceptable, only the content being under review.

The word 'graffiti' itself only enters the English language in the middle of the nineteenth century, being coined specifically to describe the inscriptions then being recorded at the Roman site of Pompeii. In its original context it had no negative connotations and was used only to describe a particular type of historic and informal inscription. And whilst a number of early modern texts do decry the creation of inscriptions in inappropriate places, as among them Thomas Dekker's seventeenth-century satirical jibe suggesting that visitors to St Paul's cathedral 'draw your knife, and grave your name (or, for want of a name, the marke, which you clap on your sheep) in great Characters upon the leades', the creation of inscriptions within medieval sacred spaces receives no such censure.

Amongst the very earliest English references to the informal inscribing of a church or place of worship is a twelfth-century text describing the life of Christina of Markyate. As a young teenager, Christina was apparently taken to visit the powerful abbey at St Albans, where she was so inspired and impressed by the devotion of the monastic brothers that she there and then made the decision to devote her own life to the service of God. As a physical symbol of her private vow of devotion and chastity, the document goes on to record that Christina inscribed a votive cross into the doorway of the cathedral church 'with her own fingernail' (Geddes 2005). Christina's act carries no overtones of destruction or vandalism, and the content of the majority of pre-Reformation church inscriptions have clear associations with devotion and belief. Many express an overt invocatory or votive function and it is clear that these early inscriptions share little with their modern counterparts beyond the method of their creation, and that any negative connotations are almost a wholly modern construct. Such questions of legitimacy are further raised by inscriptions such as that recorded at Lidgate church in Suffolk (Figure 39.1). The tiny Latin text there translates as 'John Lidgate made this, with licence, on the feast of Saints

FIGURE 39.1 Lidgate, Suffolk. Latin inscription dated on stylistics grounds to *c*.1400–*c*.1550

(© Matthew Champion)

Simon and Jude', where the use of the term 'with licence' strongly suggests an overt and perhaps even formal legitimacy to the creation of the inscription (Champion 2015b).

The study of early graffiti inscriptions in the UK has an academic pedigree that stretches back well over a century (Coulton 1915; Hine 1917; Salmon 1905). However, such studies as do exist are largely on the fringes of academic research and are most usually limited to the examination of a single site or small collection of sites (Emden 1922; Jones-Baker 1981). It was only in 1967, with the publication of Violet Pritchard's work *English medieval graffiti* that scholars began to more widely recognize the potential that early church graffiti inscriptions could have as a research subject (Pritchard 1967). However, the potential avenues of research highlighted by Pritchard and her contemporaries have gone largely unexplored until very recently. In large part this lack of further research has been the result of the difficulty in collecting meaningful quantities of good quality data. Pritchard's generation were limited by their own recording methods, which usually involved taking direct rubbings of any graffiti inscriptions and then reinterpreting the resulting images. This technique could not record the lightly inscribed graffiti which form the majority of the corpus, and was of limited use on any surface except the smoothest of stonework. Furthermore, with only a small sample of the most deeply inscribed inscriptions from each site being recorded, any analysis of distribution patterns or context became largely meaningless.

As a result the study of early graffiti inscriptions faltered. So little work has been undertaken in the intervening decades, with the exception of a handful of site-specific surveys (Graves and Rollason 2013; Peake 2012; Sherlock 1978) and a very few demonstrative articles summarizing the current position (Gardiner 2007; Meeson 2005), that Pritchard's book was recently republished in an entirely unaltered state. The very recent increase in the study of these early inscriptions has largely been the result of technological advances. The recent availability of inexpensive digital cameras now allows large-scale photographic surveys, something that was simply too costly for Pritchard's generation to undertake, and permits the mass recording of an almost wholly new corpus of medieval and early modern material. In spite of this surge of activity, however, research in the UK falls well behind that taking place across Europe. Surveys have been undertaken in a number of regions, with broadly similar results to those now taking place in the UK. Of particular note is the concordance of symbols found amongst all the graffiti inscriptions, with the same motifs being recorded repeatedly across Europe, in roughly the same proportions, and the same locations within buildings (Easton 2016). The evidence indicates that the 'language' of the inscriptions, in regard at least to their overt usage, is not confined by geographical borders, and that the same symbols occur everywhere that the medieval Christian church flourished.

Distribution

Although the recording of individual inscriptions and graffiti types are creating large amounts of research data, new emphasis has been placed upon recording the distribution patterns and the spatial analysis of graffiti within individual structures. Whilst such studies do have the potential to examine possible regional variations of styles and types of inscriptions, none of which have yet been positively identified, the analysis of distribution patterns within individual structures must be treated with extreme caution. A number of studies undertaken in cathedrals and larger religious buildings have attempted to use analysis of distribution patterns to establish relationships between graffiti inscriptions and specific activities, such as medieval pilgrimage (Champion 2013b; Jones-Baker 1987; Owen 2010). Although a single intriguing correlation has been tentatively identified at one site (Ingram 2016), the study of the inscriptions in isolation from a wider study of the building fabric raises questions about the bias introduced by centuries of fabric change and alteration. A noted lack of any such concentrations at cathedrals such as Norwich, Canterbury, St Albans, and Lincoln, all of which attracted large numbers of medieval pilgrims, and all of which have been subject to extensive fabric surveys, must raise questions as to the validity of any such studies (Champion 2013d). Such considerations are even more relevant when attempting to establish distribution patterns within more modest structures such as parish churches. Although individual stone replacement and renovations are perhaps easier to identify, it is a rare church that retains more than a small percentage of the original internal plaster surfaces (see Chapter 38). Where such plaster surfaces do survive, such as at Swannington in Norfolk, Duxford in Cambridgeshire, and Troston church porch in Suffolk there is large-scale evidence of graffiti having been also present on these surfaces (Champion 2014a; 2015b). As a result, even in the best surviving early structures, it must be accepted that the distribution patterns being recorded are inevitably incomplete and potentially misleading.

Change at the Reformation

Although it has not been possible to identify formal distribution patterns of inscriptions within individual buildings, beyond the level of superficial concentrations, it has become apparent that the types of graffiti being created do show a marked deviation and change over longer time periods. The clearest of these changes is most easily identified within church graffiti, and shows a clear link to the middle of the sixteenth century and the period of the English Reformation. Prior to this point the inclusion of actual written dates amongst the inscriptions is rare, with only a handful identified at sites such as Parham in Suffolk, and Chedworth in Gloucestershire, both of which appear to commemorate the completion of significant building works, or the well-documented inscriptions at Ashwell in Hertfordshire and Acle in Norfolk, which commemorate significant parish events including the arrival of plagues and the Black Death (Champion 2015b; Sherlock 1978). From the middle of the sixteenth century the inclusion of dates becomes increasingly commonplace, until it becomes largely the norm by the opening decades of the seventeenth century. These inscriptions invariably take the form of names or initials accompanying the dates, and show marked similarities with modern territorial or commemorative graffiti. The lack of dated graffiti prior to the period of the Reformation may be linked to the marked bias towards inscriptions of a wholly religious, votive, or spiritual nature. These range from the orthodox religious imagery, such as the enthroned Virgin and Child at King's Somborne in Hampshire, the Agnus Dei at Carlisle Cathedral, Mass vessels (Weybread and Stoke-by-Clare in Suffolk, Husborne Crawley in Bedfordshire), and hands raised in blessing (Worlington in Suffolk, Ashwell in Hertfordshire), to those reflecting aspects of lay piety in the form of the many thousands of ritual protection marks identified at churches across the country. In all these instances their religious or spiritual nature would make the inclusion of a date unnecessary and meaningless.

Another noted feature of the post-Reformation graffiti inscriptions recorded in churches is that there are periods when inscriptions are more likely to be created than at other times (Champion 2013a). Such periods are only clearly identifiable amongst the post-Reformation inscriptions due to the inclusion of written dates, but there is no reason to conclude that the practice does not hold true for the generally undated earlier inscriptions as well. These chronological hotspots coincide with recognized periods of social unrest and conflict, the most notable examples being the period of the English Civil Wars, and the First and Second World Wars (Champion 2016a). Although many of these inscriptions may simply be acts of commemoration undertaken at times of uncertainty and societal stress, drawing direct parallels with much modern graffiti, links with higher levels of mobility and a relaxing of social norms amongst the population as a whole cannot be ruled out.

General Dating

Ascribing exact dates to the majority of inscriptions, in the absence of written evidence, can be difficult (Figure 39.2). In the case of text inscriptions it is possible to ascribe a very general period based on the style and letter-form of the text itself. In relation to images of individuals, structures, or ships, the same general dating can be applied by comparing them with surviving painted or manuscript depictions. However, in some cases the building fabric is the only aid to dating. For example, at All Saints church, Litcham (Norfolk), the documentary evidence indicates that the nave arcades were rebuilt in the early fifteenth century, being consecrated on St Botolph's day in 1412 (Champion 2011a). The documentary evidence also states that the same arcades were first lime-washed during the Reformation in 1547. As a result any graffiti inscriptions now emerging from beneath the many layers of friable and delaminating lime-wash must have been created between 1412 and 1547. Similarly, inscriptions cut into the mid-fourteenth-century piers at Lidgate church (Suffolk) that are partially obscured by a parclose screen inserted in the second half of the fifteenth century can only have been created in the intervening century. In a very few cases the fabric can offer a more precise date, such as the architectural designs from Binham Priory in Norfolk that demonstrably relate to the construction of the west front in the 1240s (Champion 2011b).

FIGURE 39.2 Inscriptions, including late medieval text, from the church of St Mary, Troston, Suffolk; superimposition is one of the problems in trying to read and date graffiti

(© Matthew Champion)

The fact that certain graffiti types are relatively easy to locate on both churches and vernacular structures has resulted in a number of 'traditional' interpretations to explain them. Inscribed crosses, often located around church doorways and in church porches, have been referred to as 'crusader crosses' or 'pilgrim crosses' since at least the middle of the nineteenth century (Ditchfield 1904). These were thought to be a symbol of the vows inscribed by pilgrims or crusaders prior to setting out on their travels. In a number of churches these interpretations became more elaborate still, with crosses on one side of the doorframe being ascribed to those departing on pilgrimage, and those on the opposite side being created upon their return, neatly offering an explanation for having more crosses on one side of the doorframe than the other. Unfortunately no firm evidence has been discovered to support any of these interpretations (Champion 2015b).

GRAFFITI TYPES

The types of graffiti recorded in a medieval context have been superficially compared to the marginalia of medieval manuscripts. Whilst both may reflect an informality of approach, direct comparisons are few and far between. The grotesques and fantastic beasts, the sexual imagery, and the elaborate decorative elements of marginalia are only rarely found on the walls. The imagery found amongst the graffiti tends more towards the mundane, with windmills, simple flowers, animals, birds, and fish commonly featuring, alongside countless depictions of ordinary people. However, the vast majority of inscriptions recorded in medieval graffiti appear to have a spiritual aspect, with clear devotional or votive connotations (Champion 2016a). They relate to concepts and ideas of belief.

Ritual Protection Marks

The largest group of inscriptions, making up almost a third of everything being recorded, are those deemed to have apotropaic qualities. Some take the form of orthodox religious imagery of saints and prayers, and although relatively few in number, form an extension to traditional and orthodox devotional imagery of wall paintings and stained glass. However, by far the largest single category of inscriptions recorded are what may be termed 'ritual protection marks', more commonly inaccurately referred to as 'witch marks' (Champion 2016a; Easton 1999; 2016). A strict definition of what does, or does not, constitute a ritual protection mark is fraught with difficulties, and can depend upon a number of not entirely related factors. The same marking used in different circumstances and contexts may have widely differing meanings, not all of which can be considered apotropaic.

Broadly speaking, these markings are believed to turn away, or ward off, evil. Apotropaic markings in general are often thought of as acting as a form of sympathetic magic where, for example, the ritual scorching of newly built timbers would subsequently protect the building from fire and lightning strikes; quite literally 'fighting fire with fire' (Easton 2012). However, whilst this may apply to some ritual protection markings found in medieval churches, the vast majority appear to arise from a more complex system of beliefs. They can be considered as the physical manifestations of a system of belief that thought in multiple layers of spiritual defence; essentially each symbol can be considered a protective marking that operated in addition to, but not separate from, the prayers of the medieval church. Indeed, whilst Aron Gurevich maintains that 'traditional magic and Christianity did not form a distinct layer or separate compartments in the medieval mind', any study of ritual protection marks in the medieval church suggests that the 'magic' was already part of orthodox church belief at a parish level, lay piety as it may be termed, and couldn't have been compartmentalised even if it had occurred to them to try (Mellinkoff 2004).

Several symbols can be clearly demonstrated to have evolved from orthodox religious imagery, including the pelta or Solomon's knot (Figure 39.3). The compass-drawn designs (Figure 39.4), most particularly that known as the hexfoil or 'daisy wheel', are the single most common motif on English fonts in the eleventh and twelfth centuries, with many surviving examples found in the far west of England at sites such as at Buckland-in-the-Moor (Devon), Altarnum (Cornwall), and Combe-in-Teignhead (Devon). Other examples of these symbols are to be found in the north of England in North Yorkshire at Skelton, Marske, Bessingby, and Reighton, and further south at St Andrew's church, Bredwardine (Herefordshire), and at Egleton in Rutland, where the hexfoil

FIGURE 39.3 Pelta design in the nave of St John's church, Duxford, Cambridgeshire

(© Matthew Champion)

design features on both the early font and the eleventh- or twelfth-century tympanum. Such an association between the hexfoil and baptism is reinforced by the concentration of these motifs around the fonts at sites such as Lidgate (Suffolk) and Swannington (Norfolk), although by the later Middle Ages any direct link between the two may have been tenuous. A number of other ritual protection marks appear to cross the divide from the informal into the more orthodox canon of church decoration. Most notably the 'VV' motif, believed to have associations with Marian worship (Easton 2004), also appears as decoration on pilgrim *ampullae* associated with the shrine of Our Lady at Walsingham as well as alongside formal Marian imagery in the flint flushwork decoration on the western face of the tower of Fakenham church in Norfolk (Champion 2015b).

These same markings are inscribed into all types of medieval building, without any obvious exceptions, and are often recorded in distinct concentrations. In a church setting these clusters are sometimes associated with areas of spiritual significance, such as the font, side altars, and particular wall paintings (Champion 2012d; 2016a). In a vernacular setting they are often associated with areas that were considered vulnerable,

FIGURE 39.4 Elaborate compass-drawn design in St Mary's church, Lidgate, Suffolk
(© Matthew Champion)

such as chimneys, thresholds, and entranceways. The same symbols might also be applied to other objects that were believed to require spiritual protection, such as books, pieces of furniture (particularly beds and coffers), and individual personal items. Within a vernacular context these markings form a part of the much larger corpus of rituals, ceremonies, and actions undertaken to ensure the spiritual protection of a place (see Chapter 42). Although differing in their manner of execution, these markings belong to the orthodox practices of the parish, from the candlelight processions from room to room undertaken on Twelfth Night, and the use of holy water upon a threshold, to the informal and largely heterodox practices of ritual concealments, witch bottles, taper burn marks, and spiritual middens (Cummins 2016; Easton 2016; Hoggard 2016). They form one small part of a wider vocabulary of ritual protection (see also Chapter 40).

Architectural Graffiti

The surveys now underway are also identifying a relatively large number of inscriptions associated with the construction process. Although the majority of these are straightforward mason's marks, or setting out lines, more elaborate inscriptions relating directly to the design process have also been recorded (see Chapter 37). These rare inscriptions can vary in size and complexity, from the large-scale mason's working drawings discovered at Binham Priory in Norfolk, which were in excess of 2.4 m in height and dated from the 1240s, to small-scale schematics, such as the two window designs recorded at Weston Longville (Norfolk), which most probably dated to the fourteenth century and were only 140 mm in width (Champion 2011b; 2012c). Most of the architectural inscriptions relate to window tracery designs and share one common feature, regardless of their size. None of them appear to be completed designs, but rather working schematics or geometric exercises to establish individual elements of the overall design. The inscriptions have largely been recorded on the stone or plaster internal surfaces of churches, in the case of Swannington (Norfolk) actually incised through the surface of a surviving medieval wall painting. However, a small number have also been located on the rear of rood screens, suggesting a highly pragmatic approach to the church fabric by the medieval craftsmen; a number of these designs, such as those recorded at Blythburgh (Suffolk) and Caston (Norfolk) directly relate to the construction of the screens themselves (Champion 2012a). Although such architectural inscriptions are more usually to be found at smaller sites, where the masons would not have had access to specific workshop areas with 'tracing floors', such as that which survives at York Minster, it is notable that a number of these designs on wall surfaces have also been recorded at larger sites such as Southwark, Canterbury, and Ely cathedrals (Pacey 2007; and see Chapter 37 in this *Handbook*). In excess of forty such designs have recently been discovered, more than doubling the number of examples recorded to date, and giving insights into the little understood medieval design process (Champion 2015b).

Ship Graffiti

One of the most published types of specific inscription are those depicting ships (Brady and Corlett 2004; Buglass 2013; Champion 2012b; Champion and Cohen 2013; Pritchard 1987). Earlier scholars noted these often beautiful motifs at a number of sites, and made a number of presumptions concerning their form and function. It was believed, for example, that ship graffiti was largely confined to the coast, and that they were usually to be found either associated with fonts or low down on the walls, giving the impression that they were sailing across the floor (Jones-Baker 1981). Larger-scale studies have generally overturned these tentative conclusions. Although ship graffiti are most certainly found in concentrations at coastal sites, such as Winchelsea, Dover, or the Glaven ports on the north Norfolk coast, they regularly appear on churches throughout the country, including in those of entirely land-locked counties such as Hertfordshire and Leicestershire. Intriguingly, even those located many dozens of miles from the sea all show sea-going vessels, and no example of an obviously riverine craft has yet to be identified. Although these inscriptions can range in quality from the exceptionally crude, such as most of the examples from Winchelsea church (Sussex), to the elaborate and detailed, such as those from Cley-next-the-Sea (Norfolk) and Bassingham (Lincolnshire), almost every example of ship graffiti recorded to date, which now number over five hundred individual depictions, share certain characteristics (Figure 39.5). These include the fact that they are invariably depicted in profile, showing the full hull rather than just from the waterline upwards, are single-masted, shown with sail furled, and are very often shown with an anchor present at the end of a long line, essentially as though they are safely in port (Champion 2015a).

From the examples of ship graffiti already recorded within the UK there is a very strong argument to suggest that the creation of these inscriptions was a ritual and symbolic act. This is perhaps most clearly demonstrated by the many dozens of examples that have been recorded within the north Norfolk churches of Blakeney, Cley, and Wiveton. In Blakeney church there is a clear and demonstrable link between the ship graffiti concentration and the former site of an altar dedicated to St Nicholas, the patron saint of those in peril upon the sea (Peake 2012). Similar relationships between such ship graffiti and areas of churches dedicated to St Nicholas have also been identified at St Thomas' church in Winchelsea, and St Nicholas' chapel in King's Lynn (Champion 2013c; Dhoop et al. 2016). Such correlations suggest that the imagery was created and intended to function in the manner of an ex-voto item with an invocatory or votive function;

FIGURE 39.5 Incised late medieval North Sea cog at St Margaret's church, Cley-next-the-Sea, Norfolk

(© Matthew Champion)

perhaps in the same manner as the votive 'church ships' once known to have been present as offerings in many of our churches, with examples still to be seen in the church of All Hallows by the Tower in London (Champion 2015b).

The marked and demonstrable concentration of ship graffiti at coastal sites certainly suggests a strong link between the graffiti and maritime communities, implying that the graffiti had meaning and function that was highly relevant to these communities. However, the presence of so many newly discovered examples at sites far removed from the sea would also suggest that their meaning and function went beyond the localized settings of coastal churches; perhaps indicating a wider link to medieval concepts of transport and travel.

Text Graffiti

Although text inscriptions form only a very small percentage of early graffiti recorded, they have received proportionally more scholarly attention than any other types (Figure 39.1). In many respects this is entirely understandable: the temptation to 'read the writing on the wall' is especially strong. However, much of the graffiti text presents particular and specific problems that make transcription and interpretation difficult. At even the best-known sites, such as Ashwell in Hertfordshire, multiple interpretations are possible for each piece of text. One inscription on the easternmost pier of the south arcade has no less than four published transcriptions, varying from 'In AD 1381 the insurrection of the common people', to 'In AD 1381 he exchanged five ploughlands of the church's' (Sherlock 1978). The reason for these multiple interpretations, and in some cases a complete inability to offer any, is due to the nature of the inscriptions themselves. Many are extremely discrete, being small in size and lightly inscribed, and a large number have been heavily abraded after centuries of wear to the structural fabric. In addition, and perhaps more significantly, the majority are in heavily abbreviated and contracted clerical Latin, and do not follow the usual conventions associated with texts written on parchment or paper. In many instances the texts are so contracted as to be only understandable by the individual who wrote them. It has also been suggested that some of these texts were not designed to be read in the first place (Merrifield 1987), rather they were simply a mysterious and enigmatic text of the kind to be found on a number of medieval and post-Reformation written 'charms' (Thomas 1971; see, for example, Barroca 2011). Given the association between a number of unreadable text inscriptions and astrological symbols, such an interpretation appears attractive.

The text inscriptions that can be transcribed appear fairly formulaic, and in most cases are commemorative or memorial in nature, a theme that continues into the post-Reformation period. Some of those which commemorate individual deaths, such as that for Borthome Salemon from Horley in Surrey and the inscription asking for prayers for 'Thomas' from Harlton in Cambridgeshire, were written in Latin and even echo the form of more formal memorials.

Conclusions

Today many of these inscriptions are difficult to see except under specific lighting conditions, something that may well be a significant factor in their survival, allowing them to avoid the attention of overzealous renovation and restorations. However, it is clear that when they were first created the majority of these inscriptions would have been highly visible to even the most casual observer. The vast majority of surfaces in English medieval churches had applied pigment, either in the form of decorative wall paintings or as plain colourwash on the lower sections of the walls. When originally created these graffiti would have been incised through this pigment to reveal the pale stone or plaster beneath. In some cases the graffiti are actually cut through the main areas of decorative wall painting, with examples still visible at Swannington (Norfolk), Duxford (Cambridgeshire), and the Prior's chapel at Durham Cathedral (Graves and Rollason 2013). In the case of both Swannington and Durham several of the inscriptions appear directly related to the subject matter depicted in the murals, creating a traceable dialogue on the walls. In addition, at Swannington the surface upon which the wall painting of St Christopher is located has also been used for the creation of a large-scale architectural design for a late medieval window, with no apparent attempt subsequently to repair the damage caused to the pigment (Champion 2012a). Such actions strongly suggest a pragmatic contemporary approach to the wall surfaces within a church, despite their orthodox religious decoration, raising a number of questions concerning attitudes towards interactions with devotional religious imagery.

As with the other imagery of the late medieval church, many of these inscriptions formed a fundamental element of the visual landscape of belief (see Chapter 41). Unlike the formal imagery of wall paintings, stained glass, or alabasters, however, these inscriptions were the outcome of direct and personal physical interactions between the members of the later medieval congregation and the fabric of the building in which they worshipped. They are the physical manifestations of lay piety that go beyond offerings, prayers, and bequests, and represent the spiritual and physical appropriation of the parish space that bypassed the traditional hierarchies of the Church.

References cited

Barroca, M. 2011 'A medieval prayer finger ring from São João de Tarouca (Portugal)', in M. O. H. Carver and J. Klápště (eds), *The archaeology of medieval Europe, Vol. 2: twelfth to sixteenth centuries*, Aarhus University Press, Aarhus, 432–3

Brady, K. and Corlett, C. 2004 'Holy ships: ships on plaster at medieval ecclesiastical sites in Ireland', *Archaeology Ireland* 18(2), 28–31

Buglass, J. 2013 'Comments of the ship graffiti', in T. Robinson, 'All at sea in Ribblesdale', *Yorkshire Buildings* 41, 63–73

Champion, M. 2011a 'Medieval graffiti inscriptions found in All Saints Church, Litcham, Norfolk', *Norfolk Archaeology* 46, 199–208

Champion, M. 2011b 'Tracery designs at Binham Priory', *English Heritage Historical Review* 6, 6–21

Champion, M. 2012a 'Architectural inscriptions: new discoveries in East Anglia', *Church Archaeology* 16, 65–80

Champion, M. 2012b *Blackfriars barn undercroft, Winchelsea, East Sussex: graffiti survey record*, unpublished National Trust report

Champion, M. 2012c 'Medieval window sketch found at All Saints, Weston Longville, Norfolk', *Norfolk Archaeology* 46, 383–6

Champion, M. 2012d 'The medium is the message: votive devotional imagery and gift giving amongst the commonality in the late medieval parish', *Peregrinations: Journal of Medieval Art and Architecture* 3, 102–23

Champion, M. 2013a *Knole House: graffiti survey and interpretation*, unpublished National Trust Report

Champion, M. 2013b '"Medieval graffiti artists were 'ere": Norwich Cathedral graffiti', *Cornerstone: the journal of the Society for the Protection of Ancient Buildings* 33(1), 5–7

Champion, M. 2013c *The south porch, St Nicholas chapel, Kings Lynn: graffiti survey and interpretation*, unpublished Churches Conservation Trust report

Champion, M. 2013d 'Ecclesiastical etchings: the graffiti of Norwich Cathedral', *Current Archaeology* 277, 9

Champion, M. 2014a 'The graffiti inscriptions of St Mary's Church, Troston', *Proceedings of the Suffolk Institute of Archaeology* 43(2), 235–58

Champion, M. 2014b 'Ill wishing on the walls: late medieval graffiti curses from Norwich cathedral', *Norfolk Archaeology* 46, 61–6

Champion, M. 2015a 'Medieval ship graffiti in English churches: interpretation and function', *The Mariners Mirror* 101(3), 343–50

Champion, M. 2015b *Medieval graffiti: the lost voices of England's churches*, Ebury Press, London

Champion, M. 2016a 'Ritual protection marks in medieval churches', in R. Hutton, (ed.), *The physical evidence for ritual acts, sorcery and witchcraft in Christian Britain: a feeling for magic*, Palgrave Macmillan, Basingstoke, 15–38

Champion, M. and Cohen, N. 2013 'Victory graffiti in the undercroft?', *National Trust: Arts, Buildings, Collections Bulletin*, February 2013, 8

Coulton, G. G. 1915 'Medieval graffiti, especially in the Eastern Counties', *Proceedings of the Cambridge Antiquarian Society*, new series 13, 52–62

Cummins, A. 2016 'Textual evidence for the material history of amulets in seventeenth-century England', in R. Hutton, (ed.), *The physical evidence for ritual acts, sorcery and witchcraft in Christian Britain: a feeling for magic*, Palgrave Macmillan, Basingstoke, 164–87

Dhoop, T., Cooper, C., and Copeland, P. 2016 'Recording and analysis of ship graffiti in St Thomas' church and Blackfriars barn undercroft in Winchelsea, East Sussex, UK', *The International Journal of Nautical Archaeology* 45(2), 296–309

Ditchfield, P. H. 1904 *English villages*, Methuen and Co., London

Easton, T. 1999 'Ritual marks on historic timber', *Weald and Downland Museum*, 22–30

Easton, T. 2004 'The use of conjoined Vs to protect a dwelling', *Proceedings of the University of Spelaeological Society* 23(2), 127–32

Easton, T. 2012 'Burning issues (ritual burn markings on historic buildings)', *Cornerstone: The Journal of the Society for the Protection of Ancient Buildings Magazine*, Winter, 18–33

Easton, T. 2016 'Apotropaic symbols and other measures for protecting buildings against misfortune', in R. Hutton (ed.), *The physical evidence for ritual acts, sorcery and witchcraft in Christian Britain: a feeling for magic*, Palgrave Macmillan, Basingstoke, 39–67

Emden, A. B. 1922 'Graffiti of medieval ships from the Church of St Margaret at Cliffe, Kent', *The Mariners Mirror* 8(6), 167–73

Gardiner, M. 2007 'Graffiti and their use in Late Medieval England', *Ruralia* 6, 265–76

Geddes, J. 2005 *The St Albans Psalter: a book for Christina of Markyate*, The British Library, London

Graves, C. P. and Rollason, L. 2013 'The monastery of Durham and the wider world: medieval graffiti in the Prior's Chapel', *Northern History* 50(2), 186–215

Hine, R. 1917 'Church graffiti', *Lincolnshire Notes and Queries* 14(113), 133–44

Hoggard, B. 2016 'Witch bottles: their contents, contexts and uses', in R. Hutton, (ed.), *The physical evidence for ritual acts, sorcery and witchcraft in Christian Britain: a feeling for magic*, Palgrave Macmillan, Basingstoke, 91–105

Ingram, J. 2016 *Place and identity: medieval graffiti, place making and the constructed identity within a larger pilgrimage centre*, unpublished MA thesis, University of Southampton

Jones-Baker, D. 1981 'The graffiti of folk motifs in Cotswold churches', *Folklore* 92(2), 160–7

Jones-Baker, D. 1987 'The graffiti of England's medieval churches and cathedrals', *Churchscape* 6, 7–18

Meeson, B. 2005 'Ritual marks and graffiti: curiosities or meaningful symbols?', *Vernacular Architecture* 36, 41–8

Mellinkoff, R. 2004 *Averting demons: the protective power of medieval visual motifs and themes*, Ruth Mellinkoff Publications, Los Angeles

Merrifield, R. 1987 *The archaeology of ritual and magic*, Batesford, London

Peake, J. 2012 'Graffiti and devotion in three maritime churches', in T. A. Heslop, E. Mellings, and M. Thofner (eds), *Art, faith and place in East Anglia: from Prehistory to the present*, Boydell Press, Woodbridge

Owen, K. 2010 'Traces of presence and pleading: approaches to the study of graffiti at Tewksbury Abbey', in J. Oliver and T. Neil (eds), *Wild signs: graffiti in archaeology and history*, British Archaeological Reports International Series 2074, Oxford, 35

Pacey, A. 2007 *Medieval architectural drawing*, Tempus, Stroud

Pritchard, V. 1967 *English medieval graffiti*, Cambridge University Press, Cambridge

Pritchard, V. 1987 'Some English medieval ship graffiti', *Mariners Mirror* 73(3), 318–20

Salmon, E. F. 1905 'Masons and other incised marks in New Shoreham Church', *Sussex Archaeological Collections* 48, 145–9

Sherlock, D. 1978 *Ashwell Church: medieval drawings and writings*, Ashwell Parish Church, Ashwell

Thomas, K. 1971 *Religion and the decline of magic*, Weidenfield and Nicolson, London

Wettinger, G. 2015 *Aspects of daily life in late medieval Malta and Gozo*, Malta University Press, Msida

CHAPTER 40

AN ARCHAEOLOGY OF PILGRIMAGE

PETER YEOMAN

In poet William Langland's vivid image of a pilgrim written more than six hundred years ago,[1] a familiar figure trudges the dusty byways of medieval Britain and Europe. The pilgrim's journey still provides us with a helpful metaphor for a central theme of medieval life: the need to attain salvation. This could be achieved through the supernatural intervention of God mediated through the intercession of the saints, one of the only means that ordinary folk had of seeing their prayers answered. In an attempt to control their unpredictable lives, prayers and vows had to be channelled through the relics of the saints present at the places where they 'lived' in death, in other words, at the shrines established by the Church containing saintly relics (Figure 40.1).

These convictions were further reinforced after the Fourth Lateran Council in 1215, when it was decreed that sins had to be confessed on a regular basis in order to achieve salvation, then cleansed through penance. A chief form of penance was a pilgrimage and, as time went by, the role of the cult of saints was strengthened by the increased importance of the doctrine of purgatory, creating markets for indulgences (reducing time spent in purgatory) which could be obtained at shrines. Salvation was not the only motivation for pilgrimage, however, nor was this merely a quest for miracles of healing;

---

[1] Apparelled as a Paynim (heathen) in a pilgrim's wise.

> He bare a staff bound with a broad strip
> In bindweed wise wound about.
> A bowl and a bag he bare by his side;
> An hundred ampullas on his hat set,
> Signs of Sinai and shells of Galicia,
> Many a cross on his cloak keys also of Rome
> And the vernicle in front so that men should know
> And see by his signs what shrines he had sought.
>
> (Langland c.1380, 47).

FIGURE 40.1 Lincoln Cathedral carving of a pilgrim *c*.1400 in the spandrels of an east window of the south west chapel

(© Dean and Chapter of Lincoln Cathedral)

a pilgrim's journey could also be prompted as fulfilment of a vow to give thanks and offerings at the shrine, often on the feast day of the saint (Webb 2000, 36). The archaeology of pilgrimage, described in this chapter, allows us to bridge the gap between something as intangible as personal faith and the evidence for it in the material world. As we shall see, an interdisciplinary approach is required which integrates archaeological evidence with studies of associated documentary history.

Pilgrims in the Landscape

Pilgrims would set off on foot or on horseback, with the sick in carts or carried in a litter. Almost all shrines were on existing, often ancient, routes, which were adopted and sometimes improved, for example the Roman Watling Street which connected London with Canterbury. Chaucer, in the *Canterbury Tales*, has his twenty-nine-strong pilgrim band travel along this route from their rendezvous at the Tabard Inn at Southwark in April 1386. Their first major river crossing was the Medway at Rochester, where the timber bridge was regularly washed-away and pilgrims were forced to resort to an unsafe ferry, until a stone bridge was built in 1381 (Webb 2000, 228).

The routes to the shrine of the apostle St Andrew through the Fife countryside in eastern Scotland have been successfully charted, providing a framework for locating essential pilgrimage infrastructure, including chapels, landing places, and hospitals (Yeoman 1999, 57). The upkeep of roads and bridges, along with the endowment of free ferries, was all 'regarded as meritorious charitable work' (Webb 2000, 227). Bridge chapels were common, usually at one end of the bridge. The bridge chapel over the Calder at Wakefield is the finest survivor of this type, completed in 1356 as a chantry for the singing of Masses for the care of pilgrims and travellers. In Scotland, Queen (later Saint) Margaret established a free ferry for pilgrims across the Forth north-west of Edinburgh en-route to St Andrews. Her biographer, Turgot, writing soon after her death in 1093, records that she provided ships for the crossing as well as endowed hospitals and chapels on either side. The remains of St James's chapel can still be seen in North Queensferry. The Queen's Ferry was matched in the eastern part of the estuary by the Earl's Ferry, which carried pilgrims from North Berwick to the Fife side near Elie. This route was established by Duncan, Earl of Fife, in the mid-twelfth century, who also established hospices at either end of the crossing where pilgrims were cared for by Cistercian nuns from their convent in North Berwick on the south side of the Forth (Yeoman 1999, 58). Parts of the medieval parish church, cemetery, and hospice, located on a headland overlooking the harbour at North Berwick, have been excavated (Addyman et al. 2013, 129) (Figure 40.2).

Ships were used by pilgrims for longer journeys to shrines such as St Andrews in Scotland, Walsingham in Norfolk, and Canterbury in Kent (Webb 2000, 230). For the latter some disembarked at the Southampton 'Pylgrymesgate' dock, while Walsingham could be accessed via King's Lynn where ships carrying pilgrims offloaded at the Purfleet quay in the heart of the town. Many pilgrims heading for the shrine of the Apostle St James the Greater at Santiago de Compostela in Spain took ship from a number of ports on the south coast, including Southampton, Dover, and Winchelsea in East Sussex (see Chapter 59). The sea route, via Bordeaux or more directly to La Coruña (the port for Compostela), became more popular from the fourteenth century with the introduction of the 'cog' type of vessel, which sat higher in the water. One of these was licensed by the Crown at this time to carry 160 pilgrims (Yeoman 1999, 115).

Pilgrims were accommodated in monastic guest houses, in taverns, and inns, or as the paying guest of local householders (Webb 2000, 226). In these cases, identifying specific functions is an almost impossible task for the archaeologist, however more than one thousand medieval hospitals in Britain, many of which originated as cells of larger religious institutions, also provided food, shelter, and alms to pilgrims. Some of these offered hospitality for travellers, while others gave medical attention or were dedicated to lepers. Sometimes named Maison Dieu, hospitals like these can be found both at pilgrimage destinations as well as en route to them. Some were planned to resemble

FIGURE 40.2 Artist's reconstruction of the church, hostel, and harbour for pilgrims en route to St Andrews across the Firth of Forth

(© David Simon)

a monastic claustral plan, provided with an infirmary hall instead of a church nave, adjoining a chapel at the east end, while the domestic buildings were arranged adjacent around one or more courtyards. The infirmary usually contained two rows of screened off beds to either side, accommodating often no more than twenty individuals.

A good example, conveniently located on the Watling Street highway to Canterbury and the European mainland via Dover, is the Hospital of Blessed Mary of Ospringe, near Faversham in Kent (Smith 1979, 85). This Maison Dieu had benefitted from royal patronage from its origins in around 1230. As well as providing occasional accommodation for the king and royal household, the hospital was intended to provide temporary lodging for pilgrims as well as longer-term care for the infirm. Excavations have revealed the overall plan of sets of ranges around two courtyards, including part of the infirmary hall and its reredorter, or latrine. The hall was built of flint, about 30 m in length, with a central arcade of octagonal stone pillars. Other structures included kitchens and a bakehouse, as well as a finely decorated (possibly royal) guest chamber with an undercroft and first-floor guest hall (Figure 40.3). The principle buildings of hall and chapel were both regarded as sacred, and here conformed to a hinged plan where the hall was set at right angles to the chapel, as was also the case at St Mary's Strood and St John's Canterbury. Elsewhere, topography and water supply permitted an in-line plan for the infirmary hall and chapel, as at St Mary's Chichester, and at the Maison Dieu houses at Portsmouth and Dover. Either plan was suitable so long as it allowed the inhabitants direct access to the chapel. The Ospringe excavations produced substantial evidence of material culture, along with food remains; the hospital apparently relied on an income from selling wool, from rents in money and food, and from the raising of animals for

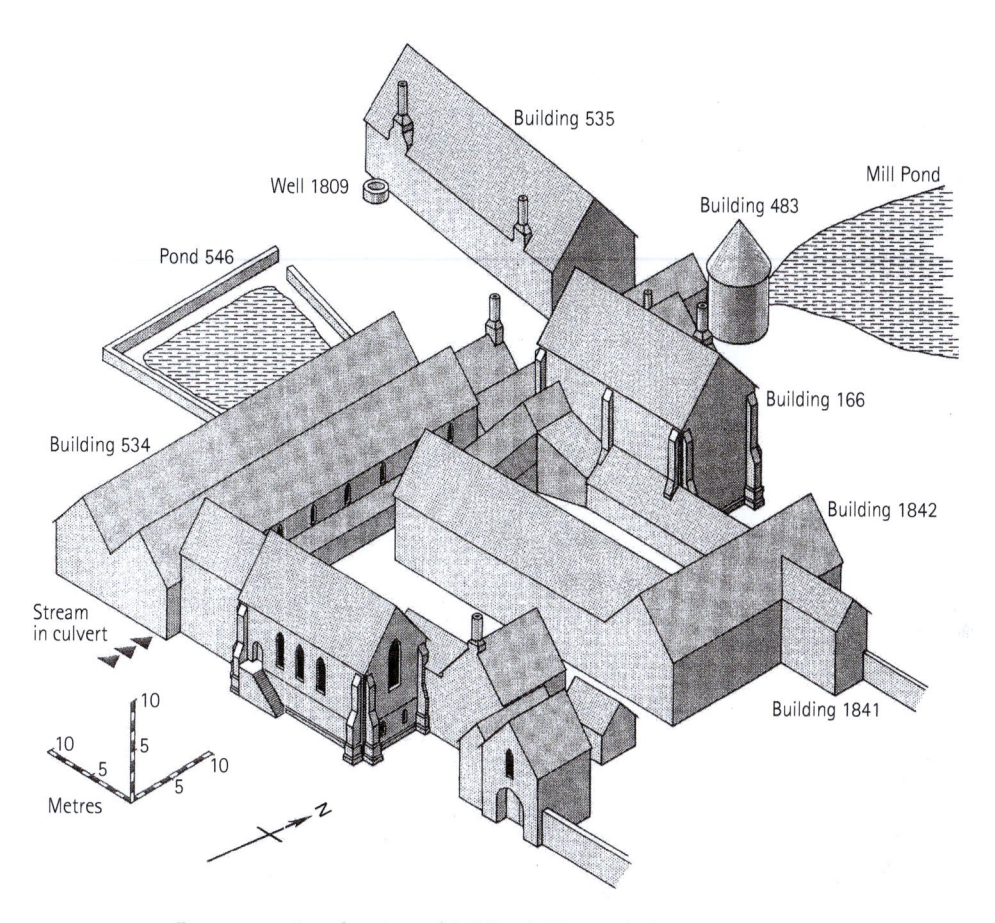

FIGURE 40.3 Reconstruction drawing of St Mary's Hospital, Ospringe, Kent, in its developed form c.1250. The chapel was on the south side fronting Watling Street, adjoining at right angles the long infirmary hall to the west (Building 534)

(© Kent Archaeological Society)

the table on their own land (Smith 1979). The best survival of a pilgrim's infirmary hall in Britain is St Mary's Chichester on a site donated by the Greyfriars in the thirteenth century. The timber-framed building consists of six massive oak-constructed bays with a chapel at the east end, all completed by 1292. The chief hospitals in London—St Mary Spital, St Barts, St Thomas's, and St Mary Bethlehem (Bedlam)—all offered accommodation and alms to pilgrims. They were run by Augustinian brethren, with lay sisters caring for the sick in wards split by gender (Barber et al. 2013, 86).

Once pilgrims reached their destination of choice, there were various opportunities for parting with their money in the cemeteries and greens around the church, or by gates and at the church door. Archaeological evidence may survive for the stalls which sold food and drink, pilgrim souvenirs, wax candles, and ex voto body parts representing ailments for which pilgrims sought cures. A seller of pilgrim badges named Adam Chapman is recorded as having leased a booth near the entrance to Westminster Abbey in the 1360s (Spencer 1998, 8).

AT THE SHRINE

An archaeological approach is helpful to understand the development and function of pilgrimage churches, along with the often fugitive remains of the shrines they once held. The majority of major shrines were in cathedrals, where offerings from pilgrims helped to finance massive building programmes; these were designed in part to provide an even more glorious setting for the cult of the saint who had chosen that place, thus creating a virtuous circle (Webb 2000, 39). The expansion of pilgrimage shrines from the twelfth century onwards attracted a broader public, allowing ordinary folk unique access to sacred spaces which were normally the preserve of churchmen and nobles. The reliquary churches provided a ritual arena within which the supernatural power of the saints could be controlled, and where the church officials could carefully control the movement and behaviour of pilgrims, who occasionally arrived in great numbers.

It is rarely possible for an archaeological approach to be taken to the relational ordering of space in the vicinity of a monastic shrine, but this is what has been attempted by Pestell at the largely destroyed Bromholm Priory, Norfolk, the site of which now lies beneath farm buildings and fields. The priory obtained a famed relic of the True Cross in 1195, following which the brethren of what was intended to be a sacred closed place had to resolve the dichotomy of how to deal with influxes of pilgrims. This issue formed part of the research design for a project based on the application of field-walking and metal-detecting which aimed to chart areas of use through 'the presence and distribution of different types of material culture', some of which can be interpreted as the casual losses of a visiting population. This innovative approach is helpful in achieving a better understanding of spatial dynamics in the wider setting of the shrine (Pestell 2006). Pilgrims, for example, often entered a reliquary church by a porched doorway on the north side of the nave. Evidence of ritual activity can be found here, in the form of incised crosses traditionally recorded as 'pilgrim crosses'. These have been attributed to pilgrims either making the vow of pilgrimage, or upon their safe return to their home parish (Matt Champion pers. comm.).[2]

The layouts of churches also provide clues. To accommodate pilgrims who came to see the famous relic of the Holy Blood, Hailes Abbey in Gloucestershire was designed with an elaborate ambulatory with radiating chapels built at the east end in 1270. Some pilgrimage churches were able to develop on two levels with a crypt or under-church, allowing a more complex sequence of controlled movement, with stops at tombs, shrines, and altars along the way. In this the pilgrims benefitted from multiple opportunities to invoke the intercession of the saint, while the church benefitted from multiple opportunities for offerings to be made. This was the case at all three shrines of the great native saints of Scotland: Columba at Iona, Kentigern at Glasgow, and Ninian at Whithorn (Yeoman 1999). Similarly, this was also true at Canterbury where the cult of St Thomas featured a prescribed route including the north transept where he had been murdered in 1170, then down to the crypt where he was originally entombed, back up to the Corona chapel at

---

[2] See also http://www.medieval-graffiti.co.uk/.

the far east end of the church to venerate the relic of the sword-sliced top of his skull, and finally to the elevated shrine in the usual location behind the high altar. The purpose-built chapel in this location was known as a feretory. Most shrines and altars were destroyed in the Reformation, but careful examination of wear patterns on floors and steps can still help us identify where key ritual activity took place. Clues can also be found in the vestiges of hooks for hangings, fixings for wall cupboards and screens, and for beams upon which reliquary containers were securely fixed, together with concentrations of graffiti, all of which can help identify foci of popular spiritual significance.

As with St Thomas, sainthood necessitated the removal of the body from its original burial place, to be translated into an elevated reliquary container. This was usually a substantial tiered stone structure, requiring a major foundation, an example of which was observed in excavations at Lichfield Cathedral, part of the lost shrine of St Chad (Nilson 1998, 49). Medieval images of the shrine of Edward the Confessor in Westminster Abbey show pilgrims crawling in and out of the lower apertures, which allowed them to touch the sarcophagus within. The polished marble base for St Margaret's shrine survives *in situ* at Dunfermline Abbey (Yeoman 1999), whereas at Lincoln Cathedral much of the architectural base of the shrine of St Hugh's head still exists at the east end of the Angel Choir. Although destroyed, *ex situ* remains of shrine bases can also be identified, for example at Canterbury where fragments of the rose-pink imported Mediterranean marble from St Thomas's shrine were recovered (Tatton-Brown 1981, 51).

Principal corporeal relics were often placed atop the architectural base in a highly decorated church-shaped chest, carved, jewelled, painted and gilded, or covered in silver plate, known as a *chasse*. The relics and their containers were often the most costly possessions of these reliquary churches, and so physical security measures were required. Evidence of these can be sought, for instance, in the ceiling fixings of ropes and pulleys which allowed the ornamental cover of the *chasse* to be removed on feast days. The Feretarius was responsible for revealing the covered shrine, as described in the Rites of Durham of the late 1500s: 'and when they had made their prayers, the clerk did let down the cover and did lock it at every corner' (Nilson 1998, 85). Occasionally a separate structure was required as in the unique circumstances at Walsingham, where a full-size timber replica of the Holy House of Nazareth was enshrined within a chapel, external to the north aisle of the nave, with stairs and a door giving access between the two. Excavations in 1961 identified the rebuilt stone chapel dated to the fifteenth century, with a raised platform in the middle upon which the House would have stood. Pilgrims could have accessed this from the church without disturbing the canons' worship in the choir and presbytery, with the west porch of the chapel providing a one-way exit (Well 1963).

Pilgrim Badges

One of the most important components of a pilgrimage was the purchase and the conspicuous wearing of badges and other souvenirs which identified the wearer as a pious pilgrim. Across western Europe, the archaeological record has confirmed that the age of pilgrimage began in the later twelfth century and this is reflected in the mass production of cheap lead-tin cast metal *ampullae* (miniature flasks) and badges at pilgrimage places, dating from this time. Brian Spencer, in leading research into this subject, has suggested that across Christendom and over a period of four centuries their manufacture ran into millions (Spencer 1998, 13). In Britain, *ampullae* appear to have been the most common pilgrimage takeaway until they were superseded by badges in the early fourteenth century. These sacred souvenirs had to display clearly the shrine or place of origin through their design, to be worn conspicuously as their credentials on the pilgrim's hat, clothing, or bag (Spencer 1998, 3). Most English badges were fitted with pins, resembling openwork brooches, often enclosed in an architectural frame, sometimes with clips for holding a backing of coloured parchment or shiny metal foil. By contrast, badges from Scottish and Continental shrines were usually solid, rectangular tokens, with fixing rings for sewing onto clothing (Spencer 1998, 4). Natural objects, imbued with the power of the shrine, can also occur in the archaeological record as pilgrim amulets, such as stones, glass, or even pottery fragments from near the shrine, or other exotic objects purchased there and curated by their owner thereafter. The pre-eminent example of this is the natural scallop shells from the Galician coast of Spain which from the later eleventh century became the insignia, universally recognized and associated with the pilgrimage to the shrine of St James the Greater at Compostela (see Chapter 59). These are typically found pierced with a pair of attachment holes drilled through the bulbous beak of the upper part of the bivalve. Spencer has suggested that the Santiago scallops were especially prized as they were evidence that their owners had undertaken this most arduous and dangerous journey, representing nothing less than a passport to heaven (Spencer 1990b, 799–801).

Badges became touch-relics having been placed on or near the shrine and thereby absorbing some of the power of the saint and divine grace (Gilchrist 2008, 129). They were considered to have apotropaic powers, which might protect the wearer on the journey, while providing benefit to others when the pilgrim arrived home again. The liquid contents of *ampullae* from the pre-eminent English shrines of Walsingham and Canterbury were objects capable of magical healing (Anderson 2010). The primary memento from the latter was the so-called 'Becket's blood', which reputedly contained a microscopic dilution of this sacred fluid to be administered as a medicine. *Ampullae* from the Marian shrine in North Norfolk were filled with water from the holy wells which still exist at Walsingham to this day.

A search of the Portable Antiquities Scheme website[3] reveals records of over one thousand pilgrim's souvenirs, with about two-thirds of these being *ampullae*, chiefly from Walsingham and Canterbury. The wide distribution of these finds serves to emphasize the point that badges are rarely found at the shrine, but end up at the home place of the pilgrim (Spencer 1990a, 799). Many hundreds have been found in excavations in London on or near the foreshore, some being thrown into the Thames possibly

---

[3] https://finds.org.uk/database.

in thanksgiving for a safe return, their owners following an established ritual practice. Indeed, an individual pilgrim might purchase a number of badges, one intended specifically for deposition in this manner. Recovery improved from 1982 when Thames Mudlarkers with their metal detectors were employed as part of excavation teams. The results of these excavations were of great importance to the wider study of badges, as the close dating of waterfront deposits through associated coins and ceramics established a chronological framework for the badges, some of which could be matched to actual moulds found at or near the distant shrines (Spencer 1998, 24, 26). Significant numbers of badges have similarly been found by the river banks at Salisbury and Canterbury, presumably as a result of the same practices (Spencer 1990b).

King's Lynn Museum in Norfolk holds a large collection of pilgrimage artefacts which originated as a bequest from Thomas Pung, a Lynn jeweller in Victorian times, who paid children to find badges in the Purfleet mud. Among its treasures are two-sided badge moulds of expensive imported limestone found at Walsingham; such moulds were usually designed with multiple matrices to cast a batch of badges in one go. Moulds are also occasionally recovered en route to, but at a distance from, the shrine. For example, part of a Walsingham mould was found in Norwich at the Cinema City excavations, in a rubbish pit at the back of a merchant's house in the middle of the medieval city. It was cheaply but well made from local fine-grained mudstone, designed to cast large openwork Annunciation badges featuring the Virgin Mary and the Archangel Gabriel within a canopied frame representing the Holy House. The earliest known Walsingham form of this type is dated *c.*1320–1400. Remarkably, a badge found at London Bridge in 1891 fits perfectly with this matrix (Wallis 2009, 480). The most likely explanation is that pilgrims from Norwich, or else travelling through Norwich possibly via the River Wensum, bought at least one Walsingham badge before setting off (Figure 40.4).

It therefore seems likely that in some pilgrimages it was essential to obtain specific badges at key points along the way, as well as at the shrine. A similar find was made at Anchor Green, North Berwick, where a fragment of a badge mould was found near the Forth crossing on the St Andrews pilgrimage route. This had been created to cast solid badges of St Andrew on his saltire cross, with stitching rings at each corner, along with at least two other matrices for casting crucifixes (Addyman et al. 2013, 80). Recently, more thought has been given to the location and disposal of these highly prized objects, suggesting that in fact there was little or no accidental loss of badges, and that the find-spot may be associated with purposeful burial. Consequently, it is no longer sufficient to study pilgrimage souvenirs as simply devotional objects, their subsequent utility when brought home must also be considered (Hall and Spencer 2012, 203).

Badges have been found in what would have been medieval fields, as well as in the vicinity of urban buildings. The Perth High Street excavations produced the greatest number of pilgrim's badges from any Scottish site, from contexts spanning the entire thirteenth century, and when recently published the authors considered their contexts in relation to their function. A Becket *ampulla*, a St Andrew's badge, together with a Compostela scallop shell, all came from a substantial hall with chambers, while a second scallop and another Becket *ampulla* came from the midden of a nearby property,

FIGURE 40.4 Fragment of mould for casting Walsingham Annunciation badges found in the Cinema City excavations in Norwich (left), together with a mould-match badge from the Thames foreshore in London (right)

(© joint copyright Norwich Castle Museum and Art Gallery and the Museum of London)

all dated to *c.*1200. It was suggested that the Canterbury *ampulla* had been attached to a bread oven constructed within the midden, the flask providing protection against fire or simply blessing the baking of the bread (Hall and Spencer 2012). Spencer has suggested that, judging from the range of find-spots on excavations, badges were buried in foundations or possibly attached to buildings to provide apotropaic protection to people and livestock, in both urban and rural locations (Spencer 1998, 18). Anderson has gone on to explore the thesis that badges were buried in fields to ensure fertility and as a magical herbicide, even as part of ceremonies to bless the fields, thereby explaining the discovery of large number of *ampullae* by metal-detectorists on rural sites (Anderson 2010).

Ampullae are usually found with their seals broken, and often in a crumpled state usually attributed to damage acquired from being in the ground, and then flattened during the conservation process. Two Canterbury Becket *ampullae* were found in this state during the excavations at Cuckoo Lane in Southampton in a stone-lined pit at the back of a merchant's house, possibly deposited *c.*1300 (Platt and Coleman-Smith 1975, 293). It has now been suggested that, once their contents were emptied, the *ampulla* may in fact have been deliberately crumpled and folded, as a ritual 'cancelling-out' and then buried again in order to anchor the magic to that particular spot (Hall and Spencer 2012, 205).

Spencer's exhaustive catalogue of pilgrim badges found in London excavations includes numerous examples from more than one hundred shrines across western Europe, the great majority in France, some of which were visited by pilgrims undertaking journeys to the major shrines of Compostela, Rome, and Jerusalem. These can helpfully identify the various routes and detours which were followed (Spencer 1998, 215–71 and fig. 13). For example, the badge of St Giles found in the excavations at St Ninian's shrine at Whithorn in south-west Scotland is likely to have been collected by a Scot travelling to Compostela by way of the Rhone region of southern France, who may have then presented this souvenir to his local saint to mark his safe return (Yeoman 1999, 48, fig. 29b). The primary purpose of foreign travel may not necessarily have been pilgrimage, and some of this activity was no doubt carried out as an adjunct to trade, in this case the wine trade, or else mercenary service.

Pilgrim Burials

Christians were meant to go unclothed into the grave, but being buried with the accoutrements of a pilgrim was the ultimate expression of identity for an individual who had sought salvation by this means, and wished to be seen as such when he or she arose fully fleshed from their grave on the Last Day. Bearing in mind the large numbers of badges which existed, it is rare for them to be found in graves. One such example, however, was the burial of an adult male outside the chapel of the hospital of St Giles by Brompton Bridge, Yorkshire. The deceased had died around the mid- to late thirteenth century and two lead badges, from pilgrimages to shrines at Lucca and Rome, had been placed on his breast before burial (Gilchrist and Sloane 2005, 97).

Pilgrim burials are commonly identified from an accompanying pierced scallop shell which had been attached to their final costume. This shell was often obtained at Compostela, or else was indicative of an avowed intention to make that pilgrimage; by the twelfth century Compostela was regarded as one of three 'great' pilgrimages, the others being Rome and Jerusalem. More than two hundred pierced natural scallop shells have been found in medieval contexts across western Europe, 90 per cent of which are from pilgrim burials. Excavations in the old village of Schleswig, Germany, produced eleven burials, each with a shell dated to the late eleventh to fourteenth centuries. Another German example was found within the church of St Dionysius, Esslingen, from the late twelfth century, where disturbed graves produced twenty-five shells, all perforated for attachment (Lubin 1990, 22; Santiago 1985, 291–3). The earliest known example in Britain is from Wallingford, Oxfordshire, where excavations at St Martin's church revealed an individual buried around 1000 with his scallop (Christie and Creighton 2013, 286). At Keynsham Abbey, Bristol, a pierced scallop was found with a burial dated to the late twelfth century, the shell having been coloured with yellow, black, and red paint (Santiago 1985, 293, no. 173). One burial in the medieval cemetery of St Helen's at Fishergate, York, was found to have a scallop close to hip level of a mature adult woman who may have been buried wearing her pilgrim's scrip (satchel) (Spall and Toop 2005). This is unusual in that the majority of burials with shells are male.

Excavations at St Mary Magdalen's hospital, Winchester, revealed the burial of a mature male pilgrim who had suffered from leprosy and had died in the later twelfth century; he was buried just outside the medieval chapel within a carefully designed anthropomorphic grave cut which included a head niche. The individual was found with a single scallop shell at his left hip; the shell had been pierced with two small holes. This had probably been attached to the pilgrim's scrip, its strap over his right shoulder (Roffey 2012, 221) (Figure 40.5). It is fascinating to note that pilgrimage may have been one mechanism by which new strains of leprosy were introduced to Britain at this time (Mendum et al. 2014). At least one individual was found buried with a scallop shell in excavations undertaken at the cemetery at Durham Cathedral (Norman Emery pers. comm.).

Two more scallop-shell burials of adult males were found in excavations beneath St Nicholas East Kirk, the principal church of the medieval burgh of Aberdeen. They had been buried under the floor of the choir, probably in the twelfth century. One burial of a young man had a pierced scallop at the left hip, while the burial of an old male had two scallops near the top of his head, which had probably been attached to a hat. Another Scottish pilgrim was found in the cemetery during the Hirsel excavations, in the cemetery close to the north-west corner of the church. Here an adult male had been buried, probably at some time in the fourteenth century, with a pierced scallop close to his head, perhaps attached to a hat worn to the grave (Cramp 2014, 285).

Scotland has also produced the most graphic post-mortem presentation of a pilgrim. Excavations at the small priory on the May Island at the mouth of the Firth of Forth, about 50 km east of Edinburgh, revealed the burial of a young man found under the floor of the church, in a place of honour in front of the high altar. What made this burial so exceptional was that his mouth had been wedged open shortly after he died with a sheep bone, to allow the upper valve of a scallop shell (*Pecten maximus L.*) to be inserted into the man's mouth (Figure 40.6). No other comparable burial accompanied by a

FIGURE 40.5 Late twelfth-century burial of male leper pilgrim with scallop shell at his hip, St Mary Magdalen's Hospital, Winchester

(© Simon Roffey)

FIGURE 40.6 Burial of young man c.1300 from St Ethernan's Priory, May Island, Fife, with a Compostela shell inserted into his wedged-open mouth soon after death

(© Fife Council Archaeological Unit)

scallop shell has come to light. It was clearly the intention that the deceased should present himself to St Peter on the Day of Judgement bearing the shell of the pious pilgrim protruding from his mouth, almost like a consecrated host (James and Yeoman 2008, 180). Of course, it is impossible to be sure that he, or any other of the individuals buried with scallops, had actually made the trip to Compostela, but the deliberate nature of the identification does make this likely. The species of the shells can provide some confirmation in that almost all are the upper convex valve of *Pecten maximus L.* which is largely an Atlantic species commonly found off the Spanish coast near Compostela, or else occasionally *Pecten jacobaeus* (e.g. the Fishergate find) which is almost completely confined to Mediterranean waters.

The most remarkably complete pilgrim burial in Europe was excavated from under the floor of the crossing at Worcester Cathedral in 1986, where a man in his 60s had been buried fully clothed and booted (Figure 40.7). The cathedral was a pilgrimage place in its own right, and home to the shrines of St Oswald and St Wulfstan. Analysis revealed that he had a strong physique, with powerful leg muscles from walking long distances, with

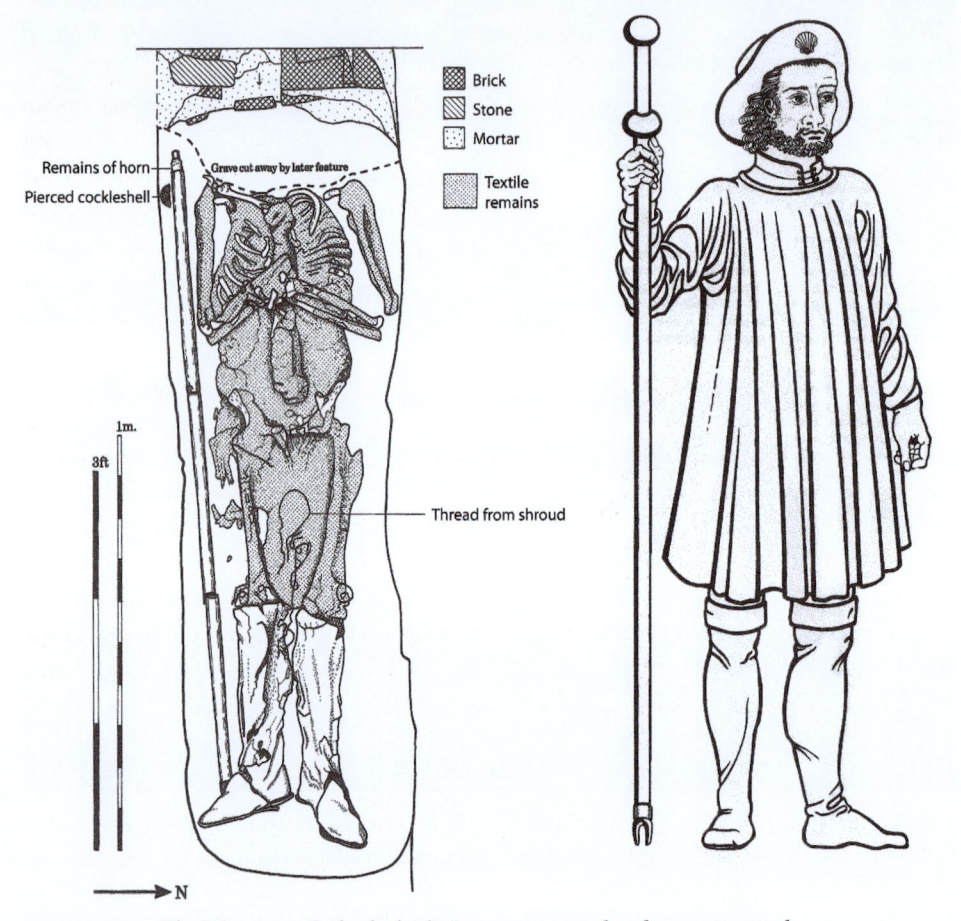

FIGURE 40.7 The Worcester Cathedral pilgrim, as excavated and reconstructed

(© Helen Lubin)

evidence of damage to his feet. The muscles on his right shoulder were particularly well developed, and his right hand very worn, possibly equated with the use of a staff, resulting in severe arthritis in later life. He was dressed in a long tunic of coarse worsted wool, and a pair of good-quality knee boots which had been cut to fit his swollen feet. Placed beside him in the grave was a 1.5 m long staff of painted ash wood, iron-spiked and horn-topped, originally with a pierced cockleshell (not a scallop) fixed to the top with a lace. Although smaller than scallops, the overall appearance of this bivalve is similar, and so served as part of his pilgrim identity (Lubin 1990).

His prestigious place of burial picks him out as a prominent member of the community, while the expensive purple colouring of his staff has given a clue to his identity. This was an expensive dye used on imported silks, leading to the suggestion that the deceased was Robert Sutton, a city dyer. Sutton's will of 1454 records his desire to be buried before the image of St James (Santiago) in the cathedral, indicating a devotion corroborated by his pilgrims' burial suit. The likelihood that he had made the pilgrimage to his patron's shrine in Galicia is increased by the fact that he also left money to the Fraternity of St James in Worcester. So, were this identification to be correct, Sutton was dressed for burial in his pilgrim garb by fellow members of his confraternity, which he had kept for many years to await this day (Lack 2005).

The Worcester pilgrim has provided so much valuable data chiefly because of his unusually good state of preservation, and elsewhere we simply cannot be sure how many pilgrim burials may have been clothed or buried with their staffs, as normally no trace would survive, except their iron points. An example of the latter was found in excavations at St Giles's Cathedral in Edinburgh, at the feet of an adult male indicating that a wooden staff had been present (Collard et al. 2006, 13). It is important, however, to be cautious in such identifications where the only evidence for a pilgrim identification is the staff, as many civic and religious officials carried a short wand or longer staff of office.

There are a small number of tomb effigies and grave slabs in which the deceased is depicted as a pilgrim. The finest of these is a late fifteenth-century effigy in St Helen's Church, Ashby-de-la-Zouch, Leicestershire. He is shown dressed in the pilgrim uniform of long cloak, with his shoulder bag or scrip by his side, and holding a long pilgrim's staff. His head rests on a broad-brimmed hat adorned with scallop shells (Adair 1978, 140). Another less well-preserved pilgrim effigy can be seen in St Mary's Haverfordwest, Dyfed. An exceptional pilgrim's grave slab is in St Tyfodwg's Llandyfodwg, Glamorgan, displaying numerous badges including the cross keys of Rome, and a scallop on his right breast, along with his boots, and tasselled scrip. He holds a wand or rod in his left hand, while his staff is grasped in his right (Adair 1978, 173).

Conclusion

Pilgrimage archaeology can help gain insights into the role of popular religion in everyday life. There is a large and growing body of archaeological evidence related to pilgrims, pilgrimages, and shrines, as well as to the materiality of pilgrimage archaeology. Research has revealed the importance of adopting new approaches to help understand behaviours at shrines, as exemplified in the analysis of spatial dynamics at Bromholm Priory, Norfolk (Pestell 2006). Further consideration of the find-spots of badges has been shown to be essential in opening up fruitful lines of inquiry into the multiple lives and uses of these powerful objects, especially in terms of their non-accidental disposal (Anderson 2010; Hall and Spencer 2012). And more can be learnt too from the pilgrim dead, who went to their graves with unique identifiers of their living experience.

Acknowledgements

The author is grateful to Tim Pestell of Norfolk Museums, Jayne Bown of NPS Archaeology, Simon Roffey of the University of Winchester, Alison Cameron of Cameron Archaeology, Elizabeth Meath Baker of Walsingham Priory, Katherine Lack, and to Matthew Champion of Norfolk Medieval Graffiti Survey, for their generous help in providing research material for this paper.

References cited

Adair, J. 1978 *The pilgrims' way*, Thames and Hudson, London
Addyman, T., Macfadyen, K., Romankiewicz, T., Ross, A., and Uglow, N. (eds) 2013 *The medieval kirk, cemetery and hospice at Kirk Ness, North Berwick: the Scottish Seabird Centre excavations 1999–2006*, Oxbow, Oxford
Anderson, W. 2010 'Blessing the fields? A study of late medieval ampullae from England and Wales', *Medieval Archaeology* 54, 182–203
Barber, B., Thomas, C., and Watson, B. 2013 *Religion in medieval London: archaeology and belief*, Museum of London Archaeology, London
Cameron, A. 2011 'Aberdeen's Mither Kirk', *Current Archaeology* 258, 12–19
Christie, N. and Creighton, O. H. (eds) 2013 *Transforming townscapes. From burh to borough: the archaeology of Wallingford, AD 800–1400*, The Society for Medieval Archaeology Monograph 35, London
Collard, M., Lawson, J., and Holmes, N. 2006 'Archaeological excavations in St Giles' Cathedral Edinburgh, 1981–93', *Scottish Archaeological Internet Report* 22, 2006
Cramp, R, 2014 *The Hirsel excavations*, The Society for Medieval Archaeology Monograph 36, London
Gilchrist, R. 2008 'Magic for the dead? The archaeology of magic in later medieval burials', *Medieval Archaeology* 52, 119–60
Gilchrist, R. and Sloane, W. 2005 *Requiem: the medieval monastic cemetery in Britain*, Museum of London Archaeology Service, London
Hall, M. A. and Spencer, B. 2012 'Devotion and belief on the Perth High Street', in D. W. Hall, G. Haggarty, A. Vince, J. di Folco, C. Martin, A. Goodall, V. Smart, M. A. Hall, J. Franklin, I. Goodall, D. Caldwell, B. Ellis, N. Q. Bogdan, J. Cherry, J. D. Bateson, A. Curteis, C. A. Morris, and D. Wright (eds), *Perth High Street archaeological excavation*

1975–77, fascicule 2: ceramics, metalwork, religious and wooden objects, Tayside and Fife Archaeological Committee, Perth, 203–20

James, H. and Yeoman, P. 2008 *Excavations at St Ethernan's Monastery, Isle of May 1992–97*, Tayside and Fife Archaeological Monograph 6, Perth

Lack, K. 2005 'A dyer on the road to St James: an identity for the Worcester Pilgrim', *Midland History* 30, 112–28

Langland, W. C. 1380 *The book concerning Piers the Plowman*, ed. R. J. M. Attwater, Dent and Sons, London

Lubin, H. 1990 *The Worcester pilgrim*, Worcester Cathedral Publications 1, Worcester

Mendum, T., Schuenemann, V. J., Roffey, S., Taylor, G. M., Wu, H., Singh, P., Tucker, K., Hinds, J., Cole, S. T., Kierzek, A. M., and Nieselt, K. 2014 '*Mycobacterium leprae* genomes from a British medieval leprosy hospital: towards understanding an ancient epidemic', *BMC genomics* 15(1), 1

Nilson, B. 1998 *Cathedral shrines of medieval England*, Boydell Press, Woodbridge

Pestell, T. 2006 'Using material culture to define holy space: the Bromholm Project', in A. Spicer and S. Hamilton (eds), *Defining the Holy: sacred space in medieval and early modern Europe*, Ashgate, Aldershot, 160–86

Platt, C. and Coleman-Smith, R. 1975 *Excavations in medieval Southampton 1953–69*, Leicester University Press, Leicester, 285–317

Roffey, S. 2012 'Medieval leper hospitals in England: an archaeological perspective', *Medieval Archaeology* 56, 203–33

Santiago 1985 *Santiago de Compostela: 1000 ans de Pèlerinage Européen*, Europalia 85 España, Keltia Graphic, Gourin (exhibition catalogue)

Smith, G. 1979 'The excavation of the hospital of St Mary, Ospringe, commonly called Maison Dieu', *Archaeologia Cantiana* 95, 81–184

Spall, C. and Toop, N. 2005 *Excavations at Blue Bridge Lane and Fishergate House*, unpublished excavation report online at http://www.archaeologicalplanningconsultancy.co.uk/mono/001/rep_cemetery.html.

Spencer, B. 1990a 'Pilgrim's badges', in M. Biddle, *Object and economy in medieval Winchester*, Winchester Studies 7ii, Clarendon Press, Oxford, 799–803

Spencer, B. 1990b *Pilgrim souvenirs and secular badges*, Salisbury Museum Medieval Catalogue 2, Salisbury

Spencer, B. 1998 *Pilgrim souvenirs and secular badges*, Medieval Finds from Excavations in London 6, Her Majesty's Stationery Office, London

Tatton-Brown, T. W. T. 1981 'The Trinity Chapel and Corona floors', *Canterbury Cathedral Chronicle* 75, 50–6

Wallis, H. 2009 'Excavations at Cinema City, Norwich 2003–06: late Saxon and medieval occupation', *Norfolk Archaeology* XLV, Part IV, 469–87

Webb, D. 2000 *Pilgrimage in medieval England*, Hambledon and London, London

Well, C. 1963 'Excavations at Walsingham Priory, 1961', *Norfolk Research Committee Bulletin* series 1 no. 14, 4

Yeoman, P. 1999 *Pilgrimage in medieval Scotland*, Batsford, London

CHAPTER 41
....

THE DEVOTIONAL IMAGE IN LATE MEDIEVAL ENGLAND

....

KATE GILES AND ALEKSANDRA McCLAIN

For contemporary writers and later iconoclasts, the later medieval visual image had particular power over its viewers. As the early fifteenth-century tract *Dives and pauper* noted: 'often man is more steryd be syghte than be heryinge or redyngge' (Barnum 1976, 82). The idea that visual images might function as a didactic tool to inspire devotion was articulated by contemporary writers such as Walter Hilton's *De adoracione ymaginum* (*c*.1380s–90s), and recognized in John Myrk's *Festial* and *Instructions for parish priests*. From Gregory the Great onwards, medieval writers argued that this was a compelling benefit for illiterate members of the laity and this function for images, seen for example in the *Biblia pauperum* or 'Poor man's Bible', has been traditionally emphasized by scholars too (e.g. Rouse 1991, 13). However, such images must also be understood within the wider context of an increase in literacy, and the growth of particular forms of affective piety amongst the laity, which were facilitated by the architectural and material transformation of late medieval parish churches (Duffy 2003; Williamson 2003).

Devotional images have increasingly been understood to have played an important role in intercessory and devotional practices which might include multi-sensory engagement, including gazing, kneeling, kissing, or touching images (Aston 2003, 69; Marks 2004, 18; Rosewell 2008, 182–8). Such an understanding has resonated with recent studies of the historicity of the senses (Biernoff 2002; Woolgar 2006; see Part VIII of this *Handbook*). The polychromatic decoration of devotional sculptures gave them particularly life-like qualities which inspired a sense of wonder or *admiratio* amongst the faithful (Boldrick et al. 2002). A compelling contemporary account of the ways in which images could inspire 'spasms of affective devotion' is provided by Margery Kempe's powerful late fourteenth-century spiritual testimony (Bale 2015).

The study of devotional images can also shed light on shifts in devotional preferences. Records and surviving examples reflect the emergence of personal, parochial, and local devotional practices, experiences associated with key biblical figures and cult images associated with miracle-working. Images of the Virgin or 'Our Lady' dominated the period, and devotional images including 'Our Lady of Boulton' at Durham, 'Our Lady of Long Melford' in Suffolk, and 'Our Lady of the Mount' at King's Lynn became centres of regional and national pilgrimage (Marks 2004, 198–203). Saints such as St George and St Christopher, St John the Baptist, and St Katherine also had national appeal and were popularized by the circulation of books such as Jacobus de Voragine's *The golden legend*, printed in 1482 by William Caxton. Other saints, such as St Cuthbert in Northumbria or St Swithin in Hampshire, offered more local foci for devotion (Riches and Gill 2007). Whilst images of individual saints could be realized across a variety of media, stained glass and wall paintings also afforded opportunities for more extended narratives of trial and suffering, such as the life and martyrdoms of saints, the Passion, or images of judgement (Rosewell 2008, 87–8). Devotional practices associated with these images were also structured and reinforced by the growth in production and consumption of Books of Hours and other devotional literature (see Clark 2014; Coleman et al. 2013 for useful recent overviews).

THE DEVOTIONAL IMAGE IN MEDIEVAL ARCHAEOLOGY

The desire to understand devotional images within their original architectural, social, and devotional contexts requires scholars to step beyond traditional disciplinary divisions and opens up the potential for archaeologists to contribute to their study. While calls for an improved integration with the discipline of history have been a staple of medieval archaeology in the past three decades, the potential of archaeological integration with art historical study has only rarely been theorized or explicitly advocated (e.g. McClain 2012; Wicker 1999). Devotional images, which sit comfortably within studies of art as well as studies of material social practice, therefore provide an opportunity to build a bridge between the two disciplines, encouraging an interdisciplinary, contextualized, and materially focused approach to religious practice in medieval society.

The primary archaeological contributions to the study of religious imagery from a methodological perspective have been in the recovery of evidence through excavation (e.g. Graves 2008a; 2015; Samuel and Schofield 2011), technical analysis and conservation (e.g. Brown 2010a; Howard 2003a; 2003b), digital visualization and analysis (e.g. Giles et al. 2012; Masinton 2006), and systematic programmes of recording (e.g. Badham 1989; Badham and Norris 1999; Gittos and Gittos 1989; McClain 2007), although the latter have been limited primarily to funerary monuments. From an interpretative standpoint, archaeology's strengths lie in analysis and interpretation beyond the piece of art itself, placing devotional imagery in its spatial, chronological, and socio-cultural contexts, and exploring the interactions and relationships between people, place, and material (e.g. Giles 2000; 2010; Graves 2000; Woodcock 2005). Archaeology can integrate the study of devotional images with a detailed examination of the development of architectural spaces within the church buildings in which they were housed, and the communities which utilized them. It can highlight their place in the devotional topography of the church, their role in liturgical practice as well as in community worship, and can also consider social motivations for devotional display, specific patrons and audiences, and bring these together with themes such as synaesthesia and sensory experience (see Chapter 42). The most consistent exemplars of this interdisciplinary approach are the *Medieval Art, Architecture, and Archaeology* conferences and transactions produced by the British Archaeological Association. Focusing on cities as a whole, regions, or individual major churches, the volumes embrace archaeology and art and architectural history, and emphasize interdisciplinary debate.

Types of Devotional Image

The following sections address some of the key categories of material evidence for religious imagery, and detail their character, use, and meaning.

Wall Paintings

Wall paintings appeared in English churches from the Anglo-Saxon period and, while examples do survive from as early as the tenth century, the vast majority date from the fourteenth and fifteenth centuries. Spatially, wall paintings could define particular liturgical spaces or settings within the church (Rosewell 2008, 167, 169–72), or serve as a physical claim on a church or space by individuals or groups of patrons, simultaneously expressing personal devotion and temporal control (Naydenova 2006). Wall paintings were also didactic and contemplative, recounting biblical and hagiographical narratives to the congregation and clergy, offering exemplars of Christian life and forming a visual focal point for prayers, sermons, and feast day celebrations (Giles 2000; Rosewell 2008, 176, 178, 181). Apart from saints' lives, frequent subjects of wall paintings included the Passion, the Last Judgment (known as a 'Doom', and often located over the chancel arch), the life of the Virgin Mary, and morality paintings such as the Corporal Works of Mercy, the Seven Deadly Sins, the Three Living and the Three Dead, and the Dance of Death (Marshall 2012).

A recent study of the wall paintings in the Stratford-upon-Avon guild chapel has highlighted the analytical value of techniques of digital modelling of medieval buildings and wall paintings from archival sources (Giles et al. 2012) (Figure 41.1). The project recreated the original scheme of wall paintings from a series of antiquarian drawings, rediscovered during nineteenth- and twentieth-century renovations, and reset them within their three-dimensional architectural context. This innovative approach allowed not only an in-depth examination of the paintings themselves, and the different antiquarian interpretations of them, but also demonstrated that wall paintings must be considered beyond the subjects depicted. They were fundamentally integrated with contemporary

FIGURE 41.1 Three-dimensional digital model of the guild chapel at Stratford-upon-Avon, focusing on the Doom painting over the chancel arch

(© Geoff Arnott)

architectural schemes, particular spaces within the church, and other decorative features, and were meant to be seen and understood in a holistic manner.

Stained Glass

Medieval stained glass in Britain is catalogued extensively in the *Corpus vitrearum Medii Aevi*, which contains more than twenty-five thousand images of stained glass from across the country, focusing on extant windows in standing buildings, rather than fragmentary finds from excavation (*CVMA* 2010). Stained glass in churches encompassed an enormous variety of themes, most commonly biblical scenes and characters, but also allegories, saints and hagiographical narratives, apocryphal stories, secular portraiture and heraldry, historical series and genealogies, geometric motifs, architectural details (real and imagined), and a wealth of marginal motifs which defy an explicitly Christian categorization (Brown 1992, 57–9). Refenestration programmes were by far the most common late medieval adaptation to the fabric of churches, and windows were a particularly attractive investment for patrons. They were a relatively quick means of updating the church to the latest architectural style, while their glass provided a conspicuous vehicle to express patronal ambitions as well as beautifying the church, and even altering the internal ambience of the building through light and colour (Giles 2007, 115). In urban parish churches, stained glass patronage seems to have been a favourite of the wealthy mercantile classes, as has been shown in the churches of late medieval York and Norwich (Barnett 2000, 76; Graves 1989, 313).

Stained glass served a variety of devotional purposes, both in the subjects depicted as well as in its role as a material element of the church building and a facet of its overall decorative scheme. Like wall paintings, stained glass images were both didactic and contemplative, and were likely used in the same way as a focus for instruction, prayers, sermons, memorial actions, or individual contemplation. They were frequently commemorative and highly personalized, depicting patrons in pious poses or actions and often flanked by their personal patron saints (Figure 41.2). Political propaganda and

FIGURE 41.2 The Corporal Works of Mercy window, All Saints North Street, York, early fifteenth century. The window likely commemorates Nicholas Blackburn Sr, Lord Mayor of York, and it is probable that the man depicted performing the acts of mercy is the patron himself

(© Steve Ashby)

social messaging sat easily beside devotional imagery, and secular messages were reinforced by their religious context (King 2008). In the hands of Anselm, Archbishop of Canterbury in the late eleventh century, stained glass also served as one facet of a coherent iconographic and philosophical manifesto, expressing his ideological position on the intersection between belief and aesthetic beauty (Heslop 2013, 77–8). Nevertheless, it is not always clear how stained glass functioned as a devotional image. Many windows, especially in great churches, were too distant for audiences to see the detail necessary to interpret its meaning or benefit from its messages. In these cases, it may have been the overall aesthetic of colour, the play of light, and the impressive scale of the glazing programme, rather than the details of the imagery, which was most effective in evoking the glory of God and the earthly Church.

Church Fixtures and Fittings

The interior decorative schemes of both great and minor churches once included wooden screens and lofts, altarpieces, retables, reredoses, statuary, hangings and tapestries, painted panels, and even architectural elements such as ceiling bosses or corbels (Williamson 2003, 376). Unlike many other devotional images discussed here, the fixtures decorating the high altar would not necessarily have been regularly accessible to the entire congregation, who were not generally allowed into the chancel area, and whose sight of the altar was often partially blocked by a screen. A sixteenth-century account of the pre-Reformation church at Long Melford, Suffolk, recounts how on the high altar there was an altarpiece featuring the crucifixion and scenes from the Passion which were 'very fair painted boards, made to shut too, which were opened upon high and solemn feast dayes, which then was a very beautiful shew' (Dymond and Paine 1992, 1). The account suggests that regular use of altarpieces as contemplative or devotional objects may well have been restricted to the clergy, and that access to and display of the fine, likely imported, altarpiece to the wider congregation was tightly managed in order to achieve the best impression on significant holy days.

Rood screens are of particular interest as devotional images, as in addition to their iconographic schemes, they also defined the spiritual topography of the church and helped control movement and sight within it. The partial blocking of sight lines into the chancel increased the mystery of the Mass, and in liturgical practice the rood screen was the point of spiritual transition between the earthly realm and the heavens—the dead were taken from the nave into the chancel through the screen, the screen was likely the point of a dramatic reveal of the body of Christ during *Corpus Christi* processions, and the congregation came to the rood screen, but not beyond it, to take communion (Lunnon 2010, 122). Although carved and pierced with tracery in earlier centuries, from the early fifteenth century rood screens began to be painted, most often with saintly, biblical, or historical figures in each of the divided panels of the screen. It has been argued that the nave-chancel/heaven-earth linking function of the rood screen meant that it was understood to symbolize the gates of heaven—a meaning which was further reinforced by the iconographic detail. On the vast majority of Norfolk screens, St Peter, the gatekeeper to heaven, occupies the panel immediately beside the screen's central opening into the chancel, and it is often flanked on the other side by angels, who are also appropriate in this context, as they acted as mediators between heaven and earth (Lunnon 2010, 123).

Reliquaries and Shrines

The cult of saints was of the utmost importance to both the practice of medieval Christianity and the economy of salvation. The physical remains of saints became both a focal point for liturgical and paraliturgical worship as well as a draw for potentially lucrative pilgrimage. Reliquaries were containers designed to hold, transport, display, and protect these remains, which were primarily fragments of bone and other body parts, scraps of clothing, or other objects purportedly associated with the holy person (Freeman 2011). Typically ornate and highly valuable, reliquaries were constructed of precious metals, ivory, or wood gilt and inlaid with gemstones. Beyond their functional role, reliquaries honoured the saint through their prestige and artistry, which also communicated to the viewing audience the significance and authenticity of the relic within, and the saint to which it once belonged (Hahn 2012, 9; see Chapter 38 in this *Handbook*). The majority of reliquaries were boxes of varying size and form, while others were shaped like crosses, and some took the form of a particular body part, such as a hand, foot, or head, although they were not always a direct representation the skeletal material contained within, as has often been assumed (Bynum and Gerson 1997, 4; Hahn 2012, 135).

In contrast to reliquaries, shrines were more architectural, ostensibly housed the complete body of the saint, and were more often focused on local saints rather than fragments of biblical personages or foreign martyrs (Crook 2011, 133). In the eleventh and twelfth centuries, tomb shrines were commonly erected over the site of a saint's burial, elevated on plinths, and integrated architecturally into new churches as part of a post-Conquest fashion for the revival of traditional local saints' cults and the translation of their relics (Crook 1998; 2011, 257). However, by the late fourteenth and fifteenth centuries, tomb shrines had often been replaced by portable wooden or metal feretories which tended to be brought out and presented on particular occasions (Malo 2013), enabling interaction with the saint to be more carefully controlled, and its use in the liturgy stage-managed. While often concealing the actual relic from view, reliquaries and shrines themselves became objects of great spiritual power, serving as conduits for the saint's intercession and benevolence. By seeing, venerating, or touching and kissing the container, supplicants could receive spiritual benefits even without physical contact with the holy relic itself.

Commemorative Art

Medieval churches featured a wide array of commemorative art, including brasses, sculpted effigies, tomb chests, and grave slabs, stained glass, chantry chapels, stone inscription panels, cloths and palls, and pulpits, fonts, and seating (Badham 2014; 2015). In the Middle Ages, there was a direct link between commemorative and devotional practice. As the deceased required the prayers of the living to progress through Purgatory, commemorative images were a means of reminding audiences of a particular individual's need for intercession, and the object gave the viewer a devotional and contemplative focus to encourage more effective prayer. As time went on, the objects themselves actively solicited devotional action, as the phrase '*Orate pro anima*' steadily replaced '*Hic iacet*' as the standardized inscriptional form all on commemoration in the late Middle Ages. Elaborate late medieval *transi* tombs, which featured effigies of both the deceased in life and in cadaverous death, encouraged the viewer to use the tomb as a *memento mori,* and to think of the health of their own souls, as well as that of the deceased. The *transi* tomb of Archbishop of Canterbury Henry Chichele (Figure 41.3) explicitly evoked the viewer's death with the inscription 'Whoever you may be who will pass by, I ask for your remembrance, you who will be like me after you die: horrible in all things, dust, worms, vile flesh' (Binski 1996, 143).

Objects of Personal Devotion

Outside of the confines of churches, a wide variety of portable objects were used as items of personal devotion, including pilgrim badges and *ampullae*, figurines, jewellry, and illustrated manuscripts such as Books of Hours. Of these objects, pilgrim signs have received the most attention from archaeologists, due to their frequent discovery by metal-detectorists (e.g. Spencer 2010; Spencer and Blick 2007; see Chapter 40 in this *Handbook*). Inexpensive and mass-produced, pilgrim badges were acquired at the pilgrimage site as souvenirs of the journey, but they also served as tangible proof, to both divine and human audiences, of the wearer's piety and his merit of the appropriate indulgence for his travels. *Ampullae* were miniature flasks used to transport holy water or oil filled from the shrine site, to be taken back to ailing relatives, or to bless a house or fields. Like pilgrim badges they were often decorated with an image from the saint's life, or a widely recognized representative emblem, such as the scallop shell of Santiago de Compostela. Pilgrim souvenirs have been found in burial contexts, perhaps as personal objects emblematic of piety, or for the amuletic properties inherent in an object which had been touched to a saint's shrine (Gilchrist 2008, 130, 152).

Other objects of personal devotion were worn as adornments, such as small gold pendant crosses which were outwardly symbolic of Christian piety, as well as containing secret compartments to hold relics or other apotropaic materials personal to the wearer (Cherry 2003, 332; see Chapter 38 in this *Handbook*). A more elaborate example of this type of devotional jewellry is the Middleham Jewel, a fifteenth-century gold lozenge-shaped pendant found near Middleham Castle, Yorkshire (Figure 41.4). It is notable for its large inlaid sapphire, and the exceptionally fine, detailed engraving

FIGURE 41.3 The cadaver tomb of Archbishop Henry Chichele, Canterbury Cathedral, c.1425

(© Xavier de Jauréguiberry)

FIGURE 41.4 The Middleham Jewel, fifteenth century, featuring an engraving of the Trinity, inset sapphire, and inscription

(© York Museums Trust, CC BY-SA 4.0)

of the Trinity, the Nativity, and fifteen different saints. The jewel was undoubtedly an aid to conventional Christian devotional practice, but its form and iconographic and inscriptional schemes suggest that it also held very specific significance to its owner (Jones and Olsan 2000). The jewel is a locket which was found with small fragments of embroidery inside, suggesting a reliquary or amuletic function. In addition, sapphires were believed to have medicinal effects, and the magical words *tetragrammaton* and *ananizapta* are inscribed around the edges of the engraved scenes, the latter being a charm against epilepsy or other seizure syndromes. Taken together with the Nativity scene and the engraved saints, some of which have connections with femininity and childbirth, it has been suggested that the jewel was commissioned as an intercessory object for a woman who may have been concerned about her health and possibly problems with pregnancy (Cherry 1994, 34).

Objects of private ritual were frequently recorded in household inventories and wills, demonstrating the widespread practice of informal worship in the household or more formalized, but still extra-parochial, practice in private chapels (Foister 2003, 334). Figurines, painted panels, rosaries, and Books of Hours proliferated amongst the wealthy classes as tangible spiritual tokens, focal points for prayer and meditation, and displays of wealth and artistic patronage. Painted diptychs and triptychs featuring biblical scenes and saints' portraits, as well as polychrome wooden and bronze figurines of saints and the Virgin Mary, were frequently imported from Germany and the Low Countries, and England's own alabaster industry also provided a great number of carved panels and miniatures (Foister 2003, 336, 342). Although finer examples with more personalization could be commissioned directly from the artist, many examples were mass-produced, putting this form of private devotional art in increasing reach of the middle classes (see Chapter 59 for exports to Spain).

Also benefitting from trends towards mass-production were Books of Hours, which were produced in vast quantities from the mid-thirteenth to the mid-sixteenth centuries. They were small illustrated manuscripts containing a series of litanies and prayers, typically including a calendar, Gospel lessons, the Hours of the Virgin, Cross, and Holy Spirit, the Penitential Psalms, the Office of the Dead, and a variety of other prayers (Wieck 1997, 9–10) (Figure 41.5). The Book of Hours became the premier tool of lay devotion, and they both facilitated the personal religious experience of their owners as well as displayed their social and cultural values to an audience of their peers (Smith 2003, 1). The imagery featured in Books of Hours was as significant as the prayers themselves, and they were designed as integrated textual and visual objects; the images informed the text, and the text influenced the viewer's contemplation of the images. Given Books of Hours' close association with the cult of the Virgin, and the female role as guardians of the family's spiritual welfare, these manuscripts became particularly significant to expressions of female piety in the late Middle Ages. The Books are also speculated to have held a role in education in the household, particularly of female children, mirroring the frequently depicted trope in Books of Hours of St Anne teaching the Virgin to read (Goldberg and Callum 2000; Rees Jones and Riddy 2006). Rather than being silently recited, the prayers in Books of Hours were often spoken aloud and in groups, embodying the textual, visual, and auditory 'multimedia' experience that was typical of medieval churches and Christian practice as a whole (Smith 2003, 4–5).

FIGURE 41.5 Christ enthroned and holding the Crucifixion, with patrons depicted praying below. Folio 33 recto from the Bolton Book of Hours, early fifteenth century

(© Chapter of York: reproduced by kind permission)

Case Study: St Botolph, Boston

St Botolph's church, Boston (Lincolnshire) is an impressive reminder of the architectural contexts in which devotional practices were structured in the later Middle Ages (Figure 41.6). Boston was one of wealthiest ports of late medieval England, attracting merchants from across Northern Europe, especially from the Baltic, to its market and annual fair. Ranked fifth in the 1334 subsidy, its changing fortunes have been studied closely by economic historians of the later Middle Ages. The rebuilding of St Boltoph's church in c.1309–90 has been seen as a symbol of civic wealth and pride, led by Margaret de Tilney, a member of one of Boston's leading mercantile families (Badham and Cockerham 2012). The parish of Boston was divided into a number of 'fees' throughout the medieval period and the town's political and cultural life was dominated, in the absence of a formal 'guild merchant', by nineteen religious guilds (Badham 2012). Most prominent of these was the guild of St Mary, which according to its return to Parliament made in 1389, was founded in 1260 by a group of prominent citizens and landowners (Brammer 1993; Giles and Clark 2011). The guild was granted a series of royal licences of incorporation granted between 1392 and 1447 and became an internationally successful fraternity, acquiring property and lands across England and as far as Calais. This was partly a result of the guild's securing a remarkable series of Papal indulgences which included the grant in 1520 of the supreme accolade of a 'Jubilee indulgence'. Visitors to the Marian feasts at Boston who completed a threefold circuit of seven altars within the church received a pardon equivalent to that obtained by visiting the *limina* of SS. Peter and Paul in Rome, or Compostela in Spain (Swanson 2007, 134–6 and 172–3).

The nave of St Botolph's church was dominated by the chapel of St Mary's guild, located in the east end of the south aisle, as well as that of SS. Peter and Paul, located in the east end of the north aisle. The west end of the south aisle also originally provided access to the now-lost chapel of Corpus Christi. Archaeological evidence suggests that St Mary's guild chapel was subdivided from the south aisle by a tall parclose screen, which was probably decorated with images of saints. The chapel preserves a sedilia for the guild priests, deacons, and subdeacons, who had their own chantry house, located near the guild's hall on South Street.

Two surviving inventories of St Mary's guild dating to 1530/1 and 1533 shed unique light on the range and scale of devotional imagery owned by the guild, all of which disappeared after its suppression at the Reformation (Badham 2012; Giles 2010). The inventories also reveal how devotional images adorned a smaller guild chapel and the objects used within its guildhall (Giles and Clark 2011). At the east end of St Mary's chapel was a 'high altar', dedicated to 'Our Lady' and this chapel also had subsidiary 'side altars' for which candlesticks and altar cloths were provided. Images of the Virgin unsurprisingly dominated the guild's devotional foci. Wooden and alabaster images of the Virgin are recorded in the chapel in St Mary's guildhall, and it seems likely that the main guild chapel had similar statues. Amongst the textiles recorded by

FIGURE 41.6 St Mary's guild chapel, St Botolph's, Boston, Lincolnshire

(© Kate Giles)

the inventories was 'a mantle for our Lady of cloth of tissue parcelled about with powder ermine of the gift of Masters Thorneborow'. Other images of the Virgin appear designed for more intimate contemplation, such as the 'little long box of ivory with an image of Our Lady of ivory there enclosed'.

Marian imagery also featured prominently on the guild's textiles. An altar cloth 'of white damask with eagles standing upon books with scriptures on their heads with a frontal of the same thereto belonging', framed by 'curtains of white satinett stained with images, the one of our Lady and the other of Gabriel with birds, standing on books' provided the backdrop for the priest, deacon, and subdeacon. They sat in their sedilia and officiated Mass resplendent in a set of matching vestments depicting 'Eagles of gold standing on books bearing scriptures on their heads and orphrays of a story of Our Lady'. The altar itself was adorned with a cross, featuring the Virgin on one 'branch', flanked by another image of St John and enamelled with a sovereign of gold. Prominently displayed as a focus for devotional contemplation was a reliquary containing 'part of the milk of our Lady', consisting of a 'case of silver and gilt with an image our Lady standing above with her child on her hand'. The inventories also record a basin decorated with a gilt rose and an image of the Virgin and a maser featuring the Virgin and lily pots. Some metalwork, such as the 'piece of silver with a print of the image of Our Lady on the bottom of the gift of William Aston of Castyr' was noted as having been delivered to the chaplains, but it had either been recycled from a previous devotional object, or had not yet found its devotional function. Devotional images of the Virgin were also moveable. The 'stained banner cloth of linen cloth with the image of our Lady and certain images of men and women kneeling before her' could have been used in guild processions, especially during the Jubilee, or during the funerals of guild members, where coffins would be draped with one of the guild's three hearse cloths, including one 'of brocade with image of the Assumption of our Lady with lily pots' and a valance of black worsted.

Another feature of the devotional imagery of the guild chapel would have been the funerary monuments of the guild's patrons set in the floor, which would have been placed there to attract prayers from the guild members frequenting the chapel. The monuments include the brasses to Thomas Flete and his wife, Athelard Bate and his two wives, and the indent of a now anonymous priest, marked only by the outline of a chalice (Badham and Cockerham 2012, 178, 182, 189). Flete was likely a lawyer who donated land and a 'booke of lawe' to St Mary's guild, probably to secure his prestigious burial location in the guild chapel (Badham and Cockerham 2012, 106). Bate's situation was less straightforward, as his slab is marked with the sign of the Holy Trinity and his will specifies a bequest to that guild, but also stipulates that if the Trinity guild would not take it, it should devolve to St Mary's. His burial place indicates that this final course of action must have been taken, and the incongruence of the iconography of Bate's brass versus its location highlights the complexity of the links between imagery, patronage, and the topography of the church.

St Mary's guild inventories and the wills and monuments of its members provide powerful evidence of the richness and diversity of devotional imagery in medieval parish churches. The reliquaries, crucifixes, banners, vestments, altar cloths, and hearse cloths of the guild provided its members with a series of devotional images of the Virgin. These would have been complemented by more permanent fixtures of St Mary's chapel, such as the polychromatic, life-like images of the saints on its stonework, screens, and stained glass. And yet less than fifteen years later, when St Mary's guild was suppressed, all of these objects disappeared from view. Understanding the loss of devotional imagery from the context of the early modern parish church and the religious lives of its parishioners is one of the greatest challenges for scholars of the Reformation.

The Reformation and Iconoclasm

The very power of the devotional image in late medieval England also made it particularly vulnerable to the reformers of the sixteenth century. During the fifteenth century, Wycliffite and Lollardian writers had criticized the potentially idolatrous qualities of devotional images. They criticized the intense sensory relationships between the devout and images of Christ and the saints, and ridiculed belief in the miraculous properties of both images and relics. Although their writings seem to have had only a limited impact on the use of images within contemporary devotional practice (Aston 2003, 69; Dimmick et al. 2002; Somerset et al. 2003), they provided an important foundation for the much wider reform movements of the early sixteenth century (Aston 1988; Duffy 1992; Kamerick 2002; Philips 1973).

Medieval archaeologists and art historians have long bemoaned the impact of the Reformation(s) on the material culture of the parish church. At one level, it has largely destroyed the artefactual evidence for the devotional practices of the late Middle Ages. The underlying narrative of the archaeology of the Reformation is one of destruction and loss, preserved in the negative evidence of ruined buildings, empty mortices, or traces of fixtures and fixings, wall scars, and disrupted floors and paving (Aston 1998; Duffy 1992; Gaimster and Gilchrist 2003; Graves 2008b). The potential to trace more subtle and nuanced accounts of individual parochial responses to successive waves of Reformation, including examples of resistance and concealment, is beginning to be recognized and told through local case studies such as that of Morebath (Devon) (Duffy 2001), Wing (Buckinghamshire) (Marks 2004, 258–75), Bradbourne (Derbyshire) (Moreland 1999), and Stratford-upon-Avon (Warwickshire) (Giles et al. 2012).

Recent theoretical shifts, particularly approaches to the 'biography' of objects and buildings, provide an opportunity to trace the histories of creation, use, destruction, and re-purposing of devotional images in the history of the church (Caple 2006; Hamling and Richardson 2010; Hoskins 1998). Whilst art historical and archaeological specialists will undoubtedly continue to analyse the particular evidence for the production and use of devotional images within disciplinary specialisms, there is more to say about the 'afterlife' of the devotional image. The particular nature of iconoclastic practices, including the targeted removal of head and hands and the gouging out of eyes, particularly of polychromatic 'lifelike' devotional images, has been noted by scholars and curators (Aston 1988, 96–143; Boldrick et al. 2002; Duffy 1992, 379ff.; Lindley 2001, 29–37; Philips 1973), and Graves (2008b) has drawn attention to the anthropological significance of these acts. The tendency for archaeologists to be interested in the *longue durée* of the parish church also affords them the opportunity to think about the enduring significance and power of devotional images, such as when they were re-discovered and recorded by clergy and antiquarians during nineteenth-century restoration works (e.g. Giles et al. 2012; Moreland 1999).

Interdisciplinary approaches to the study of the devotional image also open up new ways of curating, displaying, and interpreting them to the public. Marks (2004, 5; also Netzer 2000) notes that in museums, devotional images are inevitably abstracted from their original contexts and meaning, in order to serve the interests of art historical chronologies and taxonomies. Exhibitions such as the Tate's *Image and idol: medieval sculpture* (Deacon and Lindley 2001) and the Victoria and Albert Museum's *Gothic: art for England* (Marks and Williamson 2003) have therefore sought to re-contextualize these objects within devotional practice and the parish church. Others, such as the Henry Moore Institute's *Wonder: painted sculpture from medieval England*, have sought to use alternative forms of curatorial practice to display devotional images 'as new works, transformed rather than ruined by their fragmentation' (Boldrick et al. 2002, 28). Scholars have yet to grasp fully the possibilities of virtual-modelling techniques to support conventional scholarly narratives and curatorial strategies of the devotional image, but this is undoubtedly one area of considerable future potential within archaeological and digital humanities approaches to religious art.

References Cited

Aston, M. 1988 *England's iconoclasts*, Oxford University Press, Oxford

Aston, M. 2003 'The use of images', in R. Marks (ed.), *Gothic: art for England 1400–1547*, V&A Publications, London, 68–75

Badham, S. 1989 'Monumental brasses: the development of the York workshops in the fourteenth and fifteenth centuries', in C. Wilson (ed.), *Medieval art and architecture in the East Riding of Yorkshire*, British Archaeological Association, London, 165–85

Badham, S. 2012 '"He loved the guild": the religious guilds associated with St Botolph's church', in S. Badham and P. Cockerham (eds), *'The best and fairest of al Lincolnshire': the Church of St Botolph, Boston, Lincolnshire, and its medieval monuments*, British Archaeological Reports British Series 554, Oxford, 49–73

Badham, S. 2014 'Commemoration of the dead in the late medieval English parish', *Church Archaeology* 16, 1–19

Badham, S. 2015 *Seeking salvation: commemorating the dead in the late medieval English parish*, Shaun Tyas, Donington

Badham, S. and Cockerham, P. (eds) 2012 *'The best and fairest of al Lincolnshire': the Church of St Botolph, Boston, Lincolnshire, and its medieval monuments*, British Archaeological Reports British Series 554, Oxford

Badham, S. and Norris, M. 1999 *Early incised slabs and brasses from the London marblers*, The Society of Antiquaries, London

Bale, A. 2015 *The Book of Margery Kempe*, trans. by A. Bale, Oxford University Press, Oxford

Barnett, C. M. 2000 'Commemoration in the parish church: identity and social class in late medieval York', *Yorkshire Archaeological Journal* 72, 73–92

Barnum, P. H. 1976 *Dives and pauper, Vol. 1*, Early English Text Society original series 275, Oxford University Press, Oxford

Biernoff, S. 2002 *Sight and embodiment in the Middle Ages*, Palgrave Macmillan, Basingstoke

Binski, P. 1996 *Medieval death: ritual and representation*, British Museum Press, London

Boldrick, S., Park, D., and Williamson, P. 2002 *Wonder: painted sculpture from medieval England*, Henry Moore Institute, Leeds

Brammer, B. 1993 'The guild of the Blessed Virgin Mary', in M. Ormrod (ed.), *The guilds in Boston*, Pilgrim College, Boston, 35–44

Brown, S. 1992 *Stained glass: an illustrated history*, Studio Editions, London

Brown, S. 2010 'Stained glass conservation at York Minster: past histories, future challenges', in L. Pilosi, M. Shepherd, and S. Strobl (eds), *The art of collaboration: stained glass conservation in the twenty-first century*, Brepols, Turnhout, 57–64

Bynum, C. W. and Gerson, P. 1997 'Body-part reliquaries and body parts in the Middle Ages', *Gesta* 36(1), 3–7

Caple, C. 2006 *Objects: reluctant witnesses to the past*, Routledge, Abingdon

Cherry, J. 1994 *The Middleham jewel and ring*, Yorkshire Museum, York

Cherry, J. 2003 'Dress and adornment', in R. Marks and P. Williamson (eds), *Gothic: art for England 1400–1547*, V&A Publications, London, 326–33

Clark, R. L. A. 2014 'Spiritual exercises: the making of interior faith', in J. Arnold (ed.), *The Oxford handbook of medieval Christianity*, Oxford University Press, Oxford, 271–86

Coleman, J., Cruse, M., and Smith, K. A. 2013 *The social life of illumination: manuscripts, images and communities in the late Middle Ages*, Brepols, Turnhout

CVMA 2010 *Corpus vitrearum Medii Aevi*, http://cvma.ac.uk, last viewed 11/01/2016

Crook, J. 1998 'The architectural setting of the cult of St Edmund at Bury 1095–1539', in A. Grandsen (ed.), *Bury St Edmunds: medieval art, architecture, archaeology and economy*, British Archaeological Association, London, 34–44

Crook, J. 2011 *English medieval shrines*, Boydell, Woodbridge

Deacon, R. and Lindley, P. 2001 *Image and idol: medieval sculpture*, Tate Britain, London

Dimmick, J., Simpson, J., and Zeeman, N. (eds) 2002 *Images, idolatry and iconoclasm in late medieval England: textuality and the visual image*, Oxford University Press, Oxford

Duffy, E. 1992 *The stripping of the altars: traditional religion in England c.1400–c.1580*, Yale University Press, New Haven and London

Duffy, E. 2001 *The voices of Morebath: Reformation and rebellion in an English village*, Yale University Press, New Haven and London

Duffy, E. 2003 'Late medieval religion', in R. Marks (ed.), *Gothic: art for England 1400–1547*, V&A Publications, London, 56–67

Dymond, D. and Paine, C. 1992 *The spoil of Melford Church: the Reformation in a Suffolk parish*, Suffolk Books, Ipswich (2nd edn)

Foister, S. 2003 'Private devotion', in R. Marks (ed.), *Gothic: art for England 1400–1547*, V&A Publications, London, 334–47

Freeman, C. 2011 *Holy bones, holy dust: how relics shaped the history of Medieval Europe*, Yale University Press, New Haven and London

Gaimster, D. and Gilchrist, R. (eds) 2003 *The archaeology of Reformation 1480–1580*, The Society for Post-Medieval Archaeology Monograph 1, Leeds

Gilchrist, R. 2008 'Magic for the dead? The archaeology of magic in late medieval burials', *Medieval Archaeology* 52, 119–59

Giles, K. 2000 'Marking time? A 15th-century liturgical calendar in the wall paintings of Pickering parish church', *Church Archaeology* 4, 42–51

Giles, K. 2007 'Seeing and believing: visuality and space in pre-modern England', *World Archaeology* 39(1), 105–21

Giles, K. 2010 'A table of alabaster and the story of the doom: the religious objects and spaces of the guild of Our Blessed Virgin, Boston (Lincs)', in C. Richardson and T. Hamling (eds), *Everyday objects: medieval and early modern material culture and its meanings*, Ashgate, Aldershot, 267–88

Giles, K. and Clark, J. 2011 'St Mary's Guildhall, Boston, Lincolnshire', *Medieval Archaeology* 55, 226–56

Giles, K., Masinton, A., and Arnott, G. 2012 'Visualising the guild chapel in Stratford-upon-Avon: digital models as research tools in historical archaeology', *Internet Archaeology* 32

Gittos, B. and Gittos, M. 1989 'A survey of East Riding sepulchral monuments before 1500', in C. Wilson (ed.), *Medieval art and architecture in the East Riding of Yorkshire*, British Archaeological Association, London, 91–108

Goldberg, P. J. P. and Callum, P. 2000 'How Margaret Blackburn taught her daughters: reading devotional instruction in a Book of Hours', in J. Wogan Browne (ed.), *Medieval women: texts and contexts in late medieval England*, Brepols, Turnhout, 217–36

Graves, C. P. 1989 'Social space in the English medieval parish church,' *Economy and Society* 18, 297–322

Graves, C. P. 2000 *The form and fabric of belief: an archaeology of the lay experience of religion in medieval Norfolk and Devon*, British Archaeological Reports British Series 311, Oxford

Graves, C. P. 2001 *The window glass of the Order of St Gilbert of Sempringham: a York-based study*, Council for British Archaeology, York

Graves, C. P. 2007 'Sensing and believing: exploring worlds of difference in pre-modern England', *World Archaeology* 39(4), 515–31

Graves, C. P. 2008a 'Architectural fragments', in J. Mann (ed.), *Finds from the well at St Paul-in-the-Bail, Lincoln*, Oxbow Books, Oxford, 20–2

Graves, C. P. 2008b 'From an archaeology of iconoclasm to an anthropology of the body: images, punishment and personhood in England, 1500–1660', *Current Anthropology* 49(1), 35–57

Graves, C. P. 2015 'Stained and painted window glass', in R. Gilchrist and C. Green, *Glastonbury Abbey excavations: archaeological investigations 1904–79*, The Society of Antiquaries of London, London, 320–36

Hahn, C. 2012 *Strange beauty: issues in the making and meaning of reliquaries, 400–circa 1204*, Pennsylvania State University Press, University Park, Pennsylvania

Hamling, T. and Richardson, C. 2010 *Everyday objects: medieval and early modern material culture and its meanings*, Ashgate, Farnham

Heslop, T. A. 2013, 'St Anselm and the visual arts at Canterbury Cathedral, 1093–1109', in A. Bovey (ed.), *Medieval art, architecture and archaeology at Canterbury*, British Archaeological Association, Leeds, 59–81

Heslop, T. A. 2015 'The Norwich Cathedral Passion altarpiece ("The Dispenser Retable")', in T. A. Heslop and H. E. Lunnon (eds), *Norwich: medieval and early modern art, architecture and archaeology*, British Archaeological Association, Leeds, 201–15

Hoskins, J. 1998 *Biographical objects: how things tell the stories of people's lives*, Routledge, London

Howard, H. 2003a *Pigments of English medieval wall painting*, Archetype Publications, London

Howard, H. 2003b 'Technology of the painted past: recent scientific examination of the medieval wall paintings of the Chapter House of Westminster Abbey', in R. Gowing and A. Heritage, *Conserving the painted past: developing approaches to wall painting conservation*, Routledge, London, 17–26

Jones, P. M. and Olsan, L. T. 2000 'Middleham jewel: ritual, power, devotion', *Viator* 31, 249–90

Kamerick, K. 2002 *Popular piety and art in the Late Middle Ages: image worship and idolatry in England 1350–1500*, Palgrave Macmillan, New York

King, D. 2008 'Reading the material culture: stained glass and politics in late medieval Norfolk', in L. Clark (ed.), *Rule, redemption and representations in late medieval England and France*, The Fifteenth Century VIII, Boydell, Woodbridge, 105–34

Lindley, P. 2001 'Introduction', in R. Deacon and P. Lindley (eds), *Image and idol: medieval sculpture*, Tate Britain, London, 29–53

Lunnon, H. E. 2010 'Observations on the changing form of chancel screens in late medieval Norfolk', *Journal of the British Archaeological Association* 163(1), 110–31

Malo, R. 2013 *Relics and writing in Late Medieval England*, University of Toronto Press, Toronto

Marks, R. 2004 *Image and devotion in late medieval England*, Sutton Publishing, Stroud

Marks, R. and Williamson, P. (eds) 2003 *Gothic: art for England 1400–1547*, V&A Publications, London

Marshall, A. 2012 'Medieval wall painting in the English parish church', http://www.thepaintedchurch.org, last viewed 10/1/2016

Masinton, A. W. 2006 *Sacred space: priorities, perception and the presence of God in late medieval Yorkshire parish churches*, unpublished PhD thesis, University of York

McClain, A. 2007 'Medieval cross slabs in North Yorkshire: chronology, distribution, and social implications', *Yorkshire Archaeological Journal* 79, 155–93

McClain, A. 2012 'Theory, disciplinary perspectives and the archaeology of later medieval England', *Medieval Archaeology* 56, 131–70

Moreland, J. 1999 'The world(s) of the cross', *World Archaeology* 31(2), 194–213

Naydenova, M. 2006 'Public and private: the late medieval wall paintings of Haddon Hall chapel, Derbyshire', *The Antiquaries Journal* 86, 179–205

Netzer, N. 2000 'Collecting, re/collecting, contextualising and recontextualising: devotion to fragments of the Middle Ages', in N. Netzer and V. Reinburg (eds), *Fragmented devotion: medieval objects from the Schnutgen Museum, Cologne*, McMullen Museum of Art, Chicago (ILL), 17–30

Panofsky, E. 1927 '*Imago Pietatis*: Ein Beitrag zur Typengeschicte des "Schmerzensmanns" under der "Maria Mediatrix"', *festschrift für Max. J. Friedlander zum 60, Gerburstag*, Leipzig, 261–308

Philips, J. 1973 *The Reformation of images: destruction of art in England, 1535–1660*, California University Press, Berkeley, Los Angeles and London

Rees Jones, S. and Riddy, F. 2006 'Female domestic piety and the public sphere: the Bolton Hours of York', in J. Wogan Browne and A. Mudder Bakke (eds), *Household, women and Christianities in late Antiquity and the Middle Ages*, Brepols, Turnhout, 215–60

Riches, S. and Gill, M. 2007 'Saints in medieval society', in *Pilgrims and pilgrimage: journey, spirituality and daily life in the Middle Ages*, Centre for the Study of Christianity & Culture (3rd edn), Interactive CD-Rom

Rosewell, R. 2008 *Medieval wall paintings in English and Welsh churches*, Boydell, Woodbridge

Rouse, E. C. 1991 *Medieval wall paintings*, Shire Publications, Haverford West

Samuel, M. and Schofield, J. 2011 'Moulded stones: factual data and methodology of reconstructing the rose window', in J. Schofield, *St Paul's Cathedral Before Wren*, English Heritage, London, 265–75

Smith, K. A. 2003 *Art, identity and devotion in fourteenth-century England: three women and their Books of Hours*, The British Library, London

Somerset, F., Havens, J. C., and Pitard, D. G. 2003 *Lollards and their influence in late medieval England*, Boydell and Brewer, Woodbridge
Spencer, B. 2010 *Pilgrim souvenirs and secular badges*, Boydell, Woodbridge
Spencer, B. and Blick, S. 2007 *Beyond pilgrim souvenirs and secular badges*, Oxbow, Oxford
Swanson, R. N. 2007 *Indulgences in late medieval England: passports to paradise?*, Cambridge University Press, Cambridge
Wicker, N. 1999 'Archaeology and art history: common ground for the new millennium', *Medieval Archaeology* 43, 161–71
Wieck, R. 1997 *Painted prayers: the Book of Hours in medieval and Renaissance art*, George Braziller, New York
Williamson, P. 2003 'The parish church', in R. Marks (ed.), *Gothic: art for England 1400–1547*, V&A Publications, London, 375–423
Woodcock, A. 2005 *Liminal images: aspects of medieval architectural sculpture in the south of England from the eleventh to the sixteenth centuries*, British Archaeological Reports British Series 386, Oxford
Woolgar, C. 2006 *The senses in medieval England*, Yale University Press, New Haven and London

PART VIII

AN ARCHAEOLOGY OF THE SENSES

CHAPTER 42

OVERVIEW

The Medieval Senses

EMMA J. WELLS

To date, the medieval senses have remained largely the preserve of historians; even the most comprehensive archaeological perspectives have focused primarily on either ancient societies or how today's construct of the senses has affected our ability to study those of the past (Hamilakis 2004; 2014; Howes and Classen 2013). In terms of an *application* of a sensory theoretical methodological framework to medieval data, the field is very much in its early stages, with the majority of previous work dominated by prehistoric phenomenological analyses, such as the seminal studies by Shanks and Tilley (1992), Tilley (1994; 2004; 2010), and Ingold (2000). Complementary studies have been developed from anthropological (e.g. Brück 2005; Classen 1997; 2005; Howes 1991; 2005), geographical (e.g. Rodaway 1994), and philosophical theories, and elucidated how the embodied experience of monuments, artefacts, and landscapes are more fully understood by engaging with visual hermeneutics and sensory perceptions (Johnson 2012; Thomas 2006, 43). Gradually these types of methodological approaches transferred over to the medieval domain. The *Archaeological review from Cambridge* (Jones and Hayden 1998) first introduced the theme of perception and the senses, combining prehistoric with medieval case studies to understand the diverse ways in which people perceived and conceptualized their surroundings through analyses of material culture and the structures with which they interacted.

The olfactory has been a particular focus of archaeological analyses from a largely cultural (and prehistoric) context (Bartosiewicz 2003; Hamilton and Whitehouse 2006; Howes 2006b; Kleinschmidt 2005, 57–92), but few investigate the medieval concept of smell within a theoretical context (see Chapter 45). The meaning of scent in the early Christian era was as a vital and active symbol; a point of contact between the corporeal and incorporeal as well as temporal and spiritual worlds that other 'higher' senses could not replicate: 'to encounter a scent was to encounter proof of a material presence, a trail of existence which could be traced to its source' (Classen et al. 1994, 205; Harvey

FIGURE 42.1 Star pattern made by the vault cross-ribs above the feretory in which St Cuthbert's shrine was housed, Durham Cathedral

(© Emma J. Wells)

2006, 105). Through a holistic sacred encounter, fragrance transcended the boundaries of daily life and brought spectators into closer communion with God and his pantheon of saints, giving them a 'presence' and permeating the memory (Brazinski and Fryxell 2013, 12; Renfrew 1985, 16).

Sound has also been a major subject of sensory archaeology (see Chapter 25). Identified as archaeoacoustics (Blesser and Salter 2007, 88; Scarre and Lawson 2006), acoustemology (Feld 1996, 97; Sullivan 1986; Webb 2004), and musicology (Willis 2010), there have also been medieval research applications (e.g. Berger 2005; Hale and Campbell 2007; Kisby 2001). These studies found that sound was central to perception, arguing, for example, that 'aural and visual symbolism became tightly linked', was central to sacred edification, and thus to the construction of religious buildings, but that the acoustic properties of shrines were an accidental by-product of design (Blesser and Salter 2007, 93). The devotional infrastructures of the medieval church were actually *both* functional and aesthetic (Recht 2008, 17), as illustrated by the original eleventh-century apse of Durham Cathedral. The curved nature of the space itself, together with the cylindrical and spherical surface of the vaults (Figure 42.1), would have provided acoustics of resounding quality in addition to perfect harmonics (Reznikoff 2006, 82).

Discussions of the haptic (tactility) (Classen 2005; Howes 2005; Paterson 2007), taste (Korsmeyer 2005; Parkhurst Ferguson 2011; Sutton 2001; Woolgar et al. 2006; see Chapter 43 in this *Handbook*), artistic vision (Chapter 46), and bodily interaction are also vital for understanding the human experience of our multi-faceted cultures. This literature illustrates that analyses of the senses cross disciplinary boundaries like never before and that sensuous scholarship has become integral to an understanding of social construction in past societies (Howes 2003; 2006a).

Synaesthesia: the Interplay of Senses

The closest the field has come to understanding sites as multi-sensory entities is through the emerging concept/theory of synaesthesia which has been crucial to the progression of sensory studies. Deriving from the ancient Greek term for 'sensation' (*syn-* meaning 'together' and *aesthesis* meaning 'sensual apprehension'; Pentcheva 2006, 631), synaesthesia refers to 'the simultaneous body-mind interplay of multiple senses' (Drewal 2005, 4). In the modern sense the effect is neurological or psychological and allows sound to take on visual qualities so that one may associate certain colours with music and, essentially, 'hear colour' (Chidester 1992, 14–15). In the medieval theoretical sense, synaesthesia is more a unity or convergence of the senses.

Synaesthetic metaphors were a common staple of dogmatic vocabulary (the best example being the visual and aural concept of the Word) as religious symbolism was (and still is) grounded in sensory perception (Chidester 1992, 22). In fact, aural and visual symbolism came to be tightly linked inside the medieval church, usually being the first two senses to be engaged upon entry. This connection was then exploited further through the sensory qualities of its art and architecture (Blesser and Salter 2007, 93). Many late medieval shrines, for example, were of the rather open *foramina*-design or contained niches for pilgrims to interact with the sarcophagus. The shrine of St Werburgh at Chester Cathedral (Figure 42.2) contained six recesses where kneeling pilgrims inserted their heads whilst pleading their petition. Not only did these apertures provide acoustical properties

FIGURE 42.2 Prayer niches of the shrine of St Werburgh, Chester Cathedral

(© Charlotte Stanford)

appropriated for experience as the amplified echoes of pilgrims' prayers reverberated around the enclosed space creating an intimate encounter with the saint, but the visual isolation further contributed to the feeling of private worship, as did the small tactile space, turning the cavity into a private arena of veneration (Blesser and Salter 2007, 88).

Abundant similar approaches to the archaeology of the sacred landscape have been undertaken (Candy 2009; Jones and Semple 2012; Locker 2015) and have sought to better understand this experience from the perspective of the worshipper or pilgrim through analyses of travel, space, and accompanying art and architecture (Ashley and Deegan 2009; Lee 2008; Morris and Roberts 2002). These arguments, often structured by theological and sociological methodologies, paved the way for multidisciplinary studies on the subject of medieval religiosity and spirituality, and showed how shrines and their surroundings became sanctified, and how sensory elements were used to control response (Hahn 1997). Recent research has built upon this to show how the late-medieval English church should not only be viewed as a complete sensory structure or 'intersensorial', but that its construction was intended to affect its visitors: church architects and patrons, aware of this combined effect, chose to create spaces filled with colours, lights, sounds, smells, and tactile surfaces, wherein very rich sensory experiences could occur (Wells 2013). An increase in the sensory aspects of the decorative and architectural schemes of a cult church was a direct result of the demand by pilgrims for enhanced interaction with their devotion and hence the more forms of saintly engagement provided, the more heightened the overall experience of the cult which gave greater prestige to the church, authenticity to the relics, and subsequently enticed more pilgrims to visit (Wells 2011, 141). The church building may therefore be referred to as a theatre, with its sensory stimulants acting as the plot, and the art and architecture subassuming the role of the props (Swanson 1992, 240).

The Medieval Senses

Medieval theories and attitudes towards the senses were very different and, in many respects, far more sophisticated than our modern-day notions. Perceptions of the world, as well as belief in what was real and what was fictional, were much more intertwined and predicated on divine guarantees than the modern mind can easily comprehend. The Middle English term *sentir* or 'to sense' could be employed for thinking, tasting, or even smelling. Previous to the sixteenth century, *sense* was not generally held as a faculty of perception, but senses were often seen in combination, such as *taster/tasten* for both touch and taste (Woolgar 2006, 6). The use of *sentir* therefore refers to almost all of the senses suggesting that a distinction between the five (although defined in literary convention) was not believed in practice, and an amalgamation or unification of the senses was how experience was generated. The separation, and indeed presence, of the five senses recorded in modern western classifications was much less significant for many past societies, and even for many today (Giles 2007, 107). This is largely due to the fact that the senses functioned through either practical/physical participation in rituals and devotions, and/or mentally through ideology, imagination, and discourse. The five bodily senses or *sensus carnalis* were just one strand of the Latin term *sensus* (Rahner 1979): essentially, a metaphor based on the bodily sensory experiences used to portray heaven and hell or God and Satan, the spiritual beings external to this world. The other strand signified the inner, or spiritual, senses—the *sensus communis*—able to 'capture immaterial realities' (Caseau 2014, 90).

The difference between the medieval and the modern is that our perception and belief in reality is based on individual, empirical (and therefore physical) sensory experience. In the medieval era, not only were senses seen to 'team-up' but experience occurred through a reciprocal process which allowed transference of the tangible to the spiritual, or intangible qualities, through the bodily senses. Through faith in this belief, connection with material objects and ephemera was considered to bring people closer to what they could not effectively see, hear, taste, touch, or feel but which they considered to be real. For example, the senses established a system of communication with God and the saints; they were tools or aids to interest and teach the faithful about unseen spiritual realities (Casaeu 2014, 106). Accordingly, Christian liturgies were often based on the ability to make physical contact with the holy and involved the entirety of the senses, be it passively receiving sensations or through an active deliberate participation. Veneration posited unification between the senses and physicality of the body.

Physicality has dominated the majority of sensory scholarship thus far, whether under the auspices of archaeology or in the fields of history, anthropology, or English literature. The senses have been conveyed as more of an influence on the body, a feeling. Yet while this interpretation is correct, if it were the only perspective it is unlikely that the iconoclastic reforms that occurred throughout Europe in the sixteenth and seventeenth centuries would ever have taken place. The mutilations were directed against the head and the hands for a specific reason with some reformers treating images in the way that bodies would be treated in capital and corporal punishment (Graves 2008, 48). This was predicated on the fact that, firstly, images of the Holy Family and saints were regarded as representing their protagonists in realistic ways (i.e. saints were intercessory aids who could perform earthly miracles) and, secondly, cultural understanding was that those specific features signified more of the life-force than other bodily attributes: through the ears Christians came to hear the Word of God and through the eyes they could follow or 'see' religious events (Biernoff 2002, 137–8; Caseau 2014, 90).

A Case Study: Sensory Devotion and Spirituality

In terms of understanding medieval sensed spirituality, the church building as a material presence has been the obvious place to view how belief was structured and worship practised. Analyses have centred on how the art and architecture impacted upon the sensory attributes of the devotee; for example, how specific materials were chosen for their tactile qualities, shrines for their ability to allow bodily engagement with the holy, the use of incense to signify sanctity (Figure 42.3), or galleries added for

FIGURE 42.3 Part of a pilgrim sign, possibly a badge, made of pewter and showing a man swinging a censer for burning incense, fourteenth to fifteenth centuries. Recovered from the River Wear below Elvet Bridge in Durham

(© Gary Bankhead)

amplification (Meskell 2005; Wells 2013). It is through these types of studies that we can see how devotion and its material form developed and changed over time in relation to an impact on the senses. Margaret Aston's (2003) and Matthew Milner's (2011) work on the alleged reduction in the role of the senses, or visual apparatus of worship, caused by the iconoclasm of the Early Modern era showed just how instrumental a vessel the church can be for illustrating religious practice and change over time. The white-washing of saintly figures on the fifteenth-century rood screen at Binham Priory (Norfolk) is a significant example as it provides evidence of the sixteenth-century Reformation practice of obliterating images of saints as well as their usurpation by the Word of God, as black scripture was painted straight over the whitewashed saintly figural representations (Figure 42.4). Aston explained: 'What started with the proscription of the touchability of the holy climaxed with censorship of the seeability of the divine' (2003, 9). Yet the wash was not entirely effective and the medieval saintly faces now show through the text as if being summoned out of concealment, providing the archaeologist with significant material evidence for these momentous phases of our religious past.

But such scholarship has also flagged up the problems involved when reconstructing a church building—and particularly how worship was enacted within it—through

FIGURE 42.4 The rood screen at Binham Priory, Norfolk, showing sixteenth-century whitewash and text over the fifteenth-century figural depictions

(© David Griffith)

its material remains. Studies have generally approached the issue from two perspectives: either focused simply on the fabric, a construction-phase analysis of how the structure changed and was altered over time within the field of buildings archaeology or even art history; or, through a consideration of its materiality, be that sculpture, textiles, tombs, church treasuries, or metalwork objects which specifically relate to church function. Rather, the requirement is for interpretations that do not separate these component elements, dismissing the meaning of cues, motifs, or, more correctly, the hermeneutics behind the aesthetic of architecture so significant to the audience of the time, which leads to the sensory influence becoming overlooked (Binski 1995, 7; Kieckhefer 2004).

Medieval devotees not only visited devotional sites but experienced the vibrant array of sculpture, artefacts, and images, with interactions moving them physically, emotionally, and mentally. Participating in a venerable experience involved a holistic use of the senses. Sensory engagement was inherent, ranging from the burning of incense and candles, or the sight of vestments and paintings, to the aural sounds of the churches and monasteries: stimulation of the senses was inescapable. As a result, the sensory aspects of devotional art and architecture were not coincidental but designed for interaction and, as such, patron and artist had an underlying interest in creating works that inspired and heightened such reactions to generate an ultimate experience. Works were designed with specific interactive goals in mind so that churches could physically and mentally 'touch', communicate, and enforce understanding through assertive reciprocal performative means using images, sounds, and smells. In his *Apologia* of 1125, Bernard of Clairvaux (1090–1153) highlighted the importance of these sensory aids, stating: 'We know that the bishops ... use material beauty to arouse the devotion of a carnal people because they cannot do so by spiritual means' (Rudolph 1990, 318–19). For example, the plans of church buildings demanded movement via certain routes, while art and architecture concealed and revealed en route through both two- and three-dimensional outputs (Blick and Gelfand 2011, xxxxvii). In this way complex and theological discourses could be grasped through the sensory engagement of congregants, turning the church into an institution of performance, with the building acting as the spatial arena through which this process could evolve (Stevenson 2010).

Yet it was not only during the liturgies that theatrical spectacles were used. Devotion towards the cult of saints was also designed to convey drama and spiritual captivation. Pilgrimage was commonly described as 'seeing with the senses' (Frank 2000b, 9), deriving from the early Christian desire to visit Jerusalem in order to see and touch places where Christ was believed to be physically present. In *Flores epytaphii sanctorum*, Thiofrid, Abbot of Echternach (d. 1110), even construed relics as objects defined by the senses (Palazzo 2011, 103). Expressions of the physicality of this type of worship have also been uncovered throughout the designs of the architectural and decorative schemes, and permeating the sacred locales of the shrines of St Cuthbert at Durham Cathedral and St Thomas Becket at Canterbury Cathedral (Wells 2013). The devotional act at both sites was a very physical affair, with touching, kissing, and even crawling into the shrine structure being a common practice in order to come into direct contact with the intercessory power of the divine. Both shrines were originally constructed as eleventh- and twelfth-century tomb-shrines with porthole-esque openings and were later transformed into *feretrum*-type shrines featuring fully formed niches (Crook 2011, 1–3). The reliquaries were also revealed only at certain times of the day by pulley systems which lifted canopies decorated with bells that rang out into the entire body of the church. Moreover, ritual entrances and exits were located to create specific 'pilgrim routes' or attractions within the church building—similar to the modern theme park—while strategically placed associated art and sculpture located along the routes was designed to be seen or worshipped at (Wells 2012, 72).

Throughout these medieval cult sites there exists a repetitive theme of contact in order for a devotional experience to be achieved. As a result of her analysis of the thirteenth-century narrative *Vie de Saint Jehan Paulus*, Brigitte Cazelles confirmed this by noting that 'the spectacular is no longer a matter of *looking* at the saint's body, but of *touching* it, [which] suggest[s] a treatment of the sacred focusing on the protagonist's corporeal rather than spiritual identity' (1994, 62). These few examples demonstrate the importance of the *multi-sensory* involvement and how a theatrical environment was used to set the scene for experience by developing the material frameworks of medieval churches, primarily to preserve the *memory* of each site within the mind of the worshipper (Marks 2004, 216).

The importance of the senses to memory owes its roots to classical antiquity and requires some consideration here. Scholars such as Cicero (106–43 BC) discussed the importance of the visual in the retention of memories, suggesting that 'The most complete pictures are formed in our minds of the things that have been conveyed to them and imprinted on them by the senses' (*De oratore*, 2.87.357 (LCL 1:469), quoted in Frank 2000b, 170). Memory was central to medieval devotion as it played a significant role in conjuring up the experience of Christ, the Holy Family, and the cult of saints. Devotional events had to be sensorially 'alive' and essentially impacting the body for a memorable experience to be fully comprehended, translated into a mental picture, and retained (Hagen 1990, 103). The shrines and reliquaries of saints were thus physical and metaphorical containers through which the memories could be made manifest (Carruthers 1990, 35–42).

A problem with approaches to memory, however, has been their tendency to isolate and give predominance to vision over the other senses (Frank 2000a; Hahn 2000). Understandings of how objects, images, and buildings were received through the medieval eye have significantly expanded over the past few decades with scholars such as Michael Camille (1994) and Madeline Caviness (2001a; 2001b; 2006) leading the way. The precedence of vision-biased scholarship stemmed from the idea that, in the modern western world, vision is often primary in our mode of appropriation and this has clouded the way we consider the past—more than 80 per cent of sensory input is now visual (Brück 2005, 20; Edmonds 2006; Pallasmaa 2005; Thomas 1993). The prioritization of sight is, however, actually a product of its time (Classen 1993). Plato, Aristotle, and St Augustine suggested that 'the sense of science was to be sight' (Skeates 2010, 2), and medieval scholars, such as Roger Bacon (c.1214–c.1292) and St Bernard in the twelfth century, argued that truth could only be revealed if it was presented to the eyes (Camille 1996, 22; Palazzo 2014, 244). Medieval seeing was thought to be perceived as a cue, to provide the beholder with the sense of touching the object of vision (Graves 2007, 516; Merleau-Ponty 1962; Pentcheva 2006, 631). Examples included a need to view the Elevation of the Host during the Mass in order for Transubstantiation to occur as well as the increasing visibility of relics, some of which were displayed to the faithful in transparent crystal containers.

Subsequently, it is possible to determine why these sacred spaces were filled with ostentatious displays of materiality: they were inherently sensory. Architecture, light, and space provided a fitting aesthetic context and displays of liturgical vestments, books, and vessels were combined and placed next to paintings, glass, and shrines which reached their apogee in popularity around the mid-fourteenth century. In association were aural, visual, tactile, olfactory, and even gustatory resources, e.g. instrumental music and elaborate chants accompanied saints' feast days, Masses held at altars, candles lit, incense burned, and reflections of light cast off undulating surfaces. Together this interplay of elements formed a 'production' of atmosphere that triggered emotional connotations (Fischer-Lichte 2007, 53): the final approach to the shrine or High Altar alit the five senses and thus the perception of the sacred presence (Pentcheva 2006, 651). Devotion was essentially perfected through these means so that the dialogue between mankind and saint/God could be more easily achieved in order to draw grace from the latter, and absence from presence (Burgess 2011, 108). Through the saturation of the material and sensory, the experience created transcended the physical aspects of the church building and provided access to the intangible, invisible, and therefore spiritual plane (Pentcheva 2006, 631). This discourse encouraged people to approach devotion as an embodied, live encounter through a diverse range of media and, through it, the medieval population made sense of (and 'sensed') the architectural and decorative schemes of churches which then facilitated a divine encounter within. Accordingly, it could be argued that sensory materiality was equally important as the verbal in divine worship—its 'presence' was paramount to creating a fulfilling devotional experience.

Conclusion

The archaeological landscape of spirituality and religiosity offers a rich and relatively uncharted territory for further research towards the senses. Unravelling the sensed spirituality of late medieval devotion is only the beginning of trying to understand it, but it is a dynamic field in which great progress has been made this century. Success has come from true interdisciplinary study where all types of available evidence are equally considered. This means moving beyond the visual paradigm to an even playing field free from sensory hierarchies (Butler and Purves 2013, 3). We should not be afraid to admit that the sensual culture subject is still in its infancy and be open to suggestions and tools favoured by other related disciplines so that we may achieve a more complete or, perhaps, more proper understanding of the sensoriality of the past. The contributions to this part of the *Handbook* firmly underline this point. Recognizing the possibilities of sensory investigations will greatly expand our knowledge far beyond simple readings of material culture or built structures, as when used in combination they become more than individual texts, but rather entire novels with the possibilities of exposing the experience of medieval life!

Acknowledgements

I would like to thank Louise Hampson for providing comments in the final stages of production, for the editors' kind offer to contribute to this volume, and to Charlotte Stanford, Gary Bankhead, and David Griffith for the images.

References Cited

Ashley, K. and Deegan, M. 2009 *Being a pilgrim: art and ritual on the medieval routes to Santiago*, Lund Humphries, Farnham

Aston, M. 2003 'Public worship and iconoclasm', in D. Gaimster and R. Gilchrist (eds), *The archaeology of Reformation 1480–1580*, The Society for Post-Medieval Archaeology Monograph 1, Leeds, 9–28

Bartosiewicz, L. 2003 'There's something rotten in the State … : bad smells in Antiquity', *European Journal of Archaeology* 6(2), 175–95

Berger, A. M. B. 2005 *Medieval music and the art of memory*, University of California Press, Berkeley, Los Angeles

Biernoff, S. 2002 *Sight and embodiment in the Middle Ages*, Palgrave Macmillan, Basingstoke and New York

Binski, P. 1995 *Westminster Abbey and the Plantagenets: kingship and the representation of power, 1200–1400*, New Haven, London

Blesser, B. and Salter, L. 2007 *Spaces speak, are you listening? Experiencing aural architecture*, MIT Press, London

Blick, S. and Gelfand, L. (eds) 2011 *Push me, pull you: art and devotional interaction in late medieval and Renaissance art*, Brill Academic Press, Leiden

Brazinski, P. and Fryxell, A. 2013 'The smell of relics: authenticating saintly bones and the role of scent in the sensory experience', *Papers from the Institute of Archaeology* 23(1), 1–15

Brück, J. 2005 'Experiencing the past? The development of a phenomenological archaeology in British prehistory', *Archaeological Dialogues* 12(1), 45–72

Burgess, C. 2011 'Chantries in the Parish, or "Through the Looking-glass"', *Journal of the British Archaeological Association* 164, 100–29

Butler, S. and Purves, A. (eds) 2013 *Synaesthesia and the ancient senses*, Routledge, Oxford

Camille, M. 1994 'The image and the self: unwriting late medieval bodies', in S. Kay and M. Rubin (eds), *Framing medieval bodies*, Manchester University Press, Manchester, 62–99

Camille, M. 1996 *Gothic art: visions and revelations of the medieval world*, Weidenfeld and Nicolson, London
Candy, J. 2009 *The archaeology of pilgrimage on the Camino de Santiago de Compostela: a landscape perspective*, British Archaeological Reports International Series 1948, Oxford
Carruthers, M. 1990 *The book of memory: a study in medieval culture*, Cambridge University Press, Cambridge
Caseau, B. 2014 'The senses in religion: liturgy, devotion, and deprivation', in R. G. Newhauser (ed.), *A cultural history of the senses in the Middle Ages, 500–1450*, Bloomsbury, London, 89–110
Caviness, M. H. 2001a *Medieval art in the West and its audience*, Variorum, Aldershot
Caviness, M. H. 2001b *Visualizing women in the Middle Ages*, University of Pennsylvania Press, Philadelphia
Caviness, M. H. 2006 'Reception of images by medieval viewers', in C. Rudolph (ed.), *A companion to medieval art: Romanesque and Gothic in northern Europe*, Blackwell, Oxford, 65–85
Cazelles, B. 1994 'Bodies on stage and the production of meaning', *Yale French Studies* 86, 56–74
Chidester, D. 1992 *Word and light: seeing, hearing, and religious discourse*, University of Illinois Press, Chicago
Classen, C. 1993 *Worlds of sense: exploring the senses in history and across cultures*, Routledge, London
Classen, C. 1997 'Foundations for the anthropology of the senses', *International Social Science Journal* 49(153), 401–12
Classen, C. 2005 *The book of touch*, Berg, Oxford
Classen, C., Howes, D., and Synnott, A. 1994 *Aroma: the cultural history of smell*, Routledge, London
Crook, J. 2011 *English medieval shrines*, The Boydell Press, Woodbridge
Drewal, H. J. 2005 'Senses in understandings of art', *African Arts* (Summer), 1–6
Edmonds, M. 2006 'Who said romance was dead?', *Journal of Material Culture* 11(1–3), 167–88
Feld, S. 1996 'Waterfalls of song: an acoustemology of place resounding in Bosavi, Papua New Guinea', in S. Feld and K. H. Basso (eds), *Senses of place*, School of American Research Press, Sante Fe, 95–135
Fischer-Lichte, E. 2007 *Theatre, sacrifice, ritual: exploring forms of political theatre*, Routledge, London, New York
Frank, G. 2000a 'The pilgrim's gaze in the age before icons', in N. Nelson (ed.), *Visuality before and beyond the Renaissance: seeing as others saw*, Cambridge University Press, Cambridge, 98–115
Frank, G. 2000b *The memory of the eyes: pilgrims to living saints in Christian Late Antiquity*, University of California Press, Berkeley, Los Angeles
Giles, K. 2007 'Seeing and believing: visuality and space in pre-modern England', *World Archaeology* 39(1), 105–21
Graves, C. P. 2007 'Sensing and believing: exploring worlds of difference in pre-modern England: a contribution to the debate opened by Kate Giles', *World Archaeology* 39(4), 515–31
Graves, C. P. 2008 'From an archaeology of iconoclasm to an anthropology of the body: images, punishment and personhood in England, 1500–1660', *Current Anthropology* 49(1), 35–57
Hagen, S. K. 1990 *Allegorical remembrance: a study of 'The pilgrimage of the life of man' as a medieval treatise on seeing and remembering*, University of Georgia Press, Athens, GA, and London

Hahn, C. 1997 'Seeing and believing: the construction of sanctity in early medieval saints' shrines', *Speculum* 72, 1079–1106

Hahn, C. 2000 'Visio Dei: changes in medieval visuality', in N. Nelson (ed.), *Visuality before and beyond the Renaissance: seeing as others saw*, Cambridge University Press, Cambridge, 169–96

Hale, S. E. and Campbell, D. 2007 *Sacred space, sacred sound: the acoustic mysteries of holy places*, Theosophical Publishing House, Wheaton, Chennai

Hamilakis, Y. 2004 *Archaeologies of the senses*, Cambridge University Press, Cambridge

Hamilakis, Y. 2014 *Archaeology and the senses: human experience, memory, and affect*, Cambridge University Press, Cambridge

Hamilakis, Y., Pluciennik, M., and Tarlow, S. (eds) 2002 *Thinking through the body: archaeologies of corporeality*, Plenum/Kluwer Academic, London

Hamilton, S. and Whitehouse, R. 2006 'Three senses of dwelling: beginning to socialise the Neolithic ditched villages of the Tavoliere, Southeast Italy', *The Journal of Iberian Archaeology* 8, 159–84

Harvey, S. A. 2006 *Scenting salvation: ancient Christianity and the olfactory imagination*, University of California Press, Berkeley

Howes, D. (ed.) 1991 *The varieties of sensory experience*, University of Toronto Press, Toronto

Howes, D. 2003 *Sensual relations: engaging the senses in culture and social theory*, University of Michigan Press, Ann Arbor, MI

Howes, D. (ed.) 2005 *Empire of the senses*, Berg, Oxford

Howes, D. 2006a 'Charting the sensorial revolution', *Senses and Society* 1(11), 113–28

Howes, D. 2006b 'Scent, sound and synesthesia: intersensoriality and material culture theory', in C. Tilley, W. Keane, S. Küchler, M. Rowlands, and P. Spyer (eds), *Handbook of material culture*, Sage, London, 161–72

Howes, D. and Classen, C. 2013 *Ways of sensing: understanding the senses in society*, Routledge, Oxford

Ingold, T. 2000 *The perception of the environment: essays on livelihood, dwelling and skill*, Routledge, London

Johnson, M. 2012 'Phenomenological approaches to Landscape Archaeology', *Annual Review of Anthropology* 41, 264–84

Jones, C. J. and Hayden, C. (eds) 1998 *The archaeology of perception and the senses*, University of Cambridge, Cambridge

Jones, R. and Semple, S. 2012 *Sense of place in Anglo-Saxon England*, Shaun Tyas, Donington

Kieckhefer, R. 2004 *Theology in stone: church architecture from Byzantium to Berkeley*, Oxford University Press, Oxford

Kisby, F (ed.) 2001 *Music and musicians in Renaissance cities and towns*, Cambridge University Press, Cambridge

Kleinschmidt, H. 2005 *Perception and action in medieval Europe*, The Boydell Press, Woodbridge

Korsmeyer, C. (ed.) 2005 *The taste culture reader: experiencing food and drink*, Berg, Oxford

Lee, J. 2008 'Ad hoc pilgrimages and incidental icons: pilgrimage and exterior sculpture', *Essays in Medieval Studies* 25, 19–26

Locker, M. 2015 *Landscapes of pilgrimage in medieval Britain*, Archaeopress, Oxford

Marks, R. 2004 *Image and devotion in late medieval England*, Stroud, Sutton

Merleau-Ponty, M. 1962 *Phenomenology of perception*, Routledge and Kegan Paul, London

Meskell, L. (ed.) 2005 *Archaeologies of materiality*, Blackwell, Oxford

Milner, M. 2011 *Senses and the English Reformation*, Ashgate, Farnham

Morris, C. and Roberts, P. (eds) 2002 *Pilgrimage: the English experience from Becket to Bunyan*, Cambridge University Press, Cambridge

Palazzo, E. 2011 'Relics, liturgical space, and the theology of the Church', in M. Bagnoli, H. A. Klein, G. C. Mann, and J. Robinson (eds), *Treasures of heaven: saints, relics and devotion in medieval Europe*, British Museum Press, London, 99–109

Palazzo, E. 2014 '*Missarum sollemnia*: eucharistic rituals in the Middle Ages', in J. H. Arnold (ed.), *The Oxford handbook of medieval Christianity*, Oxford University Press, Oxford, 238–53

Pallasmaa, J. 2005 *The eyes of the skin: architecture and the senses*, John Wiley and Sons, London

Parkhurst Ferguson, P. 2011 'The senses of taste', *American Historical Review* 116, 371–84

Paterson, M. 2007 *The senses of touch: haptics, affects and technologies*, Berg, Oxford

Pentcheva, B. V. 2006 'The performative icon', *Art Bulletin* 88(4), 631–55

Rahner, K. 1979 *Theological investigations, volume XVI. Experience of the spirit: source of Theology* (D. Moreland trans.), Seabury, New York

Recht, R. 2008 *Believing and seeing: the art of Gothic cathedrals* (M. Whittall trans.), University of Chicago Press, Chicago

Renfrew, C. 1985 *The archaeology of cult: the sanctuary of Phylakopi*, Thames and Hudson, London

Reznikoff, I. 2006 'The evidence of the use of sound resonance from Palaeolithic to medieval times', in C. Scarre and G. Lawson (eds), *Archaeoacoustics*, McDonald Institute Monographs, Cambridge, 77–84

Rodaway, P. 1994 *Sensuous geographies*, Routledge, London

Rudolph, C. 1990 *Things of greater importance: Bernard of Clairvaux's* Apologia *and the medieval attitude toward art*, University of Pennsylvania Press, Philadelphia

Scarre, C. and Lawson, G. (eds) 2006 *Archaeoacoustics*, McDonald Institute Monographs, Cambridge

Shanks, M. and Tilley, C. 1992 *Re-constructing Archaeology: theory and practice*, Routledge, London (2nd edn)

Skeates, R. 2010 *An archaeology of the senses: prehistoric Malta*, Oxford University Press, Oxford

Stevenson, J. 2010 *Performance, cognitive theory, and devotional culture: sensual piety in late medieval York*, Palgrave Macmillan, New York

Sullivan, L. E. 1986 'Sound and senses: toward a hermeneutics of performance', *History of Religions* 26(1), 1–33

Sutton, D. 2001 *Remembrance of repasts: an anthropology of food and memory*, Berg, Oxford

Swanson, R. N. 1992 'Medieval liturgy as theatre: the props', in D. Wood (ed.), *The Church and the arts*, Blackwell, Oxford, 239–54

Thomas, J. 1993 'The politics of vision and the archaeologies of landscape', in B. Bender (ed.), *Landscape*, Berg, Oxford, 19–47

Thomas, J. 2006 'Phenomenology and material culture', in C. Tilley, W. Keane, S. Küchler, M. Rowlands, and P. Spyer (eds), *Handbook of material culture*, Sage, London, 43–59

Tilley, C. 1994 *A phenomenology of landscape*, Berg, Oxford

Tilley, C. 2004 *The materiality of stone*, Berg, Oxford

Tilley, C. 2010 *Interpreting landscapes: geologies, topographies, identities. Explorations in Landscape Phenomenology 3*, Left Coast Press, Walnut Creek, CA

Webb, S. H. 2004 *The divine voice: Christian proclamation and the theology of sound*, Brazos Press, Grand Rapids, MI

Wells, E. 2011 'Making "sense" of the pilgrimage experience of the medieval church', *Peregrinations Journal* 3(2), 122–46

Wells, E. 2012 'Synaesthesia in medieval pilgrimage: the case of St Neot's shrine, Cornwall', *Church Archaeology* 14, 63–77

Wells, E. 2013 *An archaeology of sensory experience: pilgrimage in the medieval Church, c.1170–c.1550*, unpublished PhD thesis, Durham University

Willis, J. P. 2010 *Church music and Protestantism in post-Reformation England: discourses, sites and identities*, Ashgate, Farnham

Woolgar, C. M. 2006 *The senses in late medieval England*, Yale University Press, London and New Haven

Woolgar, C. M., Serjeantson, D., and Waldron, T. (eds) 2006 *Food in medieval England: diet and nutrition*, Oxford University Press, Oxford

CHAPTER 43

COOKING, DINING, AND DRINKING

HUGH WILLMOTT

Of all the sensory experiences, the practices of cooking, dining, and drinking must be amongst the most developed and intense, stimulating smell, taste, sight, and even touch through comestibles and the objects used to facilitate their consumption. Studies of medieval diet have concentrated traditionally on historical texts such as the accounts of gentry households (e.g. Woolgar 1993) or ingredients and cooking recipes (e.g. Black 2012; Klemetilla 2012). Likewise, the consumption of food has been reconstructed using conduct books, amply illustrated by cooking and dining scenes from manuscripts, and cherry-picked artefacts from art historical collections (e.g. Hammond 1993). This has created a skewed view of medieval cooking and dining, only rectified more recently by cultural historians such as Sponsler (2001), who has shown how little contemporary sources reflected *actual* practice, and by the combined insights of historians and archaeologists.

Important contributions include Dyer (1983), one of the first studies to look across the social divide, emphasizing the considerable expenditure made on foodstuffs by the elite in contrast to a reliance on grains (in the form of bread and pottages), legumes, and beer for nutrition, as well as 'white meats' or dairy products by the peasantry. More recently, Woolgar (2006; 2010) has examined the sensory role of food while the full potential of archaeological data has become clearer.

Advances in excavation recovery techniques have produced more evidence for fish and, together with isotopic studies of medieval populations, this has underlined the importance of marine protein in medieval diet by the thirteenth century (e.g. Barrett et al. 2004; Müldner and Richards 2005). Residue analysis too has provided new insights (e.g. Evans and Elbeih 1984; Evershed et al. 2002, 664) as has comparative analysis. Disparities in bone assemblages from urban and rural contexts, for example, reveal a growing demand for veal in cities and towns and increasingly standardized butchery practices such as the dressing of wild birds (Albarella and Thomas 2002; Albarella 2004). Evidently, patterns of taste could change through time too, as Sykes (2014) has shown in her evaluation of the swan whose rising consumption by the secular elite she ascribes to the appropriation of the image of the swan as a chivalric symbol. As Sykes (2007) has also shown for venison, the social context for excavated faunal evidence is essential for its interpretation, and the same is true for archaeobotanical studies (see Chapter 8). It is not only faunal assemblages that can contribute to a more developed understanding of medieval taste, other environmental sources do provide insights into the sensory experience of diet in the Middle Ages. From the twelfth century onwards, more widespread archaeological evidence for the use of fennel, caraway, and parsley seeds (Livarda and Van der Veen 2008, 207) suggests the preparation of thin acidic sauces and more heavily spiced foods among the elite, although black mustard was also found on low status rural sites, demonstrating that even the peasantry had developed a taste for strongly flavoured foods.

Cooking

During the Middle Ages the kitchen was one of the most diverse spaces in the home; in the castle or monastery these could be complex and highly specialized areas consisting of several individual rooms or preparation areas, whilst in the peasant long-house they were simply an open hearth which also warmed the building. Indeed, many of the poorest may have had not access to cooking facilities at all. Those living in the poorest of urban conditions, such as the garrets of town houses or street front tenements, are very unlikely to have had ready access to kitchens or hearths (Schofield 2003). At times even the more affluent might not have had access to their own facilities, if they were travelling, for example. In larger urban centres precooked 'fast food' was readily available for purchase on the street, with a range to suit all tastes and budgets. In London, by the thirteenth century, waffles, meat or eel pasties, egg or cheese tarts, and light pastries are all recorded for sale (Carlin 1998, 29).

The ceramic 'cooking pot' is routinely recovered from archaeological excavations. This was an open-mouthed vessel usually with a flat or slightly convex base, produced in a wide range of local fabrics and found on high- and low-status sites alike. Superficially, their ubiquity seems to indicate common cooking practices but these pots served a multitude of functions, from the preparation and mixing of foodstuffs to the longer-term storage of solids, and even outside the kitchen. An early attempt to differentiate their uses was made by Moorhouse (1986, 108–11) who suggested that wear patterns might be significant. The presence or absence of sooting indicated whether a jar had been used for cooking or storage, if the pot had been placed directly in the fire or suspended over it, and even what the source of the fuel might have been. Jervis (2014a, 89–95) notes that sooting markedly decreases on cooking pots and jars after the Norman Conquest. This, he argues, resulted from a change in cooking method that saw the introduction, and widespread acceptance, of the Continental practice of suspending the pot over the fire, rather than placing it directly in the embers, which in turn reflected a developing taste for the slower cooking of meats. In many households, however, cooking pots would have fulfilled multiple roles during their lifetime, especially in rural households with less resources (e.g. Brown 1997, 86).

Despite these complications, there are some broader trends that can be detected through the analysis of ceramic assemblages (McCarthy and Brooks 1988, 102–34). It is often observed that with the Conquest there was a dramatic increase in the use of ceramics on domestic sites, even in those areas that were largely aceramic just a few decades earlier (e.g. Bryant 2004a, 118). During the late eleventh and twelfth centuries cooking pots and jars comprise the majority of ceramic assemblages, around 85 per cent in the case of Southampton (Brown 2005, 88). However, by the later thirteenth century more specialized cooking wares, such as dripping pans, became more common, whilst the fourteenth and fifteenth centuries saw the gradual introduction of newer forms such as the tripod pipkin, bung hole cistern, and the shallow pancheon (Brown 2005, 91, 94; Jervis 2008, 83). These changes in ceramic profiles reflect not just a growing access to different material forms but a developing taste for gravies, sauces, and more complex flavours.

Archaeologists have tended to view these developments in terms of status differentiation and competitive emulation. For example, Jervis (2008, 83) has suggested that the Continental form of the tripod pipkin, whilst manufactured locally in England, was more readily adopted by richer mercantile communities in Southampton than by other groups, who continued to favour traditional cooking pots or jars. However, such developments might have been as much driven by the desire to enhance sensory experience as to display social status. Whilst some late medieval elite sites, for example Bull Hall in Winchester, seem to be characterized by assemblages that include a much greater variety of food preparation vessels like mortars, Brown (1997, 92–3) has observed that these differences are not simply a result of variations in social status; rather they reflect a difference in dining habits between urban and rural environments. They may also reflect, of course, easy access to readily available wares and this requires testing with a larger selection of assemblages.

One significant problem for archaeologists attempting to reconstruct culinary practice is that the vast majority of ceramic assemblages are found in secondary contexts. There are exceptions to this: at Kirkstall Abbey, Yorkshire, spatial analysis of the ceramics revealed that the distribution of dripping pans was found grouped close to the meat kitchen and the service quarters of the infirmary, both areas where the cooking of meat might be expected (Moorhouse 1993, 10). At Worcester a group of ceramics was recovered from a kitchen belonging to an urban household destroyed by fire in 1200–50 (Bryant 2004b, 332–3). In addition to five complete jugs, six cooking pots or jars were recovered (Figure 43.1, no. 1), each of a slightly different graduated size. This suggested that they each might have been intended for the storage or cooking of a different foodstuff. Finally, excavation of a fire-damaged late thirteenth-century peasant long-house at Dinna Clerks on Dartmoor (Beresford 1979, 135–7, 147–50) revealed five cooking pots sealed by the collapse of the wattle-and-daub chimney hood and a sixth jar close by buried up to its rim, perhaps functioning as a temporary mixing or storage vessel. Next to

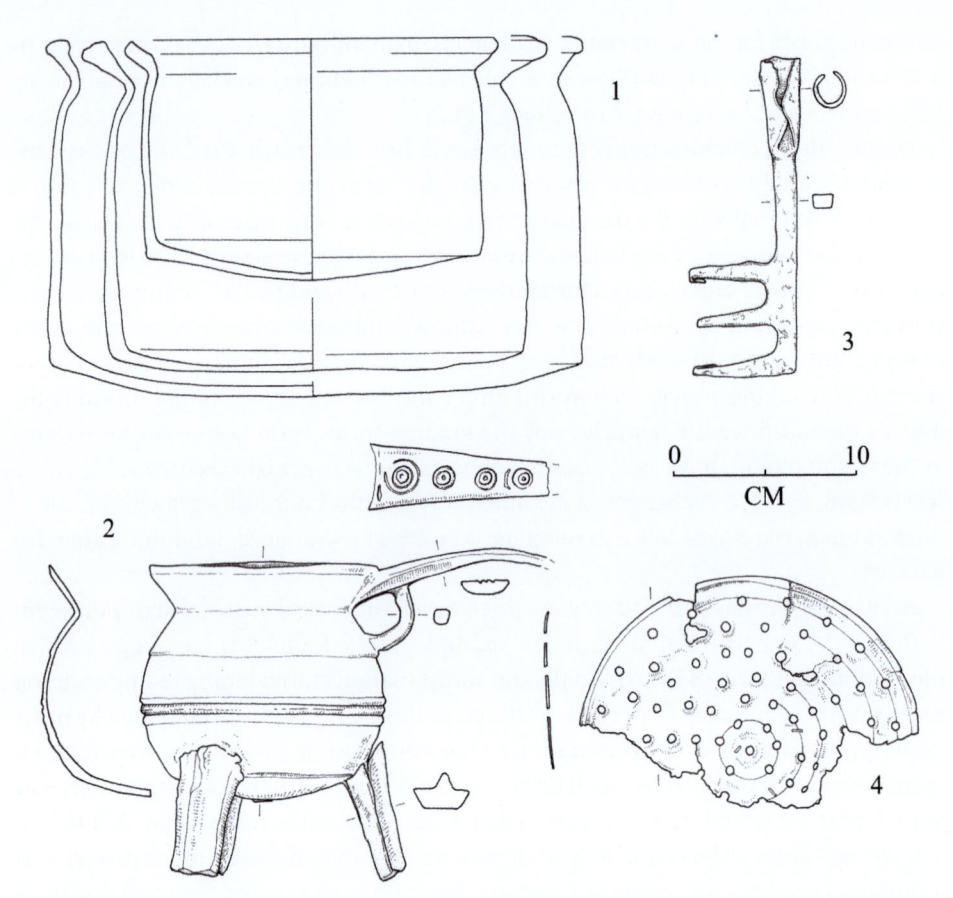

FIGURE 43.1 1) Ceramic cooking jars from Deansway, Worcester; 2) Copper-alloy skillet from Pottergate, Norwich; 3) Flesh hook from Pottergate, Norwich; 4) Skimmer from London (drawing by Jerneja Willmott)

(© Hugh Willmott)

the fire there was also a single glazed jug and the remains of two wooden bowls. The smell of cooking here must have combined with the taste of the food and the warmth of the fire.

During the later Middle Ages there was a gradual replacement of ceramic cooking pots with metal vessels (e.g. Bryant 2004a, 118) and by the late fourteenth century the *olla enea*, or copper-alloy cooking pot, was appearing in the inventories of households of every status, including cottagers. In 1368 the kitchen of the rector of St Martin Pomeroy, London, was listed as possessing six brass pots, four cauldrons, three brand irons, two griddles, one iron frying pan, two iron slices, a flesh hook, a skimmer, as well as other assorted ladles, pails, and other equipment (Thomas 1929, 91–2). Five years later, the kitchen inventory of Thomas Mockyng, a city fishmonger, included many of the above items as well as two mortars, five tubs, a fine sieve, five spits, two tripods, and a firepan. The accumulated ironwork weighed 220 lb and was valued at 1/7s 6d, whilst the brass weighed 318 lb and was worth 2/7s 6d (Thomas 1929, 155–6).

Archaeologically, metal cooking pots like these are rarely encountered, but frequent finds of folded rivets and patches used in their repair attest to their presence (Egan 1998, 176–7). Evidence for copper-alloy cooking pot production in the form of mould fragments has also been found at a number of sites, most notably at Salisbury, on a site identified in the will of John Baber, a brazier, who died in 1404 (Webster and Cherry 1973, 185). The popularity of metal is usually attributed to the growing wealth of the peasantry, on the basis that a bronze cooking pot could cost as much as two weeks wages of a carpenter (Dyer 1982, 39) and the investment was worthwhile given its extended lifespan. However, the notion that ceramics were a cheaper form of material culture only used by those who could afford little else has to be challenged (e.g. Jervis 2014a, 66; 2014b, 4–5), and it is clear that elites who had the resources to do otherwise were still choosing pottery for their cooking up until the fourteenth century. Cost was important, but so was the style of cuisine; developing culinary tastes and the slower cooking of meats in more highly flavoured sauces stimulated the introduction of new forms of metalware.

Although rare, finds of kitchen equipment are known and the most complete assemblage comes from a house on Pottergate, Norwich. Destroyed by fire in 1507, much of the household collapsed into the cellar, which was subsequently backfilled (Margeson 1993, 86–9, 94–5). Amongst the kitchen equipment were a complete copper-alloy tripod skillet (Figure 43.1, no. 2), a thin beaten copper bowl and the iron handle from a hanging bowl. Associated iron items from the fireplace were also recovered: cauldron hooks, a complete adjustable height suspension ratchet, portions of a rotary spit, and a fire pan for moving coals. There was also an iron ladle and flesh hook (Figure 43.1, no. 3), and a copper-alloy skimmer. Similar finds are also known from London's waterfront sites, and although they cannot be related to individual households, their close dating allows wider trends to be observed. For instance, the growing popularity of copper-alloy tripod skillets and cauldrons can be detected; of the nineteen different examples recovered, none pre-date the mid-thirteenth century and the majority, twelve in total, came from the period 1350–1450 (Egan 1998, 161–6). Similarly, iron flesh hooks for removing chunks of stewed meat from the pot were more prevalent during the late thirteenth and fourteenth centuries, but were largely replaced by flat pierced copper-alloy skimmers by the fifteenth century (Figure 43.1, no. 4). This was probably as a result of meat being prepared to a more sophisticated recipe prior to cooking, with the flesh now being removed from the bone, rather than larger cuts being cooked whole.

Dining

Material culture directly associated with eating, as opposed to preparation, is surprisingly rare either side of the Norman Conquest. Prior to the mid-thirteenth century, even amongst larger assemblages of ceramics, food vessels are virtually absent; in a survey of twelfth- to mid-thirteenth- century ceramics from Southampton less than 1 per cent were bowls, the remainder being jars/cooking pots and jugs (Brown 2005, 88–9). The assumption is that organic materials, and wood in particular, were used by all levels of society, although in some circumstances meals could have been consumed directly from the cooking jar. Ceramic tablewares from Spain were available from the end of the thirteenth century but had a more restricted social distribution (Gutiérrez 2012, 47–8).

Finds of wooden bowls are not uncommon on sites where there are waterlogged conditions, and yet few can be said to date to the late eleventh or twelfth centuries. Turned bowls appear in increasing numbers from the early thirteenth century onwards, especially in urban centres, with ash and alder being the most popular woods (Keys 1998a, 196). The apparent absence of wooden vessels prior to this date is probably due to excavation biases. In London, a number of group deposits of wooden bowls have been found, among them eighteen from an early fourteenth-century pit at the hospital of St Mary Spital (Thomas et al. 1997, 59–60). Along with other late medieval assemblages from Leicester Austin Friars (Clay 1981, 139) and Coppergate, York (Morris 2000, 2403–4), among others, these finds fall into two broad styles: a shallow hemispherical bowl, occasionally with a broad flange, and the flat dish or plate (Figure 43.2, nos 1–2). Given the simplicity of their form they are hard to date more precisely and it seems likely that both styles were used throughout the period.

Wooden bowls and plates are utilitarian and visually plain, but this perhaps was the intention. As an 'open' form, the bowl emphasized its contents, and the natural colouring of the wood detracted little from the food inside. Sometimes they were incised or branded on the base with initials or a personalized mark. Two bowls from Milk Street, London, were marked with a 'S' (Keys 1998a, 197), three from a pit on High Street, Southampton, were marked with a capital 'A' (Figure 42.2, no. 3), and three others from a pit at Cuckoo Lane, Southampton, part of an assemblage possibly associated with the household of the prosperous merchant Richard of Southwick, were marked with a crosshatch design (Platt and Coleman-Smith 1975, 220, 230). This personalization of everyday objects suggests first, that the bowls were portable items that might be taken outside of the home or sometimes used in environments, such as alehouses, where ownership needed to be confirmed. Second, wooden vessels were valued and establishing ownership was important. This is also suggested by the number of wooden bowls with elaborate repairs, such as one from 1–6 Milk Street, London, which had been sewn back together after breakage, even though it would probably never have been able to hold liquid foods again (Keys 1998a, 203–4).

If wooden bowls and dishes were undoubtedly the most common form of vessel for the consumption of medieval foodstuffs, metalwares increasingly played an important role. Silver and silver gilt vessels are never encountered archaeologically, but they are well documented in the inventories and wills of the elite as well as frequently being depicted in manuscript illuminations, such as the depiction of the Dukes of York, Gloucester, and Ireland dining with Richard II in the *Chroniques d'Angletere* (British Library MS Royal 14 E IV f. 265v). Despite this, even the rich would probably only have used them occasionally, and base metal flatwares, and pewter in particular, would have been a more ordinary sight at the table. Although pewter was recyclable, medieval pewterers are recorded as purchasing scrap from would-be customers (Hatcher and Barker

COOKING, DINING, AND DRINKING 703

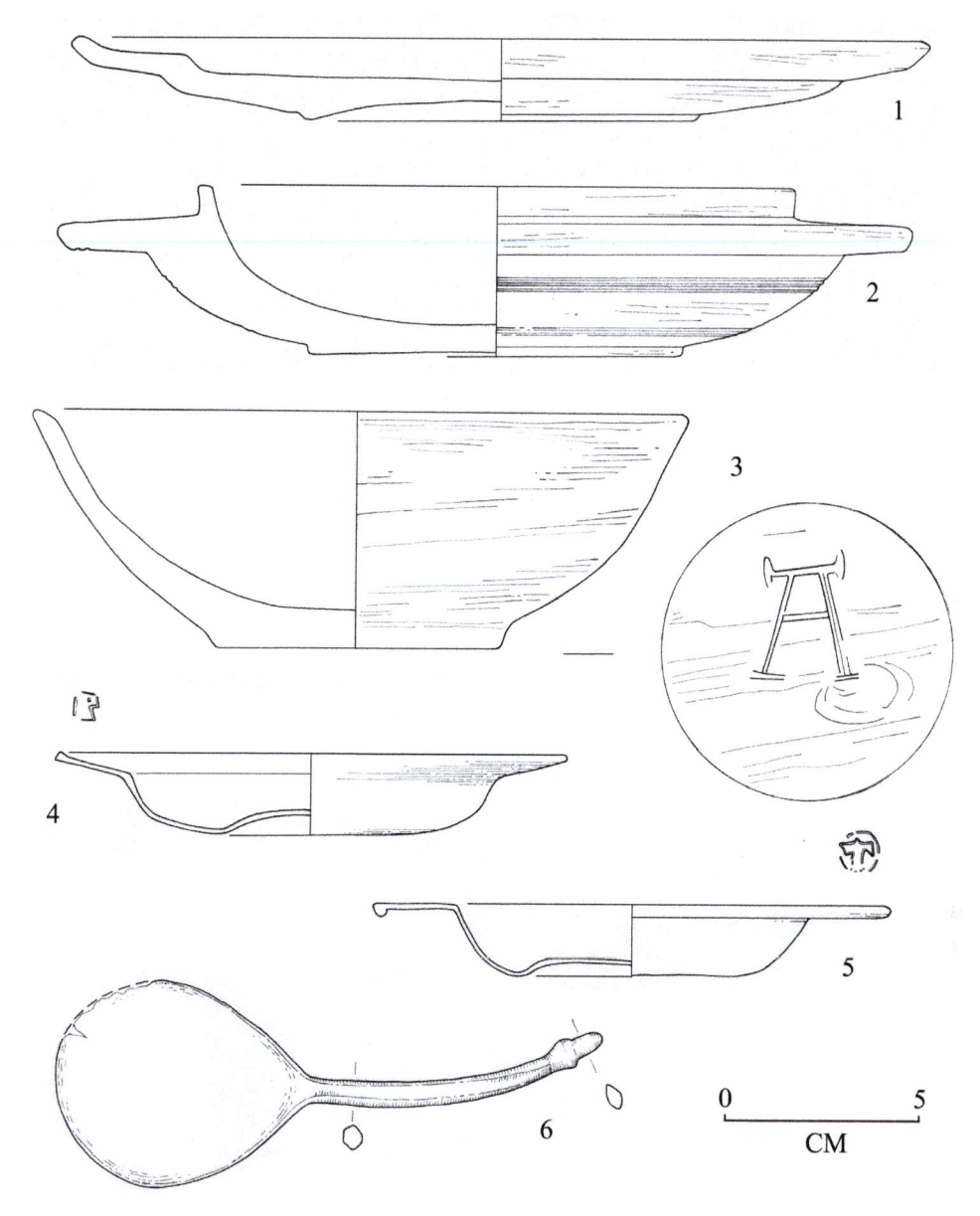

FIGURE 43.2 1–2) Wooden dishes from St Mary Spital, London; 3) Wooden bowl from High Street, Southampton; 4) Pewter saucer from Southampton; 5) Pewter saucer from Leicester Austin Friars; 6) Pewter spoon from Barentin's Manor, Oxfordshire (drawing by Jerneja Willmott)

(© Hugh Willmott)

1974, 239–40), it is occasionally found. In London, rims from at least nineteen plates or dishes have been recorded primarily from waterfront dump sites and, with one earlier exception, all date from the mid-fourteenth century onwards (Egan 1998, 184–7). More complete examples of flatware include a small shallow, rimmed bowl from a late thirteenth-century pit at Southampton (Figure 42.2, no. 4) marked with a Lombardic letter 'P' on the rim (Michaelis 1975) and two fourteenth-century date saucers from Leicester Austin Friars, both marked with a 'T' on the rim (Figure 42.2, no. 5), probably a maker's mark (Homer 1999, 7).

This archaeological evidence corresponds well with the growing organization of the Company of Pewterers, whose earliest ordinances date to 1348 and specify the range of 'disshes, Saucers, platers, Chargeours' being produced (Hatcher and Barker 1974, 38–9). Hatcher and Barker suggest that pewter was not only becoming increasingly popular during the fourteenth century, it was also replacing more traditional materials at the table. In 1391, Richard Toky, a prosperous London grocer owned 86 lb of pewter, including forty-four pieces of flatware. However, in the subsequent centuries, pewter use was clearly trickling down the social scale; in 1434 Roger Elmesly, a wax chandler's servant, owned a pewter plate, two dishes and two saucers, whilst in 1479 John Rokewood, a London squire, had six dishes, four saucers, and three platters (Hatcher and Barker 1974, 55). Even just a few pieces of polished pewter set on the table or displayed on the cupboard would have made a very dramatic visual sight, especially in low-level and artificial light sources. It is interesting in this respect that pewter platters and dishes are invariably plain in appearance, despite medieval pewterers being proficient in cast relief moulding, engraving, and hammer beating (Hornsby et al. 1989, 15–19). While the pewter may have been intended to impress the diner to some degree, it was the food that made the greatest impression.

Given the range of more saucy foods becoming increasingly popular, from the thin sour gravies favoured by the elite to simple peasant pottages, spoons were sometimes needed. These were fashioned from a wide range of organic materials, including bone, horn, and wood, though few survive. Exceptions are the eleventh- or twelfth-century examples from Goltho (MacGregor 1987), four fourteenth-century wooden spoons recovered from Perth (Curteis et al. 2012, 259–62), and seven from several different late medieval sites in York (Morris 2000). Late medieval spoons made from pewter or sometimes copper alloy were used from the fourteenth century onwards (Homer 1975). Pewter examples usually have a fig-shaped bowl, thin tapering hexagonal stem, and a detailed finial end, the most common of which was the acorn knop, such as three fifteenth-century examples found at Barentin's Manor, Oxfordshire (Figure 42.2, no. 6) (Goodall 2005, 90). Gilchrist (2012, 125–7), perhaps influenced by the early modern practice in Wales of presenting carved spoons to intended lovers, has suggested that metal spoons might have held 'special value' as symbolic wedding gifts, and points to the almost unique find of a pair of so-called 'marriage knives' from Meols, Cheshire. Their ubiquity and functional nature suggest otherwise but they were certainly intended to catch the diner's attention.

DRINKING

Material culture associated with drinking falls primarily into two broad categories: serving vessels such as jugs and pitchers, and drinking vessels which include goblets, beakers, tankards, and cups. Identifying what was being consumed is rather more difficult; traditionally it has been argued that water was avoided due to the risk of disease and that beers of differing strengths were consumed instead by the majority of people, as well as wine by those who could afford it (e.g. Hammond 1993, 91). Whether this was entirely the case is questionable, as it implies sufficient knowledge of the mechanism behind water-borne infection, yet an apparent ignorance of the benefits that prolonged boiling would have had.

Ceramic jugs are found during the Anglo-Norman period; in his study of the pottery from Southampton, Brown noted that they made up 15 per cent of the total assemblage from the town. This increased over the course of the next century so that by the middle of the thirteenth century jugs had been adopted universally in all households, in England at least (Brown 2005, 88–9, 91). At the same time variety increased and, in addition to plain and unglazed forms often of local manufacture, decorative jugs also began to appear. It has been suggested that this reflected different lifestyles as well as functions, plainer 'kitchen jugs' could have functioned in both preparation and serving roles, whilst more decorative ceramics were destined for the tables of the mercantile elite (Jervis 2008, 78–81). However, the rise in the use of jugs for serving liquids might not have been so universal. In his study of ceramic assemblages from different households, Brown (1997, 92–3) noted that prevalent jug use was restricted to urban contexts, and that even a high-status rural site such as the manor at Faccombe Netherton (Wiltshire) made relatively little use of them. This, he suggests, reflected differences in practices between the two groups, with the latter spending more time dining formally. Such divisions might in reality be slightly simplistic, or at least regionally determined. Jugs are certainly found in rural low-status contexts, and Moorhouse (1986, 103–4) has suggested that two jugs recovered from a thirteenth-century peasant house at Pennard, Glamorgan, had been conspicuously displayed upon a sideboard or a wall shelf when the building was destroyed by fire.

Ceramic jugs were not just plain utilitarian items; as early as the mid-thirteenth century polychrome wares from Saintonge decorated with pseudo-heraldic devices and beasts were imported into England as incidental ballast for the wine trade (Derœux and Dufournier 1991), and by the fifteenth century locally produced jugs could be embellished with bearded faces and other anthropomorphic elements (Figure 43.3, no. 1). The imagery on these vessels was clearly intended to not only impress and amuse, but may also have carried messages concerning perceived status and masculinity (Cumberpatch 2006). Complex jugs like these were not common; most were decorated simply, with green and brown glazes, sometimes slips and applied decoration. The use of glaze was more than just a functional addition—it was applied partially and failed to make the jugs impervious to liquid. Indeed, it may be that the application of these glazes was a very deliberate attempt to make the jug more visually appealing to the drinker through the refraction and dispersal of light, especially when viewed in the subdued artificially lit conditions experienced in the medieval house or hall (Devlin et al. 2002).

Glass jugs, though they are not identified in large quantities, begin appearing on high-status sites as early as the late twelfth century, an example decorated with opaque red

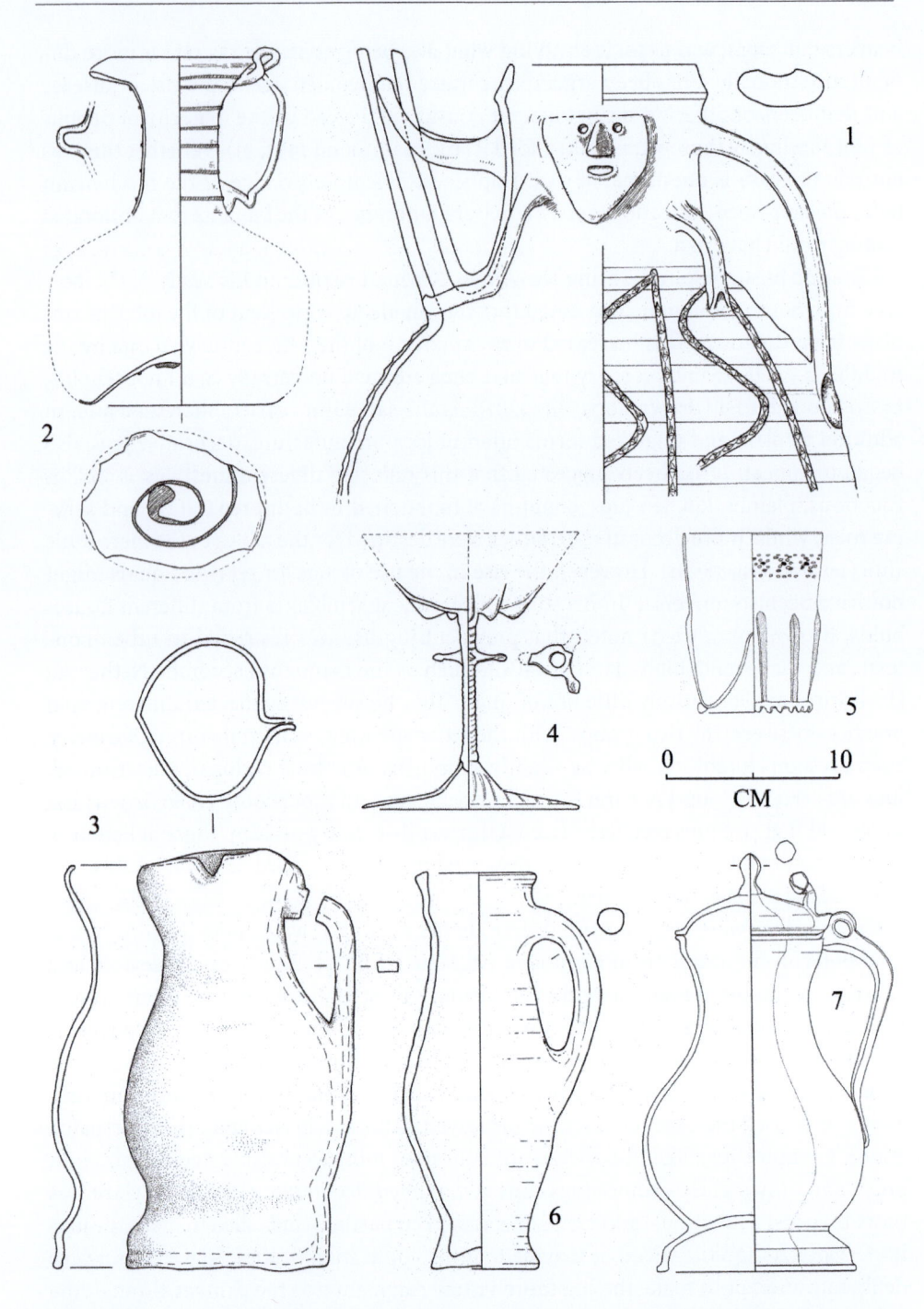

FIGURE 43.3 1) Glass jug from Southampton; 2) Ceramic 'face jug' from Hallgate, Doncaster; 3) Leather 'black jack' from Watling Street, London; 4) Glass goblet from High Street, Southampton; 5) Glass beaker from Southampton; 6) Ceramic drinking jug from Woolwich; 7) Pewter tankard from Tonbridge Castle, Kent (drawing by Jerneja Willmott)

(© Hugh Willmott)

marvered trailing was found in a pit at Southampton (Figure 43.3, no. 2) (Charleston 1975, 216) and, increasingly from the thirteenth century onwards, imported jugs are found in coloured glass, such as a blue example from Penhallam Manor, Cornwall, and the bright yellow high-lead glass at Battle Abbey, East Sussex (Charleston 1980, 69; 1985, 145). By the fourteenth century glass jugs were being produced by English glassmakers in the cheaper green potash glass, and they are found on sites of more middling status in towns (e.g. Keys 1998b, 229). Glass was not only impervious to liquids, making it easier to clean and less prone to take on aromas over time, it also permitted the drinker to view its contexts, a highly symbolic property which is explored further below.

Compared with serving vessels, ceramic cups or mugs are almost never found before the fifteenth century and, if the medieval elite might have sometimes used silver to drink from, the overwhelming majority of vessels must have been made from organic materials that simply do not survive. The Bayeux Tapestry famously depicts diners with drinking horns, and their use probably persisted through the later medieval period. By the fourteenth century in London guilds of both 'horners' and leather 'botelmakers' are recorded, and these merged during the fifteenth century (Baker 1921, 21–3). Leather was probably a common material not only for the production of storage vessels, for example costrels, but also for drinking jugs or 'black jacks', such as the very rare example excavated at Watling Street, London (Figure 43.3, no. 3) (Cherry 1991, 312–13). Wooden 'mazers' or drinking bowls are also recorded in numerous wills and inventories from the thirteenth century onwards (e.g. St John Hope 1887; Evan-Thomas 1932, 1–3) and it is entirely possible that some wooden bowls could have been used for drinking. However, the only varieties of wooden vessel that has been identified as exclusively for drinking are stave-built. At Perth, two sizes were found: mugs that were 10–11 cm in height and tankards 25–27 cm in height (Curteis et al. 2012, 226–9). Staves from similar 'tankards' have also been recovered from London's waterfront sites (Keys 1998a, 214–15) but with a capacity of between five or six pints they must have been intended for communal rather than individual use.

From the late thirteenth century onwards imported glass drinking vessels are found in relatively small numbers at elite sites, although as the fourteenth century progressed assemblages are also encountered elsewhere. This adoption of glass was not universal, however; a recent survey across the West Country has shown that glass only occurs as isolated finds and only in a single urban centre, Exeter, prior to the mid-sixteenth century (Willmott 2015, 322). Some of the earliest and most decorative drinking glasses are Italian beakers with brightly coloured enamelling depicting mythical creatures, saints, and heraldic devices; the most important group, consisting of eight or more examples was deposited in a cess pit at Foster Lane, London, between 1300 and 1350 (Clark 1983). By the start of the fourteenth century, stemmed glass goblets were used for drinking, often with a wide bowl and tall thin stem like the fragments of six examples known from in a pit at High Street, Southampton (Figure 43.3, no. 4) (Charleston 1975, 217–18). One of the appeals of glass like this was its transparency which allowed the liquid inside, particularly wines, to become part of the visual experience of drinking (Willmott 2005a, 41–3). It can be no coincidence that by the fifteenth century drinking glasses tended not to be heavily decorated (Willmott 2005b), save for small areas of gilding or enamelling, as seen in the illustrated example of a ribbed beaker from Southampton (Figure 43.3, no. 5) (Willmott 2011, 185, no. 43). Decoration was used to enhance but not obscure the contents on display, serving instead to elevate its sensory and social status.

Pottery was not a popular media for drinking vessels until the late fourteenth century. The relatively plain styles and rough fabrics of local coarsewares might have not been conducive to the drinking experience, especially when compared to polished wood, smooth metalwares, and glass (Cumberpatch 1997). After that date, imports of Rhenish stoneware drinking jugs became increasingly common, especially in urban contexts (Gaimster 1997), and drinking jugs started appearing in local glazed fabrics, such as London-type ware (Figure 43.3, no. 6) (Matthews and Green 1969; Pearce 1992, 23–9; Pearce and Vince 1988, 72). The increasing use of glazes and the high firing of more refined fabrics improved the experience of drinking and helped prevent the absorption of liquids while the use of decoration made them more visually appealing so that by the fifteenth century ceramic drinking vessels were ubiquitous (Cumberpatch 2006).

The second half of the fourteenth century also saw an increasing number of metalwares, and pewter hollow wares in particular, associated with drinking. Company ordnances refer to the production of 'pottes', 'pottes square', and 'other thinges' (Hatcher and Barker 1974, 39) and, although by no means as common as flatware, 'square pottes' appear in wills with increasing frequency during the fourteenth and fifteenth centuries. The form these took is apparent from the relatively small number that have survived; they are in fact octagonal in shape, made from individual sheets soldered together, and take the form of a lidded tankard 20–30 cm tall (Van Wijk 2014). Archaeologically, near-complete fourteenth-century examples have been found at Abbots Leigh, a property owned by St Augustine's Bristol (Homer 1999, 11) and near Tonbridge Castle, Kent (Figure 43.3, no. 7) (Hornsby et al. 1989, 52), whilst more fragmentary elements of lids and thumb rests have been found on several London sites (Egan 1998, 189–91). Pewter like this offered some obvious benefits. It was visually appealing when highly polished, easy to clean, odourless, and, perhaps most crucially, robust and difficult to break; any dents could easily be hammered out. That only handled drinking pots used for drinking beer are found, but not stemmed vessels for wine, is of little surprise: not only did the pewter alloy produce a bitter taste when it came into contact with wine, it also obscured the expensive contents.

Conclusion

Food preparation, eating, and drinking became increasingly complex and engaging activities during the Middle Ages, and the properties of food and material culture were actively exploited to stimulate the senses of sight, smell, taste, and even touch. The fourteenth century appears to have been a particularly crucial period in these developments, as has been observed by Riddy (2008, 17) who has characterized this as the century when it is possible to detect 'a material signature of domesticity'; its early decades saw the emergence of more sophisticated culinary practices, and the appearance of table glass and pewter dishes on the tables of the elite. By the end of the century these objects, alongside new ceramic tablewares, were increasingly within reach of more middling urban groups and yeoman farmers, and by the fifteenth century even the poorest were flavouring their foods, cooking in copper-alloy pots and boasted a range of eating and drinking vessels at their disposal. All of this made consumption a more engaging and complex sensory experience for every member of society.

Acknowledgements

I am very grateful to Professor John Moreland and Dr Rachel Askew who provided very constructive comment on earlier drafts of this chapter. The figures were drawn by Jerneja Willmott.

References cited

Albarella, U. 2004 'Meat production and consumption in town and country', in K. Giles and C. Dyer (eds), *Town and country in the Late Middle Ages: contrasts, contacts and interconnections, 1150–1500*, The Society for Medieval Archaeology Monograph 22, Leeds, 131–48

Albarella, U. and Thomas, R. 2002 'They dined on crane: bird consumption, wild fowling and status in medieval England', *Acta Zoologica Cracoviensia* 45, 23–38

Baker, O. 1921 *Black jacks and leather bottells*, E. J. Burrow and Co. Ltd, London

Barrett, J. H., Locker, A., and Roberts, C. 2004 'The origins of intensive marine fishing in medieval Europe: the English evidence', *Proceedings of the Royal Society of London B: Biological Sciences* 271(1556), 2417–21

Beresford, G. 1979 'Three deserted medieval settlements on Dartmoor: a report on the late E. Marie Minter's Excavations', *Medieval Archaeology* 23, 98–158

Black, M. 2012 *The medieval cookbook*, British Museum Press, London (2nd edn)

Brown, D. H. 1997 'Pots from houses', *Medieval Ceramics* 21, 83–94

Brown, D. H. 2005 'Pottery and manners', in M. Carroll, D. Hadley, and H. Willmott (eds), *Consuming passions: dining from Antiquity to the eighteenth century*, Tempus Publishing, Stroud, 87–101

Bryant, V. 2004a 'Death and desire: factors affecting the consumption of pottery in medieval Worcestershire', *Medieval Ceramics* 28, 117–23

Bryant, V. 2004b 'Medieval and early post-medieval pottery', in H. Dalwood and R. Edwards, *Excavations at Deansway, Worcester, 1988–89: Romano-British small town to late medieval city*, Council for British Archaeology, York, 281–339

Carlin, M. 1998 'Fast food and urban living standards in medieval England', in M. Carlin and J. Rosenthal (eds), *Food and eating in medieval Europe*, The Hambledon Press, London, 27–51

Charleston, R. 1975 'The glass', in C. Platt and R. Coleman-Smith, *Excavations in medieval Southampton, Vol. II: the finds*, Leicester University Press, Leicester, 204–26

Charleston, R. 1980 'Glass of the high medieval period', *Bulletin de l'Association Internationale pour l'Histoire du Verre* 8, 65–76

Charleston, R. 1985 'Vessel glass', in J. N. Hare, *Battle Abbey: the Eastern Range and the excavations of 1978–80*, Historic Buildings Commission for England Archaeological Report 2, London, 139–46

Cherry, J. 1991 'Leather', in J. Blair and N. Ramsay (eds), *English medieval industries: craftsmen, techniques, products*, The Hambledon Press, London, 295–318

Clarke, J. 1983 'Medieval enamelled glasses from London', *Medieval Archaeology* 27, 152–6

Clay, P. 1981 'The small finds', in J. Mellor and T. Pearce, *The Austin Friars, Leicester*, Council for British Archaeology Research Report 35, Leicester, 130–44

Cumberpatch, C. 1997 'Towards a phenomenological approach to the study of medieval pottery', in C. Cumberpatch and P. Blinkhorn (eds), *Not so much a pot, more a way of life*, Oxbow Monograph 83, Oxford, 125–52

Cumberpatch, C. 2006 'Face to face with medieval pottery: some observations on medieval anthropomorphic pottery in north-east England', *Assemblage* 9 (https://archaeologydataservice.ac.uk/archives/view/assemblage/html/9/cumberpatch.html)

Curteis, A., Morris, A., and Bogdan, N. 2012 'The worked wood', in D. Hall (ed.), *Perth High Street archaeological excavation 1975–1977. Fascicule 2: the ceramics, the metalwork and the wood*, Tayside and Fife Archaeological Committee, Perth, 223–316

Derœux, D. and Dufournier, D. 1991 'Réflexions sur la diffusion de la céramique très décorée d'origine Française en Europe du nord-ouest XIII–XIVe siècles', *Archéologie Médiévale* 21, 163–77

Devlin, K., Chalters, A., and Brown, D. 2002 'Predictive lighting and perception in archaeological representations', *UNESCO 'World Heritage in the Digital Age' 30th Anniversary Digital Congress* (October 2002), UNESCO World Heritage Centre (http://www.doc.gold.ac.uk/~mas01dl/CIS224b/unesco_paper.pdf)

Dyer, C. 1982 'The social and economic changes of the later Middle Ages, and the pottery of the period', *Medieval Ceramics* 6, 33–42

Dyer, C. 1983 'English diet in the later Middle Ages', in T. Aston, P. Cos, C. Dyer, and J. Thirsk (eds), *Social relations and ideas: essays in honour of R. H. Hilton*, Cambridge University Press, Cambridge, 191–247

Egan, G. 1998 *The medieval household: daily living c.1150–c.1450*, Medieval Finds from Excavations in London 6, Her Majesty's Stationery Office, London

Evan-Thomas, O. 1932 *Domestic utensils of wood from the XVIth to the XIXth century*, Owen Evan-Thomas Ltd, London

Evans, J. and Elbeih, S. M. 1984 'Medieval food residues from Exeter', in J. Allan, *Medieval and post-medieval finds from Exeter, 1971–1980*, Exeter Archaeological Reports 3, Exeter, 37–9

Evershed, R., Dudd, S., Copley, M., Berstan, R., Stott, A., Mottram, H., Buckley, S., and Crossman, Z. 2002 'Chemistry of archaeological animal fats', *Accounts of Chemical Research* 35/8, 660–8

Gaimster, D. 1997 *German stoneware, 1200–1900: archaeology and cultural history*, British Museum Press, London

Gilchrist, R. 2012 *Medieval life: archaeology and the life course*, The Boydell Press, Woodbridge

Goodall, A. 2005 'Objects of lead and pewter', in P. Page, K. Atherton, and A. Hardy, *Barentin's Manor: excavations of the moated manor at Harding's Field, Chalgrove, Oxfordshire 1976–9*, Oxford Archaeological Unit, Oxford, 88–91

Gutiérrez, A. 2012 '*Of sundry colours and moulds*: imports of early modern pottery along the Atlantic seaboard', in A. Texeira and J. A. Bettencourt (eds), *Old and New Worlds: international Congress of Early Modern Archaeology*, 37–50

Hammond, P. 1993 *Food and feast in medieval England*, Sutton Publishing Ltd, Stroud
Hatcher, J. and Barker, T. C. 1974 *A history of British pewter*, Longman, London
Homer, R. F. 1975 *Five centuries of base metal spoons*, Worshipful Company of Pewterers, London
Homer, R. F. 1999 'Pewter in medieval England', *Journal of the Pewter Society* 12(2), 2–15
Hornsby, P. R. G., Weinstein, R., and Homer, R. 1989 *Pewter: a celebration of the craft 1200–1700*, The Museum of London, London
Jervis, B. 2008 'For richer; for poorer: a study of pottery distribution in medieval Southampton within its socio-economic context', *Medieval Ceramics* 30, 73–94
Jervis, B. 2014a *Pottery and social life in medieval England*, Oxbow Books, Oxford
Jervis, B. 2014b 'Pots as things: value, meaning and medieval pottery in relational perspective', in P. Blinkhorn and C. Cumberpatch (eds), *The chiming of crack'd bells: recent approaches to the study of artefacts in archaeology*, British Archaeological Reports International Series 2677, Archaeopress, Oxford, 3–16
Keys, L. 1998a 'Wooden vessels', in G. Egan, *The medieval household: daily living c.1150–c.1450*, Medieval Finds from Excavations in London 6, Her Majesty's Stationery Office, London, 196–217
Keys, L. 1998b 'Glass vessels', in G. Egan, *The medieval household: daily living c.1150–c.1450*, Medieval Finds from Excavations in London 6, Her Majesty's Stationery Office, London, 217–38
Klemetilla, H. 2012 *The medieval kitchen: a social history with recipes*, Reaktion Books, London
MacGregor, A. 1987 'Objects of bone and antler', in G. Beresford, *Goltho: the development of an early medieval manor c.850–1150*, English Heritage Archaeological Report 4, 850–1150
Matthews, L. G. and Green, H. J. M. 1969 'Post-medieval pottery of the Inns of Court', *Post-Medieval Archaeology* 3, 1–17
McCarthy, M. and Brooks, C. 1988 *Medieval pottery in Britain AD 900–1600*, Leicester University Press, Leicester
Livarda, A. and Van der Veen, M. 2008 'Social access and dispersal of condiments in North-West Europe from the Roman to medieval period', *Vegetation History and Archaeobotany* 17 (Suppl. 1), 201–9
Margeson, S. (ed.) 1993 *Norwich households: the medieval and post-medieval finds from Norwich Survey Excavations 1971–1978*, East Anglian Archaeology Report 58, Norwich
Michaelis, R. 1975 'The pewter saucer', in C. Platt and R. Coleman-Smith, *Excavations in medieval Southampton, Vol. II: the finds*, Leicester University Press, Leicester, 250–1
Moorhouse, S. 1986 'Non-dating uses of medieval pottery', *Medieval Ceramics* 10, 85–123
Moorhouse, S. 1993 'Pottery and glass in the medieval monastery', in R. Gilchrist and H. Mytum, *Advances in monastic archaeology*, British Archaeological Reports British Series 227, Oxford, 127–48
Morris, C. A. 2000 *Craft, industry and everyday life: wood and woodworking in Anglo-Scandinavian and medieval York*, The Archaeology of York. The Small Finds 17/13, York
Müldner, G. and Richards, M. 2005 'Fast or feast: reconstructing diet in later medieval England by stable isotope analysis', *Journal of Archaeological Science*, 32(1), 39–48
Pearce, J. 1992 *Post-medieval pottery in London, 1500–1700, Vol. 1: Border Wares*, London
Pearce, J. and Vince, A. 1988 *A dated type-series of London medieval pottery. Part 4: Surrey whitewares*, London
Platt, C. and Coleman-Smith, R. 1975 *Excavations in medieval Southampton, Vol. II: the finds*, Leicester University Press, Leicester

Riddy, F. 2008 '"Burgeis" domesticity in late medieval England', in M. Kowaleski and P. Goldberg, *Medieval domesticity: home, housing and household in medieval England*, Cambridge University Press, Cambridge, 14–36

Schofield, J. 2003 *Medieval London houses*, Yale University Press, New Haven

Sponsler, C. 2001 'Easting lessons, Lydgate's "Dietary" and consumer conduct', in K. Ashley and R. Clark (eds), *Medieval conduct*, University of Minnesota Press, Minneapolis, 1–22

St John Hope, W. 1887 'On the English medieval drinking bowls called mazers', *Archaeologia* 50(1), 129–93

Sykes, N. 2007 'Taking sides: the social life of venison in medieval England', in A. Pluskowski (ed.), *Breaking and shaping beastly bodies: animals as material culture in the Middle Ages*, Oxbow Books, Oxford, 149–60

Sykes, N. J. 2014 *Beastly questions: animal answers to archaeological issues*, Bloomsbury, London

Thomas, A. (ed.) 1929 *Calendar of plea and memoranda rolls preserved among the archives of the Corporation of the City of London at the Guildhall, Vol. 2: AD 1364–1381*, Cambridge University Press, Cambridge

Thomas, C., Sloane, B., and Phillpotts, C. 1997 *Excavations of the Priory and Hospital of St Mary Spital, London*, Museum of London Monograph 1, London

Van Wijk, H. 2014 'Octagonal pewter flagons of the fourteenth and fifteenth centuries', *Journal of the Pewter Society* 39, 2–17

Webster, L. and Cherry, J. 1973 'Medieval Britain in 1972', *Medieval Archaeology* 17, 138–88

Willmott, H. 2005a *A history of English glassmaking, AD 43–1800*, Tempus Publishing, Stroud

Willmott, H. 2005b 'Tudor dining, object and image at the table', in M. Carroll, D. Hadley, and H. Willmott (eds), *Consuming passions: dining from Antiquity to the eighteenth century*, Tempus Publishing, Stroud, 121–42

Willmott, H. 2011 'Glass', in R. Brown and A. Hardy, *Trade and prosperity, war and poverty: an archaeological and historical investigation into Southampton's French Quarter*, Oxford Archaeology Monograph 15, Oxford, 182–99

Willmott, H. 2015 'Table glass in the West Country home', in J. Allan, N. Alcock, and D. Dawson (eds), *West Country households, 1500–1700*, The Boydell Press, Woodbridge, 321–38

Woolgar, C. (ed.) 1993 *Household accounts from medieval England, part 2: diet accounts (ii), cash, corn and stock accounts, wardrobe accounts, catalogue*, Records of Social and Economic History, NS 18, Oxford University Press for The British Academy, Oxford

Woolgar, C. 2006 *The senses in late medieval England*, Yale University Press, London

Woolgar, C. 2010 'Food and the Middle Ages', *Journal of Medieval History* 36(1), 1–19

CHAPTER 44

SOUND AND LANDSCAPE

STEPHEN MILESON

SOUND is a fertile but underdeveloped subject for medieval archaeologists. In the Middle Ages, as in any period, auditory perception played a vital role in structuring experience. The spoken word was the primary form of communication. In an era of restricted literacy, texts were often read out loud, and the word of God and the orders of the powerful were conveyed by sermons and public announcements. Non-verbal noises—including bird song and animal calls—were understood as part of a common heritage of ideas about the spiritual and physical world, as well as having associations with the whole range of human experiences, not least the cycle of the seasons. Words and sounds helped create a sense of place and occasion, and therefore affected patterns of behaviour. Cannons were fired and banners unfurled to signal the arrival of important visitors at the town or castle gate; the sweet song of caged birds added to the pleasurable atmosphere of royal apartments; and the sound of running water was an aid to contemplation and relaxation in monastic precinct and noble garden. Traditionally sound has been analysed primarily by specialists interested in sacred and secular music, lyric, and drama (recent studies include Butterfield 2002; Coldeway 2007; Dillon 2006; 2012; Minamino 2002; Williams 2005). Important contributions have been made by students of royal rituals and civic ceremonies (including Anglo 1969; Hurlbut 1999). Latterly sound has engaged the attention of medievalists interested in themes such as the senses and everyday life (Frugoni 2005; Woolgar 2006), and this has brought the topic closer to the core concerns of archaeologists. Nevertheless, to date, sound has not achieved a very prominent place in medieval archaeology, despite a broader interest in embodiment and materiality (e.g. Gilchrist 2012, 7–8).

Archaeologists are well placed to advance research on medieval sound. The objects found in excavations produced many of society's common noises, and the projection of sound was profoundly affected by the built and natural environment that archaeological studies have done so much to reconstruct. In recent years the framework for an 'auditory archaeology' has been set out as a way to 'stimulate alternative ways of thinking about engagement with and relationships between places, people and animals as well as considering how sound and hearing may have contributed to past understandings of them' (Mills 2014, 19). There are, of course, problems in trying to recapture something as transient as sound. The noises made in the Middle Ages have left no trace, and we have only indirect evidence of how they were received. Nonetheless, it is possible to make informed suggestions about the character of sound in well-understood medieval urban and rural landscapes through analysis of material culture and measurement of sound produced by particular activities in experimental reconstructions. To some extent, contemporary responses to specific sounds can be recovered from documents and iconography and interpreted in the light of wider knowledge of beliefs and social relations. On this basis it is possible to analyse the 'soundscapes' of different places, in other words, the range of sounds that made up the auditory environment of a town or village, monastery, or castle and the way these sounds were understood.

This chapter focuses on the social meaning of everyday sounds in medieval towns and rural settlements. Rather than attempting to build a complete soundscape for any given setting, it offers a preliminary exploration of the meaning of sound in the medieval landscape, following in some respects the qualitative approach to sound successfully adopted by historians of the early modern and modern periods (Corbin 1999; Garrioch 2003; Smith 1999). Here meaning is approached through two interrelated themes: firstly, the relationship between sound and power; secondly, actual or intended emotional responses to sound, in particular the feeling of attachment to a locality. Particular attention will be paid to the significance of church bells, instruments which did so much to shape the lives of townsmen and villagers across Britain and beyond. In the final section, bells are used to demonstrate the potential for a more quantitative experimental approach to measuring medieval 'soundmarks' (that is, distinctive and significant noises within the soundscape). The findings are based on recent fieldwork carried out in south Oxfordshire.

Sound and Power

In the Middle Ages creating and controlling noise was a significant expression of social authority. This was partly because levels of sound were considerably lower than in the mechanized modern world: with less background noise it was easier to make a sound mark. In a quieter world, loud noises were more noticeable and must have made a strong impression. Powerful, sudden, and unexplained noises such as thunder caused fear, and uncontrolled noise and din was associated with the devil and madness, a polar opposite of silence, which was linked with contemplation, order, and sanctity (Woolgar 2006, 66, 68–9, 75–6). Between cacophony and stillness was the opportunity to use sound to direct society. At the highest level, attention to royal pronouncements was commanded by cries or the blast of trumpets (Masschaele 2002, 396), the latter associated in the Bible with divine judgement. Civic authorities relied on bells and, later, striking clocks to convene judicial sessions, to regulate trade, and to mark the curfew, the time in the evening when taverns and gates were closed and the watchmen took over the quiet streets (Clanchy 2013, 274–5; Glennie and Thrift 2009, 37–40, 128–30, 186; Woolgar 2006, 74).

Ecclesiastics were especially determined to control noise in churches and beyond because of the perceived link between sound and spirituality. In the 1240s Bishop William Raleigh of Norwich attempted to restrict the use of hand bells in the streets to priests carrying the sacrament because he saw bells primarily as a means of arousing devotion (Woolgar 2006, 73). In the countryside, a wide range of activities were regulated by sound. Horns were used by shepherds and swineherds directing the common flocks; by foresters patrolling the woods and protecting deer; and sometimes to initiate the clamour of the 'hue and cry', a recognized appeal to public aid by those who were assaulted or who found a dead body. Instruments of regulatory noise became symbols of authority, including probably the ivory horn associated with Savernake Forest in Wiltshire, which was adorned in the mid-fourteenth century with silver bands depicting hunting dogs, beasts of the chase, a king facing a bishop, and a forester blowing a horn (British Museum 1975, 0401.1; Bathe 2012, esp. 175–6, 180). In many areas near forests, in Scotland as well as England, hunting horns are depicted on incised grave slabs.

Attempts to impose authority were not always successful, of course, and, in Britain as elsewhere, people sometimes actively resisted by making noise. The very democracy of sound and its humorous potential was a danger to those in authority: shouts of derision or outbursts of laughter could undermine the most carefully choreographed display of power. During civil disturbances, rebels attempted to publicize their cause in song and developed their own calls and watchwords (Wright 1839). In an appropriation of the power to control the soundscape, bells might be used to coordinate the inception of revolts and to mark their conclusion (Atkinson 2013). Ritualized inversions, including the performance of 'rough music', were carried out to ridicule unpopular rulers as well as to release communal tensions (Jonassen 1994). Local officials such as constables appear to have been particularly sensitive to verbal abuse and inappropriate gossiping (Bardsley 2003, 157–8). Aristocrats who attacked an opponent's game reserves as a way of humiliating him subverted the norms of the orderly hunt by blasting horns and shouting while slaughtering deer and destroying park fences (Manning 1993, 43). Gangs of poachers 'emasculated' foresters by taking their horns (Hanawalt 1988, 190; Marvin 1999, 233–4). Ecclesiastical views on sound were not easily enforced outside church or cloister and the conception of music as a source of virtuous harmony faced many challenges. Musical instruments such as bagpipes, fiddles, and drums became staples of popular entertainment and dancing, activities all too easily associated with sinful impropriety (Woolgar 2006, 80–3). Medieval bone, ceramic, and metal whistles have all been reported to the Portable Antiquities Scheme (e.g. LON-58D1C9; LON-5396A6; SWYOR-B284C7). Bells found many uses, some of them frivolous: miniature bells were sewn into clothes by jesters and especially after 1350 became fashionable accoutrements to clothing and horse harnesses, enabling individuals to draw attention to their appearance (Egan and Pritchard 1991, 336–41) (Figure 44.1).

Landscape archaeologists can use this kind of qualitative information to analyse the relationship between sound and power in different environments. The physical setting mattered because it greatly affected the character of the soundscape. Some places were noisier than others or were characterized by a greater duration or intensity of particular sounds. The most obvious contrast was between town and country: the town was

FIGURE 44.1 A small copper-alloy bell of the kind used as a dress accessory, found in Lewknor (Oxfordshire)

(© Portable Antiquities Scheme Object ID: BH-D7F06A, CC BY)

louder and, in particular, urban life was characterized by the more frequent ringing of a larger number of bells, which accompanied church services of many kinds and were widely used for secular purposes. The crowded nature of the urban soundscape led to conflict, as indicated by a dispute mainly about burial rights between Southwark priory and St Thomas's hospital, Southwark, in the 1220s or 1230s. The resolution included an agreement that the hospital could only have two bells weighing 100 lb (about 45 kg) in their bell tower (Bodleian MS Rawlinson D 763, f. 5v). Such bells would have weighed the same as a typical sanctus bell, a small bell rung during the Eucharist (see e.g. Sharpe

1950, 177–9). The intention, presumably, was that the hospital should not be able to make too loud a claim on the loyalties of local people.

Beyond the simple urban–rural divide, local conditions had an important bearing on the character and intensity of sound. The carry of sound was affected by topography and vegetation cover, building form and density, settlement layout and work regime, as well as by weather conditions. In terms of topography, for example, sound carried differently in the mountains than on the plains and in the woods than in the marshes, whether on a hot, dry summer day or a cold and damp winter night. A strongly human-influenced factor in geographical variation was the distribution of masonry buildings. Stone buildings allowed sound to travel in and out much less than wooden ones, so the presence and concentration of stone structures would have affected the audibility of conversations and the sense of separation between house and street. Stone buildings were much more common in town than country, amongst lords than peasants, and monks than laymen, but they were also subject to spatial zoning. In London, for example, masonry structures were clustered in certain parts of the city (Schofield 2011, 64), areas that would have had distinctive sonic properties; properties which, in turn, are likely to have affected how the status of the neighbourhood was read.

Significantly, it is clear that medieval people were aware of some of the physical influences on acoustics. In churches, sounding jars and pots were used in an attempt to amplify noise (Merrifield 1987, 121–8; Valière et al. 2013), and in some great churches and cathedrals apertures were created in galleries to allow concealed singers to project their voices out into the body of the building (Binski 2004, 111–12). In castles, the resonance of stone enhanced the communal atmosphere of the great hall, although refined manners required controls on noise levels. In more private chambers, wall hangings and soft furnishings may have been used to dampen sound as well as to enhance warmth and comfort (Woolgar 2006, 67–8). In town squares, urban authorities set up raised platforms to increase the audibility and visibility of criers making public announcements (Symes 2010, 284), though in the disordered London of the Peasants' Revolt one messenger allegedly resorted to standing on an old chair (Dobson 1970, 160). Fieldwork observation and sound recording has the potential to reveal more about the character and extent of such interventions and their possible effects on experiences and perceptions. For example, recent investigation suggests that certain hundred meeting places may have been chosen in part because of their sonic properties: some moot sites appear to have been distinguished by bowl-shaped topographical depressions which would have enhanced the audibility of the spoken voice (Baker and Brookes 2015, 16).

Sound and Meaning

The distinctive sounds of neighbourhoods would have helped people gain an impression of their character, and it has been suggested that for early modern inhabitants they formed part of the familiar setting that contributed to generating a sense of place

(Atkinson 2013, 65–9; Garrioch 2003, 14). Medieval people certainly seem to have developed attachments to localities: a fond regard for places of origin and family connection is indicated by literary texts such as Gerald of Wales's well-known late twelfth-century description of Manorbier Castle in Pembrokeshire and, later on, by bequests in wills. Dialects and regional musical traditions must also have influenced self-perception. But how might the character of sound at a more local level have played a part in shaping people's sense of belonging? The case of church bells helps to supply an answer.

The widespread erection of bell towers attached to churches, starting in eastern England in the later eleventh century (Blair 2005, 416; Stocker and Everson 2006), transformed the soundscape of the countryside (Figure 44.2). Large suspended bells were in most places the first regular source of landscape-scale sound, noise that could be heard clearly at a distance of a kilometre or more. By putting bells in towers, their long-established religious meanings and uses could be projected beyond the church and out into the surrounding area (Garceau 2011; Staaf 1996; Stocker and Everson 2006, 80–2). As a result, bells became a major tool in the ecclesiastical attempt to generate a parochial religious community. Thirteenth-century diocesan legislation makes it clear that churchmen believed that the sound of bells aroused a spirit of devotion and helped to combat sin (Arnold and Goodson 2012, 118). The loud and sonorous sound of the bells

FIGURE 44.2 The heavily restored Norman font at Belton church (Lincolnshire), showing a bell-ringer in action

(© Stephen Mileson)

reminded people of their obligation to attend church, but the bells were also used to involve the laity in the celebration of the Mass on working days when they might not be able to be present. Those outside the church, whether at home or in the fields, were enjoined to bow and pray upon hearing the Eucharist bell, which was sounded at the raising of the host (Arnold and Goodson 2012, 122).

Bells were a key element of the individual's experience of religion, and there are strong indications that they also helped shape a sense of connection with place. Their significance in both respects is indicated by financial investment. Parishioners were in theory obliged to maintain the bell tower and supply bells and ropes, but in reality the investments made were usually voluntary gifts rather than enforced payments. Individuals made bequests towards the cost of new bells and groups clubbed together to buy them, as in the parish of St Benet Sherehog in London, where, according to a proof of age, in 1412 John Barkefold 'and other neighbours bought the great bell of the church, called sweet Maria of Shorehoge' (*Cal. IPM*, 26, 87, no. 148). Investment may have been prompted partly by self-interest, since bells were widely believed to drive off demons, dissipate lightning, and prevent crop-damaging storms, as shown by inscriptions on bells themselves. Protection against demons was especially important during the funeral service, when the soul of the dead person was vulnerable to attack (Daniell 1997, 47–8), and well-off testators were careful to specify payments to bell ringers (Burgess 1987, 188). The bell not only proclaimed the death and encouraged prayers for the soul, but the length of the tolling also indicated the status of the deceased (Bainbridge 1994, 197). Bells rung in a particular parish to mark anniversaries must have had a special personal meaning for relatives of the dead person, helping generate a sense of connection between family and place through time. Yet concern for the present and future community of the parish (and a desire to be identified as a leading member of that community) is also likely to have been important. After all, the bells served the whole population, creating a common timetable for the day, marking feasts and other special occasions, and acting as a mechanism to announce public events and warn of threats such as house fires (*Cal. IPM*, 25, 392, no. 475). Spending on fabric implies an element of local pride and in some areas and periods there seems to have been a competitive urge to have the biggest bells and highest tower. In some cases it is virtually certain that investment came from ordinary inhabitants rather than lords, as for example at Berrick Salome in south Oxfordshire, where the small wooden tower has been tree-ring dated to 1429 (Miles 2013). Manorial rights at Berrick were divided between several non-resident lords as an appurtenance of Chalgrove manor, and the relative cheapness and of wood strongly suggests a grass-roots project.

The Soundmark of the Bell: A Case Study from South Oxfordshire

The Leverhulme-funded South Oxfordshire Project (completed in 2015) was an interdisciplinary investigation into rural inhabitants' perceptions of landscape over the long period from 500 to 1650 (Mileson 2012). A major question addressed by the research was how ordinary medieval people created a sense of identity in relation to the places in which they lived. The study area comprised the fourteen ancient parishes of the hundred of Ewelme, which encompassed more than 10,000 ha of mixed countryside (Figure 44.3). By 1200, the flat and open north-western part of the hundred was a landscape of mainly nucleated villages and hamlets with extensive surrounding open field systems, while the hilly and wooded Chiltern zone in the south-east was characterized by a much more dispersed settlement pattern of mainly small, scattered settlements with limited (if any) open fields and many closes. In between the two landscapes was a border area of open but undulating countryside at the scarp foot. The distinctive character of the two main parts of the study area supplied an opportunity to assess the influence of settlement and landscape type on practices and perceptions in the context of changes affecting all English rural settlements, including, in the post-Conquest period, the growth of commercial relationships from the thirteenth century and the substantial increase in migration after 1350. The project revealed significant differences in relationships and attachments across vale and Chilterns in the Middle Ages. Amongst the key findings was the greater extent of 'open' (or, to put it crudely, 'public') space in many vale settlements compared with the Chilterns, and the closer spatial integration in the vale of many homesteads with communal facilities, which had implications for sociability (Mileson 2015; 2017).

The identification of co-variant social patterns and sense of belonging in the two landscapes was strengthened by fieldwork assessment of the carry of the sound of church bells. The soundmark of bells was tested in the field by having a bell tolled for a set period of time while two members of the project team moved away from the church along public footpaths until the sound of the bell was no longer audible. The bell tolled was usually a treble, the lightest bell, but the slightly heavier bells in the usual parish church set were found not to produce significantly different results in the same conditions. The experiments were carried out on summer days in still air or light breezes. Different results might have been achieved in other weather conditions. In a few parishes, including Benson and Warborough, traffic noise from main roads led to null results in certain areas. The findings were mapped in GIS for analysis. The fieldwork suggested that wholly simulated models of soundmarks did not produce very accurate results, although some computer-generated projections were better than others (for an example of simulation of bell soundmarks see Mlekuz 2004). The soundmarks for three parishes (Brightwell Baldwin and Cuxham, in the vale, and Nettlebed, in the Chilterns) are shown in Figure 44.4.

This simple experimental technique was thought to be a fair reflection of the sounding of a bell in the late Middle Ages, since the bells rung (which were mainly of seventeenth-century or later date) were of similar weight to their medieval predecessors, even if hung somewhat differently (Sharpe 1949–53; Stocker and Everson 2006, 34–5), and were suspended in towers mainly of medieval origin. Needless to say, there are difficulties in relating the results to the medieval experience. Besides differences in the landscape the bells themselves would not all have been made at the same time, nor to the same size,

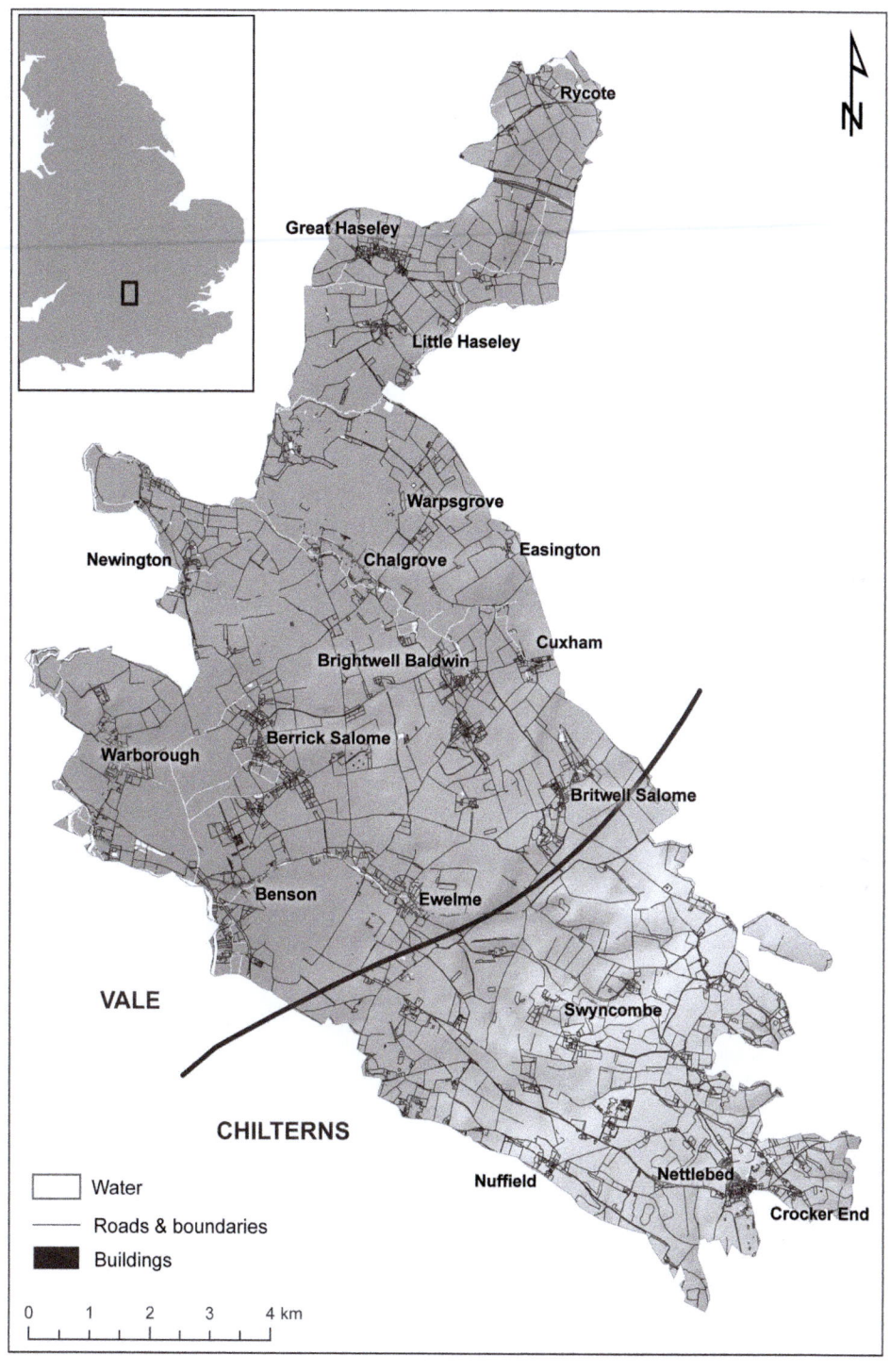

FIGURE 44.3 Ewelme hundred in south Oxfordshire, based on nineteenth-century maps. The approximate line of the Chiltern scarp is indicated

(© Stephen Mileson)

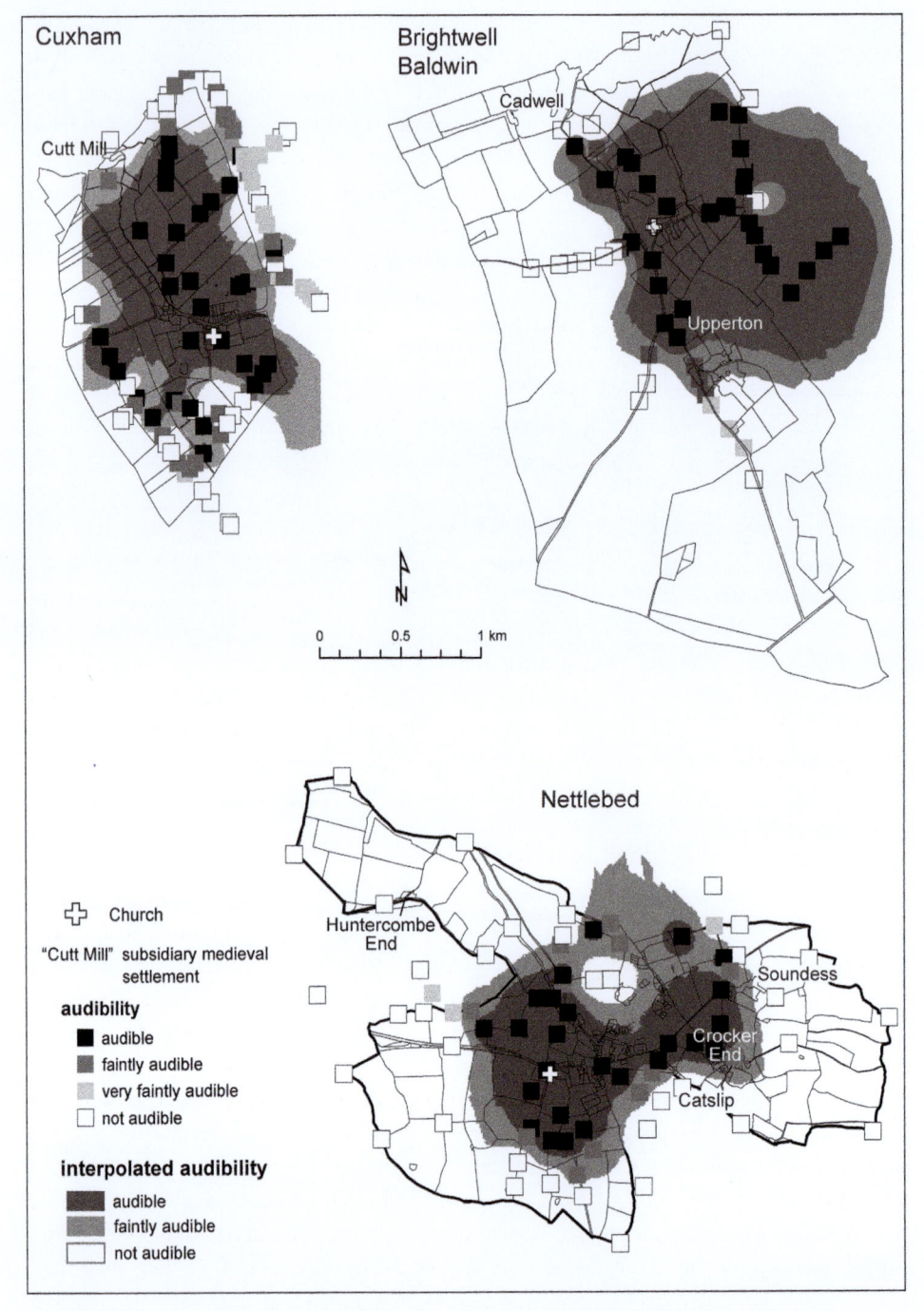

FIGURE 44.4 Selected bell soundmarks in Ewelme hundred (plotted by Stuart Brookes)

(© Stephen Mileson)

and the towers themselves would have been in various states of building and rebuilding. Nevertheless, the broad patterns observed would have applied in the Middle Ages too. These patterns are important because of the way in which bells fostered relationships with the church whence they rang: in other words, it is worth considering whether the different effects of bells in landscapes fostered different relationships.

The results suggest interesting patterns of audibility across the study area. The range of the bells does not appear to have been very strongly affected by local variations in topography and tree cover, since the soundmark in the undulating and wooded parish of Nettlebed was as extensive as those of the vale bells (Figure 44.4). However, it should be noted that Nettlebed church has a post-medieval tower measuring 15.36 m, compared to extant medieval towers or bellcotes mostly of between 8 and 13 m tall. At the margins of audibility, relief certainly did play a role: in several places the tolling of the bells became inaudible as the hearer moved down a steep slope away from the source of sound. Importantly, the nature of settlement would have had a strong effect on audibility: because the medieval population was generally clustered together fairly close to the church in vale parishes, the great majority of the inhabitants would have been in range of their home bell or bells in and around the village. In some small vale parishes, in fact, the soundmark of the bell coincides today almost exactly with the parish boundary, creating a very close match between soundmark and parochial territory. In larger parishes those working in outlying fields may not have heard the bells and, in one or two cases, there may have been hamlets out of earshot: in Cadwell today it is difficult to hear the bells of the parish church at Brightwell. In the Chilterns, the scattered character of settlement meant that a larger number of hamlets and farmsteads would have been out of bell's reach, as indicated by the experimental findings in Nettlebed (Figure 44.4).

It seems a reasonable conclusion, given these findings, that church bells would have contributed more towards a sense of parochial community in the vale than in the Chilterns. Documentary evidence shows that some people in peripheral settlements (of which there were a greater number in the Chilterns) attended churches beyond their home parish by the sixteenth century, and this was probably the case earlier. Part of the rationale may have been proximity, but the experimental findings indicate that audibility may have been a factor too. Nevertheless, there were complications in the relationship between sound and place. One of these was the presence in the vale of a few larger churches with bigger bells and taller towers that are likely to have been audible and visible across a larger area (just as they are today). These include, pre-eminently, the abbey church at Dorchester, just over the western boundary of the hundred, and, to a lesser extent and at a lower level of ecclesiastical status, the churches of Newington (with a 19 m high early fourteenth-century tower, including a locally conspicuous $c.4$ m spire), Chalgrove, and Benson. It may be that the bells of these churches to some degree created a devotional pull away from other churches, especially since the churches themselves were better supported financially (with the possible exception of Benson) and almost certainly offered more regular services and superior amenities for worship.

The reach and distinctive tone of these big bells may, along with other factors, have encouraged richer folk at least to spread their devotional attachment more widely.

FIGURE 44.5 Dorchester Abbey's tenor bell of *c*.1380, weight 843 kg. Compared with other extant medieval examples, this was a very heavy bell by local standards

(© Frank Blackwell)

That this was the case is suggested by a few sixteenth-century wills that follow pre-Reformation practices in terms of bequests towards memorial services. In 1581, for example, John Gibbs of Berrick Prior (a detached part of Newington parish) made provision for payments to be made to the ringers at Chalgrove, Stadhampton, and Drayton to ring his knell (Oxfordshire History Centre, MS Wills Oxon. 25/1/13; 186.204). John requested burial in Newington churchyard, but he evidently also wanted his passing to be marked in these other places, which surrounded Newington to the east, north, and west. Together the bells would have been audible over a large block of territory that included Newington parish. His request for burial at Newington is a further reminder of complex attachments since Berrick Prior formed the northern part of a village of parochial status with its own church (Berrick Salome), several kilometres south of Newington (Figure 44.3). John made small bequests to the church and bells at Newington, to the churches at Cuddesdon and Garsington, and a rather larger bequest towards the 'building of Dorchester steeple'. The Dorchester bells may have been regarded as having particular protective power, associated as they were with the local saint, Bishop Birinus: the heaviest bell, the late fourteenth-century tenor, given by Ralph Restwold (d. 1383), lord of Crowmarsh Gifford (8 km from Dorchester), is inscribed 'PROTEGE BIRINE QUOS CONVOCO TU SINE FINE RAF RASTWOLD' ('Birinus, protect for ever those whom I summon. Ralph Rastwold') (Sharpe 1950, 117–18, 125) (Figure 44.5).

Sound was one of several complementary ways in which medieval people related to a religious landscape that included a host of features exerting an influence across parish boundaries on practices and identities, including cathedrals, monasteries, neighbouring parish churches, chapels, hospitals, and wayside shrines. The experimental work in Ewelme hundred indicates the potential of fieldwork investigation of soundmarks, especially when combined with contextual research in documents and material culture. Such research could usefully be extended to other parts of Britain (and beyond). Medieval sound is a challenging topic, but when considered as part of sensory experiences as a whole it supplies a richer understanding of the environment and agency of people in the past, including the ordinary people whose outlook can be so difficult to reach.

Acknowledgements

I would like to thank Stuart Brookes, Paul Everson, Ian Forrest, Caroline Goodson, and Simon Townley for comments on draft versions of this chapter. John Blair kindly informed me about the dispute between Southwark priory and St Thomas's hospital.

References cited

Anglo, S. 1969 *Spectacle, pageantry, and early Tudor policy*, Clarendon Press, Oxford

Arnold, J. H. and Goodson, C. 2012 'Resounding community: the history and meaning of medieval church bells', *Viator* 43(1), 99–130

Atkinson, N. 2013 'The republic of sound: listening to Florence at the threshold of the Renaissance', *I Tatti Studies in the Italian Renaissance* 16(1/2), 57–84

Bainbridge, V. 1994 'The medieval way of death: commemoration and the afterlife in pre-Reformation Cambridgeshire', in M. Wilks (ed.), *Prophecy and eschatology*, Studies in Church History, Subsidia 10, Blackwell, Oxford, 183–204

Baker, J. and Brookes, S. 2015 'Identifying outdoor assembly sites in early medieval England', *Journal of Field Archaeology* 40(1), 3–21

Bardsley, S. 2003 'Sin, speech and scolding in late medieval England', in T. S. Fenster and D. L. Smail (eds), *Fama: the politics of talk and reputation in medieval Europe*, Cornell University Press, Ithaca, New York, 145–64

Bathe, G. 2012 'The Savernake horn', *Wiltshire Archaeological and Natural History Magazine* 105, 168–81

Binski, P. 2004 *Becket's crown: art and imagination in Gothic England, 1170–1300*, Yale University Press, New Haven

Blair, J. 2005 *The Church in Anglo-Saxon society*, Oxford University Press, Oxford

Burgess, C. 1987 'A service for the dead: the form and function of the anniversary in late medieval Bristol', *Transactions of the Bristol and Gloucestershire Archaeological Society* 105, 183–211

Butterfield, A. 2002 *Poetry and music in medieval France: from Jean Renart to Guillaume Machaut*, Cambridge University Press, Cambridge

Cal. IPM: *Calendar of Inquisitions Post Mortem*, London, 1904–
Clanchy, M. T. 2013 *From memory to written record: England 1066–1307*, Wiley-Blackwell, Chichester (3rd edn)
Coldeway, J. C. (ed.) 2007 *Medieval drama*, 4 vols, Routledge, New York
Corbin, A. 1999 *Village bells: sound and meaning in the 19th-century French countryside*, Papermac, London
Daniell, C. 1997 *Death and burial in medieval England, 1066–1550*, Routledge, London
Dillon, E. 2006 'Representing obscene sound', in N. McDonald (ed.), *Medieval obscenities*, Boydell and Brewer, Woodbridge
Dillon, E. 2012 *The sense of sound: musical meaning in France, 1260–1330*, Oxford University Press, Oxford
Dobson, R. B. (ed.) 1970 *The Peasants' Revolt of 1381*, Macmillan, London
Egan, G. and Pritchard, F. 1991 *Dress accessories, c.1150–c.1450*, Her Majesty's Stationery Office, London
Frugoni, C. 2005 *A day in a medieval city*, University of Chicago Press, Chicago
Garceau, M. E. 2011 '"I call the people": church bells in fourteenth-century Catalunya', *Journal of Medieval History* 37, 197–214
Garrioch, D. 2003 'Sounds of the city: the soundscape of early modern European towns', *Urban History* 30(1), 5–25
Gilchrist, R. 2012 *Medieval life: archaeology and the life course*, The Boydell Press, Woodbridge
Glennie, P. and Thrift, N. 2009 *Shaping the day: a history of timekeeping in England and Wales 1300–1800*, Oxford University Press, Oxford
Hanawalt, B. 1988 'Men's games, king's deer: poaching in medieval England', *Journal of Medieval and Renaissance Studies* 18(2), 175–93
Hurlbut, J. D. 1999 'The sound of civic spectacle: noise in Burgundian ceremonial entries', in C. Davidson (ed.), *Material culture and medieval drama*, Medieval Institute Publications, Kalamazoo, 127–40
Jonassen, F. B. 1994 'Rough music in Chaucer's *Merchant's Tale*', in J. E. Jost (ed.), *Chaucer's humor: critical essays*, Garland, New York, 229–58
Manning, R. B. 1993, *Hunters and poachers: a social and cultural history of unlawful hunting in England, 1485–1640*, Clarendon Press, Oxford
Marvin, W. P. 1999 'Slaughter and romance: hunting reserves in late medieval England', in B. A. Hanawalt and D. Wallace (eds), *Medieval crime and social control*, University of Minnesota Press, Minneapolis, 224–52
Masschaele, J. 2002 'The public space of the marketplace in medieval England', *Speculum* 77(2), 383–421
Merrifield, R. 1987 *The archaeology of ritual and magic*, Batsford, London
Miles, D. 2013 *Tree-ring dating of the bell tower at St Helen's Church, Berrick Salome, Oxfordshire*, unpublished Oxford Dendrochronology Laboratory report, 2013/33
Mileson, S. 2012 'The south Oxfordshire project: perceptions of landscape, settlement and society, c.500–1650', *Landscape History* 33(2), 83–98
Mileson, S. 2015 'People and houses in south Oxfordshire, 1300–1650', *Vernacular Architecture* 46, 8–25
Mileson, S. 2017 'Openness and closure in the later-medieval village', *Past and Present* 234, 3–37
Mills, S. 2014 *Auditory archaeology: understanding sound and hearing in the past*, Left Coast Press, Walnut Creek, CA

Minamino, H. 2002 'Village noise and Bruegel's parables', in L. P. Austern (ed.), *Music, sensation and sensuality*, Routledge, New York, 267–84

Mlekuz, D. 2004 'Listening to landscapes: modelling past soundscapes in GIS', *Internet Archaeology* 16 [http://intarch.ac.uk/journal/issue16/mlekuz_index.html]

Schofield, J. 2011 *London, 1100–1600: the archaeology of a capital city*, Equinox, Sheffield

Sharpe, F. 1949–53 *The church bells of Oxfordshire*, Oxfordshire Record Society, vols 28, 30, 32, 34, Oxford

Sharpe, F. 1950 *The church bells of Oxfordshire*, Oxfordshire Record Society, vol. 30, Oxford

Smith, B. 1999 *The acoustic world of early modern England: attending to the o-factor*, University of Chicago Press, Chicago

Staaf, B. M. 1996 'For whom the bell tolls', *Current Swedish Archaeology* 4, 141–55

Stocker, D. and Everson, P. 2006 *Summoning St Michael: early Romanesque towers in Lincolnshire*, Oxbow Books, Oxford

Symes, C. 2010 'Out in the open, in Arras: sightlines, soundscapes, and the shaping of a medieval public sphere', in C. Goodson, A. E. Lester, and C. Symes (eds), *Cities, texts and social networks, 400–1500: experiences and perceptions of medieval urban space*, Ashgate, Farnham, 279–302

Valière, J.-C., Palazzo-Bertholon, B., Polack, J.-D., and Carvalho, P. 2013 'Acoustic pots in ancient and medieval buildings: literary analysis of ancient texts and comparison with recent observations in French churches', *Acta Acustica united with Acustica* 99, 70–81

Williams, P. 2005, *The organ in western culture, 750–1250*, Cambridge Studies in Medieval and Renaissance Music, Cambridge

Woolgar, C. 2006 *The senses in late medieval England*, Yale, New Haven

Wright, T. 1839 *The political songs of England: from the reign of King John to that of Edward II*, Camden Society, London

CHAPTER 45

LONDON SMELLWALK AROUND 1450
Smelling Medieval Cities

HOLLY DUGAN

BUTCHERS' Bridge, Bladder alley, Lyme Street, Hog Lane, Scalding Alley, Seacoal Lane, Stinking Lane: few of us would enthusiastically volunteer to participate in an event that sought to recreate the smell of medieval London. Smellwalks are planned participatory events designed to heighten awareness of and appreciation for the role of olfaction in urban placemaking, offering their participants chances to experience the 'olfactory essences' of cities such as Amsterdam, Montreal, Pamplona, Glasgow, Edinburgh, Newport, Paris, New York, and Doncaster (Henshaw 2014, 45–7; Quercia et al. 2015, 3; 2016). Though we may acknowledge the importance of, and perhaps even revel in, the scents that define our urban environments, most of us remain hesitant to sniff those of the past. And London of the past, we imagine, is defined by malodorous stench.

Cities have unique smells, ones that emerge from a *mélange* of their animal, human, environmental, and industrial parts but also defined by signature olfactory notes. This tension, between the olfactory part and its whole, makes it difficult to talk about the smell of public spaces, let alone historicize it. For instance, data derived from twenty-first century smellwalks indicate important differences in how we talk about the smell of certain cities: Barcelona, for instance, is more often described as smelling of food and nature, whereas London most often smells of waste and car exhaust (Quercia et al. 2015, 6). Such data are fascinating as well as inconclusive, identifying molecules encountered during these events as well as implicit cultural tropes about how such molecules are perceived, coded with meaning, and described. The diagnostic tool most often used to help participants name the smells they encounter is the odour descriptor wheel (Suffet and Rosenfeld 2007, 342) (Figure 45.1). This is designed to help participants identify the odour itself rather than seeking to name its source, thus surmounting many of the challenges of describing smell in modern European languages (Henshaw 2014, 17).

No longer seen as trivial or unrecoverable, the sensory worlds of the past are also now considered by many scholars to be vital to understanding not only embodied

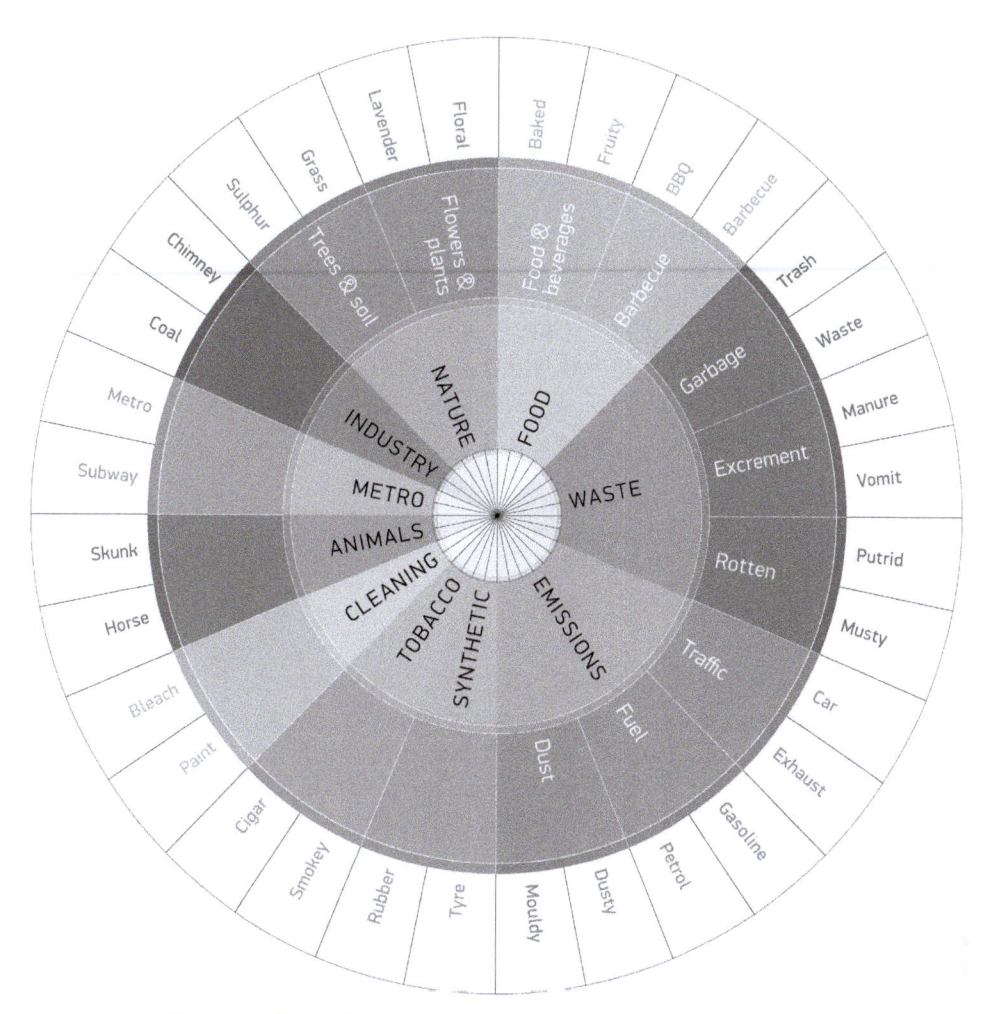

FIGURE 45.1 Urban smell wheel (from Quercia et al. 2015)

experience but also cultural, economic, material, political, and social history (Curran and Kearny 2012; Milner 2012; Stanev 2014; Waldron 2012). As recent work in geography and sensory studies reveals, mental maps of space are an important part of how urban space is experienced, connecting visceral sensation with larger cultural meanings about what smells good or bad, familiar or exotic. Our individual perceptions of localized spaces are often reworked and expanded into totalizing mental maps of environments, ones that are both personal and subjective even as they connect to broader social and urban histories. Recent neurological research also suggests that these maps might be more important than we think, allowing us to navigate space through smell (Jacobs et al. 2015).

Representational 'maps' of space are thus a key part of how we engage with our environments, raising questions about their role in the past. These should be part of our histories; though we may consider them as metaphoric (rather than material), these assumptions often reveal links between the design of a space and how it was perceived.

Archival traces of smells of the past are thus more than just evidence of what Henri Lefebvre would describe as 'representational' space; instead they index smell as it is experienced (Lefebvre 1991, 33). Such a confluence of real and imagined evidence may make them suspect sources for some historical inquiries, but it also makes them especially valuable for understanding how men and women dwelled and inhabited urban space. Though they may not offer conclusive evidence of how the past 'really' smelled, they provide a way to explore how medieval men and women perceived their environments.

This chapter draws on literary and historical sources in order to create a medieval urban odour descriptor wheel, one that demonstrates that the smell of medieval cities was both more pungent and pleasurable than we usually assume and one that will hopefully help readers orient themselves towards new understandings about the vitality of smell in the past as well as in the present.

Sensing Cities

Medieval cities, like modern ones, could be intensely crowded spaces and the phenomenological experience of crowding mattered (Munro 2005, 29). In fact, population density in medieval cities far exceeded all but our most densely populated twenty-first-century megacities. Only Tokyo is more densely populated than medieval London around the year 1300, rivalling megacities like Seoul and Beijing (c.2011) for urban population and compactness. Tokyo averages 31,150 inhabitants per square kilometre, Seoul has 21,000, and Beijing has 16,000 (Kim and Choe 2010, 59). In 1300, at its most populous, medieval London had 80,000 inhabitants in its 5.18 square kilometres, for a population density of 15,444 per km^2, almost double that of modern day Paris, which has 5962 inhabitants per km^2. Even after its population dropped by a third following plague outbreaks of the fourteenth century, London still averaged 10,193 inhabitants per km^2 (calculations based on population data found in Keene 2012, 264). Compare this, for example, with 77 inhabitants per km^2 in fourteenth-century fenlands in Deeping St Nicholas (Hallam 1961, 73). To breathe in medieval London was thus a communal affair; men and women inhaled all aspects of this crowded, shared space, including the smell of its many animal and human inhabitants, its industries, and their collective detritus.

The smell of a city, whether experienced or imagined, is an important part of its collective social history. Perception is comprised not only of our physical sensation of material phenomena but also of our memories and cultural expectations of it. Each of these renders a unique experience of shared social space that over time coalesce into collective histories, histories that include some experiences and exclude others. The smell of a city is thus intimately linked to our social understandings of who or what we imagine is integral to that space (and who or what is not).

Whether we experience those smells as pleasurable or noisome also hinges upon our unique embodied histories and past experiences of both the smell and the space in which it was encountered. For example, unfamiliar odours are often experienced (at least initially) as negative; yet for those who are neurodiverse, smells, even so-called malodorous ones, can render the space to be vastly more accommodating than seemingly deodorized, neutral space. How, then, are we to analyse something like the olfactory 'essence' of a place and its role in shaping social experience in the past? Consider, for instance, Edward III's famous (and often quoted) description of the 'abominable' stench of York in 1332:

> To the mayors and bailiffs of York, The king, detesting the abominable smell abounding in the said city more than in any other city of the realm from dung and manure and other filth and dirt where with the streets and lanes are filled and obstructed, and wishing to provide for the protection of the health of the inhabitants and of those coming to the present parliament, orders them to cause all the streets and lanes of the city to be cleansed from such filth ...
>
> (Lyte 1898, 610).

Did medieval York 'really' stink? Historians note that the medieval city lacked provisions for sanitation: despite Roman infrastructure (including stone-lined sewers), the medieval ground level was significantly higher than its Roman counterpart, suggesting that it was built upon heaps of waste (Taylor 2015, 231). But as early as 1301, public latrines were available in four quadrants of the city including on the bridge over the River Ouse (Rawcliffe 2013, 142); private, wicker-lined latrines with seats were common by the mid-fourteenth century (Taylor 2015, 231).

What about animal waste? The king mentions both dung and manure, suggesting that animals helped to define the space, both in economic terms as well as physical ones. Dung most likely referred to waste dropped by horses on city streets, but manure was a mixture of dung and earth, key to agriculture and thus invoked the smell not only of animal by-products but also of the peasants associated with such labour (Jones 2012, 148). Such 'filthy' smells of animals and humans may have seemed noisome to the king, but not to other townspeople.

Animals still comprise an important part of our urban smellscapes; the smells associated with 'skunk' and 'horse' are prominent on urban smell wheels. Yet we often imagine urban space as defined against the smell of agrarian life; the smell of horse dung marks that disjuncture and may lead to it being labelled as malodorous. That horse dung is—and has been—an integral part of urban life that reflects the ways in which our smellscapes may work to occlude some aspects of urban history. How we imagine a place should smell is often linked to who and what is allowed to inhabit it. The threshold for noisome environmental and olfactory abatement links the history of public health to the social ordering of urban space. The king's statement about the smell of York asks its mayor and bailiffs to clean the streets of all manner of filth both for the health of its inhabitants but also for those attending Parliament; though it specifically names the causes of the 'abominable' stench of York, it is not a far leap to imagine that other 'noisome' hazards could be removed in the same way.

In York, the River Ouse was a crucial resource for the labour of butchering and tanning animals (Mould et al. 2003); it was often polluted by run-off from these industries, so much so that by the mid-fifteenth century a city ordinance prohibited tradesmen from washing any manner of '"skynnez or ledir or any inmetys or corrupcion" above certain spots on the river' (Rawcliffe 2013, 246). Such evidence suggests that the king may have been right: the city certainly smelled of dung (and manure and other 'filth'), although we might wonder a little about how these smells fit into its collective urban smellscape. The city was undoubtedly defined by the smells associated with all of its industries—bread, wool, leather tanning, wood, wine—as well as by the smell of dung. Likewise, the king's sensory experience of York is hardly representative: what repulsed him may have not repulsed others, especially those who were more familiar with York. Indeed, it is possible that this ordinance was anticipatory, issued in preparation for the king's arrival and thus based on an imagined mental map of the city. Even if it was based on the king's own perception, he was newly arrived in the city and experiencing it not just as a town of industry but also as the second seat of his royal government. It is possible that the young king was making a political statement through the politics of olfaction.

The politics of smell are thus important to consider when dealing with its sensory descriptions in the past. Some of the 'filth' mentioned in this city ordinance undoubtedly came from economic industries that were vital to its prosperity. The tanners and butchers of the city (both prominent in the fourteenth century) occupied space outside the city wall closer to the River Ouse, since the tanners and the noxious scents of their labour were defined as hazardous to city life despite its economic importance. These scents were deemed so foul that the barkers and tanners often staged the 'hell' scenes in the York Corpus Christi plays (Harris 2010, 128; Higgens 1995). The abominable smell of dung thus came to represent material and metaphoric evilness on medieval stages and, over time, off stage.

It is impossible to say for certain whether or not medieval York smelled in this way; even if we could visit the space in the past, our understanding of the smell of dung is radically different from medieval men and women. Likewise, our theory of olfaction is different as well. Despite trenchant belief that there are 'five' senses, there have been many theories about how perception works as well as what constitutes its modalities. Modern science, for instance, posits as many as nine sensory modalities, including pressure, heat, and movement. Yet theories of sensation almost always involve an interface between the body and its environment.

This was especially true in the later Middle Ages in Britain. Medieval sensory perception involved both inner and outer senses, united through *sensus communis*. Believed to be located in three ventricles in the brain (according to Galen), the *sensus communis* or common senses made meaning across these differing modalities as well as connecting particular sensory perceptions of the outer material world with an inner awareness of universal truths. Galen's theory also helped solve theological questions that emerged from Aristotelian theories of sensing matter, since Aristotle located perception in the organs themselves, raising questions about the immortality of the soul and the morbidity of flesh. But there were competing theories, especially involving the number of inner senses: some posited three (Bartholomaeus Anglicus), four (Aquinas), five (Avincenna), or six (Guy de Chauliac) inner senses (in this case two for each of the three ventricles in the brain as described by Galen). The most widely accepted theory hypothesized five inner senses that directly corresponded to the five outer sensory modalities.

Whereas we might describe these as biological theories of operation, they were also spatial models. Notions of inner and outer modes of perception not only reflected but also influenced how the body was imagined in space. Indeed, the human body was often described as a built environment, likened to either a city or a house, with each of the senses functioning as a portal. Lydgate, for instance, describes the five senses as 'posternes', a fifteenth-century translator of the *Ancrene Wisse* describes them as 'gates' (Milner 2012, 55). One translator goes so far as to liken the sensory organs to 'water gates' that need to prevent dirty water, i.e. sinful vice, from infiltrating and corrupting the water supply within, i.e. virtue. The incredibly visceral aspects of this metaphor underscore not only the importance of humoural theory to medieval notions of health, but also the powerful role of clean water (and the omnipresence of foul water) within early modern built environments.

The notion that the body was an architectural space that 'housed' the soul was pervasive in theological writing: both Augustine and Abū Nasr al-Fārābī use it in their treatises on preserving virtue in Christianity and in Islam (Roazen 2008, 39). Such a notion emphasizes not only that the body was porous, influenced by its surroundings, but also that spaces were not hermetically sealed but rather were a component of a larger sensorium. The interface between the body and its surrounding was both physical and mental; a medieval smellwalk thus offers the opportunity not only to understand this interface in greater detail but also to theorize how our own 'mental' maps of space influence our perception of the world around us. To think about how a medieval built environment might have smelled involves not only our own understanding of sensory perception and its role in placemaking but also its role in shaping our mental maps of the past.

Stow's Medieval Smellwalk

It may seem specious to read a late sixteenth-century text as evidence for the smell of the medieval past. But, in the case of John Stow's *Survey of London*, the risk is worth the reward. Stow's text has been key for scholars working on pre-modern London, even as its limitation as straightforward historical evidence has been outlined. Described as a 'historical ecologist' (Collinson 2001, 34), an 'antiquarian' (Harris 2010, 96), and an archaeologist, 'sifting' patiently through 'the chaos of present detail' (Mullaney 1995, 15), Stow and his monumental *Survey of London* has come to represent an important break between the city's medieval past and its prototypical and emerging modernity (Manley 1995, 49), ironically through its extensive focus on topography rather than chronology. Capturing early modern patterns of urban navigation, Stow's *Survey* seems to provide its readers with novel ways to conceptualize the spaces of the city (Helgerson 1992, 138). He offers a mental map of London that defines the city through its built environment (and the toll it has taken on its natural environment), allowing readers to mentally inhabit the space with him. It also allows him to contemplate its ancient history: 'What London hath been in ancient time men may here see, as what it is now every man behold' (Stow 1598, Sig. A3). Perhaps because of this, Stow begins first with the wall, then its rivers, wards (moving west to east), and suburbs; he then dwells with the city's infirm, outlining hospitals and leper houses, before ending with descriptions of structures of government and economic organizations.

Almost all agree that Stow surveyed the city as he experienced it—as a pedestrian, immersed in its walls and the culture of its streets, and as a citizen, who viewed the city's increasingly 'alien warp' with trepidation (Mullaney 1995, 19). Smell doesn't factor largely into his narrative; however in key moments Stow describes an overwhelmingly malodorous city, which seems to chart a striking tale of decay. Unlike our narratives of olfaction, which usually invoke a teleology of increasing deodorization from the past to the present, Stow offers a narrative of decay: London of the sixteenth century smells much fouler than London of the past. This is important, revealing how narratives of progress or decay implicitly structure our approach to the built environment and its history, even if Stow's *Survey* cannot offer material evidence about the smell of the past.

Throughout the *Survey*, Stow compares his city with William FitzStephen's description of Norman London and finds it to be in disrepair. London is 'glorious in its manhood', says FitzStephen. In the epistle, Stow asserts 'that what London hath beene of ancient time, men may here see, as what it is now euery man doth behold' (1598, Sig. A3); later he notes that 'the alteration will be clear' (1598, Sig. D8v, p. 62). FitzStephen, he says, valued London's 'wholesome climate, its profession of the Christian faith, and the strength of its fortresses, the nature of its situation, the honour of its citizen and the chastity of its matrons' (1598, Sig. F7r, p. 79). The city's only 'plagues' are metaphorical: 'immoderate quaffing among the foolish sort'; if material, they are only 'casualties by fire' (1598, Sig. D8v, p. 62). He describes the city's thirteen large conventual churches as well as 126 parochial ones. The tower, he claims, is built with a 'cement tempered by the blood of beasts', the city's walls are 'high and thick' (1598, Sig. D4r, p. 39) and the surrounding suburbs filled with 'delightful meadows and pleasant streams', and 'an immense forest' is filled with beautified woods and 'fruitfull fields of Asia' (1598, Sig. Z6r, p. 347). Stow's London is very different from such an idealized space where all the inhabitants are polite and stylish: the city is notable 'before all other Citizens in ciuillitie of manners, attire, table, & talk'; likewise, the women 'are the very modest Sabine Ladies of Italy' (1598, Sig. F7r, p. 79).

Stow quotes FitzStephen, especially his construction of medieval London's largesse, in his segment 'Of Orders and Customs' (1598, Sig. E7r, p. 61). London is filled with food and luxury goods, as merchants from near and far were drawn to such a city: 'the Arabian's sent gold; the Sabeans sipice and frankensence: the Scithians armour, Babilon oile, Indinan purple garments, Egypt precious stones, Norway and Russia Ambergrese, & Sables, & the French men wine' (1598, Sig. E7r, p. 61). London of the past is welcoming to its visitors: a 'cookes rowe' offers roasted, sod, or fried fish, flesh, and fowl to hungry travellers. Even Smithfield seems utopic, its past pageantry drawing nobleman as well as citizens while its market offers all kinds of animals as well as all implements of husbandry (1598, Sig. E7r, p. 61). The only inconvenience of the space that FitzStephen, vis-à-vis Stow, admits is excessive drinking and frequent fires (1598, Sig. E8r, p. 63).

In comparison, Stow's London has become nothing but buildings and the filth of their inhabitants. The woods are deforested and its suburbs now enclosed, clogging the natural 'beauty' of the city with 'filthy straight passage[s]' (1598, Sig. Z6r, p. 347). Common fields, which were a source of beauty, are 'encroached' by 'filthy Cottages,' whose inhabitants, Stow recounts, throw 'filth and odure' on the street (1598, Sig. Z6r, p. 347). This olfactory narrative counteracts the many references to building and repair, in which wood bridges, vulnerable to repeated fires, were replaced by stone ones (1598, Sig. C3v, p. 30) and buildings made 'more beautiful and commodious' by repair (1598, Sig. Dr, p. 49 and 50).

A similar effect can be seen in Stow's description of the smell of water. At one point, every street and lane of the city had 'diverse fayre wels and fresh springes,' which have now 'decayed' (1598, Sig. B5v, p. 10). Wells to the north of the city known, according to FitzStephen's chronicle, for being 'sweete, wholesome, and cleare', are now 'much decayed and marred with filthinesse purposely laid there, for the heightening of the ground for garden-plots' (1598, Sig. B7v, p. 14). The same is true for the ditch, which had been 'carefully cleansed and maintained, as need required, but now of late neglected and forced either to a very narrow and the same a filthy channel or altogether stopped up for gardens planted and houses built thereon'. Here he notes that the ditch was cleansed in 1354, 1379, 1414, 1477, and then again in 1519, 1540, 1549, 1569, 1595 (1598, Sig. B9v, p. 16). Elsewhere he references 'dung' boats on the Thames, implicitly noting street cleaning though it is given no explicit mention in the Survey (1598, Sig. M3v, p. 166).

Despite this striking increase in public maintenance, however, London remains worse off than before. Stow notes, for instance, that some parts of the city near London bridge utilize forciers to divert Thames water through lead conduits to cleanse households and street sewers of urban filth, and to 'castellate ... sweet water into the street' (Stow 1598, Sig. L3r, p. 140). But there are only three such devices in the city; there was a fourth near Cornhill ward but now there 'is no such matter, through whose default I know not' (1598, Sig. L3r, p. 140). For most of the city, the history of its conduits charts a constant demand for clean water to cleanse the residue and filth produced by an ever-increasing pollution.

His description of how the River Wells became 'Turnmill' brook, or what we now call the Fleet, illustrates the text's broader investment in a narrative about how London's industrial growth threatens the health of the city. Stow cites Henry Lacy, the Earl of Lincoln's 1307 complaint, recorded in a 'fair book of Parliament', that the once wide and deep river was choked by the filth of tanners and the work of mills (Stow 1598, Sig. B6r). Despite the removal of such mills, the river remained spoiled and Stow emphasizes the failure of these measures: 'the continual incrochments upon the banks ... and casting of soilage into the streame, is now become worse', so much so that the Turnmill brook is 'cloyed and choken' more 'than ever it was before' (Stow 1598, Sig. B6v.).

All of this reveals the ways in which Stow's famous *Survey of London* is discursive and subjective, rooted in a vision of London in the past. But it also offers a unique way to approach how medieval and early modern men and women perceived a changing urban realm, including the built environment. Though it presents early modern London as the result of a cumulative and an endlessly sequential history, Stow's *Survey* is also famously a peripatetic palimpsest (Mullaney 1995, 15). Stow 'surveys' the city street by street, offering both a map of the contemporary city as well as an unearthing of its past layers, so much so that Jonathan Gil Harris argues that Stow is almost also like Nietzsche's archetype of the antiquarian, one who seeks 'to feel his way back, and sense how things were, to detect traces almost extinguished' (Harris 2010, 96).

We might, then, read Stow's *Survey* as a sensory walk. Stow's London is both real and imagined: inflected by his own experiences during his long life in London, as well as by his literary investment in a London of the past, Stow's survey is composed both through his perception of the city's built environment as well as through his interest in how such space was perceived by those who came before him. Analysed in this way, Stow's *Survey* offers a stunning snapshot not only of how one man experienced urban life but also how he created a narrative of meaning out of these experiences.

For instance, as Figure 45.1 illustrates, Stow's London consists of three distinct kinds of environments: its built environment, the natural environment (including the suburbs, gardens, fields, and fens that surround the city) and the river that traverses both spaces (including the water diverted from it and its tributaries). The built environment dominates the narrative. This makes a certain amount of sense, since Stow emphasizes the city space as one that is expansive and overwhelmingly dominated by filth. But it is also somewhat surprising since he describes more good civic smells than bad (Figure 45.2); this pattern is also

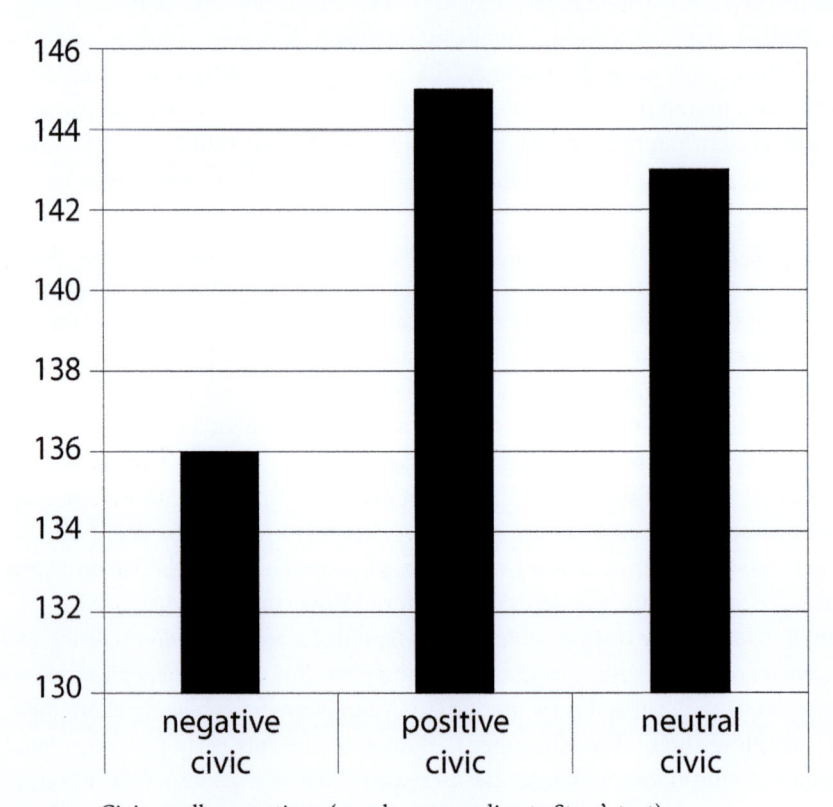

FIGURE 45.2 Civic smell perceptions (numbers according to Stow's text)

replicated across the text as a whole (Figure 45.3). As Figure 45.4 illustrates, most of these positive smells are associated with civic life, with buildings and industry far outweighing all other aspects of the built environment of the city. He, however, describes malodorous smells in much stronger terms. Negative smells of city life (Figure 45.5) are associated with its people; though Stow mentions a striking number of Londoners by name, if he mentions people in general it is because they are foreigners, Jews, aliens, or lepers.

I have coded Stow's references to the names of materials as neutral smells: wood, stone, even ale or dung, whereas positive smells include tags such as 'sweet' or 'wholesome' and negative smells 'cloying' and 'noisome.' But how should entries about gardens be coded? Nature is an enigma in the text: its references are comprised of either descriptions of private gardens or of the surrounding fens, both of which Stow describes in mostly negative terms. The same is true of London's water: the Thames dominates these references but the scarcity of water associated with the history of conduits charted in the narrative is outweighed by the attention given to them throughout the city.

Though these data are very limited, it suggests the complicated ways in which Stow's perception of the city do and do not influence his mental map of medieval London and perhaps ours as well: though his text contains many more references to mostly positive

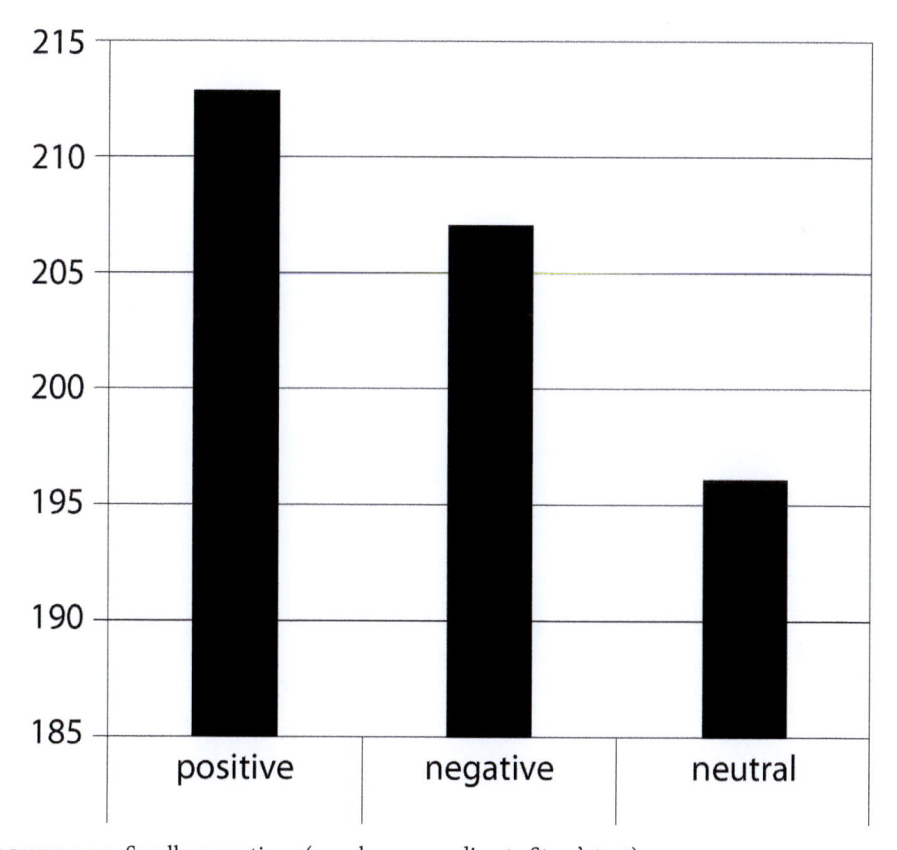

FIGURE 45.3 Smell perceptions (numbers according to Stow's text)

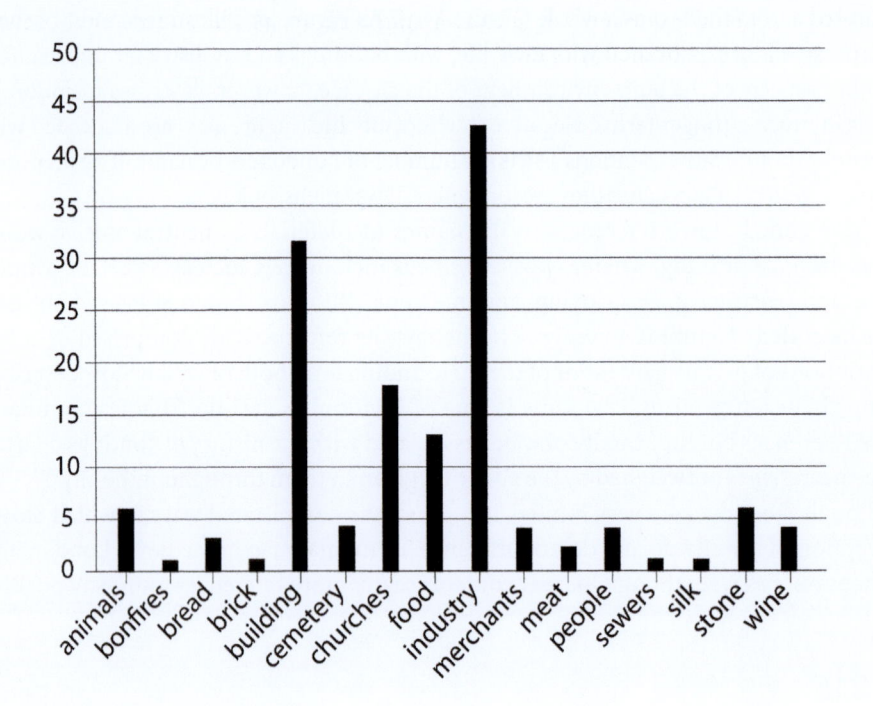

FIGURE 45.4 Positive civic smells

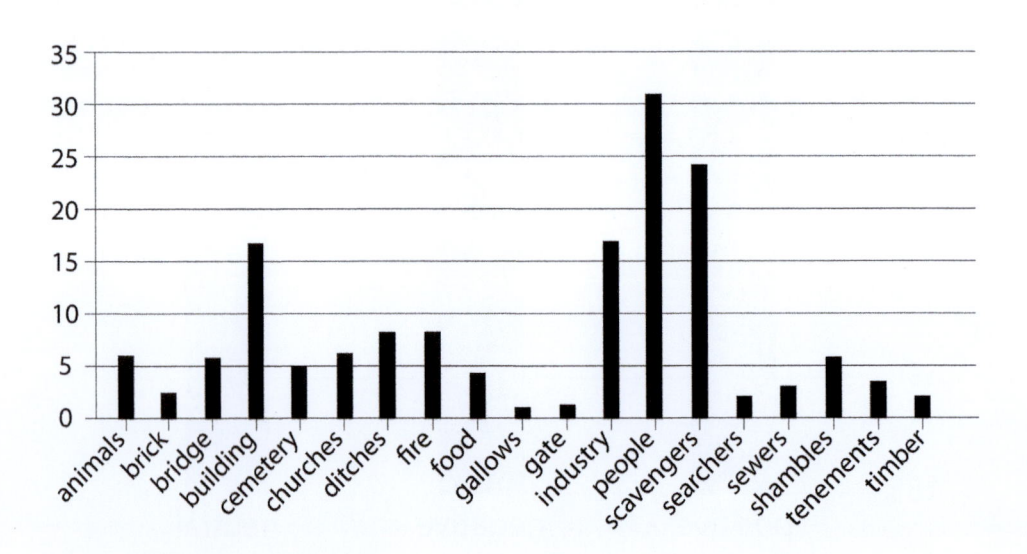

FIGURE 45.5 Negative civic smells

smells of city life, the built environment remains a filthy and debauched environment within his narrative about life in London.

ARCHAEOLOGY AND THE URBAN ENVIRONMENT

Archaeologists have generally taken a more indirect perspective on smell than the one offered here, at once more site specific and scientific in its detail. Derek Keene (1982) first reviewed the documentary evidence for later medieval rubbish disposal, with special reference to Winchester. He drew together evidence for inadequate surface drainage, sewage and cess pits, animal refuse, industrial waste, household rubbish, and much else besides, drawing attention to the potential for archaeological analysis of sediments in yards, pits, gardens, and streets: building interiors were swept clean, removing the archaeological evidence in the process. John Schofield and Alan Vince (1994, 178–203) later dedicated a revealing chapter to the 'environment of medieval towns', which summarized the evidence available from the study of soil samples, pollen, plant, and insect remains from floor layers and cess pits. This was illustrated by research ranging from the analysis of medieval diatoms extracted from the Fleet River sediments, which confirmed increasing pollution (see above), the range of small mammals present in medieval Beverley (East Yorkshire) from bank voles to weasels, to the study of human coprolites from medieval Hull (East Yorkshire). More recently, the pathoecology of medieval York has been reconstructed in detail to reveal its impacts on human health, for example the high prevalence of sinusitis and TB (King and Henderson 2014). Beetle and fly remains confirm that York's residents did indeed live in close proximity to human and animal faeces (O'Connor 2000), not to mention parasites. All these put humans at the risk of disease, a risk that was greatly increased because of the numbers of animals being kept in the city. The deposition of stable manure would have attracted decomposers, such as flies, as well as scavengers, such as rats. Taken together, this provides a vivid picture of York's urban environment between the eleventh and mid-sixteenth centuries with the promise of more detail to come as avenues in biochemical and biomolecular research develop further.

CONCLUSION

This new archaeological detail is making an important contribution to our understanding of urban environments in the Middle Ages and where more complete information is available for a single town such as York, Winchester, or London there is greater potential for the archaeologist to participate more fully in dialogues around the 'experience of living' than has hitherto been the case. The York evidence, for example, seems to indicate a trend towards greater cleanliness after the Norman Conquest, but certain areas of the city were less pleasant than others, and we can now begin to identify where these were at certain periods. As this chapter has tried to show, recent tools developed by urban geographers and computational social scientists that seek to translate visceral experiences into sensory maps of shared urban realms may also be of use to this inquiry. The impact of such research has been demonstrated to be multifaceted and future-oriented, allowing for better design of urban environments that take olfaction into consideration, including the unique challenges and opportunities of breathing and sniffing post-modern cities. It also encourages us, however, to tackle past environments and teaches us to question the role of historical perception, especially olfaction, in shaping our approach to urban history.

REFERENCES CITED

Collinson, P. 2001 'John Stow and nostalgic antiquarianism', in J. F. Merritt (ed.), *Imagining Early Modern London: perceptions and portrayals of the city from Stow to Strype, 1589–1720*, Cambridge University Press, Cambridge, 27–52

Curran, K. and Kearny, J. 2012 'Introduction: Shakespeare and Phenomenology', *Criticism* 54(3), 353–4

Hallam, H. E. 1961 'Population density in medieval Fenland', *Economic History Review* 14(1), 71–81

Harris, J. G. 2010 *Untimely matter in the time of Shakespeare*, University of Pennsylvania Press, Philadelphia

Helgerson, R. 1992 *Forms of nationhood: the Elizabethan writing of England*, University of Chicago Press, Chicago

Henshaw, V. 2014 *Urban smellscapes: understanding and designing city smell environments*, Routledge, New York

Higgens, A. 1995 'Work and plays: guild casting in in the Corpus Christi drama', *Medieval and Renaissance Drama in England* 7, 76–96

Jacobs, L., Arter, J., Cook, A., and Sulloway, F. 2015 'Olfactory orientation and navigation in humans', *PloS: One* 10(6): e0129387

Jones, R. 2012 'Understanding medieval manure', in R. Jones (ed.), *Manure matters*, Ashgate, Aldershot, 145–58

Keene, D. 1982 'Rubbish in towns', in R. A. Hall and H. K. Kenward (eds), *Environmental archaeology in the urban context*, Council for British Archaeology Research Report 43, 26–30

Keene, D. 2012 'Medieval London and its supply hinterlands', *Regional Environmental Change* 12(2), 263–81

King, G. and Henderson, C. 2014 'Living cheek by jowl: the pathoecology of medieval York', *Quaternary International* 314, 131–42

Kim, K. and Choe, S. 2010 'In search of sustainable urban form for Seoul,' in A. Sorenson and J. Okata (eds), *Megacities: urban form, governance, and sustainability*, Springer, New York

Lefebvre, H. 1991 *The production of space*, Blackwell, Malden, MA

Lyte, H. C. M. 1898 *Calendar of the Close Rolls preserved in the Public Record Office: Edward III*, Vol. 2, Her Majesty's Stationery Office, London

Manley, L. 1995 'Of sites and rites', in D. Smith, R. Strier, and D. Bevington (eds), *The theatrical city: culture, theater and politics in London*, Cambridge University Press, Cambridge, 35–54

Milner, M. 2012 *The senses and the English Reformation*, Ashgate, Aldershot

Mould, Q., Carlisle, I., and Cameron, E. 2003 *Craft, industry and everyday life: leather and leatherworking in Anglo-Scandinavian and medieval York*, The Archaeology of York 17/16, Council for British Archaeology, York

Mullaney, S. 1995 *The place of the stage: license, play, and power in Renaissance England*, University of Michigan, Ann Arbor

Munro, I. 2005 *The figure of the crowd in Early Modern London: the city and its double*, Palgrave Macmillan, New York

O'Connor, T. P. 2000 'Human refuse as a major ecological factor in medieval urban vertebrate communities', in G. Bailey, R. Charles, and N. Winder (eds), *Human ecodynamics*, Oxbow, Oxford, 15–20

Quercia, D., Schifanella, R., Aiello, L., and McLean, K. 2015 'Smelly maps: the digital life of urban smellscapes', *Proceedings of the 9th International AAAI Conference on Web and Social Media* (ICWSM), arXiv:1505.06851

Quercia, D., Aiello, L. M., and Schifanella, R. 2016 'The emotional and chromatic layers of urban smells', *Proceedings of the 10th International AAAI Conference on Web and Social Media* (ICWSM), 309–318

Rawcliffe, C. 2013 *Urban bodies: communal health in late medieval English towns and cities*, Boydell and Brewer, Suffolk

Roazen, D. H. 2008 'Common sense: Greek, Arabic, Latin', in S. Nichols and A. Calhoun (eds), *Rethinking the medieval senses: heritage, fascinations, frames*, Johns Hopkins University Press, Baltimore, 30–50

Schofield, J. and Vince, A. 1994 *Medieval towns*, Leicester University Press, London

Stanev, H. 2014 *Sensory experience and the metropolis on the Jacobean stage*, Ashgate, Aldershot

Stow, J. 1598 *A survey of London*, imprinted by Iohn Wolfe, London

Suffet, I. H. and Rosenfeld, P. 2007 'The anatomy of odour wheels for odours of drinking water, wastewater, compost and the urban environment', *Water Science & Technology* 55(5), 335–44

Taylor, C. 2015 'A tale of two cities: the efficacy of ancient and medieval sanitation methods', in P. Mitchell (ed.), *Sanitation and intestinal parasites in past populations*, Ashgate, Aldershot

Waldron, J. 2012 '"The eye of man hath not heard": Shakespeare, synaesthesia, and post-Reformation phenomenology', *Criticism* 54(3), 403–17

CHAPTER 46

MEDIEVAL COLOUR

MICHAEL J. HUXTABLE AND RONAN P. O'DONNELL

As well as being a highly significant and potentially symbolic phenomenon in medieval visual culture, colour was a serious topic for the learned concerned with its physical nature and means of perception. Of the many classical texts and Arabic commentaries that contributed to the Latin West's understanding of colour and visual perception during the Middle Ages perhaps the most important include Plato's *Timaeus* (Plato 2000), Aristotle's *De sensu et sensato* (part of the *Parva Naturalia*) (Aristotle 1984, 438b–439a), and *De anima* (Aristotle 1986) (also *De coloribus*, a work attributed to Aristotle throughout the medieval period but probably a Peripatetic text possibly written by Statius; Aristotle 1936); similarly Patristic texts including St Augustine of Hippo's *De Genesis ad litteram* and Pseudo-Dionysius's *De coelesti hierarchia* (St Augustine 1991; Pseudo-Dionysius 1987, 145–91) proved authoritative for later thinkers re-casting earlier concepts into a Christian framework. Later medieval thought on the subject thus emerged in response to certain long-standing treatments of colour and associated topics, including the role of light in divine Creation; the nature of the soul; the primacy of vision and visuality in the hierarchy of the senses; 'extramissive' versus 'intromissive' perception (i.e. actively sending out sensory 'beams' or 'species' and/or passively receiving them); and the elemental nature of the physical cosmos. The medieval contribution to a philosophical discourse on colour demonstrates par excellence a desire to synthesize, or at least to bring into line, respected pre-Christian authorities, while simultaneously shoring up matters of divine authority, religious hierarchy, and revealed Christian truth.

Hence, for example, Robert Grosseteste's treatise *De colore* (c.1225) describes a formulation of colour as a scale of embodied light (*lux incorporate*) that ascends and descends in degrees and qualities of visuality as it illuminates different bodies with differing levels of transparency (*impurum/purum*) while itself having different strengths (*multa/pauca*) and levels of clarity (*clara/obscura*) (Dinkova-Bruun et al. 2013, 17). Chromatic vision is presented in terms of 'activated light'—a thought which Christianizes both a Neo-Platonic metaphysics of emanation and an Aristotelian, elementally construed, seven-colour scale, which is described thus: 'For there are seven species of each (colours and savours), if, as is reasonable, we regard dun [or grey] as a variety of black (for the alternative is that yellow should be classed with white, as rich with sweet); while crimson, violet, leek-green, and deep blue, come between white and black, and from these all others are derived by mixture' (Aristotle 1984, 442a). Grosseteste depicts a physical hierarchy for the generation of colours that is sympathetic with the Augustinian and Pseudo-Dionysian metaphysical model of the extramissive descent of 'divine truth' from God to illuminate a world suffering in spiritual darkness. His synthetic approach is indicative of a methodology in medieval thinking which sought to combine or disentangle Christian Neo-Platonic notions steeped in the metaphysics of light with, or from, ideas drawn after the twelfth-century rediscovery of Aristotelian natural philosophy.

In less intellectually rarefied contexts colour was interpreted and evaluated according to a number of different systems. Popular understanding of the appearance of the natural world employed the Aristotelian (and earlier) tradition of the four elements: earth, air, fire, and water and their combinatory qualities of warm, moist, dry, and cold; and interpreted the body and its functions and emotions in terms of the four humours: blood, phlegm, black bile, and yellow bile, also according to the elemental approach. Some of the most formalized taxonomies of colour were to be found in medicine, notably 'uroscopy'. The inspection of urine was central to medieval medicine to the extent that the jordan, in which samples were examined, became symbolic of the physician (Jones 1998, 43–6). Typically, books on uroscopy list and illustrate twenty colours, often quite simply because these were practical books not intended to be decorative. Skin colour was also thought to derive from the humours, and was thus a guide to temperament. Most commonly, ruddiness was associated with shame or anger and paleness with fear (Woolgar 2006, 163). This could have practical applications: priests, for example, were considered to have a duty to read the complexions of penitents in order to determine if they were likely to repeat a confessed sin, as certain humeral types were drawn to particular sins. An assessment of skin colour is listed by Robert Grosseteste (c.1175–1253) as one of the responsibilities of a priest taking confession (Langum 2013).

Other popular systems for the interpretation and evaluation of colour included the liturgical colours giving religious associations between hues and the Church calendar; the colours of lapidary lore; of heraldry and blazon; alchemical associations; and poetic allusions drawn from classical and other ancient sources (Germanic, Celtic, etc.). The evaluation of colour itself, irrespective of particular hues, could also work in positive or negative terms. In *The Canterbury Tales*, for example, Chaucer's Parson attacks the sin of *superfluity*—the self-indulgent use of wealth—focusing on the contemporary (male) fashion for wearing parti-coloured clothing. He considers such costume to be sexually provocative and wasteful of resources that should go to the poor. In an impassioned section of his sermon the Parson declares:

> And mooreover, the wrecched swollen membres that they shewe thurgh disgisynge, in departynge of hire hoses in whit and reed, semeth that half hir shameful privee membres weren flayne. / And if so be that they departen hire hoses in othere colours, as is whit and blak, or whit and blew, or blak and reed, and so forth, / thanne semeth

it, as by variaunce of colour, that half the partie of hire privee membres were corrupt by the fir of Seint Antony, or by cancre, or by oother swich meschaunce

(Chaucer, *The Canterbury Tales* X (I) ll. 424–7).

The Parson is venting a criticism of colour per se that goes back at least to the Cistercians in the twelfth century: he regards bright, parti-coloured clothing as indicative of a proud and sinful nature. He argues that colourful material was especially chosen for making sexually provocative styles of clothing (especially for men) so his argument assumes a natural association between visually attractive colours and sinful behaviour (see Hodges 2005, 258–65 for a detailed consideration of Chaucer's costume rhetoric). The particular reference to white, red, and parti-coloured hose and the way they seem (to the Parson) to symbolize lust and corruption by the 'fire of St Anthony' (a venereal disease) may also have been a personal criticism of specific characters in the *Canterbury Tales*, perhaps the Merchant and the Squire. The passage also draws its rhetorical power from a political staple of the time: the use of sumptuary laws to visibly maintain the social hierarchy. Sumptuary laws described and proscribed materials in a way that would have effectively colour-coded the populace according to income, as the variable which determined access to types of dyes and pigments (Lauchard 2002, 105–23).

On the other hand, positive evaluations of colour also abound. Theophilus the monk, in his compendium of artisanal techniques *De diversis artibus* (written c.1110–40, around the same time Bernard of Clairvaux was articulating a strongly negative view of colour to his Cistercian followers), sets out the skills, crafts, and tools needed by artisans who engaged in the arts of decorating churches. In the Prologue to his third book (on the arts of the metalworker), he includes an inspiring passage describing the craftsman's seven supporting virtues (wisdom, understanding, counsel, fortitude, knowledge, godliness, and fear of the Lord) for pious inspiration:

Animated, dearest son, by these supporting virtues, you have approached the House of God with confidence, and have adorned it with so much beauty; you have embellished the ceilings or walls with varied work in different colours and have, in some measure shown to the beholders the paradise of God, glowing with varied flowers, verdant with herbs and foliage, and cherishing with crowns of varying merit the souls of the saints. You have given them cause to praise the Creator in the creature and proclaim Him wonderful in His works

(Theophilus 1961, 63).

The contrast with the Cistercian view seems stark and yet Theophilus could be said to have been drawing upon the same notions as his near contemporary. In other words, if inside a church the perceptual focus is the worship of God, then all decorations and uses of colour should lead towards that end. In Theophilus' view this meant showing the worshippers a symbolic representation of the glory and beauty of God, thereby inspiring worship. What Theophilus' views were regarding the use of colour *outside* a place of worship are unknown.

Colour, therefore, could be regarded as offering differing significations and values according to the intentions, either spiritual or secular, of the employer or bearer of the colour, and by its location either inside or outside a place of Christian worship.

Wall Paintings

Churches were covered in colourful wall paintings throughout the Middle Ages. The available palette was, however, limited technically and by cost. Throughout the period red and yellow ochre were the most common colours (Baker 1970, 59). Conversely, green and blue were only used in expensive paintings (A. M. Baker 1969, 135; Rouse 1979, 156). The principal limitation was that paints had to be compatible with the lime plaster onto which they were painted. The *secco* technique placed the paint onto the dry surface of the plaster, occasionally after revival with water. Non-lime compatible pigments were also used however, as demonstrated by blank areas in some schemes where they have since disintegrated (Figure 46.1). In more complex schemes binding agents were added to the pigment allowing a greater range to be used (Howard 2003, 201–2).

In some cases the use of colour for symbolic purposes is consistent with medieval intellectual and literary understandings of colour. For instance, the Adoration in All Saints, Shelfanger, Norfolk, depicts the Virgin Mary as the Queen of Heaven. She is clothed in white and red and has fair hair. She is thus brightly coloured such as we might expect of someone regarded as virtuous. In the same picture Christ is portrayed in gold, which, as metallic surfaces were thought to emit light and thus were potentially 'virtuous' themselves, is also appropriate (E. Baker 1969, 90). Conversely, the executioner of St Margaret at Battle, East Sussex, who is depicted as a bad character, wears a green robe along with yellow hose and black shoes (Rouse 1979, 156). In some cases the use of green had negative connotations because of its 'sub-mediary' position according to the Aristotelian colour scale (Huxtable 2011, 199), but as this idea was not universally held it is not clear that this was the artist's intention. A variation on the idea of light and purity being associated with abstract moral virtue is the depiction of Christ wearing a dark red robe at Trotton, West Sussex (Edwards 1985, 121). Red, while it was a 'mediary' rather than a pure colour, was understood liturgically to be a sacrificial colour and is thus appropriate for depictions of God or virtuous individuals. Colour could also be symbolic by itself. As we have seen, some thought of colours as glorifying the church and evoking heaven simply though the variety and vivacity of colours or general colourfulness (Woolgar 2006, 155). This is perhaps demonstrated in Salisbury Cathedral, where colours are used to differentiate the nave and the east end, understood to represent earth and heaven respectively. In this particular case the vault webs of the nave were coloured only in red whereas red, green, and black were used on the east end windows and triforium arcade (Rosewell 2008, 167). A dissenting voice, though still in line with learned approaches to colour theory deriving from Aristotle and Plato, was that of Bernard of Clairvaux who saw colours as particularly worldly and thus immoral. His extreme preference for plainness led to Cistercian monasteries being painted white inside (Figure 46.2).

FIGURE 46.1 Wall painting in All Saints and St Andrews Church, Kingston, Cambridgeshire. The white space in the shape of a human figure shows where non-lime compatible pigments have decayed

(© Ronan O'Donnell)

FIGURE 46.2 Traces of white paint at Fountains Abbey, a Cistercian monastery in North Yorkshire. The Cistercians favoured plain decoration, as a result of the views of their founder Bernard of Clairvaux

(© Ronan O'Donnell)

Medieval mural artists did not, however, always adhere to practices of colour symbolism and meaning. In a fifteenth-century painting of the life of St Eustace at Canterbury Cathedral, Kent, the colour green, while it was symbolically potent within a number of chromatic vocabularies, was used for the clothing of *all* characters, both good and bad, and so could not carry its conventional symbolic weight (Allardyce 1985). Similarly, in the Trotton doom painting the man welcoming the stranger in a depiction of the Seven Works of Mercy wears a parti-coloured garment (Edwards 1985, 120), a practice which, as we have seen, was sometimes condemned by contemporaries. Assuming symbolic meaning for colours in medieval wall paintings is therefore not a simple or verifiable matter. In many cases colours are used naturalistically. At Canterbury Cathedral, the St Eustace life contains grey stone houses, a green ground with darker green trees, pink flesh, and a dappled horse (Allardyce 1985). Indeed, the naturalism of wall paintings could sometimes go so far as to contradict philosophical understandings, for instance the rainbow mandorla painted by Giotto at the Arena Chapel in Padua in 1305–6 has colours in the sequence red, orange, yellow, blue, in contrast to the sequence given by Bartholomaeus Anglicus in *De proprietatibus rerum* which is red, green, brown, blue (Lee and Fraser 2001, 141). This suggests that artists could draw on observations of nature, perhaps more readily sometimes than they did on philosophy. The layering of pigments became more complex throughout the Gothic period (Howard 2003, 201–2) and is described in detail by Theophilus' *De diversis artibus*, which discusses a method for shading faces and the skin of nude bodies (1961, 5–8). An archaeological example may be found at Hardham, West Sussex, where water is depicted using wavy lines which blend from cream at the top to blue and crimson at the base, which was probably intended to represent increasing depth (Baker 1998, 217). Overall, while philosophical understandings of colour clearly have a part to play in the composition of mural paintings, it was just one of the aids deployed by the artist to help the viewer identify the scenes and narratives being depicted.

Clothing

Another area in which colour could be chosen symbolically, economically, or arbitrarily was for depicting or decorating clothing. Medieval literature often employs clothing figuratively suggesting that its colour could be symbolic. For instance, Sir Gowther, a 'dog-knight' of medieval romance fame, was sired by the devil and then divinely granted coloured armour, in black, then red, then white to defeat the Saracens, thus paralleling theological understanding of the virtue of the different colours (Mills 1973, 159–63). In the thirteenth century, Pope Innocent III codified the colours of liturgical vestments, adding green and violet to red and black which were already in use. White was (and indeed is) used for feasts, red for feasts of martyrs and the Holy Spirit, black for penitence, and green for Ordinary Time (Koslin 2012, 183). This is based on a particular colour spectrum developed in Salerno during the eleventh and twelfth centuries in which green is placed between black and white (Woolgar 2006, 157). More simplistic symbolism occurred in the garments of monks, whose blacks, whites, and browns required no dyeing and were thus a rejection of worldly wealth. Given Bernard of Clairvaux's denial of monastic wealth, it is unsurprising that the Cistercians wore white.

In general, a fashion for bright or deep colours during the first half of the Middle Ages was followed by a preference for darker colours and blacks from the late fourteenth century (Piponnier and Mane 1997, 72). Usually the most prized cloths were those dyed with the most expensive dyes or processes, an aspiration which motivated the fashion for increasingly deep colours. Throughout the period 'scarlet' was the most valuable cloth. Rather than referring to a particular shade, the term referred any cloth dyed with kermes, which ranged from crimson to brown to purple (Munro 1983; Piponnier and Mane 1997, 16; Bucklow 2016, 26–27). As the dye was expensive it was mostly used on high-quality wools or silks. Kermes is extracted from larvae which live on the roots of Mediterranean oak trees. Its harvesting and processing gave kermes its high value (Munro et al. 2012b). Its high value led in turn to it being specifically banned in Henry II's 1172 abortive crusade as an expression of humility (Crouch 1992, 250). It is not found in archaeological samples in Britain until the eleventh century, though it was known in Roman Britain. Subsequently it is found reasonably frequently, for instance ten samples of silk from thirteenth- to fifteenth-century contexts in London were found to be dyed with kermes (Crowfoot et al. 1992, 200), while one of seven analysed samples from Aberdeen contained kermes

(Walton-Rogers 2001). The dye only became less valuable in the sixteenth century when Mexican cochineal began to be imported to Europe (Munro et al. 2012b). Other reds are more common, indeed red is the most commonly identified colour in medieval archaeological textiles. Madder was the most commonly extractable dye from textile samples from Perth (Bowler et al. 1995, 758) and was found in 29 per cent of the twelfth- to thirteenth-century assemblage from Baynard's Castle in London and in 45 per cent of the 1330–40 assemblage from the same site (Crowfoot et al. 1992, 200). In samples from these excavations madder was used with blue dyes to create purple or black and in three of the silks analysed it was used with yellow to give an orange or brown hue (Crowfoot et al. 1992, 200). Weld, which gives a yellow tint, was also found in London but is more difficult to detect. Evidence for it in the form of seeds have been found in twelfth- to fourteenth-century contexts in Beverley (Yorkshire) and there is historical evidence for its import into Southampton in the fifteenth century (Uzzell 2012, 178). Woad is also difficult to detect but has been found at least in one sample from Aberdeen and some fabrics from London (Crowfoot et al. 1992, 200; Walton-Rogers 2001). Orchil, obtained from lichen, yields a violet or purple dye which was found in one London sample (Crowfoot et al. 1992, 200) and again seems to support the historical evidence for fashions in bright colours. Purple, in particular, is often associated with a dye extracted from shellfish and produced in the Byzantine Empire. This was particularly expensive due to the small quantities that could be extracted. It was certainly known in medieval England, and the term 'purpura' described any rich cloth (Munro et al. 2012a, 437), for instance the best cloths in many wills. Archaeologically, however, it is unknown in textiles in Britain, so its actual use was probably rare. Possible evidence of whelk dye manufacture has, however, been found in Ireland and Brittany, and some uses of purple in manuscripts have been detected recently using non-destructive analyses such as Raman spectroscopy (Biggam 2006, 36).

Coloured cloth, while popular, could also be considered immoral. We have already seen that monks and nuns wore plain garments in natural colours to show their humility. The Lollards also took this view and typically wore grey or russet. Conversely, Archbishop Arundel when he examined William Thorpe in 1407 suggested that a man who wore a scarlet gown everyday could be meeker than Thorpe in his threadbare blue gown (Woolgar 2006, 164). The choice of blue here is interesting: woad was a relatively cheap dye as it was grown domestically, but such rhetorical use of it as a symbol of poverty is rare, perhaps because the multiple dyeings required to produce fashionable deep blues could be expensive. At times this role for colour as a moral indicator could be codified into rules. In England, the 1363 Sumptuary law included the imperative: 'Also, that carters, ploughmen, drivers of the plough, oxherds, cowherds, shepherds, swineherds … and other people that have not forty shillings of goods nor of chattels, shall not take nor wear any manner of cloth but blanket and russet, of wool, worth not more than 12d, and shall wear girdles of linen according to their estate' (Myers 1994, 1153–5). Insistence on 'blanket and russet' would have determined a range of dull browns and greys for the poorest classes, and the stipulation of 'not more than 12d' in value implied that expensive dyes and decoration were out of the question. Expense was clearly a significant factor in customer choice but, once again, colour theory had its part to play.

Manuscripts

The varied and elaborate use of colour could also be found in illustrated manuscripts and, as with clothing, there was a preference for bright colours. For instance, the thirteenth-century Hatchett Psalter is dominated by bright blues, reds, and gold with tan and grey used alongside them (Schapiro 1960, 188). Like clothing too, there were also fashions for colours in manuscripts. Yellow was popular in the late Saxon and Norman periods but was later replaced with gold. From the eleventh century blue became more popular and by the Gothic period of the thirteenth to fourteenth centuries red and blue dominated. In the fifteenth century humanistic manuscript illuminators favoured white (Clemens and Graham 2007, 27, 32). Cost was again significant in determining the colour palette, so in general the most expensive manuscripts employed more valuable pigments and in greater quantities: green and red were common in English manuscripts throughout the Middle Ages as vermillion (from cinnabar) and verdigris (from copper carbonate) were cheap (Gameson 2011; Bucklow 2016). Gold was also costly, as was ultramarine made from Afghan lapis lazuli and kermes. All of these could be simulated by substituting for less expensive materials, recipes for which are found in texts such as *De diversis artibus*. Kermes could be substituted for brazilwood or madder, as it was in clothing, saffron could be used in place of gold, and tin for silver leaf (Clemens and Graham 2007, 29, 31).

Alongside price, symbol and association could influence colour choices. Gold is particularly significant in this respect because its reflective properties meant that it was thought of as a source of light and represented virtue, as for instance when it was used in haloes or on the face and hands of God (Clemens and Graham 2007, 31; Woolgar 2006, 151). Alternatively, colour mixing might be avoided where possible as colour was considered part of the natural state of any object, and thus to change it was akin to performing alchemy (Woolgar 2006, 160). Mixing and diluting were however used to produce lighter and darker shades, particularly flesh colours (Clemens and Graham 2007, 32). By the second half of the thirteenth century books had become a tool for private devotion and so were used affectively to encourage religious experience through contemplation (Lewis 1991).

Colour was also used in manuscripts in naturalistic ways. By the thirteenth century shadow was beginning to be represented, as in a Nativity scene in the Hatchett Psalter (Schapiro 1960, 188). Similarly, shading was used to mould folds in clothing and to show complexion. Finally, as an analysis of the fifteenth-century Lovell Lectionary has clearly demonstrated, even different artists working on the same manuscript could use colours in different ways. Of the three hands which painted the miniatures for this manuscript, Hand B used black for shading and orange for complexion while Hand C used the more standard browns and greens for the same (Brown and Clark 2004, 221). The choice of colour could be informed by symbolism, status display, the need for images to communicate a narrative, or by the individual choices made by an artist.

Ceramics

On the whole English medieval pottery is neither highly decorated nor strikingly coloured. Clear lead glaze was by far the most common type of surface treatment applied, often tinted with copper to produce green glaze, or with iron for brown/black, as seen on Ham Green wares from Bristol, Border Wares from London, or Cistercian Ware (McCarthy and Brooks 1988). Contrasting colours were achieved using applied clays or slips, notably for Rye (Sussex) and Cheam (Surrey) wares, usually with a red slip on a white ground. The addition of colour could be an incentive to buy pots (Hayfield 1985; Spavold 2010), but the lack of colour options limited their symbolism. The browns, olive greens, light yellows, and buffs of local pottery were only of secondary significance in the palettes of wall painting, clothing, and manuscripts that we have considered so far.

Glaze was applied to the exterior of vessels during most of the medieval period, having no real practical use (such as waterproofing the surface) so that its use seems to be merely decorative. Whereas kitchen wares were left untreated, all jugs received some colour in this way and it has been suggested that green glaze may have been symbolic of the female labour which went into the beer that jugs would have contained, while the red fabrics may have represented the combination of this female labour with male labour and the beer's consumption (Cumberpatch 1997). Certainly green could have female connotations, though numerous other symbolic associations for green are possible and, of course, not all jugs contained beer.

Colour in pottery seems to have been used functionally, simply in order to create designs, and the palette was of secondary importance. This is highlighted by the fact that the naturalistic use of colour is rare in medieval ceramics, though we have seen that it is common in paintings and manuscripts. It is possible that the brown rosettes on the Surrey polychrome jug discussed by Rackham (1972, 26), or the green birds of Saintonge Ware (Dunning 1961, 4) are naturalistic but, on the whole, potters appear to have used the colours most easily available to them. Thus, it may be significant that most ceramic decoration rarely tells a narrative as do wall paintings and manuscript illustrations and both naturalism and symbolism are less significant in a context where specific information was not being conveyed.

An exception may be that of the lustrewares produced in Spain which arrived in Britain in small but increasing quantities from the thirteenth to the fifteenth century and later (Figure 46.3). Covered in a white, opaque glaze, they were closer in appearance and feel to silver and glass than to the earthy local pottery (Gutiérrez 2012, 47). Lustrewares were finely decorated in gold and blue, with drawn, identifiable patterns which had specific symbolic meaning in the culture which had crafted them: Muslim in origin but introducing Christian symbols by the fifteenth century. The use of exotic, rare, and costly colours, such as blue and gold, would have given these vessels an added allure and, although by no means realistic, colour in this case would have been used to

FIGURE 46.3 A striking pottery vessel made in the fifteenth century in the Valencia area, Spain, decorated with gold and blue colours

(© The Walters Art Museum, public domain)

associate pottery with monetary, religious, or social values, making them special objects (Gutiérrez 2000, 188–90).

Conclusion

There is significant variation in the ways in which colour was used and understood in the Middle Ages. In general there was a preference for deep and vivid colours, for example where status was displayed through clothing. Exotically coloured imported pottery was also in demand but was expensive and of limited distribution; production was out of reach in a technical sense to local medieval potters. To some extent technical limitations also informed colour choices in wall painting but here, as in manuscript illustration, colour could be central to the narrative and more likely to be informed by philosophical understandings of colour and its arrangement into moral hierarchies. Cost too was a factor in the acquisition of pigments and dyestuffs and this led to attempts to mimic the effects of expensive materials using cheaper alternatives. Everywhere the use of colour and its understanding was contextual but strongly influenced by a set of ideas drawn from classical philosophy and its later interpretation.

References cited

Allardyce, F. A. 1985 'The painting of the legend of St Eustace in Canterbury', *Archaeologia Cantiana* 101, 115–30

Aristotle, 1936 *De coloribus* (trans. W. S. Hett), in *Aristotle: Minor Works I*, Loeb Classical Library, Heinemann, London

Aristotle, 1984 *De sensu et sensato* (trans. J. I. Beare), in J. Barnes (ed.), *The complete works of Aristotle: the revised Oxford translation I*, Princeton University Press, Princeton

Aristotle, 1986 *De anima* (trans. H. Lawson-Tancred), Penguin, Harmondsworth

Baker, A. M. 1969 'A medieval painting in Llanynys Church', *Archaeologia Cambrensis* 118, 135–7

Baker, A. M. 1970 'The wall paintings in the church of St John the Baptist, Clayton', *Sussex Archaeological Collections* 108, 58–81

Baker, A. M. 1998 'Adam and Eve and the Lord God: the Adam and Eve cycle of wall paintings in the church of Haradham, Sussex', *The Archaeological Journal* 155, 207–25

Baker, E. 1969 'The adoration of the Magi at Shelfhanger Church Norfolk', *Norfolk Archaeology* 34, 90–1

Benson, L. (ed.) 1986 *Riverside Chaucer*, Oxford University Press, Oxford

Biggam, C. 2006 'Knowledge of whelk dyes and pigments in Anglo-Saxon England', *Anglo-Saxon England* 35, 23–56

Bowler, D., Cox, A., and Smith, C. 1995 'Four excavations in Perth, 1979–1984', *Proceedings of the Society of Antiquaries of Scotland* 125, 917–99

Brown, K. L. and Clark, J. H. 2004 'Three English manuscripts post-1066 AD: pigment identification and palette comparisons by raman microscopy', *Journal of Raman Spectroscopy* 35, 217–23

Bucklow, S. 2016 *Red: the art and science of a colour*, Reaktion Books, London

Clemens, R. and Graham, T. 2007 *Introduction to manuscript studies*, Cornell University Press, Ithaca

Crouch, D. 1992 *The image of aristocracy in Britain, 1000–1300*, Routledge, London

Crowfoot, E., Prichard, F., and Staniland, K. 1992 *Textiles and clothing c.1150–c.1450*, Medieval finds from excavations in London 4, HMSO, London

Cumberpatch, C. G. 1997 'Towards a phenomenological approach to the study of medieval pottery', in C. G. Cumberpatch and P. W. Blinkhorn (eds), *Not so much a pot, more a way of life: current approaches to artefact analysis in archaeology*, Oxbow, Oxford, 125–53

Dinkova-Bruun, G., Gasper, G. E. M., Huxtable, M., McLeish, T. C. B., Panti, C., and Smithson, H. (eds) 2013 *The dimensions of colour: Robert Grosseteste's De colore: edition, translation and interdisciplinary analysis*, Pontifical Institute of Medieval Studies and Durham Medieval and Renaissance Texts 4, Durham

Dunning, G. C. 1961 'A group of English and imported medieval pottery from Lesnes Abbey, Kent, and the trade in early Hispano-Moresque pottery to England', *The Antiquaries Journal* 41, 1–12

Edwards, J. 1985 'Trotton's abbreviated doom', *Sussex Archaeological Collections* 124, 115–25

Gameson, R. 2011 'The material fabric of early British books', *The Cambridge History of the Book in Britain*, vol. 1: c.400–1100, Cambridge, 13–93

Gutiérrez, A. 2000 *Mediterranean pottery in Wessex households (13th to 17th centuries)*, British Archaeological Reports British Series 306, Oxford

Gutiérrez, A. 2012 'Of sundry colours and moulds: imports of early modern pottery along the Atlantic seaboard', in A. Texeira and J. A. Bettencourt (eds), *Old and new worlds, International Congress of Early Modern Archaeology*, Lisbon, 37–50

Hayfield, C. 1985 *Humberside medieval pottery: an illustrated catalogue of Saxon and medieval domestic assemblages from North Lincolnshire and its surrounding region*, British Archaeological Reports British Series 140, Oxford

Hodges, L. F. 2005 *Chaucer and clothing: clerical and academic costume in the general prologue to the Canterbury tales*, Chaucer Studies 34, Boydell and Brewer, New York

Howard, H. 2003 *Pigments of English medieval wall painting*, Archetype, London

Huxtable, M. J. 2011 'Aspects of armorial colours and their perception in medieval literature', in C. P. Biggam, L. A. Flough, C. J. Kay, and D. R. Simmons (eds), *New directions in colour studies*, John Benjamins Publishing Company, Amsterdam, 191–204

Jones, P. M. 1998 *Medieval medicine in illuminated manuscripts*, The British Library, London

Koslin, D. 2012 'Ecclesiastical dress post-1100', in G. R. Owen-Crocker, E. Coatsworth, and M. Hayword (eds), *Encyclopedia of medieval dress and textiles in the British Isles c.450–1450*, Brill, Leiden, 183–4

Langum, V. 2013 'Discerning skin: complexion, surgery and language in medieval confession', in K. L. Walter (ed.), *Reading skin in medieval literature and culture*, Palgrave MacMillan, New York, 141–60

Lauchard, F. 2002 'Dress and social status in England before the sumptuary laws', in P. Coss and M. Keen (eds), *Heraldry, pageantry and social display in medieval England*, Boydell and Brewer, Woodbridge, 105–23

Lee, R. L. and Fraser, A. B. 2001 *The rainbow bridge: rainbows in art, myth and science*, The Pennsylvania State University Press, Pennsylvania

Lewis, S. 1991 'The English Gothic illuminated apocalypse, *Lectio divina* and the art of memory', *Word and Image* 7, 1–32

McCarthy, M. and Brooks, C. M. 1988 *Medieval pottery in Britain AD 900–1600*, Leicester University Press, Leicester

Mills, M. (ed.) 1973 *Six Middle English Romances*, J. M. Dent, London

Munro, J. H. 1983 'The medieval scarlet and the economics of sartorial splendour', in N. B. Harte and K. G. Ponting (eds), *Cloth and clothing in medieval Europe: essays in memory of Professor E. M. Carus-Wilson*, Heinmann Educational Books, London, 13–70

Munro, J. H. and Owen-Crocker, G. R. 2012a 'Purple', in G. R. Owen-Crocker, E. Coatsworth, and M. Hayword (eds), *Encyclopedia of medieval dress and textiles in the British Isles c.450–1450*, Brill, Leiden, 436–8

Munro, J. H., Owen-Crocker, G. R., and Uzzell, H. 2012b 'Kermes', in G. R. Owen-Crocker, E. Coatsworth, and M. Hayword (eds), *Encyclopedia of medieval dress and textiles in the British Isles c.450–1450*, Brill, Leiden, 301–2

Myers, A. R. 1994 *English historical documents 1327–1485, Vol. IV*, Routledge, London

Piponnier, F. and Mane, P. 1997 *Dress in the Middle Ages*, Yale University Press, New Haven

Plato, 2000 *Timaeus* (trans. D. J. Zeyl), Hackett, Indianapolis

Pseudo-Dionysius, 1987 *The celestial hierarchy* (trans. C. Luibheid), in *Pseudo-Dionysius: the complete works*, Classics of Western Spirituality, Paulist Press, New York

Rackham, B. 1972 *Medieval English pottery*, Faber and Faber, London

Rosewell, R. 2008 *Medieval wall paintings in English and Welsh churches*, Boydell and Brewer, Woodbridge

Rouse, E. C. 1979 'Wall paintings in St Mary's Church, Battle', *Sussex Archaeological Collections* 117, 151–9

Schapiro, M. 1960 'An illuminated English psalter of the early thirteenth century', *Journal of the Warburg and Courtald Institutes* 23, 179–89

Spavold, J. 2010 'Faith made manifest: an interpretation of the decoration on Cistercian wares', *Medieval Ceramics* 31, 33–48

St Augustine, 1991 *Saint Augustine on Genesis: two books on Genesis: against the Manichees and on the literal interpretation of Genesis, an unfinished book* (trans. R. J. Teske), The Fathers of the Church 84, Catholic University of America Press, Washington D.C.

Theophilus 1961 *De diversis artibus: the various arts* (trans. C. R. Dodwell), Thomas Nelson, London

Uzzell, H. 2012 'Dyeing', in G. R. Owen-Crocker, E. Coatsworth, and M. Hayword (eds), *Encyclopedia of medieval dress and textiles in the British Isles c.450–1450*, Brill, Leiden, 175–80

Walton-Rogers, P. 2001 'Dyes', in A. S. Cameron and J. A. Stones (eds), *Aberdeen: an in-depth view of the city's past*, The Society of Antiquaries of Scotland, Edinburgh, 238–9

Woolgar, C. M. 2006 *The senses in late medieval England*, Yale University Press, New Haven

PART IX

GROWING UP AND GROWING OLD

CHAPTER 47

OVERVIEW

Archaeology and the Medieval Life Course

REBECCA L. GOWLAND
AND BENNJAMIN J. PENNY-MASON

AGE in the modern industrialized world has been conceptualized as a chronological phenomenon: the passing of time marked by the embodied processes of growth, maturation, and degeneration. Whilst ageing is often considered to be a universal process, people grow up and grow old within different cultural and physical environments and social scientists have begun to explore the role of age identity as a structuring force in society (Gowland 2006; Sofaer 2006). Within archaeology, however, these debates failed to gain traction until recently: the perception of age as little more than a chronological 'variable' persisted long after other facets of identity, such as ethnicity and gender, had been deconstructed (Sofaer Derevenski 1997). Different cultures invariably divide the life course into a series of stages, each accompanied by social attributes or expectations of behaviour appropriate for that age group. Historical evidence from medieval Britain suggests a number of different ageing schemes, though one of the most common is the six-age system: *infantia* (0–7 years), *pueritia* (7–14 years), *adolescentia* (14–21 years), *iuventus* (21–49 years), *senioris* (50–72 years), and *senectus* (72 years onwards). However, the relevance of these categories for day-to-day social behaviour and the extent to which other facets of social identity, such as gender and status, impinge upon the chronology of these age stages is less well understood.

Ethnographic studies of the life course identify some cross-cultural congruence in age categorizations, particularly those that align with biological milestones, such as teething in infancy or the commencement of puberty, but also a high degree of variation, even with respect to social definitions of the beginning and end of life (e.g. Fortes 1984; Gottlieb 2000). In gender archaeology, a separation is usually maintained between sex as a biological construct and gender as a social construct. While this distinction has long been critiqued, it serves a useful discursive purpose for archaeologists (see Sørensen 2000 and Sofaer 2006 for a discussion). Likewise, Ginn and Arber (1995, 2) have distinguished between different 'categories' of age. These include: physiological age (representing the physical ageing of the body), chronological age (corresponding to the amount of time that has passed from the moment of birth), and social age (socially constructed norms concerning appropriate behaviour and attitudes for an age group). Sofaer (2011) also highlights psychological age (how one feels, behaves, and acts) in studies of age identity. These age categories are not discrete or exclusive; behavioural norms attributed to a particular age group can have repercussions for biological milestones that are important for social age identity (e.g. learning to walk or menarche) (Gowland 2006).

Early archaeological studies of age as an aspect of social identity tended to focus on children (e.g. Crawford 1999; Lillehammer 1989). More recently, authors have argued that in order to more fully understand period-specific perceptions of a particular age group, these must be fully contextualized within the life course as a whole (Gilchrist 2000; Gowland 2006). Examples of archaeological studies that have adopted a life course approach include research by Harlow and Laurence (2002) on the Roman life course, Gilchrist (2012) on the medieval life course, Sofaer Derevenski's (1997) study of age identity in Bronze Age Hungary, and Gowland's research (2001; 2006; 2007) on age identities in fourth to sixth century England. This chapter will discuss current theories of age and the life course within archaeology, drawing upon sociological and anthropological studies of ageing. It will then focus on the historical, archaeological, and bioarchaeological evidence for understanding the medieval life course, from conception to old age.

The Life Course in Archaeology

The term 'life cycle' has commonly been used in discussions of age, though this term is now generally considered too prescriptive in its construction of life as a series of fixed chronological and biological phases (Hunt 2005). Instead, social scientists prefer a 'life course' perspective, conceptualizing age as a series of 'life pathways' and transitions over the trajectory of life from conception to death (Marshall 1996; Moen 1996, 181). The life course approach facilitates a deeper exploration of the culturally contingent nature of age identity and the fluidity and inter-sectionality of age with other aspects of identity, such as gender. The life course experience is also one that is now understood as being embedded within the social and historical matrix of a society and hence can only be interpreted in relation to this context (Hunt 2005). Importantly, it recognizes the cumulative nature of individual biographies: in other words, it explicitly considers the way in which identities and experiences in early life may impact upon later stages (Hockey and Draper 2005, 43). This is a departure from the earlier 'life cycle' approach to age, because of the explicit acknowledgement that one's identity and physiology at any moment in time is borne out of earlier phases, which may have divergent effects on individual trajectories (Levy and the Pavie Team 2005, 4). This approach has been particularly significant for bioarchaeological studies of age identity which have embraced an 'osteobiographical' approach to the study of human skeletal remains (Robb 2002). From this perspective, the skeleton is regarded as an (incomplete) archive of social as well as biological life experiences. The tissues of our bodies become saturated by the social and environmental fabric in which we exist and these interactions become fossilized within our bones and teeth (Gowland and Thompson 2013; Robb 2002; Sofaer 2006). In this respect, bioarchaeological studies are particularly informative for studies of age identity in the past; the human skeleton does not simply provide a 'snapshot' of a person at the time of death, but has a temporal dimension. For example, isotopic data retrieved from an adult skeleton may provide information relating to a variety of earlier phases of life, from infancy onwards, because different teeth form and bones remodel at different ages and rates (e.g. Beaumont et al. 2013). Likewise, some pathological lesions observed on adult skeletons (e.g. cribra orbitalia and enamel hypoplasia), as well as adult body proportions, reflect childhood stresses and provide a window into these earlier periods of the life course.

When considering age identity in the past, the cemetery context is a particularly fruitful form of evidence because of the direct link it provides between the physiological body and cultural aspects of burial practice (Gowland and Knüsel 2006). Since the 1990s, the body has been reconceptualized as a mediator of both social and biological processes (Shilling 1993). This represents an important departure from earlier models which viewed the body as a purely biological entity and largely irrelevant for interpretations of cultural practice. Finally, an important aspect to bear in mind when interpreting burial assemblages is that as people get older, not only does their identity alter, but so too does the identity of the person burying them, from parent to spouse to child. Age and gender identity are lived relationally; therefore, the variation in funerary practice accorded throughout various life course stages could reflect and reproduce the changing relationships of the deceased with age (Gowland 2001; 2006). Individuals are not monadic entities, instead strong interdependencies exist in the life course trajectories of related individuals (Levy and the Pavie Team 2005, 6). Furthermore, each individual experiences a number of different interlocking roles which lead to marked heterogeneity in age identity. A high-status medieval female will therefore experience different biological and social age milestones than her lower-status counterparts. Likewise, males and females may experience divergent social age trajectories once gender starts to become a more prominent feature of their personae.

CONCEPTION TO INFANCY

The beginnings of life and the treatment of foetal and infants remains have been a recent focus of interest (e.g. Finlay 2013; Gottlieb 2000; Gowland et al. 2014; Millett and Gowland 2015). The beginning of personhood is culturally ascribed and therefore highly variable (Kaufman and Morgan 2005, 321) and, while often marked by discrete rites of passage (e.g. baptism, or the *dies lustricus* in the Roman world), the acquisition of personhood is often, in actuality, a *process* rather than an event. Hockey and Draper (2005, 54) argued that studies of the life course have tended to be constrained by the 'twin gate-posts of birth and death'; thus omitting the significance of life before birth. Yet, as

Gilchrist (2012, 1) discusses, medieval concepts of the life course *did* include a pre-birth identity.

Medieval understandings of conception, pregnancy, and human development remained largely unchanged from those devised millennia earlier in ancient Greece and Rome (MacLehose 2010, 165; Orme 2001, 14). Aristotelian theory espoused that the father provided the 'spirit' and the mother the 'matter' for the embryo, and that foetal nourishment occurred via menstrual blood (Youngs 2006, 44). Galen's writing stated that the embryo was formed from two seeds, one from the mother and one from the father, which then developed from plant to animal form, before finally becoming human (Gilchrist 2012, 21). Once pregnant, the choice of bodily indicators that life had started is likewise culturally contingent (e.g. halted menstruation, 'quickening') (Hockey and Draper 2005). In the earlier stages of pregnancy the developing foetus was considered to exist in a vegetative, animalistic state, without a soul. The foetus then came to be imbued with a soul from forty-six days *in utero* for boys and much later at ninety days for girls, who 'lacked the heat and strength to form as quickly' (Orme 2001, 15; Youngs 2006, 44). However, some medieval writers believed that 'ensoulment' occurred later in gestation, at around six months *in utero*. At this point of the pregnancy, the now 'human' foetus acquired a social presence, but the child's soul could only be protected by the rite of baptism, which could not occur until after birth (Gilchrist 2012; Orme 2001). Tainted by the original sin, the soul of an infant who died prior to baptism was believed to live in eternal limbo, with no chance for salvation in the afterlife (Orme 2001; Youngs 2006). The time between ensoulment and baptism was therefore a spiritually precarious one and arguably one of the most tightly defined stages of the medieval life course. Loss of the infant prior to baptism resulted in their liminal status and exclusion from burial in consecrated ground (Youngs 2010). While the buried remains of these infants may have been spatially marginalized, their loss could have still invoked considerable grief in the immediate family. Murphy presents a variety of archaeological and historical data to highlight the fact that infants buried within *cillíní* in Ireland were nevertheless mourned by their families (Murphy 2011).

The spatial differentiation of infant burials in association with medieval churches is noted by a number of authors, including most recently Craig-Atkins (2014) who synthesized the evidence from sites in medieval Britain. She notes that neonates, including pre-term infants, were often buried close to church walls (within 1.5 metres). These are often referred to as 'eaves-drip' burials and interpreted as a form of posthumous baptism, with the water dripping from the eaves of the church effectively anointing the burial. However, as Craig-Atkins discusses, a number of these burials pre-date the ubiquity of more formalized ideas regarding the baptism of infants and may well have arisen from earlier traditions. The same author also notes that some young adult women, including mother/infant burials, were buried close to church walls. This has parallels with excavations from Roman sites in which infants and possible mothers were also buried close to structures (Millett and Gowland 2015). The desire to maintain the inter-connectivity between mother and infant may have been a motivating force in burial practice.

Historical evidence for medieval perceptions of infancy is biased towards the wealthier members of society (Goldberg 2010, 30; Orme 2001, 86; Youngs 2006, 63). Infants were largely restricted from moving for the first two or three months of life by the custom of swaddling. Swaddling bands were used for practical reasons in terms of restricting movements, but also because infants were considered mouldable and the practice was believed (erroneously) to promote the straight growth of long bones (Finucane 1997, 39; Hanawalt 1986, 175; Houlbrooke 1986, 132). Mortality rates were high, with a third of children not surviving infancy (the first year) (Orme 2001, 64; Youngs 2006, 34). Lewis and Gowland (2007) analysed the levels of neonatal mortality (death during first month after birth) versus post-neonatal mortality (death between one month to one year of age) from a number of rural and urban sites in medieval England. Post-neonatal mortality provides a strong indication of disease environment and diet, but tends to be lower than neonatal mortality, which is related to factors intrinsic to the mother. However, in medieval urban environments post-neonatal mortality exceeded neonatal mortality, highlighting the poor living conditions endured.

The 'average' family in later medieval England was likely to have consisted of a mother, father, two or three surviving children, with grandparents possibly also living in the same domicile or nearby (Orme 2001, 55; Schofield 2010, 58). Evidence from coroner's rolls indicates that 80 per cent of infant deaths occurred within the home (Hanawalt 2002). From the ages of 1 to 2 years, as the child began walking, talking, and weaning, they were perceived to have reached a new stage in the life course (Gilchrist 2012, 206; Lewis 2007, 6). Evidence from analysis of $\delta^{13}C$ and $\delta^{15}N$ isotope values from non-adults at Wharram Percy (North Yorkshire) suggests that most children were breast-fed until between 1 and 2 years (Richards et al. 2002, 209). The weaning diet consisted of 'pap' (porridge), or bread soaked in water or milk (Orme 2001, 71) and was provided in conjunction with breast-milk from at least six months of age. This diet, however, was unlikely to have been adequate for the developmental demands of a growing infant and at Wharram Percy this was reflected in the delayed growth of infants during the weaning and post-weaning period compared to modern values (Mays 2010, 71).

Childhood

The age of 7 years demarcated a distinct stage of transformation in the medieval life course towards a more 'rational' and responsible status as the child became more immersed in the adult world (Figure 47.1) (Hanawalt 1986, 183; Heywood 2001, 11; Houlbrooke 1986, 150; Orme 1995, 86). Seven years of age was also a significant age demarcation in the Roman period and subsequent post-medieval period in terms of child labour and legal accountability, yet it bears no relationship to any obvious biological marker. From 7 years children were encouraged to appear more adult-like and were praised for demonstrating qualities beyond their years (Young 2006, 41). It also marked a shift in gender identity, with the adoption of more strongly gendered clothing, including tunics, doublets, and belts for boys, while girls wore long-fitted gowns, with no headgear (Gilchrist 2012, 81). Medieval vocabulary also becomes gendered from this stage of maturation onwards, with boys described as 'groom', 'knave', and 'lad' and girls as 'lass', 'maid', and 'wench' (Orme 2001, 6).

FIGURE 47.1 Defining chronological, biological, and social age, in relation to medieval language commonly used to describe those under the age of 21 years old

(© R. Gowland and B. Penny-Mason)

A large-scale study of bioarchaeological evidence for medieval childhood indicates that those aged 6–11 years exhibited similar levels of disease and trauma to 0–5 year olds, suggesting that although children were developing into adult roles, the majority were likely to have experienced an extended period of childhood roles into puberty (Penny-Mason and Gowland 2014, 185). Evidence from analysis of $\delta^{13}C$ and $\delta^{15}N$ isotope values from Wharram Percy revealed that children aged 4–8 years had a distinct diet that continued to mark them out as different from adults (Mays 2010, 95). This suggests that, although they were progressing away from an infant status and towards adulthood, they were now in a separate social group of their own. Again, there are parallels here with Roman Britain: Powell et al. (2014) identified a specific childhood diet in Roman London that was clearly differentiated from both infant and adult diets in terms of content.

Adolescence

Puberty marked the physical end of childhood and a cognitive and embodied transition towards an adult identity (MacLehose 2010, 173; Orme 2001, 220; Youngs 2006, 96). The increasing divergence in physical characteristics between the sexes was further reinforced by clothing which was reflective of the ritual, identity, and performativity of adolescence. Young women were allowed to wear their hair loose up until marriage, with young men distinguishing themselves with tight-fitting tunics (Gilchrist 2012, 84). The physical changes of puberty and the adoption of more strongly gendered roles and gestures represented a shift towards a distinct socio-cultural group for adolescents. While older children were perceived to be more 'rational' than their younger counterparts, adolescence was a period of life associated with reckless behaviour, independence, and the development of passion and lust (MacLehose 2010, 173; Youngs 2006, 101).

Recent bioarchaeological studies of socially significant pubertal milestones, including menarche, have contributed significantly to understandings of medieval adolescence. Shapland et al. (2015) examined the skeletal remains of a large sample of young females aged between 14 and 25 years from medieval cemeteries. The onset of menstruation was only observed in medieval females aged 15 years and over (on the basis of osteological criteria), compared with an average of 13 years today. Puberty is strongly affected by socio-environmental conditions, with adverse environmental circumstances such as poor nutrition or high pathogen load leading to delays in growth, pubertal onset, and an extended period of maturation during adolescence and into early adulthood. These skeletal data are supported by the documentary evidence which also indicates that the age of onset of menarche was likely much lower among higher-status groups with better nutrition which included more dietary protein. The same study also found evidence of women afflicted with venereal disease from a young age (perhaps indicative of prostitution), as well as high levels of respiratory and infectious diseases.

The period of adolescence in medieval England was a protracted one and for women the transition to adult status may not have occurred until marriage, which for many did not occur until their early 20s. Whilst there is evidence for young betrothals and marriages, it was certainly not a widespread practice, nor one encouraged by the Church.

Cases are most often recorded for society's elites rather than the struggling masses (Goldberg 2004, 26; Orme 1994, 571).

THE GROWING BODY: WORK, REST, AND PLAY

Play was recognized as important in the development of a child and generally encouraged (Goldberg 2008, 262; Orme 2001, 164; Shahar 1992, 103). Material culture suggests that children's play, then as now, often imitated aspects of adult life (Crawford 2009; Orme 1995; Youngs 2006). Medieval parents considered children under five to be playful and active, although lacking in both discretion and judgement (Finucane 1997, 10). Despite this, by today's standards medieval parents adopted an attitude of benign neglect towards their offspring, often leaving them unsupervised (Goldberg 2008, 261; Gordon 1991, 163; Ward 2010, 43; Youngs 2006, 54). This is not to imply widespread indifference or even cruelty towards offspring, as inferred by previous histories of medieval childhood (e.g. Ariès 1962; De Mause 1974), but simply that they were allowed more freedom from parental constraint. Occasionally, this had fatal consequences; coroners' rolls reveal that 60 per cent of deaths during 3–6 years of age occurred as a consequence of misadventure during play (Hanawalt 2002). 'Play' continued to be a significant part of older children's lives too, but developed into more structured social group sports (Hanawalt 1993, 117), such as wrestling and mock fighting, as well as more adult pursuits such as dice and chess (Orme 2001, 178). For boys, joining the hunt was a particularly important stage in maturation (Gilchrist 2012, 92) and 'playing at war' was also encouraged, with boys as young as 7 years being taught how to shoot a bow and arrow (Orme 1995, 63).

Education could begin at home from a young age and was largely based on Christian principles, together with the customs and etiquette of medieval society (Houlbrooke 1986; Lett 1999; Ward 2010). A child's obedience to its parents was instilled in Christian teaching but only a small fraction of children received a formal education between the ages of 5 to 14 years (Orme 2001; Shahar 1992; Youngs 2006). Some churches and monasteries provided education for the younger children of the local parish (Alexandre-Bidon 1999; Lett 1999). The majority of schooling was restricted to boys, with education for girls in skills such as basic literacy a matter of parental choice (Wilkinson 2010). Peasant children would have received no formal education, and would instead have learned occupational and domestic skills through the observation and shadowing of their parents (Goldberg 2004).

Work was an additional source of potential trauma and health stress for young children and they were inculcated into domestic duties from a relatively early age (Hanawalt 1986). From around 5 years there was a gradual increase in the variety of tasks and household duties that children would be involved in (Youngs 2006). This is reflected in the increasing prevalence and variety of trauma incurred by children, including injuries in contexts away from the domestic setting, such as the father's workplace (Finucane

1997; Hanawalt 1986). Full-time employment for children tended not to begin before around 12–14 years of age and for many this meant boys taking to the fields and girls tending to the household (Alexandre-Bidon 1999; Bolton 1980). Documentary sources indicate however that girls and boys also travelled to nearby urban centres to work in domestic service, as well as a range of other occupational activities. Migration to urban centres was particularly high after the Black Death, when a wider range of occupational activities became available (Gilchrist 2012) and this exposed adolescents to a greater array of morbidity and mortality risks (Roberts 2009; Lewis 2016). Skeletal evidence for migration into towns is inferred from the excess of adolescent and young adult deaths in urban contexts (e.g. London and York) compared to rural settings (e.g. Wharram Percy). A large-scale analysis of skeletons of later medieval children also revealed that, unusually, levels of morbidity in children aged 12–16 were much higher than levels at earlier stages of life; however, levels of trauma still did not reach adult levels, highlighting this stage of life as a period of transition (Penny-Mason and Gowland 2014).

Between the fourteenth and sixteenth centuries adolescents contributed a third of the work force, a substantial portion of the economy (McKintosh 1988). Although many worked 'full time', most did not leave the household immediately, as their new finances would not permit them economic independence (Youngs 2006). The most likely children to leave home at this age were those who were taking up apprenticeships, mostly boys (Orme 2001; Houlbrooke 1986; Wilkinson 2010). Apprenticeships marked a major transition in a child's life, usually beginning between 12 and 16 years old for boys, although in the fourteenth century girls could enter domestic service from as young as 10 years of age (Orme 2001, 310; Gilchrist 2012, 145). Twelve years of age marked the first time children became independent and responsible in Common Law. Before that, any legal action taken against a child would be delayed until their maturation, or the responsibility for the action was placed upon the parents (Huscroft 2010; Young 2006). Children around 12–14 years were eligible to inherit property or make a will of personal property and by the fourteenth century children aged 14–16 years could be obliged to pay to the Poll Tax (Goldberg 2004; Youngs 2006). There is evidence that children could not give evidence in ecclesiastical court until 16 year of age, which was also around the same time they became liable to pay Church dues, becoming a full adult in the eyes of the Church (Garver 2010; Orme 2001).

Adulthood

The status of adulthood was associated with occupational skills, religious learning, and qualities such as self-control, knowledge, and wisdom; characteristics that could be attained at a wide variety of chronological ages (Youngs 2006). There was no medieval 'age of majority' and, in the absence of distinct social milestones such as marriage, there was no single point at which an adolescent entered adulthood (Youngs 2010). By the later medieval period the majority of marriages were delayed until their early 20s and this age is congruent with the final maturation of the adolescent male body and female fertility (Goldberg 2010; Shapland et al. 2015). Employment, marriage, pregnancy, establishing a household, and providing for a family all established an adult embodied identity that was reinforced through material culture. Adolescent males were depicted as beardless, but adult males grew beards, while married women covered their hair. The transition to motherhood was also marked by differences in the body and dress during pregnancy (the wearing of stomachers), and on a mother's 'churching' after delivery through the wearing of a white veil (Gilchrist 2012, 96).

Adulthood was strongly gendered. Documentary sources indicating that males ate more meat than females are supported by isotope studies from sites such as medieval York (e.g. Müldner 2009). There were also clear divisions of duties, and palaeopathological evidence from medieval sites shows that females often have different patterns of trauma and health stress when compared to males (Grauer 1991; Sullivan 2005). Female mortality also tends to peak at a younger adult age (25–35 years) than males (35–45 years), although this pattern is common to many periods and places in the past. Younger adult female mortality is often thought to be the result of 'obstetrical hazard', although this interpretation tends to be accepted too uncritically and broader archaeological reasons for younger female deaths, perhaps related to diet or activities, should also be considered (Stone and Walrath 2006).

Old Age

While medieval skeletal assemblages yield very few individuals beyond the age of 45 years, this picture is known to be influenced by taphonomic and methodological biases in osteological techniques of age estimation (Gowland 2007). Historical and epigraphic sources for the Roman and medieval worlds attest to the fact that people did sometimes reach very old ages. Only a handful of archaeological studies have sought to examine perceptions towards older people in the past (e.g. Appleby 2010; Gowland 2007; 2015). By contrast, historical studies of old age, from the classical to early modern periods, are much more plentiful (e.g. Parkin 2003; Pelling and Smith 1991; Thane 2000). In later medieval England, old age was recognized as a distinct stage of life. Some believed, for example, that the cessation of menstruation could poison an older woman's body, giving way to fornication and crime (Gilchrist 2012) but the transition to 'old age' could also allow women an increased freedom, with many experiencing greater social power (Moore 1994).

Negative attitudes towards the elderly are nothing new. Texts from both the ancient and medieval worlds supply negative descriptions of physiological decline in old age and expressions of repugnance towards the ageing body (Parkin 2003; 2011; Pelling and Smith 1991). There are some links between the ageing body and the disabled and impaired body in medieval England. Both represent an outer expression of inner sin and corruption, whilst concurrently bringing the individual closer to God, because of their proximity to suffering and death. Within a Christian world view, death marks a transition towards another, potentially more desirable, spiritual state of being and, in that context, the end stage of life may have been more greatly valued (Gowland 2016). Overall, archaeological and historical evidence suggests that individuals were cared for in their old age. This includes the sub-division of tofts to accommodate elderly kin and 'retirement' contracts, which record arrangements for older tenants to continue to be housed and fed once they had surrendered their lands (Gilchrist 2012). A number of elderly skeletons have also been recovered from medieval hospital sites. These individuals had suffered debilitating impairments but were nevertheless the recipients of institutionalized care.

Conclusions

In medieval England, males and females experienced increasingly divergent trajectories from the age of 7 years, while social status profoundly influenced biological milestones such as puberty, leading to a younger age of maturity amongst upper-class females. Life for the elderly in the medieval world was likely to have been more favourable when compared to some of the preceding periods, with family obligations and institutional care demonstrated through the archaeological and historical evidence. The influence of catastrophic events such as the Black Death profoundly altered the social fabric of society, including age norms, leading to at least temporary disruptions in family relationships in terms of the death of children and parents, as well as influencing work-related migratory patterns and the age at which occupational activities outside of the home commenced for both boys and girls. While broad age trends can be highlighted, there was a great deal of heterogeneity in experiences of the medieval life course which arose from social and environmental circumstances. In particular, the integration of bioarchaeological evidence into past biographies is proving a fruitful avenue of enquiry to unravel the medieval life experience, particularly so when it is fully contextualized with archaeological and historical data.

Acknowledgements

Thank you to Alejandra and Chris for inviting us to contribute to this volume and for their patience and editorial assistance! Thanks also to Tim Thompson and Alice Rose for commenting on earlier drafts of this paper and to Mary Lewis for providing access to her manuscripts.

References Cited

Alexandre-Bidon, D. 1999 'The child in society: twelfth–early sixteenth centuries', in D. Alexandre-Bidon and D. Lett (eds), *Children in the Middle Ages: fifth–fifteenth centuries*, The University of Notre Dame Press, Indiana, 73–138

Appleby, J. 2010 'Why we need an archaeology of old age, and a suggested approach', *Norwegian Archaeological Review* 43(2), 145–68

Ariès, P. 1962 *Centuries of childhood: a social history of family life*, Jonathan Cape, London

Beaumont, J., Geber, J., Powers, N., Lee-Thorp, J., and Montgomery, J. 2013 'Victims and survivors: identifying survivors of the Great Famine in 19th century London using carbon and nitrogen isotope ratios', *American Journal of Physical Anthropology* 150, 87–98

Bolton, J. L. 1980 *The medieval English economy, 1150–1500*, Billing and Sons Ltd, Guildford

Craig-Atkins, E. 2014 'Eaves-dropping on short lives: eaves-drip burials and the differential treatment of children one year of age and under in early Christian cemeteries', in D. M. Hadley and K. Hemer (eds), *Medieval childhood: archaeological approaches*, Oxbow, Oxford

Crawford, S. 1999 *Childhood in Anglo-Saxon England*, Sutton Publishing Ltd, Stroud

Crawford, S. 2009 'The archaeology of play things: theorising a toy stage in the "biography" of objects', *Childhood Past* 2, 55–70

De Mause, L. 1974 *The history of childhood*, Psychohistory Press, New York

Finlay, N. 2013 'Archaeologies of the beginnings of life', *World Archaeology* 45, 207–14

Finucane, R. C. 1997 *The rescue of the innocents: endangered children in medieval miracles*, Macmillan Press, Basingstoke

Fortes, M. 1984 'Age, generation, and social structure', in D. I. Kertzer and J. Keith (eds), *Age and anthropological theory*, Cornell University Press, Ithaca, NY, 99–122

Garver, V. L. 2010 'Faith and religion', in L. J. Wilkinson (ed.), *In the Middle Ages*, A Cultural History of Childhood and Family 2, 145–60

Gilchrist, R. 2000 'Archaeological biographies: realizing human lifecycles, -courses and -histories', *World Archaeology* 31, 325–8

Gilchrist, R. 2012 *Medieval life: archaeology and the life course*, The Boydell Press, Woodbridge

Ginn, J. and Arber, S. 1995 '"Only connect": gender relations and ageing', in S. Arber and J. Ginn (eds), *Connecting gender and ageing: a sociological approach*, Open University Press, Buckingham, 1–14

Goldberg, P. J. P. 2004 *Medieval England: a social history, 1250–1550*, Hodder Arnold, London

Goldberg, P. J. P. 2008 'Childhood and gender in later medieval England', *Viator* 39(1), 249–62

Goldberg, P. J. P. 2010 'Family relationships', in L. J. Wilkinson (ed.), *In the Middle Ages*, A Cultural History of Childhood and Family 2, 21–40

Gordon, E. C. 1991 'Accidents among medieval children as seen from the miracles of six English saints and martyrs', *Medieval History* 35, 145–63

Gottleib, E. 2000 'Where have all the babies gone? Toward an anthropology of infants (and their caretakers)', *Anthropological Quarterly* 73, 121–32

Gowland, R. L. 2001 'Playing dead: implications of mortuary evidence for the social construction of childhood in Roman Britain', in G. Davies, A. Gardner, and K. Lockyear (eds), *TRAC 2000. Proceedings of the Tenth Annual Theoretical Roman Archaeology Conference, London 2000*, Oxbow, Oxford, 152–68

Gowland, R. L. 2006 'Age as an aspect of social identity: the archaeological and funerary evidence', in R. L. Gowland and C. Knüsel (eds), *Social archaeology of funerary remains*, Oxbow, Oxford, 143–54

Gowland, R. L. 2007 'Age, ageism and osteological bias: the evidence from late Roman Britain', *Journal of Roman Archaeology*, Supplementary Series 65, 153–69

Gowland, R. L. 2015 'Entangled lives: implications of the developmental origins of health and disease (DOHaD) hypothesis for bioarchaeology and the life course', *American Journal of Physical Anthropology* 158, 530–40

Gowland, R. L. 2016 'That "tattered coat upon a stick" the ageing body: evidence for elder marginalisation and abuse in Roman Britain', in L. A. Powell, W. Southwell-Wright, and R. L. Gowland (eds), *Care in the past: interdisciplinary perspectives*, Oxbow, Oxford, 71–90

Gowland, R. L., Chamberlain, A. T., and Redfern, R. C. 2014 'On the brink of being: re-evaluating infant death and infanticide in Roman Britain', in M. Carroll and E.-J. Graham (eds), *Infant health and death in Roman Italy and beyond*, Journal of Roman Archaeology Supplementary Series 98, 69–88

Gowland, R. L. and Knüsel, C. (eds) 2006 *Social archaeology of funerary remains*, Oxbow, Oxford

Gowland, R. L. and Thompson, T. J. U. 2013 *Human identity and identification*, Cambridge University Press, Cambridge

Grauer, A. 1991 'Life patterns of women from medieval York', in D. Walde and N. D. Willows (eds), *The archaeology of gender*, Chacmool, Calgary, 407–13

Hanawalt, B. A. 1986 *The ties that bound: peasant families in medieval England*, Oxford University Press, Oxford

Hanawalt, B. A. 1993 *Growing up in medieval London: the experience of childhood in history*, Oxford University Press, Oxford

Hanawalt, B. A. 2002 'Medievalists and the study of children', *Speculum* 77(44), 440–60

Harlow, M. and Laurence, R. 2002 *Growing up and growing old in ancient Rome*, Routledge, London

Heywood, C. 2001 *A history of childhood: children and childhood in the West from medieval to modern times*, Polity Press, Cambridge

Hockey, J. and Draper, J. 2005 'Beyond the womb and the tomb: identity, (dis)embodiment, and the life course', *Body & Society* 11, 41–58

Houlbrooke, R. A. 1986 *The English family, 1450–1700*, Longman Group Ltd, London

Hunt, S. 2005 *The life course: a sociological introduction*, Palgrave Macmillan, Basingstoke

Huscroft, R. 2010 'The State', in L. J. Wilkinson (ed.), *In the Middle Ages*, A Cultural History of Childhood and Family 2, 127–44

Kaufman, S. R. and Morgan, L. M. 2005 'The anthropology of the beginnings and ends of life', *Annual Review of Anthropology* 34, 317–41

Lett, D. 1999 'The child in Christendom: fifth–thirteenth centuries', in D. Alexandre-Bidon and D. Lett (eds), *Children in the Middle Ages: fifth–fifteenth centuries*, The University of Notre Dame Press, Indiana, 7–69

Levy, R. and the Pavie Team 2005 'Why look at life courses in an inter-disciplinary perspective', *Advances in Life Course Research* 10, 3–32

Lewis, M. E. 2007 *The bioarchaeology of children: perspective from biological and forensic anthropology*, Cambridge University Press, Cambridge

Lewis, M. E. 2016 'Work and the adolescent in medieval England (AD 900–1550): the osteological evidence', *Medieval Archaeology* 60, 138–71

Lewis, M. E. and Gowland, R. L. 2007 'Brief and precarious lives: infant mortality in contrasting sites from medieval and post-medieval England (AD 850–1859)', *American Journal of Physical Anthropology* 134, 117–29

Lillehammer, G. 1989 'A child is born: the child's world in an archaeological perspective', *Norwegian Archaeological Review* 22, 89–105

McKintosh, M. K. 1988 'Local responses to the poor in late medieval and Tudor England', *Continuity Change* 3(2), 209–45

MacLehose, W. F. 2010 'Health and science', in L. J. Wilkinson (ed.), *A Cultural History of Childhood and Family In the Middle Ages*, 2, 161–78

Marshall, V. W. 1996 'The state of theory in aging and the social sciences', in R. H. Binstock and L. K. George (eds), *Handbook of aging and the social sciences* (4th edn), Academic Press, New York, 12–30

Mays, S. 2010 'The effects of infant feeding practice on infant and maternal health in a medieval community', *Childhood in the Past* 3, 63–78

Millett, M. and Gowland, R. L. 2015 'Infant and child burial rites in Roman Britain: a study from East Yorkshire', *Britannia* 46, 171–89

Moen, P. 1996 'Gender, age and the life course', in R. H. Binstock and L. K. George (eds), *Handbook of aging and the social sciences* (4th edn), Academic Press, New York, 181–7

Moore, H. 1994 *A passion for difference*, Polity Press, Cambridge

Müldner, G. 2009 'Investigating medieval diet and society by stable isotope analysis of human bone', in R. Gilchrist and A. Reynolds (eds), *Reflections: 50 years of medieval archaeology, 1957–2007*, The Society for Medieval Archaeology Monograph 30, London, 327–46

Murphy, E. 2011 'Children's burial grounds in Ireland (*cillíní*) and parental emotions toward infant death', *International Journal of Historical Archaeology* 15, 409–28

Orme, N. 1994 'Children and the Church in medieval England', *Journal of Ecclesiastical History* 45(4), 563–88

Orme, N. 1995 'The culture of children in medieval England', *Past Present* 148, 48–88

Orme, N. 2001 *Medieval children*, Yale University Press, Yale

Parkin, T. 2003 *Old age in the Roman world*, John Hopkins University Press, Baltimore

Parkin, T. 2011 'The elderly children of Greece and Rome', in C. Krötzl and K. Mustakallio (eds), *On old age: approaching death in Antiquity and the Middle Ages*, Brepols Publishers, Turnhout, 25–40

Pelling, M. and Smith, R. M. 1991 'Introduction', in M. Pelling and R. M. Smith (eds), *Life, death and the elderly: historical perspectives*, Routledge, London, 1–38

Penny-Mason, B. J. and Gowland, R. L. 2014 'The children of the Reformation: childhood palaeoepidemiology in Britain, AD 1000–1700', *Medieval Archaeology* 58, 162–94

Powell, L. A., Redfern, R. C., and Millard, A. R. 2014 'Infant feeding practices in Roman London: the isotopic evidence', in P. M. Carroll and E.-J. Graham (eds), *Infant health and death in Roman Italy and beyond*, Journal of Roman Archaeology Supplementary Series 96, 89–110

Richards, M. P., Mays, S., and Fuller, B. T. 2002 'Stable carbon and nitrogen isotope values of bone and teeth reflect weaning age at the medieval Wharram Percy site, Yorkshire, UK', *American Journal of Physical Anthropology* 119, 205–10

Robb, J. 2002 'Time and biography: osteobiography of the Italian Neolithic lifespan', in Y. Hamilakis, M. Pluciennik, and S. Tarlow (eds), *Thinking through the body: archaeologies of corporeality*, Kluwer Academic / Plenum Publishers, New York, 153–72

Roberts, C. 2009 'Health and welfare in medieval England: the human skeletal remains contextualized', in R. Gilchrist and A. Reynolds (eds), *Reflections: 50 years of medieval archaeology, 1957–2007*, The Society for Medieval Archaeology Monograph 30, 307–26

Schofield, P. R. 2010 'Economy', in L. J. Wilkinson (ed.), *A Cultural History of Childhood and Family in the Middle Ages* 2, 57–72

Shahar, S. 1992 *Childhood in the Middle Ages*, Routledge, London
Shapland, F., Lewis, M., and Watts, R. 2015 'The lives and deaths of young medieval women: the osteological evidence', *Medieval Archaeology* 59, 272–89
Shilling, C. 1993 *Body and social theory*, Cambridge University Press, Cambridge
Sofaer, J. 2006 *The body as material culture*, Routledge, London
Sofaer, J. 2011 'Towards a social bioarchaeology of age', in S. Agarwal and B. Glencross (eds), *Social bioarchaeology*, Wiley-Blackwell, Oxford, 285–311
Sofaer Derevenski, J. 1997 'Age and gender at the site of Tiszapolgár-Basatanya, Hungary', *Antiquity* 71, 875–89
Sørensen, M.-L. 2000 *Gender archaeology*, John Wiley and Sons, Hoboken
Sullivan, A. 2005 'Prevalence and etiology of acquired anemia in Medieval York', *American Journal of Physical Anthropology* 128, 252–72
Stone, P. and Walrath, D. 2006 'The gendered skeleton: anthropological interpretations of the bony pelvis', in R. Gowland and C. Knüsel (eds), *Social archaeology of funerary remains*, Oxbow, Oxford, 168–78
Thane, P. 2000 *Old age in English history*, Oxford University Press, Oxford
Ward, J. C. 2010 'Community', in L. J. Wilkinson (ed.), *A Cultural History of Childhood and Family in the Middle Ages* 2, 41–56
Wilkinson, L. J. 2010 'Education', in L. J. Wilkinson (ed.), *A cultural history of childhood and family in the Middle Ages*, 2, 91–108
Youngs, D. 2006 *The life-cycle in western Europe, c.1300–c.1500*, Manchester University Press, Manchester
Youngs, D. 2010 'Life cycle', in L. J. Wilkinson (ed.), *A cultural history of childhood and family in the Middle Ages* 2, 109–26

CHAPTER 48

BIRTH AND CHILDHOOD

SALLY CRAWFORD

'Childhood' is a fluid concept. Osteologists, investigating medieval cemeteries, use skeletal indicators to determine the age of the deceased. Indicators of physiological immaturity include tooth eruption and the fusion of epiphyses, which may also provide information on the probable chronological age at death. Biological childhood, however, does not map directly onto chronological age: children grow and develop at different rates, according to genetic disposition as well as environmental and health factors: growth may be promoted by good diet or restricted by disease and malnutrition, for example (Gowland 2006, 143). Biological and chronological age do not map onto one another; to add to the difficulty of discussing childhood, neither do social and cultural ages. 'Childhood' is also a cultural construct. Societies may invest more significance in developmental stages in childhood than in chronological age. Modern western society privileges chronological age for legal and educational purposes, while other cultures might recognize developmental markers—weaning, for example—as more important stages in the transitional period between birth and the time when adulthood is perceived to have been achieved. Because childhood is subject to cultural interpretation, manipulation, and construction, its study offers a particularly useful tool for understanding past societies.

Archaeologists have been relatively slow to acknowledge the importance of studying children and childhood. The discipline was born in 1989 with Grete Lillehammer's seminal paper on the child's world in an archaeological perspective (Lillehammer 1989). Though the focus of her attention was the prehistoric child, nonetheless her insistence that children and childhoods were a valid area of archaeological investigation was a call to all archaeologists to reconsider the archaeological record for evidence of childhoods. In particular, she drew attention to the link between the cultural construction of childhood and its relationship to material evidence, social identity, economics, power, and religion.

Since then, a number of medieval archaeologists have written papers giving special attention to the archaeology of childhood in c.1100–1500. Skeletal evidence from excavated cemeteries has provided information on topics such as childbirth and weaning

(Mays 2003), diet and child health in urban and rural locations (Lewis 2002), and juvenile migration (Kendall et al. 2013). The place of children in the medieval mortuary ritual, however, is still an area for further discussion and development (Hadley and Hemer 2014, 5). Children's material culture (Egan 1996; 1998; Forsyth and Egan 2005), children's play (Hall 2014; Lewis 2009), and the geography of medieval childhoods (Smith 2014) have also entered the discourse. The creation of the Society for the Study of Childhood in the Past (SSCIP) and its associated journal, *Childhood in the Past* has provided an important forum for presenting the material culture strand of childhood studies, and the active engagement of medieval archaeologists in the field has seen the publication of the monograph *Medieval childhood: archaeological approaches*, which includes four chapters specifically on post-Conquest medieval childhood (Hadley and Hemer 2014).

Birth to Death: The Cemetery Evidence

Much of our information for medieval childhood comes from cemeteries, and cemeteries, with their tangible remains of childhood in the form of burials, have been a focus of attention. Mortuary archaeology not only tells the story of juvenile disease and death: it also reveals the impact of social and cultural attitudes towards children and child-rearing. The rituals associated with the death of a child offer a particularly sharp insight into aspects of family identity, religion, and politics as well as the negotiation between private and public, personal and traditional. However, while there have been detailed studies of children's place in the furnished Anglo-Saxon burial ritual (for example Crawford 1991; 2000; Squires 2014; Stoodley 2011), there are no similarly close analyses of later Anglo-Saxon and post-Conquest juvenile burial ritual, though children's burials have been discussed in the context of wider gender and life course investigations (Gilchrist 2011; Hadley 2004). There is little to suggest that there was significant age differentiation in the burials of sub-adults, but infant burials were singled out by regularly being placed, flexed, on their sides whereas the normal position for burial was extended and supine (Gilchrist 2011, 165; Gilchrist and Sloane 2005, 155–6), and infant and child graves tend to be zoned towards the western part of the cemetery, which could be considered to be associated with the font, 'so that the efficacy of baptism could continue to protect their vulnerable souls during the dangerous journey through Purgatory' (Gilchrist and Sloane 2005, 223).

Children's burials in a later medieval context have tended to be a focus of attention when they are outside what is perceived as 'normative', either in terms of the social status of the child or the burial ritual associated with it. Well before the archaeology of childhood had developed as a discipline in its own right, Joan Tanner discussed the tombs of royal children at Westminster Abbey, London (Tanner 1953), and John Page-Phillips published a catalogue of children on medieval funerary brasses, though his rationale was expressly hobbyist rather than scholarly, as the 'Introduction' made clear: 'Because these charming groups (or single figures) are small, they can be rubbed quickly. A detail (or small brass) rubbed in half an hour can give just as much pleasure as a huge rubbing that might take four to eight hours. They are also simpler to hang as decoration, or to store in a folder for study' (Page-Phillips 1970, 8). However, the volume provides a useful illustrated catalogue, including brasses which are no longer extant.

Children appear or are named on brasses as individuals and as part of family groups from a relatively early period: the earliest surviving English brass is dedicated to Margaret, daughter of William de Valence, who died in 1276. She is commemorated by name, but without any representation of a child on her brass. She, and her brother John who died a year later, were buried in Westminster Abbey in accordance with their royal status. However, as Sophie Oosterwijk commented, neither Margaret nor her brother were 'young enough to qualify as a "child" in the modern sense of the word' at the time of death (Oosterwijk 2010).

By contrast, Katherine, the child of Henry III and Eleanor of Provence, was only 3 when she died in 1257, and her death was commemorated at lavish expense, unusual for a child's burial. In part, her funerary monuments may reflect the private and acute grief of her parents, but Henry was also interested in status and display, and his daughter's monument was integrated into a much larger rebuilding programme for Westminster Abbey (Oosterwijk 2010, 50). Royal children who die young, however, do not have a role in memorializing and validating later dynasties; Katherine's tomb was not sufficiently symbolic or relevant to later dynasties to escape re-location and damage.

One of the notable features of the earliest medieval child memorials is the 'evident discrepancy between the appearance of the effigy and the child's actual age' (Oosterwijk 2010, 53). Infants and young children were frequently depicted as idealized youths, such as William of Hatfield in York Minster, who died in 1337 before he was a year old, but whose alabaster images show him as a young adult (Oosterwijk 2010, 54). Expensive funerary monuments serve to reflect social status, prestige, and power, but dead children are a direct challenge to such narratives—only living children offer the potential for future generations: 'dead children are, to put it bluntly, ultimately a dynastic and biological failure' (Oosterwijk 2010, 59). Arguably, ostentatious display or consumption at a child's death is one way of negating the social challenge presented by the young death, off-setting the contradiction between the future possibilities offered by living children and the inescapable loss of those possibilities after death. Furthermore, representing the infant as a young adult also fitted religious conventions which identified young adulthood as a spiritually 'perfect age' (Oosterwijk 2010, 55).

Setting religious and status issues aside, funerary monuments to dead children still echo grief on the part of the family. Depictions of dead children as infants are rare before the fifteenth century (Greenhill 1976, 288), but the many examples of memorials and brasses depicting swaddled 'chrysom' infants are a poignant reminder of the emotional cost of infant mortality to medieval families (Oosterwijk 2000) (Figure 48.1). New research into medieval church graffiti suggests that, further down the social scale, bereaved parents were impelled by the same motives to memorialize their lost children. Matthew Champion has drawn attention to two examples in particular: at Gamlingay in

FIGURE 48.1 Copy of the brass of the infant Nicholas Wadham (dated 1508), St Peter's Church, Ilton, Somerset

(© Sally Crawford)

Cambridgeshire, a small undated inscription in the north aisle reads *Hic est sedes margartea vit an d(ecimo)* (Here lies Margaret in her tenth year), while another dating to 1515 at Kingston, also in Cambridgeshire, records three names, Cateryn, Jane, and Amee Maddyngley. Margaret was on the cusp of adolescence, but Champion argues that since the three Maddyngleys do not appear as adults in the parish records, they may have been infants when they died, probably victims of the bubonic plague (Champion 2015).

Juvenile and infant burials have attracted little attention in part because they appear 'normative' within the ritual. Occasionally, though, sub-adults burials appear to have had 'special' status because of their location or anomalous inclusion in burial zones otherwise exclusive to adults. At the Cistercian cemetery at Stratford Langthorne,

Essex, there was only one infant burial in the whole monastery, buried in a wickerwork basket and placed in the north transept (Gilchrist 2011, 165). At the Augustinian priory of St Mary Merton, Surrey, there were only two infants in the whole mortuary community, both from the earliest phase of the cemetery and buried next to each other (in the northern cemetery, not in the building) (Miller and Saxby 2007). Two sub-adults (one an infant) were buried in the chapter house at Sandwell Priory in West Bromwich, the Black Country (Hodder 1991), and there are further references to infant burials close to walls in northern churches: at Hartlepool Greyfriars, County Durham, there were five infants in the cemetery at the north-west corner of the nave (Daniels 1986), while at the Dominican Priory, Chester, a high proportion of the burials in the nave were of juveniles (Ward 1990, 122).

The burial of juveniles at Chester Dominican Priory points to significant memorialization of familial adult/child relationships in the burials. Five of the ten juveniles discovered during excavation were in the nave. At least two of the three in the aisle were closely associated with an adult interment, and the two juveniles at the eastern end of the nave were close to an adult female. In one case, a female aged 30 to 35 years at the time of death was buried with an infant (not neonate) at her right shoulder. In the case of some secondary interments, the intention to associate the child with an adult was deliberate and effortful, such as the case of the grave of an adult male (B2) whose central capping slabs were later removed to allow the insertion of the body of a child (B2a) (Ward 1990, 122).

The scale of investment of effort and energy into a burial is a measure of the emotional, symbolic, or religious value placed on the dead by the buriers. Not all children were accorded the status of a high-investment burial, and occasionally the archaeological evidence demonstrates the conflicting symbolism of problematic infant deaths. A woman with tuberculosis from the village of Wharram Percy, North Yorkshire, was buried with a foetus (Mays et al. 2007). Analysis of the adult skeleton indicated that she had died during childbirth, and the unusual and desperate measure of trying to remove the baby from the womb by a caesarean section had been attempted. As Simon Mays argued, the attempt to cut the baby from the womb indicates a concern to preserve the life of the baby, even after the mother had died. A parallel example of a mother with a pre-term baby comes from Wymondham Abbey, Norfolk, where one large tomb contained two lead-shrouded burials, one of an adult woman, and one of a foetus aged about 4 months. Rather than reflecting care for the baby, however, these burials may reflect the prohibition (by the Council of Canterbury 1236 and the Council of Treves 1310) against burying a woman until her foetus had been removed from her (Gilchrist and Sloane 2005, 71–2).

While a few children's burials appear to indicate the 'special dead', where some circumstance of their life, their family status, or their death has caused their inclusion in a privileged area outside the normative location for children, in other cases children's burials appear to provide evidence for conflict between social, religious, and familial attitudes to infant death and burial. By 1400, stillborn children and unbaptized infants were not allowed a grave in consecrated ground, since Church dogma decreed that they were not Christian, and that they had to be buried outside (Orme 2001, 124).

Documentary sources make it clear that parents and carers of dead infants were prepared to ignore the Church's rules: Hereford Cathedral was granted a royal licence in 1389, allowing it to surround its precinct and cemetery with walls and gates, locked at night, and amongst the reasons cited was the prevention of secret burials of unbaptized children (Orme 2001, 126). A London court case of 1493 concerning activities in the parish of St Nicholas in the Shambles refers to a midwife called Agnes Coge who helped bury the child of Alice Wanten (which had been stillborn after Alice had been beaten by one John Russell) in the churchyard of Pardon courtyard (Orme 2001, 126).

These conflicting requirements of the church and the community around the disposal of infants and neonates may be reflected in a number of non-normative burials. Prone burials have been identified at four monastic cemeteries: at Linlithgow, West Lothian, in the friary chapel dated to 1325–75; in the nave of Aberdeen Whitefriars dated to the early sixteenth century; in the western part of the cemetery belonging to the hospital of St Mary Spital, London (1235–80); and Northampton Marefair, probably dating to the twelfth century (Gilchrist and Sloane 2005, 72). There is also some limited evidence for the burial of infants outside medieval churchyards. Two coffined burials of an adult and infant, and a further infant with chalk blocks at head and legs, were found close together and ten metres to the west of the boundary walls of St Giles's cemetery, Winchester. They may be extra-mural, but may belong to an undocumented cemetery associated with St Giles's Chapel, and this is perhaps more likely given the care with which the infant burial was furnished with chalk blocks, which hardly speaks of a surreptitious, illegal burial (Nenk et al. 1997, 270).

Other infant burials are more clearly anomalous because they are not associated with churchyards at all. For example, at the long-house complex at Upton, Gloucestershire, the thirteenth century burial of a 3–6 month old baby took place in the south-east corner of a room. The baby was buried with a spindle-whorl and a large whelk shell, and a floor slab covered the grave (Rahtz 1969, 87). At the end of the thirteenth century, a baby was buried under the southern wall of a building in Westbury, Buckinghamshire. An *in utero* foetus of 5–7 months of age, showing signs of gnawing marks from rodents, was buried in association with a building on Croft 13 at the same settlement, along with two pots. Whatever was happening at Westbury was outside any officially sanctioned ritual behaviour. Nonetheless, the sense of a deliberate, intentional, and even purposeful burial was so strong that the excavator remarked that 'it is certainly possible that this burial represents some sort of foundation deposit' (Ivens et al. 1995, 145).

At the neighbouring village of Tattenhoe, Buckinghamshire, the southern wall of Building 4, archaeologically difficult to define, was marked by a line of pad-stones along the edge of an eaves-drip drainage gully. One pad-stone sealed a shallow depression containing the remains of an infant, possibly a still-born baby, with three animal bones placed over it. Again, the sense of deliberate ritual was strong enough to promote the suggestion of a foundation deposit or 'a more secretive burial of a perhaps illegitimate or deformed child' (Ivens et al. 1995, 33). The Church was clear that 'normative' burial for unbaptized infants could not take place in the churchyard, but gave no guidance on alternative ways of disposing of the baby. Settlement burials may have been one of the community's solutions.

WEANING TO ADOLESCENCE

Evidence for medieval child nutrition has traditionally come from documentary sources, but the development of scientific methods for understanding medieval diet, in particular the use of stable isotope analysis of bone collagen, is providing significant new data (Müldner and Richards 2005). For childhood, nitrogen stable isotope evidence has been particularly valuable for discussing the age of weaning. Studies of the bones from the medieval cemetery at Wharram Percy indicate that, over the six hundred years of the site's use, the age of weaning remained relatively stable at under two years, followed by a childhood diet lower in animal protein than the diet of older people (Richards et al. 2002, 210). Findings from Fishergate House cemetery in York indicate a very similar age of weaning for an urban population, although the weaned juveniles had higher nitrogen values than the adult females, suggesting larger proportions of marine fish and pork in the juvenile diets, perhaps suggesting that York parents were investing in their children's diets (Burt 2013). However, the difficulty in establishing the biological sex of juveniles from skeletal evidence means that it is not yet possible to tell if the sex differentiation in weaning practices indicated by medieval texts existed in the daily practice of a medieval agricultural population (Richards et al. 2002, 209).

Studies of isotope levels at Wharram Percy have also shown the long-term effect on women of childbirth and weaning. Medieval women at Wharram Percy, unlike modern populations, showed a rapid decline in bone density between the ages of 32 and 35, ascribed to the loss of calcium during pregnancy and breastfeeding, which a poor diet could not replace (Turner-Walker et al. 2001).

The experience of childhood, and childhood experiences, leaves traces on adult skeletons as well as juveniles. A female buried at the medieval lay cemetery of Abingdon Abbey, Oxfordshire, died when she was aged about 21. Analysis of her skeleton revealed she suffered from spondylolysis of the spine (where part of the arch of the vertebra is separated). While there are hereditary predispositions to the condition, culture and environment may contribute to its development (Wakely 1993, 38). In addition to spondylolysis, the Abingdon female had problems with her pelvis and hip which led her to keep the weight off her left leg during life. As Jennifer Wakely, who examined the bones, noted: 'the practice of swaddling... is one environmental-cultural factor likely to aggravate a pre-existing tendency to hip dislocation related to acetabular dysplasia' (Wakely 1993, 44). The practice of swaddling in medieval English society appears to have exacerbated a genetic condition, which, had she been brought up in another culture, might never have impacted so painfully on the Abingdon woman's young adult life.

The interpretation of the Abingdon woman's childhood and rearing is not simply a matter of modern archaeologists 'reading' a past onto childhood. The medieval world actively constructed child-rearing practices with the intention of shaping future adults. Gerald of Wales was alert to the medieval child's body as an arena for manipulation and for shaping cultural and political identities. Comparing Irish children to Anglo-Norman elite children, he noted that: 'They are not placed in cradles, or swathed, nor are their tender limbs either fomented by constant bathings, or adjusted with art. For the midwives make no use of warm water, nor raise their noses, nor depress the face, nor stretch the legs; but nature alone, with very slight aids from art, disposes and adjusts the limbs to which she has given birth, just as she pleases' (Wright 1894, 122).

Norman parents, attempting to build 'better' children by swaddling babies and manipulating their bodies, in fact thwarted their ambitions by their misguided actions: their overprotected children lacked the sunshine which would provide vitamin D and the exercise which would build strong bones, in contrast to the 'wild' and 'uncared for' children of the Irish. Swaddling may have contributed to the cases of infant rickets identified at the medieval cemetery of Wharram Percy, where eight burials ranging in age from 3 to 18 months at the time of death showed skeletal abnormalities consistent with rickets (Ortner and Mays 1998). Interpreting skeletal evidence for diet and stress, however, is problematic. Those whose skeletons indicate prolonged periods of nutritional challenge may actually have been relatively healthy compared to those who were unable to survive diseases and died before the impact of the disease could leave a trace on the bones—the so-called 'osteological paradox' (Wood et al. 1992).

Childhood activities may also leave a trace on the body which survives into adulthood, and this may provide information about gendered practice. Comparative studies of vertebral fractures indicate that medieval males are more likely to suffer from vertebral trauma caused by heavy shovelling before the ages of about 14–16, when the fusion processes in the vertebrae are still incomplete (Gilchrist 2012, 60; Knüsel et al. 1996). Children's skeletons are also a barometer of environmental conditions. Mary Lewis's work on skeletal material from medieval rural (Raunds Furnells, Northamptonshire) and urban (St Helen-on-the-Walls, York) sites showed that there were differences in the morbidity and mortality of non-adults from both environments, though differences between medieval urban and rural child health and nutrition were not as pronounced as those between medieval and later industrial populations, where cultural practices contributed to create significant differences (Lewis 2002).

While mortuary archaeology provides a rich vein of information about medieval childhood, settlement archaeology is also a fruitful area for research, and one which is ripe for re-investigation from the perspective of the child. Childhood experiences establish ways of seeing and interpreting an environment which shape social identity and can be exploited for political or economic gain. Sally Smith's analysis of the medieval geographies of childhood offers a case in point (Smith 2014). She examined geographies of medieval village settlements, analysing spaces and pathways used over generations and their role in reproducing social memory and community cohesion. Her comparison of the physical, social, and psychological impact of the geographies of nucleated and dispersed settlements posed questions about the experience of childhood within the village (Figure 48.2). Children within relatively stable settlements which show little change in

FIGURE 48.2 The deserted medieval village of Widford, Oxfordshire. St Oswald's church now stands isolated in the background. House platforms are visible as bumps in the field. A sunken road through the village is marked by the line of darker vegetation in the foreground

(© Tony Randall)

the organization of buildings and pathways, such as Tattenhoe in Buckinghamshire, will have trodden the same pathways as their parents and grandparents, and would expect their own children to do the same, promoting a sense of 'embeddedness' (Smith 2010, 74). Children's encounters with their environment might both challenge and reproduce ideas about private and public space, and this was a central factor in transmitting community knowledge and continuity over time. Social values could also be controlled through children's experiences of space. At Wharram Percy, the construction of the North Manor buildings around 1245 encroached on peasant tofts and agricultural fields. At least two families lost their private, domestic space. As Smith notes, the lasting impact of the experience on the children in terms of elite control and the powerlessness of their parents would have had a durable impact into the next generation (Smith 2014, 62, 70).

In addition to cases of forced relocation with their families, large numbers of medieval children experienced migration from household to household and even a period of time away from their family of origin. Factors which might lead to this migration included the death of one or more parents, the circumstances of a child's birth, particularly illegitimacy, under-age marriage, and wardship (Maddern 2010). Stable isotope analysis of earlier medieval British populations has already indicated that the archaeological evidence may be able to supply important new information about population movement (Hadley and Hemer 2011; Hemer 2014). Research on a few later medieval cemeteries is producing equally interesting results: an isotope analysis of burials from the London cemetery of East Smithfield, for example, suggested that some individuals were born much further from London than current theories arguing for relatively local migration would suggest, and that their migration occurred in their childhood. The cemetery was only in use between 1348 and 1350, so bubonic plague might have been a factor in this long-range migration.

The home itself is the core of a child's experience. How houses accommodate the dynamics of family growth and the life course in the context of changing social, economic, religious, and political factors is a relatively under-explored aspect of settlement archaeology. Yet in the past, as today, domestic material culture and domestic furniture have a dynamic interaction with human activity, with agency on both sides. Fireplaces may signify a source of heat to healthy adults, but become a locus of danger when small children are present. Staircases are accessible to normal adults, but represent geographies of danger or exclusion to the elderly, the disabled, or to small children. Evidence that house spaces were adapted to reflect the evolving needs and abilities of the inhabitants, including the needs of children, provides insight into economic strategies, private priorities, the level of care or concern exhibited by family, and social perceptions of the place of children within the domestic environment (Crawford 2014). Changes in layout, within and without the house, and the creation or loss of private and public areas, also represent a dialogue between the evolving household and society. From around 1250 onwards, the medieval rural house had a relatively fixed idea about the organization of social space, but other variations were at play to articulate ideas about social status and identity (Gardiner 2000). What happens inside domestic spaces may be private and closely linked to individual agency, but is also inflected with social imaginaries, shared sets of values, actions, and patterns of behaviour which project the identity and cohesion of a social group.

Socialization is created by the practice of taking care of the child: feeding it, clothing it, and nurturing it. What were the social consequences of the developments in vernacular building plans for children? How did changing spaces until the mid-thirteenth century—the location of fireplaces shifting from the centre of rooms to the side, the evolution of the hall, the creation of private chambers—all affect children's socialization, their sense of their place in society, their access to spaces, and their visibility? Children's experience of private gardens (Gilchrist 1999, 109–45), the separation of living spaces for family and servants (Grenville 1997), and increasing emphasis on private chambers as gendered spaces (Johnson 1997, 153) all played into children's socialization and identity, ensuring the reproduction of gendered roles, and reinforcing concepts of private and public, accessible and inaccessible spaces. Domestic space was a key tool in shaping children's perception of their environment, acting as a metaphor for social, political, gendered, religious, and personal identity.

Children's play and labour entail access to spaces and objects which help to frame and constrain social roles, gender roles, and status, as well as developing motor and physical skills. As such, children's activities represent fundamental manifestations of their socialization, but their activities have been almost invisible in current interpretations of the archaeological record (Hall 2014). Looking at the evidence with a child-centred approach, however, it is possible to begin to build an understanding of the intersection between children's agency and material culture, and to begin to understand how current adult-centric readings are hiding children's presence in the archaeological record. Experimental archaeology conducted on modern settlement sites had already established in the 1970s the significant impact of children's play and activities on the archaeological record (e.g. Bonnichsen 1973), yet the role of children in site formation is rarely considered in archaeological reports (Hall 2014, 45). New approaches to the archaeological evidence for the medieval period argue that much of the ephemeral activity and archaeological deposition on settlement sites should be considered as evidence for child's play (Crawford 2009; Lewis 2009; Willemsen 2008). Part of the problem of identifying children's interaction with their environment is that children's play is fluid and difficult to define: a toy, for a child, is more of a concept than a specific object—for children, 'plaything' is a stage many objects may pass through, particularly in the moment before final deposition into the archaeological record. Children collect, re-design, lose, hide, and cache objects which might not correspond with anything that an archaeologist would categorize as a 'toy' (Crawford 2009).

Even where objects appear to have been created with the function of toys, such as the metal miniatures mass-produced from 1200 on, they are problematic (Egan 1996). Miniatures may be toys, but they may also have had other qualities as, for example, votive objects. Hazel Forsyth and Geoff Egan's study of metal playthings from London has done much to add to the corpus of known medieval toys and to draw attention to the range and distribution of such objects (Forsyth and Egan 2005). The variety of recorded metal figures reveals much about the interplay between social ideals, the relationships between carers and their children, the creation of gender identities, and the wider medieval society. A little metal figure of a man on horseback, for example, encapsulates an ideal of chivalry, but is also a reminder of the craftsmen engaged in an industry built on appealing to children, and of a society with an established idea that buying toys for children was an appropriate and even necessary way to spend hard-earned money (Egan 1996). Any idea that medieval parents may not have invested time and emotion in their children has to be set against Geoff Egan's findings that toys were a 'widely-available, mass-produced commodity, keenly marketed from at least 1300' (Egan 1998).

Though playthings had a place in a medieval child's life, for many childhood was also a time of schooling, apprenticeship, and labour. Archaeological evidence for children's work and education in Britain is scanty, though there have been useful comparative studies from Continental archaeology (Orme 1995; Willemsen 2008). Specific studies, such as the analysis of children's fingerprints on medieval pottery, indicate the potential value of reconsidering the material culture for evidence of child agency (Mellor 2014) (Figure 48.3).

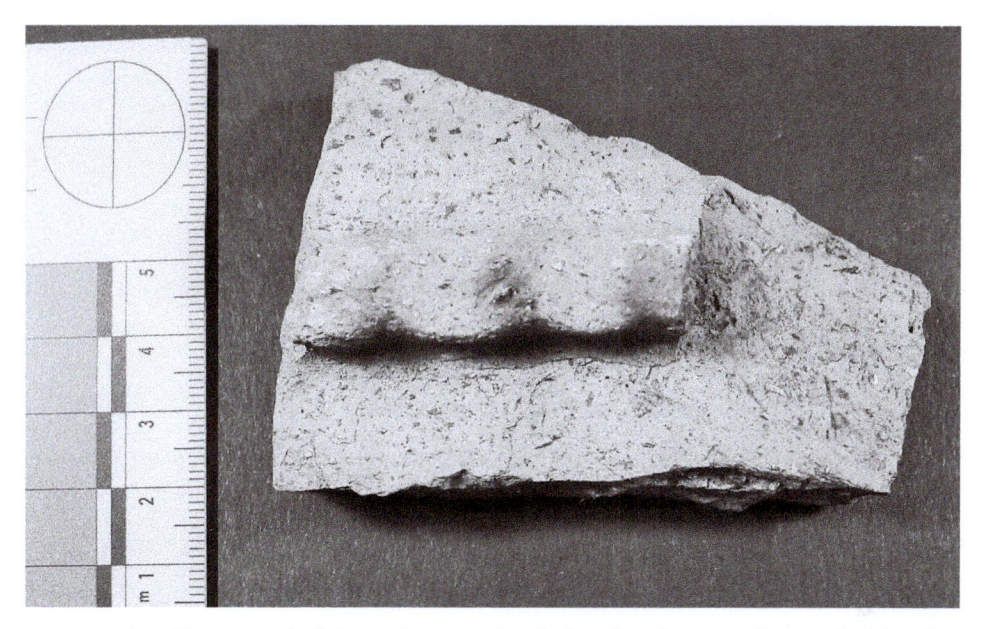

FIGURE 48.3 Finger-pinched decoration on a sherd of medieval pottery. Finger-pinching, fingerprints, and finger-nail impressions provide evidence for children's involvement in pottery production

(© Sally Crawford)

The life course of an individual may conform in a number of ways to common social practice and share values and behaviours with others in the community, but not all medieval childhoods were the same. Poor children will have different childhoods from monastic children or the children of the social elite: each group may signal its identity and relationship with other groups through its treatment of children. Gender, health, a child's place in the sibling group, and family social status all play a part in the experience of childhood. This does not undermine the value of studying the archaeology of childhood, rather it emphasizes that social identity is a matter of negotiation within the complexity of the early life course. The material culture of childhood is an important indicator of a child's relationship with adult society, and of the ways in which childhoods represent fields of negotiation over personal, political, religious, economic, and social identities. The archaeology of medieval childhood is a growing field, with huge potential to inform future studies and understanding of medieval society.

References cited

Bonnichsen, R. 1973 'Millie's camp: an experiment in archaeology', *World Archaeology* 4(3), 277–91

Burt, N. M. 2013 'Stable isotope ration analysis of breastfeeding and weaning practices of children from medieval Fishergate House York, UK', *American Journal of Physical Anthropology* 152(3), 407–16

Champion, M. 2015 *Medieval graffiti: the lost voices of England's churches*, Ebury Press, London
Crawford, S. 1991 'When do Anglo-Saxon children count?', *Journal of Theoretical Archaeology* 2, 17–24
Crawford, S. 2000 'Children grave goods and social status in early Anglo-Saxon England', in J. Sofaer Derevenski (ed.), *Children and material culture*, Routledge, London, 169–79
Crawford, S. 2009 'The archaeology of play things: theorising a toy stage in the "biography" of objects', *Childhood in the Past* 2, 55–70
Crawford, S. 2014 'The archaeology of the medieval family', in D. M. Hadley and K. A. Hemer (eds), *Medieval childhood: archaeological approaches*, Childhood in the Past Monograph 3, Oxford, 26–38
Daniels, R. 1986 'The excavation of the church of the Franciscans, Hartlepool, Cleveland', *The Archaeological Journal* 143, 260–304
Egan, G. 1996 *Playthings from the past. Lead alloy miniatures from c.1300–1800*, Jonathan Horne, London
Egan, G. 1998 'Miniature toys of medieval childhood', *British Archaeology* 35, 10–11
Forsyth, H. and Egan, G. 2005 *Toys, triffles and trinkets: base-metal miniatures from London 1150–1800*, Unicorn Press, London
Gardiner, M. 2000 'Vernacular buildings and the development of the later medieval domestic plan in England', *Medieval Archaeology* 44, 159–79
Gilchrist, R. 1999 *Gender and archaeology: contesting the past*, Routledge, London
Gilchrist, R. 2011 'The intimacy of death: interpreting gender and the life course in medieval and early modern burials', in M. C. Beaudry and J. Symonds (eds), *Interpreting the early modern world: transatlantic perspectives*, Springer, New York, 159–73
Gilchrist, R. 2012 *Medieval life: archaeology and the life course*, The Boydell Press, Woodbridge
Gilchrist, R. and Sloane, B. 2005 *Requiem: the medieval monastic cemetery in Britain*, Museum of London Archaeology Service, London
Gowland, R. 2006 'Ageing the past: examining age identity from funerary evidence', in R. Gowland and C. Knüsel (eds), *Social archaeology of funerary remains*, Oxbow, Oxford, 143–55
Greenhill, F. A. 1976 *Incised effigial slabs: a study of engraved stone memorials in Latin Christendom, c.1100 to c.1700*, Vol. 1, London, Faber and Faber
Grenville, J. 1997 *Medieval housing*, Leicester University Press, London and Washington
Hadley, D. M. 2004 'Gender and burial practices in England, c.650–900', in L. Brubaker and J. Smith (eds), *Gender in the early medieval world: east and eest, 300–900*, Cambridge University Press, Cambridge, 301–23
Hadley, D. M. and Hemer, K. A. 2011 'Microcosms of migration: children and early medieval population movement', *Childhood in the Past* 4, 63–78
Hadley, D. M. and Hemer, K. A. (eds) 2014 *Medieval childhood: archaeological approaches*, Childhood in the Past Monograph 3, Oxford
Hall, M. 2014 'Merely players? Playtime, material culture and medieval childhood', in D. M. Hadley and K. A. Hemer (eds), *Medieval childhood: archaeological approaches*, Childhood in the Past Monograph 3, Oxford, 39–56
Hemer, K. 2014 'Are we nearly there yet? Children and migration in early medieval western Britain', in D. M. Hadley and K. A. Hemer (eds), *Medieval childhood: archaeological approaches*, Childhood in the Past Monograph 3, Oxford, 131–44

Hodder, M. A. 1991 *Excavations at Sandwell Priory and Hall 1982–88: a Mesolithic settlement, medieval monastery and post-medieval country house in West Bromwich*, South Staffordshire Archaeological and Historical Society, West Bromwich

Ivens, R., Busby, P., and Shepherd, N. 1995 *Tattenhoe and Westbury: two deserted medieval settlements*, Buckinghamshire Archaeological Society Monograph Series 8, Aylesbury

Johnson, M. 1997 'Rethinking houses, rethinking transitions: of vernacular architecture, ordinary people and everyday culture', in D. Gaimster and P. Stamper (eds), *The age of transition: the archaeology of English Culture 1400–1600*, 145–56

Kendall, E., Montgomery, J., Evans, J., Stantis, C., and Mueller, V. 2013 'Mobility, mortality, and the Middle Ages: identification of migrant individuals in a 14th century Black Death cemetery population', *American Journal of Physical Anthropology* 150(2), 210–22

Knüsel, C. J., Roberts, C. A., and Boylston, A. 1996 'When Adam delved ... an activity-related lesion in three human skeletal populations', *American Journal of Physical Anthropology* 100, 427–34

Lewis, C. 2009 'Children's play in the later medieval English countryside', *Childhood in the Past* 2, 86–108

Lewis, M. 2002 *Urbanisation and child health in medieval and post-medieval England: an assessment of the morbidity and mortality of non-adult skeletons from the cemeteries of two urban and two rural sites in England (AD 850–1859)*, British Archaeological Report British Series 339, Oxford

Lillehammer, G. 1989 'A child is born: the child's world in an archaeological perspective', *Norwegian Archaeological Review* 22(2), 89–105

Maddern, P. 2010 'Between households: children in blended and transitional households in late-medieval England', *The Journal of the History of Childhood and Youth* 3(1), 65–86

Mays, S. 2003 'Bone strontium: calcium rations and duration of breastfeeding in a medieval skeletal population', *Journal of Archaeological Science* 30(6), 731–41

Mays, P., Harding C., and Heighway, C. 2007 *Wharram. A study of settlement on the Yorkshire Wolds XI: the churchyard*, University of York Archaeological Publications 13, York

Mellor, M. 2014 'Seeing the medieval child: evidence from household and craft', in D. M. Hadley and K. A. Hemer (eds), *Medieval childhood: archaeological approaches*, Childhood in the Past Monograph 3, Oxford, 75–94

Miller, P. and Saxby, D. 2007 *The Augustinian priory of St Mary Merton, Surrey: excavations 1976–90*, Museum of London Archaeology Service Monograph 34, London

Müldner, G. and Richards, M. 2005 'Fast or feast: reconstructing diet in later medieval England by stable isotope analysis', *Journal of Archaeological Science* 32, 39–48

Nenk, B. S., Haith, C., and Bradley, J. 1997 'Medieval Britain and Ireland in 1996', *Medieval Archaeology* 41, 241–328

Oosterwijk, S. 2000 'Chrysoms, shrouds and infants on English tomb monuments: a question of terminology?', *Church Monuments* 15, 44–64

Oosterwijk, S. 2010 'Deceptive appearances: the presentation of children on medieval tombs', *Ecclesiology Today* 42, 43–60

Orme, N. 1995 'The culture of children in medieval England', *Past and Present* 148, 48–88

Orme, N. 2001 *Medieval children*, Yale University Press, New Haven and London

Ortner, D. J. and Mays, S. 1998 'Dry-bone manifestations of rickets in infancy and early childhood', *International Journal of Osteoarchaeology* 8(1), 45–55

Page-Phillips, J. 1970 *Children on brasses*, George Allen and Unwin, London

Rahtz, P. A. 1969 'Upton, Glos., 1964–68', *Transactions of the Bristol and Gloucestershire Archaeological Society* 88, 74–126

Richards, M. P., Mays, S., and Fuller, B. T. 2002 'Stable carbon and nitrogen isotope values of bone and teeth reflect weaning age at the medieval wharram Percy site, Yorkshire, UK', *American Journal of Physical Anthropology* 119, 205–10

Smith, S. V. 2010 'Inhabiting settlements, inhabiting worlds: deserted medieval villages and the evidence for peasant experience', in C. Dyer and R. Jones (eds), *Deserted villages revisited*, University of Hertfordshire Press, Hatfield, 64–84

Smith, S. V. 2014 'The spaces of late medieval peasant childhood: children and social reproduction', in D. M. Hadley and K. A. Hemer (eds), *Medieval childhood: archaeological approaches*, Childhood in the Past Monograph 3, Oxford, 57–74

Squires, K. 2014 'Through the flames of the pyre: the continuing search for Anglo-Saxon infants and children', in D. M. Hadley and K. A. Hemer (eds), *Medieval childhood: archaeological approaches*, Childhood in the Past Monograph 3, Oxford, 114–30

Stoodley, N. 2011 'Childhood to old age', in H. Hamerow, D. Hinton, and S. Crawford (eds), *Oxford University Press handbook of Anglo-Saxon archaeology*, Oxford University Press, Oxford, 640–66

Tanner, J. D. 1953 'Tombs of royal babies in Westminster Abbey', *Journal of the British Archaeological Association* 16, 25–40

Turner-Walker, G., Syversen, U., and Mays, S. 2001 'The archaeology of osteoporosis', *European Journal of Archaeology* 4(2), 263–9

Wakely, J. 1993 'Bilateral congenital dislocation of the hip, spina bifida occulta and spondylolysis in a female skeleton from the medieval cemetery at Abingdon, England', *Journal of Palaeopathology* 5, 37–45

Ward, S. W. 1990 *Excavations at Chester. The lesser medieval religious houses: sites investigated 1964–1983*, Chester City Council, Chester

Willemsen, A. 2008 *Back to the schoolyard: the daily practice of medieval and Renaissance education*, Brepols, Turnhout

Wood, J. W., Milner, G. R., Harpending, H. C., Weiss, K. M., Cohen, M. N., Eisenberg, L. E., Hutchinson, K. L., Jankauskas, R., Csnys, G., Katsenberg, M. A., Lukacs, J. R., McGrath, J. W., Roth, E. A., Ubelaker, D. H., and Wilkinson, R. G. 1992 'The osteological paradox: problems of inferring prehistoric health from skeletal samples', *Current Anthropology* 33(4), 343–70

Wright, T. 1894 *The historical works of Giraldus Cambrensis*, George Bell and Sons, London

CHAPTER 49

DRESSING THE BODY

ELEANOR R. STANDLEY

STUDIES of the consumption of clothing have been absent from later medieval archaeological discourse until recently and the history of dress only claimed a respectable academic status at the turn of the twenty-first century. True enough, after the Second World War archaeologists were interested in the manufacture of material culture; these objects were at the forefront of discussions about production, trade routes, and the economy. Nevertheless, how these manufactured objects were consumed, why they were chosen, or why their styles changed, featured little. Post-war museum curators were at the forefront of studying apparel in their collections, but often it was the beautiful and exceptional rather than everyday items. One exception was June Swann's exhaustive work on footwear in Northampton Museum and Art Gallery (1969; 1981; 1996) but academic snobbery meant that the curators' work had little impact on the wider research agenda or teaching (see Taylor 2002, 64).

New ways of interpreting material culture came about with changes in archaeological thought, especially an understanding of objects as material which might be 'read' (see Chapter 3). At the same time, as more rescue and developer-led archaeology has been carried out and a greater variety of sites have been investigated, so more everyday material culture has become available for study (see the *Medieval finds from excavations in London* series and East Anglian Archaeology Reports of nearly forty Norwich excavations, especially Egan and Pritchard 2002 and Margeson 1993; see (see Chapter 1). In particular, great strides have been made in the acceptance of studying apparel and textiles, especially through new journals such as *Costume* and *Textile History*. Jones and Stallybrass's 2000 volume revealed how clothes were extremely valuable materials that were central to the making of Renaissance culture but also had roles in memory and identities. Surviving textiles, accessories, and shoes can be usefully explored to understand the people of the past, and add to a 'meaningful medieval archaeology' as advocated by Gilchrist (2009, 400).

Scraps and Offcuts

Over a thousand pieces of footwear including pattens of leather and wood, and hundreds of textile fragments have been excavated from waterlogged contexts in London (*c.*1150–1450) (Crowfoot et al. 2001; Egan 2005a, 17–32, 58–61; Grew and de Neergaard 2001). Other notable sites include Newcastle upon Tyne's Castle ditch at the Black Gate, which was used as a rubbish dump; sixteenth-century textile fragments and leather pieces found here are interpreted as cobblers' waste and domestic cast-offs (Vaughan 1981, 184–90; Walton 1981, 190–228). From High Street, Perth, 441 samples of fabrics, yarns, and cordage were also recovered. These were mostly early twelfth to fourteenth century in date and made of wool; although thirty-one silk items were found along with fibres of goat and horse hair (Dransart et al. 2012). Leather articles from the High Street in Perth numbered six thousand, including shoes, straps, sheaths, and offcuts (Thomas and Bogdan 2012) but the largest collection of clothing and footwear from a secure context anywhere in the United Kingdom belongs to the *Mary Rose* (sank 1545). In total there were 655 items of clothing, footwear, fastenings, and linings discovered in the wreck, many being associated with skeletal remains (Forster et al. 2005, 18). Most were wool and leather products including 257 pieces of footwear, of which 140 were paired. Smaller urban assemblages of wool, silk fragments, and leather footwear include those from Southampton, Winchester, York, and Oxford (Crowfoot 1975; 1990; Jones 1976; Jope 1958; Walton Rogers 1997).

Generally speaking, linen textiles are rare on archaeological sites because anaerobic and acidic environments are detrimental to plant (bast) fibres. Our physical evidence for linens comes from the processing waste of the bast fibres of flax and hemp, as well as artistic and documentary evidence. Furs suffer too, and are absent from excavations but while the exotic fur trade of Russian ermine or sable would not necessarily have left skeletal remains in Britain, we can start to identify the preparation of more common species. For example, twelfth- and thirteenth-century cat crania and thirteenth-century fox snouts from Oxford have been interpreted as the remains of killing and skinning animals for their fur (Hassall et al. 1989, 263).

These archaeological finds provide a glimpse into the later medieval textiles and shoes in everyday use, though there are challenges. The majority are scraps or offcuts; that is, the pieces thrown away after tailoring or the translation of items, such as the shoe waste deemed unusable by the cobbler. They are rarely the finished garments worn by the populace. Even the remarkable finds of the *Mary Rose* are exclusive; despite all social levels from the officers to the ordinary sailors and soldiers being present on board, the clothing is exclusively male. Another issue is that textile evidence from rural sites is practically non-existent. Were silks worn in rural settlements along with woollens? Probably they were, but the evidence is currently lacking. For higher-status sites, excavations at castles, among them Barnard Castle (Co. Durham) and Fast Castle (Berwickshire), have revealed tantalizing scraps of textile and leather but insufficient to develop a full understanding of the clothes worn by the vast array of people living and working there (Ryder and Gabra-Sanders 1992). At Barnard Castle, only three small fragments of tabby weave and two 'spun gold' threads, one forming a plait, were recovered. The threads are of a type seen in ecclesiastical embroideries, and gold plait is rare in archaeological contexts (silk examples are known from thirteenth- to fifteenth-century deposits) (Crowfoot 2007). Barnard Castle's leather finds are much more numerous with 350 manufactured fragments identified, cobblers' waste dating from the fourteenth to seventeenth centuries being the most common. The turn shoe soles of the fourteenth and fifteenth centuries indicate that practical round and small pointed toed shoe were preferred, rather than the exaggerated pointed footwear that was fashionable at the time (Mould 2007, 542).

The clothing of the religious communities is another area where relatively little is known archaeologically. The terms Blackfriars, Whitefriars, and Greyfriars suggest that the colour of their outer garments worn in public was distinctive. But what else did they wear, and did they strictly follow the regulations on dress laid down in their Rules? From excavations of religious houses a surprisingly wide range of dress accessories have been recovered, but these items may have been worn and lost by lay servants or visitors. Evidence from burials suggests that by 1100 monks were buried clothed with objects of their office (Gilchrist and Sloane 2005, 215; Standley 2013, 104); at Jedburgh Abbey (Scottish Borders) Augustinian Canons excavated in the chapter house were buried wearing leather shoes (Thomas 1995). Leather finds of footwear, belts, and sheaths at Austin Friars, Leicester, suggest that the friars were making leather goods for their own consumption (Allin 1981). Nuns' burials have also been identified from pins around the head and copper-alloy staining on the skull suggesting the head-dresses or veils that were fastened with these accessories. The nunnery of St Clement, Clementhorpe (North Yorkshire), and the Bridgettine double monastery at Syon (Middlesex) are two examples (Gilchrist and Sloane 2005, 81).

In archaeological textile reports the materials, weave pattern, twist direction of thread, and dyes are traditionally the primary focus. This information can provide evidence of production methods, trade, and possible provenances and is studied together with the remains of textile production, such as spindle-whorls, flax tools, fulling mills, and dyeing vats (Standley 2016b; Walton 1991). The scraps and offcuts that survive in Britain can be compared with whole garments, often from mainland Europe, and this helps to understand styles and trade. Extant apparel preserved in museum collections includes the hawking glove of Henry VIII in the Ashmolean Museum, Oxford (Figure 49.1), and religious vestments in the Victoria and Albert Museum in London. Pieces have also been found in tombs: for example the silk mitre, buskins, and slippers of Archbishop Hubert Walter (d. 1205) removed when his tomb was opened in Canterbury Cathedral in the nineteenth century. Most tomb remains in Britain are, however, fragmentary, such as the silks in the possible tomb of Henry de Blois (d. 1171) in Winchester Cathedral, or the tomb in Dunfermline Abbey opened in 1819 that contained a high-quality brocaded tabby silk fragment (Henshall et al. 1954–6). From the royal tombs at Las Huelgas, Burgos (Spain), late twelfth- to mid fourteenth-century

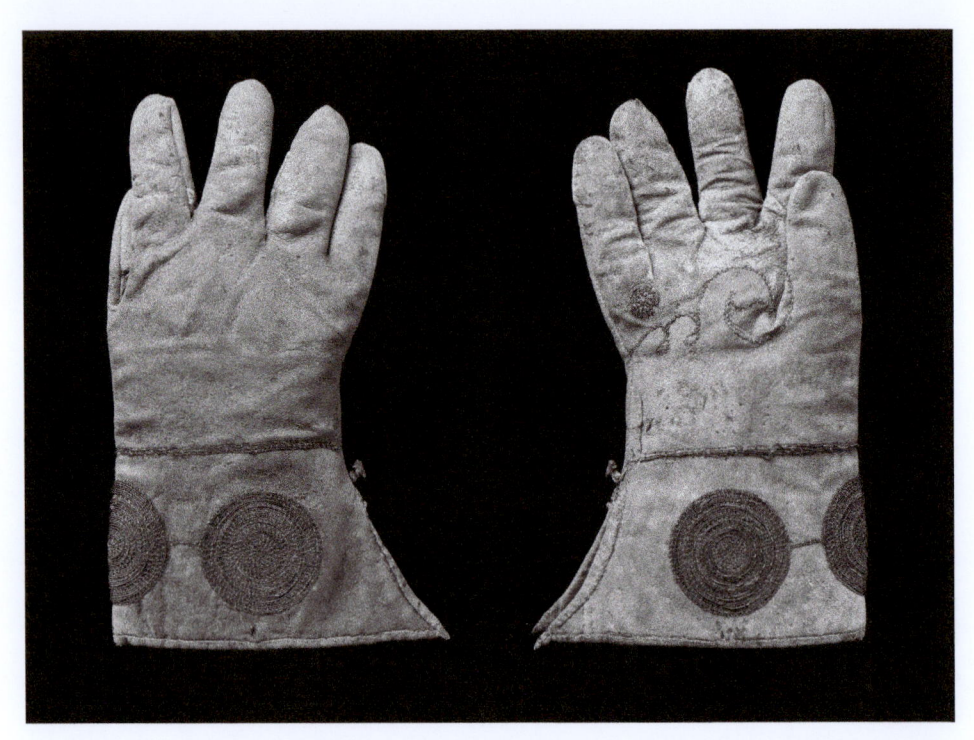

FIGURE 49.1 The right-hand hawking glove believed to have belonged to Henry VIII; probably given to John Tradescant the elder by royal warrant in 1635. Red-brown doeskin with an overlaid panel of grey-white kid or dogskin on the upper palm, and lining of white doeskin. Pink linen is also used as lining. Embroidered with silver-gilt, linen, and red, blue, and pink silk threads. A small yellow tassle with a metal thread waist is attached to the outside edge of the gauntlet. Length 285 mm, width 130 mm

(© Ashmolean Museum, University of Oxford, AN1685 B.228)

clothes and textiles have been wonderfully preserved providing comparanda for British fabrics, especially silks (Yarza 2005). Similarly, material originally from Germany can be compared with Perth's almost complete silk hair-nets, suggesting that they were imported into Scotland (Bennett et al. 2012, 49–50). Two of the delicate Perth hair-nets are embroidered with repeated designs: one of cross crosslets (Figure 49.2), the other of birds and lozenges. This embroidered netting is known as *lacis*, and the Perth finds from a context of around 1400–1410 are the first of their kind to be found in Britain.

Apparel has been found concealed in medieval and post-medieval buildings too.[1] However, there are no clear answers as to why items were chosen, their locations, or the purpose of these concealments. One suggestion is that they were protective devices like witches' bottles. Nevertheless, the occasional recovery adds to our knowledge of what was worn by, most likely, the people who were living in the buildings. The

---

[1] See the Deliberately Concealed Garments Project (http://www.concealedgarments.org).

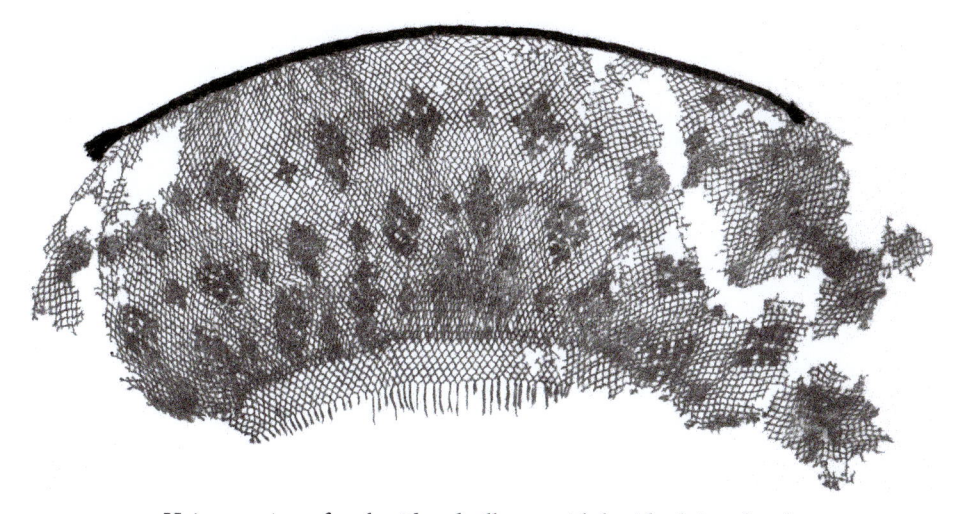

FIGURE 49.2 Hair-covering of embroidered silk net with braid edging dated to *c.*1300, excavated from Rig VI, High Street, Perth. Dimensions of net: 150 x 360 mm

(© Perth Museum and Art Gallery, Perth & Kinross Council, Licensor www.scran.ac.uk)

most regularly concealed items were shoes and the earliest cache is from Winchester Cathedral, believed to date from the early fourteenth century (Swann 1996). Other garments including corsets, doublets, and hats were concealed from the sixteenth century onwards (Eastrop 2010; Hayward 2010).

Dress Accessories

Dress accessories are ubiquitous on medieval excavations. Often made of copper- and lead-alloy and having escaped recycling, they are found as general domestic waste or, occasionally, as grave goods and special deposits. The key reference collection is from London where closely dated contexts of the mid-twelfth to mid-fifteenth century have informed the dating of buckles, brooches, mirror cases, mounts, strap ends, pilgrim badges, and much else (Egan and Pritchard 2002; Spencer 2010). Winchester, Norwich, York, Salisbury, and Perth have also produced significant assemblages. Investigations of deserted and currently occupied rural settlements are also available, with extensive investigations at Westbury (Buckinghamshire) and Meols (Cheshire), for example (Egan 2005b; Gerrard with Aston 2007; Griffiths et al. 2007; Hinton 2010; Ivens et al. 1995; Lewis 2007).

Gold and silver objects were typically recycled so their recovery is of particular consequence. Later medieval hoards such as those from Fishpool (Nottinghamshire, the jewellery dated to the mid-fifteenth century), Lark Hill (Worcester, twelfth century), and near Thame (Oxfordshire, fourteenth and fifteenth century) provide evidence of precious jewellery (alongside coins) that survived tumultuous events but was

FIGURE 49.3 Gold, amethyst, and enamel reliquary ring from the hoard found near Thame, c.1350–1400. The bezel opens to reveal a cavity that would have held a relic, perhaps a piece of the True Cross. Letters spelling DOMINE MEMANTO [sic] MEI (O Lord, remember me) are on the shoulders of hoop and openwork bezel. On the bezel's reverse is an engraved scene of the Crucifixion with the Virgin and St John with a background of red enamel. Hoop diameter 25 mm, bezel length 25 mm, width 16.5 mm

(© Ashmolean Museum, University of Oxford, AN1940.228)

never reclaimed by their owners (British Museum PE 1967.12-8.1-9; MLA.54,8-20,1-6; Ashmolean Museum AN1940.224-228; Standley 2016c; Cherry 1973). The reliquary ring from the Thame Hoard has been described as 'Perhaps the most exceptional of all surviving ecclesiastical rings' (Campbell 2009, 47) (Figure 49.3). Precious metal chance finds, often recovered through metal-detecting and processed through the 1996 Treasure Act (in England and Wales) and Treasure Trove in Scotland, also continue to test our understanding. Silver-gilt dress-hooks are a new class of Tudor accessory that came to light through the Treasure process and the Portable Antiquity Scheme (PAS)[2] (Gaimster et al. 2002) and their study underlined the efficacy of interdisciplinary approaches in historical archaeology.

---

[2] Portable Antiquities Scheme (https://finds.org.uk).

Base metal objects also have great value. Recent chance finds expose the commonality of certain object types that have so far eluded widespread recovery through excavation, for example, lead-alloy pilgrim badges, copper-alloy mirror cases, purse frames, and silver-gilt brooches decorated with rosettes. The latter were once thought to be limited to the north of Britain, but PAS results prove otherwise (Standley 2013, 41). Other exciting archaeological finds that were worn on the body include spectacles, the bone frames of which have been found at religious houses such as Battle Abbey (East Sussex), Chester Dominican Friary (Cheshire), Hailes Abbey (Gloucestershire), and Melrose Abbey (Roxburghshire). From Austin Friars, Leicester, there is also a fourteenth-century decorated calfskin case or pouch for spectacles (Allin 1981, 162); a copper-alloy reading-glass frame perhaps of the fourteenth century was a chance find from Norfolk (Ashley 2004). Cosmetic sets, mirror cases, and false hairpieces were also carried or worn (Egan and Pritchard 2002, 358–83; Crowfoot et al. 2001, fig. 99; Standley 2008) and these objects speak of the desire and lengths people went to manifest a 'desirable' appearance. Along with the lace-ends used to secure and tighten the new styles of clothing that became fashionable in the fourteenth century, they can be included in the material culture of medieval sexuality (Staniland 1997, 239; Standley 2013, 60–1).

Symbols and Saints

Self-Representation

No accessory conveyed the wearer's identity better than signet or seal rings and items of livery. These items, among them the Dunstable Swan jewel, are considered by David Hinton (see Chapter 30). Archaeological finds include a collar of forty-one silver links each formed by the letter S from the foreshore of the Thames (Museum of London 84.80). This was a suitable emblem of authority for a government official or ambassador, the *esses* probably representing the word *Souveignez* and/or *Sovereigne*. Middleham Castle (North Yorkshire) has artefactual evidence of both Houses of Lancaster and York: Ralph Neville and Richard, Duke of Gloucester, who used the castle as his powerbase before his accession to the throne. The livery accessories here were a gold ring decorated with twelve *esses* and the inscription of 'Sovereynly' once worn by a member of Neville's household (late fourteenth or early fifteenth century; York Museums Trust, YORYM: 1992.21); and a later fifteenth-century copper-alloy livery badge of a crested boar, used as an emblem by Richard. A similar but higher-value badge of silver-gilt was found in the area of Bosworth (Leicestershire) (Scott 2009).

Seal rings and pendant matrices can reveal both personal choice and elements of humour. A late thirteenth- to early fourteenth-century gold ring found in Hereford was set with a sapphire intaglio carved around the first century BC, and depicted the veiled head of a Ptolemic queen. The bezel in which it sits has the Lombardic inscription TECTA LEGE LECTA TEGE (Read what is written, hide what is read)

(Figure 49.4). This ancient gem could have been chosen because of its likeness to contemporary depictions of the Virgin Mary, or indeed to represent its female owner. Henig (2008) has argued for a well-organized, international trade in ancient gems with merchants carrying a selection for their patrons. For those without access to ancient gems or armorial privileges, a variety of motifs were chosen for personal seals, including the lamb and flag of the *Agnus Dei*, and animals referencing the hunt. Satirical images are known too, such as the inversion of the natural order in which a hare or rabbit is out hunting while riding a hound, often accompanied by the hunting cry 'Sohou!' (such as PAS YORYM-018BAF). This upside-down-world motif is taken further on a chance find matrix from Suffolk (PAS SF-1F0772), where a rabbit's body has a mitred human head, inscribed with SOHOV LEVESKE (Sohou l'evesque), suggesting the hunting of bishops.

FIGURE 49.4 Gold seal ring set with a reused sapphire intaglio carved with the veiled head of a woman. The bezel's retrograde cut inscription reads TECTA LEGE LECTA TEGE. Recovered from a well in Hereford in 1824. 25 x 24 mm

(© Victoria and Albert Museum, London, Waterton Collection, 89-1899)

Witty puns include a squirrel with the legend I CRAC NOTIS (I crack nuts), perhaps relating to sexual conquests (e.g. PAS NARC-EABB91).

Sex

Later medieval badges depicting sexual imagery can seem bizarre, even incomprehensible (Jones 1993; 2001; 2002; 2014). Purses, for example, were analogous with vulvas, and a late fourteenth- to early fifteenth-century pendant from London aptly depicts a decorated purse containing a phallus.[3] Other purse pendants were perhaps used as charms to bring good fortune or to show the wearer's charitable nature; although they too may have had sexual connotations. One from King's Lynn (Norfolk) (King's Lynn Museum PB 151) depicts the tip of a blade pointing into it. At first glance these are just two items commonly worn on a medieval belt and simply a charm against cutpurses—but daggers or swords were also metaphorical symbols of the phallus and with this knowledge the item takes on a new meaning. Possibly this was a courtship gift alongside posy rings or brooches. One such pendant is in the shape of a stylized vulva with the inscription CON POR AMOVRS (cunt for love)—leaving little to the imagination! Their use as good luck charms is another proposition and, just as phalluses and vulvas were seen as apotropaic in Roman times, this belief may have continued into the later medieval period. There may be some association with the sex trade too (Jones 2002).

Protection

Many decorative and symbolic items were made of natural materials: jet, coral, bone, ivory, wood, and semi-precious and precious gemstones. Coloured glass was used to imitate gems too, especially in cheaper base metal accessories, such as the stirrup rings that were popular from the mid-twelfth to fifteenth centuries. Many natural materials were not only deemed attractive, but perceived to hold powerful properties that could protect, heal, and cure the wearers (Evans and Serjeantson 1933). Contemporary lapidaries attest to this, and rings bearing gems often had open-backed bezels to allow the magical stone to touch the skin of the wearer, such as that in Figure 49.4.

'Pairs of beads' or rosaries used to remember and count prayers were made from a range of materials. From the Augustinian priory of St Oswald's in Gloucester, a group of eighteen amber beads were recovered from a single sixteenth-century context—perhaps a rosary or even a necklace that once adorned a statue of the Virgin Mary hidden at the Reformation; while a single jet bead from the Tudor courtier's house Acton Court (Gloucestershire) was carved with three scallop shells, suggesting its origin as a rosary

---

[3] See Kunera database of late medieval badges and *ampullae* (http://kunera.nl/Default.aspx).

FIGURE 49.5 *AVE MARIA* inscribed buckle plates from a) Suffolk and b) the deserted medieval settlement of Seacourt (Oxfordshire). The plate from Seacourt is thought to have been reused as a pendant suspended using the wire loops. a) 31 x 23 mm b) 50 x 15 mm

(© Ashmolean Museum, University of Oxford, AN1927.6257 and AN1969.91)

bead from Santiago de Compostela (Spain) (Standley 2013, 67–8). Pilgrim badges, such as scallop shells, are considered by Yeoman (Chapter 40), while Santiago as a pilgrimage destination is discussed by Gerrard and Gutiérrez-González (Chapter 59). Badges and tokens became more popular in the early fourteenth century, in preference to *ampullae*, and are often found in large numbers in riverine contexts in urban areas, notably in London and Salisbury (Spencer 2010; 1990, 58). *Ampullae*, on the other hand, are more common chance finds on cultivated land than badges (1379 *ampullae* to 448 badges in England and Wales as of April 2015; Anderson 2010).

Rings, brooches, and pendants with protective formulae and words are common finds from the thirteenth to early sixteenth centuries. The title 'Jesus of Nazareth, King of the Jews', Christ's trigram IHC, *Ave Maria*, and names of the Magi are frequently found on accessories, as well as other material culture, such as knives and ceramics (Blake et al. 2003). All these indicate devotion to the religious cults and were thought to protect wearers. Accessories that caused those who saw them to remember the Passion, Eucharist, or the martyrdom of saints acted as mnemonics, and were miniature, portable versions of the imagery that decorated churches and chapels. The late fifteenth-century Coventry ring is a powerful example of such a devotional ring: the large gold band is engraved with Christ standing in the tomb with the Cross and Instruments of Passion behind (British Museum AF.897). The Five Wounds of Christ are all represented, accompanied by the text 'The well of pitty, the well of merci, the well of confort, the well of gracy, the well of everlastingh lyffe'.

There is also evidence of modifications made to functional accessories in order to transform them into talismanic accessories. For example, late twelfth- to late fourteenth-century copper-alloy buckle plates were incised with invocations to the Virgin Mary. They have been found as chance finds throughout England, and on excavations at deserted medieval settlements, such as Seacourt (Oxfordshire) and Tattenhoe (Buckinghamshire) (Figure 49.5) (Biddle 1961–2, no. 16; Mills 1995, fig. 154.90). One possibility is that these modifications were carried out by women with the intention of

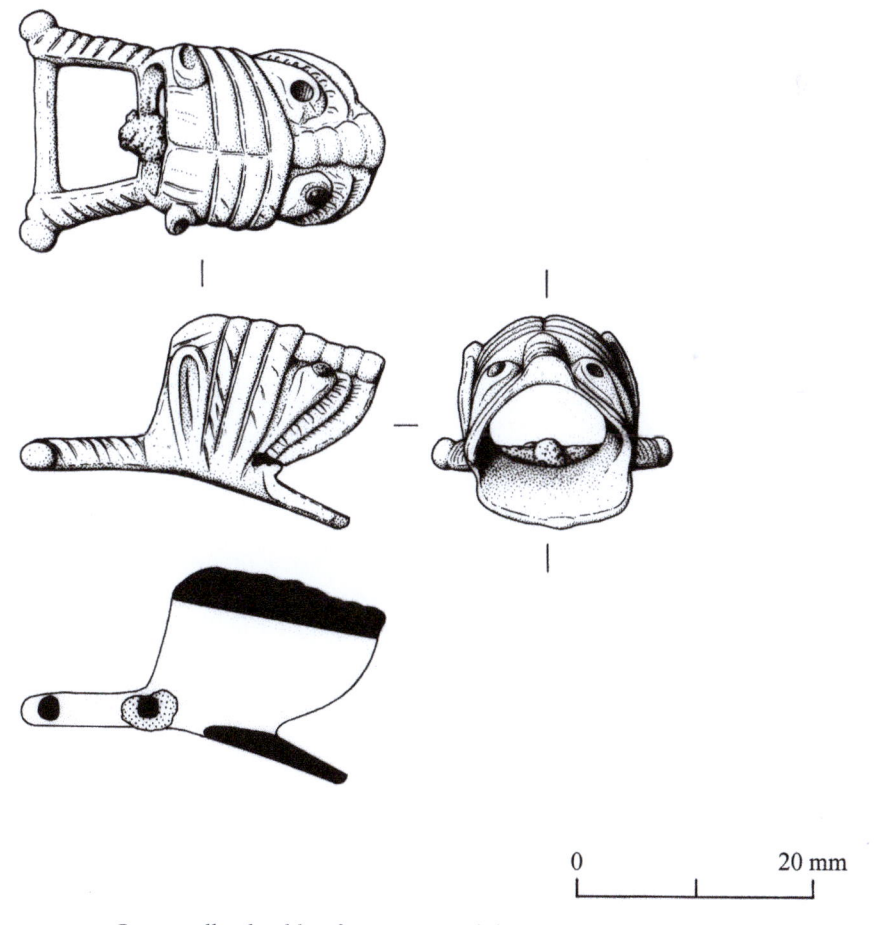

FIGURE 49.6 Copper-alloy buckle of gaping-mouth beast type with corroded fragment of an iron pin and one eye of dark blue glass. Found in the parish of Geldeston (Norfolk)

(PAS NMS-438193, illustration by J. Gibbons © Norfolk County Council, CC BY-SA 2.0)

wearing the belts during pregnancy. More elaborate buckle plates designed with devotional motifs and relic girdles were worn to protect mother and child (Standley 2013, 80–2); perhaps the inscribed buckle plates were home-made versions. The consecration of pilgrims' staves and purses was carried out at places of pilgrimage (Webb 2000, 186), and belts and attached buckle plates could well have received a similar blessing at shrines dedicated to the Virgin Mary.

Future Directions

Research into the archaeology of medieval clothing and dress accessories is far from comprehensive, but developing. For example, pinpointing accessories worn by children is difficult; simply associating the small size of objects with children is neither adequate nor accurate. Particular time periods also require further consideration, especially the eleventh and twelfth centuries (Hinton 2005, 172). Chance finds, such as the gaping-mouth beast buckles thought to be twelfth century in date, are only now beginning to fill that gap (Figure 49.6) (Rogerson and Ashley 2011). Approaches and methods need to evolve and a capacity to work with a range of sources remains an essential prerequisite (for example Hayward 2009; Heley 2009; Standley 2013; 2016a). One fruitful avenue for future study might be to develop an 'archaeology of later medieval emotion' (Tarlow 2000; 2012); many of the dress accessories discussed above are associated with fear, love, desire, joviality, lust, support, and sentimentality. Archaeological material evidence will be central to the ambitions of any project such as this.

Further Reading

Alexander, J. and Binski, P. (eds) 1987 *Age of Chivalry: art in Plantagenet England 1200–1400*, Royal Academy of Arts, London

Blair, J. and Ramsay, N. (eds) 1991 *English medieval industries: craftsmen, techniques, products*, The Hambledon Press, London

Duffy, E. 1994 *The stripping of the altars: traditional religion in England 1400–1580*, Yale University Press, London

Glenn, V. 2003 *Romanesque & Gothic: decorative metalwork and ivory carvings in the Museum of Scotland*, National Museums of Scotland, Edinburgh

Huang, A. L. and Jahnke, C. (eds) 2015 *Textiles and the medieval economy: production, trade and consumption of textiles 8th–16th centuries*, Ancient Textiles Series 16, Oxbow, Oxford

Lightbown, R. 1992 *Mediaeval European jewellery, with a catalogue of the collections in the Victoria and Albert Museum*, Victoria and Albert Museum, London

Marks, R. and Williamson, P. (eds) 2003 *Gothic: art for England 1400–1547*, Victoria and Albert Museum Publications, London

Netherton, R. and Owen-Crocker, G. R. (eds) 2005–16, *Medieval clothing and textiles series*, vols 1–12, Boydell Press, Woodbridge

Oman, C. 1974 *British rings 800–1914*, Batsford, London

Reynolds, A. 2013 *In fine style: the art of Tudor and Stuart fashion*, Royal Collection Trust, London

Sylvester, L. M., Chambers, M. C., and Owen-Crocker, G. R. 2014 *Medieval dress and textiles in Britain: a multilingual sourcebook*, Medieval and Renaissance Clothing and Textiles, Boydell Press, Woodbridge

Thomas, K. 1971 *Religion and the decline of magic*, Penguin Books, London

References Cited

Allin, C. E. 1981 'The leather', in J. E. Mellor and T. Pearce, *The Austin Friars, Leicester*, Leicestershire Archaeological Field Unit Report, Council for British Archaeology Research Report 35, 145–68

Anderson, W. 2010 'Blessing the fields? A study of late-medieval ampullae from England and Wales', *Medieval Archaeology* 54, 182–203

Ashley, S. 2004 'South Walsham (SMR 29489)', in H. Geake, 'Portable Antiquities Scheme report', *Medieval Archaeology* 48, 242–4

Bennett, H., Dransart, P. Z., and Bogdan, N. Q. 2012 'Non loom-woven fabrics', in P. Z. Dransart, N. Q. Bogdan, M. L. Ryder, and C. Thomas (eds), *Perth High Street archaeological excavation 1975–77. Fascicule 3: the textiles and the leather*, Tayside and Fife Archaeological Committee, Perth, 43–54

Biddle, M. 1961–2 'The deserted medieval village of Seacourt, Berkshire', *Oxoniensia* 26–7, 70–201

Blake, H., Egan, G., Hurst, J., and New, E. 2003 'From popular devotion to resistance and revival in England: the cult of the Holy Name of Jesus and the Reformation', in D. Gaimster and R. Gilchrist (eds), *The archaeology of Reformation 1480–1580*, The Society for Post-Medieval Archaeology Monograph 1, Leeds, 186–93

Campbell, M. 2009 *Medieval jewellery in Europe 1100–1500*, Victoria and Albert Museum Publications, London

Cherry, J. 1973 'The medieval jewellery from the Fishpool, Nottinghamshire, Hoard', *Archaeologia* 104, 307–21

Crowfoot, E. 1975 'The textiles', in C. Platt and R. Coleman-Smith, *Excavations in medieval Southampton 1953–1969, Vol. 2*, Leicester University Press, Leicester, 333–40

Crowfoot, E. 1990 'Textiles', in M. Biddle, *Object and economy in medieval Winchester Vol. II*, Clarendon Press, Oxford, 467–88

Crowfoot, E. 2007 'Textiles', in D. Austin, *Acts of perception: a study of Barnard Castle in Teesdale, Vol. II*, The Architectural and Archaeological Society of Durham and Northumberland and English Heritage, 555

Crowfoot, E., Pritchard, F., and Staniland, K. 2001 *Textiles and clothing 1150–1450*, Medieval finds from excavations in London 4 (new edition), Boydell and Brewer, London

Dransart, P. Z., Bogdan, N. Q., Ryder, M. L., and Thomas, C. 2012 *Perth High Street archaeological excavation 1975–77. Fascicule 3: the textiles and the leather*, Tayside and Fife Archaeological Committee, Perth

Eastrop, D. 2010 'The conservation of garments concealed within buildings as material culture in action', in T. Hamling and C. Richardson (eds), *Everyday objects: medieval and early modern material culture and its meanings*, Ashgate Publishing Limited, Farnham, 145–56

Egan, G. 2005a *Material culture in London in an age of transition: Tudor and Stuart period finds c.1450–c.1700 from excavations at riverside sites in Southwark*, Museum of London Archaeology Service Monograph 19, London

Egan, G. 2005b 'Urban and rural finds: material culture of country and town, c.1050–1500', in K. Giles and C. Dyer (eds), *Town and country in the Middle Ages: contrasts, contacts and interconnections, 1100–1500*, The Society for Medieval Archaeology Monograph 22, Leeds, 197–210

Egan, G. and Pritchard, F. 2002 *Dress accessories c.1150–c.1450*, Medieval finds from excavations in London, Boydell Press, Woodbridge

Evans, J. and Serjeantson, M. S. 1933 *English mediaeval lapidaries*, Oxford University Press, London

Forster, M., Buckland, K., Gardiner, J., Green, E., Janaway., R., Klein, K. L., Mould, Q., and Richards, M. 2005 'Silk hats to woolley socks: clothing remains. The textile and leather clothing assemblages', in J. Gardiner with M. J. Allen (eds), *Before the mast: life and death aboard the Mary Rose, Vol. 4*, The Mary Rose Trust, Portsmouth, 18–106

Gaimster, D., Hayward, M., Mitchell, D., and Parker, K. 2002 'Tudor silver-gilt dress-hooks: a new class of treasure find in England', *The Antiquaries Journal* 82, 157–96

Gerrard, C. M. with Aston, M. 2007 *The Shapwick Project, Somerset: a rural landscape explored*, The Society for Medieval Archaeology Monograph 25, Leeds

Gilchrist, R. 2009 'Medieval archaeology and theory: a disciplinary leap of faith', in R. Gilchrist and A. Reynolds (eds), *Reflections: 50 years of Medieval Archaeology 1957–2007*, The Society for Medieval Archaeology Monograph 30, Leeds, 385–408

Gilchrist, R. and Sloane, B. 2005 *Requiem: the medieval monastic cemetery in Britain*, Museum of London Archaeology Service, London

Grew, F. and de Neergaard, M. 2001 *Shoes and pattens*, Medieval finds from excavations in London 2, Boydell and Brewer, London

Griffiths, D., Philpott, R. A., and Egan, G. 2007 *Meols. The archaeology of the North Wirral coast: discoveries and observations in the 19th and 20th centuries, with a catalogue of the collections*, Oxford University School of Archaeology Monograph 68, Oxford

Hayward, M. 2009 *Rich apparel: clothing and the law in Henry VIII's England*, Ashgate Publishing Limited, Farnham

Hayward, M. 2010 'A shadow of a former self: analysis of an early seventeenth-century boy's doublet from Abingdon', in T. Hamling and C. Richardson (eds), *Everyday objects: medieval and early modern material culture and its meanings*, Ashgate Publishing Limited, Farnham, 107–44

Hassall, T. G., Halpin, C. E., and Mellor, M. 1989 'Excavations in St Ebbe's, Oxford, 1967–1976, part 1: late Saxon and medieval domestic occupation and tenements, and the medieval Greyfriars', *Oxoniensia* 54, 71–278

Heley, G. 2009 *The material culture of the tradesmen of Newcastle upon Tyne 1545–1642: the Durham probate record evidence*, British Archaeological Report British Series 497, Oxford

Henig, M. 2008 'The re-use and copying of ancient intaglios set in medieval personal seals, mainly found in England: an aspect of the Renaissance of the 12th century', in N. Adams, J. Cherry, and J. Robinson (eds), *Good impressions: image and authority in medieval seals*, British Museum Research Publication 168, London, 25–34

Henshall, A. S., Crowfoot, G. M., and Beckwith, J. 1954–6 'Early textiles found in Scotland', *Proceedings of the Society of Antiquaries of Scotland* 88, 22–39

Hinton, D. A. 2005 *Gold and gilt, pots and pins: possessions and people in medieval Britain*, Oxford University Press, Oxford

Hinton, D. A. 2010 'Deserted medieval villages and the objects from them', in C. Dyer and R. Jones (eds), *Deserted villages revisited*, Explorations in Local and Regional History Vol. 3, University of Hertfordshire Press, Hatfield, 85–108

Ivens, R., Busby, P., Shepherd, N., Hurman, B., and Mills, J. 1995 *Tattenhoe and Westbury: two deserted medieval settlements in Milton Keynes*, Buckinghamshire Archaeological Society Monograph Series 8, Aylesbury

Jones, A. R. and Stallybrass, P. 2000 *Renaissance clothing and the materials of memory*, Cambridge University Press, Cambridge

Jones, J. 1976 'The leather', in T. G. Hassall 'Excavations at Oxford Castle, 1965–1973', *Oxoniensia* 41, 275–96

Jones, M. 1993 'The secular badges', in H. J. E. van Beuningen and A. M. Koldeweij, *Heilig en Profaan. 1000 laatmiddeleeuwse insignes uit de collectie H.J.E. van Beuningen*, Rotterdam Papers 8, Cothen, 99–109

Jones, M. 2001 'The sexual and the secular badges', in H. J. E. van Beuningen, A. M. Koldeweij, and D. Kicken, *Heilig en Profaan 2. 1200 laatmiddeleeuwse insignes uit openbare en particuliere collecties*, Rotterdam Papers 12, Cothen, 196–206

Jones, M. 2002 *The secret Middle Ages: discovering the real medieval world*, Sutton Publishing, Stroud

Jones, M. 2014 'Sex, popular beliefs, and culture', in R. Evans (ed.), *A cultural history of sexuality in the Middle Ages*, Bloomsbury, London, 139–64

Jope, E. M. 1958 'The Clarendon Hotel, Oxford, part I: the site', *Oxoniensia* 23, 1–83

Lewis, C. 2007 'New avenues for the investigation of currently occupied medieval rural settlement: preliminary observations from the Higher Education Field Academy', *Medieval Archaeology* 51, 133–63

Margeson, S. 1993 *Norwich households: the medieval and post-medieval finds from Norwich Survey Excavations, 1971–1978*, East Anglian Archaeology Report 58, Norwich

Mills, J. M. 1995 'Tattenhoe: the finds catalogue', in R. Ivens, P. Busby, N. Shepherd, B. Hurman, and J. Mills, *Tattenhoe and Westbury: two deserted medieval settlements in Milton Keynes*, Buckinghamshire Archaeological Society Monograph Series 8, 336–42

Mould, Q. 2007 'Leather', in D. Austin, *Acts of perception: a study of Barnard Castle in Teesdale*, vol. II, The Architectural and Archaeological Society of Durham and Northumberland and English Heritage, 540–55

Rogerson, A. and Ashley, S. 2011 'Some medieval gaping-mouth beast buckles from Norfolk and elsewhere', *Medieval Archaeology* 55, 299–302

Ryder, M. L. and Gabra-Sanders, T. 1992 'Textiles from Fast Castle, Berwickshire, Scotland', *Textile History* 23(1), 5–22

Scott, W. 2009 *LEIC-A6C834: a medieval badge*, web page available at: https://finds.org.uk/database/artefacts/record/id/268787

Spencer, B. 1990 *Pilgrim souvenirs and secular badges: Salisbury Museum medieval catalogue part 2*, Salisbury and South Wiltshire Museum, Salisbury

Spencer, B. 2010 *Pilgrim souvenirs and secular badges*, Medieval finds from excavations in London 7, Boydell Press, Woodbridge

Staniland, K. 1997 'Getting there, got it: archaeological textiles and tailoring in London, 1330–1580', in D. Gaimster and R. Gilchrist (eds), *The archaeology of Reformation 1480–1580*, The Society for Post-Medieval Archaeology Monograph 1, Leeds, 239–49

Standley, E. 2008 'Ladies hunting: a late medieval decorated mirror case from Shapwick, Somerset', *The Antiquaries Journal* 88, 198–206

Standley, E. R. 2013 *Trinkets and charms: the use, meaning and significance of dress accessories 1300–1700*, University of Oxford School of Archaeology Monograph 78, Oxford

Standley, E. R. 2016a '"Best" gowns, kerchiefs and pantofles: gifts of apparel in the North East of England in the 16th century', in T. Martin and R. Weetch (eds), *Dress and society: contributions from archaeology*, Oxbow, Oxford, 130–50

Standley, E. R. 2016b 'Spinning yarns: the archaeological evidence for hand spinning and its social implications, c.1200–1500', *Medieval Archaeology* 60, 266–99

Standley, E. R. 2016c 'Hid in the earth and secret places: a reassessment of a hoard of later medieval gold rings and silver coins found near the River Thame', *The Antiquaries Journal* 96, 117–42

Swann, J. M. 1969 'Shoes concealed in buildings', *Journal of Northampton Museum Art Gallery* 6, 8–21

Swann, J. 1981 *Catalogue of shoe and other buckles in Northampton Museum*, Northampton Borough Council Museums and Art Gallery, Northampton

Swann, J. 1996 'Shoes concealed in buildings', *Costume* 30, 56–69

Tarlow, S. 2000 'Emotion in archaeology', *Current Anthropology* 41(5), 713–45

Tarlow, S. 2012 'The archaeology of emotion and affect', *Annual Review of Anthropology* 41, 169–85

Taylor, L. 2002 *The study of dress history*, Manchester University Press, Manchester

Thomas, C. 1995 'Leather', in J. H. Lewis and G. J. Ewart, *Jedburgh Abbey: the archaeology and architecture of a Border abbey*, The Society of Antiquaries of Scotland Monograph 10, Edinburgh, 114

Thomas, C. and Bogdan, N. Q. 2012 'The leather', P. Z. Dransart, N. Q. Bogdan, M. L. Ryder, and C. Thomas, *Perth High Street archaeological excavation 1975–77. Fascicule 3: the textiles and the leather*, Tayside and Fife Archaeological Committee, Perth, 147–341

Vaughan, J. E. 1981 'The leather', in B. Harbottle, M. Ellison, A. M. Donaldson, G. D. Robson, J. Rackman, J. E. Vaughan, and P. Walton, 'An excavation in the Castle ditch, Newcastle upon Tyne 1974–6', *Archaeologia Aeliana* 5th series 9, 184–90

Walton, P. 1981 'The textiles', in B. Harbottle, M. Ellison, A. M. Donaldson, G. D. Robson, J. Rackman, J. E. Vaughan, and P. Walton, 'An excavation in the Castle ditch, Newcastle upon Tyne 1974–6', *Archaeologia Aeliana* 5th series 9, 190–228

Walton, P. 1991 'Textiles', in J. Blair and N. Ramsay (eds), *English medieval industries: craftsmen, techniques, products*, The Hambledon Press, London, 319–54

Walton Rogers, P. 1997 *Textile production at 16–22 Coppergate. The Archaeology of York 17: the small finds*, Council for British Archaeology, York

Webb, D. 2000 *Pilgrimage in medieval England*, Hambledon and London, London

Yarza, J. 2005 *Vestiduras ricas. El Monasterio de Las Huelgas y su época 1170–1340*, Patrimonio Nacional, Madrid

CHAPTER 50

GENDER AND SPACE IN THE LATER MIDDLE AGES

Past, Present, and Future Routes

AMANDA RICHARDSON

STUDIES of late medieval gender and space date back over twenty years, if Roberta Gilchrist's influential *Gender and material culture* (1994) is taken as the starting point. This paper will trace its antecedents, survey developments since, and highlight possible future research directions, although readers will notice that few studies outside England are mentioned, reflecting their relative dearth to date. Space precludes outlining the rise of gender archaeology, which is anyway extensively covered elsewhere (e.g. Milledge Nelson 2006; Wilkie and Hayes 2006; see also Chapter 47 in this *Handbook*), but select studies pronouncing on privacy will feature, given that many scholars have focused on the relative 'privacy' of women. Finally, the summaries of findings presented are necessarily reductive, focusing especially on conclusions regarding gender and space, and for that I apologize to the authors.

STUDIES OF ARCHITECTURAL SPACE

Recent studies of late medieval social space derive largely from the works of late twentieth-century anthropologists, folklorists, and architectural historians, including Patrick Faulkner (1958; 1963), whose analyses of several English and Welsh castles were pioneering in their focus on domestic planning rather than defence. His methodological contribution, the planning analysis diagram, illustrated the functions and interrelationship of rooms largely as experienced by castle inhabitants—naturally, in the 1950s, implicitly male. In focusing on households, however, Faulkner established the ubiquitous late medieval spatial model of chambers, halls, and administrative areas, demonstrating the value of spatial analysis in evaluating late medieval domestic space (Coulson 1996, 179–80; Fairclough 1992, 351–2).

Further advances, based on structuralism, emanated from North America in the 1970s. Although post-medieval in emphasis they remain influential among late medieval archaeologists. In *Folk housing in Middle Virginia* (1975) the folklorist Henry Glassie analysed changes in house-plans through time ('transformational grammar'), identifying an 'evolution of individualism' from *c.*1760, when houses exhibited a heightened emphasis on privacy. The addition of vestibules made living areas less accessible to visitors and symmetrical façades ('closed architecture') obscured their layout within (Glassie 1975, 193, 88, 190). The US anthropologist James Deetz highlighted similar contemporaneous architectural transformations (1977, 86, 161–7), and each concluded that they resulted from political and social change. Glassie's eschewal of any form of documentary evidence, however, rendered women, who 'unfortunately expressed themselves in perishable artifacts', invisible (1975, 178). Indeed, gender ideologies were almost entirely neglected aside from an implication that Virginian farmers might have held their families, like themselves, 'under fearful control' (Johnson 1993, 36).

Faulkner, Glassie, and Deetz influenced the architectural theorists Bill Hillier and Julienne Hanson (1984), who presented their work at the 1985 Theoretical Archaeology Group conference. They proposed that the accessibility of each room in a building has a social meaning, equating changed patterns of access with shifts in social arrangements, developing their 'access analysis diagram' to measure such permeability. The least accessible rooms are termed 'deep', their depth measured by the number of rooms or areas traversed in order to reach them, usually from outside the building. The method has been espoused by a variety of late medieval archaeologists (e.g. Fairclough 1992; Gilchrist 1994; Richardson 2003; Schofield 1994; 1995), and remains popular in studies of gender and space (e.g. Thorstad 2015).

Hillier and Hanson's influence was evident by 1990, when they were referenced throughout *The social archaeology of houses* (Samson 1990). The rise of gender archaeology was also apparent in the eleven bibliographical entries for 'gender'. However, of the twelve multi-period chapters only two contained any late medieval content, of which gender is mentioned briefly only by Matthew Johnson (1990). By this time the processualist stress on morphological laws in archaeology had diminished (Preucel and Meskell 2004, 217) and the uncritical use of methodologies like access analysis was already being questioned, evidenced by Frank E. Brown's critique in the same volume (Brown 1990; see also Giles 2007, 108–9). The way was clear for fresh engagements with space, increasingly using contextual evidence such as written sources and the placing of imagery and since the first such study devoted to gender concerned religious spaces (Gilchrist 1994), that is where we will begin.

SACRED SPACES

The publication of several backlog excavations through the 1990s gave impetus to fresh social-archaeological approaches to religious space (Gerrard 2003, 190) including attention to gender, which have been influential across the social sciences and in studies of other domestic contexts. One still-influential reading is that religious space was consciously regulated by the Church in order to 'reinforce the ... male advantage ... [and] ... contain and marginalise women' (Tibbets Schulenberg 2006, 771–2), although recent work emphasizes women's (and men's) agency while acknowledging the restrictions placed on female religious and parishioners.

Churches and Nunneries

Social approaches to religious space are indebted to Pam Graves's influential work on interrelationships between secular and sacred spaces in fourteenth- to sixteenth-century English parish churches (Graves 1989). Graves embraced theories of agency, *habitus*, and performance (1989, 299–300) and, although focusing on social status more than gender, considered the placement of imagery and movement through space, thus highlighting the effects of material culture on social actors. She noted that the iconography of the north in churches resonated with darkness, evil, the Jews, and the Crucifixion, while the south connoted light, good, the apostles, and the Resurrection. Men and women therefore temporarily assumed the supposed traits of biblical types and antitypes through the mobile nature of the liturgy (Graves 1989, 309, 311).

Gilchrist similarly espoused the concepts of *habitus* and agency, commencing by appraising nunneries' liminality in the 'natural' landscape and their often close—yet peripheral—spatial relationship with settlements. Whereas previous scholars saw only patriarchal strategies to protect nuns' chastity, she suggested that such patterns evoked eremitic ideals associated particularly with women (Gilchrist 1994, 67, 90). Somewhat dichotomously, nunneries' dependence on priests to perform Masses and on local communities for gifts and labour prompted their spatial association with parish churches and villages, and their formal resemblance to manorial complexes (Gilchrist 1994, 90–1, 124). This interdependence is manifested also in the socially and sexually unsegregated burials in nunnery cemeteries compared with most male monasteries (Gilchrist and Sloane 2005, 68).

By the mid-1990s the feminist drive to make women 'visible' had been largely replaced by an emphasis on differences—and similarities—among and between women, men, and other social categories. Thus, while comparing female and male monastery layouts, noting the influence of the liturgical prohibitions placed on nuns, Gilchrist (1994, 224, 125) focuses on transchronological change and connections within and between social groups. Nunnery plans were found to be increasingly domestic in character from the thirteenth century, their fragmentation into 'households', comparable with the 'inner households' of seigneurial women (Gilchrist 1994, 126–7, 213). She also explores further the gendered iconography of the north observed by Graves—noting the effects of humoural theory and other contemporary philosophies—uncovering a relatively high percentage of north cloisters in nunneries; the consistent northern location of images of the Virgin in churches, and the effects of Mary's position on Christ's right in the iconography of the rood screen (Gilchrist 1994, 128–43).

Gilchrist also employed access analysis, finding dormitories to have been the deepest areas in nunneries and sacristies the shallowest, thus limiting the areas accessible by priests, while sacristies were least permeable in male monasteries, underscoring the sanctity of the priest's role in all-male environments. Perhaps not surprisingly a higher number of 'architectural steps' ran through nunnery complexes than male houses, representing nuns' greater segregation from the outside world (Gilchrist 1994, 151, 166–7). But access analysis diagrams omit important information including scale and embellishment, prioritizing relationships between visitors and inhabitants, so the placement of imagery, rendering space legible to inhabitants and visitors alike, also had to be considered, mitigating ahistoricism by interpreting space according to contemporary metaphors. At Lacock Abbey, Wiltshire, for example, male imagery appeared in the sacristy and chapter house, where male patrons and clergy were admitted, but none existed in the least permeable areas. In short, 'a spatial matrix which constructed meaning through the location and content of images' underscored nuns' gender identities, emphasized by strict enclosure and the demarcation of gendered liturgical roles (1994, 166, 160, 192). Nunneries were therefore not inferior to male monasteries, as previously inferred, but *different* (Gilchrist 1994, 191), the variations often resulting from the nuns' own agency.

Such observations have recently been extended by the historian Marilyn Oliva using thirteenth- to sixteenth-century accounts and inventories. Like Gilchrist, she notes connections with the gentry, in that nuns' bedding and furnishings displayed a similar level of comfort to gentry households. Through this, and the iconography of their hangings, they recreated the lay households they had left behind (Oliva 2008, 152–8). Oliva also considers physical movement through space, noting that nuns' furnishings, with their devotional imagery, created a continuum of domestic/sacred space, leading them 'from and through their living quarters right into the choir and chapels' (Oliva 2008, 160).

Less work has been done on gendered space in early parish churches, for which comparatively little contextual evidence survives, but another historian, Katherine L. French, has explored the allocation of seating in fifteenth-century churches. Like Gilchrist and Graves, French discusses women's association with the north, where didactic images aimed at them were frequently sited. Alongside seating arrangements by sex, this may suggest a desire to control and regulate particularly female behaviour. However, segregation allowed women (and other social groups) to enact their own boundaries, forge social relationships, and assume new identities. Moving from seats intended for maidens into those meant for wives, for example, enabled women to emulate the demeanour of their new peers (French 2008, 99, 101). Indeed, the early introduction of pews into some churches in the later fifteenth century may have resulted from a desire by groups of women to perform their piety collectively (Sterrett and Thomas 2011, 27). Either way, women appear to have been highly active in purchasing particular seats, and this was perhaps connected with the increasing prosperity and public standing of individuals of both sexes (French 2008, 103).

It is worth noting here that zoning by sex seems entirely absent in British late medieval parish church graveyards, unlike contemporary Scandinavia where men were consistently interred south and women north of churches (Gilchrist 2012, 205). However, at Raunds (Northamptonshire), tenth- and eleventh-century female burials were concentrated west and north of the church, suggesting that zoning by sex was not unknown before the Conquest, and may have been abandoned in later centuries (Gilchrist 1994, 134).

Male Religious Communities

The fluidity of gender identities features equally strongly in studies of gendered space in male religious communities. These studies have been few, no doubt due to the isolation and perceived self-containment of many orders, and the clergy's categorization as a 'third gender'—therefore not 'men' at all (Busot 2012, 4, 15–16). Perhaps not surprisingly the earliest such study involved those most 'masculine' orders, the Templars and Hospitallers (Gilchrist 1995, 62–105). Architectural and spatial similarities with nunneries were striking, particularly the resonances with manorial complexes (Figure 50.1).

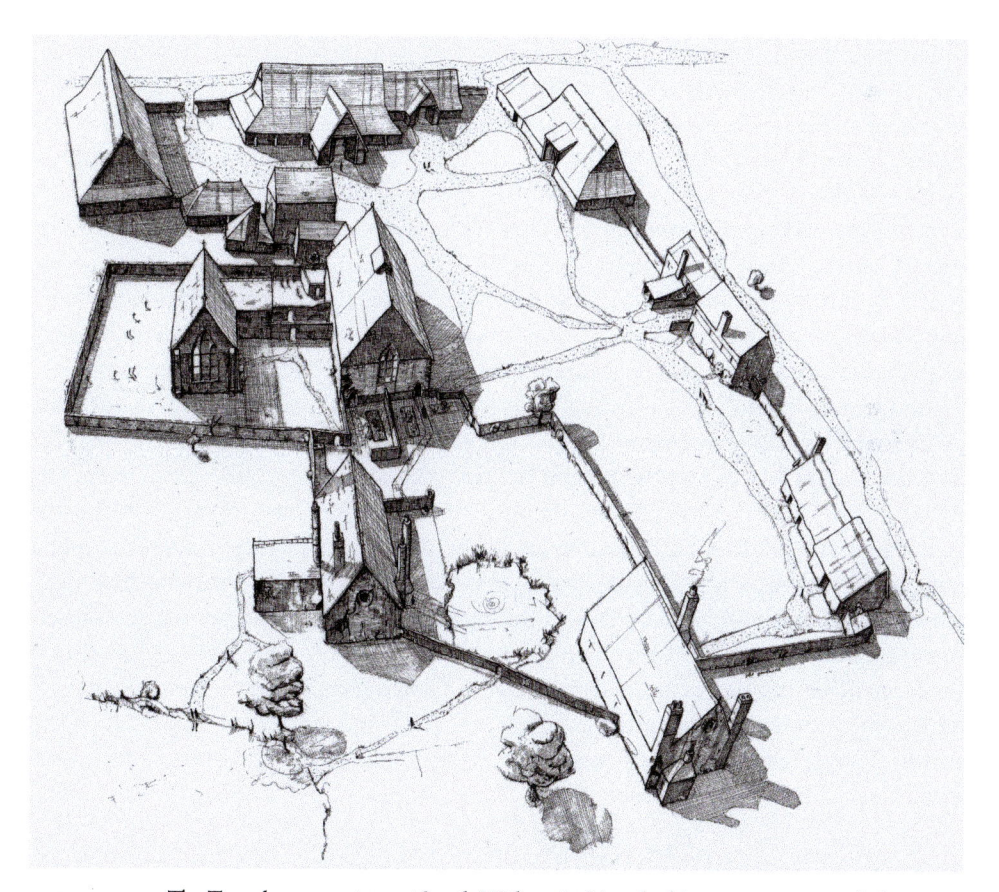

FIGURE 50.1 The Templar preceptory at South Witham in Lincolnshire as reconstructed after excavation by Philip Mayes in 1965–7. This site, and others like it, has many similarities with manorial complexes but has no cloister even though it belonged to a religious order (from Mayes 2002, 56)

(© The Society for Medieval Archaeology)

Like smaller nunneries, many preceptories (a term used for both Orders by Gilchrist) were defined by moats, signifying gentry status. Although cloisters were normally absent, conventual buildings often surrounded spaces resembling courtyards and, like nunneries, larger preceptory churches doubled as parish churches. There was a preference for first-floor halls, common in twelfth- and thirteenth-century aristocratic complexes, and the Orders' limited religious function, revealed by relatively small chapels and an absence of cloisters and choirs, bears comparison with the liturgical prohibitions placed on nuns (Gilchrist 1995, 212, 74–6, 77, 87–90, 103). These similarities—visible in other forms of material culture—deserve further exploration.

Unlike nunneries, Templar and Hospitaller architecture incorporated military iconography, most famously the rounded naves intended to evoke the Church of the Holy Sepulchre in Jerusalem (Gilchrist 1995, 215). Yet militaristic imagery was not absent from monasteries generally, for example the late fourteenth-century graffito depicting a helm, shield, and sword identified at the Cluniac priory of Bermondsey (Surrey), perhaps reflecting regular interaction with the 'outside world' and its values since the priory was on London's outskirts (Busot 2012, 56). That said, from the twelfth century novice monks were generally of seigneurial status and by the later fourteenth century they were aged at least 19, having already been socialized into hegemonic male values. Alexandra Busot argues that late medieval male religious cannot therefore represent a 'third gender', a term implying complete distinction from male and female gender ideologies (Busot 2012, 17–19, 21).

Intra-gendered connections are also evident in the Vicars Choral, introduced into English secular cathedrals to perform the liturgical duties of absent canons from the twelfth century, when they often lodged outside cathedral closes and their behaviour and morals already caused concern. From the fourteenth century these young, usually local men, were 'subjected to quasi-monastic discipline' (Hall 2005, vii) expressed architecturally in their gated residential colleges, strategically situated in cathedral closes to facilitate their strict supervision (Dobson 2005, 6; Hall 2005, vii). The effects seem to have been negligible, even producing a 'locker room' mentality. Their halls, intended for devotional readings, were often venues for ball games and occasional violent exchanges—exacerbated because so many of the vicars wore daggers—and numerous complaints survive of similar behaviour on the streets, where liaisons with women were common (Dobson 2005, 6–7). Architectural and behavioural similarities with medieval university colleges and students are obvious, and complaints regarding lax discipline in late-medieval nunneries deserve comparative theorization. Hall and Stocker's (2005) volume, setting out archaeological, architectural, and historical evidence for each of the nine Vicars Choral colleges, is an excellent starting point.

Gender and Space in Vernacular Architecture

In the *Social archaeology of houses*, Matthew Johnson decried the then extreme atheoreticism and typological obsession of studies of English vernacular architecture (1990,

245–7). All this was about to change and the subsequent twenty-five years have witnessed a flowering of spatial approaches to vernacular houses, particularly over the past decade.

In the mid-1990s two influential studies appeared. First, in *Housing culture* (1993) Johnson, like Glassie and Deetz, argued for a 'process of closure' observable over time (but much earlier) in late medieval and early modern Suffolk rural houses. Although gender was not the focus, it necessarily featured in his exploration of transformations in household dynamics (1993, vi–vii, ix, 32, 133, 137, 173). Johnson found that the hall's waning significance, evident in the rise of the parlour and removal of cooking to separate kitchens, relegated women to more peripheral areas. This shift accelerated in the 1600s but Johnson places its origins in the late 1400s. However, rather than a patriarchal desire for women's marginalization, increased awareness of their household position perhaps prompted their 'marking out' of female space (1993, 137–8). These developments, in relatively large dwellings, were not claimed to be universal and indeed in most Oxfordshire houses, comprising around two to three rooms, cooking continued in halls into the seventeenth century (Mileson 2015). This discrepancy highlights the regionality of such studies, which are only now moving towards synthesis concerning arrangements of social space, particularly regarding urban and rural comparisons.

Second, in a study of medieval and Tudor London dwellings, based on Treswell's lease-plans of *c.*1600, John Schofield (1994; 1995) similarly concluded that by Treswell's time the spatial relationship between halls and kitchens—invariably no longer directly accessible from halls—was broken. Alongside access analysis diagrams he employs structuralist readings of space, e.g. clean/dirty, public/private, and male/female, finding that the emphasis placed on privacy, already evident in thirteenth-century houses, increased in the 1300s with the multiplication of bedrooms and chambers. Due to the nature of the evidence and because little research had yet been performed on women and household economies, Schofield found it harder to pronounce on male/female space (Schofield 1994, 200, 203, 205), although it has since been argued that the socially and sexually mixed nature of urban households must have stimulated a drive towards privacy (Gilchrist 2012, 122). Schofield does, however, note that prosperous medieval women were often trained in commerce, implying that gender was a less significant organizing principle than trade, which he found to be paramount in the layout and patterns of access of larger London houses (Schofield 1994, 200).

As the historian P. J. P. Goldberg observes, writers on later medieval rural and urban vernacular housing have 'not much engaged with gender' (Goldberg 2011, 205), although recent endeavours are apparent in Kowaleski and Goldberg's multidisciplinary publication (2008, 1–13). Here Jane Grenville, exploring relationships between rural and urban architectural forms, notes the inter-visibility of the linear spatial configuration of medieval rural dwellings, affording close observation of children's behaviour, play, and work (2008, 104, 111–12). Likewise urban halls were 'safe space', allowing women to supervise children while engaged in gendered occupations like spinning and carding (Grenville 2008, 118; Rees Jones 2003, 193). This contrasts with readings of high-status halls, which are invariably identified as male space (below). Indeed, Grenville argues that the use and meanings of space in late medieval townhouses derived primarily from peasant crofts—arguably female domains for much of the year—whose halls represented both work space and social space (Grenville 2008, 117–18; Jaritz 2006, 29).

Goldberg argues that whereas peasant women were marginalized by rigid gendered labour divisions, prosperous urban wives were at least as significant in 'public' domestic areas as their husbands (2008, 136–7). He highlights the relative penetrability of bourgeois townhouses, into which visitors were regularly welcomed to consolidate business and friendship networks, contrasting peasant houses, where guests aside from immediate kin were probably discouraged. Although he found the bedchamber—that 'most intimate' household space—to be especially associated with wives (2008, 138), this need not indicate marginalization. Like Schofield, Goldberg notes such women's involvement in urban economies, affording them more household standing than their rural counterparts (2008, 137). Yet while administration was performed by both sexes in larger fourteenth- and fifteenth-century urban homes, the 'counting houses' where it took place were invariably considered male space by contemporaries. Indeed, it has been suggested that increasing numbers of rooms in townhouses by the fifteenth century encouraged replication of the binary gendered spatial divisions found in the residences of the wealthiest (Rees Jones 2003, 195, 252). Goldberg later echoed this observation for relatively spacious fourteenth- and fifteenth-century rural houses, which 'created the stage for hierarchal and gendered social relations necessitated by the presence of ... servants ... day labourers at mealtimes and ... guests' (2011, 220).

Like Goldberg and others, the literary scholar Felicity Riddy highlights women's multiple roles in mercantile households. She also contrasts such multi-room housing, where one might eat, sleep, and work in different areas, with the single-room dwellings of the urban poor. This living arrangement, she argues, would have been especially stressful for women, who could seldom escape childcare and their various work activities (Riddy 2008, 27). In the country, too, the domestic space of the poorest was 'essentially communal and not particularly gendered' since both sexes would routinely have worked and eaten outdoors, making houses essentially places of shelter and sleep (Goldberg 2011, 215). Gender and space in the most humble dwellings certainly deserves further archaeological theorization. Gilchrist, for example, notes that fourteenth-century York single rooms, rented to the poorest, were generally occupied by unmarried women and elderly men and women (2012, 120). The problem, at least regarding smaller rural dwellings, is their archaeological indiscernibility from utility buildings (Goldberg 2011, 212), explaining, perhaps, why historians currently lead the way (e.g. Dyer 2013; Goldberg 2011; Mileson 2015).

Thus, the general consensus is that increased spatial distinctions along gendered lines appeared in the fifteenth century, although the paucity of surviving buildings and related evidence before the mid-fourteenth century skews the evidence, with implications for tracing earlier continuity and change. It is indisputable though that female and male spheres frequently overlapped in towns, and that gendered space was more fluid in humbler dwellings than those of the wealthiest (Jaritz 2006, 29), where ideal male-female spatial divisions were more often realized.

HIGH-STATUS GENDER AND SPACE

Gilchrist's approach in *Gender and material culture* (1994) has influenced studies of domestic space occupied by high-status women, including an analysis of queens' apartments in English royal palaces from the twelfth to the mid-sixteenth centuries (Richardson 2003). Gendered patterns of access were clear before the sixteenth century: queens' apartments were invariably the 'deepest' areas in palace complexes—particularly their bedchambers—whereas kings' apartments were relatively shallow, symbolizing ease of access for petitioners; kings' rooms were invariably closer to great halls and other public areas, and change over time was most evident only in transformations in spatial arrangements in kings' apartments, suggesting that the queen's gender role, as manifested in architecture, remained static.

The distribution of male/female imagery in palaces is revealing. Significantly, depictions of women were largely absent from great halls throughout the entire period, with only a few more in kings' chambers—another essentially public area. In queens' chambers, 'mixed' imagery (neither male nor female, or both) was vastly predominant, with equal numbers of male and female imagery, reflecting the sexual and social diversity of their households. In direct contrast with kings' chapels, female imagery predominated in queens' chapels—due to depictions of female saints, particularly the Virgin Mary—the nature of which was largely contemplative, didactic, and maternal.

Little of this is straightforward. Spatial segregation of the sexes, demonstrated in patterns of access and the location of imagery, conveyed and replicated ideas about gender difference and the social order (Gilchrist 1999, 143) and the patterns of access therefore reveal a symbolic, not actual, marginalization of royal women. Indeed, as Tadhg O'Keefe comments in his thoughtful discussion of gender and Irish castles, 'female quarters were located not at the peripheries ... as the male view might dictate, but in the innermost spaces' (O'Keefe 2001, 77)—spaces which would have been hives of activity. As powerful landowners, queens would receive male officials on a regular basis explaining the high levels of 'mixed' imagery in their chambers.

Gilchrist (1999, 138–43) has noted further spatial patterns relating to high-status women in the castles of Portchester (Hampshire), Castle Rising (Norfolk), Chepstow (Gwent), Pickering (North Yorkshire), and Carisbrooke (Isle of Wight). Private chapels were provided in all but Chepstow, underscoring women's significant religious role as intercessors, and female associations with gardens and enclosure were evident in the proximity of courtyards and gardens to their apartments. Like most high-status castle residents they occupied upper levels, often with towers, enabling them to gaze out over castle interiors while remaining invisible. Indeed, Oliver Creighton contends that elevated views were characteristic of the chambers of elite women, particularly over enclosed gardens—in the medieval worldview a metaphor for the chaste female body (Creighton 2011, 81, and Chapter 23 in this *Handbook*; Gilchrist 1999, 142).

It is increasingly suggested that the medieval seigneurial 'spatial ideology' extended to the surroundings of residences (Creighton 2009, 7) replicating symbolic female enclosure outside high-status residences, specifically in parks (see also Chapter 25). As Naomi Sykes points out, the emphasis on young women's seclusion and enclosure makes it 'unlikely they would have been encouraged to hunt... in the open landscape' (2009, 358). Indeed, the 'debate of the heralds' (*c.*1455) mentions ladies in parks taking 'joy in shooting [deer] with the bow', and in 1550 John Coke claimed that many parks were created expressly for such female pursuits (Mileson 2009, 41; Richardson 2012, 260). This gendered association may explain the place-name 'Lady Park', scattered throughout Britain, such as that probably enclosed for Eleanor Neville, wife of Thomas, Earl of Derby, in 1470 at Lathom (Lancashire) (Neil et al. 2004, 9). There are Marian associations, noted also by Gilchrist for gardens (1999, 140–1), which deserve unpicking. Lady Park at Belper (Derbyshire), so-named from at least 1498, was associated with the 'Lady Well' spring, almost certainly linked with the Virgin in the Middle Ages and a chapel, 'Our Lady in the Park', existed in Lady Park near Liskeard (Cornwall), from the fourteenth century into the 1530s (Griffin 2008, 30; Orme 2010, 85, 100). Attention has also been drawn to parks as contested landscapes. Parkbreak (gang-poaching) was a gendered as well as a 'social crime', and there seem to have been many incidences in fourteenth-century parks owned by high-status women (Dowling 2014, 147–51; Richardson 2012, 216–63), which require further analysis.

The most likely future direction for studies of high-status gender and space may therefore involve exterior spaces. However, the late medieval / early modern transition, a key focus in studies of vernacular architecture, remains under-explored. Here Audrey Thorstad's study of four English and Welsh castles from 1485 to 1547 (2015), based on archaeology, architecture, access analysis, and documents, is an exception. Although the seigneurial apartments were securely identified only at Thornbury (Gloucestershire), that this castle was built *c.*1511 offers opportunities to uncover shifts in gendered space in the early sixteenth century. The lord's and lady's apartments exhibited equal permeability and equivalent access to the privy garden, echoing the relatively symmetrical gendered spaces in Henry VIII's new palaces such as Nonsuch, Surrey (Richardson 2003, 147–9), so that previous gendered patterns may at last have been breaking down. Of course, future work on sixteenth-century castles and country houses is necessary to calibrate such isolated findings.

Debates and New Directions

Kate Giles (2007, 106–8) has demonstrated forcefully that current spatial methodologies can impose presentist ideas on past social actors, whose perceptions of space might be very different to our own. The same can be said of conceptions of public and private largely drawn from the 'separate spheres' ideology, formulated to apply to the eighteenth and nineteenth centuries. It is now acknowledged that such a rigid model cannot be applied uncritically to all contexts, particularly for those eras when room function was largely fluid (see Goldberg 2011, 206, 227–9 regarding the use of 'public' and 'private' in late-medieval spatial studies).

Problems also exist in supplementing material remains with documents recording prescriptive patterns of use, not space as actually 'lived' by individuals (Flather 2011, 10). Accordingly, many recent interdisciplinary studies employ literary sources, thus bridging gaps between the material and the ideal (e.g. Cavalheiro 2015; Goldberg 2011; McLoughlin 2011; Morgan 2014). Sarah McLoughlin, for example, examines attitudes to bourgeois gendered space in fifteenth- and early sixteenth-century popular literature, concluding that its perceived increasing transgression prompted anxieties about women's sexuality in particular, and obsessions 'with controlling movement in and out of the house' (2011, ii, 277, 278). Importantly, McLoughlin demonstrates that the 'hermetically-sealed, perfectly ordered' gendered spaces which many of us have unwittingly implied in fact rarely existed and that where they did they were often contravened (2011, 278; Goldberg 2011, 207). This point is reinforced by the historian Anne Müller (2015), who explores claustral space as a locus for the representation of distinctive female monastic identities, focusing on boundaries and their transgression. For example in the Gilbertine double house at Watton (Yorkshire, founded 1150) the nuns, predictably, occupied the northern section. Yet a 'boundary transcending' turntable identified archaeologically in the presbytery wall allowed nuns and canons to communicate between their respective gendered spaces (Müller 2015, 313).

Studies of late medieval gendered space are therefore moving in the right direction although stagnation exists in the continued use of originally positivist methodologies, a persistent tendency to equate gender with women and the enduring pre-eminence of a few key studies, however seminal. Yet recent technologies may develop previous observations and advance new ones. For example, the many layers of data represented in GIS maps can highlight complex gendered interactions between people and places, as Mei-Po Kwan (2002) argues in advocating their use by feminist geographers.

Such opportunities have not to date been enthusiastically embraced by late medieval gender archaeologists, although one exception is a GIS project on Barking Abbey, a Benedictine female house. By integrating information from Google Earth, ArcGIS, and the ground-plan excavated in 1911, the abbey's precise position and interior and exterior parameters were established on the ground. The resulting GIS map offers opportunities for further analysis such as the exploration of links with other religious institutions and communities by displaying documented processional routes through the abbey's precincts, the church, and town. New perspectives on collective gendered self-identity might also be gained by displaying internal processional routes and other aspects of the liturgy adapted by the nuns themselves for the spaces of their church (Bussell and McNamara 2013, 177–8), possibly even exploring relationships between vision, smell, sound, and spatiality as advocated by both Giles (2007) and Graves (2007). Compared with the 2D methodologies we began with the opportunities are infinite, and Foucault's observation that an entire history of spaces remains to be written (Blake 2004, 234) is perhaps as true today as it was in the 1980s.

Acknowledgements

I am very grateful to Martha Beard, Gabriela Cavalheiro, Tom James, Rebecca Gowland, Stephen Mileson, John Schofield, Karen Stöber, and Audrey Thorstad for their helpful comments on drafts of this chapter.

References Cited

Blake, E. 2004 'Space, spatiality, and archaeology', in L. Meskell and R. W. Preucel (eds), *A companion to social archaeology*, Blackwell, Oxford, 230–54

Brown, F. E. 1990 'Comment on Chapman: some cautionary notes on the application of spatial measures to prehistoric settlements', in R. Samson (ed.), *The social archaeology of houses*, Edinburgh University Press, Edinburgh, 93–109

Busot, A. 2012 *Clergy and gender in medieval England: a bioarchaeological approach*, University of Miami Scholarly Repository Open Access Theses

Bussell, D. A. and McNamara, J. M. 2013 'Barking Abbey: a GIS map of a medieval nunnery', *Peregrinations: Journal of Medieval Art and Architecture* 4(2), 173–89

Cavalheiro, G. 2015 *'I ne have none kines thinge': secular possessions in thirteenth-century insular romance and law*, unpublished PhD in English/ Medieval Studies, King's College London

Coulson, C. 1996 'The state of research: cultural realities and reappraisals in English castle-study', *Journal of Medieval History* 22(2), 171–208

Creighton, O. H. 2009 'Castle studies and the European medieval landscape: traditions, trends and future research directions', *Landscape History* 30(2), 5–20

Creighton, O. H. 2011 'Seeing and believing: looking out on medieval castle landscapes', *Concilium Medii Aevi* 14, 79–91

Deetz, J. 1977 *In small things forgotten: an archaeology of early American life*, Anchor Books, New York

Dobson, B. 2005 'The English vicars choral: an introduction', in R. Hall and D. Stocker (eds), *Vicars Choral in English cathedrals. Cantate domino: history, architecture and archaeology*, Oxbow, Oxford, 1–10

Dowling, A. 2014 *Landscape, politics, and identity: Countess Mahaut of Artois' natural resource management, c.1302–29*, unpublished PhD thesis, University of California, Santa Barbara

Dyer, C. 2013 'Living in peasant houses in late medieval England', *Vernacular Architecture* 44, 19–27

Fairclough, G. 1992 'Meaningful constructions: spatial and functional analysis of medieval buildings', *Antiquity* 66, 348–66

Faulkner, P. 1958 'Domestic planning from the twelfth to the fourteenth century', *The Archaeological Journal* 115, 150–83

Faulkner, P. 1963 'Castle-planning in the fourteenth century', *The Archaeological Journal* 120, 215–35

Flather, A. 2011 *Gender and space in early Modern England*, Boydell, Woodbridge

French, K. L. 2008 *The good women of the parish: gender and religion after the Black Death*, University of Pennsylvania Press, Philadelphia

Gerrard, C. M. 2003 *Medieval archaeology: understanding traditions and contemporary approaches*, Routledge, London

Gilchrist, R. 1994 *Gender and material culture: the archaeology of religious women*, Routledge, London
Gilchrist, R. 1995 *Contemplation and action: the other monasticism*, Leicester University Press, Leicester
Gilchrist, R. 1999 *Gender and archaeology: contesting the past*, Routledge, London
Gilchrist, R. 2012 *Medieval life: archaeology and the life course*, The Boydell Press, Woodbridge
Gilchrist, R. and Sloane, B. 2005 *Requiem: the medieval monastic cemetery in Britain*, Museum of London Archaeology Service, London
Giles, K. 2007 'Seeing and believing: visuality and space in pre-modern England', *World Archaeology* 39(1), 105–21
Glassie, H. 1975 *Folk housing in Middle Virginia: a structural analysis of historic artifacts*, University of Tennessee Press, Knoxville
Goldberg, P. J. P. 2008 'The fashioning of bourgeois domesticity in later medieval England: a material culture perspective', in M. Kowaleski and P. J. P. Goldberg (eds), *Medieval domesticity: home, housing and household in medieval England*, Cambridge University Press, Cambridge, 124–44
Goldberg, P. J. P. 2011 'Space and gender in the later medieval English house', *Viator* 42(2), 205–32
Graves, C. P. 1989 'Social space in the English medieval parish church', *Economy and Society* 18, 297–322
Graves, C. P. 2007 'Sensing and believing: exploring worlds of difference in pre-modern England: a contribution to the debate opened by Kate Giles', *World Archaeology* 39(4), 515–31
Grenville, J. 2008 'Urban and rural houses and households in the late Middle Ages: a case study from Yorkshire', in M. Kowaleski and P. J. P. Goldberg (eds), *Medieval domesticity: home, housing and household in medieval England*, Cambridge University Press, Cambridge, 92–123
Griffin, T. 2008 *Belper Parks Project report*, Friends of Belper Park, Belper
Hall, R. 2005 'Preface and acknowledgements', in R. Hall and D. Stocker (eds), *Vicars Choral in English cathedrals. Cantate domino: history, architecture and archaeology*, Oxbow, Oxford, vii–viii
Hall, R. and Stocker, D. (eds) 2005 *Vicars Choral in English cathedrals. Cantate domino: history, architecture and archaeology*, Oxbow, Oxford
Hillier, B. and Hanson, J. 1984 *The social logic of space*, Cambridge University Press, Cambridge
Jaritz, G. 2006 'Architecture, domestic', in M. Schaus (ed.), *Women and gender in medieval Europe: an encyclopeadia*, Routledge, New York, 28–30
Johnson, M. H. 1990 'The Englishman's home and its study', in R. Samson (ed.), *The social archaeology of houses*, Edinburgh University Press, Edinburgh, 245–58
Johnson, M. H. 1993 *Housing culture: traditional architecture in an English landscape*, University College London Press, London
Kowaleski, M. and Goldberg, P. J. P. (eds), 2008 *Medieval domesticity: home, housing and household in medieval England*, Cambridge University Press, Cambridge
Kwan, M.-P. 2002 'Feminist visualization: re-envisioning GIS as a method in feminist geographic research', *Annals of the Association of American Geographers* 92(4), 645–61
Mayes, P. 2002 *Excavations at a Templar preceptory: South Witham, Lincolnshire, 1965–67*, The Society for Medieval Archaeology Monograph 19, Leeds
McLoughlin, S. A. 2011 *Gender and transgression in the late medieval English household*, unpublished PhD thesis, University of York
Mileson, S. A. 2009 *Parks in medieval England*, Oxford University Press, Oxford

Mileson, S. A. 2015 'People and houses in south Oxfordshire, 1300–1650', *Vernacular Architecture* 46, 8–25

Milledge Nelson, S. (ed.) 2006 *Handbook of gender in archaeology*, Altamira Press, Walnut Creek

Morgan, H. 2014 'Between the sheets: reading beds and chambers in late medieval England', unpublished PhD thesis, University of York

Müller, A. 2015 'Symbolic meanings of space in female monastic tradition', in J. Burton and K. Stöber (eds), *Women in the medieval monastic world*, Brepols, Turnhout, 299–325

Neil, N., Baldwin, S., and Crosby, A. 2004 *The medieval deer parks of Lathom, Lancashire*, Lathom Park Trust, Lathom

O'Keefe, T. 2001 'Concepts of "castle" and the construction of identity in medieval and post-medieval Ireland', *Irish Geography* 34(1), 69–88

Oliva, M. 2008 'Nuns at home: the domesticity of sacred space', in M. Kowaleski and P. J. P. Goldberg (eds), *Medieval domesticity: home, housing and household in medieval England*, Cambridge University Press, Cambridge, 145–61

Orme, N. 2010 *The Victoria History of the Counties of England: a history of the county of Cornwall, vol. II, religious history to 1560*, Boydell and Brewer, Woodbridge

Preucel, R. W. and Meskell, L. 2004 'Places', in R. W. Preucel and L. Meskel (eds), *A companion to social archaeology*, Blackwell, Oxford, 215–29

Rees Jones, S. 2003 'Women's influence on the design of urban homes', in M. C. Erler and M. Kowaleski (eds), *Gendering the master narrative: women and power in the Middle Ages*, New York, Cornell University Press, 190–211

Riddy, F. 2008 '"Burgeis" domesticity in late-medieval England', in M. Kowaleski and P. J. P. Goldberg (eds), *Medieval domesticity: home, housing and household in medieval England*, Cambridge University Press, Cambridge, 14–36

Richardson, A. 2003 'Gender and space in English royal palaces *c*.1160–*c*.1547: a study in access analysis and imagery', *Medieval Archaeology* 47, 131–65

Richardson, A. 2012 '"Riding like Alexander, hunting like Diana": gendered aspects of the medieval hunt and its landscape settings in England and France', *Gender and History* 24(2), 253–70

Samson, R. (ed.) 1990 *The social archaeology of houses*, Edinburgh University Press, Edinburgh

Schofield, J. 1994 'Social perceptions of space in medieval Tudor and London houses', in M. Locock (ed.), *Meaningful architecture: social interpretations of buildings*, Aldershot, Ashgate, 188–206

Schofield, J. 1995 *Medieval London houses*, Yale University Press, London

Sterrett, J. and Thomas, P. (eds) 2011 *Sacred text, sacred space: architectural, spiritual and literary convergences in England and Wales*, Brill, Leiden

Sykes, N. J. 2009 'Animals: the bones of medieval society', in R. Gilchrist and A. Reynolds (eds), *Reflections: 50 years of Medieval Archaeology 1957–2007*, The Society for Medieval Archaeology Monograph 30, Leeds, 347–62

Thorstad, A. 2015 *Living in an early Tudor castle: households, display, and space, 1485–1547*, unpublished PhD thesis, University of Leeds

Tibbets Schulenburg, J. 2006 'Space, sacred: and gender', in M. Schaus (ed.), *Women and gender in medieval Europe: an encyclopeadia*, Routledge, New York, 771–3

Wilkie, L. A. and Hayes, K. H. 2006 'Engendered and feminist archaeologies of the recent and documented pasts', *Journal of Archaeological Research* 14, 243–64

CHAPTER 51

HEALTH AND WELL-BEING

The Contribution of the Study of Human Remains to Understanding the Late Medieval Period in Britain

CHARLOTTE A. ROBERTS, JELENA BEKVALAC, AND REBECCA REDFERN

THERE has long been an interest in medieval bodies in Britain. However, early exhumations intended to recover the relics of saints were usually focused on 'the spiritual rather than the academic value of the dead' (Gilchrist and Sloane 2005, 8–11) and it was not until the eighteenth century that fuller records of tomb excavations started to be kept. Edward I, who died and was buried in Westminster Abbey in 1307, was exhumed in 1774; apart from the good preservation of his embalmed body being noted, his height was also measured (Prestwich 1997). Arguably, this curiosity about finding and examining famous people is still with us today (Richard III: Buckley et al. 2013) but in every other respect times have changed. In the 1950s and 1960s more detailed recording started to be performed on large cemeteries (Gilchrist and Sloane 2005, 11) and over the last twenty-five years bioarchaeology in Britain has seen an exponential increase in excavation, analysis, and contextually related interpretation of individual skeletons and larger populations (Roberts 2012). Bioarchaeologists can now be found both in universities and on developer-led excavations across Britain and the first national organization to represent people working in the field was founded in 1998: the British Association of Biological Anthropology and Osteoarchaeology (BABAO). While bioarchaeologists analyse skeletal remains to access demographic information, and normal variation via measurements, they also explore evidence for disease (palaeopathology) to consider morbidity (illness) and mortality (death).

THE DATASET FOR LATER MEDIEVAL HUMAN REMAINS

Late medieval burial was mainly the Christian rite of a supine, head to the west, extended inhumation in a cemetery (e.g. Waldron 2007), usually with a shroud and no grave goods

FIGURE 51.1 A late medieval skeleton in a grave prior to excavation: Hull Magistrates Court site
(© Dave Evans)

(Figure 51.1). However, crosses, staves, chalices and pattens, bullae, pilgrim badges, jewelry, coins, spindle-whorls, and medical items have all been found with burials (Gilchrist and Sloane 2005, 88–106). Specific funerary contexts include parish churchyards, battlegrounds (Fiorato et al. 2001; see Chapter 26 in this *Handbook*), abbeys, friaries, monasteries and priories (e.g. Stones 1989), hospitals (Magilton et al. 2008), church crypts (e.g. Roberts 1984), and plague burials (Grainger et al. 2008). In some cases higher status may be identified, for example for intramural burials and burials in lead coffins. In Britain there have probably been more late medieval human remains excavated and analysed than for any other period, although sites tend to be concentrated in England and particularly reflect the large quantity of urban developer-led excavations. Of the 34,797 individuals considered for a study of health and disease (palaeopathology), just less than 50 per cent (16,327 from sixty-three sites) were of late medieval date, compared to other periods (Roberts and Cox 2003, 28). While rural assemblages are far fewer in number, working in historical periods has many compensations, not least the wealth of historical data that can be used to contextualize the remains.

Late Medieval Health and Well-Being

Contextualizing evidence for health and well-being, as seen in skeletal remains, is imperative to understand the patterns seen in the past, and hence the following sections where evidence for disease is integrated with what is known about the environment in which people lived. Until *c.*1300 medieval towns developed and grew and a generally warm climate contributed to effective agricultural production to feed the population. When a cooler climate impacted food production, famines ensued, however, and the Black Death 'arrived' in the fourteenth century; this combination of circumstances affected the very survival of medieval populations (Roberts and Cox 2003, 225). Life expectancy was low, at least according to documentary records (Dyer 1989, 182). However, there are diseases seen in skeletal remains which are often consistent with old age, such as osteoporosis and tumours (e.g. Anderson 1992; Mays 1996), and joint disease is ubiquitous and usually associated with ageing. It should also be noted that age estimation of adult skeletons into the higher age categories is challenging. For example, Molleson and Cox (1993) found that methods of age estimation overestimated young adults buried in an eighteenth-/nineteenth-century site in London, and underestimated older adults by as much as 30 years (see also Milner et al. 2008 for suggested solutions to this 'methodological problem'). In the later fourteenth and fifteenth centuries, wet, cool summers and harsh winters prevailed (Lamb 1995), at the same time as people deserted rural areas to find a 'better life' in towns and cities. Nevertheless, this is a period when trade networks developed, ports were busy with outgoing and incoming trade (and disease), and people were much more mobile, especially moving from rural to urban situations. For example, it has been suggested that women in particular migrated to nearby York from the rural settlement of Wharram Percy in North Yorkshire (Mays et al. 2007, 92). This conclusion was based on a comparison of the sex ratio at this site (male>female) with that of St Helen-on-the-Walls, York (female>male). This mobility, albeit not yet much explored in late medieval contexts using isotopic analysis, potentially enabled diseases such as those caused by infectious agents to be transmitted from person to person (e.g. see Roberts et al. 2013).

Rural houses tended to be more spaced out in their settlements, but urban housing was tightly packed together, with many people sharing water supplies, latrines, and cess pits; often, poor families lived in one room with no facilities. Wattle and daub walls, sometimes with stone lower courses, earthen floors, thatched roofs, and central hearths, characterized their homes. Consequently, diseases associated with high population density were on the rise, such as tuberculosis (TB) (e.g. see Stroud and Kemp 1993 for York; Roberts and Buikstra 2003, Table 3.8 for a summary of late medieval TB in Britain), leprosy (Rawcliffe 2006; Roberts 2002), and syphilis (Roberts 1994). All these infections have been recorded from late medieval sites across Britain, including Scotland where all three were evident at Whithorn, a monastic site located in Dumfries and Galloway (Cardy 1997). Beyond basic diagnosis of infectious disease, ancient DNA (aDNA) analysis has provided more nuanced data on leprosy and TB, mostly to confirm diagnoses (e.g. Taylor et al. 1999). Houses also accommodated animals and were used concurrently for small-scale industry (e.g. see Beresford and Hurst 1990 for Wharram Percy). General environmental pollution, including of the air and water, was a common feature of late medieval life (Keene 1983; Lewis et al. 1995). Pollution may also have led to tumours, as it does today (Binachon et al. 2014). While tumours are rarely found in skeletal remains, six people buried in the Jewish cemetery of Jewbury, York, were identified with possible tumours, albeit benign (Lilley et al. 1994), and at Fishergate, also in York, many more people had evidence for tumours (Stroud and Kemp 1993). If 'pollution' was the cause, as suggested for today, this correlates well with the evidence for poor air quality (sinusitis) found in late medieval people (Roberts 2007).

Air and water pollution did lead to various initiatives to clean up urban environments (Rawcliffe 2013, 175), and there is evidence of organized waste removal, gutters, wells, aqueducts, water pipes, latrines, drains, and cess pits (see Chapter 45). Nevertheless, industry potentially caused health problems, for example zoonoses from tanning, respiratory disease from the cloth-making industry, injuries, and lead poisoning (e.g. see Budd et al. 2004). Working indoors for long periods in urban contexts or living in an environment with polluted air may have led to vitamin D deficiency (rickets) due to lack of exposure to UV light (needed to prevent 'weak' bones); there is some evidence for this condition in skeletal remains in the medieval period, even in a rural community, such as Wharram Percy, where being outdoors and exposed to good air quality and sunlight would be expected (Ortner and Mays 1998). The study of particular social groups in this period, for example monastic communities, has also shown that health and dietary patterns could differ. Skeletal data, however, do not support the suggested direct association between monastic life and the development of DISH (Rogers and Waldron 2001). Diffuse idiopathic skeletal hyperostosis is today associated with older males, Type 2 diabetes, obesity (Resnick 1995, 2081), and a 'rich' diet. Overall, it has now been found that people with DISH in late medieval populations had a reduced mortality risk, a lower disease burden, and lived longer (DeWitte et al. 2013; Mays 2006). In addition, preliminary data from stable dietary isotope analysis has shown that DISH may be related to a higher protein diet (Spencer 2008). However, the dietary isotopic differences of those with and without DISH were also seen in males, females, monastic, non-monastic, and high- and low-status people. On this basis, the suggestion that the disease is a monastic phenomenon, and one indicative of high status, is not supported.

Although diet became more varied in this period as trade networks and markets grew, most people relied on bread, porridge, and ale as staples, along with vegetables and eggs; the inclusion of meat and fish in the diet was reliant on the ability to pay. Wild animals and gathered fruits and nuts may have supplemented some people's daily diet, while others would grow vegetables and fruit. Stable isotope analysis suggests that there may have been quite a diverse range of diets, even in one location, perhaps reflecting social differentiation (Müldner and Richards 2007). However, there have been fewer isotopic studies of diet for this period than others, and there has also been a focus on northern England (Burt 2013; Fuller et al. 2003; Mays 1997; Mays et al. 2002; Müldner and Richards 2005, 2007; Richards et al. 2002; Richards et al. 2006; Spencer 2008). For example, Mays (1997) found variations in the marine component of diets in this region. While there is little evidence of *specific* dietary deficiency in late medieval skeletons, there is widespread evidence of enamel defects—this most likely suggests a dietary deficiency of some sort during childhood (or disease). Skeletons from twenty-eight cemetery sites in Britain revealed an overall average rate of 35 per cent of individuals affected (Roberts and Cox 2003, 264). Carious teeth, likely reflecting a combination of carbohydrate consumption (especially the sugar sucrose), a lack of fluoride in water and food, and poor (or no) oral hygiene, were common: forty-one sites studied produced a rate of c.50 per cent of individuals affected. When focusing on the number of teeth affected the mean rate was 5.5 per cent, with a range of 1–40 per cent. Caries rates in Scotland were generally lower for this period than in England (Lunt and Watt 1997, 573). Linked to this finding, however, virtually all people buried at the Scottish site of Whithorn had dental calculus, contrasting with nearly 60 per cent of people from twenty-seven sites documented by Roberts and Cox (2003, Table 5.18); these data suggest poor oral hygiene but also a diet high in protein, which leads to a high pH in the mouth (Lieverse 1999). More recent work has focused on the effects of dental disease on mortality, finding earlier death in those with caries and periodontal disease in late medieval London (DeWitte and Bekvalac 2010), and people with enamel defects in Canterbury (Miszkieicz 2015). This confirms the link, also identified in populations today, between dental disease and other health problems later in life (e.g. Kalladka et al. 2014)—this is explained through the developmental origins hypothesis (Barker 1994).

Overall, many health problems in this period were related to socio-economic status and general living conditions characterized by overcrowded urban environments; adult stature also declined for both men and women when compared to populations living a rural existence in the early medieval period (Roberts and Cox 2003, 396). However, provisions for addressing public health problems in towns are evident (Rawcliffe 2013), as noted above, and care and treatment are apparent in both documentary and archaeological records. For example, hospitals and practitioners were present, and there is evidence in skeletons for specific treatments such as trepanations and amputations (Roberts and Cox 2003, 251–2; and see Chapter 52 in this *Handbook*). Having now described and discussed the health of late medieval people in Britain, a focus on one site is now explored.

THE LARGEST EXCAVATED AND WELL-STUDIED LATE MEDIEVAL CEMETERY SITE

The Augustinian institution of St Mary Spital (1197–1539) was located on the outskirts of the City of London and became the largest hospital in medieval England (Connell et al. 2012; Thomas et al. 1997). In 1341 its responsibilities were described as: 'to receive and entertain pilgrims and the infirm who resorted hither until they were healed, and pregnant women ... and also to maintain the children of women who died there in childbirth until the age of seven' (*CCR 1339*, 600). Located in open space outside the City walls, the hospital had the space to accommodate the mass burials of thousands of people who died from famine (Connell et al. 2012, 229); indeed, particular famine years that affected London do correlate with mass burial at this site, along with indicators of stress in recovered skeletal remains. Four main phases of burial were identified: 1120–1200 AD (Phase 14), 1200–1250 (Ph 15), 1250–1400 (Ph 16), and 1400–1439 (Ph 17), and four burial types (A: single graves, B: a single horizontal layer of bodies comprised of two/three in a row, C: multiple burials stacked on top of each other, and D: multi-layered burials, of between eight and forty-five, comprising a number of horizontal rows on top of each other in a single grave cut). The main areas of the cemetery revealed burials of 10,516 individuals, with a total of 5,387 individuals being recorded of the total excavated. Among skeletons of both sexes and all ages, there were females who had died during pregnancy or childbirth, individuals with evidence for surgery (e.g. amputation), and those who likely required care. Being a hospital site, these particular burials correlate well with what might be expected of its function. Phases 15 and 16 comprised 78 per cent (4225) of the skeletons recorded (AD 1200–1400).

No cemetery site anywhere in the world has produced such a large sample as St Mary Spital that has subsequently undergone such a detailed contextually based skeletal analysis. It is extremely rare even to excavate over a thousand burials from late medieval cemeteries, and it was estimated that there could be as many as eighteen thousand burials there in all. Unlike most late medieval sites where only a broad time span for the cemetery is given (e.g. twelfth to sixteenth centuries AD), Bayesian C^{14} dating at St Mary Spital established four phases of use, the majority of people being interred either in single graves or as multiple burials. This phasing not only enabled bioarchaeologists to consider mortality and morbidity changes over the time-span of the cemetery, but also over shorter time ranges. This could then be linked to temporal changes in the population's socio-cultural environment, and specific historical 'events', such as famines and deteriorations in climate or living conditions. Few cemeteries associated with hospitals have been excavated in Britain, even though several hundred late medieval hospitals were founded (Orme and Webster 1995), and therefore understanding the health problems experienced by people buried at St Mary Spital provided a window on medieval care and compassion (see Chapters 47 and 52).

Analysis of the burials has revealed a very detailed understanding of the lives of the people buried there. For example, the mass pits (D burials), believed to represent people who died over a short space of time, were associated with historically documented episodes of famine in London and its environs during the twelfth and thirteenth century (Ph 14 and 15). This also appeared to coincide with reduced stature for both sexes in Ph 14, and for males in Ph 15 (Figure 51.2), and the highest rates for enamel defects

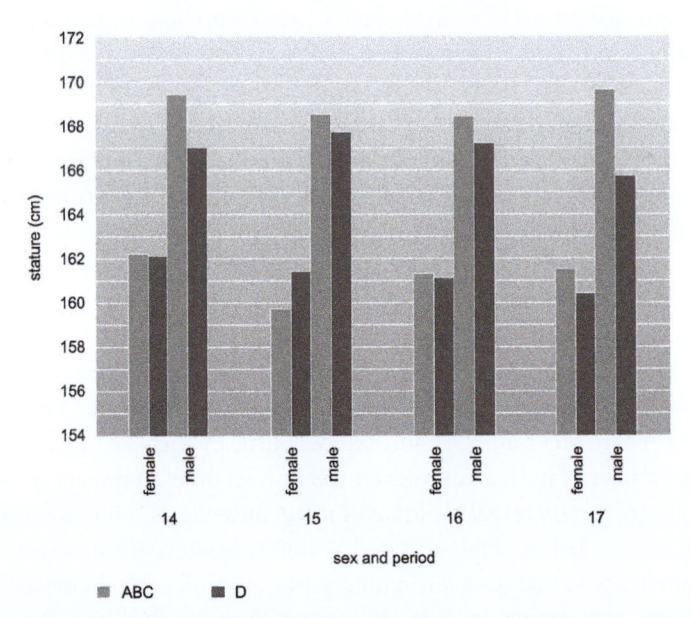

FIGURE 51.2 Stature trends over the four phases (Ph 14–17) of burials at the site of the hospital and priory of St Mary Spital (with permission of the Museum of London)

(© MOLA)

(hypoplasia) in the mass burials, most likely indicating dietary deficiency during the growth of the teeth or a childhood disease (e.g. Hillson 1996, 165–77). Nevertheless, evidence for metabolic diseases relating to dietary deficiency, such as scurvy (Vitamin C deficiency) was rare; perhaps people were dying from famine before the bone changes had a chance to develop. Equally surprising was the lack of evidence for Vitamin D deficiency, rickets being one condition that might have been anticipated in the polluted London environment.

'Specific infections', in other words, those whose causative organism can be identified based on the skeletal damage, were also lower in frequency than would be expected, particularly leprosy and TB. Bone changes in TB can occur in untreated people today at a rate of 3–5 per cent but this is much higher than that seen at St Mary Spital (e.g. sixty-four people with TB in their spine). Both infections are transmitted when exhaled droplets containing the bacteria from the lungs of one sufferer are inhaled by another individual. TB is also contracted by ingesting meat or milk from infected animals or being exposed to other products of infected animals, for example through particular occupations such as tanning. It is known that people in London at that time were living at high population density and being exposed to animals, both of which would have increased the chance of TB thriving. Indeed, the numbers affected increased in AD 1200–1400. However, there were only two people affected by leprosy, one each being buried during Ph 16 and 17. This is surprising, considering how common leprosy was supposed to be in the late medieval period (Rawcliffe 2006), but a charter associated with this site indicates that people with leprosy were excluded from the hospital and priory (Thomas et al. 1997). Finally, treponemal disease (treponematosis/'syphilis') was recorded in twenty-five skeletons, across Ph 15–17, both pre- and post- the late fifteenth century. The number of people affected increased over time, and included a 10–11 year old child born with (congenital) syphilis. The most obvious rise in the prevalence of the disease in the final period at St Mary Spital (*c*.1400–1539) may reflect documentary reports of a European epidemic from the late fifteenth century (Walker et al. 2015). This type of infection, globally ubiquitous today, likely bears witness to the increased trade, mobility, and contact occurring between London and the rest of Europe.

The Limitations of Skeletal Data

While much has been learnt about health in the late medieval period by analysing human skeletal remains from a variety of different contexts, there are a number of limitations to the data; many are discussed by Wood et al. (1992). The key areas for consideration are:

- Preservation affects the quality and quantity of data that can be recorded, e.g. compare the well-preserved remains from St Mary Spital, London (Connell et al. 2012) versus the poorly preserved remains from Ysgol Twm o'r Nant, Denbigh, Wales (Boocock and Roberts 1994);

- It can never be known how representative of the original living population the skeletal sample analyzed is, or what proportion of the funerary context has been excavated, especially in urban situations where excavation is restricted (Waldron 1994, 13); a good example is that of the site of St Helen-on-the-Walls, York, where parts of the cemetery were not excavated (Dawes and Magilton 1980);
- Disease can only affect the skeleton in a limited number of ways, bone formation and destruction, and therefore the same/similar bone changes can be seen in different diseases. It is therefore essential that distribution patterns of lesions are recorded (making good preservation important for diagnosis), and differential diagnoses considered, all related to what is known clinically about how different diseases affect the skeleton. For example, to diagnose the often-cited monastic related condition, DISH, the spinal changes alongside the non-spinal bone changes are essential for a diagnosis (Rogers and Waldron 1995, 54; 2001);
- A very small proportion of diseases affect the skeleton, but aDNA analysis is helping identify the soft tissue diseases that do not affect either bones or teeth (e.g. Schuenemann et al. 2011: late medieval plague in London);
- aDNA analysis relies on the survival of the DNA, and the use of appropriate protocols; some environmental contexts do not preserve DNA well, including late medieval cemeteries (e.g. Müller et al. 2014a; 2014b);
- An even smaller proportion of people's skeletons is affected for any one disease (e.g. leprosy: 3–5 per cent); again, aDNA analysis may provide more accurate prevalence rates where the disease is not affecting the skeleton at the time of death;
- Usually evidence of disease is chronic and healed, indicating the person's immune system was strong enough to prevent the person succumbing and dying from the disease;
- Identifying a disease that was in its acute stages, which likely killed the person with no bone changes evident at death, is not possible (again aDNA analysis can help identify these diseases);
- It is not possible to estimate sex of non-adult skeletons, or accurately age adult skeletons, thus compromising any exploration of the impact of disease on mortality for different sexes and ages; methods for ageing adults are developing (e.g. Boldsen et al. 2002; see Gowland and Chamberlain 2005 on a fourteenth century plague cemetery). Sex estimation can also be attempted using aDNA analysis, and has been undertaken in a late medieval context (see Cunha et al. 2000; and also Brown and Brown 2011, 151–65 for an overview);
- Comparison of data can be difficult because not all bioarchaeologists use the same methods of recording (Roberts and Cox 2003, 398–401), but there are now standards for data recording (Brickley and McKinley 2004);
- Individual variations in risk for disease are not generally known for the past, although susceptibility and resistance genes are now being identified for many diseases (e.g. Ozaki et al. 2016). However, while studying modern DNA samples, Barnes et al. (2011) considered an allele (variant form of a gene) associated with natural resistance to diseases such as TB. They suggested that infectious disease

became an increasingly important cause of death after the advent of urbanization (for example, in late medieval Britain), highlighting population density as a key determinant of human health and the genetic structure of populations. It is clear that aDNA analysis in the future will help to identify risk for disease in late medieval contexts.

Discussion

In discussing bioarchaeological work in the late medieval period, there are a number of areas that need attention, especially for readers unfamiliar with the field.

Training and Standards

The training and professional development of bioarchaeologists, and their presence from excavation through to archive, has meant that more datasets are produced and made available than ever before. Since establishing formal university masters courses in bioarchaeology from 1990 onwards, and the foundation of BABAO in 1998, the community of bioarchaeologists has grown and developed, and often leads the way in multi-disciplinary research projects. A key advance and integral for the field was establishing standards for recording. The driving force for this came from repatriation and reburial debates and laws in North America in the 1980s (Rose et al. 1996; Roberts 2009, 34–7), which led to the implementation of methods for recording native American skeletons should they be repatriated to their native communities and reburied (Buikstra and Ubelaker 1994); these were later followed by the standards for Britain (Brickley and McKinley, 2004). One other development in Britain is related to the excavation, retention and sometimes reburial of human remains which, at times, has provoked strong reactions (for example when the late medieval Jewish cemetery at York was excavated: Lilley et al. 1994). Ultimately, this has led to legislation, guidance, ethical codes, and policies formulated for dealing with excavation, analysis, curation, and display of human remains (e.g. APABE;[1] BABAO;[2] DCMS 2005; Giesen 2013; Human Tissue Act 2004;[3] Ministry of Justice 2008; Museum of London;[4] Redmond-Cooper 2015). It has also made bioarchaeologists realize that precise recording of human remains is essential should remains be reburied in the future.

---

[1] http://www.archaeologyuk.org/apabe/.
[2] http://www.babao.org.uk/index/ethics-and-standards.
[3] http://www.legislation.gov.uk/ukpga/2004/30.
[4] https://www.museumoflondon.org.uk/about-us/corporate-information/policies.

Advances in Analytical Techniques

Another area which deserves highlighting is the many recent advances in technology and innovations in methodology in this field. Among the biomolecular studies which target stable isotope ratios (revealing diet and mobility) and aDNA (mainly disease diagnosis) are examples of research from the late medieval period including those by Müldner and Richards (2007; diet at Fishergate, York), Roberts et al. (2013) (Figure 51.3), and Taylor et al. (2000; confirmation of leprosy in Orkney, Scotland). The application of imaging techniques also now enables researchers to 'look inside' the bones to see what cannot be accessed macroscopically. A late medieval example of this kind of analysis can be seen in the assessment of the state of fracture healing in people buried at St Helen-on-the-Walls cemetery, York (Grauer and Roberts 1996). Techniques of this kind also include micro- and macro-CT (computed tomography), where 'image slices' are taken through the 'tissue' of interest. Histological analyses examine the microstructure of sections of bones and teeth; this can help with diagnosis of disease by comparing ancient appearances with those of known diseases. An example of this type of analysis from late medieval England is a confirmed diagnosis of Paget's disease (likely caused by a viral infection) in a skeleton from late medieval Ipswich (Mays and Turner-Walker 1999).

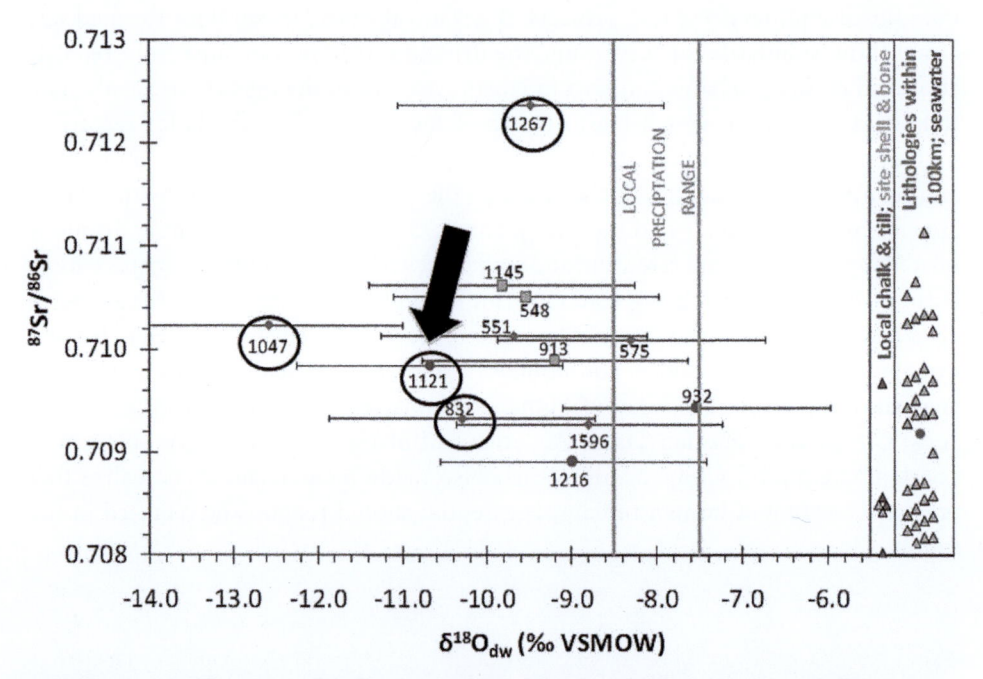

FIGURE 51.3 Stable isotope plot showing mobility histories of skeletons with evidence of treponemal disease buried at the site of Hull Magistrates Court; the circled skeleton numbers are the non-locals and the arrow signifies the only person of the four non-locals with treponemal disease in their skeleton

Contextualizing Data

In bioarchaeology the significance of contextual information should always be emphasized and a good example to demonstrate this point is the recent aDNA research conducted on individuals from the 1986 excavations at the Royal Mint, London, by the Museum of London Archaeological Services. These excavations revealed a Black Death catastrophic cemetery (East Smithfield) and the remnants of the cemetery of St Mary Graces Abbey (Grainger et al. 2008; Grainger and Phillpotts 2011). The Black Death caused the demise of vast numbers of people in the fourteenth century (Ziegler 1991), and parish churches were eventually unable to cope with burying all of their dead. In London other locations for burials had to be found to deal with the high numbers of people dying. The Black Death does not leave macroscopically discernible traces in bones or teeth so distinguishing individuals who may have died as a consequence of the disease is not possible if they were buried in the same manner as all the other burials. The causative agent of the disease resulting in so many deaths has long been debated, and with the development in aDNA techniques this cemetery provided the opportunity to answer this question. The contextual evidence from the excavations at East Smithfield cemetery corroborated that the burials, single inhumations and mass burial trenches, had taken place during 1348–51 in an emergency burial. The DNA data from these particular individuals proved that the organism causing the plague was the bacterium *Yersinia pestis*. Consequently, this was the first ancient disease genome to be reconstructed (Bos et al. 2011; 2012; Schuenemann et al. 2011).

Given the wealth of archaeological data from late medieval settlement sites, and evidence for living conditions, hygiene, work, diet and economy, and trade, contact, and conflict, it is now becoming possible to provide a nuanced view of how people's environments impacted their health and longevity. For example, recent research on leprosy in late medieval England is starting to change our views about the treatment of people with this infectious disease. By focusing on historical data (Rawcliffe 2006), and skeletal evidence within its funerary context (Roberts 2002), ideas about whether people were stigmatized and ostracized are rapidly altering. Exploring how people with evidence of leprosy in their skeletons were treated at death from a range of late medieval sites in England has suggested that people were buried 'normally' for the time period and geographical location. While there have been leprosy hospital cemeteries excavated in England, these are rare. The majority of skeletons with leprous bone changes have often been found in parish church cemeteries, or even buried at non-leprosy hospital sites. These findings are contrary to previous assumptions gleaned from historical data that have come down to us from original interpretations of leprosy in the Bible (Demaitre 2007; Rawcliffe 2006). One study, focusing on a single leprosy hospital cemetery at Chichester, Sussex (Magilton et al. 2008) explored the frequency of fractures in people buried there (Judd and Roberts 1998). Comparing fracture frequencies at this site with other contemporary sites in Scotland (Whithorn), Gloucester (Blackfriars), and York (St Helen-on-the-Walls) showed that fracture rates were much higher. While men from all sites had higher rates, at Chichester the difference was much higher compared to women. Understanding the effect of leprosy on the sensory nerves, leading to lack of feeling in the hands and feet, knowing that leprosy can affect sight, and that men with leprosy can develop osteoporosis (loss of bone mass, predisposing them to fractures), provides important insights into possible causes for the fractures.

Future Developments

There are three main areas for future development in the field of health and well-being in bioarchaeology. Firstly, palaeopathology complements very well the emerging discipline of evolutionary medicine (Nesse and Williams 1994) and, with the increasing use of aDNA analysis to track the origin and evolution of disease in our ancestors, the future is particularly bright for obtaining more nuanced understanding of disease today. For example, learning more about the history of appearance of different strains of infectious disease, and resistance and susceptibility genes through aDNA data, may help populations plan for their future health; so much more is now known about disease through modern pathogen genomics that there is a good base with which to compare ancient data (e.g. Sintchenko and Holmes 2015). There has already been research into the Black Death and TB in late medieval England (Bos et al. 2011; Müller et al. 2014b). For example, the latter study found a different strain of TB in a person buried at a site in Leicester when compared to a contemporary site in eastern Scotland. Secondly, there is much more to explore in relation to the impact of forced and free migration on health in the past (Richards and Montgomery 2012). Integrated studies of palaeopathology and mobility stable isotope data are beginning to emerge. For example, Roberts et al. (2013) found evidence that people with skeletal treponematosis buried in late medieval Hull on the east coast of England, had been born and raised away from Hull (potentially bringing their infection with them). This sort of research complements and extends what is known about the impact of mobility of people on health today.[5] However, these techniques should not be seen as 'silver bullets' to understanding the past and should be used appropriately because they are destructive in nature. Question-driven approaches are imperative. Thirdly, developing research in palaeopathology that explores the developmental origins hypothesis (Barker 2004) provides a window on early human development in the past and how problems in early life may predispose individuals to later health problems (e.g. Miszkieicz 2015 on enamel defects in early life affecting adult mortality rates in late medieval Canterbury).

Conclusion

The late medieval period was a time of considerable change and those living through it were faced with many challenges and catastrophic events that had a fundamental effect upon their lives. The implications of these were felt throughout the population and for

---

[5] http://www.who.int/hac/techguidance/health_of_migrants/en/.

generations afterwards. Bioarchaeological research for the period has achieved a great deal in learning about the health and well-being of these people at a population level, and with advances in aDNA at a genetic level. Good frameworks and strategies have been formulated and assist bioarchaeologists in targeting areas of further interest for future studies into the lives of those who lived in late medieval Britain.

REFERENCES CITED

Anderson, T. 1992 'An example of meningiomatous hyperostosis from medieval Rochester', *Medical History* 36, 207–13

Barker, D. J. P. 1994 'The fetal origins of adult disease', *Proceedings of the Royal Society B, Biological Sciences* 262: 37–43.

Barker, D. J. P. 2004 'The developmental origins of well-being', *Philosophical Transactions of the Royal Society of London B* 359, 1359–66

Barnes, I., Duda, A., Pybus, O. G., and Thomas, M. G. 2011 'Ancient urbanization predicts genetic resistance to tuberculosis', *Evolution* 65, 842–8

Beresford, M. and Hurst J. G. 1990 *Book of Wharram Percy: deserted medieval village*, Batsford, London

Binachon, B., Dossus, L., Danjou, A. M., Clavel-Chapelon, F., and Fervers, B. 2014 'Life in urban areas and breast cancer risk in the French E3N cohort', *European Journal of Epidemiology* 29, 743–51

Boldsen, J. W., Milner, G. R., Konigsberg, L. W., and Wood, J. R. 2002 'Transition analysis: a new method for estimating age-indicator methods', in R. D. Hoppa and J. W. Vaupel (eds), *Palaeodemography: age distributions from skeletal samples*, Cambridge University Press, Cambridge, 73–106

Boocock, P. and Roberts, C. A. 1994 *The human remains from Ysgol Twm o'r Nant, Denbigh, Clwyd, Wales*, unpublished report, University of Bradford

Bos, K. I., Schuenemann, V. J., Golding, G. B., Burbano, H. A., Waglechner, N., Coombes, B. K., McPhee, J. B., DeWitte, S. N., Meyer, M., Schmedes, S., Wood, J., Earn, D. J., Herring, D. A., Bauer, P., Poinar, H. N., and Krause, J. 2011 'A draft genome of Yersinia pestis from victims of the Black Death', *Nature* 478, 506–10

Bos, K. I., Stevens, P., Nieselt, K., Poinar, H. N., DeWitte, S. N., and Krause, J. 2012 'Yersinia pestis: new evidence for an old infection', *PLoS One* 7(11), e49803

Brickley, M. and McKinley, J. (eds) 2004 *Guidelines to the standards for recording human remains*, Institute of Field Archaeologists Paper Number 7, Reading (can be downloaded from the British Association of Biological Anthropology and Osteoarchaeology website: http://www.babao.org.uk/)

Brown, T. and Brown, K. 2011 *Introduction to biomolecular archaeology*, Wiley-Blackwell, Chichester

Budd, P., Montgomery, J., Evans, J., and Trickett, M. 2004 'Human lead exposure in England from approximately 5500 BP to the 16th century AD', *Science of The Total Environment* 318(1–3), 45–58

Buckley, R., Morris, M., Appleby, J., King, T., O'Sullivan, D., and Foxhall, L. 2013 'The king in the car park: new light on the death and burial of Richard III in the Grey Friars church, Leicester, in 1485', *Antiquity* 87, 519–38

Buikstra, J. E. and Ubelaker, D. H. (eds) 1994 *Standards for data collection from human skeletal remains*, Archeological Survey, Research Seminar Series 44, Fayetteville

Burt, N. M. 2013 'Stable isotope ratio analysis of breastfeeding and weaning practices of children from medieval Fishergate House, York, UK', *American Journal of Physical Anthropology* 152, 407–16

Cardy, A. 1997 'The human bones', in P. Hill (ed.), *Whithorn and St Ninian: the excavation of a monastic town 1984–1991*, Sutton, Stroud, 519–92

CCR 1339: Calendar of Close Rolls preserved in the Public Record Office: Edward III (Vol. 5) AD 1339–1341, Her Majesty's Stationery Office, London

Connell, B., Gray Jones, A., Redfern, R., and Walker, D. 2012 *A bioarchaeological study of the medieval burials on the site of St Mary Spital: excavations at Spitalfields Market, London E1, 1991–2007*, Museum of London Archaeology Monograph 60, London

Cunha, E., Fily, M.-L., Clisson, I., Santos, A. L., Silva, A. M., Umbelino, C., Cesar, P., Corte-Real, A., Crubézy, E., and Ludes, B. 2000 'Children at the convent: comparing historical data, morphology and DNA extracted from ancient tissues for sex diagnosis at Santa Clara-a-Velha (Coimbra, Portugal)', *Journal of Archaeological Science* 27, 949–52

Dawes, J. D. and Magilton, J. R. 1980 *The cemetery of St Helen-on-the-Walls, Aldwark: the archaeology of York*, The Archaeology of York: the medieval cemeteries 12/1, Council for British Archaeology, York

Demaitre, L. 2007 *Leprosy in premodern medicine: a malady of the whole body*, Johns Hopkins University Press, Baltimore

DCMS 2005 *Guidance for the Care of Human Remains in Museums*, Department for Culture, Media and Sport, London

DeWitte, S. N. and Bekvalac, J. 2010 'Oral health and frailty in the medieval English cemetery of St Mary Graces', *American Journal of Physical Anthropology* 142, 341–54

DeWitte, S. N., Boulware, J. C., and Redfern, R. C. 2013 'Medieval monastic mortality: hazard analysis of mortality differences between monastic and non monastic cemeteries in England', *American Journal of Physical Anthropology* 152, 322–32

Dyer, C. 1989 *Standards of living in the Middle Ages: social change in England 1200–1520*, Cambridge University Press, Cambridge

Fiorato, V., Boylston, A., and Knüse, C. 2001 *Blood red roses: the archaeology of a mass grave from the Battle of Towton AD 1461*, Oxbow, Oxford

Fuller, B. T., Richards, M. P., and Mays, S. A. 2003 'Stable carbon and nitrogen isotope variations in tooth dentine serial sections from Wharram Percy', *Journal of Archaeological Science* 30, 1673–84

Giesen, M. (ed.) 2013 *Curating human remains: caring for the dead in the United Kingdom*, Boydell, Woodbridge

Gilchrist, R. and Sloane, W. 2005 *Requiem: the medieval monastic cemetery in Britain*, Museum of London Archaeology Service, London

Gowland, R. and Chamberlain, A. T. 2005 'Detecting plague: palaeodemographic characterisation of a catastrophic death assemblage', *Antiquity* 79(303), 146–57

Grainger, I., Hawkins, D., Cowal, L., and Mikulski, R. 2008 *The Black Death cemetery, East Smithfield, London*, Museum of London Archaeology Service Monograph 43, London

Grainger, I. and Phillpotts, C. 2011 *The Cistercian Abbey of St Mary Graces, East Smithfield, London*, Museum of London Archaeology Service Monograph 44, London

Grauer, A. and Roberts, C. A. 1996 'Paleoepidemiology, healing and possible treatment of trauma in the medieval cemetery population of St Helen-on-the-Walls, York, England', *American Journal of Physical Anthropology* 100, 531–44

Hillson, S. 1996 *Dental anthropology*, Cambridge University Press, Cambridge

Judd, M. and Roberts, C. A. 1998 'Fracture patterns at the medieval leper hospital in Chichester', *American Journal of Physical Anthropopology* 105, 43–55

Kalladka, M., Greenberg, B. L., Padmashree, S. M., Venkateshaiah, N. T., Yalsangi, S., Raghunandan, B. N., and Glick, M. 2014 'Screening for coronary heart disease and diabetes risk in a dental setting', *International Journal of Public Health* 59, 485–92

Keene, D. 1983 'The medieval urban environment in documentary records', *Archives* 16, 37–44

Lamb, H. H. 1995 *Climate history and the modern world*, Routledge, London

Lewis, M., Roberts, C. A., and Manchester, K. 1995 'A comparative study of the prevalence of maxillary sinusitis in medieval urban and rural populations in Northern England', *American Journal of Physical Anthropology* 98(4), 497–506

Lieverse, A. R. 1999 'Diet and the aetiology of dental calculus', *International Journal of Osteoarchaeology* 9, 219–32

Lilley, J. M., Stroud, G., Brothwell, D. R., Williamson, M. H. 1994 *The Jewish burial ground at Jewbury*, The Archaeology of York: the medieval cemeteries 12/3, Council for British Archaeology, York

Lunt, D. A. and Watt, M. E. 1997 'The human dentitions', in P. Hill (ed.), *Whithorn and St Ninian: the excavation of a monastic town 1984–1991*, Sutton, Stroud, 562–92

Magilton, J. R., Lee, F., and Boylston, A. (eds) 2008 *'Lepers outside the gate': excavations at the cemetery of the hospital of St James and St Mary Magdalene, Chichester, 1986–7 and 1993*, Council for British Archaeology Research Report 158 and Chichester Excavations 10, York

Mays, S. 1996 'Age-dependent cortical bone loss in a medieval population', *International Journal of Osteoarchaeology* 6, 144–54

Mays, S. 1997 'Carbon stable isotope ratios in medieval and later human skeletons from Northern England', *Journal of Archaeological Science* 24, 561–7

Mays, S. 2006 'The osteology of monasticism in medieval England', in R. Gowland and C. Knüsel (eds), *Social archaeology of funerary remains*, Oxbow, Oxford, 179–89

Mays, S. and Turner-Walker, G. 1999 'A mediaeval case of Paget's disease of bone with complications', *Journal of Paleopathology* 11, 29–40

Mays, P., Harding C., and Heighway, C. 2007 *Wharram. A study of settlement on the Yorkshire Wolds XI: the churchyard*, University of York Archaeological Publications 13, York

Mays, P., Richards, M. P., and Fuller, B. T. 2002 'Bone stable isotope evidence for infant feeding in mediaeval England', *Antiquity* 76, 654–6

Milner, G. R., Wood, J. W., Boldsen, J. L. 2008 'Advances in paleodemography', in M. A. Katzenberg and S. R. Saunders (eds), *Biological anthropology of the human skeleton*, Wiley-Liss, New York, 561–600

Ministry of Justice 2008 *Burial law and archaeology*, Coroner's Unit, Ministry of Justice, London

Miszkieicz, J. J. 2015 'Linear enamel hypoplasia and age-at-death at medieval (11th–16th centuries) St Gregory's priory and cemetery, Canterbury, UK', *International Journal of Osteoarchaeology* 25, 79–87

Molleson, T. and Cox, M. 1993 *The Spitalfields Project Vol. 2: the anthropology. The middling sort*, Council for British Archaeology Research Report 86, York

Müldner, G. and Richards, M. P. 2005 'Fast or feast: reconstructing diet in later medieval England by stable isotope analysis', *Journal of Archaeological Science* 32, 39–48

Müldner, G. and Richards, M. P. 2007 'Diet and diversity at later medieval Fishergate: the isotopic evidence', *American Journal of Physical Anthropology* 134, 162–74

Müller, R., Roberts, C. A., and Brown, T. A. 2014a 'Biomolecular identification of ancient Mycobacterium tuberculosis complex DNA in human remains from Britain and continental Europe', *American Journal of Physical Anthropology* 153(2), 178–89

Müller, R., Roberts, C. A., and Brown, T. A. 2014b 'Genotyping of ancient Mycobacterium tuberculosis strains reveals historic genetic diversity', *Proceedings of the Royal Society B* 281, 201332236

Nesse, R. M. and Williams, G. C. 1994 *Why we get sick: the new science of Darwinian medicine*, Times Books, New York

Orme, N. and Webster, M. 1995 *The English hospital 1070–1570*, Yale University Press, London

Ortner, D. and Mays, S. 1998 'Dry bone manifestations of rickets in infancy and childhood', *International Journal of Osteoarchaeology* 8, 45–55

Ozaki, K. and Tanaka, T. 2016 'Molecular genetics of coronary artery disease', *Journal of Human Genetics* 61, 71–7

Prestwich, M. 1997 *Edward I*, Yale University Press, London

Rawcliffe, C. 2006 *Leprosy in medieval England*, Boydell, Woodbridge

Rawcliffe, C. 2013 *Urban bodies: communal health in late medieval English towns and cities*, Boydell, Woodbridge

Redmond-Cooper, R. (ed.) 2015 *Heritage, ancestry and law: principles, policies and practices in dealing with historical human remains*, The Institute of Art and Law, Builth Wells

Resnick, D. 1995 'Disorders of other endocrine glands and of pregnancy', in D. Resnick (ed.), *Diagnosis of bone and joint disorders*, WB Saunders, Edinburgh, 2076–2104

Richards, M., Mays, S., and Fuller, B. 2002 'Stable carbon and nitrogen isotope values of bone and teeth reflect weaning age at the medieval Wharram Percy site, Yorkshire, UK', *Journal of Archaeological Science* 119, 205–10

Richards, M., Fuller, B. T., and Molleson, T. I. 2006 'Stable isotope palaeodietary study of humans and fauna from the multi-period (Iron Age, Viking and late medieval) site of Newark Bay, Orkney', *Journal of Archaeological Science* 33, 122–31

Richards, M. and Montgomery, J. 2012 'Isotope analysis and paleopathology: a short review', in J. E. Buikstra and C. A. Roberts (eds), *A global history of paleopathology: pioneers and prospects*, Oxford University Press, Oxford, 718–31

Roberts, C. A. 1984 'Analysis of some human femora from a medieval charnel house at Rothwell parish church, Northamptonshire, England', *Ossa* 9–11, 137–47

Roberts, C. A. 1994 'Treponematosis in Gloucester, England: a theoretical and practical approach to the pre-Columbian theory', in O. Dutour, G. Palfi, and J.-P. Brun (eds), *L'origine de la syphilis en Europe: avant ou apres 1493?*, Editions Errance, Paris, 101–8

Roberts, C. A. 2002 'The antiquity of leprosy in Britain: the skeletal evidence', in C. A. Roberts, M. E. Lewis, and K. Manchester (eds), *The past and present of leprosy: archaeological, historical, palaeopathological and clinical approaches*, British Archaeological Reports International Series 1054, Oxford, 213–22

Roberts, C. A. 2007 'A bioarchaeological study of maxillary sinusitis', *American Journal of Physical Anthropology* 133(2), 792–807

Roberts, C. A. 2009 *Human remains in archaeology: a handbook*, Council for British Archaeology, York

Roberts, C. A. 2012 'History of development of paleopathology in the United Kingdom', in J. E. Buikstra and C. A. Roberts (eds), *A global history of paleopathology: pioneers and prospects*, Oxford University Press, Oxford, 568–79

Roberts, C. A. and Buikstra J. E. 2003 *The bioarchaeology of tuberculosis: a global view on a re-emerging disease*, University Press of Florida, Gainesville

Roberts, C. A. and Cox, M. 2003 *Health and disease in Britain: from prehistory to the present day*, Sutton Publishing, Stroud

Roberts, C. A., Millard, A. R., Nowell, G. M., Grocke, D., Macpherson, C., Pearson, G., Evans, D. 2013 'The origin and mobility of people with venereal syphilis buried in Hull, England, in the late medieval period', *American Journal of Physical Anthropology* 150, 273–85

Rogers, J. and Waldron, T. 1995 *A field guide to joint disease in archaeology*, Wiley, Chichester

Rogers, J. and Waldron, T. 2001 DISH and the monastic way of life, *International Journal of Osteoarchaeology* 11, 357–65

Rose, J. C., Green, T. J., and Green, V. D. 1996 'NAGPRA is forever: osteology and the repatriation of skeletons', *Annual Review of Anthropology* 25, 85–103

Schuenemann, V. J., Bos, K., a DeWitte, S., Schmedes, S., Jamieson, J., Mittnik, A., Forrest, S., Coombes, B. K., Wood, J. W., Earn, D. J. D., White, W., Krause, J. and Poinar, H. N. 2011 'Targeted enrichment of ancient pathogens yielding the pPCP1 plasmid of *Yersinia pestis* from victims of the Black Death', *Proceedings of the National Academy of Sciences* 108, 15669–70

Sintchenko, V. and Holmes, E. C. 2015 'The role of pathogen genomics in assessing disease transmission', *British Medical Journal* 350, h1314

Spencer, R. K. 2008 *Testing hypotheses about diffuse idiopathic skeletal hyperostosis (DISH) using stable isotope and aDNA analysis of late medieval British populations*, unpublished PhD thesis, Durham University

Stones, J. A. (ed.) 1989 *Three Scottish Carmelite friaries excavations at Aberdeen, Linlithgow and Perth 1980–86*, The Society of Antiquaries of Scotland Monograph 6, Edinburgh

Stroud, G. and Kemp, R. L. 1993 *Cemeteries of the church and priory of St Andrew, Fishergate*, The Archaeology of York: the medieval cemeteries 12/2, Council for British Archaeology, York

Taylor, G. M., Goyal, M., Legge, A. J., Shaw, R. J., and Young, D. 1999 'Genotypic analysis of *Mycobacterium tuberculosis* from medieval human remains', *Microbiology* 145, 899–904

Taylor, G. M., Widdison, S., Brown, I. N., and Young, D. 2000 'A mediaeval case of lepromatous leprosy from thirteenth-fourteenth century Orkney, Scotland', *Journal of Archaeological Science* 27, 1133–8

Thomas, C., Sloane, B., and Phillpotts, C. 1997 *Excavations at the priory and hospital of St Mary Spital, London*, Museum of London Archaeology Service Monograph 1, London

Waldron, T. 1994 *Counting the dead: the epidemiology of skeletal populations*, Wiley, Chichester

Waldron, T. 2007 *St Peter's, Barton-upon-Humber, Lincolnshire, a parish church and its community, vol. 2: the human remains*, Oxbow, Oxford

Walker, D., Powers, N., Connell, B., and Redfern, R. 2015 'Evidence of skeletal treponematosis from the medieval burial ground of St Mary Spital, London, and implications for the origins of the disease in Europe', *American Journal of Physical Anthropology* 156, 90–101

Wood, J. W., Milner, G. R., Harpending, H. C., and Weiss, K. M. 1992 'The osteological paradox. Problems of inferring health from skeletal samples', *Current Anthropology* 33(4), 343–70

Ziegler, P. 1991 *The Black Death*, Sutton Publishing, Stroud

CHAPTER 52

MEDIEVAL MEDICINE, PUBLIC HEALTH, AND THE MEDIEVAL HOSPITAL

MARTIN HUGGON

Medieval Medicine

THE medieval medical practices of Britain were, like the rest of western Europe, based upon the knowledge of the Classical medical theorists, often transmitted through Arabic scholars. Galens' humoural conception of the body was particularly significant, building upon the writings of Hippocrates (Rawcliffe 1995, 30-3). The four humours of the body (yellow bile, black bile, phlegm, and blood), associated with the four elements of the world, were linked with heat, moisture, and emotions, and had to be kept balanced to maintain good health through diet, physical intervention, and medicine. Medical theory was passed across Europe through written texts, ranging in nature from the texts on surgery by Theodoric of Cervia (1205-98) to Barton's fourteenth-century introductory work on urine and uroscopy (Goodrich 2004; Tavormina 2009). More generalized texts include John Mirfield's *Breviarium Bartholomei*, written in the late fourteenth or early fifteenth century whilst he served as a canon at St Bartholomew's Hospital, Smithfield, London, in which part of the text is given over to medicinal preparations, humoural theory, and tips for staff at a hospital (Gilchrist 1995, 34). Preventative texts like the *Regimen sanitatis Salerni*, written at the famous medical school of Salerno around AD 900, were more concerned with physical activity and diet, including recipes for the improvement of health (Bifulco et al. 2008; Horden 2007, 135; Nicoud 2008, 7). Good health was encouraged in *consilia*, practical instructions on the specific characteristics of different foodstuffs, whom they would help, dangers related to the food, and the quantity and style that should be served. They were written by both religious and secular practitioners throughout the later medieval period, either for a specific patient who displayed particular humoural characteristics or, more generally, allowing patients to engage actively with medical practice and the conditions affecting them (Horden 2007, 139; Nicoud 2008, 8).

Although practical medical intervention was discussed and implemented, it was three more generalized concepts that were central in medieval medicine: diet, regimen, and piety. This is evident in the range and number of regimen's written by physicians, such as those of the Italian physician Michele Savonarola of first Padua and then Ferrara in the sixteenth century (Nicoud 2008, 8), or those found in monastic libraries, the *Regimen sanitatis Salerni* being one of the more popular (Bifulco et al. 2008, 603). These texts indicate that medicine was not the process of diagnosis and treatment that it is considered to be today in the western world, but a treatment centred on prognosis, spiritual consequences, and improvement in the likely outcome. The greatest fear was not death alone, but a death still sinful and unworthy of heaven, and for this reason the emphasis was on religious activity, leading to the overwhelming majority of physicians being in the priesthood (Rawcliffe 1995, 112). In Britain surgeons were viewed as more practical and lay due to their status as artisans taught through apprenticeship rather than the more scholarly physicians. In addition, religious rulings, such as those of Pope Alexander III in 1163 and the Fourth Lateran Council in 1215, forbade the clergy to participate in practices that involved the shedding of blood (Egan 2007, 66; Rawcliffe 1995, 112). Also associated with medicine were apothecaries, suppliers of spices, herbs, and remedies, who often catered for the treatments prescribed by physicians, and the women who played a very important role in medical practice, occasionally maintaining a practice, treating women's maladies, serving as midwives, or nursing the sick, especially at the medieval hospital (Rawcliffe 1995). Monastic infirmarers, whose role in the monastery centred on caring for the sick and infirm of the religious community, could also care for secular patients, although their role was not solely concerned with medical treatment but with providing food, warmth, and a more leisurely setting for infirm brothers who through age, constitution, or injury, found the daily monastic routine too trying (Harvey 1993).

From the prolific nature of the historical narrative it might be expected that the archaeological record should produce some evidence to corroborate these medical practices. Instead, the material found has produced confusing, inconclusive, or individually insignificant results. An attempt by Egan (2007) to compile the archaeological evidence of medical instruments widely illustrated in the surgical treatise of Albucasis highlighted the virtually complete lack of medical tools from medieval England. In the case of the barber-surgeon's chest found aboard the *Mary Rose*, Henry VIII's flagship that sank in the Solent in 1545, almost all of the physician's tools could be mistaken for everyday items in another context: wooden jars, one of which still contained peppercorns and another frankincense, could either be medicinal or culinary ingredients; nine wooden handles for iron implements, possibly cauterizing tools and amputation knives or saws; a wooden mallet; razors; a whetstone; and some stoneware jars. The only diagnostically medical items were two metal syringes, one probably being employed for urethral conditions (Castle and Derham 2005; Egan 2007, 67). Although uroscopy (the study of urine for diagnosing ailment) was widely practised by physicians, the specialist urinals, flasks made from particularly fine and clear glass, are surprisingly lacking from hospital sites; for example, only one and possibly a second dating to the medieval period were found at the Hospital of St Mary Spital, London, while a further handful have been found across the rest of the capital, seemingly at higher-status sites (Keys 1998).

Direct evidence for material culture associated with medical practice has mostly been found in cemeteries, such as from three skeletons from St Mary Spital, London, with single examples from Merton Priory in Surrey, Stratford Langthorne Abbey, just to the east of London, and the Gilbertine Priory of St Andrew at Fishergate in York. Each one of these had a bent or folded copper or lead sheet located at the knee or elbow joints, either with holes for tying onto the body directly or possibly to cloth bandages (Figure 52.1), as some were also found with plant material attached to them, perhaps evidence of long-term binding of bandages for areas of trauma or disease. A possible surgical truss was also found at Merton Priory (Egan 2007, 70–1). In addition, the remains of distillation equipment are known from a number of contexts across Britain, especially as part of the Reformation clearance material from a number of monastery sites, most associated with the distillation of alcohols or acids which feature in some medicinal recipes (Moorhouse 1993). Whilst the virtual absence of such material need not mean that medical practice was rare in medieval Britain, the full implications of this absence need further investigation, especially in light of osteological evidence from larger cemeteries, such as at St Mary Spital, which suggests that medical intervention was carried out to set bones, amputate limbs, and carry out cranial trepanations, most of which show evidence of healing and would have required supportive post-operative care (Connell et al. 2012). One example, a male in his 40s, showed evidence of healed severe cranial trauma that had likely survived surgical intervention but probably resulted in some form of permanent soft tissue and brain damage (Powers 2005).

Archaeobotanical evidence for medicinal preparations, the examination of seeds, pollen, and residues, elucidates the composition of possible medicines and the nature of the local plant-life that may have been incorporated. This approach has been problematic, however, often because of the limited nature of sampling strategies (as discussed by Moffat 1986). Archaeological investigations carried out at the hospital of the Holy Trinity in Soutra, Scotland, specifically looking for evidence of medical treatment and medicine, produced ceramic sherds with poppy and other plant residues that could be used for a medicinal purpose (Moffat et al. 1989), but there have been some questions over the efficacy of the poppy found (Gilchrist 1995, 35). At other hospital sites, henbane, hemlock, hemp, willow, mustard, peppercorns, and other plant material were present in archaeological contexts, and medical texts list expensive imports such as ginger, cumin, and frankincense, but many of these plants are also native to Britain, growing as weeds or purposefully cultivated in monastic or food gardens, and most of them could also be used as seasoning for food (Gilchrist 1995; Thomas et al. 1997). Also at Soutra, identification of haemoglobin in the soil suggested that human blood may have been finding its way into the hospital drain, perhaps related to regular blood-letting, or phlebotomy, a common activity in monastic communities. This was a treatment for those suffering from an abundance of blood and used to relieve anxiety, fever, and inflammation

FIGURE 52.1 Lead sheet <1312> wrapped around the right shin of a 26–35 year old female, Sk 7186 (*c*.1250–*c*.1400), and (below) a copper-alloy plate <2678> found between the knees of skeleton 12441, a 36–45-year-old male (*c*.1120–*c*.1200), both from St Mary Spital, London, and possibly used for a therapeutic purpose. Interestingly Sk 12441 dates to before the hospital was founded. The function of these metal plates is unclear, but they do seem associated with healing injuries, perhaps as a brace or to hold a treatment or poultice against the affected area (Connell et al. 2012, 208–9, figs 231 and 232)

(© MOLA)

(Moffat and Fulton 1988; see Chapter 35 in this *Handbook*). Unfortunately no other sites in Britain have provided comparative data.

The apparent paucity of the archaeological record with regard to the nature of medieval medicine is linked to two misconceptions: that medieval hospitals provide the best location for evidence of practical medicine; and that the medicine discussed in the texts was available to a large enough population to be archaeologically visible. Although the medieval hospital may seem to be a logical location for material evidence of physicians and medical cures, the textual records often locate medical practitioners in secular, and especially wealthy, contexts; it was only in the mid-fifteenth century that physicians began to be paid to attend the poor at hospitals in Britain, and even then it was a rare occurrence (Carlin 1989, 30–2; Gilchrist 1995; Rubin 1989, 51). Medical practitioners were often satirized or ridiculed for the exorbitant costs of their treatments, costs that suggest the clients were mostly rich. In any case, the number of formally trained physicians that read or taught medicine at the colleges of Oxford and Cambridge between 1300 and 1499 was only 153 (Rawcliffe 1995, 105–24). Taken together, we must conclude that the likely location for material evidence of the medical care provided for the laity will lie in domestic contexts, especially high-status sites, mingled with other everyday material that will inevitably hinder the visibility of such finds. Simply put, the texts discuss medical practices that were not for the majority of the population and locate the activity in a context rarely examined from this perspective archaeologically. The role of diet in treatment may mean that animal and plant remains could be vitally important to understanding medieval medicine, especially for the poorer population, but without a clear context and with the archaeological record rarely being refined enough to show short-term dietary change, accurately labelling food as medicinal is treacherous. Ultimately, the archaeology of medicine in medieval Britain requires more archaeobotanical and residue analyses of potentially medical equipment, further evidence from elite or middle-class areas where practitioners likely resided, an expansion of the understanding of medicine to include zooarchaeological and spiritual evidence, and an acknowledgement that context is vitally important in understanding what form the evidence is likely to take.

Public Health

Black Death

The best estimates of life expectancy in later medieval Britain suggest that in the mid-thirteenth to early fourteenth centuries the population average was mid-20s, rising to the mid-30s in the next two centuries (Roberts and Cox 2003, 226). Influencing this life expectancy were famines, diseases and plagues, natural attrition, injury and accident, diet, and the nature of medical practice, amongst many other factors. The Black

Death, caused by the spread of *Yersinia pestis*, first arrived in England during 1348–9 and spread across Britain, with subsequent outbreaks throughout the remainder of the century (Horrox 1994; Theilmann and Cate 2007; Ziegler 2008). The disease possibly killed between a third and half of Britain's population in only a few years, those with underlying health issues being most at risk (DeWitte 2010). Despite almost two million deaths, however, the second half of the fourteenth century saw a trend of new town creation, civic improvement, the development of new suburbs, and a likely rise in the urban population through migration (Lilley 2015). Age estimates also imply that the population was by now living longer and there was an increase in the standard of living (DeWitte 2014).

One of the most interesting aspects of the Black Death, at least from an archaeological perspective, is actually the relative paucity of evidence for it. Only a handful of mass graves directly linked to the outbreak have so far been excavated, such as East Smithfield in London (Grainger et al. 2008; see Chapter 51 in this *Handbook*). The long trenches and rows of normal burials there were unlike the expected form of mass graves (Figure 52.2), such as the stacked bodies of Towton (Fiorato et al. 2007; see Chapter 26 in this *Handbook*) or St Mary Spital (Connell et al. 2012). The excavations investigated about half of the entire Smithfield cemetery, and it is thought the total cemetery population consisted of up to 2400 people (Grainger et al. 2008, 2), but this is a small number for one of two emergency Black Death cemeteries to cope with the crisis. A mass grave more similar to Towton, dating to the Black Death, was found in excavations in the cemetery at Hereford Cathedral (Stone and Appleton-Fox 1996). Also of importance are sites such as Charterhouse Square, London, where twenty-five individuals were found in 2013 during the Crossrail project, buried in single, double, and stacked graves in three phases, all of which held traces of *Yersinia pestis* (Dick et al. 2015). Geophysical survey of the Square suggests at least a further two hundred undisturbed individual burials in the area, and it could be argued that the nature of this cemetery may be more typical for the general treatment of the dead during the Black Death. A single Black Death cemetery in Britain has been found outside of an urban setting so far and it has been recently excavated by Hugh Willmott and Pete Townend, Sheffield University. Part of a larger cemetery that pre- and post-dated the Black Death, the pit was located next to the Hospital of St James just outside the south-west boundary of the precinct of Thornton Abbey, Lincolnshire, where forty-eight skeletons, including twenty-seven infants, were buried close together but with care and without stacking in a series of interlinked rows. The presence of *Yersinia pestis* was found in samples taken from teeth, and it seems that this mass grave represents the local rural population struggling with the crisis and looking to the hospital to provide spiritual aid to the living and the dead.

That the use of mass graves was limited, at least in emergency cemeteries, taken together with the individual nature of burial and the virtual lack of mass graves elsewhere in Britain, could have dramatic implications for the identification of large numbers of Black Death victims in the archaeological record elsewhere. Nor, it must be said, can all mass graves be assigned to the Black Death. Those excavated at the Hospital of St

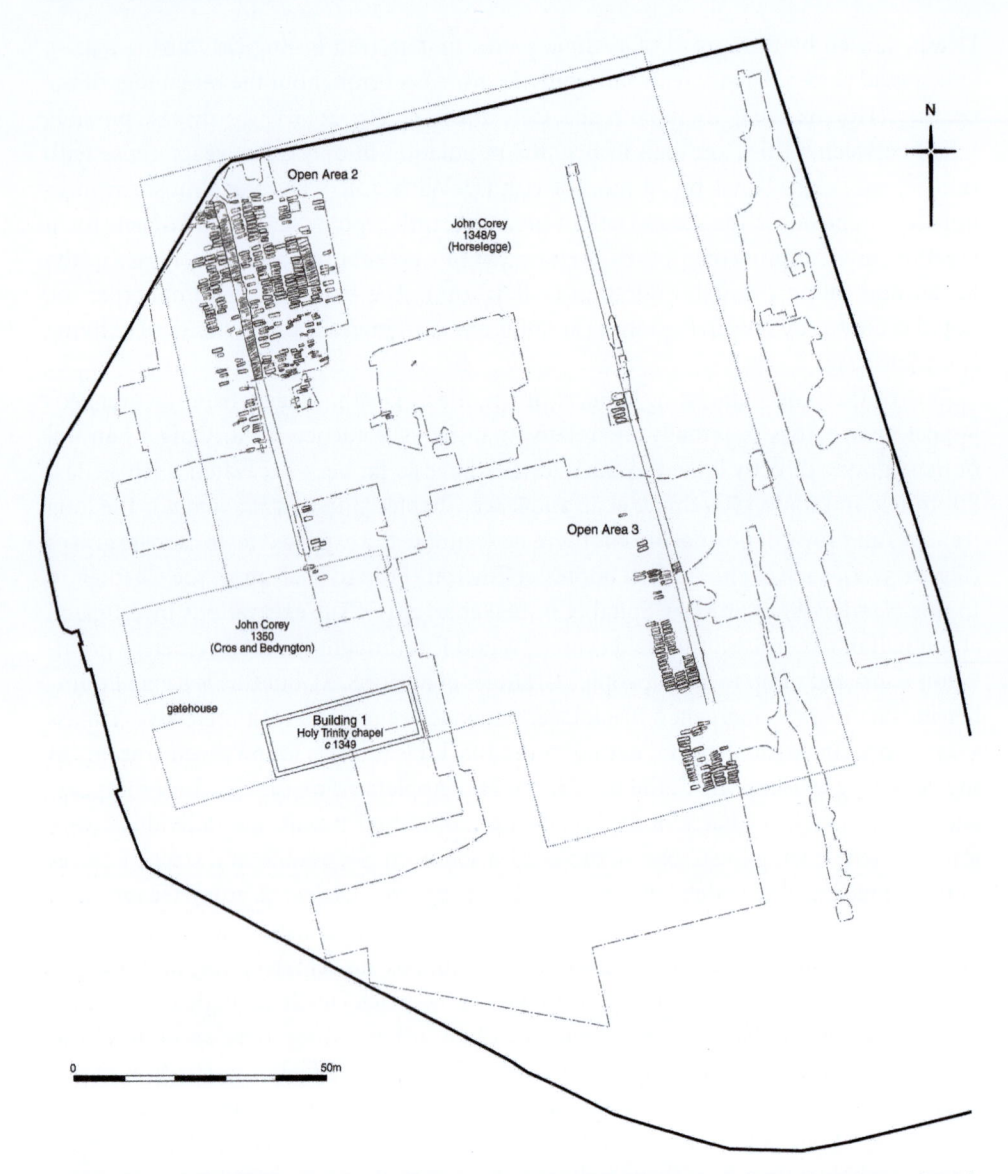

FIGURE 52.2 The Black Death cemetery at East Smithfield (OA2 and OA3) with its chapel (B1), and documented 1350 boundary. Note the individual burials and the slot trenches (from Grainger et al. 2008, fig. 8)

(© MOLA)

Mary Spital contained over one thousand individuals buried in compact areas, stacked on top of each other in several rows in a careful and respectful manner, but dated to the mid-twelfth to the mid-thirteenth century, with another one dated to the fifteenth or sixteenth century, suggesting that they were related to other periods of famine or other infectious diseases that struck London throughout the medieval period (Connell et al. 2012).

Leprosy

Another significant disease of the medieval period was leprosy (Rawcliffe 2006). Also known as Hansen's disease and caused by *Mycobacterium leprae*, this is a bacterial disease related to tuberculosis, with an incubation period of between three years and several decades, spread through close long-term association with an affected individual through droplets from the nose and mouth (Manchester and Roberts 1989; Taylor et al. 2006). The effects of the disease were often slow and cumulative, leading to anaesthesia, bone destruction, and secondary infections and gangrene (seen in the milder tuberculoid form), and in severe cases (lepromatous leprosy) blotchy and lumpy skin, rhino-maxilliary collapse, and inflammation of the eyes leading to blindness (Figure 52.3) (Magilton et al. 2008, 10; Roberts and Cox 2003, 267–8). Studies of aDNA have identified five strains of leprosy across the world, with strain 3 being associated with Europe. However, the cemeteries excavated at the medieval leprosy hospital of St Mary Magdalen in Winchester, Hampshire, an early example of a hospital catering for sufferers of the disease, showed the presence of strain 2, usually associated with Africa and the Middle East, suggesting that this may have been the original strain of the disease (Donoghue et al. 2015; Mendum et al. 2014; Taylor et al. 2006).

Roughly one-third of all hospital sites in Britain for the entire medieval period, a number in excess of three hundred, housed sufferers of leprosy (Roffey and Tucker 2012, 170; Satchell 1998). In the Middle Ages this disease was thought to be associated with sexual sin, either of the person themselves or their parents, but other believed potential causes were foul miasmas, rancid food, or the effects of the stars and planets (Rawcliffe 2006, 44–103). Ultimately the disease was seen as a sign of wickedness and sin, to be treated through piety, devotion, a regimen of food and prayer, and absolution: some medieval authors, such as poet William Langland, believed that lepers were holy penitents because they suffered their penance on earth rather than in Purgatory (Rawcliffe 2006). Kings, queens, and the elites often associated themselves with sufferers, washing feet or providing food and shelter, and although the laws of medieval society seemingly ostracized sufferers, most leprosy hospitals were located on major roads, at gates, or in suburbs, rather than being hidden away (Rawcliffe 2006, 307–14).

Although the medieval definition of leprosy may have been socially constructed, based on spiritual undesirability rather than any clinical definition (Riddle 2007, 5; Roberts and Cox 2003, 268–9), the cemeteries attached to leprosy hospitals do include significant numbers of sufferers. At the Hospital of St James and St Mary Magdalene in Chichester, West Sussex, almost a quarter of the 351 excavated individuals showed signs of the disease, over fifty from the first phase when the hospital was not opened out to the wider poor (Magilton et al. 2008). However, a broader examination indicates that osteological markers of leprosy are quite frequently found in small numbers across England (for example Roberts and Cox 2003, 270–1, Table 5.22). In the case of Scotland, only a handful of individuals have been found in the later medieval period, all in parish cemeteries (Lunt 2012), although twenty-one hospitals for leprosy are known historically from the

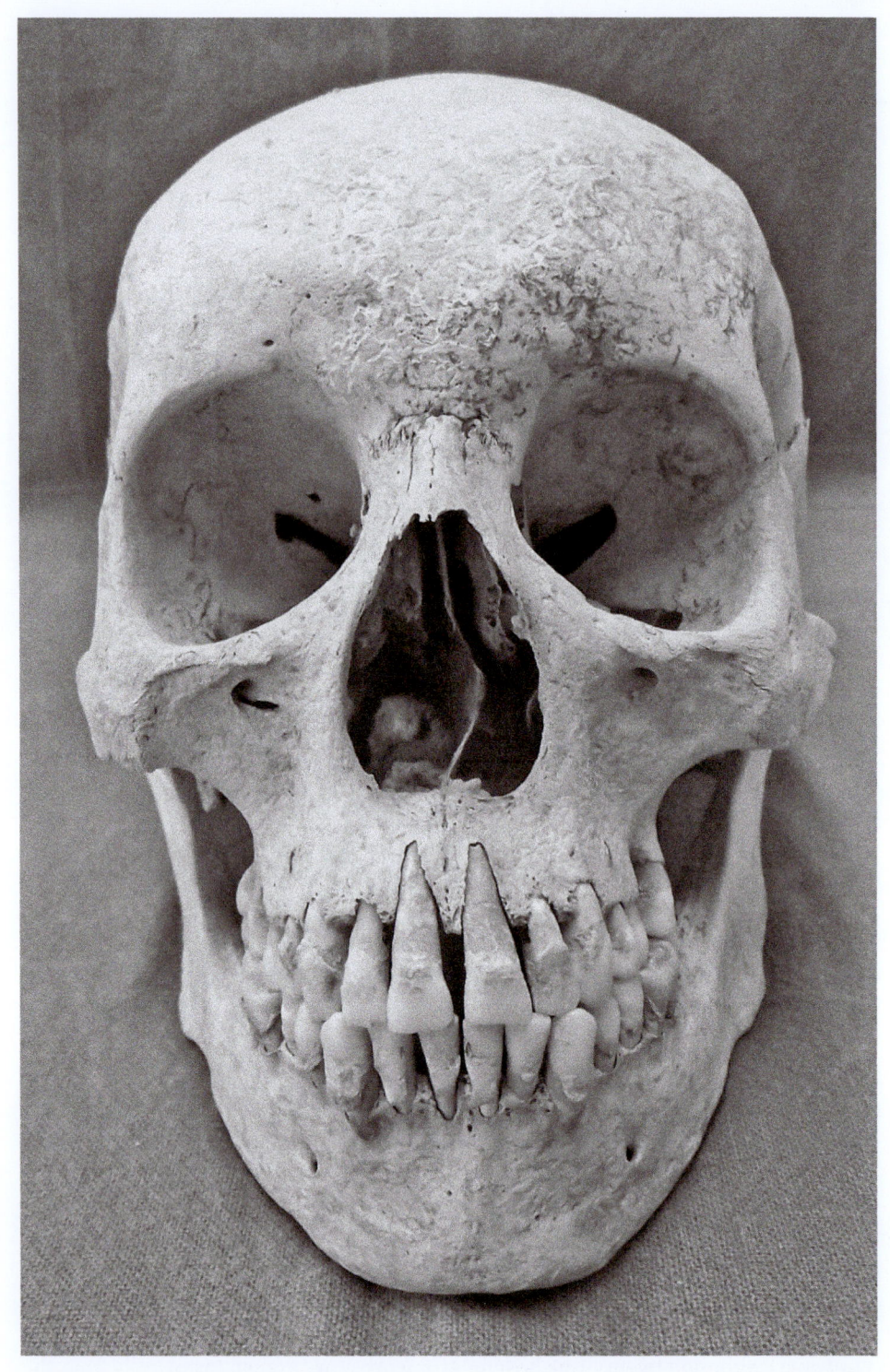

FIGURE 52.3 An example of rhino-maxillary syndrome seen on Sk 48 from St Mary Magdalen, Winchester, with widening and rounding of the margins of the nasal aperture

(© Simon Roffey and Katie Tucker, Magdalen Hill Archaeological Research Project)

twelfth century (Cowan and Easson 1976). At St Margaret's Hospital in High Wycombe, Buckinghamshire, the skeletal remains of ten to twelve individuals were found, many with signs of leprosy, such as gross tibiofibular periosteal inflammation, although bone preservation was poor (Farley and Manchester 1989). Nevertheless, most of the individuals seem to have been young adults, suggesting that poor hygiene had encouraged the aggressive infection that is usually the fatal phase of the disease. The cemeteries of St Mary Magdalen in Winchester seem to have held a higher than average number of individuals displaying signs of leprosy, suggesting that this site specialized in the care of sufferers, or perhaps that those at Winchester were better cared for allowing them to live long enough for skeletal markers to be established (Roffey and Tucker 2012).

What is clear is that those suffering from leprosy were not simply shunned (Figure 52.4). Evidence for some level of care is evident in both the historical and archaeological evidence, such as the evidence for amputation at the leprosy hospital of St Mary Magdalen, Winchester (Roffey and Tucker 2012). The proportion of the population suffering from leprosy at any one point also varied through time, although it is highly unlikely that the numbers rose above a crude prevalence rate of a few per cent of the population, with a concentration in the south and east and amongst males (as calculated by Roberts 2002). From the fourteenth century, prevalence appears to decrease and the number of leprosy hospitals drops away, with a peak of 214 hospitals in England and Wales caring for sufferers of leprosy out of a total of 602 estimated to be active in the

FIGURE 52.4 St Mary Magdalen chapel in Ripon, North Yorkshire, was built in the first half of the twelfth century as part of a hospital complex to minister to lepers, blind priests, and poor travelers. It has an unusually low, narrow window in the north wall which, according to tradition, was used to administer communion to lepers. By 1352 the leper house was deemed to be in a ruinous estate and was demolished, but the hospital became an almshouses in 1544

(© Alejandra Gutiérrez)

period 1300–50 (35.8 per cent), versus 149 of 563 (26.4 per cent) in 1350–1400, and only 46 out of 651 sites (7.2 per cent) between 1500 and the Reformation (based on Knowles and Hadcock 1971 and Cullum 1989). As leprosy declined in Britain so hospitals were adapted to care for the poor more generally, although Scotland still had cases in the eighteenth century and English records do note cases in the nineteenth century (Lunt 2012; Rawcliffe 2006; Roberts and Cox 2003, 330; Roberts and Manchester 1995).

Support for sufferers of leprosy therefore was quickly replaced by a broader concern about poverty, especially among the urban poor. Whilst this is best seen in the documentary sources, the evidence from medieval hospitals and parish cemeteries suggests a high level of enamel hypoplasia, around 35 per cent prevalence nationally, indicative of metabolic disruption due to disease, malnutrition, emotional stress, or Vitamin A deficiency (Roberts and Cox 2003). Excavations at St Mary Spital in London showed that a significant proportion of the cemetery population were 16–25 year old males, a typical trend for urban infirmaries, possibly representing migrant workers or the unemployed, as well as almost 25 per cent of the sample being children aged 11–15 (Gilchrist and Sloane 2005). Whilst care must be taken when equating the cemetery populations with residents in the hospital, these figures are probably indicative of the young, poor population of the area. The residents in the capital may have suffered higher nutritional stress compared with the rest of the country, with smaller average stature, and a higher prevalence of stress markers, whilst signs of tuberculosis have also been noted in higher percentages in the capital than elsewhere (Connell et al. 2012; Grainger et al. 2008). Osteoarthritis appears to have made up the majority of joint disease and suggests an active population, although variance in the use of terminology in osteological reports has made the picture slightly unclear. Ultimately, the most significant variable affecting public health was socio-economic status, and throughout the period the population grew, was cut in half by epidemic, restored, and then doubled, all during a time of urbanization (Roberts and Cox 2003, 281, 285).

Medieval Hospitals

The medieval hospital was based on the Christian concept of *hospitale*, hospitality provided to a guest, and served as physical embodiment of the Seven Merciful Acts of Christ, namely feeding the poor, clothing the poor, bringing drink, housing the wayfarer, visiting prisoners, nursing the sick, and burying the dead (Gilchrist 1995, 9). The infirmary of medieval monasteries is not under consideration here, although around seventy sites were housed within a monastery and over two hundred were dependencies of one, and most hospitals appear to have had canons, priests, or chaplains to oversee the spiritual needs of their residents. Key studies have focused on the history (Clay 1909; McIntosh 2012; Orme and Webster 1995; Sweetinburgh 2004), architecture (Godfrey 1955; Prescott 1992), and the archaeology of hospitals (Gilchrist 1995), but there is an ever-increasing corpus of excavated examples.

The author estimates that a minimum of 1,146 definite and possible hospitals and almshouses were operational during the medieval period in England and Wales; Derek Hall's gazetteer of Scottish hospitals lists a further 178 (Hall 2006). Incomplete documentary records sometimes mean that the dates of foundation or dissolution of hospital sites are unclear and their geographical location can be uncertain. Added to this, terminology too can vary and complicates effective comparison while the categorization of sites may be based on architectural and morphological grounds or the nature of the inmates (e.g. poor, sick, pilgrims); differences between religious hospitals and secular almshouses are inadequately critiqued; and some level of hospitality was also provided by the Military Orders (Nicholson 2012), which is not considered here. That said, if the approximate totals above can be accepted, then less than 5 per cent of medieval hospitals across Britain have undergone archaeological investigation, i.e. around forty hospitals or their associated cemeteries. Key English sites include St Bartholomew in Bristol (Price and Ponsford 1998), St Mary in Ospringe, Kent (Smith 1980; Wall 1981), St Mary Magdalen in Colchester (Crossan 2004), St Mary Magdalen in Winchester (Roffey 2012), St John the Baptist in Oxford (Durham 1991), and St Giles in Brough, North Yorkshire (Cardwell 1995). Of some twenty known Welsh sites, only the hospital at Llawhaden in Pembrokeshire has been investigated (Brennan 1995), while in Scotland few hospitals have undergone any excavation at all. Limited work has been undertaken at St Andrew's Farm in Fife (Hall 1995; Hamilton and Toolis 1999), and the hospice at Kirk Ness, Berwickshire (Addyman et al. 2013), whilst survey and excavations at Soutra, Scottish Borders, provided evidence of the layout of a hospital site and possible medicinal practice (Moffat and Fulton 1988; Moffat et al. 1989).

The most extensive excavations so far of a hospital were at St Mary Spital in London, the second largest medieval hospital in Britain with space for 180 inmates (Figure 52.5), just behind St Leonard's in York, which at its height cared for over two hundred inmates. This investigation provided a fairly complete ground-plan of a medieval hospital, as well as the skeletal remains of over ten thousand medieval Londoners, some of whom likely spent some time at the hospital itself (Connell et al. 2012; Thomas et al. 1997). The development of the ground-plan provides an insight into how the space was used by the residents, with a clear split between the religious brethren, located to the east of the site, and the inmates and the servants who cared for them, located to the west, a distinction that led over the years to the development of clearly separated claustral ranges. This separation was exemplified by the movement of the infirmary to a new position at the north-west of the church in the mid- to late thirteenth century, the blocking of the doorway connecting the north transept of the church to the infirmary hall in Period M4 (1280–1320) and in the sixteenth century by a series of new walls and a corridor linking the female quarters and infirmary with the kitchen (Thomas et al. 1997).

At St Bartholomew's, Bristol, men and women were separated into two courts with the kitchen and refectory serving as a throughway, although at certain points it seems likely that parts of the chapel accommodated the infirm and poor, possibly associated with the establishment of beds for seamen of the Fraternity of St Clement (Price and Ponsford 1998). The site of St Mary, Ospringe, clearly indicated the separation of elite areas from the infirmary hall and domestic area, with the elite royal *camera* located to the north of the chapel, and the infirmary to the north-west (Smith 1980). At this site the kitchen also served to separate the two zones. At Colchester, Essex, the Hospital of St Mary Magdalen provided evidence for the initial infirmary hall of the early twelfth to mid-thirteenth century, which was rebuilt to form the chapel, with the infirmary hall moving to the north (Crossan 2004). There is also the suggestion that an additional building was constructed to the east of the infirmary hall to provide additional accommodation, possibly

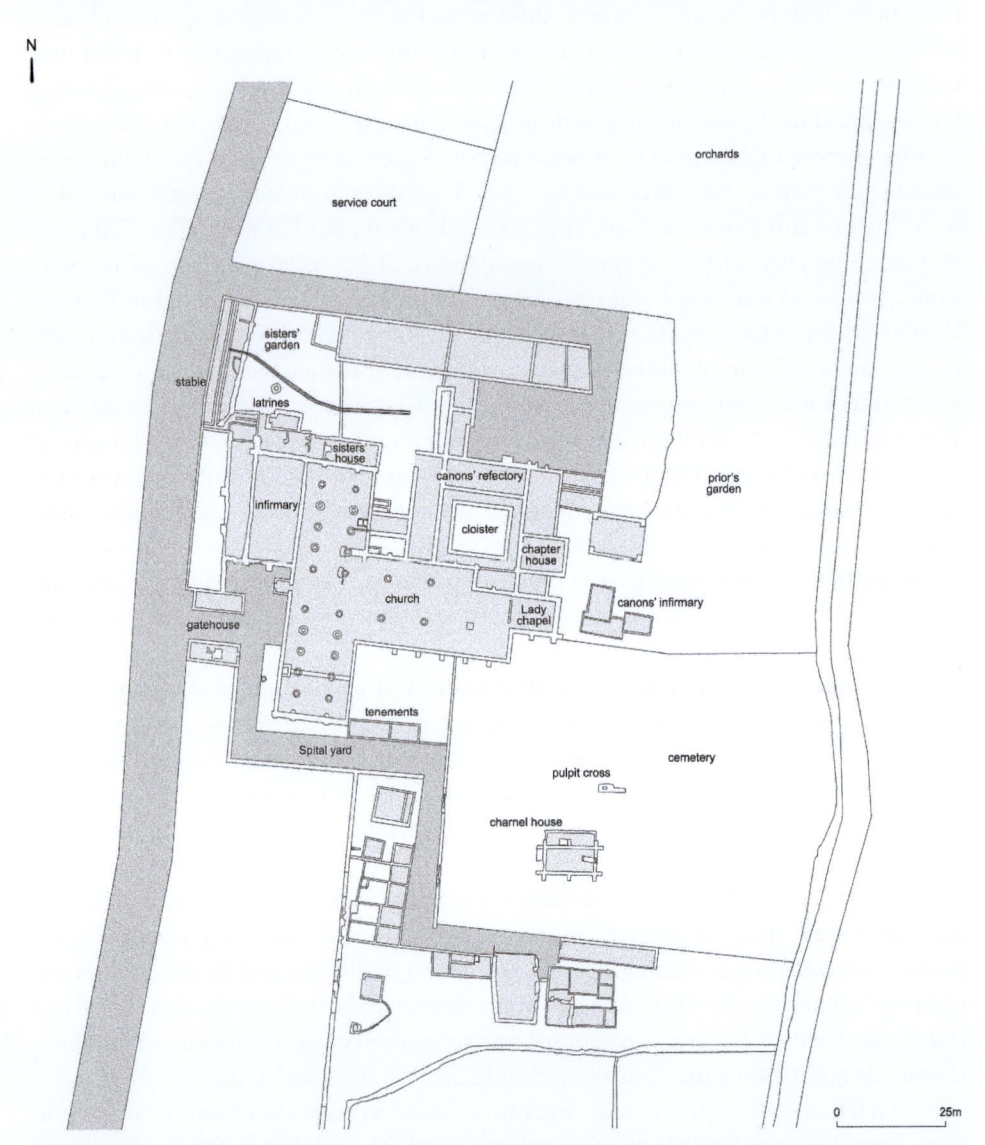

FIGURE 52.5 Plan of St Mary Spital, London, showing the known layout of the site at the time of the Dissolution. The site is clearly separated into two ranges, one for the religious community, and the other for the inmates and the sisters (from Connell et al. 2012, fig. 219)

(© MOLA)

to separate leprous and non-leprous individuals or to separate males and females. The burials at Colchester included some evidence for leprosy, especially in the earlier phases, while some phases included no indications of nutritional stress, such as enamel hypoplasia (Crossan 2004).

At St John the Baptist, Oxford, the infirmary building was located close to the ford over the River Cherwell, and the changes in the architectural plan at the east end suggest that this was the location of the chapel for the inmates (Durham 1991). A hall running off to the north along the run of the river appears to have been a hall for the staff, whilst the rest of the complex, possibly based around a large courtyard of which the infirmary and hall formed the south-east corner, spread to the north and west. The very eastern end of the hospital chapel appeared to contain tanks to hold river water; given their location the tanks may have been used for ritual cleansing or washing facilities linked to the patron saint (Durham 1991, 69). At St Mary Magdalene Hospital, Partney in Lincolnshire, although the majority of the buildings had been heavily damaged by ploughing, geophysics and excavation indicated elements of the layout of the site, located near a crossroad, with the chapel to the east and accommodation to the west (Atkins and Popescu 2010). Burials were located along the path leading up to the chapel from the east, seemingly with those of the religious community, twenty-six male adults, to the south of the path, and a more mixed population of fourteen men, women, and children to the north, as well as three next to the south wall of the chapel, and one inside the chapel building. At St Nicholas Hospital in Lewes, Sussex, more limited evidence for buildings was recovered, although pits of domestic waste suggest the kitchen range was nearby (Barber and Sibun 2010). Foodstuffs seem to have been diverse, with the animal bones suggesting cattle were the main meat supplier, supplemented with pig, sheep or goat, fish, fowl, oysters, and mussels, and the skeletal evidence of the burials suggests that most of those buried at the hospital did not suffer from nutritional deficiencies. The cemetery contained at least 103 individuals, comprised mostly of males, with some females and a small number of children or adolescents, but interestingly one individual was buried with manacles around the ankles and another appeared to have lesions consistent with sores caused by being chained up (Barber and Sibun 2010, 36).

The excavations at St Giles by Brompton Bridge, Brough (North Yorkshire) did not reveal the whole hospital complex, and much of the western side of the compound was eroded, but did suggest a likely split between activity areas, with travelers being provided with respite and spiritual assistance along the north–south road to the east, and permanent residents to the west (Cardwell 1995). Amongst the small cemetery population at least one suffered from leprosy, whilst another, buried with chalice and paten in the chapel, suffered from a slipped proximal femoral epiphysis, and corresponding information from the arms suggests the use of a crutch to move around, but altogether there were signs of high levels of disease and illness (Cardwell 1995; Knüsel et al. 1992). At St Mary Magdalen, Winchester, not only were areas of the cemeteries excavated but portions of the chapel and infirmary hall were investigated, indicating a parallel plan with the hall to the north of the chapel (Roffey 2012). This may represent a more usual layout for leprosy hospitals, with detached chapels and halls, but something similar is seen at St

Giles, Brough, which despite the presence of one individual with leprosy may have been a site more closely associated with the care of travelers and the poor. St Giles, Norwich, was a converted parish church, with its cloister to the north and the parish nave between the infirmary hall and the chapel (Rawcliffe 1999). The hospital at Thornton Abbey consisted of a chapel that appears to have been converted from an Anglo-Norman church, with a later range located to the west, possibly serving as a dormitory for residents and poorer pilgrims, one of whom seems to have lost a Tau cross of St Anthony. Overall, the majority of finds from these excavations were domestic in nature, with very little obviously associated with medical practice.

This brief summary reinforces the sense of variety amongst excavated hospital sites and helps to identify some contradictions. For example, despite the suggestion that the connection between infirmary and chapel was vital to the activities of the hospital (Rawcliffe 1984), the majority of infirmaries or housing for inmates were in fact either built detached or restricted in their access to the chapel, or else moved through the life of the site, as at St Mary Spital (Thomas et al. 1997), St Bartholomew, Bristol (Price and Ponsford 1998), and St Mary, Ospringe, Kent (Smith 1980). This may be due to the greater emphasis placed on sound in the medieval hospital, rather than vision (Horden 2001), for example the hearing of Mass through windows and doors which connected accommodation with the chapel. A better understanding of site layouts allows us to examine patterns of use, rights of access, and hierarchies of space with greater confidence and incorporate observations such as the use of mobile altars at St Mary Spital (Thomas et al. 1997, 48) into a better interpretation of how these sites operated.

Nor has the religious nature of hospital sites been sufficiently appreciated as an essential element in the medical care provided. For some the certainty of a spiritual lifestyle less strict than the monastic cloister was an enviable prospect, and one worth paying for, often leading to the giving of corrodies, an upfront payment for long term care, a practice that could become financially crippling for hospitals (McIntosh 2012; Rawcliffe 2006). In the context of this spiritual lifestyle, gardens and spaces for contemplation have been overlooked by the excavators as essential elements in the care provided, despite the ground plans of many sites showing evidence for claustral ranges, galleried gardens, orchards, and even cemeteries complete with coloured gravels and garden vegetation (Cessford 2015). There is some evidence that sites were laid out according to a common conceptual plan of use, and perhaps even with hierarchical orientations and associations of chapels to the south and east, infirmaries to the north and west. Good examples include St Mary Spital in London, St Mary in Ospringe, and the cemetery of St John's hospital cemetery, Cambridge. Faunal remains from hospital sites suggest that food was nutritional but not of the highest quality, often reducing in quality over the centuries (Thomas et al. 1997; Price and Ponsford 1998; Wall 1981). The presence of a number of small ceramic pipkins from the Hospital of St Mary Spital, vessels usually associated with food production, may suggest the making of small, individual meals or medicinal preparations (Horden 2007; Thomas et al. 1997).

The rise of the almshouse, sometimes portrayed as secular benefactors taking control of mismanaged sites from ecclesiastics (Rubin 1989), did not necessarily indicate any dissatisfaction with the operation of hospitals themselves. Even the collegiate-style secular almshouses of the fifteenth and sixteenth century, such as Browne's Hospital in Stamford, Lincolnshire, still maintained core elements of the medieval hospitals of the eleventh and twelfth century: clean living, piety, prayer, the charitable provision of clothing, food, and drink to the poor, an organized and planned layout, and a chapel (frequently at the east or south-east of a claustral range or collegiate layout). The benefactors had similar controls over the charity too; benefactions were given for specific things, hospitals only took certain kinds of people, and entry was almost always at the discretion of the master of the house. At the heart of the change in terminology appears to be a more general concern with the deserving poor, likely linked to rising urbanization and rural migration to the towns (McIntosh 2012). Accusations of corruption, mismanagement, and repeated calls for reform were also major drivers in changing fashions of benefaction (Carlin 1989; Gilchrist 1995; Orme and Webster 1995; Rubin 1989). The hospitals and almshouses of the second half of the late medieval period still provided aid to those unable to care for themselves, but only after the Reformation would the first truly medical hospitals arise, complete with their own physicians and surgeons.

Conclusion

The archaeological evidence for medicine and public health during the later medieval period is both limited and varied. The material does not match expectation, has often been overlooked and, where there is an abundance, as in the case of hospitals, excavation has been limited and sometimes lacks integration into wider historical debates. There is, however, room for optimism. New techniques such as aDNA have already provided breakthroughs in our understanding of disease and there is now greater maturity in the questions posed and our assessment of the evidence, for example the puzzling lack of medical equipment in the archaeological record. The medieval conception of medicine and health was complex but inherently centred on religion and the connection of the body with the soul, and while some of the medical preparations may have sometimes been dubious to our eyes, the environment of the medieval hospital or almshouse would have been beneficial for many and provided a calm end to life for others.

References cited

Addyman, T., Romankiewicz, T., Macfadyen, K., Ross, A., and Uglow, N. 2013 *The medieval kirk, cemetery and hospice at Kirk Ness, North Berwick: the Scottish Seabird Centre excavations 1999–2006*, Oxbow Books, Oxford

Atkins, R. and Popescu, E. 2010 'Excavations at the hospital of St Mary Magdalen, Partney, Lincolnshire, 2003', *Medieval Archaeology* 54(1), 204–70

Barber, L. and Sibun, L. 2010 'The medieval hospital of St Nicholas, Lewes, East Sussex', *Sussex Archaeological Collections* 148, 79–109

Bifulco, M., Marasco, M., and Pisanti, S. 2008 'Dietary recommendations in the medieval medical school of Salerno', *American Journal of Preventative Medicine* 35(6), 602–3

Brennan, D. F. M. 1995 *Llawhaden Hospice excavations 1992 and 1993, Vol. 1*, Dyfed Archaeological Trust unpublished report project 3577, Llandeilo

Cardwell, P. 1995 'Excavation of the Hospital of St Giles by Brompton Bridge, North Yorkshire', *The Archaeological Journal* 152, 109–245

Carlin, M. 1989 'Medieval English hospitals', in L. Granshaw and R. Porter (eds), *The hospital in history*, Routledge, London, 21–40

Castle, J. and Derham, B. 2005 'The contents of the Barber-surgeon's cabin', in J. Gardiner with M. J. Allen (eds), *Before the mast: life and death aboard the Mary Rose*, The Archaeology of the *Mary Rose* 4, Portsmouth, 189–218

Cessford, C. 2015 'The St John's Hospital cemetery and environs, Cambridge: contextualizing the medieval urban dead', *The Archaeological Journal* 172 (1), 52–120

Clay, R. 1909 *The medieval hospitals of England*, Methuen, London

Connell, B., Gray Jones, A., Redfern, R., and Walker, D. 2012 *A bioarchaeological study of the medieval burials on the site of St Mary Spital: excavations at Spitalfields Market, London E1, 1991–2007*, Museum of London Archaeology Monograph 60, London

Cowan, I. B. and Easson, D. E. 1976 *Mediaeval religious houses, Scotland*, Longmans, London (2nd edn)

Crossan, C. 2004 'Excavations at St Mary Magdalen's Hospital, Brook Street, Colchester', *Essex Archaeology and History* 34, 91–154

Cullum, P. 1989 *Hospitals and charitable provision in medieval Yorkshire*, unpublished PhD thesis, University of York

DeWitte, S. 2010 'Sex differentials in frailty in medieval England', *American Journal of Physical Anthropology* 143(2), 285–97

DeWitte, S. 2014 'Health in post-Black Death London (1350–1538): age patterns of periosteal new bone formation in a post-epidemic population', *American Journal of Physical Anthropology* 155(2), 260–7

Dick, H., Pringle, J., Sloane, B., Carver, J., Wisniewski, K., Haffenden, A., Porter, S., Roberts, D., and Cassidy, N. 2015 'Detection and characterisation of Black Death burials by multi-proxy geophysical methods', *Journal of Archaeological Science* 59, 132–41

Donoghue, H., Spigelman, M., O'Grady, J., Szikossy, I., Pap, I., Lee, O., Wu, H., Besra, G., and Minnikin, D. 2015 'Ancient DNA analysis: an established technique in charting the evolution of tuberculosis and leprosy', *Tuberculosis* 95, S140–S144

Durham, B. 1991 'The infirmary and hall of the medieval hospital of St John the Baptist at Oxford', *Oxoniensia* 56, 17–75

Egan, G. 2007 'The material culture of the care of the sick: some excavated evidence from English medieval hospitals and other sites', in B. Bowers (ed.), *The medieval hospital and medical practice*, Ashgate, Aldershot, 65–76

Farley, M. and Manchester, K. 1989 'The cemetery of the leper hospital of St Margaret, High Wycombe, Buckinghamshire', *Medieval Archaeology* 33, 82–9

Fiorato, V., Boylston, A., and Knüsel, C. 2007 *Blood red roses: the archaeology of a mass grave from the battle of Towton AD 1461*, Oxbow, Oxford

Gilchrist, R. 1995 *Contemplation and action: the other monasticism*, Leicester University Press, London

Gilchrist, R. and Sloane, W. 2005 *Requiem: the medieval monastic cemetery in Britain*, Museum of London Archaeology Service, London

Godfrey, W. 1955 *The English almshouse*, Faber, London

Goodrich, J. 2004 'History of spine surgery in the ancient and medieval worlds', *Neurosurgery Focus* 16(1), 1–13

Grainger, I., Hawkins, D., Cowal, L., and Mikulski, R. 2008 *The Black Death cemetery, East Smithfield, London*, Museum of London Archaeology Service Monograph 43, London

Hall, D. 1995 'Archaeological excavations at St Nicholas Farm, St Andrews, 1986–87', *Tayside and Fife Archaeological Journal* 1, 48–75

Hall, D. 2006 '"Unto yone hospitall at tounis end": the Scottish medieval hospital', *Tayside and Fife Archaeological Journal* 12, 89–106

Hamilton, J. and Toolis, R. 1999 'Further excavations at the site of a medieval leper hospital at St Nicholas Farm, St Andrews', *Tayside and Fife Archaeological Journal* 5, 87–105

Harvey, B. 1993 *Living and dying in England 1100-1540: the monastic experience*, Oxford University Press, Oxford

Horden, P. 2001 'Religion as medicine: music in medieval hospitals', in P. Biller and J. Ziegler (eds), *Religion and medicine in the Middle Ages*, York Medieval Press, York, 135–54

Horden, P. 2007 'A non-natural environment: medicine without doctors and the medieval European hospital', in B. Bowers (ed.), *The medieval hospital and medical practice*, Ashgate, Aldershot, 133–45

Horrox, R. 1994 *The Black Death*, Manchester University Press, Manchester

Keys, L. 1998 'Glass urinals', in G. Egan, *The medieval household*, Medieval finds from excavations in London 6, The Stationery Office, London, 252–4

Knowles, D. and Hadcock, R. 1971 *Medieval religious houses, England and Wales*, Longmans, Harlow

Knüsel, C., Chundun, Z., and Cardwell, P. 1992 'Slipped proximal femoral epiphysis in a priest from the medieval period', *International Journal of Osteoarchaeology* 2, 109–19

Lilley, K. 2015 'Urban planning after the Black Death: townscape transformation in later medieval England (1350–1530)', *Urban History* 42(1), 22–42

Lunt, D. 2012 'The first evidence of leprosy in early mediaeval Scotland: two individuals from cemeteries in St Andrews, Fife, Scotland, with evidence for normal burial treatment', *International Journal of Osteoarchaeology* 23, 310–18

Magilton, J. R., Lee, F., and Boylston, A. (eds) 2008 *'Lepers outside the gate': excavations at the cemetery of the hospital of St James and St Mary Magdalene, Chichester, 1986-7 and 1993*, Council for British Archaeology Research Report 158 and Chichester Excavations 10, York

Manchester, K. and Roberts, C. A. 1989 'The palaeopathology of leprosy in Britain: a review', *World Archaeology* 21(2), 265–72

McIntosh, M. 2012 *Poor relief in England 1350–1600*, Cambridge University Press, Cambridge

Mendum, T. A., Schuenemann, V. J., Roffey, S., Taylor, G. M., Wu, H., Singh, P., Tucker, K., Hinds, J., Cole, S. T., Kierzek, A. M. and Nieselt, K. 2014 'Mycobacterium leprae genomes from a British medieval leprosy hospital: towards understanding an ancient epidemic', *BMC Genomics* 15(1), 270

Moffat, B. 1986 *The first report on researches into the medieval hospital at Soutra Lothian/Borders Region, Scotland*, SHARP, Edinburgh

Moffat, B. and Fulton, J. 1988. *The second report on researches into the medieval hospital at Soutra Lothian/Borders Region, Scotland*, SHARP, Edinburgh

Moffat, B., Thomson, S., and Fulton, J. 1989 *The third report on researches into the medieval hospital at Soutra Lothian/Borders Region, Scotland*, SHARP, Edinburgh

Moorhouse, S. 1993 'Pottery and glass in the medieval monastery', in R. Gilchrist and H. Mytum (eds), *Advances in monastic archaeology*, British Archaeological Reports British Series 227, Oxford, 127–48

Nicholson, H. 2012 'Charity and hospitality in military orders', in I. Fernandes (ed.), *As Ordens Militares: freires, guerreiros, cavaleiros, Vol. 1*, GEsOS, Palmela, 193–206

Nicoud, M. 2008 'Food consumption, a health risk? Norms and medical practice in the Middle Ages', *Appetite* 51(1), 7–9

Orme, N. and Webster, M. 1995 *The English hospital 1070–1570*, Yale University Press, London

Powers, N. 2005 'Cranial trauma and treatment: a case study from the medieval cemetery of St Mary Spital, London', *International Journal of Osteoarchaeology* 15, 1–14

Prescott, E. 1992 *The English medieval hospital c.1050–1640*, Seaby, London

Price, R. and Ponsford, M. 1998 *St Bartholomew's Hospital, Bristol: the excavation of a medieval hospital, 1976–78*, Council for British Archaeology Research Report 110, York

Rawcliffe, C. 1984 'The hospitals of later medieval London', *Medical History* 28, 1–21

Rawcliffe, C. 1995 *Medicine and society in later medieval England*, Sutton, Stroud

Rawcliffe, C. 1999 *Medicine for the soul: the life, death and resurrection of an English medieval hospital*, Sutton, Stroud

Rawcliffe, C. 2006 *Leprosy in medieval England*, Boydell, Woodbridge

Riddle, J. 2007 'Research procedures in evaluating medieval medicine', in B. Bowers (ed.), *The medieval hospital and medical practice*, Ashgate, Aldershot, 3–18

Roberts, C. A. 2002 'The antiquity of leprosy in Britain: the skeletal evidence', in C. A. Roberts, M. Lewis, and K. Manchester (eds), *The past and present of leprosy: archaeological, historical, palaeopathological and clinical approaches*, British Archaeological Reports International Series 1054, Oxford, 213–22

Roberts, C. A. and Cox, M. 2003 *Health and disease in Britain: from prehistory to the present day*, Sutton Publishing, Stroud

Roberts, C. A. and Manchester, K. 1995 *The archaeology of disease*, Sutton, Stroud (2nd edn)

Roffey, S. 2012 'Medieval leper hospitals in England: an archaeological perspective', *Medieval Archaeology* 56, 203–33

Roffey, S. and Tucker, K. 2012 'A contextual study of the medieval hospital and cemetery of St Mary Magdalen, Winchester, England', *International Journal of Paleopathology* 2(4), 170–80

Rubin, M. 1989 'Development and change in English hospitals, 1100–1500', in L. Granshaw and R. Porter (eds), *The hospital in history*, Routledge, London, 41–60

Satchell, A. 1998 *The emergence of leper-houses in medieval England, 1100–1250*, unpublished PhD thesis, University of Oxford, Oxford

Smith, G. H. 1980 'The excavation of the hospital of St Mary of Ospringe, commonly called Maison Dieu', *Archaeologia Cantiana* 95, 81–184

Stone, R. and Appleton-Fox, N. 1996 *A view from Hereford's past: a report on the archaeological excavation of Hereford Cathedral Close in 1993*, Logaston Press, Little Logaston

Sweetinburgh, S. 2004 *The role of the hospital in medieval England: gift-giving and the spiritual economy*, Four Courts, Dublin

Tavormina, M. T. 2009 'Practice, theory and authority in a Middle English medical text: "Barton's Urines Which He Treated at Tilney"', *Journal of Nephrology* 22(S14), S33–S41

Taylor, G. M., Watson, C. L., Bouwman, A. S., Lockwood, D. J. N., and Mays, S. A. 2006 'Variable nucleotide tandem repeat (VNTR) typing of two palaeopathological cases of lepromatous leprosy from mediaeval England', *Journal of Archaeological Science* 33, 1569–79

Theilmann, J. and Cate, F. 2007 'A plague of plagues: the problem of plague diagnosis in medieval England', *Journal of Interdisciplinary History* 37(3), 371–93

Thomas, C., Sloane, B., and Phillpotts, C. 1997 *Excavations at the priory and hospital of St Mary Spital, London*, Museum of London Archaeology Service Monograph 1, London

Wall, S. M. 1981 'The animal bones from the excavation of the hospital of St Mary of Ospringe', *Archaeologia Cantiana* 96, 227–66

Ziegler, P. 2008 *The Black Death*, Faber and Faber, London

CHAPTER 53

LATER MEDIEVAL DEATH AND BURIAL

CHRISTOPHER DANIELL

THE excavation of medieval burials as a subject of academic study only began as an antiquarian interest during the eighteenth and nineteenth centuries. Skeletons and cremated remains were routinely cast aside in favour of artefacts, which were often retrieved from the graves of royalty or bishops. The serious excavation of cemeteries did not start until the 1960s and 1970s when a new methodology was worked out to analyse the cemetery as a whole, rather than individual skeletons (Gilchrist and Sloane 2005, 10). Since then there have been many works written on the subject of medieval death and burial. Hadley (2001) covers the archaeology and monuments of the medieval period—from early Anglo-Saxon to late medieval, while the urban response to death and dying between AD 100 and 1600 is analysed in a collection of cross-disciplinary papers by Bassett (1995). Daniell (1999) covered the history and archaeology of death and burial in the later Middle Ages (1066–1550) but Gilchrist and Sloane (2005) have written the most detailed archaeological summary of the period, analysing graves from monastic cemeteries. Other notable contributions include considerations of death within the life cycle (Gilchrist 2012; Youngs 2006; see Chapter 47 in this *Handbook*), daily life and mortality within a Benedictine monastery (Harvey 1993), the impact of religious change on the death ritual (Gittings 1984 and 1995 for the sixteenth century), the development of the funeral industry (Litten 2002), and the evidence from folklore for the new religious belief systems of the Early Modern Period across Britain and Ireland (Tarlow 2011).

THE ACT OF BURIAL

Compared to the rituals surrounding the death of a person and the following funeral, the act of later medieval burial was often a modest and formulaic affair (Daniell 1999; Gilchrist and Sloane 2005; Hadley 2001). After death the body was processed to the church for the funeral service; the higher in society the individual the more impressive the procession. On arrival the body would be placed before the altar on a hearse and covered by a hearse cloth, at which point the Office for the Dead was said. The number of mourners, candles, and bells was again indicative of the wealth and status of the deceased. A vigil would be held overnight and in the morning further services, including a solemn Requiem Mass.

Burial itself was rarely depicted or commented upon. The few depictions that do survive normally show a priest standing over the grave, saying prayers or sprinkling holy water over the shrouded corpse. After the burial it was widely believed that the soul of the deceased remained near or with the body in the vicinity of the grave (Daniell 1999, 61–2), thereby encouraging hauntings or 'the walking dead'. However, the soul's presence gradually faded and after a year was considered to have left the area. In the longer term, the buried body was not treated with any special respect; gravestones might be re-sold and several cemeteries in London had general clearances of earth and burials with fifty-nine loads of earth being moved from St Dunstan in the West's churchyard (Harding 1995, 128), presumably because the build-up of graves had raised the ground level too high. The collection of charnel (bones collected whilst digging a grave) was an infrequent occurrence and whilst some churches did have a 'charnel house'—notably St Paul's Cathedral in London—most did not and the collection of charnel was not specifically mentioned in the sexton's or grave digger's duties. For the most privileged in society the body might be exhumed, as was the case for Richard Duke of York in 1476, whose body was moved from Pontefract, West Yorkshire, to the more prestigious Fotheringhay Castle after his son Edward IV gained the throne (Sutton et al. 1996). Saints' bodies—or parts of their bodies which were regarded as relics—were also frequently moved, not only in England but across Europe (Robinson 2011).

Cemeteries and Burial Location

A number of considerations had to be addressed before burial could take place: the wishes of the dead person and any surviving relatives, social expectations, and the decrees of the secular or religious authorities. The degree of choice increased with wealth and power, but for the vast majority of the population there was only one real option: to be buried within the local parish cemetery. From her study of London wills, Harding (1995, 122) calculated that between 62 and 85 per cent of people wanted to be buried in their parish church.

Occasionally the location of a burial could be contested between churches, either because of the prestige or payments involved. In the countryside some regions had large number of chapels in distant parts of the parish which were associated with a parish church. However, whilst funeral services could take place in chapels, the burial had to be in the distant parish church, a cause of friction in some areas. Within towns there could also be disputes between parish churches and friaries or hospitals, which had the right of burial. In these cases it was not uncommon for a local agreement to be reached and in some cases burial at a hospital resulted in a payment to the deceased's church. In exceptional cases force was used, as in 1392 when the monks of Abingdon, Oxfordshire, not only seized the body from a funeral cortege to bury it in their own cemetery, but then dug up a further sixty-seven bodies for re-interment (Daniell 1999, 91–2).

For the wealthiest in society, like the Beauchamps (the Earls of Essex) and the Berkeleys in the thirteenth century, the continuation of power and family stability could be underlined by their choice of burial place (Golding 1985). For the same reasons Westminster Abbey became a favoured place of burial for kings and queens, while more unpopular kings were buried elsewhere, notably King John at Worcester Cathedral and Richard III at the Greyfriars in Leicester (Daniell 2008, map 51). Even for the ordinary population, the location of their burial was an important consideration. Prestige was conferred by proximity to the High Altar with invisible radiating rings of holiness through the church and out into the cemetery. Within these rings there could be 'hot spots' of particular sanctity, for example near an altar or sacred image. The prestige of being buried near the High Altar is shown by William Courtney, the Archbishop of Canterbury, who requested that the three deans buried there should be moved 'to some other honourable place' so that he could be buried there instead. The chancel was normally reserved for priests and other clergy, being near the High Altar: an analysis of 105 burial requests for burial in the chancel revealed eighty-five such requests were by rectors, vicars, or clerics (Daniell 1999, 97–8).

Initially, burial inside the church was severely restricted and in 1342 the Dean of Carlisle stated that all burials within the church walls were to be prohibited without a bishop's licence, save those of patrons and rectors. By the end of the Middle Ages, however, lay burials within the nave and aisles were common for the richer in society. Locations close to the altars of particular saints were popular (the Virgin Mary being the most sought after) as well as proximity to images. Outside, the cemetery was less differentiated (a small number requested to be near the churchyard cross) with no suggestion that south side of the church was the more favoured, at least in medieval burial requests. Spouses often requested to be buried near each other or together—or with wider family groups, such as children or parents. In archaeological terms spatial zoning is sometimes observed. In St Andrew's Fishergate (York) a line of male burials—taken to be Gilbertine monks—were located outside the east end of the church (Stroud and Kemp 1993). In other cemeteries there are occasionally more children's burials in one particular area and the Castle Green cemetery in Hereford was, after it had fallen out of use, used specifically for burial of children and infants, possibly those who had not been christened (Shoesmith 1980).

Grave Goods

Although the absence of grave goods is sometimes seen as a distinguishing feature of the Christian burial tradition, the true situation was more nuanced. St Cuthbert, for example, had a great variety of objects buried with his body and the Venerable Bede also mentions holy people being buried with grave goods. This tradition continued after the Norman Conquest and one manuscript image of Thomas Becket clearly shows his burial in his robes and mitre within his coffin. In fact, it was a commonplace for bishops to be interred with their robes on and sometimes with religious books or crosses. This has never been adequately explained theologically though in some visions of heaven bishops can be identified by the wearing of a mitre. Priests too were regularly buried with a (normally base metal) patten and chalice, though, unlike bishops, without their robes.

This tradition extended to the highest reaches of royalty and nobility, with eighteenth-century discoveries of two kings reportedly being buried in robes: King John and King Edward I. In their study of seventy-six cemeteries, consisting of over eight thousand graves, Gilchrist and Sloane (2005, 83) identified 2.6 per cent of burials with clothing or dress accessories buried with them. This finding shows that Christian burial with objects was not forbidden and could indicate an individual's status in society. The largest number of clothed burials on any site is that of the eighteen burials at the Augustinian Friary in Hull, Yorkshire, dated to the late fourteenth and early fifteenth century. The majority of these burials were in prestigious locations within the church (eight in the nave, six in the choir) and the bodies were wearing woollen garments in the latest fashions (Gilchrist and Sloane 2005, 84; the full site report is yet to be published). One unique grave, discussed by Yeoman (see Chapter 40), is that of the late Middle Ages pilgrim burial found at Worcester Cathedral. The pilgrim was wearing boots, which had been cut to allow the feet to be placed in them and he was buried with his pilgrim's staff (Lubin 1990). An excellent summary of the range of grave goods from monastic cemeteries is given in Gilchrist and Sloane (2005, 78–129): as well as clothing, a wide variety of other artefacts were included such as lead crosses, rosaries, and pilgrim badges. Plant remains have also been discovered within burials, for example, box leaves at Hull, a body wrapped in rushes at Hulton Abbey (Klemperer and Boothroyd 2004), and at Winchester Abbey a burial laid on a bed of oak.

The Body in the Grave

Osteological research is essential for understanding illnesses, indications of trauma, and more rarely the cause of death, as in the cases of the battle victims from Towton (Fiorato et al. 2000; see Chapter 26 in this *Handbook*). The analysis of DNA and isotopes too are increasingly making an important contribution, as Roberts, Bekvalac, and Redfern show in their analysis of the body in the grave (Chapter 51), and even finer detail is likely to be achievable in the foreseeable future.

An illustration of this kind of research is the discovery of the body of Richard III in the choir of the former Greyfriars of Leicester, now beneath a car park. While the burial location of the skeleton suggested a person of importance, mitochondrial DNA analysis and the examination of the skeleton in February 2013 by the University of Leicester were able to confirm that the skeleton was 'beyond reasonable doubt' that of King Richard III. The skeleton had severe scoliosis of the spine, making one shoulder higher than the other, and ten injuries consistent with injuries by bladed weapons. There were two to the skull which are likely to have been the cause of death, the location of one indicating that he was not wearing a helmet at the time. He had suffered at least one injury after death, that of a bladed injury to the right buttock (which had damaged the pelvis) and this was probably a post-death act of humiliation as the body was known to have been naked, slung on a horse and ridden into Leicester. Analysis of his stomach contents revealed that he had worms (Buckley et al. 2013) while isotopic evidence apparently could be matched to the historical records of where he had lived and journeyed. The historical records show that Richard spent much of his life in the east of England, but his isotopic signature indicated a more westerly bias—and this may have been because he ate expensive foods and wines which were imported from the Continent (Lamb et al. 2014).

Distinctive Mortuary Practices

Mortuary practices in the later Middle Ages show much less variation than the preceding Anglo-Saxon and early Norman periods. By the later Middle Ages the norm was for burial in churchyards, with graves aligned broadly east–west, and the body buried in a shroud or coffin. The relatively minor variations within this pattern are the grave goods (as described above) and the division of the body for burial in different locations. The most common practice was the separate burial of the heart or viscera, often within their own caskets, allowing a body to be sited in different places. For nobility this had the benefit of maintaining their own, or their families, influence over several sites, as well as receiving prayers for their soul from multiple churches. The practice did decline after it was outlawed by Pope Boniface VIII in 1299 in the bull *Detestande feritatus* (Brown 1981), but was persistent throughout the Middle Ages. Gilchrist and Sloane (2005, 159–60) give archaeological examples, all of which date from the late twelfth to fourteenth centuries, though other examples are known from historical records (Gill 1936; Round 1923).

Whilst heart burials were a feature of mainstream Christian practice, most distinctive mortuary practices occur either in liminal societies or under extreme social conditions. The most prominent of the liminal societies were the burials of Jews. The Jews were expelled from England by Edward I in 1290 but before this date their communities were already highly visible as 'other' in Christian communities as they were set apart by their culture and beliefs and forced to identify themselves by wearing two strips of yellow cloth. There were ten Jewish cemeteries in England but the only one to have been extensively archaeologically excavated is the Jewbury cemetery in York (Lilley et al. 1994). Jewish cemeteries were laid out as gardens, with many plants and a high surrounding wall demarcating the living from the dead. There was some grouping of burials by sex and age, including a cluster of children's graves. However, the most distinctive feature of the Jewbury cemetery in archaeological terms was the careful avoidance of the intercutting of graves, which derives from the Jewish belief that the body will rise up according to its condition in the grave. That intercutting of graves was avoided also implies that the graves must have been carefully marked in some way—probably by mounds, but perhaps by some more long-lasting method or a long-term organized system of burial. Other small areas of other Jewish cemeteries have also been excavated (for an overview see Hinton 2003).

The second distinctive liminal group were the lepers of medieval England. Leprosy was particularly feared and by the later Middle Ages leper hospitals—located on the outskirts of towns to avoid contagion—were a common feature of larger urban centres (see Chapter 52). On entering a leper hospital the leprous person was pronounced dead to the world. In France a leprous person was made to stand in an open grave, whilst in England the leprous person was led into church and had to kneel under a black cloth 'in the manner of a dead man' and after a Mass was led outside and had earth cast on their feet. So far the largest number of burials excavated from a leper hospital is from St James and St Mary Magdalene in Chichester, West Sussex. In all 351 individuals were recovered here but, apart from the eighty-three-plus leprous individuals excavated, there was no significant difference with a normal parish church cemetery (Lee and Magilton 1989; Magilton et al. 2008).

Distinctive mortuary practices are also sometimes encountered in the archaeological record when people died in battle (see Chapter 26) or during outbreaks of plague (Chapter 51), but they also occurred when an individual was condemned to death and by the later Middle Ages those put to death were often buried without care. One gallows site may have been found by a rescue excavation when two skeletons were uncovered at a crossroads between Dry Drayton and Oakington in Cambridgeshire. Their identification as executed criminals was suggested by medieval records showing that Crowland Abbey maintained a gallows there (Halliday 1997). Another similar site was excavated in Norwich, Norfolk, at the cemetery of St Margaret in Combusto. Some criminal dead buried there were orientated east–west, but others were north–south; some had their hands still bound behind them or had been thrown in face down. There had been no preparation for burial and many were still fully clothed (Ayres 1990). The practice was not uniform, however, and the Order of St John, the Knights Hospitaller, claimed papal privilege from the late thirteenth century to bury those who had given alms 'whatever ... the manner of their death'. In some areas the Hospitallers actively collected the bodies of those who had been hanged (Gilchrist and Sloane 2005, 73–4).

Heretical beliefs against religious orthodoxy could also lead to death, most frequently by burning because fire was thought to cleanse the soul. Towards the end of the Middle Ages and into the Tudor period the number of deaths by burning rose steadily as firstly Lollards and then Protestants or Catholics were burnt by the State. The historical records of heretical movements in England have been researched and mapped (Lambert 2002) and this has allowed documented burning sites to be broadly identified. In some cases memorials have been placed on the location, but it is unlikely much would remain archaeologically except for charring or burnt soil.

The Church deemed the act of suicide to be self-slaughter, though the term was graded into different types, with the worst being the loss of will to live, whereas suicide through madness was treated less harshly and juries were often reluctant to convict a person for suicide through madness as the Crown immediately seized the property and lands of the deceased. In fact, throughout most of the Middle Ages a lenient approach was taken to the burial of suicides and most were buried in the local cemetery. The harsh and stricter punishments of suicides after death, which resulted in the stake through the heart, and burial at a crossroads, were only rigorously enforced from the late fifteenth century onwards. The reasoning was two-fold: a stake would stop the body 'walking', and even if it did not, a crossroads burial would confuse the deceased into not knowing which way to go. This type of burial was not uncommon in the sixteenth century (Seabourne and Seabourne 2000; 2001) and burials at crossroads were only finally abolished by an Act of Parliament in 1823 (Halliday 1997).

Commemorative Monuments

By the end of the twelfth century the theology of Purgatory had become a prominent belief across Europe and particularly so in Britain (see Chapter 54). Purgatory was a place between heaven and hell where a person's sins were purged, allowing them—in a purified state—to reach heaven. Purgatory itself was full of horrors but a person's soul could be helped by the living saying prayers or masses for the deceased's soul. Commemoration and the need for remembrance thus became a key issue for both the dead and the living. For the most wealthy in society building a chantry chapel within a church, with one or more priests to say masses for the deceased's soul, was an attractive option. Whilst their function is well understood, there has been little research into this topic with some notable exceptions (Cook 1947; Colvin 2000; Roffey 2008; Snell 1978).

Later medieval commemorative tombs and monuments for the powerful have survived in large numbers across Britain, the majority of them within churches. Particularly fine examples survive for royalty (for example, in Westminster Abbey), nobility (for example, the tomb of Richard Beauchamp, the Earl of Warwick, in Warwick), and ecclesiastics such as the numerous bishops' tombs in cathedrals around the country. There has been considerable study of late medieval monuments with two expert societies being created to further their study: the 'Church Monument Society' and the 'Monumental Brass Society' both of which have extensive web pages with bibliographies and journals.

A broad overview of monuments in both the early and late Middle Ages is given by Saul (2009) and includes an analysis of both gender and social hierarchical issues. There is an active interest in both brasses and monuments with academic analysis becoming more specialized and targeted (e.g. for brasses Coales 1987; Norris 1995; Saul 2001). Monuments could memorialize a person across a wide area, either being placed in very important regional churches, or across the landscape, and Hall and Kratze (2005) discuss monuments associated with Cistercians across Europe. A particularly prominent form occurs with the group of Eleanor Crosses (crosses erected by Edward I to mark the route along which Eleanor of Castile's body was carried to Westminster Abbey). Shakesby (1993) considers these monuments express the grief that Edward I felt on her death, but Coldstream (1991) makes the point that, since the crosses were placed in towns, they were also a statement of royal power.

Whilst grand monuments often survive, lesser monuments are much rarer, though occasionally medieval grave-slabs and headstones are uncovered through archaeological excavation. A particularly fine series of three hundred grave-slabs were discovered when the church at Bakewell, Derbyshire, was rebuilt in 1841, and in church excavations it is not unusual to find occasional grave-slabs, for example during the Anglo-Saxon excavations of Raunds Furnell (Cramp 1996) or those at St Andrew's Priory, Fishergate, in York (Stroud and Kemp 1993). There has been surprisingly little in-depth analysis of grave-slabs, however; site reports provide individual accounts but there has been no systematic analysis on a national scale. One regional analysis is that of West Yorkshire (Ryder 1991) and Stocker has written about medieval monument markers in Kent (Stocker 1988). At a church level the Victorians undertook considerable recording of medieval grave-slabs, but there is little recent published, though Ryder (1993; 1994; 2000a; 2000b; 2002; 2003; 2005) is an exception. For the later historical periods, Mytum (2003) provides a good overview.

Small monuments within a graveyard are rarely discovered, which is either because they were not used, or else the materials they were made of (such as wood) have not survived. Some stone rounded-headed headstones have been found in monastic and parish contexts, but this practice ceased after the fourteenth century, and there are no fifteenth- or sixteenth-century headstones recorded (Gilchrist and Sloane 2005, 189–90). Given the increasing abundance of intra-church memorials during the later medieval period, the absence of cemetery headstone or monuments is puzzling.

Medieval Royal Tombs

Late medieval royal tombs are usually at the extreme end of cost, design, and status of the medieval tombs. The only modern analysis of the group is by Duffy, but there are a number of specialist studies about individual tombs or aspects of them (Duffy 1999). Duffy highlights the *Liber Regie Capelle* (written around 1448, but probably follows earlier works) which is a prescriptive account of the English royal burial ritual (Duffy 1999, 181–6), from the moment of death to burial. Only a small fraction of the ceremony and ritual would be discoverable in the archaeological record. The funeral took place over two days: during day one the coffin was placed in the hearse and an elaborate structure was constructed before the main altar to hold the coffin and candles; at Elizabeth of York's funeral her Westminster hearse had 1,016 candles. The service included the Dirige service and lessons; thereafter the mourners retired for dinner and a vigil would be held. Day two included three masses, presenting of the achievements and the offering of cloths, a sermon, censing the coffin, burial of the coffin, and the breaking of the signs of office. There were three items which were overwhelmingly important for the funeral: cloths, shields, and candles. The cloths were normally black with images or heraldic symbols on them. The burial of the body itself might be in the tomb itself (as with Henry III or Edward I), but the majority of later medieval royal burials were in vaults beneath.

Conclusion

Theoretical perspectives on the study of death and burial have hitherto been most prominent for those periods where there are no, or very few, historical resources, in particular the prehistoric and early Anglo-Saxon timeframes (Parker Pearson 2003; Williams 2010). This picture is now changing and, since the 1970s, historical and archaeological studies of death and burial in the later medieval period have increasingly run in parallel or been intertwined. The future is promising, particularly as greater efforts are made to place bioarchaeological contributions into a wider social and economic context. In terms of the archaeological evidence for death and burial practices the Norman Conquest resulted in little noticeable change, though Daniell (2002) has attempted to identify some themes. The major change from pagan to Christian burial practices had taken place gradually over the previous centuries and by 1066 the previously pagan Vikings of Normandy had converted to Christianity. At the other end of the period, although the Reformation during the sixteenth century did lead to fundamental changes to religious beliefs and social attitudes to Christianity and new Protestant beliefs from the 1540s onwards, the actual process of putting the body in the ground remained the same, making the theological shift almost invisible at least in terms of below-ground archaeology.

References cited

Ayres, B. 1990 'Norwich', *Current Archaeology* 122, 56–9
Bassett, S. (ed.) 1995 *Death in towns: urban responses to the dying and the dead, 100–1600*, Leicester University Press, Leicester
Brown, E. 1981 'Death and the human body in the later Middle Ages: the legislation of Boniface VIII on the division of the corpse', *Viator* 12, 221–70
Buckley, R., Morris, M., Appleby, J., King T., O'Sullivan, D., and Foxhall, L. 2013 '"The king in the car park", new light on the death and burial of Richard III in the Grey Friars church, Leicester, in 1485', *Antiquity* 87(336), 519–38
Coales, J. (ed.) 1987 *The earliest English brasses: patronage, style and workshops 1270–1350*, Monumental Brass Society, London

Coldstream, N. 1991 'The commissioning and design of the Eleanor crosses', in D. Parsons (ed.), *Eleanor of Castile 1290-1990*, Paul Watkins, Stamford, 55-67

Colvin, H. 2000 'The origin of chantries', *Journal of Medieval History* 26(2), 163-73

Cook, G. H. 1947 *Medieval chantries and chantry chapels*, Phoenix, London

Cramp, R. 1996 'The monumental stone', in A. Boddington, *Raunds Furnells: the Anglo-Saxon church and churchyard*, English Heritage Archaeological Report 7, English Heritage, London

Daniell, C. 1999 *Death and burial in medieval England*, Routledge, London

Daniell, C. 2002 'Conquest, crime and theology in the burial record, 1066-1200', in S. Lucy and A. Reynolds (eds), *Burial in early medieval England and Wales*, The Society for Medieval Archaeology Monograph 17, London 241-54

Daniell, C. 2008 *Atlas of medieval Britain*, Routledge, London

Duffy, M. 1999 *Royal tombs of medieval England*, The History Press, London

Fiorato, V., Boylston, A., and Knüsel, C. 2001 *Blood red roses: the archaeology of a mass grave from the Battle of Towton AD 1461*, Oxbow, Oxford

Gilchrist, R. 2012 *Medieval life: archaeology and the life course*, The Boydell Press, Woodbridge

Gilchrist, R. and Sloane, W. 2005 *Requiem: the medieval monastic cemetery in Britain*, Museum of London Archaeology Service, London

Gill, A. 1936 'Heart burials', *Proceedings of the Yorkshire Architectural and Archaeological Society* 7(4), 3-18

Gittings, C. 1984 *Death burial and the individual in Early Modern England*, Routledge, London

Gittings, C. 1995 'Urban funerals in late medieval and Reformation England', in S. Bassett (ed.), *Death in towns: urban responses to the dying and the dead, 100-1600*, Leicester University Press, Leicester, 170-83

Golding, B. 1985 'Burials and benefactions: an aspect of monastic patronage in thirteenth-century England', in W. M. Ormrod (ed.), *Symposium on England in the thirteenth century: Harlaxton Conference Proceedings*, University of Nottingham, Nottingham, 64-75

Hadley, D. M. 2001 *Death in medieval England*, Tempus, Stroud

Hall, J. and Kratzke, C. (eds) 2005 *Sepulturae Cistercienses: burial, memorial and patronage*, Cîteaux, Studia et documenta 14, Forges-Chimay, Cîteaux

Halliday, R. 1997 'Criminal graves and rural crossroads', *British Archaeology* 25, 6

Harding, V. 1995 'Burial choice and burial location in later medieval London', in S. Bassett (ed.), *Death in towns: urban responses to the dying and the dead, 100-1600*, Leicester University Press, Leicester, 119-35

Harvey, B. 1993 *Living and dying in England 1100-1540: the monastic experience*, The Clarendon Press, Oxford

Hinton, D. A. 2003 'Medieval Anglo-Jewry: the archaeological evidence', in P. Skinner (ed.), *Jews in medieval Britain*, Boydell and Brewer, Rochester, 97-111

Klemperer, W. D. and Boothroyd, N. 2004 *Excavations at Hulton Abbey, Staffordshire 1987-1994*, The Society for Medieval Archaeology Monograph 21, Leeds

Lamb, A. L., Evans J. E., Buckley, R., and Appleby, J. 2014 'Multi-isotope analysis demonstrates significant lifestyle changes in King Richard III', *Journal of Archaeological Science* 50, 559-65

Lambert, M. 2002 *Medieval heresy, popular movements from the Gregorian Reform to the Reformation*, Blackwell, Oxford

Lee, F. and Magilton, J. 1989 'The cemetery of the hospital of St James and St Mary Magdalene, Chichester: a case study', *World Archaeology* 21(2), 273-82

Lilley, J. M., Stroud, G., Brothwell, D. R., Williamson, M. H. 1994 *The Jewish burial ground at Jewbury*, The Archaeology of York: the medieval cemeteries 12/3, Council for British Archaeology, York

Litten, J. 2002 *The English way of death: the common funeral since 1450*, Robert Hale Ltd, London

Lubin, H. 1990 *Worcester pilgrim*, Worcester Cathedral Publications, Worcester

Magilton, J. R., Lee, F., and Boylston, A. (eds) 2008 *'Lepers outside the gate': excavations at the cemetery of the hospital of St James and St Mary Magdalene, Chichester, 1986-7 and 1993*, Council for British Archaeology Research Report 158 and Chichester Excavations 10, York

Mytum, H. 2003 *Mortuary monuments and burial grounds of the historic period*, Springer, London

Norris, M. 1995 'Later medieval monumental brasses: an urban funerary industry and the representation of death', in S. Bassett (ed.), *Death in towns: urban responses to the dying and the dead, 100–1600*, Leicester University Press, Leicester, 184–209

Parker Pearson, M. 2003 *The archaeology of death and burial*, Sutton, Stroud

Robinson, J. 2011 *Finer than gold: saints and their relics in the Middle Ages*, The British Museum Press, London

Roffey, S. 2008 *Chantry chapels and medieval strategies for the afterlife*, Tempus, Stroud

Round, J. H. 1923 'The heart of St Roger', *Transactions of the Essex Archaeological Society* new series 16, 1–5

Ryder, P. F. 1991 *Medieval cross slab grave covers in West Yorkshire*, West Yorkshire Archaeology Service, Wakefield

Ryder, P. F. 1993 'A medieval cross slab grave cover at St John the Baptist's churh, Staveley', *Transactions of the Hunter Archaeological Society* 17, 71–3

Ryder, P. F. 1994 'Some further medieval cross slabs in County Durham', *Durham Archaeological Journal* 10, 43–54

Ryder, P. F. 2000a 'St John's Church, Stanwick, North Yorkshire: the medieval cross slabs', *Church Monuments Society* XVII, 5–13

Ryder, P. F. 2000b 'Medieval cross slab grave covers in Northumberland 1: South West Northumberland', *Archaeologia Aeliana* series 5, 28, 51–110

Ryder, P. F. 2002 'Medieval cross slab grave covers in Northumberland 2: Newcastle and South East Northumberland', *Archaeologia Aeliana* series 5, 30, 75–137

Ryder, P. F. 2003 'Medieval cross slab grave covers in Northumberland 3: North Northumberland', *Archaeologia Aeliana* series 5, 32, 91–136

Ryder, P. F. 2005 *The medieval cross slab grave covers in Cumbria*, Cumberland and Westmorland Antiquarian and Archaeological Society, Kendal

Saul, N. 2001 *Death, art and memory in medieval England: the Cobham family and their monuments, 1300–1500*, Oxford University Press, Oxford

Saul, N. 2009 *English church monuments in the Middle Ages: history and representation*, Oxford University Press, Oxford

Seabourne, A. and Seabourne, G. 2001 'Suicide or accident: self killing in medieval England', *The British Journal of Psychiatry* 178, 42–7

Seabourne, G. and Seabourne, A. 2000 'The law on suicide in medieval England', *The Journal of Legal History* 21, 21–48

Shakesby, D. 1993 'The crosses of Queen Eleanor', *Medieval History* 3, 26–9

Shoesmith, R. 1980 *Hereford city excavations 1: excavations at Castle Green*, Council for British Archaeology Research Report 36, York

Snell, L. S. 1978 'London chantries and chantry chapels', *Collectanea Londiniensia, Studies in London Archaeology and History presented to Ralph Merrifield*, London and Middlesex Archaeological Society, London, 216–23

Stocker, B. 1988 'Medieval grave markers in Kent', *Church Monuments Society* 12, 106–14

Stroud, G. and Kemp, R. L. 1993 *Cemeteries of the church and priory of St Andrew, Fishergate*, The Archaeology of York: the medieval cemeteries 12/2, Council for British Archaeology, York

Sutton, A. E., Visser-Fuchs, L., and Hammond P. W. 1996 *The reburial of Richard Duke of York 21–30 July 1476*, The Richard III Society, London

Tarlow, S. 2011 *Ritual, belief and the dead in early modern Britain and Ireland*, Cambridge University Press, Cambridge

Williams, H. 2010 *Death and memory in early medieval Britain*, Cambridge University Press, Cambridge

Youngs, D. 2006 *The life-cycle in western Europe c.1300–1500*, Manchester University Press, Manchester

CHAPTER 54

THE MEDIEVAL AFTERLIFE

SIMON ROFFEY

A belief in the afterlife was fundamental to later medieval religious practice. Far from being an indefinable notion based on faith alone, this was a conviction that was buttressed by a raft of pious and devotional practices, vibrant liturgies, and ultimately underpinned by official church doctrine. It was further supported by diverse, and often sumptuous, architectural structures such as chapels, altars, tombs, and memorials as well as a colourful panoply of painting, sculpture, and imagery. Inside the pre-Reformation church, these spaces resounded with prayer, complex liturgies, and the mystical drama of the Mass. Outside, belief in life after death also governed people's day-to-day lives to a large degree. Many of the material aspirations of the laity, particularly the aspirational merchant classes of the late medieval period, were directed towards this end. Thus, much of how people acted and thought was indelibly linked to a sense that there was some form of existence after natural death, and that life was in many ways a preparation for this. Many churches of the period were decorated with themes such as the 'Day of Judgement', or 'Doom', above their chancel arches which marked the spatial transition between church nave and the sanctity of the sacred space of the High Altar. Here, the message was clear: this way, salvation lies. Rare survivals of 'Doom' paintings, which must represent similar arrangements once to be found at many other churches, can still be seen today at the parish churches of St Thomas's in Salisbury, Wiltshire, and North Leigh, Oxfordshire (Figure 54.1).

Central to these assertions about the afterlife was the idea of Purgatory, a transitional place which came to dominate both the world-view of ordinary people, and the religious practices encouraged and promoted by the pre-Reformation church and its artistic and architectural landscape. Moreover, it was Purgatory which was to give rise to a whole new class of medieval monument and institution: the chantry chapel.

FIGURE 54.1 Doom painting, North Leigh Church, Oxfordshire. On the Day of Judgment the dead can be seen rising from their graves to be either welcomed into heaven (left), or consigned to the gaping mouth of hell (right)

(© Simon Roffey)

Purgatory

Beliefs in an intermediate state or place where the soul was held between death and judgement can be found as early as the fourth century (McNeill 2011) and a link between intercessory prayer and purgatorial remission was already being explored in the Benedictine monasteries of late Carolingian Europe. Requests for 'soul masses' become common in wills in England from the tenth century, but it is in the late twelfth century, a period identified by the historian Jacques Le Goff as the 'Birth of Purgatory', that the concept became formalized. By the 1274 Council of Lyons, Purgatory was formally institutionalized as a place that souls 'are purged after their death, by purgatorial or purificatory penalties' where they are 'served by the suffrages of the living faithful' (Le Goff 1984, 285). Purgatory, therefore, was ultimately viewed as an assurance of deliverance of salvation, albeit one that involved a temporal period of purification and absolution, and one that relied on the services of the living.

From the later thirteenth century attempts were made to introduce a more conscious and literal mapping of Purgatory. The theologian Thomas Aquinas, for example, claimed that the location of Purgatory lay below the earth and was in direct proximity to hell (Le Goff 1984, 268–9). For some there was a close relationship between hell and Purgatory, for others it was merely an 'anteroom' to heaven. Either way, what was important was that Purgatory was existent and temporal, and that mechanisms for its relief were in place and enshrined in church doctrine. Underlying this was the belief that there was a traffic between the living and the dead. Saints also had a role to play and, when petitioned, could often intercede on behalf of the dead. This dynamic intercessory function is further revealed by the remarkable set of medieval wall paintings from South Leigh parish church, Oxfordshire (Figure 54.2). One scene on the south wall of the nave shows the 'weighing of souls'. Here the figure of the Blessed Virgin Mary is depicted surreptitiously tipping the scales in favour of a soul which is being weighed by the archangel Michael. The successful intercessory intervention of the Blessed Virgin is clear. The fact that she uses a devotional object, a rosary, to affect the balance acts, however, as a powerful metaphor to underline the devotional responsibilities of the living.

The formulation of the doctrine of Purgatory crystallized the responsibility of the living towards the dead. One important consequence from the thirteenth century was that more formal liturgical measures were developed to influence the passage of souls in Purgatory and to somehow diminish the period spent there. Central to this was the Mass, which Aquinas recommended was the most useful suffrage for the dead together with alms and prayers (McNeill 2011, 3). Consequently, Masses could be targeted and include special intercessory prayers for the dead, either individually or as a defined group providing 'a neat framework for integration of Masses into penitential practices'

FIGURE 54.2 Medieval wall painting from South Leigh Church, Oxfordshire, showing the Virgin Mary and St Michael weighing a soul. The Virgin can be seen pulling up the scales with her rosary to counteract the small devil's attempt to drag it down

(© Simon Roffey)

(Rubin 1991, 51). It is these developments that ultimately provided the rationale and impetus for the medieval chantry, a distinct type of intercessory foundation that is documented increasingly from the mid-thirteenth century. The chantry in essence was a foundation and endowment of a Mass to be celebrated at an altar, either existing or specially provided, for the souls of the founders and other specified persons (Roffey 2008, 16). However, it was the setting for such chantry Masses, often in the form of elaborate chapels and associated architectural and artistic forms and spaces, that was to make such an important contribution to the form, fabric, and material culture of the late medieval church. Although traces of its architectural form can be seen a century or so earlier than the first documented examples (Colvin 2000; Crouch 2001; Roffey 2007b; 2008), it is only in the late medieval period that we see the chantry chapel emerge as the preeminent institution, and monumental strategy, dedicated wholly to the afterlife.

Chantries, Chapels, and Memorial Spaces

The religious basis for the foundation of a chantry primarily concerned medieval beliefs in the afterlife, specifically the concept of Purgatory, and the celebration of an assigned Mass as a unit of merit (Burgess 1991; 2000a). That the chantry was probably the most common, and also one of the most distinctive, of all late medieval religious foundations further attests to the extent to which Purgatory overshadowed much of medieval life. However, far from being mere vainglorious and individualistic monuments, chantry foundations contributed to a religiously vibrant and socially active community and, through associated charitable provisions, they were also of great significance to the lives of ordinary people. Often, chantry endowment provided for the establishment of a local system of welfare, including regular almsgiving and the establishment of schools and hospitals (Roffey 2007a). At Towcester church, Northamptonshire, for example, Sponne's chantry founded in 1447 provided for one priest for preaching and another for teaching in the grammar school. Many chantries, in the form of guilds and fraternities, were corporate ventures from the outset making these financially dependent institutions more accessible to a broader spectrum of medieval society.

Chantry chapels came in all shapes and sizes. Some were founded above gatehouses and constructed on bridges, as at Wakefield, North Yorkshire, or in churchyards, as at Bray, Berkshire, and at Chew Magna in Somerset, where only the earthworks of the foundation survive (Roffey 2008, 95). The majority, however, were established within the body of parish churches, monasteries, and cathedrals. Even here, however, their specific forms were multifarious and often dependent on individual aspirations, design, wealth, and ultimately, considerations of space (Figure 54.3). Some of the great collegiate foundations of the medieval period, such as St George's Chapel in Windsor, Berkshire, and King's College, Cambridge, were very much like 'superchantries' with numerous chantries and chantry priests attached to them. At the other end of the scale, in smaller, more spatially restricted parish churches limitations on space needed to be negotiated. At St Mary's, Luton in Bedfordshire, for example, the small Barnard Chapel was founded in a tiny sunken recess in the south wall of the chancel. This late fifteenth-century feature has a lierne vault and is barely a metre deep by a couple of metres wide.

The majority of chantries, however, were intended to be temporary and generated very little in the way of physical remains; associated Masses were simply celebrated at existing altars. They were technically a service, and not necessarily visible architecturally. The architectural context for some chantries, such as a chapel and its fixture and fittings, as well as in some instances tombs and heraldic devices, may constitute the only remaining physical evidence. A number of chantries were intended from the outset to last in perpetuity, and the wealthy may also have built special altars and chapels to serve

FIGURE 54.3 Rare example of stone cage chantry chapel in a parish church. The Markham Chapel, Newark Church, Nottinghamshire, dates to the early sixteenth century. Note the small squint window cut into the chapel east wall to give a view to the altars situated in the east end of the church

(© Simon Roffey)

and to house the celebrations from which they sought to profit. These chantries often took the form of small parclosed or 'caged' areas which could also function as side chapels (Figure 54.3). These structures, although much altered with time, are still a very noticeable feature of many late medieval churches and former monastic establishments, though many more were lost during the Reformation and as a consequence of the Act of Dissolution in 1547 (Figure 54.4). Despite several outstanding examples, such as those in the cathedral at Winchester, Hampshire, and in Tewkesbury Abbey, Gloucestershire (Figure 54.5), there is often little physical trace of former chantry chapels, even in many of the English cathedrals where they might otherwise be expected to survive. At York Minster, for example, one of the great cathedral churches of medieval England, where much medieval fabric is still extant, hardly any trace survives of the seventy or so chantries that are known to have been operating in the early sixteenth century, many of which must have had some sort of physical presence (Gee 1994; Sheils 1999, 105).

Documentary references to chantry foundation, especially in wills, licences, and certificates, are likewise few in number. In particular, barely any records survive for chantries founded in monastic houses, and these arrangements are far less well understood (Wood 2010, 250). This lacuna is further complicated by the fact that there is substantial evidence

FIGURE 54.4 The elaborately decorated porch and chantry chapel of John Greenway (*c*.1517), Tiverton, Devon

(© Simon Roffey)

FIGURE 54.5 Chantry chapels of Bishop William Wayneflete, Winchester Cathedral (late fifteenth century) (left) and Sir Edward Despenser, Tewkesbury Abbey (late fourteenth century) (right)

(© Simon Roffey)

within the spaces of medieval churches for undocumented chapels, or discrete spaces, whose form, layout, and architectural elaboration were clearly designed to articulate a direct, and often individual or personalized, eschatological strategy toward an impending afterlife. Here, for example, a juxtaposition between tomb and altar might suffice to link the body and memory of the deceased with the proximity and efficacy of the Mass being celebrated at an adjacent altar. This model may raise some problems. For the medieval historian what is not a documented chantry is not a chantry per se, but to the archaeologist, concerned primarily with the physical evidence, there is often very little architecturally to distinguish between a documented chantry chapel and an undocumented one that appears to fulfil essentially the same function: that of a personal strategy for the afterlife. This may be particularly true in the case of side-chapels in parish churches, for instance. As such, it may be safer to define these as 'active memorial spaces', insomuch as they are operative and dynamic. In a wider sense, both undocumented 'privatized' spaces and documented chantries may be best viewed together as places for facilitating salvation. Likewise, there may be little to distinguish architecturally between the chapels of guilds, fraternities, individuals, families, and chantries, as well as the greater collegiate foundations, and in essence they are simply incarnations of the same intercessory impulse. What they all had in common was that they presented discrete, furnished and constructed permanent spaces dedicated, primarily and often specifically, to the spiritual welfare of the dead.

Historical and Architectural Approaches

Chantry chapels and associated monuments have received comparatively little archaeological attention (McClain 2011, 476), particularly when compared to the study of monastic or parish churches overall (Roffey 2008, 23), and their importance as medieval cultural heritage is often not sufficiently appreciated. A general survey was undertaken by Paul Biver and Frank Howard as early as 1909. Traditionally, however, chantries have long been the preserve of historians and architectural historians, and one of the earliest major studies was by the architectural historian Geoffrey Cook, a monograph largely illustrated by examples drawn from the greater churches and cathedrals (Cook 1947). Such an exclusive focus on the best recorded surviving monuments tends to bypass the lesser known, less visible architecture where archaeology has much to offer. Another issue is that chantries can be enveloped within broader studies of the history and architecture of church monuments (e.g. Binski 1996; Colvin 1991; Lindley 2011; Rosenthal 1972; Saul 2009) while historical research may be directed either towards specific status-groups or a particular class of record, such as wills. Here Michael Hicks has cautioned that breakdowns of types of benefactors are of little use without some understanding of the institutions themselves (Hicks 1985, 123). One of the earliest and most influential historical surveys of medieval chantry foundations was by Kathleen Wood-Legh (1965) who explored the history of primarily parish chantry foundations from the documents alone. Since then, a range of important urban parish church studies has been carried out by Clive Burgess, who illustrated the wider social context of chantry foundation and demonstrated the important contribution that surviving churchwardens' accounts can make to the overall study of late medieval piety and chantry foundation (2000b; 2004). Other studies focus on single ecclesiastical institutions, at St Paul's Cathedral, London (Rousseau 2011), for example, and there is an important survey which examines the possible decline of chantry foundation in the decades leading up to the Reformation (Kreider 1979). Particular forms of chantries have also been investigated, such as cage chantries (Wood 2010) and chantry priest's houses (Pantin 1959), and there are regional studies for Devon (Orme 1979) and Northamptonshire (Parsons 2000) as well as a collection of architectural and documentary papers (Luxford and McNeill 2011). With some notable exceptions, however, there is little recognition of the interrelationships between chantry chapels, memorial spaces, and the wider spatial landscape of the church, nor any understanding of the precise nature of lay interactions.

ARCHAEOLOGY

Historical sources, such as wills and churchwardens' accounts, can be used in combination with the archaeological investigation of surviving church fabric to provide an overall contextual approach to the range of surviving evidence. Here the application of theoretical approaches to the analysis of church space, topography, and structure has become increasingly influential and helps to provide a more explanatory narrative. Archaeological theory drawn largely from anthropological and social theory such as the studies of Pierre Bourdieu (1977), as well as those pioneered in North American historical archaeology, such as that applied to vernacular architecture by Henry Glassie (1975), have been combined with currents in British prehistoric archaeology, including the contextual archaeology of Ian Hodder (1986) and the phenomenological approaches of Christopher Tilley (1997). These 'positive initiatives' formed a 'full appreciation of the active role of material culture in moulding social relations' (Gerrard 2003, 229), and have included the relationship between space and ideology, both in English vernacular architecture (e.g. Johnson 1995) and ecclesiastical contexts (e.g. Gilchrist 1989; 1994; 1995; Graves 2000; Peters 1996; Roffey 2007a; 2007b; 2010) and the articulation and use of access and space in buildings more generally (e.g. Hillier and Hanson 1984; Richardson 2003). These approaches enable archaeologists to investigate how various memorial and eschatological strategies were articulated within the fabric and arrangement of church spaces, and to explain the location, positioning, and the spatial and visual relationship between tombs, chantries, shrines, and memorials, as well as defined lay and clerical areas. The aim is to interpret the various meanings and motives within a ritual topography, and understand how this may be articulated through physical accessibility, proximity, and visual interaction.

In her comparative study of churches in Devon and Norfolk, the archaeologist Pamela Graves (2000) has produced an alternative to general studies of late medieval religious piety by investigating the physical imprints of the past and how lay testators left their presence within the fabric of their churches. One of the key elements to emerge out of Graves's work was the importance of sight lines and how features such as tombs and altars were located so as to facilitate intervisibility between different parts of the church. This is crucial, for as the church historian Miri Rubin has stated, the most central element of the celebration of Mass (including chantry Masses) was the Elevation of the Host. Here all the senses were called into play, but the essence of this ritual emphasized the actual *seeing* of the host (Rubin 1991, 58, 60). The gesture of elevation came to mark the moment of consecration, and to 'offer its meaning to the audience' (Rubin 1991 51, 55). On another level, the visual participation of the laity in Masses celebrated in chantry chapels, or associated contexts, would have put them in direct contact with the architectural and metaphorical symbolism of the setting, and consequently, their founders.

A Shared Vision of Salvation

The importance of sight lines and vision (view-sheds) in eschatological ritual practice lies behind a series of recent studies which have sought to reconstruct visual relationships between discrete areas of church space, particularly chantries, tombs, and altars and to understand how architectural innovations, such as squints (small internal windows), were used inside what had become busy, cluttered, and compartmentalized spaces (Roffey 2007a). In many cases this research has shown that, far from being stand-alone monuments, many chapels, chantries, and memorial spaces were in fact part of a wider interconnected ritual 'network'. There is clear evidence for the visual relationships between altars, often facilitated by squints, in order to stagger Elevations at busy liturgical periods or to allow a view otherwise obstructed by arcades, walls, and columns. The author's own study of these essentially liturgical components has shown how common they were (Roffey 2003; 2007a; 2007b; 2008). Some squints were rather plain and basic insertions, such as those in the walls of the Hastings Chapel at Christchurch Priory, Dorset, but others were more elaborate, as at Stoke Charity, Hampshire, where a decorated double squint afforded a view from the nave to both the north-east Hampton Chapel and the chancel's high altar (Figure 54.6). Larger processional squints, such as those in the chapels of the parish churches at Avebury and Portbury, Somerset, and Sherston, Wiltshire, are effectively small internal doorways which not only facilitated lines of sight between altars but also permitted movement between the chapels and other parts of the church, thereby offering their chapels as 'gateways' for processional traffic.

Tombs and other monuments in churches and chapels were also sometimes deliberately positioned so as to obstruct, or rather intrude, on lines of sight. Such arrangements formed what Graves has termed 'presencing mechanisms' or 'intercessory triggers', which provoked a direct and intimate association between the performance of the Mass and individual memory (Graves 2000). Effigies, heraldic devices and symbols, inscribed altar cloths, and wall hangings further promoted the 'active' presence of the founder. A particularly dramatic example of this can be found in the late fourteenth-century Despenser chapel at Tewkesbury Abbey, Gloucestershire, where the painted and almost life-size effigy of Edward Despenser 'rises' up from the top of the chapel, hands clasped in eternal pious prayer to face the altar. There is clearly an implied spirituality here, but also a very real 'trigger' which serves to associate the individual not only with the Mass being taken in his own chapel but also with that being celebrated at the high altar by the community of the abbey (Figure 54.5).

Methodologically, archaeological studies like these begin to shed light on the arrangement and design of chantry chapels and the extent to which they were consciously manipulated to facilitate visual responses and evoke memory. Although chantry chapels have traditionally been viewed as wholly private monuments, the visual and spatial analysis suggests that they reflected more of a 'personalization' and not a 'privatization' of church space (Roffey 2007b). Particularly in the parishes, they were public monuments that nourished everyone's religious experience. The reconstruction of sight lines, drawing as it does on the experiential or 'phenomenological' approaches used by Tilley (1997) and GIS spatial applications (e.g. Fisher et al. 1997; Lake et al. 1998), helps us to understand why monuments were placed at particular locations and to gauge the level of visual engagement by the laity (Figure 54.6).

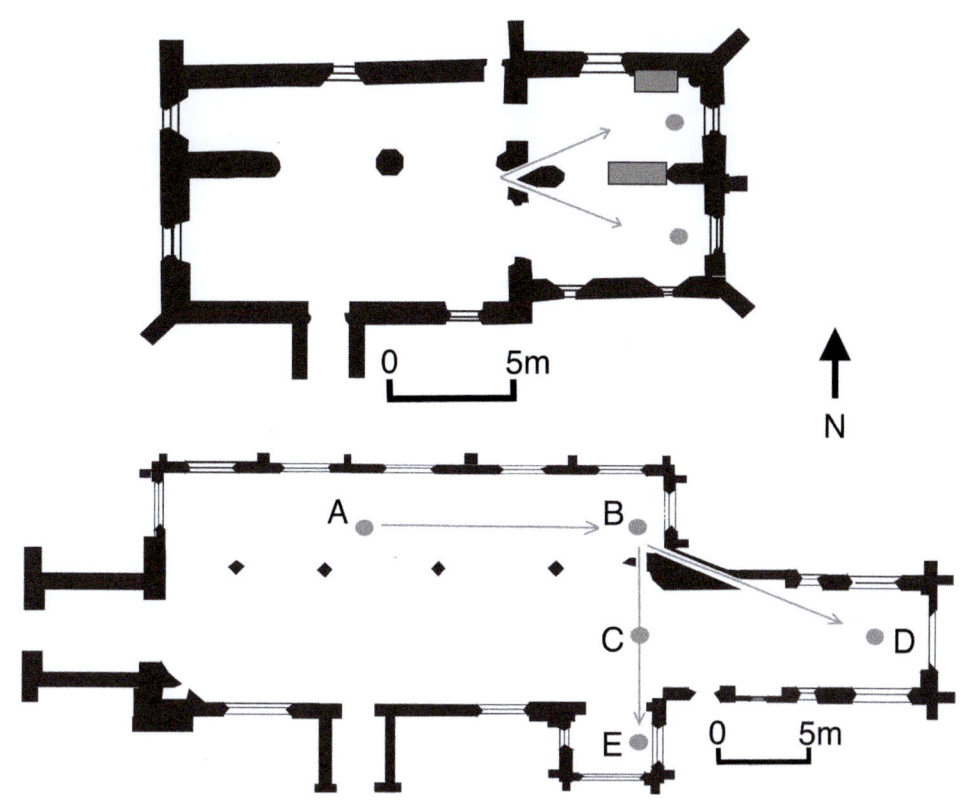

FIGURE 54.6 Reconstructed pre-Reformation view-sheds at Stoke Charity Parish church, Hampshire (top), and Holy Trinity Bradford-on-Avon, Wiltshire (bottom), not to scale. Conjectured altars are shown as grey circles. The double squint at Stoke Charity provides view into the north Hampton chapel with its tombs and memorials and to the High Altar from the north aisle. At Bradford-on-Avon, view-shed analysis illustrates the relationship between the location of the former Birde (A) and Horton chantry chapels (B) and the altars in the nave (C), chancel (D) and south transept (E). Note that the squint from the former Horton chapel cuts through several metres of masonry and is a feat of considerable engineering illustrating the importance of facilitating visual relationships within churches

(© Simon Roffey)

Shrines, Altars, and the Location of Chantry Chapels and Memorial Spaces

The veneration of saints was an important component of late medieval religion and belief and many churches would have had dedicated saint's shrines. Saints were a common subject of medieval wall paintings, stained glass, and sculptural imagery as well as being central to the devotional pious practices of the laity. At Pickering parish church, North Yorkshire, Kate Giles has shown how the cycle of wall paintings echoes the calendar of saints' feast days (Giles 2000, 50) and they were clearly an important component of ritual life in the parish church. A visit to a saint's shrine was believed to be spiritually meritorious, and close contact with the corporeal remains even more so. Thus, feretory shrines, such as those to be seen today in Salisbury Cathedral and at St Candida's church, Whitchurch Canonicorum in Dorset, contained small apertures which allowed the faithful closer proximity to the saint's body. Equally, in death, to be buried close to a shrine was of great spiritual benefit for the soul. In these circumstances the close proximal relationship between shrines and chantries, tombs, and memorial spaces, was understood to draw direct spiritual benefit from the physical remains of the saint themselves who could then intercede personally on behalf of the deceased. Just as importantly, however, this was a location that made a statement about piety and status; here the dead were in the exalted company of saints. The shrines themselves would also attract numerous pilgrims who could be petitioned to pray for the individual associated with the chantry foundation. At Westminster Abbey the great H-shaped two-storeyed chapel of Henry V (c.1422) dominated the space around the shrine of Edward the Confessor and its imposition would have caused significant changes to the layout of the area surrounding the shrine with damage inevitably being caused to some of the surrounding tombs. The giant 'H' of the chapel's design, like some form of medieval branding, would have loomed behind the shrine perhaps imposing, or 'presencing' itself, on the view of any visitor (Roffey 2008, 125)

The 'branding' of church space, to give it a modern terminology, can also be seen at Winchester Cathedral. Here, at the east end of the cathedral, the two free-standing cage chantry chapels of bishops Wayneflete (c.1480s) and Beaufort (c.1440s) once stood guard over the shrine of St Swithun; their pinnacles and minarets almost scraping the vaulting above. The shrine itself is now lost, but the imposing chapels of the two bishops must surely have reduced its architectural significance somewhat (Roffey 2008, 124). It is not the only example of the appropriation of spaces connected to the shrines of medieval saints. At St Albans, Hertfordshire, the two-storey chapel of Duke Humphrey of Gloucester is located adjacent to the shrine of St Alban, and at Salisbury Cathedral the two side-chantry chapels of bishops Richard Beauchamp and Robert Hungerford, constructed within a decade or so of the canonization of St Osmund, flanked the area where his shrine was translated sometime after 1457.

In a similar vein, the construction of chantry chapels, tombs, and memorials close to the high altar brought them near to the central religious focus of the church and, in monasteries, often close to the monks' choir, a place where regular prayer and observations would be conducted. At both Tewkesbury and Westminster abbeys clusters of closely grouped chantries and tombs ringed the site of the high altar. At Christchurch Priory the chantry chapel of Margaret de la Pole, founded around 1520, protruded out into the priory sanctuary, barely a metre or so away from the high altar. In this location the chapel would have formed a dramatic visual backdrop and also serve to 'trigger' the awareness of the monks entering the choir from the south aisle and cloister.

Conclusions

The subject of medieval chantry chapels and related memorial spaces has been largely neglected by archaeologists. New initiatives and developments in the field of archaeological theory have, however, introduced a range of methods and techniques with which to investigate church space and fabric and to provide a more interpretative and holistic framework for the investigation of church ritual space and practice. Here, archaeology can show that the traditionally defined and documented 'chantry chapel' is but one form of historically derived definition for a range of related memorial and eschatological strategies that were organized and articulated inside the late medieval church. These studies have revealed a vibrant and dynamic church space where personal and communal strategies for the afterlife could be articulated through the spatial and visual relationship between chapels, memorial spaces, altars, shrines, and tombs. The applications of archaeological theory and spatial studies have much to offer future research in church archaeology. They highlight the dynamics of church space and the way in which it was structured and manipulated through time to render a ritualized landscape that, far from being elitist or static, was vibrant, meaningful, evocative, and integral to the spiritual aspirations of a wide spectrum of medieval society.

References cited

Binski, P. 1996 *Medieval death: ritual and representation*, British Museum Press, London

Biver, P. and Howard, F. E. 1909 'Chantry chapels in England', *The Archaeological Journal* 66, 1–32

Bourdieu, P. 1977 *Outline of a theory of practice*, Cambridge University Press, Cambridge

Burgess, C. R. 1985 'For the increase of divine service: chantries in the parish of late medieval Bristol', *Journal of Ecclesiastical History* 36, 46–65

Burgess, C. R. 1991 'Strategies for eternity: perpetual chantry foundation in late medieval Bristol', in C. Harper-Bill (ed.), *Religious belief and ecclesiastical careers in late medieval England*, Boydell, Woodbridge, 1–33

Burgess, C. R. 2000a '"Longing to be prayed for": death and commemoration in an English parish in the later Middle Ages', in B. Gordon and P. Marshall (eds), *The place of the dead: death and remembrance in late medieval and early modern Europe*, Cambridge University Press, Cambridge, 44–65

Burgess, C. R. 2000b *The pre-Reformation records of All Saints', Bristol, Part 1*, Bristol Record Society Publication 53, Bristol

Burgess, C. R. 2004 *The pre-Reformation records of All Saints', Bristol, Part 2*, Bristol Record Society Publication 56, Bristol

Colvin, H. M. 1991 *Architecture and afterlife*, Yale University Press, London

Colvin, H. M. 2000 'The origin of chantries', *Journal of Medieval History* 26, 163–73

Cook, G. H. 1947 *Medieval chantries and chantry chapels*, Phoenix, London

Crouch, D. 2001 'The origin of chantries: some further Anglo-Norman evidence', *Journal of Medieval History* 27, 159–80

Fisher, P., Farelly, C., Maddocks, A., and Ruggles, C. 1997 'Spatial analysis of visible areas from the Bronze Age cairns of Mull', *Journal of Archaeological Science* 24(5), 81–92

Gee, E. 1984 'The topography of altars, chantries and shrines in York Minster', *The Antiquaries Journal* 64, 337–51

Gerrard, C. M. 2003 *Medieval archaeology: understanding traditions and contemporary approaches*, Routledge, London

Gilchrist, R. 1989 'Community and self: perceptions and use of space in medieval monasteries', *Scottish Archaeological Review* 6, 55–64

Gilchrist, R. 1994 *Gender and material culture: the archaeology of religious women*, Routledge, London

Gilchrist, R. 1995 *Contemplation and action: the other monasticism*, Leicester University Press, Leicester

Giles, K. 2000 'Marking time? A fifteenth-century liturgical calendar in the wall paintings of Pickering parish church, North Yorkshire', *Church Archaeology* 4, 42–51

Glassie, H. 1975 *Folk housing in Middle Virginia: a structural analysis of historic artifacts*, University of Tennessee Press, Knoxville

Graves, C. P. 2000 *Form and fabric of belief: the archaeology of lay experience in medieval Norfolk and Devon*, British Archaeological Report British Series 311, Oxford

Hicks, M. A. 1985 'Chantries, obits and almshouses in the Hungerford foundations 1325–1478', in C. Barron and C. Harper-Bill (eds), *The pre-Reformation church in England 1400–1530*, Longmans, London, 123–42

Hillier, B. and Hanson, J. 1984 *The social logic of space*, Cambridge University Press, Cambridge

Hodder, I. 1986 *Reading the past: current approaches to interpretation in archaeology*, Cambridge University Press, Cambridge

Johnson, M. 1995 *An archaeology of capitalism*, Wiley-Blackwell, Oxford

Kreider, A. 1979 *English chantries: the road to dissolution*, Harvard University Press, London

Lake, M. W., Woodman, P. E., and Mithin, S. J. 1998 'Tailoring GIS software for archaeological applications: an example concerning view-shed analysis', *Journal of Archaeological Science* 25, 27–38

Le Goff, J. 1984 *The birth of Purgatory*, trans. A. Goldhammer, Scholar Press, London

Lindley, P. 2011 '"Pickpurse" Purgatory, the dissolution of the chantries and the suppression of intercession for the dead', *Journal of the British Archaeological Association* 164, 277–304

Luxford, J. M. and McNeill, J. 2011 *The medieval chantry in England*, Journal of the British Archaeological Association, Leeds

McClain, A. 2011 'The archaeology of parish churches in late medieval England', in M. O. H. Carver and J. Klápště (eds), *The archaeology of medieval Europe, Vol. 2: twelfth to sixteenth centuries*, Aarhus University Press, Aarhus, 467–78

McNeill, J. 2011 'A prehistory of the chantry', in J. M. Luxford and J. McNeill (eds), *The medieval chantry in England*, Journal of the British Archaeological Association, Maney, Leeds, 1–38

Orme, N. 1979 'The Dissolution of the chantries in Devon, 1546–8', *Devonshire Association Report and Transactions* 3, 75–93

Pantin, W. A. 1959 'Chantry priests' houses and other medieval lodgings', *Medieval Archaeology* 3, 216–58

Parsons, D. 2000 *Lost chantries and chapels of medieval Northamptonshire*, Brixworth Lecture Series 3, Brixworth

Peters, C. 1996 'Interiors and furnishings', in J. Blair and C. Pyrah (eds), *Church archaeology: research directions for the future*, Council for British Archaeology Research Report 104, York, 68–75

Richardson, A. 2003 'Gender and space in English royal palaces c.1160–c.1457: a study in access analysis and imagery', *Medieval Archaeology* 47, 131–65

Roffey, S. 2003 'Deconstructing a symbolic world: the Reformation and the English medieval parish chantry', in D. Gaimster and R. Gilchrist (eds), *The archaeology of Reformation 1480–1580*, The Society for Post-Medieval Archaeology Monograph 1, Leeds, 342–55

Roffey, S. 2007a 'Constructing a vision of salvation: chantries and the social dimension of religious experience in the medieval parish church', *Archaeology Journal* 163, 122–46

Roffey, S. 2007b *Medieval chantry chapels: an archaeological approach*, Boydell, Woodbridge

Roffey, S. 2008 *Chantry chapels and medieval strategies for the afterlife*, Tempus, Stroud

Roffey, S. 2010 'Planning for the afterlife: the chantry chapels of Salisbury Cathedral', *Sarum Chronicle* 9, 19–29

Rosenthal, J. T. 1972 *The purchase of Paradise: gift giving and the aristocracy, 1307–1485*, Routledge and Kegan Paul, London

Rousseau, M.-H. 2011 *Saving the souls of medieval London: perpetual chantries at St Paul's Cathedral, c.1200–1548*, Ashgate, Farnham

Rubin, M. 1991 *Corpus Christi: the Eucharist in late medieval culture*, Cambridge University Press, Cambridge

Saul, N. 2009 *English church monuments in the Middle Ages: history and representation*, Oxford University Press, Oxford

Sheils, W. J. 1999 'The altars in York Minster in the early sixteenth century', in R. N. Swanson (ed.), *Continuity and change in Christian worship*, Studies in Church History 35, Boydell, Woodbridge, 104–15

Tilley, C. 1997 *A phenomenology of landscape: places, paths and monuments*, Berg, Oxford

Wood, C. 2010 'Cage chantries of Christchurch Priory', in C. Barron and C. Burgess (eds), *Memory and commemoration in medieval England*, Harlaxton Medieval Studies XX, Shaun Tyas, Donnington, 234–50

Wood-Legh, K. L. 1965 *Perpetual chantries in Britain*, Cambridge University Press, Cambridge

PART X

A WIDER CONTEXT: TRADE AND EXCHANGE, EUROPE AND BEYOND

CHAPTER 55

OVERVIEW

Trade and Other Contacts in Late Medieval Britain

ALEJANDRA GUTIÉRREZ

THE movement of people and goods was a constant during the later Middle Ages but subject to varying degrees of intensity, periodicity, and changing geographical scope according to political, economic, and other circumstances. The chapters in this final part of the *Handbook* present evidence for specific connections and contacts with neighbouring countries while this overview emphasizes the more general background for long-distance trade and cultural contacts.

The study of foreign trade during the Middle Ages has a long and brilliant tradition of scholarship in Britain. Dominated by economic historians, studies peaked in popularity in the first half of the twentieth century but have lost ground since (e.g. Carus-Wilson 1937; 1954; Carus-Wilson and Coleman 1963; Lewis 1913; Power 1941; Power and Postan 1933; Ramsay 1957; Rooseboom 1910; Salzman 1931; Scammel 1961; Willam 1959). Rather than archaeological research, it was the wide range of available written sources and the publication of primary texts which underpinned early interests in foreign trade. The most significant of these historical sources are the tax lists which became regularized as port books and customs accounts in 1275 in England, Wales, and Ireland, with Scotland following a little later; a single national customs system was not imposed until the middle of the sixteenth century (Gras 1918). These lists detail the boats arriving and departing and include not only the duties and rates they owed, but the quantities of goods being shipped, the name of the merchant, and sometimes the country of origin of the ship. The level of detail present, as well as the survival of evidence more generally, fluctuates significantly with those from Southampton being among the best preserved and studied (e.g. Cobb 1961; Foster 1963; James 1990; Quinn 1937; 1938; Studer 1913). Needless to say, this evidence is highly valuable but its interpretation is by no means problem-free from either an archaeological or historical perspective (Childs 1995; Gutiérrez 1995). In addition to these historical sources, archaeological excavations in ports and urban waterfronts in the 1970s and 1980s enabled the identification and dating of a wide range of imported items. Timbers preserved in waterlogged conditions were vital for fine-tuning the dating of stratified sequences (Gerrard 2003, 98, 134, 148; Hutchinson 1994).

Circuits

Trade between Britain and the Atlantic was already well established by the twelfth century with regular visits to/from Ireland in the west (see Chapter 56), and to Scandinavia, eastern, and northern Europe in the east (see Chapter 58) (Figure 55.1). Trade around

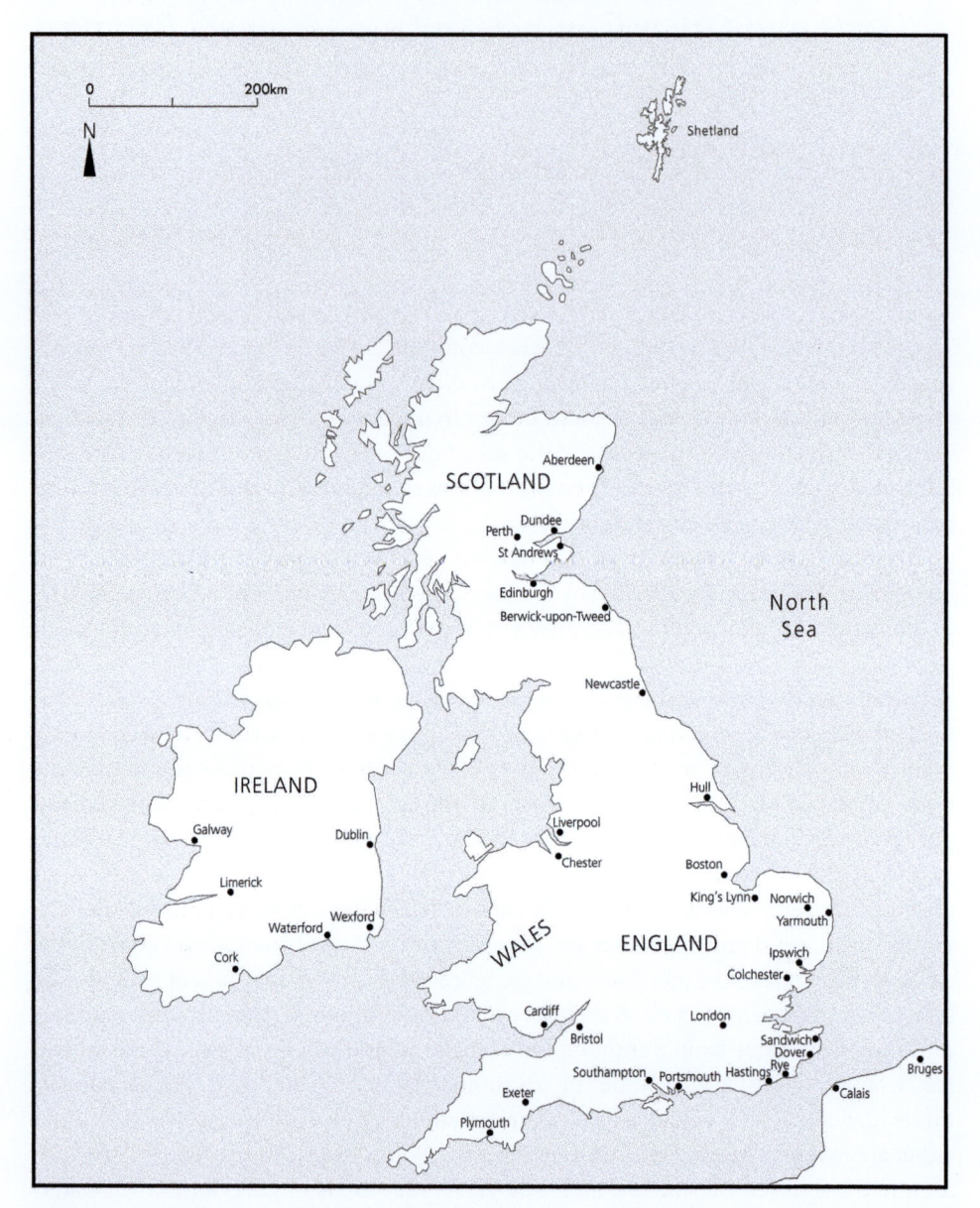

FIGURE 55.1 Main places mentioned in the text and sea routes around Great Britain in the medieval period

(© Alejandra Gutiérrez)

the northern coastline of Europe came to be dominated by the Hansa or Hanseatic League, a trading alliance of towns in Germany, North Sea, and Baltic Sea which created solid networks and important international trading centres such as Lübeck (Germany), Lund and Stockholm (Sweden), and Turku (Finland). The Hansa dominated trade in the north at least from the thirteenth century and until the seventeenth century (Wubs-Mrozewicz and Jenks 2012). Hanseatic trade seems to have been fuelled by the surplus of grain grown in Germany and Denmark and the corresponding demand for it in Greenland, Iceland, and Norway. In exchange these countries exported mainly fish, both dried and salted. Direct trips by English merchants to Iceland are documented in the early fifteenth century, their intention being to purchase local fish as well as taking a catch for themselves (Gardiner and Mehler 2007). No matter their nationality, foreign merchants here were not permitted to establish permanent trading communities and their visits seem to have been limited to coastal trading points, without venturing far inland.

During the twelfth century trade between northern and southern Europe was mainly landward and based on Roman roads and river transport (Figure 55.2). Especially important for trading contacts with the Mediterranean were the Champagne fairs in north-east France, to which Italian merchants travelled across France on an expedition which lasted as long as twenty to twenty-four days. These fairs usually lasted about six weeks and there were six each year: two in Troyes, two in Provins, one in Lagny, and one in Bar-sur-Aube. Merchants from Bruges, acting as intermediaries for most of northern Europe, would attend with their cloth; this would be exchanged for goods brought by the Italians from Alexandria and Syria. Pepper, alum, and dyestuffs, together with other spices, steel blades, lacquer, incense, drugs, silk, and sugar were all on sale here. The Champagne fairs, at least until their decline at the start of the fourteenth century, also attracted French, Spanish, English, and German merchants (Bautier 1952; Byrne 1920, 218; Face 1958; 1959; Reynolds 1931; Roger 1983).

Some maritime contact did already exist between England and Flanders and ports along the northern coast of Spain as early as the twelfth century; at the same date, Portuguese merchants were already beginning to travel north by sea. However, the Atlantic route which gave direct access to and from the Mediterranean by sea only became genuinely viable once the Islamic Empire lost its control and monopoly in Spain and Sicily. It was this political and economic transformation which opened up the possibility of direct sea travel between northern Europe and the Mediterranean, and eventually to Africa and beyond (see Chapter 59). Medieval Britain had always had access to products from Africa and Asia but, at least in the early part of the period under consideration here, had to rely on foreign traders to bring them to its shores. These goods were available to Europeans, chiefly Italians, in the markets of north Africa, particularly Cairo and Alexandria which were destinations of choice for trading routes across the Indian Ocean and Africa. It was not until the thirteenth century that Europeans ventured south around western Africa and it was not until the very end of the fifteenth century that Europeans successfully bordered Africa by sea. Portuguese seafarers were at the forefront here and settled both on Madeira (*c.*1419)

890 ALEJANDRA GUTIÉRREZ

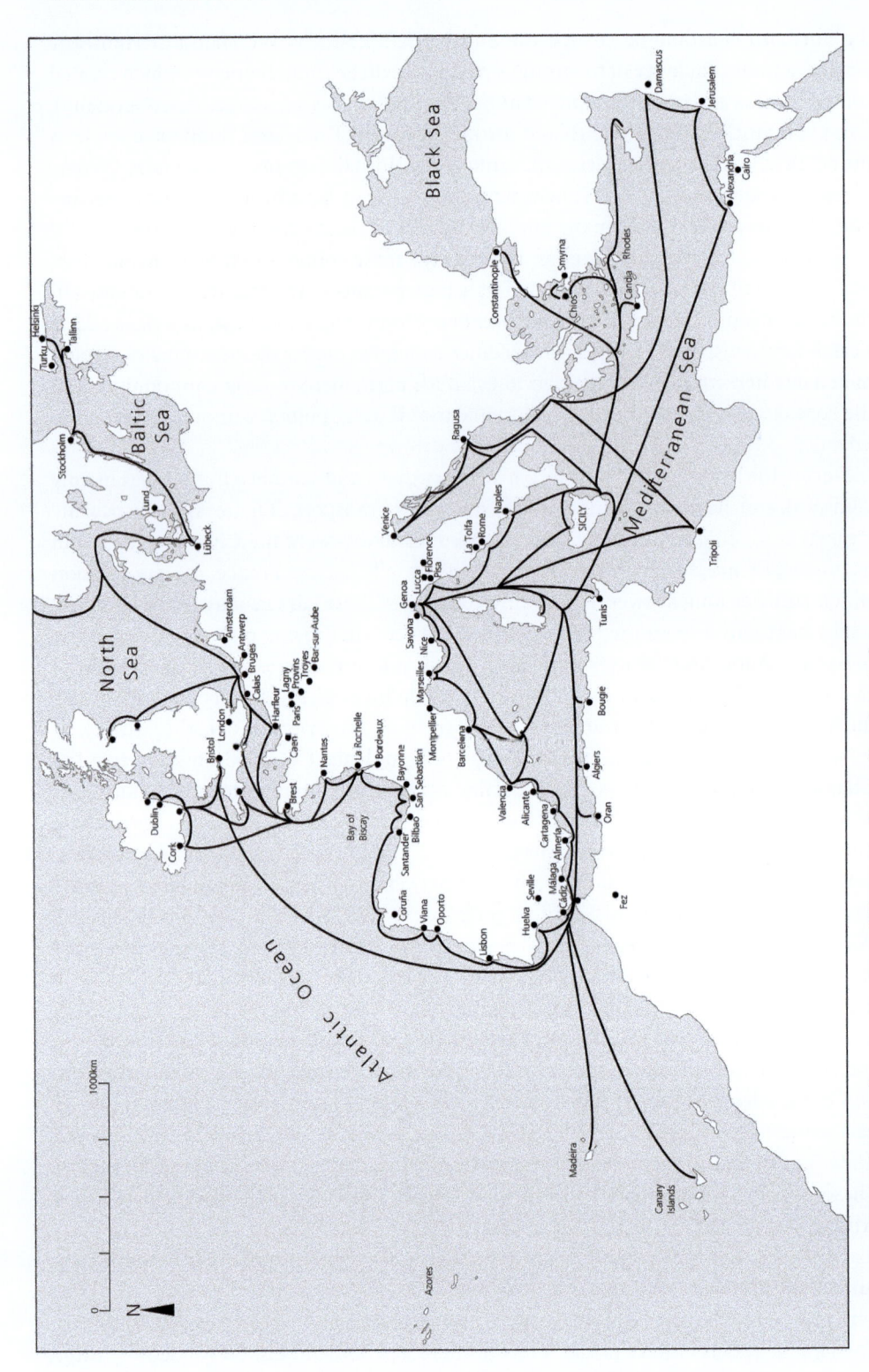

FIGURE 55.2 Main places and sea routes around Europe in the medieval period

(© Alejandra Gutiérrez)

and the Azores (c.1427), rounding the Cape of Good Hope (1488) and first completing a return trip to India via Africa in 1499. Spanish, Flemish, and Italians soon followed, with French, Dutch, and English in the next century (Newitt 2004; Russell-Wood 1992, 16). Exploration of the other side of the Atlantic also began at the same date but only became significant over the next hundred years. These events are not considered here in any detail, except to underline the participation of Bristol in early voyages of discovery (e.g. Andrews 1984).

Until direct travel to India became a reality for Europe, trade was in the hands of Muslim merchants who had established a complex network of trade routes and settlements expanding both to the east and to the west from the Arabian Peninsula and Persia, through Malabar, Coromandel, and Sri Lanka and reaching as far as southern China by the tenth century (Pearson 2010; Wade 2009; Wink 1991, 65–86) (Figure 55.3). These routes connected the Indian Ocean with the east coast of Africa and from there to the Mediterranean, with India receiving goods from Sri Lanka, China, and south-east Asia in transit to the Red Sea (e.g. Chakravarti 2012; Chaudhuri 1985; Chirikure 2014; Denbow 1990; Horton 1986; Horton and Middleton 2000). Goods travelled with Kārimī traders from the major port at Aden through the Red Sea to Fustat (Old Cairo), either across land from Al-Quizūm or along the Nile from Qūs. Meanwhile, goods from central Africa were transported down long-established trans-Saharan trade routes where major changeover points became established where routes merged, such as Zuwila, Traghen, or Murzuq (Libya). Here the caravans broke up and reformed again ready for the onward journey, north or southwards (Fischel 1958, 162–3; Magnavita 2013; Nixon 2009; Wilson 2012).

Above all, it was Italian merchants who played a significant role in European medieval trade and especially those from Venice, Pisa, and Genoa. They controlled bases not only in the Mediterranean, but also across northern Europe, the Frankish states of Syria and, after the fourth crusade of 1204, in Constantinople itself. Genoa, for example, had outposts as far as the port of Trebizond on the Black Sea coast, the preferred destination for caravans on the Silk Route from central Asia, as well as at Caffa in the Crimea, while the Venetians dominated commerce in Alexandria until the fifteenth century through treaties and agreements with the sultans of Egypt and also settled at Tana on the Black Sea. In modern-day Syria merchants followed close behind in the wake of the Crusades, establishing trading networks soon after the first crusade of 1096. These networks also included merchants from Marseilles and Montpellier in the late twelfth century and this trading network was to endure until the fourteenth century. Genoese, Pisans, and Florentines all came north regularly too, to Southampton and London from the fourteenth century, buying English cloth and selling their Mediterranean and Oriental goods. Only in the late fifteenth century did this state of affairs change radically when English merchants began to venture into the Mediterranean for themselves and the numbers of Italian boats arriving at the coast of southern England began to decline (Ruddock 1951).

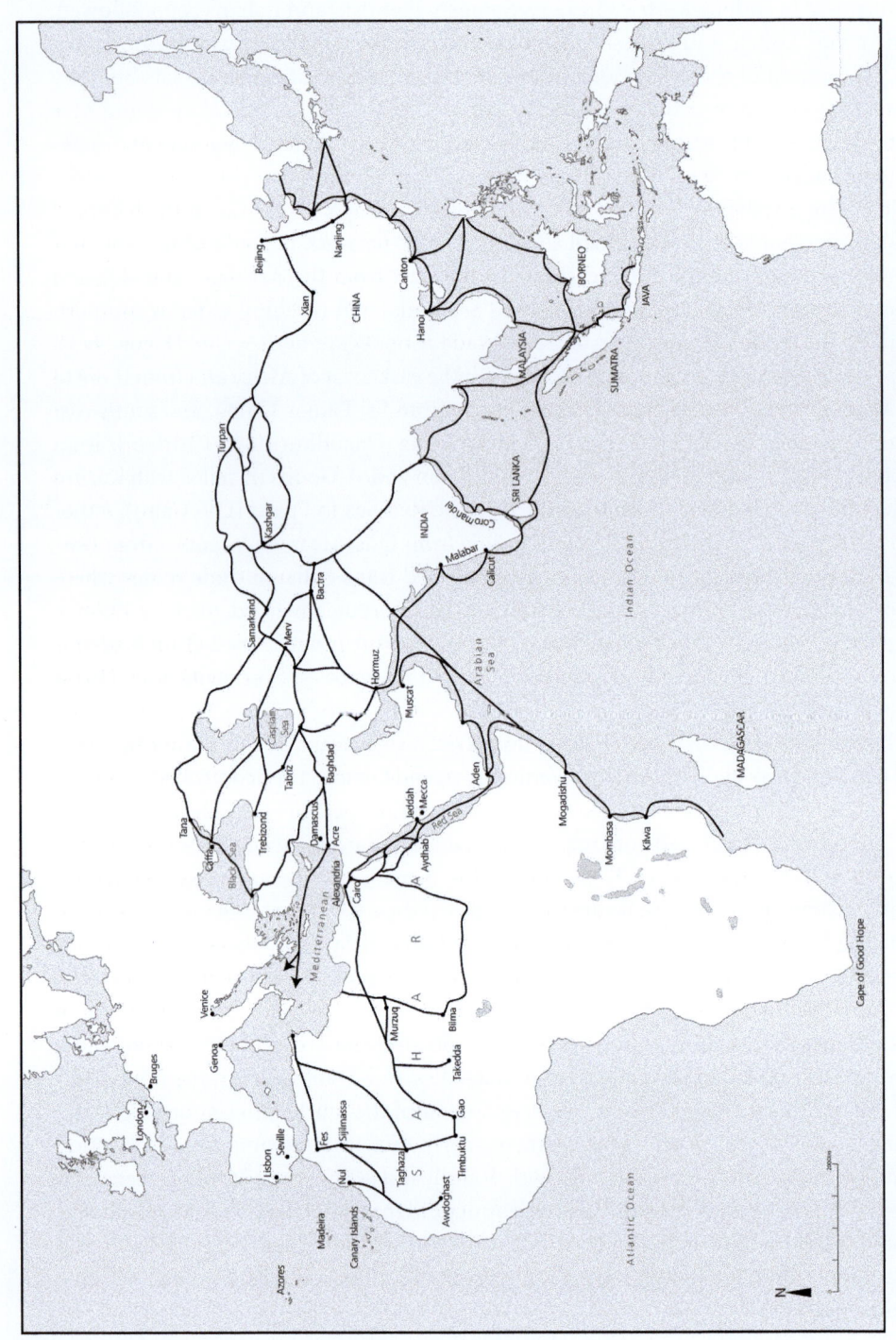

FIGURE 55.3 Some of the main medieval trading routes, links, and places mentioned in the text beyond the Mediterranean (© Alejandra Gutiérrez)

Necessities, Luxuries, Exotica, and Archaeology

The implication for the archaeologist, even from this briefest of summaries, is that almost anything and everything seems to have been available in European markets by the thirteenth century, although the price and frequency with which certain articles could be obtained varied greatly. In England, the driver behind medieval trade was, in the first instance at least, the export of wool as a raw material to Flanders, France, and Italy for the weaving of good quality cloth there. This continued until about the early fourteenth century when English exports of cloth took over (Bridbury 1982; Carus-Wilson 1987; Childs 1996; Chorley 1988). Scotland's major export was also wool, followed by hides and skins (of sheep, rabbit, marten), herring, and other fish; preserved salmon seems to have been a lucrative business and it was also traded regularly, commodities moving through Leith (the port of Edinburgh) and Aberdeen, together with major ports such as Berwick, Dundee, Perth, and St Andrews (Donnelly 1999; Grant 1930, 114–15, 311, 340; Lynch and Strang 1966; Rorke 2006). This trade was heavily directed towards the Low Countries and the Baltic, just as it was along the eastern coast of England (from Newcastle, Hull, Boston, Lynn, Yarmouth, Ipswich, and the Cinque Ports). Local merchants and the Hanse exported corn, salt (which was indispensable for drying fish), tin, lead, and coal; leather goods (bottles, buckets, bellows, belts); cereals, tallow, bacon, ox carcasses, butter and honey, although the export of non-woollens seems to have been a minor component of trade overall, perhaps 10–15 per cent of English exports by the middle of the sixteenth century (Stone 1949). Wales and southern ports of England were more directed towards Ireland, the Mediterranean, and France (Williams 1936).

Imported goods were often associated with the cloth industry. These included dyes and mordants to supplement the range available locally (Hall 1996): brasil, or red-wood, and indigo came from India; grain, red madder, and litmus from Norway; blue woad from Picardy; kermes (from the carapaces of the insect *Coccus illicis*, and also known as 'grain' to the English) from Spain, Portugal, and the eastern Mediterranean. A cheaper variety of black soap from Seville was used to wash the wool during cloth-making, while olive oil from the Mediterranean was used to moisten the wool before it was carded or combed so as to avoid breakages (Balfour-Paul 1999; Childs 1978, 111). Imported mordants used to fix the colour of the dye included alum (aluminium potassium sulphate) from Anatolia which was traded mainly by the Genoese. Small amounts of alum of lesser quality also arrived from Spain, Sicily, and north-west Africa, at least until the discovery in the 1460s of the mines at La Tolfa in the Papal States which produced alum of quality in quantity (Childs 1978, 109).

Fish, furs, and forest products (wax, bitumen, and timber) all arrived from the Baltic and Scandinavia; linen cloth and beer from Germany; copper from Hungary; wine, salt, fruit, and textiles from France; wine, oil, and iron from Spain and Portugal. Beside these major items, a multitude of smaller, varied, perhaps occasional, cargoes were also transported. In 1307/8 a Genoese merchant landed a cargo at Sandwich which included cheese, and in 1396/7, goods arriving at Lynn listed pitch, wax, and ashes, together with garlic and onions (Gras 1918, 436; Pelham 1930, 136–41). Other major imports arrived indirectly from Asia. These included a wide range of merchandise such as textiles (muslin, cotton, silk, thread, and carpets), gems and stones (pearls, rubies, and diamonds), and pepper and other spices (mace, nutmeg, cloves, cinnamon, and cardamon). With established direct routes to Asia, Portugal had a major role in distribution from the end of the fifteenth century and in spreading the taste for rich textiles to create sumptuous domestic interiors (Ferreira 2015).

Many of these cargoes have left no trace at all in the archaeological record. It has been estimated that around 95 per cent of all the imports arriving at Hull were either perishable goods or raw materials (Evans 1999). Many goods have simply not survived (for example, wine and oil), or have been consumed, transformed (e.g. ivory), or may be unidentifiable by eye as imported items (e.g. wool or dyes). Yet, determining the origin of imported goods remains highly relevant. Illustrations showing maps with direct arrows between sources of items and ports are frequently included in written reports, but they are highly misleading; sea voyages were rarely direct between the port of origin and the place of consumption. Stopping points along the way would have been necessary to top up on victuals and also on cargo, to seek out local specialties and even chance bargains like the cheese and onions already mentioned. On the voyage north, for example, most ships stopped at La Rochelle in western France to buy wine before selling it in Bruges, Southampton, London, or elsewhere, whereas Italians ships going north would anchor along the Spanish coast at Valencia, Alicante, Almería, Málaga, Cádiz, and Bilbao (Koller 1973, 679). Goods landing at ports in northern Europe would therefore have included items of wide-ranging origin, regardless of the nationality of the ship or the port of origin. One example of this is the importation of exotic animals, such as lions, leopards, and monkeys, either alive or as by-products such as pelts and elephant ivory. Although the animals mainly originated in Africa, they were often picked up at major re-distribution centres such as Valencia in Spain, or Lisbon in Portugal, from where they were transported to the north of Europe (see Chapter 10 in this *Handbook*; Pluskowski 2004). Pepper is another excellent example of this 'relay trade' (Pearson 2010). Most medieval supplies came from Malabar on the west coast of India. The long journey to the north of Europe would have begun there, perhaps as cargo in a boat setting sail from Calicut, then across the Arabian Sea and across the Red Sea to Alexandria; here it might have been collected by Italian merchants, taken to Genoa, for example, and thence re-exported to northern Europe (Constable 1994, 242; Pearson 2010, 321).

The warehouses of major European ports were well stocked with exotic goods. The role of Bruges and Antwerp as international meeting points and re-distributors of cargoes should be stressed here; a short, direct sea trip from Scottish or English shores provided access to goods from the Mediterranean, Africa, and Asia. Re-distribution was a regular part of medieval trade which emerges strongly from the written records: in 1323, for instance, London was (re)exporting Flemish cheese and Irish coney skins, while in 1303 Boston in Lincolnshire was exporting cotton and steel, products which were not produced in England at that date (Gras 1918, 119–20). Re-distribution was also the main means by which imports moved along English, Scottish, and Welsh ports. Direct exports from Flanders to Scotland may seem to have been minor (mainly spices, sugar, madder, wool), but most of the foreign supplies would have arrived from English ports (Grant 1930, 113, 312, 337).

Scientific techniques are available to help identify the origins of certain products. Chemical analysis of dyes and pigments is well developed, the latter fuelled by conservation of paintings and manuscripts (e.g. Cardon 2007; Clark 1995; Walton and Taylor 1991); the analysis of ceramics and glass beads is also widespread in order to identify their place of manufacture (e.g. Hughes and Gaimster 1999; Hughes 2016; Robertshaw et al. 2010); the analysis of metals has helped to investigate the source of gold, for instance that used for coinage (Gondonneau and Guerra 1999); and, more recently, isotope analysis is helping to identify the region of catch for cod bones found at archaeological sites (Barrett et al. 2008) and fingerprinting elephant ivory (Van der Merwe et al. 1990; Vogel et al. 1990).

Two visible and seemingly direct clues for trade are coins (see Chapter 32) and cloth seals. The latter are small items usually made of lead and consisting of two, or four, linked stamped circles which were stapled together over the cloth (Figure 55.4, no. 6). They were a mark of quality control and a guarantee that the fabrics to which they were attached complied with local stipulations of manufacture. They became increasingly popular between the fourteenth and seventeenth centuries but among the earliest in northern Europe are those found in England with the lion rampart of Flanders of the late thirteenth century (Egan 1995; 2001; Endrei and Egan 1982). The considerable collection gathered from sites in London consists of several thousand examples from across England and the Continent (Egan 1980, 185). Cloth seals, however, were also liable to be faked, especially if sent to destinations far from their sources, and they could be inserted by middlemen. Examples found in Hungary with the arms of England possibly came from the kersey cloths which were given as payment to garrison troops in the sixteenth century but the lack of parallels for such a seal in England raises suspicions as to their legality (Egan 2010, 61).

Not only is the detection of imported goods a challenge for archaeologists, evidence for them tends to be highly concentrated. Ports, urban, and high-status deposits provide much of the evidence, London being well ahead in the number and range of items identified. The variety of textiles found in the capital, for example, demonstrates a wide range of sources, dates, techniques, qualities, and uses. The silk moths which produced silk thread were originally native to China but their cultivation spread to the Byzantine Empire, Islamic North Africa and Spain, and eventually to Italy, so that silks found on London excavations in the thirteenth century include those from central Asia and China, Italian silk from Venice and Lucca, and also silk from Islamic Spain. Besides archaeological excavations, some textiles are also found as burial vestments, such as that of Hubert Walter, Archbishop of Canterbury, who died in 1205 (Crowfoot et al. 1992).

Spices and food plants are rarely found in excavations due to preservation issues, although pepper, mace, and nutmeg have all been recorded, for example, and even rice

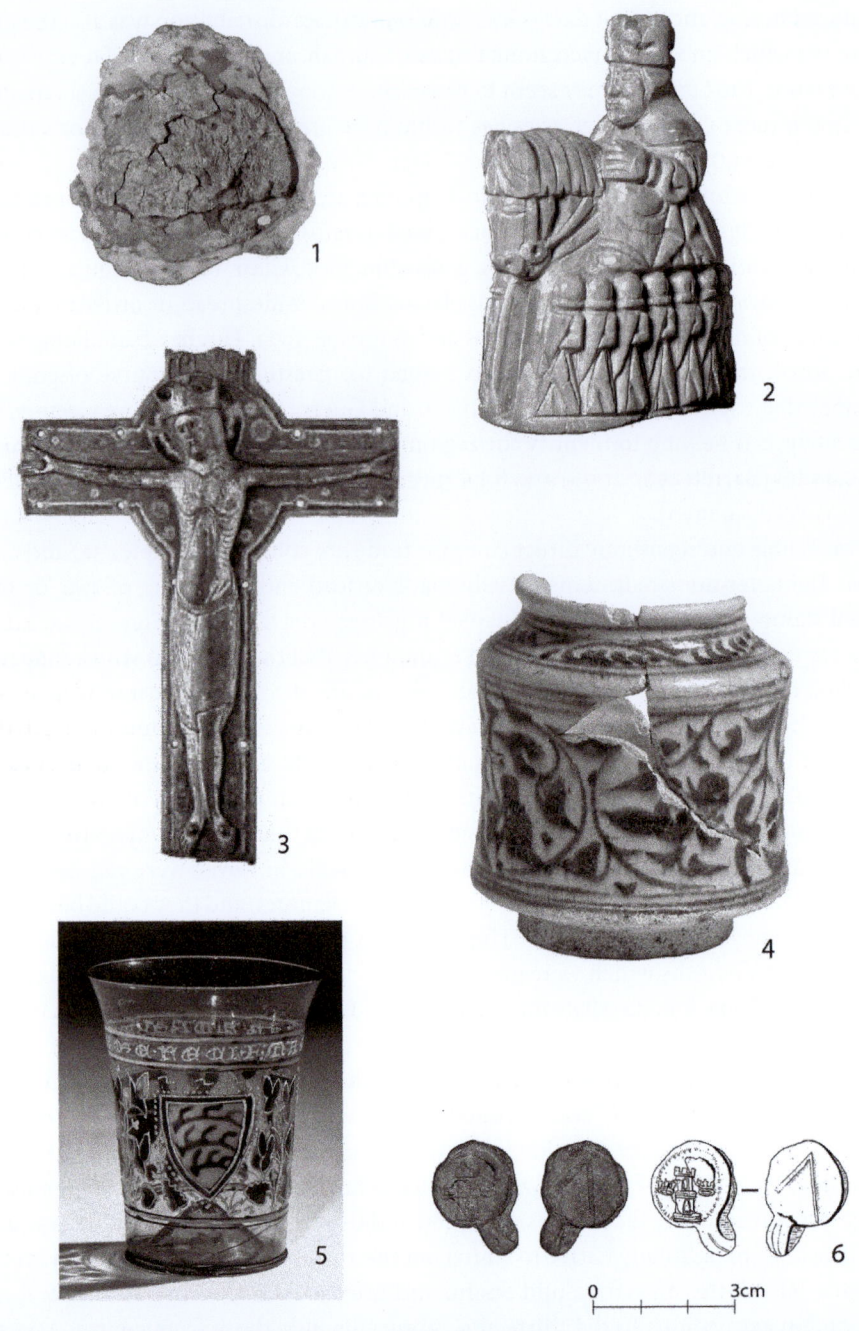

FIGURE 55.4 A range of imported items found in British contexts: (1) an scallop shell containing azurite, from Clarendon Palace; (2) thirteenth-century walrus ivory chess piece found during drainage works at Salisbury, 8.5 cm high; (3) thirteenth-century Limoges enamel crucifix found at Salisbury, 21 cm high; (4) fourteenth-century Middle Eastern fritware jar, 14 cm high; (5) mid-fourteenth-century Venetian glass, 12.5 cm high; (6) cloth seal from Tournai, sixteenth century, showing a stylized two-storey tower, symbol of the city (from the River Wear, Durham)

(© C. M. Gerrard); (With kind permission of Salisbury Museum ©); (With kind permission of Salisbury Museum ©); (© MOLA); (© The Trustees of the British Museum. All rights reserved); (© Gary Bankhead)

too in small quantities. Fruit stones or pips are more likely to survive, such as those from dates, but other spices, such as cinnamon or cardamon, are still elusive in British contexts even though they have been identified elsewhere in northern Europe (Dickson 1996, 29; Greig 1996, 227; McKenna 1987). Imported pigments and paints can be identified through analysis of the finished article, for example wall paintings or illustrated manuscripts; it is rare to find them in their raw estate but an exceptional survival is the scallop shell containing azurite found at the royal palace of Clarendon, Wiltshire, dating to the mid-thirteenth century (Figure 55.4, no. 1). It would have complemented the rich and colourful decorative scheme for the wall plasters at the palace, where lapis lazuli (blue) from Afghanistan and cinnabar (red) from the Iberian Peninsula had also been used (Beaumont James and Gerrard 2007, 74, 93; for further examples, see Howard 2006).

Precious gems are equally rare archaeological finds, but special deposits and chance discoveries provide at least a glimpse of the richness of some dress accessories decorated with glinting gems of exotic origin and diverse meaning (see, for example, the Middleham jewel, Figure 41.4, Cherry 1994; or the Thame hoard, Figure 49.3) (Campbell 1991). Although often seen in museum displays, small imported metal articles other than jewellery are unsurprisingly scant in archaeological deposits. Among the exceptions are works of Limoges enamel from France, usually found at religious sites, such as St Botolph's church, Boston, Lincolnshire, discovered during restoration work, a censer from Barnham in Sussex, a thirteenth-century cross which was found inserted in a crack in the altar at St Ninians, Shetland, and a similar reliquary found at Buckfast Abbey in Devon, together with the crucifix found under a heavy stone in the courtyard of Monpesson House in Salisbury Cathedral Close (Figure 55.4, no. 3) (Barstow 1913; Cherry 2001; Griffin 1930a; 1930b; Murray 2011).

Imported walrus, narwhal, and elephant ivory items might include combs, gaming pieces, handles, mirror cases, caskets, and oliphants or drinking and blast horns (Figure 55.4, no. 2). Some would have arrived as finished articles while others were made locally with imported raw materials; it may be difficult to determine which is the case but specialist areas of ivory carving are known in northern Italy, France, and also England and at least objects inscribed with local names or language, such as those seen on seal matrices, can help to suggest the place of manufacture (MacGregor 1985, 82, 126–7, 137, 153).

Better preserved is imported stone. That from Caen in France was used in building construction and still survives *in situ* in many places, especially churches in southern and eastern England (see Chapter 29), whereas unworked stone could also arrive as ballast from northern European boats and was also reused, for example in the building of walls as at King's Lynn (Hoare et al. 2002). Smaller stone items include hones of Norwegian mica schist (for example, from Launceston Castle, Cornwall; Riddler 2006, 361; and Dryslwyn Castle in Wales; Willmott 2007, 273, S41). Special commissions could also arrive fully formed, such as the mosaics made out of porphyry and other stones—known as Cosmati pavements—brought from Rome to Westminster Abbey at the end of the thirteenth century (Binski 1990) (see cover).

Small items, foodstuffs, and other goods would have been packed in a range of containers but most of them—baskets, textiles, leather, paper, wood, etc.—only survive under exceptional conditions and it is ceramic containers that are more often found during excavations due to their durability, those from Spain being abundant during this period (Gutiérrez 2012; Pleguezuelo 1993). They came mostly from the area around Seville, with further examples from Valencia having been identified so far only in Southampton; they would have been used to carry foodstuffs such as wine and oil. Smaller jars from a wider range of sources were used also as containers for preserves, honey, and treacle (Gutiérrez 2000, fig. 3.4 and 100–12).

Ceramic vessels and tiles other than containers were also traded, especially from south and eastern Spain, western France, Low Countries, and Germany. Trends and distribution across Britain are quite distinctive, with striking early lustrewares from southern Spain being rare and expensive in the later thirteenth and fourteenth centuries, and utilitarian German stonewares being cheaper, durable, and widespread from the mid-fifteenth century (Allan 1984; Cotter 2000, 265, 277, 367; Gaimster 1997; Gerrard et al. 1995; for prices of Spanish wares, see Gutiérrez 2000, 104–12). Netherlandish floor tiles (see below) and German stove tiles were also introduced in the fourteenth to sixteenth centuries, after which they seem to have fallen out of fashion (Gaimster 1988). They are found especially on the east coast of England and Scotland but reach as far as Cornwall on the south coast where, for example, fifty-one sherds of floor tiles were recovered from Launceston Castle (Vince 2006). Hand-painted floor tiles from Spain and the Netherlands are rare during this period but examples of fifteenth-century Valencian tiles are known from a handful of sites, mainly manor houses and palaces; sixteenth-century polychrome floor tiles (*cuerda seca*) from Seville are also found, generally at religious sites although the tiles have frequently been removed from their original settings and reused (Betts 2008; Williams 1995).

Imports of glass vessels are restricted to higher-status households, including religious houses and urban sites (Figure 55.4, no. 5). The earliest imports are late twelfth- to early fourteenth-century 'Byzantine' and Islamic beakers, colourfully enamelled, made in the eastern Mediterranean, Egypt, and Syria. These are rare in Britain; more examples are known of western European, especially Venetian, and possibly French and German glass in forms such as goblets, lids, beakers, bowls, and lamps from the thirteenth century onwards (Tyson 2000). A recent 'hoard' of probably Syrian *albarelli* and Islamic glass found during excavations in London (Pitt and Blackmore 2013) confirms that these items were traded in their own right and that they did not arrive solely as mementoes brought back from the Crusades (Figure 55.4, no. 4).

Shipwrecks also give us an insight into the transport of bulk materials, although more often than not they were salvaged when they went down and it is rare to find them with their cargoes intact. Wrecks usually corroborate the mix of geographical locations visited during voyages, with coins and pottery of different sources being found together aboard (e.g. the Newport ship in Wales, sunk *c.*1468; the Studland Bay wreck, sunk in the early sixteenth century; Nayling 2014; Gutiérrez 2003).

Exchange and Contact

Not all movement of people or goods was associated with trade. One of the reasons why people from England, Scotland, and Wales visited Europe was to go on pilgrimages to sites such as Rocamadour in northern France, Rome in Italy, or Santiago de Compostela in Spain (see Chapter 59). Trips to Compostela, for example, involved hundreds of trips and thousands of people going to and from Britain (Ferreira 1988, 609–10) and although pilgrim badges and scallop shells do sometimes appear on excavations (see Chapter 40), it is remarkable that such a large-scale traffic of people has left so little trace in the archaeological record, and apparently none at all in the ceramic record. To date, no medieval English pottery has been identified in Compostela (and vice versa), this in spite of the fact that ceramic wares could potentially have been used to fill a large gap in local manufacture, as no glazed vessels were known in Galicia at the time (Suárez et al. 1990). Elsewhere, an awareness of demand seems to have been keener. Local craftsmen in Colchester were quick to copy Flemish metalwork forms such as chafing dishes, jugs, and cauldrons in pottery and metal which were demanded by immigrant settlers working in the cloth industry by the mid-fourteenth century (Britnell 1986, 13, 72; Cotter 2000, 176).

Trade was not the only mechanism behind the movement of goods and material culture. Other forms of exchange have gone unrecorded in historical documents and are harder to detect. Gifts were a common way to construct bonds, seal alliances, and gain favour and they could be imparted in many ways and at all levels of society (Komter 1996). They usually took the form of either expensive or unusual items with which to impress and are better documented at diplomatic level and for later periods (e.g. Burchel 2013; Grinder-Hansen 2011; Heal 2008). The unspoken value of such gifts seems to have determined the difference between a mere merchant and an ambassador, and they could open—or close—doors, quite literally. When Vasco de Gama reached Calicut for the first time in 1498, he presented the Zamorin with 'twelve pieces of lambel [striped cloth], four scarlet hoods, six hats, four strings of coral, a case containing six wash-hand basins, a case of sugar, two casks of oil, and two of honey'. These offerings were rejected outright as worthless and the palace doors were closed to him denying him the chance to discuss a trade deal (Siebenhüner 2013).

Among more acceptable gifts from the royal household, the scarlet cloth that Henry III sent to his wife's French relations, to the sultan of Damascus, and to King Haakon of Norway, might sound rather plain, but this cloth, which was made at Lincoln and Stamford, was among the most expensive available at the time. King Haakon must have been pleased because in 1245 he returned the gift by sending six gerfalcons and six falcons for the English king (Carus-Wilson 1964, 187, 193). Further gifts of silver cups, gold brooches, and silk belts were given by Henry III in 1254 to French nobles during a diplomatic visit to Paris; Henry was also generous to those who helped arrange his sister's marriage to Emperor Frederick II and he gave a decorated silver cup and a basin to the emperor's chief counsellor, a belt with an attachment of silver to the Archbishop of

Cologne, silver-gilt cups to the archbishop's two clerks, and a belt of silk embroidered with silver thread for the archbishop's brother, among other items (Linley Wild 2010, 536, 545–6). Silverware and belts are recurring entries in his inventories. More awe-inspiring must have been the gifts brought to Europe by envoys from Asia, including the leopard given by the Mongols to Geoffrey of Langley for King Edward I in Tabriz in 1292 (Paviot 2000).

Other ways of acquiring objects included the commissioning of items. For example, an order for English pewter for personal use was sent by Italian merchant families to their Italians agents working in London (Bratchel 1978, 81). Direct acquisition at the place of manufacture was also sometimes possible. The possible Tunisian vessel found at Faccombe Netherton in Wiltshire, for example, could have been collected in person by the lord of the manor during his trip to the crusades in 1271–2 which included a stay in that country (Gutiérrez 2000, 165). Travel to the Crusades did provide the opportunity not only to source exotic-looking artefacts from the East and elsewhere along the way (e.g. pottery and glass, cloth, metalwork) but also as a means of introducing Europeans to Islamic and Asiatic culture and costumes. In other cases the motive and means behind the acquisition of objects are harder to untangle. The two polychrome tin-glazed tile floors installed at the Manor of the More, Rickmansworth, and at the manor house at the Vyne in Hampshire are a case in point. Both floors, probably made in early sixteenth-century Antwerp, consist of an arrangement of alternating square and oblong hexagon tiles, painted in orange, blue, and green and were a novelty at the time in England. The tiles from the Vyne are thought to have come via France with the owner (Sir William Sandys, Treasurer of Calais) (Rackham 1959).

Merchant Identities

Long-distance trade was regularly in the hands of foreign merchants who would settle abroad and manage commercial activities with the help of their agents. In England the *Carta Mercatoria* of 1303 gave them a set of privileges, including the right to trade and live where they wished in exchange for the payment of additional customs duties (Lloyd 2002). Apart from their commercial acumen, these alien merchants also brought new ideas, values, aesthetic tastes, ideology, and religious beliefs; we might ask if they are visible in the archaeological record.

It is always tempting to pinpoint groups of certain nationality, whether merchants or not, whenever concentrations of exotic material culture occur in excavations. In London, quantities of French and Rhenish pottery have been found in certain quarters where these nationalities were active (Blackmore 1999, 41). A better-documented example, if a little later, is that of the Dutch finds, including hair pins and decorated ceramics (Werra ware), linked with the arrival of Dutch immigrants settled in the east of England in the sixteenth and seventeenth centuries as a result of religious prosecution. As many as six thousand settled in Norwich and here the concentration of Dutch ceramics is higher than anywhere else in Britain. These settlers seem to have been interested in objects and tools which were not available locally, including frying pans and head-dress pins, both items that appear now for the first time in Britain (Atkin et al. 1985; Ayers et al. 1992; Margeson 1993, 236).

In most cases, however, the identification of foreign merchant groups through their material culture is not at all straight-forward and most remain elusive in the archaeological record, for example at Exeter and Southampton no special concentrations of foreign ceramics have been found (Allan 1995; Gutiérrez 2000). At those places where numbers of inhabitants of different nationalities and imports were higher, such as at major ports where the volume of foreign wares in circulation was out of the ordinary, specific links between aliens and objects need to be well documented in order not to create false associations: foreign goods were not necessarily the preferred choice of foreigners alone. Urban areas, especially towns, would have been at the forefront of new fashion and trends, promoting cultural and social change. Southampton, a major medieval port where concentrations of French pottery are high (Brown 1993), for example, was one of the first towns in England to absorb Oriental influences in textiles for the home, with 'Turkish' and Venetian carpets being a regular item in probate inventories already in the early sixteenth century (Roberts and Parker 1992).

A couple of examples which illustrate this point are the group of pottery imports aboard the *Mary Rose*, the battleship of Henry VIII, for the use of the surgeon-barber (Brown and Thompson 2004); and also the large quantity of Italian, Portuguese, and Spanish pottery and glass enjoyed by the Poyntz family at their home at Acton Court in Gloucestershire (Vince and England 2004). The Poyntz family were renowned knights and advisors to the king. Besides their 'exotic' tablewares, they are better known for the collection of floor tiles used in the chapel where Sir Robert Poyntz (1467–1520) was to be buried in Bristol. The chapel's floor was covered in colourful tiles which were made in Seville and are only rarely found in Britain. This is the single largest group ever found in northern Europe and although we do not know exactly who chose them or who brought them into the country, Robert's son Francis was an agent in Spain and he seems to be the obvious link (Gutiérrez 2012, 43). This same relationship between certain types of material culture and 'alien' or foreign identities has been used to explain the cohesiveness among the Hanse merchants in northern Europe, which encompasses not only nationality and language but also a wider cultural identification (Gaimster 2005; Immonem 2007; Mehler 2009). Whether the use of certain objects by some groups is the result of a given identity, cultural affinity, social status, or of a mix of all these, material culture was almost certainly manipulated to stress belonging with or disassociation from certain groups at different times (Barth 1994; Hodder 1986, 9).

Conclusions

Anybody visiting a major museum in the UK today might be forgiven for thinking that their medieval displays are representative of objects found in archaeological deposits.

More often than not they are viewing collections amassed in the nineteenth century (see Chapter 1). Although carved ivories, enamel metalwork, delicate textiles, ceramics, and glass were all used in medieval Britain, the vast bulk of imported goods would have been in the form of raw materials and foodstuffs destined either to be transformed or consumed. Only a small number of such products survive in archaeological deposits and this is, in itself, only a tiny percentage of the total volume of merchandise involved. We forget too easily perhaps that medieval trade established new foreign communities, that it brought new ideas and tastes, and that not all imported items were traded and written down. Here archaeology surely has a vital role in documenting the wider networks of the medieval world.

REFERENCES CITED

Allan, J. 1984 *Medieval and post-medieval finds from Exeter, 1971–1980*, Exeter Archaeological Reports 3, Exeter

Allan, J. 1995 'Iberian pottery imported into South-West England, c.1250–1600', in C. M. Gerrard, A. Gutiérrez, and A. Vince (eds), *Spanish medieval ceramics in Spain and the British Isles*, British Archaeological Reports International Series 610, Oxford, 299–314

Andrews, K. R. 1984 *Trade, plunder and settlement: maritime enterprise and the genesis of the British Empire, 1480–1630*, Cambridge University Press, Cambridge

Atkin, M., Carter, A., and Evans, D. H. 1985 *Excavations in Norwich 1981–78*, East Anglian Archaeology 26, Norwich

Ayers, B. S., Brown, J., and Reeve, J. 1992 *Digging ditches: archaeology and development in Norwich*, Norfolk Museum Service, Norwich

Balfour-Paul, J. 1999 'Indigo in south and south-east Asia', *Textile History* 30(1), 98–112

Barrett, J. H., Johnstone, C., Harland, J., Van Neer, W., Ervynck, A., Makowiecki, D., Heinrich, D., Hufthammer, A. K., Bødker Enghoff, I., Amundsen, C., Schou Christiansen, J., Jones, A. K. G., Locker, A., Hamilton-Dyer, S., Jonsson, L., Lembi Lõugas, L., Roberts, C., and Richards, M. 2008 'Detecting the medieval cod trade: a new method and first results', *Journal of Archaeological Science* 35, 850–61

Barstow, L. 1913 'Buckfast Abbey', *The English illustrated magazine* (February), 508–14

Barth, F. 1994 'Enduring and emerging issues in the analysis of ethnicity', in H. Vermeulen and C. Govers (eds), *The anthropology of ethnicity: beyond 'ethnic groups and boundaries'*, The Hague, 11–32

Bautier, R.-H. 1952 'Les principales étapes du développement des foires de Champagne', *Comptes rendus des séances de l'Académie des Inscriptions et Belles-Lettres* 96ᵉ année, N. 2, 314–26

Betts, I. M. 2008 'Spanish tin-glazed tiles from Woking Palace and other sites in south-east England', *Surrey Archaeological Collections* 94, 53–69

Beaumont James, T. and Gerrard, C. M. 2007 *Clarendon: landscape of kings*, Windgather, Macclesfield

Binski, P. 1990 'The Cosmati at Westminster and the English Court Style', *The Art Bulletin* 72(1), 6–34

Blackmore, L. 1999 'Commerce and the capital: archaeological aspects of London's trade 1100–1700', in R. Dunckel, M. Gläser, and U. Oltmanns (eds), *Lübecker Kolloquium zur*

Stadtarchäologie im Hanseraum II: Der Handel, Bereich Archäologie der Hansestadt Lübeck, Lübeck, 37–58

Bratchel, M. E. 1978 'Italian merchant organisation and business relationships in Early Tudor London', *Journal of European Economic History* 7(1), 5–32

Bridbury, A. R. 1982 *Medieval English clothmaking: an economic survey*, Heinemann Educational Books Ltd, London

Britnell, R. 1986 *Growth and decline in Colchester, 1300–1525*, Cambridge University Press, Cambridge

Brown, D. H. 1993 'The imported pottery of late medieval Southampton', *Medieval Ceramics* 17, 77–81

Brown, D. H. and Thompson, R. 2004 'Pottery vessels', in J. Gardiner (ed.), *Before the mast: life and death aboard the Mary Rose*, The archaeology of the Mary Rose 4, The Mary Rose Trust, Portsmouth, 462–77

Burchel, P. 2013 'A clock for the sultan: diplomatic gift-giving from an intercultural perspective', *The Medieval History Journal* 16(2), 547–63

Byrne, E. H. 1920 'Genoese trade with Syria in the twelfth century', *The American Historical Review* 25(2), 191–219

Campbell, M. 1991 'Gold, silver and precious stones', in J. Blair and N. Ramsay (eds), *English medieval industries: craftsmen, techniques, products*, The Hambledon Press, London, 107–66

Cardon, D. 2007 *Natural dyes: sources, tradition, technology and science*, Archetype Publications, London

Carus-Wilson, E. M. 1937 *The overseas trade of Bristol in the Late Middle Ages*, Bristol Record Society, Bristol

Carus-Wilson, E. M. 1954 *Medieval merchant venturers: collected studies*, Routledge, London

Carus-Wilson, E. M. 1964 'The medieval trade of the ports of the Walsh', *Medieval Archaeology* 6–7, 182–201

Carus-Wilson, E. M. 1987 'The woollen industry', in M. M. Postan and E. Miller (eds), *Cambridge economic history of Europe, II: trade and industry in the Middle Ages*, Cambridge University Press, Cambridge, 613–90 (2nd edn)

Carus-Wilson, E. M. and Coleman, O. 1963 *England's export trade, 1275–1547*, Oxford University Press, Oxford

Chakravarti, R. 2012 'Merchants, merchandise and merchantmen in the western seaboard of India: a maritime profile (c.500 BCE–1500 CE)', in O. Prakash (ed.), *The trading world of the Indian Ocean, 1500–1800*, Pearson Education and Centre for Studies in Civilizations, Delhi, 53–116

Chaudhuri, K. N. 1985 *Trade and civilization in the Indian Ocean: an economic history from the rise of Islam to 1750*, Cambridge University Press, Cambridge

Cherry, J. 1994 *The Middleham jewel and ring*, Yorkshire Museum, York

Cherry, J. 2001 'Enamels', in P. Saunders (ed.), *Salisbury Museum medieval catalogue, Part 3*, Salisbury and South Wiltshire Museum, Salisbury, 39–42

Childs, W. R. 1978 *Anglo-Castilian trade in the Later Middle Ages*, Manchester University Press, Manchester

Childs, W. R. 1995 'Documentary evidence for the import of Spanish pottery to England in the Later Middle Ages (13th to early 16th centuries)', in C. M. Gerrard, A. Gutiérrez, and A. Vince (eds), *Spanish medieval ceramics in Spain and the British Isles*, British Archaeological Reports International Series 610, 25–31

Childs, W. R. 1996 'The English export trade in cloth in the fourteenth century', in R. H. Britnell and J. Hatcher (eds), *Progress and problems in medieval England: essays presented in honour of Edward Miller*, Cambridge University Press, Cambridge, 121–47

Chirikure, S. 2014 'Land and sea links: 1500 years of connectivity between southern Asia and the Indian Ocean rim regions, AD 700 to 1700', *African Archaeological Review* 31, 705–24

Chorley, P. 1988 'English cloth exports during the thirteenth and early fourteenth centuries: the continental evidence', *Historical Research* 61, 1–10

Clark, R. J. H. 1995 'Raman microscopy: application to the identification of pigments on medieval manuscripts', *Chemical Society Reviews* 24(3), 187–96

Cobb, H. S. 1961 *The local port book of Southampton for 1439–40*, Southampton Record Series V, Southampton

Constable, O. R. 1994 *Trade and traders in Muslim Spain: the commercial realignment of the Iberian Peninsula, 900–1500*, Cambridge University Press, Cambridge

Cotter, J. 2000 *Post-Roman pottery from excavations in Colchester, 1971–85*, Colchester Archaeological Report 7, Colchester Archaeological Trust Ltd, Colchester

Crowfoot, E., Pritchard, F., and Staniland, K. 1992 *Textiles and clothing*, Her Majesty's Stationery Office, London

Denbow, J. R. 1990 'Congo to Kalahari: data and hypotheses about the political economy of the western stream of the early Iron Age', *African Archaeological Review* 8, 139–76

Dickson, C. 1996 'Food, medicinal and other plants from the 15th century drains of Paisley Abbey, Scotland', *Vegetation History and Archaeobotany* 5, 25–31

Donnelly, J. 1999 'An open port: the Berwick export trade, 1311–1373', *The Scottish Historical Review* 78, No. 206, Part 2, 145–69

Egan, G. 1980 'Leaden cloth seals and the trade of London', *Post-Medieval Archaeology* 14, 185–203

Egan, G. 1995 *Lead cloth seals and related items in the British Museum*, British Museum Occasional Papers, London

Egan, G. 2001 'Cloth seals', in P. Saunders (ed.), *Salisbury and South Wiltshire Museum medieval catalogue* 3, Salisbury, 43–86

Egan, G. 2010 'Medieval and later trade in textiles between Belgium and England: the picture from some finds of cloth seals', in K. De Groote, D. Tys, and M. Pieters (eds), *Exchanging medieval material culture: studies on archaeology and history presented to Frans Verhaeghe*, Relicta Monografieen 4, Brussels

Endrei, W. and Egan, G. 1982 'The sealing of cloth in Europe, with special reference to the English evidence', *Textile History* 13, 47–75

Evans, D. H. 1999 'The trade of Hull between 1200 and 1700', in R. Dunckel, M. Gläser, and U. Oltmanns (eds), *Lübecker Kolloquium zur Stadtarchäologie im Hanseraum II: Der Handel*, Bereich Archäologie der Hansestadt Lübeck, Lübeck, 59–97

Face, R. D. 1958 'Techniques of business in the trade between the fairs of Champagne and the south of Europe in the twelfth and thirteenth centuries', *Economic History Review* 2nd series 10, 427–38

Face, R. D. 1959 'The *vectuarii* in the overland commerce between Champagne and southern Europe', *Economic History Review* 2nd series 12, 239–46

Ferreira, M. E. 1988 *Galicia en el comercio marítimo medieval*, Colección de Documentos Históricos, Santiago de Compostela

Ferreira, M. J. 2015 'Asian textiles in the Carreira da Índia: Portuguese trade, consumption and taste, 1500–1700', *Textile History* 46(2), 147–68

Fischel W. J. 1958 'The spice trade in Mamluk Egypt: a contribution to the economic history of medieval Islam', *Journal of the Economic and Social History of the Orient* 1(2), 157–74

Foster, B. 1963 *The local port book of Southampton for 1443–1441*, Southampton Record Series VII, Southampton

Gaimster, D. R. M. 1988 'Post-medieval ceramic stove-tiles bearing the royal arms: evidence for their manufacture and use in southern Britain', *The Archaeological Journal* 145(1), 314–43

Gaimster, D. R. M. 1997 *German stoneware 1200–1900*, British Museum Press, London

Gaimster, D. R. M. 2005 'A parallel history: the archaeology of Hanseatic urban culture in the Baltic c.1200–1600, *World Archaeology* 37(3), 408–23

Gardiner, M. and Mehler, N. 2007 'English and Hanseatic trading and fishing sites in medieval Iceland: report on initial fieldwork', *Germania* 85, 385–427

Gerrard, C. M. 2003 *Medieval archaeology: understanding traditions and contemporary approaches*, Routledge, London

Gerrard, C. M., Gutiérrez, A., Hurst, J., and Vince, A. 1995 'A guide to Spanish medieval pottery', in C. M. Gerrard, A. Gutiérrez, and A. Vince (eds), *Spanish medieval ceramics in Spain and the British Isles*, British Archaeological Reports International Series 610, 281–96

Gondonneau, A. and Guerra, M. F. 1999 'The gold from Ghana and the Muslim expansion: a scientific enquiry into the Middle Ages using ICP-MS combined with an UV laser', in S. M. M. Young, A. M. Pollard, P. Budd, and R. A. Ixer (eds), *Metals in antiquity*, British Archaeological Reports International Series 792, Oxford, 262–70

Grant, I. F. 1930 *The social and economic development of Scotland before 1603*, Oliver and Boyd, Edinburgh

Gras, N. S. B. 1918 *The early English customs system*, Cambridge University Press, Cambridge

Greig, J. 1996 'Archaeobotanical and historical records compares: a new look at the taphonomy of edible and other useful plants from the 11th to the 18th centuries AD', *Circaea* 12(2), 211–47

Griffin, R. 1930a 'A round metal object from Boston, Lincs.', *The Antiquaries Journal* 10(2), 139–42

Griffin, R. 1930b 'Limoges enamel censer top from Barnham, Sussex', *The Antiquaries Journal* 10(3), 242–3

Grinder-Hansen, P. 2011 'Aspects of gift giving in Denmark in the sixteenth century and the case of the Rose Flower Cup', *Journal of Medieval History* 37(1), 114–24

Gutiérrez, A. 1995 'Questions of terminology in the study of Spanish medieval ceramics', in C. M. Gerrard, A. Gutiérrez, and A. Vince (eds), *Spanish Medieval Ceramics in Spain and the British Isles*, British Archaeological Reports International Series 610, 33–40

Gutiérrez, A. 2000 *Mediterranean pottery in Wessex households (12th to 17th centuries)*, British Archaeological Reports British Series 306, Oxford

Gutiérrez, A. 2003 'A shipwreck cargo of Sevillian pottery from the Studland Bay wreck, Dorset, UK', *The International Journal of Nautical Archaeology* 32(1), 24–41

Gutiérrez, A. 2012 '*Of sundry colours and moulds*: imports of early modern pottery along the Atlantic seaboard', in A. Texeira and J. A. Bettencourt (eds), *Old and new worlds, International Congress of Early Modern Archaeology*, Lisbon, 37–50

Hall, A. R. 1996 'A survey of palaeobotanical evidence for dyeing and mordanting from British archaeological excavations', *Quaternary Science Reviews* 15, 635–40

Heal, F. 2008 'Food gifts, the household and the politics of exchange in early modern England', *Past and Present* 199(1), 41–70

Hoare, P. G., Vinx, R., Stevenson, C. R., and Ehlers, J. 2002 'Re-used bedrock ballast in King's Lynn's "Town Wall" and the Norfolk port's medieval trading links', *Medieval Archaeology* 46(1), 91–105

Hodder, I. 1986 *Reading the past: current approaches to interpretation in archaeology*, Cambridge University Press, Cambridge

Horton, M. C. 1986 'Asiatic colonization of the East African coast: the Manda evidence', *Journal of the Royal Asiatic Society* 2, 202–13

Horton, M. C. and Middleton, J. 2000 *The Swahili: the social landscape of a mercantile society*, Blackwell Publishers, London

Howard, H. 2006 'Shells as palettes and paint containers in England', in J. Nadolny, with K. Kollandsrud, M. L. Sauerberg, and T. Frøysaker (eds), *Medieval painting in Northern Europe: techniques, analysis, art history. Studies in commemoration of the 70th birthday of Unn Plahter*, London, 202–14

Hughes, M. J. 2016 'Inductively coupled plasma spectrometry (ICPS) analysis of tin-glazed pottery from Glastonbury Abbey', in R. Gilchrist and C. Green, *Glastonbury Abbey excavations*, The Society of Antiquaries, London, 268–70

Hughes, M. J. and Gaimster, D. R. M. 1999 'Neutron activation analsyses of maiolica from London, Norwich, the Low Countries and Italy', in D. R. M. Gaimster (ed.), *Maiolica in the North*, British Museum Occasional Paper 122, London, 57–89

Hutchinson, G. 1994 *Medieval ships and shipping*, Leicester University Press, London

Immonen, V. 2007 'Defining a culture: the meaning of Hanseatic in medieval Turku', *Antiquity* 81, 720–32

James, T. B. 1990 *The port book of Southampton 1509–10*, Southampton Records Series 32–3, University Press, Southampton (2 vols)

Koller, E. F. 1973 'Le commerce médiéval Flandres-Espagne: une conclusion géographique', *Norois* 80, 676–83

Komter, A. E. 1996 *The gift: an interdisciplinary perspective*, Amsterdam University Press, Amsterdam

Lewis, E. A. 1913 'A contribution to the commercial history of mediaeval Wales', *Y Cymmrodor* 24, 104–63

Linley Wild, B. 2010 'A gift inventory from the reign of Henry III', *English Historical Review* 125 no. 514, 529–69

Lloyd, T. H. 2002 *England and the German Hanse, 1157–1611: a study of their trade*, Cambridge University Press, Cambridge

Lynch, M. and Strang, A. 1966 'Overseas trade: the Middle Ages to the sixteenth century', in P. G. B. McNeill and H. L. MacQueen (eds), *Atlas of Scottish History to 1707*, University of Edinburgh, Edinburgh

MacGregor, A. 1985 *Bone, antler, ivory and horn: the technology of skeletal materials since the Roman period*, Croom Helm, London

Magnavita, S. 2013 'Initial encounters: seeking traces of ancient trade connections between West Africa and the wider world', *Afriques* 4, 1–14

Margeson, S. 1993 *Norwich households: the medieval and post-medieval finds from Norwich survey excavations 1971–1978*, East Anglian Archaeology 58, Norwich

McKenna, W. J. B. 1987 'The environmental evidence', in P. Armstrong and B. Ayers (eds), *Excavations in High Street and Blackfriargate*, East Riding Archaeology 5, Hull, 255–61

Mehler, N. 2009 'The perception and interpretation of Hanseatic material culture in the North Atlantic: problems and suggestions', *Journal of the North Atlantic Special vol.* 1, 89–108

Murray, W. 2011 'The "Limoges" cross fragments', in R. C. Barrowman, *The chapel and burial ground on St Ninian's Isle, Shetland: excavations past and present*, The Society for Medieval Archaeology Monograph 32, London, 65

Nayling, N. 2014 'The Newport medieval ship, Wales, United Kingdom', *The International Journal of Nautical Archaeology* 43(2), 239–78

Newitt, M. 2004 *A history of Portuguese overseas expansion 1400–1668*, Routledge, London and New York

Nixon, S. 2009 'Excavating Essouk-Tadmakka (Mali): new archaeological investigations of early Islamic trans-Saharan trade', *Azania: Archaeological Research in Africa* 44, 217–55

Paviot, J. 2000 'England and the Mongols (c.1260–1330)', *Journal of the Royal Asiatic Society* 10(3), 305–18.

Pearson, M. 2010 'Islamic trade, shipping, port-states and merchant communities in the Indian Ocian, seventh to sixteenth centuries', in D. O. Morgan and A. Reid (eds), *The New Cambridge History of Islam, Vol. 3: the eastern Islamic world, eleventh to eighteenth centuries*, Cambridge University Press, Cambridge, 315–65

Pelham, R. A. 1930 'The foreign trade of the Cinque Ports during the year 1307–08', in I. C. Peate (ed.), *Studies in regional consciousness and environment*, Oxford University Press, Oxford, 129–45

Pitt, K. and Blackmore, L. 2013 *Medieval to early post-medieval tenements and Middle Eastern imports: excavations at Plantation Place, City of London, 1997–2003*, Museum of London Archaeology Monograph 66, London

Pleguezuelo, A. 1993 'Seville coarsewares, 1300–1650: a preliminary typological survey', *Medieval Ceramics* 17, 39–50

Pluskowski, A. 2004 'Narwhals or unicorns? Exotic animals as material culture in medieval Europe', *European Journal of Archaeology* 7(3), 291–313

Power, E. 1941 *The wool trade in English medieval history*, Oxford University Press, Oxford

Power, E. and Postan, M. M. (eds) 1933 *Studies in English trade in the fifteenth century*, Routledge, London

Quinn, D. B. (ed.) 1937 *The port book or local customs accounts of Southampton for the reign of Edward IV, Vol. I, 1469–1471*, Southampton Record Society, Southampton

Quinn, D. B. (ed.) 1938 *The port book or local customs accounts of Southampton for the reign of Edward IV, vol. II, 1477–1481*, Southampton Record Society, Southampton

Rackham, B. 1959 'Netherlands maiolica tiles', in M. Biddle, L. Barfield, and A. Millard, 'The excavation of the manor of the More, Rickmansworth, Hertfordshire', *The Archaeological Journal* 116(1), 136–99

Ramsay, G. D. 1957 *English overseas trade during the centuries of emergence*, Macmillan, London

Reynolds, R. L. 1931 'Genoese trade in the late twelfth century, particularly in cloth from the fairs of Champagne', *Journal of Economic and Business History* 3, 362–81

Riddler, I. 2006 'Stone, bone, antler and ivory finds', in A. Saunders, *Excavations at Launceston Castle, Cornwall*, The Society for Medieval Archaeology Monograph 24, Leeds, 357–80

Roberts, E. and Parker, K. 1992 *Southampton probate inventories 1447–1575*, Southampton Record Series 34–5, Southampon

Robertshaw, P., Wood, M., Melchiorre, E., Popelka-Filcoff, S., and Glascock, M. D. 2010 'Southern African glass beads: chemistry, glass sources and patterns of trade', *Journal of Archaeological Science* 37, 1898–1912

Roger, J.-M. 1983 'Un brevet des foires de Champagne du XIVe siecle', *Bibliothèque de l'école des chartes* 141(1), 117–21

Rooseboom, M. P. 1910 *The Scottish staple in the Netherlands*, Nijhoff, The Hague
Rorke, M. 2006 'English and Scottish overseas trade, 1300–1600', *Economic History Review* 59, 265–88
Ruddock, A. A. 1951 *Italian merchants and shipping in Southampton, 1270–1600*, Southampton Record Series 1, Southampton
Russell-Wood, A. J. R. 1992 *The Portuguese empire, 1415–1808: a world in the move*, John Hopkins University Press, Baltimore
Salzman, L. F. 1931 *English trade in the Middle Ages*, Clarendon Press, Oxford
Scammel, G. V. 1961 'English merchant shipping at the end of the Middle Ages: some east coast evidence', *The Economic History Review*, new series, 13(3), 327–41
Siebenhüner, K. 2013 'Approaching diplomatic and courtly gift-giving in Europe and Mughal India: shared practices and cultural diversity', *The Medieval History Journal* 16(2), 525–46
Stone, L. 1949 'Elizabethan overseas trade', *Economic History Review*, 2nd series, 2, 30–58
Studer, P. 1913 *The port books of Southampton 1427–1430*, Southampton Record Society, Southampton
Suárez, J., Gimeno, R., and Fariña, F. 1990 'La cerámica medieval en Galicia', en J. A. Gutiérrez-González and R. Bohigas (eds), *La cerámica medieval en el norte y noroeste de la Península Ibérica: aproximación a su estudio*, León, 285–301
Tyson, R. 2000 *Medieval glass vessels found in England, c. AD 1200–1500*, Council for British Archaeology Research Report 121, York
Van der Merwe, N. J., Lee-Thorp, J. A., Thackeray, J. F., Hall-Martin, A., Kruger, F. J., Coetzee, H., Bell, R. H. V., and Lindeque, M. 1990 'Source-area determination of elephant ivory by isotopic analysis', *Nature* 346.6286, 744–6
Vince, A. 2006 'Flemish floor tiles', in A. Saunders, *Excavations at Launceston Castle, Cornwall*, The Society for Medieval Archaeology Monograph 24, Leeds, 429–30
Vince, A. and England, S. 2004 'Medieval and later pottery', in K. Rodwell and R. Bell (eds), *Acton Court: the evolution of an early Tudor courtier's house*, English Heritage, London, 294–8
Vogel, J. C., Eglington, B., and Auret, J. M. 1990 'Isotope fingerprints in elephant bone and ivory', *Nature* 346.6286, 747–9
Wade, G. 2009 'An early age of commerce in southeast Asia, 900–1300 CE', *Journal of Southeast Asian Studies* 40(2), 221–65
Walton, P. and Taylor, G. 1991 'The characterisation of dyes in textiles from archaeological excavations', *Chromatography & Analysis* 6, 5–7
Willan, T. S. 1959 *Studies in Elizabethan foreign trade*, Manchester University Press, Manchester
Williams, B. 1995 'Survey of Spanish tiles imported into England: an interim note', in C. M. Gerrard, A. Gutiérrez, and A. Vince (eds), *Spanish medieval ceramics in Spain and the British Isles*, British Archaeological Reports International Series 610, 335–8
Williams, D. T. 1936 'Medieval foreign trade: western ports', in H. C. Darby (ed.), *An historical geography of England before AD 1800*, Cambridge University Press, Cambridge
Willmott, H. 2007 'Stone artefacts', in C. Caple, *Excavations at Dryslwyn Castle 1980–95*, The Society for Medieval Archaeology Monograph 26, Leeds, 272–7
Wilson, A. 2012 'Saharan trade in the Roman period: short-, medium- and long-distance trade networks', *Azania: Archaeological Research in Africa* 47(4), 409–49
Wink, A. 1991 *Al-Hind: the making of the Indo-Islamic world, Vol. 1*, Brill, Leiden
Wubs-Mrozewicz, J. and Jenks. S. (eds) 2012 *The Hanse in medieval and early modern Europe*, Brill, Leiden

CHAPTER 56

LOOKING WEST

Ireland in the Middle Ages

TERRY B. BARRY

THERE is a problem in identifying the start of high medieval settlement in Ireland. For instance, there is still an active debate over the possible existence of castles in the first half of the twelfth century before the first sustained ingress by the Anglo-Normans in AD 1169. Increasingly there is an understanding that the powerful O'Conor family constructed some kind of castle against the growing power of *Midh* (Meath). Of course, at this stage it is important to identify what we understand by the term 'castle', almost as problematic as the term 'feudal', a word not even used in the medieval period. There have been many modern definitions for this, all emphasizing the multi-functionality of these original military centres, but they all agree that castles were often the fortified dwelling places of a feudal aristocratic family of a locality, or of the Crown. There is, therefore, the very interesting question as to whether some kind of incipient feudalism existed in the O'Conor kingdom in the twelfth century, overlying the indigenous forms of land holdings that dominated Ireland until the events of 1169. The same question has also been asked about late Anglo-Saxon England where there is also some evidence that a few castles were being built before the Norman Conquest.

By the time the Anglo-Normans invaded Ireland there had already been over a century of the unrolling of the feudal landholding system by the victorious Normans in England. So it is very unlikely that the Irish kings and rulers were not influenced by this revolution in the distribution and the holding of land, much as they had been by the construction of castles. Sometimes, it seems that some scholars think of Ireland as being truly connected with the rest of Europe only after the coming of the Anglo-Normans in the latter part of the twelfth century. Logically, this is certainly not the case when it is realized the many interconnections between the Irish and the Norse in the major towns of the east coast from the tenth century onwards which were trading with much of northern Europe. Part of the problem in accepting this link probably resides in the different nature of many of the Gaelic Irish sources that did not always emphasize Ireland's view of the wider world.

Castles

When the Anglo-Norman forces landed in Ireland they found themselves in a very hostile environment, and all the contemporary accounts stress the small size of their forces. It is hardly surprising then that they decided to construct the same types of earth-and-timber campaign castles that their predecessors had built in England over a century before. The great majority of these were the motte-and-bailey castles, like those portrayed on the famous *Bayeux Tapestry*, possibly embroidered within two decades of the conquest of England in 1066, and which gives us such a rich visual image of the events surrounding that event. In Ireland we know of the existence of around four hundred examples of these castles, although there are fewer surviving baileys, as is also the case in Britain.

Far fewer ringwork castles have been identified, up to one hundred examples are known, but a major problem that researchers have in Ireland is that their morphological remains are so similar to the most numerous earthworks in Ireland, the ringforts of the first millennium AD. Nevertheless, they can usually be distinguished from each other (Figure 56.1); the main defensive elements of a ringwork castle were the perimeter fosse and the bank and palisade immediately behind it; there would also have been a significant entrance tower to defend it (Colfer 2013, 38).

FIGURE 56.1 Aerial photograph of an early medieval ringwork castle at Danesfort, Co. Kilkenny
(© T. B. Barry)

When investigating these early castles an important contemporary historical source is the *Expugnatio Hibernica*, written by a Welsh cleric, Gerald de Barry, when he visited Ireland shortly after the Anglo-Norman invasion. It is also important, however, to be aware of the geographical limits of Gerald's two visits to Ireland because they constrained his knowledge to a significant extent. Thus, when he stated that the Anglo-Normans did not build in pre-existing Irish settlement sites, Gerald was only writing about that small area of eastern Ireland that he had actually visited. This observation of his has not been supported by modern archaeological evidence as there are a number of Irish ringforts, for instance, that have provided the base for Anglo-Norman motte castles, including Rathmullan in Co. Down (Lynn 1981–2). Therefore, he was not deliberately misleading when he wrote this about the built landscape of medieval Ireland, as his knowledge was limited by the extent of his travels within the heartland of the newly established Lordship.

In this regard, it is often necessary to pay close attention to the exact Latin words that Gerald used to describe the castles. A good example of this is the construction of one of the first castles, if not the first Anglo-Norman example in Ireland by the Anglo-Normans, that at Ferrycarrig in Co. Wexford. In the critical edition by Scott and Martin, it is described as 'undoubtedly primitive and of the motte-and-bailey style' (1978, 298). But anyone who has traversed the spot at the cliff edge overlooking the River Slaney, now in the Wexford National Heritage Park just north of Wexford town, will find no trace of any mound of earth or motte. Indeed, the description by Gerald that FitzStephen 'improved by artificial means a place naturally well protected', along with his use of the word *municipium* (fortress) rather than *castrum* (castle) should have warned any reader that this was a ringwork castle (Scott and Martin 1978, 53). Archaeological excavations at Ferrycarrig confirm the presence of such a defensive earthwork there, with evidence of thirteenth-century occupation (Bennett 1984–5).

One of the biggest advances in our knowledge of castles over the last decade or so is the growing realization that the Anglo-Normans, much like their forebears in England a century or so earlier, started building in stone masonry within ten years of their arrival in Ireland. This was first brought home to the archaeological community in the mid-1990s as a direct result of a major excavation and conservation of Trim Castle in Co. Meath, one of the most impressive Norman edifices in Ireland (Figure 56.2), which examined virtually the entire area within its curtain walls (Hayden 2011). During work on the keep it was found that the putlog holes still contained extensive remains of the oak timbers of the original scaffolding of the castle. All together twelve samples were dendrochronologically dated in Queen's University, Belfast, and they conclusively showed that the base of the masonry keep was being constructed as early as the 1180s, probably less than a decade after the construction of the ringwork castle there, as recorded in *The Song of Dermot and the Earl* (Orpen 1911–20).

The other early Anglo-Norman castle with a rectangular keep, Carrickfergus in Co. Antrim in the north-east of Ireland, is sited on a base of basalt bedrock, and commanding the entrance into Belfast Lough. This masonry castle has not had the same level of archaeological exploration, especially as it is founded directly on bedrock, and also there

FIGURE 56.2 Trim Castle, Co. Meath

(© William Murphy, CC BY-SA 2.0)

is some problem with its identification in surviving contemporary historical sources. There is also no scientific dating evidence to precisely date its construction. However, McNeill has suggested, on the balance of the available evidence, that it was also built in the 1180s, probably at the behest of John De Courcey, the Anglo-Norman conqueror of Ulster (McNeill 1997).

The next major architectural development in stone castles in Ireland, as with the rest of Europe, was the construction of circular keeps. Probably the progenitor of the idea came from Pembroke Castle in South Wales, associated with many of the original Anglo-Norman families who came to Ireland. The defensibility of these keeps was enhanced by their design as they lacked any sharp corners that could more easily be reduced by siege weapons. Although they were more defensible in a siege, this advantage was more than outweighed by the interior disadvantages caused by this new plan. As the keep was often the main dwelling area in these early castles the internal layout of the rooms and chambers was often compromised. And in Ireland there is very little evidence of siege warfare throughout most of the medieval period. This should not really surprise us when it is realized how complex and expensive siege trains were in this era. Even the English Crown operating in Ireland would have been hard-pressed to provide men and money for these enterprises.

For all these many, myriad reasons the number of circular main towers or keeps in Ireland is quite low. Arguably the finest example, later largely re-built in the nineteenth century, is Nenagh Castle in Co. Tipperary. Another good example is Dundrum Castle in Co. Down, built in a stunning location on a hill overlooking Dundrum Bay in the Irish Sea. Like many other early Anglo-Norman castles, there is some limited evidence to suggest that it was sited on top of an earlier earthwork here. We also have this evidence for the complex castle site at Dunamase in Co. Laois, where excavations have revealed traces of an earlier fosse of some kind of fortification constructed by the local O'Carroll family, which is mentioned in the *Annals of Ulster* in 845 AD (Hodkinson 1999).

The final major phase of medieval castles in Ireland comprises those built without any separate keep. Now the citadel was to be found located in the heavily defended gatehouse. The best example of this was Roscommon Castle built by the Justiciar of Ireland, Robert de Ufford, in 1269. Remarkably, it was built a few years before Harlech Castle in Wales, to which it can be closely compared. All these castles were part of a massive building campaign to hold down the enemies of Edward I in Wales, Ireland, and Scotland. In addition, O'Conor has identified the remains of an outer line of defences external to the masonry walls which, if confirmed, would make it a concentric castle, like so many in Europe constructed at this time (Murphy and O'Conor 2008).

Greencastle on the Inishowen peninsular in Co. Donegal has surviving elements of polygonal towers and sandstone blocks at the quoins in contrast to the grey colour of the rest of the walls, reminiscent of Edward's mighty castle at Caernarfon in north Wales. This castle was constructed on the orders of Richard de Burgo, the 'Red' Earl of Ulster, and completed around 1305. One of its earliest names was 'Northburg' as it was constructed to defend the by-now fragmented Anglo-Irish colony in the north-west. As a testament to its continuing strategic location, one of the many Martello towers which were constructed all along the coasts of Britain and Ireland was built close to the castle about AD 1800 against a seaborne invasion by Napoleon.

This main period of medieval castle construction in Ireland came to a sudden end after the first two decades of the fourteenth century, brought about by almost a 'perfect storm' of factors which included a dramatic economic decline as well as a lack of an active strategic plan to defend the rapidly collapsing frontiers of the Lordship. This probably led to a significant reduction in the population levels within the Lordship; this and the relative poverty of the Lordship, as well as the often restricted hinterlands that these castles were served by, meant that very few earlier castles had been comprehensively repaired. Only a tiny number of sizeable castles were built in this period, among them Cahir Castle in southern Co. Tipperary. Here there is still a well preserved fortification straddling the River Suir. According to Sweetman (1999, 123–6) the core of the inner ward probably dates to the thirteenth century, but the larger outer ward is later. In 1192 Philip of Worcester was granted the lands on which the castle stands, but the original fortification was undoubtedly the impressive motte at Knockgraffon, some 6 km north.

Tower Houses

The late medieval landscape of Ireland also contained a much more complex mixture of castle and defensive sites than was originally realized. Now we know that along with the ubiquitous tower house there were also defended houses and strong houses (Sweetman

1999) and that these can be found in different regions of Ireland as geographically different as Galway in the west and Wexford in the south-east. There is potential to understand regional variations better but there have been relatively few archaeological excavations; advances in our understanding of them have been in the sphere of architecture rather than archaeology. Scholars have investigated the internal arrangements of a sizeable number and through these regional studies we can begin to get a better idea of both their chronology and functionality (McAlister 2016). Tower houses are exceptionally significant in an Irish context as they are undoubtedly the most numerous of all stone-built structures of any period to have survived throughout the island. We still do not have a completely accurate figure for all that were built throughout the later medieval period. The main reason for this lack of knowledge lies in the fact that the Ordnance Survey of Ireland firstly scientifically records their distribution only as late as the 1830s. Some studies have indicated that the military surveyors of the Ordnance Survey may have under-reported them by as much as 50 per cent (Cairns 1987). The Archaeological Survey of Ireland has a running total of around 2300 surviving examples today, so maybe a more accurate total number might be about 5000-plus tower houses. Whatever is the final total, and this is something we probably will never know with any accuracy, these stone towers and the buildings that surrounded them had a profound impact on the landscape of Ireland in the later Middle Ages. Of course, we still have no real idea how many of these tower houses were being inhabited contemporaneously, but even if all of them were, it would still possibly only represent under 10 per cent of the total population of Ireland, at a maximum.

Thus, there is no doubt as to their importance both in terms of numbers and the fact that both Anglo-Irish and Gaelic-Irish gentry dwelt in them. Indeed, some of the areas with the densest surviving distributions, such as the eastern areas of Counties Clare and Limerick, were undeniably under Gaelic-Irish control at the time. This is matched by large concentrations within the Anglo-Irish sphere of control, such as in Counties Tipperary and Kilkenny, in the Earldom of Ormond. They also have a very lengthy chronology of usage, as they arguably have their origin in the second half of the fourteenth century and they went on being built right up until the middle of the seventeenth century, when the increasing professionalism in siege artillery and warfare brought about by the Cromwellian Wars probably largely signalled their end. Nevertheless, the major construction period of tower house construction stretched over the fifteenth and sixteenth centuries.

Archaeologically, it is extremely difficult to locate evidence for the other subsidiary structures as well as the bawns marked by a defensive wall around the property that gave them added protection, unless they too were built of stone. We know from the contemporary written sources that the bawn walls would also have been constructed from wooden palisades or, indeed, from hedges. This would mean that they would be virtually untraceable today. The same is true of the subsidiary buildings, as they were typically of wooden construction. Often the tower house was the centre of an economic unit, with agricultural buildings surrounding it, both within and outside the bawn. Again, we can often only identify these from the contemporary historical record, with all the issues of the non-survival or otherwise of these documents playing an important part in this story.

Although these omnipresent tower houses dominated the late medieval Irish rural landscape, there were large zones such as the province of Ulster where the distribution is much less dense, although with some local concentrations in the Strangford Lough area of Co. Down (McAlister 2016). This also largely negates the idea that they were introduced from Scotland, especially as the Scottish examples are no earlier than the ones in Ireland.

Moated Sites

In this period only the Crown and the wealthiest aristocrats could afford not only to build but also to maintain these massive stone castles dotted throughout the Lordship. Most of the lesser nobility dwelled within earth-and-timber defensive structures, known as moated sites. There are over 750 examples known about in Ireland, with the majority concentrated along the borders of the Lordship. Counties with the densest concentration of these sites include Wexford and Tipperary, with fewer to be found in the heartland of the Colony, in counties such as Dublin. One of the major advances in our understanding of these sites in the last few years has been the identification of them in Gaelic-controlled areas (O'Conor 2000). This has been particularly marked in Roscommon, in lands controlled by the O'Conors throughout the Middle Ages. Like the tower houses that followed them chronologically, moated sites met the local needs for every ethnic background that needed secure settlements within a dispersed settlement pattern.

They can be defined as rectangular earthworks with a wet fosse on the exterior—fed by a spring or nearby river—and an internal earthen bank often surmounted with a wooden palisade. On the platform there would have been located a wooden hall and other buildings, often associated with farming. Although only a small number have been dated, they are especially to be found in the late thirteenth and early fourteenth centuries. Their chronology would, therefore, probably coincide with the high point of Anglo-Norman settlement in Ireland. Unlike the distribution pattern in lowland England, where moated sites are often located at known medieval village sites, the great majority of Irish sites are to be found in isolated locations. Their morphology is also different from most other sites in Britain and beyond, with very few examples possessing more than one platform, indicative both of the often transient nature of settlement, as well as being generally a reflection of the poorer socio-economic of much of Ireland in the medieval period.

By the late fourteenth and early fifteenth centuries it is likely that many of these moated sites were falling into disrepair, especially with the rise of the tower house. There is still a debate about the origins of tower houses, and whether they were built as early as the fourteenth century. But there is enough evidence, although limited, to at least suggest there were some tower houses existing on the Irish landscape at the end of that century, at least. What is more, a thorough investigation into what is meant by a term that often appears in late medieval documents—*fortalitia* or *fortalis*—which is usually understood to mean a small fortress, might produce some examples of this, too (Barry 2016; Lyttleton and O'Keefe 2005).

Rural Settlement

Many of the smaller nucleated settlements were deliberately given urban status in order to attract new settlers to this new frontier land in the thirteenth century. These have been described as 'rural boroughs' by Glasscock (1970, 171). But with almost fifty years of research into this phenomenon there are only a few hundred examples that have been identified so far. Thus, it is probable that the pattern of rural settlement in Anglo-Norman Ireland was much more dispersed than that of lowland England. These 'urban villages' whose traces can still be located within the modern landscape of the Lordship are especially concentrated in the better agricultural lands of the south-east. The general layout of these earthworks usually includes most of the following: rectangular house platforms, a church, a sunken way, as well as a manor house. Curiously, the more sharp the surviving earthworks, the younger the period of desertion (McAlister and Barry 2015).

Undoubtedly the best surviving medieval nucleated settlement in Ireland is Newtown Jerpoint in Co. Kilkenny. Many manorial extents and other contemporary documents survive for this rural borough which is located beside the River Nore in a very prosperous part of Anglo-Norman Ireland (Barry 1994, 75–81). Although the inhabitants were granted burgess status to try and attract settlers from Britain, many of these settlements were, in reality, villages. Newtown Jerpoint was a very small settlement, with only about twenty-two burgesses in the late thirteenth and early fourteenth century. It also has been a prime candidate for further research and geophysical survey co-ordinated by the Heritage Council (Oxford Archaeology 2007). Not only is there an impressive village earthwork, which was first completely surveyed by the Ordnance Survey in 1839, but there is also the possible site of the original medieval mill that is mentioned in the medieval extents. There are also the extensive remains of the important Cistercian abbey of Jerpoint on the other bank of the River Nore. Crucially, however, in 1375 the Provost and Commons of Newtown Jerpoint were given a grant of pontage for ten years by King Edward III so that they could levy certain tolls and customs on all saleable items that crossed their bridge. This grant ensured the prosperity of the citizens of Newtown Jerpoint until the end of the Middle Ages when other towns nearby, like Thomastown with its competing bridge across the River Nore, climbed into ascendancy as Jerpoint declined.

There have also been a limited number of excavations on other deserted medieval villages, such as Piperstown in Co. Louth, a portion of which was excavated by the present author in 1987 (Figure 56.3). This investigation concentrated upon arguably the best identifiable house platform and one large rectilinear earthen bank, the most obvious surface features among all the surviving village earthworks. With hindsight, these particular features did not produce any startling artefacts or constructional evidence to revolutionize the study of medieval settlement desertion in Ireland. It was, however, a valuable addition to the limited excavation sample of well under ten sites that is at present available for these settlements. This is especially the case given the site's location close to the eastern seaboard of the country, as most of the excavations of medieval nucleated settlements have been located in the south and west of the island (Barry 1994, 72–84).

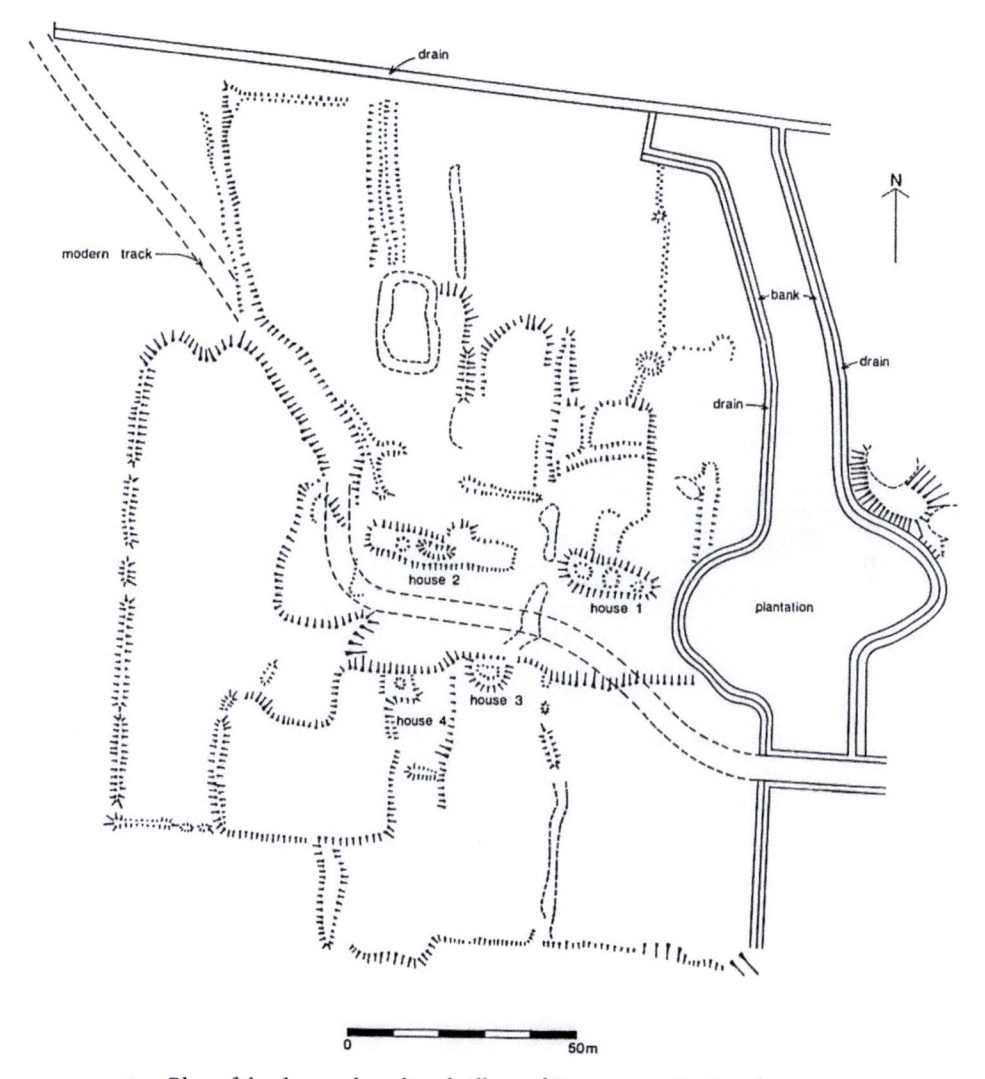

FIGURE 56.3 Plan of the deserted medieval village of Piperstown, Co. Louth

(© T. B. Barry)

Like so many other archaeological excavations of rural nucleated medieval settlements only a very small proportion of the entire earthwork complex has been investigated, and therefore it would be dangerous to be too certain in arguing that this one house platform is necessarily typical of the settlement as a whole. Nevertheless, it probably does reflect both the general chronology and the socio-economic development of the village as a whole. The artefacts strongly indicate that the village was founded sometime in the thirteenth century, probably in the latter half of that century. According to the finds evidence, some kind of settlement continued here until the early eighteenth century when it would seem that the site was finally deserted.

The desertion evidence from Piperstown has given added weight to the idea that the main period of village desertion in medieval Ireland was much later than that experienced in the English Midlands where most research on deserted medieval villages has been undertaken (O'Conor 1998). There, the archaeological evidence would indicate that the height of village desertion is associated with the switch from arable to pastoral agriculture in the fifteenth century (Beresford and Hurst 1971). In Ireland the evidence is growing to show that most village desertion is much later than this, and most often linked with the effects of the seventeenth century Cromwellian Wars on the Irish landscape and in the post-medieval period generally (Barry 1996; Corlett and Potterton 2009). For instance, at Newtown Jerpoint in Co. Kilkenny the contemporary sources for the settlement end in the middle of the seventeenth century and the earthworks, as mapped in the 1840s by the Ordnance Survey, were so sharp as also to suggest such a late desertion (Barry 1994, 76).

Towns

We also now have a much better sense of the socio-economic developments within the minor medieval towns of Ireland (Doyle and Browne 2016). This has been largely due to the research of historical geographers and economic historians rather than archaeologists. After all the archaeological research that has been lavished on our major medieval port towns, now is surely the time for attention to shift to these. The only exception to this was Wallace's excavations in the 1980s in Wexford town. This was followed in the 1990s by further archaeological excavations in Cork and Galway. Apart from Murphy and Potterton's major monograph (2010) on Dublin, however, there have been no studies that have examined the urban networks of medieval Ireland, or how the smaller towns interacted with the larger ports and cities (for buildings, see O'Keefe 2015).

Churches

Ireland also had many settlements and churches associated with the medieval Church. Indeed, for a small island, Ireland had a large number of such sites, ranging from small rural parish churches to large and impressive monasteries, religious houses, cathedrals, and abbeys (Gwynn and Hadcock 1970; Stalley 1987). In the medieval Irish Church the concept of pilgrimage was always central to the belief system of many people, with Rome and Jerusalem being the most important. The third most important destination was probably to Santiago de Compostela in north-west Spain (Taylor 2009). And many of the pilgrims to places closer to home, such as Canterbury, were also Irish, as can be shown by the finding of numerous pilgrim badges in urban archaeological sites throughout Ireland (Wallace 2015) and by artefacts of Irish origin recovered in southern England (Gerrard and Youngs 2007). There were also important pilgrimage sites in Ireland, such as Lough Derg in Co. Donegal, where there is evidence for a steady stream of European pilgrims visiting the site up until the Reformation (Haren and Pontfarly 1988).

There have also been important excavations on some of these monastic sites such as Kells, Co. Kilkenny, Tintern, Co. Wexford, and Trinity Island, Co. Roscommon (Clyne 2005; 2007; Lynch 2010). These excavations have provided much new artefactual evidence on the lifestyle of these religious communities (O'Keeffe 2001, 132–62). More than anything else the excavations of burials, particularly at the continuing community and training excavation at the Black Friary in Trim, Co. Meath, have produced much valuable information on the life expectancy and the diseases suffered by their medieval population (Dara Fleming Farrell pers. comm.).

Trade and Contact with Britain

There has also been a refining of the chronology of most of the imported medieval pottery into Ireland in the twelfth and thirteenth centuries (Le Patourel 1968). Notably among these wares, those from the Ham Green kilns near the port of Bristol have been found at high-status sites all over the Anglo-Norman Lordship and beyond. Indeed, it could almost be argued that more examples have been found in Ireland than anywhere else in these islands, apart from south Wales and lowland England. This is hardly surprising as Bristol was the English port that dominated trade with Ireland, along with Chester further north (Childs and Neill 1993; O'Neill 1987). The chronology of Ham Green wares has also been extended as a result of more recent excavations, so that we now see the first imports of this type of pottery as early as the 1170s and extending through the whole of the following century (e.g. McCutcheon 2006).

Other major types of imported pottery included Saintonge-type green-glazed and polychrome tablewares from south-west France, probably exported to Ireland either directly through the east coast French ports of La Rochelle and Bordeaux, or via the entrepots of Bristol or Chester. These have been found in sites ranging from castles to moated sites and villages, as well as in urban areas. One such high-status rural site is the Augustinian Priory of Kells, Co. Kilkenny, situated in the lush farmland of the southern half of that county. Here the rich ceramic assemblage reflected the wide geographical spread of different types of medieval pottery found in these high-status sites.

Nevertheless, of the eight thousand identifiable sherds, 94 per cent were locally made. The remaining came primarily from western England, such as Ham Green ware from near Bristol, and from France, with examples from Rouen and Saintogne being in the majority (Clyne 2007, 316–41).

The most common pottery types found were the locally made cooking wares that were fired in local kilns close to many of the main urban centres. For instance, the thirteenth-century account rolls of the important Augustinian Holy Trinity in Dublin contains much detailed economic data about its extensive land holdings, including a short reference in 1344 to potters purchasing clay in Kill O' The Grange in south Co. Dublin (Mills 1996, 55). These probably never penetrated the regional markets, but usually remained local in focus. Despite all the research over the past twenty years, we still only have limited evidence for two to three major pottery kilns in the country. Undoubtedly, the available evidence would suggest that there were probably other examples that have yet to be located. The research of O'Floinn on North Leinster Cooking Ware, one significant type which had a regional circulation, has led the way in research on a particularly important type of locally produced pottery (O'Floinn 1988).

There have also been many attempts to understand the medieval diet, especially that of the peasantry, as there are very few historical sources to assist us in this enquiry. Finds in medieval latrines and pits in Dublin and other medieval towns have indicated that wild strawberries, apples, and other local fruit were consumed. However, there are also large numbers of different foodstuffs that do not readily appear in the archaeological record (Peters 2015; see Chapter 8 in this *Handbook*).

A Frontier Society?

It is often said that medieval Ireland was a frontier society: at a macro scale this is often seen as the division between the indigenous population and the incomers, originally the Anglo-Normans who then are more commonly called the Anglo-Irish in the later medieval period. But Ireland was a much more complex place, with many micro-regional divisions and borders also in place. It is through understanding these 'internal' frontiers and the effects they had on the medieval settlement pattern that a truer picture of medieval society on the island emerges.

We also have to understand that these divisions were not impervious, in that there was never a strict line of demarcation between the two communities. Although we do not have the surviving medieval sources that would allow us to enumerate them, all the indicators would suggest that there were never enough Anglo-Normans even to completely run the Lordship without the assistance of a sizeable number of indigenous Irish. Although the Anglo-Normans were only able to ever control about two-thirds of the island of Ireland at their apogee in the thirteenth century, its erosion throughout the rest of the Middle Ages shows just how tenuous this hold really was. Sometimes our overwhelming image of the Anglo-Norman knight charging an often-unmounted

FIGURE 56.4 Earthworks of the Pale at Kilteel, Co. Kildare, as viewed from the roof of the tower house/entrance tower to the preceptory of the Hospitallers

(© T. B. Barry)

enemy gives us an incorrect impression of the solidity of the Anglo-Norman invasion and settlement. All the evidence would lead us to the understanding that the knights were always in a minority in the Anglo-Norman armies, and also in the settlement that followed. Thus, far from feeling invincible, the Anglo-Norman settlers in the Lordship of Ireland probably felt very exposed, especially on the peripheries of their colony. This undoubtedly led to the construction of a linear earthen defensive line from the late fifteenth century onwards to protect the heartland of the colony around the four eastern counties around Dublin. Some short lengths of 'The Pale' can still be identified (Figure 56.4).

Conclusion

Due largely to archaeology our understanding of the medieval past in Ireland, especially in the spheres of economy and society, is much more nuanced than it was in the last half of the twentieth century. Now we realize that medieval Ireland, although it was geographically peripheral to the English Crown who ruled over it, was anything but peripheral within the broader context of medieval Europe. For instance, Ireland's major port towns such as Dublin, Waterford, Cork, and Galway have the same broad mix of imported artefacts as are to be found in comparable medieval ports in England, Wales, and Scotland (Wallace 2015).

As a result of ongoing research into our medieval past we now can say that medieval archaeology is no longer the poor relation in Irish archaeology generally (Barry 1994; Edwards 1990). As a direct result of all this active research we can now see that Ireland was not so removed from the norm of peasant societies within medieval Europe, as had once been argued. On the contrary, it could be argued that in terms of its settlement pattern, the Lordship of Ireland was similar to those found in different areas within England, Scotland, and Wales.

In conclusion, the pattern of settlement in late medieval Ireland within the area controlled by the Anglo-Normans was, in many ways, similar to that found elsewhere in our islands. But even here it was still a frontier-like society, with many more defensive settlements located throughout the Lordship than elsewhere in these islands. And in the Gaelic-Irish areas of Ireland the pattern of settlement was even more complex, and is still not fully understood by the scholarly community in comparison to the level of research that has been applied to the Anglo-Norman Lordship. Nevertheless, this is changing, with important archaeological research organizations such as the Discovery Programme now attempting to redress this imbalance.

References cited

Barry, T. B. 1994 *The archaeology of medieval Ireland*, Routledge, London

Barry, T. B. 1996 'Rural settlement in Ireland in the Middle Ages: an overview', *Ruralia* 1, 134–41

Barry, T. B. 2016 'Reflections on the moated sites of Wexford', in I. W. Doyle and B. Browne (eds), *Medieval Wexford: essays in memory of Billy Colfer*, Four Courts, Dublin, 202–10

Bennett, I. 1984–5 'Preliminary archaeological excavations at Ferrycarrig ringwork, Newtown townland, County Wexford', *Journal of the County Wexford Historical Society* 10, 25–43

Beresford, M. W. and Hurst, J. G. (eds) 1971 *Deserted medieval villages: studies*, Lutterworth Press, London

Cairns, C. T. 1987 *The Irish tower houses: a Co. Tipperary case study*, Group of the Irish Historic Settlement, Dublin

Childs, W. and Neill, T. 1993 'Overseas trade', in A. Cosgrove (ed.) *A new history of Ireland 2: medieval Ireland, 1169–1534*, Clarendon Press, Oxford, 511–15

Clyne, M. 2005 'Archaeological excavations at Holy Trinity Abbey Lough Key, Co. Roscommon', *Proceedings of the Royal Irish Academy* 105C, 23–98

Clyne, M. 2007 *Kells Priory, Co. Kilkenny: archaeological excavations by T. Fanning and M. Clyne*, Stationery Office, Dublin

Colfer, B. 2013 *Wexford castles: landscape, context and settlement*, Cork University Press, Cork

Corlett, C. and Potterton, M. (eds) 2009 *Rural settlement in medieval Ireland in the light of recent archaeological excavations*, Wordwell, Dublin

Doyle, I. W. and Browne, B. (eds) 2016 *Medieval Wexford: essays in memory of Billy Colfer*, Four Courts, Dublin

Edwards, N. 1990 *The archaeology of early medieval Ireland*, Routledge, London

Gerrard, C. M. and Youngs, S. M. 2007 'A bronze-socketed mount and blade from Shapwick House, Somerset', *Medieval Archaeology* 41, 195–210

Glasscock, R. E. 1970 'Moated sites and deserted boroughs and villages: two neglected aspects of Anglo-Norman settlement in Ireland', in N. Stephens and R. E. Glasscock (eds), *Irish geographical studies presented to E. Estyn Evans*, Institute for Irish Studies, Belfast, 162–77

Gwynn, A. and Hadcock, R. N. 1970 *Medieval religious houses: Ireland*, Irish Academic Press, Blackrock

Haren, M. and de Pontfarcy, Y. (eds) 1988 *The medieval pilgrimage to St Patrick's Purgatory: Lough Derg and the European tradition*, Clogher Historical Society, Enniskillen

Hayden, A. R. 2011 *Trim Castle, County Meath: excavations 1995–98*, Stationery Office, Dublin

Hodkinson, B. J. 1999 'Excavations in the gatehouse of Nenagh Castle, 1996–1997', *Tipperary Historical Journal*, 162–82

Le Patourel, H. E. J. 1968 'Documentary evidence and the medieval pottery industry', *Medieval Archaeology* 12, 101–26

Lyttleton, J. and O'Keeffe, T. (eds) 2005 *The manor in medieval and early modern Ireland*, Four Courts Press, Dublin

Lynch, A. 2010 *Tintern Abbey, Co. Wexford: Cistercians and Colcloughs, excavations 1982–2007*, Stationery Office, Dublin

Lynn, C. J. 1981–2 'The excavation of Rathmullan, a raised rath and motte in County Down', *Ulster Journal of Archaeology* 44–5, 65–171

McAlister, V. 2016 'Castles and connectivity: exploring the economic networks between tower houses, settlement, and trade in late medieval Ireland', *Speculum* 91(3), 631–59

McAlister, V. and Barry, T. B. (eds) 2015 *Space and settlement in medieval Ireland*, Four Courts Press, Dublin

McCutcheon, C. 2006 *Medieval pottery from Wood Quay, Dublin: the 1974–6 waterfront excavations*, Royal Irish Academy, Dublin

McNeill, T. E. 1997 *Castles in Ireland: feudal power in a Gaelic world*, Routledge, London

Mills, J. (ed.) 1996 *Account Roll of the Priory of Holy Trinity, Dublin 1337–1346*, Holy Trinity Priory, Dublin

Murphy, M. and O'Conor, K. 2008 *Roscommon Castle: a visitor's guide*, Roscommon, Roscommon County Council

Murphy, M. and Potterton, M. 2010 *The Dublin region in the Middle Ages*, Four Courts Press, Dublin

O'Conor, K. D. 1998 *The archaeology of medieval rural settlement in Ireland*, Royal Irish Academy, Dublin

O'Conor, K. D. 2000 'The ethnicity of Irish moated sites', *Ruralia* 3, 92–101

O'Floinn, R. 1988 'Handmade medieval pottery in south-east Ireland–Leinster Cooking Ware', in G. MacNiocaill and P. F. Wallace (eds), *Keimelia: Studies in medieval archaeology and history*, Galway University Press, Galway, 325–44

O'Keeffe, T. 2001 *Medieval Ireland: an archaeology*, Tempus, Stroud

O'Keeffe, T. 2015 *Medieval Irish buildings, 1100–1600*, Four Courts Press, Dublin

O'Neill, T. 1987 *Merchants and mariners in medieval Ireland*, Irish Academy, Dublin

Orpen, G. H. 1911–20 *Ireland under the Normans, 1169–1333*, 4 vols, Four Courts Press, Dublin

Oxford Archaeology 2007 *Newtown Jerpoint County Kilkenny, Conservation Report*, Heritage Council, Dublin

Peters, C. 2015 '"He is not entitled to butter": the diet of peasants and commerce in early medieval Ireland', *Proceedings of the Royal Irish Academy* 115C, 1–31

Scott, A. B. and Martin, F. X. (eds) 1978 *Expugnatis Hibernica: the conquest of Ireland by Giraldus Cambrensis*, Royal Irish Academy, Dublin

Stalley, R. A. 1987 *Cistercian Monasteries of Ireland: an account of the history, art and architecture of the white monks in Ireland from 1142 to 1540*, Yale University Press, London and New Haven (2nd edn)
Sweetman, P. D. 1999 *Medieval castles of Ireland*, Boydell Press, Woodbridge
Taylor, L. J. (ed.) 2009 *Encyclopaedia of medieval pilgrimage*, Brill, Leiden
Wallace, P. F. 2015 *Viking Dublin: the Wood Quay excavation*, Royal Irish Academy, Dublin

CHAPTER 57

LOOKING SOUTH-EAST

France in the Middle Ages

CLAIRE HANUSSE

THIS chapter picks out selected topics in French later medieval archaeology which are relevant to a British context. An important starting point is to stress the professionalization of the discipline as a direct result of the development of 'preventive' or developer-led archaeology. This has been transformative in France and led to a redirection of human and material resources and a significant decline in research-led fieldwork and amateur involvement. On the plus side, the stripping of large open areas has produced important results, while the diachronic approach with which so many sites are now excavated has helped place the archaeology of the Middle Ages into a long-term perspective. Similarly, *archéologie du bâti*, associated with excavation work on both prestigious and more modest buildings, has greatly enriched our knowledge of the chronology and construction techniques of medieval buildings. This mass of data is yet to be fully synthesized, though there are some recent doctoral theses and published symposia offering regional overviews. One of the main challenges in this environment is to generate interdisciplinary dialogue between archaeologists and colleagues in bioarchaeological sciences, as well as more traditional partners such as art historians and historians with whom collaboration is essential. Scholarly links, dialogue, and publication are all encouraged by the national period society which, since 2013, has widened its brief to become the *Société d'Archéologie Médiévale Moderne et Contemporaine* (SAMMC) (Chapelot 2011).

COUNTRYSIDE AND AGRARIAN PRODUCTION

The study of the French countryside in the Middle Ages was shaped by the work of historians, in particular Marc Bloch and Georges Duby. Bloch encouraged the idea of a close link between farming systems and landscape forms which were synthesized into three types: Mediterranean, open field, and *bocage*, each of which was associated with specific settlement forms, either grouped or dispersed. Duby, on the other hand, stressed that the evolution of the landscape in the later Middle Ages was largely the consequence of the 'great clearings' that led to the insertion of new settlements (*habitats intercalaires*). Thus, the later Middle Ages was thought to have played a key role in the genesis of our current landscape. Over the last fifteen years these issues have largely been revisited.

Large-scale mechanical stripping, particularly in northern France, has revealed traces of plots of land, many of them very old, which demonstrate the opening up of the landscape from the first millennium BC. Thereafter, the landscape was continuously transformed but, while roads and boundaries may change in detail, antecedent structures have remained crucial (Chouquer 2000). The 25-hectare excavation led by Isabelle Catteddu at Châteaugiron (Ille-et-Vilaine), perfectly illustrates this process over the long term. The boundaries of parcels drawn on contemporary maps are some of the very oldest (prehistoric) parcels of land (Burnouf 2008). Similarly, recent studies now show that *embocagement*, in other words 'the enclosure of fields', is a relatively recent phenomenon, starting at the end of the Middle Ages and often more recently (Watteau 2005; Zadora-Rio 2010). Historians and archaeologists have also revisited the issue of open-field systems which are regarded as *the* distinctive landscape of the Middle Ages and traditionally considered to be a sign of a well-coordinated approach to medieval agrarian management. For instance, Samuel Leturcq, working on the remarkable historical texts from Toury in Beauce (associated with the abbey of Saint-Denis near Paris) together with modern terrier maps (Leturcq 2007), has revealed the origin of an open-field system that extended the cultivated area at the expense of the uncultivated in order to increase production. The provision of extensive and coherent parcels helped collective management at a community scale but did not impose either rigid crop rotation or a radical restructuring of space. Although the practice of biennial or triennial rotating crops is evidenced by medieval texts as spreading from the eleventh century, at least in several favourable regions, the extension of crop rotation at the scale of all land communities seems to be a more recent phenomenon (seventeenth to eighteenth centuries) (for comparison, see Chapter 6). Palaeobotanical data from archaeological sites demonstrate the cultivation of spring crops (oats, dressed barley, legumes, peas, vetches) and in the northern half of France attest to the practice of crop rotation over three years on parcels, including Île de France, as early as the seventh century (Ruas 2010).

This last observation illustrates the growing significance of bioarchaeology for our understanding of the medieval countryside and its cultural practices. At the village of Durfort, south of the Massif Central, a fourteenth-century granary destroyed by fire has cast light on the resources of an entire village (Ruas 2002). Various papers published in the tenth symposium of the *Société d'Archéologie Médiévale* (Chapelot and Poisson 2010) provide useful overviews on topics such as crop husbandry practices and the coping capacity of medieval communities to resource the development of their agrarian economies through very local specialisms, in the Pyrenees for example (Viader and Rendu 2014). Results to note include the disappearance of spelt after the tenth century and the persistence or recurrence of einkorn wheat in the tenth to eleventh centuries in south-western France beyond its possible continuing use as a forage plant. In the same region, millet is attested in the thirteenth century. In Languedoc, throughout the Middle Ages, wheat and barley form the basis of crop production, while rye and oats appear to be secondary.

Interest in the growing of fruit focuses on the cultural practices that are associated with consumption, the cultivation of wild cultivars such as plum, pear, and apple, and the introduction of new species such as peach and mulberry. The economic importance of vine cultivation is well understood from historical texts and wine was a significant export to more northerly countries in exchange for their wool and cloth (Childs 1978), so much so that it was a monoculture in some regions of France. By contrast, the intensive cultivation of fruit trees and the presence of orchards seem to be limited to manorial or ecclesiastical contexts. Social differentiation also emerges from the study of waste dumps in rural and urban settings. In southern France, the best documented region, a multidisciplinary study of textual sources (market taxes), French culinary treatises, and archaeobotanical data confirms a high consumption of raisins, walnuts, and hazelnuts, with increasing diversification of cultivated fruits such as fig, peach, and plum, and wild fruits like strawberry, sloes (*prunus spinosa*), raspberry, and acorn (Ruas 2006).

Archaeozoology is also opening up some exciting new perspectives which complement texts and iconography. Rural sites are not as well studied as manorial sites and urban churches in northern France but a more balanced set of results is available further south. Broadly, meat consumption was dominated by sheep/goat, beef, and pork, but the latter is no longer the elite indicator that it had been in the early Middle Ages (Rodet-Belarbi and Forest 2010). Animals 'of the barn', chickens, and geese, are also well represented. The occasional eating of duck was clearly opportunistic and other game, such as deer and hare, are linked to the provision of meat for elite tables; more unusual species such as squirrels, turtles, and brown bears in the Pyrenees are occasionally reported too (Forest 1997). In general, whereas the stature of animals had dropped from the seventh to the eighth centuries, it begins to rise again, first in the south from the thirteenth century or early fourteenth century, later in northern France after the mid-fourteenth century. These gains in weight and size are suggestive of selective breeding.

Fish remains have also received attention, in particular in the north of France through the work of Benoît Clavel (2001; 2010) who has studied fishing practices and fish consumption promoted by religious prescription. Between the twelfth and sixteenth centuries the proportion of marine species of fish remains in landfill increased by 40–80 per cent with a corresponding decline in freshwater fish. Cities far from the coast such as Beauvais, Paris, and Reims all consumed significant quantities of both salted and fresh fish, implying that effective distribution networks already existed from the early Middle Ages (Figure 57.1). Coastal fishing became more intensive (including in the English Channel) up to the fourteenth century and the size of marine fish decreased (see Chapter 9). Thereafter, there appears to have been some recovery in stock which may be linked to a reduced demand after the Black Death.

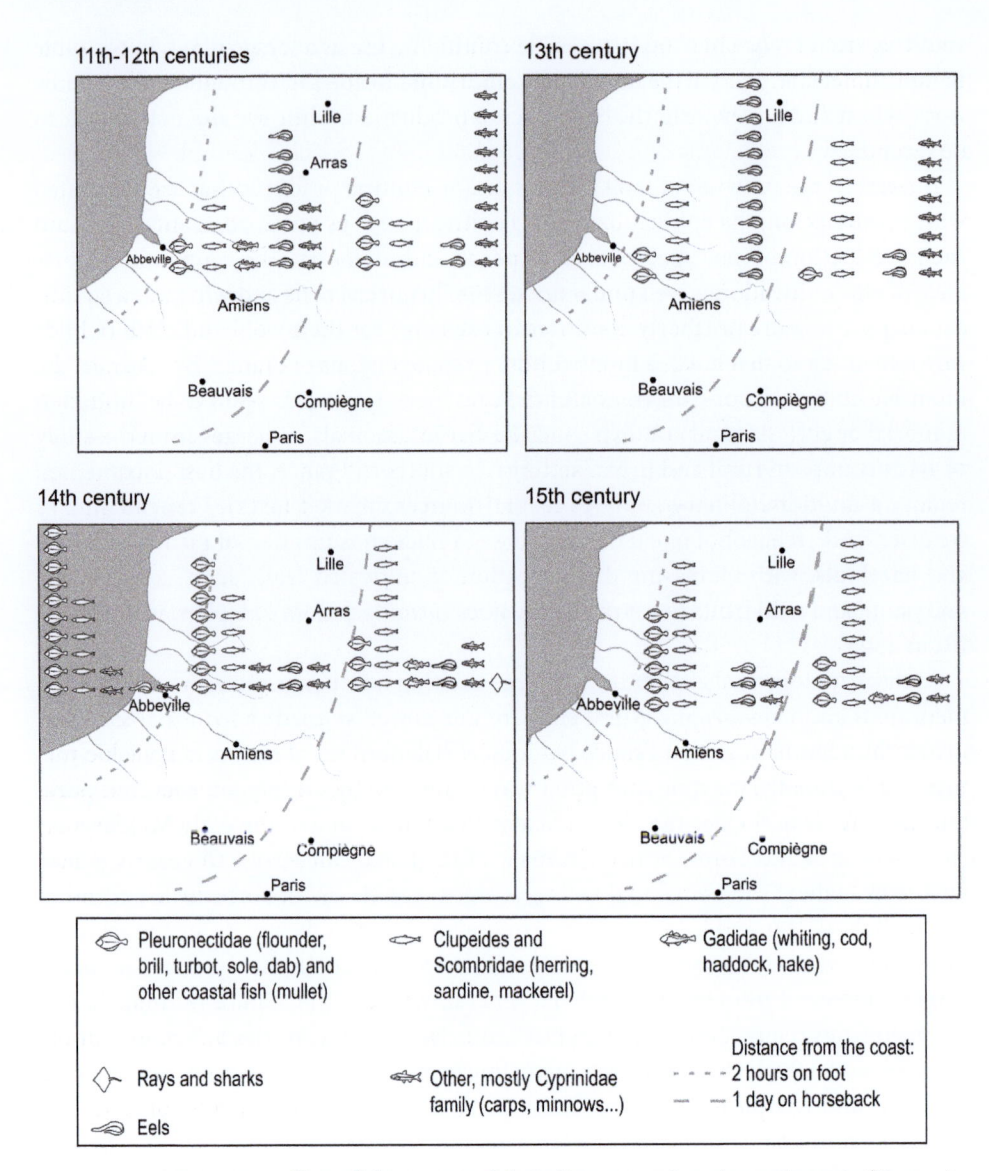

FIGURE 57.1 Frequency of large fish groups and their distance to shore in north-west of France in the fourteenth and fifteenth centuries

(redrawn by Alejandra Gutiérrez after Benoît Clavel 2001)

Villages and Rural Buildings

Recent archaeological research has also led to the reconsideration of evidence for the medieval countryside which has hitherto been based largely on documentary sources. The famous volume published in 1980 by Jean Chapelot and Robert Fossier (1980), *Le village et la maison au Moyen Âge*, reflects the state of knowledge before the data explosion associated with developer-led archaeology. On these excavations, particularly in northern France, the older site phases (fourth to twelfth centuries) have tended to be the more intensively investigated (Hanusse 2012) and the discovery of hundreds of early medieval settlements has made important contributions to the question of village origins in the tenth to twelfth centuries, a debate in France which was highly influenced by Fossier's concept of *encellulement*. Previously, the status of 'village' was thought to be an inappropriate term for eighth-century settlements, even those with a cemetery and a church, but this debate has been now overtaken (Zadora-Rio 2003).

For the later medieval period, pioneering research at Rougiers, Dracy and Brennilis and Berrien in Brittany have long demonstrated a French engagement with the topic of 'deserted villages' (see synthesis by Batt 2005). Developer-led projects are now making an important contribution here too, for example at Vallanges in Vitry-sur-Orne (Moselle) and Trainecourt (Calvados) near Caen (Taupin 1996). Research-led projects, such as the study of the abandoned village of Saint-Ursin de Courtisigny (Calvados), Normandy, remain relatively rare in northern France (Hanusse and Jarry 2007) but the situation is less negative further south where *castra* are well preserved in the current landscape (e.g. Rougiers). Research excavations of note include those at Cabaret, Durfort (Colin et al. 1996) and more recently at Vilarnau (Passarius et al. 2008). A very different case is that of the mining village of Brandes-d'Oisans in the Alps (Bailly-Maître and Benoît 2006) where survey took place within the context of a wider study of silver mines. Similarly, the study of upland settlement has opened up new perspectives about pastoralism and dispersed settlement forms such as farms and hamlets, for example, in the Massif Central, Languedoc, the region of Toulouse and Aquitaine where nucleated and dispersed settlements co-existed (Fau 2006; Rendue 2003). Surveys are made more challenging because of the long history of isolated farms on the same sites (Conte et al. 2010). This long-term perspective is also illustrated by the study of isolated sites such as Mont farm in Charny (Côte-d'Or) (Beck 1989) and Du Colombier farm in Varennes-sur-Seine (Seine-et Marne) where eighteenth-century settlement forms are also under investigation (Hurard 2012).

These investigations draw upon the gradual emergence of vernacular architecture as a topic for research in its own right. Recent work here has undermined the assumption that 'regional types' should be defined by the boundaries of current or even more ancient administrative territories (Antoine et al. 2005). Buildings in Normandy, for example, stretching from the Cotentin to the Pays de Caux, exhibit great diversity in construction materials, topographical organization, and the social composition of dwellings. Unfortunately, the lack of systematic excavations, comprehensive analysis of stratigraphy, and detailed artefact studies, especially in the context of developer-led work, inevitably limits the interpretation of sites, including the scale of housing units and associated structures (Beck 2007). Nevertheless, there is great potential for further work here.

Towns

The number of urban excavations has greatly increased over the past decade and a tremendous diversity of sites has been investigated including cathedrals, cemeteries, fortifications, townhouses, and monastic sites. Many projects combine the study of buried structures with surviving buildings. Facilitated by new technical resources, such as GIS, medieval urban space has become an important topic of investigation, not only for the interpretation of spatial data but also for the purposes of predictive risk management by State heritage services. An agenda for scientific and social issues has recently been advocated (Dufaÿ et al. 2014). The city is no longer understood as an isolated place but one which is integrated into a dynamic relationship with its periphery and seen primarily as a social construct, complex and continuously inscribed over a long period. The urban fabric (*fabrique urbaine*) is one focus of study here (Galinié 2000; Noizet 2009) in which medieval towns and cities are seen either as a social product inherited from Antiquity (*civitates*), even from pre-Roman times, or as cities which emerge in the early Middle Ages as *portus* and *vicus* in the texts and then become profoundly transformed after the twelfth century.

Towns of the twelfth century therefore inherit a number of features, first and foremost the road system and its plots which may be revealed by textual sources and planimetric data (Gauthiez et al. 2003). Organizational principles tend to be governed by either ecclesiastical interests (cathedral, monasteries) or secular authority (castle), but the overall urban structure might be described as one of multi-nucleation. For example, in Rouen and Lyon, episcopal buildings were gathered near the cathedral (later rebuilt), together with houses for canons and public buildings. There is a major national survey of these neighbourhoods (Picard 1994) as well as excavations, for instance in Toulouse (Haute-Garonne) (Cazes 1998). Many cities exceeded the limits of their ancient fortified boundaries in the thirteenth and fourteenth centuries and added new suburbs which contained hospitals, hospices, and the houses of the medicant orders. Small cities like Château-Thierry have particularly benefited from collaborative historical and archaeological research into their long-term development (Blary et al. 2013).

POWER AND BELIEF

The question of power and its expression through monuments has long focused on the castle; and its study in France was one of the founding themes of medieval archaeology in the nineteenth century. More recently, in the 1970s, historians, art historians, and archaeologists have regarded the castle mount as a marker of triumphant feudalism (e.g. Chapelot 1994; 2011). Today castles are seen to have had multiple functions, including residential, military, and economic, and various layouts which can be documented through survey and inventory (a particular phenomenon of the 1970s and 1980s in France) but more rarely by archaeological excavation (for a recent overview, see Renoux 2010). Nomenclature (*motta, manerium, domus fortis, repayre*) conceals a wide variety of forms and chronologies (Figure 57.2). In Provence, for example, the motte and bailey is abandoned as early as the late tenth century (Mouton 2008). In Maine, on the other hand, *motta* are documented in the fourteenth and fifteenth centuries and

FIGURE 57.2 The east tower of a urban fortification at Talmont, Vendée, France

(© Nicolas Prouteau, Lionel Duigou, and Teddy Bethus)

their low mounds are better interpreted as seignorial or manorial residences (Renoux 2004). These moated sites are less well fortified than 'true' castles (Mouillebouche and Bur 2002; see Chapter 23 in this *Handbook*) and represent changing taste in residential practice driven by those a little way down the social scale, although moated sites were also used by Norman bishops (Casset 2007). In contrast to the architecture of these elite residences (Sirot 2007), their surrounding landscapes have been less intensively studied but there have been some promising investigations, especially in south-west France (e.g. Barraud et al. 2006; Bourgeois and Remy 2014).

Crafts

The theme of the first conference of the *Société d'Archéologie Médiévale*, held in Paris in 1985, was 'Ceramics, production, consumption, trade' and brought together a mass of dispersed information on the topic of medieval pottery (Chapelot et al. 1987). By 1996, when the sixth congress was held in Dijon, the content of the conference had expanded to cover a greater variety of materials and, in particular, technical innovation (Beck 1998). The most recent congress of the Society, the eleventh, held in Bayeux in 2015 on the theme of 'The object during the Middle Ages and in modern times: manufacturing, trade, consumption and recycling' illustrates nicely the increased data now made available by hundreds of developer-led archaeological excavations. This is especially the case in urban contexts such as Troyes (Aube) where archaeological evidence has revealed the different zones of craft specialism including butchers and their slaughterhouses, bones, the manufacture of objects, leather tanneries, and shoe-makers (Deborde et al. 2002).

Today, pottery studies in France benefit from academic regional synthesis (e.g. in Alsace, Henigfeld 2005; in the Loire Valley, Husi 2003) and a new national research network (ICERAMM) as well as chemical and petrographic techniques which have had particular impacts in regions such as Normandy (Bocquet-Liénard and Flambard-Héricher 2009) and in Lyon for the modern period (Horry 2015). There are now detailed studies of consumption and use of pottery (Ravoire and Dietrich 2009) whereas in the 1980s the focus was largely on production and excavation (Faure-Boucharlat et al. 1996; Flambard Héricher 2002; Marchesi et al. 1997). Well-known French workshops specialized in the export of medieval pottery, the so-called 'Saintonge ware' (polychrome jugs and the more common green-glazed wares), made notably at La-Chapelle-des-Pots near Saintes in the thirteenth and fourteenth centuries, and these wares are routinely found on archaeological excavations across the UK and Ireland (Chapelot 1983). Another type of French pottery found widely across Atlantic Europe is the so-called Martincamp flasks (Normandy) which contained apple brandy or Calvados for export (Ickowicz 1993).

Understanding medieval metallurgy continues to improve thanks to multidisciplinary projects (e.g. Benoît 1997; Vivet et al. 2009). Of particular interest is research into the mining of silver deposits (Bailly-Maître 2002), the environment of production (Ploquin et al. 2010), production processes (Bailly-Maître and Bruno-Dupraz 1994) and the introduction of new technologies such as the blast furnace. There have been specific analyses of artefact categories such as weapons (Serdon 2005), locks (Linlaud 2014), and the metallographic study of iron used in the construction of churches (L'Héritier et al. 2005). Medieval glass has a long history of study (Foy 1989) with several major projects of note such as glassware production in eastern France (Anon. 1990). The website of the French

Association for Glass Archaeology (AFAV) provides further details and access to bibliography.[1] Window glass for churches and cathedrals was imported into England from Burgundy, Lorraine, Normandy, and Flanders in the fourteenth and fifteenth centuries (Marks 1991), for example from Rouen to Exeter Cathedral in 1318. Other recent studies include timber framing (Hoffsummer et al. 2011) and construction more generally (Bernardi 2011), revising earlier studies (e.g. Chapelot and Benoît 2001; Bailly-Maître and Gardel 2007). Among the natural resources exploited were salt from Guérande near the mouth of the Loire, from the Bay of Bourgneuf, in south-west France, which was exported to England. The salt was heavy and shipping by water had significant cost advantages, as it did for Caen stone which was transported long distances for building, for carving sculptural effigies and tombs, and used in the manufacture of mortars for food preparation (Dujardin 2009; see Chapter 29 in this *Handbook*). Throughout southern England and Ireland, at sites such as the Tower of London, Caen stone can be seen in columns, windows, and quoins. This stone, whose use was made possible by French patronage, was often cut to order and then shipped: at Canterbury Cathedral in 1174 William of Sens was sending 'moulds' or templates to the Caen quarries (Salzman 1967, 126; Tatton-Brown 1990, 72). Travelling in the other direction, Purbeck stone is found in France at Mont St Michel (Normandy) and Lisieux Cathedral (Basse-Normandie) among other sites (Dujardin 2009), as are high-quality English alabasters carved for devotional panels and tomb chests which were widely distributed across France (Flavigny and Jablonski-Chauveau 1997; see Chapter 29 in this *Handbook*) and are now well represented in museum collections (for example, Musée National du Moyen Âge, Thermes de Cluny, Paris).

Funerary Practices

Over the last twenty years our knowledge of religion and belief has been significantly enriched. Surviving and buried structures are now studied in their entirety and embrace topics such as origins and functional developments, as well as burials and burial practices (Treffort 2010). Important multidisciplinary studies have been undertaken at Saint-Germain at Auxerre (Yonne) (Sapin 2011), the abbeys of Cluny (Saône-et-Loire) (Baud 2003) and Marmoutier (Indre-et-Loire) (Lorans and Creissen 2014), and smaller parish churches such as Thaon (Calvados) (Delahaye et al. 2008). Improvements in the analysis of materials include a more systematic implementation of dendrochronology (Épaud 2007) and metallographic analyses which highlight the importance of iron in the construction of large buildings (L'Héritier et al. 2005). There are now both regional perspectives on the relationship between burial and buildings, for example around Lyon (Baud et Tardieu 2014), as well as more specific case studies, such as Saint-Mexme in

---

[1] AFAV: http://www.afaverre.fr/.

FIGURE 57.3 A leper's grave at Saint-Thomas d'Aizier, Eure, France

(© C. Chapelain de Séreville-Niel and M. C. Truc)

Chinon (Lorans 2006). The hierarchy of space and the notion of privileged space for burial has been the subject of symposia (Alduc-Le Bagousse 2009) following pioneering observations in Burgundy (Anon. 2011). Moreover, there have been important excavations in rural contexts which have provided long-term cemetery studies, such as Rigny (Zadora-Rio and Galinié 1992), Vilarnau (Passarius et al. 2010), Thaon (Delahaye et al. 2008) and, in an urban context, at Montpellier (Crubézy et al. 2006). These studies are characterized by greater technical application, improved taphonomic analysis, and, above all, a genuine commitment to a social and political perspective (Treffort 2010) which has highlighted new features such as deposits in graves, including pottery (Boyer-Gardner and Vivas 2014).

Perspectives

In a short contribution such as this many issues have inevitably been omitted. The dynamism of French later medieval archaeology, however, should be obvious and the significance of developer-led archaeology apparent. Theory remains the *parent pauvre* of French medieval archaeology even though there has been a move towards more multi-disciplinary and collaborative forms of research, many of which are also of interest to historians. Among these topics are the archaeology of taste (Alexandre-Bidon 2005), food consumption based mainly on ceramics (Faure-Bouchariat 1990; Ravoire and Dietrich 2009), meat consumption and the dietary practices of monasteries (Clavel 2001; 2010). The highly technical data gained in the excavation of burials and later extended by detailed laboratory analysis has led to entirely new information about, for example, the burial cemeteries of lepers, for example at St Thomas Aizier (Eure) (Chapelain de Seréville-Niel et al. 2012), the treatment of corpses (Cartron 2010), epidemics (Castex and Cartron 2007), and specific pathologies (Blondiaux et al. 2015) (Figure 57.3). As French archaeologists continue to question the tremendous dataset produced over the last thirty years, there is no doubt that they will move far beyond traditional approaches of the past.

References cited

Alduc-Le Bagousse, A. (ed.) 2009 *Inhumations de prestige ou prestige de l'inhumation? Expressions du pouvoir dans l'au-delà, IVe–XVe siècle*, Publications du CRAHM, Caen
Alexandre-Bidon, D. 2005 *Une archéologie du goût: céramique et consommation*, Picard, Paris
Anon. 1990 *Verrerie de l'Est de la France, XIIIe–XVIIIe siècles: fabrication, consommation*, 9ème supplément à la Revue Archéologique de l'Est, S.A.E., Dijon
Anon. 2011 *Le corps des anges: réflexions sur les pratiques funéraires autour de l'enfant mort au Moyen Âge. Actes de la journée d'études de Blandy-les-Tours du 14 Novembre 2009*, Silvana Editorial, Paris
Antoine, A., Cocaud, M., and Pichot, D. 2005 *La maison rurale en pays d'habitat dispersé: de l'Antiquité au XXe siècle*, Presses Universitaires de Rennes, Rennes

Bailly-Maître, M.-C. 2002 *L'argent : du minerai au pouvoir dans la France médiévale*, Picard, Paris

Bailly-Maître, M.-C. and Bruno-Dupraz, J. (eds) 1994 *Brandes en Oisans, la mine d'argent des dauphins XII–XIVe siècle*, Ministère de la Culture et de la Francophone, Lyon

Bailly-Maître, M.-C. and Benoît, P. 2006 'L'habitat de mineurs. Brandes-en-Oisans et Pampailly', in D. Alexandre-Bidon, F. Piponnier, and J.-M. Poisson (eds), *Cadre de vie et manières d'habiter (XIIe–XVIe siècle)*, Publications du CRAHM, Caen, 259–65

Bailly-Maître, M.-C. and Gardel, M.-E. 2007 *La pierre, l'eau, le métal et le feu: economie castrale en territoire audois (XIe–XVe siècles)*, éd. SESA, Carcassonne

Barraud, D., Hautefeuille, F., and Rémy, C. 2006 *Résidences aristocratiques, résidences du pouvoir entre Loire et Pyrénées, Xe–XVe siècles: recherches archéologiques récentes, 1987–2002*, Archéologie du Midi Médiéval supplément 4, Centre d'Archéologie Médiéval du Languedoc, Carcassone

Batt, M. 2005 'La maison rurale du XIIe au XIVe siècle dans les Monts d'Arrée (29): les données des fouilles archéologiques', in A. Antoine, M. Cocaud, and D. Pichot (eds), *La maison rurale en pays d'habitat dispersé: de l'Antiquité au XXe siècle*, Presses Universitaires de Rennes, Rennes, 89–98

Baud, A. 2003 *Cluny, un grand chantier médiéval au cœur de l'Europe*, Picard, Paris

Baud, A. and Tardieu, J. 2014 *Organiser l'espace sacré au Moyen Âge: topographie, architecture et liturgie (Rhône-Alpes-Auvergne)*, Publications de la Maison de l'Orient et de la Méditerranée, Lyon

Beck, P. 1989 *Une ferme seigneuriale au XIVe siècle: la grange du Mont, Charny, Côte-d'Or*, Éditions de la Maison des sciences de l'homme, Paris

Beck, P. (ed.) 1998 *L'innovation technique au Moyen-Âge: Actes du VIe Congrès International d'Archéologie Médiévale*, Errance, Paris

Beck, P. 2007 'Le bâtiment agricole en France au Moyen Âge: historiographie d'un thème second', in A. Antoine, M. Cocaud, and D. Pichot (eds), *La maison rurale en pays d'habitat dispersé: de l'Antiquité au XXe siècle*, Presses Universitaires de Rennes, Rennes, 123–31

Benoît, P. 1997 *La mine de Pampailly: XVe–XVIIIe siècles, Brussieu-Rhône*, Service régional de l'archéologie de Rhône-Alpes, Lyon

Bernardi, Ph. 2011 *Bâtir au Moyen Age (XIIIe–XVIe siècles)*, CNRS, Paris

Blary, F., Durey-Blary, V., Gély, J.-P., Ziegler, S., Racinet, P., and Bur, M. 2013 *Origines et développements d'une cité médiévale, Château-Thierry: approches archéologique et historique d'une petite ville d'accession médiévale*, Revue Archéologique De Picardie, Amiens

Blondiaux, J., Chapelain de Seréville-Niel, C., Naji, S., Bocquet-Appel, J.-P., and Colard, T. 2015 'The Leprosarium of Saint-Thomas d'Aizier: the cementochronological proof of the medieval decline of Hansen disease in Europe?', *International Journal of Paleopathology* 4, 2014

Bocquet-Liénard, A. and Flambard-Héricher, A.-M. 2009 'La vaisselle céramique en Normandie du XIVe au XVIe siècle et le PCR "Typochronologie de la céramique bas-normande Xe–XVIe siècle"', in F. Ravoire and A. Dietrich (eds), *La cuisine et la table dans la France de la fin du Moyen Âge: contenus et contenants du XIVe au XVIe siècle*, Publications du CRAHM, Caen, 215–35

Boyer-Gardner, D. and Vivas, M. 2014. *Déplacer les morts: voyages, funérailles, manipulations, exhumations et réinhumations de corps au Moyen Âge*, Maison des sciences de l'homme d'Aquitaine, Bordeaux

Bourgeois, L. and Remy, C. (eds) 2014 *Demeurer, défendre et paraître: orientations récentes de l'archéologie des fortifications et des résidences aristocratiques médiévales entre Loire et Pyrénées*, Association des Publications Chauvinoises, Chauvigny

Burnouf, J. 2008 *Archéologie médiévale en France: le second Moyen âge, XIIe–XVIe siècle*, Éditions La Découverte, Paris

Cartron, I. (ed.) 2010 *De corps en corps: traitement et devenir du cadavre*, Maison des sciences de l'homme d'Aquitaine, Pessac

Casset, M. 2007 *Les évêques aux champs: châteaux et manoirs des évêques normands au Moyen Âge (XIe–XVe siècles)*, Presses universitaires de Caen, Caen

Castex, D. and Cartron, I. (eds) 2007 *Épidémies et crises de mortalité du passé: actes des séminaires, année 2005*, Maison des Sciences de l'Homme Institut Ausonius, Paris

Cazes, Q. 1998 *Le quartier canonial de la cathédrale Saint-Etienne de Toulouse*, Centre d'archéologie médiévale du Languedoc, Carcassonne

Chapelain de Seréville-Niel C., Truc, M.-C., Guérin, T., Le Roux, F., Penna, B., and Yvernault, F. (eds) 2012 'La chapelle Saint-Thomas d'Aizier (Eure): bilan de douze années de fouille programmée', *Journées archéologiques de Haute-Normandie 2011*, Publications des universités de Rouen et du Havre, Mont-Saint-Aignan, 241–60

Chapelot, J. 1983 'The Saintonge pottery industry in the later Middle Ages', in P. Davey and R. Hodges (eds), *Ceramics and trade: the production and distribution of later medieval pottery in north-west Europe*, University of Sheffield, Sheffield, 49–54

Chapelot, J. 1994 *Le château de Vincennes: une résidence royale au Moyen âge*, Caisse nationale des monuments historiques et des sites, Paris

Chapelot, J. 2011 'L'enceinte du château de Vincennes (1372–1380): la conception d'un grand projet architectural reconstituée par l'examen du bâti et les relevés de terrain', in H. Mouillebouche (ed.), *Châteaux et Mesures*, Centre de castellologie de Bourgogne, Chagny, 100–23

Chapelot, J. and Benoît, P. 2001 *Pierre et métal dans le bâtiment au Moyen Age*, EHESS, Paris (2nd edn)

Chapelot, J. and Fossier, R. 1980 *Le village et la maison au Moyen Âge*, Hachette, Paris

Chapelot, J., Galinié, H., and Pilet-Lemière, J. 1987 *La céramique Ve–XIXe s.: fabrication, commercialisation, utilisation*, Société d'archéologie médiévale, Caen

Chapelot, J. and Poisson, J.-M. (eds) 2010 *Trente ans d'archéologie médiévale en France: un bilan pour un avenir Société d'archéologie médiévale*, Publications du CRAHM, Caen

Childs, W. 1978 *Anglo-Castilian trade in the later Middle Ages*, Manchester University Press, Manchester

Chouquer, G. 2000 *L'étude des paysages: essais sur leurs formes et leur histoire*, Errance, Paris

Clavel, B. 2001 'L'animal dans l'alimentation médiévale et moderne en France du Nord (XIIIe–XVIIe siècles)', *Revue archéologique de Picardie, numéro spécial* 19(1), 9–204

Clavel, B. 2010 'L'archéozoologie du Moyen Âge au début de la période Moderne dans la moitié nord de la France', in J. Chapelot and J.-M. Poisson (eds), *Trente ans d'archéologie médiévale en France: un bilan pour un avenir*, publication du CRAHM, Caen, 71–87

Colin, M.-G., Darnas, I., Poushtomis, N., and Schneider, L. 1996 *La maison du castrum de la bordure méridionale du Massif Central*, Archéologie Du Midi Médiéval Supplément, Centre d'archéologie médiévale du Languedoc, Carcassonne

Conte, P., Fau, L., and Hautefeuille, F. 2010 'L'habitat dispersé de l'ouest au sud-ouest du Massif central (Xe–XVe s.)', in J. Chapelot and J.-M. Poisson (eds), *Trente ans d'archéologie médiévale en France. Un bilan pour un avenir*, publication du CRAHM, Caen, 163–78

Crubézy, É., Duchesne, S., and Arlaud, C. 2006 *La mort, les morts et la ville: Saints-Côme-et-Damien, Montpellier, Xe–XVIe siècles*, Errance, Paris

Deborde, G., Montembault, V., and Yvinec, J.-H. 2002 'Les ateliers de tanneurs de la rue du Moulinet à Troyes (Aube)', in F. Audoin-Rouzeau and S. Beyries (eds), *Le travail du cuir de la préhistoire à nos jours*, Éd. APDCA, Antibes, 283–314

Delahaye, F., Niel C., Alduc-Le Bagousse A., and Blondiaux J. 2008 'L'Église Saint-Pierre de Thaon (Calvados): premières approches archéologiques et anthropologiques', in *La paroisse en Normandie au Moyen Âge, La vie paroissiale, l'église et le cimetière: histoire, art, archéologie*, Société d'Archéologie et d'Histoire de la Manche, Saint-Lô, 332–54

Dufaÿ, B., Hincker, V., and Viand, A. 2014 'Les archéologues et la lampe d'Aladin', *Les Nouvelles de l'Archéologie* 136, 3–5

Dujardin, L. 2009 'Le commerce de la pierre de Caen (XIe–XVIIIe siècle)', in M. Arnoux and A.-M. F. Héricher (eds), *La Normandie dans l'économie européenne (XIIe–XVIIe siècle)*, Publications du CRAHM, Caen, 139–54

Épaud, F. 2007 *De la charpente romane à la charpente gothique en Normandie: évolution des techniques et des structures de charpenterie aux XIIe–XIIIe siècles*, Publications du CRAHM, Caen

Fau, L. 2006 *Les monts d'Aubrac au Moyen âge: genèse d'un monde agropastoral*, Éditions de la Maison des sciences de l'homme, Paris

Faure-Boucharlat, E. 1990 *A la fortune du pot: la cuisine et le table à Lyon et à Vienne, Xe–XIXe siècles, d'après les fouilles archéologiques*, Musée de la civilisation gallo-romaine, Lyon

Faure-Boucharlat, E., Vicard, T., Maccari-Poisson, B., Maccari-Poisson, B., and Savay-Guerraz, S. 1996 *Pots et potiers en Rhône-Alpes: époque médiévale, époque moderne*, Service régional de l'archéologie de Rhône-Alpes, Lyon

Flambard Héricher, A.-M. 2002 *Potiers et poteries du Bessin: histoire et archéologie d'un artisanat rural du XIIe au XXe siècle en Normandie*, Publications du CRAHM, Caen

Flavigny, L. and Jablonski-Chauveau, C. 1997 *D'Angleterre en Normandie: sculptures d'albâtre du Moyen Age*, Musée de l'Ancien Evêché, Rouen

Forest, V. 1997 'Alimentation carnée dans le Languedoc médiéval [Les témoignages archéozoologiques des vertébrés supérieurs]', *Archéologie du Midi médiéval* 15-16, 141–60

Foy, D. 1989 *Le verre médiéval et son artisanat en France méditerranéenne*, Edition du Centre national de la recherche scientifique, Paris

Galinié, H. 2000 *Ville, espace urbain et archéologie: essai. Tours: Maison des sciences de la ville, de l'urbanisme et des paysages*, Maison des sciences de la ville de l'urbanisme et des paysages, Tours

Gauthiez, B., Zadora-Rio, E., and Galinié, H. 2003 *Village et ville au Moyen âge: les dynamiques morphologiques 1*, Maison des sciences de l'homme, Tours

Hanusse, C. 2012 'Les habitats désertés au Moyen Âge: quelques réflexions à propos d'un paradigme', in V. Carpentier et C. Marcigny (eds), *Des hommes aux champs. Pour une archéologie des espaces ruraux du Néolithique au Moyen Âge*, Presses Universitaires de Rennes, Rennes, 227–35

Hanusse, C. and Jarry, T. 2007 'Espace bâti et habitation en Normandie (Plaine de Caen) du XIIIe au XVe siècle: mise en regard des sources archéologiques et textuelles', in P. Madeline et J.-M. Moriceau (eds), *Bâtir dans les campagnes. Les enjeux de la construction de la Protohistoire au XXIe siècle*, Presses Universitaires de Caen, Caen, 133–52

Henigfeld, Y. 2005 *La céramique à Strasbourg de la fin du Xe au début du XVIIe siècle*, Publications du CRAHM, Caen

Hoffsummer, P., Touzé, R., Pariset, J.-D., Mayer, J., and Férault, M.-A. 2011 *Les charpentes du XIe au XIXe siècle Grand Ouest de la France: typologie et évolution, analyse de la documentation de la Médiathèque de l'architecture et du patrimoine*, Brepols, Turnhout

Horry, A. 2015 *Poteries du quotidien en Rhône-Alpes. XVIe, XVIIe, XVIIIe siècles. Un panorama des techniques, des formes et des décors*, Documents d'Archéologie en Rhône-Alpes et Auvergne, Lyon

Hurard, S. (ed.) 2012 *La ferme du Colombier à Varennes-sur-Seine, XVIe–XVIIIe siècles: expression matérielle de l'ascension sociale d'élites rurales en milieu humide*, CNRS, Paris

Husi, P. 2003 *La céramique médiévale et moderne du Centre-Ouest de la France (11e–17e siècle): chrono-typologie de la céramique et approvisionnement de la vallée de la Loire moyenne*, FERAC, Tours

Ickowicz P. 1993 'Martincamp ware: a problem of attribution', *Medieval Ceramics* 17, 51–60

Leturcq, S. 2007 *Un village, la terre et ses hommes: Toury en Beauce, XIIe–XVIIe siècle*, Éditions du CTHS, Paris

L'Héritier, M., Juhin, A., Dillmann, P., Aranda, R., and Benoît, P. 2005 'Utilisation des alliages ferreux dans la construction monumentale du Moyen Age. Etat des lieux de l'avancée des études métallographiques et archéométriques', *ArcheoSciences. Revue d'archéométrie* 29, 117–32

Linlaud, M. 2014 *Serrures médiévales, VIIIe–XIIIe siècle*, Presses Universitaires de Rennes, Rennes

Lorans, É. 2006 *Saint-Mexme de Chinon: Ve–XXe siècles*, Éditions du CTHS, Paris

Lorans, É. and Creissen, T. 2014 *Marmoutier un grand monastère ligérien: (Antiquité–XIXe siècle)*, Ministère de la culture et de la communication, Direction régionale des affaires culturelles du Centre, Orléans

Marchesi, H., Vallauri, L., Thiriot, J., and Leenhardt, M. 1997 *Marseille, les ateliers de potiers du XIIIe siècle et le quartier Sainte-Barbe (Ve–XVIIe s.)*, Editions de la Maison des sciences de l'homme, Paris

Marks, R. 1991 'Window glass', in J. Blair and N. Ramsay (eds), *English medieval industries: craftsmen, techniques, products*, The Hambledon Press, London, 265–94

Mouillebouche, H. and Bur M. 2002 *Les maisons fortes en Bourgogne du nord du XIIIe au XVIe siècle*, Éditions universitaires de Dijon, Dijon

Mouton, D. 2008 *Mottes castrales en Provence: les origines de la fortification privée au Moyen Âge*, Éditions de la Maison des sciences de l'homme, Paris

Noizet, H. 2009 'Fabrique urbaine: a new concept in urban history and morphology', *Urban Morphology* 13(1), 55–66

Passarrius, O., Donat, R., and Catafau, A. 2008 *Vilarnau: un village du Moyen Âge en Roussillon*, Éditions Trabucaire, Canet-de-Rosselló

Passarrius, O., Donat, R. and Catafau, A. 2010 'L'église et le cimetière du village déserté de Vilarnau à Perpignan (Pyrénées-Orientales)', *Archéologie du Midi Médiéval* 28, 219–37

Picard, J.-C. (ed.) 1994 *Les chanoines dans la ville. Recherches sur la topographie des quartiers canoniaux en France*, de Boccard, Paris

Ploquin, A., Bailly-Maître, M.-C., and Allée, P. (eds) 2010 *Mines et métallurgies anciennes du plomb dans leurs environnements. Apports des méthodes contribuant à leur étude*, ArcheoSciences 34

Ravoire, F. and Dietrich, A. 2009 *La cuisine et la table dans la France de la fin du Moyen Âge: contenus et contenants du XIVe au XVIe siècle*, Publications du CRAHM, Caen

Rendu, C. 2003 *La montagne d'Enveig: une estive pyrénéenne dans la longue durée*, Trabucaire, Canet

Renoux, A. 2004 'Aux sources du pouvoir châtelain de Geoffroi «seigneur de Mayenne, le plus fort homme du Maine» (c.1040–1098)', in D. Barthélémy and O. Bruand, *Les pouvoirs locaux en France du centre et de l'ouest (VIIIe–XIe siècle): implantation et moyens d'action*, Presses Universitaires de Rennes, Rennes, 61–90

Renoux, A. 2010 'Châteaux, palais et habitats aristocratiques fortifiés et semi-fortifiés', in J. Chapelot and J.-M. Poisson (eds), *Trente ans d'archéologie médiévale en France: un bilan pour un avenir*, Publication du CRAHM, Caen, 239–56

Rodet-Belarbi. I. and Forest, V. 2010 'Les activités quotidiennes d'après les vestiges osseaux', in J. Chapelot and J.-M. Poisson (eds), *Trente ans d'archéologie médiévale en France: un bilan pour un avenir*, Publication du CRAHM, Caen, 89–104

Ruas, M.-P. 2002 *Productions agricoles, stockage et finage en Montagne Noire médiévale: le grenier castral de Durfort (Tarn)*, Maison des sciences de l'homme, Paris

Ruas, M.-P. (ed.) 2006 *La fructiculture*, Archéologie Du Midi Médiéval 23–4, Centre d'archéologie médiévale du Languedoc, Carcassonne

Ruas, M.-P. 2010 'Carpologie médiévale en France: essor et terrains', in J. Chapelot and J.-M. Poisson (eds), *Trente ans d'archéologie médiévale en France: un bilan pour un avenir*, Publication du CRAHM, Caen, 18–21

Salzman, L. F. 1967 *Building in England down to 1540: a documentary history*, Clarendon Press, Oxford

Sapin, C. 2011 *Saint-Étienne d'Auxerre: la seconde vie d'une cathédrale: 7 ans de recherches pluridisciplinaires et internationales*, Centre d'études médiévales Saint-Germain, Auxerre

Serdon, V. 2005 *Armes du diable: arcs et arbalètes au Moyen Âge*, Archéologie et culture, Presses Universitaires de Rennes, Rennes

Sirot, É. 2007 *Noble et forte maison. L'habitat seigneurial dans les campagnes médiévales: du milieu du XIIe siècle au début du XVIe siècle*, Picard, Paris

Taupin, M.-C. 1996 'Le hameau de Trainecourt XIIIe–XVe siècle', *Ruralia* 1, 211–16

Tatton-Brown, T. W. T. 1990 'Building stone in Canterbury c.1070–1525', in D. Parsons (ed.), *Stone: quarrying and building in England AD 43–1525*, The Royal Archaeological Institute, London, 70–82

Treffort, C. 2010 'Une archéologie très «humaine»: regard sur trente ans d'étude des sépultures médiévales en France', in J. Chapelot and J.-M. Poisson (eds), *Trente ans d'archéologie médiévale en France: un bilan pour un avenir*, publication du CRAHM, Caen, 213–26

Viader, R. and Rendu C. 2014 *Cultures temporaires et féodalité: les rotations culturales et l'appropriation du sol dans l'Europe médiévale et moderne*, Presses Universitaires du Mirail, Toulouse

Vivet, J.-B., Bacheter, X., Chauvel, J.-J., and Fluzin, P. 2009 *Métallurgie médiévale et forêt en prélude aux Grandes Forges de Paimpont*, Centre régional d'archéologie, Alet

Watteaux, M. 2005 'Sous le bocage, le parcellaire...', *Études rurales* 175/6, 53–80

Zadora-Rio, E. 2003 'L'archéologie de l'habitat rural et la pesanteur des paradigmes', *Les nouvelles de l'archéologie* 92, 6–10

Zadora-Rio, E. 2010 'Planification agraire et système spatio-temporel', *Sistemi centuriali e opere di assetto agrario tra età romana e primo medioevo: aspetti metodologici, riscostruttivi e interpretativi* 7, 133–53

Zadora-Rio, E. and Galinié, H. 1992 'Fouilles et prospections à Rigny-Ussé (Indre-et-Loire) rapport préliminaire 1986–1991', *Revue Archéologique du Centre de la France* 31, 75–166

CHAPTER 58

LOOKING NORTH-EAST

Southern Scandinavia in the Middle Ages

ELSE ROESDAHL

SOUTHERN Scandinavia may roughly be defined as the medieval Danish kingdom. This consisted of present-day Denmark and what are now the Swedish provinces of Skåne, Halland, and Blekinge, as well as the northern part of Schleswig-Holstein. This chapter will also touch briefly on western Norway and its connections with Britain, which were much closer than Denmark's through most of the Middle Ages. The position of Denmark within the rest of Scandinavia will also be considered. Chronologically, this survey begins in the late eleventh century, at the end of the Viking Age and after the death in 1042 of Harthacnut, the last Danish king of England. But fairly close connections between the two countries continued for some time. The links between Denmark and England will be discussed from a mainly archaeological point-of-view (there is little evidence for links between Denmark and other parts of Britain until the late Middle Ages). The chapter ends around the time of the Reformation (in Denmark 1536).

The Danish kingdom was almost entirely surrounded by water (Figure 58.1). It consisted of Jutland with its land border with Germany, together with the islands of Fyn and Sjælland to the east and a series of smaller islands—all separated by fairly narrow sounds. To the east of Sjælland, beyond the Sound (*Øresund*, the waters between the modern states of Denmark and Sweden) were Skåne, Halland, and Blekinge. The country was, therefore, hugely dependant on ships and boats, vessels which during this period underwent dramatic developments (Bill 2011; Bill and Roesdahl 2007, 276–85; Englert 2015; Hybel and Poulsen 2007, 354–62). Denmark was the gateway through which passed the sea-going traffic between the North Sea and the Baltic, a situation which played a crucial role in the country's economy and politics.

To the south, Jutland is connected with Germany by a fairly narrow strip of land. This was defended against southern enemies by wasteland and rivers and by the massive border wall, the Danevirke, first constructed in pre-Viking times, and strengthened and rebuilt many times; its last medieval refortification being a late twelfth-century brick

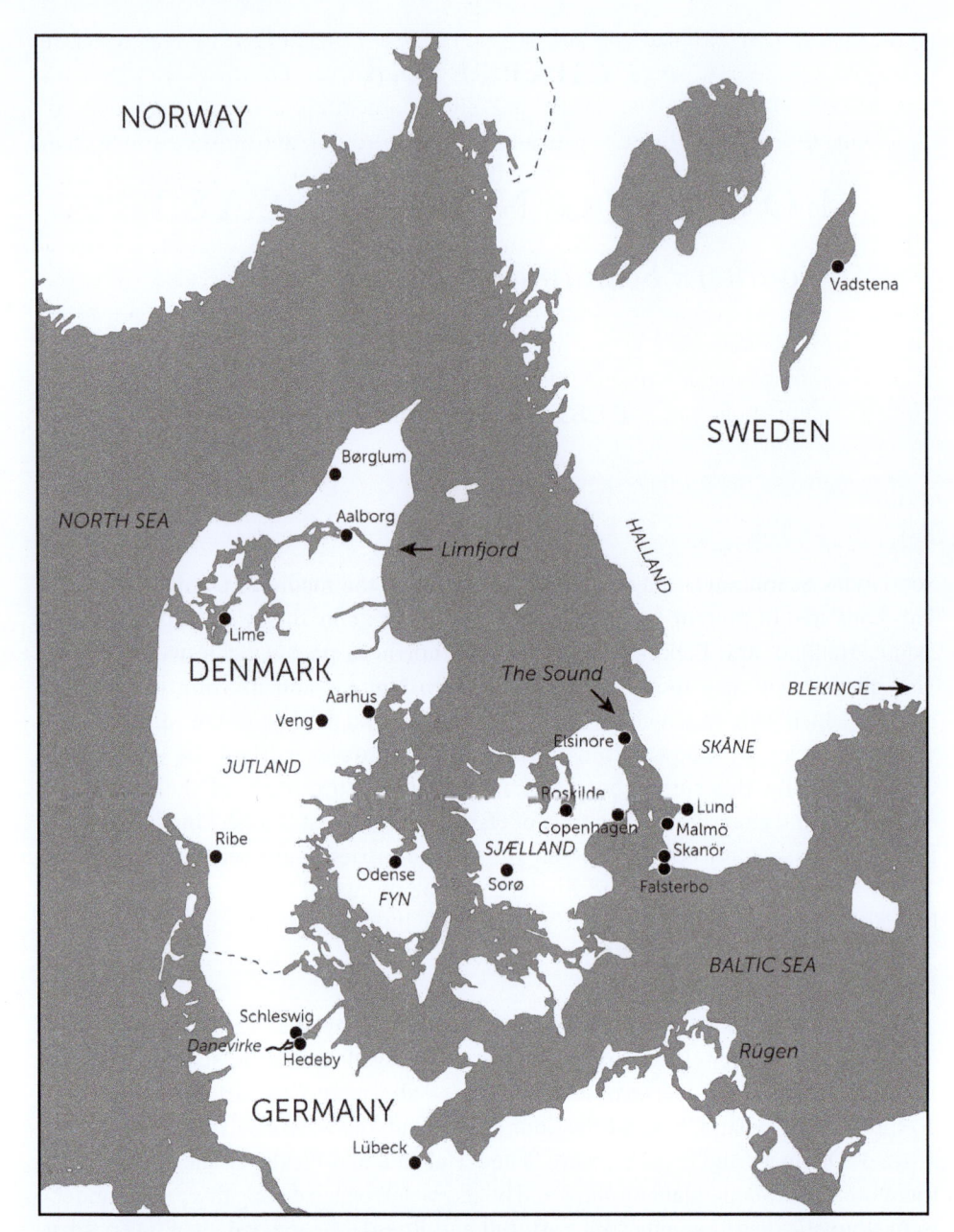

FIGURE 58.1 Denmark and part of Norway and Sweden with main place-names mentioned in the text. Modern borders between Denmark and Germany and between Norway and Sweden are indicated by dotted lines

(© Grafisk Tegnestue, Moesgaard Museum, Denmark)

wall (Andersen 1998; Dobat 2008). Beyond the Danevirke lived various peoples, each with their own language, culture, and political organization: the German Duchy of Saxony to the south, Frisians to the south-west, and the Slav lands to the south-east and along the south coast of the Baltic.

The Danish kingdom had probably largely reached its medieval extent in the eighth century or even earlier (e.g. Roesdahl 2008). By contrast, most of what is now Norway was united under one king in the early eleventh century after a long and gradual process; while most of the present kingdom of Sweden was not united until the twelfth century (e.g. Helle 2003 for an overview). All three kingdoms, however, continued to retain marked regional individuality within their individual boundaries. The many regional differences within Denmark depended on a variety of natural conditions and resources, traditions, as well as on the region's relationship to neighbouring peoples; all of which influenced density of settlement, the ownership of land, and the distribution of castles and may, for example, also be detected in church architecture, in coinage, in the types of pottery, and by the presence of goods imported from the various parts of northern Europe (Gammeltoft et al. 2008; Hybel and Poulsen 2007; Mackeprang 1944; Poulsen and Sindbæk 2011).

The main foreign influences of Denmark, Norway, and Sweden (apart from other parts of Scandinavia) arrived by different routes during most of the Middle Ages: Denmark looked to the south and the Baltic region; Norway to the west and south, and Sweden mostly to the east. Throughout the period discussed in this chapter, Denmark and Norway had for some time embraced Christianity, while Sweden was gradually converted in the mid- to late eleventh century. Much of the Saami population in northern Scandinavia, however, remained 'pagan' until the Renaissance or later.

Resources, Economy, and Chief Exports

Southern Scandinavia is flat, and, apart from the west coast of Jutland, its coastline has no tides and is dotted with fjords, inlets, and good harbours. Most of the area is fertile and had an economy based on agriculture: cattle-breeding, sheep-farming, and the cultivation of grain. Written sources indicate that agricultural produce, in particular meat and bacon, butter, fat, live oxen, and quality horses, along with herring, were the main exports (Hybel and Poulsen 2007, 373–9; cf. Carus-Wilson 1962–3). Much of these products had to be exported by sea (Bill 1991; Englert 2015), but oxen and horses from Jutland were also driven south across the border to feed and work for the growing populations of west European towns (Hybel and Poulsen 2007, 377–8). There is at present little archaeological evidence for these exports—what remains has been virtually impossible to provenance (but see e.g. Bill 1991; Søvsø 2012). New methods, however, such as strontium isotope analysis of animal bones from towns in northern Germany, the Netherlands, or England, may provide clues in the years to come.

Fishing played an increasing role in the economy. Already in the late twelfth century huge amounts of herring in Danish waters were exploited and became a major export (Hybel and Poulsen 2007, 373–6; also Chapter 9 in this *Handbook*). The vast amount of herring in the Sound gave rise to the extremely important international 'Skåne markets' at Skanör, at the south-eastern corner of Skåne. Here, herring were caught in August, then processed, cured, packed in barrels, and sold on. Lübeck and the other Hanseatic towns on the south Baltic coast were to play a major role in this trade. The Skåne market attracted merchants trading all sorts of commodities from a wide area, some of whom came from England (Carus-Wilson 1962–3, 190–1), and as this market became a main source of foreign imports, the traders also brought fresh cultural influences to Denmark. The herring fishery, the visitors' plots, and the trade itself were all regulated by the king, to whom the dues paid were of great economic importance. Royal castles at Skanör and Falsterbo, and the fourteenth-century church at Skanör (dedicated to St Gertrud, the protector of travellers), are among the relics of this trade, as are fragments of barrels, and about a thousand small, stamped lead tokens which would have been receipts for payments to the king's representative or some other form of control tokens (Eriksson 1980; Ersgård 1988; Grinder-Hansen 1997, 116–20, cat. nos 47–54; Rydbeck 1935).

All metals (lead, copper and copper alloy, pewter, etc.,) had, however, to be imported into Denmark, although some iron was produced locally. In south-western Jutland, which had little stone, tufa and other building-stones used in the construction or extensions of many churches in the twelfth to thirteenth centuries were brought from quarries in the Rhineland or Weser area to the coast where they were transhipped, presumably as ballast, on the return voyages of ships which had brought in agricultural produce. There were, of course, many other imports, including quality cloth, beer, and wine (e.g. Hybel and Poulsen 2007, 362–73; Poulsen 2010, 208–9) (see below for imports from England).

Towns, by contrast with markets and harbour sites, became increasingly important for trade and other contacts with foreign lands. Some towns, like Ribe, Hedeby, and Aarhus, had their origin in the early Viking Age, while a new wave of towns, like Lund, Roskilde, and Odense, were founded around the year 1000. A few towns were re-located around the mid-eleventh century; Hedeby, for example, moved to the site of Schleswig, while some, like Ribe, were revitalized. At the time of the European economic boom, c.1200, new towns were again founded and others expanded, while more were added during the following centuries. Norway and Sweden witnessed a similar general development. The most northern town in Scandinavia, Trondheim, became the centre of the cult of St Olav, and from 1152 the seat of the archbishopric of Norway—an archdiocese which at its height also comprised Greenland, Iceland, the Faroes, Shetland, Orkney, the Hebrides, and the Isle of Man (Andersson 2003; Clarke and Ambrosiani 1991; Kristensen and Poulsen 2016).

For much of the medieval period, Ribe was the most important Danish town for connections with England and Continental Western Europe. Situated to the south of Jutland's otherwise rather inhospitable west coast, it was within reasonable sailing distance of the north-western European trading centres such as, for example, Bruges and Antwerp (Christensen 2010; Madsen 1999). Ribe's importance was probably enhanced sometime in the twelfth century when western access to the Limfjord silted up and closed. For a long time the fjord must have been an important route for ships sailing between the Baltic and eastern Denmark and the North Sea (Roesdahl 2014, 25–6). Such traffic now had to navigate the difficult waters round the northern tip of Jutland (the Skaw); it may, consequently, have been easier for some foreign merchants to unload cargoes at Ribe and have their goods distributed via land routes.

Denmark and Neighbouring Lands, and Political History

Medieval Denmark by comparison with Britain was a small country with a small population, and the enormous accumulation of wealth by English kings, aristocracy, and the Church, which found expression by building large castles, churches, and monasteries, is not equalled in Denmark, nor indeed, elsewhere in Scandinavia. But of the three Scandinavian countries, Denmark had by far the densest population and often played a leading role in the North. From 1380 until 1814 the Danish king also ruled Norway, together with the then Norwegian lands of Iceland, the Faroes, and Greenland and, until 1468–9, Orkney and Shetland as well. Further, between 1397 and 1520 (with several breaks caused by wars or rebellion) the Danish monarch ruled all three Scandinavian kingdoms, including Finland which was then part of Sweden. This is known as the Kalmar Union, which covered a geographically immense area with vast and extremely varied resources (Etting 2004; Grinder-Hansen 1997; Helle 2003, 345–420, 679–770).

From time to time Denmark suffered from foreign raids and invasions, and also had its share of internal wars, usually triggered by competition for the throne or by the Crown's economic problems leading to heavy taxation. It reached its nadir in the fourteenth century when the country was pawned to a number of north German parties and for a short period ceased to exist. Such troubles naturally led to the building of numerous castles (Olsen 2014).

The Baltic, with its increasingly important trade routes, was always a Danish sphere of interest, although there were many competitors, including, at various times, Slav groups, Saxony, the German Order, the Hanseatic League (the Hansa), and Sweden, while at times the sea and adjacent coasts were open to piratical enterprise. In the second half of the twelfth century Denmark expanded along the south Baltic coast, beginning with the conquest of the island of Rügen in 1169, followed by Pomerania in 1185, and continuing with Estonia in 1219. Most of these lands were lost in 1227, while Estonia was sold in 1346, although in 1361 Gotland was also conquered. Finds from mass graves just outside the town wall of Visby, and hoards on the island, bear witness to the brutality and the drama of the conquest (Grinder-Hansen 1997, 192–5, cat. nos 230–9); the island held an uncertain position within the Danish kingdom for some time afterwards.

In this Baltic context it is significant that of the nineteen large and medium-sized merchant ships of which remains have been found in Danish waters and dated to 1000–1250, all but one are of Danish origin. The exception was built in western Norway (Englert 2015). During the thirteenth century, however, Lübeck and other German towns south and east of the Baltic rose to power and eventually formed, together with coastal towns in Flanders and elsewhere, the powerful trading network known as the Hanseatic League. In the fourteenth and early sixteenth centuries the League engaged in open war with Denmark. It never had a *kontor* (a counting house) there, but c.1365 a *kontor* was formally established in Bergen, in western Norway, with stock fish from the north as the all-important export commodity. Bergen became a major centre of international trade with Continental Western Europe and England, as is abundantly documented in written sources and in archaeological material such as pottery (Blackmore et al. 1994; Lüdtke 1989; Nedkvitne 2014, 31–3, 53–79, 146–86; see Chapter 9 in this *Handbook*). At the same time, however, as indeed there had been before the rise of the Hansa, there was a flourishing trade between Danish harbours and many towns in the Baltic and around the North Sea, including those controlled by the Hansa (e.g. Hybel and Poulsen 2007, 353–80).

One of the many ships which passed through the Sound in the late fourteenth century was the so-called Vejby cog, which was wrecked off the North Sjælland coast. It was found in 1976—though only the bottom had survived—and contained 109 English gold nobles from the period 1351–77, a gold coin from Lübeck (1365–71), a coin from Flanders and, in the mast step, three coins from the Teutonic Order in Prussia. Also found were pewter plates with stamps from the Dutch province of Geldern and remains of other metal vessels (including one which was probably produced in a Baltic Hanseatic town), and 18 tonnes of stone ballast. According to dendrochronology the ship was built in 1372, probably in either Gdansk or Elbląg, while the coins suggest that it sank around 1375. The ship's contents suggest that it was on its way to its Baltic home town from England via the Netherlands with a fairly light cargo, hence the ballast stones. The English gold coins would represent the profits of successful trading there. It may indeed be the very ship known from written sources to have been wrecked in 1377 on its way from Flanders to its home port of Gdansk with a cargo of cloth, oil, rice, and almonds (Bonde and Jensen 1995; Crumlin-Pedersen et al. 1976; Jensen et al. 1992, vol. 2, cat. no. 210; Grinder-Hansen 1997, cat. no. 120; Suchodolski 2012, 449–63; 2014).

Denmark's unique power at the time of the Kalmar Union was expressed in the material culture, although little of it has survived. It was at this time—in the 1420s—that King Erik of Denmark, Norway, and Sweden rebuilt a slightly older castle, Krogen, at Elsinore (Helsingør), to shape a fine castle with a Great Hall suitable for royal audiences. Krogen was again rebuilt in the 1570s–80s as the Renaissance castle, Kronborg (Nielsen 2008). From Elsinore Castle and with the castle at Helsingborg on the other side of the Sound, Erik organized, in the late 1420s, the exaction of tolls from ships taking part in the vastly increasing international and competitive sea-borne trade between Western Europe and the Baltic. Ships passed through this waterway, and Elsinore became a prosperous town with an international population (see below), while the tolls became a major source of income for the Danish crown. It was also at this time that the only post-Viking Age royal marriages between Britain and Denmark took place. The wives of nearly all other Danish kings during this period came from royal or princely houses in Scandinavia or north Germany, mirroring the prevailing politics and connections of their time.

Denmark and Britain Contrasted: The Archaeological Evidence

There are some significant differences between the medieval archaeologies of Denmark and England (see Gilchrist and Reynolds 2009; Kristiansen et al. 2015; Liebgott 1989; Roesdahl 1999). A few examples suffice. Timber was totally dominant as a building material in Denmark (by contrast with England) throughout the Middle Ages, except in building churches and, in part, castles. Timber, and later half-timbered, buildings were normal in countryside and towns, although brick-built town houses are also known. The same was true of monastic buildings until the late Middle Ages (Kristensen 2013). Even castles built of timber are well known (e.g. Kock and Roesdahl 2005). Nevertheless, very few pre-Renaissance timber buildings survive.

Surviving medieval stone and brick buildings, other than churches, are also rare. Mortared stone buildings came late to Denmark. The two earliest known are churches in Roskilde, which date back to the 1020s and 1030s and were built of easily workable calcareous tufa; the best documented of them had English architectural features, the stone from which had been re-used in a later church on the site (Olsen 1960; Johannsen and Smidt 1981, 14–19). The oldest surviving churches in Denmark were built around the year 1100 or a little earlier, although they are normally difficult to date and many have been much altered through time. Nearly all the remains of vernacular stone and brick buildings of medieval date now form part of more recent constructions. But often only the foundations survive, sometimes together with the lower part or core of walls, as stone and brick were widely re-used, because there was little native building stone (except in Skåne), while the commonly found granite Norwegian ice-borne erratics were hard to shape and were mostly used for churches. Brick production, starting in the later twelfth century, was also expensive; so expensive, for example, that bricks from the medieval royal castle of Kalø in eastern Jutland were shipped to Copenhagen in the late seventeenth century to be re-used in building the new palace of Charlottenborg. Such building practices, on the other hand, often provide excellent opportunities for excavation of demolished monuments.

More medieval church furnishings are preserved in Denmark than in many other countries, although few examples are older than the mid-twelfth century. Some furnishings still survive in their original churches, but much was transferred to the National Museum or other museums in the nineteenth century. Normally the provenance of such pieces is known, which allows for contextual studies. Most of what remained in the great churches, as that from Roskilde Cathedral, was, however, sold off shortly after 1800. Church archaeology, including excavation, remains an integral part of Danish medieval archaeology; still under the control of the National Museum, it is now often carried out in collaboration with local museums. Gradually an inventory of all churches and their furnishings is being published (Andersen 2015; *DK* 1933ff).

By comparison with England, written sources are late and few in Denmark: the earliest known charter is dated 1085, and the numbers only gradually grow. Some early histories, saints' lives, annals, etc. add to our knowledge, particularly on political matters; but a real interplay between archaeological and written sources with regard to trade, for example, is only possible from well into the thirteenth century. Danish manuscript illuminations are also late and rare, but the many church murals, especially those from the fourteenth to sixteenth centuries, are unique sources for understanding daily life. Types of objects, their forms, colours, and function are 'realistic' and show much local detail (Haastrup and Egevang 1985–92; Saxtorph 1986).

Denmark and Britain: Links

From the 990s to 1042, when Scandinavians (again) raided and then conquered and reigned England, southern Scandinavia was massively influenced from England. This is especially true during the reigns of the Danish kings, Sven Forkbeard, Knut the Great, and Harthacnut (c.987–1042), particularly after 1016 when Denmark and England shared a king except for two years. Influences encompassed coinage and the use of coins as recognized tender, all aspects of ecclesiastical matters, art and ornament, the introduction of stone buildings, as well as the importation of various types of objects, such as weapons, jewellery, pottery, and even cheap brooches. The English also probably influenced certain social institutions and the development of towns. In England, in what is often called England's second Viking Age, Scandinavian influences and imports are also evident—in art and poetry, trade, grave monuments, the occasional use of runes, and many other things. In the late ninth and tenth centuries a considerable Scandinavian population had settled in the north and east of England and in Scotland, and their presence was still a potent force in the eleventh century, when new groups of Scandinavians arrived (summaries of Danish evidence in Pedersen 2004; Roesdahl 2007; Spejlborg 2014; the English may be found scattered in various articles and books; see also Bolton 2008; Lavelle and Roffey 2016).

It is clear that Denmark's foreign contacts changed after the Viking Age and (again) came to be directed predominantly towards the Continent. But, despite the political break in 1042, the dismissal in 1051 of the English king's Danish retainers, and the Norman Conquest of 1066, trade and some of the other old links between Denmark and Britain continued, but decreasingly so, for nearly two centuries—clearly following established traditions, at first probably fuelled by family links across the North Sea and, probably for some time, by Danish dreams of a re-conquest of England. Some links may also have been triggered by Danish reactions to German power politics.

A specific group of artefacts, fragmentary elements of copper-alloy riding gear decorated in the Scandinavian Ringerike and Urnes styles, and rarely of top quality, found in increasing quantity in England and southern Scandinavia by metal-detectorists, help to demonstrate such continuing links. They show that men in the eleventh century, or probably a specific group of men, on both sides of the North Sea shared a common taste. Such riding gear may have developed from military equipment in the environment of Knut the Great, although the social meaning of these finds remains to be more closely examined (Roesdahl 2007, 22–6; Williams 1997). In England, the Scandinavian Urnes style (c.1050–early twelfth century) or local versions of the style occasionally appear also on other types of objects (e.g. Graham-Campbell 2013, 150–2).

The 30 m long war-ship found at Skuldelev in Roskilde Fjord in Denmark had been built in the Dublin region in 1042 and repaired there some twenty-five years later; it may have played a role in the upheavals in Britain around the mid-eleventh century (Crumlin-Pedersen and Olsen 2002, 141–94, 326–36). In the 1070s, following the Norman Conquest, there were several Danish raids on England, led by members of the royal family who still had ties with their erstwhile kingdom. In 1085 King Knut IV (the Holy) planned a large-scale invasion. A huge fleet was assembled in the Limfjord, but Knut was delayed at the southern border, and the fleet never sailed. The following year and during a rebellion, Knut was killed in a church in Odense dedicated to the English saint Alban, and was buried there (*DK* 1998–2001, 1729–38). The continuing links between England and Denmark (see also below) provide some background to Knut's great plan.

Written sources and coin legends tell of a number of Englishmen of various professions—often from the south-eastern part of the country—who lived and worked in Denmark in the centuries following the Viking Age. The authors of the lives of the Danish royal saints, Knut (the Holy) and Knut Lavard, canonized in c.1100 and in 1170 respectively, were Ailnoth of Canterbury, writing around 1120 (Abrams 2004), and Robert of Ely, writing in the 1130s (this life is lost, Christensen 1977, 337; Jørgensen 1960, 22–3); there were also English bishops, monks, chancellors, and chaplains to kings and princes, moneyers and goldsmiths, all known by name. English saints too were venerated, including St Alban, whose relics according to a thirteenth-century story had been taken in England and brought to Odense, but later secretly brought back by way of Ribe on an English ship. Further, five Danish churches are known to have been dedicated to St Botolph, who was particularly popular in East Anglia, while much English ecclesiastical terminology was introduced into Denmark (Biddle 2004; Jensen 2015; Jørgensen 1908; Spejlborg 2014).

The cult of Knut the Holy, centred in Odense where he was killed, was an initiative of his brothers and followers on the Danish throne. But its realization was partly carried out through the English bishop of Odense, Hubald. From Evesham, near the Welsh border, monks were recruited for a monastery attached to the new church of Our Lady, St Alban and St Knut at Odense, which was being built in stone around 1100, and Hubald also gave advice and support for the production of Knut's shrine, which was placed in the church and is partly preserved. Very little remains of the church, however, and no English features have been identified at his shrine (*DK* 1990, 75–6, 132–4, 424–58; Gazzoli 2013; Jørgensen 1908). But it has been shown that a uniquely exquisite manuscript produced by English artists and scribes in the third quarter of the twelfth century was almost certainly made for the Danish King Valdemar the Great (1157–82). Known as the Copenhagen Psalter, it is now in the Royal Library in Copenhagen (Thott 142 2°). It is also argued that it was commissioned for Valdemar's Feast at his church at Ringsted in 1170, where his son Knut was crowned and his father St Knut (Lavard) was enshrined (Stirnemann 1999; de Hamel 2016, 280–329).

Some of the eleventh- and twelfth-century bishops in Ribe, the port for England, were English. The seal matrix of one of these, Radulf, is preserved and is thought to be of English workmanship (Roesdahl and Wilson 1992, cat. no. 514). He was bishop of Ribe in around 1162–70, after a career as chaplain and chancellor to King Valdemar the Great (1157–82). Some Ribe bishops are known to have been engaged in trade with England. In 1188, bishop Omer was the contact person for the acquisition of English lead for the roof of St Geneviève in Paris—whose abbot asked the top Danish aristocracy to pay for the roof, in letters which referred to the Vikings' sack of Paris and this church in particular. In one of his letters the abbot asked the Danish archbishop, Absalon, for practical assistance in the purchase of English lead for this roof because, the letter says, he had much experience with lead for church building, the abbot's envoy having travelled directly to Ribe (Roesdahl 2010).

At this time the archbishop's family monastery was being built at Sorø in Sjælland, and stone churches were being erected all over Denmark, many of which probably had a lead roof. Unfortunately, the sources of such lead are unknown and the present lead roofs have been melted down many times. However, melted lead from the roof of Absalon's church in Sorø, caught in vaults and as drops on a tiled floor as a result of a fire in 1248, could perhaps be provenanced and may—at a guess—be English; this was said to be the best. Lead for other roofs may have come from Roman ruins in Continental Western Europe (Roesdahl 2010; cf. also Carus-Wilson 1962–3, 188–9; Hybel and Poulsen 2007, 364; Poulsen 2010, 204).

There is a fair amount of numismatic and documentary evidence for English influence on Danish coinage and for the use of English coins in Denmark. The design of Danish coins was heavily influence by English coins from *c.*995, when the Scandinavians had re-commenced their raids on England, and continued through most of the reign of Knut, until the late 1020s. At the same time many English moneyers (known from their names on the coins) were active in Denmark, and continued in this role until the 1230s; although they became increasingly less numerous after the mid-eleventh century (Jensen 1995, nos 1–5, 12, 33). The names of two late English moneyers in Denmark are recorded in the Annals of St Albans, whence they came. Anketil, a famous goldsmith, appears to have been head of the royal mint of Niels (1104–34) before 1123 and may have been responsible for the design of some rare coin types. Nicholas, son of the goldsmith John, was head of Valdemar II's mint before *c.*1237, and was probably responsible for the design and reform of the coinage of 1234 (Jensen 2005; 2015).

English coins were also well known in Denmark, particularly from the 990s until *c.*1070, when only Danish coins could be used (e.g. Jensen 1995, no. 46), and again in the fourteenth century, after the collapse of the Danish state in 1332, when the minting of Danish coins almost ceased. During this period English (and Scottish and Anglo-Irish) silver sterlings were much used, and are well known in hoards, together with French and

German coins (Jensen 1973; Jensen et al. 1992, vol. 1, 93–104, vol. 2, 314–15, and e.g. nos 203, 214).

Archaeology (and art history) adds to the evidence of contacts across the North Sea and also demonstrates that English craftsmen other than moneyers and goldsmiths worked in Denmark, and that some Danes had perhaps been apprenticed in England. Many of the architectural and artistic links may have been facilitated through English clerics in Denmark. The English influences were, however, much stronger in Norway than in Denmark (e.g. Blindheim 1958).

Some church buildings of *c*.1100 or the early twelfth century, as well as some church furnishings of the twelfth and thirteenth centuries, show Anglo-Norman or English features, although the extent of this influence has been much discussed, and has in part been denied. For a long time there was a tendency in Denmark to seek English (rather than German or other Continental) influences, and it seems that many English scholars were enamoured of such Scandinavian connections. There is nowadays more awareness of the problems of attributing stylistic features to a particular country (e.g. Johannsen 1977, 153–4; Nyborg 2014). The so-called Gunhild's Cross, for example, which is made of walrus ivory, and was long thought to be English and of late eleventh-century date, is now shown to have been made in the mid-twelfth century under German influence (Langberg 1982; Roesdahl and Wilson 1992, cat. no. 607), while the oldest known monastic church in Denmark, Veng in central Jutland, presents numerous problems: its architectural features derive from many places including England (Krins 1968, 73–84; *DK* 1988–9, 3189–3226 with note 15).

Anglo-Norman architectural features are particularly evident in Jutland, in North Sjællan and in Skåne. In village churches such features may indicate the work or influence of English masons who first worked on important early churches which are now lost. Examples include, along the Limfjord, Lime Church (Figure 58.2) and the church of Our Lady in Aalborg (where another church was dedicated to St Botolph), as well as Virring and Asferg in north-eastern Jutland, Vejby in Sjælland, and Saxtorp in Skåne (Beckett 1924, 61–4; Johannsen 1977; Mackeprang 1944, 42–3; Nyborg 2008). The round towers of a number of Romanesque churches might possibly also have been influenced from England (cf. Heywood 1988; Wienberg 2007). A small capital of Purbeck marble, from England, has been found in Ribe, and murals in two churches near Ribe, Vilslev and Farup, seem to show English features (Nyborg 2014, 97–8 and note 17).

English-influenced church furnishings include the oldest of the 'golden altars', the altar from Lisbjerg Church, near Aarhus, from around 1140, which also has the Irish St Brigid among the saints portrayed. It was, however, clearly made in Denmark (Nørlund 1926, 73–98; Roesdahl and Wilson 1992, cat. no. 467). Three walrus-ivory carvings also have English stylistic features, although presumably, like a few other artefacts of thirteenth-century date, they were made in Denmark (Nyborg 2014; Stratford 1987, 111). A small series of baptismal fonts are thought to be English-inspired or made by Englishmen in Denmark, for example the font at Tikøb in Sjælland which was carved by a mason called Alexander (Mackeprang 1941, 24–5, 357–64). A tentative study of English influences on Danish polychrome wooden sculpture of the thirteenth century concludes

FIGURE 58.2 North portal of Lime church, northern Jutland, Denmark, c.1100. The portal has an Anglo-Norman decoration of roll-billets, and the walls of the nave are built of field stones set in mortar. The latter feature is unique in Denmark, but well known in England

(© Else Roesdahl)

that English features are mainly found in the western and northern parts of Jutland and on Fyn, while a fine Virgin and Child from the former Børglum Cathedral in north-western Jutland, and dated c.1230–40 (Nyborg 2014, fig. 6), was probably imported from eastern England. But the dominant influences in Danish wood-carving are German and French.

After this period there are few architectural or artistic links or imports from England until the fifteenth century, when small altar reliefs in so-called Nottingham alabaster are known from at least six churches in Jutland, including Borbjerg and Vejrum (Beckett 1926, 149–50, note 427; *DK* 2014, 1872–87).

A variety of commodities traded between England and Denmark throughout the Middle Ages are mentioned in written sources, and Ribe clearly played an important role in this trade. It is, for example, recorded that vast numbers of quality horses were being exported from Ribe in the thirteenth century. Excavated evidence of English imports in Denmark also comes mainly from Ribe and emphasizes the town's role in the contacts with England. However, both archaeology and written sources agree that links with the Rhineland and the Netherlands were far more important for the town (Carus-Wilson 1962–3; Enemark 1958; Madsen 1994; 1999; Poulsen 2010). Two silver hoards with many English sterlings deposited in the 1240s just outside Ribe probably belonged to English merchants who had stayed over in the town. One of the hoards also contained a few non-English coins, a silver spoon of possible English origin, and some silver bits; the other hoard just held sterlings (Jensen 2006; Jensen et al. 1992, vol. 2, 15–20).

All medieval stone mortars found in Denmark were imported, and of twenty-five examples registered in present-day Denmark in 1971 seven were of Purbeck marble, or possibly of Quarr stone from the Isle of Wight, while yet another may also be of English origin. The others came from north-western France or elsewhere in the Channel region, and one from Norway. All but four of the twenty-five mortars were found in Ribe (Bencard 1971; cf. Carus-Wilson 1962–3, 188).

In 1962 little was known about Danish medieval glazed pottery, which was then thought to be 'directly influenced from England' (*EM* 1962). Today there is agreement that the main influences came from the Netherlands, although the so-called 'dancing-girl' jugs (Figure 58.3 top), which have an applied decoration representing women holding hands, were probably inspired by pottery from the English Midlands. They date to the thirteenth to fourteenth centuries and have been found in towns and castles in the eastern Danish provinces and in south-western Sweden, while others were found in Vordingborg in Sjælland, and in Aalborg in northern Jutland. Interestingly, none have been found at Ribe (Barton 1968a; 1968b; Roesdahl 1982).

Some English pottery, particularly Grimston Ware, which was produced in Norfolk, was imported into Denmark in the late twelfth–fourteenth centuries. Most sherds have been found in Ribe (Figure 58.3 bottom), others in Schleswig and other towns, but there are not many when compared with finds of the often colourful imports from Flanders and northern France (Bencard 1972; Lüdtke 1985, 66; Madsen and Stilke 2001, 599–607, 611; Vince 1996).

FIGURE 58.3 Top: reconstruction of part of a 'dancing girl' jug, height c.17cm, from Ragnhildsholmen Castle in south-western Sweden, c.1250–1310; this type of jug was probably inspired from England (redrawn after Barton 1968a). Bottom: part of an English jug of Grimston Ware, found in Ribe, rim diameter c.9.5cm, thirteenth to fourteenth century

(© Grafisk Tegnestue, Moesgaard Museum, Denmark); (© Sydvestjyske Museer, Denmark)

While the arrival of pottery was of little economic significance, the import of quality cloth into Denmark from Western Europe was of major importance, and the vast quantity of such goods is well documented in written sources. Most came from Flanders and elsewhere in the Netherlands, but there were also imports from German and Baltic towns and from England (e.g. Enemark 1963; Hybel and Poulsen 2007, 367–9). Archaeological finds of fine textiles are hard to provenance (e.g. Østergård and Rogers 2005) and the large-scale export of English raw wool adds to the difficulties of identification. But small discarded lead seals, which had been attached to cloth as quality marks, often tell where the now-missing cloth had been produced. Of the 263 cloth seals predating c.1600 known in Denmark in 1988 (many more have been found since), those which can be dated mostly belong to the fifteenth century or later, and the origin of 201 could be identified. The vast majority were from towns in the Netherlands, Germany, and also the eastern Baltic, while ten were English—two of them from Colchester (Liebgott 1975; Orduna 1995). Thus, the written sources and archaeology agree about the relative importance of the importation of cloth from England and Continental Europe. It is also significant that only two of the 278 pilgrims' badges known in Scandinavia in 1989 were English, both from Canterbury, and none of these were found in Denmark (Andersson 1989), although St Thomas was not unknown there (e.g. Liebgott 1982, 36–8, 195).

Lists of the trousseau of the English princess Philippa provide an extraordinary picture of high-quality and precious textiles brought to Denmark at the start of the fifteenth century. Philippa, the 12-year-old daughter of Henry IV of England, sailed from Lynn in eastern England with a huge entourage, in fourteen ships, and landed in Bergen, en route to her wedding in 1406 in Lund, Skåne, to Erik of Denmark, Norway, and Sweden. Philippa's extremely rich trousseau, which consisted mainly of silverware for the table (including forty-eight plates and a number of cups, candles, dishes, spoons, etc.) and for her chapel, is described in some detail in written sources. There are also lists of huge amounts of very fine textiles, as well as furs for dresses and cloaks for the princess and her followers. These were for use while travelling and for the ceremonies in Denmark. It also included rich accoutrements for her beds and wagon and so on. No jewellery is mentioned, and nothing of this great trousseau seems to have survived, but a description of her crown made by three goldsmiths in 1454 has allowed for a reconstruction (Figure 58.4) (*Diplomatarium Danicum* 4. Rk. 10, nos 455, 530, 527; Alexander and Binski 1987, 202–3; Baildon 1915–16; Etting 2001; 2004).

Philippa became an energetic and powerful queen, but died childless in 1430 and was buried in the mother house of the Bridgettine order at Vadstena in Östergötland, south-western Sweden, in which she had taken great interest. One of the 204 people who followed her to Denmark in 1406 engaged in negotiations with Vadstena, which led to the foundation by Henry V in 1415 of the only nunnery of the Bridgettine order in England, Syon Abbey in Middlesex. Seven women and two men from Vadstena went to Syon (Andersen 2014; Berglund 2009). Others among Philippa's followers in 1406 may also have played significant roles in continued Danish/Scandinavian-English relationships. King Erik's and Philippa's coats-of-arms have, since c.1410, commemorated the

FIGURE 58.4 Reconstruction of the crown of Philippa of England, based on the descriptions recorded by three goldsmiths in 1454, and also on the crown of Philippa's sister Blanche, now in the Schatzkammer der Residenz, Munich (after Etting 2001)

(© Øyvind Aasen, Copenhagen)

royal marriage at Canterbury Cathedral (Messenger 1947, 84), while the splay of a big circular window at the castle in Elsinore shows the coat-of-arms of Erik and of Philippa surrounded by those of Scandinavian dignitaries (Nielsen 2008, fig. 10).

Archaeological evidence of later connections with England are the imported alabasters mentioned above, and a handful of small, round lead 'badges' from around 1500 found in various places in Denmark. They show a Tudor coat-of-arms surrounded by a ribbon inscribed with the motto of the Order of the Garter; their function is unknown (Engberg 2003). It also appears from written sources that, because of the international competition for Baltic trade and related politics, and the behaviour of English fishermen in Iceland, relations between Denmark and England were often bad during the second half of the fifteenth century. In 1468, the Danish King Christian I even captured an English merchant fleet in the Sound. Towards the end of the century trade between the two countries was gradually resumed (Enemark 1958, 673–4; Poulsen 1996).

In 1469 the daughter of Christian I of Denmark-Norway, the 12-year-old Margrete, married James III of Scotland. She brought Orkney and Shetland to her new country as security for her dowry of 60,000 Rhenish florins, of which her father was able to pay only a small part in cash. A fine contemporary full-length portrait by Hugo van der Goes of Margrete protected by Saint George may be seen on the side panel of an altarpiece commissioned for the church of the Holy Trinity in Edinburgh; it is now in the National Galleries of Scotland.

For centuries there had been frequent contact between Norway and Scotland, but it seems that it was not until the fifteenth century that extensive relations between Denmark and Scotland were established—based on the growing Baltic trade. From this time onwards there are records of a number of Scottish residents in Danish towns, particularly in Elsinore, Copenhagen, and Malmö. Here they formed closely knit 'colonies', and many were employed in the textile industry, although others were grocers and various 'important' people. Some even taught at Copenhagen University. An early sixteenth-century altar-piece from a side altar in the main church (St Olaf's) in Elsinore (now in the National Museum of Denmark) was given to the church by the town's Scottish lord mayor; dedicated to the Scottish St Ninian, it was probably produced in a German workshop. A St Ninian's altar-piece in the church of Our Lady in Copenhagen has disappeared, and Copenhagen also had a St Ninian's guild (*DK* 1964, 131–40, figs 49–56; Appel 2012; Riis 1988; Tønnesen 1985).

Conclusion

Links between England and southern Scandinavia clearly peaked in the late Viking Age, from the 990s to the mid-eleventh century. But fairly close contacts continued on many levels, although decreasingly so, for nearly two centuries afterwards. At the same time Danish contact with Germany, the Netherlands and France grew in importance; these had been the common links from well before the Viking Age. Trade with England may be followed throughout the Middle Ages from mainly written sources. It was largely centred on Ribe, although English merchants are also known to have visited eastern Denmark, including the international Skåne markets. Archaeology agrees that Ribe's, and Denmark's, links with Germany and the Netherlands became far more important than those with England. English imports are fairly rare at Ribe and even fewer have been found elsewhere in Denmark. From around 1400, with the rapidly growing and very competitive trade between Western Europe and the Baltic, controlled by the Danish king at Elsinore, connections between Denmark and Britain again rose in importance. Of these there is little archaeological evidence, but they are emphasized by two royal marriages, and by Scottish immigrants in east Danish towns in the fifteenth century and onwards—the first comprehensive evidence of Scots in Denmark.

Acknowledgements

I am very grateful to John Cherry, Vivian Etting, James Graham-Campbell, Erla Hohler, Lars M. Sass Jensen, Jørgen Steen Jensen, Hans Krongaard Kristensen, Ebbe Nyborg, Mette H. Søvsø, Morten Søvsø, and to David M. Wilson for their help and advice with this article. David Wilson also 'cleaned up' my English.

References Cited

Abrams, L. 2004 'Ailnoth', *Oxford Dictionary of National Biography* 1, Oxford

Alexander, J. and Binski, P. (eds) 1987 *Age of Chivalry: art in Plantagenet England 1200-1400*, Royal Academy of Arts, London

Andersen, H. H. 1998 *Danevirke og Kovirke. Arkæologiske undersøgelser 1861-1993*, Jutland Archaeological Society, Højbjerg

Andersen, M. 2014 'Erik 7. af Pommern og Philippa', in K. Kryger (ed.), *Danske Kongegrave* 2, Museum Tusculanum, København, 132-47

Andersen, M. 2015 'Medieval Archaeology and the National Museum of Denmark today', in M. S. Kristiansen, E. Roesdahl, and J. Graham-Campbell (eds), *Medieval archaeology in Scandinavia and beyond: history, trends and tomorrow*, Aarhus University Press, Aarhus, 111-25

Andersson, H. 2003 'Urbanisation', in K. Helle (ed.), *The Cambridge history of Scandinavia, Vol. 1: Prehistory to 1520*, Cambridge University Press, Cambridge, 312-42

Andersson, L. 1989 *Pilgrimsmärken och vallfart*, Almqvist and Wiksell, Stockholm

Appel, L. 2012 'The Scottish and English citizens in Elsinore from the 16th to the 18th century: an archaeological approach', in H. Harnow, D. Cranstone, P. Belford, and L. Høst Madsen (eds), *Across the North Sea: later historical archaeology in Britain and Denmark, c.1500-2000 AD*, University Press of Southern Denmark, Odense, 187-94

Baildon, W. P. 1915-16 'The Trousseau of princess Philippa, wife of Eric, king of Denmark, Norway and Sweden', *Archaeologia* 67, 163-88

Barton, K. J. 1968a *Some examples of medieval glazed earthenware in Sweden*, Antikvarisk Arkiv 13, Stockholm

Barton, K. J. 1968b 'Anthropomorphic decoration on medieval jugs; some regional variations, with special reference to Swedish examples', in A. W. Mårtensson (ed.), *Res medievales. Ragnar Blomqvist Kal. Mai MCMLXVIII Oblata*, Kulturhistoriska Museet Lund, Lund, 43-52

Beckett, F. 1924 *Danmarks Kunst 1*, Henrik Koppel, København

Beckett, F. 1926 *Danmarks Kunst 2*, Henrik Koppel, København

Bencard, M. 1971 'Middelalderlige stenmortere i Danmark', *Kuml* 1971, 35-60

Bencard, M. 1972 'Medieval pottery imported into Denmark', *Chateau Gaillard* V, 13-22

Berglund, L. 2009 'Queen Philippa and Vadstena Abbey: royal communication on a medieval media platform', in M. Jönsson and P. Lundell (eds), *Media and monarchy in Sweden*, Nordicom, Göteborg, 21-32

Biddle, M. 2004 'St Alban', *Oxford Dictionary of National Biography* 1, Oxford

Bill, J. 1991 'Gedesbyskibet. Middelalderlig skude- og færgefart fra Falster', *Nationalmuseets Arbejdsmark* 1991, 188-98

Bill, J. 2011 'Sea trade: the development of ships and routes', in M. O. H. Carver and J. Klápště (eds), *The archaeology of medieval Europe Vol. 2: twelfth to sixteenth centuries*, Aarhus University Press, Aarhus, 328-37

Bill, J. and Roesdahl, E. 2007 'Travel and transport', in J. Graham-Campbell with M. Valor (eds), *The archaeology of medieval Europe Vol. 1: eighth to twelfth centuries* AD, Aarhus University Press, Aarhus, 261–88

Blackmore, L., Vince, A., Deroeux, D., Dufournier, D., Herteig, A. E., and Hufthammer, A. K. 1994 *Medieval pottery from south-east England found in the Bryggen excavations 1955–68, Vol. 2*, The Bryggen Papers: supplementary series volume 5, Bergen

Blindheim, M. 1958 'Engelsk stilinnflytelse', *Kulturhistorisk Leksikon for Nordisk Middelalder* III, Rosenkilde og Bagger, København, 638–56

Bolton, T. 2008 *The empire of Cnut the Great*, Brill, Leiden

Bonde, N. and Jensen, J. S. 1995 'The dating of a Hanseatic cog-find in Denmark: what the coins and tree rings can reveal in maritime archaeology', in O. Olsen, J. Skamby Madsen, and F. Rieck (eds), *Shipshape: essays for Ole Crumlin-Pedersen*, Viking Ship Museum, Roskilde, 103–21

Carus-Wilson, E. 1962–3 'The medieval trade of the ports of the Wash', *Medieval Archaeology* 6–7, 182–201

Christensen, A. E. 1977 'Tiden 1042–1241', in I. Skovgaard-Petersen, A. E. Christensen, and H. Paludan, *Danmarks Historie. Bind 1. Tiden indtil 1340*, Gyldendal, København, 211–399

Christensen, S. B. (ed.) 2010 *Ribe Bys Historie 1. 710–1520*, Dansk Center for Byhistorie & Esbjerg Kommune, Esbjerg

Clarke, H. and Ambrosiani, B. 1991 *Towns in the Viking Age*, Leicester University Press, Leicester

Crumlin-Pedersen, O., Jensen, J. S., Kromann, A., and Liebgott, N.-K. 1976 'Koggen med guldskatten', *Skalk* 1976(6), 9–15

Crumlin-Pedersen, O. and Olsen, O. (eds) 2002 *The Skuldelev ships I*, Ships and Boats of the North 4.1, The Viking Ship Museum, Roskilde

Diplomatarium Danicum, Det danske Sprog- og Litteraturselskab (ed), København [www.diplomatarium.dk/]

DK 1933ff *Danmarks Kirker*, Nationalmuseet, København [www.danmarkskirker.natmus.dk/] (English summaries in the latest volumes)

DK 1964 *Danmarks Kirker, Frederiksborg Amt, Vol. 1*, Nationalmuseet, København

DK 1988–89 *Danmarks Kirker, Aarhus Amt, Vol. 6*, Nationalmuseet, København

DK 1990 *Danmarks Kirker, Odense Amt, Vol. 1*, Nationalmuseet, København

DK 1998–2001 *Danmarks Kirker, Odense Amt, Vol. 3*, Nationalmuseet, København

DK 2014 *Danmarks Kirker, Ringkøbing Amt*, Nationalmuseet, København

Dobat, A. S. 2008 'Danevirke revisited: an investigation into military and socio-political organisation in south Scandinavia (*c.* AD 700 to 1100)', *Medieval Archaeology* 52, 27–67

EM 1962 *Engelsk lertøj fra Middelalderen og samtidigt dansk lertøj*, Kunstindustrimuseet, Copenhagen (exhibition catalogue)

Enemark, P. 1958 'Englandshandel. Danmark', *Kulturhistorisk Leksikon for Nordisk Middelalder* III, Rosenkilde og Bagger, København, 668–74

Enemark, P. 1963 'Handel med klæde. Danmark', *Kulturhistorisk Leksikon for Nordisk Middelalder* VII, Rosenkilde og Bagger, København, 458–65

Engberg, N. 2003 '"Skam få den, som tænker ilde herom"—fem usædvanlige danefæfund', in P. Grinder-Hansen (ed.), *Arvesølvet. Studier fra Nationalmuseet tilegnet Fritze Lindahl 2003*, Nationalmuseet, København, 55–70

Englert, A. 2015 *Large cargo ships in Danish waters 1000–1250: evidence of specialised merchant seafaring prior to the Hanseatic period*, Ships and Boats of the North vol. 7, Viking Ship Museum, Roskilde

Eriksson, H. S. 1980 *Skånemarkedet*, Wormianum, Højbjerg
Ersgård, L. 1988 *'Vår marknad i Skåne'. Bebyggelse, handel och urbanisering i Skanör och Falsterbo under medeltiden*, Lund Studies in Medieval Archaeology 4, Stockholm
Etting, V. 2001 'De tabte kronjuveler', *Nationalmuseets Arbejdsmark* 2001, 110–27
Etting, V. 2004 *Queen Margrete I (1353–1412) and the founding of the Nordic Union*, Brill, Leiden-Boston
Gammeltoft, P., Sindbæk, S. M., and Vellev, J. (eds) 2008 *Regionalitet i Danmark i vikingetid og middelalder*, Hikuin 35, Forlaget Hikuin, Højbjerg
Gazzoli, P. 2013 'Anglo-Danish connections and the origins of the cult of Knud', in A. Jennings and A. Sanmark (eds), *Across the Sólundarhaf: connections between Scotland and the Nordic World*, Journal of the North Atlantic, special volume 4, 69–76
Gilchrist, R. and Reynolds, A. (eds) 2009 *Reflections: 50 years of Medieval Archaeology 1957–2007*, The Society for Medieval Archaeology Monograph 30, Leeds
Graham-Campbell, J. 2013 *Viking art*, Thames and Hudson, London
Grinder-Hansen, P. (ed.) 1997 *Margrete 1. Regent of the North. The Kalmar Union 600 years. Essays and catalogue*, Nordic Council of Ministers & National Museum of Denmark, Copenhagen
Haastrup, U. and Egevang, R. (eds) 1985–92 *Danske Kalkmalerier 1–8*, Nationalmuseet, København
Hamel, C. de 2016 *Meetings with remarkable manuscripts*, Allen Lane, Penguin Books, London
Helle, K. (ed.) 2003 *The Cambridge history of Scandinavia Vol. 1: Prehistory to 1520* Cambridge University Press, Cambridge
Heywood, S. 1988 'The round towers of East Anglia', in J. Blair (ed.), *Minsters and parish churches: the local church in transition 950–1200*, Oxford University Committee for Archaeology Monograph 17, Oxford, 169–77
Hybel, N. and Poulsen, B. 2007 *The Danish resources c.1000–1550: growth and recession*, Brill, Leiden
Jensen, J. S. 1973 'Danish money in the fourteenth century', *Mediaeval Scandinavia* 6, 161–71
Jensen, J. S. (ed.) 1995 *Tusindtallets Danske Mønter fra Den kongelige Mønt- og Medaillesamling—Danish coins from the 11th century in the Royal Collection of Coins and Medals*, Nationalmuseet, København
Jensen, J. S. 2005 'Nicholas af Saint Albans—Valdemar Sejrs engelske mønt- og pengemand gennem 30 år', *Nordisk Numismatisk Unions Medlemsblad* 2005(2), 58–62
Jensen, J. S. 2006 'Two hoards of short-cross sterlings from Ribe, and English merchants in Denmark in the middle of the 13th century', in B. Cook and G. Williams (eds), *Coinage and history in the North Sea world, c. AD 500–1250: essays in honour of Marion Archibald*, Brill, Leiden, 471–84
Jensen, J. S. 2015 'Nicholas of St Albans, Anketil and Alfvini: three Danish moneyers of English origin from the 12th and 13th centuries', in L. Larsson, F. Ekengren, B. Helgesson, and B. Söderberg (eds), *Small things, wide horizons: studies in honour of Birgitta Hårdh*, Archaeopress, Oxford, 64–8
Jensen, J. S., Bendixen, K., Liebgott, N.-K., and Lindahl, F. 1992 *Danmarks middelalderlige skattefund c.1050–c.1550*, Det Kongelige Nordiske Oldskriftselskab, København (2 vols, English summaries in Vol. 1, 108–63)
Johannsen, H. 1977 'Engelsk stilinnflytelse, Danmark', *Kulturhistorisk Leksikon for Nordisk Middelalder*, Vol. 21 (Supplementum), Rosenkilde og Bagger, København, 148–55

Johannsen, H. and Smidt, C. M. 1981 *Danmarks Arkitektur. Kirkens huse*, Gyldendal, København

Jørgensen, E. 1908 *Fremmed Indflydelse under den danske Kirkes tidligste Udvikling*, D. Kgl. Danske Vidensk. Selsk. Skrifter, København

Jørgensen, E. 1960 *Historieforskning og Historieskrivning i Danmark indtil Aar 1800*, 2nd edn, Den danske historiske Forening, København (1st edn 1931)

Kock, J. and Roesdahl, E. (eds) 2005 *Boringholm. En østjysk træborg fra 1300-årene*, Jysk Arkæologisk Selskab, Højbjerg

Krins, H. 1968 *Die frühen Steinkirchen Dänemarks*, Dissertation der Universität Hamburg, Hamburg

Kristensen, H. K. 2013 *Klostre i det middelalderlige Danmark*, Jysk Arkæologisk Selskab, Højbjerg

Kristensen, H. K. and Poulsen, B. 2016 *Danmarks byer i middelalderen*, Aarhus University Press, Aarhus

Kristiansen, M. S., Roesdahl, E., and Graham-Campbell, J. (eds) 2015 *Medieval Archaeology in Scandinavia and beyond: history, trends and tomorrow*, Aarhus University Press, Aarhus

Langberg, H. 1982 *Gunhildkorset. Gunhild's cross and medieval court art in Denmark*, Selskabet til udgivelse af danske mindesmærker, København

Lavelle, R. and Roffey, S. (eds) 2016 *Danes in Wessex: the Scandinavian impact on Southern England, c.800–c.1100*, Oxbow, Oxford

Liebgott, N.-K. 1975 'Da klæde var en mærkevare', *Nationalmuseets Arbejdsmark* 1975, 35–46

Liebgott, N.-K. 1982 *Hellige mænd og kvinder*, Wormianum, Højbjerg

Liebgott, N.-K. 1989 *Dansk Middelalderarkæologi*, Gad, København

Lüdtke, H. 1985 *Die mittelalterliche Keramik von Schleswig. Ausgrabung Schild 1971–1975*, Ausgrabungen in Schleswig. Berichte und Studien 4, Neumünster

Lüdtke, H. 1989 *The Bryggen pottery 1: introduction and Pingsdorf Ware*, The Bryggen Papers Supplementary Series 4, Norwegian University Press, Bergen

Mackeprang, M. 1941 *Danmarks middelalderlige døbefonte*, Høst og Søn, København (with English summary)

Mackeprang, M. 1944 *Vore Landsbykirker*, Høst og Søn, København (2nd edn)

Madsen, P. K. 1994 'Byarkæologiens genstandsfund. Kilder til handels- og innovationshistorie, socialtopografiske ledetyper eller blot daglighvets tilfældige affald?', in P. Ingesman and J. V. Jensen (eds), *Danmark i senmiddelalderen*, Aarhus Universitetsforlag, Aarhus, 259–81

Madsen, P. K. 1999 'Ribe between West and East: a North Sea harbour and its Baltic connections 700–1600', in J. Bill and B. L. Clausen (eds), *Maritime topography and the medieval town*, Publications from The National Museum, Copenhagen, 197–202

Madsen, P. K. and Stilke, H. 2001 'Bleiglasierte Irdenware', in H. Lüdtke and K. Schietzel (eds), *Handbuch zur mittelalterlichen Keramik in Nordeuropa 1*, Wachholtz Verlag, Neumünster, 539–611

Messenger, A. W. B. 1947 *The heraldry of Canterbury Cathedral: the Great Cloister Vault*, The Office of the Friends Christ Church Gateway Canterbury, Canterbury

Nedkvitne, A. 2014 *The German Hansa and Bergen 1100–1600*, Böhlau Verlag, Köln

Nielsen, H. M. M. 2008 'Krogen: the medieval predecessor of Kronborg', *Chateau Gaillard* 23, 315–28

Nørlund, P. 1968 *Gyldne Altre*, Wormianum, Aarhus (1st edn 1926)

Nyborg, E. 2008 'De gulbrune kirker. Om brugen af Helsingborg-sandsten i Nordsjællands romanske kirkebyggeri, *Aarbøger for Nordisk Oldkyndighed og Historie* 2008, 213–26

Nyborg, E. 2014 'Possible English influence on Danish polychrome wooden sculpture of the thirteenth century', in N. L. W. Streeton and K. Kollandsrud (eds), *Paint and piety: collected essays on medieval painting and polycrome sculpture*, Archetype Publications, London, 93–110

Olsen, O. 1960 'St. Jørgensbjerg Kirke. Arkæologiske undersøgelser i murværk og gulv', *Aarbøger for Nordisk Oldkyndighed og Histoire* 1960, 1–71

Olsen, R. A. 2014 *Danish medieval castles*, Aarhus University Press, Aarhus

Orduna, J. R. 1995 *Middelalderlige klædeplomber—blyplomber fra klæde importeret til Danmark inden 1600*, Afd. for Middelalder-arkæologi og Middelalderarkæologisk Nyhedsbrev, Højbjerg

Østergård, E. and Rogers, P. W. 2005 'Tekstiler, reb og snor', in J. Kock and E. Roesdahl (eds), *Boringholm. En jysk træborg fra 1300-årene*, Jysk Arkæologisk Selskab, Højbjerg, 191–204

Pedersen, A. 2004 'Anglo-Danish contact across the North Sea in the eleventh century: a survey of the Danish archaeological evidence', in J. Adams and K. Holman (eds), *Scandinavia and Europe 800–1350: contact, conflict, and coexistence*, Brepols, Turnhout, 43–67

Poulsen, B. 1996 'Roundtable contribution', in T. J. Runyan, B. Poulsen, H. Wernicke, and N. Jörn, 'Roundtable. Notes on John D. Fudge', *Cargoes, embargos, and emissaries: the commercial and political interaction of England and the German Hanse, 1450–1510* [Toronto 1995] with a Response by John D. Fudge, *International Journal of Maritime History* 1996(8), 250–3 [247–58]

Poulsen, B. 2010 'Økonomi og erhverv', in S. B. Christensen (ed.), *Ribe Bys Historie 1. 710–1520*, Dansk Center for Byhistorie & Esbjerg Kommune, Esbjerg, 201–43

Poulsen, B. and Sindbæk, S. M. (eds) 2011 *Settlement and lordship in Viking and early medieval Scandinavia*, Brepols, Turnhout

Riis, T. 1988 *Should auld acquaintance be forgot... Scottish-Danish relations c.1450–1707*, I–II, Odense University Press, Odense

Roesdahl, E. 1982 'Dansepige i Ålborg', *hikuin* 8, 29–34

Roesdahl, E. (ed.) 1999 *Dagligliv i Danmarks middelalder. En arkæologisk kulturhistorie*, Gyldendal, København

Roesdahl, E. 2007 'Denmark-England in the eleventh century: the growing archaeological evidence for contacts across the North Sea', in N. Lund (ed.), *Beretning fra seksogtyvende tværfaglige vikingesymposium*, Forlaget Hikuin og Afdeling for Middelalderarkæologi, Højbjerg, 7–31

Roesdahl, E. 2008 'The emergence of Denmark and the reign of Harald Bluetooth', in S. Brink (ed.) in collaboration with N. Price, *The Viking world*, Routledge, London, 652–64

Roesdahl, E. 2010 'Danish sponsors, English lead, Vikings, and a new roof for the church of Sainte-Geneviève in Paris', in K. de Groote, D. Tys, and M. Pieters (eds), *Exchanging medieval material culture: studies on archaeology and history presented to Frans Verhaeghe* (Relicta Monografieen 4), Flemish Heritage Institute, Brussels, 285–8

Roesdahl, E. 2014 'Situation', in E. Roesdahl, S. M. Sindbæk, A. Pedersen, and D. M. Wilson (eds), *Aggersborg: the Viking-Age settlement and fortress*, National Museum of Denmark and Jutland Archaeological Society, Højbjerg, 17–30

Roesdahl, E. and Wilson, D. (eds) 1992 *From Viking to crusader: Scandinavia and Europe 800–1200*, Nordic Council of Ministers, Copenhagen

Rydbeck, O. 1935 *Den medeltida borgen i Skanör*, Gleerup, Lund

Saxtorph, N. M. 1986 *Danmarks kalkmalerier*, Politikens forlag, København

Spejlborg, M. B. 2014 'Anglo-Danish connections and the organisation of the early Danish church: contribution to a debate', *Networks and neighbours: comparisons and correlations*, vol. 2(1), 78–95

Søvsø, M. 2012 'The bishop of Ribe's rural property in Lustrup', *Danish Journal of Archaeology* 1, 4–26

Stirnemann, P. 1999 'The Copenhagen Psalter', in E. Petersen (ed.), *Living words & luminous pictures: medieval book culture in Denmark*, The Royal Library and Moesgaard Museum, Copenhagen, 67–77

Stratford, N. 1987 'Gothic ivory carving', in J. Alexander and P. Binski (eds), *The art of chivalry: art in Plantagenet England 1200–1400*, Royal Academy of Arts, London, 107–13

Suchodolski, S. 2012 *Numizmatyca średniowieczna. Moneta źródlem archeologicznym historycznym i ikonograficznym*, Trio, Warsaw

Suchodolski, S. 2014 'Den senmiddelalderlige guldskat og koggen fra Vejby strand, Nordsjælland', *Nordisk Numismatisk Årsskrift*, ny serie 1, 127–37

Tønnesen, A. 1985 *Helsingørs udenlandske borgere og indbyggere c.1550–1600*, Forlaget Misteltenen, Ringe

Vince, A. 1996 'English pottery imports in medieval Denmark', *By, marsk og geest. Kulturhistorisk årbog for Ribe-egnen* 8, 23–9

Wienberg, J. 2007 'Romanske runde kirketårne—et skandinavisk perspektiv', *hikuin* 36, 101–20

Williams, D. 1997 *Late Saxon stirrup-strap mounts: a classification and catalogue*, Council for British Archaeology Research Report 111, York

CHAPTER 59

....

LOOKING SOUTH

Spain and Portugal in the Middle Ages

....

CHRISTOPHER M. GERRARD
AND J. AVELINO GUTIÉRREZ-GONZÁLEZ

DURING the Middle Ages the Atlantic seaboard was among the most important commercial networks of medieval Europe, a contemporary to better-known economic and cultural networks in the Mediterranean and the Baltic, a rival to the land routes of the European isthmuses and a nursery of exploration for Spanish and Portuguese explorers of the fifteenth and sixteenth centuries. In this chapter we explore the archaeological contribution to our understanding of contact and trade between the Iberian Peninsula and Britain against a background of fundamental historical scholarship (e.g. for Spain, Childs 1978; Connell-Smith 1954; Ferreira 1988; for Portugal, Lomax, and Oakley 1988; Miranda 2013). We begin with pilgrimage (for which see also Chapter 40), followed by a discussion of trade in bulk foodstuffs and raw materials before considering the evidence for movement in manufactured goods and a selection of emerging themes.

PILGRIMS

....

Throughout the later medieval period Santiago de Compostela in Galicia, in north-west Spain, rivalled Rome in popularity as a pilgrim destination. Some disembarked on the west coast of France, generally on the Garonne or Bayonne estuary, and made their way on foot across the Pyrenees along the *camino francés*, over the Roncesvalles pass and westwards (Figure 59.1), while others sailed directly south from Bristol, Dartmouth, Falmouth, Fowey, Plymouth, and Poole in south-west England or from Welsh ports such as Pembroke. Their preferred destination was either La Coruña with its Roman lighthouse or smaller harbours such as Noya or Padrón.

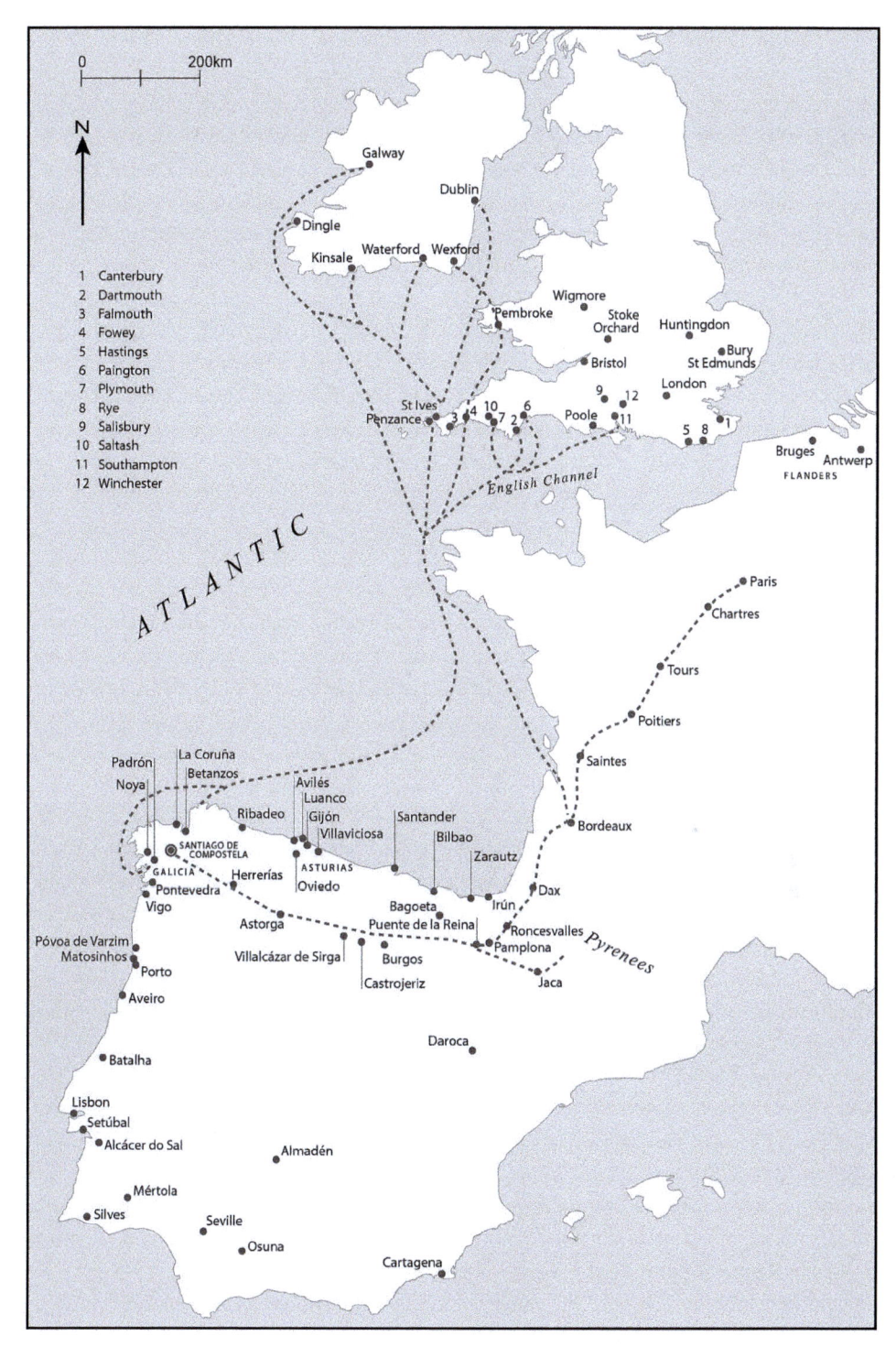

FIGURE 59.1 Main medieval routes to Santiago de Compostela and places mentioned in the text

(© Alejandra Gutiérrez)

The infrastructure required to cater for large numbers of pilgrims included everything from roads and bridges (such as that at Puente de la Reina in Navarre built in the mid-eleventh century), taverns and inns, to wayside crosses and milestones, as well as hospices and chapels; there was already a specific English hospital at Herrerías (León) before 1178 (Candy 2009; Tate 2003; Vázquez de Parga et al. 1998, 308). The geographical concentration of English silver pennies and groats in Galicia in the period 1327–1461 is one testimony to the consumer tendencies of this mass medieval tourism and the kind of direct maritime traffic which provided little opportunity for monetary exchange until landfall in Spain (Roma 2003; Suárez Otero 2004). Individual finds also have their own story to tell. The pointed oval pilgrim badge from Villasirga (Villalcázar de Sirga, Palencia) recovered from a river near Huntingdon (UK) indicates one of the many possible rest points along the *camino* (Menéndez 1992, 367). Further west at Castrojeriz near Burgos the grave of one pilgrim contained both English and French coins dating *c.*1360, presumably the purse of one traveller who never reached his destination (Rueda and Sáez 1992). Once at Santiago the throng of northerners joined other nationalities; an estimated 1400–5500 pilgrims arrived each day (Stopford 1994). At the cathedral, pilgrims were able to take confession, obtain indulgences, and leave donations, among them a silver groat and two silver pennies (one falsified) of Edward III which were discovered inside the reliquary bust containing the head of St James the Less (Suárez Otero 1998b; 1999). Sown into their clothing or packed away in their scrips, pilgrims also carried symbols of their saintly allegiances. Badges from Canterbury in England have been found at Osuna and Seville in southern Spain and at the castles of Silves and Mértola in Portugal (Ruiz Cecilia 2011; Gomes 2011, 291–3) but whether these travelled with English visitors is unclear.

On the return journey some pilgrims carried natural scallop shells (*Pecten maximus*), the emblem of St James (Köster 1983; Suárez Otero 1998a). British finds are discussed by Yeoman (Chapter 40). The familiar scallop motif was also reproduced on pendant mounts (Franco 2005a; Osma 1916) and more elaborate items such as the miniature scallops of carved jet mounted in silver attached to natural scallop shells found at Brooks Wharf, London (Spencer 1998, 244–8). Much rarer in archaeological contexts are the miniature copies of pilgrim staffs (*bordoncillos*) made out of bone or ivory (Moralejo and López Alsina 1993, 130). Quite possibly the expense of these objects was out of reach for many pilgrims who preferred smaller souvenirs such as the products of the local jet workshops established at Compostela, La Coruña, Villaviciosa, or Oviedo in Asturias, where a fifteenth-/sixteenth-century workshop has been excavated (Estrada 2014; Ferreira 1988, 209; Franco 1996; Osma, 1916, 66, 116–23) (Figure 59.2). Possible Spanish jet items found in England include a fifteenth-century jet and silver pendant from Edinburgh and parts of a jet cross from a fourteenth-century garderobe pit deposit in Winchester (Standley 2013, 85–6; Qualmann 1991, 69–71).

Galicia simply did not have the range of lucrative products to take much advantage of the constant stream of pilgrims northwards. Licences for pilgrim ships preserved in the Calendars of Close and Patent Rolls throughout the fourteenth and fifteenth centuries, however, do make mention of return cargoes of 'victuals and other merchandise'

FIGURE 59.2 Staff or *bordón* fragments (top on the right and point on the left) found during excavations in Oviedo by Rogelio Estrada in 2009. The same excavation also found evidence of jet carving and jet objects which confirm the presence of workshops in urban areas. Below are Compostela pilgrims as depicted in the *Book of Trades* of 1568, showing the typical attire by which pilgrims were identified, including the scallop shell and staffs placed both on hats and capes

(© R. Estrada); (© Deutsche Fotothek, State and University Library Dresden, public domain)

(Webb 1999, 187) and a 100 tonne capacity boat returning with only thirty pilgrims aboard certainly had space for local honey (to Southampton in 1428) and especially wine (for example, to Dartmouth in 1411). Overall, as Wendy Childs (1998) has indicated, this trade was small scale and opportunistic by comparison with the Basque trade in iron further east. Items of value did occasionally travel, however, among them corporeal relics. One of the hands of St James, apparently given to Matilda when she visited Compostela in 1125, was passed to the wealthy Benedictine abbey at Reading (UK) which had been founded by her father Henry I four years earlier. It was later visited there by Catherine of Aragon and by Philip II with his wife Mary Tudor (Iglesias 1998, 115; Vázquez de Parga et al. 1998).

The tremendous reach of St James and Compostela across frontiers is evident in heraldry, dedications, and artistic representations. In York Minster a window depicting St James was donated in 1381 in lieu of a pilgrimage to Santiago and in the chapel of St James the Great in Stoke Orchard (Gloucestershire) there is a cycle of twenty-eight scenes of mural paintings illustrating the life of St James dating c.1190–1220 (Rouse and Baker 1967). From Ivy Church Priory near Salisbury there is also part of a sixteenth century stained glass panel depicting the head of St James Major wearing a pilgrim's hat with a scallop shell (Eavis 2012, 227). Numerous other churches throughout Britain were dedicated to St James before the sixteenth century including the church at Bury St Edmunds, today the cathedral, with scallop shells as a motif on its west front (Gransden 2007), and the Augustinian house at Wigmore which was founded in 1131 following a pilgrimage to Santiago by Oliver de Merlimond. It has been suggested that a map of St James dedications marks out some of the main routes to south-western ports where pilgrims embarked for Galicia (Tate 2003, 16).

Trade in Bulk Foodstuffs and Raw Materials

The shipping of heavy goods by water had significant cost advantages and was generally reserved for the very largest vessels before being transhipped onto smaller craft upon arrival. Of particular importance in this category were wool and cloth, metal and metal ores, and bulk foodstuffs such as wine, oil, salt, and sugar. All these products are elusive archaeologically but there is an emerging 'archaeology of production' which should be noted. In the immediate hinterland of Bilbao the iron ore mines lay close to the sea and some of these have been investigated archaeologically together with the bloomeries and forges where the ore was once processed (Azcárate et al. 2011; Díez de Salazar 1983; Etxezarraga 2004; Franco Pérez 2007), for example those at Bagoeta, Álava (Figure 59.3). Documentary evidence makes clear that Spanish iron was frequently marketed in a half-finished state to be re-worked as was the case for the cramps and window-bars at St Stephen's Chapel at Westminster in 1294 (Colvin 1963, 1, 512).

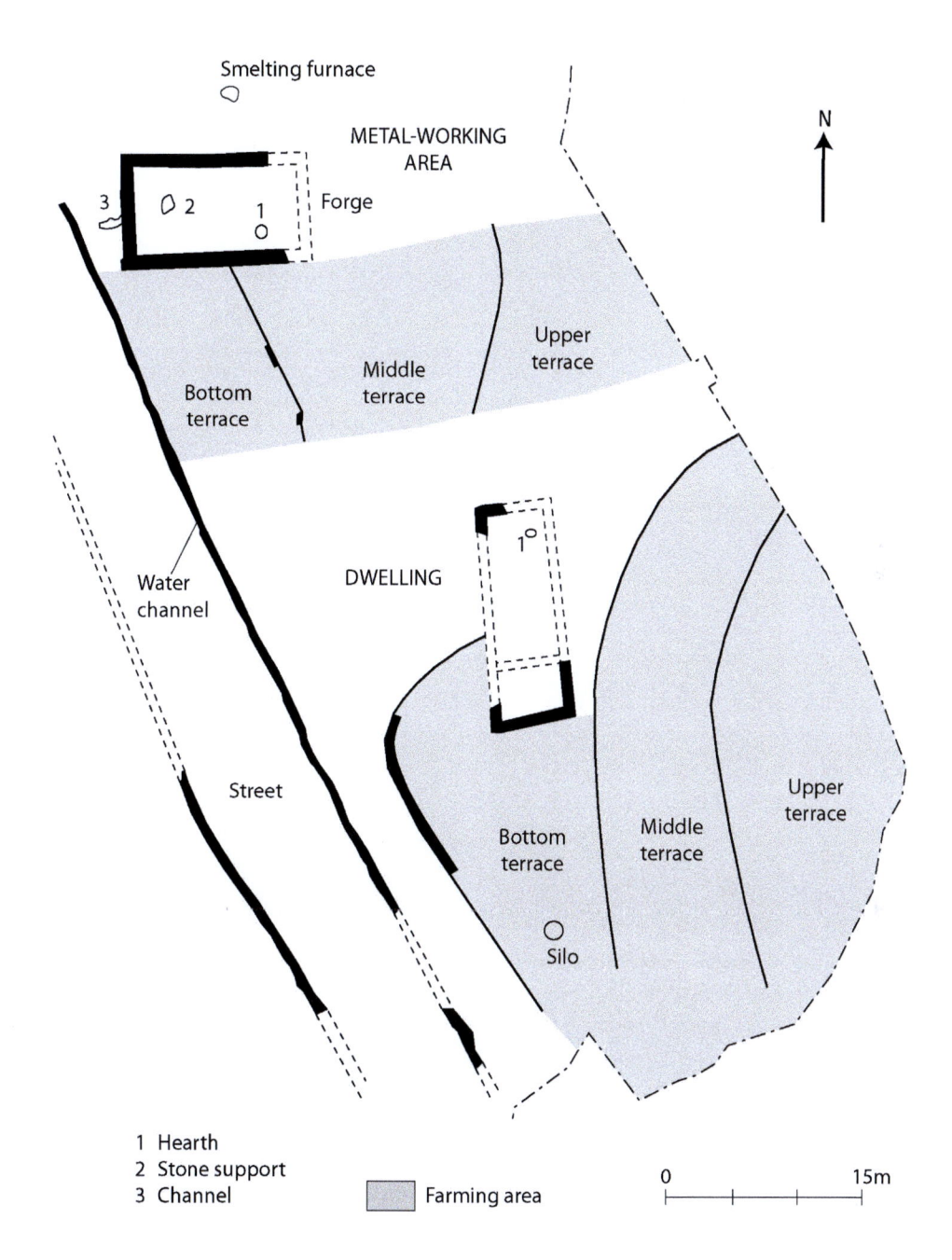

FIGURE 59.3 Excavations at Bagoeta, Álava, documented long-lived ironworks (seventh to fourteenth centuries), including domestic dwelling and workshops, bloomeries, and iron-working activities (redrawn by Alejandra Gutiérrez, after Azcárate et al. 2011, open access)

FIGURE 59.4 A fifteenth-century sugar factory under excavation in Agaete, Las Palmas de Gran Canaria, showing the main rooms (3, 4), water channel (1), wall to support the mill wheel (2), all cut by the construction of a recent road. (Below) Some of the sugar moulds as found during excavation

(© Arqueocanaria SL)

Likewise, circular or square wine presses cut into the bedrock can be found across Spain and Portugal (e.g. Almeida et al. 1999; Antunes and Faria 2002; Brochado 2001). Red and sweet wines were shipped from Andalusia while sweet Portuguese wines, said to be much like the modern *vinho licoroso* (Rose 2011, 110), tended to be traded through Porto. White wines from Galicia included those from the Miño region as well as *vinos de Viveiro* from the growing area around La Coruña from Ribadeo to Betanzos (Ferreira 1988; Miraz 2013, 151). Salt, meanwhile, also came into English ports from Setúbal in the Sado estuary and Aveiro in Portugal through Porto where the salt was stored and sold from warehouses near the quay (Morais Barros 2008). Various sites are documented, such as Alcácer do Sal, while others are inferred from the presence of rock-cut tanks such as those at Póvoa de Varzim and Matosinhos, to the north of the Duero (Fabião 1997, 46) and other remains (Quesada 1995; Urteaga 1994). Some of the best documented are those in Álava, which were in used until the twentieth century (Plata 2003; 2008–9).

The cultivation of sugar cane was introduced to the Iberian Peninsula during the Arab conquest and is documented from the tenth century although the earliest archaeological evidence dates to the fourteenth and fifteenth century in the Spanish Levant (Gisbert 1991). Production seems then to have extended along the Andalusian coast and to the Canaries and Madeira (Ouerfelli 2007). The export of sugar to Flanders, England, and France began in the middle of the fifteenth century (Childs 1992), the first known record for exported Portuguese sugar in England being April 1478; the main fifteenth- and sixteenth-century production site identified so far in Portugal is on the Tagus estuary facing Lisbon (Teixeira et al. 2015). Archaeological excavation has produced evidence for millstones to grind the canes, stone weights for presses to extract the pulp and juice, as well as the tell-tale ceramic cones needed to clarify the sugar and produce the molasses for export as powder or loaves (Barroso et al. 2014; Fábregas 2000; Malpica 1990; 1991; 1995) (Figure 59.4).

Manufactured Goods, Minor Trade, and Smaller Archaeological Objects

Many other commodities travelled north in smaller quantities. In the fifteenth century the Andalusians and Portuguese in particular came to specialize in semi-luxury goods with a fast turnover such as sweet white wine, wax, scarlet grain from Kermes, figs, honey, high-quality leather, dates, salt, and hides. By the end of the century succade (sugar-preserved fruits), marmalade, orchell, bay leaves, almonds, oranges, pomegranates, dried and candied fruit, and grain of paradise (*Aframomum melegueta*) could all be added to this list, not to mention cork (Childs 1992; Miranda 2014). West African ivory was sold in Bruges in September 1465 by the Portuguese and their first ships from Calicut in India docked in English ports in January 1504 with spices and peppers aboard. From southern Spanish ports came almonds, treacle, and pine nuts as well as less expected imports such as licorice from further north in Navarre (Childs 1978). Archaeological evidence for figs, almonds, raisins or currants, and even olives, are all known from multiple medieval sites in the UK, though their precise origins are not (Moffett 2006).

Many items seem unlikely to persist in the archaeological record. Castilian soap, sheep and coney skins exported from the north coast of Spain, the leather bought by medieval English cordwainers (Cherry 1991, 308), the Spanish silk stockings worn by Henry VIII (Walton 1991, 344), and the Spanish felts used to make hats are unlikely survivors. Others were doubtless recycled such as the tin, brass, and pewter exported from England to Spain and Portugal (Hatcher and Barker 1974). Some were rare to begin with, like the parrots or 'popinjays' arriving from Portugal by the end of the fifteenth century

(Childs 1992); although parrot bones have not been found in medieval England yet, illustrations are frequent in manuscripts from the mid-thirteenth century (Albarella et al. 2009, 89; Yapp 1981). Monkeys were imported from the twelfth century as high-status companion pets (Walker-Meikle 2012, 13). A small Barbary ape was found among the remarkable collection of artefacts recovered from Pit 14 at Cuckoo Lane, Southampton, and dated to c.1300 (Noddle 1975); further examples have also been excavated at Bristol Castle (unpublished) and London (Pipe 1992).

Two items of Atlantic exchange which have survived seem to do so because of their high value and protected context. *Opus Anglicanum* are English medieval embroideries in silk and silver-gilt thread on linen which were decorated with pearls and precious stones; these costly pieces were symbols of wealth and power in both the secular and ecclesiastical worlds. The fourteenth-century Daroca Cope (Zaragoza, Spain) is an ecclesiastical vestment that belonged to Pope Benedict XIII, it is richly decorated with scenes from the Bible, the lives of saints and venerated north European kings (including St Edward the Confessor, St Edmund of Bury, and St Olaf of Norway), and is one of several pieces known in Spain (Franco 2005b).

The other survivals are devotional panels which were carved from English alabaster. Well-known pieces are those from Cartagena (dated 1340–80) and the cathedral in Santiago, donated in 1456 by an English pilgrim (Cheetham 1984, 147; Franco 2005c). Mostly they were gilded, painted, and grouped side-by-side in a wood-mounted frieze or else rested on the altar or table top rather like the Flemish diptych paintings with which they are contemporary. While some may have been sold abroad at the Reformation, the majority were exported. In c.1390 a Dartmouth merchant ship bound for Seville had 'ymagez d'alabastre' aboard (Baildon 1896, 45). Today they are found all across France, northern Spain, and Portugal, particularly along the north coast close to sea ports and estuaries, a distribution which may suggest the occasional advantageous sale rather than a large-scale export venture (e.g. Alcolea 1971; Catálogo 1977) (Figure 59.5).

Medieval pottery imports have long caught the eye of specialists because they can be a telling archaeological indicator of commercial contact and personal exchange. Between the thirteenth and fifteenth centuries the major sources of imported pottery were along Spain's Mediterranean coastline where workshops produced fabulous lustrewares, jugs, *albarelli*, and dishes (for an overview of the major centres of production, see Gutiérrez 2000). Early Andalusian lustrewares of thirteenth- and fourteenth-century date are known from about twenty-five sites in Britain, mainly in southern England where they tend to be linked with other high-status finds such as imported glass; Valencian lustrewares of the fifteenth century are more generously recorded at over one hundred sites and their distribution reaches far inland (Gutiérrez 2012). Most of the known forms are small dishes and plates, open forms which could not be found in contemporary British workshops. Many were intended for display or used as containers for exotic imports, some being kept for surprisingly long periods. In Worcester an almost complete Valencian plate of the late fourteenth century was found in a seventeenth-century pit associated with clearing of a nearby house (Bryant 2004, 339).

FIGURE 59.5 Alabaster figures from an altarpiece made in England c.1440–60 and originally installed at the church of Campo del Tablado, Castropol, Asturias, including the Virgin and Child, St Mary Magdalene (with rosary and perfume jar), St Catherine of Alexandria (with the wheel and sword), St Margaret of Antioch (with the long cross killing the dragon), and St Apollonia (with the pliers and a large molar)

(© National Gallery of Art, Washington, open access)

In the fifteenth century there was a re-alignment in this pottery trade during which Bruges was eclipsed by Antwerp and London became the dominant English port, followed by Bristol and other south coast English ports (for overviews see e.g. Blackmore 1994; Gutiérrez 2014). In this later trade pottery was often merely a container for some other more valuable product. Globular and elongated jars suitable for transporting semi-liquids such as capers, chickpeas, honey, as well as wine and olive oil have been found at more than 150 sites across Britain and Ireland, including the Armada shipwrecks (Gerrard et al. 1995, 284). These *botijas* originated in the Seville area, as did 'Morisco' wares, the tin-glazed pottery which was exported in such massive numbers across the Atlantic to the New World in the sixteenth century, though it is less common in Britain.

The dominant pottery type exported from Portugal during this period was so-called 'Merida ware', a distinctive micaceous coarseware found on excavations from the thirteenth century onwards, particularly at ports and magnate residences. Quantities are more significant in sixteenth- and seventeenth-century contexts, numbering in the thousands of sherds at St Andrews Street, Plymouth, and Upper Bugle Street, Southampton, for example. 'Merida ware' is a term that encompasses a range of fabrics and probably sources (granitic inclusions are common to the north and west of the Iberian Peninsula); some of these wares were produced in the important port of Aveiro, but not all, and other major workshops still await discovery. Analysis of the contents of Merida ware costrels suggests a variety of possible contents, medicinal 'polypody' mixed with milk in the case of one vessel found aboard the *Mary Rose*, Henry VIII's warship sunk in 1545, while cinnabar was identified in another costrel from Carmarthen in Wales (Gutiérrez 2012). The pots themselves may, of course, have been re-used although the cinnabar, a red mercuric sulphide pigment which was used in dyes and paints, probably originated at the mines near Ciudad Real where archaeological evidence for the production of mercury has been identified at Almadén (Hernández 1996).These more pragmatic uses aside, imports from Spain and Portugal, especially the glazed finewares, became part of the cultural setting of the rich merchant, gentry and nobility, a point which is well illustrated by the assemblage from Acton Court near Bristol where 20–43 per cent of the pottery from major contexts was imported, including Merida-type wares, Valencian lustrewares, Seville tin-glazed pottery, and a variety of Italian imports (Vince and England 2004). This pottery group has been directly linked to the visit of Henry VIII and Anne Boleyn in the summer of 1535.

Decorated Spanish floor tiles were sometimes exported too, especially in the sixteenth century when the domestic industry in Britain was in decline. The largest collection (735 tiles) outside the Iberian Peninsula and the New World is in Bristol at the Lord Mayor's Chapel, with which the Poyntz family from Acton Court were also linked (Gutiérrez 2007). This is one of about thirty sites from which tiles from Valencia and Seville are currently known in Britain (Williams 1995). Most are *cuenca* or *arista* (otherwise known as 'hollow') tiles, often re-set and located in churches and monastic houses in the south and south-west of England. Very probably these tiles once formed part of a varied cargo making its way from the Guadalquivir estuary northwards, with a stopping off point at Lisbon where many similar examples are known from standing buildings and excavation (Matos 2012; Simões 1990). Archaeological evidence for production is scarce or for later periods (for example, Pérez 2008; Pleguezuelo 1992).

Discussion

There were major changes in the volume and direction of Atlantic trade during this period which can only be glossed here. The first was the 'reconnection' of the Atlantic with Mediterranean economies through the re-opening of sea routes through the straits of Gibraltar in the thirteenth century as a result of the Christian conquest. The second was the interlinking of the west coast of Africa with northern ports in the second half of the fifteenth century which brought commodities like ivory to wealthy consumers. The third was the new geographies and economies presented by the discovery of the New World and the opportunities for transatlantic commerce. Throughout the Middle Ages, however, the fortunes of merchants were never immune to economic and social trends, periods of truce, changes in political allegiance, and shifting frontiers (for examples affecting pilgrimage, see Echevarría 2007). The improved commercial relations between the English and Portuguese in the second half of the fourteenth century which brought Portuguese wines to English tables had benefitted from marriage ties between the royal families (Goodman 1994). The marriage in 1254 of Henry III's son, the future Edward I, to Eleanor of Castile, Alfonso X's sister and daughter of Fernando III of Leon and Castile, brought important cultural repercussions. Her role in the introduction of 'Spanish style' in relation to textiles, the decorative arts, and artistic exchange has been cited as an exemplar of cross-cultural exchange between England and Castile (Parsons 1977; Walker 2007). The thirteenth-century gabled tomb chests of Alfonso VIII and Leonor of England at Las Huelgas, outside Burgos, and the fifteenth-century royal tombs of D. João and Queen Philippa at Batalha in Portugal are just two enduring symbols of these royal alliances.

While these elite relationships were certainly positive for trade, the resilience of regional, national, and supra-national economies in times of crisis was impressive. Exeter, to take one example, was relatively immune to the political and economic turmoil of the 1380s–1430s because of the strength of the local carrying trade; Spanish and Portuguese products reached the city on board English sailing ships, having been stocked up at Bristol, Southampton, Dartmouth or Plymouth. Kowaleski (1995) estimates that more than 90 per cent of the trade in foreign dyestuffs, linen, foodstuffs, and spices in the 1380s and 1390s moved along the coast in this way. Nor was the movement of objects restricted to formal mechanisms of exchange. Piracy, smuggling, and raids all provided opportunity. For example in 1377 the Castilian and French naval forces plundered along the English coast: Rye was attacked, Plymouth and Hastings burnt. Eight years later, it was Londoners who apprehended Portuguese ships in lieu of full compensation for borrowed money (Miranda 2014). At other times, objects were given as gifts or travelled among the personal effects of pilgrims and here there is more work to be done in understanding how archaeological objects from far away became bound up in the construction and display of local social and cultural identities. What was the motivation behind the purchase of evidently exotic Spanish pottery for the table, for example? Of particular interest in this respect is the role of foreign merchants who lived in semi-permanent communities abroad and maintained a high degree of independence (Childs 1978, 182). In Lisbon in the fifteenth century, for example, some of the English community of merchants had spent twenty years trading in Iberia (Childs 1992). To what extent do archaeological objects provide a measure of the absorption of Atlantic cultural codes and lifestyle practices, as has been suggested for the Hansa (Gaimster 2007; Mehler 2009)?

Conclusion

Anglo-Iberian contact in the Middle Ages has left an oddly skewed signature in the archaeological record. A recent numismatic survey in the UK identified only fifty medieval coins from Portugal and slightly fewer from the Spanish kingdoms, starting with coins dating to the middle of the thirteenth century and including the Islamic gold coins referred to in English records as 'oboli de Musc' (Kelleher 2013). Most of these were apparently given as ceremonial gifts or made into plate and jewellery (Nightingale 1985, 128). This illustrates the challenges well: only a limited number of commodities, among them pilgrim badges, coins, pottery, jet, and alabasters, can be tracked with any confidence and, even here, the wider context of exchange needs to be carefully scrutinized (for coins, see Cook 1999).

Academic challenges aside, there is significant contemporary interest in the historical past of the communities living along the Atlantic coast. The redevelopment of run-down port areas for housing has encouraged both investment and discovery, the French Quarter of Southampton (UK) being one such example (Brown and Hardy 2011). In Spain, there has been major funding of public displays and purpose-built museums, as at Pontevedra in 2009 and Santander in 2006–13, as well as the expansion of existing museums at Vigo, Santiago, La Coruña, Luanco, Avilés, Gijón, Oviedo, Santander, Bilbao, Zarautz, and Irún where large new assemblages of finds have warranted the creation of additional museum space. The same could be said of Lisbon, the largest major city on the Atlantic seaboard both now and in the medieval period, where research and improved public display are beginning to make their mark. The potential exists for greater integration of coastal heritage and the development of thematic itineraries and it is in international partnerships of this kind and through the 'mining' of large archaeological and historical datasets that the future probably lies.

References Cited

Albarella, U., Beech, M., Curl, J., Locker, A., Moreno García, M., and Mulville, J. 2009 *Norwich Castle: excavations and historical survey, 1987–98. Part III: a zooarchaeological study*, East Anglian Archaeology Occasional Papers 22, Gressenhall

Alcolea, S. 1971 'Relieves ingleses de alabastro en España: ensayo de catalogación', *Archivo Español de Arte* 137–54, 174–6

Almeida, C. B. de, Antunes, J. M., and Faria, P. B. 1999 'Lagares cavados na rocha: uma reminiscência do passado na tradição da técnica vinícola no vale do Douro', *Revista Portuguesa de Arqueologia* 2(2), 97–103

Antunes, J. V. and Faria, P. B. 2002 'Lagares do Alto Douro sul. Tipologias e tecnologia', *Douro: Estudos e Documentos* 7.14, 65–77

Azcárate, A., Martínez, J. M., and Solaun, J. L. 2011 'Metalurgia y hábitat en el País Vasco de época medieval: el asentamiento ferrón de Bagoeta, Álava (ss. VII–XIV d. C.)', *Arqueología y Territorio Medieval* 18, 71–89

Baildon, W. P. 1896 *Select cases in Chancery AD 1364 to 1471*, Selden Society, London

Barroso, V., Quintana, P., and Marrero, C. 2014 'La intervención arqueológica en el ingenio de Agaete (Gran Canaria), siglos XV–XVII', in A. Viña (ed), *Azúcar y mecenazgo en Gran Canaria: el oro de las Islas, siglos XV–XVI*, Ediciones del Cabido de Gran Canaria, Las Palmas de Gran Canaria, 287–339

Blackmore, L. 1994 'Pottery, the port and the populace: the imported pottery of London 1300–1600', *Medieval Ceramics* 18, 29–44

Brochado, C. L. 2001 'A lagareta de contrapeso da Quinta da Fonte, Monção', *Douro: Estudos e Documentos* 6:12, 63–76

Brown, R. and Hardy, A. 2011 *Trade and prosperity, war and poverty: an archaeological and historical investigation into Southampton's French Quarter*, Oxford Archaeology, Oxford

Bryant, V. 2004 'Death and desire: factors affecting the consumption of pottery in medieval Worcestershire', *Medieval Ceramics* 28, 117–24

Candy, J. 2009 *The archaeology of pilgrimage on the Camino de Santiago de Compostela: a landscape perspective*, British Archaeological Reports International Series 1948, Oxford

Catálogo, 1977 *Alabastros medievais ingleses*, Museu Nacional de Arte Antiga, Lisbon

Cheetham, F. W. 1984 *English medieval alabasters, with a catalogue of the collection in the Victoria and Albert Museum*, Phaidon, Oxford

Cherry, J. 1991 'Leather', in J. Blair and N. Ramsay (eds), *English medieval industries: craftsmen, techniques, products*, The Hambledon Press, London, 295–318

Childs, W. 1978 *Anglo-Castilian trade in the later Middle Ages*, Manchester University Press, Manchester

Childs, W. 1992 'Anglo-Portuguese trade in the 15th century', *Transactions of the Royal Historical Society* 2, 195–219

Childs, W. 1998 'English ships and the pilgrim route to Santiago', *Actas del II Congreso Internacional de Estudios Jacobeos: rutas atlánticas de peregrinación a Santiago de Compostela*, Santiago de Compostela, 79–91

Colvin, H. 1963 *The History of the King's Works, Vol. 1: the Middle Ages*, HMSO, London

Connell-Smith, G. 1954 *Forerunners of Drake: a study of English trade with the Spanish in the early Tudor period*, Longmans, Green and Co., London

Cook, B. 1999 'Foreign coins in medieval England', *Local coins, foreign coins, Italy and Europe, 11th–15th centuries*, Società numismatica italiana, Milan, 231–84

Díez de Salazar, L. M. 1983 *Ferrerías de Guipúzcoa (siglos XIV–XVI)*, Haranburu, San Sebastián

Eavis, A. 2012 'Window glass', in P. Saunders (ed.), *Salisbury and South Wiltshire Museum Medieval Catalogue Part 4*, Salisbury and South Wiltshire Museum Medieval, Salisbury

Echevarría, A. 2007 'The shrine as mediator: England, Castile, and the pilgrimage to Compostela', in M. Bullón-Fernández (ed.), *England and Iberia in the Middle Ages, 12th–15th century: cultural, literary, and political exchanges*, Palgrave Macmillan, Basingstoke, 47–66

Estrada, R. 2014 'Desenterrando *istum locum, quod dicunt Oueto*: excavaciones arqueológicas en la ampliación del Museo de Bellas Artes de Asturias', *X–XI Ciclos de conferencias de la SOF*, Oviedo, 119–68

Etxezarraga, I. 2004 'Paleometalurgia del hierro en el País Vasco Cantábrico: las haizeolak. Un estado de la cuestión', *Munibe* 56, 87–104

Fábregas, A. P. 1994 'Tecnología del azúcar: el ingenio azucarero de La Palma', *IV Congreso de Arqueología Medieval Española*, Vol. III, Diputación Provincial de Alicante, Alicante, 945–50

Fábregas, A. P. 2000 *Producción y comercio del azúcar en el Mediterráneo medieval: el ejemplo del reino de Granada*, Universidad de Granada, Granada

Fabião, C. 1997 'A exploração dos recursos marinhos', in A. Moutinho Alarcão (ed.), *Portugal romano: a exploração dos recursos naturais*, Museo Nacional de Arqueologia, Lisboa, 35–58

Ferreira, E. M. 1988 *Galicia en el comercio marítimo medieval*, Universidad de Santiago de Compostela, Santiago de Compostela

Franco, Á. 1996 'Las minas de azabache asturianas y el arte', *Actas de las I Jornadas sobre Minería y Tecnología en la Edad Media Peninsular*, Fundación Hullera Vasco-Leonesa, León, 91–100

Franco, Á. 2005a 'Iconografía jacobea en azabache', in M. C. Lacarra (ed.), *Los caminos de Santiago: arte, historia y literatura*, Institución Fernando el Católico, Zaragoza, 169–212

Franco, Á. 2005b 'Arte y arqueología medievales de Aragón en el Museo Arqueológico Nacional', *Artigrama* 20, 77–109

Franco, Á. 2005c 'Un camino de ida y vuelta: alabastros ingleses en España de regreso a Inglaterra. Referencias iconográficas', in M. Cabañas (ed.), *El arte foráneo en España: presencia e influencia*, CSIC, Madrid, 237–53

Franco Pérez, F. J. 2007 'Nuevas propuestas de prospección arqueológica en la región cantábrica: el caso de las ferrerías de monte de Vizcaya', *Territorio, Sociedad y Poder* 2, 37–52

Gaimster, D. 2007 'The Baltic ceramic market 1200–1600: measuring Hanseatic cultural transfer and resistance', in H. Roodenburg (ed.), *Cultural exchange in early modern Europe, Vol. 4: forging European identities, 1400–1700*, Cambridge University Press, Cambridge, 30–58

Gerrard, C. M., Gutiérrez, A., Hurst, J. G., and Vince, A. (ed.) 1995 'A guide to Spanish medieval pottery', in C. M. Gerrard, A. Gutiérrez, and A. Vince (eds), *Spanish medieval ceramics in Spain and the British Isles*, British Archaeological Reports International Series 610, Oxford, 281–95

Gisbert, J. A. 1991 'En torno a la producción y elaboración de azúcar en las comarcas de La Safor (Valencia) y la Marina Alta (Alicante), siglos XIV–XIX', in A. Malpica (ed.), *II Seminario Internacional La caña del azúcar en el Mediterráneo*, Diputación Provincial, Granada, 211–65

Gomes, M. V. 2011 'Insígnias de peregrinação encontradas em Portugal', in R. V. Gomes, M. V. Gomes, and C. Tente (eds), *Cristãos e Muçulmanos na Idade Média Peninsular: encontros e desencontros*, Instituto de Arqueologia Portuguesa, Lisbon, 281–96

Goodman, A. 1994 'Before the Armada: Iberia and England in the Middle Ages', in N. Saul (ed.), *England in Europe*, St Martin's Press, New York, 108–20

Gransden, A. 2007 *A history of the Abbey of Bury St Edmunds 1182–1256*, The Boydell Press, Woodbridge

Gutiérrez, A. 2000 *Mediterranean pottery in Wessex households (13th to 17th centuries)*, British Archaeological Reports British Series 306, Oxford

Gutiérrez, A. 2003 'A shipwreck of Sevillian pottery from the Studland Bay wreck, Dorset, UK', *International Journal of Nautical Archaeology* 32.1, 24–41

Gutiérrez, A. 2007 'Portuguese coarsewares in early modern England: reflections on an exceptional pottery assemblage from Southampton', *Post-Medieval Archaeology* 41.1, 64–79

Gutiérrez, A. 2012 '*Of sundry colours and moulds*: imports of early modern pottery along the Atlantic seaboard', in A. Teixeira and J. A. Bettencourt (eds), *Old and new worlds, International Congress of Early Modern Archaeology*, Lisbon, 37–50

Gutiérrez, A. 2014 'Cerámica española en el extranjero: un caso inglés', *Atti del IX Congresso Internazionale sulla Ceramica Medievale nel Mediterraneo*, All'Insegna del Giglio, Venice

Hatcher, J. and Barker, T. C. 1974 *A history of English pewter*, Longman, London

Hernández, Á. M. 1996 'Hornos medievales de azogue en Almadén', *Actas de las primeras Jornadas sobre minería y tecnología en la Edad Media Peninsular*, Fundación Hullera Vasco-Leonesa, Madrid, 384–94

Iglesias, L. 1998 'Peregrinos y romeros de la Inglaterra medieval: la romería popular', *Cuadernos del CEMYR* 6, 97–124

Kelleher, R. 2013 *Coins, monetisation and re-use in medieval England and Wales: new interpretations made possible by the Portable Antiquities Scheme*, unpublished PhD thesis, Durham University

Kowaleski, M. 1995 *Local markets and regional trade in Exeter*, Cambridge University Press, Cambridge

Köster, K. 1983 *Pilgerzeichen und Pilgermuscheln von mittelalterlichen Santiago-Strassen: Saint Léonard-Rocamadour-Saint Gilles-Santiago de Compostela. Schleswiger Funde und Gesamtüberlieferung*, Ausgrabungen in Schleswig, Berichte und Studien 2

Lomax, D. and Oakley, R. J. (trans.) 1988 *The English in Portugal, 1367–1387: extracts from the chronicles of Dom Fernando and Dom João*, Aris and Phillips, Warminster

Malpica, A. (ed.) 1990 *Actas del Primer Seminario Internacional 'La caña del azúcar en tiempos de los grandes descubrimientos 1450–1550'*, Diputación Provincial, Granada

Malpica, A. (ed.) 1991 *Actas del Segundo Seminario Internacional 'La caña del azúcar en el Mediterráneo'*, Diputación Provincial, Granada

Malpica, A. (ed.) 1995 *Actas del Quinto Seminario Internacional 'Paisajes del azúcar'*, Diputación Provincial, Granada

Matos, M. A. P. (ed.) 2012 *From Flanders: the azulejos commissioned by D. Teodósio I, 5th Duke of Braganza (c.1510–1563)*, Museu Nacional do Azulejo, Lisbon

Mehler, N. 2009 'The perception and interpretation of Hanseatic material culture in the North Atlantic: problems and suggestions', *Journal of the North Atlantic Special Volume 1*, 89–108

Menéndez, F. 1992 'Emblemas de peregrinos y de la peregrinación a Santiago', in H. Santiago-Otero (ed.), *El Camino de Santiago, la hospitalidad monástica y las peregrinaciones*, Junta de Castilla y León, Salamanca, 365–73

Miranda, F. 2013 'Before the empire: Portugal and the Atlantic trade in the late Middle Ages', *Journal of Medieval Iberian Studies* 5(1), 69–85

Miranda, F. 2014 'Portuguese traders in Atlantic Europe in the Middle Ages', *E-journal of Portuguese History* 12 (1), 119–30

Miraz, M. V. 2013 *La peregrinación marítima: el Camino Inglés desde la ría de Ferrol en la Baja Edad Media*, unpublished PhD thesis, Universidad de La Coruña

Moffett, L. 2006 'The archaeology of medieval plant foods', in C. M. Woolgar, D. Serjeantson, and T. Waldron (eds), *Food in medieval England: diet and nutrition*, Oxford University Press, Oxford, 41–55

Morais Barros, A. J. 2008 'Merchants, ports and hinterlands: the building of sea ports in Early Modern Porto', *História Porto*, Series III, 9, 89–112

Moralejo, S. and López Alsina, F. (eds) 1993 *Santiago, Camino de Europa. Culto y cultura en la peregrinación a Compostela: Monasterio de San Martin Pinario*, Junta de Galicia, Santiago de Compostela

Nightingale, P. 1985 'The London Pepperers' Guild and some twelfth-century English trading links with Spain', *Historical Research* 58(138), 123–32

Noddle, B. 1975 'The animal bones', in C. Platt and R. Coleman-Smith, *Excavations in medieval Southampton 1953–1969, Vol. II: the finds*, Leicester University Press, Leicester, 332–40

Osma, G. de 1916 *Catálogo de azabaches compostelanos*, Imprenta Ibérica, Madrid

Ouerfelli, M. 2007 *Le sucre: production, commercialisation et usages dans la Méditerranée médiévale*, Brill, Leiden

Parsons, J. C. 1977 *The court and household of Eleanor of Castile in 1290: an edition of British Library, Additional Manuscript 35294 with introduction and notes*, Pontifical Institute, Toronto

Pérez, J. 2008 'Sobre la manera de fabricar la azulejería en Manises durante los siglos XIV al XVI', in *El azulejo, evolución técnica: del taller a la fábrica*, Actas del XI Congreso Anual de la Asociación de Ceramología, Onda, 83–95

Pipe, A. 1992 'A note on exotic animals from medieval and post-medieval London', *Anthropozoologica* 16, 189–91

Plata, A. 2003 'La aplicación de la Arqueología de la Arquitectura a un complejo productivo: el valle salado de Salinas de Añana (Álava)', *Arqueología de la Arquitectura* 2, 241–8

Plata, A. 2008–9 'Un nuevo reto estratigráfico: el valle salado de Salinas de Añana (Álava)', *Krei* 10, 89–110

Pleguezuelo, A. 1992 'Francisco Niculoso Pisano: datos arqueológicos', *Faenza* 88(3–4), 171–91

Qualmann, K. 1991 'A medieval jet cross from the latrine pit (F5300)', in G. D. Scobie, J. M. Zant, and R. Whinney (eds), *The Brooks, Winchester: a preliminary report on the excavations, 1987–88*, Winchester Museums Service Archaeology Report 1, Winchester, 69–71

Quesada, T. 1995 'Las salinas del interior de Andalucía oriental: ensayo de tipología', in L. Cara and A. Malpica (eds), *Agricultura y regadío en al-Andalus: síntesis y problemas*, Instituto de Estudios Almerienses, Almería, 317–34

Roma, A. 2003 'British medieval coins in Castilian archaeological contexts', *The Numismatic Chronicle* 163, 392–5

Rose, S. 2011 *The wine trade in medieval Europe 1000–1500*, Continuum, London

Rouse, E. C. and Baker, A. 1967 'Wall paintings in Stoke Orchard church, Gloucestershire, with particular reference to the Cycle of the Life of St James the Great', *The Archaeological Journal* 123(1), 79–119

Rueda, M. and Sáez, I. 1992 'Hallazgos medievales de moneda castellana y leonesa', *Numisma* 230, 205–60

Ruiz Cecilia, J. I. 2011 'Entre lo sagrado y lo profano: dos insignias medievales de plomo halladas en Osuna', *Cuadernos de los Amigos de los Museos de Osuna* 13, 54–9

Simões, J. M. dos S. 1990 *Azulejaria portuguesa nos séculos XV e XVI: introdução geral*, Fundação Calouste Gulbenkian, Lisbon

Spencer, B. 1998 *Pilgrim souvenirs and secular badges*, Medieval Finds from Excavations in London 7, Her Majesty's Stationery Office, London
Spufford, P. 2002 *Power and profit: the merchant in medieval Europe*, Thames and Hudson, London
Standley, E. 2013 *Trinkets and charms: the use, meaning and significance of dress accessories 1300–1700*, Oxford University School of Archaeology Monograph 78, Oxford
Stopford, J. 1994 'Some approaches to the archaeology of Christian pilgrimage', *World Archaeology* 26(1), 57–72
Suárez Otero, J. 1998a 'Comercio e peregrinación. Artesanía medieval compostelana en Europa', in F. Singul (ed.), *Pratería e acibeche en Santiago de Compostela: obxetos litúrxicos e devocionais para o rito sacro e a peregrinación*, Xunta de Galicia, Santiago de Compostela, 99–124
Suárez Otero, J. 1998b 'Arqueología y peregrinación: la moneda y la peregrinación marítima a Santiago', in V. Almazán (ed.), *Las rutas atlánticas de Peregrinación a Santiago de Compostela (Ferrol 1996)*, Santiago, 195–218
Suárez Otero, J. 1999 'Numismática europea bajomedieval en Compostela', (Catálogo de Exposición), Santiago de Compostela
Suárez Otero, J. 2004 'Apuntes sobre peregrinación jacobea y circulación monetaria en la Galicia medieval', *Numisma* 248, 23–48
Tate, R. B. 1993 'Las peregrinaciones marítimas medievales desde las Islas Británicas a Compostela', *Santiago, Camino de Europa: culto y cultura en la peregrinación a Compostela*, Fundación Caja Madrid, Madrid, 161–79
Tate, R. B. 2003 *Pilgrimages to St James of Compostela from the British Isles during the Middle Ages*, Liverpool University Press, Liverpool
Teixeira, A., Bento Torres, J., and Bettencourt, J. 2015 'The Atlantic expansion and the Portuguese material culture in the early modern age: an archaeological approach', in P. P. A. Funari and M. X. Senatore (eds), *Archaeology of culture contact and colonisation in Spanish and Portuguese America*, 19–38, Springer, London
Urteaga, M. 1994 'La industria de la sal en el desarrollo medieval de la villa de Leintz-Gatzaga (Salinas de Léniz), Guipuzcoa', *IV Congreso de Arqueología Medieval Española*, Vol. III, Diputación Provincial de Alicante, Alicante, 937–44
Vázquez de Parga, L., Lacarra J. M., and Uría, J. 1998 *Las peregrinaciones a Santiago de Compostela*, Gobierno de Navarra, Pamplona (1st edn 1948–9)
Vince, A. and England, S. 2004 'Medieval and later pottery', in K. Rodwell and R. Bell (eds), *Acton Court: the evolution of an early Tudor courtier's house*, English Heritage, London, 294–8
Walker, R. 2007 'Leonor of England and Eleanor of Castile: Anglo-Iberian marriage and cultural exchange in the twelfth and thirteenth centuries', M. Bullón-Fernández (ed.), *England and Iberia in the Middle Ages, 12th–15th century: cultural, literary, and political exchanges*, Palgrave Macmillan, Basingstoke, 67–88
Walker-Meikle, K. 2012 *Medieval pets*, Boydell and Brewer, Woodbridge
Walton, P. 1991 'Textiles', in J. Blair and N. Ramsay (eds), *English medieval industries: craftsmen, techniques, products*, The Hambledon Press, London, 29–40
Webb, D. 1999 *Pilgrims and pilgrimage in the Medieval West*, I. B. Tauris, London
Williams, B. 1995 'Survey of Spanish tiles imported into England: an interim note', in C. M. Gerrard, A. Gutiérrez, and A. Vince (eds), *Spanish medieval ceramics in Spain and the British Isles*, British Archaeological Reports International Series 610, 335–8
Yapp, B. 1981 *Birds in medieval manuscripts*, The British Library, London

CHAPTER 60

A LAST WORD

The Study of Later Medieval Archaeology

CHRISTOPHER M. GERRARD

IN 1987 the Society for Medieval Archaeology published an agenda for future study entitled 'Archaeology and the Middle Ages' (SMA 1987). Not long after that document emerged, the entire State-sponsored infrastructure of British archaeology found itself in a state of upheaval following the widespread introduction of developer funding (see Chapter 1). To some extent these events had been predicted but no-one could have foreseen then all the many changes to British archaeology that would ensue over the next thirty years. At the close of this volume, it is worth underlining that all the archaeological work described here sits within a wider social, economic, and political context and that this matrix of influences has directly affected the nature of research. At the same time, the transformation brought about by technological developments and the digital revolution over the past thirty years has been no less profound. Of all the recommendations made in the 1987 agenda it is the infrastructural and methodological ones which have dated least well. According to one commentator we were, even then, living only in the 'Middle Ages' of computer technology (Rawlins 1997, 59)!

That said, many of the 1987 recommendations seem prescient. The numbers of scheduled ancient monuments were substantially increased, as the agenda suggested they should be, and larger areas rather than individual sites were indeed considered for protection through the Monuments Protection Programme (in England) with other measures in Wales and Scotland. Among the academic priorities, the push for more work on middle rank and smaller boroughs, for greater consideration to dispersed settlements, the need for single large-scale landscape projects and surveys of a greater range of medieval buildings, an awareness of landscape features such as parks, warrens, and fishponds, have all been responded to and there are significant projects and publications from the last thirty years that could be placed against each one of these 'recommendations'. One in particular would command a substantial bibliography of its own today: 'the encouragement of research into human biology, physical anthropology and pathology' (Chapters 47, 51, and 52 provide a summary of developments). Other proposals strike this reader as very modern: the need to investigate complete tenements and land-units in towns, the importance of transitions between periods (for example, for industry) and the urging of thematic rather than single-site studies. All these have been mentioned as desirable developments by contributors to this *Handbook*.

Since 1987 there have been several further generations of national research priorities such as *Exploring our past* (Wainwright 1991), numerous regional research frameworks (e.g. Cooper 2006), and a wide range of suggestions put forward by other groups. These are too numerous to list here but they include the preferences of special interest groups (e.g. MSRG 2007 for rural settlement; Cranstone 1991 for mining), CBA committees (e.g. for churches), a batch of specially commissioned reviews (e.g. Mellor 1994 for ceramic studies; Roebuck and Davison 1995 for monastic estates), and a useful set of personal agendas promoted by active researchers. Among these are the recent recommendations for archaeobotany in medieval Britain (Van Der Veen et al. 2013) and others for science in medieval archaeology and for medieval rural settlement (Astill 1993; 1998). In this final chapter of the *Handbook* we too consider the future. The first section below addresses what might be thought of as infrastructural issues; the second section outlines what are here called 'the grand challenges'.

INFRASTRUCTURE

Mining Archaeological Data: The Challenge of Unpublished Reports

For many of the themes addressed in this *Handbook* the challenge of synthesis depends upon ready access to information, with far better online availability than currently exists. As our contributors have found, it is currently virtually impossible or else too time-consuming to provide a comprehensive summary for any aspect of the unpublished later medieval dataset from developer-led excavations. Grey literature online rarely contains the fullest possible analysis of discoveries; financial and time constraints often mean that site reports are written without the benefit of dating evidence. Here, and elsewhere, there is an inevitable tension between the site-specific contents of reports of the kind that must be generated for clients or for the purposes of 'development control' and any attempt to address broader research questions.

At present there is no equivalent for the later medieval period of the assessment of the contribution of commercial archaeology to our understanding of the Roman period (Fulford and Holbrook 2011). Similar challenges do exist, however, among them the uneven geographical distribution of UK excavations with far fewer in the south-west, northern England, Wales, and Scotland, and a predictable dominance of urban centres such as London and York. That said, strengths in the archaeological record differ in their detail so that while the City of London provides rich evidence for medieval buildings until the fourteenth century and deep waterfront deposits, small towns may contain proportionately more standing buildings but have shorter archaeological sequences (Chapter 19). These biases exist for every class of evidence; very few manor houses or moated sites have been examined in their entirety (Chapter 16), castles in State care are very rarely excavated at all (Chapter 23), far more is known about watermills than windmills (Chapter 31), and far less is known about the precincts of some religious orders than it is for others (Chapter 35). The list of the desired and the indispensible could be greatly extended. Medieval archaeologists, it must be said, are remarkably fast to take advantage of any opportunity and, as a result, there are some remarkable new themes such as the study of pilgrim burials, graffiti, and the medieval afterlife, all of which are addressed in contributions here (Chapters 39, 40, and 54). Nevertheless, there are disappointments. A recent review of archaeobotanical remains in Britain revealed only eight waterlogged later medieval sites in Wales, nine in Scotland, but 270 from England. Such a disparity mars any meaningful comparative analysis (Van Der Veen et al. 2013).

What kind of information would researchers like to see made more easily available? The enormous quantity of unpublished 'grey literature' outside the mainstream academic debate is one routine complaint (Evans 2015), another being the list of unpublished (often large-scale) excavations from the 1960s–1980s which the Society for Medieval Archaeology has made a priority in its monograph programme over the past fifteen years (for example, South Witham, excavated 1965–7, Mayes 2002; Launceston Castle, dug 1961–83, Saunders 2006). But that is not all, it can be hard to find out about community projects, redundant websites and blogs, conference proceedings, and academic theses too (both masters-level and doctoral). There are sometimes barriers to accessing online sources, among them subscription firewalls, and websites requiring routine updates can easily fall by the wayside when priorities change. On the positive side, archaeologists can be ingenious innovators: the East Midlands Research Framework is available as a wiki so that regional research priorities can be constantly updated (East Midlands Heritage 2015) while the People's Collection Wales (PCW) accepts data of all kinds relating to the history of Wales. Above all, the Archaeology Data Service has become an indispensible resource for preserving and disseminating medieval research.

Using Meta-Data: The Challenge of Synthesis

Medieval studies entered the age of Big Data several years ago and we are faced with ever higher volumes of information as a direct result of our ability to record, store, and disseminate (Hardman and Evans 2010). Every major archive seemingly has its own digitization project with high resolution images; one scholar recently claimed that more images of folios from medieval manuscripts have been 'tweeted' and uploaded on Facebook in the past year (2016) than most scholars have seen *in situ* in their entire careers. British archaeology too is moving ever faster in classifying and re-using meta-data. The Excavation Index held by the Archaeological Data Service (ADS) incorporates the Archaeological Investigations Project (AIP) and OASIS, a vital source of information for all kinds of archaeological fieldwork in England up to 2011. A search for 'medieval' in The Library of Unpublished Fieldwork Reports available through ADS returns 7381 entries. Museums are also putting their archives online; through the Museum of London portal researchers can now view medieval pilgrim souvenirs and leather shoes as well as consult the London Archaeological Archive and Research Centre which holds summaries of 7500 sites in the capital and archives for half of those.

Other useful information online includes the metadata on terrain and nineteenth-century rural settlement created for Brian Roberts and Stuart Wrathmell's *An atlas of rural settlement in Britain*. These are available for downloading in GIS format through the Historic England website so that the data can be re-visualized and re-worked (Lowerre 2010). Elsewhere it is possible to find the zooarchaeological meta-analysis undertaken on archaeological cod remains from ninety-five sites in London which revealed changing patterns of supply (Orton et al. 2014), the digitized plans and relational database for medieval monastic cemeteries created by Roberta Gilchrist and Barney Sloane, the Exeter Archaeology Archive project which provides online access to excavation data in that city between 1970 and 1990, the aerial photographic plotting for English Heritage's National Mapping Programme (Winton and Horne 2010), and the Vernacular Architecture Group's database on dendrochronology; all these are available through ADS. The database which is most frequently flagged up in this *Handbook* is the Portable Antiquities Scheme (for example, Chapters 32 and 49) whose results are now routinely incorporated into research projects on coinage and dress accessories. At present, there is nothing to match the ambition of the European earthquake catalogues provided by AHEAD (Archive of Historical Earthquake Data; Locati et al. 2014) and SHEEC (SHARE European Earthquake Catalogue 1000–1899; Stucci et al. 2013) with their open access online platforms and tools for geographical and chronological interrogation. However, the English landscape and identities project (EngIaID), now underway at the University of Oxford, which has amassed nearly one million digital records and aims to produce a history of the English landscape from 1500 BC to AD 1086, will surely have lessons for later periods (Cooper and Green 2016).

Cross-Disciplinarity: The Challenge of Collaboration

In many of the contributions in this *Handbook*, later medieval archaeology is triangulated between the complementary archaeologies of the humanities, sciences, and professional practice. To take a single example, the Corpus of Scottish Medieval Parish Churches project run by the universities of St Andrews and Stirling assessed the fabric of 105 parish churches in pre-Reformation Scotland and has directly informed their future management and conservation and associated policy.[1] Research and teaching has tended towards the multi- or interdisciplinary with ever closer links to art/visual culture, architecture, the biological and material sciences as well as historical texts. So often do medieval archaeologists claim partnerships and interdisciplinary thinking that it is in danger of becoming a commonplace. As we have seen, geographers, historians, ecologists,

---

[1] arts.st-andrews.ac.uk/corpusofscottishchurches/sites.php.

scientists, and many others have been involved in our discipline from its earliest days, and many collaborations are claimed and encouraged throughout the *Handbook* and outside of it, particularly for landscape and rural settlement themes. While the combination of detailed documentary study in close relation to physical archaeology and architectural study is widely considered to be essential (Chapter 24) and the challenges of inter-disciplinarity have been widely celebrated (e.g. Albarella 1999), difficulties do remain. Archaeologists may understand better that written evidence must be interpreted with great care but do not always do so (Dyer 2011). Nor are the debates and data of archaeologists always taken up by other disciplines, as Draper (Chapter 4) laments, and we would all recognize that there is work to be done in communicating our message. Medieval archaeology is too often equated with excavation and excavation alone, many excavation monographs still isolate the archaeology from the historical evidence, while art historians and specialists in visual culture successfully pick over what others would regard as archaeological evidence. As exemplars of what can be achieved when stepping beyond traditional disciplinary divisions, the reader is referred to the contributions here by Giles and McClain (Chapter 41) and by Huggon (Chapter 52).

Methodologies: The Challenge of New Techniques

There have been significant changes over the last decade in the kinds of skills which later medieval archaeologists are expected to acquire, or at least grasp in outline. Non- (or less) destructive techniques such as geophysics and more surgical interventions such as intensive test-pitting within currently occupied medieval settlements are emphasized throughout this volume (Dyer and Everson 2012). In spite of the past successes of field-walking in East Anglia and elsewhere in mapping the evolution of settlement (see Chapter 12), its popularity with archaeologists has declined, as has earthwork survey (but see Jecock et al. 2011 for Byland Abbey, North Yorkshire), while new techniques such as LiDAR have not had the impact of aerial photography. In some parts of Britain, such as the Scottish Highlands, it is still hard to tell medieval remains apart from their later counterparts. Among the dating techniques applied to the historic periods, dendrochronology has had the greatest effect while the radiocarbon-dating of lime mortars holds great potential for masonry buildings. Access analysis continues to be used to good effect to untangle the plans of castles and other buildings where survival is good.

All the most sophisticated applications of recent years have been made possible by leaps in computing power and memory capacity. They include developments in geophysics, spatial technology, remote sensing, and the faster processing speeds needed to interrogate meta-data sets. Geographical Information Systems (GIS) are, for example, fundamental to Historic Landscape Characterization (whose merits are debated by several authors in this *Handbook*) and the Scottish Historic Land-Use Assessment project (1996–2015) as well as to the mapping of archaeology across towns, cities, and landscapes (for example the UADs, Urban Archaeological Databases, and the extensive urban surveys of smaller towns which have substantially enhanced HERS). All archaeologists now have to engage with multimedia presentation on digital platforms and open access technologies and a particular trend at present is the move towards the 3D-modelling software. Photogrammetry has long been considered best practice for standing buildings like parish churches but the ability to construct 3D images from 2D images is now having an impact on the ways in which archaeology is recorded on excavations and objects are presented in museums (e.g. medieval pilgrim badges from the British Museum collections). While the analytical methods required to exploit the sophistication of these models still lag behind (Shott 2014), it is already possible to generate models of excavations from archive photographs and to reconstruct excavation evidence.

Archaeological science is a fast-moving field; Fradley (Chapter 2) refers to specialist reports 'stepping out' from the appendices. This includes everything from the identification of residues in ceramics, to results emerging from research into faunal assemblages and botanical remains (e.g. Chapter 8). Again, while some techniques have barely registered in later medieval archaeology, for example large-scale DNA studies of cemetery sites (though see Richard III), inventive applications of stable isotope analysis show what can be achieved with adequate samples and strong research questions (Chapter 9). One significant challenge for the future is that many archaeological scientists now work freelance or for larger archaeological units without the benefit of reference collections, libraries, and their specialist journals.

Outreach and Impact: The Challenge of Public Archaeology

During the 'rescue' projects of the 1970s members of local societies were routinely involved in survey and excavation work. A typical collaborative project then might have involved the labour, logistical, and public relations skills of a local society, funding from the State for the appointment of a field archaeologist, a museum which acted as a base, maps and sometimes financial support from a county planning department, and a university as employer with its extra-mural students working up documentary research projects through a local record office. For example, a review of evidence for medieval and post-medieval Liverpool was the result of a partnership between university, museum, and the Merseyside Archaeological Society (Nicholson 1981).

More recently almost all continuing education or extra-mural education programmes in universities have closed and the professionalization of archaeology has led to fewer opportunities for involvement. Public interest, however, has not declined; television series such as *Inside the medieval mind* (2008) and *The Normans* (2010) are watched by around three million viewers. Building on the political agenda for localism, other kinds of 'open archaeology' have come to fill the 'participation gap' ranging from online viewing (e.g. at Oystermouth Castle in Wales),[2] to training and crowdfunding opportunities (e.g. through DigVentures at Leiston Abbey, Suffolk, in 2015). The most significant community of new users are the many heritage projects being undertaken by

[2] digoystermouth.blogspot.com.

local communities under the supervision of, or in co-production with, universities or museums, as well as projects undertaken by societies, special interest groups, and metal-detecting clubs (Bonacchi and Moshenska 2015). The latter are now more frequently involved in archaeological fieldwork and the success of the PAS underlines an important shift in the relationship between archaeologists and metal-detectorists (Thomas 2012).

All the emphasis has been upon enabling communities so that, for example, the Thames Discovery Programme was a collaboration between the UCL Institute of Archaeology and the Museum of London to identify threatened sites on the Thames foreshore and record them using trained volunteers. A second is the 'Dig Hungate' project by York Archaeological Trust (2006–11) in which members of the local community joined a commercial excavation on York's largest ever excavation, uncovering medieval cess pits, wicker-lined wells, and bread ovens. Finally, the Newport Medieval Ship Project integrated several public collaborations facilitated by Heritage Lottery Funding (2006–8) after the discovery of a medieval ship on the riverside of the Usk in Newport in south-east Wales (Nayling and Jones 2014). The impact of the Heritage Lottery Fund has been extremely significant, particularly in some regions. Among the projects deemed suitable for funding are the preservation of medieval landscapes such as traditional meadows, the reinterpretation of monuments, and parish heritage projects such as the excavation of a medieval mill building by Coquetdale community archaeology and the investigation of a pele tower and manor house in Radcliffe, Greater Manchester.[3]

The importance of public archaeology, in all its different forms, will continue to be significant in the future and medieval archaeologists will need to embrace its possibilities. At its best, community archaeology can change people's appreciation of the past, bolster protection for sites, and create opportunities for dialogue. It can also affect community values and identity positively, bring together those with common interests and teach new skills such as management and presentation. We must wait to see now whether the interpretative benefits can also be fully explored.

The Interpretative Toolkit: The Challenge of Theory

As Mileson (Chapter 25) affirms, 'real advances in understanding require new thinking as well as new facts' and throughout this *Handbook* a new engagement with social theory and the impact of post-processual approaches becomes evident (Chapter 3). The spaces, layouts, and visual clues in medieval buildings reinforce hierarchies and roles (e.g. Chapter 15) while the exploration of the relationship between an object and its user(s) can open up discussions about archaeological 'memory' (e.g. Van Dyke and Alcock 2003), material mnemonics (Lillios and Tsamis 2010), and biographies of artefacts (Gosden and Marshall 1999). Several medieval case studies are now available

---

[3] www.radcliffeheritage.co.uk.

(Gilchrist 2009; McClain 2012), including those for the medieval life course (Gilchrist 2012; Chapter 47), symbols on artefacts (Blake et al. 2003), objects found 'out of context' (Gerrard 2007), and for dress accessories (Standley 2013). In each case, the object or building 'biography' is revealed through a combination of archaeological and historical evidence; Giles and McClain (Chapter 41) explain here how the same approach can be applied to the destruction of devotional images. There are also recent studies of later medieval 'special deposits' such as Caple's (2012) investigation of the hidden twelfth-century apotropaic symbols inscribed on threshold stones by labourers at the southern entrance to Nevern Castle, Wales, or the bent silver pennies found embedded in medieval walling (Chapter 38). Research into medieval graffiti is also now being taken far more seriously with important implications for the archaeology of medieval identity and symbolism (e.g. Meeson 2005; Oliver and Neal 2010; Chapter 39 in this *Handbook*).

Several contributions to this *Handbook* make a persuasive argument that medieval archaeology can expose the daily lived experience of the sensory, sensual, and experiential past. This has been a topic of interest for some time. Both Cumberpatch (1997) and Brown et al. (1997), for example, stress the colour, texture, and decoration of medieval pottery against a backdrop of cloths, bedding, and cushions inside the medieval household while Barnwell (2007) shows how the castle at Peak in Derbyshire, a site long associated with local legend, was designed to maximize its visual impact in the landscape. Within the wider context of phenomenology, Gardiner and Kilby (Chapter 14) discuss the perceptions of late medieval people and the different ways they viewed their surroundings, highlighting gaps in our understanding; Antrobus (Chapter 20) draws attention to the medieval street scene as a three-dimensional space which invited the purchaser in. Part VIII of the *Handbook* picks up the theme again, inspired by a handful of recent publications such as Altenberg (2003 for landscapes), Woolgar (2006), Nichols and Calhoun (2007), and Day (2013) which trace scientific ideas about sensory experience and explore how objects and spaces could define and control the senses. Medieval archaeology is rich in possibilities, from smells and hygiene (Chapter 45) to the acoustic world of liturgy and prayer (Chapters 42 and 44). Unlike other archaeologists, medievalists have the advantage of both documentary evidence and standing architecture to help understand the interplay of the senses with different religious and domestic environments.

The Grand Challenges

The 'grand challenges' described below are deliberately set at the broad scale rather than being site-based or regional initiatives or, indeed, ones that focus upon particular events. Several candidates emerged from a reading of *Handbook* contributions, among them cultural landscapes, bioarchaeology, the European dimension, and the impact of archaeological theory. I have restricted myself to just four.

Social Complexity

This is a broad theme which emerges repeatedly across several contributions. Beginning with medieval elites, how do 'leaders' emerge, maintain themselves, and transform society? We have seen how the manipulation of landscape, fauna, flora, architecture, etiquette at the table, and symbols of power are central to performance. In his discussion of castles and elite landscapes, Creighton (Chapter 23) shows how park creation, settlement planning, road diversions, and the patronage of churches and monasteries are among the hallmarks of lordly influence in the countryside. Likewise, in Chapter 33, Hall discusses chess boards and gaming in the context of aristocratic life in castles. Several authors, particularly in Part X, underline the importance of memory and the use of the past in the past and in the emergence of macro-scale European elite identities. Others stress the need to tackle in greater detail the relevance of traditional divisions of culture history (e.g. the Norman Conquest and the Reformation) as moments of transition in social complexity.

Insufficient attention has been paid by archaeologists to how and why social inequalities change through the Middle Ages. Medieval societies experienced great differences in wealth and power embedded in the hierarchies of Church and State, and medieval archaeologists could provide more coherent accounts of transformations through time and within social groups (e.g. Smith 2009), for example by addressing the material changes caused by the Black Death. Another challenge is to examine social complexity across different kinds of settlement, most notably between town and countryside (e.g. Chapter 21). Medieval cities, in particular, have proved especially rich in information about their urban fabrics and one of the major challenges is to sift and analyse the very large quantities of data now available in order to explore the size and nature of urban hinterlands, the exchange of goods between town and country, differences between inland and coastal towns, and towns as centres of consumption (Giles and Dyer 2005). Some scholars are now enlisting a bundle of theoretical approaches, which includes social practice theory (SPT), to consider urban lifestyle and the role of the individual, identity, gender, and agency in everyday life (e.g. Christopherson 2015; Giles 2000).

Resilience

This theme has broader relevance to other disciplines such as geography and history as well as having modern resonance. What hazards were medieval societies exposed to? While archaeologists cannot simply ignore the ever more nuanced climate data now being offered, no claims are made here for environmental determinism (Dawson et al. 2007; Gerrard and Petley 2013). As Roberts et al. (Chapter 51) explain, many health problems for example were related to socio-economic status and general living conditions, they were not imposed, and most scholars would support this view more generally. Students of risk, they might say, must first be students of society and culture (Oliver-Smith 1986, 25). Other core questions include: how did medieval communities react in the aftermath of disaster and plan to combat 'risk' in the future? To what extent did natural disasters such as flooding and severe weather lead to cultural and economic transformation? As Brown (Chapter 11) shows, there is significant potential in re-thinking how societies coped with short-term extreme weather events such as fire (Dyer 1992), high winds, and flooding (Galloway and Potts 2007) in order to understand the effect of these events on medieval society (for example, famine, economic downturn) and the reactions they provoked (Keene 2011). Were religion and belief always at the core of contemporary interpretations of events? The deliberate folding and deposition of coins, the physical embodiment of a protective religious vow struck with the saints, may have been one of these reactions, and new evidence from the Portable Antiquities Scheme has greatly expanded the corpus of examples for study (Chapter 32).

The study of resilience, however, need not be restricted to natural hazards and responses to them. It should include the development of insurance mechanisms and the importance of credit in the medieval economy. Several traditional features of the medieval agrarian and household economy also served to buffer risk and provide food security, particularly from routine 'slow-onset' hazards such as harvest failures. Archaeology can provide evidence for the diversification of crops, the mixing of crop types to reduce the risk of failure, the consumption of so-called 'fall-back foods', the scattering of arable strips across different soils to help share risk, as well as the management and sharing of resources such as woodland and pasture. Crops, field systems, and animal husbandry, all themes discussed in this *Handbook*, require more even regional coverage to understand how resilience differed between, for example, the livestock husbandry of the uplands (Chapter 7) and lowland field systems (Chapter 6). How did medieval communities cope in extreme environments such as mountains or shoreline?

Behaviour and Identity

What social identities can be identified in the archaeological record in the Middle Ages? How did these identities form and how might they best be characterized? In this volume the theme of identity is explored through dress, architecture, household objects, urban design, among others. Quite a straightforward relationship can sometimes be argued between objects and their households, for example between the large quantities of imported goods, including Low Countries pottery from the Netherlands, and the presence of immigrant communities living in south-east England in the fifteenth century (Chapter 55). At other times, because personal and group identities are created and asserted, this one-to-one relationship is far from clear. For example, a detailed study of assemblages found in the port of Southampton reveals that Italian merchants used no more Italian pottery than their neighbours (Brown 1993). This particular merchant community chose not to emphasize their identity through their pottery but perhaps they had other ways of doing so which are not so visible archaeologically, such as the way they dressed? The presence of Flemish colonists in south-west Wales and Anglo-French incomers in Aberdeenshire during the later medieval period provides further opportunity to investigate the fluidity of identity. Other fruitful areas for further study are the archaeology of childhood (Chapter 48) and a more balanced approach to gender (Chapter 50). Where we seem to see the agency of material culture with much greater clarity in shaping social interaction and experience is through food and eating. To take one example, Pluskowski (Chapter 10) discusses the re-introduction of the peafowl after the Norman Conquest, almost exclusively on high-status sites. The peacock was a symbol of renewal, resurrection and immortality popular in Christian symbolism but their display at lavish banquets in the fourteenth century was probably intended to signify dynastic longevity. At the other end of the social scale Hinton (Chapter 27) points to the possible mockery by peasants of their social superiors in their purchases of aquamaniles and puzzle-jugs.

Humans and the Environment

Rising and falling population numbers have fundamental impacts on all aspects of the archaeological record. In particular, a surge in population in the last two decades of the twelfth and the thirteenth century such as is now being suggested (e.g. Langdon and Masschaele 2006) has major implications for the expansion of open fields, the balance of dispersed and nucleated settlement, trade and exchange, and architectural developments. For bioarchaeologists there can hardly be a more important question if nutrition, diet, disease, and differences in well-being between urban and rural environments are to be better understood.

It comes as a surprise to find that some medieval landscapes are not at all well explored. Gardens are a good example of this, although now we have a better idea about where 'dead' medieval gardens might survive, as oppose to 'living' gardens which continue to be maintained. Battlefield archaeology too is in its infancy for this period (Chapter 26). HERs can even be deficient in information about industrial and extractive sites such as quarrying and mining of stone and metal ores although they have important implications for the exploitation of woodland, the distribution and function of settlement and infrastructure, and much else besides. Experimental archaeology still has an important role to play in understanding medieval technology, although there is nothing in Britain to rival the *de novo* thirteenth-century castle construction project at Guédelon in Treigny (France).

The late medieval period represented a time of significant ecological transformation in Britain but how did fauna and flora change in the Middle Ages? When do we start to see selective breeding? What was the impact of new cultivation techniques such as crop rotation? What transformations were brought about by the Norman Conquest and the Black Death? All these questions require larger datasets to work with (Van Der Veen et al. 2013) if we are to understand how the regions of Britain differed one from another in terms of the composition of landuse and settlement type. As Rippon et al. (Chapter 12) point out, the nucleated villages of central England with their open fields laid out to either side should be considered the exception; pollen analysis has not yet been conducted on a large enough scale to see the picture across Britain. Taking these questions forward will require both carefully targeted research agendas as well as satisfactorily dated contexts. Rippon et al. (2014) illustrate what can be achieved using zooarchaeological and archaeobotanical evidence, but as Fradley (Chapter 2) points out, there is little in the way of faunal data from monastic sites, for instance, and well-stratified material from rural settlement sites is far harder to come by than it is for medieval towns.

Conclusion

Later medieval archaeology has flourished in Britain over the past thirty years and the next thirty years are surely equally full of promise. Like the 1987 agenda I hope parts of the text above will quickly become dated, though other sections may enjoy a longer life. Very likely there will be technological drivers to science and methodology which we cannot now imagine as well as waves of political and economic change which will affect us all through developments in our cities and countryside. Whatever the future holds, I hope that this volume demonstrates how later medieval archaeology thrives, the opportunities it presents, and the distinctive perspectives it can offer on the past to students and researchers across Europe and the world.

References cited

Albarella, U. 1999 'The mystery of husbandry: medieval animals and the problem of integrating historical and archaeological evidence', *Antiquity* 72, 867–75

Altenberg, K. 2003 *Experiencing landscapes: a study of space and identity in three marginal areas of medieval Britain and Sweden*, Almquist and Wiksell, Stockholm

Astill, G. 1993 'The archaeology of the medieval countryside: a forty-year perspective', in H. Andersson and J. Wienberg (eds), *The study of medieval archaeology*, Lund Studies in Medieval Archaeology 13, Stockholm, 131–48

Astill, G. 1998 'Medieval and later: composing an agenda', in J. Bayley (ed.), *Science in archaeology: an agenda for the future*, English Heritage, London

Barnwell, P. S. 2007 'The power of Peak Castle: cultural contexts and changing perception', *Journal of the British Archaeological Association* 160, 20–38

Blake, H., Egan, G., Hurst, J., and New, E. 2003 'From popular devotion to resistance and revival in England: the cult of the holy name of Jesus and the Reformation', in D. Gaimster and R. Gilchrist (eds), *The archaeology of Reformation 1480–1580*, The Society for Post-Medieval Archaeology Monograph 1, Leeds, 175–203

Bonacchi, C. and Moshenska, G. 2015 'Critical reflections on digital public archaeology', *Internet Archaeology* 40, http://dx.doi.org/10.11141/ia.40.7.1

Brown, D. 1993 'The imported pottery of late medieval Southampton', *Medieval Ceramics* 17, 77–81

Brown, D., Chalmers, A., and MacNamara, A. 1997 'Light and the culture of colour in medieval pottery', in G. De Boe and F. Verhaege (eds), *Method and theory in historical archaeology*, pre-printed papers of the Medieval Europe Brugge 1997 Conference, Zellik, Vol. 10, 145–7

Caple, C. 2012 'The apotropaic symbolled threshold to Nevern Castle–Castell Nanhyfer', *The Archaeological Journal* 169(1), 422–52

Christopherson, A. 2015 'Performing towns: steps towards an understanding of medieval urban communities as social practice', *Archaeological Dialogues* 22(2), 109–32

Cooper, A. and Green, C. 2016 'Embracing the complexities of "Big Data" in archaeology: the case of the English Landscape and Identities project', *Journal of Archaeological Method and Theory* 23, 271–304

Cooper, N. J. 2006 *The archaeology of the East Midlands: an archaeological resource assessment and research agenda*, University of Leicester Archaeological Services Monograph 13, Leicester

Cranstone, D. 1991 'Mining sites in Britain: priorities for research and preservation', *Institute of Mining History and Archaeology Newsletter* 3, 6–8

Cumberpatch, C. G. 1997 'Towards a phenomenological approach to the study of medieval pottery', in C. G. Cumberpatch and P. W. Blinkhorn (eds), *Not so much a pot, more a way of life*, Oxbow, Oxford, 125–51

Dawson, A. G., Hickey, K., Mayewski, P. A., and Nesje, A. 2007 'Greenland (GISP2) ice core and historical indicators of complex North Atlantic climate changes during the fourteenth century', *Holocene* 17(4), 427–34

Day, J. 2013 *Making senses of the past: towards a sensory archaeology*, Southern Illinois University, Center for Archaeological Investigations Occasional Paper 40, Carbondale

Dyer, C. 1992 'The great fire of Shipston-on-Stour', *Warwickshire History* 8, 179–94

Dyer, C. 2011 Review of *Caldecote: the development and desertion of a Hertfordshire village*, *Speculum* 86(1), 162–4

Dyer, C. and Everson, P. 2012 'The development of the study of medieval settlements, 1880–2010', in N. Christie and P. Stamper (eds), *Medieval rural settlement: Britain and Ireland, AD 800–1600*, Windgather Press, Oxford, 11–30

East Midlands Heritage 2015 *An updated research agenda and strategy for the historic environment of the East Midlands*, http://archaeologydataservice.ac.uk/researchframeworks/east-midlands/wiki/

Evans, T. N. L. 2015 'A reassessment of archaeological grey literature: semantics and paradoxes', *Internet Archaeology* 40, http://dx/doi.org/10.11141/ia.40.6

Fulford, M. and Holbrook, N. 2011 'Assessing the contribution of commercial archaeology to the study of the Roman period in England, 1990–2004', *The Antiquaries Journal* 91, 323–45

Galloway, J. A. and Potts, J. S. 2007 'Marine flooding in the Thames Estuary and tidal river c.1250–1450: impact and response', *Area* 39(3), 370–9

Gerrard, C. M. 2007 'Not all archaeology is rubbish: the elusive life histories of three artefacts from Shapwick, Somerset', in M. Costen (ed.), *People and places: essays in honour of Mick Aston*, Oxbow, Oxford, 166–80

Gerrard, C. M. and Petley, D. 2013 'A risk society? Environmental hazards, risk and resilience in the later Middle Ages', *Natural Hazards* 69(1), 1051–79

Gilchrist, R. 2009 'Medieval archaeology and theory: a disciplinary leap of faith', in R. Gilchrist and A. Reynolds (eds), *Reflections: 50 years of Medieval Archaeology 1957–2007*, The Society for Medieval Archaeology Monograph 30, Leeds, 385–408

Gilchrist, R. 2012 *Medieval life: archaeology and the life course*, The Boydell Press, Woodbridge

Giles, K. 2000 *An archaeology of social identity: guildhalls in York, 1350–1650*, British Archaeological Reports British Series 315, Oxford

Giles, K. and Dyer, C. (eds) 2005 *Town and country in the Middle Ages: contrasts, contacts and interconnections, 1100–1500*, The Society for Medieval Archaeology Monograph 22, Leeds

Gosden, C. and Marshall, Y. 1999 'The cultural biography of objects', *World Archaeology* 31, 169–78

Hardman, C. and Evans, T. 2010 *GLADE: grey literature, access dissemination and enhancement. The pilot assessment phase final report*, http://archaeologydataservice.ac.uk/attach/research/GLADEreportv5.pdf

Jecock, M., Burn, A., Brown, G., and Oswald, A. 2011 *Byland Abbey, Ryedale, North Yorkshire: archaeological survey and investigation of part of the precinct and extra-mural area*, English Heritage Research Report 4/2011, London

Keene, D. 2011 'Crisis management in London's food supply, 1250–1550', in B. Dodds and C. D. Liddy (eds), *Commercial activity, markets and entrepeneurs in the Middle Ages: essays in honour of Richard Britnell*, The Boydell Press, Woodbridge, 45–62

Langdon, J. and Masschaele, J. 2006 'Commercial activity and population growth in medieval England', *Past and Present* 190, 35–82

Lillios, K. T. and Tsamis, V. (eds) 2010 *Material mnemonics: everyday memory in Prehistoric Europe*, Oxbow Books, Oxford

Locati, M., Rovida, A., Albini, P., and Stucchi, M. 2014 'The AHEAD portal: a gateway to European Historical Earthquake Data', *Seismological Research Letters* 85(3), 727–34

Lowerre, A. G. 2010 'The *Atlas of Rural Settlement in England* GIS', *Landscapes* 11(2), 21–44

Mayes, P. 2002 *Excavations at a Templar preceptory: South Witham, Lincolnshire, 1965–67*, The Society for Medieval Archaeology Monograph 19, Leeds

McClain, A. 2012 'Theory, disciplinary perspectives and the archaeology of Later Medieval England', *Medieval Archaeology* 56(1), 131–70

Meeson, R. 2005 'Ritual marks and graffiti: curiosities or meaningful symbols?', *Vernacular Architecture* 36, 41–8

Mellor, M. 1994 *Medieval ceramic studies in England: a review for English Heritage*, English Heritage, London

MSRG (Medieval Settlement Research Group) 2007 Policy statement, https://medieval-settlement.com/about/policy/

Nayling, N. and Jones, T. 2014 'The Newport medieval ship, Wales, United Kingdom', *International Journal of Nautical Archaeology* 43(2), 239–78

Nichols, S. G. and Calhoun, A. 2007 *Rethinking the medieval senses*, John Hopkins University Press, Baltimore

Nicholson, S. 1981 *The changing face of Liverpool 1207–1727*, University of Liverpool, Liverpool

Oliver, J. and Neal, T. (eds) 2010 *Wild signs: graffiti in archaeology and history*, British Archaeological Reports International Series 2074, Oxford

Oliver-Smith, A. 1986 'Disaster context and causation: an overview of changing perspectives in disaster research', in A. Oliver-Smith (ed.), *Natural disasters and cultural contexts*, Studies in Third World societies 36, College of William and Mary, Williamsburg, 1–34

Orton, D. C., Morris, J., Locker, A., and Barrett, J. H. 2014 'Fish for the city: meta-analysis of archaeological cod remains and the growth of London's northern trade', *Antiquity* 88, 516–30

Rawlins, G. J. E. 1997 *Slaves of the machine*, MIT Press, Cambridge MA

Rippon, S., Wainwright, A., and Smart, C. 2014 'Farming regions in medieval England: the archaeobotanical and zooarchaeological evidence', *Medieval Archaeology* 58, 195–255

Roebuck, J. and Davison, A. 1995 *Medieval monastic sites: priorities for research*, English Heritage, London

Saunders, A. 2006 *Excavations at Launceston Castle, Cornwall*, The Society for Medieval Archaeology Monograph 24, Leeds

Shott, M. 2014 'Digitizing archaeology: a subtle revolution in analysis', *World Archaeology* 46(1), 1–9

Smith, S. 2009 'Materialising resistant identities among the medieval peasantry: an examination of dress accessories from English rural settlement sites', *Journal of Material Culture* 14(3), 3009–32

SMA (The Society for Medieval Archaeology) 1987 'Archaeology and the Middle Ages', *Medieval Archaeology* 31, 1–12

Standley, E. 2013 *Trinkets and charms: the use, meaning and significance of later medieval and early post-medieval dress accessories*, Oxford University School of Archaeology, Oxford

Stucchi, M., Rovida, A., Gomez Capera, A. A., Alexandre, P., Camelbeeck, T., Demircioglu, M. B., Gasperini, P., et al. 2013 'The SHARE European Earthquake Catalogue (SHEEC) 1000–1899', *Journal of Seismology* 17, 523–44

Thomas, S. 2012 'Archaeologists and metal-detector users in England Wales: past, present and future', in R. Skeates, C. McDavid, and J. Carmen (eds), *The Oxford handbook of public archaeology*, Oxford University Press, Oxford, 60–81

Van Der Veen, M., Hill, A., and Livarda, A. 2013 'The archaeobotany of medieval Britain (c. AD 450–1500): identifying research priorities for the 21st century', *Medieval Archaeology* 57(1), 151–82

Van Dyke, R. M. and Alcock, S. E. 2003 *Archaeologies of memory*, Blackwell, Oxford

Wainwright, G. 1991 *Exploring our past: strategies for the archaeology of England*, English Heritage, London

Winton, H. and Horne, P. 2010 'National Archives for National Programmes: NMP and the English Heritage Aerial Photographic Collection', in D. C. Cowley, R. A. Standring, and M. J. Abicht (eds), *Landscapes through the lens: aerial photographs and historic environment*, Occasional Paper of the Aerial Archaeology Research Group 2, Oxbow Books, Oxford, 7–18

Woolgar, C. M. 2006 *The senses in late medieval England*, Yale University Press, London and New Haven

Index

Note: Figures are indicated by an italic *f* following the page number. The index is not exhaustive.

Aalborg (Jutland) 953
Aarhus (Denmark) 944
abandoned villages *see* deserted villages
Abbey Church, Llantony (Abergavenny) 4*f*
Abbey of Fors (Jervaulx Abbey), Wensleydale (North Yorkshire) 145–6
Abbey Row, 30–50 Church Street, Tewkesbury (Gloucestershire) 313, 317
Abbeygate Street, Bury St Edmunds (Suffolk) 317
abbeys *see* monasteries
Abbot's Staith, Selby Abbey (North Yorkshire) 344
Abbots Leigh (Bristol) 708
Abbotsbury (Dorset) 497, 498*f*, 501
Aberconwy (Clwyd) 297, 570
Aberdeen (Aberdeenshire) 14
    Aberdeen Cathedral 582, 590, 591
    animal remains 109, 134
    architecture of churches 605
    brewing industry 443
    Broad Streets 319
    buildings 301
    dyes 748–9
    Gallowgate 319
    port 893
    salterns 184
    shops 319
    St Nicholas East Kirk church 652
    vegetable remains 119
    Whitefriars 779
    wolf hunting 146
Aberdeenshire
    animal remains 111
    Bishop's Loch, Loch Goil 186
    buildings 306
    Castle Hill, Strachan 363
    castles 363
    Fetternear 382
    Forvie, storm (1413) 159, 164
    Garioch 176, 180
    immigration 180, 991
    Invernochty Castle 185
    Old Rayne 111
    Rattray 111, 306, 363
    settlements 176, 177, 180
    Wardhouse Castle 180
    see also Aberdeen (Aberdeenshire)
Abingdon (Oxfordshire) 306, 345–6, 858
Abingdon Abbey (Oxfordshire) 121, 780
Abou-El-Haj, B. 617
Absalon (Danish archbishop) 950
Abū Nasr al-Fārābī 733
Abu Ya'qub Yusuf I 514*f*
Acklum, William of Wharram le Street 58
Acle (Norfolk) 629
acoustemology 683
Act of Dissolution in 1547 873
Acton Burnell (Shropshire) 250
Acton Court (Gloucestershire) 121–2, 243, 250, 253, 797–8, 974
Adderbury (Oxfordshire) 457, 458
Addyman, Peter 11
aDNA *see* ancient DNA
analysis 826–7, 829–30, 843
adolescents 44, 765–6, 767
    employment 767
Adoration of the Magi Mural, All Saints Church, Shelfanger (Norfolk) 745
adulthood 767–8
aerial photography 8, 25–7, 26*f*, 172, 465, 466*f*, 910*f*
    of monasteries 567
aerial survey 25–7, 26*f*

Afforestable Land Survey 172–3
Afghanistan 897
Africa 371
　coins from 514f
　ivory 971, 975
　leprosy 843
　silks 895
　trade with 150, 889, 891, 893, 894, 971, 975
　see also individual countries
afterlife
　belief in 868, 869f
　Purgatory 641, 665, 775, 862, 870–1, 871f
Agaete, Las Palmas (Gran Canaria, Spain) 970f
ageing 759–61, 768–9
　and disease 820
　perceptions 774
Agincourt Battle [France, 1415] 404, 410
Agnus Dei 162, 796
Agnus Dei at Carlisle Cathedral 630
agricultural buildings 259–60, 260f, 262, 263–6, 264f
agriculture 74
　chronological changes 74–5
　climatic effect 79–80
　equipment 196
　environmental approach 77–80
　family labour 475
　food production 262–3
　layout of holdings 266–70, 267f, 269f
　methods 95
　open fields 334
　processing and production 477–8
　tools 261–2
　see also arable landscapes
Ahrensfelde (Germany) 494
Ailnoth of Canterbury 949
Ailsworth (Northamptonshire) 220
alabaster 335, 439, 458, 471, 606, 953, 972, 973f
Álava (Spain) 968, 969f, 971
Albucasis 837
Alcácer do Sal (Portugal) 970–1
Alcester (Warwickshire) 201
Aldeburgh (Suffolk) 316
ale 443
Alexander III (Italian Pope) 837
Alexander III (King of Scotland) 514f

Alfonso VIII (King of Castile) 975
Alfonso X (King of León and Castile) 538, 975
Alhambra (Granada, Spain) 373
All Hallows-by-the-Tower Church (London) 637
All Saints and St Andrew Church, Kingston (Cambridgeshire) 746
All Saints Church, Litcham (Norfolk) 630
All Saints Church, Shelfanger (Norfolk) 745
All Saints Church, York (North Yorkshire) 662f
Almadén (Spain) 974
Almohad half dinar of Abu Yaʿqub Yusuf I 514f
almshouses 847, 850–1 see also infirmaries
Alnhamsheles (Northumberland) 196
Alnwick (Northumberland) 31, 280, 574
Alsace (France) 932
Alsted (Surrey) 481
Alston Grange (Leicestershire) 460
Altarnum (Cornwall) 632
altarpieces 663
altars 584, 590, 598, 599–600, 606–7
Althrey Hall (Flintshire) 252
amber 485
Amberley (Sussex) 503
Ambion Hill (Leicestershire) 408
ampullae 162f, 201, 548–9, 633, 648, 649–50, 665, 798
analytical earthwork survey (archaeo-topographical survey) 23, 25
Anarchy-period castles 361
Anastis Rotunda, Church of the Holy Sepulchre, Jerusalem 40
Anchor Green, North Berwick (East Lothian) 649
ancient DNA (aDNA) 117, 124, 826–7, 829–30, 843
Ancient Monuments and Historic Buildings Directorate 9
Ancient Monuments Laboratory (London) 10, 102
　Report series 103
Ancient Woodland Indicator Species (AWIS) 33
Andernach (Germany) 502
Angel Choir 589, 647 see also Lincoln Cathedral; Lincoln (Lincolnshire)

Angers (France) 307
Anglesey (Wales) 135
Anglo-Normans, invasion of
 Ireland 909–12, 920–1
Anglo-Saxon Chronicle 516
animal bones 60, 251, 332
 assemblages 103
 burial pits 107–8, 107f
 cat 108–9
 disease 107
 dog 109
 horse 109
 size 105–6
animals
 carcass products 482–4, 483f
 cause of smells 731–2, 739
 exotic imported 900, 971–2
 farmed in France 927
 farming 78–9
 grazing settlements 180–2
 imported exotic 148–9, 150, 894
 wild *see* wild animals
'animalscapes' 367
Anketil, a famous goldsmith 950
Annales Cambriae 147
Annales school, France 70
Annals of Ulster (845 AD) 913
Annandale (Scotland) 184
Anne Boleyn (Queen of England) 974
Anne of Bohemia (Queen of England) 376
Anne of Cleves (German princess and Queen
 of England) 378
anoxic burial environments 117
antler carving 483–4, 483f
Antwerp (Belgium) 944, 974
anvils 482
APABE (Advisory Panel on the Archaeology
 of Burials in England) 827
Apologia (Bernard of Clairvaux) 689
apothecaries 837
apprenticeships 767
apses 598, 611f, 683
Aquitaine (France) 929
Arabian Peninsula 891
arable landscapes 86
 chronological changes 92–8
 effect of Black Death 96–8

 regional variation 86–92, 88f, 89f, 90f
archaeoacoustics 683
Archaeological Data Service (ADS),
 University of York 103, 293, 984–5
Archaeological Investigations Project
 (AIP) 984
Archaeological Journal (AJ) 5, 6
archaeological societies 5 *see also individual
 society names*
Archaeological Survey of Ireland 914
Archaeology and the Middle Ages
 (SMA agenda) 982
archaeo-topographical survey
 (analytical earthwork survey) 23, 25
architecture
 agricultural buildings 259–60, 260f, 262,
  263–6, 264f
 cathedrals 582–90, 587–8f
 churches 554–5, 600–5, 603–4f, 611f
 Denmark 947, 951–3, 952f
 European influence on Normans 373
 Gothic 3–6, 229, 375, 555, 586, 602,
  747, 750
 graffiti 634–5
 layouts of buildings 805–6, 809f, 810
 manor complexes 266–70, 267f, 269f
 manor houses 243–6, 245f
 monasteries 566–7, 566f, 571, 572–5
 peasants' houses 201–2, 204, 205–7,
  206f, 226–38
 Romanesque 371–5, 601–2
 shops 313–15, 313f, 314f, 321
 structuralist approach 40–1
 surge in interest 6
 tripartite plan 246–9, 246f
 vernacular 810–12, 929, 985
Archive of Historical Earthquake Data
 (AHEAD) 985
archives
 of aerial photographs 25–6
 online 984–5
Arden Forest (Warwickshire) 87, 95, 213
Arena Chapel, Padua (Italy) 747
aristocracy 329, 366–8
 board games 533, 535
 designed landscapes 386, 395–7
 in Ireland 915

aristocracy (*cont.*)
  location of burials 858
  pleasure gardens 393–4, 397
  space and gender 813–14
  tournaments 394
Aristotle 690, 732, 742–3, 745, 762
Armada shipwrecks 974
arrowhead, as charm 616
artefacts
  from battlefields 408–11, 409f
  biography of 45
  biological 250–1
  changing emphasis over time 5
  coins as 513–15
  destruction of 5, 45
  domestic setting 43
  evidence of trades and crafts 326
  illegal removal 414
  increased understanding of 15
  from moated sites 250
  movement across the Channel 5
  numbers of finds 20
  recycling 5
  from sieges 411–13, 412f
  storage 14, 439
  symbols of resistance to power 427–8
  urban 291
Arthur (King of the Britons) 419
artisans, symbols of resistance to power 427
Arts and Humanities Research Council 11, 414
artworks
  commemorative 664–5
  depicting chessboards 532
  symbols of power in 418, 420f
  wall paintings 660–1, 661f, 745–8, 746–7f, 879–80
Arundel, Thomas (Archbishop of Canterbury) 421, 749
Asferg (Jutland) 951
Ashmolean Museum, University of Oxford (Oxfordshire) 791, 792, 794
  coin collections 512
Ashwell (Hertfordshire) 629, 630, 637
Asia, trade with 889, 891, 894 *see also individual countries*
assarting 93–4, 95, 96
Assize of the Forest 142

Association for Environmental Archaeology (AEA) 102
Association of European Archaeologists 448
Aston, Mick 11
At Risk Register 414
Athelhampton (Dorset) 247, 247f
Attleborough (Norfolk) 608
Atwell, George (surveyor and mathematician) 159
Aubrey, John (antiquarian) 373–5, 591
auditory perception *see* sounds
Audley (of Walden), Thomas Audley, Baron 405
Audun-le-Tiche (France) 494, 496
Augsburg (Germany) 532
Augustinian brethren 645
Augustinian canons 791
Augustinian Friary in Hull (East Riding of Yorkshire) 859
Augustinian Holy Trinity (Dublin) 920
Augustinian house, Wigmore (Herefordshire) 968
Augustinian monasteries 569, 571, 577
  estates 576
Augustinian priories 581
Augustinian priory of Kells (Co. Kilkenny, Ireland) 919
Augustinian priory of St Mary Merton (Surrey) 439, 778
Auldhame (East Lothian) 547
aumbries 607
Austin Friars of Hull (East Riding of Yorkshire) 571
Austin Friars, Leicester (Leicestershire) 702, 703f, 704, 791, 795
authority, studies of 44
Avebury (Wiltshire) 878
Aveiro (Portugal) 970, 974
Avilés museum (Spain) 976
Azores (Portugal) 891

BABAO (British Association of Biological Anthropology and Osteoarchaeology) 819, 827
Baber, John (brazier) 701
Bacon, Roger (philosopher and scientist) 691
badges, as symbols of resistance to power 428

badges of royalty 421–3, 422f
Bagoeta, Álava (Spain) 968, 969f, 971
baileys 361, 363
Bakewell (Derbyshire) 863
Ballyine (Co. Limerick, Ireland) 500, 500f, 501
Balsall (Warwickshire) 244
Baltic coast 336, 942, 944, 945
Baltic Sea 128, 444, 889, 941, 964
Baltic states 442
   coins 524
   Estonia 446, 945
   herring from 131, 134
   trade with 131, 134, 147, 670, 893, 943,
      945–6, 955–7
Baltonsborough Mill, Glastonbury
   (Somerset) 499
Bamburgh Castle (Northumberland) 5, 6f
Bampfield mine, North Molton (Devon) 463
bandages 838, 839f
Bangor Cathedral (Gwynedd) 584
Bannockburn, Battle of [Stirling,
   Scotland, 1314] 402, 404–5, 410
baptism 762, 775
baptismal fonts 608–10, 609f
Barcelona (Spain) 728
Bardney (Lincolnshire) 570
Bardowick (Germany) 500f, 501
Barentin family 427
Barentin's Manor (Oxfordshire) 243, 251, 253,
   703, 704
Barenton, Brittany (France) 221
Barkefold, John (15th century) 719
Barker Tower, York (North Yorkshire) 346
Barking Abbey, (London) 815
Barlings Abbey (Lincolnshire) 566
Barnack (Northamptonshire) 244, 329, 332
Barnack quarry (Cambridgeshire) 438, 457
Barnard Castle (Co. Durham) 14, 103, 104,
   105, 111, 358, 363, 790–1
Barnard Chapel, St Mary's Church, Luton
   (Bedfordshire) 872
Barnet, Battle of [Hertfordshire, 1471] 405,
   408, 411
Barnham (Sussex) 897
barns 196–7, 263–5, 264f, 266–8, 270
Barra, Outer Hebrides (Scotland) 185
barrel-coopering 478

Barrow upon Soar (Leicestershire) 460
Bartholomaeus Anglicus 747
Barton Blount (Derbyshire) 155, 197, 506
Barton Farm, Bradford-on-Avon
   (Wiltshire) 265, 269, 269f
Basel (Switzerland) 301
basket houses 226
Basque trade 968
Bassingham (Lincolnshire) 635
bastles 365
Batalha (Portugal) 975
Bate, Athelard 672
Bath (Somerset) 346, 373
   Bath cathedral 581
   bishop palace 382
   monasteries 569
Batsford (East Sussex) 496, 497, 498f, 499,
   500, 500f
Battle (East Sussex) 745
Battle Abbey (East Sussex) 707, 795
battlefields 401–2
   artefacts found 408–11, 409f
   conservation management 413–15
   contamination with modern items 414–15
   evidence 404–8, 407f
   records of 402–4, 403–4f
   see also individual battles
Battlefields Inventory 413
Battlefields Register 414
Battlefields Trust, Resource Centre 402
Bawtry (South Yorkshire) 344
Bay of Bourgneuf (France) 933
bay divisions 301–2
Bayeux Tapestry 405, 418, 419, 420f, 707, 910
Baynards Castle (London) 749
BBC documentary 7
beads 485, 797
bears 146, 148–9, 149f
Beauchamp, Richard (Bishop of
   Salisbury) 620, 880
Beauchamp, Richard de (13th Earl of
   Warwick) 862
Beaufort, Henry (Bishop of Winchester) 880
Beaulieu (Hampshire) 502, 573
Beaumaris (Anglesey) 5
Beaumont-le-Richard (France) 244
Beauvais (France) 927

Beckamoor Combe, Dartmoor (Devon) 464
Becket, Thomas (á) (Archbishop of Canterbury) 347, 423, 859
Becket ampulla, Canterbury 649, 650
Becket's blood 648
Beckside (East Yorkshire) 500
Bedern, The, York (North Yorkshire) 481
Bedfordshire
  Bedford 346
  Chicksands Priory 566–7
  Dunstable Priory 571, 620
  Husbands Crawley 630
  Leighton Buzzard 24
  Luton 610, 872
  pottery in 332
  Stratton 122, 123
  Tempsford Park 243
Beer quarry (Devon) 457
Beguine movement 550
Beijing (China) 730
Belchamp (Essex) 263
bell-casting 481
bell foundries 439
bell-ringers 718f, 719
bell towers 584, 598, 718, 719, 723
bells 715, 716f, 716–17
  church 555, 718–25, 724f
  for communication 715
Belmont on Unst, Shetland (Scotland) 464–5
Belton church (Lincolnshire) 718f
Ben Lawers Landscape Project (Scotland) 173, 175, 176f, 178, 181
Benedict XII, Pope 376
Benedict XIII, Pope 972
Benedictine abbey, Reading 968
Benedictine monasteries 569–70, 571, 577, 581
  belief in Purgatory 870
  cloisters 572
  estates 575–6
  medical conditions 575
Benedictine nunneries 815
Benedictine Rule 571, 573
Benson (Oxfordshire) 720, 721f, 723
Bere (Gwynedd, Wales) 288
Bere Alston (Devon) 184, 463
Bere Ferrers (Devon) 175, 437, 461, 462f
Bergen (Norway) 441, 446, 946

Bergmann's Rule 106
Berkeley Castle (Gloucestershire) 54
Berkeley family (13th century) 858
Berkshire College, Cambridge (Cambridgeshire) 377
Bermondsey Abbey (London) 14, 810
Bernard of Angers (11th-century author) 531–2
Berrick Prior (Oxfordshire) 719, 724
Berrien, Brittany (France) 929
Berwickshire
  Berwick port 643, 893
  Coldingham 570
  Eyemouth 134, 183
  Fast Castle 790–1
  The Hirsel 547, 652
  Kirk Ness 847
Bessingby (North Yorkshire) 632
Bethersden (Kent) 218
Beverley (East Yorkshire) 14, 119, 120, 300, 302, 306, 500, 739, 749
  board games 533
Bewdley (Worcestershire) 327f
bezels 797
Bible 621
Biblia pauperum (Poor Man's Bible) 658
Bicker Haven (Lincolnshire) 469
Big Data 72, 984
Biggar (Lanarkshire) 180, 605
Bignor (Sussex) 471
BioArCh team, University of York 105
Bilbao (Spain) 968, 976
Bilney (Norfolk) 460
Bilson, John (18th-century scholar) 592
Binham Priory (Norfolk) 630, 635, 688, 688f
bioarchaeology 60–1, 819, 824, 827, 926, 992
  analytical techniques 828
  data analysis 829–30
  future research 830–1
biographical studies 44–5
biographies, archeological 988–9
biomolecular archaeology 15, 32
birds, wild 144–5
Birmingham (West Midlands) 438, 439, 549
birth 762
Bisconis, Andreas de (15th-century cleric) 626
Bishop Auckland (Co. Durham) 382

bishoprics 372, 372f
bishops 581
Bishop's Loch, Loch Goil (Aberdeenshire) 186
Bishops Waltham (Hampshire) 382
Bishopsgate (London) 341
Bishopstone (East Sussex) 129
Blackburn, Nicholas Sr (Lord Mayor of
 York) 662f
Black Death (1348–50) 147, 154, 325, 376, 377,
 820, 840–2
  catastrophic cemetery
   (East Smithfield) 829
  commemorated in church inscriptions 629
  dwellings rebuilt after 232, 239
  effect on ageing norms 769
  effect on arable landscapes 96–8
  effect on fishing industry 135
  effect on housing 305
  effect on monasteries 576
  effect on population 285
  effect on shops 320
  effect on work practices 767
  studies of 60–1
  and urban change 289
black earth 333
Blackfriars, Gloucester
 (Gloucestershire) 469, 829
Blackfriar's Barn, New Winchelsea
 (East Sussex) 314–15
Black Friary, Trim (Co. Meath, Ireland) 919
Black Gate, Newcastle upon Tyne
 (Tyne and Wear) 790
Black Sea 891
blacksmiths 481–2
Blairgowrie (Perthshire) 182
Blakeney (Norfolk) 601, 601f, 636
Blanche's Crown 420–1
Blekinge (Sweden) 941
blood-letting 838–40
Blythburgh (Suffolk) 635
boar, symbol 422–3, 422f
board games 531–8, 532f, 534f, 536f
Boarstall (Buckinghamshire) 201, 331
Bodiam Castle (East Sussex) 23, 42–3, 55,
 253, 357
Bodleian Library, University of Oxford
 (Oxfordshire) 54, 285, 287

Bodmin Moor (Cornwall) 41, 93, 95, 463
Bohemian glass-making 443
Bohun family 422
Bollingen (Württemberg, Germany) 517
bones
  abnormalities 780, 781
  ageing process 761
  animal *see* animal bones
  charnel 857
  evidence of morbidity in children 767
  examining 859–60
  fracture rates from leprosy 829–30
  human 60–1, 819–30 *see also* burials
  limited diseases affecting 826
  objects made from 483–4
Boniface VIII, Pope 860
Book of Sainte Foy, The (Bernard
 of Angers) 531–2
Books of Hours 659, 668, 669f
Boothby Pagnell (Lincolnshire) 244, 245
Borbjerg, Jutland (Denmark) 953
Bordeaux (France) 444, 514, 919
Border wares from London 751
Bordesley Abbey (Worcestershire) 163, 437,
 478, 482, 567, 568f, 569
 watermill 495f, 495, 496, 497, 499f, 499,
  500, 501, 502
Boreham Airfield (Essex) 246
Børglum Cathedral Jutland (Denmark) 953
Bornish, South Uist (Scotland) 131
Boston (Lincolnshire) 132, 133, 342, 345,
 670–2, 671f
  Boston stump *see* St Botolph's Church,
   Boston (Lincolnshire)
  imports and exports 894–5, 897
Bosworth, Battle of [Leicestershire, 1485] 401,
 405, 408, 409f, 411, 414, 418, 795
Boteler's (or Oversley) Castle
 (Warwickshire) 366
botijas or 'olive jars' 974
Bottisham (Cambridgeshire) 608
Boulogne area (France) 458
Bourges (France) 496
Bourne (Lincolnshire) 331
Bovey Tracey (Devon) 608
box-framing timber tradition 229, 234, 234f
Brabant region 590

Bradbourne (Derbyshire) 673
Bradford-on-Avon (Wiltshire) 265, 269f, 481, 879f
Bramber (West Sussex) 458, 468, 470
Bramford (Suffolk) 608
Brandes-d'Oisans (France) 929
Brandon (Suffolk) 218
brasses 862
Brassington (Derbyshire) 205
brass-rubbings 775–6, 777f
Bray (Berkshire) 872
Brayford Pool, Lincoln (Lincolnshire) 345
breastfeeding 763
Breckenborough (North Yorkshire) 517
Brennilis, Brittany (France) 929
Breviarium Bartholomei (by John Mirfield) 836
brewing industry 443, 477
brickmaking 443
bridge chapels 643
bridge estates 348
Bridge Masters 346
bridges 345–8, 347f
Bridge Street, York (North Yorkshire) 316
Bridgettine order 955
Bridgewater Without (Somerset) 505
Bridgnorth (Shropshire) 280
Bridlington (North Yorkshire) 132, 504
Brightwell Baldwin (Oxfordshire) 720, 721–2f
Brikar, Thomas (15th-century carpenter) 442
Brill (Buckinghamshire) 201, 331
brine springs 484–5 *see also* salt production
Brinklow (Warwickshire) 280
Briquebec (France) 244
Bristol 284, 285, 287, 290
  Abbots Leigh 708
  bridges 346, 347
  Bristol Castle 972
  dyes 479, 480f
  houses 297, 301, 306, 307, 317
  Keynsham Abbey 566, 651
  Lord Mayor's Chapel 5, 974
  market stalls 319
  ports 135, 291, 342, 344, 919, 964, 974, 975
  pottery 444, 751, 919–20, 974
  Poyntz family 901, 974
  quarries close to 471
  Redcliffe area 479, 480f
  shop-houses 318, 486
  St Bartholomew's Hospital 847, 850
  St James's Priory 525
  St James the Less Church, Iron-Acton 901
  tanning 482–3
  textile industry 479, 480f, 482–3
  trade route to Ireland 919
  urban regeneration 12, 14, 275
  waterfronts 279, 343
  wine 330, 446
British Archaeological Association 5–6, 14, 593, 660
British Association of Biological Anthropology and Osteoarchaeology (BABAO) 819, 827
British Geological Survey 471
British History Online website 53
British Library (London) 54, 253, 702
British Museum 6, 7, 12, 380, 422, 518, 607, 615–16, 715, 794, 799, 987
  coin collections 512
Brittany (France) 39
Broad Streets, Aberdeen (Aberdeenshire) 319
Bromholm Priory (Norfolk) 646, 656
Brompton Bridge (Yorkshire) 651
brooches 615–16
  coins as 524–5
  see also pilgrim badges
Brook Street, Winchester (Hampshire) 304, 304f, 308
Brooks Wharf (London) 966
Brora (Sutherland) 184
Brown Willy, Bodmin Moor (Cornwall) 93, 95
Browne's Hospital, Stamford (Lincolnshire) 851
Bruegel, Pieter (16th-century artist) 538
Bruges (Belgium) 944, 971, 974
Buckfastleigh (Devon) 608
Buckland-in-the-Moor (Devon) 632
Bucklersbury (London) 315
buckle plates 798f, 799f, 800
buckles 203f
building industry 200
Buildings at Risk Register 382
buildings
  agricultural 259–60, 260f, 262, 263–6, 264f

on bridges 347–8, 347f
copied designs 213
designed to be impressive 212–13
fronting 306–7
lordly 212–13
manor complexes 266–70, 267f, 269f
privacy 216
standing *see* standing buildings
stone 301, 317, 456–60
tripartite plan 246–9, 246f
urban 298–308, 299f, 303f, 304f
views from 213–15, 214f
vocalized 211–12
waterfront 342–4, 345, 441
Bulkington (Wiltshire) 445f
Bull Hall, Winchester (Hampshire) 699
Burgo, Richard de ('Red' Earl of Ulster) 913
Burgundy (France) 933, 935
burials 44
 cathedrals 585
 children 775–80, 777f
 coins in 525
 commemorations 426–7, 426f, 862–3
 criminals 861
 crossroads 862
 data analysis 829–30
 evidence of battlefields 405–8, 407f
 exhumations 819, 820f, 827, 857
 and funerals 856–7
 gender segregation 808–9
 grave goods 858–9
 infant 762–3
 limitations of data 825–7
 locations 857–8
 mass graves 841–2, 842f
 monasteries 575
 mortuary practices 860–2
 pilgrims 651–5, 652f, 653f, 654f
 position of bodies 819–20, 820f
 royal tombs 863–4
 sex and age estimation 826
 St Mary Spital hospital cemetery 823–5, 824f
 studies of bodies 859–60
 tomb shrines 664–5, 666f
 see also Wharram Percy (North Yorkshire)
Burnham (Lincolnshire) 553

Burton (Wiltshire) 608
Burton Agnes (Yorkshire) 244
Burton Dassett (Warwickshire) 506
Burton on Trent (Staffordshire) 161, 335, 570
Bury St Edmunds (Suffolk) 320, 342, 476–7
 Abbeygate Street 317
 cathedral 968
 coin-making 476, 514f
 Moyse's Hall 213
 stone 332
 windows 314
Butcher's Row, Shrewsbury (Shropshire) 317
butchery
 carcass products 482–4, 483f
 practices 697
 in smallholdings 198–9
 written documents 60
Buzzart Dykes (Perthshire) 185, 382
Byland Abbey (North Yorkshire) 567, 574, 986

Cabaret, Durfort (France) 929
Cade, William of London 418
CADW, Welsh historic environment service 11
Cadwallader (Northumberland historian) 6
Caen, Normandy (France) 332, 458, 459f, 470, 897
Caen stone 445–6, 933
Caernarfon (Gwynedd) 284, 287, 913
Caesarius of Heisterbach 535
Cahir Castle (Co. Tipperary, Ireland) 913
Cairngorms (Scotland) 141
Calais (France) 515
Caldecote (Hertfordshire) 62, 173
Calicut (India) 971
Calstock (Cornwall) 463
Cambridge (Cambridgeshire) 334–5
 animal remains 109
 museums 512, 514
 River Cam 221
 St John's Hospital 405, 850
 stone 332
 University 25, 54, 377, 567, 840, 872
Cambridgeshire
 Barnack quarry 438, 457
 Bottisham 608
 burial of criminals 861

Cambridgeshire (*cont.*)
  Chesterton 460
  Duxford 460, 629, 633*f*, 638
  Ely *see* Ely; Ely Cathedral
  Gamlingay 776–7
  Harlton 637
  Hayley Wood 33
  Hemingford Grey Manor House 244
  Histon 460
  Kingston 746*f*, 777
  Peakirk Church 606
  Peterborough 220, 331
  Peterborough Abbey 438, 567
  Peterborough Cathedral 582, 586, 593
  Ramsey Abbey 438, 441
  St Neot 43
  Yaxley 460
  see also Cambridge (Cambridgeshire)
Cambuskenneth Abbey (Stirling) 184
Camp Shiel Burn (Peeblesshire) 181
Campbells of Glenlyon (Perthshire) 615
Campo del Tablado Church, Castropol (Spain) 973*f*
canals 345
Canaries Islands (Spain) 971
candles 436
Canmore database 184, 185, 402
canons 581
Canterbury (Kent) 320, 643, 644, 955
  ampulla 648, 649, 650
  Christ Church 265
  dental health 823, 830
  monasteries 569
  Northgate 161
  St Augustine's Abbey 377–8, 458, 470, 573
  St John's Church 644
  stone buildings 301, 470
Canterbury Cathedral, Canterbury (Kent)
  artwork 747
  construction of 346, 582, 583*f*, 586, 592, 933
  inscriptions 635
  pilgrimages to 43, 619, 629, 643, 646–7, 919, 955, 966
  planning 583*f*, 585
  Priory 571, 573
  royal marriage 956
  shrines 584, 643, 646–7, 648, 689, 955

  tombs 426, 665, 666*f*, 791, 858, 895
Canterbury Tales, The (Chaucer) 643, 743–4
Cape of Good Hope (South Africa) 891
Capetian kings 372, 376
Capon, William 378
carcass products 482–4, 483*f see also* butchery
card games 537
Cardigan Bay 228
Cardinal College (Christ Church), Oxford University 577
Care of Cathedrals Measure 593
Carisbrooke Castle (Isle of Wight) 60, 367, 813
Carlisle (Cumbria) 337
Carlisle Cathedral (Cumbria) 581, 589, 590, 630
Carmarthen (Wales) 974
Carmelite friary 439
Carolingian empire 571, 615
Carrick (Argyll) 532
Carrickfergus (Co. Antrim, Ireland) 911–12
Carse of Gowrie (Perthshire) 182
Carta Mercatoria (1303) 900
Cartagena (Spain) 972
Carter, John (18th-century draughtsman) 3
Cartergate, Grimsby (Lincolnshire) 132–3
Carthusian monasteries 569
Carthusians, cloisters 574
cartography *see* mapping
carvings 318
Cashel Cathedral (Ireland) 445
castellology *see* castles
Castile (Spain) 975
Castle Acre (Norfolk) 212, 213, 358, 532, 534–5
Castle Combe (Wiltshire) 288
Castle Donington mill (Derbyshire) 496, 498, 502
Castle Eden (Co. Durham) 91
Castle Green cemetery (Hereford) 858
Castle Hill, Strachan (Aberdeenshire) 363
Castle Mall, Norwich (Norfolk) 359
castle-palaces 371
Castle Rising (Norfolk) 813
Castle Studies Group 8, 355
castle-towns 279–80, 284
castles
  association with chess 532
  design 212–13

earth-and-timber castles 361–3
earthwork castles 185
　in France 930–2, 931f
　gardens surrounding 394
　gender and space 813, 814
　in Ireland 909–13, 910f, 912f
　layout 805
　'military v. symbolism' debate 357–8
　motte-and-bailey castles 356, 358, 910, 911, 930
　'origins of the castle' debate 41–3, 356–7
　plant remains 121
　projective and reflective views 366–7
　studies of 355–6, 358–68
　siege castles 361
　surge in interest 5, 7
　towns built next to 329
　see also individual castles
Caston (Norfolk) 635
Castor (Northamptonshire) 216
Castrojeriz, Burgos (Spain) 966
catastrophic events 154, 156–9, 157f, 158f
　mitigating the damage 159–61, 160f
　protection from 161–4
cathedrals 581–2
　architecture 582–90, 587–8f
　burials 585
　design and construction 582–6
　furnishings 590–1
　plans 583–6, 583f
　studies of 591–3
　see also individual cathedrals
Catherine of Aragon (Queen of England) 968
Catpund quarry (Shetland) 440f
cats 108–9
cattle 332
cattle stalls 262
cattle-farming 74, 79, 110–11
　calf slaughter 104–5
　disease 106–8
　grazing 333–4
　leather-working 105
　living conditions 262
　size of cattle 105–6
　on smallholdings 197, 199
　vellum production 104–5
Caus (Shropshire) 325

Causeway Lane, Leicester (Leicestershire) 108
Caxton, William 659
Cefn Graeanog (Gwynedd) 171, 179
cellars 318
Central Province 87
ceramics
　albarelli 898
　assemblages 698–700, 700f
　colour 751–2, 752f
　dripping pans 699
　imported 898
　jugs 705, 706f
　pipkins 850
　traditions 441
　see also pottery
cereals 118, 120, 121, 123, 197
Chalgrove (Oxfordshire) 427, 616, 719, 723, 724
chalk 460
chamber blocks 244
Champagne fairs 889
chancel areas 598, 599, 607–8
Chancery records 53
chantries 600, 872–5, 873f, 876, 878
chantry chapels 872, 874–5f, 875–6, 878–81
Chapel Hill, Ballachly (Caithness) 464
Chapel of our Lady of the Pew, Westminster Abbey (London) 378, 380
chapels 220, 552–4, 597, 600
　on bridges 348, 643
Chapman, Adam (seller of pilgrim badges) 645
chapter-houses 573, 585
charcoal 435–6
Charlemagne 615 see also Carolingians
Charles I (King of Great Britain and Ireland) 379, 419
Charles the Bold (Duke of Burgundy) 523
Charlottenburg Palace, Berlin (Germany) 947
charnel 857 see also bones
charring 117, 120
Chartered Institute for Archaeologists (CIfA) 13
Charterhouse Square (London) 841
'chases' (deer reserves) 388
chasses 647
Châteaugiron, Ille-et-Vilaine (France) 926

Château-Thierry (France) 930
Chaucer, Geoffrey 523, 643, 743–4
Cheam (Surrey) 486, 751
Cheapside (London) 283, 315, 319, 320, 321, 341, 481
Cheddar (Somerset) 371
Chedworth (Gloucestershire) 629
Chellaston (Derbyshire) 335, 458
Chelmsford (Essex) 346
Chepstow Park (Monmouthshire) 184
Chepstow Castle (Monmouthshire) 14, 318, 363–5, 364*f*, 813
Chertsey (Surrey) 380
Cheshire
  Buerton 25
  College Fields 25
  Combermere Abbey 566
  Darnhall 570
  Meols 159–60, 704, 793
  monasteries 570
  Nantwich 469, 484
  Newhall Tower 26, 26*f*
  Norton Priory 437, 567, 572
  Old Abbey Farm 243
  Poulton 570
  salt working 469, 484
  Stanlaw on the Mersey 570
  Tatton 205
  Vale Royal 570
  see also Chester (Cheshire)
chessboards 531–3, 534, 536, 537–8, 990
chess pieces
  chalk 534
  found on Isle of Lewis 15, 46
  ivory 484, 896*f*
  Northampton 483*f*
Chester (Cheshire) 11
  buildings 301, 303, 306, 316, 320
  Chester Cathedral 573, 590, 683–4, 684*f*
  Chester Rows 318–19, 487
  Dee Bridge 346
  Dominican Priory 778, 795
  Earls of 276
  monasteries 569, 570, 778
  shops 318–19, 320, 487
  streets 316, 341, 342
  trade route to Ireland 919

  urban landscapes 281, 285, 286*f*, 325
  Watergate 316
Chester's Pentice, Felsted (Essex) 316
Chesterton (Cambridgeshire) 460
Chestnut Wood, Borden (Kent) 25
Chew Magna (Somerset) 872
Chichele, Henry (Archbishop of Canterbury) 426, 665, 666*f*
Chichester (West Sussex)
  bell-casting 481
  Bishop's Palace 380–2
  Chichester Cathedral 163, 582, 584
  St James and St Mary Magdalene Hospital 829, 843, 861
  St Mary's Hospital 644, 645
Chicksands Priory (Bedfordshire) 566–7
childbirth, death in 778
children 44, 61, 763–5, 774–5, 780–5
  burials 775–80, 777*f*, 858
  as craftworkers 443
  education 767
  infants 761–3
  morbidity 767
  physical labour 781
  play 537–8, 766–7, 784
  socialization 783–5
  work 766
Chillingham (Northumberland) 105, 107
Chilmark limestone 586
Chilterns 720, 721*f*, 723
Chilvers Coton (Warwickshire) 201, 331
chimneys 307
China 891
Chingley Forge (Kent) 464, 496, 497, 498*f*, 499, 500, 500*f*, 502
Chrétien de Troyes 148
Christ Church, Canterbury (Kent) 265
Christ Church, Oxford University 577
Christ Church, York (North Yorkshire) (York) 551
Christchurch Priory (Dorset) 878
Christchurch Priory, Twynham (Hampshire) 615
Christian I (King of Denmark, Norway, and Sweden) 956–7
Christianity 371–2, 375–6
Christina of Markyate 627

Christmas festivities 621
Chronicles (Froissart) 532
Chroniques d'Angletere 702
Church
    association with landscape 545–6
    resistance to 428–9
    and State 371–2
Church of the Holy Sepulchre,
        Jerusalem 40, 810
Church Monument Society 862
church records 53–4
Church Street, Tewkesbury
        (Gloucestershire) 313
churches
    acoustic modelling 550–1
    aesthetics 554–6
    architecture 554–5, 600–5, 603–4f, 611f
    bells 555, 718–25, 724f
    board games in 535–7, 536f
    chapels 552–4
    components 598–600
    Denmark 949, 950, 951–3, 952f
    design and construction 600–1
    details and furnishings 605–10
    fixtures and fittings 663–4
    Gothic architecture 375–6
    graffiti inscriptions *see* graffiti inscriptions
        in churches
    interplay of the senses 683–5
    Ireland 918–19
    and landholders 555–6
    landscapes 551–6
    parish *see* parish churches
    plans 598–9, 599f, 646
    studies of 610–12
    in towns 549–50
    wall paintings 745–8, 746–7f
    see also monasteries
Cicero 690
Cinema City excavations, Norwich
        (Norfolk) 649, 650f
cinnabar 974
Cinque Ports 132, 446
circular keeps 912
Cirencester (Gloucestershire) 598, 605
Cistercian monasteries 569, 570, 573
    cloisters 574, 575

    estates 576
Cistercian nuns 643
Cistercian Ware 751
Cistercians 744, 745, 747, 748
    architecture 586
    monuments 863
Ciudad Real (Spain) 974
Clarendon Palace (Wiltshire) 371, 376, 377,
        380, 381f, 382, 383, 896, 897
Clarendon Park (Wiltshire) 39, 373, 375, 389f
clay dabbins 205
Cleeve Abbey (Somerset) 566, 566f
Clement VI, Pope 376
Clerkenwell nunnery (London) 14
Clermont-Ferrand Cathedral (France) 589
Cley-next-the-Sea (Norfolk) 635, 636, 636f
Clifford, Rosamund (mistress of Henry II)
        373
climate 154–6
    effect on agriculture 79–80
    effect on animal size 105–6
    effect on cattle 107–8
    effect on health 820–1
climate change 76
Cloere Brien prison (Berkshire) 60
cloisters 572–5
Cloontycarthy (Co. Cork, Ireland),
        watermill 492f
cloth-making 335
cloth-working 441–2
clothing 336, 789
    colours 748–9
    dress accessories 793–800, 794f, 796f,
        798f, 799f
    finds 790–3, 792f
    future research 800
    production 199, 200
    religious 791
cloth seals 895, 896f
Cluny Abbey, Saône-et-Loire
        (France) 301, 933
Clwydian Hills (Wales) 70
Clywd-Powys Archaeological Trust 415
coal 436
coal mining 465–6, 466f, 467f
coastal areas 71
    ship graffiti 635

coastal areas (*cont.*)
  specialized settlements 182–3, 183*f*
  storms 159
coats-of-arms 423, 955–6
Cobham, John de (builder) 211
cochineal 749
Cockersand (Lancashire) 221
cod 129, 130–1, 132–6, 332, 895, 985
Coflein database 11, 402
Coge, Agnes (midwife) 779
Coggeshall (Essex) 298
coins 199–200, 235, 511–12, 514*f*
  collections 512–13
  dating 515–17, 516*f*
  Denmark 950–1, 953
  as documents and artefacts 513–15
  folded 160–1, 160*f*, 525, 616, 989
  forgeries 516
  future research 525–6
  hoards 517–19, 518*f*
  from Iberian Peninsula 976
  imported 521–4, 522*f*
  mutilation 525
  production 476
  as sacred relics 616–17
  Scandinavia 946
  secondary use 524–5
  single finds 519–21, 521*f*
  Spain 966
Colchester (Essex) 298, 325, 334, 519, 847, 848–9, 899, 955
Coldingham (Berwickshire) 570
Coleham Island, Shrewsbury (Shropshire) 347
Coleorton (Leicestershire) 465–6, 466*f*, 467*f*
collaborations between disciplines 985–6
College Fields (Cheshire) 25
Cologne Cathedral (Germany) 615
Colomby (France), watermill 494, 495*f*, 495, 496, 500*f*
colour 742–5
  ceramics 751–2, 752*f*
  clothing 748–9
  detail in churches 605–6
  manuscripts 750
  in wall paintings 745–8, 746–7*f*
Colwyn Castle (Powys) 184

Combe Martin (Devon) 461
Combe-in-Teignhead (Devon) 632
Combermere Abbey (Cheshire) 566
commemorations 426–7, 426*f*, 664–5, 862–3
commerce 444–6, 445*f* *see also* trade
Common Law, age of responsibility 767
Common Pleas court, Westminster 53, 379
communication, sounds 715
community archaeology 987–8
community projects 11–12, 22–3, 173*f*
Company of Pewterers 704
compass arms 496
compass-drawn designs 632, 634*f*
Compostela *see* Santiago de Compostela (Spain)
computed tomography 828
computer recording systems 102–3
Conan IV (Duke of Brittany) 145–6
coneygarths 391
Coney Street, York (North Yorkshire) 304
Conflict Archaeology International Research Network (CAIRN) 401
Conques (France) 549
conservation management of battlefields 413–15
Constantinople (Turkey) 621*f*, 891
Conwy (Wales) 276, 284, 287, 301
cooking 697, 698–701, 700*f*
Cooling Castle (Kent) 211
Copenhagen (Denmark) 957
  Copenhagen Psalter 950
  University of Copenhagen 957
copper
  mining 463
  transportation 470
copper alloy 336
  cooking pots 700–1
  from Scandinavia 948–9
Coppergate, York (North Yorkshire) 476, 702
Coquetdale community archaeology 988
Corbett, Peter (Marcher lord) 146
Corcannon (Co. Wexford, Ireland) 493
Corfe Castle (Dorset) 25, 29*f*, 484
Cork (Ireland) 444, 918
Corn Street (Bristol) 319
Cornwall 96, 205
  Altarnum 632

INDEX

Bodmin Moor 41, 93, 95, 463
  Calstock 463
  chapels 552, 553
  churches 605
  copper mining 463
  field systems 90f, 91
  fishing industry 135
  Fovey 506
  hamlets 174
  Launceston Castle 11, 13, 79, 102, 104, 106, 111, 358, 366, 532, 897, 898, 984
  Liskeard 814
  Penhallam 242, 244, 248, 250, 707
  St Michael's Mount 412–13
  tin mining 463
Coromandel Coast 891
Corona chapel, Canterbury 646–7
Coronation Chair, Westminster 419
Corporal Works of Mercy, All Saints North Street, York (North Yorkshire) 660, 662f
Corpus Christi play cycle 551
Corpus Christi processions 621, 663
Corpus of Scottish Medieval Parish Churches project 985
correspondence, private letters 54
Cosmati pavements 897
COST (European Cooperation in Science and Technology) 136
Cotswolds 441, 480
Council Chamber, York (North Yorkshire) 347
Council for British Archaeology 7, 9
Council of Canterbury (1236) 778
Council of Lyons (1274) 870
Council of Treves (1310) 778
countryside surveys 70–1, 73–4
  chronological changes 74–5
  environmental approach 77–80
  theoretical approaches 75–6
  see also rural landscapes
County Clare (Ireland) 914
County Durham (England)
  field systems 91
  silver mining 461
County Kilkenny (Ireland) 914
County Limerick (Ireland) 914
County Meath (Ireland), windmills 503

County Tipperary (Ireland) 914, 915
County Wexford (Ireland) 915
Couper Angus Abbey (Perthshire) 182
Courcey, John de 912
Court Hall, New Winchelsea 315
court rolls 54, 55, 58, 62, 218
courtyard houses 302, 303f
courtyards 266, 267f, 365
Coventry (Warwickshire) 120, 201, 276, 277f, 284, 285, 287, 290, 292f, 304, 325, 342, 439
  churches in 549
Coventry Cathedral 581
Covington (South Lanarkshire) 180
Cowthorpe (North Yorkshire) 607
Crabhouse Priory (Norfolk) 159
craft production 199, 326, 436, 475–7
  animal products 483–4, 483f
  France 932–3
  rural households 477–8
craftworkers 442–4, 442f
crannogs 185–6
Crawley (West Sussex) 464
Crécy Battle [France, 1346] 404, 421
creel houses 226–8
Cricklade (Wiltshire) 28f
criminals, burial practices 861
Croft (Lincolnshire) 607
crofts 176
Cromarty Medieval Burgh Community Archaeology Project 12
Cromwellian Wars 914, 918
Crondon Park, Stock (Essex) 391
crop rotation 926
'Cross-and-Crosslets' coinage 516–17
cross-heads 548
Crossrail project (London) 841
crossroads burials 862
cross-trees 504–5, 506
Crowe, John (14th-century peasant) 218
Crowland Abbey (Lincolnshire) 221, 861
Crowmarsh Gifford (Berkshire) 361
crowns 419–21, 420f
  Imperial State Crown 419
  Philippa of England 956f
crucifixes 896f
cruciform plans of cathedrals 583, 583f
cruck-trusses 226, 227f, 228–9, 231f, 233f, 235

INDEX

Cruggleton (Dumfries and Galloway) 363
Crusades 900
Cuckoo Lane, Southampton (Hampshire) 650, 702, 972
Cuddeson (Oxfordshire) 724
Cumberland, copper mining 463
Cumbria 228, 461
Cuppin Lane, Chester (Cheshire) 341
Curia Regis Rolls 53
curiae 266, 267*f*
Currently Occupied Rural Settlements (CORS) project 11–12
Custom House, Hull (East Riding of Yorkshire) 344
cutlery 704
Cuxham (Oxfordshire) 720, 721–2*f*

dabbins 228
Dalkeith (Midlothian) 605
Dalyngrigge, Sir Edward (builder of Bodiam Castle) 55
dams, construction 498
Danbury (Essex) 486
Dance of Death 660
dancing-girl jugs 953, 954*f*
Danesfort (Co. Kilkenny, Ireland) 910*f*
Danevirke 941–2
Danish Scanian fishery 132
Darenth (Kent) 608
Darnhall (Cheshire) 570
Daroca Cope 972
Dartmoor (Devon) 41, 78, 230, 326, 464
   Dinna Clerks 699
   granite 502
Dasing (Germany) 494, 496, 500
data, storage 984–5
data analysis, from burials 829–30
data collection 102–3
   plant remains 116–18
   techniques 986–7
dating techniques 986
David I (King of Scotland) 184, 185, 523
Dean Court Farm, Abingdon Abbey (Oxfordshire) 121
Deansway, Worcester (Worcestershire) 120, 700*f*

death
   funerals 856–7, 933–5, 934*f*
   post-neonatal 763
   studies of 856
Decorated period 602
decoration
   in churches 605–6, 663–4
   in royal palaces 379–80, 381*f*
deductive approach 38–9
Dee Bridge, Chester (Cheshire) 346
de Elsyng, Richard (14th-century London mercer) 318
Deeping St Nicholas (Lincolnshire) 730
deer 372
deer-farming 111
deer-hunting 142–4, 149–50, 388–91
deer parks 185, 373, 382
defences, urban 281
Degannwy (Gwynedd) 375
Dekker, Thomas (17th-century writer) 627
demesne farming 97, 108, 477
Denbigh (Denbighshire) 315, 319
Denbigh Moors (Denbighshire) 182
dendrochronology dating techniques 31, 32, 59, 59*f*, 297–8, 566–7, 985
Dene, Robert (Stoneleigh) 58
Denmark 135, 261, 941–3, 942*f*
   architecture 947, 951–3, 952*f*
   churches 949, 950, 951–3, 952*f*
   contrasted with Britain 947–8
   craftworkers 443
   import of metals 944
   produce 945–6
   relationship with Britain 948–56
   relationship with Scotland 957
   research in 259
dental health 822–3
depositions 46
Derby (Derbyshire) 348
Derbyshire 344
   Bakewell 863
   Barton Blount 155, 197, 506
   Belper 814
   Bradbourne 673
   Brassington 205
   Castle Donington mill 496, 498, 502
   Chellaston 335, 458

Derby 348
Drakelow 221
Needham Grange 97
Norbury 598
Peak (or Peveril) Castle 210–11, 368, 989
Peak District 93, 97, 145, 205, 332, 463, 502
River Dove 519
Royston Grange 22
silver mining 461
Deritend (Warwickshire) 201
Deserted Medieval Village Research Group (DMVRG) 7–8
deserted villages 155, 172, 179, 200, 204, 782f, 916–18, 917f
France 929
desiccation 117
Despenser, Sir Edward le 875f, 878
Despenser chapel, Tewkesbury Abbey (Gloucestershire) 878
detectorists *see* metal-detecting
de Ufford, Robert (Justiciar of Ireland) 913
developer-led archaeology 12–14, 21
Devon 77–8, 96, 228, 239, 332
 Beer quarry 457
 Bere Alston 184, 463
 Bere Ferrers 175, 437, 461, 462f
 Bovey Tracey 608
 Buckfastleigh 608
 Buckland-in-the-Moor 632
 chantries 876
 chapels 552
 Combe Martin 461
 Combe-in-Teignland 632
 field systems 90–1, 90f
 fishing industry 135
 Frithelstock 608
 Great Beere 7
 hamlets 174
 Harberton 608
 Hound Tor 230
 Marwood 608
 Morebath 673
 North Molton 463
 Okehampton 196–7, 358
 Ottery St Mary 598
 Plymouth 974, 975
 rivers 461–2, 463

silver mining 461
Tavistock 437f
tin mining 463
Tiverton 874f
see also Dartmoor; Exeter
de Voragine, Jacobus 161
devotional images 658–60, 670–2
 after the Reformation 673–4
 senses 686–91
 types 660–9, 661f, 662f, 667f, 669f
devotional panels 972
dice 534
diet 123, 697–8, 836, 837
 aristocratic 150
 of calves 105
 childhood 765, 774, 775, 780, 781
 deficiencies 825
 effect on neonatal mortality 763
 at Launceston Castle 145
 marine 129, 822
 meat 103, 571
 and medicine 840
 in monasteries 571, 572, 822
 peasant 200, 202, 920
 of pigs at Dudley Castle 79
 weaning 763
 see also food
Dieulacres (Staffordshire) 570
diffuse idiopathic skeletal hyperostosis (DISH) 575, 822
Dig Hungate project by York Archaeological Trust 988
DigVentures excavation, Leiston Abbey (Suffolk) 12, 987
dining practices 701–4, 703f
Dinna Clerks, Dartmoor (Devon) 699
dioceses 581
diseases 739, 744, 820–3, 829–30
 analytical techniques 828
 animal bones 107
 dietary deficiencies 822, 825
 limited data from burials 826–7
 spread 825
DISH (diffuse idiopathic skeletal hyperostosis) 575, 822
Dissolution 577
ditches 120–1

Dives and pauper 658
D. João, royal tomb 975
DNA analysis 124, 826–7, 829–30
dogs 109
  as saints 620
Dolforwyn (Powys) 358
Domesday Book 53, 130, 359, 365, 468, 471, 476–7, 485
domestic environments 43, 58
Dominican Priory, Chester (Cheshire) 778, 795
Doncaster (South Yorkshire) 343, 439, 441
Donington-Le-Heath (Leicestershire) 244
'Doom' (Last Judgement) wall paintings 660, 661*f*, 868, 869*f*
doorways 315, 317
  monasteries 567
Dorchester (Oxfordshire) 723
Dorchester Abbey (Oxfordshire), church bell 724*f*, 724
Dore (Herefordshire) 570
Dornoch (Moray) 581
Dorset 331
Douglas standard 408
Dover (Kent) 570, 635, 644
Dover Castle (Kent) 383, 506
Dowglen (Eskdale) 177
Dragon Hall, Norwich (Norfolk) 306, 447*f*
Drakelow (Derbyshire) 221
draughtsmen 3–5
Drayton (Oxfordshire) 724
dress accessories 793–800, 794*f*, 796*f*, 798*f*, 799*f*
dress-hooks 794
drinking practices 705
drinking vessels 704–8, 706*f*, 932
dripping pans 699
Droitwich (Worcestershire) 485
droveways 181
Dryburgh Abbey (Scottish Borders) 181
Dryslwyn (Carmarthenshire) 111, 358, 532
Dryslwyn Castle (Carmarthenshire) 14, 59, 121, 123, 897
Dublane Cathedral (Stirling) 586
Dublin (Ireland) 915, 918
  imported pottery in 444
  potter's district 441

Duchy of Lancaster 548
Du Colombier farm, Varennes-sur-Seine (France) 929
Dudley Castle (West Midlands) 79, 103
Dugdale, Sir William 54
Dumfries (Scotland) 345
Dumfriesshire (Scotland) 177
Dunadd (Argyll and Bute) 419
Dunamase (Co. Laois, Ireland) 913
Dunbar (East Lothian) 109
Duncan (Earl of Fife) 643
Dundee (Scotland) 109, 605, 893
Dundonald (Ayrshire) 358, 532
Dundrum Castle (Co. Down, Ireland) 912
Dundry stone 444, 471
Dunfermline (Fife) 306
Dunfermline Abbey (Fife) 184, 647, 791
Dunkeld Cathedral (Perth and Kinross) 590
Dunrod and Bombie (Kircudbrightshire) 252
Dunstable Priory (Bedfordshire) 571, 620
Dunstable Swan jewel 795
Dunster (Somerset) 329
Dunwich (Suffolk) 130, 132, 157–8, 164, 345
Dunwich Bailiffs 131
Dupplin Moor Battle [Perth and Kinross, 1332] 402
Durfort (France) 926, 929
Durham (Co. Durham) 301, 346
Durham Cathedral 683
  burial site 652
  construction 583, 583*f*, 584, 585, 586, 587*f*, 682*f*
  furnishings 590, 591
  graffiti 638
  kitchen 121*f*
  pilgrimages to 43
  Purbeck marble 458
Durham Priory 573, 574
Dussindale, Battle [Norfolk, 1549] 405
Duxford (Cambridgeshire) 460, 629, 633*f*, 638
dye-houses 479–80, 480*f*
dyes 120, 748–9
  imports 893, 895
dykes 163
dynamic entanglements 340

Eadgar the Peaceful (King of the English) 515
Earlspark (Co. Galway, Ireland) 395–6

Earldom of Ormond 914
'Early English' interior design 602
Early Medieval Corpus (EMC) 513
earth-and-timber castles 361–3
earthwork castles 185
earthwork survey 986
earthworks 361, 363
  monasteries 567
  around watermills 497
Easby (North Yorkshire) 574
Easebourne (East Sussex) 471
East Anglia 172, 313, 332, 336–7, 548, 605, 608, 610
  field systems 89–90, 89f
  textile industry 480
East Dereham (Norfolk) 610
East Haddesley (West Riding of Yorkshire) 243
East Midlands 94, 228
East Midlands Heritage 984
East Midlands Research Framework 984
East Riding of Yorkshire 602
  Beverley 119, 300, 739, 749
  burials 859
  gardens 571
  Hull 341, 739, 859
  Keyingham 159
  Ravenser Odd 157
  Weedley 503
East Smithfield cemetery (London) 60–1, 783, 829, 841, 842f
East Stoke, Battle [Nottinghamshire, 1487] 406
Eastbourne (Sussex) 506
Easter Sepulchre/Tomb of Christ 607
Eastgate Street, Chester (Cheshire) 341
Eastgate, Beverley (East Yorkshire) 300
ecology 32–3
Écouen château (France), artefacts from 5
Edinburgh 306, 605
Edinburgh Castle 14, 377
Edington, William (Bishop of Winchester) 591
education 766
Edward I (King of England) 146, 284, 287, 288, 318, 394, 421, 426, 514f, 517, 523, 619, 819, 860, 863, 864, 913, 975

  gift of leopard 900
Edward II (King of England) 142, 144, 375, 376, 519, 533, 589
Edward III (King of England) 285, 374, 375, 376, 379, 394, 421, 422, 514f, 515, 731, 732, 916, 966
Edward IV (King of England) 514f, 517, 523, 857
Edward VI (King of England and Ireland) 378
Edward the Black Prince 376–7, 395, 419, 514f
Edward the Confessor 418, 419, 514f, 647, 880
Egglestone stone (Co. Durham) 458
Egleton (Rutland) 632
Egypt, trade with 889, 891
Eifel region (Germany) 470
Eldbotle (East Lothian) 176, 183, 205
Eleanor of Castile (Queen of England) 863, 975
Eleanor of England (Queen of Castile) 975
Eleanor of Provence (wife of Henry III) 776
Eleanor Crosses 863
Elevation of the Host 691, 877
Elgin (Moray) 13, 109
Elgin Cathedral (Moray) 582, 586, 593
Elias of Dereham 444
Elizabeth I (Queen of England and Ireland) 377
Elizabeth of York (wife of Henry VII) 863–4
Elmesly, Roger 704
Elmley Castle (Worcestershire) 218
Elsdon (Northumberland) 92f
Elsinore Castle, Helsingør (Denmark) 946, 957
Elton (Huntingdonshire) 218
Elvet Bridge, Durham (Co. Durham) 346, 348, 687
Ely (Cambridgeshire) 325, 331, 332, 344
Ely Cathedral (Cambridgeshire) 581, 582, 584, 586, 589, 590, 593, 635
embocagement (enclosure of fields) 926
emeralds 161
English Bridge, Shrewsbury (Shropshire) 347, 348
English Civil War 517
English Episcopal *Acta* 53
English Heritage 23, 24, 102, 405, 413, 566, 567, 985 *see also* Historic England

English Historical Documents series 53
English landscape and identities project (EnglaID) 985
Environment Agency 27
environmental archaeology 76–80
episcopal palaces 371–3, 372f
Erasmus 538
Erik VII (King of Denmark, Norway, and Sweden) 946, 955–6
Essex 213, 336
  Belchamp 263
  Boreham Airfield 246
  Chelmsford 346
  Coggleshall 298
  Colchester 298, 325, 334, 519, 847, 848–9, 899, 955
  Danbury 486
  Felsted 316
  Great Barfield 608
  Havering 93, 97
  Horham Hall 248
  Leigh-on-Sea 182
  Maldon 298, 460
  North Shoebury 611f
  Rochford 346
  Romford 346
  Saffron Walden 280, 314
  Salcot 184
  Sible Hedingham 331, 441
  Southchurch Hall 243, 248, 250, 253
  St Osyth's 571
  Stebbing 608
  Stock 391
  Stratford Longthorne 777–8, 838
  Temple Cressing 268
  Thaxted 336, 487
  Walden 487
  Waltham Abbey 457, 569
  Writtle 145, 184, 373, 388
Essex marshes 326
estate churches 365
estate management, ordered 260, 266–70
Estonia 446, 945
etiquette 43
Eton College, Cambridge (Cambridgeshire) 377, 443, 457
Ettrick forest (Scottish Borders) 177, 181, 184

Europe
  cathedral designs 582
  industrial sites 438
  influence on architecture by Normans 373
  iron imported from 470
  pilgrim badges 651
  silver mining 461
  stone buildings 301
  timber buildings 301
  trade with 130, 131, 132, 133–4, 336, 889–91, 890f, 893–8, 900
  see also individual countries
European coastal regions 71
European Cooperation in Science and Technology (COST) 136
European Gothic tradition 229
Everswell, Woodstock (Oxfordshire) 373, 393
Ewelme hundred (Oxfordshire) 720, 721–2f, 723
excavation, as a methodology 20–2
Excavation Index 984
Exchequer Rolls for Scotland (1326–1600) 53
Exeter (Devon) 108, 297, 302, 325, 341, 361, 427, 439, 975
  chapels 552
  churches 549
  drinking vessels 707
  Exeter Bridge 346, 347
  Exeter Castle 356
  Exeter Cathedral 598, 933
  faunal assemblages 102
Exeter Archaeology Archive project 985
Exmoor 230, 461f
Exning (Suffolk) 606
exorcism 620
exportation of goods 444–6, 445f, 470–1, 893, 895
  alabaster 972, 973f
  fish 130, 131
  to Ireland 919
  stone to France 933
Expugnatio Hibernica (de Barry) 911
Extensive Urban Surveys (EUS) 275
extinctions 141
Eyemouth (Berwickshire) 134, 183
Eynsham Abbey (Oxfordshire) 5, 14, 121, 567

Faccombe Netherton (Wiltshire) 705, 900
Fairford (Gloucestershire) 606
Fakenham church (Norfolk) 633
Falkland (Fife) 372
Falsterbo (Denmark) 944
families, buried together 858
famine 823
farming *see* agriculture
farming equipment 196
farmsteads 173, 174
Farnham Castle (Surrey) 244
Faroe Islands 944, 945
farriers 481
farthings 517
Farup (Denmark) 951
Fast Castle (Berwickshire) 790–1
Fauld near Hanbury (Staffordshire) 458
faunal assemblages 108
    data collection and analysis 102–3
    evidence of farming 110–11
    wild animals 141
Faxton (Northamptonshire) 8, 9*f*
Feast of Fools 621
Feet of Fines 53
Felsted (Essex) 316
Fenland 71, 94, 546
Fernando III (King of Leon and Castile) 975
Ferrers, Sir Thomas de 346
ferries 346
Ferrycarrig (Co. Wexford, Ireland) 911
Fetternear (Aberdeenshire) 382
field boundaries 33
field-names 25, 56, 215
field survey 22–4, 179
field systems 86
    chronological changes 92–8
    effect of Black Death 96–8
    regional variation 86–92, 88*f*, 89*f*, 90*f*
field-walking 22–3, 33, 93, 171–2, 261, 986
Fields of Conflict (FOC) 401, 402
fields, open 87, 174–5, 334, 926
Fife (Scotland) 643
finger-rings 428, 444
Finlaggan, Islay (Inner Hebrides) 185, 616
Finland 945
fire damage 158–9
fireplaces 307

First Barons' War (1215–16) 375
First Edition Ordnance Survey maps 176, 177
First Edition Survey Project 15, 177
fish
    consumption 129, 130, 133, 697
    exporting 130, 131, 893
    imports 133–4, 889
    remains 129
    trade between towns 332–3, 335–6
    see also individual species
Fishergate, York (North Yorkshire) 651–2, 780, 821, 828, 863
'fish event horizon' 128–9
fishing 74, 128
    coastal settlements 183
    in France 927, 928*f*
    freshwater 129–30
    Scandinavia 943–4
    sea 128–9, 130–3, 135–6
fishponds in monastic gardens 572
Fishpool (Nottinghamshire) 421, 519, 793
Fish Street, Worcester (Worcestershire) 120
FitzAlan, Brian (Lord of Bedale) 426*f*
Fitz Drogo, Richard 317
Fitz Stephen, William 321, 734–5
Fitzwilliam Museum, coin collections 512, 513, 514
Five Wounds of Christ 799
Flambard, Ranulf (Bishop of Durham) 346
Flanders 414, 933, 946, 953, 955, 971
Flemish settlers 180
Flete, Thomas 672
Flintshire (Wales) 160*f*, 461
Flodden, Battle [Northumberland, 1513] 405, 410, 411
flooding events 156–7, 157*f*, 159
    Bodmin Moor (Cornwall) 463
    damage 163, 348
    protection from 162–4
floor coverings 520
floor tiles 5, 15, 43, 380, 381*f*, 423, 441, 444, 486, 898, 900, 901, 974–5
Flores epytaphii sanctorum (Thiofrid, Abbot of Echternach) 689
foetuses 762
    burials 778, 779
fold courses 90, 91, 97

folded coins 160–1, 160*f*, 525, 616, 989
Folkestone (Kent) 570
fonts 591, 608–10, 609*f*, 718*f*
food 697–8
　considered healthy 836
　cooking 697, 698–701, 700*f*
　dining practices 701–4, 703*f*
　exports 893
　imports 895–7, 898
　in infirmaries 849, 850
　production 198, 262–3
　storage 238
　symbol of power 421
　trade between towns 333–4
　transported between royal palaces 380–2
　see also diet
footwear 790, 791, 859
foramina 535–6, 536*f*
Fordington (Dorset) 606
Forest of Arden (Warwickshire) 213
Forest of Dean (Gloucestershire) 144, 330, 332, 470
forests 177, 181, 184–5
　as hunting grounds 387–8, 390*f*, 393
　wild animals in 145
fortalitia or *fortalis* 916
Forvie (Aberdeenshire) 159, 164
Foss Dyke (Lincolnshire) 345
Foster Lane (London) 707
Fotheringhay Castle (Northamptonshire) 857
Fotheringhay Church (Northamptonshire) 604*f*
Fountains Abbey (North Yorkshire) 439, 478, 497, 574, 585, 747
Fourth Lateran Council (1215) 606, 641, 837
Fowey (Cornwall) 506
Fowler, Peter 11
Fowlis Easter (Perthshire) 607
Fox, Richard (Bishop of Durham) 348
Framwellgate ('Old') Bridge, Durham 346
France 331, 332, 605, 953
　bay divisions 302
　castles 930–2, 931*f*
　Champagne fairs 889
　chessboard finds 532
　coins from 523
　craftworking 932–3

　dating of houses 298
　funerary practices 933–5, 934*f*
　Gothic architecture 376
　import of sugar 971
　industrial sites 438
　jetties 307
　pilgrim badges 651
　pottery 901, 919–20, 932
　regional studies 70
　royal houses 372
　rural landscapes 925–9
　shops 321
　symbols of power 930–2
　timber buildings 301
　towns 929–30
　villages 928–9
Fraternity of St Clement 847
Fraternity of St James, Worcester 655
Frauncey, Adam 321
Frederick II (King of Germany) 899
Freeby (Leicestershire) 460
French Association for Glass Archaeology (AFAV) 932–3
French Quarter of Southampton (Hampshire) 976
French Revolution 5
French Street, Southampton (Hampshire) 313
freshwater fishing 129–30
Freswick Links (Caithness) 183
Friars of the Sack and Pied Friars 576–7
Friday Street (London) 317
Frisians 942
Frithelstock (Devon) 608
fritware jars 896*f*
Frosterley quarry (Co. Durham) 458
fruits 118–19, 121, 197
fruit trees 927
Fuggerhäuser (Jacob Fugger) 532–3
Fulford, Battle of [Yorkshire, 1066] 410
Fuller's Hill, Great Yarmouth (Norfolk) 156
fulling 479
functionalist approach 38, 42
funding 11–12
　developer-led 12–14, 21
　for monument excavations 13
　for universities 11, 21
funerals 856–7, 933–5, 934*f*

fur trade 108–9, 146–7, 483, 790
furnaces 486
Furness Abbey (Lancashire) 437
furniture 237, 300
　shops 314f, 315–16
Furzehill (Hampshire) 463
Fyfield Down (Wiltshire) 93
Fyn (Denmark) 941

Gadlys (Glamorgan) 253
gadoids 183
Galen 732, 762, 836
Galicia (Spain) 648, 966, 970
Galilee Chapel, Durham Cathedral 458
Gallowgate, Aberdeen
　(Aberdeenshire) 319
Galten (Denmark) 496
Galway (Ireland) 918
galy hapens (silver *soldini*) 524
gambling 533
gaming boards 531–8, 532f, 534f, 536f
Gamlingay (Cambridgeshire) 776–7
gardening 197
gardens 366, 367f, 393–4, 397, 992
　gender and space 814
　monastic 571–2
　royal 376
Garioch (Aberdeenshire) 176, 180
Garsington (Oxfordshire) 724
Garth, Hugh 221
Gascony wine trade 130, 132, 446, 893
Gatesgarth, Buttermere (Cumbria) 111
Gdansk port (Poland) 946
Geldeston (Norfolk) 799
gemstones 161, 470, 615–16, 897
gender 44, 806
　and education of children 766
　identity in children 763
　in medicine 837
　and migration 821
　and mortality 768
　and religious space 806–10
　roles 768
　space in aristocratic dwellings 813–14
　and spatial analysis 814–15
　in vernacular architecture 810–12
Genoa (Italy) 891

Geographical Information Systems
　(GIS) 15, 71–2, 73, 281, 282f, 290, 293, 366,
　815, 986
geophysical survey 27–9, 367, 375, 382, 405,
　567, 612, 841, 916
Gerald of Wales 61, 718, 781, 911
German Order 945, 946
Germany 955
　coins from 523
　connection with Jutland 941, 942f
　dating of houses 298
　import of quernstones 502
　industrial sites 438
　trade with 130, 131
　urban and rural boundaries 330, 331
Gibbs, John (of Berrick Prior) 724
Gibraltar (UK) 975
gifts, exchanges with foreign
　countries 899–900
Gijón museum (Spain) 976
Gilbert of St Leonard (Bishop of
　Chichester) 160
Gilbertine monks 858
Gillingham (Kent) 93, 94
Gimbscheim, River Rhine (Germany) 501
Giotto (painter) 747
girdle settlements 179, 179f
Girdlergate Street, York (North
　Yorkshire) 483, 484
GIS *see* Geographical Information Systems
Glamorgan, silver mining 461
Glasgow (Scotland) 345, 646
Glasgow Cathedral 158–9, 158f, 586, 589, 590,
　592f, 593, 594
glass 307
　drinking vessels 705–8, 706f
　exportation 445
　imported 896f, 898
glass-making 485
glass-working 443, 439
　France 932–3
Glastonbury (Somerset) 345, 499, 545
Glastonbury Abbey (Somerset) 15, 56–8, 57f,
　268, 567
Glaven ports (Norfolk) 635
glaze on pottery 751
Glenlyon brooch 615–16

Gloucester (Gloucestershire) 330, 332, 344–5, 420
  churches in 549
  cloisters 573, 574
  monasteries 569
Gloucester Castle 532
Gloucester Cathedral 589, 593
Gloucestershire 262
gloves 791, 792f
Glyn Dŵr revolt (1400–15) 97
goats, horn cores 109–10, 110f, 111
Gogar (Edinburgh) 547
gold 750
  jewellery 793, 794f, 795–6, 796f
  mining 460–1
  vessels 702
Golden Ball Street, Norwich (Norfolk) 359
Golden legend, The (de Voragine) 161, 659
Golden Section 582
Goldicote (Warwickshire) 200, 201
goldsmiths 950–1
Goldsmith's Hall (London) 481
Goltho (Lincolnshire) 103, 155, 217, 243, 356, 365, 482, 704
Goodramgate, York (North Yorkshire) 487
Gothic architecture 3–6, 229, 375, 555, 586, 602, 747, 750
Gotland (Sweden) 945
Gough, Richard ('Gough Map') 3, 285–8, 287f
government records 53
Gozo (Malta) 626
graffiti boards 535–6, 536f
graffiti inscriptions in churches 626–30, 627f, 631f, 633f, 634f, 636f, 638, 989
  dating 630–1
  types 631–7
Grafisk Tegnestue, Moesgaard Museum (Denmark) 942
Grampian Mountains (Scotland) 146
granaries 265
Grand Pont, Oxford (Oxfordshire) 346
Grandmontine priories 577
Grandson and Murten, Battle [Switzerland, 1476] 408
Grantham (Lincolnshire), churches in 549, 550
grave goods 820, 858–9

grave-slabs 863
grazing settlements 180–2, 333–4
Great Bardfield (Essex) 608
Great Beere (Devon) 7
Great Chalfield (Wiltshire) 426–7
Great Coxwell (Oxfordshire) 266
Great Cressingham (Norfolk) 218, 601f
Great Famine (1315–17) 325
Great Gate, Bury St Edmunds (Suffolk) 320
Great Hall, Blenheim Palace, Woodstock (Oxfordshire) 373
Great Hall, Stirling Castle 383
Great Hall, Westminster 379
Great Limestone Belt, Somerset to the East Riding 555
Great Linford (Buckinghamshire) 193–4, 194f, 197, 200, 217, 217f, 504, 504f, 505, 506
Great Malvern (Worcestershire) 570
Great North Road 344
Great Replanning 75
Great Seal 420, 423
Great Tower, Chepstow Castle (Monmouthshire) 363–5, 364f
Great Yarmouth 132, 134–5
Green Man imagery, Perth (Scotland) 45
Greencastle, Inishowen peninsular (Co. Donegal, Ireland) 913
Greenland 944, 945
Greenway, John 874
Greenwich (London) 494
  watermill 495, 496, 497
Gregory I (Gregory the Great) 658
grey literature 21, 23, 72, 77, 103, 250, 281, 283, 358, 435, 983–4
Greyfriars 645
Greyfriars Carmarthen, Wales 535
Greyfriars in Leicester 858, 859–60
Grimes, William 8, 12
Grimm, Samuel 3, 4f
Grimsby (Lincolnshire) 132–3, 134, 291, 423, 441
Grimston (Norfolk) 331
Grimston Ware 953, 954f
Grittenham (Wiltshire) 471
Grose, Francis 5
Grosseteste, Robert 742, 743
ground-penetrating radar (GPR) 28–9

Guadalquivir estuary (Spain) 975
Guédelon, Treigny (France) 992
Guérande (France) 933
Guild of Butchers 60
guild of St Mary, Boston (Lincolnshire) 670–2, 671f
Guildford Castle (Surrey) 373
Gunhild's Cross 951
Guy of Warwick 148
Gwent Levels (Wales) 15, 182, 183f
    reclamation 94

Haakon IV (King of Norway) 148, 899
habitus 807
hachure survey 23–4
Hackness (North Yorkshire) 570
Haddenham (Buckinghamshire) 460
Haddington (East Lothian) 605
Hadleigh (Suffolk) 336
Hafod Nant y Criafolen, Denbigh Moors (Denbighshire) 182
Hailes Abbey (Gloucestershire) 646, 795
hair-nets 792, 793f
Halesowen (West Midlands) 288
halfpennies 517
Halghton Hall (Flintshire) 252
Halland (Sweden) 941
Hallgate, Doncaster (South Yorkshire) 706
Hallhill, Dunbar (East Lothian) 109
hall-houses 232–8, 234f, 236f, 239
    and shophouses 318
halls, open 302, 303f, 304, 306
Ham Green Ware (Bristol) 444, 751, 919, 920
Hambleden (Buckinghamshire) 481
hamlets 174, 178
Hampton Court, King's Lynn (Norfolk) 316, 377
Hanbury (Worcestershire) 93, 95
Hanley Castle (Worcestershire) 201
Hanse merchants 524, 901, 976
Hanseatic League 131, 132, 133, 333, 470, 945–6, 889, 945, 946, 976
Hansen's disease *see* leprosy
Harberton (Devon) 608
Hardham (West Sussex) 748
hardi d'or coin 514f
Harlech Castle (Wales) 229, 913

Harlton (Cambridgeshire) 637
Harold II (King of England) 419, 420f
harrows 261
Harrying of the North 180
Harthacnut (King of Denmark and last Danish king of England) 941, 948
Hartlepool (Co. Durham) 14, 104, 289, 290, 298, 302, 439, 441
Hartlepool Greyfriars (Co. Durham) 778
Hartzhorn, Battle [Germany, early 3rd century] 410
harvesting 263
harvesting tools 262
Hastings, Battle of [East Sussex, 1066] 401–2, 405, 410, 414–15
Hastings Chapel, Christchurch Priory (Dorset) 878
Hatch Beauchamp (Somerset) 608
Hatchett Psalter 750
Haverfordwest (Pembrokeshire) 301
Haverfordwest Priory (Pembrokeshire) 571
Havering (Essex) 93, 97
Hawton (Nottinghamshire) 607
Hayley Wood (Cambridgeshire) 33
Hazlewood quarry (North Yorkshire) 457
health 836, 840–6
heart burials 860
Hebrides (Scotland) 205, 552, 944
    remains of dwellings 226
Heckington (Lincolnshire) 607
Hedeby (Denmark) 944
hedgehogs 147
hedges, study of 33
Hedon (East Riding of Yorkshire) 276
heirlooms 45, 615–16
Helen-on-the-Walls, York (North Yorkshire) 20
Helsingborg Castle (Denmark) 946
Hemingford Grey Manor House (Cambridgeshire) 244
Hen Caerwys (Flintshire) 171, 179, 205
Hen Domen (Powys) 21, 356, 358, 359f
Hen Gwrt (Monmouthshire) 250, 252, 253
Henry I (King of England) 148, 372–3, 514f, 515, 516, 968
Henry II (King of England) 343, 373, 374, 387, 393, 422, 476, 514f, 516, 748

Henry III (King of England) 148, 374, 375, 380, 514*f*, 519, 523, 864
　burial of daughter Katherine 776
　gifts abroad 899–900
Henry IV (King of England) 422, 955
Henry V (King of England) 377, 422, 423, 880, 955
Henry VI (King of England) 377, 514*f*, 523, 619
Henry VII (King of England) 377, 422, 525
Henry VIII (King of England) 377–8, 423, 517, 597, 791, 792, 814, 971, 974
Henry of Blois 372, 373, 791
Henry of Eastry (Prior of Christ Church, Canterbury) 265
Henry of Huntingdon 130, 211
Henry of Yevele 346
herbs 119, 120, 121
Hereford (Herefordshire) 14
Hereford Cathedral (Herefordshire) 582, 779, 841
Herefordshire 601
heretics 861–2
Heritage Council 916
Heritage Lottery Fund 11, 382, 988
Heritage at Risk programme 11
hermits 221, 548, 554
Herrerías (León) 966
herring 129–32, 134–5, 183, 200, 943–4
Hesdin (Artois, France) 376
Hessel (Denmark) 496
hexfoil design 632–3
Hextalls (Surrey) 212
High Altar, prestige of burials near 858
high altars 584
High Bridge, Lincoln (Lincolnshire) 348
High Farming period 261
High Speed 1 railway (Kent) 15
high-status settlements 184–6
High Street (Bristol) 319
High Street, Salisbury (Wiltshire) 302
High Street, Perth (Scotland) 109, 111, 441, 534, 649, 790, 793
High Street, Southampton (Hampshire) 702, 703, 706, 707
High Street, Winchester (Hampshire) 317
High Tower, Launceston Castle (Cornwall) 366

Higham Ferrers (Northamptonshire) 426
Highlands and Islands (Scotland) 181
　rural settlements 175, 176*f*, 177, 178
Highlight (Glamorgan) 252, 253
Hilborough (Norfolk) 601
Hildenley (North Yorkshire) 457
Hilton, Walter 658
hinterland 330, 331
Hippocrates 836
Hirsel, The (Berwickshire) 547, 652
Histon (Cambridgeshire) 460
Historic England 23, 265, 275, 414, 448, 471, 985 *see also* English Heritage Archive, Swindon 25
Historic Environment Records (HERs) 8, 25, 72, 357
　Wales 402, 415
Historic Environment Scotland (HES) 11, 25
Historic Land-Use Assessment Project 177
Historic Land-Use Assessment, Scotland 31, 73 *see also* Historic Landscape Characterization
historic landscape analysis 73
Historic Landscape Characterization (HLC) 11, 24, 31–2, 73, 986
Historic Rural Settlement Group, Scotland 8
Historic Towns Atlas (HTA) 284
Historic Urban Character Areas (HUCAs) 275
historical ecology 32–3
history, relationship with archaeology 40
holdings, division of 94–5
holiness 615
Holme-Cultram (Cumberland) 91
Holworth (Dorset) 196
Holy Blood relic, Hailes Abbey (Gloucestershire) 646
Holy House of Nazareth 647
Holy Rood cult 616
Holyrood Abbey, Edinburgh (Scotland) 184
holy sites 219–20
Holy Trinity, Bradford-on-Avon (Wiltshire) 879*f*
Holy Trinity chapel, Salisbury Cathedral (Wiltshire) 535–6, 536*f*
Holy Trinity church, Edinburgh (Scotland) 957

Holy Trinity, Coventry (Warwickshire) 606
Holy Trinity, Dublin (Ireland) 445, 920
Holy Trinity, Micklegate, York (North Yorkshire) 551
Holy Trinity Hospital, Soutra (Scotland) 838
Holywell (Flintshire) 617–18, 618f
Holywell (Oxfordshire) 95
holy wells 648
honey 968
Horham Hall (Essex) 248
horizontal watermills 492–3, 492f, 501
Horley (Surrey) 637
horns 483
   for communication 715
   as drinking vessels 707
Horold, John 216
Horseland (Glamorgan) 252
Horseman's Green (Flintshire) 252
horses 109
Horsham at the Weald and Downland Museum, Singleton (West Sussex) 313
Hospital of Blessed Mary of Ospringe, Faversham (Kent) 644–5, 645f
Hospitallers 82, 577, 809, 810, 861, 921
hospitals *see* infirmaries
hosts, in churches 606–7
Hound Tor (Devon) 230
houses 174f
   adapted for children 783
   burials in 779
   gender and space 810–12
   layout 806
   peasants 226–39, 231f, 233–4f, 236f
   rural settlements 193–207, 206f, 327–8
   survival 226–35, 227f, 231f, 297–8
   urban 298–308, 299f, 303f, 304f, 327–8
Housing and Planning Bill (2015–16) 14
Hoxne (Suffolk) 610
Hubald (Bishop of Odense) 949
Hugh de Hemeleseye 348
Hugh de Puiset (Bishop of Durham) 346
Hull (East Riding of Yorkshire) 14, 132, 135, 289, 341, 343, 344, 441, 739, 830, 894
Hull Magistrates Court, burial site 820f, 828, 828f
Hulton Abbey (Staffordshire) 13, 859
human geography 39

Human Tissue Act (2004) 827
Humber estuary 94, 213
humours 743, 836
Humphrey (1st Duke of Gloucester) 880
Hundred Rolls (*Rotuli Hundredorum*, 1274–5/1279–80) 53
Hundred Years' War 404
Hungary 438, 760, 895
Hungerford, Robert 880
hunting 387
   culture in the countryside 73–4
   forests 184
   grounds 375, 387–93, 389f, 390f, 392f
   horns 424–5, 424f, 715
   legislation 142–4
   lodges 185, 373
   wolves 145–6
Huntingdon (Cambridgeshire) 966
Huntington (Welsh Marches) 396
Hurstpierpoint (West Sussex) 24
Husbands Crawley (Bedfordshire) 630

Iberian Peninsula 119, 897, 964, 965f
   see also Portugal; Spain
Iceland 135, 889, 944, 945
iconoclasm 45
icons *see* devotional images
identity 44, 991–2
   age 760–1
   during puberty 765
   gender in children 763
   pre-birth 762
   and sounds 718
Île de France 586, 926
Ilton (Somerset) 777
imaginative memory 615
imaging techniques 828
immune systems 826
Imperial State Crown 419
importation 205, 470–1, 893–5, 896f, 897–8, 901
   coins 521–4, 522f
   exotic animals 148–9, 150, 894
   fish 133–4
   from France 932–3
   pottery 972–5
   sugar 971

Inchadney Well (Perthshire) 619
Inclesmoor (Lincolnshire-Yorkshire boundary) 548
India, trade with 890f, 891, 894
Industrial Revolution 455
industrial settlements 183–4
industrial sites 436–42, 437f
industry, evidence of 455–6
infants 761–3
   burials 778–9
   swaddling 780–1
   weaning 780
infirmaries 571, 643–5, 645f, 823–5, 837, 845f, 846–51, 848f
infrastructural issues in archaeology 983–9
Inglebard, Philip 159
Innocent III, Pope 748
insignia, royal 421–4
International Council for Archaeozoology (ICAZ) 102
Invernochty Castle (Aberdeenshire) 185
Iona (Inner Hebrides) 570, 616, 646
Iping (West Sussex) 471
Ipswich (Suffolk) 828
Ireland 135, 921–2
   castles 909–13, 910f, 912f
   churches 918–19
   coins 514f, 523
   as a frontier society 920–1
   hunting grounds 393
   imports and exports 444–6
   mills 491–3
   moated sites 915–16
   remains of buildings 228
   rural settlements 916–18, 917f
   tower houses 913–15
   towns 918
   trade with 471, 919–20
   windmills 503
iron
   cooking equipment 701
   mills 568f
   mining 464–5
   from Spain 968, 969f
   transportation 470
iron-smelting furnaces 439
Irún museum (Spain) 976

Isbell, Adam 218
Islam 371, 733
Islamic coins 524, 976
Islamic culture 900
Islamic Empire 889
Islamic glass 898
Islamic influences in architecture 376
island dwellings (crannogs) 185–6
islands on moats 253
Isle Abbots (Somerset) 608
Isle of Lewis (Scotland) 181
Isle of Man 944
Isle of Purbeck (Dorset) 439
Isle of Skye (Scotland) 178
Isle of Thanet (Kent) 265
Isle of Wight 458, 953
isotopes 79, 112, 117, 129, 130, 131, 133, 141, 332, 406, 455, 697, 761, 763, 765, 768, 780, 782, 783, 821, 822, 828, 828f, 830, 859, 860, 895, 943, 987
Italy 331
   coin collections 512
   craftspeople 475
   drinking vessels 707
   trade with 891
ivory 484, 896f, 897, 966, 971
   walrus 951
Ivy Church Priory, Salisbury (Wiltshire) 968

James I (King of Scotland) 377, 622
James III (King of Scotland) 957
James IV (King of Scotland) 383
James V (King of Scotland) 377
Jarrow (Tyne and Wear) 570
Jarvis Brook (East Sussex) 464
Jedburgh Abbey (Scottish Borders) 184, 791
Jennings Yard, Windsor (London) 109
Jerusalem 549, 651, 919
Jervaulx Abbey (Abbey of Fors), Wensleydale (North Yorkshire) 145–6
jet 439, 444, 466–8, 485, 797
   items in Spain 966, 967f
jettied houses 301, 307
jetties 343
jewellery 439, 441, 615–16, 793–4, 794f, 795–800, 796f
   coins as 524–5, 616–17

devotional 665–8, 667f
imported 897
royal 422
Jews, burials 860–1
Jew's House, Lincoln (Lincolnshire) 314
Jewbury, York (North Yorkshire) 821, 827, 860–1
John (King of England) 373, 374, 375, 388, 418
buried at Worcester Cathedral 858
as Lord of Ireland 523
John II (King of France) 376
John of Gaunt's palace, King's Somborne (Hampshire) 382
Johnson, Samuel 5
Joydens Wood (Kent) 242
jugs 705–7, 706f
Justinian of Ramsey Island 220
Jutland (Denmark) 941, 944, 951

Kalmar Union 945, 946
Kalø Castle (Jutland) 947
Kells (Co. Kilkenny, Ireland) 919
Kelso Abbey (Scottish Borders) 181, 183, 184
Kempe, Margery 658
Kempley (Gloucestershire) 605
Kenilworth Castle (Warwickshire) 42, 185, 253, 377, 411
Kennington Palace (Surrey) 377, 395f
Kent 132, 201, 265, 601
churches 605
field systems 91
grave-slabs 863
tanning 483
textile industry 480
Kent Archaeological Society 645
kermes 748–9, 750
Keyingham (East Yorkshire) 159
Keynsham Abbey (Bristol) 566, 651
keys 439
Kidwelly (Carmarthenshire) 297
Kill O'The Grange (Co. Dublin, Ireland) 920
kilns 265, 437, 460, 485–6
Kilscanlan, near Old Ross (Co. Wexford, Ireland) 503
Kilteel (Co. Kildare, Ireland) 921f, 921
Kiltyrie (Scotland) 176f
Kinewards Bridge (Somerset) 499

King John's Hunting Lodge, Writtle (Essex) 145
King's Bench court, Westminster (London) 53, 379
Kings Clipstone (Nottinghamshire) 382, 383
King's College, Cambridge (Cambridgeshire) 377, 872
King's College Chapel, Aberdeen Cathedral (Scotland) 591
King's Knot, Stirling (Scotland) 366, 367f
Kings Langley (Hertfordshire) 380
King's Lynn (Norfolk) 12, 108, 109–10, 132, 133, 306, 314, 315, 331, 332, 343–4, 468, 478, 503, 649, 797, 897
King's Lynn Red Register 315
King's Mills, Leeds (West Yorkshire) 499
King's Norton (Leicestershire) 382
King's Somborne (Hampshire) 382, 630
Kingston (Cambridgeshire) 746f, 777
Kingston Deverill (Wiltshire) 59, 59f
Kingston upon Hull see Hull (East Riding of Yorkshire)
Kingston-on-Thames (Surrey) 486
King Street, King's Lynn (Norfolk) 315
King Street, Norwich (Norfolk) 306
Kirk Ness (Berwickshire) 847
Kirkcaldy (Scotland) 306
Kirkstall Abbey (West Yorkshire) 502, 699
Kirkwall Cathedral (Orkney) 584, 594
Kisimul Castle, Castlebay (Scotland) 185
kitchens 236, 698–701, 700f
Knaresborough Castle (North Yorkshire) 380
Knockgraffon (Co. Tipperary, Ireland) 913
Knox, John 622
Knut the Great (King of Denmark) 948, 949
Knut IV the Holy (King of Denmark) 949
kontors (counting houses) 946
Kristian I (King of Denmark, Norway, and Sweden) 956–7
Krogen, Elsinore (Helsingør) 946
Kronborg Castle (Denmark) 946

La Coruña (Spain) 970, 976
La Rochelle (France) 919
La-Chapelle-des-Pots, Saintes (France) 932
Lacock Abbey (Wiltshire) 808
Lacy, Henry de (Earl of Lincoln) 735

Lady Chapel, Wells Cathedral (Somerset) 589
Lady Park, Belper (Derbyshire) 814
Lady Park, Liskeard (Cornwall) 814
Lady Row, Goodramgate, York (North Yorkshire) 304, 317
Lakenheath, Mildenhall (Suffolk) 216, 218, 219
Lambeth Palace (London) 29
Lamington (Scotland) 180
Lamport (Northamptonshire) 504
Lanarkshire (Scotland) 180, 330, 504, 605
Lancashire 221, 570
   chapels 552
   field systems 91
   Furness Abbey 437
   Lathom 814
Languedoc (France) 927
land access 219
land boundaries 216–18, 217f
land ownership 142
land use disputes 218–19
landholders 555–6, 597
landraces 123
Landscape Character Assessment 73
landscape management 142
Landscape Movement in gardens 3
landscape studies 71–4
   chronological changes 74–5
   environmental approach 77–80
   theoretical approaches 75–6
landscapes
   animals added to 367
   aristocratic 386, 395–7
   association with Church 545–6
   churches in 551–6
   designed 366–8
   monastic 575–6
   pleasure gardens 393–4, 397
   see also rural landscapes; urban landscapes
Lark Hill (Worcester) 793
Las Huelgas, Burgos (Spain) 791–2, 975
Lastingham (North Yorkshire) 570
Last Judgement ('Doom'), wall paintings 606, 660, 661f
Last Supper 573
Lateran Council (1215) 606, 641, 837
lathe-turning 478
Lathom (Lancashire) 814

latrines 300–1, 731
   food waste found in 121–2
Launceston Castle (Cornwall) 11, 13, 79, 102, 104, 106, 111, 358, 366, 532, 897, 898, 984
Lavenham (Suffolk) 313f, 335, 486
Laverstock (Wiltshire) 443, 485
Laxton (Nottinghamshire) 365
Lay Subsidies 24, 285, 477, 486
Layerthorpe Bridge, York (North Yorkshire) 346
lead-iron round shot 412f, 413
lead mining 461, 462f, 463
lead roofs 950
lead seals 955
leat tunnel 437f
leather
   drinking vessels 706f, 707
   offcuts 790, 791
leather-working 105, 441–2, 482–3
lecterns 591, 607
legumes 118
Leicester (Leicestershire) 333, 334
   animal remains 104–5, 108
   Austin Friars 702, 703f, 704, 791, 795
   burial sites 830, 858, 859–60
   Department of Local History 70
   Greyfriars 858, 859–60
   Leicester Castle 244
   Manor Farm 504
   urban excavation 325
   vegetable remains 119
Leicestershire 329
   Alston Grange 460
   Ashby-de-la-Zouch 655
   Barrow upon Soar 460
   Bosworth *see* Bosworth, Battle of
   coalfield 456, 466f, 466, 467f
   Coleorton 465–6, 466f, 467f
   Donington-le-Heath 244
   Freeby 460
   graffiti 635
   King's Norton 382
   Lyddington Bede House 372, 372f
   Owston Abbey 572
Leigh-on-Sea (Essex) 182
Leighton Buzzard (Bedfordshire) 24
Leiston Abbey (Suffolk) 12, 987

leisure activities of peasants 202
Leith, Edinburgh (Scotland) 134, 893
Leland, John 174, 345, 556
Lendal Tower, York (North Yorkshire) 346
Leominster (Herefordshire) 570
leper houses
leprosy 821, 825, 828, 829–30, 843–6, 844f
   burials 652f, 934f, 935
   fear of 861
   leper houses 643, 734, 845f, 861
   leper pilgrims 652f
Letterston (Pembrokeshire) 180
Lewes Castle (Sussex) 5, 572
Lewes, Battle [East Sussex, 1264] 410
Lewis chessmen 15, 46
Lewknor (Oxfordshire) 716
Lewmote (Kent) 250
ley farming 91
Library of Unpublished Fieldwork
   Reports 985
licences 55
Lichfield (Staffordshire) 581
   chapels 554
   Lichfield Cathedral 647
LiDAR (Light Detection and Ranging) 27, 28f, 71, 363, 986
Liddesdale (Roxburghshire) 181, 185
Lidgate (Suffolk) 633, 634f
Lidgate church (Suffolk) 627–8, 627f, 630
life course 44–5, 759–61, 769
   conception to infancy 761–3
   childhood 763–5, 780–5
   burials of children 775–80
   adolescence 765–6
   adulthood 767–8
   old age 768–9
life expectancy 840
lightning
   damage 158–9, 158f
   protection from 161–2
Lilleshall Abbey (Shropshire) 317
Lillingstone Dayrell (Buckinghamshire) 22
lime 457
Lime church (Jutland) 944, 951, 952f
limestone 436, 458, 460, 555, 586
limestone blocks 260f
Limfjord, Lime Church (Jutland) 944, 951

liminal societies 860–2
Limoges enamel from France 897
Lincoln (Lincolnshire)
   animal remains 60, 79, 102
   architecture 301, 314, 321
   bishops of 372
   bridges 348
   churches in 549
   metalworking 439
   pottery 485
   quarries 460
   stone buildings 301, 314
   textile industry 480, 899
   waterways 345
Lincoln Cathedral (Lincolnshire) 642f, 647
   construction 583, 585, 586, 593
   furnishing 590, 591
   inscriptions 629
   stone benches 535
   windows 589
Lincolnshire
   Bardney 570
   Barlings Abbey 566
   Bassingham 635
   Boothby Pagnell 244, 245
   Boston see Boston (Lincolnshire)
   Bourne 331
   burial sites 329
   Burnham 553
   churches 547, 602
   Croft 607
   fens 217
   Foss Dyke 345
   Goltho 103, 155, 217, 243, 356, 365, 482, 704
   Heckington 607
   North-West, survey 70
   Partney 849
   quarries 332
   salt working 469
   South Witham 503, 575, 809f, 984
   Spalding 161
   spires 555
   Stamford see Stamford (Lincolnshire)
   Tattershall 214
   Thornton Abbey 163, 567, 571, 841, 850
   Wainfleet St Mary 469, 485
   Wolds, excavation of villages 7

Lindisfarne (Northumberland) 570
Linlithgow (West Lothian) 15, 377, 605, 779
lions 148
Lisbjerg Church, Aarhus (Denmark) 951
Lisbon (Portugal) 975, 976
Lisbon museum (Portugal) 976
Lisieux Cathedral, Basse-Normandie (France) 933
Little Ice Age 106, 111, 154–5
Little Saxham (Suffolk) 248
Little Trefgarn (Dyfed) 570
Lived Experience in the Later Middle Ages project 42–3
Liverpool (Merseyside) 987
livery accessories 795
living conditions 990–1
Llandaff Cathedral (Glamorgan) 584
Llanrwst (Denbighshire) 608
Llanthony Priory (Monmouthshire) 5
Llantrissent (Glamorgan) 87
Llantwit Major (Glamorgan) 606
Llawhaden (Pembrokeshire) 847
Llay Hall (Denbighshire) 252
Llys Edwin (Flintshire) 253
Llysworney (Glamorgan) 253
local records 54
Lochaber (West Highlands) 228
Lochbuie brooch 616
Loch Clunie (Perthshire) 185
Loch Doon (Dumfries and Galloway) 185
Loch Finlaggan (Islay) 185
Loch Goil (Aberdeenshire) 186
Loch Leven Castle (Fife) 185
loch settlements 185–6
Loches (Indre et Loire, France) 365
Lochindorb Castle (Moray) 185–6
lock technology 438
Lodsworth (West Sussex) 471
lofts in churches 608
Loire Valley (France) 932
London 279, 285, 291, 298, 299f, 300, 301, 302, 305f, 307, 326, 342, 376, 460
    availability of food 698
    Battle [1554] 405
    board games 533
    cattle-farming 105
    churches in 549
    commerce 446
    cooking practices 700f
    dental health 823
    dining practices 702, 703f
    dress accessories 793
    fish-bone finds 129, 130
    grain trade 334
    import of fish 133
    imports and exports 894
    market stalls 319
    monasteries 567
    pavers 341
    plant remains 119
    population 730
    ports 344, 974
    rodents 147
    royalty in 371
    shops 317
    smells 728, 730, 733–9
    sounds 717
    textile industry 479
    trades 477
    urban projects 14
    waterfront buildings 342–3
London Archaeological Archive and Research Centre 985
London Bridge 315, 321, 347, 348, 649
London Guildhall 14
Long Crendon (Buckinghamshire) 239
Long Cross coinage 516–17, 523
Long Melford (Suffolk) 335, 663
Longthorpe Tower (Northamptonshire) 214
Lord Mayor's Chapel (Bristol) 5, 974
lords, creators of new towns 280
Lorne brooch 616
Lorraine (France) 933
Lost Islands of Somerset project 173f
Loudon Hill Battle [East Ayrshire, 1307] 402
Lough Derg (Co. Donegal, Ireland) 919
Louis IX (King of France) 148, 375
Lounge site, Coleorton (Leicestershire) 465–6, 466f, 467f
Lovell Lectionary 750
Low Countries 331, 336, 443, 523, 550, 590, 617, 893
Lower Berse (Denbighshire) 252
Lower Brockhampton (Herefordshire) 253

Lower Harford (Gloucestershire) 197
Lowlands (Scotland), rural settlements 175–7
Lowther, Richard 537
Loxton (Somerset) 608
Luanco museum (Spain) 976
Lübeck (Germany) 298, 301, 889, 943–4, 945, 946
Ludgershall (Wiltshire) 358
Ludgershall Castle (Wiltshire) 11, 20
Ludlow (Shropshire) 276, 306, 321, 328f, 361, 607
Lumburn Leat water course 463
Lund (Sweden) 889
Lund, Skåne (Denmark) 944, 955
Lurk Lane, Beverley (East Yorkshire) 306
lustreware (Spain) 751, 752f, 898, 972, 974
Luton (Bedfordshire) 610, 872
Luttrell Psalter 262, 425, 427, 620, 621f
Lyddington Bede House (Leicestershire) 372, 372f
Lydgate, John 314f, 321
Lydgate (Greater Manchester) 733
Lyminge (Kent) 261
Lymington (Hampshire) 485
Lyng (Somerset) 173f
Lynn *see* King's Lynn (Norfolk)
lynx 146
Lyon (France) 930, 932, 933
Lyveden (Northamptonshire) 184, 331

machar shell sand 178
MacNeils of Barra 185
madder 480, 749, 750, 893, 895
Maddyngley children, burials 777
Madeira (Portugal) 889, 971
Magna Carta 375, 418
magnetometers 27, 28, 29f
Magnus the Martyr (Earl of Orkney) 134
Magor Pill wreck, Severn Estuary 15, 470
Main Street, Pembroke (Pembrokeshire) 301
Maine (France) 930–1
Maison Dieu, hospital 643, 644–5
Maison Dieu, Ospringe (Kent) 645f
Malabar (India) 891
Maldon (Essex) 298, 460
Malham (North Yorkshire) 553
Malmesbury (Wiltshire) 475, 574

Malmö (Denmark) 957
malt kilns 198
Malvern Hills (Worcestershire-Herefordshire) 70
'Managing a Masterpiece' Project 22–3
Manchester 607
manor complexes 266–70, 267f, 269f
Manor Farm, Humberstone, Leicester (Leicestershire) 504
Manor Farm, Kingston Deverill (Wiltshire) 59, 59f
Manor of Hextalls (Surrey) 243, 246
manor houses 242–3
   future research 249–52
   moats 252–4
   plant remains 121
   presentation of 243–6, 245f, 247
   tripartite plan 246–9, 246f
Manor of the More, Rickmansworth (Hertfordshire) 900
Manorbier Castle (Pembrokeshire) 718
Manorial Documents Register 54
manorial records 54, 55, 58, 59, 62
manuscripts, colour 750
map-based studies 72–3
mapping
   of earthwork surveys 23–4
   towns 281–8, 282f, 286–7f, 290–3, 292f
maps, regressive analysis 56
marble 439
'marbles' (limestone) 458
Marches (Wales) 142, 145, 178, 229, 236, 237, 252, 388, 396, 547, 570
Marcher landscape 358
Margaret of Denmark (Queen of Scotland) 957
Margaret of York 421
Margary of the Buttershops, Chester (Cheshire) 322
Marham (Norfolk) 94
Marian feasts at Boston 670
Marian shrine (North Norfolk) 648
maritime regions 71
market places 290
market stalls, becoming shops 319
market towns 288, 329–30, 336
Markham, Gervase 104

Markham Chapel, Newark Church (Nottinghamshire) 873f
Marlborough castle (Wiltshire) 375
Marlow, William 347
Marlstone Rock Bed 457
Marmoutier, Indre-et-Loire (France) 933
Marquise, Boulogne area (France) 470
Marquise oolite 458, 470
marriage practices 765, 767–8
Marshall's Inn, Oxford (Oxfordshire) 316
marshes, reclaimed 182
Marske (North Yorkshire) 632
Martincamp flasks (France) 932
Marwood (Devon) 608
Mary Rose 135, 537, 790, 837, 901, 974
Mary Tudor 577, 968
masonry castles 363
masonry dwellings 230
masons 586, 600–1
masons' marks 600, 601f, 634
mass graves 841–2, 842f
    evidence of battlefields 405–8, 407f
Masses 582, 584, 585, 590, 599–600, 606, 870–1, 877
Massif Central, Languedoc (France) 929
Masterby, Battle of [Sweden, 1361] 402, 410
Matilda (daughter of Henry I) 968
matrices ecclesiae 554
May Island (Scotland) 652, 653
Mayen quarry (Germany) 502
Mayfield (Sussex) 377
meat consumption
    France 927
    wild birds 144–5
meat production 104, 108–9, 111, 198–9
medical evidence 61 *see also* bioarchaeology
medical practices 836–40
    availability for the poor 840
    equipment 837–8, 839f
    herbal preparations 838, 840
    infirmaries *see* infirmaries
    public health 840–6
Medieval Climate Anomaly (*c.* 900–*c.*1300) 105, 111, 154, 155
Medieval European Research Council (MERC) 448
Medieval Genealogy website 53

Medieval Pottery Research Group 8
Medieval Settlement Research Group (MSRG) 7, 983
Medieval Warm Period (*c.*900–*c.*1300) 105, 111, 154, 155
Melksham Forest (Wiltshire) 481
Mellifont Abbey (Louth, Ireland) 446
Melrose Abbey (Roxburghshire) 181, 570, 574, 589, 795
memento mori 665
memorial spaces 878
memories, and the senses 690
menopause 768
mensas 606
menstruation, onset 765
Meols (Cheshire) 159–60, 704, 793
merchants, identity 44, 900–1, 991
mercury 974
merels (Nine Men's Morris) 532, 532f, 534, 535
Merida Ware 974
Merlimond, Oliver de (12th-century pilgrim) 968
Mértola castle (Portugal) 966
Merton Priory (Surrey) 14, 572, 838
metal-detecting 23, 414, 511–12, 519, 649
    clubs 988
metals
    cooking pots 700–1
    drinking vessels 708
    imported into Denmark 944
metal-working 205, 335, 439, 480–2
    France 932
methodologies
    aerial survey 25–7, 26f *see also* aerial photography
    collection of plant remains 116–18
    dendrochronology 31, 32, 59, 59f, 297–8, 566–7, 985
    excavation 20–2
    field survey 22–4, 179
    geophysical survey 27–9
    Light Detection and Ranging (LiDAR) 27, 28f, 71, 363, 986
    scientific 32–3
    study of standing buildings 29–31
Michelmersh (Hampshire) 485
middens 182

Middleham Castle (North Yorkshire) 795
Middleham Jewel, Middleham Castle (Yorkshire) 665–8, 667f, 897
Middleton Stoney (Oxfordshire) 365
Midland Field System 86–7, 90, 91
migrations 821
Mildenhall (Suffolk) 218, 219
military battlefields *see* battlefields
Military Orders 847 *see also* Hospitallers and Templars
'military *v.* symbolism' debate 357–8
Milk Street (London) 702
mill system 491
millponds 497
mills 198, 265–6, 438, 479
millstones 470, 502–3
Milton 457
Minepit Wood (Sussex) 481–2
mineral replacement 117
mining 199, 437
   base metals 463–5
   coal 465–6, 466f, 467f
   precious metals 460–3, 462f
   transport of goods 469–71
Ministry of Justice 827
Ministry of Works 7, 512
Miño region, Galicia (Spain) 970
mints (coin production) 476
Minute Book (Dunwich Bailiffs) 131
miracles 159, 525
Miracles of St Augustine 470
moated houses 373
moated sites 121–2, 213, 250–1, 252–4, 302
   France 931
   Ireland 915–16
Moated Sites Research Group 252
Mockyng, Thomas 700
moles 147
Mølleån (Denmark) 501
monasteries 329, 565
   architecture 566–7, 566f, 571, 572–5
   board games in 535
   burials 575
   cloisters 572–5
   DISH (diffuse idiopathic skeletal hyperostosis) 822
   earthworks 567

   estates 575–6
   flooding 159
   gardens 571–2
   identity in 44
   industrial sites 437–8
   infirmaries 837
   Ireland 919
   layout 807–8
   militaristic imagery 810
   plant remains 121
   precinct plans 571–2
   Scottish 184
   shrines 646
   site selection 569–70
   studies of 566–9, 568f
   surge in interest 5
   use of waterways 344
monastic records 54
Monasticon Anglicanum (Dugdale) 54
moneyers 950–1
Mongols 900
Monk Bretton Priory (South Yorkshire) 573
monkeys, imported 148, 150, 972
monks, clothing 748, 791
Monkwearmouth (Tyne and Wear) 570
Monmouthshire
   buildings 228
   Chepstow Castle 14, 318, 363–4, 364f
   Chepstow Park 184
   Hen Gwrt 250, 252
   Llanthony Priory 5
   Monmouth 14, 87
   Monnow Bridge 347
   Severn Estuary 178–9
   Trellech 288, 465
Monpesson House, Salisbury Cathedral Close 897
Mont farm, Charny (France) 929
Mont St Michel (France) 573, 933
Montpellier (France) 935
Monumental Brass Society 862
monuments 13, 14
Monuments Protection Programme 11, 982
Moot Hall, Aldeburgh (Suffolk) 316
Moray (Scotland) 14, 181
Morebath (Devon) 673
Morett (Co. Laois, Ireland) 496, 501

Morisco wares (Spain) 974
Morow, John 589–90
morphological approach 74
mortality
　children 774–5
　gender differences 768
mortars 332, 333f, 470, 484
Mortimer's Cross, Battle of [Herefordshire, 1461] 411
mortuary practices 860–2
Mote of Urr (Dumfries and Galloway) 363
motte-and-bailey castles 356, 358, 910, 911, 930
mottes 361–3
moulding profiles 601f
moulds for pilgrim badges 649
Moulton (Northamptonshire) 460
Mount Grace Charterhouse (North Yorkshire) 571
Mount House (Oxfordshire) 243
Moyse's Hall, Bury St Edmunds (Suffolk) 213
Muchelney (Somerset) 174f
Murzuq (Libya) 891
Musée National du Moyen Âge, Thermes de Cluny, Paris (France) 933
Museum of County Antiquities, Lewes Castle (Sussex) 5
Museum of London 382, 795, 827, 985, 988
　Archaeological Services 309, 829
museums
　online archives 985
　Portugal 976
　Spain 976
Museums Act (1845) 5
music 715
musicology 683
Mycobacterium leprae 843 see also leprosy

Nanmor (Dafydd) 160
Nant Col (Gwynedd) 61
Nantwich (Cheshire) 469, 484
Nassington Prebendal manor house (Northamptonshire) 248
National Archaeological Survey 173
National Archives of Scotland (NAS) 53
National Archives, The (TNA) 53, 54, 55
National Association of Mining History Organisations (NAMHO) 471, 472

National Buildings Record 8
National Collection of Aerial Photography (NCAP), Scotland 25
National Galleries of Scotland 957
National Mapping Programme (English Heritage) 985
National Monument Records 357
National Museum of Denmark 947, 957
National Planning Policy Framework (NPPF) 13
Nativity scene 667f, 668
Navarre (Spain) 971
nave areas 598, 599, 607–8
Neath (West Glamorgan) 570
Needham Grange (Derbyshire) 97
neighbourhoods 290
Nenagh Castle (Co. Tipperary, Ireland) 912
Nendrum Mill 1 (Co. Down, Ireland) 493
Netherlands 605, 953, 955
　immigrants from 900–1
　trade with 898
Nettlebed (Oxfordshire) 720, 721–2f, 723
Nevern Castle (Pembrokeshire) 363, 532, 989
Neville, Eleanor (first wife of Thomas Stanley, Earl of Derby) 814
Neville, Ralph 795
Neville Screen, Durham Cathedral (Co. Durham) 590
New Archaeology 23–4, 39, 102
New Bodleian Library extension, Oxford (Oxfordshire) 12
New College, University of Oxford (Oxfordshire) 267, 268
New Hall (Denbighshire) 252
New Romney (Kent) 156, 157f
New Winchelsea (East Sussex) 278f, 280, 303, 314–15, 318
New World 975
Newbattle Abbey (Midlothian) 184
Newcastle upon Tyne (Tyne and Wear) 24, 343, 346, 441
Newcastle-under-Lyme (Staffordshire) 24
Newfoundland (Canada) 135
Newgate, York (North Yorkshire) 317
Newhall Tower (Cheshire) 26, 26f
Newington (Oxfordshire) 439, 482, 723, 724

Newport (Wales) 119, 988
  medieval ship 15, 898, 988
Newport Street (Worcester) 119–20
Newtown Jerpoint (Co. Kilkenny, Ireland) 916, 918
Niedermendig (Germany) 502
Niels (King of Denmark) 950
Nijmegen (Holland) 301
Nine Altars Chapel, Durham Cathedral, Durham 458
Nine Men's Morris (*merels*) 532, 532*f*, 534, 535
Nonsuch Palace (Surrey) 378, 814
Norbury (Derbyshire) 598
Norfolk 33, 332
  churches 546
  dress accessories 795
  pottery from 953, 954*f*
Norfolk Archaeological Unit 359
Norfolk Marshland 172
Norfolk Medieval Graffiti Survey 11
Norman Conquest of England (1066) 142–3, 145, 180, 290, 329, 341, 346, 423, 523, 949
  castles 356, 359
  cooking practices 698–9
Norman rulers 371
  European influence on architecture 373
Normandy 929, 932, 933
  exports of marble to 471
  masons from 586
Norse settlements 175
North Berwick (East Lothian) 643
North Downs (Surrey) 457–8
North Gate Bridge (Cork) 502
North Leigh Church (Oxfordshire) 868, 869*f*
North Leinster Cooking Ware 920
North Marston (Buckinghamshire) 619–20
North Molton (Devon) 463
North Pennine mines 461
North Queensferry (Fife) 643
North Raunds (Northamptonshire) 460
North Shoebury (Essex) 611*f*
North Sjælland (Denmark) 946, 951
North Yorkshire
  Bedale 426*f*
  Benedictine abbeys 570
  Bessingby 632
  Breckenborough 517
  Bridlington 132, 504
  Brough 651, 847, 849–50
  Byland Abbey 567, 574, 986
  chapels 553, 845*f*, 872
  Clementhorpe 791
  Cowthorpe 607
  Easby 574
  Fountains Abbey 439, 478, 497, 574, 585, 747*f*
  gardens 571
  Hackness 570
  Hazlewood quarry 457
  Hildenley 457
  high status women 813
  hospitals 847, 849
  Jervaulx Abbey 145–6
  Knaresborough Castle 380
  Lastingham 570
  Malham 553
  Marske 632
  metal smelting 463
  Middleham 665–8, 795
  monastic houses 39
  Mount Grace 571
  Northallerton 316
  nunneries 791
  Pickering 813
  Reighton 632
  religious symbols 632
  Richmond Castle 146, 213–14, 214*f*
  Rievaulx Abbey 437, 586
  Ripon 549, 845*f*
  Scarborough 132, 331
  Selby Abbey 344
  Skelton 632
  Swale valley 213–4, 214*f*
  Swaledale 463
  Vale of Pickering 87
  Wakefield 95, 218, 348, 872
  wall paintings 879
  Wharfedale 463
  Whitby 132, 439, 466, 468, 485
  see also Wharram Percy; York
Northallerton (North Yorkshire) 316
Northampton (Northamptonshire)
  antler carvings 483*f*
  Battle of [1460] 405, 411, 414

Northampton Marefair 779
Northampton Museum and Art
    Gallery 789
Northamptonshire 201, 332, 334
  agriculture 77
  Ailsworth 220
  Barnach 244, 329, 332
  Castor 216
  chantries 876
  chapels 552
  churches 547
  Faxton 8, 9f
  Fotheringay 604f, 857
  Higham Ferrers 426
  Lamport 504
  Longthorpe Tower 214
  Lyveden 184, 331
  Moulton 460
  Nassington Prebendal manor house 248
  North Raunds 460
  Oundle 331
  Raunds 71, 172, 174, 605, 808–9
  Raunds Furnell 781, 863
  Salcey Forest 94
  Towcester 872
  Stanion 331
  Stanwick 460
  Sulgrave 356
  Tansor Crossroads 504, 505
  Weldon 332, 464
  West Cotton 97, 122, 123, 195, 195f, 198, 334,
      502, 503, 533–4
  Whittelwood Project 14, 22, 70, 94, 95, 97,
      175, 261, 547
  see also Northampton (Northamptonshire)
Northern Crusade 524
Northern Isles (Scotland) 552
Northfleet (Kent) 493
Northgate, Canterbury (Kent) 161
Northumberland 91, 92f, 436
Northwold (Norfolk) 607
Norton, Anthony 537
Norton Priory (Cheshire) 437, 567, 572
Norway 135, 332, 333, 943
  commerce 444
  exportation to 446
  imports of fish 133–4

relationship with Scotland 957
  towns 944
Norwegian mica schist 897
Norwich (Norfolk) 13, 14, 458, 789
  animal remains 332, 333
  board games 533
  bridges 346
  buildings 297, 301, 302, 303, 306
  churches in 549, 662
  Dragon Hall 306, 447f
  dress accessories 793
  household artefacts 307, 336
  immigration 900
  land use 334–5
  market places 290
  monasteries 572
  Pottergate 700f, 701
  reclamation 343
  stained glass windows 662
  St Giles Church 850
  St Margaret Westwick Church 601, 861
  St Mary Coslany Church 601
  St Peter Mancroft Church 610
  Stranger's Hall 316
  streets 341
  trades 477
  urban landscape 275, 281, 284, 285, 287
  Walsingham 633, 643, 647, 648, 649, 650f
Norwich Castle 21, 358, 359, 360f, 650
Norwich Cathedral 591, 629
  close 14, 382, 550–1
  construction 458, 582, 583, 583f, 584
  graffiti 535
  Priory 438
  spire 163
Notley Abbey (Aylesbury) 46, 548
Nottingham 300, 334, 335
Nottingham alabaster 953
Nottinghamshire 344, 602
nucleated villages 175, 178, 180, 326, 916–18
nucleated workshops 476
nucleation 74–5
numismatic study 511–12
  collections 512–13
  future research 525–6
  see also coins
nunneries, spatial analysis 807–8, 815

nuns, clothing 791
nuts 118

O'Carroll family 913
O'Conor family 909, 915
O'Neil, Bryan 7, 9
Oakham Castle (Rutland) 244–5, 245f, 248
OASIS 984
oast houses 265
Oatlands (Kent) 377
objects of personal devotion 665–9, 667f, 669f
Ockwells Manor (Berkshire) 247
Odense (Denmark) 944, 949
Odiham Park (Hampshire) 388
odour descriptor wheel 728, 729f, 730
Office for the Dead 857
Okehampton (Devon) 196–7, 358
Old Abbey Farm (Cheshire) 243
Old Baile, York (North Yorkshire) 356
Old Flinder 180
Old Lodge, Chepstow Park (Monmouthshire) 184
Old Manor House, Walmer (Kent) 213
Old Rayne (Aberdeenshire) 111
Old Sarum (Wiltshire) 28–9, 244, 382
Old Scatness 131
Old Soar (Kent) 244
Old Winchelsea 157
olfactory senses 681–2, 728–40, 729f, 733
olive jars 974
olla enea, or metal cooking pots 700–1
Omer (Bishop of Ribe) 950
open fields 87, 174–5, 334, 926
open halls 302, 303f, 304, 306
opus anglicanum 972
opus dei (the work of God) 581, 590
Orate pro anima (pray for the soul) 665
orchil 749
Order of St John, the Knights Hospitaller 861
   see also Hospitallers
Order of the Garter 421
ordered estate management 260, 266–70
Ordnance Survey (OS) 8, 27, 56, 281, 282f
   First Edition maps 174, 176, 177
   of Ireland 914, 916, 918
oriel windows 247, 247f
'origins of the castle' debate 41–3, 356–7

Orkney 133–4, 136, 178, 181, 549, 828, 944, 945, 957
   chapels 553
   churches 547
ornamentation 202, 203f
Osney Island 345
Ospringe, near Faversham (Kent) 644–5, 645f
Ossett (West Yorkshire) 218
osteoarthritis 846
Osuna (Spain) 966
Otterburn, Battle [Northumberland, 1387] 408
Ottery St Mary (Devon) 598
Oundle (Northamptonshire) 331
Our Lady, devotional images 658–9
Our Lady of Bolton, Durham 659
Our Lady church, Aalborg 951
Our Lady church, Copenhagen 957
Our Lady of Long Melford (Suffolk) 659
Our Lady of the Mount, King's Lynn (Norfolk) 659
Our Lady shrine, Walsingham 633 *see also* Walsingham (Norfolk)
Ouse Bridge, York (North Yorkshire) 321, 347, 347f
Outer Hebrides 178
overshot waterwheels 496
Oversley (or Boteler's) Castle (Warwickshire) 366
Oviedo, Asturias (Spain) 966, 967
Oviedo museum (Spain) 976
Owain Glyndŵr's Revolt 239
Owston Abbey (Leicestershire) 572
Oxford (Oxfordshire) 290, 332, 341, 346, 380, 460
   footwear 790
   University of Oxford 423, 448, 985
   waterways 345
Oxford Archaeology 916
Oxford Blackfriars 572
Oxfordshire 284, 332, 334
   Abingdon 121, 306, 345–6, 780, 858
   Adderbury 457, 458
   Barentin's Manor 243, 251, 253, 703, 704
   Benson 720, 721f, 723
   Berrick Prior 719, 724
   Brightwell Baldwin 720, 721–2f

Oxfordshire (*cont.*)
  Burford 457
  Chalgrove 427, 616, 719, 723, 724
  Cuddeson 724
  Cuxham 720, 721–2*f*
  Dorchester 723, 724*f*, 724
  Drayton 724
  Ewelme hundred 720, 721–2*f*, 723
  Eynsham Abbey 5, 14, 121, 567
  Garsington 724
  Great Coxwell 266
  Holywell 95
  Lewknor 716
  Middleton Stoney 365
  Mount House 243
  Nettlebed 720, 721–2*f*, 723
  Newington 439, 482, 723, 724
  North Leigh Church 868, 869*f*
  River Cherwell 849
  River Thame 548
  Seacourt 798, 799
  South Leigh parish church 870, 871*f*
  Stadhampton 724
  Swalcliffe 264*f*, 266
  Thame 421, 793, 794
  Vale of the White Horse 22, 93, 96
  Wallingford 280, 283, 346, 358, 651
  Wallingford Castle 31, 60, 361, 362*f*
  Warborough 720, 721*f*
  Widford 782*f*
  Witney Palace 109, 457
  Yarnton 93
  see also Oxford; Woodstock
Oystermouth Castle (Wales) 987

pad-stones 779
Paget's disease 828
Painted Chamber, Westminster
    (London) 378, 379–80
Painted Seld, Cheapside (London) 321
paints, imported 897
Palace of the Popes, Avignon (France) 376
Palace of Westminster (London) 589
palaces 371–83, 374*f*
  gender and space 813, 814
Palatine Hill, Rome (Italy) 371
Pale, Kilteel (Co. Kildare, Ireland) 921*f*, 921

Palermo (Sicily) 373
Papal records 53
parchment 104–5
Parchment Street (Flesmangere Street),
    Winchester (Hampshire) 483
parenting practices 766–7, 781
Parham (Suffolk) 629
Paris (France) 730, 927, 950
parish-based studies 71
parish churches 545, 546–7, 597–8, 617
  burials 857–8
  and chapels 552–4
  components 598–600
  gendered space 808
  in towns 549–50
parkbreak (gang-poaching) 814
parks 148
  and gender 814
  as hunting grounds 388–91, 389*f*, 390*f*, 392*f*
parrots, imported from Portugal 971–2
PAS database *see* Portable Antiquities Scheme
Paschal Candle 591
Passion wall paintings 660, 663
Paston Letters 54, 248
Pastscape database 402
Patrick Street, Dublin (Ireland) 494*f*, 496,
    497, 498*f*, 499
Patrishow (Brecknockshire) 608
patron saints 160
pavage 340–1, 443–4
Paver, John 341
Paver, Miles 341
pays 70–1
peafowl 145
Peak, or Peveril Castle (Derbyshire) 210–11,
    368, 989
Peak District (Derbyshire) 93, 97, 145, 205,
    332, 463, 502
Peak Forest 141
Peakirk Church (Cambridgeshire) 606
peasants
  consumption 238–9
  disputes 216–19
  furniture 237
  hall-houses 232–8, 234*f*, 236*f*, 239
  households 193–207, 206*f*
  housing 226–39, 231*f*, 233–4*f*, 236*f*

kitchens 236
perceptions 215–19
privacy 216
property boundaries 216–18, 217f
Peasants' Revolt (1381) 239, 392, 717
peg-holes 238
Pelican in her Piety 607, 610
pelta (Salomon's knot) 632, 633f
Pembroke (Pembrokeshire) 276, 912
Pembrokeshire 179, 555
pendants 795–6, 797
Penhallam (Cornwall) 242, 244, 248, 250, 707
Penmaen (Glamorgan) 363
Penn (Buckinghamshire) 486
Pennant Melangell (Powys) 549, 610, 611f
Pennard (Glamorgan) 156, 164, 705
Pennines 335
Penrith (Cumbria) 337
Pensford (Somerset/Wiltshire) 325
People's Collection Wales (PCW) 984
pepper, trade 894
Perceton (Ayrshire) 123, 250–1, 252
Permian limestone 470
'Perpendicular' period 602, 604f
Perpignan (France) 376
Persia 891
personal names 24, 476, 477
personhood, acquisition of 761
Perth 109, 110, 120, 134, 162, 288, 300, 327–8, 345, 605, 616, 617, 704, 749, 792
  board games 533, 534f
  dress accessories 793
  drinking vessels 707
  High Street 109, 111, 441, 534, 649, 790, 793
  Perth Museum 622
  port 893
  survey 70
Perthshire 175
Peterborough (Cambridgeshire) 220, 331
Peterborough Abbey (Cambridgeshire) 438, 567
Peterborough Cathedral (Cambridgeshire) 582, 586, 593
Petrus Alphonsi 43
pewter 335, 481, 900
  drinking vessels 706f, 708
  eating vessels 702–4, 703f

pheasants 144–5
phenomenological approach 41–2, 76, 210–11, 989
Philip II (King of France) 523
Philip II (King of Spain and Portugal) 968
Philip of Worcester 913
Philippa of England (Queen of Denmark) 955–6
Philippa of Hainault (Queen of England) 380
Philippa of Lancaster (Queen of Portugal) 975
Phillips, Charles 8
photogrammetry 987
phytoliths 118
Pickering (North Yorkshire) 813
Picturesque in painting 3
piecemeal enclosure 96–8
piers 343
Piers Plowman 270, 443, 523
pig farming 79, 111, 334
pilgrim badges 647–51, 650f, 665, 687f, 798, 955, 966
pilgrim burials 651–5, 652f, 653f, 654f, 859
pilgrim crosses 646
pilgrim staffs (*bordoncillos*) 966, 967f
pilgrimages 549, 619–21, 641–5, 642f, 644f, 899, 919
  badges *see* pilgrim badges
  and graffiti inscriptions 629
  to holy wells 618–19
  'seeing with the senses' 689
  shrines *see* shrines
  unwelcome by locals 617
  see also Santiago de Compostela (Spain)
Pilton (Somerset) 268
Pinkie, Battle [Scotland, 1547] 405, 406, 410, 411
Piperstown (Co. Louth, Ireland) 916–18, 917f
Pipewell Gate, Winchelsea (East Sussex) 211–12
piscinas 607
pit-wheel segments 500–1, 500f
pivot stones 501
place-names 24, 177, 180–1, 184, 215, 220–1, 253
  historic 25
  indicative of bridges 346
  involving water 342

place-names (*cont.*)
  quarrying 460
  reference to battles 402
plan analysis 31–2
planned villages 180, 184
planning-led archaeology 12–14
Planning Policy Guidance Note 16
    (PPG16) 13, 21, 447
Planning Policy Statement 5 (NPPG5)
    Planning for the Historic
    Environment 13
plant remains 262–3
  data collection 116–18
  pollen 78, 118, 122
  possible uses 120–1
  preservation 117
  research 122–4
  types and places 118–22
Plantagenet era 245
plaques 211
play 530–1
  board games 531–8, 532*f*, 534*f*, 536*f*
  children 537–8, 766–7, 784
Plato 690, 742, 745
plot repletion 289
plough pebbles 261
ploughs 259, 261–2
Plymouth (Devon) 975
poaching 144
Poitiers, Battle of [France, 1356] 376
Poll Tax 285, 767
pollen 78, 118, 122
'polluter pays' principle 13
pollution 821–2
Pomerania 945
Pontefract (West Yorkshire) 554, 857
Pontevedra museum (Spain) 976
Pont's maps 185
Pool (Orkney) 131
Poole (Dorset) 344, 439, 446
population, urban 730
population changes 992
population studies 78, 285
Port Wall (Bristol) 343
Portable Antiquities Scheme (PAS) 9, 23, 161,
    162*f*, 199, 337, 428, 442, 447, 512, 513, 521,
    525, 548, 648, 715, 716, 794, 795, 985, 991

Portbury (Wiltshire) 878
Portchester (Hampshire) 358, 376, 813
Porth Strinian (Wales) 220
Portland (Dorset) 470
ports 344, 974
  fishing in 135
  plant remains in 119
  sea-fishing 132
  see also trade
Portsmouth (Hampshire) 484, 644
Portugal 331, 964, 965*f*
  coins from 524
  sugar industry 971
  trade with 446, 889, 890*f*, 893, 894, 970–1,
    974, 975–6
post-mills 503–6, 504*f*
post-processual approaches 41–6
Postwick (Norfolk) 460
Pottergate, Norwich (Norfolk), cooking
    practices 700*f*, 701
pottery
  from abroad 900
  on assarts 94
  Bedforshire 332
  Bristol 444, 751, 919–20, 974
  Border wares from London 751
  Cistercian Ware 751
  colour 751–2, 752*f*
  in domestic settings 43
  drinking vessels 708
  dripping pans 699
  Dublin (Ireland) 444
  found in castles 363
  fritware jars (Syria) 896*f*
  France 901, 919–20, 932
  glaze on pottery 751
  Grimston Ware 953, 954*f*
  Ham Green pottery (Bristol) 444, 751,
    919, 920
  imported from Iberian Peninsula 972–5
  imported in Ireland 444, 919–20
  Lincoln 485
  lustreware (Spain) 751, 752*f*, 898, 972, 974
  Martincamp flasks (France) 932
  Merida Ware 974
  Morisco wares (Spain) 974
  Norfolk 953, 954*f*

North Leinster Cooking Ware 920
olive jars 974
repairs 204
Rhenish stoneware drinking jugs 708
Saintonge Ware (France) 751, 932
Scandinavian 953, 954f
sooting of cooking pots 698
trade between towns 331–2
tripod pipkins 699
Werra ware (Germany) 900
in windmills 504–5
Woolwich, drinking jug 706f
Worcester, cooking jars 700f
see also ceramics
pottery industry 445f
pottery production 172, 177, 181, 184, 200–1, 443, 485–6
by children 784–5, 785f
villages 441
Poulton (Cheshire) 570
poverty 329
Póvoa de Varzim y Matosinhos (Portugal) 971
power, resistance to 427–8
power symbols 418–25, 420f, 422f
in France 930–2
see also status symbols
Powys (Wales) 239
Poyntz family 901, 974 see also Acton Court (Gloucestershire)
Prague (Czech Republic) 301
prayer, objects of 668
prayers 160, 161
prebendaries 581 see also canons
preceptories 809f, 810
precious metals 460–3
precious stones 161, 470, 615–16, 897
pregnancy 762, 768, 780
Premonstratensian monasteries 570, 574, 581
Premonstratensians, estates 576
presence culture 420
preservation of plant remains 117
Prest, Hugh 218
Prestwich (Greater Manchester) 408
Priest's House, Muchelney (Somerset) 174f
Prior of Coventry 260
Prior of Lewes 321

priors 581
Prior's Chapel, Durham Cathedral (Co. Durham) 638
Priors of the Benedictine Abbey of St Mary's, Coventry 276
privacy 196, 216
and space in houses 811
processions, Christian 620–1
processual approaches 39–40
projective view 212, 366–7
property boundaries 216–18, 217f
protection, jewellery for 797–800, 799f
Provence (France) 930
Prussia 946
Pseudo-Dionysius 742, 743
puberty 765
public archaeology 11–12, 22–3, 173f, 987–8
public education 7
public health 840–6
Public Record Office 380
publication of investigations 13
pulpits 591
Pung, Thomas 649
Purbeck (Dorset) 332, 470
Purbeck marble 458, 469, 471, 535, 586, 951, 953
exported to France 933
Purfleet quay, King's Lynn (Norfolk) 643
Purgatory 641, 665, 775, 862, 870–1, 871f
Pusey, William (Pusey Horn) 424–5, 424f
Puxton (Somerset) 172
Pyx Chapel, Westminster Abbey (London) 515

Quantocks (Somerset) 93
Quarr stone (Isle of Wight) 332, 458, 953
quarries 332, 335, 437, 439, 440f, 456–60, 459f, 471
stone working workshops 484
quays 343, 344
Queen Street/Castle Street, Oxford (Oxfordshire) 341
Queen's University (Belfast) 911
querns 470, 471, 484
quernstones 502
quicklime 460
Quoygrew (Orkney) 77, 131, 183, 205, 206f

rabbits 146–7, 150
Radcliffe (Greater Manchester) 457, 988
Raddun (Wiltshire) 93
radiocarbon dating 177, 181, 250
Radulf (Bishop of Ribe) 950
Ragnhildsholmen Castle (Sweden) 954
Raleigh, William (Bishop of Norwich) 715
Ramsey Abbey (Cambridgeshire) 438, 439, 441
Ranworth (Norfolk) 606, 607
Rathmullan (Co. Down, Ireland) 911
rats 106, 147
Rattray (Aberdeenshire) 111, 306, 363
Raunds (Northamptonshire) 71, 172, 174, 605, 808–9
Raunds Area Project 22
Raunds Furnell (Northamptonshire) 781, 863
Ravenserodd (East Yorkshire) 132, 133, 157–8
Rayonnant architecture 589
Reading (Berkshire) 159, 332
reclaimed land 94, 182–3, 183f, 343
Record Commission 53
Records of the Exchequer 53
rectories 598
Redcliffe area (Bristol) 479, 480f
Redenhall (Norfolk) 607
refectories 573
Reference Collection of Medieval Pottery, British Museum 12
reflective view 212, 366–7
Reformation 556, 576, 593, 610, 621–2
 and devotional images 673–4
 effect on graffiti inscriptions 629–30
Regensburg (Germany) 301
regimens, medicinal 837
regional groups 8
regional surveys 69–73
regional variation 171, 178, 180
regressive map analysis 56
Reigate district (Surrey) 332
Reigate stone 457–8
Reighton (North Yorkshire) 632
Reims (France) 589, 927
relics 614–17, 646–7 *see also* reliquaries
religion 545
 in Scandinavia 943
 spatial analysis and gender 806–10

 see also Christianity; Islam
religious images, destruction of 45
religious rituals 161–2
reliquaries 664, 690
 jewellery 794f, 794
 see also relics
reports, unpublished 983–4 *see also* grey literature
Requiem Mass 857
reredoses 606
RESCUE 13
research projects 983
resilience 990–1
resistance metres 27–8
Restwold, Ralph (Lord of Crowmarsh Gifford) 724–5
revisionism 42
Rhedynog-felen (Conwy) 570
Rhenish stoneware drinking jugs 708
Rhine Valley, chessboard finds 532
Rhineland (Germany) 331, 332, 336, 438, 953
rhino-maxillary syndrome 844f
Rhuddlan (Wales) 276, 375
Rhygyfarch 220
Ribe (Denmark) 944, 949, 950, 951, 953, 954
Richard of York (3rd Duke of York) 857
Richard I (King of England) 374
Richard II (King of England) 144, 348, 376, 377, 380, 395, 420, 421–2, 532, 702
Richard III (King of England) 377, 405, 408, 415, 418, 422, 819, 987, 795
 buried at the Greyfriars in Leicester 858, 859–60
Richard of Southwick 702
Richmond Castle (North Yorkshire) 146, 213–14, 214f
Richmondshire (Yorkshire Dales) 554
rickets (vitamin D deficiency) 781, 822, 825
Rickman, Thomas 6, 591
Ridgewardine (Shropshire) 27
Rievaulx Abbey (North Yorkshire) 437, 586
Riga (Switzerland) 301
Rigny (France) 935
Ringerike style 948
Ringsted 950
ringworks 356, 357, 910–11, 910f
Ripon (North Yorkshire), churches in 549

Rites of Durham 647
ritual protection marks, church graffiti 632–4
rituals 161–2, 622
    board games 534
    private, objects of 668
River Adur (Sussex) 468, 470
River Aire (Yorkshire) 548
River Avon 343, 345, 617
River Blythe (Midlands) 345
River Brue (Somerset) 345
River Calder (West Yorkshire) 643
River Cam (Cambridgeshire) 221
River Cherwell (Oxfordshire) 849
River Conon (Easter Ross) 183
River Don (South Yorkshire) 548
River Dove (Derbyshire) 519
River Eden (Cumbria) 348
River Fleet (London) 739
River Foss, York (North Yorkshire) 345
River Frome (Dorset) 343
River Great Ouse (East Anglia) 343–4
River Humber (Yorkshire–Lincolnshire) 548
River Idle (Nottinghamshire) 344
River Nore (Ireland) 916
River Ouse (North Yorkshire) 344, 345, 346, 548, 731–2
River Rhine (Germany) 502
River Severn (Bristol) 574
River Slaney (Ireland) 911
River Suir (Ireland) 913
River Tamar (Devon–Cornwall) 461–2
River Tavy (Devon) 463
River Tay (Scotland) 441
River Thame (Oxfordshire) 548
River Thames 345–6, 371, 617, 795
    pilgrim badges in 648–9, 650f
    salt working 468
    smell 737
    at Surbiton, Surrey 376
River Trent 548
River Usk, Newport (Wales) 988
River Wear (Co. Durham) 687
River Wensum (Norfolk) 649
River Witham (Lincolnshire) 345
rivers
    building on waterfronts 343–4, 345
    crossings 345–8

pilgrim badges in 648–9
rubbish deposits 345
Roach Smith, Charles 5–6
roads *see* streets
Robert the Bruce (King of Scotland) 616
Robert of Ely 949
Roberton (Scottish Borders) 180
Rocamadour (France) 899
Rochester Castle (Kent) 213
Rochester Cathedral (Kent) 619
Rochford (Essex) 346
Rockingham Forest (Midlands) 72, 94, 97, 146
rodents 147
Roel (Gloucestershire) 197
Rogation processions 218
Rogationtide processions 620–1, 621f
Roger of Pont-l'Évêque, Archbishop 586
Rokewood, John 704
roll-billets 952f
Roman buildings 301
Roman Empire, collapse 371
Roman London Excavation Council 7
Roman and Medieval London Excavation Council 7, 12
Roman period 763
Roman van Walewein 533
Roman Watling Street 643
romance, board games 537
Romanesque architecture 371–5, 601–2
Romantic Movement 555
Romanticism in poetry and fiction 3
Rome (Italy) 550, 651, 899, 919
Romeyn, John de (Archbishop of York) 160
Romford (Essex) 346
Romney Marsh (Kent/East Sussex) 94, 163, 199
rood screens 663–4, 688, 688f
roofing 302, 315
rosaries 797–8
Roscommon Castle (Ireland) 913, 915
Roskilde (Denmark) 944, 947
Roslin (Midlothian) 600
Rotherfield (East Sussex) 464
Rotherham (South Yorkshire) 348
Rouen (France) 307, 920, 930, 933
Rougiers, Dracy (France) 929
Round Table 376, 394, 421

Rowley, Trevor 11
Rows of York 317
Roxburgh (Scotland) 275, 283, 288, 325
Royal Archaeological Institute 356
Royal Commission groups 8, 23, 70, 75, 163, 252, 253, 300, 303, 567
   Inventories 592
Royal Commission on the Ancient and Historical Monuments of Scotland (RCAHMS) 15, 70,
Royal Commission on the Ancient and Historical Monuments of Wales (RCAHMW) 11, 25
Royal Forests 94
royal houses 371, 372–83, 374f
Royal Library in Copenhagen 950
Royal Mint (London) 829
Royal Numismatic Society 518
royal treasure 419–21, 420f
royalty
   burials of children 775, 776
   commemorative monuments 862
   foreign gifts 899–900
   foreign marriages 975
   grave goods 859
   images on coins 513, 514f
   insignia 421–4
   location of burials 858
   tombs 863–4
Royston Grange (Derbyshire) 22
rubbish deposits 345
rubbish pits 333, 476
Rügen island (Germany) 945
run-rigg 91, 95
rural landscapes 193–207
   board games 533–4
   chronological change 326
   France 925–9
   housing 327
   effect of industry 438
   Ireland 916–18, 917f
   sounds 715–17
   space and gender 811–12
   vs. towns 327–37
   workshops 477–8
Rye (East Sussex) 297, 751, 975
rynd-and-spindle assemblies 501

Saami population in northern Scandinavia 943
sacrality 614
   after the Reformation 621–2
   pilgrimages 619–21
   places 617–19, 618f
   relics 614–17, 646–7
   rituals 622
Sacrament Houses 607
sacred spaces 219–20, 221
Saffron Walden (Essex) 280, 314
Saint-Germain, Auxerre, Yonne (France) 933
Saint-Mexme, Chinon (France) 933–5
Saint-Thomas d'Aizier, Eure (France) 934f
Saint-Ursin de Courtisigny (France) 929
Sainte-Chapelle, Paris (France) 376
Saintogne (France) 705, 920
Saintonge Ware (France) 751, 932
saints 619–21
   celebrated in Denmark 949
   cults 220
   interment 647
   relics 614–17
   role in Purgatory 870
   shrines to 643, 646–7, 654, 879–80
   transport of bodies 857
   whitewashed images 688, 688f
   see also individual names
Salcey Forest (Northamptonshire) 94
Salerno school of medicine 836
Saliba, Jacoba 626
Salisbury (Wiltshire) 275, 276, 297, 300, 302, 303, 321, 341, 342, 345, 550
   Bishops 382
   cooking practices 701
   dress accessories 793
Salisbury Cathedral (Wiltshire) 31, 163, 444, 535–6, 536f, 581, 582, 584–5, 586, 588f, 591, 745, 880
Salisbury Museum 896
salmon fishing 134, 135
Salomon's knot (pelta) 632, 633f
salt production 184, 484–5
salt trade 933, 970–1
salt working 184, 468–9, 484–5
Saltcot (Essex) 184
saltmarshes, reclaimed 182

Salwarpe valley (Worcestershire) 469
Samsonshelis, Channelkirk (Scottish Borders) 181
Sandal (West Yorkshire) 21, 358
Sandonbury (Hertfordshire) 266, 267f, 268
Sandwell Priory, West Bromwich (West Midlands) 567, 778
Sandwich (Kent) 14, 297, 302–3, 303f, 304, 318, 344, 605
Sandys, Sir William (Treasurer of Calais) 900
sanitation 739
Santander museum, Spain 976
Santiago de Compostela (Spain) 549, 617, 643, 648, 651, 798, 899, 919, 964–5, 965f, 967f, 972
  museum 976
  scallop shells *see* scallop shells
  shrine 643
  see also St James the Greater
Savernake Forest (Wiltshire) 27, 424, 715
Saxony (Germany) 942, 945
Saxtorp, Skåne (Denmark) 951
'scalingas' (shieling huts) 181
scallop shells 648, 649–50, 651–5, 652f, 653f, 665, 967f
  with azurite 896f, 897
  carved in jet 797–8, 966
  depictions in art 968
Scandinavia 80, 941–3, 942f
  coins from 523
  fishing industry 132–3, 135
  gender segregation 808
  import of fish from 133–4
  produce 943
  trade with 893
  see also individual countries
Scanian fishery (Denmark) 132
Scarborough (North Yorkshire) 132, 331
Schatzkammer der Residenz, Munich (Germany) 956
Schleswig-Holstein (Germany) 651, 941, 944, 953
Schorn, John 619–20
scientific approach 32–3, 39–40, 102
scientific data 455
Scolland's Hall, Richmond Castle (North Yorkshire) 213–14, 214f

Scone Palace (Perthshire) 377
Scotland
  agricultural buildings 265
  agricultural tools 261
  architecture 206f
  battlefields 402
  bridges 345
  castles 356–7, 358
  cathedrals 582, 584, 589–90, 593–4
  chapels 554
  churches 546, 605, 607
  coastal settlements 182–3
  coins 514f, 523
  conservation management 414
  dental health 822
  Dissolution 577
  exports 893
  field systems 91, 97
  fishing industry 133–4, 135–6
  grazing settlements 181
  hunting grounds 184, 393
  hunting legislation 142, 144
  infirmaries 847
  iron mining 464–5
  island settlements (crannogs) 185–6
  leprosy 843–5, 846
  meat production 109
  moated sites 252
  monasteries 437, 565, 570
  mountainous areas 145
  parish churches 597
  pilgrim burials 652, 653f
  pilgrimages 619
  planned villages 180
  reclamation of saltmarshes 182
  Reformation 622
  relationship with Denmark 957
  relationship with Norway 957
  remains of buildings 226–8, 230
  royal houses 372, 377
  run-rigg 91, 95
  rural settlements 175–8, 176f, 204
  saints 646
  salt production 184
  sea-fishing 131
  settlements 172
  surveys of palaces 382

Scotland (*cont.*)
  tournaments 394
  urban housing 306
  urban mapping 288
  villages 176–7
Scottish Archaeology Internet Report (SAIR)
    series 103
Scottish Chancery records 53
Scottish Highlands 986
Scottish Historic Land-Use Assessment
    project 986
Scottish Wars of Independence 402
scurvy (vitamin C deficiency) 825
scythes 262
Seacourt (Oxfordshire) 798, 799
sea-fishing 128–9, 130–3, 135–6
seal matrices 442, 442*f*, 950
seal rings 795–6, 796*f*
seals, royal 421, 423–4
seasonal settlements 172, 181, 182
security 196
sedilia 607
seeds 118, 119
Selby Abbey (North Yorkshire) 344
Selden Society 53
selds 319, 320, 321
senses 685–6, 691–2, 989
  colour *see* colour
  devotion and spirituality 686–91
  number of 732–3
  smells 728–40, 729*f*
  sound *see* sounds
  studies of 681–3
  synaesthesia 683–5
  taste 697–8
  visual 690–1, 877–9, 879*f*
sensory archaeology 43
sensus communis or common senses 732
Seoul (South Korea) 730
Seton (East Lothian) 605
settlement patterns
  coastal areas 182–3, 183*f*
  grazing 180–2
  high-status settlements 184–6
  industrial settlements 183–4
  planned villages 180
  rural 173–9, 176*f*

  studies of 171–3
Setúbal (Portugal) 970
Seven Deadly Sins 660
Seven Merciful Acts of Christ 846
Seven Works of Mercy, painting of 747
Sevenhampton (Wiltshire) 216, 218
Severn Estuary (Monmouthshire) 178–9, 470
Seville (Spain) 966, 974
sewage 300–1, 341
sexual imagery 626, 797
Shaftesbury Abbey (Wiltshire) 265, 269, 269*f*, 481
Shakespeare, William 418
Shapwick (Somerset) 22, 33, 56–8, 57*f*, 93, 95, 96, 107–8, 107*f*, 122, 172, 174, 204, 439, 547
SHARE European Earthquake Catalogue (SHEEC) 985
shearmongers 476
Sheen (Surrey) 376
sheep 332
sheep-farming 74, 90, 91, 97, 111, 177, 181, 334
  living conditions 262
  on smallholdings 197–8, 199
sheepcotes 262
Sherborne Old Castle (Dorset) 382
Sheremoiners Lane (London) 476
Sherston (Somerset) 878
Shetland (Scotland) 178, 181, 944, 945, 957
  chapels 553
shielings 181
Shillamill Wood, Tavistock (Devon) 437*f*
ship-building and repairing 484
ship graffiti 635–7, 636*f*
ship names 423
ships, for pilgrimages 643
shipwrecks 15, 470, 898, 946, 949
  Armada 974
  Mary Rose 135, 537, 790, 837, 901, 974
  Newport 15, 898, 988
  Studland Bay wreck 898
Shootinglee (Scottish Borders) 177
shop-houses 318, 486–7
shop-keeping 321–2
shops 300, 306, 312, 328*f*
  architectural detailing 313–15, 313*f*, 314*f*, 321
  chronological changes 319–20

evolved from market stalls 319
furnishings and fittings 314f, 315–16
layout 320–2
signage 321
types 316–19
Short Cross coinage 517, 523, 525
Shrewsbury (Shropshire) 14, 297, 306, 321, 346, 347
Shrewsbury Abbey 119
Battle [1403] 410
shrines 616, 643, 646–7, 664, 879–80
interplay of the senses 683–5, 684f
pilgrim badges of 648
pilgrim burials at 651–5, 654f
sensory involvement 689–91
Shropshire 23, 297
timber-framed houses 31
Sible Hedingham (Essex) 331, 441
siege castles 361
sieges 411–13, 912
silk 895
silver
Denmark 953
eating vessels 702
jewellery 793
mines 175, 184, 437, 461, 462f, 929
silver-gilt spoon 419
Silves castle (Portugal) 966
Simnel Street, Southampton (Hampshire) 318
Simonsbath (Exmoor) 184
Singleton (West Sussex) 313
sinusitis 821
Sir Gawain and the Green Knight 556
Sir Gowther 748
Siston (Gloucestershire) 608
Sites and Monuments Records (SMR) 8
Sjælland (Denmark) 941
Skåne (Sweden) 941, 947, 951
markets 943–4
Skanör (Denmark) 943, 944
Skeldergate, York (North Yorkshire) 344
Skelton (North Yorkshire) 632
skin colour 743
Skuldelev, Roskilde Fjord (Denmark) 949
Slackshaw Burn, Mauchline (East Ayrshire) 181
slag-tapping 464

slate 332
Slav groups 945
Slav lands 942
Smailholm (Roxburghshire) 365
smallholdings ('crofts') 176, 197–9
smells 681–2, 728–30, 729f, 733
smelting 463, 464, 470, 481–2
Smithfield cemetery *see* East Smithfield cemetery (London)
smoke blackening 117
Snettisham (Norfolk) 608
social identities 44
social inequality 990
social practice theory (SPT) 990
social space
aristocratic dwellings 813–14
and gender 814–15
role of religion and gender 806–10
studies of 805–6
vernacular architecture 810–12
social status 239
Society of Antiquaries (London) 285, 512
Société d'Archéologie Médiévale Moderne et Contemporaine (SAMMC) 925, 926, 932
Society for Landscape Studies 33
Society for Medieval Archaeology (SMA) 7, 809, 982, 984
1981 Conference 39–40
Society for the Study of Childhood in the Past (SSCIP) 775
sociological studies 44–5
soldini 524
Solway plain (Cumbria) 205, 228
Somerset 605
silver mining 461
Somerset Levels, reclamation 94
Song of Dermot and the Earl, The (Orpen) 911
Sonman, Hugh 218
sooting of cooking pots 698
Soper Lane (London) 318
Sorø, Sjælland (Denmark) 950
soul, acquisition of 762
soul masses 870
Sound, the (Denmark–Sweden) 943, 946
soundmarks 720–2, 722f
sounds 683, 713–14
amplification 717

sounds (*cont.*)
  and meaning 717–25
  and power 714–17
South Creake (Norfolk) 220
South Downs 547
South Leigh parish church
    (Oxfordshire) 870, 871*f*
South Mimms (Hertfordshire) 361
South Oxfordshire Project 719–25, 721–2*f*
South Witham (Lincolnshire) 503, 575,
    809*f*, 984
Southampton (Hampshire) 12, 109,
    129, 301, 313, 320, 330, 331, 342, 484,
    699, 749
  commerce 446
  dining practices 701, 703*f*
  drinking vessels 705, 706*f*, 707, 708
  footwear 790
  foreign trade records 887
  ports 344, 901
Southchurch Hall (Essex) 243, 248, 250, 253
Southwark (London) 321
Southwark Cathedral (London) 635
Southwark priory (London) 716–17
Soutra (Scottish Borders) 838, 847
souvenirs, foreign 900
Spain 331, 964, 965*f*
  board games 533
  coins from 524
  pottery from 751, 752*f*, 972–5
  trade with 446, 889, 890*f*, 893, 894, 898,
    966, 968–75
Spalding (Lincolnshire) 161
spatial analysis 39, 805–6
  aristocratic dwellings 813–14
  and gender 814–15
  role of religion and gender 806–10
  vernacular architecture 810–12
spatial syntax 247
special deposits 989
specialist interest groups 8
spectacles 795
spices, imports 895–7
spindle-whorls 478–9
spindles 501
spinning 477, 478–9
spires 555, 602, 604

spirituality
  board games 534
  and the senses 686–91
Spitalfields (London) 14
spolia 373
Spon Street, Coventry (West Midlands) 317
spondylolysis 780
Sponne's chantry, Towcester church
    (Northamptonshire) 872
spoons 419, 704
spores 118
springs, holy 617, 618*f*
Spynie (Moray) 358
squints 878, 879*f*
Sri Lanka 891
St Alban 949
St Albans (Hertfordshire) 427, 550, 570
St Albans II, Battle
    [Hertfordshire, 1461] 408, 411
St Albans Cathedral and Abbey Church
    (Hertfordshire) 162, 163, 441, 573, 583*f*,
    586, 591, 627, 629, 880, 950
St Aldates, Oxford (Oxfordshire) 616
St Andrew (the apostle) 643, 649
St Andrew Priory, Fishergate, York (North
    Yorkshire) 129, 838, 858, 863
St Andrews (Fife) 109, 184, 276, 288, 306, 893
  pilgrimage to 643, 644*f*, 649
  St Rule's Church 584
St Andrews Cathedral (Fife) 550, 582, 586,
    589, 591, 593
St Andrew's Church, Bredwardine
    (Herefordshire) 632
St Andrew's Farm (Fife) 847
St Andrews Street, Plymouth (Devon) 974
St Andrews University (Fife) 985
St Anne 668
St Ann's Street, King's Lynn (Norfolk) 314
St Anselm (Archbishop of Canterbury) 663
St Anthony 554, 850
St Apollonia 973*f*
St Augustine of Canterbury 733
St Augustine of Hippo 690, 742
St Augustine's Abbey (Bristol) 319, 708
St Augustine's Abbey, Canterbury (Kent)
    377–8, 458, 470, 573
St Barbara 160

St Bartholomew's Hospital (Bristol) 847, 850
St Bartholomew's Hospital, Smithfield
    (London) 645, 836
St Bees (Cumbria), Lady 32
St Benet Sherehog Church (London) 719
St Bernard 691
St Bernard of Clairvaux 689, 744, 745, 747, 748
St Birinus 724
St Botolph 630, 949, 951
St Botolph's Church, Boston
    (Lincolnshire) 670–2, 671f, 897
St Brigid 951
St Bueno 618
St Candida's Church, Whitchurch
    Canonicorum (Dorset) 880
St Catherine of Alexandria 973f
St Catherine's Church, Winchester
    (Hampshire) 549
St Chad 647
St Christopher 638, 659
St Clement nunnery, Clementhorpe (North
    Yorkshire) 791
St Columba 646
St Cuthbert 584, 585, 617, 659, 682, 689, 859
St Cuthbert Cathedral (Durham) 583, 584,
    585, 682f, 689
St David 220
St David's (Pembrokeshire) 220
St David's Cathedral (Pembrokeshire) 220,
    586, 590
St Dionysius Church, Esslingen
    (Germany) 651
St Dunstan-in-the-West Church
    (London) 857
St Edmund of Bury 972
St Edward the Confessor 972
St Ethernan's Priory, May Island
    (Fife) 652, 653f
St Eustace 747
St Faith's church, Winchester
    (Hampshire) 549
St Geneviève, Paris (France) 950
St George 659
St George's Chapel, Windsor Castle
    (Berkshire) 457, 620, 872
St Gertrud 944
St Giles 651

St Giles's Cathedral, Edinburgh
    (Scotland) 655
St Giles Church, Norwich (Norfolk) 850
St Giles's Church, Winchester
    (Hampshire) 549, 779
St Giles Hospital by Brompton Bridge, Brough
    (North Yorkshire) 651, 847, 849–50
St Giles Mill, Reading (Berkshire),
    watermill 495, 495f, 497, 498f,
    499–500, 500f
St Gregory's Church, Bedale (North
    Yorkshire) 426f
St Guinefort (dog) 620
St Guthlac 221
St Gwenfrewi (Winefride) 617–18, 618f
St Helen on the Walls, York (North
    Yorkshire) 329, 781, 821, 826, 828, 829
St Helen's Church, Ashby-de-la-Zouch
    (Leicestershire) 655
St Helen's Church, Fishergate, York (North
    Yorkshire) 651–2
St Helen's Church, Winchester
    (Hampshire) 549
St Hugh 647
St Ives 348
St James the Greater 648, 655, 966, 968 see
    also Santiago de Compostela (Spain)
St James the Less 966
St James Church, Chichester (West
    Sussex) 843
St James's Church, Southam
    (Worcestershire) 260f
St James Hospital (Lincolnshire) 841
St James's Priory (Bristol) 525
St James the Less Church, Iron-Acton
    (Bristol) 901
St James and St Mary Magdalene Hospital,
    Chichester (West Sussex) 829, 843, 861
St John the Baptist 607, 659, 672, 794f
St John the Baptist Hospital, Oxford
    (Oxfordshire) 847, 849
St John's Church, Canterbury (Kent) 644
St John's Church, Duxford
    (Cambridgeshire) 633f
St John's Hospital, Cambridge
    (Cambridgeshire) 405, 850
St Joseph, Kenneth 8, 25

St Katherine 554, 659
St Kentigern 646
St Kilda (Outer Hebrides) 105
St Knut Lavard 949, 950
St Leonard's Hospital, York (North Yorkshire) 847
St Margaret 643, 647, 745
St Margaret of Antioch 973f
St Margaret's Church, Cley-next-the-Sea (Norfolk) 635, 636f
St Margaret's Church, Combusto (Norfolk) 861
St Margaret's Hospital, High Wycombe (Buckinghamshire) 845
St Margaret Westwick Church, Norwich (Norfolk) 601f, 861
St Martin Pomeroy (London) 700
St Martin's Church, Wallingford (Oxfordshire) 651
St Martin's Seld (London) 319
St Mary Bethlehem hospital (Bedlam, London) 645
St Mary church, Troston (Suffolk) 631f
St Mary Graces Abbey 829
St Mary's, Coventry (Warwickshire) 276
St Mary, Ospringe (Kent) 847–8, 850
St Mary Coslany Church, Norwich (Norfolk) 601
St Mary Magdalen chapel, Ripon (North Yorkshire) 845f
St Mary Magdalen, Colchester (Essex) 847, 848–9
St Mary Magdalen Hospital, Winchester (Hampshire) 652, 843, 844, 845, 847, 849–50
St Mary Magdalene 973f
St Mary Magdalene Hospital, Partney (Lincolnshire) 849
St Mary Magdalene, Chichester (West Sussex) 843
St Mary Merton (Surrey) 439, 778
St Mary Spital hospital (London) 14, 15, 645, 702, 703f, 779, 823–5, 824f, 841–2, 838, 839, 846, 847, 848f, 850
St Mary, Happisburgh (Norfolk) 609f
St Mary, North Shoebury (Essex) 611f
St Mary, Taunton (Somerset) 605

St Mary's Abbey, York (North Yorkshire) 548
St Mary's Church, Hickling (Norfolk) 536
St Mary's church, Lidgate (Suffolk) 633, 634f
St Mary's Church, Adderbury (Oxfordshire) 457, 458
St Mary's guild, Boston (Lincolnshire) 670–2, 671f
St Mary's Guildhall, Lavenham Market Place 313f
St Mary's Haverfordwest (Pembrokeshire) 655
St Mary Hospital, Chichester 644, 645
St Mary's, Enville (Staffordshire) 149f
St Mary's Church, Luton (Bedfordshire) 872
St Mary's, Strood 644
St Michael 870, 871f
St Michael's Mount (Cornwall) 412–13
St Modwenna 221
St Monance (Fife) 184
St Neot (Cambridgeshire) 43
St Nicholas 636
St Nicholas East Kirk, Aberdeen (Aberdeenshire) 652
St Nicholas Hospital, Lewes (Sussex) 849
St Nicholas in the Shambles 779
St Nicholas of Myra 554
St Nicholas's chapel, King's Lynn (Norfolk) 636
St Nicholas Church, Blakeney (Norfolk) 601f, 636
St Nicholas's Church, Keyingham (East Yorkshire) 159
St Nicholas's Church, New Romney (Kent) 156–7, 157f
St Ninian 646, 957
St Ninian's shrine, Whithorn (Scotland) 651
St Ninians, Shetland (Scotland) 897
St Olaf of Norway 972
St Olaf's church, Elsinore (Denmark) 957
St Olav 944
St Osmund 535–6, 536f, 880
St Oswald 654
St Oswald's Church, Widford (Oxfordshire) 782f
St Osyth's (Essex) 571
St Paul 423
St Paul's Cathedral (London) 263, 264, 589, 857, 876

St Paul's manor of Sandonbury
    (Hertfordshire) 266, 267f, 268
St Peter 654, 664
St Peter Mancroft Church, Norwich
    (Norfolk) 610
St Peter's Church, Felsted (Essex) 316
St Peter's Church, Ilton (Somerset) 777
St Petrog 160
St Queran's Well, Cargen (Dumfriesshire) 619
St Rule's Cathedral, St Andrews
    (Scotland) 584
St Sampson's Church, York (North
    Yorkshire) 317
St Serf's Abbey, Loch Leven (Scotland) 186
St Stephen's Chapel (Westminster) 376, 378,
    379, 589, 968
St Swithin (Hampshire) 659
St Swithun 880
St Thomas 646–7, 955
St Thomas Aizier (Eure) 935
St Thomas Aquinas 870
St Thomas Becket, Canterbury Cathedral
    (Kent) 584, 585, 619, 689
St Thomas's, Salisbury (Wiltshire) 868
St Thomas's Church, Winchelsea (East
    Sussex) 636
St Thomas's Hospital, Southwark
    (London) 645, 716–17
St Tudwal's Island (Caernarvonshire) 231f
St Tyfodwg's Llandyfodwg (Glamorgan) 655
St Werburgh shrine, Chester Cathedral
    (Cheshire) 683–5, 684f
St William of Perth (Scotland) 619
St William's chapel, York (North
    Yorkshire) 347, 347f
St Wulfstan 654
stable isotope plotting 828, 828f
Stadhampton (Oxfordshire) 724
Stafford, Humphrey (1st Duke of
    Buckingham) 405
Stafford Castle (Staffordshire) 363
Staffordshire 335, 463
stained glass windows 661–3, 662f, 968
stalls in cathedrals 590
Stamford (Lincolnshire) 220, 320, 329, 331,
    332, 485, 515, 570, 851
    limestone quarries 458

textile industry 480
standing buildings 29–31, 226–7, 227f,
    229–35, 297–8
    and written documents 58–60
Stanion (Northamptonshire) 331
Stanlaw on the Mersey (Cheshire) 570
Stanley (West Yorkshire) 218
Stanwick (Northamptonshire) 460
Stapeldon, Walter de (Bishop of Exeter) 590
status symbols 418, 420f, 422f, 425–7 see also
    power symbols
Statute of Merton 95
steatite/soapstone 440f
Stebbing (Essex) 608
Stedham quarry 471
steeples 555
Stephen (King of England) 373, 376, 514f,
    515, 516
Stewart, William (Bishop of Aberdeen) 591
Stigand (Archbishop of Canterbury) 419
stillborn infants 779
Stirling 301, 345, 605
    castle 377, 383
    University of Stirling 985
    wolf hunting 146
Stock (Essex) 391
Stockholm (Sweden) 889
Stoke Charity (Hampshire) 878, 879f
Stoke Orchard (Gloucestershire) 968
Stoke-by-Clare (Suffolk) 630
Stoke-sub-Hamdon, near Yeovil
    (Somerset) 396
Stokesay (Shropshire) 185
Stone (Staffordshire) 120
stone 333f, 335
    bridges 346
    buildings 301, 317, 456–60
    effect of sound on 717
    imported 897
    quarries 456, 471
    to and from France 933
    trade between towns 332
    transportation 469–70
stone-built blocks 244
Stoneleigh Abbey (Warwickshire) 58, 95,
    233f, 239
stonemasons 346, 444, 586

Stone of Scone 419
stone working 484
storage facilities 439
storm damage 156–7, 157f, 159–60, 161
Stothard, Charles 378
Stour valley on the border of Essex and Suffolk 335
Stow, John 347, 729, 733–9
Strand Street, Sandwich (Kent) 302–3, 303f
Stranger's Hall, Norwich (Norfolk) 316
Strangford Lough area (Co. Down, Ireland) 915
Strasbourg (France) 582
Strata Florida Abbey (Ceredigion) 159, 545, 570
Strata Marcella (Powys) 570
Stratford Langthorne (Essex) 777–8, 838
Stratford-upon-Avon (Warwickshire) 201, 330f, 673
  guild chapel, wall paintings 660, 661f
Stratton (Bedfordshire) 122, 123
street-names 24, 290, 320, 342
streets 340–2
Stroud valley (Gloucestershire) 335
structuralism 40–1, 806
Studland Bay wreck 898
Stumpe, William 475, 480
suburbs 289
Sudbury (Suffolk) 336
Sudeley Castle (Gloucestershire) 27
Suffolk 41, 96, 97, 213, 217
  churches 546
Suffolk Archaeology 22–3
sugar cane 971
sugar factory 970f
suicide 862
Sulgrave (Northamptonshire) 356
sumptuary laws 744, 749
supernatural 220–1
Surbiton (Surrey) 376
surgery, instruments of 837
Surrey 331
Survey of London (Stow) 733–9
Sussex 132, 284
  field systems 91
  iron mining 464
Sussex Archaeological Society 5

Sussex Weald 326
Sutton, Robert 655
Sutton Valence (Kent) 460
Sven Forkbeard (King of Denmark) 948
swaddling of infants 763, 780–1
Swalcliffe (Oxfordshire) 266
Swalcliffe Tithe Barn (Oxfordshire) 264f
Swale valley (North Yorkshire) 213–14, 214f
Swaledale (North Yorkshire) 463
Swan Lane (London) 305f
Swannington (Norfolk) 629, 633, 635, 638
swans 145, 698
Swansea (Wales) 281, 283, 606
Sweden 942f, 943, 945, 953
  commerce 444
  research in 259
  towns 944
Swinfield, Richard (Bishop of Hereford) 380
Sydenhams Moat (Warwickshire) 243
symbolic system 40
symbols of power 418–25, 420f, 422f
symbols of resistance to power 427–8
symbols of status 418, 420f, 422f, 425–7
Symington (South Ayrshire) 180
synaesthesia 683–5
Syon (Middlesex) 791, 955
syphilis 821, 825
Syria 891, 898

Tagus estuary, Lisbon (Portugal) 971
Talmont, Vendée (France) 931f
Tamar Valley sites 184, 461–2
Tamar Valley Project, University of Exeter 471
Tamworth (Staffordshire) 493
Tanner Street, Winchester (Hampshire) 482
tanning 120, 441–2, 482–3, 825
Tansor Crossroads (Northamptonshire) 504, 505
Tantallon Castle (East Lothian) 412, 464
taphonomy 103
Tate Gallery 674
Tattenhoe (Buckinghamshire) 203, 779, 782, 799
Tattershall (Lincolnshire) 214
Tatton (Cheshire) 205
Taunton (Somerset) 605
taxation records 476

Taylor, Christopher 11
Taynton quarry, near Burford (Oxfordshire) 457
Teampall na Trionad ('Trinity Church') (N. Uist) 30f
Tees valley (Co. Durham) 458
televised archaeology 7, 22, 987
Templars 24, 40, 577, 809, 809f, 810
　preceptories: South Witham (Lincolnshire) 21
Temple Cressing (Essex) 268
Temple fee, Redcliffe area (Bristol) 479
Temple Guiting (Gloucestershire) 24
Tempsford Park (Bedfordshire) 243
Tenby (Pembrokeshire) 291, 297
test-pitting 22, 173f
Tewkesbury (Gloucestershire) 304, 487, 570
Tewkesbury Abbey (Gloucestershire) 873, 875f, 878, 880
Tewkesbury, Battle [Gloucestershire, 1471] 414
text graffiti 637
textile industry 441–2, 478–80, 480f, 487
　Denmark 955
　exports 893
　imports 893
textiles 790–3
Thame (Oxfordshire) 421, 793, 794
Thame hoard 46, 897
Thames Discovery Programme 988
Thames Mudlarkers 649
Thankerton (South Lanarkshire) 180
Thaon, Calvados (France) 933, 935
thatch 120, 123–4, 262, 302
　survival of base layers 226
Thaxted (Essex) 336, 487
thegnly fortifications ('proto-castles') 356
Theodoric of Cervia 836
Theophilus the monk 744, 747–8
Theoretical Archaeology Group conference (1985) 806
Thervay (France) 494, 496, 500f
Thetford (Norfolk) 332, 514
Thiofrid (Abbot of Echternach) 689
third gender 810
Thirty Years' War 517
Thomas (2nd Earl of Lancaster) 519

Thomastown (Co. Kilkenny, Ireland) 916
Thornbury (Gloucestershire) 814
Thornton Abbey (Lincolnshire) 163, 567, 571, 841, 850
thoroughfare towns 329
Thorpe, Harry 8
Thorpe, Sir Robert 214
Thorpe, William 749
Threave (Dumfries and Galloway) 358
Three Living and the Three Dead 605, 660
Three Magi (Jaspar, Melchior, and Balthazar) 615, 616
threshing 264
Tidenham (Buckinghamshire) 506
Tikøb, Sjælland (Denmark) 951
tile-making 441
tiles 444–5
　imported 898, 900
　production 486
　from Spain 974–5
　see also floor tiles
Tilney, Margaret de 670
timber, survival 250
timber buildings 301, 947
timber-framed houses 335
timber-framed shops 316–17
timberwork 260
Time Team projects 22
tin 205
　mining 463–4
　transportation 470
Tintern (Co. Wexford, Ireland) 919
Tintern Abbey (Gwent) 5, 437, 470, 570, 573, 574
Tiptoft, John (1st Baron Tiptoft) 396
Tironensian priories 577
Tisbury estate, Shaftesbury Abbey (Wiltshire) 481
tithe barns 264f, 265
Tiverton (Devon) 874f
Toky, Richard 704
Tokyo (Japan) 730
Tolbooth, Northallerton (North Yorkshire) 316
Tomb of Christ/Easter Sepulchre 607
tomb shrines 664–5, 666f
Tonbridge Castle (Kent) 706, 708

tools 196, 261–2
tooth decay 822–3
Toppe, Robert 447, 447f
Torrin (Isle of Skye) 181
Totternhoe stone 457
Toulouse (France) 929, 930
tourism, archaeological 5
Tournai (Belgium) 458, 591
tournaments 394
Toury, Beauce (France) 926
Tovstrup (Denmark), watermill 495f, 495, 496, 500
Towcester church (Northamptonshire) 872
Tower of London 14, 148, 356, 371, 373, 378, 383, 537, 933
tower-houses 357, 363, 365
  Ireland 913–15
Town Hill, Wrexham (Clwyd) 315
tower-mills 506
town plans 276–9, 277–8f, 298, 299f, 327f
towns *see* urban landscapes
townscapes 320–2
township-based studies 71
township splitting 177
townships, Scotland 176–7
Towton, Battle of [Yorkshire, 1461] 401, 405, 406–8, 407f, 410, 411, 414, 841, 859
toys 784
trade 205
  between town and country 331–7
  buildings for 300
  with Denmark 953
  foreign 887–98, 888f, 890f, 892f
  with Ireland 471, 919–20
  with Portugal 446, 889, 890f, 893, 894, 970–1, 974, 975–6
  with Spain 446, 889, 890f, 893, 894, 898, 966, 968–75
trades 326, 476–7
Tradescant, John 792
Traghen (Libya) 891
Trainecourt (France) 929
transformational grammar 806
transhumance 74, 181
transi tombs 665
transport of goods 444, 469–71
transubstantiation 590, 606, 691

Treasure Act (1996) 9, 517, 518, 794
Treasure Trove laws 517
  in Scotland 794
trees, studies of 33 *see also* dendrochronology dating techniques
Trelech (Monmouthshire) 14, 28, 288, 465
trepanation 61
treponemal disease (syphilis) 825, 828, 830
Trim Castle (Co. Meath, Ireland) 911, 912f
Tring (Hertfordshire) 606
Trinity, the 667f, 667
Trinity Guildhall, Felsted (Essex) 316
Trinity Island (Co. Roscommon, Ireland) 919
tripartite plan 246–9, 246f
tripod pipkins 699
Trondheim (Norway) 438, 446, 944
Tropenell, Sir Thomas 426
Troston church porch (Suffolk) 629
Trotton (West Sussex) 745, 747
trousseau 955
Troyes (Aube) 932
True Cross, relic of 646
Trunch (Norfolk) 610
tuberculosis (TB) 821, 825, 830
Tudor palaces 374
tumours 821
Turku (Finland) 889
turriform churches 356
Turweston (Buckinghamshire) 506
Tusser, Thomas 106
Tutbury (Staffordshire) 329, 519
Tutivillus (demon) 605
Twomileborris (Co. Tipperary, Ireland) 497, 499, 501
Tyddyn Llwydion (Powys) 205–6, 232–5, 233–4f, 236, 238
Tyne Bridge, Newcastle 348
Tynemouth (Tyne and Wear) 570
Tyson, R. 485, 898
Ty-uchaf, Llanwddyn (Wales) 179f

Ufford (Suffolk) 610
Ugadale brooch 616
Uists (Scotland) 178
Ulster (Ireland) 915
umland 330, 331
undercrofts 318–19

undershot waterwheels 493–6, 494f, 495f, 501
universities, archeology departments 11, 21
University of Bradford 29
University of Cambridge 25, 54, 377, 567, 840, 872
University College London Institute of Archaeology 988
University of Copenhagen 957
University of Exeter 29f, 471
University of Leicester 860
University of Oxford 448, 985
University of Southampton 28–9, 382
University of Stirling 985
University of York 103, 105, 293, 382
Unst (Shetland) 178
Upper Beeding (West Sussex) 468
Upper Bugle Street, Southampton (Hampshire) 974
Upper Greensand (Reigate stone), North Downs (Surrey) 457–8
Upper Hem, Forden (Montgomeryshire) 236f
Upper Merrivale, Dartmoor (Devon) 464
Upton (Gloucestershire) 779
Upwich, Droitwich (Worcestershire) 469
Urban Archaeological Databases (UADs) 986
urban archaeology 7
urban castles 359
urban development 276–9, 277–8f, 298, 299f
urban landscapes 275–9, 277–8f
    artefacts 326–7
    board games 533
    bridges and river crossings 345–8, 347f
    buildings 298–308, 299f, 303f, 304f
    chronological change 289–91, 325
    churches in 549–50
    comparative approach 283–5
    effect of industry 438
    France 929–30
    housing 327, 328f
    impact of industry 438
    Ireland 918
    mapping 281–8, 282f, 286–7f, 290–3, 292f
    modelled on other towns 550
    newly formed 279–82
    place-names 24
    plant remains 119–20
    pollution 821–2
    population 730
    Scandinavia 944
    smells 728–40, 729f
    sounds 715–17
    space and gender 811–12
    specialized industries 487
    spread of disease 821
    streets 340–2
    vs. rural settlements 327–37
    waterfronts 342–4, 345
    waterways 344–5
    wild animals 147
    written accounts of 283
urban migration 767
urban projects 14
urban regeneration schemes 12–13
urban regulations 300
urbanization 275, 279–82, 334, 336
Urnes style 948, 949
uroscopy 743, 837–8
Usk (Wales) 178

Vadstena, Östergötland (Sweden) 955
Valdemar I the Great (King of Denmark) 949–50
Valdemar II (King of Denmark) 950
Vale of Glamorgan (Wales) 162f, 178, 555
Vale of Pickering (North Yorkshire) 87
Vale of the White Horse (Oxfordshire) 22, 93, 96
Vale Royal (Cheshire) 570
Valencia (Spain) 752
Valencian pottery 751, 752f, 898, 972, 974
Vallanges, Vitry-sur-Orne (Moselle, France) 929
Valle Crucis (Clwyd) 570
Valor Ecclesiasticus (1535) 53, 597
van der Goes, Hugo 957
Vasco de Gama 899
veal 697
vegetables 119, 122
Vegetius (Publius Flavius Vegetius Renatus) 405
Vejby, Sjælland (Denmark) 951
Vejby cog 946
Vejrum 953
vellum production 104–5

Venerable Bede 859
Veng church (Jutland) 951
venison 698
Vere family 422–3
Verjeslev (Denmark) 500
vernacular architecture 810–12, 929
Vernacular Architecture Group 985
Vernacular Buildings Group 260
vertical watermills 493–6, 494f, 495f, 501
Vesey, William de 443
Vézelay (France) 617
Viborg Søndersø (Denmark) 438
vicars 581
   residences 585
Vicars Choral 550, 810
Vicar's Choral community college, York (North Yorkshire) 535
Victoria and Albert Museum (London) 380, 606, 674, 791, 796
Victoria County History 9, 54, 62
Vienna (Austria) 582
viewing platforms 394
Vigo museum (Spain) 976
Viking Age 941, 944, 949
   second 948
Vilarnau (France) 929, 935
villages
   boundaries 217
   children in 781–2
   chronological change 326
   deserted 155, 172, 179, 200, 204, 782f, 916–18, 917f, 929
   excavation 7
   formation 75, 77
   in France 928–9
   nucleated 175, 178, 180, 326, 916–18
   planned 180, 184
   Scotland 176–7
   test-pits 22
Villasirga, Palencia (Spain) 966
Villaviciosa, Asturias (Spain) 966
Vilslev (Denmark) 951
Vineyards Farm (Dorset) 25
Virgin and Child 973f
   at King's Somborne (Hampshire) 630
Virgin Mary 870, 871f
   wall paintings 660

Virring (Jutland) 951
Visby, Battle of [Sweden, 1361] 406, 945
visual perception *see* colour
visual senses 690–1, 877–9, 879f
vitamin deficiencies 822, 825, 846
Vitry-sur-Orne (Moselle, France) 929
Vives 538
Voragine, Jacobus de 659
Vordingborg, Sjælland (Denmark) 953
Vyne, The (Hampshire) 900

Wace (historian) 221
Wadham, Nicholas 777f
Wainfleet St Mary (Lincolnshire) 469, 485
Wakefield (North Yorkshire) 95, 218, 348, 872
Walden (Essex) 487
Wales
   architecture 205–7
   assarting 93
   battlefields 402
   castles 363–5, 364f
   cathedrals 584
   chapels 553
   field systems 91
   fishing industry 135
   funding for excavations 7
   granite from 502
   grazing settlements 181–2
   hunting grounds 393
   hunting legislation 142
   industrial settlements 184
   infirmaries 847
   iron mining 465
   Midland Field Systems 87
   moated sites 252, 253
   monasteries 565, 570
   mountainous areas 145
   piecemeal enclosure 97
   planned villages 180
   reclamation of wetlands 182, 183f
   remains of buildings 228, 230, 231f, 232–5, 233–4f, 236, 236f
   royal palaces 375
   rural settlements 178–9, 179f, 204
   settlements 171, 172
   urban mapping 287–8
walkways 315, 394

wall paintings 660–1, 661f, 879–80
  colours 745–8, 746–7f
Wallaces's House, Elderslie (Renfrewshire) 252
Wallingford (Oxfordshire) 280, 283, 346, 358, 651
Wallingford Castle (Oxfordshire) 31, 60, 361, 362f
Walmer (Kent) 213
Walmgate, York (North Yorkshire) 120
Walpole St Peter (Norfolk) 468–9, 601
Walsall (West Midlands) 487
Walsham (Suffolk) 216
Walsingham (Norfolk) 633, 643, 647, 648
  pilgrim badges 649, 650f
Walter of Henley 95, 107, 263
Walter, Hubert (Archbishop of Canterbury) 791, 895
Waltham Abbey (Essex) 457, 569
Wanborough (Surrey) 526
Wanten, Alice 779
Warandashales (Shropshire) 25
Warborough (Oxfordshire) 720, 721f
Wardhouse Castle (Aberdeenshire) 180
Ward-Perkins, John 7
Ware (Hertfordshire) 525
warehouses 344
Warkworth Bridge (Northumberland) 347
warrens 391
Wars of the Roses (1455–87) 402, 404, 411, 422, 519
Warwick (Warwickshire) 201, 862
Warwickshire, churches 547
wash-houses 479
water
  holy 648
  as sacred place 617–19, 618f
  symbolism 253–4
  transport of goods 968, 975–6
Waterford (Ireland) 444
waterfronts 342–4, 345, 441
Watergate, Chester (Cheshire) 316
watermills 265, 491
  components 499–502, 500f
  construction 497–9, 498f, 499f
  types 492–6, 492f, 494f, 495f, 501
Waternish (Isle of Skye) 178

water-power 482, 491, 568f see also watermills
waterways 342, 344–5
Watling Street (London) 644–5, 645f, 706, 707
Wattisham (Suffolk) 514
Watton (East Riding of Yorkshire) 574, 815
Wayneflete, William (Bishop of Winchester) 875f, 880
wayside crosses 548
Weald of Kent 439, 485
  iron mining 464
Wealden house (Kent) 239
weaning 780
weapons, as status symbols 425–6
weather 154–6
  effect on agriculture 79–80
  catastrophic events 156–61, 157f, 158f, 991
  effect on cattle 107–8
  prayers for 160, 161
  protection from hazards 161–2, 163–4
weaving 478–9
Weedley (East Riding of Yorkshire) 503
Weeting 'Castle' (Norfolk) 213
weld 749
Weld estate (Dorset) 33
Weldon (Northamptonshire) 332, 464
Well, C. 647
Wells (Somerset)
  bishop palace 373, 382
  cathedral 581, 582, 585, 589
wells, holy 617–19, 618f
Welsh Bridge, Shrewsbury (Shropshire) 347, 348
Welys, John and Johan 315
Werra ware (Germany) 900
West Colliford reservoir, Bodmin Moor (Cornwall) 463
West Cotton (Northamptonshire) 97, 122, 123, 195, 195f, 198, 334, 502, 503, 533–4
West Country 605, 608
  drinking vessels 707
  field systems 90, 90f
  fisheries 135, 136
West Highlands (Scotland) 616
West Midlands 232, 502
West Riding of Yorkshire 552
West Sussex, stone quarries 471
West Walton (Norfolk) 598

West Whelpington
(Northumberland) 263, 519
West Yorkshire 335
  burials 857, 863
  chapels 552
  grave-slabs 863
  Ossett 218
  Sandal 358
  Stanley 218
  textile industry 480
  Wakefield 95, 218
Westbury (Buckinghamshire) 203, 478, 479, 779, 793
Westerham (Kent) 605
Westminster Abbey (London) 14, 109, 375, 378–80, 379f, 379–80, 420, 444, 458, 567, 645, 647, 775, 776, 819, 880
  great hall 373
  royal burials 858
  stone used in 457
Westminster Palace 371
Weston Longville (Norfolk) 635
Wexford town (Ireland) 918
Weybread (Suffolk) 630
Whalley (Lancashire) 570
Wharfedale (North Yorkshire) 463
Wharram le Street (North Yorkshire) 58
Wharram Percy (North Yorkshire) 7–8, 10f, 21, 174, 196, 197, 199, 200, 230, 243, 428, 460, 486, 547, 610, 763, 765, 778, 780, 781, 782, 821
  assarting 94
  burial sites 202–4
  consumption of fish 133
  Data Sheets (Rahtz) 39
  of Black Death on 96
  field system 97
  life span 329
  lordly building 212
  mill site 497–8
  vitamin D deficiency 822
  written documents 58
whetstones 470
whistles 715
Whitby (North Yorkshire) 132, 439, 466, 468, 485
White Tower, Tower of London 14, 31

Whitefriars 24, 791
Whitefriars, Aberdeen (Aberdeenshire) 779
Whitefriars, Coventry (Warwickshire) 520
whitewashing of saintly images 688, 688f
Whithorn (Dumfries and Galloway) 570, 646, 821, 822, 829
Whithorn Cathedral (Dumfries and Galloway) 581
Whitland (Glamorgan) 570
Whittlewood Project (Northamptonshire) 14, 22, 70, 94, 95, 97, 175, 261, 547
Widford (Oxfordshire) 782f
Wigmore Castle (Herefordshire) 24, 968
wild animals 141–2, 149–50
  bone finds 143f
  carnivores 145–6
  fur trade 146–7
  habitats 142–4
  hunting legislation 142–4
  imported exotics 148–9, 150
  small commensals 147
wild birds 144–5
wild boar 144
Willey (Shropshire) 392f
William the Conqueror 372, 373, 514f, 515, 516
William II, Rufus (King of England) 373, 378, 516
William the Englishman 582
William of Hatfield 776
William of Hirsau 161
William of Namur 523
William of Sens 582, 586, 933
William de Valence (1st Earl of Pembroke), burial of children Margaret and John 776
William de Wollechirchehawe 341
William of Wykeham 376, 380
William FitzOsbern (1st Earl of Hereford) 365
Willis, Robert 6, 591–2
Wilton Diptych 380, 422
Wiltshire 284
Wiltshire Dendrochronology Project 59
Wiltshire and Swindon Archives 59
Winchelsea (East Sussex) 211–12, 276, 635
Winchester (Hampshire) 12, 21, 95, 290, 301, 302, 304–5, 304f, 308, 341, 372, 380, 420, 515, 516, 966
  bell-casting 481

board games 535
churches in 549
dress accessories 793
footwear 790
horn belonging to 424–5
monasteries 569
smells 739
tanning 482–3
textile industry 479
trades 477
Winchester Bible 373
Winchester Castle (Hampshire) 421
Winchester Cathedral (Hampshire) 373, 458, 582, 583–4, 590, 591, 593, 791, 793, 873, 875f, 880
windmills 265–6, 491, 503–6, 504f, 505f
windows 213–14, 214f, 247, 247f, 305f, 307
   cathedrals 586
   in churches 602, 603f, 604
   imported glass 933
   making 485
   in shops 314
   stained glass 606, 661–3, 662f
Windsor Castle (Berkshire) 371, 376, 380, 421, 443
   stone used in 457
windstorms 163
wine 968
wine trade 130, 132, 446
   Spanish 970
Wing (Buckinghamshire) 673
Winslow (Buckinghamshire) 216
Wiston (South Lanarkshire) 180
Witham Valley (Lincolnshire) 548
Witney Palace (Oxfordshire) 109, 457
Wiveton church (Norfolk) 601, 636
woad 749
Wodehouse, Sir William 536
Woking Palace (Surrey) 382
Wolsey, Cardinal Thomas 377, 577
wolves 145–6, 149
Wolvesey, Winchester (Hampshire) 372, 373, 380
women
   board games 537, 538
   in the brewing industry 443
wooden drinking vessels 707

wooden eating vessels 702, 703f
Wood Hall (Yorkshire) 250
Woodstock (Oxfordshire) 371, 373, 380, 383, 393, 457
   hunting park 375
   walled park 373
wool 441, 478
Woolwich, drinking jug 706f
Worcester (Worcestershire) 201, 213, 300, 464, 972
   bell-casting 481
   chapels 554
   churches in 549
   cooking practices 699, 700f
Worcester Cathedral 581, 858, 859
   pilgrim burial 654–5, 654f
   Priory 574
Worcestershire, salt working 469
Word of God 688
workshops 438–41, 475–7
   domestic 486–7
   stone working 484
Worlington (Suffolk) 630
Wrexham (Clwyd) 315
written documents 52, 61–3, 283
   as evidence 56–61, 57f
   finding 52–4
   interpreting 55
   reading 54
Writtle (Essex) 184, 373, 388
Wychwood (Gloucestershire) 94, 95
Wye (Wales) 178
Wykeham, William (Bishop of Winchester) 426
Wymondham Abbey (Norfolk) 778
Wynford, William 376

Y Ferwig (Ceredigon) 160
Yarmouth *see* Great Yarmouth
Yarnton (Oxfordshire) 93
Yaxley (Cambridgeshire) 460
Yeavering (Northumberland) 371
Yersinia pestis 841 *see also* Black Death
Yevele, Henry 444
York 13, 102, 103, 119, 235, 275, 281, 284, 285, 287, 290, 302, 304, 307, 320, 341, 344, 346, 348, 439, 441, 470, 515

York (*cont.*)
  board games 533
  churches in 549
  dress accessories 793
  eating practices 704
  ferries 346
  fish-bone finds 129, 130
  fish consumption 133
  footwear 790
  layout of shops 320–1
  migrations to 821
  single occupancy dwellings 812
  smells 731–2, 739
  stained glass windows 662
York Archaeological Trust 988
York Cathedral 43, 582, 586, 589, 590, 591
York Minster 635, 776, 873, 968
York Museums Trust 795
York Mystery Plays 551
York Palace (Whitehall) 377
Yorkshire 601
  architectural details 601, 602
  Burton Agnes 244
  ceramic assemblages 699
  coal 465
  copper mining 463
  East Haddesley 243
  East Yorkshire *see* East Yorkshire
  Fulford 410
  Gilbertine priory 574, 815
  Hedon 276
  Knaresborough Castle 380
  Midland Field System 87
  military hoards 517
  mill dams 498
  North Yorkshire *see* North Yorkshire
  pilgrim burials 651
  quarry sites 457
  South Yorkshire 344, 573
  Towton 401
  West Yorkshire *see* West Yorkshire
  windmills 503
  Wood Hall 250
  see also Wharram Percy (North Yorkshire)
Yorkshire Dales 554
Yorkshire Moors 141
Yorkshire Wolds 198, 230 *see also* Wharram Percy (North Yorkshire)
Ysgol Twm o'r Nant, Denbigh (Wales) 825
Ystad (Sweden) 77

Zaragoza (Spain) 972
Zarautz museum (Spain) 976
zooarchaeology 60, 79
Zürich (Switzerland) 301
Zuwila (Libya) 891